THE EMPEROR

AND THE WOLF

STUART GALBRAITH IV

ff FABER AND FABER

NEW YORK • LONDON

THE EMPEROR
AND THE WOLF

THE LIVES AND FILMS OF

AKIRA KUROSAWA

AND TOSHIRO MIFUNE

Faber and Faber, Inc.
An affiliate of Farrar, Straus and Giroux
19 Union Square West, New York 10003

Faber and Faber Ltd
3 Queen Square
London WC1N 3AU

Owing to limitations of space, all acknowledgments for permission to publish previously published material can be found on page 825.

Library of Congress Cataloging-in-Publication Data
Galbraith, Stuart, 1965–
    The Emperor and the wolf : the lives and films of Akira Kurosawa and Toshiro Mifune
  / Stuart Galbraith IV.
        p.   cm.
    Includes bibliographical references and index.
    ISBN 0-571-19982-8 (alk. paper)
    1. Kurosawa, Akira, 1910–   2. Mifune, Toshiro, 1920–   3. Motion
  picture producers and directors—Japan—Biography.   4. Motion picture actors
  and actresses—Japan—Biography.   I. Title.

PN1998.3.K87   G35   2001
791.43'0233'092—dc21
[B]
                                                                                2001023825

Designed by Jonathan D. Lippincott

            1   3   5   7   9   10   8   6   4   2

FOR THE KUROSAWA-GUMI

CONTENTS

A NOTE ABOUT
THE TEXT AND A FEW
PERSONAL REMARKS

I believe it necessary to preface this work with a few explanatory comments pointing out the challenges particular to this project, resulting in a work somewhat different from other biographies.

First was the decision to write a joint biography. To those already familiar with the works of Kurosawa and Mifune, the reason should be clear. Beyond the reasons stated in the introduction, I found it impossible to write a Kurosawa biography or a Mifune biography without going into considerable detail on the separate career of the other. And because the life and career of Mifune without Kurosawa (as opposed to the reverse) has been so completely disregarded in the West, bringing the two together seemed not only desirable but essential.

Second, if this were, say, a biography of John Ford and John Wayne, references to other actors and other films could be mentioned with a minimum of comment. Everyone has at least heard of Warner Bros. Most readers are familiar with Henry Fonda or Shirley Temple or the Academy Awards, and know a little something about the Alamo and Abraham Lincoln. Such is not the case with Japanese films (aside from those of Kurosawa and the *Godzilla* series), Japanese actors, Japanese history, Japanese production and releasing methods, and so on. Therefore, I've attempted to make this book accessible to everyone, even those whose knowledge of Mifune is limited to John Belushi's imitation of him on *Saturday Night Live*, or whose closest encounter with Kurosawa was seeing *A Fistful of Dollars*.

In order to achieve this, I opted to depart from the standard format of filmmaker/actor biographies in some respects. For example, this book emphasizes the distribution and exhibition of their films far more than the typical biography because the limited, erratic manner in which the films reached American shores directly impacted both their careers in Japan, in the pictures Mifune subsequently made abroad and in the financing Kurosawa received on his later works.

One simply cannot understand the peaks and valleys of their careers and marketability abroad without understanding how their films were released and received in the West. In the 1950s and '60s, at least, no market was more important than the United States, and nearly all their most famous films were first funneled through one of two theaters in the United States: the Toho La Brea Theater in Los Angeles and, to a lesser extent, the Toho Cinema in New York. This manner of distribution-exhibition was unique—no other contemporary foreign cinema enjoyed the benefits and endured the pitfalls of such an arrangement, and its ultimate failure is mourned by fans and scholars of Japanese cinema to this day.

Similarly, plot synopses, actor biographies, and especially the filmography are more expansive than in most biographies, because such information has rarely, if ever, been published in English. Many of Kurosawa's most famous films, the ones readily available on home video in the United States, have skimpy translated credits when they have credits at all. This is an egregious oversight. To understand the filmmakers and actors who worked on these films, one must first be able to identify them, and every effort has been made to make the filmography in the back of the book as complete and useful as possible.

In addition, Western reviews of the films are quoted at greater length than in most biographies of foreign filmmakers. In the course of my research I was surprised, as I'm sure you'll be, by these contemporary reviews. Especially during the 1950s, but continuing today, many writers for major newspapers and magazines proved alarmingly uninformed about their work. This was not a simple case of liking or not liking a certain film: many critics were recklessly ignorant about the nature of these pictures and the culture and industry from which they sprang, while these same critics simultaneously dismissed them, usually out of a kind of cultural jingoism. They insistently imposed Hollywood standards on non-Hollywood films and, later, expected Kurosawa's last works to be exactly like those that had come before. Since these films had such limited distribution to begin with, a single review could greatly affect a film's success or failure in the United

States. In a sense, if this book has a villain, it's the *New York Times* critic Bosley Crowther; and if there's a hero, it's the *Los Angeles Times*'s Kevin Thomas. This book is, in a minor way, a tribute to Thomas's thoughtful commentary and tireless promotion of Japanese cinema, at least for several generations of Angelenos. Similarly, after reading dozens of condescending American reviews of *Seven Samurai* that invariably criticized its (already shortened) length and accused it of being little more than a "Made in Japan" knockoff of superior Hollywood "gun-and-gallop" Westerns, the author was surprised to come across a review by the late Arthur Knight that understood Kurosawa's film so clearly, so precisely, that his eloquent words proved deeply moving. Such is the power of good film criticism.

Between them, Kurosawa and Mifune worked on more than 150 movies, plus various television programs and commercials. Much of this work has never been seen (nor is likely to be seen) in the United States. Indeed, the majority of Mifune's films have not been available, even to the Japanese, since their initial release. For that reason my plot summaries of many of the films tend to be longer than those found in other books, mainly for the historical record.

The reader will also note that most of the interviews done especially for this book were almost entirely with Japanese personnel, rather than Americans and Europeans who might have worked for, or were influenced by, Kurosawa and Mifune. This was deliberate. Japanese actors and filmmakers had, obviously, the longest-running, closest relationships with these filmmakers, while Americans, with a few notable exceptions, were peripherally or fleetingly linked to them; also, their comments have been well documented elsewhere. I have thus chosen to quote from interviews made at the time of their association, as, I believe, contemporary accounts are more likely to be accurate.

Conducting interviews for a biography like this one presents its own case of *Rashomon*. Can memories be trusted when discussing events of thirty, fifty, even sixty years ago? How does one handle interview subjects with their own agenda? In a book like this, the problem is even more complicated, as most of the interviewees spoke only Japanese. Thus most of the questions were asked in English, translated into Japanese, answered in Japanese, and translated back into English. Every effort has been made not to lose the subtlety of comments, and because of the vagaries inherent in translation, I have paraphrased some of the speakers' words in the interest of clarity, without changing the intent.

What struck me most about the interviews is the profound impact both

Kurosawa and Mifune had on those who knew them. I believe I was able to see bits and pieces of Kurosawa and Mifune reflected in those closest to the two men, from eighty-seven-year-old Senkichi Taniguchi, who knew Kurosawa back in the 1930s and directed Mifune's screen debut, to forty-four-year-old Yoshitaka Zushi, who played the little boy in *Red Beard* and the teenager in *Dodes 'ka-den* and who lived in Kurosawa's home for several months in the mid-1970s. The reality of doing a book like this is that you want to talk to all these people for days, which just isn't possible. But quite unlike in more conventional celebrity interviews, there was an urgency in their comments. They made a concerted effort to get across the essence of Mifune and Kurosawa, for they seemed to have a need to express the professional and personal impact the two had had on their lives, so much so that for them, it seemed, these interviews became a kind of catharsis.

Sadly, several of the people I interviewed for this book did not live to see its publication. Still others were not able to complete the interview process due to failing health. A few subjects agreed, in fact insisted, I meet with them in spite of ill health, even after I, realizing their condition, tried to beg off. I came to realize that Kurosawa and Mifune had so affected their lives that their own waning strength was less important to them than helping any serious researcher, especially someone from outside Japan who might be writing about their *sensei*, men whose impact extended far beyond the industry in which they worked.

In Japan, very nearly everyone was extremely polite and generous with their time. Every interview seemed to end the same way, with the same comments. At first I thought these words, heard time and again, were merely polite ways of saying goodbye and wishing me luck. I soon realized they were something more, something that drove home the responsibility of the task before me. The interview subject would stop me as I turned to leave, look into my eyes, and say, "Please, please write a good book." I always promised to do my best.

ACKNOWLEDGMENTS

This book could not have been written without the hard work and support of many individuals. First and foremost is Yukari Fujii, tireless translator of hundreds of articles, faxes, and letters. She squinted at blurry film credits, translated Japanese television documentaries, and helped set up most of the interviews in Japan. When I found myself without an interpreter in 1999, Yukari took a tremendous professional risk by quitting her job in Los Angeles to accompany me to Japan for my final research trip. When she returned to the United States, her future was a great unknown, and especially for this tremendous sacrifice, I am in her debt. Yukari is one of the most dedicated, hardworking, and fundamentally kind persons I know, and I am proud to call her my friend.

When East Coast–based Anne Wasserman learned about my project, she volunteered her services and generously and greatly supplemented my research, sending pounds of photocopied articles, some of which she even had translated from other languages. She did all this at her own expense, refusing to accept any compensation. Like many others too numerous to list here, she simply wanted to see this book exist but, more than anyone else, worked hard to make it happen.

Atsushi Sakahara acted as my interpreter for my 1996 trip to Japan, but he was more than that. He guided me through Tokyo's labyrinthine subway system, making sure I arrived at each and every interview on time. An extremely talented and ambitious man, Atsushi's life changed forever when he became a victim of the infamous sarin gas attack shortly before I met him, and our adventures together were, I think, the beginning of his new outlook on life.

Sergei Hasenecz, Stephen Bowie, and Steve Ryfle, all talented, busy writers, took time out from their own schedules to make suggestions and corrections to the manuscript. Each had their own strengths: Sergei as a dramatist very knowledgeable about Japanese films and refreshingly blunt in his comments; Stephen as an experienced film and television historian; Steve as an excellent author and journalist with an eye on the big picture. They complemented one another beautifully. They all were, quite thankfully, merciless in their remarks, and made this book much better than it would have been without them. Their overall support for this project and deep concern for my mental well-being during this daunting task must also be acknowledged.

Tony Sol spent many hours at the Academy of Motion Picture Arts and Sciences Library when I couldn't get there, sifting through thousands of clippings. He also spent many weeks working his way through forty years of *Kinema Jumpo* articles on my behalf. Like Anne Wasserman's, Tony's love of Japanese film made it a pleasant task, but I can't deny that it was also time-consuming and occasionally frustrating. Thank you, Tony. Ted Newsom offered more of the same—thanks.

James Bailey generously provided audio cassettes of interviews with Kurosawa, members of his staff, and Donald Richie.

Linda Hayashi offered great moral support. Her carefully considered view of Kurosawa in many ways mirrored my own, and talking with her for hours put my own approach to this book into perspective.

Filmmakers Yuko Yoshikawa and Yoshifumi Hosowa took time out during the production of their film *Home Sweet Hoboken* to help me track down contact information for many of the interview subjects, translate faxes, introduce me to filmmakers and actors, and do other miscellaneous but important work. Chris D generously made videotape copies of several extremely obscure Mifune films I might otherwise not have seen, while Tomoko Koizumi translated several articles and credits when Yukari's workload became overwhelming.

Also adding support and encouragement were Izumi Hasegawa, Lianne X. Hu, David Kalet (All Day Entertainment), Bill and Beverly Warren, Patience Winthrop Gordon-Brown, and my family, Stuart (III) and Mary Galbraith, Kim Hunsanger, and Melissa Galbraith.

I would also like to thank my agent, Peter Rubie, for getting this project off the ground in the first place; my editor at Faber and Faber, Denise Oswald, for her patience, good judgment, and support; and Chandra Wohleber, also of Faber and Faber.

In Japan, I am indebted to Shiro Mifune (Mifune Productions Co., Ltd.) for his tremendous generosity and kindness. In the hours we spent together, he himself retrieved box after box, scrapbook after scrapbook, allowing me to look through anything I asked for. His warm, gentle, and helpful nature suggested the man his father was, and I am grateful to him for greeting me and my project so kindly.

Mike Y. Inoue, Akira Kurosawa's nephew, was equally kind and generous with his time, and extremely helpful in coordinating my interviews with Kurosawa's staff and in giving the green light to actors of Kurosawa's stock company for interviews. My thanks also to Hisao Kurosawa and Kazuko Kurosawa (Kurosawa Production Co., Ltd. and Kurosawa Film Studio Co., Ltd.), and their employees.

Mikayo Nagao and her husband, actor-comedian Shunji Fujiyama, were extremely generous with their time. Ms. Nagao not only arranged my interview with actor Akira Terao but also provided me with many hours of Kurosawa and Mifune television tributes which aired after their deaths.

I would like to thank my wife, Yukiyo, for her moral support as this project neared its completion.

Among those also providing assistance in the United States: Tak W. Abe (Kurosawa Enterprises USA, Inc.), Leith Adams, Miyako Araki (Asmik Ace Entertainment, Inc.), Norihiko Asao, Dennis Bartok (American Cinematheque), Peter Beckman, Jeff Briggs, Mila and Antonio Carlin, Andy Chua, Ned Comstock (University of Southern California Cinema-Television Library), Bill and Satoko Ferguson (Neptune Media), Carlos A. Gutierrez (Mexican Cultural Institute), Barbara Hall (the Margret Herrick Library of the Academy of Motion Picture Arts & Sciences), Phil Hallman (University of Michigan), Yoshikazu Ishii, Anne Kaneko, Kurando Mitsutake, Aleks Nelson, Christopher Potter, David W. Renwick, Luisa Ribeiro, Donna Ross and the UCLA Arts Library Special Collections, Takefusa Sano (NHK), Scarecrow Press, Gary Teetzel (M-G-M), Ichiro Takase (Shochiku Films of America, Inc.), Brad Warner and Atsushi Saito (Tsuburaya Productions), and Faye Wong.

Finally, my thanks to those persons who worked with Mr. Kurosawa and Mr. Mifune, whose interviews are really the heart of this book: Tak Abe, Donna Kei Benz, Richard Fleischer, the late Yu Fujiki, Kinji Fukasaku, the late Jun Fukuda, Eiji Funakoshi, Akira Hakube, Mie Hama, Shinobu

Hashimoto, Kaizo Hayashi, Kimi Honda, Yuriko Hoshi, Akira Ifukube, Mike Y. Inoue, Mr. and Mrs. Jerry Ito, Kyoko Kagawa, Takeshi Kato, Yuzo Kayama, the late Momoko Kochi, Hiroshi Koizumi, Takashi Koizumi, Tsugunobu "Tom" Kotani, Akira Kubo, Hisao Kurosawa, Shue Matsubayashi, Tatsuo Matsumura, Shiro Mifune, Rentaro Mikuni, Kumi Mizuno, Yoshiro Muraki, Mie Nakao, Minoru Nakano, Yosuke Natsuki, Terumi Niki, Kazuto Ohira, Mariko Okada, Kihachi Okamoto, Tomio Sagisu (P Production), Kenji Sahara, the late Henry G. Saperstein, the late Masaru Sato, Yoko Sugi, Akira Takarada, Senkichi Taniguchi and Kaoru Yachigusa (Taniguchi), Akira Terao, Yoshio Tsuchiya, Hitoshi Ueki, Yoji Yamada, Michio Yamamoto, Noriaki Yuasa, Izumi Yukimura, Charlie Ziarko, and Yoshitaka Zushi.

THE EMPEROR

AND THE WOLF

INTRODUCTION

When Akira Kurosawa died on September 6, 1998, tributes to the director of *Rashomon*, *Seven Samurai*, and *Yojimbo* poured in from around the world. Steven Spielberg called him "the pictorial Shakespeare of our time,"[1] while Martin Scorsese noted, "His influence is so profound as to be almost incomparable. There is no one else like him." In a eulogy he wrote for *Time*, Scorsese added, "[He was] one of the great treasures of film history."[2]

When asked to name his favorite Kurosawa film for a Japanese video documentary, an amused Francis Ford Coppola said, "Well, so many of them are great, I mean, you could ask yourself which are the great ones, and which are merely very, very excellent."[3]

At Kurosawa Production in Yokohama, 4,000 friends, relatives, and colleagues had been invited to a memorial service to be delivered from the "Gold Room" set left standing from *Ran*.

Thirty-five thousand showed up.

Reporters frantically covered the steady procession of famous faces entering and leaving the late director's studio. Tatsuya Nakadai, the star of *Kagemusha* and *Ran*, who had gotten his start as an extra in *Seven Samurai* forty-five years earlier, wistfully recalled his last conversation with the director—they had talked, he said, of doing one last picture together. Filmmaker Nagisa Oshima was there; the "New Wave" director whose own visionary, radical work had helped unseat Kurosawa in the eyes of many Japanese critics was now frail himself and distraught before reporters: "He looked like he had reached a heavenly peace . . . I respected Mr. Kurosawa for his lifetime devotion to his work."[4]

"Kurosawa's death marks the end of an era, but we must carry on," said director Nobuhiko Obayashi, as if rallying after a natural catastrophe. "He was a father figure in the world of film."[5]

Spielberg told a Japanese news service, "I'm not sure [that there are any other] contemporary filmmakers from the Golden Age of Filmmaking who [were] ever great in their late seventies."[6] In his eulogy Scorsese had marveled how, at eighty-two, Kurosawa was still climbing ladders on his sets. In his seventies and eighties he had, amazingly, directed five noteworthy, increasingly meditative features.

But the Kurosawa so admired in the West had been, it was perceived, all but rejected by his own country for most of the last three decades. After his falling out with star Toshiro Mifune—with whom he made most of his best films—the box-office failure of *Dodes'ka-den* (1970), and a subsequent suicide attempt, an unfathomable dichotomy lingered about the worth of his later works.

Who was this man who ruled his sets with such autocratism he was nicknamed *Tenno*, the Japanese word for "emperor"? In his 1982 *Something Like an Autobiography*, Kurosawa himself wrote: "I believe that what pertains only to myself is not interesting enough to record and leave behind me. More important is my conviction that if I were to write anything at all, it would turn out to be nothing but talk about movies. In other words, take 'myself,' subtract 'movies,' and the result is 'zero.' "[7]

But the life of Akira Kurosawa and the actor with whom he is most closely associated is fraught with drama and mystery. Why, for example, did Kurosawa and Mifune end their artistically lucrative collaboration? And how could the subsequent careers of these two giants of world cinema come crashing down so completely in the 1970s? Why did Kurosawa's two Hollywood projects fall apart so disastrously? Why, in 1971, did Kurosawa try to kill himself? How could, as the Western media claimed, the Japanese so reject the later work of this master filmmaker in light of the nearly unanimous acclaim he received in every other corner of the globe? Was it his increasingly expressionist style? Was it Japanese resentment of his Western influences?

As for Mifune (pronounced "Mee-foo-nay"), if his screen persona and fame express, as writer Michael Atkinson argues, "postwar ideas of Japanese-ness—'inscrutable,' unscrupulous, and ready for battle,"[8] how did (or could) the real Mifune measure up, and how did he cope with the unenviable task of symbolizing, for the rest of the world, the postwar Japanese ideal?

In the West very little is known about Mifune's personal and professional life; incredibly, until now an English-language biography did not exist. Newspapers and magazine articles reported only that he grew up in Manchuria, China, born of Japanese parents, and didn't set foot on Japanese soil until he was twenty years old. He became an actor almost by accident: an aerial photographer during World War II, Mifune went to Toho Studios after the war hoping to get a job as an assistant cameraman. Somehow he wound up applying to the studio's "New Face Contest," and was nearly rejected by a panel of judges who were insulted by the actor's apparent disrespect. Actress Hideko Takamine, director Kajiro Yamamoto (Kurosawa's mentor), and Kurosawa himself saw a raw and unusual talent in this obstinate, unpretentious wanderer. He achieved stardom with Kurosawa's *Drunken Angel* (1948), in what was just his third film. It was as if he had sprung out of nowhere, a concept the actor perpetuated in almost every interview he ever gave.

Most of Mifune's 126 features and 17 television films have had little or no distribution in the United States. Outside of a handful of films he did for director Hiroshi Inagaki (the "Samurai" trilogy), Mifune's career in Japan is singularly linked to the sixteen films he did for Kurosawa. Sadly, American media coverage upon his death focused less on his pictures with Kurosawa than on his co-starring role in the American miniseries *Shogun* opposite Richard Chamberlain. His films for other great directors like Kenji Mizoguchi, Kihachi Okamoto, Yoji Yamada, and Masaki Kobayashi were virtually ignored.

For many in the press, Mifune was an Asian knockoff of the Duke (indeed, he was frequently referred to as "the Japanese John Wayne"), trading in six-shooters for a sword and becoming the archetypal screen samurai in these "Japanese Westerns." As Clyde Haberman wrote in *The New York Times*: "Just as Wayne at some point stopped being merely an actor who knew how to get on a horse and became *the* American cowboy, so Mr. Mifune is *the* shogun, an image that people in the Japanese film world believe he likes to encourage."[9] Clint Eastwood, who became a star parroting Mifune's moves in Sergio Leone's remake of *Yojimbo*, *Fistful of Dollars*, readily acknowledges Mifune's influence: "[He] was definitely an inspiration for me. He will always be the great samurai for us."[10] The comparisons between Mifune and Wayne, though, were usually grossly overstated and unconsidered, and Mifune himself once said, "John Wayne was a *real* star—a giant. He loomed so large. I'm just stardust at his feet."[11]

Nevertheless, no other Japanese actor is as well known in the West. John Belushi's uncanny imitation of Mifune's *Yojimbo* character on *Saturday*

Night Live seemed less a parody than a tribute from a longtime fan. In an appreciation for *The Washington Post*, writer Stephen Hunter said, "Whether or not his name was instantly recognizable, [Mifune] was a movie star like no other."[12]

Mifune himself liked to say, "I'm not always great in pictures, but I'm always true to the Japanese spirit," and a 1984 poll in a Japanese magazine named Mifune "the most Japanese man."[13] But this also dismisses some of his best work. A chameleonlike thespian more akin to De Niro, Jack Nicholson, or Marcello Mastroianni, Mifune was equally at home in contemporary roles, perhaps best personified as company executives in *High and Low* and *The Bad Sleep Well*. Writer Michael Jeck recalled how a college classmate had attended a Kurosawa/Mifune double bill of *The Lower Depths* and *Record of a Living Being*. In the latter film Mifune, then thirty-five, starred as a seventy-year-old man obsessed with fear of a nuclear holocaust. When Jeck enthusiastically asked his classmate how he liked Mifune's performance, the classmate replied, "Oh, was he in [that one, too]?' "[14]

This is understandable, for few actors (when given good direction) had the range or intensity of Toshiro Mifune. He has played an automotive mogul and a mechanic, a Mexican peasant, lowly Army privates and celebrated Imperial Navy admirals. As a swaggering samurai wannabe in *Seven Samurai*, Mifune is alternately foolish, courageous, incredulous, outrageous, and ultimately almost unbearably tragic. Contrasting this rigorously physical role is *High and Low*, with Mifune the wealthy executive who must decide whether to sacrifice his life's earnings—at a time when he needs his powerful resources most—to save his chauffeur's son from a psychotic kidnapper. In this role, Mifune displays all the excruciating complexities of this difficult decision almost entirely visually. No face was more expressive, no actor more economical. (Mifune would have been a huge star in silent films.)

As Mifune's power rose in Japan, he formed his own company, Mifune Productions, which co-financed many of his later starring features, twenty in all. He opened an acting school and even directed a film, *The Legacy of the 500,000* (1963). He went to Mexico to star in *The Important Man* (1961), and his bankability outside Japan led to offers to appear in films made all over the world.

In his forties, Mifune tried unsuccessfully to shed his hard-drinking, off-screen image for one more business-like, though like Frank Sinatra he remained the epitome of hip machismo for the rest of his life. Despite his marriage in 1950 and two sons, Mifune openly had a longtime mistress nearly half his age, with whom he fathered a daughter while in his sixties. His subsequent separation from his first wife resulted in a tabloid free-for-all echoing his 1950 film for Kurosawa on yellow journalism, *Scandal*. The 1980s and '90s saw the actor receiving nearly every international award possible: his office was littered with prizes from around the world, including an Emmy nomination and an honorary degree from UCLA (Laurence Olivier was the only other actor so honored). Amid rumors of Alzheimer's disease and failing physical health, the actor continued working, taking small roles in small films like *Picture Bride* (1994) and *Deep River* (1995), and while he was clearly dying—in the latter film he is shockingly gaunt and aged—his commanding screen presence never diminished.

Toshiro Mifune starred in sixteen of Akira Kurosawa's thirty films. No pairing—neither Buñuel and Fernando Rey nor Ingmar Bergman and Max von Sydow, nor Scorsese and De Niro—can match their incredible track record. (Director Yasujiro Ozu and actor Chishu Ryu in some ways eclipse Kurosawa and Mifune in terms of their cinematic output, but Ryu's roles were typically less central to Ozu's films.) And just as Kurosawa has influenced several generations of directors and screenwriters, Mifune's screen persona paved the way for thirty years' worth of roaming, warrior rogues. Could there have been a Clint Eastwood or a Harrison Ford or a Chow Yun-Fat without Mifune?

In my interviews with actors, directors, and others who worked with Mifune, the actor's offscreen personality is often likened to that of a wolf or a lion. Like Kurosawa, Mifune was a heavy drinker, and much like the characters he often played, he was, certainly in his early years, outsized and larger-than-life. Reviewing his performance in *Rashomon*, *The* (London) *Times* wrote: "Toshiro Mifune capers about the screen like a ferocious, demented Puck, bellowing with maniacal laughter."[15] Though his performances were largely instinctive, he was also the consummate professional; always thoroughly prepared, he brought a quiet intensity to every set.

Kurosawa, who rarely admitted an admiration for film actors, was amazed by Mifune's uncanny ability to generate rich characterizations from the most economic of gestures. "Mifune had a kind of talent I had never encountered before in the Japanese film world," he said in his autobiography. "It was, above all, the speed with which he expressed himself that was astounding. The ordinary Japanese actor might need ten feet of film to get across an impression; Mifune needed only three feet."[16] Coupled with his amazing talent were his rugged, working-class good looks and virile, fierce demeanor at a time when most leading men in Japanese films had delicate,

even androgynous features. Against such competition, Mifune was exhila-
ratingly, refreshingly magnetic, and he became a screen idol almost
overnight.

As his popularity rose, Mifune was threatened with typecasting in gangster parts, but Kurosawa, recognizing his talent, cast him in a wide range of
roles. Yet at the very height of their abilities, Kurosawa and Mifune went
their separate ways. After *Red Beard* in 1965 they never worked together
again. "[Kurosawa] still has a lot of energy and spirit," Mifune said in 1983,
"and I'd like to do two or three films [with him] before he goes on to another world."[17] But it was not to be. And though he would star in a few interesting Japanese features here and there, Mifune spent much of the rest
of his career adding class to an array of inferior Japanese "epics," or frittering away his talents in small roles in mediocre international productions
like *Inchon!* (1982) and *Shadow of the Wolf* (1993). As Mifune complained to
the *Los Angeles Times*, "In the Japanese society, they're all young people now.
They do not have the intellectual level for that sort of film. They are into
rock groups. All they do is watch television."[18]

Kashiko Kawakita, the late director of the Kawakita Memorial Film Library in Japan, told *The New York Times* in 1982, "[Mifune] is gifted, but without Kurosawa he has not performed as well. He has many concerns, with
his business interests, and in a way it is a pity. He cannot concentrate on his
acting as much."[19] Despite some bright moments, his later years sadly
echoed those of other great actors like Olivier, Orson Welles, and Henry
Fonda, who cheapened their body of work by trading in on their fame with
hopes of financing other, better films or building up their estates for their
families. To raise cash, both Mifune and Kurosawa wound up pitching beer,
whiskey, mattresses, and pharmaceutical products in Japanese television
commercials.

Like Mifune, Kurosawa had been lured to the West, to direct his script
of *Runaway Train* for B-movie mogul Joseph E. Levine, and subsequently the
Japanese half of an initially ambitious filming of the attack on Pearl Harbor:
Tora! Tora! Tora! (1970). Both films were eventually made without Kurosawa. 20th Century-Fox, the studio that produced the impressively
mounted, yet generally artless war film, viciously blamed Kurosawa's departure on mental illness. These accusations only seemed to be confirmed
after the box-office failure of his next film, *Dodes'ka-den*, and the director's
subsequent suicide attempt.

Partly because his films were so expensive (by Japanese standards), it
took the financial assistance of the Soviet Union to produce his next film,

Dersu Uzala, and the intervention and financial assurance of George Lucas and Francis Ford Coppola to make *Kagemusha* five years later. And though these films, as well as the French-financed *Ran*, won numerous international awards and proved popular worldwide, the director seemingly could not escape has-been status in his own country. For many Japanese critics, Kurosawa simply had nothing new or substantial left to say. This attitude culminated in 1985, when, in spite of the resounding success of *Ran*, Japan's Movie Producers Association appeared to snub the director, submitting another film as Japan's official entry in the Foreign Film category in that year's Oscar race. An outcry from the Directors Guild of America led to a grass-roots nomination for Kurosawa as Best Director, but by then the damage had already been done.

Kurosawa and Mifune died less than nine months apart, and in the West, obituaries and tributes likened their work, as had been the case for decades, to American Westerns. But their films together, and many of those done separately, strike much deeper. Kurosawa's films were, first and foremost, deeply humanist pictures, films which effortlessly transcended cultures and centuries.

Coppola's distinction between Kurosawa's great works and those that were "merely very, very excellent" is not inappropriate. For a filmmaker to produce one great work is an achievement, but Akira Kurosawa co-wrote and directed a dozen such masterpieces, and even his weakest films have moments of superb craftsmanship and inventiveness. The late John Kobal's 1988 poll of international film critics for his book *Top 100 Movies*, which attempted to rank the greatest films ever made, not only found *Rashomon* placing 10, *Seven Samurai* at 24, and *Ikiru* at 34, but *Dodes'ka-den*, *Kagemusha*, *High and Low*, and *Ran* were also nominated by Kobal's panel. *Drunken Angel* (1948), *Stray Dog* (1949), *Throne of Blood* and *The Lower Depths* (both 1957), *The Hidden Fortress* (1958), *Sanjuro* (1962), and *Dersu Uzala* (1975) are similarly regarded as masterworks.[20]

This is the first English-language biography of Kurosawa (or Mifune, for that matter), something long overdue. Kurosawa's films have been written about extensively, Donald Richie's *The Films of Akira Kurosawa* being the best example. Richie's book, along with his writings on director Yasujiro Ozu, represent what is probably the most thorough, thoughtful analysis of any single director's oeuvre. By design, however, Richie did not (nor has anyone else) detail the production history of his films, especially the unfinished projects; provide background on his collaborators or his relationships with various studios; examine his place within the Japanese film industry as a whole, the financing, budgets and grosses of his films; provide information on his career as an assistant director and screenwriter; or detail the peripheral projects. He did not explore how Kurosawa's films came to be shown abroad, their critical reception in and outside Japan, the deeply personal impact he had on those he was closest to, or the reaction of those who saw his films when they were new. These aspects, until now, have been largely ignored. The director himself penned *Something Like an Autobiography* (published in the United States in 1982), but for personal reasons he chose to tell his life's story only up through the year 1950, stopping at the very moment he first won international acclaim and began the most fruitful period of his career. Mifune, on the other hand, has been almost completely ignored: many of the films covered in this book have never been discussed in the West, and his career beyond his work with Kurosawa has never been written about at any length.

Every biography of an artist assumes the primacy of his role as an author/auteur, but this book deliberately avoids placing Kurosawa's work in the context of the auteur theory. With the possible exception of Chaplin, no director exerted more control over every aspect of his work than Kurosawa, yet like all great filmmakers, Kurosawa relied on a handful of collaborators (especially his co-screenwriters and assistants like Teruyo Nogami and Ishiro Honda, to say nothing of his art directors, actors, and composers) to make his films what they are. Likewise, I deliberately avoid other branches of cultural theory set down by the likes of Noël Burch, Jean-Louis Baudry, Laura Mulvey, or *Cahiers du Cinéma*.

I very much wanted to interview Mifune and Kurosawa, but by the time I first went to Japan in late 1994, Mifune was already in poor health. Again like Sinatra, his hard living had finally caught up to him, and rumors of an Alzheimer's-like senility were flying in the Japanese media.

I had arranged an interview with Kurosawa through the widow of one of his closest and oldest friends, the director Ishiro Honda, who had known Kurosawa since the mid-1930s. But when the time came, the great director, already in his mid-eighties, was too ill to receive me. When I returned in 1996, another interview was set up, but again Kurosawa canceled at the last minute. Ultimately, my one, brief, but rewarding interview was conducted over a fax machine a few months later, through the kindness of his daughter.

All was not lost, however, as nearly all the forty-five or so actors, directors, and other artisans I interviewed on these early trips had worked with Kurosawa, Mifune, or both at some point in their own careers and had a lot to say on the subject. These interviews laid the groundwork for this book.

Kurosawa's best films transcend motion picture art—he was one of the few filmmakers whose work has an almost religious effect on moviegoers. Surely one of his greatest films, *Ikiru*, about a dying government worker coming to terms with his own life and death, is, for many, a life-changing experience. For all the praise heaped on his films by critics and film theorists who admire his use of color, telephoto lenses, editing, staging, and multiple cameras, nearly all fail to mention the deeply personal impact of his films. Writer Bill Warren ran into Kurosawa and his interpreter in front of the library of the Academy of Motion Picture Arts & Sciences. He was so overcome during this unexpected meeting that he soon realized that, as his admiration for the director poured out (while remembering the many hard years Kurosawa had endured), tears were streaming down Warren's face. When he noticed that the interpreter wasn't translating anything, he asked why. The interpreter's response: "He knows exactly what you're saying."[21]

This impact has never been explored before in an English-language book and is something which has been ignored even by Japanese film scholars like Donald Richie. In 1990 Richie admitted to writer James Bailey, "Do I feel anything emotional about his films, anything warm? No, not very much. My problem I think is I have become so closely associated with him in people's minds and in actual fact I'm not close. Nobody is. He has a great use for people, men and women, who are of use to him. He is a born user, like Orson Welles or von Stroheim. He's very much like the both of them."[22] But just as there are many who find in Kurosawa's films a visceral, sometimes epiphanic profundity, there are those for whom the impact of working closely with him, the emotional bond, was equally strong.

It has been said that in Alfred Hitchcock's films, Cary Grant represented an idealized facet of Hitchcock's own personality, while James Stewart depicted the director's darker side. Similarly, John Ford and François Truffaut had paternal working and personal relationships with John Wayne and Jean-Pierre Léaud, respectively. The bond between Kurosawa and Mifune was similar and no less strong. As Richard Corliss said of Mifune, which could just as easily apply to Kurosawa, "In a society of soft voices and deep bows, [he] played the insurrectionist, an explosion of ego and id. [He] was a one-man action film . . . [His] display of mercurial moods—sinking into mopery, then geysering into rage—made the audience feel that this, for better or worse, is a man."[23]

For many, this writer included, Kurosawa was a *sensei*, a teacher, perhaps self-consciously so in his later films, whose life lessons influenced not just other filmmakers but moviegoers around the world, regardless of class, race, and cultures. For Kurosawa, Toshiro Mifune was less an alter ego than an instrument through which his screenplays were best interpreted. Their faith in one another resulted in their own self-discovery. In this work, it is my hope to uncover the essence of these two great artists.

ONE

FRAGMENTS

One of the effects of the Second World War, often overlooked by those in North America and other parts of the world who emerged relatively unscathed, was the devastating loss of history. Centuries-old buildings of great architectural beauty were bombed out of existence, paintings by great Masters were reduced to ashes. Thousands of motion pictures, all produced and stored on highly flammable nitrate stock, ignited into white-hot bursts of fire and were lost forever. Historical documents—birth certificates, college diplomas, medical records, real estate certificates, bank accounts, personal letters and photographs—were lost as well.

In the last year of the war Japan was pummeled nearly out of existence. Allied forces began dropping their bombs on June 15, 1944, from B-29 Superfortresses flying out of bases in the Mariana Islands. By early 1945 each plane was able to drop up to 10 tons of explosives, and as many as 600 bombers might take part in a single attack. Special incendiary bombs were developed that created firestorms on their targets that were extremely difficult to extinguish. Yokohama, the port city adjacent to Tokyo, was almost completely destroyed in a single attack, and it took just three major raids to flatten the heart of Tokyo. Before the dropping of the atomic bombs on Hiroshima and Nagasaki, upward of a thousand Allied planes were making daily runs. By the war's end, sixty of the country's predominantly industrial cities were annihilated. A million and a half Japanese soldiers were killed, and several generations of men were nearly wiped out. The number of civilian casualties was never accurately determined because all records of the civilian dead had been destroyed in the bombings.

Akira Kurosawa, Toshiro Mifune, and their families were not excepted. Kurosawa lived in the Ebisu section of Shibuya-ku, Tokyo, during the war, and when the Allied bombing intensified, he moved to the relative calm of the western suburb of Setagaya, near Toho Studios, where he was employed. The next day his house went up in flames, and his wedding photos were lost less than twenty-four hours after he was married.

Mifune was born and raised in China. The relative peace of his childhood was turned upside down after the Japanese invaded Manchuria in 1931, and the discord accelerated when fighting broke out on July 7, 1937, at the Marco Polo Bridge in Peiping; then the atrocities against Chinese citizens began in earnest. He spent more than five years in the Japanese Imperial Air Force, and though he avoided combat, he nonetheless lost many friends during the war and trained countless others for what was certain death. When the fighting ended and he was discharged, Mifune was left with nothing but the clothes on his back.

Records of the early lives of Akira Kurosawa and Toshiro Mifune are fragmentary. Until they began their respective film careers, both at the age of twenty-six, their histories are composed mainly of their own personal recollections. Most of their relatives, including all of Kurosawa's siblings, are dead, and their classmates are deceased or scattered across Asia. In the books on Kurosawa and Mifune published in Japan after their deaths, information on their early lives remains scant. The majority of what I have written about Kurosawa's childhood and early adult years, for example, has been reprinted from the anecdotes he compiled for his autobiography. As for Mifune, he rarely discussed his childhood; his years before joining Toho Studios have, even in Japanese books about him, been passed over in as little as a sentence or two. Following are the fragments which remain.

Akira Kurosawa was born on March 23, 1910, in Oi-cho, in the Omori district of Tokyo. He was the youngest child of Isamu* and Shima Kurosawa. His mother, Shima, from a merchant's family in Osaka, was forty years old when Kurosawa was born, and Isamu was five years her senior. Isamu had been born in Toyokawa Village, a remote, northern community in the Senboku-gun district of Akita Prefecture. The Kurosawas were a family of

---

*Not Yutaka, as reported elsewhere.

former samurai, and Isamu had worked at the Army's Physical Education Institute. By the time Akira was born, Isamu was the director of its junior high school. There he established facilities for training in the martial arts, including judo and *kendo* swordfighting. He embraced Western athletics as well, including baseball, and oversaw the construction of what may have been Japan's first swimming pool.[1]

The Kurosawa family was not poor. They had a servant in their household, and might have been considered wealthy if not for Isamu's many dependents. Akira, the youngest sibling, had three older brothers (one of whom died before he was born) and four older sisters, Shigeyo, Haruyo, Taneyo, and Momoyo. At the time of Akira's birth, his oldest brother and sister were already adults, living outside the home and starting families of their own; Kurosawa spent his youth with the three younger sisters and his older brother Heigo, who was born in 1906.

Akira Kurosawa began school in April 1916, at Morimura Kindergarten in Shimagawa. His earliest recollection of seeing motion pictures dates from that same year. Kurosawa was raised in the Taisho period (1912–26), an era of unusual openness toward the West, when Soviet literature, European modernism, and American moviemaking began to seep into the lives of Japanese citizens. Kurosawa's father viewed these foreign influences with an open mind, especially motion pictures. "Looking back and reflecting on it," Kurosawa wrote, "I think my father's attitude toward films reinforced my own inclinations and encouraged me to become what I am today. He was a strict man of military background, but at a time when the idea of watching movies was hardly well received in educators' circles, he took his whole family to the movies regularly. Later in more reactionary times he steadfastly maintained his conviction that going to the movies has an educational value; he never changed."[2]

The following year Kurosawa entered Morimura Gakuen Elementary. He found his first years of schooling miserable. "I don't like to think I was a retarded child," he wrote, "but it is a fact I was slow."[3] This changed after his family moved to 6 Nishi, Edogawa-cho, Koishikawa-ku, also in Tokyo, in August 1918, upon his father's retirement.[4] The following month Kurosawa was transferred to the Kuroda Primary School, where he met one of the first big influences on his life, a sympathetic, progressive teacher named Seiji Tachikawa, who saw in the young boy an intelligence and talent waiting to be nurtured. It was he who helped Kurosawa discover a love of drawing, and his two years as Kurosawa's mentor made a lifelong impact.

Two other important relationships blossomed during Kurosawa's Kuroda Primary School days. He became friends with another young boy, Keinosuke Uekusa, later a famous playwright and occasional collaborator on Kurosawa's early screenplays, in whom Kurosawa saw a mirror image of his own, forming personality.

At the same time, he was drawn closer to his older brother Heigo, who would look after him during recess and who impressed him with his intelligence during their long walks to school. Heigo was gifted yet self-destructive and darkly cynical, more adult than child, even in his early teens. He placed third in the Tokyo-wide academic-ability examination given to all fifth-grade primary-school students, and first the following year, but failed a middle-school entrance examination for the top-ranked, state-controlled middle school, which would have ensured his future and won him a place at the prestigious Tokyo Imperial University.

Heigo "seemed willing to throw his academic career to the winds," Kurosawa wrote. Heigo chose instead to pursue an intense love of foreign literature, but outside of the formal requirements of academia. His relationship with his father became strained, and Kurosawa could only watch as his brother grew more and more estranged from his family.

In 1920, when Kurosawa was ten years old, his youngest sister, Momoyo, died suddenly after a brief illness. "Little Big Sister," as he called her, "was the prettiest of my three sisters who lived at home, and she was almost too gentle and kind. Her beauty was something of a glass-like transparency, delicate and fragile, offering no resistance. When my brother fell off the balance beams and injured his head at school, it was this sister who sobbed and said she wanted to die in his place. Even as I write about her now, my eyes burn with tears and I keep having to blow my nose."[5] Memories of this youngest sister were later to be reflected in "The Peach Orchard" segment of his 1990 film *Dreams*.

As he settled into his new school, young Kurosawa's confidence grew. He became captain of the school's *kendo* club and that same year began taking Japanese calligraphy lessons after school at his father's insistence.

When he was thirteen, he graduated from the Kuroda Primary School and in April 1923 entered Keika Junior High School. But five months into the school year, on September 1, 1923, Tokyo and Yokohama were devastated by the Great Kanto Earthquake, in which more than 100,000 people died. Kurosawa was in the street near his house when it struck and grabbed onto a telephone pole as the earth violently shook beneath him. "[It] was a terrifying experience for me," Kurosawa wrote, "and also an extremely important one. Through it I learned not only of the extraordinary powers of nature, but extraordinary things that lie in human beings."[6] It was here he saw "the ability of fear to drive people off the course of human behavior," especially as a witness to the massacre of Korean residents by mobs of racist Tokyoites who blamed them for the earthquake.

As the dust began to settle, Heigo took the young Akira out to inspect the ruins of central Tokyo. "Amid this expanse of nauseating redness lay every kind of corpse imaginable. I saw corpses charred black, half-burned corpses, corpses in gutters, corpses floating in rivers, corpses piled up on bridges, corpses blocking off a whole street at an intersection, and every manner of death possible to human beings displayed by corpses. When I involuntarily looked away, my brother scolded me, 'Akira, look carefully now.'"[7]

When he returned home, Kurosawa was prepared for a sleepless night, or perhaps one plagued with unspeakable nightmares. Neither happened. "This seemed so strange to me that I asked my brother how it could have come about. 'If you shut your eyes to a frightening sight, you end up being frightened. If you look at everything straight on, there is nothing to be afraid of.' Looking back on that excursion now, I realize that it must have been horrifying for my brother too. It had been an expedition to conquer fear."[8]

Throughout the 1920s and early '30s, Kurosawa pursued his love of literature and painting, and he wrote essays that were published in his class magazine. He became a leading student in these fields, while failing in subjects such as mathematics and compulsory military training.

At the same time, the economic growth Japan had enjoyed in the 1910s gave way to runaway inflation and industrial unrest in the 1920s. The Great Kanto Earthquake was preceded by nationwide rice riots. Takashi Hara, leader of the "Taisho Democracy," was assassinated, and as older Meiji-era statesmen died off, the country became conservative and militaristic. Kurosawa's father, though a military man and an anti-socialist, was appalled by the changes that were taking place. He was horrified by the 1923 murder of anarchist Sakae Osugi by militant extremists and the 1928 assassination of Manchurian warlord Chang Tso-lin by Japanese Army officers, along with the subsequent arrest of Japanese Communist Party members.

Kurosawa might well have been pressed into military service himself if not for the sympathetic Army physician who remembered and respected his father. Upon his conscription examination in 1930, Kurosawa received the Japanese equivalent of 4-F status. Deemed physically unfit, he was never drafted, even in the last, desperate days of the Pacific War, when young boys and old men were pulled into active duty. "I often wonder what would have happened if I had actually been drafted," Kurosawa reflected in his autobiography. "I had failed military training in middle school, and I had no certificate of officer's competence. There would have been no way for me to stay afloat in the Army. . . . Even thinking about it now makes me shudder. I have that officer who administered the Army physical to thank for sparing me. Or maybe I should say I have my father to thank."[9]

But as Japan slipped further into economic depression, his family's finances grew worse, and they moved again, this time to the Ebisu section of Shibuya, in Tokyo. Only gradually did it dawn on Kurosawa that each time his family moved, it was invariably to a smaller house, reflecting the worsening of their fortunes. In the late 1920s, oblivious to their situation, Kurosawa had decided that he wanted to become a painter. His father did not discourage him, but insisted he apply to art school. Kurosawa resisted such formal training, though, and failed to pass the entrance examination for the one art school to which he applied.[10]

During this time, he began fully embracing the arts, especially Japanese and Western theater and motion pictures. He prowled art galleries, and in 1929 he joined the Proletarian Artists' League. He contributed to a radical newspaper and was nearly arrested on several occasions. In spite of his dangerous activities, he never considered himself a Communist. "I had tried reading *Das Kapital* and theories of dialectic materialism," he wrote, "but there had been much that I couldn't understand. For me to try to analyze and explain Japanese society from that point of view was therefore impossible. I simply felt the vague dissatisfaction and dislikes that Japanese society encouraged, and in order to contend with these feelings, I had joined the most radical movement I could find. Looking back on it now, my behavior seems terribly frivolous and reckless."[11] He was quickly disenchanted with their politicking of the arts, and it proved to be a brief flirtation, lasting until the spring of 1932, when he drifted away from the movement completely.

In the late 1920s, Heigo took up a career as a *benshi*, or silent-film narrator. *Benshi* was an art form all its own, and in their day *benshi* frequently received better billing than the pictures they narrated. Indeed, *benshi* leaders like Musei Tokugawa were stars in their own right, earning fees comparable to those of Japan's leading film actors. Joseph Anderson and Donald Richie, in their book *The Japanese Film—Art and Industry*, contend that the popularity of the *benshi* in Japan and not in the West was partly due to a Japanese need for explicit definition. "The Japanese, then as now," they wrote, "were constantly afraid of missing the point, of not understanding everything, and demanded a complete explanation. This the *benshi* gave them, usually expanding his services to the extent of explaining the obvious."[12] They point to the continuing influence of *benshi* long after their passing—for instance, all the sign-language scenes in *The Man of a Thousand Faces* (1957) were subtitled, and in Jacques-Yves Cousteau and Louis Malle's *Le Monde du silence* (1956), the names of all the sea life were superimposed, "even in the straight lyrical sequences where there was no narration at all. The fact that the titles were so scientific that very few in the audience could even read them disturbed no one."[13] Similarly, it was the Japanese who established the practice, in war movies, of superimposing the names and titles of military leaders on the screen as characters are introduced, a practice which continues to this day.

Heigo rose quickly through their ranks, yet, in spite of his growing fame, he chose to live in slumlike conditions similar to those later reflected in Kurosawa's 1957 film *The Lower Depths*. Kurosawa subsequently moved in with his brother, and the two became inseparable. But the darker side of Heigo's personality increased with the coming of talking pictures and the gradual firing of *benshi* nationwide.

Led by Heigo, the dwindling number of active *benshi* went on strike. When the strike failed, Heigo, who had always told his family he would die before the age of thirty, attempted suicide. Soon thereafter, on July 7, 1933, he treated Kurosawa to dinner, and afterward the two young men said their goodbyes in a taxi in front of the Shin Okubo train station. Heigo went up the steps, turned, and walked back to the taxi. "I got out of the cab and walked over to him," wrote Kurosawa, who asked his brother, " 'What is it?' He looked at me very hard for a moment and then said, 'Nothing. You can go now.' He turned back and went back up the stairs. The next time I saw him he was covered with a bloody sheet."[14]

On July 10, Heigo ended his life at a hot springs inn on the Izu Peninsula. (Exactly how Heigo took his life is unknown, though it is generally assumed he slashed his wrists and throat, as his brother would nearly forty years later.)* Kurosawa and his father, along with another relative, went there to retrieve the body and have it cremated. Kurosawa was inconsolable. Four months later, his oldest brother, Masayasu, died too, leaving

*According to Senkichi Taniguchi, a longtime colleague of Kurosawa's, Heigo committed double suicide with a woman, presumably a lover. While this has not been confirmed, it suggests that perhaps Heigo's suicide was not prompted by the failure of the *benshi* strikes at all.

Kurosawa his family's only surviving son. His ambitions to become an artist had gone almost nowhere, and he began to have doubts about his abilities. The economy and his personal finances were so bad he could not even afford paints and canvases. Japan had invaded China, and political turmoil was brewing all over the world.

Kurosawa spent the next two years aimless about his future. Then, one day in late 1935, he saw an ad in a newspaper that would change the direction of his life. Photo Chemical Laboratories (or, as it was known, P.C.L.), a new film studio, was hiring assistant directors.

Toshiro Mifune, who late in life earned the title "the most Japanese man," was actually born in China on April 1, 1920. His parents were Japanese nationals living in Tsingtao (now Qingdao, and pronounced *Ching dow*), a port and manufacturing city of 500,000 on the Yellow Sea, in the Shantung region of central eastern China, about midway between Shanghai and Tientsin. The southern tip of Korea stood between Tsingtao and the Japanese mainland, about 500 miles to the east.

Much of the city had been built late in the nineteenth century by German settlers, who developed it for the coal resources nearby. In 1914, after the start of World War I, the Japanese invaded Tsingtao and took control of the city. The Japanese built and operated cotton textile mills there, but in 1922, when Mifune was two years old, the Japanese agreed to return Tsingtao and the rest of Shantung to China. Mifune grew up in a Japanese enclave and had little contact with the Chinese people themselves, though according to Akira Takarada, another Toho star born in China to Japanese parents, Mifune did speak Mandarin.

Mifune was the oldest son of Tokuzo and Sen Mifune. Their family was small compared to Kurosawa's; Mifune had a younger brother, Yoshiro, and a sister, Kimiko, his youngest sibling. Tokuzo Mifune was, like Kurosawa's father, originally from Akita Prefecture, at the edge of the Koshaisen Mountains near Yamagata Prefecture. Tokuzo's father was a physician specializing in herbal medicine and had sent his son to study medicine in Tokyo. But Tokuzo was drawn to the nascent world of still photography and emigrated to China instead.

Like Kurosawa's father, Tokuzo was already a middle-aged man, some forty-eight years old, when Mifune was born. Sen was Tokuzo's second wife after a childless marriage. Tokuzo owned his own business in Tsingtao, called Star Photography Studio (Star shashinken), and he earned his living not only as a portrait photographer, shooting Japanese neighbors, but also by selling photographs he took of the Chinese countryside, and he traveled to Europe during World War I to photograph the conflict there. He self-published one collection of his images in a 1910 book called *Views of Southern Manchuria*.[15] At least one more book, *Santo meisho shashincho*, was published in 1929.[16]

Mifune entered Dairen Junior High School in 1933 and graduated five years later. In school, he was adept at karate, archery, and swordsmanship. When he was a child, his father's business was good, with many employees working under Tokuzo, and Mifune spent much of his free time going to the movies. However, as worldwide economic depression spread in the 1930s, the family business foundered. Simultaneously, Mifune became interested in his father's work and helped around the studio. In 1938 the Japanese Army returned to Tsingtao, as part of their invasion of China, and held on to the city until the war's end. In March 1940, Mifune was drafted into the Japanese military, the Kanto Aviation Training Team in Manchuria. As the war escalated and the Japanese began planning their attack on Pearl Harbor, the Kanto Aviation Training Team was moved to Japan, to Yokaijo City in Shiga Prefecture.

And so, at the age of twenty-one, Toshiro Mifune set foot on Japanese soil for the first time, and his feelings of being a stranger in his feverishly nationalistic homeland were compounded by his father's death that same year. Mifune's experience with photographic equipment led to his assignment to an aerial photography unit instead of going headlong into combat. Like Kurosawa, Mifune was saved, albeit indirectly, by his father.

"During the war," said Shiro, Mifune's oldest son, "one of my father's superiors asked him to photograph his family. He did, and the superior really liked the result . . . and told my father to stay in the division because of his skills as a photographer. His buddies went to the front and died, but he was able to live because of that incident. He was sent to an aerial photography division that flew to the front and took pictures, from which maps were made."[17]

Shiro's account is supported by surviving photos of Mifune, his head shaved in a military-style crew cut, standing bravely next to a plane, wearing a flight suit and parachute, which suggests that he flew dangerous missions. But such was not the case.

One of the few survivors of that period is Tomio Sagisu, a draftee trained by Mifune who later became his closest and oldest friend. "Once he entered the Air Force he found the rules extremely hard," Sagisu said, "especially the Japanese Air Force, which was very strict. Some people killed themselves, some tried to escape. Of course, Mifune wasn't comfortable with the situation he found himself in and started to fight with his superiors. For someone in the service as long as he was—nearly six years—he should have been promoted, but because he was so rebellious, his rank stayed the same. The regulations in the service required that aerial photographers be a certain rank. The lower ranks took the film, developed it, and produced the reconnaissance maps, which is what he did."[18] Mifune, then, wasn't a flier but a ground engineer.

And because he had access to cameras and films, Mifune became something of a hustler, earning cash by taking pictures of his comrades wearing borrowed flight uniforms, to send back to their families. The photograph of Mifune standing boldly next to a Japanese fighter plane, Sagisu insists, was one he faked for himself, to send back home to his family. "He wasn't supposed to wear that pilot's uniform. He was hiding out, waiting until he could sneak near the plane and have his picture taken. In the days before he was an actor, he had lots of this still printed up and would autograph and give them to his comrades."[19]

P. C. L. AND YAMA-SAN

Photo Chemical Laboratories had been founded in 1929 by Yasuji Uemura. Originally, Uemura's plan was simply to provide laboratory services to the other burgeoning movie companies—Shinko, Nikkatsu, Shochiku—but with the coming of talking pictures in Japan in the early 1930s, P.C.L. expanded its operation, building soundstages and recording facilities, intending to rent them out to production companies struggling with the silent-to-sound transition. As the production of talkies increased, P.C.L. began making its own feature films, starting in 1933. These first films were made mainly to hawk the products of P.C.L.'s investors, which included the Meiji Candy Company and Dai-Nippon beer. It was for the latter that they produced their first feature, *Intoxicated Life* (Horoyoi jinsei), a 77-minute feature about the joys of beer drinking.

P.C.L. made just two films in 1933, but expanded to eight the following year, and double that in 1935. Because of their state-of-the-art sound equipment, most of P.C.L.'s early films were musicals, partly to get the jump on their technically primitive rivals, partly because these early efforts were financed by record companies wanting to promote their most popular singers, a symbiotic tradition that continues at the studio (and later at all the majors) to this day. Among the studio's first roster of contract talent were Heihachiro "Henry" Okawa, who had appeared in American silent films; Kamatari Fujiwara, later a member of Kurosawa's stock company of actors; actress Sachiko Chiba; and a broad comedian named Kenichi

Enomoto, better known to moviegoers by the affectionate abbreviation of his name (as said in the Japanese surname-first fashion), "Enoken."

P.C.L.'s growing success came to the attention of railroad magnate Ichizo Kobayashi. A former managing director of the Arima Electric Railway Company and one-time chairman of the Hankyu Electric Railway Company, Kobayashi made a fortune in real estate along the Tokyo-Osaka railway line. Key to his plans was diversification, which included building a chain of theaters and department stores at key train stations.[1] Most famous of these were the Takarazuka Grand Theater, built in 1924 in the hot springs resort city of Takarazuka, and the Tokyo Takarazuka Theater. Before the coming of sound, Kobayashi's main interest in his theaters was in his "all-girl opera" troupe, which toured the country, performing Japanese versions of Western musicals and light operas. They were a wholesome, family-oriented alternative to Kabuki, where men played both male and female roles, or films, where women had been shut out until the early 1920s.

To provide product for his growing theater chain, Kobayashi gained full control of P.C.L. and merged it with J. O. Studios, another laboratory-turned-production-house that made its first feature, *Chorus of One Million* (Hyakuman nin no gasho), in 1935.* Kobayashi's solid financial backing, combined with the companies' cutting-edge equipment, began to attract major talent for the first time. Director-screenwriter Kajiro Yamamoto left Nikkatsu to join P.C.L. in the spring of 1934, and director Mikio Naruse abandoned Shochiku for P.C.L. a year later. P.C.L. officially became a production-distribution organization in February 1935, but Shochiku, the country's leading production-releasing organization, began threatening theater owners who booked P.C.L. films.

With the number of movie houses available to P.C.L. dwindling, Kobayashi found himself in a bind. He resorted to aggressively luring away talent from the other major studios, and by 1938 had acquired the services of major stars, including actor Denjiro Okochi, actress Takako Irie, and prestigious yet commercially proven directors like Mansaku Itami and Sadao Yamanaka. But the most controversial of these acquisitions was P.C.L.'s luring of popular star Kazuo Hasegawa from Shochiku. In the fall of 1937, after he had joined the company, Hasegawa was attacked with a razor by a hood who had ties to Shochiku. Hasegawa survived, and despite his being left with a permanent facial scar, the surrounding publicity only

---

*"J. O." was short for "Jenkins," the name of the sound recording system the company employed, and Yoshio Osawa, its founder.

increased his star status and bolstered the company's profits. On August 27, 1937, P.C.L., J. O., and the other smaller production units Kobayashi had brought in were consolidated into a company known as Toho.[2]

"It had never occurred to me to enter the film industry," Kurosawa wrote, "but when I saw that advertisement, my interest was suddenly aroused." Prospective assistant directors were put through a series of tests. The first of these was a written composition on "the fundamental deficiencies of Japanese films." If the deficiencies were fundamental, Kurosawa replied in his essay, then there was no way to correct them.[3] Nonetheless, P.C.L. was impressed by his obvious and extensive knowledge of both the Japanese and foreign films his father and brother had taken him to, as well as traditional arts and literature.

A few months later he was called to P.C.L.'s studio, located in the then-rural southwestern Tokyo suburb of Seijo, in Setagaya-ku. When he arrived there were "more than 130 people assembled in the [studio] courtyard for the second round. I knew that out of all these only five people would actually be hired. I no longer felt like taking the second test."[4] But he stayed and completed sample screenplay pages, followed by an oral examination. There he met the man whom he would come to regard as the best teacher of his entire life: Kajiro Yamamoto.

"I really wanted [to hire] someone who first understood motion pictures," Yamamoto said, "and then, a person who understood music and, after that, a person who understood literature. I needed those three qualities which none of the assistant directors had at the time. I don't know exactly how many applicants there were, but we interviewed ten people among them and picked three out of those ten. Kurosawa-kun dressed so poorly for the first four or five years. It was incredible. I couldn't believe he would come to an interview wearing such awful clothes. He was wearing a shirt, tattered pants and sandals. He apparently failed the entrance exam. 'You seem to like paintings.' 'Yes, I do.' 'What kind of paintings do you like?' 'Well, I like Van Gogh.' I thought he was genuine. While we were talking about painters, the person who seemed to be a manager of the general affairs section seated next to me asked him, 'How much do you want to get paid?' He looked embarrassed, his face turned red and he said, 'As much as I can get.' Everybody laughed. The company was reluctant to hire him but I asked, 'Please hire him no matter what!' "[5]

Kurosawa was indeed hired, on February 26, 1936, at ¥28 a month (about $560), along with future directors Hideo Sekigawa and Seiji Maru-yama, but almost immediately he began to have second thoughts. His first assignment was a minor film called *Paradise of the Virgin Flowers* (Shojo hana-zono), directed by Shigeo Yagura and released on June 11, 1936. Neither the film nor its director endeared Kurosawa to his new occupation, and af-ter this one film he was ready to quit. But his colleagues insisted that the life of an assistant director wasn't always as boring as his experience with Yagura might have suggested. He decided to stick it out, and his second film was *Enoken's Ten Million* (Enoken no senman chojya, 1936), directed by Yamamoto.

"I was lucky enough to be favored with an [unsurpassed] teacher, the fa-mous director Kajiro Yamamoto," Kurosawa said in the 1960s. "Shortly after I entered P.C.L., on more than one occasion I tried to quit. I was disgusted with the job of assistant director. Each time it was my colleagues who com-pelled me to change my mind, but it was Yamamoto who influenced me to make my home in this world of the cinema."[6]

Compared with Yagura, working for Yamamoto was like a breath of fresh air. "I learned there are many kinds of films and many kinds of directors," wrote Kurosawa. "The work in the Yamamoto 'group' was fun. I didn't want to work for anyone else after that. It was like the wind in a mountain pass blowing across my face. By this I mean that wonderfully refreshing wind you feel after a painfully hard climb. The breath of that wind tells you you are reaching the pass. Then you stand in the pass and look down over the panorama it opens up. When I stood behind Yama-san in his director's chair next to the camera, I felt my heart swell with that same feeling—'I've made it at last.' The work he was doing was the kind that I really wanted to do. I was standing in the mountain pass, and the view that opened up be-fore me on the other side revealed a single straight road."[7]

In Yamamoto's group, Kurosawa became friendly with his two senior as-sistant directors, both of whom would become major filmmakers in their own right and important personal friends and collaborators. The first of these, Yamamoto's chief assistant, was an irascible, balding, and bespecta-cled man named Senkichi Taniguchi (b. 1912), who joined the company at its inception.

"Kurosawa and I were so close and had such strong ties, everyone was really surprised by it," Taniguchi said. Early in their friendship, Kurosawa broke into Taniguchi's home, looking for a place to live. " 'You got into my house without my permission!' " Taniguchi said to him. " 'What are you going to do if I say no?' He said, 'Please let me stay, I can't get to sleep without your futon.' In Japan we put the futon on the tatami and sleep on it. My mother had made a special longer futon because I was so tall. He was as tall as I was and thought he'd sleep better on the longer futon." Kurosawa stayed. "Neither of us ever took showers or changed our clothes," Taniguchi said. "When we walked through the studio, actresses would change their direction because we were so stinky. Toho gave us meal tickets, but that wasn't enough. While we were waiting in front of the studio commissary, an old actress with whom we were acquainted said, 'Go to my house and talk to my maid. There should be something to eat in the cupboard.' Kurosawa and I ran to her house and ate until we were stuffed. We spent many years together at the bottom."[8]

Kurosawa's other close friend was Yamamoto's second assistant, Ishiro Honda (1911–93), a man who, like Kurosawa and Taniguchi, towered over most of his contemporaries. All three stood nearly six feet tall and were notably handsome and distinguished-looking. But where Taniguchi was carefree and short-tempered, Honda, born into a family of monks, was quietly dedicated and serious, gentle and sweet-natured, with a refined sensibility. He was born in Yamagata Prefecture and at the age of twenty entered the art department of Nihon University; he joined P.C.L.'s production department two years later, the same year Taniguchi joined the company.

"I entered P.C.L. before [Kurosawa] did, but I was drafted and had to go to war," Honda said. "He was hired while I was in the army. After I returned from [China], we started working together. On our first film together, Mr. Senkichi Taniguchi was the chief assistant director, I was the next AD, Kurosawa-kun was next, and then [Shin] Inoue-kun, who has since passed away. I was exhausted after work. Many of the actors we worked with on this first film together were from the Kabuki, and shooting didn't begin until after their nightly stage performances. The daytime and the nighttime we spent during the production was flip-flopped."[9]

They called one another by nicknames after the Kanji characters in their family names: "Kuro-chan" ("Blackie"), "Sen-chan" ("Dear Sen," ironic, given his temperament), and "Ino-chan" ("Piggy"). Kurosawa especially admired Honda's dedication, and also referred to his friend as "Keeper of the Grain." "He was then second assistant director, but when the set designers were overwhelmed with work, he lent a hand. He would always take care to paint following the grain of the wood on the false pillars and wainscoting, and to put in a grain texture where it was lacking, hence his nickname. . . . His motive in drawing in the grain was to make Yama-san's work look just that much better."[10]

"Mr. Yamamoto was a free-spirited person," Honda recalled, "rare at that time. For instance, he never sent his assistant directors out to fetch cigarettes. He didn't ask anybody to do anything, in fact. In other words, he didn't want 'Yes-Men' around him. We always went drinking with him, though. But he was never an autocrat. It was the policy of P.C.L., with Mr. Iwao Mori [Toho's vice president in charge of production] as well. Since [Mr. Yamamoto] was so knowledgeable, his stories were always interesting. He was also frank on the set and would ask me to write parts of the script. And then he'd use it."[11]

Yamamoto would even allow the quality of his own work to slip so that his assistants might learn. According to Kurosawa, Yamamoto always used the second-unit footage his assistants shot, even if it proved less than imaginative. "His attitude was that in order to train his assistant directors it was worth sacrificing his own pictures. At least, that seems to me the only possible interpretation."[12]

After Kurosawa had worn out his welcome with Taniguchi, he moved in with Honda. "We drank every day," Honda said. "When I had ¥1.5, we were able to drink until we were feeling really good! . . . When we drank, we talked exclusively about movies."[13]

Assistant directors in Japan, then as now, function in a manner quite unlike their Hollywood counterparts. Both work closely with the director in production planning, preparing locations, readying and directing extras, and supervising second-unit filming. But where assistant directors in Hollywood often spend their entire careers as ADs, or become producers themselves, in Japan they have always been seen as directors-in-training. In Hollywood, assistant directors almost never become directors.

After luring talent away from the other studios, Toho's plan was to train a new, homegrown generation of filmmakers. The new ADs under Yamamoto were assigned myriad tasks far beyond the scope of Hollywood's ADs. "[We] were required to gain a thorough mastery of every field necessary to the production of a film," Kurosawa wrote. "We had to help in the developing laboratory, carry a bag of nails, a hammer and a level from our belts and help with scriptwriting and editing as well. We even had to appear as extras in place of actors and do accounts for location shooting."[14]

But among Toho's staff of experienced filmmakers, no one recognized the long-term value of such training more than Yamamoto. Part of this may have been due to his age. Born in 1902, he was less than a decade older than his assistants. Then again, Naruse and Yamanaka were even younger than he was. The entire studio was in fact filled with artists born well into the twentieth century, but only Yamamoto had the utter selflessness that served aspiring artists like Kurosawa so well. Yamamoto directed his first film, *Bomb Hour*, at Nikkatsu when he was just twenty-three years old. At no point was he considered a great artist. Rather, he was always viewed as a reliable, sophisticated craftsman. His reputation at Toho was solidified by his popular comedies with Enoken, which encompassed about half his yearly output, as well as a two-part film known collectively as *A Husband's Chastity* (Otto no teiso) released in April 1937 and one of P.C.L.'s first big hits. He would go on to direct several popular war movies for the studio in the 1940s, but after that his assignments were almost always routine. However, nearly all of Yamamoto's assistants during the 1930s and early '40s went on to long careers at the studio and, like Kurosawa, were unanimous in their boundless praise of him.

By 1937, Kurosawa had worked on eleven films, most for Yamamoto, with Taniguchi and Honda as his seniors. Over that summer, however, Taniguchi was transferred to another division of the company, and Honda, the obvious choice to replace him, was called back to active duty. According to Taniguchi, he "had really bad luck. He was drafted when he was young, and just at a time when he could have learned so much about making movies. I think he was in the military for seven or eight years. I went to war as well, but came back earlier than he did. When I returned, Kurosawa had gotten married and many changes had occurred at the studio."[15]

That summer, though, Yamamoto needed a new chief assistant. But who could replace Taniguchi and Honda, then considered the best ADs on the lot?

"There was a real pecking order at the studio," Taniguchi said. "Once you passed the test to work as an assistant director, you'd start out as a third assistant, which was called *kachiko*, the lowest rank. I became an assistant director to Kajiro Yamamoto, who was supposed to be the best of the twenty or so directors there." Taniguchi may have been respected on the lot, but in the front office it was a different story. The executive board grew increasingly worried about production expenditures and abruptly transferred Taniguchi to Toho's planning division. "Since you know how much a piece of wood costs," they told him, "we want you to go to the head office and teach the workers there. We need someone who knows how much money it really costs to make a film, to teach this to the executive staff immediately."[16]

At the time, Taniguchi was Yamamoto's chief assistant director. "He asked me, 'Who can fill your position?' I finally mentioned Kurosawa to him, and he became Mr. Yamamoto's chief assistant director.

"There were forty or fifty assistant directors at Toho at the time. We were usually promoted based on years of employment. Most of them were waiting for the chance to become Yamamoto's chief assistant, but Kurosawa—who nobody paid any attention to and who had less experience—was chosen. They all complained about it, saying, 'There are so many assistant directors waiting for this position. Why was this person, who had no experience as even a third or second assistant director, being promoted to chief assistant?'

"Yamamoto said, 'Well, I decided to hire whoever Taniguchi suggested. It's all his fault, not mine.' "[17]

And so, beginning with Yamamoto's *The Beautiful Hawk* (Utsukushiki taka), released that October, Kurosawa suddenly jumped through the ranks, becoming Yamamoto's right-hand man barely a year after he had been hired.

As Kurosawa's confidence in his position grew, Yamamoto began giving him greater responsibilities. His own natural talent began to blossom, too, and his contemporaries were amazed by his limitless enthusiasm and dedication to what would become his life's craft.

At the same time, Kurosawa began writing. "Yama-san said: 'If you want to become a film director, first write scripts.' I felt he was right, so I applied myself wholeheartedly to scriptwriting."[18] His first efforts were forgettable, but as his understanding of the language of cinema grew, so did the quality of his screenplays. One early, never-filmed effort was *A German at Daruma Temple* (Daruma-dera no doitsujin), based on the life of architect Bruno Taut. Like many of his early scenarios, it was deemed unsuitable by film and government censorship boards; others were too expensive to be filmed once the Pacific War broke out. However, most of these were published in film magazines like *Eiga hyoron* or won prizes, and this built his reputation in the film community at large.

"Kurosawa used to say the script was most important," Taniguchi recalled, "as it determined whether the film would be any good or not. He always said Japanese filmmakers wasted time, concentrating on other aspects like casting. I agreed with him, but he was always so noisy about it and would complain about the same things over and over again.

"I'm not saying I was jealous of him, but Kurosawa was unusual and different from any of us. For example, some of the studio's hair stylists used to live in an apartment across the street from my house and they'd give me sake. I drank what I wanted and then gave Kurosawa the rest. I got drunk and went straight to sleep, but he didn't. When I woke up in the middle of a night, I found him writing a script. There were many movie magazines at the time and they often had script contests. His scripts started to win and mine never did. One day, as I passed through Toho's front gate, a security guard asked me, 'Mr. Taniguchi! Is Kurosawa *sensei* [Teacher Kurosawa] on the lot?' I never imagined he was referring to the Kurosawa I knew, and I replied, 'No, we do not have a Kurosawa *sensei* here.' " A week later, the same guard asked Taniguchi if he knew who had been visiting Kurosawa *sensei*. "I said, 'How should I know?' " and the guard told him, "The script that Kurosawa *sensei* wrote will be filmed by Daiei Studios."

"This is when I first realized that he was way ahead of me," admitted Taniguchi. "Every time we passed each other in the studio, he told me about a script that he was working on and asked me for advice. When I was in a good mood, I'd give him my opinion, but he kept bothering me. I also told him, 'If you win, you have to share the prize money because a lot of your script came from me,' and he agreed. I think less than a year after that I saw him in the garden of the studio after I had returned from location shooting. He handed me an envelope, and when I asked what it was, he replied, 'I made a promise to you.' It contained a lot of money, something I rarely saw, and I was taken aback. But my pride prevented me from accepting it. I said, 'Take care of your parents with it!' but I was really jealous. After that, he kept winning awards and I started to think, He's not an ordinary filmmaker. We were always together, and he didn't look like he was studying that much, but I guess he was. I guess I'm not as serious about making films. Each of us had different ideas about making films, but we got along. At the same time, I envied him as much as I liked him."[19]

Although he worked mainly for Yamamoto, Kurosawa did a handful of pictures for other directors. He worked with Shu Fushimizu and Mikio Naruse one time apiece. Naruse, he felt, did everything for himself, delegating very little to his assistants. But he impressed Kurosawa with his ability to build upon brief shots during editing, one upon another, and with his wasteless energy, even during meals. Once Kurosawa began his own directing career, he spent dinnertime with his cast and crew reviewing the day's events, and perhaps this grew in part out of his brief association with this greatly underrated director.

Kurosawa was also impressed by Fushimizu's dedication and talent for musical comedy, believing he would inherit Yamamoto's expertise in the genre, which none of his other disciples ever did. But in 1942, after directing a dozen films for Toho, Fushimizu died in the wake of a brief illness. He was only thirty-two years old, the same age as Kurosawa.

As chief assistant director, Kurosawa worked on two films directed by

Eisuke Takizawa, whom he had worked with more than any other director aside from Yamamoto in his first year. But as a director, Takizawa did not make much of an impression; Kurosawa said almost nothing about him in his autobiography, and even less about acclaimed director Shiro Toyoda, for whom he did one picture. He also served as chief assistant on a film directed by Hiromitsu Karasawa, who goes completely unmentioned in his book.

By the end of the decade, Yamamoto and Taniguchi were not alone in their belief that Kurosawa was something special. Toho and the other major studios began to recognize that a major new talent was emerging. But Kurosawa's rise coincided with horrible events happening around the globe, events which would greatly impact even the remote dream factory Kurosawa now called home.

THREE

TREADING
THE TIGER'S TAIL

When Toshiro Mifune was drafted in March 1940, he expected to serve two years, but after the bombing of Pearl Harbor on December 7, 1941, he was forced to serve until the war's end. For Mifune it was worse than being in prison. His sentence was indefinite, and he served his time under leaders infected with a zealous nationalism. This was something he could not fathom. He had been raised in China and could not understand the anti-Chinese, anti-Korean, anti-American, anti-everything-but-Japanese fervor of many of his comrades raised with such stark xenophobia. "There I was, a naïve man of twenty," Mifune said. "[I] and the other bewildered young recruits were stirred up to a blood lust. What a nightmare!"[1]

In interviews after he became a star, Mifune disliked talking about his time in the military, usually dismissing those five long years of his life with "I was in the Japanese Air Force, but I didn't see any action."[2] This much is true. His knowledge of still photography had spared him from combat. He did not fly dangerous reconnaissance missions, nor was he cannon fodder in the Japanese infantry. But even in the relative safety of Yakaijo City, he witnessed the ugliness of Japan's militarism.

"In the military," said Tomio Sagisu, "superiors would strike the lower ranks, but Mifune couldn't watch that without complaining. He'd yell, 'What are you doing?!' But he wasn't supposed to say things like that. He'd say to his superiors, 'I don't care. Take your stripes off. You and me. Let's fight as men, one-on-one.' He had such powerful eyes that his superiors would usually back down."[3]

"Near the end of the war," said Shiro, Mifune's oldest son, "he was sent to another division in Kumamoto and was teaching fifteen- and sixteen-year-old boys how to attack when the [Allied] invasion force came, but by then it was almost the end of the war." Their supplies had run out. There were no guns, no ammunition left for them to train with. "The military taught its soldiers to say '*Banzai*' when they died, but he told them to say '*Okaasan*' ['Mother']. The next day the young boys went to war, and they never came back."[4]

In 1940, Kurosawa was working on his last film as chief assistant director, a drama for Kajiro Yamamoto about a young girl and her relationship with a beloved horse. Yamamoto happened upon a radio broadcast of a horse auction. He noticed that amid all the noise of the auction were the sobs of a young girl, who became the model for the film's heroine, Ine.[5] This picture, *Horse* (Uma), put Kurosawa another step closer to the director's chair and marked his own first encounter with the increasingly irrational government censors who now ruled the film industry.

The story, set in the present day, concerns a young woman, Ine (Hideko Takamine), who raises a colt from birth. Inevitably the time comes when the horse is sold at auction to the Army, and this loss breaks her heart. Toho came to regard *Horse* as a prestige picture; it had been in the planning stages as far back as 1937. The film took three years to plan and was shot over much of 1940 and early 1941. As the film followed the relationship between the girl and her horse over the course of two years, four cameramen were employed to capture each of the four seasons.

The film would require extensive second-unit shooting in northeastern Japan. When it was ready to commence production early in 1940, Yamamoto and Kurosawa were tied up shooting a quartet of money-making comedies, three starring Enoken, the fourth toplining another popular star, Roppa Furukawa. Probably for this reason Yamamoto first chose Ishiro Honda as *Horse*'s chief assistant. "I was an assistant director until the scene of the horse auction," Honda recalled, "but while on location I was called back into active duty and had to return to the war. Kurosawa-kun became chief assistant director after me. I didn't get to see the completed movie until the following year, when I was at the front."[6] For the rest of the war Honda would complete a tour of duty, come back to Tokyo to briefly work as an assistant director, then be pressed back into service. Kurosawa, with his 4-F status, was able to stay behind at Toho and build on his burgeoning career.

Kurosawa took Honda's place, while Yamamoto spent much of the film's production moving back and forth between *Horse*'s location and Toho Studios, where he simultaneously cranked out more reliably commercial pictures. Yamamoto directed four films in 1940 and wrote screenplays or treatments for three others which he did not himself direct. That he would leave so much of the film in Kurosawa's hands led to speculation that Kurosawa all but directed the picture himself, in addition to collaborating on its screenplay and doing the editing.

"During the filming of *Horse* Yama-san did indeed come to the location set-ups," according to Kurosawa. "But usually after spending one night there he would say, 'Take care of it,' and go back to Tokyo. It was in this way that I was trained, before becoming a director, to handle the crew and to coach the actors."[7]

By 1940, Yamamoto was so comfortable with Kurosawa's abilities that he began referring to him as "my other self." With *Horse*, his chief assistant went one step further. "Kurosawa took over much of the production," Yamamoto remembered. "He had advanced so quickly that while I was working in Tokyo, shooting a musical comedy, he assumed complete responsibility of the second unit and shot location footage for *Horse* in northeastern Japan. This must have been strenuous practice for him. When we both got back [and resumed principal photography], I found him much tougher, much more exacting than I generally was. He would order retakes for scenes I thought acceptable. At first the crew was flabbergasted, but they soon realized his instincts were right and obeyed his instructions. People began talking about this young man's prospects, and by the time the film was finished, everyone regarded him as a full-fledged director."[8]

When the film was completed, Kurosawa had his first of many run-ins with military government censors. Although they had approved the film's script and had a representative present during the entire production, once the film was edited, the Army's Equestrian Affairs Administration demanded the entire auction scene be cut. Some of the extras were shown drinking, which was in conflict with the ban on daytime alcohol consumption. Kurosawa refused to give in, and while shots of the drinking extras were ultimately excised, the auction scene remained.

Horse was a popular and critical success when it opened on March 11, 1941. It helped establish Hideko Takamine as one of Japan's great film actresses, while the picture itself made the "Best Ten" list of the year in Japan's leading film magazine, *Kinema Jumpo*, placing second behind Yasujiro Ozu's *The Brothers and Sisters of the Toda Family* (Toda-ke no kyodai).

"There was realistic photography," noted Joseph Anderson and Donald Richie in their groundbreaking book *The Japanese Film—Art and Industry*, "and a very careful documentation of horses and horse-breeding. This film greatly influenced the rising Japanese documentary movement and the relation of feature films to reality."[9]

Horse was briefly released in the United States in 1986. " 'Horse' is an unsentimental tale," wrote *The New York Times*, "about a young girl and the colt she raises from its birth. It's also about the struggle of farmers on the edge of poverty, about family love and loyalties (which go mostly unexpressed), and about the cyclical nature of life as expressed through the changing of the seasons. Mr. Kurosawa's second-unit work contains a lot of striking shots that are forerunners of material contained in his own later, greater films, including 'Throne of Blood.' Here his fascination with horses . . . is cast in a somewhat more conventional form, though the composition and imagery are often as fine as anything he was to do afterward. . . . The film's last, long-held image—that of a line of horses being led away to war—might once have looked patriotic. The generals could be pleased. Today, it's haunting in an entirely different way."[10] (Much more haunting is the cut back to Takamine's face, as she strains to hear the fading hoofsteps of her beloved horse.)

The Village Voice called it "a neorealist kid's film, something like a cross between *La Terra Trema* and *National Velvet*. . . . *Horse* exudes a low-key naturalism. The narrative is leisurely, anecdotal, and synched to the cycles of nature. . . . [But] for those familiar with [Hideko Takemine's] later work, her youthful presence in *Horse* may prove more haunting than the film's traces of early Kurosawa."[11]

Following the release of *Horse*, Kurosawa spent the next year and a half writing nearly a dozen scripts. Some were done for Toho and the newly formed Daiei Studios; others were entered in various screenwriting contests sponsored by the government's Information Ministry and prominent film magazines. Two of these scripts were produced at Toho in 1942. The first, *Wind Currents of Youth* (Seishun no kiryu), was based on two stories by Jun Minamikawa, "Construction of Life" and "The Life Plan." The picture was directed by Shu Fushimizu, the last film he made before his untimely death. It starred Japan's leading film actress, Setsuko Hara, with Toshiko Yamane, Houden Onichi, and an up-and-coming leading man named Susumu Fujita.

This was followed by *The Triumphant Song of the Wings* (Tsubasa no gaika), directed by leftist filmmaker Satsuo Yamamoto (no relation to Kajiro), which Kurosawa wrote with Bonhei Sotoyama. Judging by its cast, *Wings* was a lesser war movie, starring Joji Oka and Takako Irie, with Heihachiro "Henry" Okawa and Seizaburo Kawazu, though it featured elaborate special effects by Eiji Tsuburaya.

"They were stories that the times required," Kurosawa wrote, "about the aircraft industry and boy aviators. Their aim was to fan the flame of the national war spirit, and I did not undertake them out of any personal inclination. I just dashed them off in the suitable formulas."[12]

"I offered no resistance to Japan's militarism," Kurosawa admitted. "Unfortunately, I have to admit that I did not have the courage to resist in any positive way, and I only got by, ingratiating myself when necessary and otherwise evading censure. I am ashamed of this, but I must be honest about it."[13]

For Daiei he wrote *Wrestling Ring Festival* (Dohyosai), which was produced after the success of his first film and directed by Santaro Marune. Another Daiei script, *The Story of a Bad Horse* (Jajauma monogatari), was never produced. Neither were *A Thousand and One Nights in the Forest* (Mori no senichiya), *The San Paguita Flower* (San Paguita no hana), *Beautiful Calendar* (Utsukushiki koyomi), *The Third Harbor* (Daisan Hatoba), *All Is Quiet* (Shizukanari), or *Snow* (Yuki), despite the fact that the latter two were awarded prizes by the Information Ministry. Kurosawa did, however, receive substantial cash awards of ¥300 ($6,000) and ¥2,000 ($40,000) respectively, and he welcomed this sudden income.

"He was twenty-two or twenty-three years older than I am," said Yoshio "Mike" Inoue, the oldest son of Kurosawa's older sister Taneyo. "I used to read his scripts. I still remember some of the wonderful scripts. He was always winning contests, winning big money."[14]

Kurosawa wanted to make a film of what he thought was the best of his screenplays, *A German at Daruma Temple*, but during preproduction it was rejected by the military censors, who by this time had become so strict that something as innocent as a shot of a crying baby was forbidden.

> At that time the censors in the Ministry of the Interior seemed to be mentally deranged [Kurosawa wrote]. They all behaved as if they suffered from persecution complexes, sadistic tendencies and various sexual manias. They cut every single kiss scene out of foreign movies. If a woman's knees ever appeared, they cut that scene, too. They said that such things would stimulate carnal desires. The cen-

sors were so far gone as to find the following sentence obscene: "The factory gate waited for the student workers, thrown open in longing." What can I say? . . . They were the people who really should have been put behind bars. . . . Toward the end of the war I even made a pact with some of my friends: If it came to the point of the Honorable Death of the Hundred Million and every Japanese would have to commit suicide, we vowed to meet in front of the Ministry of the Interior and assassinate the censors before we took our own lives.[15]

Kurosawa thought he had finally written (with Toho staff writer Hideo Oguni) a censor-proof script in *Three Hundred Miles Through Enemy Lines* (Te-kichu odan sanbyakuri), about the Tatekawa reconnoitering party during the Russo-Japanese War. By then, however, the present conflict had escalated to the point where Toho simply could not afford to produce it. "If only I had let you make that movie," producer Nobuyoshi Morita told Kurosawa years later, "but I felt bad about it even at the time. I really had no choice."[16] The film was eventually made by director Kazuo Mori in late 1957.

"I just had a gut feeling that 'This is it,' " Kurosawa recalled when first seeing a newspaper ad for a forthcoming novel by Tsuneo Tomita called *Sanshiro Sugata* (Sugata Sanshiro). "There was no logical explanation for my reaction, but I believed wholeheartedly in my instinct and did not doubt for an instant."[17]

Convinced, sight unseen, that this would be the perfect property in which to make his directorial debut, he begged Toho to buy it for him. He recalled going to see producer Morita, who was understandably reluctant to purchase the screen rights for a story that had not yet been published. Although today such practice is common—film rights to novels are commonly bought in the galley stage—Kurosawa was forced to wait until *Sanshiro* had reached bookstore shelves before they would commit to its production. By his own admission, Kurosawa obsessed over the unread work, haunting bookstores morning, noon, and night, until one evening in Shibuya he found a copy, took it home, and read it immediately. His instincts were right: it was commercially appealing, he could easily adapt it to his own interests, and most important, it would without question meet the military's stringent guidelines. In the middle of the night, he returned to Morita's home, and the producer wearily agreed to send someone from the story department to Tomita's house the next day.

Tomoyuki Tanaka, who would go on to co-produce several of Kurosawa's later films, was at the time working in Toho's story department. His account concurs with Kurosawa's, though he remembered it was Keiji Matsuzaki, *Sanshiro*'s producer, and not Morita whom Kurosawa had pestered that evening in late 1942. At other times, Kurosawa said it was producer Iwao Mori's home he went to. In any event, Tanaka said, "I . . . rushed to see Mr. Tomita, and was surprised to learn that both Daiei and Shochiku had already approached him about adapting it. Mr. Kurosawa was an assistant director to Kajiro Yamamoto, but everyone expected that he would become a director, and the other companies paid attention to him because of his excellent scripts. I was surprised to learn that Mr. Tomita had heard of him. I remember him saying that Kurosawa could make a good adaptation. But I couldn't negotiate with him about it because he was already negotiating with the other companies. Two days later I was invited to his house, and we negotiated terms. We settled on a fee of ¥100 [about $1,500], which was the going rate at the time."[18] Years later Kurosawa claimed it was Tomita's wife, who he said had read about the aspiring director in film magazines and recommended him to her writer husband. "So at least in a way I owe the start of my career as a director to the wife of the author of the novel *Sanshiro Sugata*," he said.[19]

Toho may have bought the film rights, but they weren't necessarily committed to having Kurosawa direct the adaptation. Masahiro Makino, in his autobiography, claims that he was asked by Nobuyoshi Morita to direct *Sanshiro Sugata*. He declined, but recommended Kurosawa.[20]

In any case, Kurosawa adapted the novel "in one sitting," and took his work to Kajiro Yamamoto for advice. Yamamoto was then on location, completing work on Toho's first big war movie, *The War at Sea from Hawaii to Malaya* (Hawai • Maree oki kaisen, 1942). When he arrived at the naval air station on the Chiba coast, Yamamoto was having dinner with an admiral and his officers. Kurosawa recalled going to bed in the barracks where the camera crew was being housed and didn't expect to see his *sensei* until morning. When Kurosawa awoke in the middle of the night, he peered into Yamamoto's room and saw him carefully reading Kurosawa's screenplay.[21]

Ishiro Honda likewise remembers Kurosawa's enthusiasm. "I can vividly recall Kurosawa-kun telling me about *Sugata Sanshiro* before shooting began. . . . I think Toshio Komatsu got married around that time and we went to his house to celebrate the wedding.[22] The whole time we were there, all we did was discuss movies. Kurosawa-kun couldn't stop talking about *Sanshiro Sugata*. I guess he was really excited about it and just couldn't hold that enthusiasm inside him any longer. Everybody listened to his story and said, 'How interesting!' He had already planned each shot. Since he had been a painter, he had the complete film structure mapped out in his mind. The way he talked was fresh, strong, and attractive. I was impressed by his exacting vision of how he was going to shoot it."[23]

Sanshiro's story is simply plotted and its presentation refreshingly straightforward. In 1882, Sanshiro Sugata (Susumu Fujita) is a skilled but immature tough in search of a *sensei* to instruct him in the martial arts. He witnesses the spectacular dispatching of jujitsu bullies (led by Yoshio Kosugi as Kodama) by a martial-arts teacher, Shogoro Yano (Denjiro Okochi). Using the then-new form of judo, Yano tosses them one by one into an adjacent river. Sanshiro becomes Yano's pupil. Time passes, and Sanshiro uses his newly found judo skills to break up a village festival where he gets into one merry fight after another. But while Yano admires Sanshiro's abilities, he is dismayed by his pupil's lack of discipline. Yano is ready to dismiss him. "To teach judo to you . . . is like giving a knife to a madman," he says. Sanshiro disagrees, and suddenly jumps into a lotus pond to prove his strength and loyalty (a gesture visually linked to Yano throwing the jujitsu men into the river). Clinging to a stake in the middle of the icy cold pond, Sanshiro sits determinedly for a day and a night. When he sees the opening of a lotus blossom at dawn, he suddenly understands what the teacher has been trying to teach him: self-realization. He jumps out of the pond, humbles himself, and asks Yano's forgiveness.

Sanshiro is then put through a series of tests. He must face Kodama, the jujitsu thug; Hansuke Murai (Takashi Shimura), the older but wiser judo man with whom he becomes friends and with whose daughter (Yukiko Todoroki) he falls in love; and Gennosuke Higaki (Ryunosuke Tsukigata), the worldly, highly experienced judo master. But like all such tests in Kurosawa's films, the matches themselves are not especially important. Rather, the director is interested in testing Sanshiro's growing spirit, his *kokoro*, his *zen*. Nonetheless, the three matches are directed with great flair, particularly the climactic duel, set against a windswept field as clouds race through the sky above.

Tomita's book and Kurosawa's adaptation is basically a variation on Eiji Yoshikawa's serialized biographical novel, *Musashi Miyamoto* (Miyamoto Musashi), published between 1935 and 1939. Yoshikawa's story had been one of the hottest literary properties of the late 1930s and early '40s, and this may account for why all the studios had clamored for Tomita's book as

soon as it was published. Both stories revolve around the spiritual enlightenment of a highly skilled but untamed man (Musashi is an expert swordsman) who is tested and humbled (Musashi is tied and suspended from a tall
tree, Sanshiro broods in a muddy pond, the latter an invention of Kurosawa, not Tomita) before his real training can begin. After submitting themselves completely to their *sensei*, both are put through a series of tests and
challenges from opponents at various levels of ability.

Tomita was a thirty-eight-year-old judo-master-turned-novelist. His father, Tsunejiro Tomita, was an acclaimed student of the Kodokan School,
and its *sensei*, Harugoro Yoshino, served as the basis for Yano's character.
Sanshiro Sugata was based on one of the elder Tomita's colleagues, the celebrated judo expert Shiro Saigo (1866–1922).

Much of Kurosawa's unique visual style is already present in his maiden
work. For example, his use of the vertical wipe, in which a line moves
across the screen as transition from one shot to the next, rather than a simple cut. In American films, wipes were most commonly used in serials (but
also in features of the 1930s) to show the passage of time or a sudden shift
in locale. But Kurosawa uses wipes for punctuation, this in lieu of other
cinematic transitional devices, such as fades and dissolves, which, by the
1950s, he rarely deployed at all. Instead, to show the passage of time in
Sanshiro Sugata, he does something unexpected for a film from this period.
When Sanshiro eagerly becomes Yano's pupil, he kicks off his wooden clogs
and becomes Yano's impromptu rickshaw driver (the real driver having fled
during the fight with Kodama and his men). We then follow the clog, not
Sanshiro, in a series of cuts as it is kicked about the road, chewed by a dog,
tossed up onto a fence pole, and, eventually, as it floats down the river. It is
a simple but effective device.

With *Sanshiro*, Kurosawa likewise introduces one of his common
themes, that of parallel education (i.e. physical or intellectual *and* metaphysical): while learning the art of judo, the protagonist tries to educate
himself, spiritually, through the guidance of an older, wiser master. This is
what happens to Sanshiro, and this is what would happen to Kurosawa's
doctors, his detectives, his samurai. Sanshiro is an ordinary man in search
of his self. There are other parallels in *Sanshiro Sugata* as well: the thugs
thrown in the river are linked to Sanshiro immersing himself in the pond;
images of Kodama's daughter are likened to Murai's daughter.

In *Sanshiro Sugata*, we also see the beginnings of what would become the
"Kurosawa-gumi" or Kurosawa stock company of actors. Many of these
were already under contract to Toho, but Kurosawa came to like several

members of his cast in particular and would use them over and over again. Fujita, Shimura, Kosugi, Kokuten Kodo (as the temple priest where Yano lives) would appear in film after film. Other performers, like star Denjiro Okochi, would gradually fade from view.

Sanshiro Sugata made a star out of Susumu Fujita; this was his first significant role, though he received second billing to Okochi, a far bigger star at the time. Fujita (1912–87) had been at Toho as early as *The Lady Ties a Ribbon* (Ribon wo musubu fujin), directed by Satsuo Yamamoto and released in 1939. He was starring in films by the following year, when he toplined *The Naval Bombing Unit* (Kagun bakugekitai), the first in a series of war pictures, the genre with which he was most associated early in his career. He appeared in Shiro Toyoda's *Ioko Okumura* (Okumura Ioko, 1940) and Mikio Naruse's *Mother Never Dies* (Haha no shinazu, 1942), but prior to *Sanshiro*, Fujita was no more than a rising talent at the studio. He acted in the Kurosawa-scripted *Wind Currents of Youth* for director Shu Fushimizu and in Kajiro Yamamoto's *The War at Sea from Hawaii to Malaya*, both of which Kurosawa had surely seen.

Fujita was Kurosawa's regular leading man until Fujita's departure from Toho in the late 1940s, which coincided with Toshiro Mifune's rising popularity. Fujita had soft, expressive eyes that belied an imposing physicality— one not unlike Mifune's. But Fujita was stockier and less athletic than Mifune, nor did he have Mifune's range or willingness (or perhaps ability) to throw everything he had into his performances. Where Mifune at times was over the top, Fujita by contrast could be rather stiff and inexpressive. Both had working-class looks, but under Kurosawa's direction Mifune could get away with playing the kind of roles which Fujita could not.

Outside of his films for Kurosawa, Fujita became typed playing war heroes, and when the war was lost, he struggled to find a new screen persona. He left Toho during the strikes of the late 1940s and moved to Shintoho, which further derailed his career as a leading man. By the early 1950s he was back at Toho, but by then the studio had built up a stable of new stars. Fujita was reduced to featured billing in supporting roles, often as generals, policemen, and other authority figures. Kurosawa gave him small but memorable roles in *The Hidden Fortress* (1958), *The Bad Sleep Well* (1960), and *Yojimbo* (1961), but Fujita spent most of the 1960s in Toho war movies.

While on location for *Sanshiro Sugata*, Kurosawa discovered Fujita had been sleeping with a local woman. When Kurosawa learned of the tryst, he used Fujita's embarrassed expression for the scene where Sanshiro is scolded by Yano. Fujita, even into his seventies, was fairly notorious as a ladies' man. According to one of his neighbors in later years, Sook-Yeoung, Fujita was vain but warm. She suggests his unabated virility may have been a response to the enormous guilt he expressed to her about having played so many fearless soldiers (known as *gunshin*, or "military gods") during the Pacific War. These propaganda films were so powerful that he felt responsible for fanning the flames of a hopeless, brutal conflict which ended in death for so many soldiers who modeled themselves after Fujita's characters. In fact, he very nearly retired after the war because of this overwhelming feeling of culpability.

Toho, with Yamamoto's encouragement, had generously groomed Kurosawa as a star director, and he wasn't about to let them down. Eager to please, *Sanshiro Sugata* is, first and foremost, commercial entertainment that's always engrossing. Not only is it full of action but Kurosawa's remarkably lean adaptation and editing further emphasize the narrative momentum. There are imaginative touches evident throughout, though the greatness he would achieve in less than a decade is only suggested here. Like the later *Rashomon*, Kurosawa's first film was so influential that the freshness of it when it was new is lost to some degree on audiences seeing it today: many of its innovations have been copied again and again, lessening its impact, if only through familiarity. *Sanshiro Sugata* is more than a curiosity, but less than a masterpiece, despite several extraordinary moments.

Filming on *Sanshiro Sugata* began on December 13, 1942, when Kurosawa was thirty-two years old. The first scene shot turned out to be one of the best in the entire picture: Sanshiro and Yano observe Murai's daughter praying at a shrine for her father. This sequence was filmed at the Asama Shrine in Yokohama, about an hour's drive from Toho. Kurosawa by now had worked on so many films, and had done so much second-unit work, that the transition to full director was fairly effortless. However, he recalled that when he said, "*Yoi, staato!*" ("Ready, action!") for the first time, his voice sounded rather odd.

Two days later the production went on location for Yano's riverside fight with Kodama's jujitsu men. According to a diary kept by cinematographer Akira Mimura, the temperature was near zero at the location, the Handa River in Aichi Prefecture. As star Okochi threw the men into the water one by one, they had to be rushed by car back to the crew's hotel to warm up, and at one point Okochi himself fell into the ice-cold waters.[24]

After a New Year's break, shooting resumed on January 13, 1943, at the studio. "The [climactic fight] scene was described as follows," wrote

Mimura. "Sanshiro is quietly standing while surrounded by broken clouds which run through the moonlight like ice and the sky like a wild animal in the rolling wind. No one expected to be able to find such a location. We thought we wouldn't be able to shoot this scene without special effects, so we built a set, painted clouds, and created the winds with large fans."[25]

Kurosawa, however, didn't like what he saw. "I felt that what we could shoot [on the set] would not only fail to be more impressive than the other fight scenes, it would look tawdry enough to ruin the whole picture."[26] He asked for and got permission to go out on location once more, but only for three days. That February, the crew drove to the Sengokuhara plain in Hakkone, and Kurosawa readied his crew for the windswept finale. The first two days the weather was unusually calm, but on the third and final day of shooting, a tremendous windstorm struck the location.

"It was miraculous!" said Mimura. "I guess the winds must have been blowing at 17 or 18 meters per second. The clouds ran across the sky just like a plane. . . . Of course we were all freezing, but everyone was impressed by the two lead actors playing their roles in mere judo costumes. I was glad nobody complained about the hard work."[27]

"People often ask me how I felt directing my maiden work," wrote Kurosawa, "but . . . I simply enjoyed it. I went to sleep each night looking forward eagerly to the next day's shooting, and there was absolutely nothing painful in the experience. . . . The whole task was carried out with a feeling of ease."[28]

Getting the film past the military censors was another matter. The film had every reason to be passed without question. It embraced Japanese views on martial arts and spirituality, its villain was singularly Western in dress and manner—more specifically, a Japanese corrupted by Western influence. The board reviewing *Sanshiro* consisted of several filmmakers, including Tomotaka Tasaka and Yasujiro Ozu, but was composed mainly of government and military censors. According to Kurosawa, he was instructed to sit in a single chair across from and facing them all. "It was really like being on trial. . . . It seems I had committed the heinous crime called *Sanshiro Sugata*."[29]

He became livid as he heard them charge his first film with being too "British-American," particularly in the love scenes with Fujita and Todoroki, a ludicrous claim. He had risen to lash out at them when Ozu simultaneously stood up and, according to Kurosawa, praised *Sanshiro* as an important artistic achievement. The film was passed.

In Japan, *Sanshiro Sugata* was a critical and commercial success. The latter was perhaps partly due to the dwindling number of films in release as the war raged on, but the novel had been a bestseller, and Kurosawa's unique telling captured the imagination of audiences. On March 27, at the prime minister's residence, *Sanshiro Sugata* shared the National Incentive Film Prize, which included a cash award of ¥500. It also won the Sadao Ya-manaka Prize (named for the late director) and ranked second on *Eiga Hyo-ron*'s (*Film Review*'s) list of the year's best films.

After the war, it was discovered that portions of *Sanshiro Sugata*'s original negative had been lost. Approximately 17 of the film's original 97 minutes had inexplicably vanished, and the film was reconstructed in 1952 (for theatrical reissue) to its present form. Because of the lost footage, wordy titles fill in the blanks of its narrative.[30] While the addition of explanatory title cards is admirable, it does little to enhance the incomplete film, which perhaps would have been better without them. All the critical scenes appear intact, though supporting characters do tend to come and go rather abruptly at times.

It would be more than thirty years before American audiences would have the opportunity to see the film. It was finally released in the West (retitled *Judo Saga* in some markets) in 1974. "Even in this elliptical version," wrote *The Wall Street Journal*, " 'Sanshiro Sugata' makes for compelling film experience, providing us both with considerable evidence of the cinematic genius that would one day form into the creation of 'Rashomon,' 'Ikiru,' and 'The Seven Samurai,' and with rich material out of which to build an understanding of Japanese character and values. . . . Everything here is played out through images of exquisite precision and through compositions totally cinematic in their conception. . . . But as persuasive as this articulation of the beauty, the grace and nobility of the martial arts may be, so also it is somehow terrifying—and all the more so in the face of the growing number of Western devotees to Kung Fu movies and karate and adherents to the slow-motion bloodletting in films like those of Sam Peckinpah and Robert Aldrich. And though I suppose we can have a poetics of destruction—we can, for instance, see rose petals in bomb bursts—what kind of sensibilities does such a poetics finally serve?"[31]

"[This cut version] . . . has not lost its genius," argued Judith Crist in *New York* magazine. "[It has all] the hallmarks of the great artist in his first work. . . . It is Kurosawa's techniques, the subtle marking of the passage of time, the backflash and foreflash, the wipes and dissolves and the remarkably telling indirection in the narrative, and, above all, the final duel in the windswept field under darkening cloud-laden skies, that are so impressive in their origins in the work of a 33-year-old film-maker [sic] in 1943."[32]

The New Yorker thought the film was "like 'The Karate Kid' made by an artist. . . . [It] shows off the talents of a vivid, audacious, mystical—but also down to earth and humorous—director in first bloom."[33]

The *Los Angeles Times* agreed. "Obviously a must for Kurosawa admirers, it seems today something of a museum piece, often static and remote but possessed of much charm and some stunning sequences that make it worth the effort. . . . Fragmentary, elusive yet steadfastly appealing, 'Judo Saga,' so much more than mere entertainment, is clearly the work of a man who was to become a great director."[34]

On the heels of *Sanshiro Sugata*, Kurosawa was approached by the Information Section of the Japanese Navy, which asked him to make a film about Zero fighter planes and their pilots. This was not surprising, as Kajiro Yamamoto, his mentor, had abruptly shifted away from lighthearted comedies to large-scale war films. His *The War at Sea from Hawaii to Malaya* (1942), with its unprecedented use of elaborate miniatures by cinematographer-turned-special-effects artist Eiji Tsuburaya, had been Toho's biggest hit of late 1942 and early 1943, and was named by *Kinema Jumpo* as the year's best film. Yamamoto and Tsuburaya followed its success with *Colonel Kato's Fighting Squad* (Kato shun sentotai, 1944), which was released five weeks prior to Kurosawa's *The Most Beautiful* and which confirmed Susumu Fujita's screen persona as a star of such films, much as John Wayne's war movies added an important facet to his screen image. "But it was already evident that Japan was going to lose the war," Kurosawa recalled, "and the Navy's ability to carry on was reaching the bottom. They really couldn't have spared any Zero fighters to make a movie with, and I never heard anything more about the project."[35]

Evidence that the war was indeed being lost could be seen within the very walls of Toho. Supplies and even food were starting to run dangerously low. Film production had dropped enormously. In 1941 the studio produced 45 films; in 1944 just 13 were made. Industry-wide, it was much the same: 232 films in 1941, just 46 in 1944. The situation was so bad that, in order to save film, the government ordered that pictures be released without opening titles. Casts and crews received no onscreen credit: Toho's logo and title cards alone introduce these late wartime films.

So instead of the Zero fighter film, Kurosawa made *The Most Beautiful* (Ichiban utsukushiku), a story of young women—all in their teens or early twenties—working in a heavily regimented lens factory. Filmed in a semi-documentary style, the picture is without a linear narrative and is instead a collection of anecdotes set over several months in the factory. The women are drafted to aid in the war effort and struggle to meet production goals. The film's theme is exceedingly simple: personal sacrifice for the common good. The women persevere, banding together for a cause larger than themselves. One woman with a chronic fever conspires with Tsuru (Yoko Yaguchi), the girl leader, to hide her condition so that she can continue working. Another falls from the dormitory roof, breaking her feet, but soon returns to work. Their labor, grinding and checking precision lenses used in binoculars and targeting scopes, is exhausting. They miss their families and must endure a military-style dorm life.

The picture's central character, Tsuru, is its driving force, keeping the girls focused and united. She constantly exhorts the others to press on. "Keep trying," she says throughout the film. "Do your best." Her job is to look for flaws in lenses used in combat, and when she is distracted by a dispute among two of the girls, she mistakenly sends a lens through the system without checking it. Her sense of duty and concern that soldiers may die because of her carelessness—while avoiding stating explicitly that the lenses are themselves being used as weapons—is such that without hesitation she spends many sleepless hours at a microscope. Going through hundreds of lenses in the middle of the night, she searches for the one she missed. At the end of the film, the company's managers want to send her home after receiving word that her mother is dying, but she concludes that she's needed at the factory and bravely decides to stay.

The Most Beautiful was shot from January through March 1944, much of it on location at Nippon Kogaku, a real factory in Hiratsuka. For technical reasons, some of the film had to be shot at Toho. One such scene is a beautiful vignette in which one of the girls wanders out of the dormitory, gazes at the moon, and, upon hearing a single, distant train whistle, begins weeping. A brief scene involving the dorm mother (Takako Irie) visiting a sick girl sent home was shot in the snowy mountains and offers a brief, visually stunning respite from the drab factory settings.

With this film, Kurosawa established a practice he would continue to employ more or less for the rest of his career. To obtain natural performances from his cast, especially in how they react to one another and perform their jobs, he had them live in the real factory's dormitory. They were sent off to different sections of the plant to learn how to use its equipment, and he had them organize a fife-and-drum corps (like that seen in the picture) and parade around the factory grounds. Additionally, many of the actresses were given character names not far removed from their own. Thus, actress Sachiko Ozaki became "Sachiko Yamazaki," Isuzu Miyakawa became "Shizue Miyazaki," and so forth.

The experiment was a success. "Their makeup lost its artificiality," Kurosawa wrote, "and at first glance, and even at a harder second look, they appeared to be in all respects a healthy, active group of ordinary girls."[36] From here on, Kurosawa would continue to have the families in his movies live together as a unit during preproduction and shooting. They would address one another by character name only, and during rehearsals, especially in his period films, Kurosawa directed his actors in full costume and makeup.

The result of all this hard work is that the young girls in *The Most Beautiful* rarely seem to be acting. When they work with the lens grinders, they do so with the slightly bored expression of women who have been doing such tasks for many months. They appear not as actresses playing factory workers but as factory workers chosen by Kurosawa to act in his film.

The scenario is little more than war propaganda, politically no better or worse than similar movies being made in America at the same time, but less explicit than those pouring out of Hollywood. Nor was its script unique among Japanese films, as the market was flooded with similar films about civilians banding together for the war effort. Shortly after it was completed, Kurosawa's experiences with Communist and anti-Communist forces within Toho would disenchant his naïve views of collective action, as well as the very Japanese notion which frequently places the group over the individual, the inclination toward the common cause over individual needs. *The Most Beautiful* is alone among Kurosawa's films in that he has unreserved faith in the group. From here on, he reserved his faith for a belief in individuals like Tsuru.

But where his script is unremarkable, his direction is energetic and consistently inventive. Had Kurosawa embraced Japan's militarism, he might have been as dangerously influential as Germany's Leni Riefenstahl—his editing in particular recalls her style. This is most apparent as the girls play volleyball as part of their physical exercise. These scenes are cut at an extraordinarily quick pace, and Kurosawa alternates long, spontaneous shots with rhythmic inserts and much more obviously staged but very dynamic tight shots of the girls' happy faces. And, like Riefenstahl, he often cuts away to inanimate objects to reflect on or punctuate a particular scene, especially to signs about increasing production, which are all over the factory.

If the cutting suggests Riefenstahl, then the compositions exhibit the influence of Russian cinema, such as Alexander Dovzhenko's classic film about collective farming in the Ukraine, *Earth* (Zemlya, 1930), and that country's later "dynamic" documentaries. All of the film is extremely well crafted, but does little to hint at the direction Kurosawa's career was to take in the next few years. What's more interesting are innovations particular to Kurosawa's oeuvre, early examples of ideas he expanded and improved upon in later work. For example, the film is for its time remarkable for what it does not show, what the director emphasizes and what he throws away, which remain some of the most interesting aspects of his abilities as a writer-director.

When Tsuru loses that precious lens, we are not shown how it was lost until much later, in an exquisitely cut, remarkably tight flashback that incorporates shots we've seen before with new ones that fill in the blanks. Later, as she examines lens after lens throughout the long night, Kurosawa cuts between shots of a clock showing it getting later and later and Tsuru in tighter and tighter focus as she sings the group's "battle song" in an effort to stay awake. With each cut back to Tsuru, her singing gets slower and sleepier, to good effect.

Another potent instance of enhancing the drama by not showing the audience what they expect to see comes when one of the girls accidentally falls from the domitory roof. The scene begins with the girl relaxing on the roof, talking with a friend at one of the dorm's windows. The friend at the window turns to leave as the girl on the roof begins to climb back inside. We cut to the dorm hallway as she steps out. Not hearing the girl behind her, the friend walks back into the room. We then see the same shot through the window, with the girl nowhere in sight. The friend looks around, and in a POV shot looking down, we see the girl supine and silent on the ground below. Cut to the fallen girl's point of view, looking up at her friend, then a quick cut to a much tighter shot of the friend's horrified reaction, followed by a horizontal wipe to the injured girl now in bed, surrounded by the other workers. At no point do we see or hear the girl actually fall; on the soundtrack we hear only the distant singing of the other girls. The result is a marvelously shocking bit of action, in a style Kurosawa would use again and again throughout his career.*

There is little in the way of characterization because the girls aren't so much individuals as part of a larger collective. Kurosawa relies on his actresses' faces rather than their characters to tell them apart. Beyond Yoko

---

*The names of these characters are undetermined. The only English-subtitled source available to the author was a Hong Kong DVD in which all the girls were given Chinese names.

Yaguchi's Tsuru, none stand out and none were any more than budding starlets at Toho. Undoubtedly, Kurosawa wanted actresses not well known to the general public, which is probably why, as a concession, bigger names appear as peripheral characters. Takashi Shimura plays the head of the factory, Soji Kiyokawa and Ichiro Sugai play section leaders, and Takako Irie is the girls' dorm mother. But their roles are even less defined than the girls', and they're given nothing in the way of personality. They're also disconnected from most of the action, as their scenes appear to have been shot almost exclusively on stages at Toho, not at the factory.

Yoko Yaguchi, however, is as idealized a heroine as Kurosawa ever conceived. She is the most beautiful (of the title), not because of her looks—Tsuru is not unattractive, but not conventionally beautiful, either—but rather because of her *kokoro*, her spirit and dedication to the cause. Just as Kurosawa worked on his scripts late into the wee hours of the morning, so too does Tsuru stay up determined to find that lens. She, like many a Kurosawa hero, is unstoppable: if she works hard enough, long enough, she knows she will succeed in finding it.

Yaguchi was born Kiyo Kato on August 27, 1921. She was the daughter of wealthy Japanese parents living in Shanghai, where her father was an executive at a shipping company. While Kato was in the fourth grade, her family returned to Japan, and she was raised in the Nakano section of Tokyo. In 1936, while a sophomore at the Showa High School for Girls, her sister secretly applied to the Shochiku Girls Musical Troupe on her behalf. The application was accepted, and Kato dropped out of high school. She made her professional debut in 1937, taking the stage name Terumi Wakazono. Two years later, while visiting her sister, who was working on a film at P.C.L., she was invited to join the studio as an actress.

Again she changed her stage name, this time to Yoko Yaguchi, and late that same year she made her film debut, in a leading role opposite Setsuko Hara in Yasujiro Shimazu's *Until the Day You Marry* (Tsuguhi made), released in March 1940. She made nine more films before *The Most Beautiful*, including Kunio Watanabe's *Kingoro the Heartless* (Kingoro ai no mujo, 1940); *Triumphant Song of the Mother-in-Law* (Shutome musume no gaika, 1940); *Ivy* (Tsuta, 1940), with Isuzu Yamada; *Diary of a Female Student* (Jogakusei niki, 1940), with Hideko Takamine and directed by Takeo Murata; and Shiro Toyoda's *A Record of My Love* (Waga ai no ki, 1941).

Yaguchi discovered that Kurosawa demanded more from her as an actress than had ever been expected of her before. She sneaked off the set to visit Takako Irie, who was spared the bother of living at the factory because of a new baby, and Yaguchi asked the more experienced actress for advice. The two became close, and Yaguchi's confidence, like her character, steadily grew.

Indeed, just as Kurosawa put a lot of himself in the character of Tsuru, so too did he discover much of his own strong-willed personality in the actress playing her. "At that time she represented the actresses and frequently came to argue with me on their behalf. She was a terribly stubborn and uncompromising person," Kurosawa wrote, "and since I am very much the same, we often clashed head on."[37] Irie, by now trusted by them both, acted as an intermediary.

The production of *The Most Beautiful* had a lasting impact on its cast. Working and living in the factory made many of the actresses re-examine the direction of their lives. They had been in a world of make-believe as the real world was crumbling around them. None had lasting careers after the film, and most retired and married.

Yoko Yaguchi married her director.

Kurosawa had no interest in making a sequel to *Sanshiro Sugata*, but after that film's great success, Toho pressured him into making one early in 1945. Undoubtedly he felt obligated. The company had, after all, given far more than it had taken, leapfrogging Kurosawa from third to chief assistant director after just one year at the studio, and he was now writing and directing films at a time when few were being made. But, as he wrote, "it was still a question of refrying to a certain extent. . . . [It] was not a very good film. Among the reviews was one that said 'Kurosawa seems to be somewhat full of himself.' On the contrary, I feel I was unable to put my full strength into it."[38]

In 1887, five years after the beginning of the first film, Sanshiro (Susumu Fujita) has returned from his travels. As the picture opens, he witnesses a burly American sailor (Osman Yusef, a Turk) taunting a young rickshaw driver, Daisuburo (Ko Ishida). In an obvious mirroring of the first scene in the original *Sanshiro* (and overtly propagandistic to boot), the villain is thrown into a river. Sanshiro is invited to fight an American boxer at an exhibition of American and Japanese fighting styles. When they arrive, however, Sanshiro is appalled at the brutality of American boxing and watches with great sadness as a down-on-his-luck jujitsu man is pummeled by the hulking American fighter. When Sanshiro asks the jujitsu man why he would subject himself to such humiliation, the man implies that it is because of judo's rise in popularity and jujitsu's subsequent fall—and partly therefore because of Sanshiro's own popularity—that he has fallen to such depths.

Meanwhile, the father of Sayo (the ingenue from *Sanshiro Sugata*) has died, and though Sanshiro fought him fairly, he can't help but feel guilty about the man's death. At the same time, Sanshiro's old rival, Gennosuke Higaki (Ryunosuke Tsukigata), is now similarly bedridden after his own defeat by Sanshiro. His two younger brothers rush to challenge Sanshiro: the vicious Teshin (also played by Tsukigata), a highly skilled but undisciplined man, and his insane, pasty-faced younger brother, Genzaburo (Akitake Kono). Where *Sanshiro*'s climax took place in a windswept field, *Part Two* ends on a snowy mountainside. Teshin is defeated, and when Sanshiro looks after the beaten man, Genzaburo pulls out an ax, planning to kill Sanshiro as he sleeps. But Genzaburo is taken aback when a dreaming Sanshiro suddenly smiles in his sleep. The next morning, the brothers appear reconciled to their defeat, and Sanshiro is beaming.

Sanshiro Sugata, Part Two (Zoku Sugata Sanshiro) is widely regarded as Kurosawa's weakest film. Donald Richie considered it "very bad," concluding, "In it we have what the original *Sugata* might have been had an ordinary director done it."[39] Mitsuhiro Yoshimoto, in his book *Kurosawa—Film Studies and Japanese Cinema*, wrote: "It might be said that among Kurosawa's works, this film is least satisfying artistically and perhaps most overtly propagandistic. . . . In fact, rather than a sequel to *Sanshiro Sugata*, *Sanshiro Sugata, Part Two* is more like a bad remake of the former."[40]

Part Two is indeed pure melodrama. The scenes between Sanshiro and Sayo have little of the warmth of the first film, and with one exception are clichéd and dependent on our knowledge of the couple from the first film. The snow-filled climax is just a rehash of the original. The final reels show some damage due to the unstable nitrate film stock used at the time, and the battle between Sanshiro and Teshin, possibly because of this, is difficult to make out. The men appear to have been backlit against the white snow, which creates a silhouette effect, and in presently available prints they are opaque most of the time, appearing almost like empty mattes.

"I had a difficult time shooting that climax," Fujita recalled. "We shot it in Shiga-Kogen and I had to be barefoot in the snow. On the other hand, Mr. Tsukigata, who played Teshin, wore a pair of shoes made of barley. After each shot my feet were numb. I was carried to a bonfire. I thought I was going to die. They used a stuntman for the scene where I threw Teshin down the mountainside. After he was thrown he couldn't get up. The still photographer skied down to him and picked him up. I was so scared. It was a 'shoot to the death.' "[41]

The younger brothers have none of the subtlety of Gennosuke's character from the first film. Teshin, with his coyote-like howling and rolling eyes is like something out of a cartoon—he even looks into a mirror and growls at himself. Genzaburo is a character straight out of Japanese Noh (a form of traditional Japanese theater), but unlike Kurosawa's similar use of Noh influences in later films like *Throne of Blood*, Genzaburo just looks silly. At Shogoro Yano's *dojo*, where the brothers make their first appearance, Genzaburo dances about the tatami in a fit of rage, twirling about in Noh fashion, unable to control his rage, but the effect is lacking in any subtlety, appearing foolish rather than frightening, even for Japanese audiences.

Curiously, it was this character which most intrigued Kurosawa. "I spent a great deal of effort on [Genzaburo's] costume and makeup," he wrote. "We put him in a tousled long black wig like those used in the Noh drama. He wore white makeup all over his face, and bright red lipstick. We put him in a white costume and had him carry the 'bamboo grass of madness' that crazed characters in Noh plays hold."[42]

Richie, like Yoshimoto, criticized the film for pandering to wartime propaganda needs. Referring to its opening scene: "It escaped no one in the 1944 audience [sic] that the hero was protecting a poor, helpless Japanese from a big, brutal foreigner. The first *Sugata* managed to avoid all of the clichés of the wartime Japanese film; the second subscribes to most of them."[43]

In fairness, Japanese films like *Sanshiro Sugata, Part Two*, while clearly anti-American, depicted the enemy with restraint compared to Hollywood's films. As Kyoko Hirano states in her excellent book, *Mr. Smith Goes to Tokyo*, "American war films carefully manipulated and juxtaposed contrasting images to portray 'our side' as the heroic guardian of humanity. They took the same care to show 'our enemy' as cold-blooded, treacherous, and inhuman. They thus tried to inspire their audience to fight for the good cause by destroying the enemy."[44] The Westerners in *Part Two* may be brutish and ignorant of Japanese ways, but by no means are they comparable to the inhuman monsters the Japanese became in Hollywood films.

After the bombing of Pearl Harbor, racism against both the Japanese people and Japanese-Americans went hand in hand with opposition to its military regime. Japanese-Americans lost nearly everything they owned and were summarily shipped to concentration camps, quite unlike German-Americans. Songs like "When Those Little Yellow Bellies Meet the Cohens and the Kelleys," "You're a Sap, Mr. Jap," and "We're Going to Find the Fellow Who Is Yellow and Beat Him Red, White, and Blue" became popular. Where Hollywood films portrayed Germany's leaders as demented and its soldiers as either evil (and often sadistic) or foolish, ordinary German citizens were viewed in a much more sympathetic light. Not so with the Japanese. Japanese men and women, in films like *Objective, Burma!* (1945) and especially *Gung Ho!* (1943), were depicted in the most vile, despicable manner imaginable. Buck-toothed and half-witted, they wore thick, Coke-bottle glasses and generally were something less than human. This Hollywood image of the Japanese people made so deep an impression that postwar films like *Breakfast at Tiffany's* (1961), with its grotesque characterization by Mickey Rooney, continued to perpetuate this image. As late as the 1990s, Jerry Lewis still donned false teeth and thick-lensed glasses for comedy routines.

In *Part Two*, Richie found fault with the boxing sequences in particular. The audience is filled with cigar-chomping American men and large-nosed, unrefined American women; even the boxer is nicknamed "The Killer." But while Richie is correct in stating, "This view of things foreign and Japanese quite agreed with aims of the Japanese wartime propaganda department," it might also be viewed in a more specific sense. Admittedly, these scenes pander to anti-American propaganda, but they offer something beyond that, a condemnation of boxing itself. Take away the film's opening scene and what *Part Two* does in its boxing sequences isn't so different from what happens in postwar American films like *The Set-Up* (1949) and especially *The Harder They Fall* (1956), which likewise condemn the barbarity of the sport. Sanshiro looks at this brutality with extreme, even moving sadness. He has never even heard of boxing before, and while this was probably not Kurosawa's intention, the nightmarish close-ups of the bloodthirsty crowd might be viewed as Sanshiro's subjective exaggeration of the savageness he perceives. In both films Sanshiro is something of a rube, an innocent, and in this scene his innocence is lost. It's the best scene in the picture.

Sanshiro's subsequent fight with the boxer later in the film is entertaining in an empty sort of way, though even this is undermined by the scene's humor. Kurosawa tries to add a little life to the fight by freezing the action (and deadening the sound) for nearly 30 seconds after Sanshiro throws the boxer, knocking him momentarily unconscious. This was accomplished not, as Richie claims, by optically printing freeze frames, but rather by having the actors and extras stand still. Unfortunately, some extras can be seen blinking, breathing, etc., so the effect becomes artificial and forced.

The director experiments, more than in any other film, with the kind of flashy dissolves common in Japanese films of the period but rare in Kurosawa. The best use of these comes when the rickshaw boy who joins Sanshiro's school is seen sitting and bowing in a series of lap dissolves. With each shot his posture improves, his confidence builds. In a nice touch, the last shot ends with the boy eyeing some pebbles on the tatami; he picks them up and flicks them to one side. Another effective sequence has San-shiro saying goodbye to Sayo at a shrine. In a series of dissolves he walks several steps, looks back, and finds her still standing there. Each time she bows he acknowledges her. (This sort of thing is very common in Japanese etiquette, a show of respect for the departing person.)

Susumu Fujita is still relegated to second billing after Denjiro Okochi, even though Okochi is in the film for less than 15 minutes. That this sequel is inferior is in no way Fujita's fault. He's even better in *Part Two*, giving a more relaxed, confident performance, though the character as written is less spiritual. Indeed, in *Part Two* Sanshiro comes dangerously close to be-coming a "lovable dumb lug."

Wartime conditions worsened during the making of *Part Two*. Negative cut-ter Yoshie Yano recalled that rushes were printed on inferior recycled film stock. During editing, Yano, script supervisor Hachiko Toi, and Kurosawa had to work with film so poor they could barely make out the actors. Post-production was completed in late winter, when frequent power outages forced them to work in ice-cold buildings. When there was power, it fluc-tuated greatly. When they heard air raid sirens, the three would have to grab all their film and run to the nearest shelter.[45]

Sanshiro Sugata, Part Two premiered on May 3, 1945, one of only five films Toho released in the three months before the Japanese surrender. By then, there were few theaters left standing to show it. More than three-quarters of Toho's theaters had been damaged by air raids, and more than half had been completely destroyed.[46]

As Kurosawa was finishing *Sanshiro Sugata, Part Two*, he and Yoko Yaguchi de-cided to get married. She had been engaged before, but her fiancé had died during the war. Kurosawa himself allegedly had been engaged once himself, though whether or not this is true and to whom may never be known.

Years later, Yoko told her children that Kurosawa wooed her with love letters, but he remembered events much less romantically:

> It all began with my parents' evacuation to the country. Nobuyoshi Morita, who was then head of the Toho production division, saw that I was having a difficult time taking care of myself in my day-to-day

life. He suggested that I give some thought to getting married. "But who?" I asked, and Morita immediately replied, "What about Miss Yaguchi?" "Well, that does make sense," I thought to myself, but since she and I had done nothing but fight all the way through *The Most Beautiful*, I told Morita I thought she was a little too strong-willed. But he countered with a big grin, "But don't you see that's exactly what you need?" I had to admit he had a point, and I made up my mind to ask her hand in marriage.

My proposal went something like this: "It looks as if we are going to lose the war, and if it comes to the point of the Honorable Death of the Hundred Million, we all have to die anyway. It's probably not a bad idea to find out what married life is like before that happens."[47]

Yoko eventually said yes and retired from acting. Her decision to marry Kurosawa might also have been due to the fact that she was two months pregnant with his child. In any case, the couple was married on May 21, 1945, eighteen days after the premiere of *Sanshiro Sugata*, *Part Two*. The ceremony was held at the wedding hall of the Meiji shrine in Tokyo. Kajiro Yamamoto and his wife acted as official matchmakers. The day after they wed, the bombing of Tokyo intensified.

During the early part of the Pacific War, Kurosawa lived next door to his parents, who shared their house with his older sister Taneyo. Her husband had died in the late 1930s, and their seven-year-old son, Mike Inoue, moved in next door with his uncle. But as the war escalated in 1943, Kurosawa's parents, sister, and nephew were evacuated out of Tokyo to Isamu Kurosawa's birthplace in Akita Prefecture. For this reason they missed their son's wedding, but shortly after the wedding, Kurosawa took Yoko to Akita to meet them. Kurosawa recalled, "I had to part with them under conditions that meant we might never meet again. I was on a lonely road that stretched off into the distance from the front gate of the house. I kept looking back over my shoulder at my parents standing there to see me off. It was my mother who immediately turned and hurried back into the house. My father kept standing there perfectly still, looking in my direction, until he appeared as small as a bean . . . . I believe that things were the opposite of what they appeared on the surface. My father was actually the sentimentalist, and my mother the realist."[48] Kurosawa's father stayed in Akita after the war, and the two never saw each other again.

As the war drew to its horrifying climax, Mike Inoue was admitted to the Japanese Naval Academy as a cadet, which led to another difficult, heartbreaking good-bye. He said, "It was in March 1945 when I was about 15 years old. I still remember when my grandparents (Kurosawa's parents) decided to evacuate from Tokyo taking me and my mother, Taneyo, with them to Akita Prefecture where Akira's father was born. So I went to junior high school in that area. On the way to the Naval Academy in the Hiroshima area, I stopped over in Tokyo to visit my uncle at the Toho studio where he was directing *Sanshiro Sugata, Part Two*. After our visit, he brought me to the rear gate and I started walking away. A few minutes later I looked back and he was still there waving his hand. Like his father, he looked severe, but was himself a sentimentalist."

Kurosawa spent most of the rest of 1945 lodging at his friend's home in Soshigaya close to the Toho Studio. (It was not his new home.) Despite everything, Toho and Kurosawa pressed on. "The war was hurtling Japan along the road to defeat at breakneck speed," Kurosawa wrote, "and yet the Toho studios, employing the hands of people with empty stomachs, continued to show remarkable vitality in the production of motion pictures. But those who were not running around frantically trying to complete a picture were sitting on their heels in the central courtyard talking. They were so hungry it was painful for them to stand up."[50]

Kurosawa was, to his relief, one of the frantic ones. His next film was to be *The Lifted Spear* (Dokkoi kono yari), a *jidai-geki* (historical drama) covering events he would later dramatize in his 1980 film *Kagemusha*. The script required horses for a massive battle scene, but Toho simply did not have the resources any longer. Nor, by the war's end, did Japan have enough horses for the film.

"In great haste," according to Kurosawa, he threw together an alternative project, *The Men Who Tread on the Tiger's Tail* (Tora no o fumu otokotachi), based on the Kabuki play *The Subscription List* (Kanjincho) and the Noh drama *Ataka*. Both were themselves based on a historical anecdote. Kurosawa's script, supposedly written in one day, was intimate: most of the 59-minute film was shot on a single set. It was a period film, like *The Lifted Spear*, but required little in the way of location work and had no expensive battle sequences. It also had no women—most of Toho's actresses and female staff had been evacuated out of Tokyo. With its story of feudal loyalty, it was readily accepted by the Japanese military censors.

The Men Who Tread on the Tiger's Tail concerns twelfth-century lord Yoshitsune (Hanshiro Iwai), fleeing from his brother with a handful of retainers, all of whom disguise themselves as traveling monks. To escape they must pass through a barrier, or *sekisho*, heavily guarded by the brother's forces and commanded by Togashi (Susumu Fujita). Kurosawa departs from the plays by adding the character of a porter, Kyoryoku (Kenichi "Enoken" Enomoto), who alerts them that Togashi is already aware the band is traveling in disguise. The lord's chief retainer, Benkei (Denjiro Okochi), decides to press on to the checkpoint. Through little more than sheer bravado, he hopes to convince Togashi that they are genuine monks. When Togashi asks Benkei to read his order's subscription book, Benkei boldly, convincingly, reads from an empty scroll. Togashi is impressed by all this and allows the ersatz monks to pass. As they depart, a suspicious messenger (Yasuo Hisamatsu) recognizes Yoshitsume, disguised as a porter. Benkei saves him by berating the lord as he would a real porter, going so far as to beat his own master. No retainer, Togashi surmises, under any circumstances, would do such a thing, and he allows them to continue their journey. Togashi sends the fake monks some sake, Benkei tearfully apologizes to his lord for his inexcusable act, and the lord easily forgives him. They get drunk and continue their journey, leaving Kyoryoku behind.

The core of the film—and Kurosawa's main interest in the material—is the implication that Togashi is well aware he is being deceived but is so impressed with Benkei's performance that he knowingly allows him to pass through the barrier station. There is nothing in the dialogue to suggest this; it is only implied. The inference comes mainly through the marvelous performance of Susumu Fujita, who spends most of the film seated stoically, listening to Okochi's ad-libbed reading of the religious subscription. He sits, stares unemotionally, closes his eyes, and even nods off (or appears to do so) for long stretches. Then, on occasion, he smiles, Sanshiro-style, faintly hinting he is not only aware of the deception but is enjoying it immensely. This much-debated aspect of the Kabuki and Noh plays has been interpreted in numerous ways, in much the same way Western theater has approached the question of Hamlet's madness. Togashi in *Tiger's Tail* remains enigmatic, though most critics have taken the position that he is indeed aware of the monks' deception.

Richie, and especially Yoshimoto, make much of the film's debt to Kabuki and Noh, the two indigenous, highly stylized forms of Japanese theater. The picture is filled with Noh music (incorporating traditional instruments such as the *kotsuzumi* and *fue*), particularly in the barrier camp scene, and ends with Benkei's drunken exit, which incorporates music from Kabuki. Denjiro Okochi's performance is in the Noh tradition, and so forth. But in the end the matter is beside the point. The film's Kabuki and

Noh references are there solely to provide the dramatic premise, its time and place, which Japanese audiences would have already been familiar with. Rather, the film is almost pure entertainment, a kind of psychological anecdote with music.

Although the film's look is obviously compromised, with patently studio-bound sets standing in for heavily forested exteriors (though some of the early scenes were filmed outdoors), *The Men Who Tread on the Tiger's Tail* is something of a remarkable achievement. Through the compactness of its narrative and Kurosawa's refusal to surrender to its physical limitations, *Tiger's Tail* becomes an entertaining little gem.

It is to Kurosawa's credit that although half the film is confined to one, albeit large, set, *Tiger's Tail* never seems stagy. Indeed, he uses his cameras so ingeniously that their effect becomes invisible. This is the very opposite of most of today's Hollywood movies, where often elegant cinematography is ruined by showy, self-conscious dollying, awkward if striking compositions, and trite slow-motion effects. *Tiger's Tail* opens with angles subtly favoring Enoken, but as the motives and bravery of the retainers, especially Benkei, become clear, the camera is placed in not-quite-subjective positions from their point of view. This works to involve the audience with the extreme tension felt by the retainers as they risk their and their lord's lives. Again, all of this is practically invisible; one is almost never aware of the camera.

In the middle of production, on August 15, 1945, Kurosawa was summoned to the studio to listen to a radio address, the first ever, by the Japanese Emperor, whom many still revered as a deity. The war had clearly come to an end, and Kurosawa, like most Japanese, expected the worst, that all Japan would be compelled to commit suicide. "I will never forget the scenes I saw as I walked the streets that day," Kurosawa remembered. "On the way from Soshigaya [where he had moved in April] to the studios in Kinuta the shopping street looked fully prepared for the Honorable Death of the Hundred Million. The atmosphere was tense, panicked. There were even shopowners who had taken their Japanese swords from their sheaths and sat staring at the bare blades."[51]

Only weeks before, Kajiro Yamamoto had taken most of Toho's prominent actresses to the heavily bombed Tateyama City, to shoot a film called *Straight to the Americans* (Amerika yosoro). The film was commissioned by the government to prepare audiences for the mass suicide upon the now-inevitable American invasion. On August 12, Yamamoto was hand-delivered a secret letter from studio head Iwao Mori. He instructed Yamamoto that, should an "emergency" arise, he was to "stop shooting and first of all send the actresses back to Tokyo as soon as possible; second . . . make sure that no one in the crew acts carelessly in the confusion or attempts suicidal actions; and third, [remember] that the safety of the crew is the first priority, and do not worry about the possible loss or destruction of their equipment."[52]

On the fifteenth, all Japan listened with great relief as the Emperor implored his subjects to lay down their swords. "When I walked the same route back to my home after listening to the imperial proclamation," wrote Kurosawa, "the scene was entirely different. The people on the shopping street were bustling about with cheerful faces as if preparing for a festival the next day. I don't know if this represents Japanese adaptability or Japanese imbecility. In either case, I have to recognize that both these facets exist in the Japanese personality. Both facets exist within my own personality as well."[53]

Conversely, actress Hideko Takamine, on location in Tateyama, remembered that evening sadly listening to Japanese pilots crashing their Zeros into the Pacific off Tateyama's shores.[54]

Incredibly, as American forces began their seven-year occupation, Toho's executives opted to continue as before. "Although the war has ended," Mori told his employees, "we do not have anything to do but continue filmmaking. Let's continue our daily work without being confused."[55] Barely skipping a beat, *Tiger's Tail* went back into production, this in spite of the fact that by the war's end food shortages were so bad much of Japan was starving to death. "When we recorded the chorus," Kurosawa said, "nobody could sing very loud because we were all starving. I sang, too."[56]

"There was no film or raw materials available at that time," remembered Susumu Fujita. "Everything was shot on a soundstage. I want to say that *The Men Who Tread on the Tiger's Tail* is Akira Kurosawa's best film. Enoken gave a great performance, and Denjiro-san created a remarkable character. But I looked so bad. I didn't think I performed well, but director Kurosawa said of my performance, 'It's good.' Mr. Enoken and Mr. Okochi were everything in that movie, though."[57]

Kurosawa was less complimentary to Shubo Nishina, known later as Hanshiro Iwai, cast as Yoshitsune. "He was a scary director," said Iwai. "I was scolded by him many times."[58]

American soldiers frequented the set of *Tiger's Tail*, including director-turned-Navy lieutenant commander John Ford, though Kurosawa was not aware of his presence until he formally met Ford in London a dozen years

later. Another visitor was British filmmaker Michael Powell. "I don't remember exactly when," Kurosawa recalled, "but it was during postproduction, and I remember that he came to the wardrobe office. I guess Sen-chan
[Senkichi Taniguchi] or somebody else brought him and introduced me to
him. I showed him the film, and he was impressed by it, and kept saying,
'It's wonderful.' "[59]

Tiger's Tail represents, for most Americans, their single encounter with
the comedian known as Enoken. He was born in 1904 and began his career
at eighteen as a member of an Asakusa operetta troupe. The following year,
however, came the Great Kanto Earthquake, and in the wake of the massive
destruction the company was disbanded. He had small roles in a few silent
films, but made little impact. In 1929, he joined a new company, Kajino
fori (Casino Follies), in which he employed a style of humor influenced by
American vaudeville and silent-film comedy, and quickly became its biggest
star. He was signed by P.C.L. in 1934, appearing in its sixth release, and by
the late 1930s was making five to six features for the studio every year.
Enoken's films were Toho's bread and butter, along with other modestly
budgeted films starring comedians like Kingoro Yanagiya and the team of
Achako (Hanabishi) and Entatsu (Yokoyama). Because they were so cheap
to produce, Toho's comedies consistently reaped big profits and helped finance more expensive, ambitious films for directors like Kurosawa, Shiro
Toyoda, and Mikio Naruse. Their films dominated Toho's production schedule more than any other almost from Toho's inception and established its
identity more than any other genre.

Enoken remained popular until his death in 1970, but in the late 1950s
a new generation of postwar comedians—Frankie Sakai, Hitoshi Ueki, Hajime Hana, the Drifters—began to dominate, and Enoken was relegated to
guest-star status by the 1960s. With his rubbery features, wide mouth, and
broad delivery, his comic style was closest to that of American comedian
Joe E. Brown, who, like Enoken, came into prominence in the film world
in the early 1930s. In *Tiger's Tail*, some of his reactions, particularly when he
is panicked, are equally reminiscent of Stan Laurel. Unlike Laurel, who co-
wrote, directed, and edited his films with Oliver Hardy in all but name,
Enoken, like all Japanese comedians, relied on writers and directors to
shape the films in which he starred. These pictures were helmed by a wide
range of house directors, notably Nobuo Nakagawa and Torajiro Saito
(though even Mikio Naruse had his hand in a few), but it was Kajiro Yamamoto, with Kurosawa as his chief assistant, who set the standard with
the Enoken comedies of the late 1930s.

Modern audiences may find Enoken's mugging hard to take, but his persona—the neurotic overreactor—was quite appropriate for the story, and his broad style nicely contrasts with the demeanor of his grim patrons. Okochi and Fujita were already big stars who ensured the film's box-office success, and there were so few films being released at this time that virtually anything was making money. Kurosawa added the porter character to make his story less remote; Enoken provided the audience's perspective, if one exaggerated to great comic effect. He is a commoner who is witness to this event. But he is not us, because, as Donald Richie noted, "we are brighter than that; but, perhaps, the man sitting next to us."[60]

Japanese censors had objected to Enoken's character because, in one sense, the porter reacts as we might to the extreme ritual and formality around which the feudal world revolved. In that sense the film was seen by some as a criticism of feudalism. But, as Richie argues, "one would not expect Kurosawa to uphold the feudal thesis of *Kanjincho* and he does not. But neither does he denigrate it. What he does do is uphold the drama, the story, the fable—and to show us its strength."[61]

Denjiro Okochi, normally an inexpressive actor who made little impression as Sashiro's teacher, is excellent as Benkei, expressing with great subtlety the inner workings of this clever retainer. Okochi was born in Fukuoka in 1898. He made his film debut at twenty-six, at Nikkatsu, and became one of its biggest stars in several films as Jirokichi Nezumikozo, before switching to Toho by way of J. O. Studios in 1937. He remained one of Toho's top stars well into the 1950s, though few of his starring films, other than those he did with Kurosawa, were ever released outside Japan. He died in 1962.

The other monks were played by members of Kurosawa's growing stock company: Takashi Shimura, Yoshio Kosugi, Masayuki Mori. The roles are essentially small, but they bring considerable individuality to them, as each of the "monks" reacts to the deception as it is played out. Have they been discovered? Has their lord been identified? Will they be forced to draw their swords? Theirs is a perfect example of effective ensemble acting.

The picture was completed in September 1945, but as the Japanese military censors passed their reports to the GHQ, they failed to file one on *Tiger's Tail*, quite possibly willfully and out of spite for all the conflicts they had had with the intractable director.

"At the end of the Pacific War I was an assistant director, but had directed a puppet film called *A Girl at Dojo Temple* (Musume Dojoji)," said Kon Ichikawa. "Right after completing the film, the war ended. Because the script hadn't been investigated by the Occupation Army, the film wasn't released. When we set out to make it, there was no such system. At the same time, I heard that Kuro-san (I always called him 'Kuro-san' out of respect) couldn't release *Tiger's Tail* for similar reasons. My film was an experimental short, but Kuro-san's film was a magnificent theatrical film, so it became a big problem. I was disappointed in not being able to see it, but heard about a special screening that would be held at the studio and sneaked in to watch it. It was less than an hour and made with hardly any money. But I was surprised that you couldn't see how difficult it had been to make. All of Kuro-san's films pulled the audience into its stories from the very beginning. I respect Kuro-san with all my heart because of his skillful storytelling and structure."[62]

Kurosawa placed the blame for the banning of *Tiger's Tail* at the feet of the Japanese censors. In truth, it was the Occupation Forces, concerned over the film's alleged "pro-Feudalism," which held up its release. In April 1951, Toho and Daiei requested that seven films banned by the GHQ, including *Tiger's Tail* and *Sanshiro Sugata* (which Toho wanted to rerelease), be reconsidered. They were both approved the following February, and Toho released them a few months later.

It was another eight years before *Tiger's Tail* reached American shores. The picture was released by Brandon Films as part of a nine-film package that included several other Kurosawa titles. Reviews were generally positive, mainly on the grounds that it offered a rare glimpse of filmed Kabuki. "[It] is a peculiar but interesting mélange of Kabuki solemnity and Oriental variations on Mack Sennett comedy," said John McCarten in *The New Yorker*.[63] "For the present-day U.S. audience," said *Variety*'s "Anby," "[the] film offers a unique opportunity to see a Kabuki type of drama (a highly stylized presentation in which dance and song are used to move the plot along) translated in screen terms. Satirical or not, it also evokes a quaintly attractive mood of long ago and far away."[64]

Kurosawa spent most of the rest of 1945 at his new home in Soshigaya, relieved that the war had ended and that conditions were beginning to improve. He wrote a one-act play, *Talking* (Shaberu), but spent much of that fall and early winter with his family. "She was very beautiful," Mike Inoue said of Yoko Kurosawa. "I have never seen such a good-looking lady in my life. She had a lot of patience, she respected her husband."[65]

Kurosawa's parents remained in Akita, but Yoko's mother and father moved in with him, and he enjoyed their company enormously. When they first married, Yoko could not even cook rice, but retiring from acting soon changed this. Almost immediately, Kurosawa began inviting the Kurosawa-gumi to his home for *daienkai* (Japanese-style large parties) several times a month, bringing as many as forty people over at a time. And eventually Yoko became quite a gourmet. She also became a mother. On December 20, 1945, she gave birth to a son they named Hisao.

The Pacific War was over, but another kind of war, one far more directly destructive, was on the horizon.

FOUR

NEW FACES OF 1946

Kurosawa's first postwar film remains his most elusive. *Those Who Make To-morrow* (Asu o tsukuru hitobito, 1946) has not been seen in Japan since its initial release and has never been shown in the United States. It is not mentioned in Kurosawa's autobiography, and even Donald Richie, author of *The Films of Akira Kurosawa*, has never seen it.[1] It was produced amid labor unrest at Toho and made to promote the union's inroads in the entertainment industry. The picture was quickly thrown together and co-directed with Kajiro Yamamoto and Hideo Sekigawa. Set in a theatrical company, it starred Hideko Takamine, Takashi Shimura, Masayuki Mori, and Seizaburo Kawazu, among others.

Like *Sanshiro Sugata, Part Two*, it was a film Kurosawa did not want to make, but unlike in that film, he had little opportunity to rise above the material given him. He completely disowned *Those Who Make Tomorrow*: he excluded it from his official filmography and almost never discussed it. Perhaps in deference to him, the picture was never released to home video in Japan or anywhere else. And the chance that Toho will ever make it available for screenings in the West are slim.

The film revolves around a family whose very structure is based on (and critical of) Toho's production and acting divisions. The father (Kenji Susukida) is an anti-union white-collar worker. One of his daughters (Chieko Nakakita) is a script girl at a film studio, the other daughter (Mitsue Tachibana) a revue dancer. And a boarder in their home (Masayuki

Mori) works for a railroad conglomerate—a rather obvious allusion to Toho's parent company.

The railway workers go on strike, and unionists at the movie studio join the picketers. The studio goes unnamed, but is clearly Toho, as actors like Susumu Fujita, Seizaburo Kawazu, and Hideko Takamine play themselves. When one of the revue dancers is fired by a brutish stage manager (Takashi Shimura), the girls decide to organize. The father is opposed to his daughters' activities, but then he's fired himself, and the film ends with everyone, including Papa, on strike and singing pro-union songs.[2]

Those Who Make Tomorrow was the direct result of increasing labor strife in Japan. As detailed in Hirano's *Mr. Smith Goes to Tokyo*, workers' rights had been legalized by the Occupation Forces, which, in the fleeting days prior to the Cold War, initially encouraged labor unions and pro-labor films. Toho's union demanded improved working conditions and themselves went on strike on March 20, 1946, shortly before the release of *Those Who Make Tomorrow*. After fifteen days, the company acquiesced to the union's demands. They agreed to a minimum monthly salary of ¥600 (plus overtime) and allowed the union to create committees which would exert considerable power over which scripts would be filmed and help determine what new talent would be hired by the studio.

Based on existing information (the author was unable to view *Those Who Make Tomorrow* for this book), the picture is very likely overtly polemic at the expense of any subtlety. Similar to *The Most Beautiful*, it is filled with militant signs like DEMOCRATIZATION OF CINEMA IS FOR THE PEOPLE and LET'S WIN OUR DAILY BREAD THROUGH STRUGGLE AT THE STUDIO. Characters complain about how the film studio is interested only in profits, how they don't think of the audience's needs or the economic security of its employees. "Rather than effectively dramatizing the unionists' struggle," concluded Kyoko Hirano, "the film resorts to clichéd dialogue and relies for its effect on close-up shots of strikers singing militant songs. It is too simplistic in dividing the world into exploitative capitalists and noble, hardworking employees."[3]

Kurosawa did not contribute to its screenplay, and it is unclear what portions of the film he may have directed, though it seems likely, based on how quickly it was thrown together and its patchwork script, that one director probably helmed the dance revue sequences, another the movie studio material, and a third all the domestic scenes.

"This film cannot be described as mine more than anyone else's," Kurosawa insisted in a *Kinema Jumpo* interview years after its production. "In sum, it is a film made by [a] committee and it is a good example of how un-interesting such films can be. It was made in a week, and even now, when I hear their songs on May Day, it reminds me of this film and makes me sleepy. However, I guess it wasn't too bad for a picture shot in a week."[4]

Into the midst of this growing chaos came Toshiro Mifune, a civilian once again after the war's end. Mifune was given two blankets when he was discharged; at the time, he was so poor that he fashioned them into a crude jacket and a pair of slacks. "At the end of the war he went to Kumamoto," said Tomio Sagisu, "and when the war was over I went to Kumamoto, too, looking for him, but there was nothing left of the city."[5]

"Right after the war he lived in Isagao, in Yokohama," said son Shiro, "and he got a part-time job carrying tanks of Coca-Cola syrup for the American Navy."[6] Mifune's mother had died during the war, but his sister and his brother joined him in Yokohama. The sister quickly married a second-generation Japanese living in Hawaii. Mifune's brother attended Meiji University and eventually became an official in the Army.

Mifune, however, had no idea what he wanted to do with his life. He was desperate for work, though, and went to Toho with the hope of getting a job as a cameraman. He thought he had an "in." Tomio Sagisu had worked for the studio's special-effects department under Eiji Tsuburaya on *The War at Sea from Hawaii to Malaya* and other war pictures prior to being drafted, while another comrade, Nenji Oyama, had been a cameraman. "When they were in the Air Force together," Sagisu said, "Oyama told Mifune, 'If you want to be a cameraman, I'll be back at Toho once your tour of duty ends, so please come and see me.' Mifune was supposed to be discharged the following year, but the war was getting worse and he wasn't able to. He wasn't happy about it."[7]

"I was friends with a soldier named Nenji Oyama, who was a cameraman at Toho," Mifune recalled. "I was going to ask him to put me in the cinematography division in 1946. I sent my résumé to Toho but it was sent to the first New Face auditions."[8]

Toho's New Face program was an ambitious attempt to replenish the studio's acting stable, which had diminished during the war years. Some of the leading men had died at the front, while many of its actresses, like those in *The Most Beautiful*, had gotten married and retired. For its New Face program, promising talent would be selected from among nearly 4,000 applicants. They would be given six months of intensive training, which included not only acting lessons by its leading actors, directors, and cameramen (mainly Eizo Tanaka and Yoshio Kosugi) but also lessons in the art of moviemaking, film theory, traditional Japanese dance, and theatrical and film makeup. Actors were then gradually slipped into Toho's productions, first in bit parts, and if they continued to show promise, they would be built up by the company's aggressive publicity department. When Toho's biggest stars walked out during the company's second strike late that same year, Toho's investment proved doubly invaluable; not only did they have a roster of fresh talent to choose from, they were also able to avoid charges that the company had hired "scabs" to star in its pictures. For the next two decades, the studio held annual New Face auditions, and most of its major stars emerged from this program.

Just how Mifune came to the June 3, 1946, audition has become steeped in legend. Mifune always perpetuated the notion that he simply got into the wrong line, or that his résumé was sent to the acting division by mistake. But in fact, Mifune was desperate for work. He was willing to do anything to make a living.

"After the war . . . I went back to work at Toho's Kinuta Studio," Sagisu said, "and at that time Toho was looking for new faces and looking at new applicants. After the war, Mifune went to Nenji Oyama for help, but many veterans were returning from the war and the studio was practically full. Mr. Oyama wanted to have Mifune start in the camera department as an assistant, but he couldn't get him in. Since he had promised to help Mifune, Oyama put him in the New Face contest. 'Once you get in you can transfer to my division.' When I was going to the studio in Seijo on the Odakyu [train] line, I saw a man who was wearing his uniform, and it looked like Mr. Mifune. I approached this man, and indeed it was him. When I asked what he was doing there, he told me he was going to the studio to take a test. So I helped get him to Toho, to Stage 3. I dropped him off and went back to work. But I was concerned about the audition, so during the lunch break I visited the stage and asked around. The committee was Kajiro Yamamoto, Hideko Takamine, Susumu Fujita, and some of the union people were there, too, as well as some of the producers and cameramen. During the audition they asked him to laugh, and he said, 'Why do I have to laugh?' He's a shy man, and couldn't get into character immediately, so he became so violent—screaming and yelling—and he failed the test. I was very disappointed."[9]

"They told me, 'You have a gangster's face, you ought to do well in this,' " Mifune recalled. "But then they told me to cry, and I said, 'How can I cry when I'm not sad?' Then they asked me to get angry, and I got too angry and failed the test."[10]

Kurosawa was at that time shooting his next picture, *No Regrets for Our Youth* (Waga seishun ni kuinashi). The studio was abuzz with would-be talent and speculation about who would be hired and about the angry applicant who refused to cooperate with the panel of judges.

> During lunch break I stepped off the set and was immediately accosted by actress Hideko Takamine [Kurosawa remembered]. "There's one who's really fantastic. But he's something of a roughneck, so he just barely passed. Won't you come have a look?" I bolted my lunch and went to the studio where the tests were being given. I opened the door and stopped dead in amazement.
>
> A young man was reeling around the room in a violent frenzy. It was as frightening as watching a wounded or trapped savage beast trying to break loose. I stood transfixed. But it turned out that this young man was not really in a rage, but had drawn "anger" as the emotion he had to express in his screen test. He was acting. When he finished his performance, he regained his chair with an exhausted demeanor, flopped down and began to glare menacingly at the judges. Now, I knew very well that this kind of behavior was a cover for shyness, but the jury seemed to be interpreting it as disrespect.
>
> I found this young man strangely attractive, and concern over the judges' decision began to distract me from my work.[11]

Kurosawa wrapped shooting early that day and went to visit the judges. Kajiro Yamamoto had recommended that Mifune be hired, but the voting was stacked against him. Kurosawa recognized that the union was throwing its weight around, offended by Mifune's audition without understanding it. The director argued that the unionists were less qualified to judge Mifune's performance than the experienced directors and actors on the panel. "It's like appraising a gemstone," Kurosawa wrote. "You wouldn't give a greengrocer's appraisal the same weight you would a jeweler's." Mifune "squeaked through," and Yamamoto agreed to take responsibility for the decision.[12]

Mifune was one of sixteen men and thirty-two women hired from the original four thousand applicants. He immersed himself in Toho's regimented six-month program and kept detailed notes of his lessons. As these notes illustrate, for the first few of those months he continued to hope he might be transferred to Toho's camera division. He made intricate sketches of cameras and lenses, but gradually was drawn into the world of film acting. "Since I came into the industry very inexperienced," he admitted, "I don't have any theory of acting. I just had to play my roles my way."[13] Within a year, changes at Toho would steer him toward a leading part in his first film.

Meanwhile, Kurosawa was completing production on *No Regrets for Our Youth*. The original screenplay was written in collaboration with play-wright-turned-screenwriter Eijiro Hisaita (1898–1976). Hisaita's script was based on the persecution of Yukitoki Takigawa, a liberal professor at Kyoto Imperial University in the early 1930s, and Hotsumi Ozaki, an expelled student (but not Takigawa's) wrongly executed for treason in 1944, just two years before *No Regrets* went into production. Both men came to be revered as martyrs.

Hisaita had known Kurosawa since the days of *Sanshiro Sugata*. "It was 1943," Hisaita recalled. "A longtime acquaintance, producer Keiji Matsuzaki, suggested going to Gotemba to meet Mr. Kurosawa. When I got there, he was having a meeting with four or five assistant directors."[14]

Matsuzaki, who produced *Sanshiro Sugata* and *Those Who Make Tomorrow*, had been a student of Takigawa's at Kyoto Imperial University. It was he who had initiated the project and, after bringing in Hisaita, imposed his own aspirations on the script. Matsuzaki went so far as to conduct research for the project himself, traveling to Kyoto and interviewing Takigawa's student followers, and contributed to the screenplay without credit.

"I actually took twenty days to write it," Hisaita said. "We decided upon the theme of the film, discussed the characters, and wrote the first draft. . . . I was impressed with Kurosawa's concentration, which lasted for two or three hours at a stretch. While he was working, he never accepted any telephone phone calls or visitors. He concentrated all his energy into the tip of his pencil. I was very excited about it. He'd lie on his stomach and ask me to massage his back after work. He'd take a bath and would spend a couple of hours finishing his whiskey. . . . He used to take sleeping pills so he could get to sleep. He was so excited that the whiskey didn't affect him. I'd get drunk after two or three shots of whiskey-and-water, but I listened to him because his stories were so interesting. I should have taken notes."[15]

Hisaita, Kurosawa, and Matsuzaki were enthusiastic about their work, but there was a problem. One of the results of the first Toho strike was the creation of the Scenario Review Committee, a Communist-dominated board. All scripts were now subject to their approval, and they rejected the Hisaita draft on the grounds that another script, covering similar territory, had been written by Kiyoshi Kusuda. "This committee decided that the script for *No Regrets* required changes," Kurosawa recalled, "and the film was shot from a rewrite. . . . I felt, however, that although the two scripts were based on similar material, they treated it in entirely different ways. The result, I was sure, would be two entirely different films. Anyway, this is what I said before the Review Committee, but my opinion was rejected. . . . Eijiro Hisaita's first script for my film was such a beautiful piece of work that it still pains me to remember that it was shelved at the hands of such thoughtless people."[16]

But the demands placed on Kurosawa were ultimately fortunate. Most of the changes made to *No Regrets for Our Youth* come in the film's second half, as its focus falls more directly on its heroine, Yukie. It is this second half—more personal, more cinematic than the historically based but ham-fisted polemics of the first half, that remains eminently more interesting, more alive and memorable.

The story begins with the dismissal of the Takigawa character, here called Yagihara (Denjiro Okochi), and the student revolt it inspires. His daughter, Yukie (Setsuko Hara), is courted by two of Yagihara's students, Noge (Susumu Fujita) and Itokawa (Akitake Kono). Yukie lives in a care-free, bourgeois world oblivious to the tumultuous events that surround her. Noge is expelled for his anti-militaristic activities, while the weak-willed Itokawa chooses the opposite path, joining the military government as a public prosecutor. Yukie follows Noge to Tokyo, becoming first his secretary, then his wife. Noge is arrested again and dies in jail, presumably tortured to death. She returns briefly to her parents before deciding to take her husband's remains to his rice farmer parents (Haruko Sugimura and Kokuten Kodo). Because of their son's infamy, the parents are ostracized from the village community and forced to eke out a living during the night. The mother curses her son. But Yukie's selfless decision to work in their rice paddies like an ordinary peasant, refusing to hide in the shadows, gradually impresses Noge's parents. When their neighbors viciously trample their rice crop, Yukie determinedly starts over, in spite of total exhaustion and fever—she will not give up. The war ends and Yukie again returns home, where she realizes that her life as a peasant had more meaning; she returns finally to live with Noge's parents.

Production began in the spring of 1946. Japan was still recovering from the effects of the war and food was still in short supply. "To tell the truth, I was starving," said assistant director Hiromichi Horikawa. "I stayed at Kurosawa's home at the time. I remember I'd feel dizzy on the way there coming from work. We went to Kyoto for location shooting. We shot the scene of the demonstrations in front of the main gate of Kyoto University. Except for Setsuko Hara, Susumu Fujita, and Akitake Kono, all the students were played by the assistant directors to cut down on the film's costs. That's why the students didn't look all that young. No university would allow us to shoot there now, but back then they would cooperate with us."[17]

Haruko Sugimura concurred. "The scene where I buried my son's remains in a secret grave was shot on a set at Toho. It was hard for us to make such a deep hole using shovels because we had no food and were always hungry. Of course, we had no energy. One day, around lunchtime, we were shooting. I was very hungry and my stomach started growling. Everyone was quiet during the take, but then the recording person said, 'Who the hell is hungry?' The shot was NG [no good]. I couldn't bring myself to admit it was me. I've never forgotten that. I wish I could've confessed."[18]

Electrical service was likewise recovering from the war. "In the scene where Setsuko Hara and Susumu Fujita were reunited at the office in Tokyo, there were shots of them with [Fujita in the foreground, and Hara in the background]," recalled Horikawa. "I remember Mr. Kurosawa asking the director of photography Mr. [Asakazu] Nakai, 'Why can't you focus on both of them?' Because of power shortages, we weren't able to get enough light to stay in focus."[19]

No Regrets for Our Youth is a mixed bag. The first half is a superficial, romanticized view of the student-teacher rebellions and postwar social consciousness. It wears its heart on its sleeve without much explanation; we never really know why the professor loses his job or specifically what Noge is fighting for, other than out of a vague sense of pacifism and ideals about free speech. More than any other Kurosawa film, *No Regrets* relies on audience knowledge of—and nostalgia for—their historical counterparts. Unlike postwar American films such as *The Best Years of Our Lives* (1946), which used the universality of soldiers returning home to their families for its foundation, or later Kurosawa films like *Dersu Uzala* (1975) and *Kagemusha* (1980), which were rooted in historical events but had their own universality about them, *No Regrets* leans heavily on specific incidents from then recent Japanese history that are lost on non-Japanese audiences.

The characters played by Fujita and Kono are simple extremes and not very interesting, and Denjiro Okochi's passive teacher is almost invisible. Setsuko Hara's Yukie is so naïve in the early parts of the film, skipping through the hills, pounding furiously on the family piano, or tearing apart a flower arrangement when emotionally torn, that the character borders on the comical. Once Fujita's character is arrested and murdered, however, the film shifts more directly toward Yukie's story and her enlightenment, which is the film's emotional center. Here *No Regrets* shows its true colors and plays up to Kurosawa's strengths. Ultimately, the film isn't about the idealism of the students, the passiveness of the dismissed teacher, the persecution of Noge, or even the noble spirit of the peasants (who are shown in a very unflattering light, quite the opposite of the Communist idealization of them), but rather the indomitable spirit of the individual who teaches others while coming to understand her "self" through example. Yukie so immerses herself, literally and figuratively, in the mud of the rice paddies that the emptiness and meaninglessness of her aristocratic life are washed away.

Her determination reaches extraordinary heights. The peasants, who in very Japanese fashion consider the parents as reprehensible as their "spy" son, maliciously trample the rice paddies where Yukie and Noge's mother have labored for backbreaking days. The mother breaks down at the loss, the father sits stoically. But Yukie will not give up. Without hesitation she goes straight back to work, inspiring the mother to do likewise. Even the father, who has said not a word to this point, jumps into the paddies, angrily disposes of the Spies Go Home signs littering the paddies, and sets to work. "Mr. Kodo's performance was excellent," recalled Sugimura. "He entered the rice paddies without hesitation and uprooted the signs, saying, 'Shit! Shit!' His performance was so powerful that Hara and I were really impressed."[20]

These scenes in the second half of the film are consistently powerful: Yukie's arrest and refusal to betray her husband; her disallowing Itokawa to visit her husband's unmarked grave; her growing courage and refusal to be intimidated by the hostile peasants who resent and mercilessly persecute her; her gradual apathy toward them, in spite of their relentless maliciousness; the meaningful planting of the rice; and her incredible yet completely believable physical transformation from bourgeois Kyoto girl to weather-beaten peasant. "The second draft of the script . . . was a forced rewrite of the story, so it became somewhat distorted," Kurosawa wrote apologetically. "This shows in the last twenty minutes of the film. But my intention was to gamble everything on that last twenty minutes. I poured a feverish energy into those two thousand feet and close to two hundred shots of film. All of the rage I felt toward the Scenario Review Committee went into those final images."[21]

Late in the film the professor, reinstated, addresses his students and pays tribute to the fallen Noge. This epilogue mirrors the first scenes in the picture, but given Yukie's much more dramatic self-realization, the professor's words carry little weight, perhaps by design. Like Mr. Watanabe in *Ikiru*, the bravest acts go unnoticed, unacknowledged. And for Yukie, like Watanabe, the professor's words are simply irrelevant.

No Regrets is significant as Kurosawa's only work, apart from *The Most Beautiful*, in which a woman is its central figure. The film is quite similar to Mizoguchi's superb, unapologetically feminist *My Love Has Been Burning* (a.k.a. *My Love Burns*, 1949), a superior work due to Mizoguchi's better grasp on the suffering of women in Japan and a superlative performance by star Kinuyo Tanaka. Mizoguchi's and Kurosawa's films represented a growing acknowledgment of the increasing importance of women in Japanese society. By the end of 1945, women were given the right to vote, and the following year thirty-nine were elected to the Japanese Diet. Kurosawa readily confessed he didn't understand women's roles in his pictures, and this is obvious from his often contradictory portrayal of Yukie in the film's early scenes. As much as Yukie is the heroine of the film, at times she still falls back into traditional Japanese roles for women. There's no clear explanation why she chooses to work the paddy fields rather than get an education after the war, other than that such activity is "honest work" and that living with a deceased husband's parents was the traditional place for a Japanese woman. For these reasons Hara's character was criticized as much as her performance was praised.

Kurosawa argued, "At that time I believed the only way for Japan to make a new start was to begin by respecting the 'self'—and I still believe that. I wanted to show a woman who did just that."[22] Yukie, then, does what must be done for her own personal salvation, but her actions don't hold up against scrutiny—her motives, at times, are hard to fathom.

Setsuko Hara made her film debut at the age of fifteen, at Nikkatsu Studios, in 1935, but soon thereafter joined Toho via J. O. Studios when the two companies merged. Hara came into prominence in the first Japanese-German co-production, *The New Earth* (Atarashiki tsuchi, 1937), directed by Arnold Fanck. Fanck used Hara in much the same manner he had Leni Riefenstahl in their mountain films of the late 1920s/early '30s. Hara may have been cast by Fanck because (many believe) one of her grandparents was German; and indeed, her appearance—tall, large eyes, prominent nose, sculpted rather than flat features—is Eurasian. And, as Kyoko Hirano points out in *Mr. Smith Goes to Tokyo*, she differs from most of Kurosawa's women, who tend to be short, with plumper bodies and very Japanese features. Despite anti-Western sentiment, Hara became Toho's biggest star of the late 1930s through the 1940s. Indeed, she was revered in Japan for her extraordinary beauty, and after the war she came to symbolize the indomitable spirit of the postwar Japanese woman, especially in her many films for Yasujiro Ozu. Compare Hara to Chieko Nakakita, the female lead in Kurosawa's next film, *One Wonderful Sunday*. As Hirano says, "The Western resemblance hints at a Western-style liberal feminism almost unknown in Japan."[23]

For reasons unknown, Hara did not especially want to portray Kurosawa's heroine. Despite her fame, she found acting in films generally unrewarding. She abruptly retired in 1962 and has since lived a Garbo-like reclusive life in Kamakura. She is never interviewed, and rarely is she seen in public. Before she retired, though, Hara cemented her reputation in an unforgettable string of Ozu masterpieces: *Late Spring* (Banshun, 1949), *Early Summer* (Bakushu, 1951), *Tokyo Story* (Tokyo monogatari, 1953), *Tokyo Twilight* (Tokyo boshoku, 1957), *Late Autumn* (Akibiyori, 1960), and *Early Autumn* (a.k.a. *The End of Summer*; Kohayagawa-ke no aki, 1961). "If the Japanese film had anything at all approaching a 'woman's woman,' " wrote Richie and Anderson, "it would probably be Setsuko Hara. Like Joan Crawford, her approach is almost consistently feminist and presumably best-loved roles tend to illustrate the idea that mother, or more often, wife knows best. . . . But, unlike Joan Crawford or Greer Garson, she is almost excessively subtle in her attacks on men, her main complaint being that they fail to understand, one, her business talent and two, her true feminine delicacy. This type of role, very close to that of Maria Schell, has not unnaturally made her enormously popular with middle-aged women, whose spokeswoman she has become."[24] *No Regrets for Our Youth* helped establish Hara's postwar persona as a strong-willed woman devoted to her husband and family. Simultaneously, it moved her away from her glamorous image during the war years. For audiences in 1946, seeing Hara sweaty, without makeup, and knee-deep in mud must have been almost shocking.

Against Hara's strong performance, Denjiro Okochi makes little impression, and Fujita is miscast as an intellectual. However, Akitake Kono is fine as Itokawa. Kono (1911–78) had appeared in all of Kurosawa's films to this point, memorable as the crazed, Noh-like brother in *Sanshiro Sugata, Part Two*. After *No Regrets*, Kono gave a fine performance in Toshiro Mifune's first film, *Snow Trail* (Ginrei no hate, 1947), but left Toho in the early 1950s. He did several films for Kenji Mizoguchi, including *Sansho the Bailiff* (Sansho dayu, 1954) and *New Tales of the Taira Clan* (Shin Heike monogatari, 1955), and continued working in films at least through the late 1960s, but by then his pictures were routine. Kono brings a remarkable subtlety to the unsubtle role of Itokawa. It's probable that this leftist actor based his character on men he had known during the 1930s who, like Itokawa, surrendered their ideals to the tide of Japanese militarism.

Equally fine is Haruko Sugimura as Noge's mother. "Since actors were under exclusive contracts at the time, we couldn't borrow talent from the other studios," said Hiromichi Horikawa. "In the case of Mrs. Haruko Sugimura, we were able to get her because she was a young stage actress. I met her for the first time and was surprised by how young she looked. 'I guess I won't need wrinkles, eh?' she said. 'Don't be so hard on yourself,' Mr. Kurosawa replied. She had no makeup and played an old woman by using her entire body."[25] Sugimura was only three years older than Susumu Fujita. She made her film debut at twenty-three, yet despite her age was quickly typecast as older women.

Reflecting on this in 1993, she said, "I think there was no one who could play old women at the time. I started playing old women when I was in my early twenties. I had no choice."[26]

The film's casting drips with irony. Less than two years earlier, Susumu Fujita and Denjiro Okochi had epitomized the heroic officer and enlisted man in Toho's war movies; now they played the fiercely anti-war teacher and radical student. Virtually overnight, Toho, the studio that complied with wartime propaganda demands more than any other, abruptly reversed its position, kowtowing to the Occupation Forces, producing "democratization films," of which *No Regrets* is the most representative. Noriaki Yuasa, son of film actor Hikaru Hoshi and later himself a director at Daiei, recalled, "When I was young, after Japan had lost the war, the adults I looked up to suddenly went from being very militaristic to anti-militaristic. Because of this hypocrisy I felt as if I couldn't trust adults any longer."[27]

The irony of the film's casting continued with the second Toho strike, which began on October 25, 1946, four days before *No Regrets* was released. Setsuko Hara, Denjiro Okochi, and Susumu Fujita, who had all played hard-core liberals in Kurosawa's film, walked out on Toho as part of the Society of the Flag of Ten, an alternate union founded in protest against the more militant unionists who had taken control of the studio and all but ground Toho to a halt. Akitake Kono, the anti-liberal, pro-government symbol of the picture, remained at the studio as one of its leftist unionists.

Toho's second strike dragged on during the fall of 1946 and was far more devastating than the first. The studio released no films in November and just one in December, both lacking any star talent. By the end of the year most of Toho's theaters had to shut down. The walkout by the Flag of Ten, besides Okochi, Hara, and Fujita, included virtually all of Toho's stars: Kazuo Hasegawa, Hideko Takamine, Isuzu Yamada, Takako Irie, Toshiko Yamane, Ranko Hanai, and Yataro Kurokawa. Two of the company's most prolific directors, Kunio Watanabe and Yutaka Abe, also walked out, as did 445 other employees. The strike lasted fifty-one days, ending December 3, 1946, but few were satisfied with its resolution, and the strike wound up crippling Toho.

No Regrets for Our Youth went into release during the second strike, on October 29, 1946. Predictably, many contemporary critics hated the film. It was disliked by both the left and the right. One review in the *Eiga Times* was typical of the reaction of the leftists: "The devious heroine looks like a mad person. It is ironic that she simply looks like a hysterical girl. The film is proud of itself as progressive; however, it is fatal that the film in reality praises conventional morality. The theme that a woman has to stay with her husband's family even after he dies is very obsolete. When Yukie Yagihara rushes to plant rice despite her fever, it is as if she were saying, 'No regrets for a mad person.' "[28] However, *No Regrets for Our Youth* did place second on *Kinema Jumpo*'s list of the year's best films, behind Keisuke Kinoshita's *The Morning of the Osone Family* (Osone-ke no asa), released earlier in the year and also written by Hisaita.

Even Toho's unionists hated it. "After my film was completed," Kurosawa said, "it turned out that the other film was totally uninteresting." (Kusuda's film *As Long As I Live* [Inochi aru kagiri] was released on August 1. It too featured Akitake Kono.) "Therefore, they began to say that they should have let me make my film as I had wanted to. I yelled at them, 'What are you talking about now?' The unionists and the communists were really lording it over us then. A communist screenplay writer was repatriated, and he insisted on incorporating the device of syllogism into screenplay writing. However, I replied that an uninteresting screenplay is uninteresting, despite all such devices. I argued often because I was young."[29]

Still, audiences embraced the picture, partly because there were so few new films to see to begin with, partly because of its romanticized view of the past. More urgently, its stark freedom of expression was a revelation to high school and college students who had never known such freedom. More than any of Kurosawa's earlier films, it influenced the next generation of filmmakers, including Nagisa Oshima, Kei Kumai, and Yoshishige Yoshida. The phrase "No regrets for our . . ." entered Japanese pop culture for a time, and the picture enjoyed a large profit.

In the United States, *No Regrets for Our Youth* wasn't shown until it became part of a retrospective of postwar Japanese films in 1978, and it wasn't officially released until 1980.

Japanese film scholar Joan Mellen wrote of the film's revival: " 'No Regrets,' one of Mr. Kurosawa's most deeply felt films and one infrequently screened abroad, is fresh in its awareness that it is not enough to survive; living meaningfully may entail the sacrifice of comfortable continuity for less certain paths."[30]

The *Los Angeles Times* thought *No Regrets* "superb," that it "[accumulates] tremendous power through a deliberate gradualness."[31] Observed Vincent Canby:

> Because of the passage of time . . . [Kurosawa's] movie operates on several levels that didn't exist at the time it was produced. There's not a frame of this film that is not informed by our awareness of the body of work that the then comparatively young (36) director would go on to create. Then, too, one is acutely aware of the conditions under which "No Regrets for Our Youth" was made. . . . The film's continuing impact says more about the force of Kurosawa's talent than it does about the film's politics, which could have been learned at Stanley Kramer's knee. The performances are rather simple and uncomplicated, unlike the film itself, which, in telling a heroic story, also manages to raise some disturbing questions about the nature of democracy imported from the West along with swing music, short skirts and Coca-Cola. This is not to underrate the drama . . . but to emphasize that Mr. Kurosawa is incapable of making anything as simple as a straight propaganda film.[32]

The Village Voice thought Kurosawa's film "a much more relevant event" than the belated release of Mizoguchi's *My Love Has Been Burning* earlier that same year. "Both films deal with a modern Japanese woman's liberation at a time of repressive government." [This is not accurate, as *My Love* is set at the turn of the century.] "The Mizoguchi, however, merely added [this] narrowest ideological perspective to a canon of glorious feminine images. The Kurosawa, severely breaking form with his male-centered universe, not only reveals his first major heroine but also represents his first major personal film. *No Regrets* is the first true beginning of a still prospering career. . . . *No Regrets* confirms Kurosawa as an artist true to his own adamantly unfashionable identification with loners going against the system, and the shock for most fans of the director will be that the first true Kurosawa hero was a heroine."[33]

FIVE

THREE GANGSTERS, A DAY OUT, AND CAYENNE PEPPER

As part of Toho's settlement with the unionists, the studio adopted a "closed-shop" system modeled after that of the American auto industry. This shut out the 400-plus employees who had walked out with the Flag of Ten and refused to go along with the first union's demands. The Flag of Ten group, working with Toho's executives as investors, formed Shintoho ("New Toho"), a separate production entity yet bastard child, whose films would be released through Toho. The parent company provided Shintoho with outlying studio facilities. Its first production was *1,001 Nights with Toho* (Toho senichiya), directed by Kon Ichikawa and released on February 25, 1947.

The film signaled a short-lived period of friendly and not-so-friendly rivalry between the union-controlled Toho and the Flag of Ten–led Shintoho. Toho's productions during 1947—all made under the watchful eye and tight control of the unionists—were well received by film critics. Six of their films made *Kinema Jumpo*'s "Best Ten" list, but the unionists also drove their costs to twice that of the previous, pre-strike year, and Toho ended up ¥78.2 million in the red in 1947.[1] They also made fewer films. Of its twenty-seven releases, just twelve were exclusively in-house productions, a drop from eighteen the previous year. In 1947, three of Toho's releases were co-productions, eleven were made at Shintoho, and the last was an independent.

1,001 Nights with Toho was intended as a showcase for Shintoho, featuring as it did most of the Flag of Ten stars. Toho, by contrast, had no stars, so it opted to play up its pool of acclaimed directors—Shiro Toyoda, Mikio Naruse, Teinosuke Kinugasa, and Kurosawa. All of them had a hand in one of Toho's first poststrike features, *Four Love Stories* (Yotsu no koi no mono-gatari), released two weeks after *1,001 Nights*, which also heavily promoted its New Faces, among them Ryo Ikebe, Yoshiko Kuga, and Setsuko Wakayama. Other non-exclusive talent like Takashi Shimura and stage actors like Haruko Sugimura buttressed the anthology film, of which Kurosawa wrote one segment. Unfortunately, *Four Love Stories* was never released in the United States, nor has it been made available on home video in Japan.

Mifune did not appear in *Four Love Stories*. Instead, he received top billing in his very first film, *Snow Trail* (Ginrei no hate), in production as *Four Love Stories* went into release. Both films were part of Toho's almost militarylike strategy to regroup after the second strike. Late in 1946, Kurosawa, Taniguchi, Yamamoto, and the other contract directors joined the staff of screenwriters and producers at a hot spring resort on the Izu peninsula south of Tokyo. After several highly charged meetings, which Kurosawa remembered as "most pompous," a slew of ambitious titles were announced. Kurosawa himself committed to an "insane schedule," writing one of the segments for *Four Love Stories*, co-writing all of Taniguchi's film *Snow Trail* and his own *One Wonderful Sunday* (Subarashiki nichiyobi, 1947). After meeting with his old friend Keinosuke Uekusa, with whom he would write *One Wonderful Sunday*, Kurosawa turned his attentions to *Snow Trail*.[2]

Remaining at the inn after everyone else had gone, Kurosawa and Taniguchi had made virtually no progress during their first three days of work writing *Snow Trail*. Panicking and deciding "there was no way out of it but a frontal attack, I wrote out something like a newspaper headline: 'Three Bank Robbers Escape to Mountains of Nagano Prefecture; Investigation Headquarters Moves to Base of the Japan Alps.' [Which is exactly how the finished film begins.] Then I had three bank robbers hide out in the snows of the Japan Alps, sent a police inspector after them, and, adding in Sen-chan's mountaineering experiences and general knowledge, we wrote a little every day. At the end of three weeks we had a complete script for [the picture], with a story that was not bad at all."[3] Kurosawa then dashed off his script for his segment of *Four Love Stories* and returned to work on *One Wonderful Sunday*.

Taniguchi, meanwhile, began casting *Snow Trail*. Takashi Shimura and Yoshio Kosugi would play two of the three criminals, with Kokuten Kodo and Akitake Kono as innocent men at the shuttered hot springs resort where the robbers hole up. Setsuko Wakayama, a Toho New Face, would play the ingenue. But the newly appointed director had trouble casting the most treacherous of the three bank robbers. On the train in and out of Seijo, he conferred with producer Tomoyuki Tanaka. "I was standing in the overcrowded train and we were discussing the trouble we were having casting this role," Taniguchi remembered. "Toho was losing patience waiting for the shooting to begin. It was my first film. I looked across the train and saw a mean-looking guy with a thick chest. It was Mifune. I said to [Tanaka], 'I want a guy like him.' And he said, 'Oh, he works for the company.' I said, 'What do you mean?' And he said, 'He works for Toho. He should be coming to the studio tomorrow.'

"I met him at the studio's garden the next day and introduced myself. 'I am Senkichi Taniguchi and I'm about to start my first movie. It's going to be about a mountain. Would you like to be a part of my film?' And then he said something very interesting.

" 'No. I am a man. I understand why actresses use their faces to get parts, but as a man I don't like that at all.'

"So I said, 'Well, okay. But why don't you do it anyway?'

" 'I want to be a cameraman. I don't want to be an actor. I don't want to have to rely on my face to make money. I wasn't even supposed to be in the New Face class, but my friend told me not to quit if I ever wanted to be a cameraman.'

"I was so busy preparing the film the only time I'd see him after that was on the train. Since he hadn't accepted the role, I thought I'd better try to calm him a little." Taniguchi noticed that Mifune had been wearing the same clothes day after day, even when he slept. It was the cheap suit he had fashioned out of blankets after his discharge. "That was all he had. And I offered to buy him new clothes if he would be in my film. So finally he agreed, and I bought the new clothes for him—that was his salary."[4]

However, even after accepting the role, Mifune remained apathetic. He told Taniguchi, " 'I'm not interested in acting at all, but I guess I could do it if you teach me how.' He didn't have common sense, but he listened to me as I instructed him." Still, Taniguchi was enthralled with the young man's natural ability. "I fell in love with him," he said.[5]

"I think the reason I got the part," Mifune said years later, "was because of the physical risks involved. Because the big stars had left Toho from the strike, I was chosen as a co-star in *Snow Trail*. Mr. Kurosawa worked on the script and editing. I had to climb the mountain with a bag called a *kurobitsu*. It was a really hard location. Mr. Kurosawa ordered shooting of additional scenes or reshoots by telephone. It called for a great deal of mountain climbing, and I believe the studio felt an unknown actor was more expendable."[6]

Shooting began in mid-January 1947—the middle of winter—at Mt. Hakuba, in Hokkaido. Location filming was difficult for everyone except the director, who, with his love of mountaineering, was having a grand old time. "There was no hotel, just a kind of shed built by the government. We all brought sleeping bags with us, and the temperature was always below freezing. But I think the extreme working conditions made everyone work harder. The crew was tense because we faced death from one shot to the next. I was scared that somebody would fall to their death or be seriously injured. I taught them about things like tying ropes around one another, but that was back in Tokyo, and none of them knew anything about mountain climbing."[7]

Also on the set was a young assistant director named Kihachi Okamoto. "I did *Four Love Stories*," Okamoto said. "I worked on the segment directed by Shiro Toyoda, called 'First Love.' Then, because I was a good skier, I was switched from Toyoda's team and did *Snow Trail*." Of Mifune the assistant director said, "Once he got drunk he was wild, but he was quiet on the set."[8] The unit sent to the mountains was small, so small in fact that Mifune himself carried upward of 100 pounds of equipment, including the unit's tripod, and assisted Takashi Shimura up and down the mountain every day. The two became fast friends.

The picture took three months to shoot. Kurosawa's involvement extended beyond co-writing the script. Although he was shooting *One Wonderful Sunday* at the time, he would watch *Snow Trail*'s dailies and send telegrams to Taniguchi telling him the footage was no good. He urged him to reshoot much of it, but Taniguchi ignored Kurosawa's advice. After Taniguchi returned, the two worked closely together during editing.

Escaping into the mountains, three bank robbers, Nojiri (Shimura), Eijima (Mifune), and Takasugi (Kosugi) find refuge at a hot springs resort. But guests are getting suspicious of the men, particularly Nojiri, whose right hand, missing several fingers, is a dead giveaway to his identity. Police close in, sending the trio higher into the Alps. At the same time, the fury of a barking police dog panics Takasugi, who accidentally fires his pistol, triggering an avalanche that carries him away. Continuing on, Nojiri and Eijima find a shuttered inn, half-buried in the snow and closed for the season. They're greeted by a kindly mountaineer named Honda (Akitake Kono), an old man (Kokuten Kodo), and his granddaughter, Haruko (Setsuko Wakayama). Unaware of the robbers' identity (their radio doesn't work), the people at the inn welcome the two men with open arms, and over the next few days Nojiri is impressed by their kindness, while Eijima grows increasingly irritable.

Eijima threatens Honda, who agrees to take the two robbers farther up and over the treacherous range. As Honda expertly ascends the mountainside, Nojiri and Eijima struggle and Eijima slips, sending both men, connected by a lifeline, dangling from a cliff ledge. Honda by now knows they're the bank robbers, but abides by the code of the mountains: Never cut the rope. As a result, the force of the fall snaps Honda's forearm, though he bravely hangs on to the criminals anyway. In spite of this sacrifice, Eijima, now safely back on the trail, wants to leave the incapacitated Honda behind. Nojiri is outraged. They struggle, and Eijima's pistol goes off, shooting Honda in the leg. The snow gives way, and Eijima falls to his death. Nojiri carries Honda back to the hut and turns himself in.

Snow Trail is a perfect combination of an excellent hard-boiled thriller and Kurosawa's classic humanism. Taniguchi's expert handling of the Alp sequences recalls the Arnold Fanck–Leni Riefenstahl mountain films of the twenties and thirties with its stunning, often harrowing shots of the actors high above the clouds, while its human story—Nojiri's gradual redemption—is played with honest sentiment, faintly echoing Raoul Walsh's *High Sierra* (1941) and anticipating Nicholas Ray's superb *On Dangerous Ground* (1952). Shimura is excellent, his performance predicting similar work in Kurosawa's *Scandal* (1950) and *Ikiru* (1952), as well as Keigo Kimura's *The Life of a Horse-Trader* (Baku rou ichidai, 1951). Initially sinister with his dark sunglasses, cigarette holder, and black gloves, the latter to hide his missing fingers, Nojiri is moved by Haruko's kindnesses. She resembles his own deceased daughter. She gives him honey-laced tea, which reminds him of springtime, and without hesitation she forgives him when he returns with the injured Honda and gives himself up.

An odd and sentimental but nonetheless effective motif used for the film is the song "My Old Kentucky Home," which Nojiri and Eijima hear as they first reach the hut. Nojiri listens nostalgically to Haruko's record of the song later, asking her, "What is Kentucky?" He is touched by the song's unashamed warmth, the universal feeling of the music. In a wonderfully old-fashioned touch, as the police escort Nojiri away from the cabin, Haruko plays the record for him one last time. The shots of Shimura in profile, chin on chest, listening to the music, are memorably sentimental in the good sense.

Snow Trail received excellent reviews when it opened on August 5, 1947, and the picture ranked seventh on *Kinema Jumpo*'s list of the year's best, just behind Kurosawa's *One Wonderful Sunday* and ahead of *Four Love Stories*. It was Taniguchi's second film (not the first, as he often claimed), following *Toho Show Boat* (Toho sho boto), released the previous fall. For the next few years, Taniguchi was considered as formidable a talent as Kurosawa, but in retrospect critics have downplayed his skills, citing the fact that Kurosawa co-wrote his early scripts and that, in his later films, written without Kurosawa's help, Taniguchi failed to measure up. But his direction of *Snow Trail* is often excellent. An early scene of Mifune, Shimura, and Kosugi huddled in an abandoned hut, their faces illuminated only by the small fire they have built, is effectively moody. The performances are uniformly good, and a tense pace is maintained throughout, partly through Kurosawa's editing, but also because of the raw materials provided him by the director.

The use of "My Old Kentucky Home," as well as "O, Susanna," was Kurosawa's idea. They are certainly unlike anything one might expect from the film's composer, Akira Ifukube. Born in 1914, Ifukube was a friend of his better-established contemporary Fumio Hayasaka, who encouraged Ifukube to get into film music for its easy money. Ifukube's score is impressive, alternately thrilling and ominous. He got into an argument with Taniguchi over the former's insistence on using a haunting, mournful cue for a skiing sequence, but Ifukube won out in the end, and the result is quite effective and evocative. The composer would soon gain fame for his archetypal music for Toho's monster movies, and several of *Snow Trail*'s cues, particularly its main title theme and the skiing montage, were later reworked with minimal changes into these fantasy epics. At the wrap party Ifukube recalled Yoshio Kosugi chastising the young composer about arguing with the director, but Takashi Shimura stepped in, saying, "I never heard of a composer who'd fight with a director. That's great!"[9] For his efforts, Ifukube recalled with a laugh, "When the film came out I discovered that my name was put at the very end of the staff list, even after those of the set dresser and wardrobe mistress!"[10]

Though Shimura's character is the picture's center, Mifune got top billing. Toho needed new stars, and in *Snow Trail* he exhibited tremendous screen presence and considerable promise. Though a bit stiff here and there, most of what would become his familiar persona is already present in his debut: the cynical laugh, the contemptuous shrug, the primal outbursts of physicality. Indeed, there are scenes in *Snow Trail* that augur memorable characters yet to come. In one sequence, for example, Shimura's Nojiri is listening rapturously to "My Old Kentucky Home" when Mifune's Eijima storms down from upstairs and demands that the music be stopped. His character here—cynical, brutish, and unsentimental—reminds one of Kikuchiyo in *Seven Samurai*. Though Eijima's character is one-dimensional— a greedy thug—Mifune lends it a marvelous intensity.

After Kurosawa and Mifune solidified their international reputation in the 1950s, Toho tried to sell *Snow Trail* to the American market for years. They pushed the film well into the 1960s, but found no buyers, and the film was never released in the United States, which is unfortunate. Mifune and Shimura, in their first film together, are, as already noted, playing characters very much like those they would play in subsequent films directed by Kurosawa, and *Snow Trail* is at least as inventive as the films Kurosawa himself directed during the 1940s. It shows off Taniguchi's considerable talents to great effect, offering an impressive performance by a heretofore unknown, lighting up the screen in his very first film.

When Mifune returned to Toho, he made a brief appearance as a gang boss in Kajiro Yamamoto's comedy *These Foolish Times* (a.k.a. *New Age of Fools*; Shin baka jidai, 1947), released in two parts that October. The film starred Enoken and longtime Toho favorite Roppa Furukawa. Mifune's role was minor. Yamamoto had remembered him from the notorious New Face audition and liked Mifune's work in Taniguchi's film. Again he played a gangster, but here he played his scenes with, as Kurosawa described it, "an opposite kind of cruel refinement."[11] A surviving photograph of Mifune, in a scene with Enoken, shows him with his hair slicked tightly back. He wears a smart, conservative suit and a pencil-thin mustache. Such is the contrast to his role in *Snow Trail* that even this one still, which shows his dress and his manner, confirms that while Toho may have typecast Mifune as nothing more than a gangster actor, he already was showing a wide range.

Taniguchi, however, claimed to have not even been aware that Yamamoto was making the film. "I didn't know Mifune was in *sensei*'s movie. Toho was too big a studio for everyone to be aware of what was happening all the time."[12] Though popular in its day, *These Foolish Times* is now nearly forgotten. It's been little heard from since its release more than fifty years ago and has never been shown in the West.

Almost in response to the chaos that befell Toho, Kurosawa's *One Wonderful Sunday* is resolutely apolitical. It is a sweet, uncomplicated story: Yuzo (Isao Numasaki) and his fiancée, Masako (Chieko Nakakita), are a typically poor postwar couple, still dating and not yet married. One Sunday, their only day off each week, they try to enjoy their time together with just ¥35— very little money—between them. They visit a modest (but by their standards, luxurious) house for sale, play stickball with some neighborhood boys, go to the zoo (nearly devoid of animals on account of the war), encounter a war orphan, and go to a coffee shop and fantasize about opening one of their own. They try to buy tickets to a concert of Schubert's *Unfinished Symphony*, but black market scalpers (prevalent during the postwar era) have bought all the remaining seats, and Yuzo is beaten when he demands they sell him two tickets at the legal price. That evening they go to an abandoned bandshell and pretend to enjoy Schubert's symphony in the ruins. Yuzo drops Masako off at the station, and they promise to meet again the following Sunday.

One Wonderful Sunday, much more than the polemic-driven *No Regrets for Our Youth*, has Kurosawa returning to his strengths. It is a delightful film, charming in its rich characterizations, while simultaneously capturing the flavor of postwar Japan and the Japanese in much the same way as the director would again in *Stray Dog* (1949). Neither Numasaki nor Nakakita, in both physical terms and in the characters they play, are idealized in the manner of Hara's and Fujita's roles in *No Regrets*—they're ordinary people. That this couple, mainly Masako, refuse to give up (just like Yukie) when beset with one minor disaster after another makes them all the more remarkable, real, and even inspiring. Masako is a typically devoted, hardworking, self-sacrificing postwar woman, full of dreams and aspirations, simultaneously struggling with torn nylons and worrying about her meager finances. Numasaki seems to have been cast, in part, because he reminded Kurosawa of his cheerful and adamantly upbeat friend Ishiro Honda—Numasaki even closely resembles Honda especially in his facial features.

But where Honda looked sophisticated, Numasaki by contrast looked perfectly ordinary. "The story called for them to be the kind of young couple you might see anywhere in Japan at that time," Kurosawa wrote, "so in that sense they were perfect for the parts. And for that reason they seem to me, as I think about them today, to be like a couple I met by chance . . . and became friends with, rather than protagonists of a movie."[13]

One Wonderful Sunday was Numasaki's sole film for Kurosawa. He had been with Toho as early as 1943, appearing in Takeshi Sato's *The Joy of Youth* (Wakakihi no yorokobi) that summer. He co-starred opposite Susumu Fujita and Setsuko Hara in *Hot Wind* (Nepu) and appeared in *Four Love Stories,* both released earlier in 1947. After *One Wonderful Sunday,* Numasaki had a supporting role in Teinosuke Kinugasa's *Actress* (Joyu, 1947) and Fumio Kamei's *The Life of a Woman* (Onna no issho, 1949), but left the studio by the end of the decade. He had a supporting role in the independently produced *Vacuum Zone* (Shinku chitai, 1952), directed by Satsuo Yamamoto, but died suddenly the following year at the age of thirty-seven.*

Twenty-one-year-old Chieko Nakakita had been at Toho as early as 1944's *Daily Flight* (Nichijo no tatakai). She appeared in both comedies and dramas, and had worked with Kurosawa before as an extra, one of the student workers in *The Most Beautiful,* and she had a bit part in *No Regrets for Our Youth,* playing one of Setsuko Hara's flower-arranging classmates. She was the script-girl sister in *Those Who Make Tomorrow,* though apparently did not work directly with Kurosawa. *One Wonderful Sunday* elevated her to star status, however fleetingly. By the following year, she was reduced to character parts in films like Toshio Takagi's *The Happy Chair* (Shiawase no isu), which also featured Numasaki. She married producer Tomoyuki Tanaka, a man more than sixteen years her senior, and he kept her busy in supporting parts in films that he produced. But Nakakita was a fine character actress, a favorite of many of Toho's house directors, especially Mikio Naruse, with whom she worked on pictures like *Mother* (Haha, 1952) and *When a Woman Ascends the Stairs* (Onna ga kaidan o agaru toki, 1960). She had major supporting parts in *Drunken Angel* and *The Quiet Duel* (both 1949), then vanished from the Kurosawa-gumi, though she remained active in films as late as the Mifune film *The Ambush: Incident at Blood Pass* (Machibuse, 1970).

"After the second strike . . . Toho and the planning council made great films, even though the studio had no stars," Nakakita recalled in 1993. "I think there was a lot of enthusiasm to make high quality films since the great directors were still there. Mr. Kurosawa was younger than a lot of the other excellent directors—Tadashi Imai, Mikio Naruse, Kajiro Yamamoto, Fumio Kamei—but he was very skillful and had a lot of energy. . . . I was

*According to one source, Numasaki committed suicide.

very lucky. Thanks to the strike, new actresses like myself were suddenly given good roles. . . . The script was well-written and easy to act out. I just naturally played myself. Because the character I played was a typical girl who could be seen anywhere, she and I matched perfectly. Numa-chan, who played my boyfriend, was a delightful actor, but didn't have much range. Since Mr. Kurosawa was preoccupied with Numa-chan, I didn't get yelled at."[14]

Kurosawa wrote *One Wonderful Sunday* with his childhood friend Keinosuke Uekusa. The two had seen each other only sporadically since their youth. Uekusa, like Kurosawa, spent much of the 1930s wandering, searching for a career in which he could truly immerse himself. He even worked as an extra on several Toho features of the late 1930s, including *Tojuro's Love* (Tojuro no koi, 1938), a Kajiro Yamamoto film on which Kurosawa had been chief assistant director. Uekusa found his niche as a playwright, and within a few years was writing occasional filmscripts. His first was Yasujiro Shimazu's *A Mother's Map* (Haha no chizu), produced by Toho in 1942 and starring Setsuko Hara. Earlier in 1947, Uekusa wrote *Once More* (Ima hitotabino) for director Heinosuke Gosho, a story involving a well-bred girl in love with a doctor who works in a slum. *Once More* placed third on *Kinema Jumpo*'s "Best Ten" list, while *One Wonderful Sunday* placed sixth. More important, it shared elements Uekusa and Kurosawa would address again in their collaboration on *Drunken Angel* (1948). After that film, Uekusa wrote mainly for the stage, returning to films infrequently, but those he took on were always surprising. He penned a Hibari Misora musical for Shochiku in 1951, followed by *The Outsiders* (Mori to Mizuumi no matsuri), an early Ken Takakura film with Kyoko Kagawa, directed by Tomu Uchida in 1958. Uekusa then worked on one of Toei's earliest animated features, Osamu Tezuka's *The Journey West* (Saiyu-ki, 1960), badly Americanized a year later and released as *Alakazam the Great*.

Kurosawa said of him, "As weak as he is, he puts on a show of strength; as romantic as he is, he puts on a show of being a realist."[15] Perhaps it was Uekusa's contradictory nature that led to *One Wonderful Sunday*'s audacious—if not successful—climax. As Masako tries to cheer Yuzo in the bandshell after being denied tickets to hear Schubert's *Unfinished Symphony*, she suggests they pretend. At first her bit of inspiration works, but the sadness of the long day begins to wear on Yuzo and the imaginary music stops. Then, suddenly, Masako addresses the movie's audience, looking straight into the camera. With tears running down her cheeks, she pleads with the audience to clap its hands, à la *Peter Pan*. "Please, everyone," she says, "if you feel sorry for us, please clap your hands. If you clap for us, I'm sure we'll be able to hear the music." After an excruciatingly long silence, Schubert is heard at last.

Uekusa's idea for the scene differs slightly from that in the finished film. He proposed that after Masako's pleas, clapping would gradually be heard on the film's soundtrack. The camera would then show other like-minded couples sitting in the shadows of the bandshell. Perhaps Uekusa was simply hedging his bets, but the idea would have emphasized the couple's universality, that Japan was filled with Yuzos and Masakos. Kurosawa, however, wanted to meet the experiment head-on. "[It] proved to be a failure in Japan," he admitted. "The Japanese audience sat stock still, and because they couldn't bring themselves to applaud, the whole thing was a failure. But in Paris it succeeded. Because the French audience responded with wild applause, the sound of the orchestra tuning up at the tail end of the clapping gave rise to the powerful and unusual emotion I had hoped for."[16] Most audiences, though, in both Japan and America, met Masako's plea with rigidly folded arms and squirming in their seats. Screenwriter Sergei Hasenecz recalled a screening of *One Wonderful Sunday* in Los Angeles in the mid-1980s. Bemused by the picture's go-for-broke ending, he and his companion tried to make sense of it. On their way out of the theater, they saw a group of old Japanese women weeping in the very back row of the theater. His companion turned to him and said, "*That's* why it works!"

Reviews focused on this notorious climax, often dismissing the simple beauty that preceded it. Donald Richie, who otherwise was quite charmed by the picture, wrote: "This [sequence] is enough to ruin the entire picture and that it does not says a good deal for the strength of Kurosawa and the extreme skill of Chieko Nakakita—she almost makes this riot of kitsch believable."[17]

More than any Kurosawa film preceding it, *One Wonderful Sunday* was stylistically rooted in American films, which only now were returning to Japan after a long absence. Kurosawa admitted to basing it on a film he saw as a child, D. W. Griffith's unabashedly sentimental *Isn't Life Wonderful* (1912), and it also has the innocence of Frank Capra. Richie likens the couple to those played by Jean Arthur and James Stewart in Capra's films, an apt comparison.

By the time *One Wonderful Sunday* reached American shores in 1982, the picture was deemed "something of an archeological find" by Vincent Canby. "Though [it] looks simple, it's a carefully composed, elegant, sometimes prescient work, a small-scale love story set against a background of tumultuous social and political change. . . . It seems to have much more to do with the sort of sentiments one might find in D.W. Griffith, but Griffith, reportedly, was one of Kurosawa's inspirations for this film. It also suggests the unashamed lyricism of F. W. Murnau, another influence on Kurosawa."[18]

"Despite some lyrical urban interludes, I found much of the film clumsy and cloying," wrote J. Hoberman. "The most striking thing about *One Wonderful Sunday* is how totally it seems the missing link between F. W. Murnau's *Sunrise* and [Francis Ford] Coppola's own *One from the Heart*. Not just the film's quasi-musical quality but . . . the magical junkyard where the couple enact their fantasy of opening what the subtitles call 'Hyacinth: A Popular Cake Shop' has obvious echoes in the Coppola opus."[19]

The film's mixed reviews mattered little to Kurosawa and Uekusa. Shortly after its release, Kurosawa received a postcard from an old man deeply moved by what he saw. It was from Seiji Tachikawa, their beloved teacher at Kuroda Primary School.

Before *Drunken Angel* (Yoidore tenshi), widely regarded as Kurosawa's first major work, nearly all his films had been compromised in one way or another. His earliest pictures had to meet the military government's strict guidelines, while *No Regrets for Our Youth* had to be rewritten due to unionist demands; even *One Wonderful Sunday* had to meet with their approval. By late 1947, however, the unionists' power was eroding in the wake of unprofitable releases, and their input on the film was minimal. Kurosawa still had to comply with the Occupation censors, but despite this, he came to regard *Drunken Angel* as an important step in his career. "In this picture I finally found myself," he said. "It was *my* picture. I was doing it and no one else."[20]

Kurosawa and co-writer Uekusa built the film around a pre-existing set, the black market neighborhood constructed for Kajiro Yamamoto's *These Foolish Times*. They decided to pit a *yakuza* hood against "a young, humanist doctor who was just setting up his practice in the area."[21] But as the gangster came to life in their pages, the character of the doctor remained an enigma. "He was so perfect," wrote Kurosawa, "that he had no vitality. The gangster figure, on the other hand, had become almost real enough to breathe; his every move reeked of flesh and blood. This immediacy arose from the fact that he was based on a real-life model, whom Uekusa was meeting with regularly. . . . Day after day I sat glaring in my mind's eye at the puppet-like image of the doctor who refused to grow into a real character. After about five days Uekusa and I had a sudden revelation at just about the same moment." During their research, wandering Tokyo's black market districts, they had come across an unlicensed, alcoholic doctor who surprised them with his arrogant demeanor. This was their man. "The marionette-like young doctor who was the picture of humanitarianism was blown to bits."[22]

Most of the film's action occurs in the vicinity of a large, oily sump. It is here that Dr. Sanada (Takashi Shimura), a resigned alcoholic, cares for his neighbors. One night he's visited by a gangster, Matsunaga (Mifune), who has been shot in the hand. Sanada has great contempt for his type, so much so that he refuses to give the hood anesthetic as he stitches his wound. Sanada suspects Matsunaga has tuberculosis and urges him to get X-rayed. When the X rays confirm that Matsunaga has an advanced case of TB, Sanada, despite his contempt for the gangster, insists on treating him. Matsunaga, however, is proud of his position as neighborhood gang boss, and the two are constantly at each other's throats. Matsunaga continues to smoke, get drunk, and sleep with his girlfriend (Michiyo Kogure). However, as his condition worsens, his old boss, Okada (Reizaburo Yamamoto), is released from prison and moves in to reclaim his old territory. Matsunaga briefly surrenders himself to Sanada's treatment, but is pressured to keep up with Okada's lifestyle of whiskey, cigarettes, and women. His fall from power begins to consume him—he's lost his identity, his reason for being. He loses his girl, his fortune, and the respect (albeit through intimidation) of his contingents. Okada simultaneously pressures Sanada to give up his nurse (Chieko Nakakita), who was once the old gangster's mistress. (It is suggested that she came under Sanada's care after he infected her with syphilis, but this is never explicit.) Barely able to breathe and coughing up blood, Matsunaga confronts Okada. Partly out of revenge, partly to save the nurse, partly for his own redemption, Matsunaga tries to kill the gang boss. But he himself is killed, and Sanada is bitter at the life that has been wasted.

Although Kurosawa began writing the film as an exposé on the rising power of the *yakuza*, *Drunken Angel* is essentially about the relationship between the doctor and the gangster. Sanada loathes Matsunaga because he symbolizes the kind of corrupt parasites that dominated the urban scene immediately after the war. But he also reminds the doctor of the man he himself once was—selfish, concerned only with living for the moment. Sanada's been paying for his foolhardiness for years, living in a humid, mosquito-plagued slum and reduced to drinking medicinal alcohol intended for his patients. He sees himself in Matsunaga, a man not only plagued with TB but corrupted by the temptations of chaotic postwar Japan.

As an alcoholic, Sanada is himself diseased, further cementing their connection. One of the picture's few faults is that while Sanada is almost militant in his fight against disease—yelling at children not to play in the sump lest they be infected with typhoid, urging a teenage girl (Yoshiko Kuga) to rally in her own fight with TB—not once does he discuss his battle with alcoholism. Clearly, he had given up years ago, but why he chooses not to fight it now is left unsaid. Extremely hypocritical in his actions, at one point he spies one of his own alcoholic patients (Senkichi Omura) drinking at a local bar and berates him—then, without skipping a beat, settles down for a drink himself.

Both men are also afflicted with tremendous self-loathing. When Sanada tells the nurse, "[Matsunaga] acts tough but I suspect he's lonely inside," he's talking about himself as much as the gangster. But his contempt for Matsunaga is stronger than his own self-hatred. It's not too late for the gangster, yet here he is, throwing his life away. Through his work, Sanada at least finds some vindication in his fight against disease. It may be too late for him, but not for others. Although he may at first seem pathetic, eking his way through life taking what work an alcoholic doctor can get, Sanada is truly a drunken angel. He does not passively bemoan the state of the world, he actively fights against it. In spite of his open contempt for many of them, he worries about his patients. Even the teenage girl, an ideal patient if ever there was one, is grilled by Sanada about her treatment, though he clearly adores her. Sanada is a character Kurosawa would return to again and again, culminating with the not dissimilar title character of his 1965 film *Red Beard*.

Sanada is never intimidated by Matsunaga, because he recognizes in the gangster the fear and loneliness that he himself feels. He bullies and berates Matsunaga with the same contempt the gangster has for him. From the very first scene, wherein after stitching the gangster's wound, Sanada injures his own hand in a fight with Matsunaga, the two characters are linked visually as well as thematically—they are two sides of the same coin.

Kurosawa and co-writer Keinosuke Uekusa employ this Hitchcock-like parallelism throughout *Drunken Angel* (a device Kurosawa would take to even greater lengths in *Stray Dog*). Both men simultaneously look up to and resent their more successful counterparts—Matsunaga to Okada, Sanada to a wealthier, more esteemed colleague (Eitaro Shindo) from his medical school days. Matsunaga is loved by a bar girl (Noriko Sengoku), while

Sanada is cared for by Nurse Miyo, whom he regards as "his woman," though their relationship is never sexual.

Matsunaga is paralleled by other characters as well. Like the nurse, he is tied to the old gang boss, but she's stronger than Matsunaga and resists the temptation to return. He is also affiliated with the teenage girl, similarly stricken with TB, but who, because of her youth, hasn't lost her simple innocence the way Matsunaga has. The doppelgänger motif is foregrounded in a scene where Matsunaga doubles himself. In a strange, singularly European-looking dream sequence, a dapper *yakuza* Matsunaga chops open a seaside coffin containing the living body of his true, disease-ridden self, which then chases him along the shoreline.

Tying everything together is the polluted sump. It symbolizes the psychological world both Sanada and Matsunaga find themselves in. Huge and all-encompassing, it serves as a constant reminder of the overwhelming desolation of their world. Kurosawa's camera frequently pans across it, often revealing the reflections of characters looking into it, seeing themselves. This is most clearly demonstrated when Matsunaga, hopeful that Sanada might cure him, is confronted by his old gang boss at the sump's edge. Okada's return is too much for the young hood, and Matsunaga takes a fresh carnation from his lapel and tosses it into the dirty pond—figuratively throwing his life away.

Like the heroine in *No Regrets for Our Youth*, Matsunaga finds a kind of redemption in the end. He has failed to kill the gang boss, but he has found the strength to at least fight the corruption, the disease in his boss and within himself. But, like Yukie, Matsunaga must do it alone, unappreciated. This is reinforced in the film's bittersweet coda, where neither the doctor nor the bar girl who loved him understand what Matsunaga achieved in his final moments.

Preproduction on *Drunken Angel* began in November 1947, and shooting commenced later that month. Toho pressured Kurosawa to get the film completed, partly out of a desire to have more films in release, partly because yet another strike was brewing. Kurosawa was beset with both production and personal problems, however. Keiko Orihara was originally cast as Shimura's nurse, but fell ill shortly after the start of production, and in January 1948 he decided to replace her with Chieko Nakakita.

The following month, during the final weeks of shooting, Kurosawa's father, Isamu, died at the age of eighty-three. "I received a telegram that he was failing quickly," Kurosawa wrote, "but I was so pressured to get the picture done for the fixed release date that I couldn't go to be at his side in Akita Prefecture."[23] Did completing *Drunken Angel* mean more to him than seeing his dying father? Any extenuating circumstances leading to this decision will probably never be known, but Kurosawa did complete *Drunken Angel* on time: shooting wrapped on March 10, 1948, and the picture was released six weeks later.

Shimura is excellent as the alcoholic doctor—loosely basing his performance on Thomas Mitchell's character in *Stagecoach*.[24] But it was Matsunaga's story, thanks to Mifune's intensely physical performance, that got all the attention. "Shimura played the doctor beautifully," Kurosawa said, "but I found I could not control Mifune. When I saw this, I let him do as he wanted, let him play the part freely. At the same time, I was worried because, if I didn't control him, the picture would turn out differently from what I'd wanted. It was a real dilemma. Still, I did not want to smother that vitality. In the end, [even] though the title refers to the doctor, it is Mifune that everyone remembers."[25]

Mifune agreed that Kurosawa gave him considerable latitude. "Since he was paying attention to me [during the editing of *Snow Trail*], he chose me for the lead in *Drunken Angel*. . . . It was a lucky beginning for me. He never told me how to play a scene—he wanted to see what I would come up with. What I did was simply guess what the person I played would do in each situation and play him that way. Sometimes he said, 'That is good.' Sometimes he said, 'Why don't you do it this way?' I don't remember ever being nervous on his sets."[26]

Because of this latitude, Mifune's performance has a raw energy almost unseen in Japanese films up to that time. The young man Kurosawa saw seventeen months earlier "reeling around the room in a violent frenzy, [like] . . . a wounded or trapped savage beast trying to break loose" has been brought directly to the screen.[27] He capers about like a wolf, leaps at Sanada in rage, lies prostrate on the floor, struts in his loose-fitting *yakuza* fashions like a peacock, and dies like an animal. The nakedness of Mifune's emotions stunned Japanese audiences in much the same way Marlon Brando's did in *A Streetcar Named Desire* three years later. Mifune never considered himself a Method actor like Brando; Mifune instinctively drew from himself, whereas with Brando it was a process (though the end result was much the same). And unlike Brando's, Mifune's raw talent was, by Kurosawa and Mifune's own admissions, untamed and results in him literally flinging his body about nearly every set in the picture. Kurosawa would suppress this with mixed results in his next film, *The Quiet Duel*, before cultivating this extraordinary power in *Stray Dog* and *Rashomon*. For now, unrefined Mifune was enough.

Shimura and Mifune were not alone in receiving Kurosawa's praise. "I had never seen eyes as frightening as [Reizaburo Yamamoto's]," Kurosawa said, "and when I met him I was afraid to get close enough to carry on a conversation. When I finally did talk to him, though, I was surprised at what a fine human being he was."[28] They would go on to work together again in *Stray Dog*. Yamamoto died in 1964.

The film's other notable casting is Michiyo Kogure, one of Japan's great film actresses, as Mifune's opportunistic lover. Kogure (1918–90) had been in films since the age of nineteen, and first made an impression in Heinosuke Gosho's *Wood and Stone* (Bokuseki, 1940). More than any other Japanese film actress, Kogure had an amazing chameleonlike quality, inhabiting a diverse range of characters. She was so good, in fact, that the star-driven studios had a hard time casting her, but a handful of directors recognized her great skill—Tadashi Imai in *Blue Mountains* (Aoi sanmyaku, 1949) and especially Mizoguchi in *Street of Shame* (Akasen chitai, 1956). In that film Kogure was cast as a married prostitute, one who regarded her scandalous vocation with the same kind of slightly bored resignation as that of a career secretary or bookkeeper.

Drunken Angel marked not only Kurosawa's first film with Mifune but also his first with composer Fumio Hayasaka, who would score all but one of Kurosawa's future films until his death in 1955, after a long battle with tuberculosis. Thirty-four-year-old Hayasaka had been scoring films since his mid-twenties, beginning with *The Lady Ties a Ribbon* (Ribbon o musubu fujin) for Satsuo Yamamoto in 1939. He wrote mainly for Toho in the 1940s, cranking out up to a half-dozen scores each year. Kurosawa hit it off with Hayasaka immediately and they became close friends. In the 1950s Hayasaka wrote for a variety of directors at both major studios and for the growing number of independent productions. Outside of his work for Kurosawa, he is best remembered for his fine scores for the late films of Kenji Mizoguchi, including *Ugetsu* (Ugetsu monogatari, 1953), *Sansho the Bailiff* (Sansho Dayu), and *Crucified Lovers* (Chikamatsu monogatari, both 1954). All this work was composed while Hayasaka suffered symptoms not unlike those experienced by Matsunaga in *Drunken Angel*.

Memos written by Kurosawa and published in the April 1948 edition of *Eiga Shunshu* (Films of the Spring and Fall) reflect their likemindedness. "When we met," Kurosawa wrote, "we completely agreed with one another." Kurosawa, admitting to being "too casual" about film music in the past, consciously attempted to create with Hayasaka a "turning point" in Japanese film music. "Music was considered during the writing stage, mapped out, and tied to the images and what kind of role it would play. [For example,] the song played by the *yakuza* Okada was named 'Song for

Murder.' When we were writing the script, we wanted to use the suite from *Die Dreigroschenoper*, particularly the Mackie Messer music, but the legal department found that it was copyrighted and would be too expensive to use. . . . Anyway, we wanted to use it to expose Okada's cruelty. . . . We wanted to use the 'Cuckoo Waltz' for counterpoint near the end, for the film's saddest scene [where Matsunaga is spurned by the neighborhood businesses]." Kurosawa and Hayasaka supposedly shook hands when they realized they had thought of the same idea at the same time, but separately.[29]

"The foundation for all film music," Hayasaka said, "is that it functions differently from simple music. By combining it with the images onscreen, the music can remind the audience of something, or mean something quite different from what is being shown. . . . Mr. Kurosawa has the intuition to find music which matches these onscreen images. When we work together, Mr. Kurosawa is the Music Director, and I am just a composer."[30]

Kurosawa, working with recordist Wataru Konuma, does an excellent job integrating ambient sounds with Hayasaka's music. The neighborhood may be crawling with *yakuza* and pollution, but it is still bustling with activity. Music emanates from run-down dance halls, as buyers and sellers haggle, stores pitch their wares through distorting loudspeakers (still prevalent in the Japan of today). The integration is so complete that Okada plays (on a guitar) his own motif.

The film received rave reviews when it opened on April 27, 1948. Hailed as Kurosawa's first true masterpiece, it was awarded Best Film by both *Kinema Jumpo* and the *Mainichi Eiga*. For the latter it also won prizes for Best Cinematography (Takeo Ito) and Best Music.

Toho promoted *Drunken Angel* throughout the 1950s, but it didn't make its way to the United States until January 1960, when it was licensed by Brandon Films as part of the nine-film package that included *The Men Who Tread on the Tiger's Tail*. " 'Drunken Angel' . . . is certainly one of the most effective and searching views of contemporary Japanese life to reach these shores," wrote *Variety*'s "Anby." "In technique and style, 'Angel' would seem to owe a lot to some of the great neo-realist films which came out of postwar Italy. The sharp eye of the camera delights in catching the details of squalor, of oppressive heat and creeping disease, but the details are carefully selected and integrated to contribute to the single overall theme, which is one of human nobility in a chaotic, amoral world. . . . [The] film is beautifully acted by Toshiro Mifune and Takashi Shimura . . . in a series of hard-hitting scenes which vividly delineate a milieu that would have been Godforsaken without the noble old doctor."[31]

The release of *Drunken Angel* coincided with a third, climactic strike that once again crippled Toho's operations, this time for more than six months. It began with the appointment of staunch anti-Communist Tetsuzo Watanabe as Toho's new president in December 1947. Watanabe was singularly ignorant about film production; he claimed not to have seen any films at all since the French detective film *Zigomar* was released in Japan in 1911. He likewise knew little about the Communism he so despised. Reportedly, when he first visited the studio and was greeted by unionists waving red flags and singing the "Internationale," he turned to his aide and asked, "I don't like red flags, but I like that nice song. Is it Toho's company song?"[32]

Watanabe, working with a much-hated aide, Takeo Mabuchi, restored the power of section chiefs and abolished the shop steward system. They vetoed film projects proposed by unionist leaders, and in April 1948 announced the firing of 1,200 employees, including nearly 300 working at the studio, all of whom were admitted or suspected Communists. In protest, the unionists that same month occupied the studio grounds, erecting barbed-wire barricades and bringing production to a halt. The studio officially closed the lot down on June 1 and stopped paying salaries. The front and rear gates of the studio became a veritable war zone, with the unionists using fire hoses to keep the Japanese police, American tanks, and anti-Communist leaders at bay. "The greatest work of genius," Kurosawa cynically wrote, "was the fans: They set up two big wind machines just inside the front and back gates of the lot, facing outward like heavy artillery. In the event of a storming of the gates, they were ready with a huge amount of cayenne pepper to toss in front of the fan blasts and blind the oncoming enemy."[33] The studio remained occupied for 134 days that summer.[34]

Kurosawa, in an effort to continue making money, directed a stage production of Chekhov's *Proposal* and an adaptation of *Drunken Angel*, with Mifune and Shimura performing key scenes from the recently released film.

> When I look back on it now [Kurosawa wrote in 1978], this third strike has all the appearances of a children's quarrel. It was like two siblings fighting over a doll, snatching it away from each other head by arm by leg until it's in pieces. . . . The point when the management launched its punitive attack, the union and the film directors had already heard the criticisms on the sets where the films were being made, and they were well aware that the situation had gotten out of hand. They themselves were already imposing a better discipline, and the production of films was beginning to proceed smoothly again. Just at this sensitive juncture the management came in with

force. This was a tremendous blow to us. . . . My personal experiences in this strike . . . were only bitter ones. . . . Far from learning from experience with their blunders in the second strike, the management were heaping more errors on top of what they had done. They were tearing to shreds the cooperating work force of precious talent we had nurtured for so long. . . . [When the strike ended,] what had vanished was the feeling of devotion we had once had toward the studio. . . . I had come to understand that the studio I had thought was my home actually belonged to strangers.[35]

Over the next three and a half years Akira Kurosawa would make five films, but none would be produced by Toho.

SIX

STRAY DOGS

Kurosawa was itching to get back behind the camera. "Not only had the 195-day strike put my family's kitchen accounts into terrible straits," he said, "but I was desperate to get back to filmmaking."[1]

Prior to the third strike, Kurosawa joined several prominent names within the studio to form a production company called Film Art Association (Eiga geijutsu kyokai). Kurosawa, Taniguchi, Kajiro Yamamoto, director Mikio Naruse, and producer Sojiro Motoki were its founders. *The Quiet Duel* was its first feature, a co-production between Film Art Association and Daiei Studios, and Kurosawa's first directorial effort outside the confines of Toho. Daiei had filmed his script of *Wrestling Ring Festival* and had wanted to film more. After the strikes, according to Kurosawa, Daiei was simply the studio that made the first offer.

The Quiet Duel was an adaptation by Kurosawa and Taniguchi of a contemporary play by Kazuo Kikuta, about a young doctor infected with syphilis during an operation. Adapting an established play rather than writing an original script, the new company was hedging its bets. The play had a presold audience and was thus less risky financially, and filming it would seemingly be more straightforward. Minoru Chiaki, who starred in the play as the doctor, would soon become one of the most prominent members of Kurosawa's stock company of actors. Kurosawa, however, opted not to use him. He wanted Mifune.

"Since his debut," Kurosawa said, "Mifune had been playing almost nothing but gangster roles, and I wanted to give him a chance to broaden his artistic horizons." While it's true that Mifune had played gangsters in his first three films, two of these were directed by Kurosawa himself. It was partly the director's skill that had created Mifune's image as a heavy. "Turning his type-cast image around," Kurosawa continued, "I conceived a role for him as an intellectual with sharp reasoning powers. Daiei expressed surprise over this role, and there were many in the company who were frankly worried about it."[2] Kurosawa then came to regard the film chiefly as a vehicle for Mifune, one which would stretch his acting muscles and display his range.

"Because this was my first picture filmed outside of Toho, it felt like a second maiden work," he wrote. But Kurosawa found the move to Daiei an easy one. "The studio itself retained the old flavor of people who made the 'flickers,' and its inhabitants were stubborn but generous." Production on *The Quiet Duel* went smoothly, and Kurosawa could not find fault with Daiei's crew. "Everywhere at that time, at every shoot for every studio, no matter how much the atmosphere of one studio differed from the next, the people working on the set were all inveterate movie lovers."[3]

The film opens in 1944. Mifune plays an exhausted Army surgeon, Kyoji Fujisaki, working in deplorable conditions on a South Pacific island. During an operation, Kyoji absentmindedly removes a glove, cuts his thumb on a scalpel, then sticks his hand back into the wounded man's abdomen. The wounded soldier, Nakada (Kenjiro Uemura), turns out to have syphilis, and Kyoji realizes he may have infected himself. Kyoji has his blood tested, and after several weeks learns the awful truth.

After the war Kyoji returns home and works in the small, adjacent hospital run by his obstetrician father, Konosuke (Takashi Shimura), a widower. Before the war, Kyoji had been engaged to Misao (Miki Sanjo). Given his condition, however, he decides to break the engagement, but will not tell her the reason. Confused by his remoteness toward her, she continues to help out, fixing meals for the two doctors in their hospital-home, all the while hoping she will learn the reason for the change in Kyoji's personality. She confronts Konosuke; he feels guilty about his son's behavior toward her but doesn't understand the reason, either.

A nurse's apprentice, Minegishi (Noriko Sengoku), catches Kyoji giving himself an injection of salvarsan as part of his treatment, and later she hears him discuss his predicament with his father. Minegishi, a former prostitute (subtitled prints call her—ahem—a "dancer"), thinks Kyoji had been unfaithful to his fiancée during the war. A bitter, downtrodden woman,

Minegishi had attempted suicide when she became pregnant, but Kyoji saved her, gave her a job at the hospital, and encouraged her to have her baby. When she sees Kyoji and Misao together and he treats Misao coolly, Minegishi calls him a "beast."

Misao continues to plead for an explanation, but Kyoji refuses to budge. She offers to wait for him, but this only furthers his resolve. He reckons that it will take three to five years for him to be completely cured and cannot bring himself to ask her to wait.

Among the hospital's patients is a boy with appendicitis. After the operation, the boy is anxious to eat again, but he is told he must wait until he begins passing gas. Sometime later the boy farts and the other patients celebrate his accomplishment.* During the jubilation, Kyoji asks Misao not to come to the hospital anymore.

When the boy is discharged, Minegishi tells Kyoji that the boy wants to say goodbye to him. Kyoji reaches into a cabinet and finds a baseball mitt to give him. With this, Minegishi has a change of heart and realizes the young doctor is a kind, selfless man after all. She becomes resigned to having her baby and decides to study nursing as a career.

Soon after, Kyoji has a chance encounter with Nakada, the man who infected him. Unlike Kyoji, Nakada has not been treating his own syphilis, and the young doctor warns him about its effects and his responsibility to others. Nakada, living in a world of self-deception, has married, and his wife is pregnant. Worried that the baby may be stillborn or deformed, Kyoji urges Nakada to come to the hospital and have his wife, Takiko (Chieko Nakakita), examined. Kyoji reveals that he, too, has been infected, but Nakada refuses to believe him.

Later Takiko turns up at the hospital alone and in labor. She gives birth to a deformed, stillborn baby. Nakada shows up drunk. Minegishi, by now in love with Kyoji, is livid at the man's irresponsibility to both Kyoji and Takiko and attacks him. However, Nakada's syphilis and heavy drinking have caught up with him: he is terminally ill and the disease has affected his brain.

Misao comes to the hospital to tell Kyoji that she will be getting married the following day. She hopes that by telling him this he will decide to marry her, or at least explain why he will not. But Kyoji does neither. He politely congratulates her and sends her on her way. After she's gone, Kyo-

---

*Flatulence also plays a major role in Ozu's *Good Morning* (Ohayo, 1959). Who says all Japanese movies are highbrow?

ji's anguish bubbles to the surface. He breaks down in front of Minegishi, who bursts into tears herself. Saying she has no plans to remarry, she offers herself to Kyoji, but he declines. He regains his composure and returns to work.

As winter becomes spring, he receives a letter from Misao, who has found happiness in her new marriage. Minegishi assures Takiko that the syphilis that has infected her can be cured, just as it will someday be cured in Kyoji. In a series of fast cuts, we see Kyoji continuing his work at the hospital, helping those less fortunate than himself.

Though financially successful, *The Quiet Duel* is largely an artistic failure, albeit one with scenes and ideas that anticipate better films to follow. The setup for the drama, Kyoji's decision not to marry Misao or reveal his condition, is established ten minutes into the film. Artificial and strained, this device drags on endlessly and ultimately goes nowhere. Misao begs Kyoji to tell her why they cannot marry; he refuses. He has done nothing wrong, and his refusal to say anything perpetuates the conflict rather than working to resolve it. He never falters, never weighs his options. His obstinance is irritating, because without it, there would be no conflict and no story; it is a convenience of plot.

Another problem is the circumstance surrounding his infection. That this doctor would remove his glove, then immediately cut himself *and* stick his bloody finger back into a man's insides borders on the absurd.

After the war, Kyoji suffers, but we get little else from the film. It is implied that he works through his suffering by burying himself in caring for others, but Kurosawa does not show us how this might heal him, and there is little interaction between doctor and patient. He does not learn from his patients' suffering, nor does he seem to derive any satisfaction from helping others. He is simply a dedicated physician, much like the dull character originally envisioned for *Drunken Angel*. It's also clear that he was already devoted to his profession as the story begins, so the character never changes, his suffering just intensifies. Someone refers to him as a saint, but saints aren't very engaging dramatically unless they question their own actions and consciously consecrate themselves in spite of their own suffering.

Minegishi says people suffer two different ways. "Some cry with pain," she says, "others sweat it out." Up to now, Kyoji has clearly been sweating it out. But when he finally admits his bitterness, there's no emotional punch because Kurosawa and Taniguchi's script is maudlin and mechanical.

"When I remember this film," Kurosawa said, "it seems to me that only the early scenes in the field hospital have any validity. This is because I didn't describe things too well in this picture. When the locale moved back to Japan, somehow the drama left the film."[4]

He's right. Kurosawa is uncharacteristically clumsy for much of the film, but the wartime opening is done with flair and imagination. The operation sequence, for all its improbability, is tightly directed and the primitive conditions are emphasized quite well. The fan used to keep insects away blocks the camera (and thus our) view, and when rain begins dripping in, an attendant holds a pan under it. The ping-ping-ping of the drops on the pan adds to the tension, and both devices work to keep the viewer off balance.

After the war, when Konosuke overhears his son discussing his affliction, Kurosawa does not show Takashi Shimura's face. Rather than the camera conventionally focusing in on him in a tight shot, we see only his back, his hands clasped behind him. When he hears the news, his hands come apart, and slumping slightly, he walks away. This invites the viewer to infer Shimura's reaction and is rather clever.

In one of the few really effective scenes in the picture, Konosuke thinks his son had been unfaithful to Misao. When Kyoji explains how he became infected, his father, feeling guilty, apologizes and offers his son a cigarette. Then each tries to light the other's cigarette. Looking up simultaneously, they break into wide smiles. This is the only natural, relaxed, and unforced moment in the entire film.

Mostly the film's use of symbolism is obvious and clumsy. We first see Kyoji just prior to Nakada's operation, slumped against a wall of the operating room, where he rests with one gloved hand on his elbow, pointing toward the ceiling, bluntly foreshadowing the infection to come. Outside the hospital is a wrought-iron gate, and Kurosawa predictably shoots Mifune through it, like prison bars, to reflect Kyoji's emotional state.

When Takiko's baby is stillborn, Kyoji and Takiko wheel her away from her dead infant. When Nakada shows up, we hear a baby crying offscreen and think perhaps the baby isn't dead after all. In fact, it is Minegishi's baby. Kurosawa was making a halfhearted attempt to link the two infants together thematically, but the result is confusing.

Adding to the film's artifice is the fact that nearly the entire picture, including its exteriors, was shot on a soundstage. Where Kurosawa's later *Stray Dog* beautifully captures the atmosphere of postwar Japan using real locations, *The Quiet Duel* has the look of an overwrought Bette Davis melodrama. This is best exemplified by Kurosawa's use of the same wrought-iron gate to show the passage of time. As the seasons change, we see snow on the gate, snow melting, branches in bloom behind it. These ham-fisted transitions are an attempt at lyricism, but contradict the frank intentions of the story.

With its VD issues, *The Quiet Duel* recalls *Dr. Ehrlich's Magic Bullet* (1940) and cautionary educational films of the time. Admirably, the film is more blunt in its treatment, but this is undermined by its mawkish, old-fashioned drama. In addition, Kurosawa and Taniguchi's frankness about the disease worried the Occupation Forces, whose censors compelled them to change their original ending, where, like Nakada, Kyoji was to have gone mad. The GHQ, mindful of the widespread outbreak of syphilis after the war, feared the scene would so frighten audiences as to have the very opposite effect of what was intended. Like Nakada, it was felt, people would avoid treatment. The original plan of having Kyoji become insane was no better than the ending used in the film, but the imposed change irked Kurosawa. The softened conclusion further steered *The Quiet Duel* toward a conventional, tragic love story, and Kurosawa lost interest, which is all too evident in the finished product.

Kurosawa himself says little about the film in his autobiography. Its chapter mainly discusses a nostalgic anecdote about filming the scene where Mifune's doctor breaks down and his nurse bursts into tears. Kurosawa shot a five-minute take, and while the camera rolled, he was moved to the point of shaking with emotion, while his cameraman, Shoichi Aisaka, broke into tears behind the viewfinder.[5] But what makes *The Quiet Duel* interesting is how many of Kurosawa's favorite themes and ideas, done better in later films, are introduced here. Much of what doesn't initially work in *The Quiet Duel* he tried again with better results in *Stray Dog*. The film's theme of selflessness, self-sacrifice, as well as certain plot elements and its setting, would be revisited in *Red Beard* (1965), especially the scenes with Takiko and Minegishi at the end of the film. In both pictures a psychologically scarred young woman is saved by a doctor's kindness. She, in turn, becomes kind herself, and this kindness is transferred to someone equally unfortunate. In *The Quiet Duel*, Kurosawa goes overboard. There are close-ups of a flower as Shimura walks in carrying Minegishi's baby, bluntly implying renewal. Minegishi's counterpart in *Red Beard*, a young girl named Otoyo, is more subtly handled and more emotionally real. The depths of the characters in *Red Beard* are earned in a way those in *The Quiet Duel* are not.

We can also see Kurosawa's growth as a filmmaker in the way he uses the hospital interiors in both films. In *The Quiet Duel*, the hospital sets always look artificial, and except for an interesting tracking shot of Takashi Shimura walking through its halls, Kurosawa films them in drab medium shots. As many inexperienced directors tend to do when adapting plays, Kurosawa shoots much of the picture in an artificial, stagy way, relying on static medium shots, as if filming a live performance. By the time he made *Red Beard*, Kurosawa knew the importance of detail and was extremely skillful at conveying a setting's geography. The least important scenes in *Red Beard* have a realness lacking in all of *The Quiet Duel*.

Music for *The Quiet Duel* was written by Akira Ifukube, who had scored *Snow Trail* two years earlier. Ifukube didn't endear himself to Kurosawa. "Unfortunately the script was not very good," Ifukube said. "It was very illogical, and however wonderful Kurosawa may [have been], the outcome of the affair was obvious. . . . But, as a director, I think Kurosawa is very great."[6]

Likewise, this was Miki Sanjo's only appearance in a Kurosawa picture. Sanjo (b. 1928), with her tiny voice and delicate features, is well cast, but Misao is a character that carries little weight. The actress is very good in her early scenes with Mifune but has no opportunity to be better than serviceable. Sanjo worked at Daiei in the late 1940s, when she earned the nickname "Daiei's Treasure." But by the mid-1950s Sanjo was playing ingenues in program pictures helmed by Motoyoshi Oda at Toho, films like *The Invisible Man* (Tomei ningen, 1954). She continued in character parts, however, appearing in several of Kon Ichikawa's mysteries, such as *The Inugami Family* (Inugami-ke no Ichizoku, 1976), and in films as recently as 1997. "*The Quiet Duel* was produced at Daiei," she remembered, "but Mr. Kurosawa and most of the crew were from Toho. Only Mr. Kenjiro Uemura and I came from Daiei. We shot the film there, but the rest of the work, such as the rehearsals, took place at Toho."[7]

Where Kyoji doesn't change, Minegishi changes dramatically. Her character and the actress playing her are the best things about the film. Though her scenes are as trite as everyone else's, Minegishi is at least compelling. Noriko Sengoku (b. 1922) played the bar girl in *Drunken Angel*, and would go on to play the gunman's moll in *Stray Dog*, Mifune's friend in *Scandal*, and lesser roles in *The Idiot, Seven Samurai*, and other Mifune films not directed by Kurosawa. A versatile actress, Sengoku was cast by prominent directors from every studio. She worked for Mizoguchi in *The Life of Oharu* (Saikaku ichidai onna, 1954), Masaki Kobayashi in *Kwaidan* (Kaidan, 1964), and Yasuzo Masamura in *The Blind Beast* (Moju, 1969). She was also a favorite of directors Hiroshi Inagaki and Shiro Toyoda, and worked into the 1990s as well, appearing in *Okoge* (1992), a film about homosexuality. Sengoku's Minegishi is a woman as hard as Sanjo's Misao is delicate. Her transformation lacks subtlety, but it's effective nonetheless. Sengoku plays her matter-of-factly, and the script does not beg sympathy for her, the way it does for the two leads. When Minegishi watches Kyoji's breakdown, Mifune, at this point in his career at least, is out of his depth. But Sengoku surmounts the material given her, and when Kurosawa pans to her weeping, the film has its only moment of real emotion. Mifune makes a believable doctor, just as Kurosawa had predicted, but the part offers him little else. Unlike Sengoku, Mifune wasn't experienced enough to bring more to it than the script offered. Takashi Shimura is wasted as his father. He's capable in the scenes he's in, but the character has little function beyond giving the leads someone to talk to.

The Quiet Duel was not released in America until 1979, by which time the film appeared far more dated than it was when it was new and was of interest mainly as a stepping-stone in Kurosawa and Mifune's careers. "The movie's 'problem' seems remote to us now," wrote Vincent Canby, "not only because syphilis is not quite the lifelong sentence it was when the film was made, but also because the codes of honor being acted on appear to be designed to increase and perpetuate guilt rather than alleviate it. The film's most effective scenes are not those of renunciation and sacrifice but those occasional explosions in which the condemned young doctor questions the fate that has given him the punishment for a crime he has never committed. . . . Mifune gives a fine, restrained performance, while the late, great Takashi Shimura . . . has a much smaller role as the young man's extremely understanding father."[8]

The Quiet Duel was well received. It ranked eighth on *Kinema Jumpo*'s "Best Ten" list. Daiei, prominently billing Kurosawa in the film's advertising, made a profit. This perhaps says less about the quality of the picture than about the state of the film industry, still recovering from the war, and the public's hunger for entertainment.

After *The Quiet Duel*, Taniguchi saw Mifune's availability ebbing under Kurosawa's influence, and he didn't like it. "I was in love with [Mifune]. I wanted to work with him for a long time, but then Kurosawa took him. I couldn't argue with that, because he had helped me a lot. I guess Kurosawa must have asked to borrow Mifune after my fifth or sixth film with him. After that, Kurosawa was constantly busy and kept using Mifune. I guess he fell in love with him just as I did. I guess he was a better director, and he helped me in many ways—I just couldn't turn him down."[9]

However, all three—Kurosawa, Mifune, and Taniguchi—collaborated on *Jakoman and Tetsu* (*Jyakoman to Tetsu*). Taniguchi and Kurosawa wrote the script, Taniguchi directed, and Mifune starred, just as they had done for *Snow Trail* two years earlier. Like that film, *Jakoman and Tetsu* was another hard-boiled action picture, based on a story by Keizo Kajino. In Hokkaido, Jakoman (Ryunosuke Tsukigata, the villain in *Sanshiro Sugata*), a one-eyed outlaw, wreaks havoc in a herring-based seaport. Tetsu (Mifune), the son of the president of a local fishing company, decides to battle Jakoman. The picture failed to make *Kinema Jumpo*'s "Best Ten" list but was popular enough to be remade by Kinji Fukasaku in 1964, with Ken Takakura and Tetsuro Tamba in the roles played by Mifune and Tsukigata.

Jakoman and Tetsu opened on July 11, 1949, just as Kurosawa began production on *Stray Dog* (*Nora inu*), his ninth film in little more than six years. The story concerns a police detective, Murakami (Mifune), whose pistol is stolen. The gun is used in a robbery and a murder, and Murakami becomes obsessed with finding the gun and the murderer before he kills again. Working with Chief Detective Sato (Takashi Shimura), he finds the odds are stacked against them. Tokyo is still recovering from the war, *yakuza* lord over entire neighborhoods, and crime runs rampant. Murakami, however, is determined, much like the student worker in *The Most Beautiful* and Yukie in *No Regrets for Our Youth*. Disguised as a returning soldier, he gradually traces the pistol to a pickpocket (Noriko Sengoku), a teenage showgirl (Keiko Awaji), and her gangster boyfriend (Isao Kimura).

The film has three major attributes. First, it builds upon the marvelous postwar atmosphere Kurosawa captured in *One Wonderful Sunday* and *Drunken Angel*. Second, it explores his fascination with the machinations of crime-solving, how detectives build clue upon clue in their efforts to capture a criminal, something he would expand upon even further in *High and Low* (1963). Finally, it re-examines not only Kurosawa's favorite character type—the indefatigable individual who stays determined in his task until a problem is solved—but also expands upon the Hitchcockian doppelgänger structure he first introduced in *Drunken Angel*.

This is shown in many ways. The loss of the pistol unnerves Murakami. He feels a tremendous guilt not only because another man uses it for robbery and murder but also because, in this postwar world, the pistol has become his very identity. Returning from the war, he was just one of thousands of discharged veterans, no better or worse than Yusa, the man who stole the gun, who is himself a veteran. Without his pistol, Murakami is just another displaced man, a stray dog. The title, then, refers not only to Yusa but also to Murakami. Kurosawa emphasizes this by having Murakami blame himself for the crimes committed with his gun. More directly, he identifies with the murderer. As a veteran himself, Murakami knows that war can turn good men bad. When Murakami finally confronts Yusa in the woods at dawn, the two struggle in the mud until both are covered in black muck. They have become indistinguishable. Kurosawa attempted something like this before, in *Drunken Angel*, when Mifune's gangster and his ex-boss grapple in a hallway, knock over several cans of white paint, and their dark clothes become angel-white as they slip and slide in their death struggle. But *Stray Dog* goes one better: after Murakami handcuffs Yusa, the two men lie on their backs in the deep grass, exhausted after the long chase. The off-camera distant singing of children on their way to school is heard. The murderer looks up at the summer blossoms and begins to cry. It is a beauty he knows he will not see again. Only choice separates Murakami from Yusa. As Shimura's Sato tells him, we have all been victimized. We have all felt outrage at the injustices of the world. Only this ability to choose separates us from the animals, from the stray dogs.

Kurosawa had heard about a real-life detective who had lost his pistol, and he wrote a novel around it. The novel, written over six weeks, probably during Toho's third strike, was never published, but the director saw the cinematic possibilities of the idea. It also afforded him the opportunity to direct his first crime thriller, a genre that he loved. "I am very fond of Georges Simenon," he once said.[10]

By the time he was ready to write the screenplay of *Stray Dog*, he found he needed a new collaborator. Keinosuke Uekusa had returned to his wandering. "After we finished writing *Drunken Angel*," Kurosawa said, "[he] disappeared again."[11] Senkichi Taniguchi, meanwhile, was occupied with another project, *Escape at Dawn* (Akatsuki no dasso), which was mired in censorship problems with the Occupation government. So Kurosawa turned to a thirty-five-year-old writer, Ryuzo Kikushima. Kikushima had never written a script, but Kurosawa recognized his talent and took him under his wing. By the time Kurosawa was making films like *Yojimbo* and *Sanjuro* in the 1960s, he appointed Kikushima his producer. They would write a dozen scripts together before they had a bitter parting of the ways in 1969. In the chapter on *Stray Dog* in Kurosawa's autobiography, Kikushima goes unmentioned.

Kurosawa thought fashioning the completed novel into a workable screenplay would be easy enough, but just the opposite proved true, and he struggled with adapting his own material. However, the experience proved useful, for in adapting his novel he learned to express ideas with a minimum of action and clutter by narrowing its focus. For instance, he initially planned to edit the opening scenes in chronological order, with the young detective leaving marksmanship practice, boarding the bus, having his pistol stolen, and then reporting its loss to his superior. "The effect was terrible," Kurosawa wrote. "As an introduction to a drama it was slow, the focus was vague and it failed to grip the viewer. Troubled, I went back to look at the way I had begun the novel. I had written as follows: 'It was the hottest day of that entire summer.' Immediately I thought, 'That's it.' I used a shot of a dog with its tongue hanging out, panting. Then the narration begins, 'It was unbearably hot that day.' After a sign on a door indicating 'Police Headquarters, First Division,' I proceeded to the interior. The chief of the First Detective Division glares up from his desk. 'What? Your pistol was stolen?' . . . This new way of editing the opening sequence gave me a very short piece of film, but it was extremely effective in drawing the viewer into the heart of the drama."[12]

Stray Dog was a co-production of Shintoho and the Film Art Association. Due to lingering post-strike resentment, the film was not shot on Shintoho's stages but rather at Oizumi Studios (now Toei-Tokyo Studios), in the Ikebukuro section of Tokyo. Though away from his home studio, Kurosawa again found the experience an enjoyable one, recalling how, after a long day's shoot, his enthusiastic crew often suggested working into the night.

Kurosawa reserved special praise for Ishiro Honda, who returned from the war and enthusiastically became *Stray Dog*'s chief assistant director. "I had Honda do mainly second-unit shooting. Every day I told him what I wanted and he would go out into the ruins of postwar Tokyo to film it. There are few men as honest and reliable as Honda. He faithfully brought back exactly the footage I requested, and almost everything he shot was used in the final cut of the film. I'm often told that I captured the atmosphere of postwar Japan very well in *Stray Dog*, and if so, I owe a great deal of that success to Honda."[13]

The people that you see onscreen were just like those in the city at that time [Honda recalled]. The postwar period was one of poverty. Around that time, a black market sprang up around the big train stations where people went looking for food, clothes, and work. The most famous places were the west exit of Shinbashi Station, the

north exit of Ikebukuro Station, and the Ameya side street of Ueno.
. . . The crew stayed in the dormitory there. They couldn't get there
otherwise because of the food and transportation situation.

Since the sets didn't look real enough, we decided to shoot in
and around a real black-market neighborhood. Director of Photography Kazuo Yamada and I planned on taking a camera to Ueno, to
Yamashita Street and the Ameya side street. Even newsreel cameramen couldn't shoot there because of [threats of violence]. I put
on my demobilization clothes, played Mifune's role, and walked
through the crowd. Yamada-kun put a hand-held camera in a box and
followed me around. The first five or six shots went fine, but as I was
about to enter the side street from Yamashita Park, somebody said,
"Here he comes," and a man blocked my path. He showed me his
[yakuza] tattoo. The boy who said, "Here he comes," had apparently
seen Yamada and me conferring. The man wasn't frightening at all.
He said that he was desperately trying to survive. When I gave him
some of my lunch, he seemed impressed. "White rice!" he said.[14]

A large portion of the film is layered with the sounds of the black market, much like the city scenes in *Drunken Angel*, only taken one step further.
Achieving the results Kurosawa was after in the dubbing stage was as difficult as it was to shoot. "We used about twelve songs for the scene where
Mr. Mifune's feet were shown in close-up in the black-market," said Masaru
Sato, assistant to composer Fumio Hayasaka. "We took two or three days
selecting the songs. We'd put the good ones aside and kept going through
songs. When we edited them together, all we could do was put a mark right
on the records we wanted to use and record them. Since the film was moving at 24 frames per second, it was impossible to match the cuts with the
frames precisely."[15]

"There was no tape at that time," said Kurosawa's longtime script supervisor, Teruyo Nogami. "The first day of dubbing didn't go very well so we
stopped and decided to try again the following day. Mr. Kurosawa went
back to the waiting room but the soundman, Mr. Fumio Yanoguchi, didn't
join him there, even though Mr. Kurosawa waited a very long time. When
he went back to the dubbing room, he found Mr. Yanoguchi crying by himself. I guess he was completely exhausted from all of the complex dubbing
work."[16]

The result of all this work was a montage of Mifune (often seen only
from the waist down, which is where Honda doubled him) prowling the

black market. This sequence runs for nearly ten minutes and has been criticized as excessive. "The atmosphere is caught, to be sure," wrote Donald Richie, ". . . but it is so long that one expects summer to be over and autumn begun by the time it finally stops."[17] But this long, exhilarating sequence does more than simply capture postwar Tokyo and black-market seaminess. Its length comes close to the breaking point because it needs to. Murakami's determination must exceed our own; the montage serves to illustrate this, while putting the audience inside his very psyche.

Mifune's performance is an improvement over his work in *Drunken Angel*. Partly because of Kurosawa's script, partly due to Mifune's growing abilities, Murakami offers a much greater complexity than any character Mifune had played before. Kurosawa allows Mifune's primal acting instincts and physicality to shine, but together they learned to keep it in check.

Most reviewers, however, singled out Takashi Shimura's delightful portrayal of Mifune's superior. "When you learn [Sato] is a skilled detective," Shimura said, "you imagine that his personality must be intimidating. Quite the contrary. The character I played had a calm demeanor and ate ice cream with the woman he was questioning. I was impressed with Mr. Kurosawa's skillful direction. I guess it was the first Japanese film about an ordinary detective searching for clues to find a criminal."[18]

Making her film debut as Yusa's girlfriend is Keiko Awaji, who became one of Toho's biggest stars of the late 1950s and early '60s. "Every time I remember that picture, I am impressed by how childishly I behaved. . . . I was fifteen or sixteen years old at the time, and still a student of S.K.D. [Shochiku's dance troupe]. The audition had been whittled down to ten students, including me. I knew neither Mr. Kurosawa nor Mr. Mifune. I didn't think they were anybody. They asked us, 'What kind of roles do you want to play?' While the other students answered, 'I want to be a princess' or 'I want to be a prima donna,' I said that I wanted to play an enchantress. I guess they thought I was strange for saying that, but was hired anyway." Mifune took her under his wing, played catch with her, and nicknamed her "Boku-chan, because I looked like a boy."[19] "Boku-chan" has no direct English equivalent, but suffice to say that Mifune is essentially nicknaming her as a very young tomboy.

"Messrs. Mifune, Shimura, [director of photography Asakazu] Nakai, [soundman Fumio] Yanoguchi, and I went to Mr. Kurosawa's room and drank every night. I would eat something while listening to their conversation. One day after work, I was surprised to see the film's poster. Here I was, squatting down on my heels. 'This is me!' Only then did I realize that appearing in the film was a big deal."[20]

"This ingenue was spoiled enough to be a full measure of trouble," confirmed Kurosawa. "She was only sixteen years old, had never acted before, and all she really wanted to do was dance. She would fret and fuss no matter what she was asked to do, and in places where she was supposed to cry she would burst out laughing out of pure contrariness. As time went by and the crew befriended her, it seems Awaji began to find the work more and more interesting. Unfortunately, by that time her job was finished. We all gathered at the studio gate to see her off. After sitting in the car, she burst into tears. Then she said, 'I couldn't cry when I was supposed to, and now look at me.' "[21]

Awaji gave up dancing and pursued film acting. She appeared in supporting roles at Toho during the mid-1950s, mostly in comedies and musicals, but with occasional forays into drama, in films like *Downtown* (Shitamachi, 1957) and *Samurai Saga* (Aru kengo no shogai, 1959), both of which starred Mifune, and Naruse's *When a Woman Ascends the Stairs* (Onna ga kaidan o agaru toki, 1960). In the mid-1960s she switched to Daiei, appearing in films such as *Illusion of Blood* (Yotsuya kaidan) and *Hoodlum Soldier* (Heitai yakuza), both 1965. She returned to the stage after that, to films infrequently, including *Tora-san Goes North* (Otoko wa tsuraiyo— Shiretako bojo, 1987), in which she played Mifune's middle-aged love interest.

Production wrapped in September, and *Stray Dog* was released the following month with great success. The Mainichi Eiga Concourse awarded prizes to Takashi Shimura, Asakazu Nakai (for his and Yamada's cinematography), Fumio Hayasaka, and Shu Matsuyama for his and Yoshiro Muraki's art direction. *Stray Dog* placed third on *Kinema Jumpo*'s "Best Ten" list, behind Ozu's *Late Spring* and Imai's *Blue Mountains*.

Stray Dog was not released in the United States until 1963.

Commercial whimsy has dictated a peculiar pattern for the American release of the films of Akira Kurosawa [observed *Newsweek*]. His films are welcome, of course, but it has become a problem to trace Kurosawa's development as a film-maker. . . . There is a crude vigor to the work in 'Stray Dog.' . . . The purity of the obvious is the strength of [the picture]. The old business about the young cop learning from the weary experience of the old cop is winningly unpretentious. And the enumeration of the bullets—the thug has only seven—to structure the chase is as charming as a *quattrocento* dinner-plate halo. Everything is on the surface, but then Kurosawa's fondness for surfaces is part of his genius. When Mifune is advised that he may get a lead by hanging around the amusement section of town, Kurosawa puts him there in a montage that goes on without a word for eight minutes. In an Italian of the '50s, this would be precious. In Kurosawa, in the '40s it was thrillingly crude—and all the finer art for it.[22]

" 'Stray Dog,' made in 1949, has taken a long time to get here, but it is by no means an immature work," agreed the *Motion Picture Herald*. "A delightfully expert detective thriller, it is, in fact, very close in subject and quality to the Japanese master's latest film, 'High and Low.' . . . Not only Mifune and Shimura are presented as complex, believable people, but all the minor characters are as well. . . . The story . . . is slight; the characters are not. . . . [The atmosphere points] up the tension and lethargy of the times. Subtly, without preaching, Kurosawa makes a comment on the poverty, the debasement of values, the Americanization of post-war Japan."[23]

More recently, the Pacific Film Archives' notes on the film make several interesting observations. "Kurosawa has acknowledged his debt to Simenon, whose . . . Maigret is a Murakami-like seeker grown grey (and not resigned to the fact that the bad sleep well). But *Stray Dog* is typical of Kurosawa's uncanny ability to mold genre to his own concerns. More than a hard-boiled thriller, *Stray Dog* is a Dostoyevskian saga of guilt, and expiation, by association."[24]

The *LA Weekly*'s Henry Sheehan wrote, if somewhat erroneously, "Although Kurosawa sometimes tends toward tinny allegory with such material, here he opens it up, and the cop's sense of responsibility becomes a rich and capacious metaphor for any number of ideas: the vicarious thrill of crime, personal responsibility for social violence, the individual's place in the mass, and finally—in the most obviously autobiographical aspect—an apprentice's inadequacy in the face of professional obligation. Western in its genre and story line, the film is Japanese in its meditative contemplation, and the combination has guaranteed the film a less than enthusiastic reception in both the East and West."[25]

Stray Dog was remade in 1973 by director Azuma Morisaki at Shochiku, and starred Tetsuya Watari and Shinsuke Ashida in the Mifune and Shimura roles, respectively. (Noriko Sengoku appears in both versions, though not in the same role.) According to San Francisco's newspaper *Hokubei Mainichi*, "The original Kurosawa screenplay is kept essentially intact except that, in the current version, the culprits are a gang of young Okinawans, and some attempt is made to incorporate a social statement with regard to discrimination against Okinawans in present-day Japan, a question of some importance since the reversion of Okinawa to Japan in 1972. Like most remakes of earlier classics, this new 'Stray Dog' suffers by comparison with its original; however, on its own merits, it is still an exciting detective story with . . . interesting new twists, such as the concealment of the gun in a gift-wrapped box of incinerated human bones."[26]

Today, *Stray Dog*'s status in the Kurosawa oeuvre has been elevated through frequent theatrical revivals and, more directly, home video availability in the United States, a luxury that, until recently, *Drunken Angel* has been denied. Both films found Kurosawa and his new star at the cusp of greatness, which both would find in a decade of incredible revitalization.

SEVEN

A NEW DECADE

In the course of Toshiro Mifune's training, he became acquainted with a fellow New Face: a petite eighteen-year-old woman named Sachiko Yoshimine. Unlike Mifune, she was interested in pursuing an acting career. Both worked hard during the six-month program, with Sachiko winning bit parts in a couple of Toho's 1946 releases. When she graduated from the New Face program, Toho was eager to sign her, but her father, a conservative Tokyo dentist and budding politician, would not allow it, and Sachiko never accepted the studio's offer.

By this time, Mifune had fallen for her. While stranded in the North Alps during the production of *Snow Trail*, he wrote her love letters, and when he returned to Tokyo, they decided to get married.* Mifune moved out of his small apartment in Isobo, in Yokohama, and temporarily moved in with Kihachi Okamoto, one of *Snow Trail*'s assistant directors. Okamoto lived near Toho in Seijo, which put Mifune closer to Sachiko as well.

Senkichi Taniguchi remembered Sachiko Yoshimine as "very sincere" and always wondered why she ever wanted to become a New Face. "When Mifune decided to marry her, he came to me for advice," Taniguchi recalls. "I wasn't very reliable in those days and told him, 'Sure, whatever.' Her father

*Mifune was not alone in finding love during *Snow Trail*'s production. Director Taniguchi and in-genue Setsuko Wakayama fell in love during filming, and they were married in 1949. The couple divorced, but Taniguchi married another Toho actress, Kaoru Yachigusa, who has remained at his side ever since.

was a dentist and a member of the government. He didn't like the idea of her getting married to another actor. So Kurosawa and I visited Sachiko's father and really complimented Mifune. She was very grateful."[1]

The young lovers moved into a small house near Toho, just down the street from Mr. and Mrs. Takashi Shimura. In fact, RSVPs to their wedding invitations were mailed to Mifune in care of the Shimuras. The older couple became surrogate parents for Mifune. And while he may have sought approval from Kurosawa, Shimura offered a warm, fatherly friendship which wasn't rooted in whatever film they were working on. "When I was a child," said Shiro, Mifune's oldest son, "Mr. Shimura was a kind of father figure for him. . . . The first place my mother and father lived had no bath, and they used to take baths in [the Shimuras'] home [nearby]. I used to call them Grandma and Grandpa. I thought [my grandfather] *was* Mr. Shimura."[2]

Mifune and Sachiko were married on January 5, 1950. He was twenty-nine and she was twenty-one. The Christian ceremony was extremely lavish for the time, as much of the country was still in ruins. But Mifune, his friends and co-workers, and to a lesser extent Sachiko's family were comparatively wealthy. A boisterous reception followed. The Kurosawas, the Shimuras, and Kajiro Yamamoto all attended, as well as several of Toho's rising stars, who, like Mifune, were trained in New Face programs, Ryo Ikebe and Masumi Okada among them. Nenji Oyama, the cameraman who brought Mifune to Toho, also attended the service and reception.

Not quite eleven months later, on November 27, 1950, Sachiko gave birth to Shiro. Mifune couldn't have been happier. During the Occupation, most Japanese struggled to meet their rent, to buy enough food. Mifune, by contrast, had enough money to take care of his siblings while comfortably starting a family of his own. It was the beginning of a new year, a new decade, and a new career.

But as his popularity rose, as the gap between Mifune the star and Mifune the person widened, he became increasingly uncomfortable with his abilities as an actor and his star status. Unlike many of the actors he worked with, Mifune had risen to stardom with no training at all beyond his months in Toho's New Face program. His personal life became the subject of fan magazines, he was frequently recognized in public and spoke at publicity events, all of which made him feel uneasy. He began drinking heavily, veering toward full-blown alcoholism, though his ability to work was never affected.

"Our house was very near Toho Studios," Shiro remembered. "He used to have an English sports car, a 1953 MG, and it was really loud, so when he came back from work, we could hear him coming. When he got home he'd take a bath because of the makeup, and then we'd eat dinner, and he'd want to know what we did that day. Then he would drink a lot of alcohol— every night [laughs]. He was a very strong drinker. Almost an entire bottle of whiskey or brandy or Japanese rice wine each night. Sometimes he'd bring home people from the studios, sometimes they'd work until midnight, sometimes until early in the morning. During the rainy seasons they might not work for two or three days. When I was a child, Mr. Kurosawa's team, the actors and staff, would have a party after they'd finish the film which included the families, and then we'd go to Mr. Kurosawa's house and we'd play with Mr. Kurosawa's son and daughter, like one big family."[3]

Three days after Mifune's wedding, a new film scripted by Kurosawa and Taniguchi premiered, *Escape at Dawn* (a.k.a. *Desertion at Dawn*; Akatsuki no dasso). The picture had been a long time in coming. It was based on Taijiro Tamura's 1947 novel, *The Story of a Prostitute* (Shumpuden). Kurosawa and Taniguchi had completed a first draft more than two years before it was made. The story, suggested by Tamura's seven years of service in China, concerns a Japanese soldier, Mikami (Ryo Ikebe), who is captured by the Chinese. When he returns to his unit, he is ill-treated because he allowed himself to be captured, an act considered reprehensible by the Japanese military. He falls for an Army prostitute (Yoshiko "Shirley" Yamaguchi), but when they try to desert, they're shot dead by a sadistic officer (Eitaro Ozawa).

As detailed in Kyoko Hirano's landmark book on Japanese films of the Occupation period, *Mr. Smith Goes to Tokyo*, Kurosawa and Taniguchi's script was subject to intense scrutiny by the Civil Information and Education Section (CIE). The American censors demanded rewrite after rewrite, and at least seven drafts were prepared over the next eighteen months. By the time Taniguchi directed the film late in 1949, the prostitute had become a "singer," her nationality changed from Korean to Japanese. The latter change may have come not at the insistence of the CIE, but rather of producer Tomoyuki Tanaka, who was concerned that the depiction of Korean women as prostitutes might fan long-standing anti-Korean sentiment (still prevalent in Japan, especially in its southern prefectures, to this day).

American censors rejected Kurosawa and Taniguchi's first script in September 1948, and a second two months later. In a third draft, dated December 30, 1948, Taniguchi decided to take the CIE head on, adding a preface to the script in which he emphasized its anti-war aspects "through the contrast between the love of a woman from a despised vocation for a soldier of the lowest rank, and his faith in his army, which never rewarded him but cruelly killed him instead."[4] He added that the depiction of prostitution and the Japanese military would in no way be treated sensationalistically. Nevertheless, the CIE demanded eleven sections of the script be revised. With that, Kurosawa had had enough and left Taniguchi to continue the battle alone.

By the time Taniguchi's cameras rolled, Kurosawa and Taniguchi's first script had changed dramatically, and much of its potency had been diluted. Its long preproduction, expensive exterior sets, and tangled red tape to secure permission for use of military hardware for filming (machine guns, etc.) made it the most expensive Japanese feature to that point. *Escape at Dawn* received mixed reviews from the critics, but most applauded its uncompromised depiction of ruthlessness within the military regime, and it was selected as Japan's official entry at the 1951 Cannes Film Festival.[5]

Nineteen fifty was a prolific year for Kurosawa. Aside from *Escape at Dawn*, two more of his scripts were filmed. *Tetsu of Jilba* (Jiruba no Tetsu) was directed by Isamu Kosugi, while Masahiro Makino helmed *Fencing Master* (a.k.a. *Swordplay Choreographer*; Tateshi danpei) at Daiei. Both films endured the same kind of scrutiny Kurosawa had experienced on Taniguchi's film; *Fencing Master* was rewritten twice before the American censors allowed it to be filmed.

Mifune, meanwhile, made time for his new bride by accepting supporting rather than starring roles on his next two films. *Conduct Report on Professor Ishinaka* (Ishinaka sensei gyojyoki) was a comedy about college intellectuals, directed by Mikio Naruse and starring Ryo Ikebe. Mifune played a farmer in a provincial town. It was a popular film, and besides Ikebe, Mifune worked with two New Face actresses with whom he would remain friends for many years, Setsuko Wakayama (from *Snow Trail*) and Yoko Sugi.

Escape from Prison (Datsugoku, 1950) was Mifune's second film for Kurosawa's mentor, Kajiro Yamamoto; the picture starred Takashi Shimura and Eitaro Ozawa, the latter having just appeared as the murderous officer in *Escape at Dawn*. Like *Tetsu of Jilba* and *Fencing Master*, *Escape from Prison* has fallen into obscurity and is all but forgotten today, even in Japan. Details about this film remain frustratingly elusive.

From his very first film, *Sanshiro Sugata*, Kurosawa's work was criticized by some Japanese reviewers for being "too Western." And in America and Europe, to this very day, Kurosawa is still referred to as "the most Western of Japanese directors." Kurosawa's films would frequently be compared to American Westerns and noir thrillers, sometimes inaccurately so, and almost always in an overstated manner. In *Scandal* (Shubun—Sukyandaru, 1950), however, shot in late 1949 and completed in January 1950, the influence of Hollywood is undeniable. For the first and only time, Kurosawa simply and obviously imitates rather than transcends his influences, trying to work through several major themes amid a patchwork of ideas.

This is not to say *Scandal* is without merit. Indeed, there are inventive moments throughout, and parts of the film anticipate better ones to come, especially in *Ikiru* and *The Bad Sleep Well*. But *Scandal* is an inconsistent, unbalanced work, starting out as an uncompromising attack on tabloid journalism and ending with a man's melodramatic salvation.

A famous singer, Miyako Saijo (Yoshiko Yamaguchi), stranded in the mountains, meets a young painter, Ichiro Aoye (Mifune). They learn they are staying at the same hotel, and he offers her a ride back into town on his motorcycle. She accepts, and Aoye later visits her in her hotel suite. Each has just taken a bath, and Aoye hangs his towel next to hers on the balcony. A tabloid photographer sees this and, assuming a tryst, snaps away. Soon enough their faces are plastered all over Japan in a two-bit rag called *Amour*.

Aoye isn't happy about this at all and punches *Amour*'s editor in chief, Hori (once again, Eitaro Ozawa, this time at his most smug), but this only generates more publicity. He decides to sue and is approached by a shabby-looking attorney, Hiruta (Takashi Shimura). Neither Aoye nor his friend and model (Noriko Sengoku) know what to make of the downtrodden lawyer, and she warns Aoye not to trust him. Regardless, Aoye visits the lawyer's house, deep in *Drunken Angel* territory. Although Hiruta is not there, his gentle daughter, Masako (Yoko Katsuragi), a bedridden young girl stricken with tuberculosis, is, and Aoye is enormously impressed by her. Continuing on to Hiruta's office, a shack on the roof of an office building, Aoye is impressed again when he sees a small photograph of a smiling Masako hanging near the door. He signs Hiruta on as his attorney.

Hiruta visits Hori, but the editor quickly senses Hiruta's vulnerability, and soon the weak-willed attorney is on Hori's payroll, providing information about his client. Hiruta uses some of the money he gets from Hori to buy his sick daughter elaborate presents, but she knows that something's up and gently tells him so. Although he feels tremendous guilt, Hiruta finds himself trapped, and his lack of confidence and self-loathing take up much of the rest of the picture. At the very end of the trial, following Masako's sudden death, Hiruta breaks down and spills the beans, thus spelling victory for Aoye and Saijo. Asked by reporters about Hiruta's sudden revelation, Aoye says, "We just saw a star being born . . . compared to that our victory is nothing." However, given that Hiruta's daughter is dead and that he will certainly be disbarred and possibly thrown in jail, Aoye's statement comes off as too callous to be believed.

Metaphorically, stars dominate the film as a symbol of idealism and purity. Aoye refers to Masako as being "as pure as the stars," and since the picture is set in December, we see a lot of them on Christmas trees. (Christmas is a secular but extremely popular holiday in Japan.) In one of the picture's odder moments, Mifune barrels down the street with what appears to be a two-meter-tall Christmas tree—fully decorated—on the back of his motorcycle. In another, more subtle scene, Aoye and Hiruta, both drunk, the latter despondent, walk past a sump—recalling *Drunken Angel*—and see the reflection of stars (and themselves) in it.

Scandal, far more than any other film Kurosawa made, is directly influenced by the Hollywood pictures Kurosawa and the rest of postwar Japan were now able to see. The sudden influx of American movies after the war, with their lush production values and relative artistic freedom, was as influential on Japanese filmmakers as the Italian neorealist films they also consumed with great passion. "We were hungry, literally hungry," said director Nagisa Oshima. "And American movies were more than just movies. They were like food. That lasted for a long time. Even if we were opposed to the United States and the Americanization of Japan, we were passionately keen on American films."[6]

The second part of Kurosawa's film rather obviously apes Capra in general and *It's a Wonderful Life* (1946) in particular. There are close-ups of ornaments on trees, Shimura goes around yelling "Merry Kurisumaas! Merry Kurisumaas!" at no one in particular, and his courtroom scenes recall both Lionel Barrymore in Clarence Brown's *A Free Soul* (1931) and Claude Rains in Capra's *Mr. Smith Goes to Washington* (1939). Finally, in a run-down bar adorned with the tiniest bit of tinsel, Shimura drunkenly leads everyone in a Japanese rendition of "Auld Lang Syne."

Though it's easy to misjudge this sequence as the height of cloying sentiment, Kurosawa here transcends his material. At first everyone laughs at Hiruta and a drunken companion (Bokuzen Hidari) as they vow to become better men in the New Year and then break into song. The establishment's third-rate band joins in, and slowly all the other patrons and bar hostesses begin to think of their own discontent and weepily join in.

In a way, the profound impact of Hollywood films on Japanese filmmakers, certainly not just Kurosawa, can partially be explained by the fact that, after being banned during the war, films from Hollywood, as well as the other Allied countries, were finally pouring in, flooding the market along with the cultural consciousness.

In addition, after years of stringent military censorship, the Occupation Forces were encouraging free speech in Japan (only to limit it again by the time of *Escape at Dawn*). But for celebrities (and popular culture) free speech had its downside in the proliferation of tabloid papers that recklessly fabricated stories for an insatiable public all too ready to believe whatever appeared in print. As the number of these publications grew, competition reached stratospheric heights, and the stories they printed became even more outlandish. Kurosawa was outraged by this development, particularly after a film actress, who goes unnamed in his autobiography, was accused of having an illicit affair. "I reacted as if the thing had been written about me," he wrote. "This was not freedom of expression, I felt, it was violence against a person on the part of those who possess the weapon of publicity. I felt that this new tendency had to be stamped out before it could spread. Someone had to come out and fight back against this violence, I thought; there was no time for crying oneself to sleep."[7] *Scandal* thus began as a crusade against yellow journalism.

In later years, Kurosawa gregariously gave many interviews, appeared in television commercials, and welcomed, if only for the publicity it generated, reporters to his sets. But during the 1950s he avoided such attention. Though he makes no mention of it in his autobiography, Kurosawa was romantically linked in the tabloids to Hideko Takamine, the star of *Horse*. This, combined with the chaos at Toho—the strikes, the New Face contests, the unhappy stars now at Shintoho—generated titillating copy for the tabloids.

But for all of Kurosawa's earnestness, as he and Ryuzo Kikushima began writing the script, Hiruta's character began to dominate the film. And with the introduction of Hiruta, both Mifune and Yamaguchi fade into the background, becoming supporting, even minor characters in their own story. This is just as well, as they're little more than victims. Yamaguchi's singer prefers to maintain a low profile during the breaking scandal, while a more naïve Mifune forges ahead, taking action. When Mifune suddenly addresses the court during the final statements, we are almost surprised to be hearing from him, as the character has been nearly forgotten.

Kurosawa realized sometime later that he had based Hiruta on a man he'd met in a bar in the early 1940s. Like Hiruta, this drunken man's daughter was bedridden with TB, and the gentleman, full of self-contempt, went on and on about how pure and innocent his daughter was, and what a wretch he was by comparison. Although the bar's owner was embarrassed by the man's intrusive behavior with the patrons, Kurosawa was both fascinated and moved by his story, and it stayed with him, ultimately becoming the real focal point of *Scandal*.

Unfortunately, Kurosawa's portrait of him teeters on the maudlin. Though Hiruta dearly loves his daughter, he's weak, and his confession is only that: he isn't empowered by this act, and when we last see him, he is simply wandering through the busy streets unnoticed. Takashi Shimura, surprisingly billed sixth in the credits, gives the character everything he's got, but in the end he's unable to elevate Hiruta above the material. Still, there are several charming moments early in the picture, particularly Hiruta's entrance. He peers through the broken window of Aoye's studio home, then comes through the door and, in a bit of beautiful timing, stares at Mifune as if fascinated by him. He talks incessantly, intermittently waving the wet, smelly socks he has just removed. As the trial begins, Shimura turns up—as newsreel cameras roll—in a hilariously outdated ceremonial robe that only makes him look more foolish. For all the picture's preachiness, these bits of characterization are endearing because they are well acted and enhance the characters with a minimum of exposition. Once he has sold his soul to Hori, Hiruta's guilt is overdone. Shimura and Kurosawa would have far better luck with a similar character in *Ikiru* two years later, and in some ways *Scandal* can be viewed as a dry run for that film.

Scandal was the first of five films Mifune made opposite Yoshiko Yamaguchi. Just six weeks older than Mifune, like him, Yamaguchi grew up in China. Though born of Japanese parents, she became famous playing Chinese women in propaganda films during the Japanese occupation of the Chinese mainland. Using the name Li Xianglan (or Ri Ko Ran, as she is still remembered in Japan), Yamaguchi fooled an entire nation into believing she was genuinely Chinese. In nearly every film she played a Japanese-hating Chinese woman who invariably falls in love with a Japanese soldier, sees the error of her thinking, and realizes that the Japanese invaders are swell folk after all. Once the Japanese were defeated, though, the Chinese branded Yamaguchi a traitor—by their reckoning, Li Xianglan had conspired with the enemy. To escape almost certain execution, Yamagushi declared that, ahem, she wasn't Chinese after all but a Japanese national who loyally served her country. According to Yamaguchi, at first the Chinese didn't believe her claim, and it was only the last-minute discovery of her birth certificate that proved once and for all she was Japanese and saved her from the firing squad.

Though reviled in China, her popularity in Japan soared. She joined

Toho Studios in 1948 and became one of their very few bona fide stars after the Flag of Ten moved to Shintoho. She debuted at the studio with *The
Happy Chair* (Shiawase no isu) and *Danshichi, the Black Horse* (Kurouma no
Danshichi), both 1948, the latter for Hiroshi Inagaki. The following year
she appeared in *Human Patterns* (Ningen no moyo) for Kon Ichikawa and,
earlier in 1950, starred opposite Ryo Ikebe in Senkichi Taniguchi's *Escape at
Dawn*. Yamaguchi left Toho in the mid-1950s for rival Shochiku Studios, but
by then had made several films in America and was firmly established as
Japan's first postwar international star.

Using the name "Shirley Yamaguchi," she made her American debut in
King Vidor's *Japanese War Bride* (1952). Though she starred in *Shangri-La* (a
Broadway musical version of *Lost Horizon*), was romanced by Yul Brynner,
and appeared on American television, she was never more than an exotic
curiosity, and a nationally displaced one at that. As Ian Buruma noted in his
informative if condescending article for *Interview*, "It was fitting . . . that her
main companion in America was Yul Brynner, then starring in another Oriental fantasy, *The King and I*. These were all variations of the Chinese
rumba; the stars' mixed identities had become a form of kitsch, displaced
images: Eurasian fantasy."[8]

Clearly, at least some of this was Yamaguchi's own doing. In article after
article she informed reporters that she had come to America "to learn how
to kiss."* By the time she appeared in Sam Fuller's *House of Bamboo* (1955),
starring Robert Stack, and *Navy Wife* (1956), Yamaguchi had to film her
scenes in Japan—she was denied an entry visa because she was suspected of
being a Communist. During the 1950s she married and subsequently divorced Isamu Noguchi, one of the most important sculptor-designers of
the twentieth century. Mifune appeared opposite Yamaguchi one last time,
in the all-star *Holiday in Tokyo* (1958), and after shooting was completed,
she wed diplomat Hiroshi Otaka and retired from films.

To say Yamaguchi failed to become a typical Japanese housewife would
be a gross understatement. In the 1960s she took a job as a television reporter who covered the Vietnam War, and even wrangled an exclusive interview with hijacker and Palestinian terrorist Leila Khaled. After that, she
had a successful career as a Liberal Democratic Party member of the Upper
House of the Japanese Diet from 1974 to 1992. In this position she social-
ized with the likes of King Faisal and Margaret Thatcher.

---

*In Japan to this day, onscreen kissing is rare, and during the early fifties, when it was finally in-
troduced, it was one of the major subjects of discussion in the very same tabloids depicted in
Scandal.

It is also more than ironic that in making his film about the press, Kurosawa, who had never used Yamaguchi before nor would again, should cast Japan's most scandalous, most notorious movie star as an innocent victim of yellow journalism. For her part, Yamaguchi didn't relish working with Kurosawa. "As soon as I came on the set, I was terrified," she said in 1974. "I don't mean to suggest that director Kurosawa was himself frightening, but the atmosphere on the set was so incredibly intense you could hear a pin drop. . . . He was nice to me, but a perfectionist to the point that no mistake was lost on him. . . . He never compromised a single shot until it was perfect. In that way I think he was like Mr. [Charles] Chaplin. This film was unique in my career, because never once did I laugh on the set."[9]

Kurosawa himself had to admit *Scandal* did nothing to control the tabloids, which continue unabated to this day, and in the years to come, Kurosawa, and especially Mifune, would themselves fall victim to them, as have so many others in the Japanese film community. Famed director Juzo Itami, who wrote and directed some of Japan's best film comedies (*The Funeral*, *Tampopo*, *A Taxing Woman*), jumped off a building in December 1997, just days before Mifune's death, killing himself, allegedly after learning a tabloid was going to report that he was cheating on his wife, actress Nobuko Miyamoto. Itami's tragic death, however, only served to sell even more papers. As Eitaro Ozawa's Hori says, "Right or wrong, the public will love it." In the age of *The National Enquirer* and *The Star*, "entertainment news" cable and syndicated shows, and Internet gossip, the message of *Scandal* remains as timely as its melodrama appears quaint.

The free-for-all atmosphere of the tabloids covering the scandal and the public galloping to the newsstand to read about it is well done, if less polished than the director's masterful handling of similar material in *The Bad Sleep Well*. Though critics have likened *Scandal* to Capra, the influence of *Citizen Kane* (1941) is clear here, too (however, Donald Richie states Kurosawa had not yet seen the film). There is an excellent montage as the scandal breaks, with headlines screaming "Love on a Motorcycle!" and "Passion on Two Wheels!," echoing the rise of Kane's newspaper and the fury surrounding Kane's own scandal. Kurosawa films this sequence in a similarly breakneck style, and Fumio Hayasaka's music echoes Bernard Herrmann's. (And, also as in *Kane*, we're treated to a fake newsreel.) Though overstylized, in the midst of this montage are witty shots of Ozawa and Mifune completely surrounded by arms thrusting microphones and cameras at them. Perhaps most arresting is the final shot of the film—a large wall where posted bills advertising the scandal are already peeling off, awaiting new ones to take their place.

Today, *Scandal*'s place in the Kurosawa-Mifune oeuvre has been buried deep in the shadow of *Rashomon*, released later that same year, even though *Scandal* placed sixth right behind *Rashomon* on *Kinema Jumpo*'s annual "Best Ten" list. Having been made at Shochiku, a studio with much less success releasing its films abroad compared to that of Toho or Daiei, *Scandal* wasn't shown in the United States until July 1964 and is rarely revived.

In Los Angeles, the film was initially paired with Ozu's *An Autumn Afternoon* (then called *The Widower*), prompting the *Los Angeles Times*'s Kevin Thomas to write that the double bill "provides a unique opportunity to compare the completely different styles of two of the greatest directors of all time. The presentation of a Kurosawa picture new to American audiences is in itself an important occasion, but the premiere of a film by Ozu, the least known of the top Japanese directors . . . makes this double feature . . . a major event for anyone who enjoys good films. . . . Fast-moving and exciting, *Scandal* belongs to Kurosawa's series of films protesting the moral chaos of postwar Japan. . . . The scenes between [Shimura] and his daughter are straight out of *The Old Curiosity Shop*."[10]

Scandal was reissued in 1980 by Entertainment Marketing. It received a somewhat wider exposure, though not necessarily good reviews. "The film belongs in the same company as *Sarah and Son* and *Stella Dallas*," said *Variety*'s "Robe," "but is worth seeing just to watch the talented cast wring every tear out of the terrible story."[11]

Vincent Canby, in *The New York Times*, offered a surprising view, saying that Kurosawa was laying on the sentiment "so thickly that the film quickly turns into a parody of Hollywood that, simultaneously, satirizes the willingness of the postwar Japanese to accept without question a Western culture completely alien to them. . . . Like all Kurosawa films, *Scandal* is motivated by considerations of humanity and justice, but rarely has the director been so witty or even as subversive as the movie must have seemed to thinking Japanese in 1950."[12]

Even Donald Richie considered the film "shallow," writing: "The picture looks like a more than usually well-made Japanese programmer and few of the excellences of *Stray Dog* or *Rashomon* are visible."[13]

Filled with promising moments and flashes of charm, *Scandal* was all too much a protest film, an unbalanced work whose focus shifts away from its intended purpose to a not uninteresting but peripheral character. Kurosawa would revisit elements of *Scandal* in other films made later that decade, and his growth as a filmmaker during this time would prove extraordinary.

EIGHT

GATE TO THE WORLD

MARGE SIMPSON *(Trying to get her husband to see a subtitled film)*: C'mon, Homer, you liked *Rashomon* . . .
HOMER SIMPSON: That's not the way *I* remember it!
—from the television series *The Simpsons*

In his next film, Kurosawa examined the relative nature of truth. *Rashomon* opened the doors of Japanese cinema to the rest of the world. Its very title has entered our consciousness, its name synonymous with contradictory versions of reality.

The project originated with a Daiei screenwriter with whom Kurosawa would have one of his most valuable, longest-running collaborations, Shinobu Hashimoto (b. 1917). "[Director] Mansaku Itami was my *sensei* at the time," Hashimoto said. "He was a pioneer of the prewar era, and Mr. Kurosawa, who was an assistant director at that time, respected him. During the war Kurosawa wrote *A German at the Daruma Temple*, and when Mr. Itami read it, he figured Kurosawa would be a big name in the Japanese film industry."[1]

Looking for a story to adapt, Hashimoto sifted through the works of short-story writer Ryunosuke Akutagawa (1892–1927), famed for his eerie, psychologically haunting adaptations of classic folktales. "None of Akutagawa's stories had ever been filmed," Hashimoto said, "so I read six or seven of them. The one that interested me the most was 'In a Grove,' and I wrote a script based on it. Because Mr. Kurosawa respected Mr. Itami, whom I was working under, Mr. Kurosawa read the seven or eight scripts I had written thus far, one of which was 'In a Grove,' and decided to make a film of it."[2]

Hashimoto met with Kurosawa at his home, spending many hours discussing the script, then titled *Male-Female* (Otoko-onna). "He seemed to have substance," Kurosawa said of Hashimoto, "and I took a liking to him."[3]

Kurosawa wanted to make *Rashomon* as early as 1948, and according to Donald Richie, the project was originally going to be financed elsewhere. As Richie states, the Toyoko Company, a short-lived independent production company, as well as Toho, had both rejected it on the grounds that its unusual structure made producing it financially risky.[4] Regardless of where *Rashomon* originated, Kurosawa met with opposition at every turn. Even at Daiei, where the film would eventually be made, company executives, specifically studio head Masaichi Nagata, were reluctant to finance it. But Kurosawa liked what he read. The one problem as far as he was concerned was that the script was too short. "We only had 90 pages," Hashimoto recalled, "that's why we decided to add [Akutagawa's] 'Rashomon.' After that the script was too long and didn't work well, either. We were supposed to revise the script together, but then I got sick."[5] Despite concerns over its length, once elements of "Rashomon" were added, serving as wraparound scenes (and as a kind of Greek chorus to the main tale), Daiei granted Kurosawa its approval.

With Hashimoto unavailable due to illness, Kurosawa traveled to a hot springs *ryokan* (a traditional Japanese-style inn) in Atami and finished the script himself. He was joined there by Ishiro Honda, who was working on a script of his own, *The Blue Pearl* (Aoi shinju, 1951), which would mark his own directorial debut.

Rashomon's story is exceedingly simple. It is set in the eleventh century. A woodcutter (Takashi Shimura) and a priest (Minoru Chiaki) wait out the pouring rain under the half-ruined, ancient *Rashomon* (Rajoman Gate). They meet a commoner (Kichijiro Ueda), and the woodcutter tells him a baffling, deeply troubling tale. A samurai (Masayuki Mori) has been killed and a bandit (Toshiro Mifune) arrested for the crime. At the inquest, the bandit claimed—shown in subjective flashbacks—that the samurai's wife (Machiko Kyo) made advances toward him, and she convinced him to kill her husband. The wife testifies that she was raped by the bandit, after which her husband rejected her and she fainted. When she awoke, the wife says, she found him dead. The slain samurai, speaking through a medium (Fumiko Homma), agrees that she was raped, but asserts that his wife then asked the bandit to kill him. He was so shamed by her actions that he committed *seppuku* (ritual suicide). Finally, the woodcutter, also witness to the events, offers yet another version. He says that after the rape the wife egged the two men on to fight each other, resulting in an almost comic duel in which the husband was killed. (Quite unlike the usual *chambara*, the violent genre where swordfights are choreographed like ballets, the two men are terrified of doing battle.) As the three men at the gate ponder all this, they discover an abandoned newborn. The commoner begins stealing the baby's meager possessions. The woodcutter is outraged, but the commoner accuses him of hypocrisy, correctly guessing that the woodcutter stole the dagger that fatally wounded the husband. Overcome with shame, the woodcutter decides to adopt the baby into his already large family, thus restoring the priest's faith in humanity.

No one—not in Japan, not in America, not anywhere in the world—had seen a film quite like it before. And its critical and (relative) commercial success in the West opened the market for Japanese films in Europe and the Americas. But for all its historical significance, *Rashomon* is today a victim of its own worldwide impact. In its day *Rashomon* was a completely new type of filmmaking. Critics had never seen a commercial feature which so successfully abandoned the conventional, objective narrative form. Such experimentation was virtually unheard of. Indeed, some moviegoers were completely baffled by it. Likening it to conventional mysteries, many believed there was an actual solution hidden somewhere in the bush. For 1950 audiences, it was comparable to D. W. Griffith's use of parallel editing (i.e., intercutting between simultaneous actions) in the early silent era. It was as if Kurosawa had discovered a new way of making movies.

But since its release, *Rashomon* has been directly adapted as a Broadway play and remade as a Western. It paved the way for other films which similarly toyed with non-linear and multiple point-of-view techniques, such as *The Killing* (1956), *Last Year at Marienbad* (1961), and *Four Times That Night* (1973). Today such films are not uncommon (c.f., *Reservoir Dogs, The Usual Suspects*, and *Run Lola Run*), and writers have lifted *Rashomon*'s premise as the basis for hundreds of episodic television programs, from Hitchcock's "Incident at a Corner" (1960) to episodes of sitcoms like *Growing Pains* and science-fiction dramas like *Star Trek: The Next Generation*.

Because these groundbreaking elements have been so widely absorbed into modern filmmaking, the effect that *Rashomon* has on audiences today is markedly different from the effect it had on those who first saw it in Japan in 1950 and subsequently in the West. As a result, Kurosawa's film has become more historically than aesthetically significant. Aside from its impact on narrative forms, and spurring general interest in Japanese film in the West, it bolstered the careers of Kurosawa and Mifune in particular. And in this regard *Rashomon*'s importance cannot be overestimated.

As a film *Rashomon* is technically flawless, but lacks the resonance of Kurosawa's later works. Kurosawa and Hashimoto knew they were treading unfamiliar waters and boiled their scenario down to the bare essentials. Any more would have been too much for audiences of the time to handle. For *Rashomon*, Kurosawa reached back to the silent films he so loved in his youth, relying on visual storytelling more than ever before. There are long stretches without a word of dialogue, which doubtlessly helped it gain acceptance outside Japan. Kurosawa later recalled, "Since the advent of the talkies in the 1930s, I felt, we had misplaced and forgotten what was so wonderful about the old silent movies. I was aware of the aesthetic loss as a constant irritation. I sensed a need to go back to the origins of the modern motion picture to find this peculiar beauty again; I had to go back to the past."[6]

"Many of my friends sought to dissuade me from making *Rashomon* for Daiei," Kurosawa recalled. "They thought the picture's theme too unusual and wondered why I should take such a risk while free to take my pick of other types of stories. I could see what they meant, but I was not to be shaken from the venture, because I was tired of mannerisms in most Japanese pictures. I wanted something new, something with an idea a bit ahead of all others. Unless you are ambitious and have courage enough to do something nobody has done before, you cannot go a step forward. Besides, I never thought the *Rashomon* theme unusual. If you are observant, you can find such things everywhere in the world."[7]

However, according to Kurosawa, Daiei's executives weren't especially observant. "Daiei . . . did not understand it and kept asking: But what is it about? Actually, Daiei was adamant in its refusal to understand . . . it."[8]

Indeed, Masaichi Nagata, head of the studio, walked out of the first screening and promptly disowned the film: unlike in Daiei's other prestige pictures, his name is nowhere to be found in the credits. "[Nagata produced] all of Daiei's big budget movies," said actor Eiji Funakoshi, one of Daiei's biggest stars of the 1950s. "He introduced Japanese films to people all over the world and was one of the great producers in the history of the Japanese film industry, but as a manager, well, maybe he should have done something else."[9]

Nagata had no idea how to market *Rashomon*. One of the things that bothered him was the acting, which he felt was inexplicably exaggerated, particularly in the performances of Mifune and Machiko Kyo. He had his publicity men shoot stills of the cast mugging outrageously. Nagata's still photographer then had the cast pose for comic-book-like action shots, suggesting the film was a more traditional *jidai-geki*, which *Rashomon* was anything but. Finally, glamour shots of Kyo, posing seductively (in a bathing suit no less), were inserted into the film's press materials, playing up the film's "exotic" nature.

If the acting style in *Rashomon*, which Kurosawa would use again in films like *Seven Samurai*, didn't spring from contemporary Japanese films, then where did it come from? Again, Kurosawa was harking back to the style common in silent-film acting. By the early 1950s, the broad gestures and extreme facial expressions of silent cinema had, to Japanese as well as Western audiences, become rather comical. In *Singin' in the Rain* (1952), set during the silent-to-sound transition in Hollywood, Debbie Reynolds's Kathy Selden pokes fun at Don Lockwood's (Gene Kelly) Fairbanksesque mannerisms, which by then were considered shameless overacting. But *The Saturday Review* (presumably an uncredited Arthur Knight), reviewing *Rashomon* when it came to America, instinctively picked up on precisely what Kurosawa was after:

> It is more like silent film acting than anything else I can think of, and how people will judge it is anybody's guess. In the 1921 "Tol'able David," there is a scene in which Ernest Torrence, the villain, prepares to fight the hero. As he nerves himself to the attack, a muscle in his face twitches uncontrollably. When this film is shown nowadays at the Museum of Modern Art, most audiences react to the face-twitching with laughter. They have forgotten—the conventions of present-day acting have made them forget—that under stress of fear or anger, a man loses control of his nervous system. His pulse pounds, his heart beats faster, adrenaline pumps through him, he is apt to make unintelligible noises . . . and since dialogue dominates most film today the ability of silent screen actors to exhibit naked emotion has become a forgotten art which is not even recognized as an art, when occasionally resurrected. "Rasho-Mon" [sic] is a reminder of what it was like at its best, and this is no accident. It is part of the design of the film. . . . Whoever Akira Kurosawa is, however he came into his greatness as a film director, it was by more than knowing his lenses and his cameras. He knows how difficult it is to live, how necessary to love.[10]

Another inspiration for the performances came to Kurosawa accidentally. "We were staying in Kyoto," Kurosawa said, "waiting for the [gate] set to be finished. While we were there we ran off some 16mm prints to amuse ourselves. One of them was a Martin Johnson jungle film in which there was a shot of a lion roaming around. I noticed it and told Mifune that was just what I wanted him to be. At the same time [Masayuki] Mori had seen a jungle picture in which a black leopard was shown. We all went to see it. When the leopard came on Machiko was so upset that she hid her face. I saw and recognized the gesture. It was just what I wanted for the young wife."[11]

Considering its small cast and three simple locations, *Rashomon* was not a cheap film, at least by Japanese standards, costing an estimated $140,000 (about twice the usual budget), much of it poured into the construction of the Rashomon Gate set.[12] Even at this figure, however, Kurosawa, perhaps wary of Daiei's open distaste for the project, kept it within budget, something he rarely did at this phase of his career. Moreover, he filmed it very quickly. Thanks to careful preproduction planning, the film was shot in just a few weeks. It's also possible that Kurosawa wanted to get out of the Nara Mountains, where much of the story was filmed as, incredibly, while on location the cast and crew were besieged by mountain leeches, which were so prevalent they would drop from the trees above.[13]

For all of Daiei's trepidation, *Rashomon* was a hit, becoming their fourth-highest-grossing film that year. It was less popular in rural areas, where worried theater managers went so far as to hire long-retired *benshi* to narrate and decipher the film for confused patrons. But in the larger cities, helped no doubt by Daiei's saturation booking in its urban theater chains, *Rashomon* was popular. Reviews were mixed, but it made *Kinema Jumpo's* "Best Ten" list, ranking fifth behind Tadashi Imai's *Until We Meet Again* (Mata au hi made), Hideo Oba's *Return to the Capitol* (a.k.a. *Homecoming*; Kikyo), the Kurosawa-scripted *Escape at Dawn* directed by Taniguchi, and Shin Saburi's *Reprieve* (a.k.a. *The Deferment*; Shikko yuyo). *Scandal* ranked just behind *Rashomon*, placing sixth.

Much of the film's praise went to Daiei's star cinematographer, Kazuo Miyagawa (1908–99). Miyagawa joined the industry in 1926, when he was just eighteen, and his long, varied career stretched over a remarkable seven decades, from silents to sound, from black-and-white to color, standard to wide screen, with Miyagawa a master of them all. He shot the most prestigious of features and the lowliest of programmers, enhancing everything photographed through his lenses. He worked with every major director of the sound era: he filmed most of Mizoguchi's later films, including *Ugetsu* (Ugetsu monogatari, 1953), *Sansho the Bailiff* (Sansho Dayu, 1954) and *Street of Shame* (Akasen chitai, 1956), as well as Ozu's *Floating Weeds* (Ukikusa, 1958). For Daiei, Miyagawa lensed many of Kon Ichikawa's best films, including *Conflagration* (Enjo, 1958) and *Odd Obsession* (Kagi, 1959), and was one of the key cinematographers on Ichikawa's epic documentary *Tokyo Olympiad* (Tokyo Orinpitsuku, 1965). As the golden period of Japanese film came to an end, Miyagawa found steady employment lensing a half-dozen "Zatoichi" films, the long-running *chambara* series about a blind swordsman starring Shintaro Katsu. In his last working years, he shot three features for Masahiro Shinoda: *MacArthur's Children* (Setouchi shonen Yakyudan, 1984), *Gonza the Spearman* (Yari no Gonza, 1986), and *The Dancer* (Maihime, 1989). Because he was employed by Daiei, Miyagawa had little opportunity to work with Kurosawa, but the director was able to secure his services again for *Yojimbo* and later on for *Kagemusha*. Though they rarely worked together, in later years Miyagawa and Kurosawa became close friends, and Kurosawa remained Miyagawa's biggest fan.

That most of the film is *photographed* from the point of view of a third rather than a first person is partly what baffled so many moviegoers. Kurosawa wisely chose to limit the number of subjective camera angles, rendering those he and Miyagawa employed powerfully effective. The ones film scholars remember most involve the woodcutter's walk through the forest, in which Miyagawa's camera points up through the high trees where the sun, shining directly into the camera, flickers in and out. It is quite unlikely that such cinematography had never been attempted before, even though Miyagawa is often credited as the first person to do so. More significantly, this and Miyagawa's use of roaming dolly shots work marvelously to put the viewer into the characters' minds, rather than locating them geographically by subjective angles.

Miyagawa also worked closely with Kurosawa's preoccupation with climate as cinematic punctuation. As critic Michael Jeck notes in his audio commentary for the laserdisc and DVD versions of *Seven Samurai*, the weather in Kurosawa's films is never accidental. If there's rain in his films— and there is a lot of rain in *Rashomon*—it wasn't because they filmed on rainy days: Kurosawa put it there. Rain and also wind in Kurosawa's pictures typically reflect narrative shifts in his scenarios. His characters frequently endure gut-wrenching periods of enlightenment during rainstorms (as in *Rashomon*), while fierce winds usually foreshadow turning points in his stories, often signaling the arrival of key characters. Weather changes are a device Kurosawa would use in nearly every film he made, right up until his last screenplay, appropriately named *After the Rain* (Ame agaru).

Rashomon was Miyagawa's first encounter with Toshiro Mifune:

> My impression when I met Mifune for the first time was "He doesn't talk." I don't talk too much myself but he really is a quiet person. So at that time, I was wondering what he was thinking. Though he was a quiet man, he expressed himself more with action. He was an actor who understood how the camera moves. When I'm looking into the lens, he often looks like he wants to talk with me or ask for a suggestion. Maybe he had some questions about his own acting sometimes. I am known as someone who shoots with a lot of camera movement, so he might have been curious about what I was doing.
>
> What made Mifune outstanding was his body. He has a thick chest, muscular arms and shoulders. It was really clear from the lens. So it also helped *Rashomon* to be very real; regular acting can't create that feeling. I also have to talk about his eyes. His eyes were really serious when he was acting, but off-camera, they turned out to be very warm.[14]

Rashomon made an unlikely star of Machiko Kyo. Kurosawa cast her in part because of her physique. She had an earthy sexuality about her, and some in the Japanese press likened her to Jane Russell. At various times she was dubbed not only the "Jane Russell of Japan" but "Japan's Marilyn Monroe" and the "Girl with the Most Beautiful Legs."[15] Partly this was Nagata's doing. Taking a cue from Hollywood, he fashioned her into a veritable sexpot when she joined the studio in 1949. Until then, Japanese actresses had always been presented as sweet and wholesome. They were girl-next-door types, everyone's ideal mother or sister or girlfriend. Kyo might be considered Japanese cinema's first "bad girl," and Nagata lavished attention and publicity on her buxom features, rather as Howard Hughes did with nearly every woman under contract to RKO.

Born in Osaka in 1924, Kyo joined that city's Shochiku Girls Opera as a dancer at the age of twelve but languished in minor roles until she was called to Tokyo after appearing in blackface and covered head to toe in feathers in a routine entitled "Turkey Boogie." She made her film debut at twenty, in *Three Generations of Danjuro* (Danjuro sandai) in 1944. *Rashomon* was her breakthrough role, and she had the good fortune to land starring parts in both *Ugetsu* and *Gate of Hell* (Jigokumon, 1953) afterward. All three films made a big splash in the United States, and Kyo, it was assumed in America, must be Japan's leading actress. In Japan, however, she was still thought of as more of a Julie Newmar than a Julie Harris, and her work was rarely taken seriously. Daiei, however, wasn't about to question Occidental tastes and cast her in plum roles over the next several years. Kyo's best screen part came in Mizoguchi's sublime *Street of Shame* (Akasen chitai, 1956), in which she played a hilarious, hip-swaggering, money-grubbing hooker. That same year Kyo flew to Hollywood to star opposite Glenn Ford and Marlon Brando in *Teahouse of the August Moon* (1956), a painfully unfunny comedy adapted from the John Patrick play.

"Her friends, directors and fellow actors describe her as being a reserved, simple, and naïve but self-possessed person," reported *Asia Scene* in 1957. "She seldom goes out, except on studio command, because of the large crowds and rabid fans. . . . Her life has been free of the usual romantic gossip that afflicts most movie stars. . . . Miss Kyo usually makes from six to seven movies a year, rarely taking off more than a week between pictures. After work she usually rests, studies her scripts, or knits, while any extra spare time is usually taken up with her favorite hobbies of fishing or seeing movies."[16]

By the time she made *Teahouse of the August Moon*, Kyo's stock in Japan had begun to wane, but during the late 1950s and throughout the 1960s, Kyo turned in good supporting performances in many A-list Daiei films as varied as *Odd Obsession* (Kagi), *Floating Weeds* (Ukikusa), both 1959, *Buddha* (Shaka, 1962), Shiro Toyoda's *Sweet Sweat* (Amai ase, 1964), for which she won *Kinema Jumpo*'s "Best Actress" Award, and Hiroshi Teshigahara's *The Face of Another* (Tanin no kao, 1966). In the 1970s Kyo began turning up on Japanese television, returning to features only sporadically, in films such as *Tora-san's Heart of Gold* (Otoko wa tsuraiyo—Torajiro junjo shishu, 1976) and *Make-Up* (Kesho, 1984).

After *Rashomon*, Kyo was immediately reteamed with Mifune and Takashi Shimura in Keigo Kimura's *The Life of a Horse-Trader* (Baku rou ichidai, 1951), but she never again worked with Kurosawa. Nonetheless, Kurosawa held her in high esteem, recalling in his autobiography, "During rehearsals before shooting I was left virtually speechless by [her] dedication. She came in to where I was still sleeping in the morning and sat down with the script in her hand. 'Please teach me what to do,' she requested, and I lay there amazed. The other actors, too, were all in their prime. Their spirit and enthusiasm were obvious in their work, and equally manifest in their eating and drinking habits."[17]

International recognition of *Rashomon*, and for that matter Kurosawa and Mifune, might have been stalled for years if not for the intervention of an Italian woman named Giulliana Stramigioli, then head of Italiafilm's Japanese office. The twelfth annual Venice International Film Festival had formally invited the Japanese industry to submit a film for competition the following August, long after *Rashomon* had completed its run. Kurosawa's film was not even considered and was, as far as Daiei was concerned, already forgotten, despite its favorable reviews in film magazines like *Kinema Jumpo*. But Ms. Stramigioli remembered seeing *Rashomon* in Japan and recommended it. It was only through Stramigioli's tenacity that Daiei and Masaichi Nagata reluctantly struck and shipped an Italian-subtitled print to Venice.[18]

Rashomon was shown there on August 24, 1951. Seventeen days later, on September 10, 1951, Kurosawa's modestly produced film stunned the film world. The first Japanese film ever entered at Venice had won its Grand Prize. Kurosawa's film beat out twenty-eight competing movies from fourteen countries, including Jean Renoir's *The River*, Robert Bresson's *Diary of a Country Priest* (Le Journal d'un Curé de Campagne), Elia Kazan's *A Streetcar Named Desire*, and Billy Wilder's *Ace in the Hole*.[19]

On September 12, Italian diplomatic representative B. Lanza d'Adenta sent a letter to Nagata informing him of *Rashomon*'s victory. "May I add to this," the Italian wrote, "my personal feelings of felicitation on the distinguished acknowledgment made in Venice of the outstanding characteristics of the Japanese motion picture." Soon thereafter, the award, a gold reproduction of the Lion of San Marco, was shipped to the studio.

"We were very surprised that it won," Hashimoto remembers. Kurosawa was especially surprised; he was not aware *Rashomon* had even been entered.[20] Less surprising, perhaps, is that once *Rashomon* began winning awards abroad, Nagata had no reservations about taking all the credit, and he kept the Venice prize for himself.

Decades later, long after Nagata had driven Daiei into bankruptcy and Kurosawa's fame had far eclipsed the controversial studio head's, the director remained bitter about the experience and made no bones about his feelings. In the epilogue to his autobiography, Kurosawa recalls seeing Nagata on Japanese television when *Rashomon* was first broadcast: "This man, after showing so much distaste for the project at the outset of production, after complaining the finished film was 'incomprehensible,' and after demoting the company executive and producer who had facilitated its making, was now proudly taking full and exclusive credit for its success! He boasted how, for the first time in cinema history, the camera had been boldly pointed directly into the sun. Never in his entire discourse did he mention my name or the name of the cinematographer whose achievement this was, Kazuo Miyagawa. Watching the television interview, I had the feeling I was back in *Rashomon* all over again."[21] Kurosawa did not refer to Nagata by name, but his identity was obvious to everyone in the industry who read this book.

Variety's "Mosk" had seen *Rashomon* in Venice and reported back to the American trade paper: "Direction is excellent. Shot completely outdoors, the camera work is flawless." So unknown were both Kurosawa and Mifune at the time, "Mosk" completely mangled the names of the cast and crew, mixing the two components as well. "Seinobu Haseimoto [sic] gives a searing performance as the vermin-ridden bandit. Toscio Mifume [sic!] supplies a role of dramatic intensity. Achira Curosawa [sic!!] lends an impassive, glowering presence to the part of the husband." Nonetheless, *Variety*'s comments may very well have tipped the scales to spur an American release of the picture. "Brilliance of conception, technique, acting and its theme of passion make this a good art house bet in the U.S. Exploitation values are there and crix should go for it," "Mosk" concluded.[22]

Daiei struck an English-subtitled print of *Rashomon*, which they ran for American servicemen in Japan in mid-October. Executives were still uncertain whether American audiences would be able to follow its story. Reassured by their positive reaction, Daiei then shipped its print to Los Angeles, to the Linda Lea Theater in Little Tokyo, for a brief limited run beginning December 6, 1951.[23] Within a few days the American studio-distributor RKO announced that they had acquired the U.S. distribution rights. RKO, which had been negotiating with Daiei as early as October, was the most logical choice to handle the film. The deal was engineered by James A. Mulvey, president of Samuel Goldwyn Productions. Goldwyn's films were then being distributed by RKO, while RKO's films were distributed in Japan by Daiei. Nevertheless, the move was highly unusual. After the coming of sound, foreign language films in America were almost never acquired by major studios. Rarer still was the concept of exhibiting such a film with English subtitles instead of simply dubbing it. Indeed, the only foreign language film RKO ever released with subtitles prior to *Rashomon* was René Clair's *Man About Town* (*Le Silence est d'ôr*, 1947), but that starred Maurice Chevalier, who had been a Hollywood star in the 1930s.[24] Moreover, the French film was partly financed by RKO, and in most markets, the company released the film not with subtitles but with an English narration spoken by its star.[25]

As the deal was finalized, *Rashomon* formally premiered in New York on December 26, at the newly refurbished Little Carnegie Theater. It was the first Japanese film shown there since Naruse's *Wife! Be Like a Rose* (*Tsuma yo bara no yi ni*, 1935) more than a dozen years earlier. "I do not have any idea how this picture will be accepted in the United States," Kurosawa said of the film's American release. "I do believe that human nature is the same the world over and *Rashomon* is a drama of human beings."[26]

American critics were impressed, if bemused, by what they saw. Consider Bosley Crowther's review for *The New York Times*. He called *Rashomon*

> an artistic achievement of such distinct and exotic flavor that it is difficult to estimate it alongside conventional story films. On the surface, it isn't a picture of the sort that we're accustomed to at all.
> . . . Whether this picture has pertinence to the present day—whether its dismal cynicism and its ultimate grasp at hope reflect a current disposition of people in Japan—is something we cannot tell you. But, without reservation, we can say that it is an artful and fascinating presentation of a slice of life on the screen.
>
> Much of the power of the picture—and it unquestionably has hypnotic power—derives from the brilliance with which the camera of director Akira Kurosawa has been used. The photography is excellent and the flow of images is expressive beyond words. Likewise the use of music and of incidental sounds is superb, and the acting of all the performers is aptly provocative. . . . Toshiro Mifune plays the bandit with terrifying wildness and hot brutality.[27]

"I don't know what I expected of a Japanese film," wrote William Whitsbait of *The New Statesman and Nation*, when *Rashomon* opened in London. "Something tawdry in color, I dare say, about paper houses and geisha girls; but *Rashomon* took me quite by surprise. . . . What is revealed is native, cruel, poetic and alive. How am I to convey this impact? . . . Who is Akira Kurosawa? What are his other films, and does he stand alone as the exponent of a strong and sophisticated art, or are there in Japan others like him?"[28]

Ed Sullivan wrote:

If you haven't seen 'Rashomon' . . . drop into the Little Carnegie
Theater. You'll find it an exciting evening, because the direction, the
photography, and the performances will jar open your eyes. . . . Director Akira Kurosawa also wrote the screenplay and his characters
emerge with startling impact. These are creatures of flesh and bone,
possessed of emotions that come raging out of the film. The photography is by Kazuo Miyagawa and it is spellbinding. In some fashion,
he achieves visual dimensions that I've never seen in Hollywood
photography. Most of it is shot through a relentless rainstorm that
heightens the mood of the somber drama. It is superb photography,
sensitive and moving. Moviegoers who see 'Rashomon' come away
with a new understanding of the Japanese—and a further appreciation of the art forms of the Far East.[29]

But some critics, such as *Newsweek*'s unnamed, uninformed reviewer,
were already setting a bad precedent by suggesting that Japan's film factories traditionally imitated Hollywood, just as its electronics industry copied
our transistor radios. "The Japanese film industry has been well known for
a sad aping of Hollywood's less admirable habits, but this picture is something else again. It represents the legendary esthetic powers of the Japanese
at a high pitch. It is a stunning work of art."[30] Such backhanded compli-
ments were typical. In this case, for instance, it's extremely unlikely that
Newsweek's scribe had ever even seen a Japanese feature prior to *Rashomon*,
but such unfounded criticisms were common in the 1950s, and when writing about Japanese cinema, few ever noticed such egregious errors.

The *New Yorker*'s critic dissented, saying, "Perhaps I am purblind to the
merits of 'Rashomon,' but no matter how enlightened I may become on the
art forms of Nippon, I am going to go on thinking that a Japanese pot-
pourri of Erskine Caldwell, Stanislavski, and Harpo Marx isn't likely to
provide much sound diversion."[31]

But the combination of mostly good reviews, word-of-mouth, and the
film's novelty resulted in excellent box office. At the Little Carnegie alone
Rashomon earned about $35,000 in its first three weeks, an astounding
gross for a single theater at that time.* Its success prompted RKO to ac-

---

*RKO also produced and apparently released in some markets a dubbed version of the film,
making it quite possibly the first Japanese feature ever looped into English. The extent of this
version's market is unknown; however, it was released in America on laserdisc along with the
subtitled version. Predictably, the dubbing is poor, though not as bad as that of most films of its
kind.

quire another foreign film the following month, the English-language *Faithful City*, made in Israel.

Meanwhile, the same print of *Rashomon* made its way to Washington, D.C., on February 25, then moved to Los Angeles on March 13, earning excellent reviews wherever it played. RKO's pressbook played up the film's reviews, quoting them at length.[32]

The National Board of Review named *Rashomon* the Best Foreign Film of the Year, and Akira Kurosawa Best Director. On March 20, 1952, at the RKO-owned Pantages Theatre in Hollywood, *Rashomon* was given a special honorary Oscar (the Foreign Film category was not yet in place) by the Academy of Motion Picture Arts & Sciences as "the most outstanding foreign language film released in the United States during 1951." Members of the Japanese consulate in Los Angeles accepted the prize, profusely praising Nagata while not once mentioning Kurosawa.[33]

However, a few months later, on June 21, *Rashomon*'s director was feted at a dinner in Tokyo celebrating the acclaim the film had earned abroad, and the benefits he would reap from its international release stretched far beyond the trophies and plaques that were initially denied him.[34]

Rashomon's success overseas stunned the Japanese film industry. The studios, especially Daiei and Toho, had very particular views about which of their films were "suitable" for export. *Rashomon*, it was felt, was as inappropriate for non-Japanese audiences as could be imagined. Specifically, studio executives were surprised that a film with a historical setting could ever be accepted outside Japan. Of course, these same executives failed to understand that *Rashomon*'s setting was irrelevant and went on to produce increasingly lavish historical films over the next decade. In subsequent years, mediocre historical films specifically made with the export market in mind would make little impact abroad, while extremely well-crafted, often innovative work (e.g., films with modern settings, as well as the more inventive program pictures) deemed unsuitable for Western audiences would languish unseen outside Japan indefinitely.

Rashomon's influence extended to the Broadway stage, where it was adapted by Fay and Michael Kanin in a production directed by Peter Glenville and bankrolled by David Susskind and Hardy Smith. The play *Rashomon* premiered at Broadway's Music Box Theatre on January 27, 1959, with Rod Steiger as the bandit, Noel Willman as the husband, Claire Bloom as the wife. Akim Tamiroff, Oscar Homolka, and Michael Shillo played the woodcutter, commoner, and priest, respectively. Although the play followed the film very closely, its credits claimed it was based not on Kurosawa's film but "on stories by Ryunosuke Akutagawa." The movie *Rashomon* was grievously short-changed, the only mention of it buried near the end of the show's program, where the following statement was made:

> *Rashomon*, the Japanese film which won many world-wide honors in 1951, was, like this play, based on the stories of Akutagawa. It was written by Shinobu Hashimoto and Akira Kurosawa and was directed by the latter. The playwrights respectfully acknowledge the cinematic contributions of these two men which have carried over into this play.[35]

Nonetheless, it was clearly Kurosawa's film they had adapted, and certainly not an idea springing independently from the Kanins after they had coincidentally read the same two Akutagawa stories. There are a few minor differences—the commoner has become a wigmaker, for instance, as in Akutagawa's original story—but the play's true source is obvious.

The Kanin *Rashomon* was itself adapted into a television drama directed by Sidney Lumet, and then a film was produced in 1964, under the title *The Outrage*. Directed by Martin Ritt, its setting was moved to the Old West—Claire Bloom, who had played a Japanese woman in ancient Kyoto on Broadway, now played a nineteenth-century woman in America. Though earnest, *The Outrage* is self-conscious and self-important. Despite excellent cinematography by James Wong Howe and fine supporting performances—Howard Da Silva as the woodcutter (now a prospector), Edward G. Robinson as the commoner (now a con man)—the leading roles were fatally miscast, especially Paul Newman as the wild-eyed Mexican bandito who assumes Mifune's role. At least this version more readily acknowledged its source, albeit in type so tiny that, when seen on television today, it is nearly unreadable.*

Rashomon had a great influence on art houses. The Italian neorealist movement so popular (outside Italy) in the early postwar years was winding down, and movies from Japan would dominate the art-house market for most of the fifties. In addition, interest in Japanese culture skyrocketed in America, spurred as much by GIs returning from World War II and the Korean War as the flurry of Japanese films that debuted in the early fifties.

---

*Yet another official remake was put into development by Harbor Light Entertainment in 2001. The $40 million feature is intended to become a contemporary thriller, tentatively called *Rashomon: Where Truth Lies*.

In Hollywood, filmmakers were influenced by Japanese movies as well, especially by their early color cinematography, and they began imitating many of their techniques. Interest in Asia in general and Japanese movies in particular led Hollywood to begin shooting movies on location in Asia for the first time, including such pictures as *The Bridges at Toko-Ri* (1954), *House of Bamboo* (1955), *Sayonara* (1957), *The Barbarian and the Geisha* (1958), and *The Last Voyage* (1960).

In the more than fifty years since its debut, *Rashomon* reliably turns up on lists of the most important films of the millennium. It is widely available on video all over the world and is frequently revived. Grove Press first published the screenplay in English in 1969, including an interesting if unconvincing argument by writer James F. Davidson that suggests that *Rashomon* reflected the postwar Japanese psyche and that Mifune's bandit symbolized the *gaijin* (foreigners) that had invaded their country.[36] As J. Hoberman noted in a retrospective review for *The Village Voice*, "*Rashomon* seems one of the key global-village syntheses of post–World War II movies. Where Kurosawa claimed to have found inspiration in French silent cinema, Hollywood . . . would remake *Rashomon* with cowboys. By transposing the Western classics—Shakespeare, Dostoyevsky, Dashiell Hammett—to weirdest Japan, Kurosawa blazed a trail of defamiliarization broad enough for acolytes as disparate as Sergio Leone and George Lucas to reinvent traditional genre entertainment. Or at least that's one way of telling the story."[37]

Of *Rashomon*'s success, Mifune said, "Our own people didn't understand it and it wasn't popular at home till it won the top prize at the Venice Film Festival. Then it became an epic turning point for everybody."[38]

This was certainly true of Kurosawa, whose international fame Toho immediately latched onto. They lured him back to the studio, where he would work almost exclusively for the next fifteen years. Between *Rashomon*'s Japanese release and its discovery by the world, however, he would make one last film during his nomadic period, an ambitious, ill-fated adaptation of one of his favorite writers.

NINE

MISSTEP

"This *Idiot* was ruinous."
—Akira Kurosawa

After *Rashomon*, Kurosawa's next film was a big step in the wrong direction. *The Idiot* is a faithful adaptation of Fyodor Mikhailovich Dostoyevsky's novel, one that Kurosawa had wanted to adapt for many years. "There is no other author," Kurosawa said in 1990, "who is so gentle; I mean the gentleness that makes you want to avert your eyes when you see something really dreadful, really tragic. He has this power of compassion. And he refuses to turn his eyes away. He looks straight into it and suffers with the victim; he is more God than human."

Quite unlike with his later screenplays based on the works of Shakespeare, pulp novelist Ed McBain (i.e., Evan Hunter)[1] and others, when adapting *The Idiot* Kurosawa was archly faithful to its source. And though its narrative has been greatly condensed and its characters have been transported to modern-day Hokkaido, at times the film script approaches a literal transposition.

Traveling by train to snowy Hokkaido, Denkichi Akama/Rogozhin (Toshiro Mifune) has a chance meeting with Kinji Kameda/Myushikin (Masayuki Mori). Akama is struck by the man's peculiar if saintly and compassionate demeanor. Kameda had been mistaken for a war criminal and came close to execution before it was determined that he was the wrong man. The ordeal drove him mad; suffering from epilepsy, he spent time in an asylum and was released after being declared an "idiot."

Akama is in love with Taeko Nasu/Nastasya (Setsuko Hara), to whom he once gave a diamond, but she has agreed to an arranged marriage with Mitsuo Kayama (Minoru Chiaki). Kayama, in turn, agrees to marry her in exchange for ¥600,000, and in so doing must sacrifice the woman he really loves, Ayako/Aglaïa (Yoshiko Kuga). Ono (Takashi Shimura), a distant relative of Kameda and Taeko's father, invites Kameda to stay at his home. There Kameda falls in love with both Taeko and Ayako. The women fall in love with him as well. He prefers Taeko, however, and she eventually gives herself emotionally to him. Akama, jealous that he cannot have Taeko for himself, stabs her. He and Kameda, driven to insanity, sit near her dead body under a blanket, amid flickering candles.

Kurosawa adapted *The Idiot* with Eijiro Hisaita, his collaborator on *No Regrets for Our Youth*. When approached with the project, Hisaita said, "I hurried to reread the original novel again because I hadn't read it since I was a student and had already forgotten the story. Since it's a big novel and translated from a very literary writer, I had a hard time comprehending it. I hardly understood its characters' emotions." Kurosawa, then, took the lead in fashioning it into screenplay form, leaving Hisaita little to do but make suggestions here and there. "Once I reread it," he said, "I went to the *ryokan* in Atami. Mr. Kurosawa by then had read it seven times. Whenever I had time in Atami I would read it, but Mr. Kurosawa's image of the work was much stronger, so he took the lead. He has a very strong personality but is also generous in listening to other people's opinions. In other words, if he believes in your opinion, he'll happily use it for the film. It made me feel that I was able to contribute something to the picture."

"I believe the script wasn't perfect," he concluded. "Besides, the movie's reception wasn't good, because of the altered nationalities. He fell in love with the book and wanted to make the film with a Japanese cast, in Japan. I know it wasn't natural, but filming with Japanese actors in Japan meant so much to Mr. Kurosawa and me."[2]

Kurosawa typically wrote his scripts with a pencil and notepad, but *The Idiot* was special, and he regarded it with an almost religious solemnity. As Kajiro Yamamoto related, "He never wrote with a writing brush [used for traditional Japanese calligraphy], but [for *The Idiot*] he used one, writing the script on two-meter-long rolled letter paper."[3]

Kurosawa's cut of the film ran four hours and twenty-five minutes, and was presumably intended to be shown in two parts, a common practice at the time. Sensing disaster, Shochiku insisted the film be cut. With great reluctance Kurosawa edited his work down to three hours, but even this did not satisfy the studio. Ray Falk reported in *The New York Times*: "The director argued that if butchered it would really live up to its title."[4] But Kurosawa's three-hour version was shown only at its premiere engagement, at the Togeki Theater in late May 1951. Without Kurosawa's participation, Shochiku further cut the film to its present two-hour forty-six-minute length.

"[Kurosawa] sent me a long letter," said Yamamoto, "in which he literally poured out his anger [with the studio]. It seemed as though he could not control it. He went so far as to write that if they wanted to cut it, they might as well do so lengthwise—from beginning to end. When it was finally released—in its cut form—I have literally never seen Kurosawa so furious."[5]

Indeed, the radical and obvious cutting of most of the film's first few reels is disastrous. Most of the extreme editing appears to have been done here, and much of the deleted action is explained through the incessant use of intertitles. For those not familiar with Dostoyevsky's novel, the effect is maddening and hopelessly confusing. There are many awkward transitions throughout, resulting in peculiar continuity flaws, and the rhythm of the narrative is often out of sync in the picture's first half.

But even with 99 minutes shorn from its original length, *The Idiot* is tough sledding. Possibly this is due to all the cuts that were made, but unlike cut versions of films as varied as *Lawrence of Arabia* (1962) and *A Star Is Born* (1954), where one can still perceive a great film lurking between the splices, here this is not the case. In later adaptations, Kurosawa freely departed from his original sources to pursue his own interests, diluting the most cinematic elements of the original work, those which best fit his own particular style. But he adored Dostoyevsky and felt, as Donald Richie suggests, that simply photographing the novel alone would best serve his *Idiot*. The problem this creates is twofold: while Kurosawa clearly throws himself into the film with all the fervor of his best work, the novel's assets are mainly internal and psychological, rendering *The Idiot*, if not completely unfilmable, then certainly the most difficult of Dostoyevsky's celebrated works to translate to celluloid. *Crime and Punishment*, for instance, can be turned into a reasonably decent if unspectacular film, like Josef von Sternberg's 1935 version with Peter Lorre, but not so *The Idiot*.

The other problem is that by determinedly sticking so reverentially to his source, Kurosawa simply transposes the characters, lock, stock, and barrel, to postwar Hokkaido. Its characters, their actions, behavior, and motivations remain singularly Russian, singularly un-Japanese. Hokkaido is to mainland Japan what Alaska and Hawaii are to Americans, a weird blend of the familiar and the exotic. There Japanese culture is freely integrated with Western influences. People sit in chairs and at tables rather than on tatami; the architecture is Russian-influenced. They behave in ways that strike mainlanders as Western and un-Japanese-like. Perhaps Kurosawa thought the extremely un-Japanese behavior of his own characters would be accepted within this setting. Such extremes, however, fooled no one. Even to Western audiences unfamiliar with Dostoyevsky's work and Japanese culture, the film looks odd and, ultimately, works neither as Dostoyevsky nor as Kurosawa.

This is most obviously reflected in the actors' performances, several of which are well below Kurosawa's usual standard. Masayuki Mori, the husband in *Rashomon*, gives an enigmatic performance that consists mainly of maintaining an unblinking Christlike demeanor at all times. Characters react to his purity with great emotion, but regrettably none of Kameda's saintliness ever reaches the film's audience. (Compare Mori's acting with Terence Stamp's similar but riveting portrayal in *Billy Budd*, 1962.) We are constantly told how good, how innocent Kameda is, but Kurosawa is able only to lift pages directly out of the novel; we never see beyond the surface, or really come to know the characters in ways that are real or believable. Mifune, never good in hot-blooded lover roles, is so unrestrained and obviously uncomfortable in the part he's difficult to watch at times. When he lapses into insanity at the end, his wide-eyed, cackling portrayal is hammy and unconvincing (though the character in the novel is much the same). But the main problem is Setsuko Hara. With her batting, long eyelashes, flowing cape, and flamboyant gestures, Hara borders on camp. As Donald Richie states, "Casting her in this film was like casting Joan Crawford in *The Brothers Karamazov*. Matters were made worse in that either she or Kurosawa had seen and been impressed by Cocteau's *Orphée* [1950]. Her makeup, her hairstyle, her cape, her whole manner, is that of Maria Casarés and, right as it was for the Cocteau picture, it is absolutely ludicrous in the Kurosawa."[6] Writer Sergei Hasenecz disagreed with Richie, "if only because Hara's beauty would affect others the way her character does. Richie can't see beyond her Ozu-depicted virginity. She was cast against type and it wasn't accepted. If the film had been better, it might have worked."

Hara was then at the peak of her popularity. Indeed, she had by 1951 become a Japanese screen icon nicknamed "the eternal virgin" after the purity of her onscreen persona, typified by her fine work for Ozu (his *Early Summer* [Bakushu], Hara's next film, was named "Best Picture" of the year). She assured *The Idiot*'s success at the box office, but reviews were mixed to poor and the film failed to crack *Kinema Jumpo*'s "Best Ten" list—Kurosawa's only work of the 1950s that managed not to.

The supporting performances fare somewhat better. Yoshiko Kuga is fine and eminently more believable as Ayako, and Minoru Chiaki and Takashi Shimura are serviceable in underdeveloped roles. Kuga saw a contrast between the relative ease in which she filmed her part in *Drunken Angel* to Kurosawa's feverish direction of her in *The Idiot*. In particular she remembered a scene in which her character plays the piano. He spent an entire day on the scene, shooting her over and over, finally telling her, "Kuga-kun, why didn't you tell me you could not do it in the beginning? I would not have hired you! I say this not because you can't do it, but because you're just not trying!" On the next take she pounded the keys with great emotion and the director was finally satisfied. Shooting wrapped for the day, and at the studio gate she was met by Kurosawa, assistant director Yoshitaro Nomura, and Fumio Hayasaka. Kurosawa told her, "Kuga-kun, I know you had a hard time today. You have to come to work early tomorrow morning. Why don't you take a bath and get some rest?" Kuga burst into tears. "If you don't mind my saying so," Kuga said in 1974, "I really thought 'Shit!' [during shooting]. The more he scolded me, the more I thought 'Shit!' When I look back on my career, I believe that 'Shit!' has helped me."[7]

Aside from the performances, the picture has other problems, along with a few significant assets. Fumio Hayasaka, undoubtedly at Kurosawa's direction, so overloads the film with Russian classical music that its incongruity at times becomes comical. However, the location photography in Hokkaido by Toshio Ubukata (with help from Asakazu Nakai) is often stunningly beautiful. The long dialogue scenes, well blocked by the director, are shot with the usual inventive *mise-en-scène* and good use of long lenses, which optically flatten the depth-of-field, and which Kurosawa would put to even greater use in subsequent films. And while the film's innumerable close-ups of Setsuko Hara and Masayuki Mori have little impact within the context of the film, the photography of them is never less than striking.

When *The Idiot* reached America in May 1963, the reviews were no better than they had been in Japan twelve years earlier. "Its pace is glacierlike," said *The New Yorker*'s Brendan Gill. "I didn't so much enjoy it as feel drugged by it, and I wouldn't risk recommending it except to fervent admirers of Kurosawa and Dostoevski."[8]

"I was grateful for the chance to see it," wrote Stanley Kauffmann in *The*

New Republic, "but my gratitude diminished as time wore on. . . . It displays none of the special power and style that Kurosawa had developed by that time."[9]

Time, wrongly thinking that the 165-minute version was Kurosawa's cut, and that Shochiku had edited it down to 90 minutes in Japan, wrote: "[Kurosawa] demonstrates that the energy of genius can make a miss almost as exciting as a hit. . . . [But] the trouble seems to be that Kurosawa got fascinated with Dostoevsky's genius and forgot about his own. He follows with nearsighted assiduity every thread of the novelist's intricately woven tale. What's more, he too often tells the story in the author's words; he forgets to translate the words into correlatively compelling images."[10]

Even the *Los Angeles Times*'s Kevin Thomas was uncharacteristically harsh: "In its present form 'The Idiot' is hard to evaluate and is of interest only to the director's most ardent admirers. . . . As it stands it's a resounding artistic flop and a crashing bore."[11]

The Idiot was too close, too personal for Kurosawa ever to admit, publicly at least, that it failed to live up to its great ambitions. "I think I succeeded pretty well in doing what I wanted to do," he insisted. "I distorted [it] to be sure, but I don't think I have ever put more of myself into any other picture. . . . People have said it was a failure. I don't think so. At least, as entertainment, it is not a failure. Of all my films, people wrote me most about this one. If it had been as bad as all that, they wouldn't have written me."[12]

Soon after Kurosawa lost his battle with Shochiku over *The Idiot*, *Rashomon* premiered in New York and earned him rave reviews. Interest in his work prompted Ray Falk of *The New York Times* to meet with Kurosawa in his home that December, for the first known interview with him published in the West. "He sat on the straw-matted floor of his large upper class home in front of a charcoal brazier," Falk wrote, "and from the long sleeves of his black *kimono* he fished out cigarettes which he lit on the graying embers. Several layers of underwear peeped out as is the home fashion of better class Japanese. Green tea was served in earthen cups. An amply decorated Christmas tree stood in the corner."

Kurosawa was markedly blunt. "He is diffident in his answers," Falk wrote. "Told that his international prize-winner 'Rasho-Mon' had opened . . . in New York, the first Japanese post-war film so honored, he accepted the statement without question, without comment. But he was ready to sail into his Japanese contemporaries." Perhaps reflecting on his troubles on *The Idiot*, Kurosawa told him, " 'Our directors aim at small accomplishments.

The scale is very small. We must take up big subjects and not be afraid of failure. Japanese directors lack the courage. They imitate each other. And they are not ashamed of this condition. The tendency is encouraged by management which fears new developments.' . . . Mr. Kurosawa finds that since the death of the silent picture and the advance of Technicolor, films have become more and more complicated. He feels the form of expression should be simpler." (Kurosawa cited *All About Eve* as one of the more complicated. This is understandable, as Joseph L. Mankiewicz's wonderfully acerbic, dialogue-driven work would doubtlessly not have translated well into Japanese.) "I can't think of any American film using the simplified technique," Kurosawa added, "but I do find Roberto Rossellini of Italy trying for simplification."[13]

Kurosawa saw this notion of simplification as an important aspect of modern art, and therefore something he needed to apply to his own filmmaking. More precisely, he was looking for a way to make his films leaner, to make every frame count, to make every shot add to the viewer's understanding of character. From *Rashomon* on, extending to films made from scripts after his death, the leanness of his art became one of his greatest achievements.

Sandwiched between the productions of *Scandal* and *Rashomon*, Mifune put in an appearance in writer-director Keisuke Kinoshita's *Engagement Ring* (Konyaku yubiwa, 1950), which starred Kinuyo Tanaka and Junkichi Uno. From the time *Rashomon* wrapped, through the production of *The Idiot*, and up to Mifune's next work for Kurosawa, in *Seven Samurai*, the actor appeared in an astonishing eighteen features in less than three years, mostly for Toho. Unfortunately, most of these early films have fallen into almost total obscurity. Only two have ever been shown in the United States, and one of those has rarely been seen in more than forty years. Likewise, in Japan few of his films from the early 1950s have been available since their release. Almost none are available on home video and rarely are they revived. Even Mifune's son Shiro has been unable to see several of his father's early films.

Most of these eighteen features were program pictures, genre films designed to fill out Toho's calendar of new releases and keep theaters steadily supplied with new product. Though Toho would subsequently make several of these available to the international market, there was no interest in the United States, and they did little business outside Japan. By the time Toho had established its own modest chain of theaters in the United States, these earlier black-and-white films languished in company vaults in favor of splashier wide-screen and color films. In Japan, where production grew to unparalleled heights during the 1950s, only the biggest and most famous films were ever reissued. And by the time the home-video market emerged in the 1980s, these early Mifune films had been all but forgotten.

The first thing one might conclude from these early films, however, is that Mifune's stock at Toho had risen to the point where the studio was able to earn additional income by loaning him out to other studios. During this time, he appeared in films made by Shochiku, Daiei, and Shintoho. The practice was common in Hollywood. Companies like Universal, Paramount, and Warner Bros. might loan out one of their biggest stars at a premium, pay the actor his going rate, and pocket the difference. Or, in Toho's case, they may have loaned him out to obtain the services of a star of equal status contracted to one of these studios.

Among the more interesting films from this time was *Beyond Love and Hate* (Ai to nikushimi no kanata e, 1951), a Film Art Association production for Toho, written by Kurosawa and Senkichi Taniguchi and directed by the latter. The film, based on the story "Fugitive" by Kotaro Samukawa, was another melodrama about an escaped convict, along the lines of *Snow Trail*. Ryo Ikebe starred as a prisoner who believes his wife (Mitsuko Mito) has been unfaithful and, after escaping, flees to the mountains. The story also featured Takashi Shimura and Kichijiro Ueda.

Mifune and Shimura were paired again in supporting roles in *Elegy* (Erejii, 1951). The picture, which starred Ken Uehara and Mieko Takamine (Hideko's sister), was directed by Kajiro Yamamoto, and much of the crew were men and women usually associated with Kurosawa, including cinematographer Asakazu Nakai and art director Shu Matsuyama.

Hiroshi Inagaki's *Pirates* (Kaizukusen, 1951) was not, as its title and director suggest, a period film but a modern-day noir thriller, with Mifune in another tough guy role. That same year he appeared in Inagaki's *Kojiro Sasaki* (Kanketsu Sasaki Kojiro—Ganryu to ketto), the third film in a trilogy about the famed swordsman. Yuzaemon Otani played Kojiro in all three films, produced from 1950 to 1951. Mifune was cast as Kojiro's even more legendary rival, swordsman, and zen master, Musashi Miyamoto, who kills Kojiro in a famous, real-life duel on Ganryu Island. For Mifune it was a warm-up of sorts: he would soon star as Musashi in his own trio of acclaimed films for Inagaki made during 1954–56.

Daiei reunited three of the stars of *Rashomon*—Mifune, Machiko Kyo, and Takashi Shimura—in Keigo Kimura's *The Life of a Horse-Trader* (Baku rou ichidai, 1951). Though Mifune had only a supporting role, the now almost total obscurity of this film is especially sad. According to actor Yoshio Tsuchiya, soon to join the Kurosawa-gumi (Kurosawa's stock company) and become close friends of both Mifune and Shimura, "Mr. Mifune was just like an older brother to me. Every night we went on the town drinking, roaring like lions! Mr. Shimura was a very fine actor and just like an uncle. In fact, I always called him 'Uncle' and never Shimura-san. For me, he was the epitome of an actor. He gave superb performances in *Seven Samurai* and *Ikiru*, but in my opinion, his finest work on film was the Daiei production *The Life of a Horse-Trader*. Shimura's character was a kind of good/bad guy. Deep down he is good, but on the surface he is a bit of a bad guy—a very twisted characterization. And every time I saw Mr. Shimura I'd say, 'Hey, Uncle! Act like you did in *The Life of a Horse-Trader*! He loved it every time I mentioned that film."[14]

Mifune finished out the year with a Kajiro Yamamoto melodrama, *Who Knows a Woman's Heart* (Onnagokoro dare ka shiru), perhaps only significant in that it teamed him, for the first time, with the actress with whom he is most associated, Kyoko Kagawa.

While Kurosawa was occupied with a new project, *Ikiru*, in which Mifune does not appear, he kept his leading player busy in films he wrote but did not direct. The first of these was the leading role in *Vendetta for a Samurai* (Araki Sauemon—Ketto kagiya no tsuji, or "Sauemon Araki—Duel at the Key-Maker's Corner," 1952), directed by Kazuo Mori. The story concerns a famous swordsman, Mataemon Araki (Mifune), coming to the aid of Kazuma Watanabe, who is seeking vengeance. Again it featured Takashi Shimura (just prior to beginning work on *Ikiru*), as well as Minoru Chiaki and Daisuke Kato.

Much more is known of the second film written by Kurosawa and starring Mifune, *Sword for Hire* (Sengoku burai, 1952). Kurosawa wrote the screenplay with director Hiroshi Inagaki. It was based on Yasushi Inoue's acclaimed serialized novel published in the *Sunday Mainichi*. This convoluted *jidai-geki* opens with Kotani Castle under attack. Among those defending its walls are warriors Hayatenosuke Sasa (Mifune), Jurota Tachibana (Rentaro Mikuni), and Kagami Yaheiji (Danshiro Ichikawa). During the fighting, Hayatenosuke is visited by Kano (Shinobu Asaji), a chambermaid and his lover, and he tells her that he will meet her in Shinano, leaving her in the care of Jurota, and both Hayatenosuke and Yaheiji slip out of the castle during the night. They sneak into the enemy camp, where they are separated and

Hayatenosuke is wounded and knocked unconscious. When he revives, he sees a young woman, Oryo (Shirley Yamaguchi), looking at him. She finds herself attracted to him and helps him escape the melee by boat. Hayatenosuke recovers as Oryo's love for him grows, but months later the civil war rages on. When Oryo's father discovers his daughter's comb in Hayatenosuke's tent, he becomes enraged and strikes him. In the process, Hayatenosuke accidentally stabs and kills him. Panicked, Hayatenosuke flees the camp. Meanwhile, Yaheiji has become leader of a band of pirates who capture Oryo. Distraught over the death of her father and her capture, she falls unconscious, and Yaheiji becomes attracted to her. Jurota, on the other hand, has changed his allegiance, and both he and Kano, Hayatenosuke's chambermaid lover, continue searching for him.

The following year a battle erupts with Hayatenosuke and Jurota on opposite sides, and when Jurota's side suffers a defeat, he decides to become a *ronin* (masterless samurai) and marry Kano. Kano is kidnapped by another warrior but rescued by Yaheiji, who reveals to Oryo where Hayatenosuke is presently residing. She rides horseback through a fierce storm to return to him, with Yaheiji and Kano in hot pursuit.

Hayatenosuke, now resigned to his belief that Kano and Jurota have been married, awaits death as a watchtower guard at the castle. Jurota is shot, and Hayatenosuke is reunited with Oryo. The two would-be lovers and Yaheiji find the wounded Jurota, who, in his dying breath, admits to Hayatenosuke that he never married Kano at all. Oryo, realizing Hayatenosuke's undying love for Kano, tells him to return to her, then accidentally falls off a cliff. Hayatenosuke and Kano are reunited as the film ends.

Despite a classical lavishness, the hallmark of Inagaki's films of the 1950s and '60s, *Sword for Hire* was a tough sell to American audiences. *Rashomon, Seven Samurai*, and Mizoguchi's *Ugetsu* made it to the United States first, and all were better movies. Inagaki's *Samurai* (Musashi Miyamoto, 1954) would find considerable success abroad, but that was due largely to the film's exquisite color photography, which made licensing *Sword for Hire*, filmed in black-and-white and, because of a rapid modernization of equipment and style in Japanese cinema during the decade, already starting to look dated by the mid-fifties, even more difficult to push. Perhaps taking a cue from *Samurai*, which supplemented its English subtitles with English narration to explain certain cultural aspects, Toho gave *Sword for Hire* the same treatment. Bob Booth, a foreigner living in Japan who appeared in the studio's films from time to time, was brought in to narrate.

This was enough to finally sell the movie in America to a minor outfit called Topaz Films, which gave it an extremely limited release. In Los Angeles it was paired with an Italian sex comedy *Girl in the Negligee*, ran briefly in New York the following year, then pretty much vanished until it was shown in 1982 as part of a Mifune retrospective in New York.

Foghorn (Kiribue, 1952) reteamed Mifune with Shirley Yamaguchi and director Senkichi Taniguchi. The film, based on the novel by Jiro Osaragi, had been adapted once before by director Minoru Murata. Set in the Meiji period, the story concerns a love triangle between a foreigner (Bob Booth, *Sword for Hire*'s narrator), his mistress (Yamaguchi), and their footman (Mifune). The picture was not well received and today is almost completely forgotten.

Mifune had better luck when he was loaned out to Daiei for a small role in Kenji Mizoguchi's *The Life of Oharu* (Saikaku ichidai onna, 1952), which won the Grand Prize at the Venice Film Festival and placed ninth on *Kinema Jumpo*'s "Best Ten" list for the year.

Mizoguchi was Daiei's most important director, and Mifune, already nervous about working among strangers at another studio, found Mizoguchi's autocratism not unlike that of Kurosawa. "Mizoguchi was a stickler for props," Mifune said of his work on the picture. "If an object was used in his movie for tea time, he might look at it and say, 'This is a reproduction!' He would close the set and order the original from Kyoto. . . . Mizoguchi was an artist, a professional."[15]

Like much of Mizoguchi's work, the film depicts the immeasurable suffering of women in Japan's feudal age. Told in flashback, it traces Oharu (Kinuyo Tanaka) as she falls from distinguished lady-in-waiting to pathetic, aged prostitute, all because she dared to love a low-ranking page (Mifune). Made late in the director's career—he died in 1956—it is an exquisite if devastating work, and Tanaka's luminous performance, astonishing in its range, is one of the finest in all Japanese cinema.

Mifune's role, however, is small, virtually a cameo, all of ten minutes in the 135-minute film, and shows his limited abilities as an onscreen lover. So while the film itself is remarkable, Mifune is less so, and he rarely discussed it.

Jewels in Our Hearts (Tokyo no koibito, or "Tokyo Sweetheart," 1952) was an ensemble "tragicomedy" about people struggling for a living in postwar Japan, including a woman who paints portraits on a street corner, a trio of shoeshine boys, an imitation-jewelry maker, and girls working in a pachinko parlor. The film reunited Mifune with Setsuko Hara and was directed by Yasuki Chiba. Chiba (1910–85) had been in the industry since he was twenty years old and had worked at Nikkatsu, Toho, Daiei, and Shin-toho during the 1930s and '40s before being contracted indefinitely by Toho in the early 1950s. He garnered a reputation for his frank love stories and would go on to direct many of the studio's lavish romances filmed abroad, such as *A Night in Hong Kong* (Hon Kon no yoru, 1961) and *Honolulu • Tokyo • Hong Kong* (1963). He would direct Mifune in three more films, only one of which, *Downtown* (Shitamachi, 1957), received distribution in the United States.

While Kurosawa was busy editing *Ikiru*, Mifune had starring turns in films by two colleagues. The first was *Swift Current* (Gekiryu, 1952), another Senkichi Taniguchi action movie that had no lasting impact. The other was the third feature by Kurosawa's friend from his assistant-director days, Ishiro Honda. *The Man Who Came to Port* (Minato e kita otoko, 1952) was a modern, seafaring melodrama, with Asami Kuji as Mifune's love interest. Produced right after production on *Ikiru* had wrapped, the film co-starred Takashi Shimura, Bokuzen Hidari, Kamatari Fujiwara, and Akira Tani, all from *Ikiru*, and featured a new young talent, Hiroshi Koizumi. It was one of Toho's last attempts to cast Mifune as a romantic leading man. Koizumi, with his sensitive features and more restrained manner, was better suited to such roles.

Movies like *Swift Current* and *The Man Who Came to Port* were A-level program pictures, designed to provide Toho-owned theaters with product and rebuild the company's stable of stars. If these pictures failed to win any major awards, they did help to increase Mifune's star status and keep him in the public eye. Kurosawa knew that while making *Ikiru* he could leave his most valuable actor in the capable hands of old friends like Taniguchi and Honda, or directors like Inagaki and Chiba, whom he respected. Although he may not have known it at the time, Kurosawa would have big plans for Mifune over the next dozen years, plans that would mold the actor's persona into a screen icon.

TEN

TO LIVE

"After the current *Rashomon* was completed at Daiei Studios," reported the movie's English pressbook, "Kurosawa turned his attention to a film as yet untitled, which takes up the problem of a bureaucrat suffering from a malignancy; his reactions, both under pressure of bureaucratic protocol and approaching physical infirmity, serve as Director Kurosawa's strong but simple story line."[1]

That story became *Ikiru* ("To live"), which to this day is considered one of the finest films from one of the world's great filmmakers. The screenplay was an original story, written by Kurosawa and Hashimoto, who were joined by a new collaborator, Hideo Oguni. Oguni was born in 1904 in Aomori and, after graduating from Baptist Seminary, joined Nikkatsu Uzumasa in 1929; later he was transferred to that company's Tamagawa studio. Like Kurosawa, Oguni had been writing scripts since he was in his late twenties, first at Nikkatsu and then at Toho, beginning in 1938. There he was viewed as little more than a reliable scenarist of action films directed by Masahiro Makino and comedies by Torajiro Saito. In his first year alone he wrote seven screenplays. On several films he collaborated with Kajiro Yamamoto or adapted Yamamoto's treatments into full-blown scripts. He wrote one of the segments of *Four Love Stories* and penned the Kajiro Yamamoto–directed *These Foolish Times* (1947), as well as the Mifune films *Elegy* and *Pirates*, the latter written the previous spring.

None of Oguni's early screenplays were remarkable, but Kurosawa knew he was an expert in story construction and character development. By the time Kurosawa made *Sanshiro Sugata*, he was already asking Oguni for advice. Their relationship endured, on and off, through *Ran* (1985), which they co-wrote, until Oguni's death in 1996 at the age of ninety-two.

"We hit it off," Oguni said. "I also lived close to him. Since he is a tall man, I'd see him over my hedges. One day he said that he would no longer listen to my advice. When I asked him why, he told me that he wanted to write a story about a person who learns he's dying but finds something to live for in his last days. He said he wanted more than mere advice. He wanted to use Tolstoy's *The Death of Ivan Ilyich* as its basis and asked me to write with him. . . . When I agreed to do it, he took me to Hakkone in the middle of winter. . . . Why he brought me to such a cold place, I'll never understand. My gloves were frozen solid in the bathroom."[2]

According to Hashimoto, when they were writing *Ikiru*, "Oguni was late getting to the *ryokan*, so Mr. Kurosawa and I started writing without him. We finished almost 30 to 40 pages, and when he arrived, he read what we had written and said, 'No, this is no good.' Mr. Kurosawa got really mad. 'Why!? Why isn't it any good?' he demanded. Oguni told him, and Kurosawa got so angry he grabbed the work he had done and ripped it to shreds, yelling at Oguni, saying, 'It's your fault because you're late!' Oguni was older than Kurosawa and a very famous, skilled writer. Since he was older, he was able to say whatever he wanted to Mr. Kurosawa. Ryuzo Kikushima and I were the beginners. One day during drinks after work Oguni told Kurosawa, 'For the artist, reputation is the punishment given by God.'

"The way Kurosawa thought of the script was very simple: a man has seventy-five days left to live. That's the theme, and he thought in terms of that one thread. Anybody—an artist, a *yakuza*—could be that person. And it was just a casual decision that we made him a government worker. I wanted to make him a *yakuza*, but he had already done something similar in *Drunken Angel*. I wrote the first draft, and in that draft Takashi Shimura's character died at the end. Then when Mr. Oguni came and joined us at the *ryokan* we changed the screenplay's structure so that he died in the middle."[3]

Oguni's idea proved to be one of *Ikiru*'s greatest assets, and Kurosawa came to trust Oguni's instincts more than any other collaborator's. "I cried," Oguni said, "when I read what he wrote about me in *Kinema Jumpo*: 'Oguni is regarded as a hack writer but that's entirely wrong. His skills are misunderstood.' When we stayed in Atami to write *Tora! Tora! Tora!*, producer Elmo Williams came to visit us. He was curious about how we wrote together. Kurosawa said to him, 'I write a script as the writer-director, but

Oguni is like a navigator. He stops me from going in the wrong direction and puts me back on course.' "[4]

"I don't think anybody is capable of writing the same way Kurosawa did," Hashimoto said. "He never compromised. Most importantly, he concentrated on writing good scripts. He directed actors, of course, but he also directed the writers, and that was the hardest thing for him, because they're stubborn, difficult people to direct. For him, the script was the foundation of a film."[5]

Ikiru opens with a shot of an X ray. A narrator states that the X ray is that of the film's hero, Kanji Watanabe (Takashi Shimura), a man as yet unaware that he is dying of cancer. Watanabe is a minor government official in the city's Citizen's Section. He whiles away his time year after year, accomplishing little and, like workers in all the other city departments (and in what seems a universal stereotype), is forever passing the proverbial buck, never accepting responsibility for those seeking his aid. This is seen in a clever montage in which a group of women, after being turned away by Watanabe, are passed from one department to the next in a fruitless attempt to get a polluted sump in their neighborhood drained. Finally, they are back where they started, having achieved nothing.

Watanabe learns he is dying, and the first hour of the film details his attempt to find some measure of happiness and meaning once he learns the dreadful news. A middle-aged widower, Watanabe lives with his adult son and daughter-in-law, but while he sacrificed everything to raise him after his wife's death, the son and his wife are selfish and ungrateful. Watanabe drowns his sorrows in alcohol, but the cancer precludes much drinking. Finding no solace, he decides to live only for the moment, to enjoy the pleasures of life he previously eschewed. At a bar he meets a "writer of cheap novels" (Yunosuke Ito) and asks the writer to show him how to enjoy the ¥50,000 he has withdrawn from the bank. Inspired by Watanabe's rebellion ("Man finds truth in misfortune!" the writer declares), the writer whisks Watanabe all over town: to pachinko parlors, a beer hall, a strip club. But these diversions provide little comfort. Rebellion will not stop the inevitable, and empty pleasures are not enough. Watanabe is absent from work for several weeks, and one of his employees, Toyo (Miki Odagiri), finds him outside his home. She needs his official stamp on her resignation letter. Watanabe is drawn to the young woman's vivacious energy and youth. Perhaps through her, he thinks, he will find some comfort, some validation. He buys her stockings (replacing the worn ones she wears), takes her out to restaurants and to an amusement park. But eventually she grows uncomfortable. Though their relationship is never sexual, she's concerned that he's beginning to regard her as a kind of mistress and she starts a new and rewarding job at a toy factory making wind-up rabbits, finding little time for him. Watanabe reveals his terminal illness and pleads with her to teach him how to be like her. Neither really understands what this means, but she suggests that he find a job somewhat like hers. She feels that when she makes toy rabbits, "it's as if all the children of Japan were my friends." Suddenly Watanabe knows what he must do. He has found an answer. Returning to work, he finds the ladies' petition about draining the sump and dashes out of the office with several employees to make an inspection.

Abruptly the narrative jumps ahead five months. Watanabe is dead. At his home, relatives and colleagues, along with a contingent of government officials, gather to pay their respects at an all-night wake. A park has been built where the sump once was, though the deputy mayor (Nobuo Nakamura) and various department heads take all the credit and downplay Watanabe's role in its completion. The press arrive and the deputy mayor dismisses claims that Watanabe was responsible for the park. But then the women petitioners arrive, weeping, and their tears reveal the truth of the matter. The enormity of Watanabe's act becomes clear, causing no end of embarrassment for the bureaucrats. They depart, and Watanabe's employees begin to piece together his final months. Gradually they realize that Watanabe must have known he was dying, and that it was he alone, using all his remaining energy, who pushed the project to completion. Only through his absolute refusal to quit was the park built. They recall how he humbled himself at every step, bowing deeply to even the most minor worker, but always refusing to take no for an answer. They remember how at the park's dedication Watanabe's name wasn't even mentioned. How sad he must have been, they speculate. Then a policeman arrives and admits he saw Watanabe in the park the night he died. In flashback we see him in the park, on a swing, content in the gentle snow as he reprises an old love song heard earlier:

> *Life is so short,*
> *Fall in love, dear maiden,*
> *While your lips are still red,*
> *And before you are cold,*
> *For there will be no tomorrow.*
> *Life is so short,*

Fall in love, dear maiden,
While your hair is still black,
And before your heart withers,
For today will not come again.

Inspired, the department vows to continue Watanabe's work with the same tenacity, but soon the Citizen's Section is back to where it started. The myriad of red tape has returned. Only one worker (Shinichi Himori, very good in the role) seems to have maintained the spirit Watanabe's employees showed at the wake, and the film ends with only the faintest hope that he will, perhaps, carry on.

The effect *Ikiru* can have on audiences is almost religious. Is it possible to watch *Ikiru* and not have it change you? Or is its effect much the same as Watanabe's impact on his co-workers? What does it mean to truly be alive? The film, ultimately, is about Watanabe's search for some kind of affirmation in his last months. He regains his self by finally taking responsibility for the needs of others.

From the very beginning of the picture, Kurosawa explores the differences between existing and living. The narrator tells us that Watanabe is "barely alive," that he's "like a corpse," and that, in essence, he's already been dead for the past twenty-five years. Toyo nicknames him "The Mummy," and Shimura's expressions are like that of a tortoise. Early on, the camera shows us a city improvement plan he prepared that now sits in a desk drawer collecting dust, a symbol of the last time there was really any life left in Watanabe. In short, the man exists, but little else. He has forgotten how to live, how precious it is to be alive, and how existence is meaningless unless one uses it for something better than himself.

The most obvious—though very effective—use of this motif comes in a nightclub scene at the conclusion of Watanabe and Toyo's conversation about Toyo's job. Throughout the scene, there is a group of young girls in the background preparing a surprise birthday party for one of their friends (a cake is brought in, they giggle in anticipation, etc.). Watanabe, inspired by Toyo's comments about making toy rabbits, suddenly dashes off. At the same time, the birthday girl arrives. In a low-angle shot we see an inspired Watanabe walking down the stairs just as the guest of honor runs up. Seeing their friend arrive, the girls begin singing "Happy Birthday (to You)." But the girl is out of frame: we see only Watanabe and the chorus of girls above and behind him. This is, of course, intentional, for in a sense this is the moment of Watanabe's rebirth.

"It was the most important scene in *Ikiru*," said script supervisor Teruyo Nogami. "I remember that the script didn't provide any details about the birthday party other than it was in the background. . . . It was hard work getting the girls to act. I remember that we spent an entire day rehearsing. They were from the Toho New Face class and were very enthusiastic in their work. Some of them stayed in the Kurosawa-gumi and worked on all of his films, some as late as *Madadayo*."[6]

Ikiru is also, as the cliché goes, a celebration of the human spirit, more specifically the spirit of the determined individual. Kurosawa was wise in rejecting Hashimoto's suggestion to make Watanabe a *yakuza*. For *Ikiru* to work, for his act to be so meaningful and so moving, he must be an ordinary man. Watanabe is no judo master like Sanshiro Sugata; he's not the superhumanly ethical doctor of *The Quiet Duel*. He's just an ordinary, middle-aged bureaucrat, no better or worse than us all.

Ikiru is really two films: one about a man in search of validation and the other a biting indictment of the impersonal bureaucracy that serves as its background. In this regard, *Ikiru* is the very opposite of *The Most Beautiful*, in which Kurosawa believed that a common good could be achieved through collective effort. In *Ikiru*, Watanabe must fight alone and unappreciated every step of the way. With still-relevant accuracy the director portrays Watanabe's employees and his superiors as they are in nearly every workplace: gossipy, ambitious, lazy, petty, political, back-stabbing.

Thematically, these two halves come together in the final thirty minutes of the picture, during Watanabe's wake, where we see the illusion, and in flashbacks the reality. By having Watanabe die in the middle of the film, rather than at its end, both serve each other. Through the irony of the politicians and bureaucrats taking credit for Watanabe's work, Kurosawa exposes what is true and what is false. As in so much of his other work, Kurosawa is exploring the differences between perception and reality.

And just as *One Wonderful Sunday* and *Stray Dog* so beautifully capture the atmosphere of the immediate postwar years, *Ikiru* does likewise with the essence of an urban Tokyo bouncing back from almost total annihilation. It is cheery, thrilling, chaotic, Western-influenced, vulgar. By contrast to the first half of the film, the wake is visually the opposite, simple and stagelike. In its production *Ikiru* is faultless. Asakazu Nakai's camera re-creates the vibrancy of 1952 Tokyo and seamlessly blends the location work with that shot in the studio. There are unforgettable images throughout: when

Watanabe briefly admires a gorgeous sunset—the first time he has done so in years—the effect is overwhelming; so good is this shot that orange-red colors seem to jump out of the black-and-white film.

As usual, Kurosawa presents all this with remarkable brevity. All of *Ikiru*'s themes and nearly all its major and supporting characters are introduced and defined within the first ten minutes. When the women shuttle from one department to the next, vainly trying to have their neighborhood sump drained, we are introduced to all the bureaucrats who will later take credit for Watanabe's actions.

An early scene at the doctor's office is particularly unsettling. In the waiting room, an older patient (Atsushi Watanabe) details the symptoms of stomach cancer and how doctors will lie and tell their patients they are suffering from an ulcer (which, even now, is a common practice in Japan). When Watanabe finally sees the doctor, his worst fears are realized: the doctor tells him exactly what the patient has said. Watanabe asks for the truth, but the embarrassed physician is incapable of being so frank. (The scene is superbly directed. Neither the doctor nor the nearby nurse and intern will look directly into Watanabe's eyes and frequently turn away from him.) There is an excellent use of silence as Watanabe leaves the hospital, stunned at the news of his terminal illness. As he wanders the streets oblivious to everything around him, there is no sound at all, yet behind him are the flashes of welding at a construction site. As he crosses the street, there is a sudden burst of traffic noise as he's nearly run over. The effect puts us inside Watanabe's mind and emotions, which Kurosawa does again and again throughout the film's first half.

Another excellent scene, accompanied by Fumio Hayasaka's beautiful score, shows a series of flashbacks as Watanabe recalls his most vivid memories in raising his son. We see him twenty years earlier with his young boy in a car, following a hearse on the way to his wife's burial. The hearse begins to pull away, and the son yells, "Hurry! Mother is leaving us behind!" He remembers watching his son play baseball, going into surgery for an appendectomy, leaving for the war. As he remembers all this, he quietly calls out his son's name over and over: "Mitsuo! Mitsuo!"

The effectiveness of this scene and the film in general is due in no small way to the performance of Takashi Shimura, in what is arguably the best of his career. Shimura was born Shoji Shimazaki in Hyogo, on March 12, 1905. When he was twenty-four, he formed his own theater company and turned professional a year later. He joined Shinko Kinema Studios in 1934 and made his film debut the following year. Shimura was longtime friends

with producer Nobuyoshi Morita, and it was Morita who suggested the actor audition for *Sanshiro Sugata*. Shimura had read Kurosawa's unproduced
scripts for *A German at Daruma Temple*, *Snow*, and *All Is Quiet*, and thought his
work unusually intelligent. They met in front of Toho's big, central fountain and liked each other immediately. "Mr. Shimura is more than just an
actor to me," Kurosawa said years later. "Since I met him, he's been 'Oji-
chan' ['dear Uncle'] to me."

During his long career Shimura made films at every studio in every
genre. He sang in musicals, played gangsters in crime films, scientists in
monster movies (he starred in the original *Godzilla*). He played Buddhist
priests, historic generals, samurai in *jidai-geki*, fathers, uncles, and grandfathers in home dramas.

In one sense, Shimura in *Ikiru* was living the part. "Prior to shooting," he
recalled, "I was having trouble with my cecum [the pouch at the beginning
of the large intestine]. I told Mr. Kurosawa about it, and he said, 'Why
don't you have surgery to correct it?' He didn't want me to be hospitalized
during shooting. I had surgery and lost weight. . . . He told me not to gain
the weight back, but the more I was told, the more weight I gained. I took
steambaths to try and keep the weight off. I was playing a man who had
cancer over a six-month period, and my own stomach wasn't feeling well,
either. After we finished shooting, I went to see a doctor. He said I was suffering from an inflammation of the stomach and had to take medicine for
quite a while."[7]

Shimura's performance is in turn empathetic, endearing, heartbreaking,
inspiring. Never before or since has an actor so eloquently expressed the
terrible dread and loneliness that accompany terminal illness. "There's a
scene in a coffee shop," he remembered, "where I tell [Toyo] that I didn't
have long to live. She suggested I do what I want to do, and I said, 'It is too
late.' I spent a week thinking about that one line."[8] Kurosawa's direction to
Shimura about singing the song also proved difficult. "I knew of 'Song of
the Gondola' because it had been popular when I was young, but didn't
learn it until I met with Mr. Fumio Hayasaka and one of his musicians. Mr.
Kurosawa instructed me, 'Sing the song as if you are a stranger in a world
where nobody believes you exist.' Of course, I hadn't a clue how to sing
like that. I thought it a rather difficult request. I made three kinds of
recordings and had him listen to them. He picked one out of those three."[9]
The final shot of Watanabe singing on the swing is among the most haunting, emotionally charged images of Kurosawa's oeuvre.

At times, Shimura is also very funny. His reaction upon seeing the stripper's performance—childlike shock—is priceless. In another scene, as he works his way through the red tape to get the park approved, he must contend with a *yakuza* gang boss (Seiji Miyaguchi) who wants to build a tavern on the site. In a government hallway, the *yakuza* ambush him, grab him by the collar, and, when he says nothing, demand, "Say something! Do you value your life?" Watanabe finds this funny and can only look up at the gang boss and grin, leaving the *yakuza* bewildered by his reaction.

Preproduction and rehearsals on *Ikiru* began in mid-January 1952, and shooting commenced on March 14. There was a break in shooting in early June, when Toho's employees were given a short summer vacation, but production resumed on June 17 and the film wrapped in mid-September.

Miki Odagiri was in 1952 a first-year student at Haiyu-za, the Tokyo-based theater company. One of her colleagues had auditioned for the role of Toyo, and Odagiri accompanied her, merely to provide her friend with some company. She won the role. "I forgot what we were asked," Odagiri said, "but everyone stared at us and this made us uncomfortable. I'd seen Mr. Kurosawa's films and heard he was a great director, but I wasn't intimidated by him." Perhaps this was because Odagiri had been in films before; as a child she appeared in Satsuo Yamamoto's *Pastoral Symphony* (Denen kokyogaku) at Toho in 1938. "I was a little surprised when I was hired later. He always told me to present myself as I really was. I got a perm and wore lipstick for the first time. . . . He never scolded me in terms of my performance, but chastised me when I went to see the other actors do their scenes. In the scene where I told Mr. Shimura, 'It would be great if you were to do such a thing,' I was able to act well because his performance was incredible. When he said, 'Teach me! How can I be like you?' I was really frightened by his powerful playing.

"When the film opened I went to a theater in Hibuya to see it. There I saw the completed *Ikiru* for the first time. The surprise and impression it made upon me was indescribable. . . . *Ikiru* is my life's treasure."[10]

Kin Sugai (b. 1926) played one of the petitioning women. It was her first of five films for Kurosawa, and she recalled shooting the scene where Watanabe inspects the construction of the park in the pouring rain: "The lead actor, Mr. Shimura, stood in the rain, and I gave him my umbrella. This was to show how much I appreciated Watanabe, who had made the building of the park possible. Two or three fire engines came to make the pouring rain. We ran through the scene several times, all the while my costume was getting wet. Before the take, it was completely soaked. By then, I was oblivious to the rain and the camera—I acted without even thinking about it. I could hear the director say 'Okay!' When Mr. Kurosawa said, 'Sugai-san! It was good, really good!' I couldn't stop crying."[11]

The picture was an enormous commercial and critical success in Japan. It was deemed "Best Picture" by *Kinema Jumpo* and won numerous other prizes. But in the midst of its success, less than a month after it had opened, Kurosawa's mother, Shima, died at the age of eighty-two. At the same time, his family moved into a new home in Komae City which reflected his increasing wealth and prosperity. The seven-bedroom house included one room for a live-in housekeeper; one for Teruko Kato, Yoko's sister; and still another for Yoko's mother and father. It was large enough that Kurosawa could invite guests to stay for months at a time, and afforded him room to practice his golf game and play catch with Hisao.

Meanwhile, the impact of *Ikiru* was being felt abroad. Shortly after the release of *Seven Samurai*, on June 19, 1954, *Ikiru* was awarded the Silver Bear at the fourth Berlin International Film Festival.

Perhaps due to its subject matter or the fact that it wasn't a period film, and hence not "exotic" enough for American tastes, *Ikiru* was a long time in reaching American shores. Nevertheless, early test screenings in the United States were well attended and generally well received. The first was held in May 1956, under the terrifically awful international title given it by Toho: *Doomed*. "As the first of a series of five films at UCLA Sunday night," reported the *Los Angeles Times*, "[the picture] aroused amazing public interest, even though it was an interminably long production. This is one of the modern-life cinemas [sic] about Japan. . . . The picture . . . is exceptional in any number of respects. . . . Royce Hall was packed for the showing."[12]

Despite this, it was nearly four years before *Ikiru* was officially released. Eventually picked up by Brandon Films, it opened in New York in February 1960, as part of the distributor's "Season of Japanese Films." Company president Thomas Brandon held a press conference on January 29 claiming that U.S. customs officials had detained his print of the film after its inspector "questioned one or two scenes." A customs spokesman countered that Brandon "was looking for some free publicity" and then, after re-examining the film, released it to Brandon without cuts.

The official's charge against Brandon is not without merit. The film was released with the most ludicrous of advertising, which featured not, as one might expect, images of Takashi Shimura, but rather the high-heeled stripper Watanabe sees during his night on the town. (Lasa Saya was a real stripper whom Kurosawa and producer Motoki had discovered in Asakusa.) Ads made no mention of the film's subject matter but hinted at some kind of Japanese girly show: "See It Now! Complete! Uncut!" screamed the ads. "Go Now—Lest You Repent Later!" The tacky pressbook suggested theater owners "Stage a Contest for 'The Most Deserving Civil Servant,' " on the eve of the film's opening.[13]

When *Ikiru* was at last released, its theme of redemption was lost on many critics, who appeared more interested in its "varied and detailed illustration of middle-class life in contemporary Japan," as Bosley Crowther wrote in his review of the film for *The New York Times*. He commended it as "strangely fascinating and affecting . . . most expressive in its cinematic style," but added, "If it weren't so confused in its story-telling, it would be one of the major postwar films from Japan."

Crowther simply didn't get it. He completely mistook the film's remarkable structure, calling its last third "an odd sort of jumbled epilogue in which the last charitable act of the deceased man is crudely reconstructed in a series of flashbacks that are intercut with the static action of a tedious funeral . . . It's that long-drawn, funereal maundering by the dead man's family and dull associates, all of them drinking and talking and showing their pettiness, that is the anti-climactic death of the film."[14]

The *Los Angeles Mirror*, while calling *Ikiru* "one of the best from Japan," agreed with Crowther. Referring to Watanabe's act: "Does he get any credit? Not immediately, and that is director Kurosawa's error. He belabors this ingratitude for another 30 minutes."[15]

"The film's faults," said a condescending *Time*, "along with its Asiatic strangeness and its painful subject, will surely scare away most U.S. moviegoers. Director Kurosawa is in such raging and relentless earnest that he labors almost every point he makes. And the film maintains its intensity at much greater length than the average spectator can be expected to tolerate. Shimura, though at moments transcendently right and revealing, rather too continuously resembles a Japanese Jiggs who has just been beaned by the eternal rolling pin and is about to say tweet-tweet."[16]

The Hollywood Reporter was equally grim about the film's appeal in America: "It is possible to admire what has been achieved in Toho's 'Ikiru' without wishing to view it . . . It perhaps should be a good bet for the art houses, but it will take the most devoted patrons of the arts to sustain interest in it. It's doubtful there are many of them around, and 'Ikiru' does not seem likely to be a popular attraction. . . . The story is told with care and intelligence but its low key tempo is likely to lose most western viewers, and its lack of sympathy for the central figure casts a cold spell. The spectator is likely to feel after a time that Kurosawa's direction is based on the theory of water dropping on a stone, with the spectator the stone."[17]

" 'Ikiru' is a very deeply affecting study of a life, a death, and a final desperate attempt to bring a meaning into both of them," countered the *Los Angeles Times*. " 'Ikiru' must be put into that small category of film masterpieces. Its director, the noted Akira Kurosawa, has combined bleakly honest reportage with a kind of mute visual lyric poetry which has reminded more than one reviewer of the black and white camera work of Ingmar Bergman. . . . Takashi Shimura, a magnificent actor, gives a really harrowing performance as the dying bureaucrat; his pained eyes fix us through and through; he wastes like a candle, glowing more brightly, more transcendently as it gutters lower and lower to extinction."[18]

In *The Saturday Review*, Arthur Knight, also likening the film to Bergman, wrote:

> [*Ikiru*] is to this viewer Kurosawa's most notable achievement in a long line of masterpieces. . . . Inevitably, today Kurosawa must be compared to Ingmar Bergman. Not that there is any particular spiritual affinity between the mystic Swede and the hyper-realistic Japanese. (Indeed, so far as film *style* goes, Kurosawa rather strikingly resembles our own John Huston.) But Bergman has emerged as the symbol of the individualist director, the complete filmmaker who originates a story that is meaningful to him and illuminates it through his own special handling of the camera and sound track. Kurosawa is no less personal, even to the extent of building, like Bergman, his own stock company of actors—notably Takashi Shimura and Toshiro Mifune. . . . Kurosawa, Bergman, India's Satyajit Ray, de Sica, Fellini the list is not a long one, of these men who create films to their own vision of life and art. This provides all the more reason, therefore, to seek out each of their works as they come along.[19]

Two years later *Time* recanted, calling *Ikiru* "one of the cinema's rare great works of art; [Kurosawa] revealed a rugged realism, an exquisite humanity, a sense of what is sublime in being human."[20]

More recently, *Ikiru* has taken its rightful place as one of the cinema's greatest films—a profound and deeply moving work which addresses and even dares to answer that most basic of human questions: How might I find meaning in my existence?

Toshiro Mifune made two pictures early in 1953, *The Last Embrace* (Hoyo) and *Love in a Teacup* (Himawari musume). *The Last Embrace* was a romance melodrama/crime film co-starring Shirley Yamaguchi, who had just returned from Hollywood, where she had made *Japanese War Bride*. The film was directed by Masahiro Makino and featured Mifune in a dual role. He is first seen as Shinkichi, a forester who rescues Yukiko Nogami (Yamaguchi) during a blizzard. Amidst the snowy mountains they fall in love and plan to be married. Shinkichi, however, goes out to get a lily for Yukiko; there's a snowslide, and he is killed.

Haunted by her memories, she leaves the mountains and accepts a job at a bar. On Christmas Eve she spies a man in a crowd named Hayakawa (also Mifune), a dead ringer for her former lover, and follows him into the bar. Once inside, she loses Hayakawa, finding only regular patrons Sampei (Hiroshi Koizumi), Kuro-chan (Ren Yamamoto), Nabe-chan (Takashi Shimura), Sandaime (Akihiko Hirata), and Saboten (Sachio Sakai), all struggling painters or poets. Kuro-chan, in love with Yukiko but realizing she will never forget her lost lover, commits suicide.

The following Christmas Eve, Yukiko, now working as a singer at a nightclub, runs into Sandaime, who has just returned from France. They visit their old friends at the bar and he proposes to her. Then Hayakawa reappears, and Yukiko learns that Shinkichi's double is a gangster fleeing both the police and his gangster past. When he arrives, two of his former comrades (Seiji Miyaguchi and Kazumi Tezuka) appear, wanting to bring Hayakawa back into the fold. With Yukiko's help, he escapes from the gangsters, who apparently want to kill him, and Sandaime wishes Yukiko good luck with this "phantom lover."

Hayakawa listens to Yukiko's story about Shinkichi, and they decide to return to the mountain where her first lover was killed. Yukiko begins to fall in love with Hayakawa, but the gangster, realizing the police are after him and that Yukiko may be arrested as an accomplice, sneaks off. Yukiko runs after him, and the two wind up in a snowy cave. As the police draw near, they realize their love for one another; Hayakawa fires a pistol, creating another avalanche that encases the two lovers in the cave, where they will be together forever.

From this brief description, it's obvious that *The Last Embrace* (scripted by Toshio Yasumi, one of Toho's most prolific screenwriters) is pure and outrageous melodrama, though it does bear a superficial resemblance to Hitchcock's *Vertigo* (1958). Toho prepared an English-subtitled version in the mid-1950s, but the film received little, if any, release in America. Still, the film did afford Mifune his only dual role, and the scenes with Shimura and relative newcomers Hirata, Sakai, Koizumi, and Yamamoto—all to become prominent character players at Toho—were probably amusing, as they reliably were in their later work.

Japanese audiences could see Mifune again when *Himawari musume* ("Sunflower Girl"), marketed for release abroad as *Love in a Teacup*, opened two weeks later (though apparently it was never released in the United States). Directed by Yasuki Chiba, *Love in a Teacup* was Mifune's first "salaryman comedy," a genre unique to Japan, and Toho's bread and butter for the next two decades. Since Toho's audience mainly consisted of middle-class urbanites, the studio learned that as Japan recovered from the war and American occupation the countless white-collar women and especially men (still called "salarymen" in Japan, owing to their regular paychecks) were drawn to lighthearted films centering around the workplace. These films lampooned bosses and company presidents (or *shacho*) and reflected the aspirations and frustrations of salaryman life in and outside the office. For Toho, they were also very cheap to produce: real exteriors could be used, and unlike with *jidai-geki*, no money had to be spent on wigs and period costumes. Because one office looked much like any other, sets could be recycled from film to film. As stars like Keiju Kobayashi and Hisaya Morishige established themselves in such films, the genre began to dominate Toho's schedule. By the 1960s, half of Toho's output would be these salaryman comedies, and Morishige, virtually unknown outside Japan, became a Toho star whose popularity was rivaled only by Mifune's.

In *Love in a Teacup*, Setsuko Fujino (Ineko Arima, a former star of the Takarazuka stage, making her film debut) is a newly hired office worker in the General Affairs Section at Tokyo Chemical Industry. She is taken around the office by the much-liked department head Ippei Hitachi (Mifune). Hitachi has been nicknamed "Mr. Benkei" because he was once confronted by a gangster who tried to blackmail the company, beat him up, and threw him out of the office.

Setsuko enjoys making tea for her hardworking boss, but the other women think it degrading and decide to go on strike. This leads to a confrontation on the office's rooftop garden (a common break and meeting area for white-collar workers all over Japan's big cities), where the leader of the strikers, Eiko Ishii (Sumiko Abe), punches Setsuko in the nose. An older female employee, Naoko, is sympathetic to Setsuko, and the next day surprises the strikers by pouring tea for everyone at the office. The company's executives hold an emergency meeting, and the strike ends when tea serving by the women employees is made voluntary.

Ryosuke Tanabe, heir apparent to the firm, falls for Setsuko and invites her to his birthday party. She goes to the party chaperoned by Hitachi, and there Setsuko and Ryosuke dance and seem to be having fun, but Eiko, long in love with Ryosuke, is disheartened.

However, Hitachi and Setsuko decide to ditch the party; neither care for the bourgeoisie atmosphere and instead go to a comfortable drugstore, and by the time they reach her home, the two are falling in love. However, Ryosuke's parents make a formal marriage proposal to Setsuko's family, complicating matters. Finally, Setsuko and Hitachi are together as the picture ends.

During the period between *The Idiot* and *Seven Samurai*, Toshiro Mifune appeared in a wide range of films that solidified his star status and screen persona but did little else. Under contract to Toho, he appeared in those pictures that were assigned him. It is difficult to assess his growth as an actor during this time—his choices, approaches, and interpretations—because so few of the films are available today, even in Japan. Perhaps one day his early work will be revived; until then, one can only speculate.

ELEVEN

THE MAGNIFICENT
SEVEN

"After *Ikiru*," Shinobu Hashimoto said, "we wanted to write a screenplay about a single samurai. We decided to show one day of a samurai's life, from the time that he woke up, prayed with incense, spent time with his family, went to the castle, and so on. At one point during the day he would make some kind of mistake, and at the end of the story he would commit *seppuku*."[1]

Kurosawa's ancestors, a mere hundred years earlier, were themselves samurai, and he was always intrigued by what their daily lives must have been like. One thing was certain, the lives of real samurai were quite different from the movies. Up to that point, Japanese filmmakers had depicted them as glamorous, highly stylized supermen.

The historical samurai were a feudal warrior class that ruled Japan from late in the twelfth century until their dissolution under the Meiji Restoration in 1868. They were experts in horseback riding and archery, and were often highly educated. But it was their swords, so integral to their survival, that came to be regarded as a samurai's very spirit. Samurai followed a strict code, the "Way of the Warrior," known as the *bushido*, built on loyalty to their lord, self-discipline, and spiritual growth. Even the lowest class of samurai—guards, foot soldiers, clerks—socially far outclassed the vast majority of the civilian population. During World War II, films about samurai were encouraged by the Japanese military government because the *bushido* mirrored government nationalism in many ways. For this same reason, *jidai-geki* and *chambara*, films often centered on the lives of samurai, were suppressed by the Occupation government. But the ban did not lessen the continuing Japanese fascination with samurai. By 1953, the time was right for a samurai epic.

"We did a lot of research," recalled Hashimoto, "the producer [Sojiro Motoki], the assistant producer [Hiroshi Nezu], and myself, but it was all so vague. We could never really determine specifics of their day-to-day life. For example, when a samurai shaved his beard or combed his hair, did someone do it for him? Did he do it himself? What kind of razor did he use? What kind of food did he eat for breakfast? Did he bring his lunch to the castle? Books only detailed the historical events—the day, the year, and so forth, but there was nothing about the samurai's daily life. So I told Mr. Kurosawa that I wouldn't be able to write the script, and he got really angry because he had already been waiting for three months.*

"So the project was canceled, and we debated about what we were going to try next. Kurosawa said, 'How about the Japanese masters of fighting, such as the Yagyu clan?' We picked the most interesting parts of their lives, and we did a lot of research. Then I wrote the story, which at the time was about eight people, but it wasn't very good. Mr. Kurosawa read it, thought very deeply, and said, 'We can't make a film like this, either.'"[2]

Poring over their research materials, Kurosawa came across a small article about a real-life incident in which peasant farmers hired a samurai to protect their village from roaming bandits. "Mr. Kurosawa and I met with producer [Sojiro] Motoki," remembered Hashimoto, "and discussed an idea about ronin who travel the country, but because they don't have enough traveling money, they go from dojo to dojo [fencing school], challenging the masters. If they win, they can stay over, eat breakfast, and get some rice for lunch, before setting out to look for the next dojo. But what if they can't find a new dojo? Well, let's say there is a village where the farmers have to protect themselves from bandits, so the farmers hire the samurai to protect them. When I heard that, I realized that was our story. We decided on the number of samurai, seven, and based the characters on these real-life masters; for instance, Kambei, played by Takashi Shimura, was based on Isanomukami Koizumi. In a sense, then, every samurai in the film actually existed. So I started to write the script, and Mr. Kurosawa told me to write freely, not in the strict script format. The result was 500 pages long."[3]

*All was not lost, though. Hashimoto's efforts became the basis for another screenplay, the superb Harakiri (Seppuku, 1962), directed by Masaki Kobayashi and starring Tatsuya Nakadai and Rentaro Mikuni.

This was in November 1952. The following month, Hashimoto, Kurosawa, and Hideo Oguni went to the Minaguchi-en *ryokan* to write the
actual screenplay.[4] "I was very impressed by [Kurosawa]," Hashimoto remembered: "He would bring along a notebook and would flip through it,
and he'd write very precise, detailed information about the seven samurai—their height, the way they walked, the way they'd tie their shoes, how
they'd answer when people spoke to them. It was an unbelievable effort. I'd
never had that kind of person in my life."[5]

Their only visitor at the inn was Toshiro Mifune, who later recalled,
"There was no Kikuchiyo [Mifune's character] in the beginning. There were
six samurai. I heard that I was supposed to play Kyuzo, who was eventually
played by Seiji Miyaguchi. Mr. Kurosawa, Shinobu Hashimoto, and Hideo
Oguni were writing it at Minaguchi-en in Atami at that time, and I used
to stop by there. I saw that they got together in the evenings to discuss
the work they had done. During one discussion they decided that if all
the samurai were serious, the story wouldn't be as interesting. And then
Kikuchiyo was born. Kurosawa said, 'This is your role. You can do anything
you want with the character.' "[6]

Kurosawa and his screenwriters worked longer on *Seven Samurai* than on
anything that had preceded it. They didn't leave the inn—or venture much
beyond their room—for more than six weeks, working well into 1953.
Like *Ikiru*, the team played off each other's strengths. Kurosawa and
Hashimoto were competitive and masters of technique; Oguni was the
script's soul, and he played devil's advocate with his collaborators, challenging their ideas and script-doctoring plot and character motivations that
needed work.[7]

"When we wrote together, we'd stay at a *ryokan* and sit at a long table,"
Hashimoto recalled, "where each of our positions were already decided."
Kurosawa and Oguni would always face each other, with Hashimoto at one
end of the table. (When Ryuzo Kikushima joined them on later films, he
would sit opposite Hashimoto.) They would all work independently on the
same scene, then pass their work counterclockwise to one another, reading
their pages when they were done and pooling their best ideas. As with
Ikiru, Oguni had veto power over everyone, including Kurosawa. "If Oguni
said no," Hashimoto said, "everyone would have to start over."

"[Kurosawa] used to say, 'Writing a script is like a marathon, one step at
a time; if you keep writing you'll finish it eventually.' We started to write at
10:00 in the morning and stopped at 5:00. We always finished right at
5:00—we never overworked. He told me that if we keep at it, someday the
script will be completed. I don't think he was a literal genius, but he was a

genius in terms of the effort he put into his writing. He said a screenplay is like architecture and that we shouldn't compromise—once you start compromising you can't stop."[8]

During the forty-five days they spent writing *Seven Samurai*, the three men accepted no telephone calls and, with the exception of Mifune, no visitors. As he had in his assistant director days, Kurosawa abused his body, working as hard as he did. His tall frame wasn't built for the hours he sat cross-legged on the tatami mats. After a few weeks he would ache all over, and Hashimoto would stand on Kurosawa's back, loosening it for another day's work.[9]

"The reason why we had a difficult time writing it was because Kurosawa was sick," said Oguni. "We gave each other massages every night. Kurosawa wasn't feeling well for a long time, and Hashimoto was worried he might have cancer. We called his wife and put him in the hospital. He had roundworms [a common problem at the time due to unsanitary conditions in the years after the war]. When he fasted and finally took a laxative, a lot of long roundworms came out of his body."[10]

"When we finished writing *Seven Samurai* I thought I'd never be able to write anything as good ever again," Hashimoto recalled. "On the other hand, I thought since writing it was so difficult, and I survived, I could write anything."[11]

The picture's core narrative is actually quite elementary, which has made it easily adaptable to other genres, and the film has been subsequently remade, officially and unofficially, into Westerns and science-fiction movies. A rural farming village learns bandits plan to invade and steal their crop. They hire seven *ronin* to protect them: Kambei (Takashi Shimura), their leader; Kikuchiyo (Toshiro Mifune), a wild but brave warrior; Heihachi (Minoru Chiaki), a samurai with limited ability but whose affability will boost morale; Kyuzo (Seiji Miyaguchi), an expert swordsman; Shichiroji (Daisuke Kato), who with Kambei survived many battles; Gorobei (Yoshio Inaba), a wise samurai; and Katsushiro (Isao Kimura), disciple to Kambei. The samurai teach the farmers how to protect themselves, and the bandits are vanquished. But the price of freedom is heavy. Homes are lost and several farmers die in the attacks, as do four of the samurai.

Although the story is simple, its execution is anything but. The characters, from the leading samurai to the lowliest farmers, are richly developed, far more so than in its famous American remake, *The Magnificent Seven* (1960). The relationships among the various samurai, and the samurai with the farmers, are likewise complex.

Significantly, *Seven Samurai* is not called "Shichinin no ronin" ("Seven

Ronin"), even though the seven are, in fact, masterless samurai. This is because all of them, including Kikuchiyo, a peasant aspiring to be one of them, are samurai in the true, spiritual sense. Each samurai is distinctive, and the four who die are all killed the same way—by gunfire, symbolic of the Western influence that corrupted the *bushido*, or samurai code. *Seven Samurai* was a major departure from the *chambara* genre, which until then had consisted of clichéd melodramas along the lines of B-Westerns, and whose action scenes were choreographed with all the realism of Kabuki, the art form in which it was rooted. In *chambara*, duels are like ballet, elegant and highly stylized but never real. In *Seven Samurai*, people kill one another, and the line between good and evil is markedly blurred. *Seven Samurai* presents a world of uncompromised, chaotic violence, with deeply flawed, emotionally scarred characters choosing to fight and endure in the harsh world in which they live.

"Japanese films all tend to be light, plain, simple but wholesome, just like green tea over rice," Kurosawa said, ". . . but I think we ought to have both richer foods and richer films. And so I thought I would make a film which was entertaining enough to eat, as it were."[12]

But *Seven Samurai* is so much more than thrilling entertainment. Like all truly great films, it is rich in character, exquisitely structured, technically adroit. Like the samurai, the viewer comes to question whether the farmers are really worth saving, and to what end? Like the farmers, the viewer questions the samurai's motives. On the surface, the film may appear just a great adventure, but the questions *Seven Samurai* poses its audience are far more complex than its simple premise suggests. It is a subtler and more mature work than the more overtly intellectual *Rashomon*.

Most important, *Seven Samurai* is universal. Like Mizoguchi did in his period films, Kurosawa creates a world so believably real and lived-in that it becomes contemporary, one so emotionally true that its time and place become our time, our place. Using everything that he has learned as a filmmaker, Kurosawa's greatest success with the film is that he puts us in the thick of it.

This remarkable film—Kurosawa and Mifune would make none better—is, even at more than three hours, lean. As only a great filmmaker can, every line of dialogue, every gesture, every shot of *Seven Samurai* have been carefully considered by Kurosawa and his collaborators, ultimately adding to its whole. In every minute of the film the audience learns something new, something important about the film's characters. When the seven samurai are together, the audience must watch them carefully: when one samurai speaks, not only is more disclosed about his character, but the reactions of the other samurai reveal more about them, too. A good example of this comes early in the film, when Kikuchiyo, in a drunken rage, shows them a tattered scroll to prove he is a true samurai. Looking the paper over, Kambei is amused: according to the document, obviously bought or stolen, Kikuchiyo is thirteen years old. How each of them responds to Kikuchiyo's claims exemplifies Kurosawa's meticulous care and attention to detail for each character.

And, as Michael Jeck points out in his audio commentary on the film in its American laserdisc and DVD release, Kurosawa's attentiveness extends to the smallest detail, including even Kambei's hair. In a remarkable feat of continuity, Kambei shaves his head when the character is introduced, and Kurosawa uses the slow regrowth of his hair to note the passage of time.

Seven Samurai is also a masterpiece of structure. At the village, Kurosawa crafts an elaborate sequence in which the samurai survey the land they are to protect. Takashi Shimura as Kambei makes and carries a map of the village, and the camera cuts back and forth between sections of the village and its corresponding place on the map. Kurosawa provides his audience with a clear understanding of the village's layout. Once the battle begins, the audience will always know where scenes are in relation to everything else.

The first battle between the samurai and the bandits doesn't even occur until roughly ninety minutes into the film. In delaying the action Kurosawa has by this time so carefully defined and established the characters that once the bandits arrive, the audience never forgets the function of the various samurai and farmers, nor does it have difficulty distinguishing one from another, their relationship to one another, or their psychological state at any given moment. Compare *Seven Samurai* to the average Hollywood war movie, where it is often impossible to know where characters are, or even at times to tell one soldier from the next.

As Hashimoto noted, the rich character detail of not only the samurai but of the farmers grew out of Kurosawa's desire to make every role important. Like the notes he kept on his samurai, Kurosawa went so far as to create a registry of the village's 101 residents, made up of twenty-three families. He created a kind of family tree and gave this to his extras, whom he instructed to work and live together like real families during the production. He spent time annotating every character, no matter how minor, believing that anyone could be central in a particular shot.[13] Only a few of the farmers—the tragic Rikichi (Yoshio Tsuchiya), the suspicious Manzo (Kamatari Fujiwara), foolish Yohei (Bokuzen Hidari), pragmatic Mosuke

(Yoshio Kosugi), and the village elder (Kokuten Kodo)—could be called major characters. But in *Seven Samurai*, like in all of Kurosawa's best films, his extras are never really extras but *individuals*. Throughout the film, there is detailed background action that in itself is unimportant but that adds tremendously to the picture's realism. Because of this background action, which most viewers would not consciously notice, the audience can subconsciously perceive still more action just around the corner, just beyond the frame. Thus, when viewers see the farmers in the background carrying on with their day-to-day lives, and their varied reactions to the samurai, the characters become real and vaguely familiar people to them. With this attention to detail, and the heightened sense of reality that is thus achieved, every death becomes more powerful, every man's struggle more important, adding to the film's incredible power.

As he did in *Stray Dog* and would again in *High and Low*, Kurosawa interlinks his characters, even to the point of paralleling shots hours apart: the samurai to the bandits, the bandits to the farmers (in their savagery), Kikuchiyo to the farmers, and so forth. Offhand remarks are recalled reels later in ironic resolutions. As the samurai ready the village for attack, Kambei decides that three outlying houses, including Mosuke's hut and the elder's mill, being separated from the rest of the village by a small river, will have to be sacrificed. The normally pragmatic Mosuke is horrified, and suddenly he urges everyone to fight for their home. Quickly Kambei runs at him, his sword drawn, and gets Mosuke and the other would-be deserters back into line. Kambei is kindly and wise—but he means business. "We can't endanger twenty [houses] for three," he tells the villagers. Later, the bandits set fire to the huts and mill across the river. The farmers start wailing at this loss, but Mosuke cries out, "Forget those worthless shacks!" That he is referring, in part, to his own burning home is quite moving, yet the setup has been so carefully planned it's treated as a throwaway line.

And just as Kurosawa uses every moment to enrich his characters, so too does he use the natural elements. As in *Rashomon* and *Ikiru*, the director uses rain to punctuate the contemplation of his characters (such as the farmers' despair when they are initially unsuccessful at finding samurai) and wind to echo the narrative's emotional peaks, often as a metaphor of impending, fundamental change (for example, the arrival of Kambei).

Mifune's hot-blooded portrayal of Kikuchiyo is breathtaking, a performance light-years away from his roles in the programmers he made for Toho, one more intricate than even in his other films for Kurosawa thus far. What begins as comic relief—Kikuchiyo's pomposity, his wild gesturing and jumping about like a lunatic—gives way to a tragic figure of immense self-loathing, a desperately lonely man laid bare. He is a man who finds the very meaning of his existence. So vivid is his performance that, like the children of the village, we come to love him, and his death is devastating. Mifune had never played such a physically demanding role. Kikuchiyo is a man desperate for validation and acceptance, something very much like the real Mifune. And so in a sense, the relationship between Kikuchiyo and Kambei becomes much like the one between Mifune and Kurosawa and, in a larger sense, between Mifune and the world. His is a character of enormous psychological complexity.

Mifune stayed in character throughout the long production, a practice he employed from the earliest days of his career. Kurosawa encouraged him to dig deeper with every performance, and Mifune found preparing for his key scenes in *Seven Samurai* deeply unnerving. In one of these, Kikuchiyo remembers that the elder's son and daughter-in-law (with an infant in her arms) had rushed to the elder's mill across the river to rescue him. Kikuchiyo and Kambei race to the burning mill, only to find the elder and his son dead, and the mother, wading through the water, speared. She hands her baby to Kikuchiyo as she dies. In one of the film's most powerful moments, Kikuchiyo, holding the infant, breaks down in the river as the mill burns behind him. Vividly recalling his past, he weeps: "I was just like this baby." Actor Yoshio Tsuchiya recalled that Mifune drank a lot of sake that day. For him, baring one's soul as nakedly as that required some distancing, even if it was artificially induced. Mifune's greatest strength as an actor was the way he threw himself so completely into whatever role he played. As Kikuchiyo, he was never more passionate.

In the end, the glamorous trappings of a samurai's life hold no meaning for Kikuchiyo, as they had when the character was introduced. A series of circumstances have brought him back to his very roots, and confronted with his own past and taught by his six companions, Kikuchiyo, a farmer's son, dies not as a farmer but as a true samurai. But for Kurosawa this is an ignominious end: Kikuchiyo, born in a world of millet and mud, dies in this same world.

Aided by composer Fumio Hayasaka's apish motif for the character, a delightful orchestration of bassoon, piccolo, and bongos, Mifune is very funny early on, with Shimura superbly playing straight man to Mifune's ridiculous, would-be samurai. And, as always, Mifune adapted himself well to the more physically demanding aspects of the role. As one watches him exert himself throughout the film—during his drunk scene, the hand-to-hand combat, the climbing, riding, and falls—it seems amazing that he didn't seriously injure himself. By now, however, Mifune had been acting for seven years, and his physical training, which included studying *kendo, iai* (i.e., quick-draw swordplay), and horsemanship culminated with this film.[14]

Minoru Chiaki's cheerful Heihachi was a man not far removed from the actor's own self, one of tremendous humor and charm, though Chiaki was decidedly more mischievous and, for a Japanese man, uncharacteristically blunt. He remembered Mifune as "a great but really strict person. He adored Mr. Kurosawa very seriously, and he never made fun of anybody. [Mifune] was a good drinker, he often drank whiskey straight, sometimes mixed with beer. But he would never get drunk in front of other people, in public." In Kurosawa's presence Mifune was like a nervous student around the director's larger-than-life *sensei*, a relationship much like the one between John Wayne and John Ford. "When Mr. Kurosawa wasn't around," Chiaki said, "Mifune would be relaxed, but never completely."[15]

Takashi Shimura's Kambei is a pillar of strength, one of the best roles of his career and a nice contrast to his Watanabe in *Ikiru*. Through Kambei, *Seven Samurai* is both hopeful and without illusions. He expects nothing from the world; all he can do is hope that his own actions can positively impact those around him. Kambei is the first samurai who agrees to help the farmers, thus setting the story in motion. The poor farmers can offer him nothing but rice, yet he agrees to fight on their behalf because they are offering the best they have. But many of the farmers turn out to be much less innocent than they appear, and by the end of the film, Kambei is disillusioned. He had hoped these farmers might be different, and with the selfless example of the seven samurai, he thought he might make a lasting impression upon them. But the last scene of the picture makes clear he has done nothing of the sort. Soon after the last battle, the samurai are already being forgotten. As Donald Richie wrote: "To be disappointed in the farmers was to have hoped, and this is something which, until now, he has not allowed himself. Yet he had hoped to win, and further had hoped that this winning would somehow change something. He has become human enough to confuse ends and means and forget that everything is means and that there is no end."[16]

Kurosawa had a bad habit of singling out one actor on each of his films and abusing him mercilessly. He always knew exactly what he wanted and was impatient with those who couldn't fulfill his wishes immediately, which explains why he used the same actors in film after film. The malleable ones, like Mifune, could be fashioned in his image; after a few films Mifune instinctively knew exactly what Kurosawa wanted—long discussions rarely were required. Actors like Masayuki Mori and Takashi Shimura had plenty of experience with other directors, good and bad. They appreciated Kurosawa for the rich characters he provided them and knew how to listen and anticipate what was required of them.

Among the samurai, Yoshio Inaba (1920–98) was the only actor Kurosawa hadn't worked with before. And on *Seven Samurai* Kurosawa's wrath fell on him. "It's hard to find an actor who can play a humble and mature man," Kurosawa said. "That's why I hired Inaba. But, as it turned out, he didn't have a lot of guts."[17] The heavyset thespian was primarily a stage actor, having come to the film from Haiyu-za (The Actors' Group), which is also where Yoshio Tsuchiya was discovered. *Seven Samurai* was quite possibly Inaba's first film; regardless, Kurosawa pounced on his lack of experience with the camera. (Kurosawa's tendency to single out an actor for abuse, though unfortunate, was not uncommon among directors; John Ford and Otto Preminger did the same thing.) Watching Kurosawa bark at everybody, Inaba panicked. Shooting interiors at Toho, Inaba would become so pale that Kurosawa ordered his beefy samurai to run around the entire lot. When he returned, exhausted, Inaba was still nervous, and Kurosawa had him sing "Tanko-bushi," a song about coal miners, to ease his tension. But they never warmed to each other. *Seven Samurai* would be Inaba's only substantial role in a Kurosawa film (he had a bit part in *Throne of Blood*), and he was the only one of the seven samurai to thereafter have a film career limited to insignificant character roles. Mifune must have liked him, however, for he worked with Inaba on and off in supporting roles through the 1980s.

The showier role of expert swordsman Kyuzo, the part originally intended for Mifune, boosted the film career of Seiji Miyaguchi. Miyaguchi (1913–85) had been, like Inaba, primarily a stage actor. He had won the first Mainichi Theater Prize and even published his own theater magazine. He made his screen debut in Kurosawa's *Sanshiro Sugata, Part Two*, but his parts before *Seven Samurai* were usually limited to bit roles. Although he would appear in many A-pictures throughout the rest of his career, including *Throne of Blood* (1957), *The Ballad of Narayama* (Narayama bushi-ko, 1958), *Pale Flower* (Kawaita Hana, 1964), and Mifune's *Admiral Yamamoto* (1968), he never rose above supporting-player status. Oddly, this seems due, in part, to Miyaguchi's resemblance to another, more prominent character actor, Yunosuke Ito, who had a similarly long, gaunt face and played the kind of roles that might have been perfect for Miyaguchi. In any event, by the 1970s and '80s, Miyaguchi's role in *Seven Samurai* had nevertheless elevated him to a kind of cult status, which filmmakers like Yoji Yamada tapped into, casting him in several "Tora-san" comedies. Miyaguchi was later reunited with Inaba and Mifune in *The Challenge* (1982), which cast Miyaguchi and Inaba simply because they were two of the original seven samurai.

Despite his theater background, Miyaguchi contended, "The man who made me as an actor is Kurosawa. . . . When he wanted me as the swordsman in *Seven Samurai* I couldn't even carry a sword, much less use one. . . . During the shooting, which took a long time, over a year, I became friendly with him, got to know him—not just the strong side that makes some people call him 'the Emperor.' It was he, I now know, who created that performance for me. With pure skill he somehow got the very best out of me."[18]

By contrast, portly, round-faced Daisuke Kato (1911–75) was a tremendously popular character player, one whose appeal and familiarity might be likened to that of Claude Rains or Charles Coburn in the 1940s. Like Rains, Kato rarely carried a film, usually playing the second or third lead. Born of a Kabuki family, Kato abandoned his theater roots when he was very young, making his first film at twenty-two. But it wasn't until the 1950s that his popularity soared, and he came to be loved by audiences in much the same way Takashi Shimura was. Although he spent much of his early career in period films, it was by portraying a mid-level salaryman that he won his lasting fame, starring opposite Hisaya Morishige in Toho's long-running "*Shacho*" comedies of the 1950s and '60s. Actor Tatsuo Matsumura warmly recalled how when he first got into film acting in the 1950s, Kato immediately treated this neophyte as an equal. "His character was very gentle, very warm," Matsumura said. "He was wonderful. When I first met him, I was an unknown and he was already a famous actor, and yet he acted like he had known me for years, shaking my hand. I still remember that."[19]

Kato's skills weren't limited to comedies. He often worked for Mikio Naruse (*When a Woman Ascends the Stairs*), Mizoguchi (*Street of Shame*), and Ozu (*Early Spring, An Autumn Afternoon*). In 1961, Kato starred in *Snow in the South Seas* (Minami no shima ni yuki ga fura), a film based on his autobiographical account of entertaining Japanese troops during the war. Kato had worked with Kurosawa before, appearing in a small role in *Rashomon* and as a gangster in *Ikiru*. Probably because he was so much in demand, Kurosawa was able to acquire his services only once more, but memorably so. In *Yo-jimbo*, Kato played the very opposite of Shichiroji, the grotesque, piggish Inokichi.

Isao Kimura had appeared as the gunman in *Stray Dog* and as an intern in *Ikiru*, but Katsushiro in *Seven Samurai* was his biggest role in a Kurosawa or Mifune picture. He had made his film debut in Kajiro Yamamoto's *The War at Sea from Hawaii to Malaya* (1942), and though he doesn't look it, Kimura was already thirty years old when *Seven Samurai* began shooting. As Kambei's young disciple, Kimura has just the right balance of agility, youthful innocence, and aristocratic air. *Seven Samurai*'s chief assistant director, Hiromichi Horikawa, would cast Kimura the following year as the second lead in *Tomorrow I'll Be a Fire-Tree* (Asunaro monogatari, 1955), which Kurosawa scripted, and he would appear as one of the detectives in *High and Low*. Despite his plum role in *Seven Samurai*, however, Kimura never quite became a film star. He received good parts in several Kon Ichikawa satires of the early 1950s, but Toho didn't quite know how to capitalize on this theater-trained actor, starring him in throwaway programmers. Kimura was never able to transcend that phase of his career the way other theater-rooted actors like Tatsuya Nakadai and Tsutomu Yamazaki did. Outside of his role in *Seven Samurai*, Kimura is probably best known in the United States as the detective who matches wits with female impersonator Akihiro Maruyama in Kinji Fukasaku's cult film *Black Lizard* (Kurotokage, 1968). Kimura made his last film in 1978 and spent the final years of his life paying off debts on a trouble-plagued theater company he ran.[20] When the debt was paid, Kimura died. He was only fifty-eight years old.

Keiko Tsushima (b. 1926), who plays Katsushiro's farm-girl lover, was a former dancer and a graduate of the Toyo Music School. She was discovered by director Kozaburo Yoshimura of Shochiku and joined the studio at twenty-one. The director cast her in his *A Ball at the Anjo House* (Anjo-ke no butokai, 1947), and Ozu gave her the part of a decidedly modern, postwar Japanese woman in *The Flavor of Green Tea Over Rice* (Ochazuke no aji, 1952). She appeared in Tadashi Imai's *The Tower of Lilies* (Himeyuri no to) just prior to starting work on *Seven Samurai*, her first picture as a freelance actress. Kurosawa apparently cast her without a formal interview, as the actress remembered meeting him for the first time on location in Horikiri of Izu, Nagaoka. "I went to the first location with my mother," she recalled, "where we shot part of the last scene of the rice-planting. The weather was not good so we were able to have a lot of meals with director Kurosawa and the crew when shooting was delayed. Thanks to that, I felt more relaxed. While

I was at Shochiku I had heard he was a scary person, but he never scolded me. Actually, that made me even more frightened of him. I used to think he had given up on me."[21]

Among the farmers, the key role was that of Rikichi, the man obsessed with ridding his village of the brigands after they kidnap his wife. The part went to a twenty-six-year-old medical student turned stage actor named Yoshio Tsuchiya. "It was my first film role," he said. "I was acquainted with the studio chief at Toho and was advised to visit the shooting of the films there. One day, when I was still a theater student, I heard about the auditions for the role of Rikichi, but frankly, I'd rather see films than be in them, and the very day of the audition I skipped it and went to a pachinko parlor. About the time the auditions were finished I went back to the studio and went to the lavatory. There was this huge guy in the urinal next to me doing his thing. A few days later I was invited by Toho to meet with Mr. Kurosawa, and when I met him, he turned out to be the big guy in the men's room!"[22]

Tsuchiya brought to the role a remarkable intensity. After *Seven Samurai*, Toho groomed him for stardom, but Tsuchiya, a deliriously eccentric man, spent most of the next fifteen years in character parts. Partly this was his own doing, as he eschewed leading-man roles, preferring to play bizarre, often tortured characters. He frequently portrayed aliens or men possessed by aliens in Honda's sci-fi thrillers, and these were the kinds of roles he loved. But it was the actor's almost religious devotion to his characters that won over Kurosawa. Only Mifune threw himself into his roles to the degree that Tsuchiya did, and Kurosawa and Tsuchiya became very close.[23]

"I had no idea how long it took to shoot a movie from beginning to end," Tsuchiya said, "and asked one of my older acquaintances at Haiyu-za. 'Well, I think a movie needs about one month, but in his case, I guess it will take about two months.' Two months passed. Three months passed. We still had a lot to shoot. I started to want to leave and go mountain climbing. I told the chief of the acting section that I wanted to take ten days off. He panicked and told the studio head, and the studio head told Mr. Kurosawa. Kurosawa said, 'What are you thinking?! You can't run off and do anything like that on your own. Everybody is working hard.' He taught me the rules of filmmaking. He also understood the attraction of going mountain climbing more than anyone else. Naturally, we started talking about mountains. A few days later he said, 'Why don't you stay at my house? You can stay there as long as you'd like. And there will be good food there for you to eat.' I said, 'But . . . I have my own house. Besides, I'm trying not to gain any weight.' 'No! I'm worried about your leaving me. You can go to the studio with me each day. Yes. It is better.' "

And so Tsuchiya moved in, staying for nearly two years (director John Ford would also take in members of his stock company), joining Kurosawa, Yoko, their son, Hisao, Kurosawa's maid, and Yoko's parents. Tsuchiya described Mrs. Kurosawa as "cheerful, beautiful, and warm. . . . She had played the lead in *The Most Beautiful* and was now the lead in the Kurosawa family. She dedicated herself to letting her husband make good films. . . . Mr. Kurosawa couldn't be stronger than she was in the household."[24]

Each morning a chauffeur would pick them both up. "When we passed the gates of the studio, people would bow toward the car. It was interesting to me and I waved to the people just like a member of the Imperial Family. Mr. Kurosawa said, 'Don't be arrogant. They're bowing at me, not you.' I said, 'But I feel like the emperor,' and waved my hand again. And he said, 'I am the emperor.' "[25]

After a time, Tsuchiya began feeling guilty about the free room and board. "I was aware I was doing nothing around the house and tried to help out sometimes. Mr. Kurosawa said, 'No, talk with me instead,' and he never let me do anything. I saw Yoko's father sweeping in the garden. I said, 'I should be doing this.' Mr. Kurosawa said to me, 'No, he needs the exercise.' "[26]

The other key farmers were played by Kamatari Fujiwara, Kokuten Kodo, and Yoshio Kosugi, all members of the director's stock company, but it is Bokuzen Hidari, as the slow-witted Yohei, who steals every scene he's in. Yohei's bewildered peasant is a patsy to Mifune's straight man, and their scenes together are priceless. Yet he's more than a rube to be laughed at. We come to love him as we do Mifune, and his death is among the most painful. Hidari (1894–1971), with his Emmett Kelly face, seems to have been born a sad-looking old man. In his youth, Hidari fell in love with the ballet and opera at the Imperial Musical Theater and dreamed of studying ballet in Moscow.[27] He had been acting as early as 1920, though he didn't appear in motion pictures until 1949. It was largely through Kurosawa's films that he became a typecast but much-loved character actor, almost always playing doddering grandfathers and peasants. He was in constant demand throughout the 1950s and '60s, appearing in films of every genre, and for a variety of studios. His parts ranged from major supporting roles to tiny bit parts—the kind of walk-ons directors knew would get a surefire laugh. In *Giant Monster Gamera* (Daikaiju Gamera, 1965), Hidari's role as a man who sees the giant extraterrestrial turtle fly across the nighttime sky is only twenty seconds, but that's all that was needed. The very notion of Hidari—the archetypal funny old man—seeing such a thing was humorous in and of itself. The director of *Gamera*, Noriaki Yuasa, used Hidari in subsequent films and remembers him as an eccentric man whose equally eccentric, fiercely protective wife steered him into odd, New Age rituals such as falling to the ground and breaking into convulsive chants. "When he did that," Yuasa said, "it had a tendency to alarm the crew." By the late 1960s and early '70s, Hidari reached the age of the characters he always played, and while his popularity never dimmed, as Yuasa joked, "The executives at Daiei always told me to hurry up with my scenes with Hidari before he dropped dead."[28] His tiny frame, wrinkly, expressive features, and slow, turtly voice were guaranteed to elicit affection, and decades after his death, Hidari is still remembered, still missed.

Once the script for *Seven Samurai* had been completed, Kurosawa spent three months on preproduction.[29] Much of this time was spent looking for locations, especially the village whose geography was so crucial to the story. In the end, the village had to be re-created using five separate locations, though the main part of the village, a reclaimed field, was a veritable backlot of its own: some twenty-three houses were built, and forty horses were brought in. Because other locations would also represent outlying parts of the village, moving the horses proved to be a logistical nightmare. Finally, somebody thought of simply using local horses at each location and coloring them to look like those used on the main village set.[30]

Kurosawa ordered four weeks of rehearsals. As before, he made his cast practice in full costume and, when they weren't needed, had his villagers eat together and address one another by their character's name. He put not only the thirteen leading players through his methods; even bit players with a single line were expected to attend his readings.[31] *Seven Samurai* commenced shooting on May 27, 1953, beginning with the fight between a disheartened Rikichi and Manzo, just prior to Kambei's entrance.

To lend an air of authenticity to the film, many of the bit parts were filled by non-actors. An ancient woman the samurai visit was discovered by assistant director Sakae Hirosawa at a nursing home in Tokyo. She was a widow; her husband had died in a B-29 attack during the war.[32]

Nearly two months into shooting, in mid-July 1953, Kurosawa was sent to Kinoshita Hospital, a few minutes from Toho in Seijo. He had so devoted his energies to his new production that he had worked himself to the point of total exhaustion. This was a recurring pattern for the rest of his professional life. During shooting he would allow himself to get run down and became susceptible to any number of ailments. For many of the films that followed, shooting would have to be stopped while Kurosawa recuperated—a few days here, a few weeks there. During *Seven Samurai*'s production, he suffered from exhaustion and the effects of roundworm, which ironically he got from eating infested beef, food he ate for the strength it gave him.[33]

It's likely that it was during Kurosawa's hospitalization that he allowed Mifune to make a brief appearance in Ishiro Honda's *Eagle of the Pacific* (Taiheiyo no washi, 1953), his sole film appearance between March 1953 and April 1954, when *Seven Samurai* opened. *Eagle of the Pacific* was something of a big event. The Occupation Forces gone, Toho revived its war-movie genre with this picture, an all-star naval epic centering on Admiral Isoroku Yamamoto (Denjiro Okochi). Yamamoto, who died in a plane crash before the war's end, had opposed the attack on Pearl Harbor but remained loyal, and his fatalistic attitude about Japan's chances made for compelling drama while skirting the larger issue of glorifying Japan's part in the war. This and subsequent war movies from Toho had all the spectacle, bravery, and nationalism of the wartime propaganda films, with the wisdom of hindsight. By the end of the 1960s, their war movies had become routine special-effects extravaganzas. Honda's film, however, and later work by Shue Matsubayashi capture the tragedy of Japan's warmongering and the price it paid.

The picture also revived the career of special-effects director Eiji Tsuburaya (1901–70), whose work on such pictures during the war was so realistic that the Occupation Forces mistook many of his elaborate miniatures for the real thing.* The film's success not only predicated the annual all-star war epics from Toho which the studio produced into the early 1970s but inspired producer Tomoyuki Tanaka to reteam Honda and Tsuburaya for the giant monster movie that eventually became *Godzilla* (Gojira, 1954).

As drama, *Eagle of the Pacific* is something of a dud. Honda's direction is

---

*Apparently believing it to be genuine, a 2001 National Geographic documentary on Pearl Harbor for NBC likewise included footage faked by Tsuburaya.

flat and morose, and Toho, not sure if a large-scale war film would fly at the box office, loaded it down with stock footage from the company's wartime films, which by 1953 were already looking dated. Okochi's performance as Yamamoto is stiff, and the character is so deified that he becomes unrealistic. Mifune's role, a pilot named Tomonaga, is brief. In the two-hour film he appears for less than ten minutes, though his face would dominate ads, second only to that of the star, Okochi.

Meanwhile, *Seven Samurai* was slated to wrap on August 18, 1953, with postproduction scheduled to finish a month later, so that Toho could release the film at the beginning of October. The opening was to take place in six weeks, yet Kurosawa had shot less than one-third of his script.[34] He returned to Toho on August 1 and resumed filming, but there was no way around it. He was in trouble. Then it got worse.

He had exhausted the film's budget, which initially probably hovered around $150,000 to $200,000. By the beginning of September 1953, Kurosawa had just ¥70,000,000 (about $19,000) left to complete his movie. He had never expected to finish on time or within budget, but with less than one-third of the film shot, he was already almost out of money.[35]

While producer Iwao Mori continued to support his director, the film was now out of his hands. "It was a very serious problem for Toho at that time," Mori recalled. "The entire studio was against me. Even Kurosawa said, 'Oh my God! Toho might go broke if I keep working on this film. I'll have no choice if they decide to replace me.'"[36]

Production had fallen far behind partly due to the extensive location work. The weather had been uncooperative—June was the rainy season—and the hundred or so cast and crew members spent much of the month idle. But it was also Kurosawa's perfectionism that had led, in part, to this crisis. His unparalleled success, now on an international scale, had evolved into a growing arrogance. Budgets and schedules were no longer his concern, and now he was at risk of being removed altogether.

Perhaps the greatest humiliation was his possible successor, director Kunio Watanabe (1899–1981), known for cranking out B-movies like so many sausages. Watanabe had been in the business since joining Nikkatsu in 1924. He became a director in 1927, and had been with Toho since 1937, supervising as many as nine features a year. In the time Kurosawa had spent on *Seven Samurai*, Watanabe had prepped, shot, and released two complete films, and that was just at Toho. He worked even more prolifically at Shintoho, which he had helped establish, and served there as production chief and on their board of directors.

Watanabe was a hack, but that wasn't the only thing that worried Kurosawa. He was also fiercely anti-union, anti-leftist, anti-Communist, and in the years after the war upset much of the industry with his McCarthy-like witchhunts. He accused six Toho films of being "Communist propaganda," including Kurosawa's *One Wonderful Sunday* and *Those Who Make Tomorrow*.[37] He was not the man to take over a film about the working poor banding together.

By September 1953 the money for *Seven Samurai* was gone, production was suspended, and Kurosawa had little choice but to wait and see whether the studio would back him, replace him with Watanabe, or shelve the film altogether. He knew he needed rest, so he went fishing in the Tama River. He was visited by Minoru Chiaki, who was taken aback by Kurosawa's demeanor, now strangely calm. Sitting by the river for several days, he became convinced the studio would back him. "Toho isn't going to waste the money they've already spent," he told Chiaki. "They're going to listen to me as long as my movies keep making money."[38]

Luckily, Kurosawa was right. Production resumed under his command on October 3. But if Toho's executives thought that Kurosawa's near-firing would temper his arrogance, they were mistaken. If anything, it boosted his self-confidence, and in no time he returned to his autocratic ways. While he was shooting the battle at the bandits' fort, Toho's publicity department invited some reporters to watch the filming. Chairs were set up for them some distance from the set, as it would be going up in flames. According to Yoshio Tsuchiya, Kurosawa was livid. "You idiots!" he growled at the publicity men. "Show them the completed picture! You're not supposed to show it to them *while* we're making it!" Throwing his script down, he announced, "I'm going home!" and walked away.[39]

The next morning he returned. By then the weather had become unusually dry. Tsuchiya, as Rikichi, was to approach the flames, desperate to rescue his kidnapped wife from the burning building. Quickly he realized that something was very wrong. "The fire unexpectedly spread very quickly," Tsuchiya said, and the heat from the flames was far more intense than anyone had imagined. Nonetheless, he withstood the flames until they became unbearable. Kurosawa, standing next to the camera some distance from the fire, could only see Tsuchiya missing his marks.

According to Kurosawa, "Mifune said, 'What the hell is he doing?' I wondered what he was doing, too. And then we saw Tsuchiya jump into the pond and burst into tears." In the middle of the take, Kurosawa yelled "Cut!" and Tsuchiya sobbed uncontrollably as the set burned to the ground. He had become so devoted to Kurosawa and the film that he was racked with guilt over spoiling the take. "While I was telling him it was okay," Kurosawa said, "his face began to swell—it was blistering up with burns."[40]

Tsuchiya and other members of the cast culled from the legitimate stage likened working with Kurosawa to the intensity of life in the theater, where casts and crews lived and breathed their current production, blurring their professional and personal lives. Kurosawa loved shooting on location because it generated an atmosphere like that of a theatrical troupe on the road. Everyone worked together, ate together, slept at the same inn. He got better performances out of people like Tsuchiya, and more devotion from his crew. On *Seven Samurai*, his cast and crew stayed at the Sakanaya Ryokan, and when they had put in a full day's work, they would return to the traditional-style inn and have dinner together in its banquet hall. Much like John Ford did in his legendary dinners and nighttime bridge games with his casts and crews, Kurosawa would hold court, drinking Johnnie Walker to unwind, and review the day's events often until midnight before sending everyone to bed.

"He had to do it," Chiaki said. "He had to eat and drink and talk to us all every night."[41]

Some, like Tsuchiya, hung on every word. Others, like Chiaki and Mifune, would duck out, only to be chastised the following morning. Most just wanted to get some sleep, but stayed.

Shooting dragged on into 1954, and Toho wondered if the film would ever be finished. They began pressuring Kurosawa to wrap it up, but he refused to be rushed. By that point, Kurosawa's cast and crew had become so devoted that replacing him might have resulted in a mutiny. Kurosawa delayed shooting the final battle until the last days of the production. "I waited until the end to shoot the climax on purpose," he said. "I knew Toho would have said, 'That's it. You're done shooting,' even if I had only shot a portion of the scene." He withheld this part of the script from his actors; he and Kikushima and Oguni continued to make changes right up until the end, including moving Kikuchiyo's death from a rooftop to a muddy bridge.[42]

During this last battle, the rain pours down on a scale unequaled in any other Kurosawa film. For Kurosawa, it was a chance to set the film apart from American Westerns. Because California was so dry, he reasoned, his water-soaked climax would be comparatively novel.

By the time he was ready to film the climactic battle, it was the middle of winter. "It snowed," said Tsuchiya, adding in English, "*All snow!* The staff and cast removed all the snow, working together. We operated seven water pumps to remove it, then stepped into the icy water to make the mud. We could hardly move, but somehow during the takes we could run on it. However, as soon as Mr. Kurosawa said, 'Cut!' our feet became immobile again."[43]

The cast and crew risked frostbite shooting in the freezing, artificial rain, and Kurosawa was a veritable slave driver, yelling at everyone indiscriminately. "I'm sure that my crew doesn't like me ordering them about," Kurosawa said later. "I don't plan on being mean to anybody. I don't dislike anyone. But it's like I'm following someone or something's command. It's like I hear a voice from the heavens. I guess all of us are possessed by something."[44] Almost miraculously, the cast and crew members had remained committed and passionate until the bitter end. For one grueling year, they had all but given their lives to Kurosawa. They were exhausted.

"On the set, it was just like a war," said Mifune. "He was shooting with a fierce expression on his face. He kept screaming the whole time."[45]

"It was probably the toughest movie I ever made," Mifune added. "Isn't it funny how one remembers the hardest experiences so clearly, but forget the happy ones? . . . Kurosawa [was] the world's toughest taskmaster, never satisfied until everything was absolutely perfect. . . . That final battle scene in the rain and mud—we spent nearly two months shooting it, in January and February. That rain was freezing cold, and I was wearing practically nothing at all. After we finished, I had to go into the hospital for a couple of weeks, just to recover."[46]

As production wrapped, Kurosawa met with an ailing Fumio Hayasaka, who had turned down innumerable offers to concentrate his limited energies on Seven Samurai's score. Hayasaka's tuberculosis had gotten much worse, and the director would consult with him at the composer's home. Hayasaka wrote 300 orchestral sketches over a two-month period, which so tired him that he would often lie on his bed, inhaling oxygen from a nearby tank, while discussing the music with arranger Masaru Sato.[47]

Hayasaka's condition didn't compromise the director's vision. Hayasaka had prepared several possible cues for the main "Samurai Theme." But every time Sato began playing, Kurosawa would bluntly say, "No. This isn't what I want." Time after time: "No. That's not it." Hayasaka was soon at a loss. Then he remembered one cue that he'd rejected prior to Kurosawa's arrival and had Sato pluck it from the trash. To the composer's surprise, Kurosawa exclaimed, "That's it! That's what I want!"

As a testament to Hayasaka's work, the film's opening titles single him out—his name appears alone—a credit unheard of for a Japanese film composer at the time.

The music was recorded over two weeks in the spring of 1954. Ailing, Hayasaka made the trip to Toho's scoring stage and music editing room. Out of respect for the ill composer, the music department had declared its recording booth a non-smoking room, but Kurosawa chain-smoked around him anyway. He didn't think twice about halting shooting for his own sake but was oblivious to other people's health.

The director, working with his assistants and Toho's publicity department, cut together a tautly edited coming-attractions trailer that likened the film to *Gone With The Wind* in its epic scope, even acknowledging its lengthy production, which, by now, had become scandalous. In an effort to make the expensive film more appealing to both men and women, Keiko Tsushima and Yukiko Shimazaki, the latter cast as Rikichi's wife, were given third and fourth billing (over five of the seven samurai), despite the fact that Shimazaki, a minor actress, appears in the picture for all of two minutes.

During the 1950s, most Japanese features were shot in four to six weeks. *Seven Samurai* was in production for nearly a year, of which 148 were shooting days. At three hours and twenty-seven minutes, it was the longest Japanese feature yet produced. It was also the most expensive. *Seven Samurai* had cost the studio ¥210,000,000—almost $560,000 in American money—five to eight times the cost of an average feature. (At the time, Japanese films cost about one-quarter the negative cost of American features, while Japanese salaries were one-tenth that of American casts and crews.) Kurosawa's film, combined with Hiroshi Inagaki's color production of *Musashi Miyamoto* (which cost $500,000) and Ishiro Honda's *Godzilla* ($167,000), with its unprecedented and untried man-in-a-monster-suit effects, nearly crippled the studio. But *Godzilla* begat a franchise as big as its monster, *Musashi Miyamoto* would be Toho's first great success in America, winning the Oscar as Best Foreign Film, and *Seven Samurai* would become one of the greatest films ever made.

It was a popular success, too, earning ¥290,000,000 in ticket sales, most of which were purchased at Toho-owned movie theaters, which, in turn, meant greater profits for the company.[48] It was the year's biggest money-earner (both *Musashi Miyamoto* and *Godzilla* made the Top Ten as well), if not hugely profitable. The film received good reviews, but as is sometimes the case, its popular appeal worked against its critical acceptance. The film actually placed third on *Kinema Jumpo*'s "Best Ten" list, behind Keisuke Kinoshita's excellent *Twenty-four Eyes* (Nijushi no hitome) and his *The Garden of Women* (Onna no sono). But then again, 1954 was a banner year for Japanese film. *Seven Samurai* beat major works by Mizoguchi, *The*

Crucified Lovers (Chikamatsu monogatari) and *Sansho the Bailiff* (Sansho Dayu); Naruse's *Sounds of the Mountains* (Yama no oto) and *Late Chrysanthemums* (Bangiku); and films by Minoru Shibuya, Heinosuke Gosho, and actor-turned director So Yamamura. Years later, in a 1989 critics' poll of the 150 best Japanese movies of all time, *Seven Samurai* was ranked at the very top. Ozu's *Tokyo Story* placed second, but the gap between them was huge. Kurosawa's film received almost twice as many votes.

Because of its extreme length, the complete *Seven Samurai*'s run was limited to its first few weeks, and only in Japan's biggest cities. In rural areas and in subsequent runs it was cut to a more manageable, if compromised length. "It was a big hit in Japan," Hashimoto remembers, "but I learned that some of the rural theaters were booking the film in two parts [an audience might watch it over two nights], not the complete film. I didn't tell Mr. Kurosawa about this, because I knew he'd be mad if he found out about it."[49]

But Kurosawa had other things on his mind. The week the picture opened, something happened that turned his attention away from film. On April 29, during *Seven Samurai*'s completion party, Yoko went into labor with her second child, more than nine years after Hisao's birth. It was a girl. Kurosawa remained at the party, getting drunk with the Kurosawa-gumi. Not that he didn't care: quite the opposite, cohorts like Mifune and Minoru Chiaki's children were all boys and Kazuko's birth finally provided the Kurosawa-gumi with a little girl to fuss over. (Mifune's wife, Sachiko, gave birth to their second and last child the following year, a boy named Takeo.) Kurosawa was overjoyed to have a new daughter.[50]

"I looked at a piece of paper he was writing on," Tsuchiya recalled. "The sheet was filled with girls' names. 'Which name do you think is best?' he asked me. I said, 'There are too many to choose from.' He went through the names and picked out two of them. They were 'Keiko' and 'Kazuko.' He finally settled on 'Kazuko.' I asked him, 'Why didn't you choose the other one?' 'Keiko is too good to be her name. I go for the simple and common names.' I didn't know why 'Keiko' was too good, and never remembered to ask him about it again."[51]

Kurosawa adored his daughter, so much so that he couldn't bear to watch when she needed immunization shots or other injections. When the doctor came to visit her, he would run out to the courtyard and practice his putting.[52] As she grew, Kazuko was shy but given to sudden bursts of crying so explosive that Kurosawa nicknamed her *"Genbaku musume"* ("Atomic Bomb Girl"). Years later, when he directed the young actress Terumi Niki in a critical breakdown scene on a bridge in *Red Beard*, he recalled how Kazuko would suddenly burst into tears and instructed Niki to do likewise.[53]

Toho knew they had a winner in *Seven Samurai*, but they were worried that its length might be even more off-putting to foreigners than to the rural Japanese. Perhaps they had read a brief mention of the film in a June 1954 edition of *The New York Times*, where an uncredited reporter, after seeing the film in Japan, wrote: "The film's running time is three and a half hours, much too long for the plot. Mr. Kurosawa could have told his story just as well in half the time, but his intense desire to recreate life rather than create an illusion has, as in his past pictures, got in the way of his cutting-room scissors."[54] This is an absurd statement, but comments like these always seemed to worry the studio, so prior to entering the film at the Venice International Film Festival, Toho set its editors to work. When they were done, nearly an hour had been chopped out. Nevertheless, on September 8, 1954, it was the shortened version that was awarded the Silver Lion Prize.

Reviewing the film in Italy, *Variety*'s "Mosk" said: "High adventure and excitement are stamped all over this solid-core film," but even at 155 minutes, he argued, "the lone drawback is its length, which can be sheared."[55] The Hollywood majors seemed to agree, and Toho's representatives left Venice without a buyer. The following January, the Foreign Press Association held an invitation-only screening of *Seven Samurai* at the Hotel Ambassador in Los Angeles, but one year after its Japanese release, interest in the film seemed to be waning.[56]

Then, in August 1955, Columbia Pictures, in want of product, established a special department to acquire and perhaps even partly finance foreign films for release in America. Films from Austria, France, and Italy had been acquired and were awaiting release through the department, and *Seven Samurai* topped the list.[57] Or did it? Nearly a year after that, *Seven Samurai* had still not reached American screens.

"When I got older," Hashimoto said, "I realized that Mr. Kurosawa and I had made a mistake. When *Seven Samurai* was released abroad we used subtitles, but if we had dubbed the film into English, perhaps people would've accepted it more widely, and instead of its playing in small theaters, more people would have seen it. And when I look back, I think our eyes were not open to the entire world."[58]

Still uncertain of its future, Toho, or perhaps Columbia, took a print of the picture to a downtown Los Angeles movie theater, the Linda Lea, where *Rashomon* has similarly been test-screened. The picture ran just six days in July 1956 to meet the Academy of Motion Picture Arts & Sciences rules for Oscar consideration. Finally, the decision was made to officially open the film at the Guild Theater in New York that November.

When it officially emerged, *Seven Samurai* had a new title: *The Magnificent Seven*. Critics praised the film, but the praise was tainted with a kind of cultural condescension. The same critics who didn't quite know what to make of *Rashomon*, praising it as much for its "exoticism" as its daring structure, were now applying another postwar stereotype: the Japanese as clever imitators of American product.

A condescending *Cue*, for instance, had this to say: "The Japanese lately have been full of surprises. Having for some years watched Hollywood mystery films, they turned out a picture called 'Rasho-mon.' . . . Then, having viewed the Occidental colorfilm technique, they promptly matched our best films with 'Samurai.' . . . Now, having been treated to many U.S. gun-and-gallop Westerns, our Oriental cinema cousins have ground out a Far Eastern Western that may well turn out to be the daddy of them all."[59]

The New Yorker's critic added: "The well-known Japanese talent for imitation is readily discernible in the movie. . . . [But] this is not to say that it isn't a sprightly enterprise."[60] *Time* admired its universal depiction of violence and its "sensuousness," but said: "Rarely does the story seem to drop through the floor of everyday reality into the moral hell that war really is. Unlike some of his Japanese colleagues, director Kurosawa is not centrally concerned with spiritual statement. He would rather make a social comment, and in *The Magnificent Seven* he makes a biting one."[61]

Bosley Crowther, while calling it "extraordinary" and "brilliant," went on to add: "To give you a quick, capsule notion of the nature of this unusual film, let us say it bears cultural comparison with our own popular Western 'High Noon.' That is to say, it is a solid, naturalistic, he-man outdoor action film."

In fairness, the film was substantially cut for American release, losing nearly fifty minutes of critical character development in the process. It's hard to imagine where to remove one minute, let alone fifty.* And yet

*Most of the footage cut concerned Rikichi's mysterious behavior, Manzo's cutting of Shiino's hair, and the entire subplot about the old peasant woman (and her vengeance). (This may account for the lack of characterizations with the farmers in the American remake, *The Magnificent Seven*.) Among other scenes deleted were Kikuchiyo's drunk scene with the samurai, and several scenes with Kyuzo which destroy the parallel character development between Kikushiyo and Katsushiro.

Crowther still complained: "It is much too long for comfort or for the story it has to tell. The director is annoyingly repetitious. He shows so many shots of horses' feet tromping in the mud in the course of battle that you wonder if the horses have heads. And his use of modern music, which is as pointed as the ballad in 'High Noon,' leads you to wonder whether this picture is any more authentic to its period of culture than is the average American Western."[62]

Crowther back-pedaled somewhat, writing another review of the film five days later, which re-examined Kurosawa's Western-genre influences. "There is nothing wrong with Mr. Kurosawa using this format consciously. Several American directors have used it and made tremendous films. . . . What is artistically important is that Mr. Kurosawa has done what Mr. [John] Ford and Mr. [Fred] Zinnemann and Mr. [George] Stevens did to make outstanding Western films."[63]

But Arthur Knight genuinely understood Kurosawa's influences and intentions: "It is in the wealth of detail, the richness of characterization, and the robust quality of its physical action—as well as in the sheer technical virtuosity with which Kurosawa has managed each sequence—that lies the ceaseless fascination of the film. For he has taken a theme as familiar and standardized to Japanese audiences as our own Westerns are to us and treated it with a freshness, a directness, a sensitivity to texture and tempo and psychological truth that impart new excitement and meaning to the old form. . . . Long before it is over we have forgotten that this is an isolated incident in a distant era. Kurosawa has made it part of a ceaseless struggle of the weak and humble against their predators in every age and every land."[64]

The following spring, in 1957, the Oscar nominations were announced. *Seven Samurai* was nominated for its art direction and costume design, eventually losing in both categories. It was not among the five nominees for Best Foreign Film—Fellini's *La Strada* won, the Japanese nominee being Kon Ichikawa's *Harp of Burma* (Biruma no tategoto, 1956). (Many historians have confused *Seven Samurai* with Hiroshi Inagaki's *Samurai*, which also starred Mifune and which won the 1955 Best Foreign Film Oscar. Even Kurosawa Production's press materials on films as recent as *Ame agaru* state that *Seven Samurai* won the Oscar.) This wasn't surprising; *Seven Samurai* ran less than a week months earlier at an inconvenient downtown theater, and because Columbia apparently had only one print, the Los Angeles release didn't begin until well after the awards were handed out.

The same evening *Seven Samurai* lost at the Oscars, Yul Brynner won for his performance in *The King and I*. Shirley Yamaguchi's former beau was approached by Anthony Quinn, who in turn had been offered *Seven Samurai*'s remake rights by producer Lou Morheim, who had bought them from Toho for the ludicrously low sum of $250.[65] Originally Quinn was to star in a Western remake, with Brynner directing and possibly taking a supporting role. But once the script was written, Quinn was out and Brynner was now starring in the role originally played by Takashi Shimura.

"Despite our mutual disrespect," Quinn recalled in his autobiography, "Brynner and I jointly purchased the American rights to . . . *Seven Samurai*. . . . We both wanted to remake Kurosawa's film as a Western, and could not see the point in bidding each other up and inflating the price, so we became partners. As it turned out, I did not have the same scheming head for business as my new associate. In the months ahead, Brynner would dupe me from my share of the picture. . . . I never forgave him his trickery."[66] The remake was eventually filmed by the Mirisch Company and the Alpha Corp. (director John Sturges's company) for release through United Artists.[67]

"One time, on a flight back to Japan from Paris, I ran into Yul Brynner," Hideo Oguni recalled. "I was bored so I went to him and said, 'I am the one who wrote *Seven Samurai*.' He got very excited and we kept talking until we arrived in Japan. He asked me, 'Does Mr. Kurosawa drink as much as Mr. Oguni?' He gave me a bottle of Napoleon brandy as a souvenir."[68]

Following the release of Brynner's Western, also called *The Magnificent Seven*, Kurosawa's film once again became known throughout the world as *Seven Samurai*. The American Western was released in Japan in 1961, becoming the biggest imported film of the year (two other action films, *One-Eyed Jacks* and *The Guns of Navarone*, placed second and third).[69] In the decades since, numerous films in nearly every genre unofficially copied *Seven Samurai*'s premise, from *The Dirty Dozen* (1967) to the outer-space adventure *Battle Beyond the Stars* (1980) to the computer-animated *A Bug's Life* (1998).

As Kurosawa's stature grew, so too did interest in the uncut *Seven Samurai*. There was much speculation about what exactly had been cut for the film's American release. *Films in Review*, for example, blasted Columbia's cut version, not realizing that it was Toho who had cut the picture in the first place: "What Americans now see is half of Kurosawa's idea, and hence the travesty of it," wrote T. S. Hines. Amusingly, Hines mistakenly believed most of the cut footage came *after* the final battle, where the villagers exploit their saviors. "Why [was it cut]? Because the corruption of the samurai is a cynical truth which offended the importer's commercial instincts and/or political allegiances."[70]

In Japan, it was the cut version that was shown when the film was reissued there in 1955 and 1967, but in 1975 Toho rereleased the complete version on a roadshow basis. Much as MGM had done in 1967 with its hugely successful retooling of *Gone With The Wind*, Toho remixed *Seven Samurai* to four-track stereo, opening it in a single Tokyo theater. And in just two weeks in that one theater, the new *Seven Samurai* earned nearly $160,000.[71] Toho reissued the long version again in 1991, and it did even better. Toho's spokesmen estimated the thirty-seven-year-old film would earn roughly $2.2 million in that year alone.

In America, an uncut version of the film was allegedly shown briefly in Los Angeles in 1969, and in the early 1970s PBS ran *Seven Samurai* as one in a series of foreign films. Despite this, it was not until 1983 that *Seven Samurai* was given a legitimate theatrical reissue in its original form in America.

Kurosawa and co-writers Hideo Oguni and Shinobu Hashimoto saw none of this money and sued Toho for certain rights to the film and money the studio earned when they sold the American remake rights. In 1978, the Tokyo District Court sided with the trio, ruling that Toho hadn't paid them enough money "to claim perpetual ownership of the movie."[72] The court also found fault with MGM, which now owned the Western remake, ruling that Kurosawa, Hashimoto, and Oguni had "granted a 'one-picture license' to produce 'Seven Samurai,' with no sequel or remake rights."[73] In other words, Toho didn't have the right to license the rights to Yul Brynner in the first place, nor did United Artists have the right to produce any of *The Magnificent Seven*'s three sequels.

Hashimoto claims never to have seen *The Magnificent Seven*, but Kurosawa was quoted on the film in 1980, saying simply, "Gunslingers are not samurai."[74]

In 1991, MGM countersued Toho and Kurosawa Production. Two years later, the dispute was settled out of court, with Toho paying MGM about $50,000. "Kurosawa and the writers retain ownership to the copyright and all other rights to the screenplay," reported *Variety*. "Toho retains its ownership and copyright in the motion [picture], and MGM . . . [is] entitled to make sequels and remakes of the screenplay . . . 'but only in the Western genre.' All other remake and sequel rights are reserved to Kurosawa Production and the writers."[75]

By now critics the world over had come to regard *Seven Samurai* as one of the greatest films ever made. "The vivid action film techniques that the director invented for this film—multiple camera photography, slow-motion footage of violence, teeming crowd scenes compressed and intensi-fied by 'long lens' photography—have exerted an enormous influence upon several generations of filmmakers," said the *Los Angeles Herald-Examiner*. "Kurosawa's trademark devices have become basics for gifted 'Samurai' devotees like Arthur Penn, Sam Peckinpah, Walter Hill, Francis Coppola, George Lucas and George Miller. Nevertheless, the tumultuous original is still the most richly satisfying, deep-dish entertainment in the history of the medium."[76]

"*Seven Samurai* is an epic all right," Donald Richie wrote. "It is an epic of the human spirit because very few films indeed have dared to go this far, to show this much, to indicate the astonishing and frightening scope of the struggle, and to dare suggest personal bravery, gratuitous action, and choice in the very face of the chaos that threatens to overwhelm."[77]

And Kevin Thomas of the *Los Angeles Times* called *Seven Samurai* "one of the great epics of the screen, right up there with 'The Birth of a Na-tion,' 'Gone With the Wind,' and 'Alexander Nevsky.' . . . 'Seven Samurai' celebrates more than brotherhood, for in the heroism that emerges . . . Kurosawa allows us to see in his people what we all might be. 'Seven Samurai' has endured not because of its bravura style but because that style serves to reveal and proclaim a profound, if ironic, affirmation of life and humanity."[78]

If the initially mixed reaction by American critics to *Seven Samurai* gave Toho any pause, it certainly was offset by the film's Academy Award nomi-nations and the desire of Hollywood to remake it. Kurosawa's reputation (and, to a lesser extent, Mifune's) was now firmly international in scope, and *Seven Samurai*'s financial and critical success in Japan ensured the direc-tor a level of independence enjoyed by only a handful of filmmakers world-wide.

TWELVE

THE GOLDEN AGE

Hiroshi Inagaki's *Samurai* (*The Legend of Musashi*; Miyamoto Musashi, 1954) was a landmark period drama in Japanese cinema, less because of its cinematic virtues (though it has many) than because of the impact it made on American audiences in the mid-1950s, and its rather surprising longevity along with its two sequels.* In terms of both style and content, Hiroshi Inagaki's samurai saga is classical, the polar opposite of *Seven Samurai*. But its combination of straightforward storytelling and exotic "Japaneseness" was, ironically, more in tune with American tastes of the period than Kurosawa's film. American film critics of the 1950s didn't understand *Samurai* any better than they understood *Seven Samurai*, but they got behind Inagaki's film in a manner denied Kurosawa's, and their influence continues to be felt. The trilogy is still highly regarded in America, deemed worthy of deluxe laserdisc and DVD releases, and has been resissued on VHS several times. The trilogy can be found even in mainstream video stores and are among the most accessible Japanese films in the West.

This is not to say that *Samurai* is a bad film. It's quite entertaining in a "Classics Illustrated" sort of way—colorful, lively, and uncomplicated— and Japanese audiences were very much primed for it. A film about

---

*The film was called *Miyamoto Musashi* in Japan, the name of the main character; Toho initially called the film *Master Swordsman* for the international market. Today the picture is known in America as *Samurai I: Musashi Miyamoto*.

Musashi Miyamoto is to the Japanese what a film about Robin Hood or Wyatt Earp is to Americans—by 1954, when the film was released, there had already been numerous other motion picture versions of the same story, based on both a popular novel and historical events. *Miyamoto Musashi*, Eiji Yoshikawa's book on which this and most film versions have been based, was originally published between 1935 and 1939, in serial form, in the pages of the *Asahi Shimbun*, one of the country's leading newspapers, and studios hastened to film it even before the story had played out. Those companies that couldn't get the rights filmed the story anyway, basing their versions on the real-life, historical Miyamoto (c. 1584–1645).

Indeed, *Samurai* was itself a color remake of a three-part 1941–42 version Inagaki had directed, all prints of which were seized and taken out of Japan by the U.S. Occupation Forces and long assumed destroyed. Kenji Mizoguchi himself made one, also called *Musashi Miyamoto* (Miyamoto Musashi) in 1944, starring Chojuro Kawarasaki. The same year *Samurai* was released in Japan, Rentaro Mikuni (who plays Matahachi in Inagaki's film) starred as Miyamoto Musashi in Toei's film of the same name. Seven years later, Toei launched a Musashi Miyamoto series of its own, lasting six films. This acclaimed series, directed by Tomu Uchida and starring popular actor Kinnosuke Nakamura (and featuring, yet again, Rentaro Mikuni), was immensely successful, easily cracking the year's top-ten-grossing domestic films.

The 1954 *Samurai*, based more on Yoshikawa's novel than on historical fact, focuses on Musashi Miyamoto's spiritual awakening. In the year 1600, Takezo Shimmen (Toshiro Mifune) is a wild, ambitious youth, an outcast from his family who, seeking fame and fortune, leaves his hometown of Miyamoto with childhood friend Matahachi (Rentaro Mikuni), joining the Toyotomis in the Battle of Sekigahara. The Toyotomis are defeated in the bloody battle, in which some 70,000 men lose their lives. Matahachi is wounded, and the two make their way to the peaceful, rural home of Oko (Mitsuko Mito) and her daughter, Akemi (Mariko Okada). Spending several weeks there, Matahachi, despite being betrothed to Otsu (Kaoru Yachigusa), makes advances to Akemi, who by now loves Takezo.

Bandits raid Oko's house, where she and her daughter have eked out a living stripping dead samurai and selling their armor. Takezo fights the bandits, who retreat. Oko begs Takezo to stay on and makes sexual advances, which he refuses. In revenge, Oko tells Matahachi that Takezo tried to rape her, prompting Matahachi, Oko, and Akemi to flee to Kyoto, unceremoniously leaving Takezo behind.

The three are subsequently attacked on the road, and Matahachi, despite his cowardice, dispatches the bandits and marries Oko. The three then start a new life in Kyoto.

Takezo, meanwhile, tries to return to Miyamoto. But when he is stopped by border guards, he charges through, launching an intense manhunt. Takezo seeks refuge at the home of Matahachi's mother, Osugi (Eiko Miyoshi), but thinking Takezo left her son for dead on the battlefield, she betrays him, much to Otsu's horror. Otsu, meanwhile, receives a letter from Oko telling her that she has married Matahachi.

The search intensifies, and the wise town priest, Takuan (Kuroemon Onoe), seeing the ridiculousness of it all, decides to take matters into his own hands. Otsu, wanting to learn more about Matahachi from Takezo, joins the priest. Together they build a campfire deep in the mountains above Miyamoto, the warm fire and hot food lure Takezo out of the night. They bring the bound Takezo back and leave him hanging from a large tree at the temple. Takuan uses his influence with the Himeji court to assume responsibility for Takezo, who, after several days of hanging from the tree, begins a spiritual awakening. However, Otsu, feeling pity then love for Takezo, cuts him down. The two flee. The manhunt begins anew, but Takuan tricks Takezo into entering a small, book-filled room at Himeji castle, where he locks him in. Forced to stay at the castle, Takezo finally learns about morality and virtue and, three years later, is renamed Musashi Miyamoto and allowed to leave the castle to wander the countryside as part of his training. As he departs, he sees Otsu near the Hanada Bridge. She begs him to let her join him and he agrees. But as she gets her things, he wanders off, carving his apologies on the wooden bridge.

Hiroshi Inagaki (1905–80) was a journeyman filmmaker, more artisan than auteur. He was an actor in silent films who turned to directing in 1927, working first for a company created by actor Tsumasaburo Bando. He moved to Nikkatsu, directing *The Great Bodhisattva Pass* (Daibosatsu toge) there in 1935. When P.C.L. was formed in the mid-1930s, much of Nikkatsu's talent, both behind and in front of the camera, were lured to the new company with its modern facilities, but Inagaki stayed behind.

Inagaki's niche was period drama. He was comparable to a Michael Curtiz or a Victor Fleming, which is to say he was a competent director who occasionally transcended the genres in which he worked. He knew how to use a camera and cut film, but, as Joseph Anderson and Donald

Richie wrote in *The Japanese Film—Art and Industry*: "It has been said that [Inagaki's] greatest importance was in spurring [directors like Mansaku Itami and Sadao Yamanaka] to greater heights," rather than adding his own personal stamp to the genre.[1]

Inagaki emigrated to Shintoho in the late 1940s, and when most of that company's talent moved back to Toho he joined them. There he made costume pictures almost exclusively, often remaking his earlier glories. *Samurai* gave Inagaki all but carte blanche to Toho's resources, including the novelty of color and the opportunity to adapt Hideji Hojo's play, also from Yoshikawa's novel. Indeed, much of the film seems like a play, though Inagaki and co-writer Tokuhei Wakao have opened it up considerably. Most of the film was shot outdoors, on location, a contrast to the two sequels, which are far more studio-bound.

The exterior shooting also shows off Jun Yasumoto's excellent photography, which is quite unlike anything done before anywhere in the world. Even in the digital age of today, where film stocks offer far more flexibility, his work is still impressive.

If the film itself is unexceptional, it afforded Mifune one of his best roles of the 1950s. Takezo is an intensely physical character, a wild, immature man, and Inagaki cuts Mifune loose. What may seem hammy to some is actually in keeping with the character, and Mifune expertly conveys Takezo's raw, untamed energy. Particularly notable is the scene where Takuan and Otsu lure him out of the woods. Starving and hunted for days, Takezo has become like an animal, and Mifune expresses the character's desperation quite well. He is equally impressive at the end of the picture, when Musashi emerges from the castle transformed. More than just the new samurai wardrobe he wears, it is Mifune's performance that captures the change of Takezo to Musashi. He really looks like a man who, locked in the castle reading books for three years, has undergone a spiritual metamorphosis. Yet, in his final scene with Yachigusa, bits of Takezo's tenderness bubble to the surface, thanks to Mifune.

Kuroemon Onoe (b. 1922), by contrast, makes little impression as Takuan. A former Kabuki actor who spent three years in Los Angeles, appearing at the Pasadena Playhouse from 1949 to 1951, Onoe's film career was limited to *Samurai* and its first sequel, after which he apparently returned to the stage. Unfortunately, what appeal the character has comes from the script rather than from Onoe's performance, and it's a shame someone like Takashi Shimura wasn't tapped for the role (at the time he was busy making *Godzilla*).

Also miscast is Rentaro Mikuni as Matahachi. With his long face and large, placid eyes, Mikuni had become a popular player with younger audiences, in spite (or perhaps because) of his reputation on the set as a rebellious troublemaker along the lines of Marlon Brando. Beautiful Kaoru Yachigusa (b. 1931) joined Toho in 1951, coming from the Takarazuka Girls Opera Company. Her first few years at the studio were unremarkable, despite leading roles. She had starred opposite Tomoemon Otani in Inagaki's *Traveling with a Breeze* (Tabi wa soyo kaze) the year before, and Toho began to think her virginal beauty might have an international appeal. Immediately after completing work on *Samurai*, Yachigusa was cast in another expensive color film, *Madame Butterfly* (Chocho fujin), an elaborate though ill-conceived adaptation of Puccini's opera filmed in Italy as a co-production among Toho, Rizzoli Films, and Gallone Productions. Soon after that, she starred with Shirley Yamaguchi in another international production, *Madame White Snake* (Byukufujin no yoren), a Toho/Shaw Brothers (Hong Kong) fantasy bolstered by Eiji Tsuburaya's special effects, and one of several films Yachigusa made for director Shiro Toyoda. *Madame Butterfly* and *Madame White Snake* failed to set the international film market afire, but it gave Yachigusa a tremendous visibility, landing her prominent and popular films for the rest of the decade.

She then married director Senkichi Taniguchi, a man twenty years her senior. It was nevertheless a happy union; unlike the fate of most film actresses of the day, her marriage didn't preclude a successful, ongoing career. She continued to work and remained popular in films and television long after Taniguchi's own career fizzled in the early 1970s. When his health began to fail in the late 1990s, she remained fiercely protective of him.

As Otsu, Yachigusa is saddled with the kind of role that plagued her career: the self-sacrificing virginal beauty willing to forfeit everything, up to and including her own identity, for the man she loves. She spends most of the film crying and pleading, first with Matahachi, then with Takuan, and finally with Takezo. That she does more of the same in the sequels—years of waiting for Takezo on that damned bridge—borders on the comical.

Mariko Okada (b. 1933), with her large, almond-shaped eyes, was one of the studio's biggest stars of the early and mid-1950s. She made her debut at eighteen, in Naruse's *Dancing Princess* (Maihime, 1951), and made a big splash in Toho's first color film, Kajiro Yamamoto's *The Girl in the Orchard* (Hana no naka no musume tachi, 1953), and as *Geisha Konatsu*, a Toshie Sugie film made immediately prior to *Samurai*. Toho seized on her popularity—she appeared, mostly in starring roles, in a whopping ten features in

1953 alone. She wasn't especially happy at Toho and moved to Shochiku in 1957. She continued in leading parts well into the 1970s and remains active in films and in television dramas.

Mitsuko Mito (1919–81) was loaned out from Daiei. She may have been brought over because of her prominent role in Mizoguchi's *Ugetsu*, and the hope that her appearance might help sell the film abroad. She had been in films as early as 1937, and while her career was unremarkable, she lent the movie a seductive quality quite different from the more innocent appeal of Okada and Yachigusa.

Musashi Miyamoto was Toho's second film in color. That, combined with its long production schedule, the large number of costumed extras, and location shooting drove the film's cost upward of $500,000, making it, according to press materials, the "second most expensive motion picture to be produced in Japan."[2] Shooting began on April 15, 1954, just prior to *Seven Samurai*'s premiere, and took several months due to inclement weather. The mountain and battle scenes were filmed in Nikko, 150 miles north of Tokyo, and, according to press materials, "other exteriors, such as Shippo Temple and Himeji Castle, were photographed on actual location [sic]. It might be noted that the castle is the same one where Musashi was actually imprisoned. The bridge outside Himeji where Musashi and Otsu meet for the last time was photographed at the actual site of that meeting. The message carved by Musashi in the bridge rail is actually still legible."[3]

Jun Fukuda was Inagaki's chief assistant director: "There were something like 210 warriors on horseback, and 800 samurai extras—I supervised them for those sequences. I learned a lot from director Inagaki, especially how he handled extras and the relationships between characters. Filming it in Eastman Color took longer to shoot than black and white, but we had a large budget; it took six months to shoot the film. That was during the Golden Age of Japanese film. When I became a director in 1959, Japanese films were already in decline."[4]

Despite weather problems and the logistics of finding both horses and riders for the battle scenes, Inagaki was well versed in this kind of film. Like Kurosawa, he knew exactly what he wanted, expressed himself clearly during rehearsals, and thus rarely filmed more than two takes of a given shot.

One visitor to the set was American actor William Holden, an Asiaphile who had spent much of 1954 in Tokyo filming *The Bridges at Toko-Ri*, which featured Keiko Awaji, on loan from Toho. Holden's postwar career bore a certain resemblance to Mifune's (both played rugged, cynical anti-heroes, were ill used late in their career, had personae cultivated by autocratic directors, etc.), though it was Holden's off-screen personality—a hard-drinking world traveler, a man to whom acting was just one facet of his career, a man who had business interests and property spread out all over the world—that most impressed Mifune.

Holden in turn was greatly impressed by what he saw, and his contribution to introducing Japanese film in America has been almost completely overlooked—most biographies of the actor don't even mention it. According to the film's press material, "During his stay in Japan [Holden] spent considerable time at Toho Studios in Tokyo. When he saw the calibre of the production of 'Samurai,' he determined to become responsible, in part at least, with its presentation to motion picture audiences in the United States." What dazzled Holden and American critics was its striking use of color. Teinosuke Kinugasa's *Gate of Hell* (*Jigokumon*, 1953), a rather undistinguished Daiei production, had similarly fascinated American audiences with its inventive use of color technology. All Hollywood's Technicolor films made during 1933–1949 were under the strict, almost dictatorial supervision of Natalie Kalmus, who generally imposed a bright garishness on color productions. With few exceptions, films made under her auspices, regardless of genre, had all the photographic subtlety of a Betty Grable musical. The Japanese, by contrast, were far more restrained and realistic, at least in their period dramas, reserving splashy colors for ornamental robes and kimono, and their cinematographers quickly learned to use color for dramatic punctuation, rather than ostentatiously throughout. So impressed were they that some of Hollywood's best talent, from John Huston to Sam Fuller, would direct films shot on location in Japan mainly to experiment with this seemingly new palette.

Samurai was unquestionably a novelty. It was only the fourth Japanese feature to get a national release in the United States, following *Rashomon*, *Ugetsu*, and *Gate of Hell*. Working with partner Robert Homel, Holden himself recut the picture and supplemented it with English subtitles and some explanatory narration. Holden got behind the film, now retitled *Samurai* (*The Legend of Musashi*), to the extent of appearing onscreen in its American pre-release trailer, and invested in a special screening held on October 2, 1955, at the Academy Award Theatre in Hollywood. The gamble paid off: Holden's sincere efforts had impressed his industry friends and colleagues. The following March, the picture won an Honorary Oscar at the twenty-eighth annual Academy Awards as "the best foreign language film first released in the United States during 1955," a year that saw the release of such foreign titles as *Mr. Hulot's Holiday* (Les Vacances de Monsieur Hulot, 1953), *Ugetsu*, *Umberto D* (1952), and Buñuel's *This Strange Passion* (Él, 1952).

The picture went into a somewhat wider release the following month, to good, if not rave reviews. "Many of the shortcomings of a film as colorful as 'Samurai,' a medieval [sic] Japanese legend, can be forgiven simply because it is so colorful and lovely," said the *Los Angeles Times*. "Even the antics of some of its players, antics which somehow recall Errol Flynn's better days, can be overlooked. . . . William Holden, who certainly has taken on an Oriental bent lately, narrates unobtrusively . . . filling in here, explaining there. . . . Toshiro Mifune portrays the great fighter with a vigor and intensity which come through even the film's language barrier. . . . The nearest Western comparison to the fantastic warrior is probably Beowulf. . . . Some of the customs of medieval Japan may annoy and revolt western audiences, but enough action is mixed with the travelogue scenes to make its 100-minute running time seem astonishingly short."[5]

John McCarten, writing in *The New Yorker*, was less impressed, calling the film "noisy. . . . The actors . . . are uniformly overwrought. In contrast, the scenery is serene and at all times beautiful. After 'Gate of Hell,' I was hopeful that the Japanese would keep up the good work. But 'Samurai' would seem to indicate that the Hollywood-B virus has infected them."[6]

Bosley Crowther agreed, saying: "It would be this reviewer's guess that it will entertain more people as a cultural exhibit than as a deeply emotional experience or esthetic display. . . . [It] is essentially a bit of first-class pandering to the tastes of the Japanese mass audience." Going further, he presumptuously added: "Its drama is largely a conglomeration of contemporary Japanese romantic clichés, very much on the order of the conventional situations that occur in Hollywood Western films. And its general performance is in such a fulsome, fustian style, by our standards of reasonable restraint in acting, that it is likely to strike the American viewer as quite absurd. . . . It may have an academic interest, but not a great deal more."[7] Of course, comparing *Samurai* to an American Western is a bit like comparing *Open City* to *Three Coins in the Fountain*.

But industry trade papers saw *Samurai* as more appealing to the masses, with *Variety*'s "Brog" calling it "a distinguished film, likely to take its place with such other arties as 'Rashomon,' 'Gate of Hell,' and 'Ugetsu' as strong sure-seater filmfare. In some ways it is an easier pic for stateside audiences to follow, having a universally-recognizable plot, good English subtitles and clear narration by William Holden. . . . [The film] does remarkable things with color and photography. Scene composition is artistry of the highest order, yet never interferes with the story-telling."[8]

Considering the film is pretty much a warm-up to Parts II and III, filmed in 1955 and 1956, it's somewhat surprising that American audiences had to wait a dozen years to see the last two-thirds of Miyamoto's story. Critics who subsequently reviewed all three films mistakenly believed that Holden's version was either a severely trimmed down adaptation of the entire series, or at least a heavily compromised cut of the first picture. Neither was true, and while *Samurai* is hardly an artistic masterpiece, it is an engrossing, classically told tale from one of Japan's master craftsmen. And we have William Holden to thank for introducing it to American audiences.

As production wrapped on *Samurai*, Mifune was rushed into four films of varying quality for release in late 1954 and early 1955. He had a supporting role in director Senkichi Taniguchi's *The Surf*, the first of several film versions of Yukio Mishima's *The Sound of the Waves* (Shiosai).

Filmed on location in the Shima Peninsula in Mie Prefecture, home of Japan's famous women pearl divers, the picture tells the story of Shinji (Akira Kubo), a lonely teenager living on a remote island in Ise Bay. One day on the beach he meets a beautiful young pearl diver, Hatsue (Kyoko Aoyama, later the sympathetic daughter in *I Live in Fear*), and soon the two are in love. However, Hatsue is loved by another teenager, Yasuo (Yoichi Tachikawa, later in the Malcolm role in *Throne of Blood*), and as gossip about Shinji and Hatsue spreads, Yasuo counters with vicious gossip of his own. Because of this, Hatsue's boat-owner father, Miyata (Kichijiro Ueda), forbids Hatsue to continue seeing Shinji. Some of the women on the island, sensing the purity and innocence of their love, try to convince the father to let the two young lovers marry, but are not successful. Nevertheless, he hires Shinji and Yasuo, both expert sailors, for his boat, and when Shinji rescues Miyata's passengers during a storm, he finally gives Shinji and Hatsue his blessing.

Mifune's role in this much-praised film is as the skipper of the *Utashima-maru*, an older man sympathetic to Shinji and Hatsue's love. Director Taniguchi was glad to get Mifune, if even for only a few days, and his scenes with Kubo and Aoyama have a genuine tenderness and poignancy.

Akira Kubo, then eighteen, was a rising star at Toho. He recalls, "*Tomorrow Is Too Late* (Domani é troppo tardi, 1949), with Pier Angeli, had been a really big hit in Japan. Each of the studios—Toho, Shochiku, Toei, Shintoho, Daiei—all tried to make that kind of film in Japan. They wanted to use real sixteen-year-olds for the film, looking in schools, on the street. It was really difficult to find someone who fit with [Taniguchi's] concept for the role. Three years earlier, I had worked with [Seiji] Maruyama on an educational film. He had completely forgotten about me and chatted with his wife about who would be good for the leading role, and his wife said, 'How about Yamaguchi?' (Yamaguchi is my real name.) 'That's really a great idea!' And so I went to Toho Studios, and when he saw me he said, 'Oh, you're the guy! Yeah, you'd be perfect!' That was really the beginning of my career at Toho."

Kubo says of Mifune, "He is *the* great actor. When he was young, he looked like a wolf! We did six or seven films together. Usually the top stars look down upon the lesser-known, younger actors, but not Mifune." Kubo remembers Mifune as being "very quiet, not talkative. Sometimes he would crack a joke, but generally kept pretty quiet—except when he drinks, then he was quite boisterous!"[9]

The picture was well received in Japan. Anderson and Richie called it "an exceptionally tasteful film . . . distinguished by its . . . restraint. This was particularly true of the nude love scenes between the two youngsters, which was a far cry from the obviousness of the usual teen-age sex picture. In this film Taniguchi showed a delicacy of touch which had never been suggested in previous pictures, and this was instrumental in making [*The Surf*] Taniguchi's best film since *Escape at Dawn*."[10]

The film's success, however, couldn't turn the tide on the director's sagging career, and as Toho came to regard him as more of a straightforward action director, he found himself directing more and more routine projects. The man who had once been considered Kurosawa's equal would now be sadly relegated to second-rate material.

Mifune, meanwhile, moved on to the leading role in *The Black Fury* (Mitsuyu-sen, 1954), a quickly made programmer directed by the prolific Toshio Sugie. The film capitalized on Japan's growing fascination with crime films and cast Mifune as a harbor policeman who goes undercover to thwart a ring of Yokohama dope smugglers.

After a ship, the *Fukuryu-maru*, explodes in Yokohama Harbor, tough narcotics officer Eiichi Tsuda (Mifune) launches an investigation so brutal and uncompromising he incurs the disfavor of his fellow officers. Tsuda is driven to extremes because his younger brother died of an overdose and his mother, grief-stricken, died soon thereafter. Tsuda infiltrates a band of smugglers (including several Chinese and a Western character played by

Bob Booth), but his hatred and ruthlessness nearly destroy him in the process, and the picture ends with an elaborate boat chase.[11] The film, never released in the United States (though an English-subtitled version was produced) and largely forgotten in Japan, appears to have been marginally interesting at best, if only for Mifune's portrait of the tortured officer.

Mifune followed *The Black Fury* with yet another gangster melodrama, *A Man Among Men* (Dansei No. 1), directed by a slumming Kajiro Yamamoto. Mifune is Maki, a gangster whose racket is ticket scalping. He learns that another hood, Ken (Koji Tsuruta), is muscling in on his territory, and the two agree to a tenuous compromise. Ken eventually double-crosses Maki to get money for his mother, who dreams of owning a restaurant but has been reduced to scrubbing floors. However, Ken soon loses this money when the trust company he has it deposited in suddenly goes bankrupt.

Ken's gang boss then persuades him to fix a boxing match involving a champion backed by Maki. When Maki realizes what Ken has done, he nearly beats Ken to death. But Ken and Maki discover that their gang bosses are in collusion, playing them off against each other, and together they raid their bosses' headquarters and eventually abandon their evil ways.

"I spent a lot of time with [Mifune]," said co-star Yu Fujiki. "He's number one. [*A Man Among Men*] was a 'January' movie—we have different film seasons in Japan. ['January' films capitalized on the New Year's holiday, much like Memorial Day in America.] I did this film with Mifune, Mariko Okada, Koji Tsuruta. I played a kind of homeless kid picked up and trained as a championship boxer, and Mifune was the kid's trainer. He let Koji Tsuruta win for the money or whatever. As a January movie it was really pretty good, and had a great cast."[12]

Mifune then starred in an all but forgotten two-part film based on a story by Keita Genji, *All Is Well* (Tenka taihei; or "A World of Peace"). Directed by Toshio Sugie, the film co-starred Asami Kuji, Akira Takarada, Yoko Tsukasa, and Chishu Ryu, and was released in January and February 1955.

That spring the baseball/family drama *No Time for Tears* (Otoko arite) featured Mifune in a supporting role. The film was directed by forty-one-year-old Seiji Maruyama. Educated at Kyoto University, Maruyama directed his first film, *The Story of Santa* (Santa monogatari), in 1951 for Geien Productions, joining Toho that same year. He made his studio debut with *My Son's Bride* (Musuko no hanayome) in 1952. At the studio, Maruyama specialized in family dramas, though late in his career he would helm two of Toho's biggest war movies, *Admiral Yamamoto* (1968) and *Battle of the Japan Sea* (1969), both with Mifune.

The picture stars Takashi Shimura as Shimamura, coach of the Sparrows, a team down on its luck. They acquire a new pitcher, Onishi (Yu Fujiki), and Shimamura takes him into his home, where the new player becomes intimate with Shimamura's daughter, Michiko (Mariko Okada).

During a big game in Tokyo, Onishi manages an important victory by stealing home. In doing so, however, Onishi has ignored Shimamura's instructions, and after the game, the coach slaps him. Michiko is appalled at her father's actions, and the coach begins feeling lonely and dejected. Later, when a Sparrows player is called out at second base, an infuriated Shimamura loses his head and strikes the umpire. He's suspended for a month, and during this time he begins to think about the great sacrifices his family, especially his wife, have made on his behalf. The suspension is overturned, and Shimamura returns to his team, now away in Kyushu. Upon his arrival, he receives word of his wife's sudden death. While mourning, he receives a final, desperate call from his team and returns for their last game of the season. A reserve player is injured; Shimamura, a veteran player himself, steps in to replace him and the Sparrows win. Shimamura, however, has lost virtually everything in the process, and he sadly visits his wife's grave as the picture ends.[13]

No Time for Tears isn't really about baseball. Rather, it's more in keeping with the kind of domestic dramas Maruyama specialized in. Mifune's role once again is in support; he was brought in for marquee value. He portrays one of the Sparrows' star players, though his character's role in the narrative is unclear. The picture offered a terrific part for Shimura, as well as for Fujiki, then a rising talent at Toho, but its quality is difficult to ascertain based on available material. Although the film was subtitled into English by Toho soon after it was finished, it may never have been released in America.

Mifune's next appearance came in the second part of Hiroshi Inagaki's Musashi Miyamoto trilogy, known in the United States as *Samurai II—Duel at Ichijoji Temple* (Zoku Miyamoto Musashi—Ichijoji no ketto, 1955). The picture has several outstanding action scenes, but as a drama plays very much like the second act of a three-act play. The picture opens with Musashi's duel with Old Baiken (Eijiro Tono, impressively menacing), a chain-and-sickle weapon master. This is the best sequence in the film; it is beautifully choreographed, and like much of the picture, it atmospherically contrasts its human struggle with the unstoppability of nature, in this case a howling wind. Musashi defeats Baiken, but his victory is questioned by an old priest (Kokuten Kodo), who accuses Musashi of being a brute, an unenlightened man "too strong" for his own good and certainly one not true to the samurai spirit.

Arriving in Kyoto, Musashi challenges members of the Yoshioka school and, later, the school's master, Seijiro Yoshioka (Akihiko Hirata). Yoshioka, however, is away, courting a reluctant Akemi (Mariko Okada), who still loves Musashi. Yoshioka eventually rapes her and she runs off, only to meet the mysterious Kojiro Sasaki (Koji Tsuruta), a cunning master swordsman who carefully observes Musashi's actions from a distance, already aware that they will eventually meet in a historic duel.

In the meantime, Seijiro's brother, Denshichiro (Yu Fujiki), returns to Kyoto and, shocked by the cowardice of his brother who has lost face in the family, himself challenges Musashi. But Denshichiro is killed, and spurred by Akemi's confession to Seijiro that she still loves Musashi, a final duel between Seijiro and Musashi is set into motion near Ichijoji Temple. However, Yoshioka's men, against their leader's wishes, prepare an ambush, and Musashi must battle virtually the entire school, some 80 men. Musashi kills dozens of thugs (the action well staged in a rice paddy) before escaping, but as he makes his way through the forest, he meets Seijiro. Having finally escaped his own protectors, Seijiro apologizes for his school's enormous breach of the samurai code. They fight, but just as Musashi is about to strike a fatal blow, he recalls the words of the old monk (among others) and walks away.

He returns to Otsu, but in a moment of passion he suddenly tries to take her and she becomes frightened. As a result, Musashi returns to his wandering and his training, swearing off women in the process. Meanwhile, Kojiro waits in the wings for the inevitable showdown.

The film's three duels, all well done, are set against a complex series of chance encounters in which Otsu meets Akemi, Akemi meets Kojiro, Kojiro meets Musashi, Musashi meets Seijiro, and so on. The many coincidences that drive the melodrama strain credibility, bordering on the soap operaish at times. And, of course, not very much happens anyway, as the picture is still another buildup, this time to Part III, the climactic duel between Musashi and Kojiro.

Samurai II is notably studio-bound compared to its predecessor. It was shot in the spring of 1955, but the colors are muted, with most of the film (again shot by Jun Yasumoto) looking dull brown, in contrast to the bright hues of the first film and Kazuo Yamada's astonishing camera work on *Samu-*

rai III. That so much of the film was shot at Toho probably had to do with the leading actors' schedules. After *Seven Samurai,* Toho was anxious to get Mifune into as many films as possible before rehearsals began on Kurosawa's next film, *Record of a Living Being,* that June. Koji Tsuruta and Mariko Okada likewise could ill afford to be tied up on a production as lengthy as Inagaki's first *Samurai.*

Mifune's performance in *Samurai II* is unremarkable, though the script does little to help him. To his credit, there is some nuance in his early scenes, such as the fencing match at the Yoshioka school, where Mifune really looks like a man possessed. In this film Musashi's spiritual growth is rather muddled, and Mifune spends most of the film looking uneasy in the arms of Yachigusa and Okada and, in a not terribly believable manner, alternately brutish or wise the rest of the time.

Some of the more interesting aspects of the picture are Mifune's scenes with a renowned courtesan, played by the great actress Michiyo Kogure. In contrast to the immature, conniving Akemi and the simpering Otsu, Kogure's Lady Yoshimo is an adult, and she reads Musashi like a book. She is also mature enough to let him go even though she loves him. In the film's second action set piece, Musashi's duel with Denshichiro, Inagaki makes an interesting choice, cutting away to Yoshino's courtesan singing in the courtyard as the snow falls around her. It's one of the picture's few moments of lyricism, something the film could have used more of.

This was the second of many pairings of Mifune with Toho star Koji Tsuruta. They, along with Mariko Okada, had toplined Kajiro Yamamoto's *A Man Among Men* earlier that year, but that film received no distribution in the United States. Tsuruta was born in 1924 and during the war was drafted into a kamikaze squadron. He survived, and made his film debut in the late 1940s. He appeared in all types of films—*jidai-geki,* comedies and musicals, gangster films and war movies (often playing doomed pilots). In *Samurai II* and its sequel, Tsuruta's androgynous features (to Western eyes; in Japan he was considered quite sexy) and understated performance provide a sharp contrast to Mifune's working-class looks and intensely physical acting (as someone says in the picture, Kojiro "looks more like an actor than a swordsman"). The two were frequently paired, often making a guest appearance in the other's starring film. In 1961, Tsuruta moved to Toei, typically starring as the patriarchal *yakuza* leader in that studio's innumerable gangster films. He remained popular until his death in 1987, as much for his career as an *enka* singer (a genre known for its mournful, stylized ballads) as that of an actor.

Akihiko Hirata had appeared with Mifune in a supporting role in Makino's *The Last Embrace* (1953), and by 1955 he was recognized by Toho as one of its leading character players. His looks projected an air of intelligence and sophistication, and he was almost always cast in that type of part. His role as the tortured, eye patch–wearing scientist, Dr. Serizawa, in *Godzilla* led to his being typecast as intelligent weaklings in films like this and *Saga of the Vagabonds* (Senyoku gun to-den, 1959), but he re-emerged in the 1960s playing James Bondian villains in spy pictures, thoughtful samurai in *jidai-geki*, and company executives in salaryman comedies and dramas. He also appeared in countless *kaiju eiga* (monster movies) in films and on television, and it is this genre for which he is most fondly remembered. At Toho, he was a much-loved personality and was constantly in demand until his death in 1984.

No Time for Tears and *Samurai II* were among the first films of actor Yu Fujiki. "As a fencing student at the university, in 1951, I was an all-Japan champion. . . . Toei offered me a job in films as a *chambara* actor. I didn't have any ambitions in that regard, so at first I refused. After graduation I visited my older brother [Ichiro Sato], who was a producer at Toho. I consulted with him, and he suggested I join as an advertising or PR person. I applied, but they asked me, 'Why don't you become an actor for us?' I was trying to change my career, to move away from acting, but somehow I ended up spending forty-two years at it!"[14] Fujiki continued appearing in films of all types—dramas for Naruse, *jidai-geki*, and war movies, but he found his niche in broad comedies as a foil in salaryman films. He frequently appeared in slapstick features starring Hitoshi Ueki and the Crazy Cats (a musical-comedy team), usually as a middle-management type who falls victim to the outrageous shenanigans around him.

Rentaro Mikuni had no interest in reprising his role as Matahachi, so the role went to Sachio Sakai (1925–98), a busy character actor at the studio since the late 1940s. Sakai's casting may have been intended as a slap in Mikuni's face. Sakai's odd features—big ears, pushed-in, button nose, heavy jaw—couldn't have flattered Mikuni. Then again, *Samurai II*'s cast wasn't cheap. Mifune, Tsuruta, and Okada were at the peak of their popularity, and Kogure was on loan from Shochiku, so the casting of a relatively minor actor may have been as much a budgetary decision as anything else. Matahachi's scenes are peripheral to the already herky-jerky script, but amusing in their own right. Cast off by both Akemi and Oko, the weak-willed Matahachi returns to his deliciously unscrupulous parents, played by Akira Tani and, as Matahachi's evil old toad of a mother, Eiko

Miyoshi.* There is a terribly funny scene where Matahachi, having stolen Kojiro's fencing diploma, encounters the famous swordsman, claiming to be the very man he is talking to. Sakai was especially good at this kind of broad comedy and was in demand for pictures of all types from Ishiro Honda fantasies to Kurosawa movies.

Released in July 1955, *Samurai II* was a popular success, ranking sixth in the year's top-grossing films. Only *So Young, So Bright* (*Janken musume*), the first of the "*Sannin musume*" ("Three Young Girls") films, starring singers Hibari Misora, Izumi Yukimura, and Chiemi Eri, made more money for the studio.

But while *Samurai I* received considerable exposure in the West, including an Academy Award, Toho had difficulty finding a foreign distributor for Parts II and III. Beginning in the mid-1950s and continuing through at least the late 1960s, Toho produced lavish English-language sales booklets to market their films in America and other English-speaking countries. According to these, Toho first tried to sell the film as *Duel at Ichijoji Temple*, but found no takers. Then, in the late 1950s, the studio rechristened their international version *Bushido*, combining it with *Samurai III*. No running time is provided, so it's not clear how much, if any, of the two films was cut, though it's likely both were left intact and were intended to be seen in two parts. Given the popularity of CinemaScope in the middle 1950s, it's also possible that Toho optically converted both films to their anamorphic widescreen process, Toho Scope, to make them more commercially viable.

But all of this was for naught. Neither film was shown in America until 1967, at which point they were more than ten years old.

---

*The actress's range was highlighted in 1955, when she also appeared as Mifune's long-suffering wife in Kurosawa's *Record of a Living Being*.

THIRTEEN

I LIVE IN FEAR

In this post–Cold War era, many people have quickly forgotten the paralyzing fear of nuclear holocaust once felt across the globe. Not long ago, the entire planet faced complete annihilation at the touch of a button—the world we knew could at any time have come to an end in less than an hour. Like the Tokyo residents going about their business during the opening titles of *Record of a Living Being* (1955), most of the world took on a weary, fatalistic acceptance.* For others, though, this sword of Damocles was simply unbearable, haunting them in their dreams, triggering adrenaline-fueled panic with every sonic boom, wail of a siren, or civil defense test.

Not that the threat is over, even today. Nuclear testing still goes on, uranium-powered reactors continue to operate despite protests, countries on nearly every continent remain unstable, and in September 1999 Japan experienced its worst nuclear accident ever, when a leaking reactor sent three workers to the hospital and left hundreds of thousands of area residents fearing contamination.[1] Despite protests from anti-nuclear groups, there were more than fifty reactors operating in Japan in 2000 (providing about one-third of that country's energy needs), with more on the way.

In the Japan of 1955, the specter of nuclear terror was even greater. The

---

*The film's title, *Ikimono no kiroku*, means "Record of a Living Being," and the film is generally known by this title. However, the picture was first released in the West as *I Live in Fear* and made its television debut under that title in 1999.

Korean War renewed fears of nuclear attack, the Rosenbergs were in the news, and, just ten years after the bombing of Hiroshima and Nagasaki—during which nearly 300,000 Japanese were killed—the United States, the Soviet Union, and Great Britain were regularly conducting nuclear tests in the Pacific. These tests begat radioactive rainstorms in Japan and subtly affected weather conditions all over the Northern Hemisphere. The hydrogen bombs developed in 1952 were 750 times more powerful than those dropped in 1945, and one such test, dubbed "Operation Bravo," would turn Japan upside down.

On March 1, 1954, a hydrogen bomb was exploded by the American military near the Bikini Atoll. The bomb's power was much greater than expected, sending radioactive clouds drifting over a 7,000-square-mile area of ocean. Wandering into this deadly cloud was a Japanese fishing boat, the *Lucky Dragon No. 5* (Dai-go fukuryu maru). The twenty-three men aboard were soon covered in radioactive ash and developed nausea, headaches, and discolored skin. Two weeks later, news reports of this disaster began to leak out, triggering a nationwide recall of tuna. Ironically, the day after the *Lucky Dragon* incident, the Japanese government approved funding for the development of its very first nuclear reactor, and the number of nuclear tests conducted by the United States tripled in 1955 to eighteen from the previous year's six. A grass-roots protest against nuclear testing began in Japan, and by the time *Record of a Living Being* was released in November 1955, more than 32 million signatures had been collected.

The Japanese film industry had produced several films about "the bomb" and its effects just as the Allied Occupation of Japan was ending, notably Kaneto Shindo's *Children of Hiroshima* (Genbaku no ko) and Hideo Sekigawa's *Hiroshima*, both in 1952. Nevertheless, Japan was already becoming resigned to the doomsday specter. The *Lucky Dragon* disaster, and the immoral efforts by the American government to downplay their role in it, renewed Japanese concern and fury.

In the midst of all this, Toho produced two very different films with fear of the Bomb at their center. *Godzilla* (Gojira, 1954), the first in a long line of *kaiju eiga*, is about a mutated dinosaur that becomes the very symbol of nuclear horror via atomic testing. Directed by Kurosawa's old friend Ishiro Honda, the film took its subject matter very seriously, quite unlike the many sequels that followed and, albeit, within the context of a commercially viable genre film, with uncompromising and vivid images cleverly supervised by special effects master Eiji Tsuburaya. There were scenes echoing the *Lucky Dragon* incident (sailors die of radiation burns), commuters griping about having survived Hiroshima only to face yet another atomic threat, fear of radioactive exposure, and one especially unsettling moment when a woman, about to be killed by the monster, cradles her small children, telling them they'll soon be reunited with Papa. While the film was inspired mainly by the monster-on-the-loose spectacles made in Hollywood, especially *King Kong* (1933) and *The Beast from 20,000 Fathoms* (1953), *Godzilla* rose well above the genre and couldn't have been more immediate. It was an enormous success and joined *Seven Samurai* and *Musashi Miyamoto* among Toho's biggest hits of 1954. Even when the film was reworked for its American release, as *Godzilla, King of the Monsters!*, with American character actor Raymond Burr cleverly cut into the action, Honda and Tsuburaya's powerful handling of the material could not be subdued.

The second film was Kurosawa's *Record of a Living Being.* If the children of *Ikiru* are apathetic to their father, the family of *Record of a Living Being* are unsympathetic when not downright ruthless in the treatment of theirs, a man consumed by a fear no less terrifying than Watanabe's terminal illness, which they, too, fail to understand. It is this, combined with the general apathy toward the looming threat of total destruction, that is the heart of the picture. (Throughout the film, there are fatalistic lines like "Life is precious . . . but people die sooner or later.") Unlike *Ikiru* and *Seven Samurai*, where moral dilemmas are presented and solutions offered, *Record of a Living Being* asks many questions but doesn't pretend to have any answers.

In the film, the family of a moderately wealthy factory owner, Nakajima (Mifune), petition the court to have him declared mentally unsound. The seventy-year-old man lives in fear of the bomb and is attempting to use his considerable assets to move the family to Brazil, where he believes air currents will protect him in the event of a nuclear war. (There was much emigration to Brazil at the time and, concurrently, the widely held misconception that South America would somehow be spared any deadly fallout from such a conflict.) Most of the family, including the families of his former and present mistress, will have none of it: they have no interest in leaving Japan and don't want to see the family fortune drained by this seemingly mad scheme.

In desperation the father burns down his own factory, trying to force the issue. He finally goes mad, believing himself to be on another planet, safe from the terror on Earth. A psychiatrist (Nobuo Nakamura) at the mental hospital contemplates the film's message: "Is [Nakajima] a lunatic, or am I a lunatic?"

In many ways the film is a precursor to Kurosawa's *Ran*, for *Record of a Living Being* is, essentially, a modern-dress *Lear*, with Nakajima and his family destroying one another, not so much for money or power as for security—to maintain a standard of living and a sense of normalcy that, if you believe Nakajima, may not be living at all. The film gives us a rich range of characters: we have the mother (Eiko Miyoshi, one of the women protesters in *Ikiru* and the tinker's dying wife in *The Lower Depths*), who is sadly manipulated by her own children; Ichiro (Yutaka Sada), the timid first son; Jiro (Minoru Chiaki), the openly selfish second son; the youngest daughter (Kyoko Aoyama), who is fully aware of her siblings' treachery; the present mistress (Akemi Negishi), whose callous father (Kichijiro Ueda) wants his daughter added to Nakajima's will before he dies, and so forth. Interestingly, Chiaki's Jiro appears to be the only one actively pushing for the court ruling. Without his influence, perhaps none of this would be happening at all. Several family members appear perfectly willing to do what Father tells them, but are as passive in family matters as they are about the bomb and so yield to the much more aggressive Jiro. In the end, they respond to warnings of an undeniable urgency by silencing the messenger. The film isn't so much a warning against nuclear testing as it is an admission of our own apathy toward it.

The picture also has certain echoes of *Rashomon* in that the domestic court representatives—three men—once again act as a kind of Greek chorus, weighing arguments for and against ruling Nakajima insane. One of these, a dentist, is played by Takashi Shimura, again portraying a common man trying to understand the truth and the moral good. He, more than anyone else, begins to realize that perhaps Nakajima isn't so crazy after all. His son doesn't feel all that different from Nakajima's family (when Nakajima appeals to a higher court, the dentist's son says, "Very good. You're no longer responsible"), and when the dentist reads an explicit book on the effects of the atomic bomb, *Ash of Death*, it becomes plain that Nakajima's fears are not without merit.

Toshiro Mifune was thirty-five years old in 1955, yet his portrayal of a man twice his age is completely convincing. Perhaps the best evidence of this is in scenes with Nakajima's wife; Mifune is playing opposite an actress nearly twenty-five years his senior, and yet they make a perfectly believable couple. The excellent makeup is subtle, avoiding the mounds of wrinkled rubber usually used for such portrayals. Mifune's head is shaved on the sides, dyed gray, and longer on top (a style common to that generation), and he's given a pair of glasses with thick lenses to lessen the impact of his

strong, youthful eyes. (The glasses also suggest, in the few close-ups of Mifune, magnifying glasses: Nakajima may be viewing the world more clearly
than everyone else.) Nakajima is an old but seemingly robust man, at least
early on, and he is strong-willed. Mifune stiffens his shoulders and walks in
a slightly slouched manner, but never overdoes it. After his defeat in court,
Nakajima seems to age considerably, and the actor is subtle yet effective in
displaying the character's physical and mental decline.

The first production meeting was held on May 19, 1955, nearly eleven
months after the release of *Seven Samurai*. Kurosawa opted for a month's
worth of rehearsals with the actors. Readings and rehearsals were conducted with the entire cast, despite the fact that, aside from a few key
scenes, most would be paired opposite Mifune in small groups. The rehearsals began on June 20, in the throes of an unusually hot summer, then
were delayed for several weeks in early July, when Kurosawa was hospitalized for an undisclosed ailment.

Character actress Haruko Togo (b. 1920) played Nakajima's oldest
daughter. At the time she worked mainly for Hiroshi Inagaki and Yasuki
Chiba at Takarazuka, the stage-affiliated subsidiary of Toho. It was during a
break in shooting for one of these productions that Togo auditioned for her
role, and she recalled that Kurosawa sat through the interview smiling
broadly. This took her by surprise: she was well aware of the Emperor's
reputation. "After the start of shooting," Togo recalls, "he said nothing to us
women. I saw him yelling at one of the men at the studio. When I asked
Ms. [Noriko] Sengoku, 'Why isn't he saying anything to us?' she suggested,
'Why don't you go up and ask him?'

"[When I approached him, Mr. Kurosawa told me,] 'I don't know very
much about women. You should talk to [director] Keisuke Kinoshita.' " At
a wardrobe meeting Kurosawa also deferred to the female cast, allowing
them to pick out clothes they thought suitable, then had the wardrobe department fashion similar outfits for shooting.

During rehearsals Kurosawa instructed the actors who played the Nakajima family to call each other by their character's name; Togo, who was the
same age as Mifune, kept calling him "Daddy." "We all went to the studio
commissary and ate *zarusoba* [cold buckwheat noodles] together. . . . Mifune would ask us what we wanted, and he would bring the food to us.
Most of us ate *zarusoba* every day. He really took care of us. Mr. [Yutaka]
Sada was really shy, and couldn't bring himself to let Mr. Mifune serve him
and stayed out of all that. We used to try and make him come over and join
us. However, he was well cast as Ichiro, since the character was supposed to
be timid." (Sada's timid nature would again be tapped—to great effect—in

his best role in a Kurosawa film, and of his career, as the chauffeur in *High and Low*.)

Finally, Kurosawa was satisfied. "One day," Togo remembers, "he saw us and said, 'You guys look like a real family now.' "[2]

Shooting commenced on August 1, 1955, with scenes in Takashi Shimura's dental office. The film's production moved at a comparatively swift pace, lasting only six weeks. But then, three days before the picture was to wrap, word came that Fumio Hayasaka had died.

After *Seven Samurai*, Fumio Hayasaka had scored *The Black Fury* (Mitsuyu-sen), the Toshio Sugie–directed Mifune picture released in November 1954. He then went to Daiei to work with Mizoguchi on two films, *Princess Yang Kwei-Fang* (Yokihi) and *New Tales of the Taira Clan* (Shin Heike monogatari), both 1955. In spite of his advancing tuberculosis, Hayasaka then returned to Toho to score *Tomorrow I'll Be a Fire-Tree* (Asunaro monogatari), Hiromichi Horikawa's film of Kurosawa's script, itself adapted from a story by Yasushi Inoue. That film was released on October 5, six weeks before *Record of a Living Being* and ten days prior to Hayasaka's death. (It was never released in America.) Sugie's *Beyond the Stars* (Shiawasewa ano hoshi no motoni), released the following February, was the last film to feature a score by Hayasaka. Like the music for *Record of a Living Being*, it was completed by Hayasaka's assistant, composer Masaru Sato.

Hayasaka died just as Kurosawa was filming Mifune's breakdown after the foundry fire. The news cast a pall over the company—Hayasaka was only forty-one years old—and Kurosawa felt he had failed with this critical sequence because his heart just wasn't in it anymore.

Masaru Sato had no telephone at the time and received word by telegram. "I entered the gate of his house and smelled incense," Sato recalled. "Inside, the house was quiet and the horrible reality hit me. My whole body froze. I prepared myself and entered his study. He lay on the bed by the wall. I saw a white piece of cloth covering his face, smoke from incense by his pillow, and a pair of scissors on his chest.* Those scissors made me realize he was dead."[3]

Kurosawa arrived in the middle of the night, and the next day people from all over the industry paid their respects. Hayasaka's funeral was huge, which surprised his survivors, and was more on the scale of a popular film star than of a man who wrote movie music. As the hearse carrying his body left his home, music from *Seven Samurai* was heard. Sato, however, insists

---

*I have been unable to find any religious or cultural significance regarding the scissors, but have regardless chosen to include this description for its vivid imagery.

that no recording existed of the score at the time and that everyone re-membered hearing the music simply because they wanted to so badly.

Hayasaka's death was a devastating blow to Kurosawa. Beyond his talent as a composer, Kurosawa deeply respected Hayasaka's knowledge of film-making in general, his instinctively solid ideas regarding the use of sound as well as film music, and he was widely regarded as a wise and gentle man. "He was the composer he was closest to," said Mike Inoue, Kurosawa's nephew. "After he died, we were forbidden to mention his name around Kurosawa."[4]

Hayasaka respected Kurosawa's authority but never hesitated to tell him when he was wrong. To their mutual credit, Hayasaka often had to admit that, with hindsight, Kurosawa's ideas were often better than he had thought. But that didn't prevent Hayasaka from disagreeing with him, and Kurosawa respected him for it. As the most powerful filmmaker in Japan, Kurosawa enjoyed the company of genuine disciples like Tsuchiya, but also insulated himself, perhaps unconsciously, with "yes men." When Hayasaka died, he had one less person to rein him in.

Moreover, it was Hayasaka himself who had suggested the project in the first place.

He had inspired the film during one of Kurosawa's visits to the dying composer. "When he said to me that a dying person could not work," Kuro-sawa remembered, "I thought he meant himself. But he didn't, it turned out. He meant everyone. All of us. The next time I went to see him, he sug-gested we do a film on just this subject."[5]

Hayasaka and Kurosawa were thinking of a satire, though gradually Kurosawa and co-screenwriters Shinobu Hashimoto and Hideo Oguni (the latter penning many Toho comedies) begged off due to the controversial nature of the subject matter. (*Dr. Strangelove*, released nine years later, received harsh criticism for even *attempting* a satire about nuclear war.) However, the film's roots in dark comedy can still be seen in several scenes, especially when the court officials applaud Mifune's land-swap idea rather than view it as a symptom of madness, much to the family's shock. Similarly amusing is when the unnamed Old Man from Brazil (Eijiro Tono) shows up with a film projector to show sunny footage of the land Nakajima is considering. With his shock of white hair, white suit and hat (an obvious parallel to Mifune in dress if not manner), and sporting a deep tropical tan, he looks to the bemused family as if he were from another planet.

One of the film's best scenes, both funny and touching, vividly captures the contrary nature of parent-child relationships. While the court officials debate Nakajima's fate, the family wait in the hall on benches, sweating and wiping their brows in the stifling heat. Someone wonders where Father went, and just then Nakajima appears. He has returned with orange sodas for the very people trying to declare him incompetent. Mother weeps, the others just sit there looking embarrassed, while Nakajima guzzles away. Clearly he's a man who rarely shows affection, yet in this moment we realize how much he cares for his family. And it's this caring that gets in the way of his emigration from Japan. But when his fear becomes all-consuming, he finally breaks down and does something virtually unthinkable for a Japanese patriarch: he begs them for their understanding.

If he wasn't to score a satire, then Hayasaka felt that at least the music shouldn't bellow the picture's message, opting for an unexpected jazzy title cue (bookended by uncharacteristically long exit music) incorporating a lazily played saw against a meandering tenor sax.

When the film was released on November 22, 1955, audiences reading daily reports of Cold War tensions and nuclear tests responded to *Record of a Living Being* much as Nakajima's family do: they rejected its message. The film's advertising, in which a boiling-hot sun looms over Mifune's sweaty features, reminded them of the long hot summer they had just endured. Given the Japanese indifference, Toho made little effort to exhibit the film abroad. "It was the kind of a story Japanese people resented," said Mike Inoue, "they didn't even want to listen to or see things about the atomic bomb."[6] *Record of a Living Being* wasn't seen outside Japan until it was finally shown at a Kurosawa retrospective in Berlin in 1961 (where it was highly regarded). It didn't premiere in the United States until 1963, as part of the New York Film Festival. For some reason the American distributor, Brandon Films, didn't actually release the film until four years later, and it didn't play in Los Angeles, where it would qualify for Academy Award consideration, until late 1971.

Reviews were mixed. Many critics seemed reluctant to address the film's anti-nuclear theme, preferring to limit their comments to the film as a family drama and Mifune's performance. "It is inexcusable that a film of this quality has taken some 12 years to get a commercial showing in New York," complained *Cue*. "Mifune, literally disguised with a makeup job, some of it not very professional-looking, gives a strong performance as the troubled man. . . . Thank you, Thomas Brandon, for releasing this overdue film."[7]

"Like Federico Fellini, Japanese film director Akira Kurosawa is too talented a filmmaker to turn out a dull film even when his ideas seem a bit fuzzy," said *Variety*'s "Anby," adding that Mifune's performance was played "in his familiar grunt-and-groan style. . . . The ruggedly handsome hero of Kurosawa's samurai tales and here caked over with a lot of not very effective makeup. . . . One might understand the old man's fears on a more personal and petty level, but as written anyway, one suspects he is incapable of such God-like vision which makes him weep for all the world. . . . His relations with his family are beautifully and touchingly realized."[8]

Newsweek agreed, calling the film "difficult but strangely moving. . . . It is early and often shaky Kurosawa, but early Kurosawa is still more interesting than recent works by lesser directors. Once the film is out of sight, some of its scenes still refuse to be put out of mind. . . . Not even the great Mifune can get away with playing a man twice his age, even though his mouth seems to have been slashed crooked by a stroke and his body can barely withstand the weight of his years and fears. . . . Much of the plot is shamelessly soap-operatic. Yet the merciless heat of summer and the mindless threat of extinction are almost tangible, and the film should be seen if only for its final moment with Mifune."[9]

The *Motion Picture Herald* damned the film with faint praise: "An interesting but slow-moving film. . . . Audiences familiar with Oriental films may be accustomed to a leisurely telling of the story. But to Western eyes and ears, the pace is often maddeningly slow. If patrons' attention-spans are sufficiently long, there is much of worth to be gained by watching. . . . But the message is a long time coming."[10]

Perhaps most on the mark was Judith Crist, then writing for the New York *World Journal Tribune*. She called the film "an absorbing drama, distinguished not only by the Japanese director's skill in treating a superhuman subject in throbbingly humanistic terms but also by a remarkable character performance by Toshiro Mifune. . . . [It] constitutes a highlight of this remarkable actor's career. . . . Through Mifune's perceptive performance we see a strong man crumble before our eyes, we see the transition from fear to terror, the concern extend beyond the household and family to all of humanity—and finally the borderline of sanity is crossed. The director's brilliant camera eye finds the inhuman in a son's blank-eyed reaction to his father's agony, the compassionate in a young girl's outreached hand."[11]

Back in 1955, the picture was also well received by Japanese critics, placing fourth on *Kinema Jumpo*'s "Best Ten" list that year, behind Naruse's *Floating Clouds* (Ukigumo), Toyoda's *Marital Relations* (Meoto zenzai)—both were Toho releases—and Kinoshita's *She Was Like a Wild Chrysanthemum*

(Nogiku no Gotoki Kimi nariki). An impressed Nagisa Oshima, then an assistant director at Shochiku, said seeing the film was like being "struck on
the back of the head with an iron rod."[12]

Record of a Living Being was a commercial failure and Kurosawa's first
film to lose money during its initial release. But concern over the Bomb
continued to preoccupy his mind, and he would return to this theme in
several of his later films.

Mifune spent the remainder of 1956 making Samurai III, the last installment
of Hiroshi Inagaki's trilogy. The film opens not with Musashi but with rival
Kojiro Sasaki (Koji Tsuruta again); indeed, Kojiro shares nearly equal
screen time, and Tsuruta (if one were to read the opening titles in the traditional Japanese manner) is actually top-billed. As it turns out, Kojiro is
more dominant than Musashi this time out, though Musashi goes through
more compelling changes than he did in either Samurai I or II. Conversely,
Kojiro remains a bit of an enigma.

Akemi (Mariko Okada) is still with Kojiro as he contemplates his destiny. Despite his obvious skill, Kojiro's narcissism and lack of humanity
frighten Akemi, especially when he kills a bird in mid-flight with his sword,
and she runs off. Musashi, having won sixty consecutive duels, is first seen
witnessing a fencing match where bullish priest Agon (Kichijiro Ueda),
overenthusiastic, taunts the crowd of spectators, who are reluctant to challenge him. A boy, Jotaro, who has become Musashi's disciple, urges him to
challenge the priest, but Musashi refuses. Jotaro goads the priest, and when
Agon attacks them both, the priest and Musashi begin dueling. But an old
priest, Nikkan (Kokuten Kodo, also in Samurai II), observing Musashi's earlier reluctance, stops the fight. Nikkan praises Musashi's spiritual growth;
he has now achieved a balance of his incredible skills with a sense of justice
and a deep humanity. However, when Nikkan asks him if he's ever been in
love, it becomes clear to the priest that one aspect of Musashi's life is yet
unresolved.

Kojiro, meanwhile, desires to become a fencing master under Lord
Yagyu in Edo, but during a demonstration of his skill, he permanently crip-
ples one of the lord's vassals. His brutality costs him the position, but he
also feels, perhaps for the first time, some guilt about what he has done and
visits the man he has injured. (This scene recalls Sanshiro Sugata, where the
hero likewise visits the opponent he has seriously injured.) Despite this,
Kojiro brutally slays four men from the nearby Kobata Military Academy,

all with single strokes and for no other reason than for his action to serve as a calling card to Musashi. Out of respect, Musashi delivers the bodies back to the school, but the *dojo* master, fearing the shame their deaths might bring, denies the dead students were ever his. Disgusted, Musashi buries the men and, disillusioned by the *dojo*'s actions, travels to Shimosa, resolved to become a farmer and reconsider his life's direction. Before he leaves Edo, Kojiro challenges Musashi to a duel, but Musashi puts it off for a year, as it might appear that he is fighting only to preserve the school's name.

Joined by Jotaro and Kumagoro (Haruo Tanaka), a ruffian-turned-Miyamoto disciple, Musashi builds a modest hut and farms the land. But the village, much like that in *Seven Samurai*, is frequented by bandits. Otsu (Kaoru Yachigusa) makes her way to the village, and Musashi, recalling his unrequited sexual advances on her, still feels guilty and avoids her. Meanwhile, Akemi, now working as a geisha, entertains Kojiro one night during which he reveals Musashi's whereabouts. On the way to Musashi's village, however, she meets the bandits. One of the brigands is Gion (Daisuke Kato), who joined the bandits to save his own life after they killed his lover (and Akemi's mother), Oko. They force Akemi to lie to the villagers and say they have been arrested, and to then set fire to Musashi's hut as a signal for an attack.

At the village Otsu, shunned by Musashi, tries to drown herself. Musashi rescues her, just as Akemi arrives. Akemi makes one last-ditch effort to win Musashi's affections, but he refuses her. Meanwhile, Akemi's news that the bandits have been arrested leads to a celebration. But at Musashi's hut Akemi confronts Otsu, attacking her with an ax. During the struggle an oil lamp tumbles into the hay, and the hut is set afire. Seeing this, the bandits attack, but Musashi's training of the villagers (again, à la *Seven Samurai*) surprises the brigands and they retreat, although Kumagoro is killed. As the hut becomes engulfed in fire, Akemi, finally seeing the errors of her ways, rescues Otsu when she is attacked by Gion. Akemi fatally stabs him with a spear, and he in turn cuts her down, causing her death.

With the stage set for the inevitable showdown between Kojiro and Musashi, the two agree to meet at dawn on Ganryu Island. Otsu pleads with Musashi to run away with her, but he surprises her by—in a backhanded sort of way—proposing to her. Musashi and Kojiro meet on the beach at sunrise and, using only a quickly carved wooden sword (which the real-life Musashi limited himself to in later duels), Musashi kills Kojiro. As he climbs back aboard the boat that will take him home, Musashi weeps for his dead opponent, the greatest swordsman he will ever know.

Samurai III is more successful than either Parts I or II in getting inside the heads of Musashi and Kojiro. The script by Inagaki and Tokuhei Wakao is better structured, because we're able to contrast the external and internal conflicts between the two characters. Kojiro's senseless killing of a swallow is contrasted with Musashi's refusal to duel Akon; Kojiro's murder of the four students is followed by Musashi's compassion for the dead strangers. Musashi uses his skills nobly, helping the defenseless farmers, while Kojiro goes to work for the shogunate.

The film is also less episodic, more story- and character-driven than those that had preceded it. There are subtle allusions to other characters and incidents we've seen before, and the picture has a lyricism largely absent from the first two films. After Otsu's arrival at the village, for instance, she plays her flute that night as if to musically lure Musashi to her, much as she did in *Samurai I*. There's also an effective montage of numerous farmers, fearing the brigands, fleeing the village. Inagaki shows this in long, wide-angle shots with music but no sound effects, giving it the poetry of a silent film. And the trilogy's payoff, the climactic duel, is expertly staged and beautifully photographed.

Mifune's role has interesting parallels and antecedents to some of the other characters he played. His scenes in the village recall *Seven Samurai*, while one comic bit has Musashi, challenged by ruffians, stoically responding by picking flies out of the air with chopsticks. This amazes the thugs and anticipates the warrior rogues Mifune would later play in films like *Yojimbo*.

The cast consists mainly of carryovers from the previous films, though Michiko Saga has a rather thankless, underdeveloped role as Kojiro's lover and Takashi Shimura turns up in a few scenes as a court official. A real cheat in Toho's advertising is Minoru Chiaki (the woodcutter swordsman from *Seven Samurai*), who, although prominently billed, turns up in a tiny role as the boatman who takes Musashi to the island.

Very amusing is Haruo Tanaka (1912–92) in a broadly comic role as Kumagoro, the horse dealer and self-described "tough guy" who becomes an unabashed disciple of Musashi. As early as 1938, Tanaka appeared in pictures of all kinds, though he seemed to specialize in period adventures and broad comedies, often starring Enoken. He had small roles in several Kurosawa films—*No Regrets for Our Youth*, *Ikiru*, and *The Lower Depths*—and continued working until at least 1985, when he made a brief appearance as one of the old mourners in Juzo Itami's comedy *The Funeral* (Ososhiki).

Mifune plays Musashi with deadpan confidence most of the time, and tortured uneasiness in his scenes with Yachigusa and Okada. At least the love triangle is finally resolved, as Yachigusa's weeping and Okada's conniving have long ago become more irritating than effective. Musashi's training is at an end, and this makes him strong, confident, but also a little dull. Unfortunately, the character is basically humorless (except for that scene with the flies) and cold, giving Mifune scant opportunity to enrich his part with enough real warmth to justify these two women following him around for so long.

Kojiro thus becomes more intriguing. He is awed by Musashi's abilities but never grasps that it is Musashi's humanity that truly makes him great. Kojiro becomes a tragic character, a skillful man whose ambitions and single-mindedness blind him to the point of destruction. Discussing his life-or-death duel, he tells Omitsu (Saga), "Win or lose, in either case you'll always remember me as your lover." Yet Kojiro isn't exactly conceited. He is frank, honest, and uninterested in material wealth, and like Musashi he is in pursuit of spiritual achievement; but he is also so self-absorbed he's willing to commit murder to better his skills.

As previously stated, the photography—by Kazuo Yamada—is excellent, the final duel on the beach at dawn being the highlight. Fewer of the exteriors were shot on soundstages than in *Samurai II*, though shooting in the fall of 1955 did necessitate some interior filming, and the final duel is compromised by the use of rear-process screens for some shots. But from a technical standpoint, *Samurai III* is generally a well-made film.

And so the Mifune-Musashi story ends, partly because it is here that Eiji Yoshikawa's novel, on which the trilogy is based, comes to its conclusion. *Samurai III* was also much less successful at the box office, giving Toho's executives little incentive to continue the series. The real Musashi, a far more brutal man than depicted here, went on to more battles, including the purge of Christians in Kyushu. In his last years he withdrew from public life and wrote *A Book of Five Rings* (Go rin no sho), which is often compared to Sun Tzu's *The Art of War* and remains a bestseller today, 350 years after Musashi's death.

Like *Samurai II*, the third part of Inagaki's trilogy took eleven years to reach America's shores, making its debut when all three films were shown, uncut, as a triple bill. Kevin Thomas raved about the opportunity to see the entire saga. "Taken in its entirety," he said, "it is truly a remarkable achievement that must take its place as one of the screen's great epics. Technically, it is superb, with breathtaking color and a stirring score [by Ikuma Dan], and the myth it projects has a universal appeal." But Thomas did have reservations about Part III. "The [trilogy] would have been better if it had been split into only two parts and got to the fine climax faster. Part III has been spread pretty thin, spending far too much time on the two weepy females . . . who have been following Musashi around for so long and relying too heavily on coincidence in bringing characters together."[13]

Variety's "Robe," who inexplicably likened the film to "a Japanese 'Cool Hand Luke,' " praised what he called "a lengthy, colorful buildup to a big gunfight (or sword, in this instance) at the Ganryu Corral. . . . It's a commercial attempt, and as such, it's successful." However, "Robe" was unimpressed by Koji Tsuruta, who so dominates the film. "His role is indifferently played . . . [and he] never strikes the creative spark that young Jap [sic] actor Tetsuya Nakadai always manages in scenes with Toshiro Mifune."[14]

Less than three weeks after *Samurai III* opened, Mifune had another film in theaters, Senkichi Taniguchi's *Rainy Night Duel* (Kuroobi sangokushi, 1956), a standard, convoluted action film with Mifune as a judo expert. Although Toho produced an English-subtitled version, it is unlikely that it was released in the West.

The film is set in Kyushu roughly during the same period as *Sanshiro Sugata*. Mifune plays Masahiko Koseki, who rescues a young woman, Kikuko (Mariko Okada), from a boxer named Kotetsu (Yu Fujiki). This leads to a challenge by another boxer, Hachiro Iba (Hideo Saeki), but Koseki defeats him, too. All this fighting results in Koseki's judo master, Masazumi Amaji (Shin Saburi), expelling him from the school, despite the fact that the teacher's daughter, Shizue (Kyoko Kagawa), is in love with him.

A depressed Koseki heads for Tokyo and is approached by a racketeer, Joji (Haruo Tanaka), who persuades Koseki to work for him in Hokkaido, but there he discovers that Joji is running a slave-trafficking organization. Disillusioned, he joins forces with Shiro Katahara (Akio Kobori), a detective trying to arrest Joji, but Joji's gang learns about this. In the end, Koseki and Katahara are saved when a young woman, Oyo (Asami Kuji), sets off a stick of dynamite in Joji's lair.

Meanwhile, Amaji is challenged to a duel by karate master Shunsuke Iba (Akihiko Hirata). During the fight, Koseki's judo master goes blind. Koseki decides to return to Kyushu, but Joji, having survived the dynamite blast, pursues him. Oyo tries to intercept Joji, but he stabs her. Koseki, meanwhile, duels Iba, wins, and is reunited with Shizue.

Mifune's third film role of 1956 was a small, supporting part in Kajiro Yamamoto's *The Underworld* (Ankokugai), a noirish *yakuza* thriller starring Koji Tsuruta. Such films were becoming the mainstay at Nikkatsu and Toei, but Toho had only a passing interest in the genre, and they remained a small fraction of the studio's output. *The Underworld*, by its very novelty, was popular enough to warrant an unofficial series of "Underworld" thrillers, but this initial offering is nebulous at best and positively antiquated compared to the films that followed just a few years later. *The Underworld* would be Ya-mamoto's only film in the series; the later, more vital films were directed by a new generation of filmmakers, including Kihachi Okamoto and Jun Fukuda.

Fukuda, in fact, was chief assistant director on *The Underworld*; at thirty-three he was seen as a hot new talent, perhaps the best to come along since Kurosawa and Taniguchi nearly twenty years earlier. The film's stark, ener-getic location work bears his stamp more than Yamamoto's, and gives this otherwise routine crime melodrama what power it has.

Gang boss Tsunejiro Furuya (Takashi Shimura) has heart trouble. Re-turning from the hospital, he meets with his chief henchmen. During his absence, Furuya's concerns—pachinko parlors and mahjong dens—have all lost money. Only his dance hall, managed by Takao Shoji (Tsuruta), has turned a profit. Spending a clandestine evening with Furuya's mistress, Natsue (Akemi Negishi), Shoji hits upon an idea: a hot springs resort with the service of blind masseurs included in the cost of a room. He pitches the idea to Furuya, who is developing a growing respect for his protégé.

But Furuya has other things on his mind. While in the hospital he met a young, virginal intern, Yumiko (Kyoko Aoyama), and he begins calling on her with the pretense that he's still in need of medical attention. Yumiko's hospital is in want of an X-ray machine for its TB patients, and Furuya sends Shoji off to Kamakura with Yumiko to fetch one. Eventually, Shoji gives Yumiko the money needed to buy the machine, but it's cash he got from Natsue, Furuya's mistress, and the gang boss's other henchmen, jeal-ous of Shoji's favoritism, reveal to their chief that Shoji and Natsue have been double-crossing him. The hoods gang up on Shoji, shooting him sev-eral times. Trying to avoid police attention, Furuya has Yumiko picked up to attend to Shoji's wounds. He also tries to rape her, but the wounded Shoji prevents this. Eventually, the police (led by Mifune) show up and arrest Fu-ruya and his gang. Yumiko and her fiancé (Hiroshi Koizumi) are reunited and Shoji, now confined to a police hospital, looks out a window as Natsue leaves him for an older, wealthier man.

The Underworld is a modest, reasonably entertaining film, though it lacks any real depth. Seiichi Endo's stark black-and-white photography at times recalls the best American noir films, and Ikuma Dan, the high-profile but often unimaginative composer of the "Musashi Miyamoto" trilogy, con-tributes a nice little waltz motif, played on an accordion. And though Tsu-ruta, Negishi, and Aoyama play their roles strictly by the book, Takashi Shimura has an interesting, atypical role as an aging gang boss who, when

Aoyama's around, becomes putty in her hands. Shimura, so much the leader in *Seven Samurai*, so wise as the scientist in *Godzilla*, is a delight as a *yakuza* chief who is also a foolish old man.

Mifune's inconsequential role is that of Chief Inspector Kumada, a cop investigating Furuya's illegal activities. Mifune introduces the film, sets the story into motion, then disappears for long stretches until he saves Tsuruta and Aoyama in an anticlimactic rescue. Tsuruta's character is simply too nice a *yakuza*, too much of a lightweight compared to the rest of the gang (especially his chief rival, *Seven Samurai*'s master swordsman, Seiji Miyaguchi). Mifune tries to inject the role with what little he can. When the character is introduced, he goes over Furuya's holdings with some reporters, congenially serving them rice crackers at the end of his little speech. And his meeting with Shimura is mildly amusing, too: Shimura's trying to hide the fact that he's got Tsuruta and Aoyama locked up in a nearby room, while Mifune, catching on, is all smiles, feigning blissful ignorance.

As Kurosawa prepared their next collaboration, Mifune continued cranking out films for his studio. *Samurai III*, *Rainy Night Duel*, and *The Underworld* were released in the first two months of 1956, and four more films followed before the year was out. He had a supporting role in *Settlement of Love* (Aijo no kessen), helmed by actor-director Shin Saburi. The romantic melodrama starred Setsuko Hara and Keiju Kobayashi and featured Kaoru Yachigusa.

More significant was *A Wife's Heart* (Tsuma no kokoro), Mifune's second and last film for Mikio Naruse. Like so many of Naruse's later films, *A Wife's Heart* is an uncompromising examination of the postwar Japanese family that starred his favorite actress, Hideko Takamine. Regrettably, the picture has had no release in the United States. Along with Kurosawa, Naruse was Toho's finest postwar director, yet very few of his films have ever been available in the West.

Scoundrel (Narazumono) was, by contrast, a throwaway program picture directed by the prolific Nobuo Aoyagi, who made seven other films in 1956 alone. Mifune was paired with Mariko Okada, and also featured were Yumi Shirakawa, Takashi Shimura, and Minoru Chiaki in supporting roles. Mifune and Okada were together again in *Rebels on the High Sea* (Shujinsen, or "Prison Ship"), a lesser Inagaki adventure based on "The Story of the Hokokumura Ship" ("Hokokumura no hanashi") by Kazuo Kikuta.

Immediately after *Scoundrel* and *Rebels on the High Sea* wrapped, Mifune joined rehearsals on Kurosawa's new film, one which would bring him more international acclaim than his last six films combined.

FOURTEEN

TWO PLAYS

The last time two new films by Kurosawa were released in a single year was 1957. Both films were adaptations of plays, though near-opposites in their cinematic design and fidelity to their source. The first was a loose adaptation of Shakespeare's *Macbeth*, released in the West as *Throne of Blood* but in Japan as *Kumonosu-jo* ("Castle of the Spider's Web") or, more commonly, *Cobweb Castle*. Kurosawa once stated that he and his collaborators wrote the film with the intention of turning the script over to a younger director (perhaps Hiromichi Horikawa), but this rings false. He was, several months after the release of *Record of a Living Being*, ready to make another film and had wanted to make a film of *Macbeth* as far back as the late 1940s, when, he said, Orson Welles's own expressionistic adaptation, produced by Republic Pictures in 1947, forestalled any serious plans he may have had. Critics and film theorists (to say nothing of film and literature students) have frequently compared and contrasted *Throne of Blood* to Shakespeare's play, though such exhaustive efforts are to some degree beside the point. *Throne of Blood* is more suggestive than adapted. It follows *Macbeth*'s framework rather closely, but departs from its source in a number of ways. While whole scenes from the play appear intact, the film, which is aggressively cinematic and richly visual, is as much an original work as it is an adaptation. In any case, unlike in *The Idiot* or Kurosawa's next film, *The Lower Depths*, its source is not even acknowledged in the credits.

And, also unlike with *The Idiot*, Kurosawa and co-writers Hideo Oguni,

Shinobu Hashimoto, and Ryuzo Kikushima didn't bother to bring copies of *Macbeth* with them to the *ryokan* when they began writing the film in early 1956. "We had already read *Macbeth* when we were young," Hashimoto said, "so we didn't refer to it . . . when we wrote the script."[1] (Which by no means suggests a cavalier attitude about adapting it; rather it speaks to the power of Shakespeare's play.)

Hideo Oguni remembered it somewhat differently: "Kurosawa and I used to read Shakespeare, but the other two did not. We were concerned that Shakespeare's story wouldn't be accepted by the current generation, but decided to give it a try. Many years later, in November 1972, I was invited to the Los Angeles Exposition of Screenwriters. People there were surprised to learn that I had written 300 scripts. How could I write so many? A list of my screenplays was prepared, and one of the writers stood up and said, '*Macbeth* has been adapted many times, all over the world, but *Throne of Blood* was the best.' The film wasn't a hit in Japan, but had a very good reputation abroad."

Once again, the four holed up in Kurosawa's favorite *ryokan*, writing scenes separately and then sharing their work and pooling their best ideas. Hideo Oguni described the sleeping arrangements during their stay: "Since I was the oldest, I was accorded my own, special room. When I had slept with Kurosawa, I couldn't sleep because of his loud snoring. Kikushima snored as much as Kurosawa did, so they slept together. However, each complained about the other's snoring."[2]

Despite the relative commercial failure of *Record of a Living Being*, Toho was sold on the idea of *Throne of Blood*. Toei Studios, less than ten years old, and Nikkatsu, which had resumed production during the 1950s, were now edging Toho, Shochiku, and Daiei out of the annual list of top-grossing films. Toei catered to teenagers (who became adults fiercely loyal to Toei output) with *jidai-geki* and underworld thrillers. Nikkatsu was less structured, but their films were mainly geared to the youth market as well, and many were *jidai-geki* and contemporary films about troubled youths. By 1956, the four top-grossing films had been produced by Toei, and the fifth by Nikkatsu. Undoubtedly Toho wanted to reclaim its position, and who better to secure it than the man who had directed the immensely popular *Seven Samurai*? That film wasn't as profitable as Toho might have hoped, but it was an immensely popular and prestigious release. Kurosawa's production, then, would be lavish, on a par with *Seven Samurai*.

But where *Seven Samurai* presented a *jidai-geki* world set mainly in a world of peasants, *Throne of Blood* presented a world of lords and warriors.

And this is precisely one of the film's remarkable achievements. As with *Seven Samurai*, *Throne of Blood*'s script, art direction, props, and costumes are used in ways never before seen in *jidai-geki*. Compare it to the prettified, Eastman-colored splendor of Inagaki's "Musashi Miyamoto" movies. *Throne of Blood* is darker, uglier, chaotic.

Washizu (Mifune) and fellow warrior Miki (Minoru Chiaki), having won a fierce battle, are on their way back to their lord's castle when they encounter a witch (Chieko Naniwa), who predicts that Washizu will assume control of the castle but that Miki's son (Akira Kubo) will subsequently rule. When they return to the castle, another of the witch's predictions, that Washizu and Miki will be rewarded fiefs, immediately comes true. Washizu tells his wife, Lady Asaji (Isuzu Yamada), about the predictions, and she goads him into killing the lord (Takamaru Sasaki) when he visits Washizu's mansion. When Lady Asaji becomes pregnant, Washizu sends an assassin after Miki and his son, but the latter survives. Washizu is haunted by Miki's ghost. When Asaji's baby is stillborn, she goes mad. Washizu visits the witch again; she tells him he will never lose a battle until the Cobweb Forests (Birnam Wood) come to the castle. The prophecy is fulfilled when forces loyal to the murdered lord advance on the castle, hidden behind cut tree branches and shrubbery. Washizu's own troops, by now aware that their master engineered the lord's murder, turn on him and shoot him full of arrows.

In *Record of a Living Being*, Kurosawa asked his characters (and, by extension, his audience) to consider the world as seen by Kiichi Nakajima, that his world might in fact be real while ours is false. In *Throne of Blood* all the film's characters inhabit a world very similar to the one seen through Nakajima's eyes, a world utterly without hope. The entire story is told in flashback, long after all its characters are deceased. Dreamlike, fog-shrouded images of death haunt every scene, yet Kurosawa keeps his audience at a distance, especially from its main characters. The picture has no emotional impact, perhaps because, given the nature of the story, for him to pull his audience in further would be unbearable (though he goes on to achieve just that in *Ran*). It is therefore a formal experiment in which everything is fated, and indeed, Kurosawa himself regarded it in exactly those terms. As Jack F. Jorgens states in his book *Shakespeare on Film*, Kurosawa has "stripped the poetry from the lines and infused it in the movements of characters and camera, contrasting settings and costumes, and beautifully composed images."[3]

If *Throne of Blood* lacks the humanism of Kurosawa's best work, it is nevertheless a superbly crafted film. In terms of production—the photography, the sets, the costumes—it is nearly faultless. The director succeeds in his lifelong quest for "pure cinema," creating a dark, treacherous world. Asakazu Nakai's black-and-white photography is so beautiful that it is impossible to imagine the film in color, any more than it would be to imagine *Ran* in black and white. As Donald Richie notes: "There has rarely been a blacker and whiter black and white film. [Kurosawa] purposely restricts himself. The only punctuation he allows is the simple cut and the simple wipe. There are no fades, no dissolves, nothing soft, nothing flowing."[4] That is, with one very interesting exception: his use of fog for dissolves. This is seen clearly at the film's beginning and end, when we see a stone marker and the foundation stones of Cobweb Castle. Fog consumes the markers, and we are suddenly in medieval Japan. As the story shifts back and forth in time, it is the mist that serves as transition, and throughout the picture it is within the murky fog where time and space shift, enhancing its nightmare-like imagery.

Yoshiro Muraki's incredible castle set—built on the black, volcanic slopes of Mt. Fuji—and the equally fine interiors are magnificent, yet Kurosawa's direction never draws attention to their lavishness the way so many Hollywood epics do. The castle never overwhelms the actors; he shows us only what we need to see, and in doing so heightens the realism. The costumes are, like Inagaki's films, historically accurate, yet they have a lived-in, functional quality that Inagaki's films rarely achieve. Part of Kurosawa's goal was to make the *jidai-geki* genre meatier, more cinematically modern, but with a respect for history. Toho limited its *jidai-geki* to a handful of films each year, mainly large-scale productions like Inagki's films. But the other studios—Daiei, Nikkatsu, Toei—were each churning out dozens annually, almost always as lightweight, instantly forgettable soufflés, typified by Toei's *jidai-geki* musicals starring singer Hibari Misora and heart-throb Kinnosuke Nakamura. If Kurosawa's more historically immediate, more intimately psychological *Throne of Blood* failed to change the genre's course, aesthetically at least Kurosawa achieved exactly what he set out to do: *Throne of Blood* is like no other *jidai-geki* of its period. It is also a masterpiece.

Casting and rehearsals began in the late spring of 1956. For Takeshi Kato, *Throne of Blood* would be his first film with Kurosawa. He recalled, "I went to an audition. I was just a student of the theater at the time. All the acting students went to Toho to appear at the auditions. We went to the director's office, sat down, and, while we were waiting for him, we were all so nervous that we were shaking. He came in and was so tall—he was very cool—he looked like Gary Cooper. He smiled and appeared very nice. Of course the audition wasn't for the main cast, just for the smaller roles. He asked us to wear helmets, and he checked each of us. And he said, 'Okay, I'll announce the casting later on,' but I was just very excited to meet him. We heard he concentrated on one production at a time and was called *Tenno*. I had seen all his films since *Sanshiro Sugata*, and I was so excited about the opportunity to be in one of his films. As a result, I got the role of one of the king's guards, and I drank poison sake, and Mifune killed me!

"Before the shooting started, all of us—the entire cast, no matter how small the role—got together and read the script, even though I had only one scene. We all had to speak so loudly, by the time we were done our voices were gone. And after that we rehearsed in full costume and we ran through the entire script again. The costume was extremely heavy."[5]

Shooting began on June 29, 1956, and took up the entire summer and fall. Location work in Gotemba and Nara Prefecture was shot during the early summer, then the crew returned to Tokyo and began shooting on the backlot in July, August, and September. In October the crew returned to Gotemba, shooting scenes at Washizu's mansion in Nagaoka, in Izu, the following month. Postproduction, including all dubbing and music recording, was completed in January 1957, and the film opened on the fifteenth.

"It was summertime at the open set," Kato said. "I was hot, and the lighting was hot, and bugs were swarming all over me, but I couldn't move until I was killed. I worked for about a week. I kept hoping Mr. Mifune would kill me as soon as possible."[6]

When he did, Kato might have preferred to wait in the heat. "Three cameras shot Mr. Mifune coming at me with the sword. I put a piece of wood up my sleeve for safety when he stabbed me. However, Mr. Mifune was so quick and powerful that he broke right through the wood and really stabbed me! It was so painful. I was not acting in that scene and I still have a scar under my arm."[7]

Akira Kubo, in the Fleance role, approached his debut with Kurosawa with some trepidation. "*Throne of Blood* was made when I was very young, in my twenties. At the time I had heard that he was very, very scary, but not once did I see him get pissed off about anything. In his eyes I was just a kid, and he didn't get angry with me." The actor was thrown by Kurosawa's practice of always using the first take of everything he shot, saying, "His way of shooting is different from other directors—using three cameras at the same time, etc. Because he'd do only one take, I asked him if he was pleased with my performance, and he'd say, 'Because we spent so much time on rehearsals, I usually need only one take.' Rehearsals were very important to him. We spent at least a month on rehearsal. Toho is different from Toei in that we didn't regularly make samurai movies, and the actors therefore didn't have that much experience making *jidai-geki*. . . . Kurosawa's idea was to make everything more believable by having us become accustomed to our props and costumes. If we were in the samurai costumes long enough, we would begin to look and act like real samurai. In samurai movies, real swords are never used—Kurosawa's movies were the exception, so that even when we walked, the weight of the sword would be felt."[8]

During this time, Michio Yamamoto was newly hired at Toho as an assistant director. "The first job for an assistant director was like being a best boy [i.e., chief assistant to the head electrician], and there was a strict code of protocol. On *Throne of Blood* we'd scurry around the mountains with radios on our backs. I thought, Why did I ever bother to go to college? But in the middle of the production I was asked to prepare lunch for Kurosawa and had a chance to listen to him and came to learn about him as a human being. I came to know what film is. He was in his own world, [engrossed in the filmmaking process] rather than hard on his staff." Yamamoto was duly impressed during the filming of the climax, where Washizu is shot to death by arrows. "They were shooting real arrows at him. He'd run a few steps, and they'd shoot more arrows at him. Even with the armor he was wearing, it really stung. They'd fire off the arrows, which were hollowed out and ran along a piece of wire to ensure they hit their target, and it was my job to cut the wire as soon as the arrow was fired. I was scared during that. Right after we shot that scene, Mifune had a nightmare that he was being bombed."[9]

"Those were real arrows," Mifune said, "and that's real fear in my eyes! I'm not really acting at all. And until I stopped him, Kurosawa wanted to use a bunch of amateur archers . . . just extras . . . to shoot the arrows!"[10]

Throne of Blood does not attempt to re-create the poetry of Shakespeare; its best scenes are those that are vigorously cinematic in their execution and that expand the skeleton of *Macbeth*'s plot. There is a sequence of eerie foreshadowing in which Miki's horse, on the day its master is murdered, bucks and refuses to be saddled. After Miki's death, the riderless horse runs back to Miki's fort, heading straight for its stall. There is also an amusing tangential scene, yet another bit of Greek chorus, in which Washizu's servants (Ikio Sawamura, Sachio Sakai, Senkichi Omura, and Akira Tani) consider another bad omen: like a sinking ship, all the rats have fled Washizu's castle. But the best of these expanded sequences are the first scenes with Washizu and Miki as they try to find their way out of the Cobweb Forest. To Masaru Sato's underrated, atmospheric score, they charge their horses through the thick fog and dense foliage in a series of tightly cut telephoto shots, before arriving at the hut where the witch appears. The charging horses were shot on location, the hut scenes on a soundstage, but this is not immediately apparent due to Kurosawa's clever, seamless editing.

"My biggest memory of *Throne of Blood* is the never-ending horseback riding," said Chiaki. "It helped that Mr. Takashi Shimura, Mifune-kun, and I bought a horse and became crazy about riding when we made *Seven Samurai*. Horses are living animals and sometimes they don't obey like a car will. . . . [But] even though I enjoyed riding horses, on *Throne of Blood* Mifune-kun and I had to wear suits of armor, have flags put on our backs and swords at our sides. Wearing this heavy costume, we rode our horses through the forests in Nara." Shooting the racing horses with particularly long lenses proved problematic for cinematographer Asakazu Nakai. "The director of photography seemed to have trouble shooting us. He kept saying, 'You're not in the frame. No good. One more time!' I told him he must be hung over."

These early scenes end with Washizu and Miki on the plain a mile or so from the castle, where the fog is much thicker, and the action proved even harder to catch on film. "It was difficult for the horses to run in the sand in Gotemba," Chiaki said. "Besides, we waited until the fog came in to obstruct our view. In this deep and thick fog, we had the horses gallop. The director of photography couldn't see anything. We were dependent upon him yelling, 'Hey! We're here!' and we had to guess where they were. We rode our horses at top speed straight for the camera. . . . It wasn't easy to get the horses to run together. In the forest and in the fog, we rode our horses for much longer than they appear onscreen. These were strong animals, but by the time we were finished, they were exhausted."[11]

The scenes with the witch are vivid and otherworldly, aided by the manipulation of Naniwa's voice, which was given a strange, reedlike quality by Toho's sound department. Dressed in white with matching hair and facial makeup suggest a Noh mask, the *yaseonna* ("old woman"), Naniwa sits at a spinning wheel, the hut bathed in white light to suggest its unearthliness.

There are similarly haunting images throughout the film. Mifune's second visit to the witch doesn't measure up to the stark visuals of his first, but Kurosawa is innovative in having the witch take the form of phantom samurai, played by three great actors nearly unrecognizable in their heavy makeup: Nobuo Nakamura, Isao Kimura, and Seiji Miyaguchi. That Kurosawa would cast such eminent actors in this brief scene was audacious and set a precedent for future films. There is also an inspired sequence in which crows, fleeing the forest as it is cut down, chaotically fly inside the castle, yet another bad omen.

Mifune's Washizu is flawed only because he plays him—as directed by Kurosawa—at fever pitch from beginning to end. From the moment the character is introduced, he seems on the verge of coming unhinged, and to a certain degree this constant intensity loses its impact on the audience by the final reel. It is accentuated, too, by Mifune's makeup, which exaggerates his features and purposely suggests a Noh warrior mask (*heida*). As Donald Richie asserts, Kurosawa wanted to simplify the character and erase the ambiguities usually seen in other Macbeths. He is the paranoid product of his own hellish world, seeking power, in part, because of the protection he thinks it will afford him, rather than, as Richie suggests, as a means of self-realization. In the feudal world, as today, to show one's fears was to show one's weaknesses. Washizu, a respected warrior, cannot do this, and so the fear becomes buried in ambition and spurred by his *very* ambitious wife. She knows exactly what she wants from the start and has no hesitation in doing away with anyone who might stand in her way. Washizu, as Mifune plays him, and as is made clear in Kurosawa's script, would just as soon stay right where he is.

Mifune's wide-eyed, teeth-grinding, hyperventilating Washizu is contrasted with Isuzu Yamada's Lady Macbeth. In stark contrast to Mifune, Yamada is directed in one of the most formal manners imaginable. Her entire performance is, like that of the witch (with whom she is thematically linked), based on Noh: her makeup much more directly than Washizu's is aggressively reminiscent of a Noh mask (specifically, the *shakumi*); she walks about the rooms of the castle in a formal Noh heel-to-toe manner (complete with squeaking sounds as her feet glide across the polished wooden floors). Her mannerisms, even the way she is photographed while seated, borrow directly from the Noh.

Though not a Noh actress per se, Isuzu Yamada had extensive theater credits by the time she made her first film with Kurosawa. Along with Kyoko Kagawa, she was the greatest of his leading ladies. "I worked with [Yamada] in other films and on the stage. She was born to become an actress," said colleague Kyoko Kagawa. "As a human being, she was very humble and didn't insist on trying to make herself look good. She was extremely nice and took care of younger actresses."[12]

"Even though [Kurosawa] was known for his strict rehearsals," Yamada said, "he didn't do this for the scene where I was trying to wash the blood off my hands. He said, 'I don't know about women,' and was completely reliant on me. After I got home, I practiced with tapwater."[13]

Yamada had worked with Kurosawa before, when he was chief assistant director on *Chushingura, Part II* (1939). She was born on February 5, 1917, in Osaka, the daughter of actor Kazuo Yamada. She made her film debut at thirteen, and before she was twenty she had starred in several early Mizoguchi masterpieces, including *Osaka Elegy* (Naniwa erejii) and *Sisters of the Gion* (Gion no shimai), both 1936. By the end of the 1930s she had begun an association with actor Kazuo Hasegawa, and made a series of unambitious films with him at Toho during the war years. Nevertheless, it was through these films that she established herself as one of Japan's most popular and respected film actresses. She is best known in the West for her postwar films with Kurosawa, though she did excellent work for other major directors, appearing in Mikio Naruse's *Flowing* (Nagareru, 1956), Shiro Toyoda's *A Cat, Shozo, and Two Women* (Neko to Shozo to futari no onna, 1956), and Yasuki Chiba's *Downtown* (Shitamachi), the latter co-starring Mifune and made immediately after *The Lower Depths*.

In her forties, Yamada was becoming typecast in *jidai-geki* epics like Toho's *Daredevil in the Castle* (Osaka-jo monogatari) and Daiei's *Buddha* (Shaka), both 1961, and so she shifted her focus to the stage, rarely doing films after 1962. She continued to remain active in the theater well into her eighties.

Throne of Blood turned a modest profit but was not the blockbuster Toho had hoped for. Neither it nor Kurosawa's next film, *The Lower Depths*, made the year's list of top-grossing films, which was instead dominated by the very *jidai-geki* programmers to which *Throne of Blood* was a response. Critical reaction was mixed to positive. It tied for fourth place (with Yuzo Kawashima's *Saheiji Finds a Way*) on *Kinema Jumpo*'s "Best Ten" list, behind Tadashi Imai's *Rice* (Kome), *A Story of Pure Love* (Junai monogatari), and Keisuke Kinoshita's *Times of Joy and Sorrow* (a.k.a. *The Lighthouse*; Yorokobi mo kanashimi mo ikutoshitsuki).

Throne of Blood was well received in America when it opened in 1961. As usual, Bosley Crowther led the dissenters, saying it "hits the Occidental funny bone. . . . The action is grotesquely brutish and barbaric . . . with Toshiro Mifune as the warrior grunting and bellowing monstrously and making elaborately wild gestures to convey his passion and greed. . . . To our western eyes, it looks fantastic and funny . . . and the final scene, in which the hero is shot so full of arrows that he looks like a porcupine, is a pictorial extravagance that provides a conclusive howl."[14]

"From a purely cinematic standpoint," countered *Variety*'s "Tube," "[*Throne of Blood*] is noteworthy for the remarkable manner in which it explores and extends the possibilities of the medium as an instrument for exciting the nerves, the senses, and the emotions of the audience. It is all motion picture, an achievement of mood and photographic invention that deserves to be seen for academic purposes alone by every student of the cinema, from novice through professional."

"No doubt about it now," added *Time*, "Japan's Akira Kurosawa must be numbered with Sergei Eisenstein and D. W. Griffith among the supreme creators of cinema. . . . [*Throne of Blood*] is a nerve-shattering spectacle of physical and metaphysical violence, quite the most brilliant and original attempt ever made to put Shakespeare in pictures."[15]

Throne of Blood was immediately followed by another adaptation, Maxim Gorky's 1902 play *The Lower Depths* (Na dne). The screenplay was written by Kurosawa and Hideo Oguni and, unlike with *The Idiot*, transposing its characters to Edo-period Japan proved remarkably easy. "We were of one mind and didn't have to stop to say anything," Oguni recalled. "We decided to follow the original story and finished writing it in two weeks."[16]

Like the play, *The Lower Depths* is a nearly plotless examination of a group of destitute people sharing a slum dwelling. Like *Rashomon* before it, *The Lower Depths* is an examination of illusion and reality, a theme present in many of Kurosawa's films and one he would directly address again in the very similar *Dodes'ka-den*. Its characters include a thief (Toshiro Mifune) who sleeps with the landlord's wife, Osugi (Isuzu Yamada), but loves her younger sister, Okayo (Kyoko Kagawa); a cynical gambler (Koji Mitsui); an actor (Kamatari Fujiwara), whose career has been ruined by alcoholism; and a tinker (Eijiro Tono) who buries himself in his work, ignoring his dying wife (Eiko Miyoshi). Two tenants live in a world of fantasy to escape the hellish reality that surrounds them. One is a prostitute (Akemi Negishi) who dreams of a supposed lost love, while another (Minoru Chiaki) fancies himself a *ronin*, recalling with great nostalgia his alleged days as an important samurai.

This self-deception extends to the comparatively wealthy landlord (Ganjiro Nakamura), a hypocrite who regards his tenants as his children, even as he conspires to make them fall further and further into his debt.

The younger sister, Okayo, prefers not to trust anyone or anything, rather than face facts about the poverty that surrounds her. When the thief earnestly proposes to her, she instinctively distrusts him, and when he kills the landlord, she assumes the worst: that the thief and her sister have conspired against her.

Though, as in *Throne of Blood*, Mifune and Yamada receive top billing, *The Lower Depths* is a repertory piece. The film has no central character, but a good deal of the action does revolve around a wizened old pilgrim (Bokuzen Hidari) who lacks the bitterness or fatalism of the other tenants. He is the only character besides the gambler who can face the world as it actually is. Unlike the gambler, he has faith in the individual spirit. He is also a source of hope for the other characters: he tells the actor about a temple where his alcoholism might be cured, listens attentively to the prostitute's stories of her fantasy lover, provides comfort for the dying old woman in her last, miserable days, and encourages the thief and Okayo to run off and start a new life together. But once he moves on, the story's characters, like those in *Ikiru*, revert back to their old ways. The thief and the landlady are arrested for the landlord's murder; Okayo runs off, possibly driven to madness; the actor becomes despondent and commits suicide.

Interestingly, the performance singled out in Japanese reviews was that of Koji Mitsui, who won the Tokyo Blue Ribbon Prize for Best Supporting Actor. As Yoshisaburo, the cynical gambler, it is his oboe-like voice that leads the group in song at the end of the film, as the tenants briefly find a sense of camaraderie in their suffering. He is the only character in the story who holds no illusions of hope. Rather, he is amused by the fantasy worlds the others cling to. For this reason, ironically, he is also the most at peace. In a brilliant bit of cutting, at the height of the tenants' joyous singing—meticulously rehearsed, though it plays as if it were improvised—word comes that the actor is dead; the gambler petulantly comments while looking straight into the camera, "The idiot . . . just as the fun was beginning." There is an abrupt cut to black, accompanied by a single, piercing snap of a *hyoshige*, the wooden clapper used at the beginning and end of traditional Japanese stage performances, followed by a purposely brief *owari* (the Kanji character for "The End"). This sudden finale—all completed within a few seconds—is always shocking, always devastating when viewed. Mitsui's delivery of that final line is absolutely on target: ironic, cruel, funny, horrible.

"Koji Mitsui was fabulous," recalled co-star Kyoko Kagawa. "He was great at the very end, with his close-up—an outstanding performance. Another one of his films was *Christ in Bronze* [Seido no Christ, 1955], from Shochiku and directed by Mr. Minoru Shibuya. It was about anti-Christians and he played a menacing office worker and was terrific in that, too. He also played a reporter in *High and Low*. He was great in any role."[17]

Mitsui was born in 1910 and acted in films as early as 1933's *Dragnet Girl* (Hijosen no onna). He appeared in Ozu's *A Story of Floating Weeds* (Ukikusa monogatari) the following year, as well as in its remake, *Floating Weeds* (1959). He worked for a wide range of directors in such films as Masaki Kobayashi's *The Human Condition I* (Ningen no joken I–II, 1959), Hiroshi Teshigahara's *Woman in the Dunes* (Suna no onna, 1964), and Susumu Hani's *Inferno of First Love* (Hatsukoi jigokuhen, 1968). Mitsui died in 1979.

Mitsui was a Shochiku actor, on loan to Toho. Kurosawa liked him and borrowed his services for small but memorable roles in *The Hidden Fortress*, *High and Low*, *The Bad Sleep Well* (again playing a reporter), and *Red Beard*. His last role for the director was as the foodstand owner in *Dodes'ka-den*.

Kurosawa also borrowed Ganjiro Nakamura for the role of Isuzu Yamada's jealous husband. Nakamura's long film career began in 1941, with *The Life of an Actor* (Geido ichidai otoko), and he alternated his stage career with leading parts in movies. His prominence in films began in the late 1950s. Besides *The Lower Depths*, he did excellent work in several Ozu movies, including a starring turn in *Floating Weeds* and, that same year, in Kon Ichikawa's *Odd Obsession* (a.k.a. *The Key*; Kagi, 1959). Like Mitsui, Nakamura made films for a wide range of directors, including Mizoguchi, Masaki Kobayashi, Mikio Naruse, Shohei Imamura, and actress-director Kinuyo Tanaka. He died in 1983.

Mesmerizing, too, is Kamatari Fujiwara's alcoholic ex-actor, a role that, along with his parts in *The Hidden Fortress*, *Seven Samurai*, and *The Bad Sleep Well*, displays his wide range. For his character here he visited the alcoholic wards of Tokyo hospitals, and his performance is a flawless portrait of a man in the final stages of the disease. Fujiwara had false teeth and he removed them (leaving what seems like two teeth in his mouth) to increase the pathetic nature of the character. Bokuzen Hidari, Yohei in *Seven Samurai*, gives a likewise rich performance as the pilgrim. The part gave him more dialogue than all his other films for Kurosawa combined, and he's never less than enchanting. "*The Lower Depths* was perfectly suited to him," said an amused Kyoko Kagawa, "and it was hard to tell sometimes where the character ended, and where the real man began."[18]

In addition, there were fine background performances from twenty-six-year-old Yu Fujiki as the unhinged Unokichi, Haruo Tanaka as Tatsu, and real-life sumo wrestler Fujitayama as the potbellied Tsugaru. Their characters are minor, but Kurosawa and his actors make them memorable.

Yu Fujiki, a relative unknown, was positively star-struck. "It was pretty difficult," he said. "When I was working with Mr. Kurosawa, he was always with Toshiro Mifune. You see, he would voice his ideas about the film through Mifune. Kurosawa only had to give Mifune a smile—they understood each other completely; Mr. Kurosawa's heart was in Mr. Mifune's body. Mr. Kurosawa was pretty hard on the other actors, though! [laughs]. There were tons of great stars in the film—Mifune, Ganjiro Nakamura, Kyoko Kagawa, Isuzu Yamada—and I was so awestruck by everyone. I was just a kid! Kurosawa would say, 'Hey, Fujiki! Quit acting so shy, get out of here! You don't have to rehearse today!' That drove me crazy, because I wanted to rehearse, but that was the way Kurosawa readied me for my role."[19]

Tatsu was Haruo Tanaka's biggest part in a Kurosawa film, and assistant cameraman Takao Saito remembered the actor's difficulty learning his dialogue for the final scene. "He had so many lines he wrote his dialogue on the back of the dried squid [used in the scene]. When Kurosawa caught on he said, 'No wonder he keeps looking at the squid! What a brilliant idea! He's good at cheating, but this isn't going to work.' So he took the squid away from him. . . . I never see actors like Tanaka anymore."[20]

As for Mifune, that he is excellent in a film brimming with exquisite performances is a testament to his abilities. The character suits both his skills as an actor and his screen persona. Sutekichi may be down on his luck, but he has great charisma and charm; he is cynical, driven, and passionate. So good is Mifune that Donald Richie argues that his performance is "not only Mifune's finest single role but also one of the great pieces of acting in Japanese cinema. . . . His mimicry is flawless: every one of the recognized details of the *yakuza* is there; the mock-toughness, the little-boy angularity of gesture, the abrupt shift of his kimono skirt, the calculated vulgarity of his squat, the sudden warmth of his smile—the nastiness, the sexiness, the innocence, the danger. All of this is continually before us; yet, as in any great performance, it is varied by the person with whom he is acting. Here Mifune's timing seems almost miraculous."[21]

The Lower Depths marked the Kurosawa debut of the actress most identified with his canon: Kyoko Kagawa. Born on December 5, 1931, in Ibaragi, Kagawa won a "New Face Nomination" contest sponsored by the *Tokyo Shimbun* and joined Shintoho Studios at seventeen. She made her screen debut in *Jump Out of the Window* (Mado kara tobidase) in 1950. During the seven short years between her debut and *The Lower Depths*, Kagawa had already emerged as one of Japan's leading film actresses. She had major roles in Ozu's *Tokyo Story* (Tokyo monogatari, 1953), Mizoguchi's *Sansho the*

Bailiff (1952), and Mikio Naruse's *Mother* (Haha, 1952), giving accomplished performances in all of them before she was twenty-two years old. She proved equally adept at both period and modern films, a rare feat for Japanese actresses, who are usually typed in one or the other. Between more prestigious assignments she contributed her considerable skill to a wide range of genre films, often light comedies or melodramas, including *Who Knows a Woman's Heart* (Onnagogoro dare ka shiru, 1951), her first of thirteen films with Mifune. Outside of their work with Kurosawa, they were usually paired in Hiroshi Inagaki *jidai-geki* like *Secret Scrolls* (Yagyu Bugeicho, 1957–58) or the subsequent *The Three Treasures* (Nippon tanjo, 1959). She appeared, always memorably, in four more Kurosawa films, including his last, *Madadayo* (1993), as well as Mifune's final film, *Deep River* (Fukai kawa, 1995).

"*The Lower Depths* was my first film with Mr. Kurosawa," Kagawa said. "He was very tall, slim, and he had a wonderful smile. Of course, he looked intimidating during the shooting, but once he said okay, his smile became very warm, very refreshing.

"He was a director who took time for rehearsals. Before shooting, we all got together and read the script, and rehearsed in our costumes, despite the fact that they were so dirty because of the slum life of the people. . . . We took our time." She likened her maiden work for Kurosawa to that of an earlier master: "The most difficult film for me to make, and the one where I got the most training, was *Crucified Lovers* [Chikamatsu monogatari, 1954] by Kenji Mizoguchi. He never told me how to play the role. His approach to acting was, if you become the character itself, you can act quite naturally. I think Mr. Kurosawa's way was similar. He told me, 'I wish I could direct actors like Mizoguchi.' It's not that Mr. Kurosawa didn't talk to us—he did, and not just to me but to the other actors as well. But I would just act according to my own instincts, and if he said okay, then it was okay."[22]

Rehearsals for *The Lower Depths* began in May 1957, four months after the release of *Throne of Blood*. Kurosawa invited famed comic storyteller Shinsho Kokintei to the studio so his cast could better understand the anecdotal lives of the characters living in the slum. Kokintei regaled Kurosawa's actors with old stories from the same period as the picture's setting that expressed the mood the director was trying to achieve.[23]

The slum itself was a "long house" (a specific type of tenement endemic to Japan at this time) composed of two impressively designed sets built on the Toho lot and virtually a character in and of itself. One set was an interior built on a soundstage that could accommodate Kurosawa's multiple-camera technique, especially important here because so much of the film hinged on the performances. A masterpiece of contrived dilapidation, the entire set leans at a 75-degree angle, as if it might collapse at any moment. So effective is its design that many Western critics accused the production of being threadbare, when in fact building the set in the right way was quite expensive. (During certain moments in the picture, hidden cameras actually face one another, and the set had to be engineered to allow for filming in a seamless fashion. That you never notice this speaks to the intimacy and attention to detail brought to the production by art director Yoshiro Muraki.) The other set, an exterior, had a similarly unique design. It and the landlord's house were surrounded on all sides by stone and tile walls, as if in a bowl. The exterior set is used to especially good effect in the film's opening shots: under the titles the camera, at a low angle, pans nearly 360 degrees around the prisonlike walls (which the film's characters never go beyond), concluding with a shot of two peasants high above dumping dead leaves into the pit.

In sum, Muraki's art direction, Kurosawa and Oguni's screenplay, the unilaterally vivid performances, and Kurosawa's direction merge into a faithfully and effectively adapted work that has little in the way of cinematic flourishes and instead, by its own design, is more like a record of the performance of a play. With his multiple-camera technique, Kurosawa does much more subtly and effectively what was later attempted in films like the Richard Burton *Hamlet* (1964), which used a videotape-to-film technology called Electronovision to record what was an actual theatrical performance.

Mainly, though, the picture is a superb character study, dependent on the acting. In many ways, the film was really an experiment for Kurosawa, who wanted to see how far he could go with his rehearsal methods and his use of multiple cameras, while also attempting to combine the theatricality of the film's dialogue and performances against the uncompromised realism of its set and costume design. The experiment is an unqualified success. The characters, even the minor ones, are richly adapted from the original material, and though almost the entire film takes place in a single room, the scenes are at all times artfully blocked. While there is no flashy camerawork per se, Kurosawa achieves a remarkable range of dolly shots within the slum, and his choice of angles is often uniquely arresting. During the dialogue between the pilgrim and the dying woman, the latter is almost never seen—the camera stays in medium shot on the pilgrim—emphasizing Hidari's dialogue and performance while increasing the horror of what the unseen woman must look like in her final hours.

Despite what might seem like the unrelieved despair of its characters, the film still has moments, however fleeting, of affirmation, and Kurosawa would argue that *"The Lower Depths* isn't all gloomy. It is very funny and I remember laughing over it. That is because we are shown people who really want to live and we are shown them—I think—humorously. People are just supposed to relax and enjoy this picture as they would any programmer."[24]

Filming began on June 24. The rehearsals with both the actors and Kurosawa's cameras paid off, and the entire picture, shot mostly in sequence, was completed in just four weeks. *The Lower Depths* was test-screened on September 1, 1957, and opened on a roadshow basis sixteen days later, before going into wide release at the end of the month. Like those of *Throne of Blood*, reviews for *The Lower Depths* were mixed, though the film did earn numerous awards. It ranked tenth on *Kinema Jumpo*'s "Best Ten" list, and Isuzu Yamada was awarded Best Actress for the combination of her work here, in *Throne of Blood*, and in Yasuki Chiba's *Downtown*, all of which co-starred Mifune.

As *The Lower Depths* went into wide release in Japan, Kurosawa traveled to Europe for the very first time. He went to London during the last two weeks of October 1957 for the opening of the National Film Theatre, where *Throne of Blood* was met with great enthusiasm. There he had the opportunity to meet with director John Ford, who was in England making the ill-fated *Gideon of Scotland Yard* (1958). "You really love rain," Ford told him. "You really have seen my films," replied Kurosawa. Upon his return from England, Kurosawa began, much like Ford, to wear sunglasses and a wool cap on the set (he did not, however, stuff his mouth with handkerchiefs), such was his admiration of him. The influence of John Ford on Kurosawa's life—if indirectly on his films—was immense. Japanese books on Kurosawa, many of which include detailed chronologies that slavishly note the birth and death dates and chronologies of his life, always note his two encounters with Ford and, alone among Westerners, the date of August 31, 1973: the day John Ford died.

The Lower Depths was released in America in 1962, where it received mostly favorable reviews. "That Akira Kurosawa is one of the world's greatest cinema directors is evident in 'The Lower Depths,' " said the *Los Angeles*

Times. "This famous play of Maxim Gorky has now been proven to be universal in its application. Misery disturbs all souls in the same way. . . . One cannot overrate this production. . . . Toshiro Mifune, as the thief, and Isuzu Yamada, as the landlord's wife, are magnificent, as one would expect after having seen them in 'Throne of Blood.' Another outstanding performance is that of Bokuzen Hidari, as the pilgrim. In his small, superannuated frame he carries tremendous dignity."[25]

"Director Akira Kurosawa has kept virtually intact Maxim Gorky's Russian drama," said *Show Business Illustrated.* "But *The Lower Depths* also succeeds as an emotional experience with its vulture-eye view of the misery of down-and-outs in a squalid room—fighting, drinking, dying and, most of all, dreaming of escape. As the purely intellectual pleasure of watching Kurosawa's camera skill begins to wane, the Oriental hellhole ignites and the film takes off on a cinematic tour de force that builds to a near-orgiastic climax in its simultaneous pathos and exhilaration."[26]

Flavia Wharton wrote a bizarre review for *Films and Filming:* "Akira Kurosawa . . . succeeds less and less in his attempts to translate classics of Western literature into Japanese films. His translation of Dostoevsky's *Crime and Punishment* [actually, *The Idiot*] seemed, in my Western eyes, an interesting attempt. His filming of *Macbeth* (*Throne of Blood*) was for me indistinguishable from a routine Samurai picture; and *The Lower Depths* is even more of a bore than was Renoir's inept filming of Gorky's book 25 years ago. *The Lower Depths* was produced by the Toho Co. on the cheap. I don't think there are more than half a dozen camera set-ups, and the sets are among the most inexpensive in movie history. . . . Some of the hopeless inertia and instinctual folly of Gorky's characters comes over, but it does so in inexcusably static cinema."[27]

Wharton's review notwithstanding, *The Lower Depths* was a captivating departure from the starkly cinematic visions of *Throne of Blood*, and remains one of Kurosawa's most intriguing and underrated films. It is to his credit that one remembers most its talented ensemble cast, including Mifune, who gives one of the best performances of his career.

Sandwiched between *Throne of Blood* and *The Lower Depths*, Toho rushed their number one star through three more conventional releases and another multipart Inagaki *jidai-geki.* The first was Senkichi Taniguchi's *A Man in the Storm* (*Arashi no naka no otoko*), an uninspired knockoff of *Sanshiro Sugata,* with Mifune a Meiji Era judo expert at odds with judo master Akio

Kobori and karate veteran Jun Tazaki. Kyoko Kagawa played Mifune's love interest in this action-filled but ultimately empty film. Toho dubbed it into English, but couldn't find a distributor who wanted it. In 1969, they released it themselves in America, where it received scant, mixed reviews.

Be Happy, These Two Lovers (Kono futarini sachi are) was directed by Ishiro Honda and written by Zenzo Matsuyama. Mifune had a supporting role in the film opposite Keiko Tsushima, *Seven Samurai*'s ingenue. But they were not the two lovers of the title—Hiroshi Koizumi and Yumi Shirakawa were—and Mifune's role appears to have been an undemanding guest appearance.

He had an even smaller role in *A Dangerous Hero* (Kiken na eiyu), which starred novelist Shintaro Ishihara (brother of Nikkatsu actor-singer Yujiro Ishihara). Ishihara's novel *Season of the Sun* (Taiyo no kisetsu) was the hottest book in Japan in the mid-1950s, launching a wave of youth-rebellion films (called *Taiyozoku*, or "Sun Tribe" films, after the novel), much as James Dean and *Rebel Without a Cause* had done in America at this same time. Ishihara's novel was given the prestigious Akutagawa Award, and Toho signed him to a long-term contract that ultimately included his writing, directing, and in some cases starring in pictures the studio hoped would capture the youth audience. However, Ishihara was just a hired hand on *A Dangerous Hero*: it was written by Eizo Sugawa and directed by Hideo Suzuki, neither great auteurs, and Mifune's guest appearance was brief.

Toho tried to duplicate the success they had enjoyed with *Samurai* (*The Legend of Musashi*) with another Inagaki-Mifune *jidai-geki*. *Secret Scrolls* was a two-part film about the Tokugawa-era Yagyu clan and based on Kosuke Gomi's *Yagyu bugeicho*, published in serial form during 1956–59. The story revolves around three scrolls which, if put together, would spell ruin for the Yagyu clan and bring about an end of relative peace in the country. One of the scrolls is stolen by the sinister Princess Yu (Yoshiko Kuga). A magician-samurai from a rival clan, Tasaburo (Mifune), is dispatched along with his brother (Koji Tsuruta) to retrieve it.

Mifune appeared in the sequel, *Secret Scrolls (Part II)* (Yagyu Bugeicho—Ninjitsu, 1958), also known abroad as *Ninjitsu*, after completing *The Lower Depths*. Like *Samurai III*, Mifune played second fiddle to Koji Tsuruta in the sequel, which continues the search for the missing scrolls and concludes with them safely back in the hands of the Yagyu clan. Despite Inagaki's usual craftsmanship and an excellent cast in both films (including Kyoko Kagawa, Mariko Okada, Denjiro Okochi, and Nobuko Otowa), the two pictures, like the second and third *Samurai* films, failed to find an outside distributor.

Both were eventually distributed by Toho themselves in the late 1960s. They were released to little fanfare and, though technically they are on a par with the *Samurai* films, enjoy none of that trilogy's popularity in the West. They have never been released to home video.

Prior to shooting his scenes for *Secret Scrolls (Part II)*, Mifune starred opposite Isuzu Yamada once again for Yasuki Chiba's short (57 minutes) *Downtown* (Shitamachi), based on a story by Fumiko Hayashi. Set immediately after the war, the plot concerns a lonely widow (Isuzu Yamada) and her young son, who take up with a struggling laborer (Mifune). Together they regain a measure of the happiness and optimism lost during the war, until the laborer dies suddenly in an accident. This simple but moving film was little shown outside Japan, but as stated in the program notes for a rare New York screening in 1984, it "beautifully captures the feeling of postwar Japanese life, as lived by common people attempting to build new lives for themselves. In Mifune's performance there is none of the ferocity or bravado so often associated with his roles in other films. Here he is seen as a simple, rather ordinary fellow, a character he played often in the 1950s films that are rarely seen outside Japan."[28]

Anderson and Richie agreed, calling it "an excellent adaptation. . . . The feeling of the period just after the war was beautifully captured and . . . the impermanence of love and the tragedy of being a woman [in early postwar Japan] were emphasized."[29]

Mifune also made cameo appearances in three 1958 releases. The first was in Kajiro Yamamoto's *Holiday in Tokyo* (Tokyo no kyujitsu), released in mid-April 1958, a film designed mainly to show off Toho's vast resources, as well as its still-novel use of color (which had come into vogue just a few years earlier) and Toho Scope photography. The picture marked Shirley Yamaguchi's return to the studio; the actress was cast as May Kawaguchi, a famous fashion designer living in New York. As the picture opens, she returns to Tokyo with a group of ordinary tourists, hoping to remain anonymous. However, she is instantly recognized by reporters and, à la *Scandal*, soon finds herself on the front pages of newspapers across Japan. Eventually, she's coaxed into holding an elaborate fashion show.

In reality, the film was mostly a low-rent Cinerama travelogue, showing off Tokyo as a neon-lit metropolis fully recovered from the ravages of the Second World War, with Toho's stable of stars doing their thing in up-to-the-minute fashions for the Toho Scope lens. Mifune joined popular stars Izumi Yukimura, Ryo Ikebe, Keiju Kobayashi, and Hisaya Morishige in cameo parts; his role demanded no more than a day or two. And in spite of all the hoopla, the film would be Yamaguchi's last before her retirement.

A gag cameo followed in Yasuki Chiba's *The Happy Pilgrimage* (Yajikita dochu sugoroku, 1958), also known as *Yaji and Kita on the Road*, a comedy based on the popular classic *Dochu Hizakurige*, a story that falls somewhere between Chaucer's *Canterbury Tales* and Laurel and Hardy's *Sons of the Desert*. Toho had already made a series of pictures in the mid-1950s, based on the story, that starred Itoshi Yumeji and Koichi Kimi, a *manzai* comedy team (i.e., lowbrow humor dependent on fast-paced dialogue and physical humor; a Western equivalent would be Abbott and Costello), but the technical marvels of color and Toho Scope seemed to cry out for a newer, bigger adaptation.

In this version, Yaji (Daisuke Kato) and Kita (Keiju Kobayashi) decide to get away from their wives and make the pilgrimage from late-eighteenth century Edo to the Great Shrine at Ise. Along the way they have a series of comic adventures. At a bathhouse they find a woman's kimono, which turns out to belong to a female impersonator. A winking woman they think is flirting with them turns out to merely have a nervous tic. They finally bed down with another woman, who is revealed as a thief and steals their belongings. Mifune and Ryo Ikebe appear briefly as men mistaken for the two leads.

Later that year Mifune made a brief guest appearance in Toshio Sugie's *Theater of Life* (Jinsei gekijo—seishun hen), which was a remake of a popular Tomu Uchida film of the same name. Based on a story by Shiro Ozaki, the film concerns a young man (played by a not very young Ryo Ikebe) sent off to college, only to be disillusioned by life's inequities. The remake was a flop, and Mifune's part small, but he would return to the material years later, in Kinji Fukasaku's 1983 film based on the same story; again Mifune's role was minor.

In the midst of all these cameos, Mifune starred in *The Rickshaw Man* (Muhomatsu no issho, 1958), first released in the United States under Toho's international title, *Muhomatsu, the Rikishaw Man* [sic]. It was one of his most famous roles, though the film is not one of his best. The film's Gold Lion award at the nineteenth International Venice Film Festival that September seemed to confirm that European critics had no more understanding of Japanese cinema than those in America.

Like Inagaki's films of Musashi Miyamoto and Kojiro Sasaki, *The Rickshaw Man* was a color remake of an earlier work, this time a 1943 film of the same name made for Daiei, with Tsumasaburo Bando as the title character. Seven years later, in 1965, Daiei produced another version, directed by Kenji Misumi and co-starring Ineko Arima, Mifune's leading lady in *Love in a Teacup*. It starred Shintaro Katsu, an actor who, with his tendency to play lovable if brutish ruffians, was seemingly born to play Matsu.

Set at the turn of the century, Matsu (Mifune) is a rickshaw driver, illiterate and working-class. His gestures are apish; he has a deep tan owing to his profession, thick eyebrows, and, because of his social stature, the kind of built-in, instinctive bowing motion one still finds in Japan's lower classes. (These physical characteristics indicated a life marked by hard, physical labor and not one of leisure. Pale skin, by contrast, was a sign of a life of prosperity and, thus, upper-class status.) He is known as "Wild Matsu" or "Matsu the Untamed." An intensely physical man, Matsu is something of a local character, a beloved rogue, and this is demonstrated in the very first scene. At the time, rickshaw men were traditionally given free tickets to theatrical performances (though no one seems to remember why), but as the film opens, Matsu is denied a pass. He somehow comes up with two first-class seats, and with another rickshaw driver creates pandemonium in the theater by cooking a smelly, smoky mix of garlic and leeks at the grill in his theater box (a standard fixture in theaters at the time). The neighborhood's wise elder (Chishu Ryu) acts as an intermediary in the dispute between Matsu and the theater men. The boss is impressed by Matsu's straightforward apology. Matsu may be a ruffian, but he's also extraordinary in his genuineness.

While working, Matsu comes across a young boy, Toshio (Kaoru Matsumoto), who has hurt himself trying to climb a tree. Matsu takes the boy home. His parents, Kotaro Yoshioka (Hiroshi Akutagawa), an officer in the military, and his wife, Yoshiko (Hideko Takamine), try to give Matsu some money for his trouble, but he refuses. The family end up hiring the rickshaw man to shuttle Toshio back and forth to the doctor. Matsu becomes something of a friend of the family, but he remains all too aware of their different status, never feeling quite at home when he's with them. Then suddenly Kotaro falls ill and, virtually overnight, is dead.

Yoshiko, now a widow, is concerned that Toshio, already "physically and psychologically weak," is in real trouble with no father around. She asks Matsu to act as a surrogate father to the boy, and over the years Matsu becomes the family patriarch in all but name. He comes to regard Toshio as his own child and falls deeply in love with Yoshiko, all the while knowing he can never really be part of the family.

This becomes apparent as Toshio, now a young man (played by Kenji Kasahara), goes off to college. Finding new friends, he is embarrassed in Matsu's company. Matsu's heart is broken when Yoshiko tells him that Toshio no longer wants him to address him as *Bon-bon* (the equivalent of "Sonny"). Matsu asks Yoshiko what he's supposed to call him, and she tellingly suggests "Toshio-san" (Mr. Toshio). Yoshiko never remarries, having devoted herself to raising the boy, and although she's alone herself and quite lonely, she never considers marrying Matsu.

Once again, Mifune plays a contradictory character, one who is wild but tender, uneducated but wise, poor but rich. Part of the film's appeal hinges on wild Matsu's broad manner, and Mifune plays him exactly so and with great humor in these scenes. There is, for example, a foot race in which Matsu joins in, waving at the crowds as he rounds the track, that illustrates his popular appeal as well as the growing admiration developing within young Toshio. There is also a scene in the center of town where an older Matsu takes over a large *gion* drum; his spirited performance brightens up hundreds of spectators who had assumed there was no one left alive who could play it in the traditional manner.

But Matsu's relationship with the widow and her son is an almost total dramatic failure. Matsu is something of a Japanese Falstaff, with Toshio his Prince Hal. But Falstaff never sees Hal's inevitable rejection coming. He lives only for the moment, deceiving himself into believing it can last forever. Matsu, however, knows from the very beginning that he will never really become part of the family he so dearly loves. Mifune reacts to every kindness with embarrassment, looking at the floor, shifting his body nervously. The problem is that Matsu's emotions are always internalized, always repressed. He never discusses his feelings with anyone, and Yoshiko, unbelievably, never seems aware of them. When Matsu, after his exhilarating performance on the *gion* drum, works up the courage to tell Yoshiko his true feelings, he pulls back at the last minute, disgusted with himself, and runs out the door. Only then does Yoshiko become at least somewhat aware of what the last ten years have meant to him, but she does nothing and they never see each other again. Yoshiko never reflects on her relationship; Toshio isn't around to reflect on his. Matsu becomes a drunk like his father (Yoshio Kosugi) and simply wanders off into the snow and dies. When he dies, essentially of a broken heart, Yoshiko weeps and everyone mourns the poor old rickshaw man. But there's no drama.

Like the Musashi Miyamoto films, *The Rickshaw Man* is a handsomely mounted, colorful picture with elaborate sets and hundreds of costumed extras, effectively evocative of the period. Kazuo Yamada's photography is quite lovely at times, particularly the location work in the snowy countryside where Matsu finally dies. But Inagaki's old-fashioned, straightforward approach is often ungainly. He uses, rather obviously, the wheels of the rickshaw to show the passage of time, and in a hopelessly clichéd device, even for a film made in 1958, the wheels stop when Matsu dies. These shots are photographed against a myriad of bright backgrounds, and the novelties of shooting in color and wide-screen get in the way of the drama. As Matsu stumbles about in the knee-high snow, Inagaki and Yamada use a strange sequence to take us into his psyche. Inagaki cuts away from Matsu to a flashback of balloons, confetti, and streamers, with portraitlike shots of Yoshiko, all jarringly edited back and forth between positive and negative printing. Rather than take us inside Matsu's deepest emotions, it plays like a demonstration film from AgfaColor's advertising department.

And despite the accolades he received, Mifune wasn't pleased about the film. "I was not very happy with it, but I was under contract and had to fulfill certain obligations. I do not like remakes, because the audience that saw the original version also sees the second. It usually suffers by comparison . . . if only because the time-lapse makes everything seem better."[30]

FIFTEEN

100 PERCENT ENTERTAINMENT

After the bleakness of *Throne of Blood* and *The Lower Depths* Kurosawa said, "No heavy themes [on the next film]. I want to make a 100% entertainment film, full of thrills and fun."[1] And so he did. *The Hidden Fortress* (Kakushi toride no san-akunin, or "Three Bad Men in a Hidden Fortress") remains Kurosawa's lightest film, a rousing, often hilarious comedy adventure bordering on fantasy that subverts the genre it simultaneously embraces. The basis for the story, written during the production of *The Lower Depths*, came from Ryuzo Kikushima. Kikushima grew up in Yamanishi Prefecture, the site of an actual hidden fortress, and Kurosawa built his script around it. "Kikushima told us that Shingen Takeda made a hidden fortress in Koshu which still exists," recounted co-writer Hideo Oguni. "That's how we started the story. It was a Western-like movie."[2]

The film also had roots, albeit vaguely, in two earlier works. *The Hidden Fortress* shares story elements with *The Men Who Tread on the Tiger's Tail*, and its premise is not unlike that of a script Kurosawa wrote in 1942, just prior to *Sanshiro Sugata*, called *Three Hundred Miles Through Enemy Lines* (Tekichu odan sanbyaku ri). After years on the shelf, Daiei had finally made a so-so film of *Three Hundred Miles*, directed by Kazuo Mori and called *Advance Patrol* (Nichi-Ro senso shori no hishi—Tekichu odan sanbyaku ri), which was released late in 1957.* But Kurosawa wasn't especially happy with *Advance*

---

*Hideo Oguni is credited as co-writer, though it is unclear whether his contributions were made after Daiei greenlighted the film or years earlier, when the film was in development. Also, it should be noted that director Mori's first name is often mistranslated as Issei.

Patrol or the wartime censorship and budgetary restrictions on *Tiger's Tail* (which he had considered remaking in close collaboration with composer Fumio Hayasaka) and was now thinking that elements from both films might be incorporated into an original, escapist *jidai-geki*.

The resulting film is set in the sixteenth century. A princess (Misa Ue-hara) and her retainers are on the run from forces that would overthrow her. The only way she and her clan can survive is to cross a heavily guarded border into safety. The general guarding her (Mifune) comes up with an ingenious plan. With the help of two greedy country bumpkins (Minoru Chiaki and Kamatari Fujiwara), oblivious to the general's and princess's identities, they pretend to be firewood dealers, hiding the clan's gold in hollow sticks of firewood. They are eventually captured, but a sympathetic warrior (Susumu Fujita) employed by the enemy suddenly frees them, joining them as they escape across the border.

According to Kurosawa, the manner in which the script was written deviated from his usual methods: "Every morning I created a situation which allowed no escape for the general and the princess. Then the other three writers [Kikushima, Oguni, and Shinobu Hashimoto] made desperate efforts finding a way out. This is how we wrote day by day. I wanted to make an invigorating historical spectacle."[3] And indeed it is. The film boasts huge, elaborate sets, a stirring score, thrilling vignettes, and charming performances, all beautifully photographed in Toho's still-new anamorphic wide-screen process, Toho Scope.

From a production standpoint, it took the wide-screen revolution five years to travel from Hollywood to Japan. In an effort to bring back postwar audiences, who had stopped going to the cinema in favor of spectator and participatory sports, or simply stayed at home with their families to watch free television, Hollywood had turned to new technologies. Studio knowhow would give them something they couldn't get on their tiny black-and-white television sets, namely movies in "glorious Technicolor, breathtaking CinemaScope, and stereophonic sound," as the Cole Porter song goes. Wide-screen processes like Cinerama and CinemaScope seemed like the answer. They offered high-fidelity, magnetic stereo sound, and screen shapes twice as wide as the old standard-size ratio of pre-1953 films. *This Is Cinerama* (1952) and *The Robe* (1953) were worldwide box-office hits, and by early 1954 theaters in Japan exhibiting foreign films were being converted to CinemaScope. Toho itself converted two theaters, the Teiko-ken in Tokyo and the OS Theater in Osaka, to show the technically complex Cinerama.

Commercial television in Japan was several years behind America, and movie attendance was actually on the rise. But during the production of *The Hidden Fortress*, the number of TV sets in Japan cracked the one million mark, or about 8 percent of Japanese homes, nearly double that of the previous year. In addition, Japanese studios had to contend with the growing influence and popularity of foreign films.

Shintoho, meanwhile, had its worst year ever in 1955, losing money on every picture it made, mostly due to limited distribution opportunities. Up to this point they had been competing with Toho for the urban, white-collar audience. During that year, desperate to turn the tide, they hired theater owner Mitsugu Okura to run the studio. He immediately transformed Shintoho, changing its target audience to children and uneducated laborers with a policy of violent *chambara*, "nudie" films, ghost stories, and serial-like fantasies.

In 1957 Okura sunk $560,000—Shintoho's entire capital—into what Anderson and Richie called his "suicide charge": a wide-screen war epic called *The Emperor Meiji and the Great Russo-Japanese War* (Meiji tenno to Nichi-Ro daisenso). With the use of anamorphic lenses acquired in France, the film's image was too wide to be projected in Okura's movie houses and had to be exhibited in theaters showing Hollywood films and thus converted for CinemaScope. The film was a huge success, taking in $1.3 million.[4] It was the highest-grossing film of 1957, making more than twice that of Toho's biggest earner, *On Wings of Love* (Oatari sanshoku musume), a musical starring the singing trio of Hibari Misora, Chiemi Eri, and Izumi Yukimura, and Toho's first wide-screen feature, and far more lucrative than either of Kurosawa's two 1957 releases.

Toei and Shochiku immediately jumped onto the wide-screen band-wagon, converting to what they called Toeiscope and Shochiku Grand-Scope, both virtually identical to CinemaScope. Like their Hollywood counterparts, these early films filled the screen with grainy color, travelogue-like vistas, and all-star casts. Toho, which had been developing its own anamorphic system since the release of *The Robe*, was initially more cautious. *On Wings of Love* was released in July, but of Toho's remaining forty-one releases that year, only eight were in Toho Scope.* That August, the studio also began releasing many of their films in Perspecta Stereo-

---

*All these wide-screen formats used essentially the same technology as CinemaScope, and all rendered a screen image that was 2.35 times as wide as it was tall. Anamorphic Panavision is a refinement of CinemaScope and is still used in Hollywood today.

phonic Sound, a three-channel directional system that was an inexpensive alternative to the four-channel magnetic stereo employed on most CinemaScope films. The system was already widely used in Hollywood by MGM and Paramount. While Perspecta was phased out by 1960 in America, Toho continued using it as late as 1965. Beginning with *The Hidden Fortress*, nearly all Kurosawa's films through *Red Beard* were released in stereo, though in the United States, both in theaters and on home video, these films have, until recently, been released with monaural sound.

By 1958 Japan had embraced anamorphic wide-screen far more completely than Hollywood ever did, shooting virtually everything, including newsreels, in some form of anamorphic wide-screen. In the second half of 1958, Toho shot 84 percent of its films in scope; by 1959 it had risen to 96 percent.

Joseph Anderson and Donald Richie argue in *The Japanese Film—Art and Industry* that wide-screen "was particularly troublesome to Japanese filmmakers because the proportions did not lend themselves well to Japanese sets. The rooms of Japanese houses are small and hence difficult to photograph, the wide angles always wanting to take in more than is actually there."[5] While this was certainly true of Yasujiro Ozu's films, for he alone among filmmakers of his generation continued shooting "flat," filmmakers in Japan otherwise embraced anamorphic wide-screen like those in no other country in the world.

The older generation of Hollywood directors generally disliked anamorphic wide-screen, and most 'scope films from Hollywood in the 1950s showed little imagination with the format imposed upon them. In Japan, however, directors and cinematographers quickly learned to take full advantage of 'scope and used it to bring arresting, energetic compositions to crime films and musicals. *Jidai-geki* and *chambara* took advantage of the majesty CinemaScope allowed while simultaneously opening up the choreography of swordfighting sequences. Filmmakers like Mikio Naruse and Masaki Kobayashi began using the extreme width of anamorphic wide-screen in their blocking of actors, creating thematic compositions that would have been difficult if not impossible to replicate on the standard screen. The result was that wide-screen films in Japan became uniformally striking, far more so than in America—in Japan, even low-budget program pictures, the schlockiest of schlock, had impressive wide-screen photography.

Kurosawa was eager to direct in this new format. As good as his compositions and blocking are in his standard-screen films, his 'scope films have an electric visual energy that exceeds his earlier work. His inclination for long takes blossomed with his use of Toho Scope. And far more than in his standard-screen films Kurosawa uses diagonal lines in blocking and in his sets, and multiple planes of action through deep-focus photography, all of which became even more pronounced in this format. He was able to balance characters (or, by design, throw characters off balance), visualize their isolation, and create claustrophobic environments in ways that were simply unattainable with the standard screen shape. Examples of this can be seen in *The Hidden Fortress*'s opening shots. As the two peasants are introduced, they are shocked as a bloody samurai (Takeshi Kato) steps backward into the frame and is slaughtered by soldiers on horseback, right in front of them. When the peasants are captured and made slaves at the ruins of a castle, Kurosawa and cinematographer Kazuo Yamasaki shoot the slaves' revolt with all the richness and vitality of David Lean's best work. In comparison, Kurosawa's last six features were all shot in cropped wide-screen, a non-anamorphic process, known in Japan as "VistaVision size," with aspect ratios that are much less wide. Though all these last films are artfully photographed, *Kagemusha* and *Ran* in particular lack the kinetics Kurosawa brought to his 'scope films of the 1950s and '60s.

In 1958 Kurosawa was delighted with the new technology. "I have been feeling that the standard screen is a little too narrow from the viewpoint of composition, to my way of filming," he said. "I find wide screen rather easier for me, so there will be no difficulty as far as I am concerned, I hope."[6] But he still resisted shooting in color. "I am not yet contented with the color of Japanese pictures," he said. "Color pictures are apt to have a shallower focal-length so they do not suit my style of direction. Also, color film is too expensive to use when you're shooting a lot of film."[7]

One of Kurosawa's first priorities on *The Hidden Fortress* was the casting of the princess. Despite Toho's bloated roster of pretty young talent, he insisted, "She should not be an experienced actress but a girl with a fresh and princess-like dignity, and she should have the intensity of a samurai's daughter." Many hundreds of young women auditioned for the role, including Toshiko Higuchi (ultimately cast as the slave girl the princess rescues) and future Toho bombshell Akiko Wakabayashi. Kurosawa rejected them all, and put out a call through the Toho organization, including its nationwide theater chain, to keep an eye out for his princess. The woman he finally chose was twenty-year-old Misa Uehara.

"On the way back to my hometown of Fukuoka I stopped in Nagoya to visit Professor Tokugawa, at the college of Bunka Joshi," Uehara remembered. "He used to be president of the college and he invited me to visit him. We went to see *The Antarctic Continent* (Nankyoku tairiku, 1957) at a Toho theater. Later I learned that Toho employees were looking for applicants to play Princess Yuki. A Toho employee was looking at me because Professor Tokugawa, who was very famous in Nagoya, had brought me there. The manager of the theater called Toho's main office, somebody there contacted Professor Tokugawa, and he contacted me. It was a surprising series of events. When I returned to Tokyo, Mr. [Hiroshi] Nezu of the Kurosawa team got hold of me and asked me to come to the studio. Mr. Nezu picked me up by car, and by the time I got to the studio everything was ready. I was surrounded by a lot of people who took a lot of pictures of me."[8]

Kurosawa was struck by Uehara's elegant beauty, especially what he dubbed her "miraculous eyes."[9] "What was funny," Uehara says, "was that Mr. Kurosawa entered the makeup room with a big picture of Elizabeth Taylor, put it by my mirror, and tried to imitate that look. I guess he already had something in mind. Anyway, in the end he decided to base the princess's look on a Noh mask, and the makeup was created using a book on Noh he had found during his research."[10] Uehara was given riding lessons and coached by actress Eiko Miyoshi, who turned up in the film as the princess's elderly lady-in-waiting.

Uehara, whose career lasted barely three years, remembered the making of the film with great fondness. "I had fun shooting every day," she says, "and had only one bad experience. For the scene where the princess stood at the top of the rocky mountain weeping [for the double executed in her place], I just couldn't get myself to cry, no matter how hard I tried. The scene was shot at the Ikuta open set near the studio by the chief assistant director, [Mimachi] Yanagase. Mr. Kurosawa wasn't there. The assistant directors crushed an onion and put it under my eyes, but I couldn't cry. While I was trying, the sun started to go down. All of a sudden I became very sad and couldn't stop crying when I realized the crew wouldn't be able to go home. This is one of my good memories."[11]

Years later, in 1981, Uehara appeared on a Fuji-TV program with Kurosawa, Minoru Chiaki, and Kamatari Fujiwara to discuss the film. Uehara, long since retired from acting, had maintained a deep respect for Kurosawa. A transcript of her appearance shows her extremely polite toward her former director, almost to a fault.

Chiaki, with his cherubic, flabby features, and Fujiwara, with his spindly, tiny frame, played the two rascals with tremendous charm. They are utterly without scruples, always greedy and constantly bickering. Much like Laurel and Hardy, they care deeply for each other, but rarely display it. Their playing is likewise delightfully broad and amusingly overdone, but without Laurel and Hardy's childlike innocence. They are ludicrous, incompetent, endearing rubes. And their incessant, selfish bellyaching is all the funnier because Kurosawa places them in a world of realistic violence and danger.

This charm is seen when the band of refugees flee the enemy. The general, pretending to be a mercenary, tells them the princess is a deaf-mute peasant (thus hiding her obviously royal manner of speech), and they assume she's his woman. Chiaki and Fujiwara want the gold for themselves and are constantly trying to run off with it. At one point they even try to steal the horse carrying the gold. Thinking she cannot hear their plans, they openly discuss them in front of her, pantomiming that they are taking the horse to water it. To Masaru Sato's droll music, Chiaki and Fujiwara mimic a drinking horse to a woman who knows exactly what they're up to while pretending not to understand. It's a priceless moment.

Chiaki was born in Hokkaido on July 30, 1917, and had starred in the stage version of *The Quiet Duel*. He made his film debut as the girly show director in *Stray Dog* and appeared in eight Kurosawa films prior to *The Hidden Fortress*. He made a believably disillusioned priest in *Rashomon*, and portrayed the humorously easygoing samurai in *Seven Samurai*, a role perhaps closest to the actor's own personality. Firmly cemented in the Kurosawa-gumi, Chiaki had given strong performances in both *Throne of Blood* and *The Lower Depths* the year before. After *The Hidden Fortress*, he appeared in more routine pictures like *Saga of the Vagabonds* (1960) and *The Youth and His Amulet* (1961) before tapering off his film work to return to the stage. His last appearance for Kurosawa was in a very brief role, a cameo really, as a reporter in *High and Low*. Chiaki outlived Mifune to become the last survivor among the *Seven Samurai*. In poor health for many years, having suffered a cerebral hemorrhage in 1975, he still managed to win a Japanese Academy Award for his last film appearance, in *Gray Sunset* (Hana ichimonme, 1985), as a man battling Alzheimer's disease. He died in 1999, of acute respiratory and coronary failure.

Kamatari Fujiwara, unlike Chiaki, was a prolific character player at Toho from its very inception. He starred in P.C.L.'s first release, *Intoxicated Life* (Horoyori jinsei, 1933), and several of the films on which Kurosawa

worked as chief assistant director, including *Horse* (1941), in which Fujiwara played Hideko Takamine's father. He appeared in several of Mifune's
earliest films, including *Conduct Report on Professor Ishinaka* (1950) and *Kojiro
Sasaki* (1951), but was so busily employed at Toho Kurosawa didn't have a
chance to direct him himself until *Ikiru* in 1951. Starting with *Ikiru*, Kurosawa used Fujiwara more frequently than he did any other actor, including
Mifune and Takashi Shimura. With the exceptions of *Throne of Blood* and
Dersu Uzala, he appeared in all of Kurosawa's films through *Kagemusha*.
Between assignments for the director, Fujiwara had supporting roles in
every kind of picture Toho made: B-thrillers like *The Invisible Man* (Tomei
ningen, 1954), college romances such as *Bull of the Campus* (Daigaku no
wakadaisho, 1961), samurai dramas, and salaryman comedies. And although he was known primarily as a comic actor, his work for Kurosawa
brought him to the attention of other leading filmmakers. He acted in Nagisa Oshima's *The Sun's Burial* (Taiyo no hakaba, 1960) and Masahiro Shinoda's *Double Suicide* (Shinju ten no Amijima, 1969), and was even flown to
America for a non-speaking role in Arthur Penn's New Wave–influenced
Mickey One (1965). Fujiwara died in 1985, shortly after making a brief but
memorable appearance in *The Funeral* (1984).

The antics of Chiaki and Fujiwara's characters are made all the funnier
when contrasted with Mifune's imposing general, who functions mainly as
a straight man. He is fearless and determined; they are cowardly and stupid. The importance of the straight man is usually underestimated in legitimate comedy teams, so it would be easy to do likewise with Mifune's
performance. But he gives an admirably restrained portrayal and, while
top-billed, never draws the audience's attention away from the lovable buf-
foons who are at the film's center. Mifune's face is made up much as it had
been in *Throne of Blood*, and he is daunting and strikingly physical. The film
does afford him several standout action scenes, including an impressive
lance duel between the general and his old friend (Fujita), now working for
the enemy. In this scene, Mifune is able to take a few simple shots, as he
tests a series of lances, and, through his amused reactions to their varying
quality, make them memorable. There is a thrilling chase on horseback,
with Mifune standing in his stirrups, sword drawn, as he charges after his
opponents (director John Milius replicated this in *The Wind and the Lion*,
1975). In the end, though, the film really belongs to Chiaki and Fujiwara.
By making them the central characters instead of the general and his
princess, Kurosawa most obviously subverts the genre.

Shooting began on May 27, 1958, in Arima, in Hyogo Prefecture. The
cast and crew then moved their unit to Gotemba, about 90 miles west of

Tokyo, on August 1. They were originally scheduled to wrap at the end of the month, but the set was plagued by bad weather. "I was supposed to finish shooting in Gotemba in about ten days, but I took a hundred," Kurosawa recalled in a 1981 television appearance. "Three typhoons came and destroyed all the trees. We had to change locations three times."[12] The film didn't wrap until December 11, with the final scenes at the princess's castle shot on the studio's open set. Toho wanted to get the film out as a New Year's release, and Kurosawa obliged them, finishing postproduction on December 23. Prints were struck, and the film premiered five days later.

Though Masaru Sato had written the scores for *Throne of Blood* and *The Lower Depths*, he really came into his own with *The Hidden Fortress*, which features rousing, richly orchestrated music. One of Japan's best and most prolific composers, Sato (1928–99) was a short, stocky man with then wild hair and a prominent gold-capped front tooth. He had been a protégé of Fumio Hayasaka, orchestrating much of the music on *Seven Samurai* and completing Hayasaka's work on *Record of a Living Being*. By the late 1950s he was writing regularly for Kurosawa—and just about everyone else. "One year I wrote eighteen complete scores; that's my record," he liked to say. "No one could break that record now—that was during the Golden Period." Sato would eventually write music for more than 300 features and was to Japanese film music what Ennio Morricone would be to Italian. "I went to see [Hayasaka] a week or so before my graduation from music school. I chose him as my mentor. Because of his work in films and especially his score for *Rashomon*, I thought he would be the very best person to apprentice with. At first he refused, but he was really surprised by my understanding of his work and finally accepted me as his student."[13]

After Hayasaka's death, Kurosawa turned to Sato, using him exclusively for the next ten years. Sato explained, "Mr. Kurosawa had very strong feelings about Hayasaka, and since I was his student, I was kind of spiritually linked.

"Kurosawa was a director who liked music. If he'd had the talent, he probably would have done it himself. I tried to anticipate what he wanted beforehand. Usually a composer would write music scene-for-scene, but for him I was writing music from a script and for individual lines of dialogue. I paid a lot of attention to this. He didn't give me any direct advice. He would say, vaguely, 'Could you please try something a little bit different?' He wanted to do a lot of improvisation, not realizing that with an orchestra this was very difficult—someone has to write the notes down! In that sense, he was the only demanding director in Japan."[14]

Also making his first significant contributions to a Kurosawa film was swordplay choreographer Ryu Kuze (1908–85). "I think [he] was a nice action director who recognized the nature of film expression," said his son-in-law, special-effects artist Minoru Nakano. "Prior to working with Kurosawa on *The Hidden Fortress*, he worked with Inagaki and Masahiro Makino. . . . For *The Hidden Fortress*, Kurosawa had originally hired a *Kendo* master, and while the choreography was correct for *Kendo*, it wasn't cinematic. . . . For his films with Mr. Kurosawa, he did not only the swordplay choreography but also the movements of the various hierarchies. For example, the samurai usually walked on the left side of the road because of the way the sword is drawn. And there are many rules about the position of the sword—how it's worn, where it's positioned—so he had to think about these things constantly. In the eyes of some historians, Kurosawa's films are full of historical inaccuracies, but it is the truth in terms of cinema."[15]

The Hidden Fortress was Kurosawa's first smash hit since *Seven Samurai*, and it earned ¥362,640,000 in Japan (just over $1 million). It ranked second on *Kinema Jumpo*'s list of the year's best films (behind Keisuke Kinoshita's *The Ballad of Narayama* [Narayama bushi-ko]). Shinobu Hashimoto was given its screenwriter award for his work on the film, along with his other scripts produced that year. The film was awarded the Tokyo Blue Ribbon Prize as Best Picture and the following year won the International Film Critics Prize and the Silver Bear at the ninth Berlin International Film Festival.

As with *Seven Samurai*, Toho fretted over the picture's length (139 minutes) as it readied the film for release in the West. It was screened in San Francisco in November 1959, and perhaps spurred by *Variety*'s comment that the film "might find limited appeal in U.S. arties if trimmed a bit," Toho had lopped 13 minutes off by the time it officially opened in America in October 1960.

"The realism and the *kabuki* stylization kill each other," said *Esquire*. "The film illustrates Kurosawa's two weaknesses: a tendency to overlabor and repeat and the mingling of incompatible genres; both are traits of a director who is unsure of his style. . . . Kurosawa makes it a class matter: the two peasant soldiers are like Shakespeare clowns—earthy, without inhibitions or dignity—while the princess and her general are frozen, withdrawn, contemptuous. But these are really, to a Westerner, two types of hysterical behavior, the open and the closed kind, as when the general's rigidity is shattered by strong feelings and he barks like a cougar."[16]

Esquire, along with the majority of American critics, missed the point of the film. It was always intended as a lighthearted, comic romp, but many insisted on comparing it unfavorably to earlier, more serious works. "Director Akira Kurosawa often elicits a surprising amount of suspense . . . but *The Hidden Fortress* is hardly up to his memorable *Rashomon* and *Seven Samurai*," wrote the *Los Angeles Mirror*.[17] The *Hollywood Citizen-News* agreed, saying, "Unfortunately, [it] doesn't quite compare with its predecessors." And they still complained about the length, the *Citizen-News* adding, "Although much good can be said for this lusty, sprawling saga of Japan's medieval days, it nonetheless could stand a good job of editing for it is poorly paced and almost ponderous in content for the first half of it."[18]

And so *The Hidden Fortress* was cut even further—to an alarmingly brief 90 minutes—when it was reissued in 1962. Not until 1984 was the film released at its original length, an arrangement engineered by Audie Bock (who did double duty retranslating the subtitles) and Michael Jeck, two Japanese film critics who also worked at the time in Japanese film distribution in the United States.

During the interim, critics had taken note of the similarities between Kurosawa's film and the plot of *Star Wars* (1977), George Lucas's box-office gargantua. When *The Hidden Fortress* was reissued, Lucas admitted that Minoru Chiaki and Kamatari Fujiwara were indeed the basis for the bumbling robots, C-3PO and R2-D2, and the princess in both films is a tough, strong-willed character. Beyond this, though, Lucas's sci-fi adventure is only incidentally similar, just as Kurosawa's was derivative of any number of Japanese *jidai-geki* and Hollywood adventures. Of *Star Wars* Kurosawa said, "I'm not a critic, I just like it."[19]

"I asked [Lucas] which aspects were inspired by my film. He said that he used the first scene, where Kamatari and Chiaki were walking. There was the scene where the small robot and the gold one were walking and fighting. It was very similar. The last scene was also similar."[20]

Though some have tried to link all the major characters to *Star Wars* (e.g., is Mifune Han Solo or Obi-Wan Kenobi?), the similarities are usually overstated. In point of fact, another Japanese fantasy, released to American television as *The Magic Serpent* (Kai tatsu daikessen, 1966), follows the plot of *Star Wars* much more closely, but it is likely that this is merely another example of genre-bred coincidence.

In any event, the popularity of the Star Wars series boosted interest in Kurosawa's picture, and Mike Schlesinger's review was typical: "It's an exceptionally fine film. . . . Kurosawa acknowledged his debt to John Ford when he made the picture, so in a sense *Star Wars* has brought the film full circle. But as much fun as [*Star Wars*] is, it just ain't the same as the original."[21]

J. Hoberman's review in *The Village Voice* was less enthusiastic. "That it is being shown for the first time in its complete . . . version may have less to do with its merits, though, than its inspiration for George Lucas's *Star Wars*. As such, *The Hidden Fortress* has more to answer for than live up to; on its own terms, though, Kurosawa's entertainment has style to give away."[22]

And, as Donald Richie summed it up, "The result is . . . an action-drama . . . so beautifully made, one so imaginative, so funny, so tender, and so sophisticated, that it comes near to being the most lovable film Kurosawa has ever made."[23]

If *The Hidden Fortress* lacks the weight of his previous efforts, it is also a refreshing departure, a grand adventure that demonstrates just how far Kurosawa could rise above the similarly escapist *jidai-geki* then pouring out of all the Japanese major studios. Like most great comedies, the fulsomeness of its characters is easy to overlook, as is its superb craftsmanship. And escapist though it may be, it is not without the same kind of humanism found in most of Kurosawa's films from this period. Part of the film's resonance, and something lost on most contemporary reviewers, is that much of it deals with the princess's spiritual awakening. Because of her royal blood, she has been raised at a far remove from the peasants under her rule. Her adventures with the general and the two peasants provide her with a different view of the world she lives in. When she is captured and faces execution, she is oddly at peace, telling her general something that might equally apply to Kurosawa: "I have seen people as they really are, in all their beauty and ugliness, with my own eyes. I thank you."

Well before *The Hidden Fortress* opened in America, its director was busy setting up his own production company, Kurosawa Production, officially established in April 1959. Kurosawa's team used offices on the Toho lot. "Toho enjoyed a lot of income from Kurosawa's films," said nephew Mike Inoue, "but they were always afraid because of the budgets he needed. So I think the executives at Toho decided to make Kurosawa form his own production company and then participate [financially] in the films he'd make."[24] According to Tetsu Aoyagi, Kurosawa Production's managing director of the late 1960s, Toho owned 55 percent of the company's shares. In spite of the box-office success of *The Hidden Fortress*, its high negative cost (much of it sunk into the terrifically expensive set of the ruined castle, used only briefly) limited Toho's profits. From now on, Kurosawa, making films in association with Toho rather than producing them in-house, was given more freedom to make the films that he wanted, but he needed to keep an eye on the bottom line, since he would now sink much of his own money into each production.

While Kurosawa began forming his own production company and prepping his next two scripts, Mifune spent 1959 appearing in no less than five varied features. He starred in two period films, *Samurai Saga* (Aru Kengo no Shogai) and *Saga of the Vagabonds* (Sengoku gunto-den); had a supporting role in another *ankokugai* (underworld) film, *The Big Boss* (Ankokugai no Kaoyaku); and made a brief appearance in Kihachi Okamoto's wry war movie *Desperado Outpost* (Dokuritsu gurentai). He then starred in Toho's biggest film of the year, the all-star religious epic *The Three Treasures* (Nippon tanjo).

The first to be released was *The Big Boss*, an excellent film directed by Kihachi Okamoto and toplining Koji Tsuruta. The story mainly concerns the relationship of gangster Ryuta (Tsuruta) and his younger brother, Mineo (Akira Takarada), who's trying to go straight after taking part in the murder of a loan company executive. Mineo is trying to start a new life as a singer in a "jazz coffeeshop," and Ryuta is torn between his loyalty to the gang and his blood ties to his brother. In the end, Ryuta is forced to lead his brother's gang execution, but at the last minute he turns on the triggerman. Mineo escapes, Ryuta dies of gunshot wounds, and the "Big Boss" (Seizaburo Kawazu) dies in a fiery car crash.

Mifune is quite good in his guest-star role, playing an honest auto mechanic menaced by the *yakuza* hoods. For a change, he is intimidated rather than intimidating, playing the part with an effective uneasiness. Director Okamoto gives the film a wonderful energy; its style combines American noir, Japanese *yakuza* thrillers, and homegrown *manga* (Japanese comic books). His editing, use of angles, and *mise-en-scène* is always vivid, and he makes excellent use of Toho's pool of contract supporting and bit players. *The Big Boss* is a surprisingly sophisticated work in an unsophisticated genre, to crime films what *The Hidden Fortress* was to *jidai-geki* and what *Yojimbo* would be within the *chambara* genre.

The film also serves as a reminder of how much Toho was changing by the end of the decade. In terms of style, the film is light-years ahead of Kajiro Yamamoto's *The Black Fury* and *The Underworld*, while it features several actors (Takarada and Yosuke Natsuki as Mifune's assistant) who would shortly supplant Mifune and Tsuruta as leading men in Toho's modern action films of the 1960s. It is significant therefore as a transitional work, demonstrating how the talent involved, then at the peak of their abilities, could transcend even routine crime thrillers like *The Big Boss* and make them memorable.

Mifune was soon working for Okamoto again in *Desperado Outpost*, a darkly cynical, comic tragedy set on the northern Chinese front during World War II. Makoto Sato starred as Sergeant Okubo, a war correspondent out to avenge his brother's death on the front lines. After killing the sadistic officer (Tadao Nakamaru) who murdered his brother, and following the death of his prostitute lover (singer Izumi Yukimura, in a rare dramatic role), as well as the annihilation of his comrades by the Chinese, Okubo deserts, joining a group of bandits (led by Koji Tsuruta and *The Hidden Fortress*'s Misa Uehara, as Tsuruta's sister).

With its extensive location work and taut battle sequences incorporating hundreds of extras, the film exemplifies Toho's growing confidence in their thirty-five-year-old director. Deeply cynical, darkly ironic war movies were another of Okamoto's specialties, and the film proved an enormous critical and commercial hit. Six sequels followed, including the Mifune-starring *Fort Graveyard* (Chi to suma, 1965), the last film of the series. It also made a cult star of Makoto Sato, whose flat, slyly derisive features and grinning, Cheshire-cat mouth made him visually suited to psychotic villain roles, typified by his work in films like Okamoto's *The Big Boss* and Tai Kato's *The Executioner* (Minagoroshi no reika, 1968). His unusual looks generally limited him to supporting parts. Even in *Desperado*'s thematically similar but narratively unrelated sequels, Sato played second fiddle to other, more bankable talent.

Mifune was brought in to lend *Desperado Outpost* star power, and while his name helped sell tickets, his role was small and not terribly memorable. He plays the outpost's unhinged battalion commander, apparently driven mad after a head wound, but he disappears after the first thirty minutes, during which he appears in all of two brief scenes.

Mifune followed his part in *The Big Boss* with leading roles in two period films, one a curious but not ineffective adaptation of an acclaimed Western work, the other an enjoyable retooling of an English legend. *Samurai Saga* (Aru kengo no shogai, 1959) was a direct lifting of Edmond Rostand's *Cyrano de Bergerac*, the classic French play about the great duelist and romantic cursed with an outrageously long nose. Director Hiroshi Inagaki adapted it to seventeenth-century Japan, transposing the protagonist's features in the process. In Japan wide, flat noses rather than long pointy ones are considered ugly, so while Mifune's makeup is rather jarring, it lacks the outrageousness of other film versions of *Cyrano*, like the 1950 José Ferrer film, in which the makeup goes to Pinocchio-like extremes.

In *Samurai Saga*, entire scenes from Rostand's play are borrowed, such as Cyrano's beating a cruel man's would-be insults to the punch, while at the same time amusing a crowd with an endless stream of self-effacing, witty acknowledgments of his extreme proboscis. Like *Cyrano*, samurai Heihachi (Mifune) and Jurota (Akira Takarada) both love the same woman, Princess Chiyo (Yoko Tsukasa). The eloquent, romantic Heihachi channels his love through the handsome but inarticulate Jurota by speaking through him, as he woos the princess in her garden, under the moon. Like the play, the story ends with the princess aware as he dies in her arms that for the past decade she has in fact loved the ugly little man.

Mifune's performance in the early portion of the film, during its high comic moments, is quite good, but he is less convincing as the refined, if ugly, doomed lover. However, it is difficult to fully assess his performance as the poetic language of such a dialogue-driven film is lost in translation. The English subtitles on the only presently available version of the picture are too literally translated, unlike, for example, Anthony Burgess's excellent translation for the 1990 French film with Gérard Depardieu.

Mifune's busy year continued with *Saga of the Vagabonds*, released in late August 1959. After the resounding success of *The Hidden Fortress* the previous December, Toho wanted to produce another such picture, and Kurosawa obliged them, penning a script adapted from the 1937 Takizawa film of the same name on which he had been third assistant director. The job probably appealed to Kurosawa for several reasons: it was easy money that could be funneled into his new production company, it offered an excellent vehicle for Mifune, and its story was based at the foot of Mt. Fuji, a location that had impressed him twenty-two years earlier and that he frequently returned to in such films as *Throne of Blood* and *The Hidden Fortress*.

Saga of the Vagabonds was directed by the venerable Toshio Sugie, though he was something of an odd choice. Sugie had joined Toho back in its P.C.L. days the same year Kurosawa did, and he, like Kurosawa, may well have worked on the 1937 film. But after directing Mifune in *The Black Fury* and *All Is Well*, Sugie had found his niche at Toho helming musical comedies starring, in various combinations, Toho's *Sannin Musume*, or "three young girls"—Hibari Misora, Chiemi Eri, and Izumi Yukimura. These three women all had beguiling and distinctive charm, and their films were among Toho's most popular. By the late 1950s, however, Misora had moved over to Toei, and Eri had settled into a film series based on Machiko Hasegawa's phenomenally popular *manga* (comic book) character Sazae-san. Yukimura successfully made the transition to other modern musical comedies and occasional dramatic parts in films like *Desperado Outpost*. But Toho knew they were on to something and had Sugie supervise a brand-new series of comedies known as the "Three Dolls" movies, which starred Reiko Dan, Sonomi Nakajima, and Noriko Shigeyama, playing similar roles. Sugie had done the first two of these, *Three Dolls in College* (Daigaku no oneichan) and *Three Dolls in Ginza* (Ginza no oneichan) earlier in 1959. Still, given the general lighthearted nature of *Saga of the Vagabonds*, and the fact that Sugie could work quickly at a time when Toho in general and Mifune in particular were cranking out features at a furious pace, that the picture doesn't look rushed is an achievement.

Saga of the Vagabonds is a kind of Japanese *Robin Hood*, the inverse of *Seven Samurai*, with Mifune this time a bandit. It reunited him with Misa Uehara and Minoru Chiaki, all happily playing characters quite unlike those they had played in *The Hidden Fortress*. The story has Lord Taro (Koji Tsuruta) entrusted to deliver a large chest of war funds to the rural governor, but the gold is stolen by a band of lusty thieves led by Jibu (Minoru Chiaki). One of the new recruits, the braggart Rokuro (Mifune), makes off with the gold, burying it. Taro and Rokuro meet accidentally and unwittingly become friends. When Rokuro becomes impressed by Taro's honesty and determination, he decides to give the gold back.

Meanwhile, Taro's weak-willed but greedy and ambitious brother Jiro (Akihiko Hirata, typecast again) and his even more ambitious vassal (Seizaburo Kawazu) accuse Taro of stealing the gold himself. Disgusted, Taro joins the thieves, and they become the "Crimson Band," who, as they say, rob from the rich and give to the poor.

Taro's motives are called into question when a young mountain woman (Yoko Tsukasa) questions the band's morals. Moments later her suspicions are confirmed when Jibu and a fallen priest-turned-bandit (Yoshifumi Tajima) try to rape her. Taro decides to call it quits, but by the following morning Jibu has betrayed his fellow thieves and Jiro's soldiers set fire to their lair. Some of the men escape and reunite a month later.

Jiro, however, has other problems. At his vassal's urging, he pushes his own father (Takashi Shimura) off a cliff, and despite Taro's long absence from the castle and fall from grace, Jiro cannot convince Princess Koyuki (Misa Uehara), Taro's betrothed, to love him instead. She commits suicide, Jiro goes mad, and just as the vassal prepares to kill *him*, Taro, Rokuro, and the former bandits raid the castle.

The picture is a grand, old-fashioned adventure epic, quite like, though much superior to, the CinemaScope epics made by the Hollywood majors just a few years earlier (*King of the Khyber Rifles* [1953], *Knights of the Round Table* [1953], *Garden of Evil* [1954], *King Richard and the Crusaders* [1954], etc.). *Saga of the Vagabonds* may not have much on its mind beyond simply telling a good adventure story, but what's there is adequately done and reasonably diverting, and memorable in a way that similar CinemaScope epics from Hollywood, which emphasized pageantry and little else, are not.

Technically, the picture is wonderful, with gorgeous cinematography by Akira Suzuki, making excellent use of the Toho Scope lens and oversaturated AgfaColor. Particularly good are its opening shots, over the main titles, where the bandits are seen in silhouette riding their horses against a crimson sunset with Mt. Fuji in the background. Later scenes of galloping horses and the thieves, now dressed in crimson themselves (right down to their bows and arrows), are similarly impressive.

The picture is helped enormously by Mifune's delightful comic performance as the larger-than-life Rokuro. Somewhere between *Seven Samurai*'s Kikuchiyo and *Yojimbo*'s Sanjuro, Rokuro is wily, boastful, honorable, subversive. There's little doubt that Kurosawa wrote the screenplay with Mifune in mind, for his scenes are always amusing. Mifune is delightfully broad in the Japanese manner—only he (and, sometime subsequently, actors like Shintaro Katsu and brother Tomisaburo Wakayama) could get away with such outrageous playing. Later in life, Mifune would almost always play stoic, veteran warriors, and to see him clearly relishing such a broad, physical role is a genuine pleasure. He alone makes the film worth watching.

The much more interesting first half is really a comedy of errors. When we first see him, Mifune stops thief Kenzo Tabu's runaway horse and steals it himself. Mifune immediately tries to sell it, only the potential buyer is the horse's real owner; thus Mifune is forced to make a hasty retreat. Later, he shares drinks with Taro and, unaware of whom he's talking to, claims to be a childhood friend of the lord. Later still, as Taro tells Rokuro of his plight and his sincere efforts to return the gold, Mifune bobs his head up and down in a wonderful kind of tortured amusement; the gold is buried ten feet away and he really wants to keep it, but in the end Rokuro is an honest thief. He decides to give it back, first making Taro promise not to get angry. Like Kikuchiyo, Mifune plays him as someone who truly enjoys playing warrior. As the soldiers set fire to the bandits' lair, Mifune starts eating large rice balls, and he continues to do so even as hot embers begin raining down from the burning roof. Panicking, the thieves begin pouring out of the engulfed building in little clusters, and most are hit by gunfire. Mifune, however, strolls out leisurely, cocking his body slightly in fascination as a bullet whizzes by him, craning his neck to see where it went. Later there is a scene reminiscent of the comical moment in *Seven Samurai* when Mifune sits next to one of the bandits in the forest and pretends to be one of them, carrying on a conversation before killing him. Rokuro tracks down a drunken Minoru Chiaki, who's not quite sure if Mifune knows whether he betrayed him or not. Mifune has brought a musket with him, and he asks Chiaki how to work it. The result is a scene both humorous and suspenseful, with Mifune pointing the gun at Chiaki and Chiaki pushing it away. Later, during the final raid on the castle, in the middle of the melee, Mifune eyes the lord's throne and promptly sits on it, trying it out for size.

The first half of the picture is brimming with moments like these, and not just with Mifune. Two of Jibu's bandits (Kenzo Tabu and Ren Yamamoto) try to figure out how to use a musket, and their speculation is amusing. After stealing all the signboards (the equivalent of "wanted" posters), the thieves decide to shoot arrows at it, aiming for certain Chinese characters. However, most of the thieves can't read, which creates much confusion.

Unfortunately, the picture's other subplots are less interesting. Kurosawa's script doesn't have much to do with either the princess or the peasant woman (Tsukasa, described in the subtitles as a "mountain monkey" because of her prowess in the wilderness), both of whom fall for Taro. The princess simply kills herself, and Tsukasa's romancing of Tsuruta never goes anywhere; neither is especially interesting. This, combined with the odd casting of Tsukasa and Uehara (who probably should be playing each other's role), adds up to an extraordinarily flat subplot. Unnecessary, too, is all the court intrigue, which has little to offer except to underscore the fact that the rulers are no better than the thieves themselves. As Mifune tells the thieves, "I grant you we're only bandits, a band of ruffians. But Toki and his son are the lowest of rascals! We're like innocent girls compared to them!"

Saga of the Vagabonds opened in Los Angeles in November 1960. Yet again, American critics likened this period film to American Westerns, but the reaction was mostly favorable, with Mifune's performance singled out. *The Hollywood Reporter*'s James Powers went so far as to suggest that the film might appeal to a mainstream audience, saying: "The Western used to be a form of motion picture that was purely American. No more. The Italians are doing chariot Westerns; now the Japanese have displayed . . . that the far east has its elements for the outdoor action film. In fact, the Toho production has enough action, movement and color to make worthwhile considering putting it in general run. It would need some trimming, but in the present product shortage it might be worth it. . . . Toshio Sugie's direction is first-rate, and so is the camera work by Akira Subuki [sic] in characteristically limpid AgfaColor and Toho Scope."[25]

Frank Mulcahy of the *Los Angeles Times* argued: "In this picture the viewer merely substitutes the powerful warlord as the mean old cattle baron. . . . The outstanding performance is that of Toshiro Mifune. . . . Beautifully photographed in Eastmancolor [sic]."[26]

Others were less impressed, and no one seemed to agree about the color. "The Japanese filmmakers are masters in the use of color," said S. A. Desick of the *Los Angeles Examiner*. "They demonstrate it again in 'The Vagabonds,' a lustrously tinted film. . . . It is not only lustrous; it is, to use Hemingway's favorite word, true. . . . The cast is no less impressive. Headed by Toshiro Mifune, probably one of the finest actors in the world today, it is steeped in skill down to the smallest bit part. It is therefore all the sadder to have to report that all this technical and acting talent is deployed for such a mediocre story. . . . There is plenty of hard riding, and some rousing combat, but such stories have by now become corpulent clichés."[27]

The Three Treasures, known in Japan as *Nippon tanjo*, or "The Birth of Japan," was billed as Toho's 1,000th production. A three-hour, all-star epic, the film was an acknowledged variation on Hollywood biblical spectacles like *The Ten Commandments* (1956) and *The Robe* (1953). Unlike Hollywood, which had moved away from the studio system by 1959, Toho and the other Japanese majors were still using this method of production, and films like *The Three Treasures* gave them a chance to show off their resources, in terms of both talent and technical wizardry.

In terms of talent, *The Three Treasures* has it all: respected film and stage actors like Kinuyo Tanaka, Setsuko Hara, Ganjiro Nakamura, Takashi Shimura, Nobuko Otowa, and Kyoko Kagawa; stars like Yoko Tsukasa, Misa Uehara, Akira Takarada, and Koji Tsuruta. Even popular comedians like Enoken, Keiju Kobayashi, and Norihei Miki were pressed into service, to say nothing of the dozens of contract character and bit players.

The technical aspects were equally lavish. Eiji Tsuburaya's special-effects supervision of Toho's monster movies had brought in foreign money from all over the world. A three-hour film about the birth of Shintoism, Japan's oldest religion, would have limited appeal outside Japan, but Tsuburaya's technical wizardry, it was reasoned, might help sell the film abroad. Shinto stories of Japan's birth included volcanic eruptions and, significantly, a duel with an eight-headed serpent, something right up Tsuburaya's alley.

Toho had made all-star films before—*Eagle of the Pacific* and *Holiday in Tokyo* are just two examples—but *The Three Treasures* went far beyond anything the studio had ever attempted. It was crammed with virtually every star and character player under contract, and to accommodate this, the picture was shot over twelve months in spite of the studio's already tight production schedule. The film cost $1 million, the studio's most expensive feature to date—nearly twice *Seven Samurai*'s final tab—and publicity materials boasted its use of "some 5,000 costumes, including 800 suits of authentic armor, 1,200 swords forged for the picture and 16,000 bows and arrow sets—all reproduced by experts."[28]

Based on the *Kojiki* and *Nippon Shoki*, Japan's oldest surviving historical documents, the film is set circa A.D. 300. Mifune stars as Prince Ousu, son of Emperor Keikoh. The Emperor's chief vassal, Otomo, wants Keikoh's second son, Ouso's stepbrother Waka, to ascend to the throne, this despite Ouso's popularity. Trying to get Ouso out of the way, he convinces the Emperor to send Ouso on a suicidal mission to subjugate the powerful Kumaso clan near Yamato and the Imperial Court.

However, Ouso is victorious and, taking the name Yamato Takeru, returns to the Emperor's castle. Despite the accolades, he is immediately dispatched on an even more dangerous mission. Before leaving, Yamato visits his aunt (Kinuyo Tanaka), chief priestess of the Grand Shrine of Ise, for advice. There he meets and falls in love with Princess Tachibana (Yoko Tsukasa). He asks her to join him, but she refuses on religious grounds. She is in the service of the gods, and mortal love is prohibited. She changes her mind, however, and joins Yamato on the battlefield. Otomo, still plotting, has his men ambush Yamato, but he escapes. Learning of Otomo's treachery, Yamato returns to the castle by sea, but en route Yamato's forces encounter a ferocious storm that threatens to capsize the entire fleet. Princess Tachibana, believing the storm to be the gods' wrath at her love for Yamato, jumps into the raging waters to calm them, which they do as she drowns. Yamato is ambushed once again by Otomo's forces and is killed. However, the gods transform him into a swan and trigger the eruption of Mount Fuji, annihilating Otomo's forces as the prince-turned-swan ascends into the heavens.

Interspersed throughout the film, and notably absent from Toho's own synopsis, are various Shinto tales, including a long humorous anecdote in the first act featuring Toho's top comedy stars, including Enoken, Norihei Miki, Kingoro Yanagiya, and Daisuke Kato. In the second half, Mifune appears in a different role, as a god named Susano, and grapples with an eight-headed dragon created by Eiji Tsuburaya's effects crew. The gangly serpent, its heads obviously dangling from wires, is patently phony. The creature was built on a much smaller scale than Tsuburaya's usual men-in-suit monsters. Standing about waist-high, it pales when compared to the picture's other visual effects, especially those set in the heavens, which are surreal and resplendent, quite unlike anything done in the West.*

Billed in Japan as "The Greatest of Toho's Great Films of Special Effects Photography," *The Three Treasures* was released on November 1, 1959, to excellent box office if not rave reviews, raking in more money than any other film that year save for Toei's equally lavish *Chushingura*. While Inagaki brought to the picture the same sure-handed craftsmanship he exhibited on the Musashi Miyamoto trilogy, he was too tasteful a filmmaker, lacking the grand, lurid tackiness that made Cecil B. DeMille's later films so entertaining. Scenes with the various gods and the special-effects set pieces are done on an epic scale and are generally involving, but ultimately Yamato's story is just another *jidai-geki*. Mifune is serviceable, but his role is nothing new.

For release abroad, Toho cut *The Three Treasures* down to 111 minutes, thus losing more than an hour's worth of narrative.† Still, when the film opened in Los Angeles in December 1960, it garnered favorable reviews, nearly every critic likening it—as Toho had done in their own print ads—to a DeMille epic.

> Toho . . . has mounted a lavish, yet visually meticulous account of Japan's mythological heritage. Western audiences . . . will have to admire the artistry and painstaking photographic mastery of the craftsmen who designed and manufactured this film. . . . The film should attract art house attention beyond the Japanese sphere and, being physically and culturally superior to recent costume imports

---

*The creature did serve as the genesis for the later, much more fully realized Ghidrah—the Three-Headed Monster that battled Godzilla in numerous sequels.

†It was probably cut for general release in Japan as well. As was standard practice when preparing general release or edited reissue versions of its films, editors cut from the original negative, and like so many Japanese movies, the home video version had to be cobbled together from several prints of varying quality.

from Europe, could even, with proper handling, make some sort of a showing as a general release attraction. . . . It is Eiji Tsuburaya's special effects that steal the picture. His execution of the story's demanding visual aspects . . . are spectacularly lifelike. These purely cinematic achievements may be the lesser art to the philosophical stature of a simple, human story, but within the narrow horizon of technical physique, *The Three Treasures* is a fine accomplishment.[29]

S. A. Desick of the *Los Angeles Examiner* also admired the visuals: "But the studio failed to include one important ingredient," he wrote, "a story to grip your interest. . . . [But] this grand scale shows itself in the use of stunning color, in the artistry of many individual scenes, and in such spectacular special effects as an eight-headed dragon and an earth-heaving volcanic eruption."[30]

SIXTEEN

WIND

The Last Gunfight (Ankokugai no taiketsu) was Toho's and Toshiro Mifune's first film of the 1960s. It was a typically busy year for the actor; that year alone Mifune appeared in six features. Filmed by director Kihachi Okamoto in late 1959, *The Last Gunfight* was yet another *ankokugai* (underworld) film, a genre at which the younger generation of directors at Toho like Okamoto and Jun Fukuda excelled.

After a political scandal, Detective Fujioka (Mifune) is demoted and transferred to a police station in the crime-ridden city of Kojin. There two gangs, the Okas and the Kozukas, are fighting over territory. Fujioka becomes friendly with gang boss Oka (Seizaburo Kawazu) while investigating the murder of the wife of Kozuka gangster Tetsuo Maruyama (Koji Tsuruta). Tetsuo doesn't cooperate, but it's soon apparent that she was murdered by someone within the Oka clan. The two gangs have a shootout over rights to haul sand from the Kojin River, and the Kozuka gang is wiped out, with the single exception of Tetsuo, who is saved by Fujioka. The two become uneasy allies, à la *A Man Among Men* (1955), and Tetsuo learns that the man who killed his wife is also dead. However, Tetsuo still holds Oka responsible and seeks vengeance. He confronts the gang boss and, despite the pleas of Fujioka, kills him. Fujioka is forced to shoot his friend, and it is then revealed that Fujioka's demotion was a ruse—he had actually been transferred to clean up crime and corruption in Kojin.

The Last Gunfight had little, if any, release in the United States when it was new. Decades after it was made, the picture turned up in New York as part of a Japan Society film series called "Crime and Passion in Japanese Cinema." Writing in *The Village Voice*, Elliott Stein called *The Last Gunfight* "a good example of the genre. . . . It's good-naturedly enjoyable, but that's about all. What's most interesting about the movie is that Mifune's morally ambiguous cop is something of a Japanese Dirty Harry—years before *Dirty Harry*."[1]

Another program picture, *The Gambling Samurai* (Kunisada Chuji, 1960), followed. Senkichi Taniguchi directed this *jidai-geki*, with Mifune playing a kind of Japanese Robin Hood. Indeed, when the film was released in America, Toho played up this very angle, much like *Saga of the Vagabonds*. "The Robin Hood of Japan!" cried the ads. "His Startling Swordplay Helped the Weak and Killed the Strong!"

The story concerns Chuji Kunisada (Mifune), a gambler returning home after a two-year absence. He discovers his mother long dead and the farmers there oppressed by corrupt officials. Chuji's sister (Kumi Mizuno) has been raped by a magistrate (Susumu Fujita) and has gone mad. She wanders about Chuji's home, playing with flowers. When the sister's fiancé (Ko Mishima) dies after trying to avenge his lover, she grabs his sword and kills herself. Seeking vengeance, Chuji goes to the magistrate's residence, but the magistrate escapes.

With the help of his comrades (Daisuke Kato, Yu Fujiki, Yosuke Natsuki), Chuji begins robbing from the rich and giving to the poor, forcing him to hide deep in the (Sherwoodesque) forests of Mt. Akagi. After three long years, Chuji does avenge his sister's death, but in so doing he must leave behind his fiancée, Toku (Michiyo Aratama), though he vows to return.

Costume melodramas were never director Taniguchi's strong suit. *The Gambling Samurai* is competent but resolutely unmemorable. It has none of the historical richness of Inagaki's films, or the agreeable breeziness of *Saga of the Vagabonds*, and the promise Taniguchi showed in his early work is absent here. Screenwriter Kaneto Shindo, a talented writer-director capable of greatness in his own endeavors, such as the excellent *Onibaba* (1964), would crank out hack scripts for others when he felt obliged to. *The Gambling Samurai* proved a simple program picture and nothing more.

Less than a month after *The Gambling Samurai*'s release, Mifune was back in theaters in another picture, in a role taken on, possibly, during *Gambling Samurai*'s production. He was one of a dozen male stars to populate Toho's war epic *Storm Over the Pacific* (Taiheiyo no arashi, 1960), the company's biggest such film since *Eagle of the Pacific* seven years earlier. Since that time, the other studios, mainly Shintoho, had cashed in on the nostalgia of veterans. Toho had produced Ishiro Honda's *Farewell, Rabaul* (Saraba Rabauru, 1954), but the success of the Honda-Tsuburaya monster films and their popularity abroad had sidelined the production of war movies for most of the decade. In 1959, Shue Matsubayashi's modestly produced *Submarine E-57 Never Surrenders* (Sensuikan I 57 kofukusezu), starring Ryo Ikebe and filmed in black-and-white, had been a big hit and convinced Toho that the time was right for another all-star war film.

Storm Over the Pacific revisited the attack on Pearl Harbor and the defeat at Midway, as had *Eagle of the Pacific*, but this time in color and Toho Scope and on a scale not seen since *The War at Sea from Hawaii to Malaya* in 1942. Unlike in *Eagle of the Pacific*, no stock footage was used. Tsuburaya was given carte blanche with his use of miniatures, and Matsubayashi's live-action sets, notably carrier decks and the like, were constructed on a scale comparable to later, more expensive American films like *Tora! Tora! Tora!* Toho built a special-effects "pool" in the back of the studio to shoot the miniature naval battles, though some of the miniatures were so large that the effects footage involving them had to be shot outside the pool, on real, untamed waters.

Shue Matsubayashi (b. 1920) brought to the film a unique perspective: he had been a naval officer himself, which explains why a director known mainly for his "Shacho" ("Company President") comedies with Hisaya Morishige was assigned *Submarine E-57* and *Storm Over the Pacific* in the first place.

"Filmmakers who were not in the Army have been able to capture that feeling and atmosphere reasonably well," he said, "but I think the spirit of the Imperial Navy is much more difficult to achieve. It's a much less tangible thing to grasp—it is almost impossible. I'm the only Imperial Navy officer to have become a director." But it was not just his naval spirit. Matsubayashi had experienced the terror of war firsthand. "American planes dropped bombs on us, and I was directing the fleeing sailors. Our ship capsized. One plane got so close I could see the face of the American flier who was doing the shooting. He was about twenty-five years old—I still remember him waving at us. On the deck of the ship that came to our rescue I could see many bodies piled up and that I had lost many of my men. . . . A lot of my colleagues died during the war; as a movie director, I wanted my [war] films to serve as a memorial to my comrades."[2]

The film focuses on one Navy flier, Lt. Koji Kitami (Yosuke Natsuki), a navigator-bombardier who is part of the successful Pearl Harbor raid. He returns home a hero and becomes engaged to a childhood sweetheart, Keiko (Misa Uehara, the princess from *The Hidden Fortress*). He is then, like many of his fellow fliers, swept up in the early, easy victories, buying wholesale Japanese nationalism, until the stunning defeat at Midway forces him to re-examine his dedication.

The film walks a fine line between glorifying the heroics of the pilots and mourning the folly of Japan's militarism: the battles are exciting, even exhilarating, but Matsubayashi and screenwriters Shinobu Hashimoto and Takeo Kunihiro balance this with a much bleaker second half. Hashimoto worked on the film in the midst of *The Bad Sleep Well* with Kurosawa, just as he had done a few years earlier with *Eagle of the Pacific* during the making of *Seven Samurai*. Whereas *Eagle of the Pacific* had been little more than a text-book history of the war and its battles, with Admiral Yamamoto as a central character, *Storm Over the Pacific* was much more personal and far more immediate with its everyman protagonist.

Hashimoto wrote in the script's preface: "Nobody thinks of war positively, but the history of war is the history of man. This fact brought inexpressible, deep sadness to us all. Why does mankind do such sad things?"[3] Unlike *Eagle of the Pacific*, Hashimoto and Kunihiro presented the war in very real, personal terms, with Natsuki's small-town life and his marriage to Keiko interrupted by a call to duty playing a larger part of the drama than in earlier war films, or those that followed.

The film boasted the biggest all-star cast, mostly in cameo parts, since *The Three Treasures*, including such names as Makoto Sato, Takashi Shimura, Daisuke Kato, Akira Takarada, Hiroshi Koizumi, Keiju Kobayashi, Tatsuya Mihashi, Seizaburo Kawazu, Ken Uehara, and even Enoken. Ryo Ikebe, Koji Tsuruta (as Natsuki's mentor-pilot), and Mifune were given special "guest star" billing.

The picture was one of the very few Toho war movies ever released to home video in America and provided viewers with a rare opportunity to see again the promise Misa Uehara had shown in her film debut in *The Hidden Fortress*. After Kurosawa's film, Toho had kept her busy in films like *Saga of the Vagabonds* and *Desperado Outpost*, but like so many actresses of her day, she abruptly vanished. After appearing in one more film, Kihachi Okamoto's *The Spook Cottage* (*Daigakuno Sanzokutachi*, 1960), she retired.

However, it was Eiji Tsuburaya's effects that sold the picture and were its biggest attraction. "Look at the Special Effects Crew!" declared the ads, "The Big Battles of Hawaii and Midway, Seen from the Sky and the Sea!

The Biggest War Movie Ever, with an All-Star Male Cast!" Tsuburaya's work surely warranted co-director billing. The visual effects are truly awesome, with highly detailed re-creations of battleships, carriers, planes, and the American bases at both Pearl Harbor and Midway. They are filmed in imaginative, sometimes poetic fashion: when the low-flying planes approach Pearl Harbor, they create a tailwind that gently rustles the trees below. Both Tsuburaya's effects and Matsubayashi's live-action scenes proved so good that they were recycled as stock footage in Toho's war movies as late as *Imperial Navy* (Rengo kantai, 1981), also directed by Matsubayashi. Footage from *Storm Over the Pacific* even turned up in a few American films, such as Universal's *Midway* (1976).

Matsubayashi had great respect for Tsuburaya. "He's number one. After the Japanese defeat at the end of the war, Japan didn't have any aircraft— no warships, nothing—it was all at the bottom of the ocean. Everything was done with miniatures, and yet they don't look like miniatures in the film. There's nobody like Mr. Tsuburaya anywhere in the world. I respected Mr. Tsuburaya and his techniques, so I let him do everything, including shooting some of the drama. . . . Together we were able to express the sadness of war. That was what was so meaningful to me about working with him."[4]

Storm Over the Pacific had the distinction of being released in the United States in two different formats. Toho's international division exhibited it with English subtitles, while Parade Releasing, a minor company created by the American distributors of *Godzilla, King of the Monsters!*, dubbed it into English and distributed it on the exploitation circuit as *I Bombed Pearl Harbor*. Despite the ingeniously crude title, Parade knew it was treading a thin line with its subject matter. In trying to head off attacks from the American Legion and other conservative groups, Parade stated in its press materials that the picture "does not attempt to justify or excuse the attack on Pearl Harbor."[5]

Parade substantially recut the film, deleting about 15 minutes, and rearranged scenes. Sadly, the dubbing and adaptation of the script were very poor, retaining the exploitable action at the cost of the film's more mournful moments.* An unnecessary prologue and epilogue were added, featuring Franklin Roosevelt's radio address after the Pearl Harbor bombing and

---

*The worst casualty of the Americanization is undoubtedly director Matsubayashi, whose name is buried in the credits, appearing in tiny type below that of the assistant editor of the American version.

an incessant narration by Natsuki's character. "We were told we were invincible, then we were told to expect the unexpected," Lt. Kitami says, with clipped accent. "It tests my reasoning too much!" Such dialogue made the film foolish and simplistic.

Mifune's voice was dubbed by character actor Paul Frees (1920–86), who, for that matter, looped nearly everyone else as well. Frees had appeared in such films as *The Thing (from Another World)* (1951) and *The War of the Worlds* (1953), but by the late 1950s he had found his niche as a voice-over artist and dubbing director. He was the voice of Boris Badenov on *Rocky and Bullwinkle*, Professor Ludwig von Drake on *The Wonderful World of Disney*, and was heard in countless other animated films. He directed the dubbing of innumerable foreign-language films, narrated coming-attraction trailers, and provided voices and narration for movies like *Spartacus* (1960), *The Manchurian Candidate* (1962), and *Patton* (1970). His association with Mifune, minor though it was, lasted for decades. In both Japanese and international productions featuring Mifune, Frees often wound up looping the actor. Here, because he's dubbing almost the entire cast, everyone sounds alike; most are given pseudo-Japanese accents that are borderline cartoonish.

Mifune's role occupies about 20 minutes of the film. He plays Admiral Yamaguchi (not Yamamoto, as credited elsewhere), the first of countless admirals and other high-ranking military leaders he would play well into the 1980s. Like the seasoned samurai role that would also come to haunt him, these parts were often thankless, asking little other than that he look imposing when giving orders or stoically grim when not. Despite Mifune's top billing over Natsuki in the American version, several key scenes, his best in the film, were cut. The first is a meeting between Yamaguchi and Admiral Yamamoto (Susumu Fujita) that follows Natsuki's aborted wedding. They drink sake and discuss the critical shortage of oil. Yamamoto gives Yamaguchi orders to attack Midway, and the scene has an intriguing, fatalistic air.

I Bombed Pearl Harbor ends with the sinking of Mifune's aircraft carrier. In this riveting sequence, the carrier, hit by Allied torpedoes, lists but will not sink. Dozens of men have been trapped belowdeck, while Mifune and another officer, played by Jun Tazaki, have tied themselves to the wheel, determined to go down with the ship. The Japanese Navy orders the ship scuttled rather than fall into enemy hands. Those fortunate enough to be rescued, including Kitami, watch helplessly from the deck of a nearby cruiser as their own carrier is torpedoed and sinks against a brilliant sunset.

But the Japanese version doesn't end here. The camera slowly descends deep into the ocean, and the distant voices of the trapped crew can be heard, their spirits singing a military song. The camera moves toward the not-quite-distinct shapes of Mifune and Tazaki, still tied to the wheel. In spectral, Noh-like tones, we hear Tazaki say, "I fear that from this day forward, many more will die and the Pacific will become a massive graveyard." Mifune's replies, "I don't want to see any more."

The film then moves to a barracks in Kyushu where the surviving pilots, including Natsuki, await further orders. Though they have returned safely, the military has cut them off from the rest of the world, not allowing them to contact family and friends to let them know they're alive. In a sense, the military renders them dead as well. The following morning, given new orders, they fly off to parts unknown, their fate unquestionably sealed.

In addition, a scene of Kitami's wife and mother listening to a radio announcer falsely reporting triumphant victories has been moved from the final minutes of the film to earlier in the picture, thus robbing it of its irony. It is grievously unfortunate that this last section of the movie was so bluntly lopped off the American version as its bleakness eloquently conveys the great tragedy for which Matsubayashi and Hashimoto strived.

Storm Over the Pacific was tremendously successful in Japan. General Minoru Genda, who planned the Pearl Harbor attack, the widow of Admiral Yamamoto, and veterans who participated in the raid attended the premiere on April 23, 1960. "The general tone was one of nostalgia for the defunct 'armada,' " reported UPI. "Younger people in the audience applauded thunderously when the screen depicted pilots radioing a report that 'the surprise [Pearl Harbor] attack succeeded!' "[6]

Though he doesn't play Yamamoto, Mifune's character echoes the real-life admiral's concern that the Navy's failure to destroy the American carriers at Pearl Harbor and Japan's overconfidence after its early victories will lead only to defeat. Duty forces him to carry on. Yet his is a stock character, lacking any real depth and relying heavily on Mifune's screen presence in a series of impressive three-quarter-angle shots, with the actor looking fierce, like a cigar-store Indian, as his aides scurry about him. Nonetheless, it was the first time a Mifune film had such wide exposure in the United States, even if it did mean playing drive-ins.

In Los Angeles alone *I Bombed Pearl Harbor* was saturation-booked into twenty-four theaters and drive-ins, a week shy of the Pearl Harbor anniversary, while, on that same day, a complete subtitled version opened at a single Los Angeles theater. Of the wide release, *Variety*'s "Tube" predicted "a swift, short-lived, but sufficiently potent kick at the box office, especially [with its] multi-opening, 'spray-and-scram' basis."[7]

Kay Proctor of the *Los Angeles Examiner* summed up blow-by-blow the mixed reaction to the film in the United States: "It is impossible for Americans to view the English language version without mixed emotions, and strong ones at that! Rage will be your first response; you will all but blow your top during the opening third of the film. Next will come mounting excitement, tinged with a few flashes of pity; basically, however, you still will be angry and indignant. Then comes the final third with all its fury and fiery tragedy; surprisingly you may find much of your original wrath melted away in the compassionate realization that there must be two suffering sides—in terms of human beings—in any war."[8]

But like *The Three Treasures*, it was Tsuburaya's effects, not Mifune, that garnered the most copy. Proctor admired "the spectacular sequences of the Dec. 7 sweep down the mountainous approach to Pearl Harbor; the subsequent aerial dogfights, and the battle of Midway Island. Photographed in Technicolor [sic], they are superb in their realism, even though filmed (of necessity) in miniature."[9]

"The film . . . is very well made," concurred the *Los Angeles Times*'s Charles Stinson, who also noted how differently the two versions ended. "The miniatures of both U.S. and Japanese planes and ships and the terrain around Honolulu are done with the usual scrupulous and admirable Japanese attention to detail. In fact, their excessive tidiness betrays their clever artificiality."[10]

Variety's "Tube" agreed, writing: "[Miniature work is] a field in which the Japanese screen artisans excel. But, impressive as this work is, these models simply cannot completely convey to the critical eye the illusion of reality. However, the Toho craftsmen have come about as close as possible to this elusive goal. It's quite an achievement."[11]

"What makes this picture so authentic," added the *Mirror*'s Margaret Harford, "are the special effects—the authentic miniatures—by veteran director Eiji Tsuburaya, who can match the best of Hollywood's film magicians when it comes to fooling the public." Harford also complained about the dubbing. "Although [it] is far superior to most foreign pictures shown in English, you may prefer to hear the actors' own voices speaking Japanese, the gist of which is well translated in titles."[12]

While Mifune's part hardly taxed him, it was in a well-produced and sincerely made effort. Asked if any of the characters were specifically based on people he knew, director Matsubayashi said, "Yes, of course. All of them, really. They are all reflected in my work. . . . Pure heart in film is everything."[13]

After filming his modest role in Matsubayashi's war picture, Mifune was back at work on another Taniguchi picture, *Man Against Man* (Otoko tai otoko, 1960), a modern thriller. While no masterpiece, it was a step up from *The Gambling Samurai* in that Taniguchi had returned to the genre in which he made most of his best films. The story concerns two wartime buddies, Kaji (Mifune) and Kikumori (Ryo Ikebe), now working as a marine transport chief and cabaret manager, respectively. Conflict arises when a gang of drug traffickers wants to use Kaji's boats to transport narcotics, with Kikumori's cabaret serving as a front. Dock workers are killed in a series of "accidents," and the owner of the cabaret (Takashi Shimura) is murdered. Kaji and Kikumori begin blaming each other for the crimes, and tension between them mounts. Kaji is forced to ship volatile explosives to save his company, and Kikumori is blackmailed into shooting Kaji and destroying his boatload of explosives. At the last minute Kikumori has a change of heart and tries to kill the gang boss (Jun Tazaki) instead. During the struggle, Kikumori is shot, and when Kaji tries to come to his aid, Kikumori takes another bullet for Kaji, who then guns down the gangsters.

Man Against Man is of interest mainly as a symbol of the changing face of Toho Studios. Senkichi Taniguchi was being phased out of the genre. Younger directors like Kihachi Okamoto and Jun Fukuda were bringing a hipper, more electrifying energy to such films, and Taniguchi's subsequent assignments became increasingly routine. At forty-two, Ryo Ikebe was beginning to lose his legion of young female admirers, and he, too, found himself being moved from starring parts in A-pictures to programmers like Honda's *Battle in Outer Space* (Uchu daisenso, 1959) and cameo parts in Toho's war movies. As with Koji Tsuruta, who left Toho for Toei in 1961, Ikebe saw greener pastures elsewhere. In 1964 he left Toho for Shochiku, where he found better assignments in Masahiro Shinoda's *Pale Flower* (Kawaita hana, 1964) and Minoru Shibuya's *Twilight Path* (Daikon to ninjin, 1964), the latter adapted from a story by Ozu.

At the same time, *Man Against Man* marked the film debut of twenty-three-year-old Yuzo Kayama (b. 1937) as Toshio, the gullible son of the cabaret owner. An ambitious singer-bandleader, Toshio is tricked by his girlfriend (Akemi Kita), actually a member of Tazaki's gang, into turning over shares of the cabaret's stock. The real-life son of actor Ken Uehara, Kayama was pushed into film work by his father. In only a few years, Toho groomed Kayama into one of Japan's biggest recording and film stars, his popularity at Toho rivaled only by Mifune, and he came to symbolize the new generation of performers and films Toho nurtured. He would go on to make several films opposite Mifune, including two for Kurosawa, *Sanjuro* (1962) and *Red Beard* (1965).

Kurosawa himself was busy preparing his next film, *The Bad Sleep Well* (Waruiyatsu hodo yoku nemeru, 1960), the first co-production between his new company and Toho. The project originated from an unlikely source, Kurosawa's nephew Mike Inoue. Late in the Allied Occupation, Inoue had graduated from Waseda University's Department of Political Economics, but his passion lay elsewhere: "When I went to college I wanted to be a scriptwriter. I wrote a script and gave it to my uncle to read. Of course, he received scripts from all over. I wrote my name on the script, and every time I went to see him the script was always under a big pile, and each time I would move it to the top of the stack. One day I went to his birthday party and his wife rushed out to meet me at the front door and said, 'You'll be very happy to know your uncle had nothing to do while he was waiting for the guests to arrive, and he started reading your script.'

"Later on he said, 'You know something, you always write about political and bureaucratic corruption. Why don't you write a script about avenging these corrupt men?' That gave me an idea. I spent about six months writing it, titling it 'Bad Men's Prosperity.' When I took it to his house, he read it right away and told me, 'The story is very interesting. I might take up the subject for a film, but I'd have to refine the script you wrote. You don't mind, do you?' "[14]

Kurosawa followed much of Inoue's basic story, reworking it with Eijiro Hisaita (with whom he co-wrote *The Idiot*) at an inn in Izu. He invited Ryuzo Kikushima to join them, but Kikushima was tied up with other projects, and arrived after the first forty or so pages of the script were completed. Hideo Oguni and Shinobu Hashimoto also contributed material, joining them later at another inn at Hakone. Kurosawa was attracted to Hisaita's political and social ideology, which he felt had contributed to both *The Idiot* and *No Regrets for Our Youth*. (Some believed that Hisaita's contributions had begun to dominate the contributions of the other writers.) After seeing the finished picture, director Yasujiro Ozu pointedly asked Kikushima, "Hisaita and Kurosawa must have written the script when they were angry, didn't they? You and Hashimoto must have been sleeping."[15]

"There was so much corruption going on [at the executive level of Japanese industry] at the time," Kurosawa said, as if to counter Ozu's claim. "The investigations were always dropped when some assistant manager would kill himself. That made no sense. What would happen if somebody investigated the corruption and followed it through to the end? 'Let's make a thorough story about it!' I thought. That was how we started. It was difficult writing the script. . . . It would have been easier if we had a model for our story. If we had based it on a true story of a real company's corruption, though, the studio wouldn't have allowed us to make it."[16]

Inoue had mixed feelings about surrendering his work. "Some of the scenes I spent ten pages on he replaced with only one line. I had many sleepless nights writing those scenes, but I have to admit their version was much better, and it wasn't my script anymore." Although Inoue did not receive screen credit for the story's genesis, Kurosawa was forthcoming about its source. Inoue recalled a business trip to Paris years later. "I was going out to dinner," he said, "and I saw a very tall man in the distance and realized it was my uncle. He said, 'What are you doing here?!' He suggested that I come to his room for drinks with three men from the Japanese Television Network and Ms. Teruyo Nogami, his assistant. As we kept drinking, my uncle said, 'Listen, I'm going to tell you something very interesting. This is the man who wrote *The Bad Sleep Well!*' Everybody stood up and got very excited! I said, 'Wait! Wait! He's been drinking, he doesn't know what's he's saying.' "[17]

The script finished, Kurosawa joined producers Sanezumi Fujimoto and Tomoyuki Tanaka at a press conference on January 26, 1960, to announce that shooting would commence on March 1.[18]

The screenplay opens at a large wedding reception, of a kind still very popular in Japan, mixing traditional Japanese and Western elements. Koichi Nishi (Mifune), secretary to Iwabuchi (Masayuki Mori), the vice president of a government housing company, has married his boss's pretty but handicapped daughter, Yoshiko (Kyoko Kagawa). Amid the formality, an undercurrent of intrigue becomes apparent. With newspaper and tabloid reporters watching close by, it is revealed that the company is embroiled in scandal, and one of the company executives, Wada (Kamatari Fujiwara), is about to be arrested. Yoshiko's brother, Tatsuo (Tatsuya Mihashi), in his speech to the wedding party, threatens to kill his new brother-in-law if he fails to make his sister happy. Then, chaos erupts when the wedding cake is wheeled into the hall. The cake is baked in the shape of a large office building, with a black rose sticking out of one of the miniature windows. The executives are shocked. Five years earlier, one of their own, the scapegoat of an earlier scandal, had committed suicide by jumping out the window of that very building. As one of the reporters says flatly, "Funny wedding."

The wedding sequence is followed by a lengthy, thrillingly edited and scored montage as the scandal rips wide open. An accountant, Miura (Gen Shimizu), is arrested. After weeks of questioning, neither he nor Wada will talk. A company lawyer (Nobuo Nakamura) passes a message to Miura, and he promptly commits suicide. Lacking evidence to charge him, Wada is released. He too plans to kill himself—by jumping into a volcano, no less—but is stopped by Nishi.

Wada learns that Nishi is the illegitimate son of the company man who had been driven to suicide five years earlier. Since then Nishi has been meticulously plotting revenge, going so far as to marry the vice president's daughter to infiltrate the company's inner circle.

Faking Wada's suicide and observing the subsequent funeral, Nishi then uses Wada's apparent death to get to the two men working directly under Iwabuchi: Shirai (Ko Nishimura), whom Nishi drives mad, and Moriyama (Takashi Shimura, his hair dyed an oily black), whom he kidnaps and blackmails.

Nishi's plans begin to fall apart after Iwabuchi learns his son-in-law's true identity. And while Nishi married Iwabuchi's daughter for the sole purpose of engineering his revenge, he now realizes that he genuinely loves her, and she him. Trusting her father's claims that he wants to help Nishi, Yoshiko reveals the location of Nishi's hideout and Iwabuchi has both Nishi and Wada murdered. The film ends with the hero dead, the corrupt executive unpunished.

The Bad Sleep Well is one of Kurosawa's most underrated films. It is a difficult, challenging picture, and while it doesn't always work, much of it is impressive. Part of the problem is that the first 25 minutes of the 151-minute film (the wedding and the scandal montage) are so striking—and as good as anything Kurosawa ever directed—that the rest of the film pales by comparison. Yet, while the second and third acts lack the first part's vibrancy, they too have a power and complexity all their own. In some ways, many of the best and weakest elements are just the opposite of what the director had intended.

As he did so expertly in *Seven Samurai* and again in later films like *Yojimbo*, *High and Low*, and *Red Beard*, Kurosawa establishes the large cast of characters and their relationship to one another in the engaging, defining introductory scenes. The wedding reception is suspenseful, funny, and ironic. Nothing is what it seems to be. What begins with stifling formality comes crashing down into near-farce. This is followed by an exciting montage of newspaper headlines and newsreel-like footage of the subsequent scandal. Men are arrested, witnesses are questioned, headlines bleat outrage at the events. This sequence is helped enormously by composer Masaru Sato's "corporate underworld" motif. "I was trying to depict the ruthless corporate environment," Sato said in 1996, "and I remembered the expression 'It's a jungle out there,' and so I tried to create a jungle-like atmosphere in the music."[19]

It might be said that Nishi is Mifune's Hamlet. The film is inspired by Shakespeare (if not to the degree of *Throne of Blood*), and like Hamlet, Nishi pretends to be something he's not in an intricately plotted vengeance story against a surrogate father responsible for the real father's death.* Where Hamlet feigned madness only to teeter on the border of genuine insanity, Nishi becomes so "bad" himself that to get to the bad men, he veers toward becoming one of them. It is no easy task and Nishi knows it, particularly when his feelings for Yoshiko become more complex than he had anticipated. Men like Iwabuchi find peace and serenity despite their viciousness, but this is something Nishi is incapable of doing (though Donald Richie argues just the reverse): being so single-minded about his revenge plot proves extremely injurious to Nishi's soul. Like the film's title, one lacking in conscience can sleep better than one who isn't. Nishi is ruthless, but he has a soul, and it is his basic decency that proves his undoing.

Kurosawa seemed to realize his inability to satisfactorily depict this inner struggle. In his later film *High and Low*, the director much more successfully portrays similarly complex internal conflicts. In that picture Mifune's torment is both realistic and universal, and the story never lapses into the melodramatic, which *The Bad Sleep Well* occasionally does. The fundamental difference between Mifune's Nishi in *The Bad Sleep Well* and his Gondo in *High and Low* is that Nishi is incapable of being completely evil. Gondo, by contrast, chooses, in spite of everything, to be good.

Kurosawa falls short in his efforts to blur Nishi's morality, specifically in questioning whether his actions are morally any more justifiable than the acts of the very men he seeks vengeance upon. Much of Mifune's dialogue consists of Hamlet-like monologues that address this, but like Hamlet,

---

*Helmut Kautner's *The Rest Is Silence* (Der Rest ist Schweigen), starring Hardy Krüger and Peter Van Eyck and released in 1959, also adapted *Hamlet* to a modern corporate world.

Nishi remains an enigma. While the audience is cued by the conventions of the corporate thriller to be on Nishi's side, these scenes never really get inside the character.

Reflecting on the film, Kurosawa remarked, "I was simply not telling and showing enough. Like the final scene with [Masayuki] Mori on the telephone. This is the last of several calls, all apparently to the same person, someone very high in the Japanese government. That suggests, but is not explicit enough, [that] an even worse man is at the other end of that telephone line, but in Japan if you go any further then you are bound to run into serious trouble. This came as a big surprise to me, and maybe the picture would have been better if I had been braver. At any rate, it was too bad that I didn't go further. Maybe I could have in a country like America. Japan, however, cannot be this free and this makes me sad."[20]

However, it is not the ambiguity of this scene that weakens the film's impact. Indeed, it has just the opposite effect, which is to enhance its universality. Rather, it is in the scenes immediately prior, which so insist on tragedy, which so demand that in Nishi's decision to no longer be bad he must then inevitably perish, that the film becomes artificial and forced. These last scenes are not without a certain power (Takeshi Kato as Nishi's friend and Kagawa as Nishi's wife descend into a kind of madness), but here Kurosawa allows his drama to lapse into dogma.

More interesting is how Kurosawa explores loss of identity and how several of the main characters exist in a kind of purgatory between life and death. Nishi, for instance, is Iwabuchi's son-in-law, but all the while he uses his friend's identity. When Nishi is murdered, so too is the real Nishi's "identity" murdered. Wada pretends to be dead and witnesses his own funeral.

The film is much more successful with the Claudius-like Iwabuchi, a character who is both a bad man and a good father. One minute he is warmly treating his children to a barbecue in the back yard, gently blowing on a hot sweet potato to cool it for his daughter, the next plotting the murder of one of his employees. This type of character would become a cliché in corporate-world thrillers, but at the time Kurosawa's approach was relatively novel.

A chameleon of an actor, Masayuki Mori, in his last film for Kurosawa, is virtually unrecognizable as the same man who played the husband in *Rashomon* and the title role in *The Idiot*. Born Yukimitsu Arishima in 1911, in Sapporo, Hokkaido, Mori was the son of writer Takeo Arishima. He was educated at Imperial University in Kyoto and began a long and much-acclaimed career on the stage at the age of eighteen. He made his film debut in 1942, and first worked for Kurosawa in *Sanshiro Sugata, Part Two* three years later. Although Western audiences know him best for his work in *Rashomon* and as the potter in Mizoguchi's *Ugetsu* (1953), Mori is best known in Japan as a master of contemporary roles, especially in his work for Mikio Naruse. For him Mori gave memorable performances in such films as *Floating Clouds* (Ukigumo, 1955; for which he won *Kinema Jumpo*'s Best Actor prize) and *When a Woman Ascends the Stairs* (Onna ga kaidan o agaru toki, 1960). He worked for a wide range of postwar directors, including Keisuke Kinoshita (*Broken Drum* [Yabure taiko, 1949]), So Yamamura (*The Crab-Canning Ship* [Kanikosen, 1953]), Hiromichi Horikawa (*The Path Under the Platanes* [Suzukake no sanpomichi, 1959]), but is most closely associated with Mizoguchi and, after that director's death, Naruse. Actress Kyoko Kagawa said of him, "I admired him so much as an actor. . . . He was an actor who could play any role, from an intelligent lawyer to a *yakuza*."[21] Mori worked steadily in films and in the theater until his death in 1973.

Kurosawa also succeeds in an unexpected way that is rarely mentioned in other writings on the film: the love scenes between Nishi and Yoshiko. With the exception of *Madadayo* (1993), their moments together have a tenderness unmatched in Kurosawa's entire oeuvre. Over time, Nishi develops deep feelings of love for Yoshiko, but suppresses them—or tries to. In one remarkable scene, Tatsuo all but begs Nishi to be good to his sister, for as a child it was Tatsuo who crippled Yoshiko in a bicycle accident. Yoshiko, bringing Tatsuo a drink, overhears their conversation and begins weeping. She drops a glass and stumbles. Hearing this, Nishi and Tatsuo rush to her aid. Nishi reaches her first, lifting her in his arms like a doll. Seeing this instinctive behavior, Tatsuo quietly beams, for he now knows Nishi really does love her. Yoshiko also realizes that Nishi loves her, but then, remembering his goal, he leaves her, and once again she weeps. It's a powerful scene, partly because every emotion is left unsaid. (It also parallels a brief moment during the wedding reception when Yoshiko also stumbles. There it is the brother alone who runs to her aid.)

Later, Wada secretly takes Yoshiko to Nishi's hideout. Nishi finds that Yoshiko loves him in spite of her awareness of his identity and his plans against her father. The two finally, passionately, embrace. (Kurosawa ingeniously separates them by a bench-high stone divider; they must lean over it to reach each other.) It is a deeply felt moment, unique in Kurosawa's work.

Kagawa makes the most of these scenes, giving a heartbreaking performance. As she often did with her characters, Kagawa worked hard to make Yoshiko's physical handicap believable. "It was very difficult wearing the special shoes, which were taller on one foot, to make it appear that I was lame. [Actress Hideko] Takamine had once played a character who injured her leg, and she advised me to wear a knee brace so I wouldn't be able to walk naturally, freely. This helped me quite a bit."[22]

Though equally believable, Mifune makes, oddly, little impression in the film. Partly this is by design: as Iwabuchi's secretary, he's supposed to be all but invisible. When Nishi's motives become clear, the single-mindedness of the character similarly works against a deeper understanding of this tragic figure.

Mifune is also up against a half-dozen superb supporting performances. Besides Mori and Kagawa, the excellent cast includes Takashi Shimura, Ko Nishimura, and Kamatari Fujiwara. Tatsuya Mihashi (b. 1923), on the verge of stardom playing hip, Bondian spies (he was the lead in the "International Secret Police" series that Woody Allen lampooned in *What's Up, Tiger Lily?*), is well cast as the guilt-ridden playboy/brother-in-law. By the time he made *The Bad Sleep Well*, Mihashi had already worked with Kagawa many times before. She recalled, "We played brothers and sisters in so many films that offscreen I thought of him as a brother."[23] Mihashi remembered Kurosawa telling Toho star Kyoko Anzai (Mihashi's wife) that he wanted a performer whom the audience might suspect was behind the acts actually committed by Nishi in the earliest scenes.[24]

Takeshi Kato (b. 1929), the "real" Koichi Nishi with whom Mifune trades identities, had appeared in small roles in *Throne of Blood* and *The Hidden Fortress*. It was Kato who played the bloody samurai who backs into the frame at the beginning of *The Hidden Fortress*, shocking the two peasants. A stage actor trained at the Bungakuza Theatre Company (Haruko Sugimura was one of its founders), Kato was becoming known in films in the new decade, mainly in supporting roles at Nikkatsu. *The Bad Sleep Well* was his first big role in a Kurosawa film, and his inexperience made him the target of Kurosawa's wrath. Once again, the director was singling out an actor for abuse.

Production began three weeks late, at the N. I. Motors office set, on March 28. "During rehearsals, I kept being scolded by Mr. Kurosawa. All the time," Kato said. "On the first day there was no shooting, just on-set rehearsals. We had kidnapped Kamatari Fujiwara and put him on the second floor of the car dealership. There was a long scene, maybe five or six minutes with Mr. Mifune and Mr. Fujiwara, and then I entered that room. It all had to be done in a single take. But every time I entered the room, Mr. Kurosawa would say, because of my facial expression, 'No good. Cut!' [laughs].

"Back then, foreign car dealerships were rare, so it was a very fashionable business. My character drove a Studebaker, an automatic, but I didn't even have a driver's license. My character should have had a very relaxed, cool demeanor, with his modern suit, his Dunhill lighter, his cigarette case. But I was just a poor student, eating bread every day. And this reality became obvious in my performance. I had never worn such clothing—it took three days to decide on the suit I wore. Mr. Kurosawa ordered me to wear the suit all the time to get used to it. So on the outside I looked great, but inside I still looked poor and I realized that because of this I wasn't relaxed, and the more Mr. Kurosawa told me to relax, the less relaxed I became.

"We were supposed to be on the second floor of a car dealership, but actually it was shot on the third floor of the Toho Haiyu Kaikan Building, and so he told me to run up and down the steps to relax myself. Finally shooting began, but I still wasn't relaxed, and I was supposed to enter the office, eating fried rice with Mr. Fujiwara, and should have been the coolest of the three. We did the scene over and over, and each time: 'Cut!'

"I so appreciated Mr. Mifune, because he never looked angry, and every take he gave a great performance. I heard later on that because of Mr. Kurosawa's deep-focus photography, they had to use a lot of lights, and because of this Mr. Mifune and Mr. Fujiwara should have been mad at me, being under such hot lights. Mr. Fujiwara kept pretending to go to bathroom, but actually he left to go throw up [because of the heat generated by the lights]. That's why even now I still remember and appreciate them. He was getting sick because of me! To this day, every time I see that scene, I want to throw up! [laughs]."

Kato was well aware of the kind of treatment Japan's biggest movie stars expected. Mifune, Kato said, was different. "You know, Mr. Mifune always played tough, dynamic roles, but off the set he was very delicate, a caretaker. Usually at that time the big stars had a *tsukibito* [a personal assistant], who was supposed to follow the star around with a chair, light their cigarettes, and so on, but he never had one. He'd carry a chair around by himself. I was just a new face, and just standing around, and Mr. Mifune found *me* a chair to sit in!"[25]

"Even on his films with Kurosawa, he'd go to the studio alone," remembered son Shiro. "Other actors would have their assistants and managers helping them, but he didn't like to have people helping him like that. He wanted to do everything himself. He never had an agent. He would negotiate his contracts himself."[26]

Tomio Sagisu concurred. "He was a big star, [yet] he was the only one not to have [a tsukibito]. He did everything himself. I think it was because of his six years in the Navy."[27]

"I was always worried about him being exhausted, because he took care of other people too much," confirmed Kyoko Kagawa. "He would bring people chairs. If the costume designer was carrying a heavy bag, he would help her. . . . He drove himself, he did everything himself. He was called 'Mifune of the World,' but I don't think he was aware of it. He was so humble. That's what everybody thought of him.

"I never saw him with a script," she added. "He always knew his lines. He was a hard worker, and made a lot of effort, but he didn't show it. I don't think it was false modesty, though. I think he was embarrassed that he was proud of himself." After watching Mifune and Kurosawa working together, Kagawa said, "They knew everything about each other, and Mr. Kurosawa wrote the scripts with Mr. Mifune in mind, pulling Mr. Mifune into the character. Working together they were able to bring out the best in each other."[28]

The film also marked the Kurosawa debut of Ko Nishimura (not Akira Nishimura, as he is usually billed), as Shirai. Nishimura (1923–97), in films after 1951, was one of the industry's busiest character actors. He was as much in demand as Takashi Shimura, and his status was nearly as great. Appearing in everything from Zatoichi movies at Daiei to science-fiction films at Toho, Nishimura is best remembered in Japan for the TV drama *Mito Komon*. Nishimura wrote:

> I never have vivid memories of the films I do, but [*The Bad Sleep Well*] is an exception, because both the finished film and being on the set were so powerful . . . . I had to be surprised all the time in the film. Well, I really had no choice because there were surprises in every scene. When I met Mr. Kurosawa for the first time, I was surprised when he told me, "Nishimura-kun, you will be surprised twenty times in this film. All of your reactions should be different. You think about it." There aren't that many different ways to look surprised, I thought. He also ordered me to save my biggest reaction for the last scene. This was the scene where I'm surprised when a lot of money turns up in my briefcase as I open it in Mifune-chan's room. At first, I glanced into the bag and closed it. He didn't like it. "Closing your bag quickly means you knew what was inside it," he said. "You aren't

supposed to know that. You don't expect money in there at all. You look at it and *then* you get scared." The script said my reaction was supposed to be as if I had been struck by lightning. Thanks to his good advice I think I did a good job.[29]

The wedding reception was shot over two weeks, from April 22 through early May. Around this time, Mifune played host to Charlton Heston, in Japan for the opening of *Ben-Hur*. Heston wrote of Mifune: "My God, what a presence. If he could act in English, he'd conquer the world."[30] He regarded Mifune as "Japan's greatest actor," and the two exchanged Christmas cards every year until Mifune's death.[31]

The scene in which Nishi and Wada take Shirai to the building where Nishi's father had committed suicide was shot at the New Maru Building on the evening of May 15. "We were shooting the scene where Mifune-chan shoves a handkerchief into my mouth," remembered Nishimura. "His performance was very physical. Mr. Kurosawa yelled, 'Take it easy!' but Mifune-chan couldn't take it easy once he started acting. He finally cut the back of my lip, and blood was all over the handkerchief. He apologized profusely. Then we shot the scene where he shoves me out the window. It was the real window of the building, and my body was tied to a rope which was firmly attached to a steam heater. But Mifune-chan attacked me with his unusual power. That was frightening."[32]

On June 10, the cast and crew drove to Mt. Aso to shoot Wada preparing to jump into the smoky volcano. The production then moved to an open set [backlot] on June 23 for Nishi and Wada observing Wada's staged funeral. The picture wrapped soon after, with the music recorded in late July and the first test screenings held on August 22.

In the midst of production, Kurosawa was approached to direct a documentary on the 1964 Tokyo Olympics, still some four years away. The film would be produced by the Organizing Committee for the Games of the XVIII Olympiad, with support from Toho. Kurosawa was intrigued by the idea, and he flew to Rome that fall to see the 1960 games, stopping at several film festivals on his way back.

Meanwhile, advertising was prepared, declaring, "A Fearless Man Takes on a Huge, Evil Institution—the Japanese Underworld. The Great Master Brings His Ambitious Skill to the Present Age."

The Bad Sleep Well received favorable reviews in Japan and ranked third behind Kon Ichikawa's *Her Brother* (Otoko) and Hiromichi Horikawa's *The Lost Alibi* (a.k.a. *Black Book*; Kuroi gashu) on *Kinema Jumpo*'s list of the year's best films. The picture was neither a flop nor a hit at the box office. It

294 STUART GALBRAITH IV

earned its money back and then some, but in the end turned a smaller profit than the Kurosawa films that immediately followed. Indeed, the ten top-grossing films of the year were dominated by Toei (with five in the year's top ten) and Nikkatsu (with four), both of whom had made remarkable strides over the past decade. Only Mikio Naruse's *Daughter, Wife, Mother* (Musume • Tsuma • Haha) made the list for Toho, ranking eighth.

Because of its limited success in Japan, its modern setting, and the studio's belief that its story was singularly "Japanese," Toho had little faith in the film's box office outside Japan, even after *The Bad Sleep Well* became the hit of the Berlin Film Festival. As a result, the picture was not shown in the United States in 1960 or 1961. But Kazuto Ohira, a Toho employee living in Los Angeles, loved it, and with the help of James Silke, a professor at UCLA, arranged a special screening on the Westwood, California, campus on October 5, 1962. The screening proved extremely successful, with students cramming the aisles and prompting a second, unscheduled showing. This was enough to spur Toho into releasing the picture three months later, albeit in a truncated form running 16 minutes shorter than the Japanese version. Perversely, the love scenes between Mifune and Kagawa were cut, as was the scene where Moriyama visits Nishi's stepmother and thus learns his identity.

When the film opened in New York, reviews were hostile. Bosley Crowther, as he so often did with Japanese films, damned *The Bad Sleep Well* with faint praise:

> Akira Kurosawa made it and he is a director with great ingenuity and style. But, if you inspect it closely and with some knowledge of the oldies, you will see that it is actually an imitation, in form and melodramatic incidents, too, of some classic American gangster pictures. . . . This is usual with Kurosawa. He is great at "borrowing" and applying the cinema styles of other countries to a Japanese milieu. . . . Fortunately, his new picture . . . is a forceful, suspenseful realization of the gross power it is meant to expose, and it is well played by Toshiro Mifune and other of Kurosawa's favorites. But it is still an imitation, which the director himself would probably admit. For, again we note, imitation is the sincerest form of plagiarism in films.[33]

The film was officially released in the United States in early 1963, following American distribution of both *Yojimbo* and *Sanjuro*, Kurosawa's next

two films. But reviews remained mixed to negative. "The last picture by
Akira Kurosawa . . . is not very good," wrote Stanley Kauffmann in *The New
Republic*. "It is so remote in every way from the mainstream of his work
that, except for the opening sequence and the presence of some of his
'stock company,' there is no internal reason to believe that Kurosawa did it.
It could have been made by any experienced, tamely imaginative director
of films or television. . . . The picture's one reward is in seeing Toshiro
Mifune young, handsome, and sprucely double-breasted. Those who have
watched him as a tigerish medieval bandit, a staunch old general, a frenzied
Nipponese Macbeth, a deft nineteenth-century thief, or, lately, as a solitary
and pragmatic samurai, will at least enjoy marveling at this leonine actor's
magnificent range."[34]

Fritz Blocki of the *Hollywood Citizen-News* thought the film "a well produced, excellently directed and enacted suspense melodrama," adding, "It is
unfortunate they did not dub the entire film into English, instead of merely
using subtitles, because the Japanese names of characters are complicated
and difficult to understand."[35]

It was Kevin Thomas of the *Los Angeles Times* who rightly noted: "Far too
many critics are writing off the new Akira Kurosawa film . . . as second rate
in comparison to his celebrated period dramas. Perhaps they are disappointed that, despite skyscrapers and sport cars, Kurosawa has not come up
with a really 'contemporary' drama. This is a grave injustice, for Kurosawa
perceives that the world of high finance and corporate intrigue is material
for classic tragedy acted in the grand style with a hero who has imagination
and courage far beyond the usual Man in the Gray Flannel Suit."[36]

Time said: "Kurosawa, a superb director with a burning concern for social problems, addresses himself in this angry, ironic, sometimes unfair but
always violently exciting story of corruption in high places. His story is cir-
cumstantial, but his theme is universal. . . . The suspense is terrific, but
Kurosawa generates more than suspense. In his big boss (Masayuki Mori)
he develops a masterly portrait of the power complex, and in scene after
scene he examines with incinerating irony a way of life in which profits
come first and people last. . . . Within his conventions Kurosawa is a realist,
and when he does a caricature he does it in acid. *The Bad Sleep Well* is not
quite as strong as his strongest pictures, but it has a vulgar energy, the cutting relevance, the mortal moral seriousness of first-rate journalism."[37]

More recently, the film's status has been raised appreciatively, and its
examination of characters both good and evil became more influential on
filmmakers such as Francis Ford Coppola and Martin Scorsese than some of

his better known works. Indeed, the entire wedding reception in *The God-father* mirrors in many ways the one in Kurosawa's film. Coppola himself wrote: "The first 30 minutes of *The Bad Sleep Well* seem to me as perfect as any film I have ever seen. The clear and formal build-up of the elements of this modern story unfold in a poetic unveiling of a mysterious tragedy. . . . Kurosawa interprets life. This is the most any artist can do. And why he can be ranked among the great dramatists of history."[38]

It was at this time that Toho, having limited success selling its product abroad beyond the Ishiro Honda–Eiji Tsuburaya monster films, embarked on an entirely new strategy of foreign distribution. If they couldn't get their films distributed in America, then they would distribute them there themselves. The company purchased a former art-house theater, the Art La Brea, located in midtown Los Angeles, at 857 La Brea Avenue, a few blocks south of the "Miracle Mile" section of Wilshire Boulevard. It was a strange place to open a Japanese movie house, several miles northwest of what was then the largest concentration of Japanese-Americans in the city. The La Brea was also southwest of the studios in Hollywood (Paramount, Columbia) and east of the deal makers in Beverly Hills and Culver City (including the Fox and M-G-M lots). Still, it was otherwise centrally located to most of the city, and at 640 seats an ideal size for the kind of pictures it would show.

The Toho La Brea, as it became known, was the first of a half dozen or so theaters the company would own and operate outside Japan. Over the next four years, Toho theaters would open in São Paulo, New York, Okinawa, Rio, and Honolulu, but the La Brea remained the most visible. Toho International's main office was on its second floor.

Toho saw its future in America in establishing a chain of theaters throughout the country, much as it did in Japan. Since the mid-1950s, the studio had been subtitling or dubbing one- to two-thirds of its yearly product, usually around forty features a year, plus the occasional short subject. Subtitling and shipping prints abroad was not cheap, costing approximately $3,500 per title, and to Toho's way of thinking, the more theaters they could show them in the better, even if they did have to show them in theaters they had to manage themselves.

At first the Toho La Brea struggled to determine its own identity and purpose, and to find an audience. Originally, the studio had hoped to use the La Brea to exhibit and market not only its own product but that of the other Japanese majors as well. Toho spokesmen initially told the Japanese press, "It's a display window not only for Toho, but also for five other Japanese studios." But the other studios either declined Toho's offer or couldn't come to terms, and one of the effects this lack of industrywide support had was that the La Brea soon ran out of films to show. This resulted in Toho subtitling more of their own films than originally intended, forcing them to exhibit less popular films for longer runs. Its managers also had to acclimate themselves to American tastes. *Throne of Blood*, for example, which was not a blockbuster in Japan, ran for five weeks in Los Angeles and could have played several more. The subsequent success of Kurosawa's *Yojimbo* in America helped establish a regular audience at the La Brea, but the company still had to spend more money on advertising than for a Toho theater in Japan, often going to the expense of flying out guests like Mifune for their biggest releases.[39]

At the same time, several other studios began operating theaters in Los Angeles. Daiei, which had established itself in America earlier thanks to *Rashomon*, moved from the small Kinema Theater downtown to the Kokusai. A larger theater than the La Brea, and also located in central Los Angeles (near a Japanese enclave), the Kokusai stood at the corner of Crenshaw and Adams. Toei and Shochiku operated smaller theaters in downtown Los Angeles, near the city's "Little Tokyo" neighborhood: the vacated Kinema and the Linda Lea, respectively. But the population of Japanese-Americans in Los Angeles was not large, less than 40,000, and the number of non-Japanese who regularly attended such films was substantially less than that.

The La Brea's first manager was Kazuto Ohira. "In 1956, when I graduated from Waseda University, I passed Toho's test and joined the company," he said. "That was the best time for Japanese films. After the San Francisco Peace Agreement, Toho planned to expand their business all over the world, including in America. The La Brea was the first part of this plan, in 1959. In January 1960, Toho sent five workers to Los Angeles, and another to Hawaii. . . . Previously, International Toho [as Toho International was then known] had an office in Little Tokyo, in Los Angeles. There was already one person from Japan working there, as well as two assistants.

"The purpose of the La Brea, which was in a white neighborhood, was to directly invite American audiences to come and see Japanese films. Of course, we were planning to distribute our films to the entire nation, but thanks to the La Brea, our films came to the attention of the directors and producers in Hollywood."[40]

Ohira saw the La Brea as an operation quite different from older Japanese movie theaters in America, such as the Linda Lea. "The target audience at the La Brea was American, in addition to Japanese-Americans. On the other hand, the Linda Lea operated on a smaller scale, showing anything they could get, including independent Japanese films. For the major films, 60 percent of the Toho La Brea's audience was American. I was impressed that for the Kurosawa films Americans drove in from outside the Los Angeles area to see them, as well as [Zenzo Matsuyama's] *Happiness of Us Alone* [Namonaku Mazushiku Utsukushiku, 1961]. For the program pictures, the audience was about 80 percent Japanese-American, 20 percent Caucasian. We tried to slip Japanese films into American culture so that Americans would gain a better understanding of Japanese film, and so that we'd acquire Japanese film fans, which ultimately contributed to the film prosperity of the 1960s."[41]

The Rickshaw Man was selected to open the Toho La Brea, and president Masashi Shimizu asked Mifune to join him for the grand opening on August 3, 1960. With them were Toho starlets Kumi Mizuno (Mifune's sister in *The Gambling Samurai*) and Misao Kamijo, along with Nagamasa Kawakita, director of Toho's foreign department, acting as an interpreter. Arriving in Los Angeles, Shimizu told reporters, "Japan has surpassed America in annual film production, but we still consider Hollywood the spiritual capital of the motion picture industry." He also announced plans to build Toho theaters in New York and Chicago, to bring Toho's Nichigeki Dancers to Radio City Music Hall, and that other Toho stars, including Izumi Yukimura, Yoko Tsukasa, and Reiko Dan, would also be making personal appearances in the coming months.[42]

Ohira asserted that Shimizu's plan to build a theater in Chicago wasn't financially feasible, and Toho wasn't serious about it. Nonetheless, Ohira remembered Shimizu as a man "who earnestly tried to expose the [world of Japanese film] abroad. The response was so positive. No other company in Japan was so successful. But beyond the financial success, he helped introduce the world to Japanese film, especially Kurosawa's, and helped them understand Japanese culture through film."[43]

The opening of the La Brea and other Japanese movie houses did help the industry. By 1962 the market for Japanese films in America had increased 30 percent from 1959, and Toho made plans to expand its American chain, hoping to open a dozen theaters in the United States over the next several years.[44]

Mifune returned to Japan to star in Toho's big New Year's release for 1961, Hiroshi Inagaki's *Daredevil in the Castle* (Osaka-jo monogatari). The film was a historical spectacle set in the early seventeenth century, with Mifune leading the large cast as Mohei, a samurai who has lost his entire family in the Battle of Sekigahara. His wandering leads him to Osaka, where he joins the Toyotomis and wins their respect with his unwavering bravery. Mifune battles monks and Portuguese opportunists at sea, as well as thousands of Japanese soldiers in and around an occupied Osaka Castle, the latter splendidly re-created by Eiji Tsuburaya's special-effects crew.

Produced on a huge scale, the picture climaxes with several thousand costumed extras storming Osaka Castle. Mohei and his comrades try to fend off the siege against a very large and quite believable miniature of the fortress superimposed behind them. Toho wasn't misleading the public with the film's advertising, which promised "Bigger Film Entertainment Than Ever Before!"

The prestigious cast included Kyoko Kagawa, Isuzu Yamada, Takashi Shimura, and a teenage starlet newly acquired from Takarazuka, Yuriko Hoshi (b. 1945). "That was my *jidai-geki* debut. I played the princess," Hoshi proudly recalled. "At the time I was sixteen years old. Isuzu Yamada was doing a play, and so we shot our scenes at night. I was still a student and had to go to school during the day—I was very sleepy. . . . [Inagaki] was my favorite director. He cherished me like a granddaughter. Toho didn't make many *jidai-geki* compared to the other studios. Inagaki's films were an exception, and he put me in more of his later films than any other actress." Of the film's star Hoshi said, "Mr. Mifune was very gentle, very quiet. We had common friends in Hawaii, and I had several opportunities to visit his house and have dinner."[45]

Daredevil in the Castle did respectable if not spectacular business in Japan. In America, the picture was seen as just another Eastern Western. "Aside from its seventeenth-century trappings and samurai swashbuckling," said *The New York Times*, "*Daredevil*—like, say, *Samurai*, its 1956 counterpart—could accommodate the rugged talents of John Wayne, Randolph Scott and company. Is that bad? Not exactly, but *Daredevil*, which is as action-filled as any horse opera, is a confusing business despite a plethora of English subtitles that often are unintentionally funny. Telling the good guys from the bad guys sometimes becomes a difficult assignment to handle. . . . As indicated there is hardly the simplicity and delicacy of a flower arrangement here, but there is, amid all the grunting and grimacing, no end of hand-to-hand swordplay as well as a climactic battle where Mifune, like the Seventh Cavalry, saves the besieged garrison almost single-handedly."[46]

"As Mohei," said the *Los Angeles Times*, "Toshiro Mifune proves to be an excellent performer who develops character generally deeper and stronger than the garden variety of leading man. He's not handsome, but he is rugged."[47]

"Unlike his films for Kurosawa, which depended on strong scripts," said *Variety*'s "Robe," reviewing the film when it was reissued in America in 1969, "the Hiroshi Inagaki efforts are concerned with only one thing—action. When the John Wayne of the Japanese cinema is not wiping up the ground with dozens of opponents, Inagaki fills in with the special effects work of Eiji Tsuburaya. . . . The result is a film that will delight samurai buffs and probably bore more serious filmgoers to death. . . . As the Japanese continue to add Western gimmicks—the pre-title sequence, the Westernized music, the fast cutting, etc.—they lose something of that special quality that made the earlier efforts of Kurosawa, Ozu, etc., truly works of cinematic art. Only such actioners as Inagaki's samurai efforts still retain a touch of the original, and that's gradually disappearing."[48]

SEVENTEEN

MULBERRIES, CAMELLIAS, AND CACTI

Mifune's next film would be the picture that deeply etched his screen persona, to both good and bad effect, for the rest of his life. In *Yojimbo* ("Bodyguard"), Kurosawa toys with the *chambara* genre, amusedly turning it inside out, much like Mifune's self-satisfied title character. Kurosawa had subverted the genre's conventions before, in *Rashomon*, *Seven Samurai*, and *The Hidden Fortress*, although playing with the genre had been a secondary concern. By contrast, *Yojimbo*, a black comedy, is a direct response to the mindless *chambara* Toei, Daiei, and Nikkatsu were churning out with great success and reckless abandon.

The story opens in 1860. Mifune, a *ronin* named Sanjuro, is seen wandering under the opening titles in tight close-ups. His journey is interrupted by the appearance of a farmer's son (Yosuke Natsuki), a youth sick of the rural life, in want of fame and fortune. His father tries to dissuade him. But the farmer's son wants a "short and exciting life" and runs off. Soon thereafter, Sanjuro reaches a small, hellish town. Windows slide open, and geisha and thugs stare at him suspiciously.

As he walks down the dusty, windswept road, a diminutive but sprightly man, Hansuke (Ikio Sawamura) runs out and tells Sanjuro that the town is torn by civil strife. Two factions are fighting for control of the village. One is led by the local sake merchant, Tokuemon (Takashi Shimura), and his gang boss, Ushitora (Kyu Sazanka); the other by the silk merchant, Tazaemon (Kamatari Fujiwara), and *his* henchman, Seibei (Seizaburo Kawazu).

For the price of one *ryo*, Hansuke advises Sanjuro to join Seibei's band. Hansuke says he would like to introduce Sanjuro to him but cannot: he's the town constable.

Sanjuro then sets about—to his great amusement—playing one side against the other, until the two sides destroy each other and the town is littered with bodies.

Yojimbo not only redefined the *chambara* genre; its influence was felt all over the world, and its basic story and antihero concepts have been reworked in a myriad of genres and countries. For Japanese audiences, *Yojimbo* was unlike anything that had come before. Its overwhelming popularity proved tremendously influential. It begat countless imitations in Japan as well, but none better than the original. The hundreds of imitative *chambara* films made since have only slightly lessened *Yojimbo*'s startling impact on audiences today. Though it lacks the weight of Kurosawa's best films, *Yojimbo* is undeniably a showcase for his technical virtuosity and the indelible screen presence of its star. It's a dazzling visual and aural feast, and immensely entertaining.

As in *Seven Samurai* and *The Hidden Fortress*, Kurosawa plays with the genre and the audience's expectations, filling the film with tough *yakuza* who are cowards and a *ronin* who is uncouth and unkempt. Yosuke Natsuki, as the farmer's son, had already become known for playing the kind of clichéd heroes the director lampoons here. In *Yojimbo*, Kurosawa sends him home, crying for his mother. Everyone talks big, but ultimately they are as ridiculous as the samurai and bandit in *Rashomon*. *Yojimbo* is brimming with point-of-view shots, exemplified by Mifune looking down at his villains from high atop a fire tower. In this, the *yojimbo* is really Kurosawa, amused by the ridiculousness of the world around him.

Kurosawa's revolutionary approach extended to the film's swordplay choreography, music, and sound effects.

[In *chambara* films], you used to hear only the sound of the sword or the samurai's yell [explained script supervisor Teruyo Nogami]. But our director, Kurosawa, asked the experienced sound mixer Ichiro Minawa, "Don't you think there would be some kind of sound when somebody is cut with a sword?" I heard they discussed this while standing in front of the Toho commissary. It was hard to find anyone willing to participate in this experiment. Anyway, Mr. Minawa thought about it, and made more than ten sound effects. I remember him hitting and stabbing cuts of pork and beef that he bought

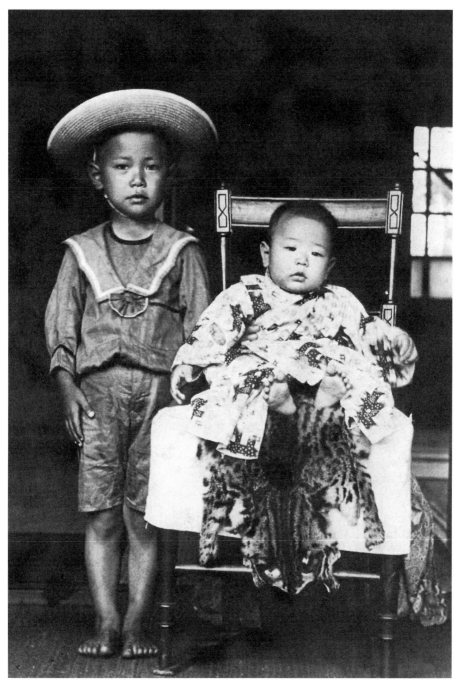

Six-month-old Kurosawa (seated) with brother Heigo, taken in the Kurosawa's hallway on August 3, 1910. (Courtesy of and reproduced with the permission of Kurosawa Production K.K. of Yokohama, Japan)

The Mifune family, circa 1925, in China. His uncle, Toshiro, father Tokuzo, brother Yoshiro, mother Sen, and sister Kimiko. (Courtesy of Mifune Productions Co., Ltd.)

Kurosawa and Ishiro Honda during their assistant director days. (Courtesy of and reproduced with the permission of Kurosawa Production K.K. of Yokohama, Japan)

Director Kajiro Yamamoto (center), flanked by two disciples, Senkichi Taniguchi and Kurosawa. (Courtesy of and reproduced with the permission of Kurosawa Production K.K. of Yokohama, Japan)

Mifune the wartime aerial photographer—a shot faked to impress his family and friends.
(Courtesy of Mifune Productions Co., Ltd.)

Kurosawa directs Yoko Yaguchi on the set of *The Most Beautiful* (1944). They would marry the following year. (Courtesy of and reproduced with the permission of Kurosawa Production K.K. of Yokohama, Japan)

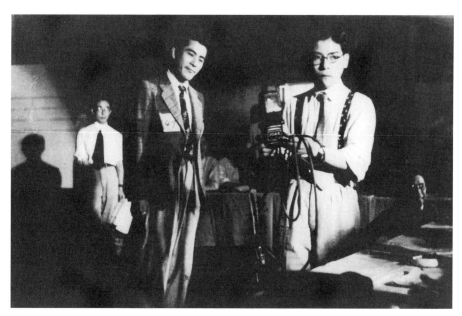

June 3, 1946. Mifune auditions to a skeptical panel at Toho's New Face Program. (Courtesy of Mifune Productions Co., Ltd.)

Kurosawa meets Frank Capra at a sukiyaki party thrown in Capra's honor. (L–R) (bottom row) directors Torajiro Saito (2nd from left), Kurosawa, Capra, Eisuke Takizawa, an unidentified man, and Hiroshi Inagaki; (top row) Senkichi Taniguchi, Shiro Toyoda, two unidentified men, Yasuki Chiba, Nobuo Nakagawa, and Yuzo Kawashima. (Courtesy of and reproduced with the permission of Kurosawa Production K.K. of Yokohama, Japan)

Mifune, Masayuki Mori, Machiko Kyo, and Kurosawa during preparation for *Rashomon* (1950). (Courtesy of and reproduced with the permission of Kurosawa Production K.K. of Yokohama, Japan)

Takashi Shimura in *Ikiru* (1952). (Brandon Films publicity still)

THE ACCLAIM IS UNANIMOUS! THE ENGAGEMENT IS AGAIN EXTENDED!

"ONE OF THE WORLD'S GREAT PICTURES! GO NOW—LEST YOU REPENT LATER!

"UNQUESTIONABLY A GREAT PICTURE IN THE BREADTH AND DEPTH OF ITS SUBJECT. THE WILD NIGHT OF DRUNKEN-NESS IS A TREMENDOUS CAMERA VISION OF NIGHTLIFE. IT IS A SHARPLY IRONIC STATE-MENT FROM BEGINNING TO END; HUMANLY SIGNIFICANT, UNFORGETTABLY INCISIVE... EXACTLY THE KIND OF PICTURE MANY A SERIOUS MOVIE-GOER WILL REGRET HAVING MISSED, SEARCH FOR, AND FAIL TO FIND."
—Archer Winsten, N.Y. Post

"A MASTERWORK! THE FINEST ACHIEVEMENT OF JAPAN'S MOST VIGOROUSLY GIFTED MOVIEMAKER." —Time Magazine

AKIRA KUROSAWA'S MASTERPIECE

Little **CARNEGIE**
57th Street, East of 7th Ave
CI6-3454

("TO LIVE!") 東宝

A TOHO PICTURE
RELEASED BY BRANDON FILMS

at: 1:10, 3:30, 5:50. 8:10, 10:35

Lurid art for Brandon Films' release of *Ikiru* in 1960. (Brandon Films Ad Mat)

Mifune with sons Takeo (top) and Shiro, around 1958. (Courtesy of Mifune Productions Co., Ltd.)

The Toho La Brea at the time of its purchase in 1960. (Courtesy of and reproduced with the permission of Kurosawa Production K.K. of Yokohama, Japan)

The first of many admirals: Mifune, Ryo Ikebe, and Koji Tsuruta in *I Bombed Pearl Harbor* [a.k.a. *Storm Over the Pacific*] (1960). (Parade Releasing publicity still)

At the hot springs inn, writing *The Bad Sleep Well* (1960). (L-R) Eijiro Hisaita, Shinobu Hashimoto, Kurosawa, Hideo Oguni, and Ryuzo Kikushima. (Courtesy of and reproduced with the permission of Kurosawa Production K.K. of Yokohama, Japan)

Shooting Wada's suicide attempt in *The Bad Sleep Well*. (L-R) (bottom row) Kamatari Fujiwara, Mifune, Takao Saito, Hiroshi Nezu, Yuzuru Aizawa, Kurosawa, Shiro Moritani, Fumio Yanoguchi, Kiyoshi Nishimura, Yoshimitsu Sakano, Senkichi Nagai; (top row) Shigeo Yamabayashi, Shoji Ogawa, Tokoroi, Ichiro Inohara, Teruyo Sato, Yoichi Matsue, and Koichi Hamamura. (Courtesy of and reproduced with the permission of Kurosawa Production K.K. of Yokohama, Japan)

On the open set of *Yojimbo* (1961). (L-R): Eijiro Tono (smoking), Mifune, and Shimura. Note the latter's contemporary glasses and wristwatch. (Courtesy of and reproduced with the permission of Kurosawa Production K.K. of Yokohama, Japan)

Aerial view of the open set of *Yojimbo* during shooting of the clash between the sake and silk merchants. Note Mifune on the firetower. (Courtesy of and reproduced with the permission of Kurosawa Production K.K. of Yokohama, Japan)

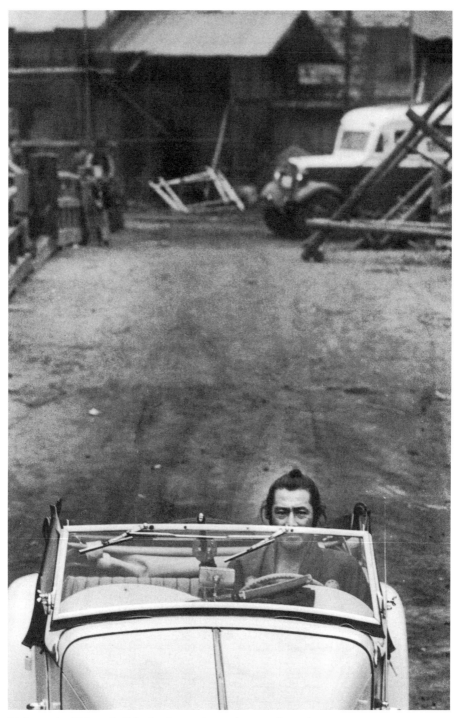

Mifune in his MG on the Toho lot during the production of *Yojimbo*. (Courtesy of and reproduced with the permission of Kurosawa Production K.K. of Yokohama, Japan)

El Hombre Importante (1961). Mifune as Animas Trujano. (Publicity still)

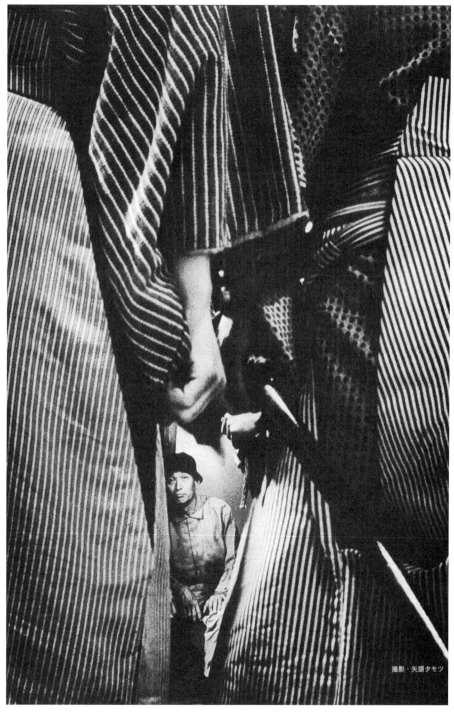

撮影・矢頭タモツ

Kurosawa framed by two samurai in *Sanjuro* (1962). (Courtesy of and reproduced with the permission of Kurosawa Production K.K. of Yokohama, Japan)

Japanese theater exhibiting
High and Low (1963).
(Courtesy of and reproduced
with the permission of Kurosawa
Production K.K. of Yokohama,
Japan)

The Toho Cinema in Manhattan, January 1963. (Courtesy of and reproduced with the permission of
Kurosawa Production K.K. of Yokohama, Japan)

from a butcher. He said it was expensive buying big cuts of meat. And so, the meat he attacked became food for the crew. According to Mr. Minawa, beef and pork were too soft to make a sound. He needed something bony. Finally, he put some chopsticks in a whole chicken and then attacked it with a sword. . . . On TV or in movies, they always use this kind of sound effect now, but *Yojimbo* was the first.[1]

The new sound effects were combined with graphic makeup. When the *yojimbo* cuts down one of the thugs, blood spurts onto the wall behind him. When Sanjuro kills Unosuke (Tatsuya Nakadai), the *yojimbo*'s pistol-carrying archrival, a puddle of blood spreads beneath him. This level of graphic realism, particularly in contrast with its comic elements, was unprecedented in Japan or anywhere else, and years before *Bonnie and Clyde* (1967) and *The Wild Bunch* (1969) shocked American audiences. Ryu Kuze's unprecedented, violent swordplay choreography—the very opposite of that in films like Inagaki's "Samurai" trilogy—and the degree of its violence stunned Japanese audiences. "Believe it or not," said Kuze's son-in-law, Minoru Nakano, "the first reaction was laughter. They hadn't seen this type of bloodshed in *jidai-geki* movies. Before *Yojimbo*, the *jidai-geki* was a kind of child of Kabuki, with very formalized movements and samurai mannerisms. So the first reaction was surprise. They didn't know how to react."[2]

The wall-to-wall music was also unlike anything heard in a *chambara* film before. With *Yojimbo*, Masaru Sato established himself as one of Japan's top film composers. "Up to that point *chambara* films had a very particular style of music [i.e., *faux*-traditional, mainly incorporating Japanese instruments]. It was total nonsense to my ears. It had no sense of universality. Mr. Kurosawa said, 'Write whatever you like, but please don't write *chambara* music!' So I started from scratch, with elements from Westerns mixed with traditional Japanese instruments. I tried to reflect the barbarism of the period. Since then, *chambara* music has changed quite a bit."[3]

Outstanding is his main title theme, and all the early music as Mifune arrives in the corrupt town, especially his cue for the unsettling, yet hilarious bit where Mifune, surveying the empty, dusty streets, encounters a happy-go-lucky dog bouncing down the road—with a severed hand in its mouth.

Sato admitted his style was greatly influenced by Henri Mancini: "[He's] one of my favorite composers. He changed American film music, and made it popular to the masses." Shortly after *Yojimbo*'s release, Sato had the opportunity to meet his American counterpart. "He asked to see me, and when we met he was surprised by how young I was. 'Have you been composing film music since you were born?' he asked. I remember he asked me a lot of questions about *Yojimbo*'s score, such as how long it took to compose and record, things like that."[4]

Kurosawa's characters are often likened to those of Dickens. Western audiences need look no further than *Yojimbo* for the obvious parallel. This is a story, like *Great Expectations*, *David Copperfield*, and *Oliver Twist*, filled with grotesque caricatures. There is, for example, Daisuke Kato's very funny Inokichi. The "Ino" of Inokichi, like Ishiro Honda's surname, means "boar," and the rotund Kato is boarlike in his appearance, heavily made-up, with a single, bushy eyebrow and protruding, gnarled teeth.

The town's cheery undertaker (Atsushi Watanabe) is a character straight out of *Oliver Twist*, a man happy only when there are coffins to make and bodies to bury. There are the Mutt and Jeff giant and his diminutive cohort, thugs played by Namigoro Rashomon (!) and Akira Tani. Their scenes guarding a beaten Mifune are quite amusing. Also, the vulgar geishas kept by Seibei's wife (Isuzu Yamada), the slimy Tokuemon, and the diminutive Hansuke are all delicious caricatures, exaggerations in the Dickensian mode—unscrupulous villains and pathetic victims, but Mifune's *Yojimbo* is a conspicuous anomaly.

Yojimbo redefined Mifune's screen persona. Up to now his samurai roles outside of Kurosawa's films were more along the lines of Musashi Miyamoto. *Seven Samurai*'s Kikuchiyo was grounded in reality. In *Yojimbo*, Kurosawa and Mifune created a myth, one no less significant than that of Shane or Ethan Edwards or the Wild Bunch.

"Shrugging and scratching myself were my own ideas," Mifune told the *Film Daily*'s George E. Eagle. "I used these mannerisms to express the unemployed samurai, penniless, wearing dirty [kimono]. Sometimes this kind of man felt lonely, and these mannerisms characterize the loneliness."[5]

From here on, Mifune's samurai would more frequently be sardonic, disreputable, unkempt loners whose motivations are increasingly ambiguous. Why does the *yojimbo* clean up the town and help an innocent family escape? Not for money. To amuse himself, perhaps? He is on the side of good, but outwardly plays the greedy bad man. Without Kurosawa, however, Mifune's redefined samurai heroes would have little of the humor found in *Yojimbo* or its sequel. This was usually lost on filmmakers who aped the film's style. They failed to remember that *Yojimbo* was, first and foremost, a comedy, and nearly a parody at that.

Mifune is glorious. His reactions to the hand-carrying dog or the mallet-brandishing giant are priceless. Unshaven, pulling his arms deep inside his kimono to keep warm, sauntering down the town's dusty streets with a toothpick in his mouth, Mifune and Kurosawa's creation was a new kind of antihero, whose influence spread the world over.

Like *The Hidden Fortress*, *Yojimbo* and its follow-up, *Sanjuro*, were physically taxing for Mifune, now in his early forties. Actress Yoko Tsukasa (playing the beautiful woman held as a sex slave by Tokuemon) remembered shooting the scene where Sanjuro kills the six people guarding her. The lights were so hot, so intense for Kurosawa's deep-focus photography, they nearly set Mifune's back afire. "I was so impressed by his hard breathing after he killed those . . . people," she added. "He moved his shoulders up and down and regained his composure. I thought he risked his life for his performance."[6]

"I did a scene where I had to kill thirty people at once," Mifune said of a similar sequence in *Sanjuro*. "I was young then, but I thought my heart would explode."[7]

In Unosuke, Tatsuya Nakadai (b. 1932) created an archetypal villain. The character became the mold for cocky, psychologically unhinged villains as deadly as their heroic counterparts, villains with superior, modern weapons. Referring to Unosuke's name, the character is likened to "a rabbit, but with a wolf inside." With his large, glassy eyes and crazy grin, Nakadai's Unosuke kills men with his pistol as if showing off a new toy.

Initially, though, Kurosawa was reluctant to cast him. "Mr. Nakadai had received the Rookie of the Year Award for *Untamed* [Arakure, 1957]," remembered Haruyo Nogami, "and worked on *The Human Condition* [Ningen no joken], directed by Masaki Kobayashi, beginning in 1959. His skills were widely recognized. I remember that . . . Moritani had suggested him to director Kurosawa and that Kurosawa decided to meet with him.[8]

" 'I don't like Nakadai,' " he told chief assistant director Shiro Moritani. " 'If the director doesn't like an actor, he shouldn't cast him as one of the leads.' " To this Moritani replied, "I thought it was strange. I asked him which of Nakadai's movies he had seen. He hadn't seen any of them; he doesn't usually watch domestic films. But then he watched all of Nakadai's movies and finally said, 'How about Nakadai for *Yojimbo*?' He likes Nakadai now."[9]

"During preproduction," recalled Nogami, "he spent time with Nakadai

to create the character's personality. Unosuke's muffler was one of Kurosawa's suggestions. . . . We didn't think a muffler in a *jidai-geki* was appropriate, but . . . he chose a red muffler made in Scotland. 'Isn't this good?
Foreigners wear this, too. Unosuke got it somewhere,' Kurosawa said,
laughing. 'Actually, the muffler is a good effect and helps explains Unosuke's *yakuza* personality.' "[10]

There was only one problem with using Nakadai. He was scheduled to
go before Masaki Kobayashi's cameras for the third part of *The Human Condition* trilogy. Kobayashi decided to let Nakadai make *Yojimbo* first. "If you
play the same character for too many years," Kobayashi told the actor, "your
screen persona may become fixed. I think it's a good idea for you to play a
totally different character for Mr. Kurosawa."[11]

The scenes with Nakadai and Mifune are electrifying, as one critic
noted, like a face-off between Elvis Presley and John Wayne. They are
memorable in spite of the fact that the two actually share little in the way of
screen time together. Before the picture was released, Toho and Kurosawa
began to capitalize on their magnetism. A coming-attractions trailer was
prepared with footage not part of the finished film. One bit, shot specifically for the trailer, has them against a neutral background on a soundstage,
facing off. The trailer also contains a shot from the climactic battle, in
which the two approach each other and Nakadai says, "Don't come too
close." In the trailer, none of Ushitora's men are in sight, just Mifune and
Nakadai, quite unlike the finished film. (As with all of Toho's trailers from
the period, it was put together using alternate takes and angles, apparently
to save lab and printing costs. Viewing the footage, one can see how adeptly
Kurosawa uses his multiple-camera technique and his choice of angles and
takes.)

Smiling broadly, Kurosawa told Nakadai, "Sanjuro and Unosuke are like
a stray dog and a snake. There are so many movies where the villain is over-
powered by the main character from the start. But that's no fun. The villain
should be his equal, in fact he should be more powerful than the main char
acter." Nakadai was thankful for the opportunity. "In those days, it was said
that a movie star should carefully maintain the image he creates through his
characters. I hoped that I could be an actor who was continually challenged
with different characters. My master [Kurosawa] gave me many opportunities to play different roles. . . . When I look back, I was very lucky to have
had many chances to play unique characters, thanks to him."[12]

Once again Kurosawa used the natural elements to accentuate the mood
of his story. In this case, it is a violent, dust-filled wind that punctuates *Yo-*

jimbo's hellish setting. Eight wind machines were used during filming, and the fierce winds they created posed problems when shooting the climax. "Once they were turned on, we couldn't hear anything," Nogami remembered. "It was like a helicopter flying over our heads." For the final duel between Mifune and Nakadai, Kurosawa ordered his two leads not to blink, and between takes the actors would have to rinse the sand out of their eyes.[13]

"I still remember Mr. Kurosawa having fun on the set," recalled Nakadai. "Of course, it wasn't just fun and games. It was fun combined with perfectionism, without compromise. . . . At a very young age I learned to be deeply passionate about filmmaking. I cannot measure the happiness I derived working with the great one."[14]

One actor who didn't care for Kurosawa's personality was Yosuke Natsuki. "Mr. Kurosawa was a gentleman, like Mr. [Ishiro] Honda, but there was an intimidating atmosphere that surrounded him, so much so that no one wanted to go near him," Natsuki said. "When we went on location I would have dinner with Mr. Mifune and Mr. Kurosawa in Kurosawa's room. He was very kind, but once he was working he'd sell his soul to the devil for a good shot. The stage was filled with tension. No one talked about anything except the work at hand. It was very quiet. He was called 'Emperor Kurosawa'—what he said and did was always right. The word 'compromise' didn't exist in his dictionary."[15]

Isuzu Yamada, in her last film for Kurosawa, is magnificently unscrupulous as Orin, Seibei's conniving wife. "He seemed to want a woman who was pushy, almost a bitch," Yamada recalled. "He didn't want an actress who couldn't be that. I was the wicked woman he imagined. I was disappointed in my performance because it might have been better if I had played that up more."[16] But the actress need not have been disappointed. She is marvelous, both funny and frightening, all smiles and charm to Sanjuro one minute, coldly plotting his murder the next.

Stealing every scene he's in is Ikio Sawamura (1905–75), playing Hansuke, the corrupt constable and timekeeper. The tiny actor with the wonderful falsetto voice had been a popular stage performer before joining Toho in 1954. He quickly garnered a reputation as a surefire laugh getter, much like Bokuzen Hidari before him. He seemed to turn up in nearly every Toho picture, in every genre, including many of Mifune's films without Kurosawa. He had small roles in Kurosawa's films, beginning with *Throne of Blood*, and would later appear as the eccentric trolley man in *High and Low*. Kurosawa's friend Ishiro Honda especially liked Sawamura. The actor had featured parts in most of Honda's sci-fi fantasies, including *Terror of Mechagodzilla* (Mekagojira no gyakusha, 1975), made as Sawamura was dying of cancer.

Shooting began on January 14, 1961, with scenes at the sake shop in which much of the story is centered. The production then went on location to Kofu, in Yamanishi Prefecture, to shoot the opening scenes under the main titles and those at the farmer's house. By early February Kurosawa's crew had moved to the open sets on the Toho lot to shoot the extensive exteriors.

Much of the picture's success has been attributed to cinematographer Kazuo Miyagawa, Kurosawa's cameraman on *Rashomon*. The picture undeniably bears his stamp, with beautifully framed wide-screen compositions throughout. However, Miyagawa conceded that Takao Saito, Kurosawa's assistant cameraman since *One Wonderful Sunday*, deserved much of the praise.

"Kazuo Miyagawa manned camera 'A' and Taka-chan [Saito] camera 'B,' " according to Kurosawa. "I left Taka-chan alone most of the time because he understands me very well. He shoots things in unexpected ways. That was interesting to me. Miyagawa asked me to use more of Taka-chan's footage than his own."[17]

Saito concurred, claiming that "at least 70 percent of all the shots used in the film were mine. It was the same time that rookie player [Shigeo] Nagashima joined the Yomiuri Giants [baseball team and Kurosawa] said to me, 'Kazuo Miyagawa is like [veteran baseball star] Kawakami. You are like Nagashima. We don't know if you should be the third batter or the fifth batter or what. We can count on Mr. Miyagawa just like we did on *Rashomon*. You can shoot whatever you want."[18]

Miyagawa, being Daiei's top cinematographer, hadn't worked with Kurosawa since *Rashomon* eleven years earlier, but they resumed their symbiotic relationship without missing a beat—Miyagawa likened it to a wife returning to her old husband. "We used three cameras," Miyagawa recalled, "but we used them simultaneously only for the teashop scene. We used two cameras for about a third of the picture, and one camera for another third. Some of the younger crews use multiple cameras to save time, but Mr. Kurosawa uses them so he won't have to interrupt an actor's performance."[19]

In March, Kurosawa filmed Mifune's escape from gang boss Ushitora, followed by scenes at a small temple where Sanjuro hides out near the end. Then, on April 10, the spectacular fire at Seibei's place and the climactic battle were filmed. Shooting wrapped on April 16. Because of Kurosawa's practice of editing during production, and the Japanese industry's habit of rushing films through postproduction, *Yojimbo* premiered just four days later, on April 20, 1961.

Kurosawa's reputation once again dominated the film's ads: "Everything Great About Motion Pictures Gathered Together in One Film. The Great Master Re-creates a Lawless Land." The public agreed. *The Lower Depths, Throne of Blood*, and *The Bad Sleep Well* had been marginally successful at the box office. *Yojimbo*, on the other hand, was an enormous hit. It earned ¥350,000,000 (about $1 million) in Japanese rentals alone, making it even more profitable than *Seven Samurai*, and the year's third-biggest domestic money earner. Mifune was awarded *Kinema Jumpo*'s Best Actor prize (for this and *Daredevil in the Castle*), and the picture placed second on their "Best Ten" list, just behind Susumu Hani's *Bad Boys* (Furyo shonen).

Surprisingly, the film received mixed reviews when it opened in the United States in 1962. Bosley Crowther dismissed the film with blunt cultural jingoism. "Beyond any question," he insisted, "a straight transposition of Western film clichés, which in turn may be dubious reflections of the historical and cultural truth of our frontier. Still, they stem from our tradition, not that of the Japanese." Of Mifune he said, "Always an interesting actor, commanding and apt at imagining strain. He passes well in this picture for a Japanese Gary Cooper or John Wayne." In the end, Crowther wrote, "as in most Westerns, the dramatic presentation is not deep. . . . Kurosawa is here showing more virtuosity than strength. 'Yojimbo' is a long way (in the wrong direction) from his brilliant 'Rashomon.' "[20]

But *The Saturday Review* begged to differ: "Kurosawa has, in effect, taken a familiar tale of violence and made from it a magnificent ironic parable; for Sanjuro, symbol of force and power that he is, becomes a plague on both houses. This extra dollop of significance helps give the film its glow of distinction, but it is not all. The action, and there is a lot of it, is staged with energy and style, and the strong mood of the film is further enhanced by a curious and effective musical score. 'Yojimbo' is helped, too, by Toshiro Mifune. . . . His Sanjuro is a virtuoso blend of confidence, high humor, and agile theatricality; a man immune to fear, but cautious as well as quick; a fearsome swordsman who can nevertheless be slightly startled when a dog walks by, a human hand in its jaws."[21]

Dorothy Masters of the New York *Daily News*, finding the picture "seldom relieved by comedy," preferred Mifune's performance in the Mexican-produced *The Important Man*, a film made immediately after *Yojimbo* but released in New York first. "In 'Yojimbo' . . . Mifune has less range. . . . Violence and gore dominate the presentation."[22]

S. A. Desick, reviewing the picture for the *Los Angeles Examiner*, wrote that the film "hardly carries the philosophical content of 'Rashomon'; nor does it have the epic character of 'Seven Samurai'; but it is a thoroughly satisfying action film that clangs with resounding swordplay. And Kurosawa has directed it at a spanking pace and with an artistic hand (he started out as a painter). When his combatants line up for pitched battle, they do so with all the geometric felicity of a *corps de ballet*."[23]

Geoffrey Warren of the *Los Angeles Times* was harsher, saying, "Director–co-author Kurosawa has come up with quite a good piece of movie making. But it is a far cry from his famous and great 'Seven Samurai' of a few years back. There is much in this film that is good. In fact, there are moments of the same kind of greatness, but there is also much that is contrived and sheer hokum. Mifune, also from 'Seven Samurai,' gives a performance far above what one would expect in this kind of a show."[24]

Closest to the mark was *Time*'s unnamed reviewer, who pegged the film "both a wow of a show and a masterpiece of misanthropy. Kurosawa emerges as a bone-cracking satirist who with red-toothed glee chews out his century as no dramatist has done since Bertolt Brecht. . . . All the players play with successive intensity, but Mifune, a magnificent athlete-actor, dominates the scene. Looped in a soggy kimono, crusted with stubble and sweat, gliding like a tiger, scratching like an ape, he presents a ferocious and ironical portrait of a military monk, a Galahad with lice. Behind Mifune stands a script that develops with an intricate symbolic logic and violent inevitability of a folk epic, and behind the script, behind the actors, behind the camera stands a major talent and a massive moral force: Kurosawa."[25]

Yojimbo was a big success in American art-house theaters, so much so that Seneca International, a small distribution firm, saw a wider, mainstream market for the picture. They picked up the U.S. distribution rights, making it available with English subtitles and in a new, English-language version dubbed by Peter Reithof, an award-winning looper of foreign films. They called both versions, redundantly, *Yojimbo, the Bodyguard*, and premiered the dubbed version at the Kimo Theater in Kansas City.[26]

Two years later, in late 1964, an Italian/West German/Spanish co-production premiered in Italy. It was the second feature of Italian director Sergio Leone, a screenwriter and second-unit director on a number of Hollywood films shot in Italy, including *Helen of Troy* (1955), *Ben-Hur* (1959), and *Sodom and Gomorrah* (1961). Leone had made his directorial debut with *The Colossus of Rhodes* (Il Colosso di Rodi, 1961), one of countless Italian "sword and sandal" movies (the genre known as *pepla* in Italy) that flooded the international market. But it was this second film, a Western called *Per un Pugno di Dollari* ("For a Fistful of Dollars") that would launch not only his career but also that of brilliant Italian composer Ennio Morricone and American TV actor Clint Eastwood, the film's star. *A Fistful of Dollars*, as the film became known in the United States, was the first of the "Man with No Name" or "Dollars" trilogy, a series of increasingly epic, operatic films that launched the "Spaghetti Western" genre, which begat more than 300 films over the next ten years. Leone's film, however, was also an unequivocal steal of *Yojimbo*, albeit transposed to the American West. Even *Yojimbo* composer Masaru Sato noted similarities to his own music in Ennio Morricone's otherwise archetypal score.[27] Indeed, this was apparent to critics as soon as the film opened in Italy. Producers Arrigo Colombo and Giorgio Papi had apparently tried to get permission to adapt the material, but never did, and made their film anyway. Perhaps they hoped that moving it to the American West (combined with Leone's changes) would be enough to either disguise it or make the film its own entity.

In later years, Leone would downplay *Yojimbo*'s influence. But as biographer Christopher Frayling makes clear in *Sergio Leone—Something to Do with Death*, Leone directly used Kurosawa's film as the model for *A Fistful of Dollars*.

According to Frayling, Leone had seen *Yojimbo* in late 1963, approximately one month prior to completing his first draft of *Dollars*. Leone's wife, Carla, recalled, "I remember going to see *Yojimbo* with him, and he got the idea of turning it into a Western there and then."[28] Director Sergio Corbucci recalled Leone "slaving over a moviola machine and copying *Yojimbo*, changing only the setting and details of the dialogue."[29] And during the *Dollars* production, word came down from Jolly Film (one of the production companies bankrolling the picture) to "refrain under any circumstances from mentioning the word *Yojimbo*."[30] Leone himself pleaded ignorance, saying that he had always been prepared to acknowledge *Yojimbo* and that there was simply some mixup regarding the payment of royalties. He may have been oblivious to the legal hurricane he was creating, but the money men clearly were not.

When a print of the film was seen by Toho executive Sanezumi Fujimoto, he immediately filed a complaint with the International Federation of Film Producers.[31] A lawsuit followed, filed by Toho and Kurosawa Production, that dragged on through the production, release, and promotion of *Red Beard* in 1964–65. Partly this was because the Italian producers had shamelessly and absurdly countered that Kurosawa had in turn based *Yojimbo* on an Italian play, *Arlecchino servitore di due padrone*.

But Tonino Valerii, who years later would direct Mifune in *Shatterer* (1987) and was head of postproduction at Jolly Film in 1964, admitted, "Papi and Colombo had first viewed *Yojimbo* with Sergio, very early on, at a private screening in a secret location. . . . I had the invoice for this screening in my possession. When the court case began, I still had this piece of paper. Remember, I was being paid by Papi and Colombo and I was by then friends with Leone. So I adopted the only correct position in the circumstances. I went back home and tore up the invoice."[32]

For his part, Kurosawa liked Leone's film, but, in a letter to Leone, was firm in his assertion that he be financially compensated. Valerii explained, "It was addressed to Sergio and it said, 'Signor Leone—I have just had the chance to see your film. It is a very fine film, but it is my film. Since Japan is a signatory of the Berne Convention on international copyright, you must pay me.' Now Sergio was so naïve that he waved this letter around to everyone. The letter was really offensive, with its accusation of plagiarism, of copying Kurosawa's film, but he didn't seem to realize it. He couldn't get beyond the fact that the great director Kurosawa had written him, and called his work a very fine film. He was so thrilled about this. When anyone tried to get him to put the letter away, he kept asking 'Why?' "[33]

Finally, a year after its Italian premiere, an out-of-court settlement was reached whereby Kurosawa would receive 15 percent of *Fistful*'s worldwide receipts, with a guarantee of around $100,000.[34] A subsequent lawsuit was filed by Toho and Kurosawa regarding the picture's American release. Jolly Film and UNIDIS, the co-producer and Italian distributor of the film, filed their own suit against Leone and Eastwood over the sequel, *For a Few Dollars More*, which was produced without their participation. All this further delayed United Artists' release of *A Fistful of Dollars* in America until 1967.[35] When the film was finally shown in the United States, no screenplay credit was given at all.

In 1992, New Line Cinema legitimately purchased the remake rights to *Yojimbo*. Originally, this version was to have been set in the near-future at the turn of the millennium, with a script by Harry Bean and a projected budget of $10 million, an A-picture by New Line's standards of the time.[36] Even before the script was written, the company was confident about the value of the material and put their money where their mouth was. "We bought [the option to remake it] outright," said New Line's Sara Risher. "We didn't option the rights because we believed this film would get made."[37]

They shouldn't have bothered. The film that was made, *Last Man Stand-*

ing, proved execrable, devoid of humor but brimming with stylized, brain-numbing violence, director Walter Hill's stock-in-trade. To add insult to injury, the picture's budget went out the window as soon as star Bruce Willis was signed. He alone received "$16 million, with another $500,000 in perks" for his services.[38] The film bombed when it was released in 1996.

Hill's film was set in the 1930s, recalling Dashiell Hammett's 1929 novel, *Red Harvest*, itself the basis (though likewise uncredited) for *Yojimbo*. Although *Red Harvest* isn't even mentioned in Donald Richie's essay on *Yojimbo* in *The Films of Akira Kurosawa*, there is little doubt that Kurosawa owed much to Hammett's story: his film is even closer to the novel than Hill's.

As Maurice Charney, an English professor at Rutgers University and the author of *All About Shakespeare*, wrote: "The foundations [of *Yojimbo*] are undoubtedly in world folklore. It's a very old story: Someone pits two evil forces against each other, who then destroy each other. Kurosawa was very interested in exploring these kinds of folklore fragments." In fact, by the time *Last Man Standing* went into production, legal claims to the material had become so convoluted that Hill refused to discuss his version's influences in press interviews.[39]

In the end, it's the original *Yojimbo* that stands above the rest. It is as funny and thrilling as ever, one of the great joys of the Kurosawa canon and Kurosawa's most internationally popular picture.

As shooting on *Yojimbo* got under way, Mifune announced that he had been invited to star as a Zapotec Indian peasant in a Mexican film, *The Important Man* (Animas Trujano [El Hombre Importante], 1961). The press briefing was held on January 31, 1961, at Geihinkan, a banquet hall, at a big affair sponsored by the Mexican Embassy. Mifune, sporting his scraggly beard for Kurosawa's film, wore a tuxedo and posed for pictures wearing a serape.[40]

The offer to play a non-Japanese character was not Mifune's first. According to the actor, during the production of *Seven Samurai* he had been asked to appear in an Italian film, probably either *Cavalleria Rusticana* (U.S. title, *Fatal Desire*, 1954), a non-singing version of Mascagni's opera directed by Carmine Gallone, the same man behind the Japanese-Italian co-production of *Madame Butterfly*; or possibly *Attila* (also 1954). In any case, both films were made with Anthony Quinn instead. A few years later, Quinn filled another role first offered Mifune: *The Savage Innocents* (1960), Nicholas Ray's Eskimo drama featuring Yoko Tani and Anna May Wong, and filmed with Italian, French, and British money. "Originally, [*The Savage In-*

nocents] was supposed to be a co-production with Toho," Mifune said, "but it didn't work out." Apparently Mifune was also approached to appear in such Hollywood pictures as *Escapade in Japan* (1957) and Disney's *Swiss Family Robinson* (1960), the latter in the Sessue Hayakawa role of a pirate who threatens the family of castaways.

That Mifune was asked to appear in a Mexican-made feature may have surprised the Japanese film community, but it also made sense. He had appeal in Mexico, which he never fully achieved in the United States, where his audience was limited to the art-house crowd. In Mexico, Mifune's hard-boiled action films were given a much wider release than in the United States and were as familiar to Mexican audiences as his films with Kurosawa. Mifune was excited about the opportunity to finally work outside Japan, and for the first time outside of Toho in nearly a decade. And as part of the deal, Mifune controlled the Japanese rights to the film. He eventually sold these to Toho, which released the picture in 1962 as *Kachi aru otoko* ("The Worthy Man").

"The director of the film [Ismael Rodriguez] was a very enthusiastic person," Mifune said. "He first asked me to do it [in 1959], but I ignored him. When I went to Los Angeles [the following year], he tried to make a deal with me again and again. As I was leaving for New York, he called my hotel and asked for my decision. I said, 'Since I can't decide here, I'd like to talk about it when I get back to Japan.' And, last October [1960], he came to Japan. . . . I showed the script to Mr. Kurosawa and Mr. [Ryuzo] Kikushima. They said it sounded interesting. Meanwhile, the director said he wasn't leaving Japan until I signed the contract. We met every day for two weeks."[41]

"To begin with," Rodriguez said, "it seemed odd that everybody criticized me for casting a Japanese as a Mexican farmer . . . and I answered, 'Why not?' The countryside is the same here as it is in China and the arts have no frontiers. Toshiro Mifune was the type I needed, and I wouldn't think twice."[42]

Rodriguez (b. 1917) was born in Mexico City and had been a child actor as early as 1929. In the mid-1930s, while still working as an actor, he helped pioneer the coming of sound in Mexican films by developing his own sound amplification system, which was adapted in theaters throughout the country. He began writing and directing films before he was twenty-five and formed his own production company, Rodriguez Films, S.A. (Películas Rodríguez, S.A.) in 1939. By the time he made *The Important Man* he was a veteran of thirty-five features, including *Tizoc* (1956), which won the Silver Bear at the Berlin Film Festival.

Mifune's departure was a media event for Toho. Yuriko Hoshi, one of his co-stars from *Daredevil in the Castle*, saw him off. Mifune, having grown a bandito-style mustache, left Japan in the company of Nagamasa Kawakita, president of Toho's foreign distribution subsidiary, Towa, on April 22, 1961.

"We agreed that we would record his dialogue in Japanese, and that he would be dubbed [into Spanish] afterward," Rodriguez said. "Just before he arrived, [I received a letter] saying that Mr. Mifune had a surprise—he had learned all his lines in Spanish! Of course—and it goes without saying—with a terrible accent."[43]

The picture began shooting on May 11, with Columba Dominguez, the director's wife, as Mifune's long-suffering spouse. Shooting went smoothly, despite Mifune's inability to communicate to the crew without an interpreter, and he got along well with Rodriguez, even though he was upset that the lines he had so carefully memorized were often changed by Rodriguez at the last minute.

The film was based on a novel by Rogelio Barriga Rivas titled *La Mayordomia*, concerning a poor, illiterate Indian, Animas Trujano (Mifune), who dreams of becoming the *majordomia* of his village. Every year the Indians hold an annual festival, and the *majordomia*, the most respected man in the village (and the one who usually pays for the festival, often going broke in the process), has the honor of offering the festival to the Indians' patron saint. Animas Trujano (the name means, roughly, "wishful fool") lives in a world of self-deception, however. He's a drunk who can't hold down a job and is abusive to everyone around him, yet he has a beguiling sense of humor and a certain brutish charm.

As the film begins, Animas and his wife, Juana (Dominguez), watch as their youngest son dies. Because Animas is poor—the family lives in a one-room shack with a dirt floor—one of the neighbors pays for the funeral, a celebration really, because the soul of an innocent has gone to heaven. Animas feeds on being the center of attention (he's almost joyous), until the arrival of Tadeo (Antonio Aguilar), a generous, gregarious man recently appointed *majordomia*, whom everyone at the funeral warmly welcomes. Animas boils with drunken rage, telling Tadeo, "You've come to ruin my party! You're worse than a woman—you're a bitch!" Animas is so belligerent that he's kicked off the neighbor's property.

Animas also has a lust-hate relationship with Catarina (Flor Silvestre), a prostitute who simultaneously arouses and disgusts him. He pursues her, but Catarina has already turned her attentions to Tadeo.

The next morning Animas finds a small amount of money Juana has left for him. We see that Animas is a superstitious man and a chronic gambler, and soon the money is gone. Juana, meanwhile, has learned that the local distillery needs workers, and she urges her husband to join her there. Despite his constant yelling and complaining about it, Animas does in fact go to work at the distillery, and everyone is amazed at his hard, if clumsy, efforts. However, Animas feels contempt for his wife, who, being able to read and write, works at a higher level and reports directly to the distillery owner, a Spaniard. Later, Animas finds his daughter, Dorotea (Titina Romay), embracing the son of the owner, whom he attacks and wounds with a pitchfork. This lands him in prison, where he must pay 1,500 pesos or spend one year incarcerated. (The corruption of the Mexican legal system is hinted at in this scene.)

Juana diligently begins raising the money; the entire family pitches in, working odd jobs. Eleven months into Animas's sentence, she has raised the 1,500 pesos, but on her way to the prison she sees a sign advertising some land for sale (land that we've seen for sale throughout the film, only now the price has been lowered). Because Animas has only one month to go, she buys the land instead, figuring it's a better investment for the entire family.

Meanwhile, Dorotea has a child by the son of the distillery owner. However, she has returned to the arms of Carrizo (Jaime J. Pons), a childhood sweetheart, a man Juana had earlier discouraged her daughter from seeing because he is uneducated. Because Dorotea's child is light-skinned, she and Carrizo realize no one will believe the child is theirs and decide to start a new life in another village. They leave the infant in Juana's care.

When Animas is released, he's furious that Juana didn't get him out of prison. "You love a piece of land more than you love your own husband!" he screams. He sells the land at once and goes on a spending spree, flaunting his wealth with the greedy Catarina, now openly his mistress. He gambles at the cockfights, winning even more money, but loses it all on the last fight. Since he is now broke, Catarina leaves him, and no one in the town respects him. At the ruins of a church, Animas offers his soul to the devil for the privilege of becoming majordomia, but there is only silence. "Even the devil despises me," he says. A fortune-teller overhears this and instructs Animas to ask the Golden Cock for his wish. He tells Animas to go to the local cemetery with six chickens and, if he hears the cock crow at midnight, to leave the chickens as an offering and wealth will await him at home. At midnight Animas hears a cock's crow, leaves the chickens behind, and races home to his supposed wealth. The fortune-teller grabs the chickens and runs off—Animas has been suckered again.

And so the film ends—or does it? Apparently Spanish television stations air only this truncated version, but in its original theatrical release the picture continues on with a densely plotted third act. Returning home, Animas learns that the distillery owner wants to "buy" his grandchild, whom he sells for 10,000 pesos. Now rich beyond his wildest dreams, Animas is appointed *majordomia*. At the festival the villagers enjoy the free food and drink, but Animas is no more respected than when he was poor. Catarina tries to become his mistress again, but Juana stabs her. Animas asks his wife, "Why am I so important to you?" She replies, "Because I love you." Reflecting on this, Animas tells the authorities that he, not Juana, stabbed Catarina and convinces the villagers to go along with his deception. Animas is taken away, but now, at last, he has the respect of his people, something that had eluded him his entire life.

As a Mexican peasant, Mifune is completely believable. His approach to the character is broad, lustful, and larger-than-life, much like the salt-of-the-earth characters often portrayed by Anthony Quinn. Everything Animas does is accentuated with self-important, sweeping gestures, such as his constant guzzling of mescal. Mifune's performance recalls those in both *Rashomon* and *Seven Samurai*, though his interpretation here comes dangerously close to making the character completely reprehensible and without any redeeming values, for the film's script is in no way forgiving of his brutish actions, which include physically abusing his wife and children. Animas is a bum, but this is a product of his lack of education, bad luck, alcoholism, a lack of self-awareness, and, to some degree, racism against the Indian population. All of this is implied when Juana visits Animas in prison; it's clear that she loves him and that he loves her, though he is incapable of expressing such emotions, so much so that when Juana kisses his hand, he instinctively wipes it on his trousers.

During the festival, while still flush with cash and with Catarina on his arm, Animas comes upon a fortune-teller who uses a remarkably well-trained little bird that pulls fortunes for customers, as if selecting from a deck of cards. The fortune the bird pulls for him reads: "In love and sport you're the best, and you'll find yourself lucky today, though you will try to hide it." But of course, after the cockfights, Animas is broke and Catarina is gone. Furious, he snatches the little bird from its owner and, away from the festival, makes the following confession to it:

You cursed one. Now I'm going to tell you about *your* luck. If only you hadn't lied. Do you want to fly? Do you want to fly? Damn bird,

you bumped right into bad luck. But don't believe it. Animas Trujano doesn't harm no one. No species.

(*His anger shifts to sorrow . . .*)

Nobody loves me. My own son doesn't love me. If God knows
I'm a good person, why does he let my rooster lose? Why? Why?
What's wrong with me? What's wrong with everybody?

(*Turning his attention back to the bird . . .*)

I wish you nothing bad. Go.

He opens his hand and the bird falls to the ground. During his passionate confession, Animas has crushed it to death.

There is humor in the character that comes from Animas's occasional
optimism, his naïve belief in good-luck charms (in prison he trades his
blanket to an inmate for a supposedly charmed rock, which turns out to be
a simple magnet), and his laughable attempts to be manly. He constantly
plays with his chest hair, twirling it around his finger, something considered
very sexual in Mexico. (This effect is undermined by the fact that Mifune
had no chest hair. The sloppy makeup looks as if someone had poured syrup
on his chest, sprinkling it with scraps of hair gathered from a barbershop
floor.)

When production wrapped, Mifune joined his wife and two children
for an extended vacation. They went to Acapulco, then flew to Europe to
meet with Takashi Shimura and his wife and Kyoko Kagawa and attend the
Berlin Film Festival. Mifune also flew his family to Paris and Rome. "But,"
Mifune said, "they liked Mexico more than anywhere else."

When Mifune returned home, *The Important Man* was hurried into release, having earned a great deal of press in Japan, and was in Tokyo theaters several months before it opened in Mexico.* Promoting the film, he
wrote a brief speech that was reprinted in *Kinema Jumpo*: "I agree with Mr.
Ismael Rodriguez when he says, 'We have to understand one another
through our films,' and so I went to Mexico. Shooting the movie gave me
cold sweats. Besides the quality of the picture, I believe that my appearance
in a Mexican film helped relations between Japan and Mexico a little bit. I
am proud of that. I think more Japanese film actors should appear in foreign films."[44]

An unexpectedly wide American release was prompted when *The Important Man* was nominated for an Academy Award as Best Foreign Film. It

---

*It is entirely possible, even likely, that Mifune's own voice was heard in the Japanese version.

lost to Ingmar Bergman's *Through a Glass Darkly* (Sasom I en Spegel, 1961), but the publicity surrounding the nomination had sparked enough interest for release beyond the art-house circuit.

The Important Man was picked up for U.S. distribution in 1962 by Lopert, which released it through United Artists exchanges. Apparently the film was shown on a limited basis, with English subtitles, though most theaters ran English-dubbed prints. Lopert didn't exactly give the film first-class treatment; it played mostly in second-rate theaters, and its release was much less extensive than that of mainstream Hollywood films, but it was the first time a Mexican feature had been given such a wide showing outside the Spanish community.

The Hollywood Reporter went so far as to call *The Important Man* "one of the best films ever made in Mexico. . . . Some traces remain in Mifune's performance of a different style of acting than is customary in the west, but he is totally believable in the total picture."[45]

The *Los Angeles Times* agreed, saying, "[Mifune,] garbed in Zapotec Indian clothes and sombrero, blends into the sun-baked backgrounds of Oaxaca like a native. And once again, he displays his genuine quality as an actor in a blunt, forceful portrayal."[46]

The film won numerous accolades, including a Best Picture award at the San Francisco Film Festival, the Silver Plaque in Turin, a Palenque Head Award from the Mexican Review of Festivals, the Mexican Press Gold Medal, and the Screen Actors Guild of Mexico Diamond Pendant.

The Important Man did help Japanese-Mexican relations, in their respective film communities at least. For Mifune, it was a personal triumph, one that he would speak of with great fondness the rest of his life. It proved he could do good work outside Japan, appearing in an internationally acclaimed film not directed by Akira Kurosawa. If its financial success outside Central America was limited, it was a success nonetheless. While today the film is all but forgotten outside Mexico, the clout it brought Mifune was tremendous.

As he readied *The Important Man*'s release in Japan, Mifune moved on to other projects. He appeared in a children's fantasy film called *The Youth and His Amulet* (Gen to Fudo-Myoh, 1961). His role, small as it was, kept his name in theaters during the seven-month gap between *Yojimbo* and *The Important Man*. Toho's biggest hits of the summer were *Yojimbo* and the Ishiro Honda–Eiji Tsuburaya–directed *Mothra* (Mosura), a lighthearted giant monster/fairy tale/musical satire about a giant moth wreaking havoc in Tokyo. For this reason it was understandable that the studio wanted to combine Mifune's star power with Tsuburaya's visuals, as had been done with *Storm Over the Pacific*, even if only for a film as quickly made as *The Youth and His Amulet*, which Hiroshi Inagaki threw together during July and August.

This simple picture is about a lonely boy, an orphan named Gen (Toru Koyanagi), who has as an imaginary friend the curly-haired god Prince Fudo-myo (Mifune). Fudo-myo pops in from time to time, glowing and looking for all the world like the personification of blind justice.

While shooting, Mifune took time on July 15, 1961, to participate in the groundbreaking of a new stage, No. 11, devoted to Tsuburaya's special-effects team. Mifune and Kurosawa may have been earning Toho a sackful of international film prizes, but it was Tsuburaya's films that were bringing Toho much-needed foreign currency. By 1961 Tsuburaya was more important to the studio than his usual collaborator, director Ishiro Honda, and in his own way, he was as big a star on the Toho lot as Mifune.

Before *The Youth and His Amulet* opened in Japan, Mifune flew to Venice in late August to receive the Best Actor Prize for his work on *Yojimbo*. He returned to Tokyo on September 7, and Kurosawa and producer Iwao Mori were at Haneda airport to welcome him back. That same day, Masashi Shimizu, Sanezumi Fujimoto, and Yoshitaku Inoue were sent off in the opposite direction—to attend a Toho Film Festival at the Toho La Brea in Los Angeles.

When *The Youth and His Amulet* opened ten days later, Mifune invited a large group of orphans to a free screening at the Chiyoda Theater in Hibuya, offering them words of encouragement.

For the rest of the year, the actor attended numerous parties thrown in his honor, celebrating his work on both *Yojimbo* and *The Important Man*. In December, he was fêted at a prerelease party for *The Important Man*, held at the Tokyo Kaikan Hall, where the Ambassador of Mexico gave a speech promoting Japanese-Mexican relations.

He also received *Kinema Junpo*'s highest acting honor for his work in *Yojimbo*. The publication noted: "*Yojimbo* couldn't have been made without Toshiro Mifune. As Sanjuro, he threw himself into the role with an open heart, a sensitive personality, and a strong sense of justice. He has tremendous acting skill derived from Kurosawa's hard training."[47]

But Mifune was less than happy about being connected so closely to Kurosawa and that his labors on *The Important Man* went unacknowledged. In accepting the prize, he made his feelings clear: "In the beginning I wondered why I got the honored prize for *Yojimbo* alone. I would like to accept this prize [for *Yojimbo* along with] my work on *The Important Man* in Mexico. While I was in Mexico, it was difficult, but I realize that it was worth it. I'm very happy. I am also glad that I had the opportunity to encourage people to work in other countries." Then, perhaps realizing he had gone too far, his comments returned to the film he was actually being honored for. "I worked on *Yojimbo* with Mr. Kurosawa and the crew for about a hundred days. This film is one of my most memorable projects. Sanjuro Kuwabatake was the creation of Mr. Kurosawa's direction and the crew's assistance. I would like to thank all of them and share in their happiness. I would not have been able to work in Mexico without Mr. Kurosawa's hard training."[48]

Mifune's frankness was hardly surprising. During his career, he had worked for more than twenty different directors, yet, in publications like *Kinema Jumpo*, he was still joined to Kurosawa's hip; few thought he could achieve greatness on his own. "What is lucky for [Mifune] is that he has a great master in Akira Kurosawa," said one typical article, "a director who is alternately a strict teacher and a kind brother." The unnamed critic did have telling praise for Mifune: "Japanese actors tend to go in the wrong direction once they become famous, but that's not the case with Mifune. He is known within the industry as a gentleman. . . . He has a wide range befitting Kurosawa's varied films. That's Mifune's appeal. Some critics are jealous of his success and try to find something bad to say about him. They complain about his mumbling, but I have to say they are completely wrong; he speaks his lines very eloquently, very clearly. Any mumbling is a conscious decision on his part and Kurosawa's."[49]

Mifune was nevertheless back to work for Kurosawa, in a stand-alone sequel to *Yojimbo*. "It's called 'Sanjuro Kuwabatake' or 'Sanjuro Tsubaki,' " Mifune said. "It's in preproduction now and I will have to be in Venice until September 3 or 4. I think I'll start shooting as soon as I return."[50]

Sanjuro, as the picture became known in the United States (in Japan it was *Tsubaki Sanjuro*), is a delightful follow-up. Where *Yojimbo* put Sanjuro in a world of *yakuza* thugs and corrupt local officials, *Sanjuro* places him among the elite samurai class. Sanjuro is himself a samurai, of course, but amid the refined ladies, shimmering kimono, and formal etiquette, Sanjuro is as out of place as a stray mutt at a blue-ribbon dog show.

After the opening titles (with the theme from *Yojimbo* playing over them), the story begins with nine inept samurai, led by Iiro Izaka (Yuzo Kayama), secretly meeting in a deserted shrine. Izaka has returned from a meeting with his uncle, the chamberlain, where he petitioned the lord to allow the samurai to clean up the rampant corruption while he is away. The chamberlain has refused, saying, "Perhaps I'm behind it all. You never know. After all, people aren't always what they seem." Izaka and his samurai begin to suspect that this is indeed the case. Frustrated, Izaka has turned to the superintendent, Kikui, a distinguished official. Izaka tells the samurai that Kikui has agreed to help them.

Behind them they hear a loud yawn, and out of the darkness steps Sanjuro (Mifune). Having overheard their conversation, Sanjuro believes that the chamberlain is honest and the superintendent corrupt. He's convinced Kikui is setting the samurai up, and sure enough, Sanjuro looks out a window of the small shrine to find that Kikui's men have surrounded them.

Sanjuro hides the nine samurai, then steps out to greet Kikui's men, demanding to know why he's been so rudely disturbed. With brute force he knocks down several of the men like bowling pins, then kills a dozen of them with his lightning-fast sword. Out of the group of attackers, Muroto (Tatsuya Nakadai) steps forward. Since they weren't after Sanjuro to begin with, he orders his men to stop. "Besides," he adds, "it would take a long time to kill him." Instead, Muroto offers Sanjuro a job, working for Kikui.

Kikui's men leave, and Sanjuro returns to the young samurai, whom he had hidden under the floorboards. The samurai express their gratitude, and Sanjuro tells them rudely, "Forget it. Just give me some money." Realizing the chamberlain has been kidnapped by Kikui, but not knowing where he's being held, the samurai decide to first rescue the man's wife and daughter, likewise threatened by Kikui. Hearing their plans, Mifune decides to join them, saying, "You can't take care of yourselves."

They make their way to the chamberlain's house, the young samurai following Sanjuro "like a centipede," much to the ronin's chagrin. (The film's trailer includes an alternate take, in which Sanjuro likens the line of samurai to a "trail of goldfish dung.") In a nearby barn, they speak to a servant, Koiso (Toshiko Higuchi, the female slave from The Hidden Fortress), who agrees to get the men guarding the women drunk. Sanjuro uses her bravery to further insult Izaka and his men. "She's a samurai," he says. "More reliable than you kids." One of the samurai, Terada (Akihiko Hirata), suggests using his house as a base, despite the fact that it's next door to one of the traitors' homes. Sanjuro agrees, and has Terada, Izaka, and Yasukawa join him in rescuing the women, ordering the others to try and find out where the chamberlain is being hidden.

Preparing for the raid, Sanjuro orders the three samurai not to draw their swords. "You might cut me in the back," he says, barely concealing his contempt for them. Sanjuro kills two of the three men guarding the women, sparing one, Kimura (Keiju Kobayashi), to find out where the chamberlain is hidden. They rescue the chamberlain's wife (Takako Irie) and her daughter, Midori (Reiko Dan). Hiding out in the barn, the wife inquires about the man who rescued her. "It's hard to explain," Izaka says, "but he's our friend."

The women stare in fascination at Sanjuro; they've never seen his like before. There is now a beautiful, even touching, scene where the mother, never having been in a barn in her life, joins her daughter in wonder over the simple smell of the hay; the two women lean back against it in an almost dreamlike state.

"I shouldn't say this after you saved us," the wife dreamily tells Sanjuro, "but killing people is a bad habit. You're too sharp, that's your trouble. Like a drawn sword. Sharp, naked, without a sheath. But good swords are kept in their sheaths." Sanjuro is notably uncomfortable hearing this. And despite the danger her family's in, the wife is, by contrast, extremely calm, if not downright serene. The samurai are blunt with her, saying the chamberlain will be forced to write a false confession and commit *seppuku*. But she's not worried in the slightest, for her husband, she says, is a "shrewd old fox."

The samurai try to make Kimura talk, but it becomes clear that he knows nothing. Sanjuro wants to kill him, but the chamberlain's wife absolutely forbids it.

As Kikui's men return, Sanjuro realizes they'll have to flee to Terada's house. The old woman agrees, adding, "But please don't use too much violence." To escape the approaching men, the group must climb over a wall. The samurai easily hop over, but the women are reluctant—it just isn't proper. Mifune has to beg the old woman, suggesting she use him as a footstool. In the most polite language imaginable, the woman apologizes to Sanjuro as she steps on his back. (Unfortunately, the extreme formality of the language, and thus much of the great humor of this scene, is lost on non-Japanese speakers.)

At the house of Kurofuji (Takashi Shimura), one of the conspirators, Superintendent Kikui (Masao Shimizu), Kurofuji, and Takebayashi (Kamatari Fujiwara), another traitor, come to realize that the chamberlain (who is kept off camera) is indeed a shrewd old fox.

Eventually the inept samurai, led by Sanjuro, rescue the uncle (Yunosuke Ito). But as they reflect on their victory, Sanjuro is nowhere to be found. The chamberlain's wife asks her samurai to search for Sanjuro. They find him in a field, preparing to face off against Muroto, who insists they duel.

"Must we fight?" Sanjuro asks. "It's not worth it." But Muroto is adamant. As the young samurai watch, Sanjuro and Muroto face each other as if frozen in time, for an excruciatingly intense 26 seconds. (It seems longer.) Then, like lightning, they simultaneously draw their swords. Instantly, blood sprays out of Muroto's chest. (According to *Variety*'s "Tube," it "gushes across the screen with the sudden furious force of Old Faithful."[51])

The samurai (as well as the audience) are stunned. Not knowing quite what to do, Izaka blurts out, "Splendid!"

Sanjuro is furious at this response. "Idiots! You don't know anything! . . . [Muroto] was exactly like me. A naked sword. He didn't stay in his sheath. The lady's right. Good swords are kept in their sheaths. You'd better stay in yours. Don't follow me or I'll kill you!"

The samurai drop to their knees, confused and dejected. Several burst into tears.

As at the end of *Yojimbo*, Sanjuro says simply, "*Abayo*" ["Bye"], walking off as the film fades to black.

Sanjuro began as a script Kurosawa developed for one of his former assistant directors, Hiromichi Horikawa, who had launched a successful career as a director in 1955. According to Kurosawa, Toho pressured him into directing it himself, and whether or not this is true is unknown. The story was based on *Hibi Heian* ("A Break in the Tranquillity"), by Shugoro Yamamoto, a writer with whom Kurosawa would be associated, on and off, for the rest of his life. A draft of the screenplay, by Kurosawa, Hideo Oguni, and Ryuzo Kikushima, had been prepared prior to the shooting of *Yojimbo*, but according to Kurosawa, the hero wasn't terribly skilled and used his brains more than his sword. When Kurosawa took the project over, the story was rewritten by the trio for the character of Sanjuro.

If *Yojimbo* plays off the conventions of the typical *chambara* film, then *Sanjuro* may be seen as a lampoon of the typical *jidai-geki*, placing Mifune's scruffy, unkempt *ronin* in a world of pomp and circumstance. In his scenes with Takako Irie, Mifune is so out of place, it's as if Sanjuro had wandered onto a Kabuki stage in the middle of a performance. He finds himself in a world of manners and elitism, where civility supersedes expediency. Sanjuro was much more at home in the Hadean landscape of *Yojimbo*.

Sanjuro is a movie, like *The Bad Sleep Well*, in which nothing is what it seems. The incongruity is in and of itself funny, but *Sanjuro* offers something more. On the surface, the young, well-dressed samurai appear straight out of the *Loyal 47 Ronin*, but they're inept, inexperienced, and foolish. Tsubaki Mansion is beautiful, but within its walls exists wholesale treachery. Sanjuro himself is nothing like the typical samurai. He looks like a bum, yet ultimately he is wiser than the nine younger samurai put together—a real samurai, a real man. To some degree, the myth Kurosawa and Mifune created in *Yojimbo* is brought back down to earth, while simultaneously being reinforced, much as George Roy Hill and Sam Peckinpah would later do in *Butch Cassidy and the Sundance Kid* and *The Wild Bunch*, both 1969, respectively.

In *Yojimbo*, Sanjuro is like a Greek god toying with the mortals around him. In *Sanjuro*, he chastises the youths and, by extension, the samurai code, saying at one point, "This is not a game!" It's difficult to imagine the Sanjuro of *Yojimbo* saying such a line, and it's here that *Sanjuro* is critically different from its predecessor: Sanjuro is a fantastic swordsman, to be sure, but here he's more down-to-earth, more human, flawed, and learns something about his nature in the course of the picture. And yet the young samurai, his students, do not learn from him. While a comedy, the film's ending surprises with its sadness. The villain is dead, yet Sanjuro mourns him. He thought he had taught his young students the meaninglessness of *bushido* (the samurai code), but realizes that, in the end, he has taught them nothing.

This theme is emphasized by the film's casting, especially by Yunosuke Ito's homely chamberlain. The character looks like a villain, but he is an honest, decent man. (Ito typically played villains. He would soon have the role of one of Mifune's rivals in *High and Low*, and the parts he most commonly played are best exemplified by that of Kenmotsu Hashino in a later Mifune film, *Samurai Assassin*.) The chamberlain's wife, who appears hopelessly naïve and out of touch with the realities of the *bushido* and samurai politicking, is wisest of all. When Sanjuro calls her a fool, he's actually praising her wisdom—he knows she is wiser than he—though the younger samurai don't realize this.

Mifune's character, heavy on slovenly confidence, is a refinement of his role in *Yojimbo*. For most of the film, he keeps his hands deep inside his kimono, except when scratching his chin or reaching for his sword. In *Sanjuro*, we see a bit more of his character, especially when the chamberlain's wife compares his life of violence to a naked sword. Mifune is excellent here, expressing his uneasiness through gestures more than dialogue, and his constant annoyance at the ineptitude of his reluctant followers is consistently funny.

In both *Yojimbo* and *Sanjuro*, the mythical nature of the character is accentuated in a scene where the *ronin* is asked his name. Looking around, he says, "Sanjuro [thirty years old] . . . , going on forty." Then, eyeing the nearest vegetation, he adds, as his family name, "Tsubaki [Camellia]." (In *Yojimbo*, he called himself "Sanjuro Kuwabatake [Mulberry Field]."

Nakadai once again portrays Mifune's archnemesis, this time an expert swordsman so steeped in *bushido* philosophy that he simply cannot understand Sanjuro's newfound wisdom. The character, fiercely loyal to the samurai code, is far removed from the psychotic gunslinger Nakadai played in *Yojimbo*. Rather, he is more in line with classical samurai adversaries such as Kojiro Sasaki, Musashi Miyamoto's chief rival. That Sanjuro deeply regrets having to fight a fatal duel with him, at least by genre conventions, is to Muroto unthinkable, and it further emphasizes Sanjuro's transformation. Much like the chamberlain with his rivals, he will no longer kill indiscriminately. But whereas the chamberlain is resigned to the conflict as a sad part of his place in the Japanese pecking order, the more rebellious Sanjuro responds quite differently. After killing Muroto, Sanjuro finds himself in a "bad mood." He is just beginning to understand the depth of the lady's words.

The young samurai posed problems for Kurosawa, one of which he may not have been aware of. He tries to give the characters individual personalities; when they sit in deference to Sanjuro, it is in order of their varying degrees of respect and distrust. Akihiko Hirata's Terada, while not the leader, is obviously more experienced and wiser than Izaka. (He even calls Izaka an "idiot" at one point.) Kunie Tanaka's Yasukawa is the mistrusting hothead of the group. However, the samurai are simply funnier when they act and move as a group, as in the "centipede" scene, so Kurosawa couldn't make them too distinct without losing some of the humor in the process.

Most fascinating and easily overlooked is the character of the chamberlain's wife, played by former Toho star Takako Irie (1911–95). At first glance she seems to be nothing more than a doting dowager. But she's no fool. The scene of her and Chidori relaxing in the hay, taking in its pleasant smell, is the most evocative in the picture. Irie's delicate, dreamy voice is exquisite, and an engaging contrast to Mifune's unkempt *ronin*. Irie's career stretched back to the late 1920s, including a leading role in Mizoguchi's *Metropolitan Symphony* (Tokai kokyogaku, 1929). She was one of Toho's biggest stars when Kurosawa became an assistant director there. She played the female lead in several Kajiro Yamamoto films on which Kurosawa worked, including the two-part *A Husband's Chastity* (1937) and *Kojuro's Love*

(1938). For Kurosawa, she was the dorm mother in *The Most Beautiful* (1944), but after leaving Toho as one of the Flag of Ten, she didn't work with him again until *Sanjuro* nearly two decades later. The actress continued working in films until at least the late 1970s, appearing in *The House of Hanging* (Byoinzaka no kubikukuri no ie) in 1979.

Quite good is Keiju Kobayashi as the samurai kept, for much of the film, in Terada's closet. He had appeared with Mifune going back to the early 1950s, but by the early 1960s was firmly established as one of Toho's biggest comedy stars, his status confirmed by second-billing credit in *Sanjuro* despite his small role. "I was originally supposed to be the leading actor, when Hiromichi Horikawa was going to direct it," Kobayashi recalled. "I had an offer to appear in the film but couldn't do it because I was making Salaryman movies.

"I thought I'd be nervous [working with Kurosawa], but wasn't. [Nevertheless, he] wasn't satisfied with just a verbal performance; he wanted us to act with our entire body. Of course, this is not easy. You can see what he's after by watching Mr. Mifune."[52]

Reiko Dan saw both sides of the director. "Working with the Kurosawa team was considered a big deal and a kind of honor," she said. "When I went to the set, I had goose bumps and my body shook. But he smiled and wasn't scary as most people believe. However, once shooting started, he became a different person and very intimidating."[53]

Sanjuro began filming on September 25, 1961, at Toho, with the shrine interior set. The picture was shot more or less in sequence. In early October, the production moved to interiors of the barn, followed by scenes inside Terada's house and in the Tsubaki mansion.

"We built [the houses] on the open set," said art director Yoshiro Muraki. "We built the interiors and the tea room at the studio. When we constructed the houses outside, we put roofs on them to protect them from the rain, just like real houses. The shrine at the beginning of the film was a real shrine in Gotemba [it still stands], and we put a big Japanese cedar there.

"The chief retainer's house, the pond in front, and the garden were built on the biggest stage at Toho. The tea room was built on one corner of Stage 7, which wasn't very big, and it was shot from the other end of the stage using a 100mm telephoto lens. . . . The house and the police officer's house were left on the open set until we made *Red Beard*. Mr. Kurosawa said, 'Can't I destroy it since I was the one who had it built?' And so we pulled it down, destroying it to shoot the earthquake scene in *Red Beard*."[54]

One visitor to the set was a reporter from *Time*.

To look at [Kurosawa], nobody would believe it. Tall, lithe, springy, togged in a sports shirt and a battered sailor's cap turned inside out, Kurosawa at 52 looks more like a golf pro than a genius. . . . With his crew Kurosawa is curt; with his cast he is patient. He never scolds an actor—though once, when an actor infuriated him, he turned to a horse that was standing nearby and bellowed in the poor brute's ear: "Idiot!" . . . Kurosawa despises the traditional Japanese esthetic of "artless simplicity." His method and values are more Western, more active, more individual. . . . In the individual Kurosawa sees all humanity, and his passion for the individual has made him both an incendiary and a firebringer, a revolutionary not in politics but of morals. "I am interested," he says simply, "in producing a better quality of man." The man he means is a man of large humanity who loves evil as well as good, who sees life drunkenly and sees it whole, who laughs with a grand laughter that accepts and brothers everything that breathes. But men cannot win such wisdom without suffering, and in his films Kurosawa shows them what to suffer: the world as it is, themselves as they are.[55]

Kurosawa was short-tempered when it came to one aspect of the production: the camellias. Everyone, including the director, worked hard to make them look just right. "All of the camellias in the film were man-made, not real," Muraki explained, "and the leaves were not real camellia leaves. If we had used camellia leaves with the fake flowers the leaves would have [photographed] unnaturally old. Instead, we used leaves of the *sakai* plant, and the crew changed the leaves every morning before shooting."[56]

Akira Kubo, who plays one of the inept samurai, fondly remembered, "[Kurosawa] wasn't a good businessman, and with *Yojimbo* and *Sanjuro* he said, 'Okay, I'm going to make some fun movies,' though even here he didn't compromise. It was a great learning experience. It was an honor."[57]

Shooting moved outdoors on November 1, to exteriors of the back yard, Mifune's battle outside the shrine (also filmed in Gotemba), and exteriors of the Tsubaki mansion. In mid-December came Mifune's duel with Nakadai. The assistant who operated the pressure cooker–like controls that sprayed fake blood from Nakadai's chest was extremely nervous about getting it right on the first take. He continued building up pressure so that, when the cameras rolled, the blood burst out like cannon fire, delighting Kurosawa.

Another aspect of the violence is made clear by a frame-by-frame examination of the slaying of Nakadai's character. An impressed Minoru Nakano explains, "A man cannot be killed instantly with just one blow of the sword. At least two strokes are needed, and to kill as many men as Toshiro Mifune does required tremendous speed. That was the most fantastic aspect of Mifune. He was able to do the swordplay as quickly and as precisely as my father and Mr. Kurosawa needed."[58]

Because so much of the film was shot at Toho or nearby locations, the production of *Sanjuro* proceeded smoothly, with the picture wrapping on December 20, less than three months after it had begun. Kurosawa obliged Toho by sailing through postproduction, with Masaru Sato recording the music two days later and Toho's sound men dubbing the film's sound effects over Christmas. Kurosawa and Toho's ad men prepared a unique trailer for the film. Masaru Sato wrote a delightful piece of music not used in the film, a bouncy variation of his inept samurai theme with trumpet, accordion, and xylophone. The trailer also touted Kurosawa's growing reputation and, for the first time, included footage of the director on the open set, rehearsing with his cast.

Sanjuro was test-screened by December 27 and opened on New Year's Day, 1962. In Japan, it proved even more popular than *Yojimbo*. Its high production cost, approximately $500,000, was offset by box-office revenues, which exceeded ¥450,000,000 (about $1.25 million in rentals).[59] It was a critical success as well, placing fifth on *Kinema Jumpo*'s "Best Ten" list for the year.

The Hollywood Reporter noted that Masashi Shimizu, "and two of Toho's top stars, Reiko Dan and Yuko Hama [sic; presumably Mie Hama]," flew to America for the U.S. premiere at the Toho La Brea, where a festival celebrating the studio's films was held June 14–18, 1962. There was a press reception the first day of the festival at the Beverly Hilton Hotel, and *Sanjuro* was greeted with some of the best American reviews of Kurosawa's career.[60]

"The charm of this fascinating Toho production," said *Variety*'s "Tube," "stylishly directed by Akira Kurosawa, is the personality of this hero powerfully played by Toshiro Fifune [sic]. . . . Although an invincible swordsman, it is not this aspect of his identity that gives him his greatest appeal. Unlike many of the mighty adventure heroes of the west, he is endowed with an incredible sense of logic—a Gestaltian way of reasoning invariably correct in drawing the simplest, most natural conclusions when others have jumped to theirs emotionally and illogically. The character is also very human—especially in his appreciation of little things such as *sake*, sleep, and money. In short, a well-rounded figure: physically epic, mentally agile, emotionally normal—a kind of cross between Robin Hood and a typical Humphrey Bogart character."[61]

Stanley Kauffmann was the significant dissenting voice; he apparently missed the entire point of the film: "In execution the film cannot be faulted. It seems to me flawlessly directed, excellently acted. . . . But the content of the film is so slight as to be transparent. It has even less texture than its predecessor, is even more cheery an action film: good guys, bad guys, and the 'lone gun'—a seeming bad guy with a heart of gold. One wonders how the people who could make a film so superbly could be content to make one so shallow."[62]

Conversely, *The Hollywood Reporter* called it "a superb picture and should be seen by everyone in Hollywood interested in films. . . . Good subtitles make certain that the film is perfectly clear even though the spectator does not understand Japanese."[63]

Bosley Crowther disagreed about the subtitles, blaming them for his failing to instantly recognize *Sanjuro* as a comedy: "Finally one senses from the action and from the English subtitles (which are poor) that the great Kurosawa is being humorous, that he is really poking fun. . . . But, unfortunately, this startling realization of the nature and intent of the film is greatly delayed in getting to us because we can't understand the implications and inflections of the dialogue, and the English subtitles are so ponderous and skimpy that they provide no introductory clues." Crowther made the case that if one reviewer couldn't figure this out, all the more reason to dub the film, presumably with funny voices. "Dubbed English dialogue is what most foreign films should have," he insisted.[64]

Judith Crist disagreed: "The subtitles are literate and charming. . . . There's no overt fun-poking or pushing of the innate comedy, subtly underlined by an excellent music score. . . . Mifune is beyond compare as he wriggles his shoulders and flexes his muscles and walks tall and alone."[65]

Sanjuro's impact went beyond good notices. Having lost control of his remake of *Seven Samurai*, Anthony Quinn signed onto an American reworking of *Sanjuro*. In 1965 the rights were purchased by Columbia Pictures, and David Swift, a former Disney animator who had recently directed *The Parent Trap*, was named as its producer-director. An October start was announced, with filming on the remake, now a Western, to be done in New Mexico and Colorado. But the film was never made.[66] Yet another *Sanjuro* adaptation reared its head in 1989, when independent producer William Allyn acquired an option on *Sanjuro*'s story,[67] and again, no film materialized.

Sanjuro lacks *Yojimbo*'s momentum, and its script doesn't allow the kind of showy set pieces that made *Yojimbo* so memorable. But it is as funny and at times has an exquisiteness that transcends the more visceral moments of its predecessor. It is a lightweight film, but as lightweight films go, it is something of a masterpiece.

As Kurosawa prepared his next picture, Mifune and director Hiroshi Inagaki revisited elements of their internationally lauded *The Rickshaw Man*. Their new film was *Tatsu* (Doburoku no Tatsu, 1962), with Mifune playing another illiterate brute with a heart of gold. Set deep in the Japanese wilderness just after World War II, the story concerns a group of rough, hard-drinking gang laborers who eke out a living moving from one dangerous job to another. One of them, Tatsu (Mifune), is encouraged to rape the proprietress of a remote drinking establishment. He drags the woman (Chikage Awashima) into another room, shutting the door. There is much yelling and screaming, but in fact Tatsu is feigning the rape because he is, at heart, a gentle soul, despite his outward brutality. After he rescues the girl, the two begin to fall in love, just prior to Tatsu and the other laborers finding work as road builders in the forests of Hokkaido. The workers are paid in advance, but the work is dangerous and they find themselves in a "pen[itentiary] system" of labor. They must sign on for six months and risk being shot if they try to run out on their contract. One man escapes, but is captured and nearly beaten to death. Tatsu protests to the foreman, Shaguma (Tatsuya Mihashi), creating a rift between them.

Tatsu also becomes infatuated with a young woman, Shino (Junko Ikeuchi), working in the mess hall, but she rejects his clumsy advances. When the foreman tries to rape her, Tatsu steps in and the two begin dueling with axes. Shino turns out to have a husband, newly released from prison, and he joins the other workers. The foreman becomes jealous and assigns the husband the most backbreaking of labors. Tatsu plans to run off with the couple, but in the end escapes on his own. He returns to the drinking establishment and considers renewing his romance with the proprietress, but learns that workers at a rival construction site, angered by a swindle arranged by the vicious foreman, are about to raid his old camp. Tatsu returns to the construction site and saves the day.

The picture was a big success in Japan, premiering in 200 theaters for three- to five-week showings during the Golden Week of May 1962, an unusually wide distribution and long run for a Japanese film of the time.[68] Only *Sanjuro* and *King Kong vs. Godzilla* (Kingu Kongu tai Gojira) made more money for Toho, with *Tatsu* ranking eight in the year's top-grossing Japanese films.

The picture was well reviewed in America, too. "Hiroshi Inagaki has an appropriately simple style reminiscent of John Ford," wrote Kevin Thomas of the *Los Angeles Times*. "In the title role, Toshiro Mifune possesses all the virtues of a classic western hero. The hardest drinker and the toughest fighter, 'Hooch' Tatsu, for all his coarseness, has a strong sense of justice and looks out for the underdog. In the hands of a lesser actor Tatsu might have emerged as an insufferable, one-dimensioned stereotype, but Mifune, one of the world's great screen performers, invests his role with a marvelous sense of the comic."[69]

A singularly odd review, written by "ELGEE" of the *Hollywood Citizen-News*, illustrates the ignorance of Japanese film that Western critics occasionally displayed. ELGEE seemed to think *Tatsu*'s contemporary setting was a new-fangled innovation, as if the Japanese had never before thought of giving their films a modern setting. "The Japanese film industry has come a long way," ELGEE wrote, "since it began with traditional stories of their samurai and other historical and legendary incidents. For here is a modern drama of contemporary Japan. . . . There is no circumspect story of Oriental blandness [sic?]. It is as up to date as American colloquialisms and slang of which, incidentally, the subtitles are full, although badly translated, no doubt [sic]."[70]

Simultaneously, Toho's executives turned 1962—the company's 30th anniversary—into one gigantic party. Neither Kurosawa nor Mifune was left out, whether they wanted to participate in all the hype or not. Six films produced that year were singled out as "30th Anniversary Productions": Ishiro Honda's big special-effects extravaganza *King Kong vs. Godzilla*; Mikio Naruse's biographical drama about writer Fumiko Hayasaka, *Lonely Lane* (Horoki); Hiroshi Inagaki's remake of *Chushingura*, which featured Mifune; Yasuki Chiba's domestic melodrama *Born in Sin* (Kawano hotoride); Shiro Toyoda's *Madame Aki* (Yushu heiya); and Kurosawa's *High and Low*. (The latter two would not open until early 1963.)

Production-wise, by far the biggest of these films was Inagaki's *Chushingura*, a three-and-a-half-hour, all-star adaptation of the eighteenth-century story of the loyal forty-seven *ronin*. This classic tale—a fundamental Japanese epic—follows a group of samurai seeking vengeance for their incorruptible Lord Asano (Yuzo Kayama). Asano was unjustly compelled to commit *seppuku* after striking an imperial retainer, Lord Kira (Chusha Ichikawa), who tried to pressure Asano into bribing him.

To everyone's surprise, Asano's chamberlain, Oishi (Kabuki actor Koshiro Matsumoto), surrenders the Asano castle to authorities and seems utterly uninterested in avenging his dead master, despite the protestations of his loyal samurai. Of course, Oishi is plotting all along, and much of the story's suspense is piqued when various members of Asano and Oishi's followers plead with him to tell them what he *really* intends.

Oishi manages to keep his true intentions secret for two long years, until the snowy night of January 30, 1703. Asano's loyal samurai, now *ronin*, are called together for an attack on Kira's mansion. Forty-seven of them attack Kira's home, kill him, and march through the streets with his head, as awed spectators look on. While their raid is successful, they also know it will mean their own death: although true to the *bushido*, their act is technically illegal, and the shogunate demands they too commit *seppuku*. Their loyalty and bravery continue to fascinate to this day, and the temple where they and their master are buried remains a site of pilgrimage for many Japanese.

Although Mifune's role is peripheral and occupies less than fifteen minutes of screen time, his name is set alone in the credits. He is the very last actor listed, giving him "special guest star" billing in a film filled with stars. Given the sheer number of leading actors appearing in *Chushingura*, Toho was acknowledging Mifune as their greatest commodity. For this same reason, his role is spread across the long narrative. Early in the story, Kira forces Asano to replace hundreds of tatami mats overnight. The rush to produce new tatami results in a desperate hiring of every mat maker within miles of the castle. One of Asano's samurai, Gorobei (Tatsuya Mihashi), finds a tatami maker, Otokichi (comedian Kingoro Yanagiya), in the midst of a drinking match with a tough *ronin*, Genba Tawaraboshi (Mifune). Genba refuses to cancel the drinking challenge, even for Lord Asano's sake, so Gorobei takes Otokichi's place in the dusk-to-dawn binge, thus relieving him to do his part for the Asano clan. Genba and Gorobei become fast friends. Later, when Genba is suspected of working as a bodyguard for Kira, the loyal *ronin* send Gorobei to kill the highly skilled lanceman as a precaution. But Genba himself has spread the rumor, to determine whether the Asano *ronin* were really plotting to avenge their master. Gorobei's appearance confirms this. Knowing Gorobei's fate, Genba asks that he join him for one last drink before the raid. Later, during the attack on Kira, Genba turns up outside the mansion, preventing officials from interfering with Oishi's vengeance.

Chushingura was the umpteenth remake of what many regard as the greatest story in Japanese literature. Since the Ako Vendetta (as it is also known), the story has been adapted by such preeminent playwrights as Chikamatsu Monzaemon and Takedo Izumo. Hundreds of novels, comic books, and radio plays have since followed. Film versions date as far back as Masahiro Makino's 1913 adaptation (which he then remade in 1927) and Tomiyasu Ikeda's 1926 silent picture, but it's likely that there are other films, presumably lost, dating back even further. Teinosuke Kinugasa had directed Kazuo Hasegawa in the first all-talkie adaptation, released in 1932. Shochiku produced its own all-star, four-hour adaptation (apparently the first in color) in 1956; that film also starred Koshiro Matsumoto and was directed by Tatsuo Osone. Daiei followed suit in 1958, with *The Vendetta of the 47 Loyal Ronin* (Chushingura), a 138-minute epic directed by Kunio Watanabe and starring Kazuo Hasegawa, Raizo Ichikawa, Shintaro Katsu, and Machiko Kyo. And the following year, Toei produced its own version, *Chushingura*, a three-hour film directed by Sadatsugu Matsuda, marketed abroad as *The Great Revengers*.

Prior to Inagaki's film, the most acclaimed adaptation of the story had been Kenji Mizoguchi's two-film adaptation released in 1941–42 and known collectively today as *The 47 Ronin* (Genroku Chushingura—zenpen and Genroku Chushingura—kohen), made during the war and commissioned by the military government to tie the samurai's *bushido* to Japan's own wartime nationalism.

In 1960, Toho filmed a two-part comic version of the story, *Salaryman Chushingura* (Sarariman Chushingura, 1960, and Zoku Sarariman Chushingura, 1961; also known as *The Masterless 47*). The comedy was billed as "Toho's 100th Salaryman Movie," with prolific screenwriter Ryozo Kasahara adapting it to the white-collar age.

The two-part story made up the thirteenth and fourteenth "Shacho" ("Company President") movies, one of Toho's most profitable and longest-running (forty features) series. Starring Hisaya Morishige, these pictures revolved around a company president whose underlings, played by Daisuke Kato, Keiju Kobayashi, Norihei Miki, and Frankie Sakai, were constantly trying to get their boss out of trouble. They portrayed different though similar characters from film to film, and in *Salaryman Chushingura*, the story was adapted with Morishige as Oishi, Eijiro Tono as Kira, and Ryo Ikebe as Asano.

"After the war, Japan was in ruins," director Shue Matsubayashi said of this uniquely Japanese genre. "The Japanese people worked very hard in the postwar period, from morning till night, and for very little money. Everybody worked for companies like the one in the series. And what I tried to do was to show the Japanese people what the company president was like, in a comic manner, and to present the joy company life could be. . . . One of the famous film critics said the series was 'the engine of the white-collar age.' Many salarymen coming home from work would stop off at a cinema and watch these films."[71]

Big film that it was, Toshiro Mifune joined its all-star cast in a small role as businessman Kazuo Momoi. Unfortunately, the U.S. release, like *all* of Japan's comedies from that period, was limited to Japanese-owned theaters like the Toho La Brea—when they were shown at all. Most were considered so insignificant as to be rarely reviewed in the United States, and none have turned up on home video outside Japan. Mifune wouldn't do another flat-out comedy for years, nor did he believe the genre translated well to the West. "The Japanese sense of humor just doesn't lend itself well to a feature comedy," he argued. "Oh yes, you get probably our best films [in America], and some bad ones, even as we do yours. Sometimes the very social backgrounds of films rule out their practicality as imports to another country."[72]

Since Inagaki's 1962 *Chushingura*, there have been numerous television miniseries adaptations, often spread out over an entire year, including an epic NHK television version produced in the late 1970s, with a cast rivaled only by Inagaki's film. In 1994, director Kinji Fukasaku combined *Chushingura*'s story with Japan's other internationally famous Kabuki play, the *Yotsuya Ghost Story*, in a film for Shochiku released abroad as *Crest of Betrayal* (Chushingura gaiden—Yotsuya kaidan). That same year Kon Ichikawa directed his own, more conventional version for Toho, *47 Ronin* (Shi-ju-shichi nin no shikaku, 1994), which starred Ken Takakura, Kiichi Nakai, Rie Miyazawa, Tatsuo Matsumura, Hisashi Igawa, Ko Nishimura, and Hisaya Morishige.

But it is Inagaki's version that remains the best version of the story thus far. His mastery of the *jidai-geki* form was never better. Its classicism has been criticized by some Japanese film scholars who prefer Mizoguchi's more cerebral adaptation, but Inagaki's approach is undeniably effective, resulting in an epic film as intimate as it is huge, much like David Lean's best work. At 204 minutes, the film is never less than fascinating, often deeply moving, rich in characterization, with a thrilling climax. It manages to both glorify and criticize the *bushido* and the intractable regimentation of Japanese society. And in sheer production alone, its scope has never been equaled. For Toho, the 1962 *Chushingura* was a culmination of everything they had built in the postwar era. Never again would they produce a film on this scale.

"The studio threw everything into this production," remembered Yuriko

Hoshi, who played the lover of a samurai (Yosuke Natuski) who obtains blueprints of Kira's mansion. "Mr. Inagaki did a great job. Everybody worked on it. The studio's wealth was reflected in its Genroku period setting—the costumes, the props—and Mr. Inagaki had a lot of money to shoot the film. It was really great."[73]

Yu Fujiki, who played one of the 47, said of Inagaki, "He was an actor when he was a kid, so he knew all about film acting. He lets the actors act, then he tactfully points out what changes he wants to make. He did so very indirectly, through an assistant director."[74]

Akira Ifukube composed a beautiful, equally epic score for the picture. He recalled, "During the Occupation, the Army censored samurai films; *Chushingura* was made shortly after the ban was lifted. It was a kind of propaganda film to show the rich production values of each of the companies." He remembered Inagaki, with whom he had worked many times, as "a superb film director, though he sometimes inserted strange cuts. A bit old-fashioned, but still a superb director." Ifukube approached the film's music differently: "When the 47 samurai were ordered to commit *seppuku*, and for the main titles as well, I used my well-known tone poem. Most film versions tried to match the Kabuki interpretation, but I tried to make it very solid, with straightforward motifs."[75]

Nearly every star and bit player on the lot put in an appearance—the opening titles tout more than a hundred names in the cast. Unlike *Around the World in 80 Days* (1956), *The Greatest Story Ever Told* (1965), and other Hollywood counterparts, where the all-star cameos seem forced when not downright ludicrous, *Chushingura*'s complex story and numerous—though always compelling—subplots lend themselves well to what was admittedly stunt casting. And it's doubtful that American audiences, to whom most of the actors remain completely unknown, would imagine Japanese audiences reacting to the picture the way they would to similar homegrown epics. ("Hey, there's Hisaya Morishige! Look! It's Setsuko Hara!")

Ads for the film proclaimed, "Toho has confidently created the best *jidai-geki* ever!" *Chushingura* drew long lines at the box office. It was Japan's tenth-highest-grossing film that year, and Toho's biggest money earner after *Sanjuro, King Kong vs. Godzilla*, and Inagaki's other 1962 release, *Tatsu*.

Just before *Chushingura* opened, Masashi Shimizu presided over the company's official 30th anniversary party, and when the picture premiered at the Tokyo Takarazuka Theater, thirty-four employees were recognized for twenty-five years or more of service. They were brought onstage by Toho president Shimizu to thunderous applause. Three weeks later, Sanezumi Fujimoto and Tsuneyuki Amamiya held another big party, perplexingly called the "Toho 60th Reunion Party," in which longtime contract staff, including Kajiro Yamamoto, were given honorary red caps.

For *Chushingura*'s U.S. premiere, Toho ballyhooed the film not only as a thirtieth anniversary "event," but also to celebrate the tenth anniversary of Toho's international division. On October 10, 1963, the picture opened at the Toho La Brea, where Shimizu was joined onstage by co-stars Yoko Tsukasa and Kumi Mizuno. The three then attended the New York premiere. At a luncheon for the trade press at the New York Hilton Hotel, Shimizu stated that 20 percent of the sixty features Toho planned to produce that year would be suitable for export, and plans for a national release of *Chushingura* would be considered, depending on the public's response.[76]

Incredibly, Toho chopped their epic down to 108 minutes for release in America, losing nearly half the original film in the process. To bridge the large gaps of lost material, an English-language narration was added to supplement the frantic and confused subtitling. Nonetheless, the film received mostly favorable reviews. "While there is nothing particularly awesome about Toshio Yasumi's screenplay," wrote the *Hollywood Citizen-News*, " 'Chushingura' offers the type of Japanese film diversion which has appealed to American audiences: swashbuckling samurai adventure. . . . The truly outstanding aspect . . . is the brilliant color photography by Kazuo Yamada, one of Toho's best lensmen. The final scenes, shot with a background of snow-covered streets and housetops, are breathtaking."[77]

"Toho Co. . . . has turned out a powerful, attention-holding drama which may attract more patrons than either 'Rashomon' or 'Samurai,' " predicted *Variety*. "This vehicle has been so deftly subtitled that it no longer is handicapped by having all the dialogue in a foreign tongue. Anyway, this is one of those rarities among foreign pictures—a production where action speaks louder than words. Pic seems assured of being the most profitable Toho release to be distributed in the U.S."[78]

While *Variety*'s reviewer didn't seem to miss the nearly two hours cut from the film, *Newsweek* found the picture practically incoherent in its short form, disliking the very element the *Citizen-News* found so appealing: "[It] virtually ignores the ritual and history surrounding the story. Perhaps something has been lost in translation . . . because the latest 'Chushingura' turns out to be simply a swashbuckling story about sacrifice a bit too supreme for American credibilities."[79]

Predictably, Bosley Crowther found even the cut version overlong. "[It's] another of those stately legend-dramas that is so exquisite pictorially that it almost compensates the patient viewer for its paucity of drama and its heavy pace. . . . It makes for dull drama for my remote occidental taste, and, by our standards, it is weirdly played by a cast of distinguished Japanese artists. . . . This is the most tastefully, subtly designed Japanese film since the memorable 'Gate of Hell.' But, unfortunately, it has none of the sensitive and intense human tension that was in that film. It stands as a cold and clumsy drama in the Japanese epic style."[80]

The picture did reasonably well in its Los Angeles and New York engagements. However, Edward Landberg, president of the Berkeley Cinema Guild and a staunch supporter of Japanese film, picked up the U.S. distribution rights after *Chushingura* had finished its limited run. He wanted to give the complete *Chushingura* a chance and acquired the original 208-minute version from Toho. Landberg owned four San Francisco Bay–area theaters and opened the complete *Chushingura* at his Cinema Theatre in Berkeley, instituting a money-back guarantee: patrons who didn't want to stay for the second act could get their money refunded. To audiences of mostly U.C–Berkeley students, the film ran an amazing forty-one weeks. In late 1965, the complete version began making the rounds in other parts of the country.[81]

The picture reopened in New York in October 1966, and *Chushingura* took on a second life; it ran for months, and every major critic rereviewed the picture—except for Bosley Crowther, "who 'stood pat' on his original review and, reportedly, has not seen the film being presently shown." The trades were fairly amazed by *Chushingura*'s resurrection. *Variety* noted: "The experience . . . is something of a phenomenon in the U.S. film industry as it is, possibly, the only film, restored to its original shape from dismembered parts, to be successfully exhibited."[82] (The complete version was released to home video in the United States and Japan in the late 1990s.)

With Toho producer Iwao Mori, Mifune flew to New York on January 21, 1963, for a reception in his honor. That same month in Japan he was starring in Toho's big New Year release, *Attack Squadron!* (Taiheiyo no tsubasa, or "Wings of the Pacific"), a follow-up to *Storm Over the Pacific*. Again directed by Shue Matsubayashi, with special effects by Eiji Tsuburaya, the film was another big-budget, all-star war epic, this one focusing on an elite group of fighter pilots.

Mifune stars as Commander Senda, who, near the end of the war, is opposed to the idea of sending Japan's remaining fighters on kamikaze missions. He wants to regain control of the skies and wins approval to compile an elite task force of the country's best surviving pilots. He recruits three squadrons, led by Teppei Yano (Makoto Sato), stationed in Rabaul; Nobuo Odaka (Yosuke Natsuki), presently in Okinawa; and Shiro Taka (Yuzo Kayama), now fighting guerrillas in the Philippines.

After various adventures, the three squadrons are brought together at the Matsuyama Air Base in southern Japan. At first the pilots are scorned by the more openly nationalistic kamikaze, who think the three squadrons cowardly, especially after Senda, wanting to protect his fighters, orders his men to fly away during an air raid. But the commander's careful handling of the pilots and their planes eventually results in several successful missions, where the Allies suffer huge losses, their first in many months, while Senda's attack force loses nary a plane. Because of these successes, Senda is ordered to cover a much wider part of Japan—half the country, in fact— thus spreading his squadrons too thin to be effective. At the same time, the pilots and their planes are not being replaced as they're shot down, and the odds against them become overwhelming. Yano dies after making an emergency landing, and Odaka is killed after disobeying orders by providing air cover for the doomed battleship *Yamato*. As the number of pilots dwindle, Senda orders Taka to "stay alive." During a mission, however, Taka watches from above as dozens of B-29 bombers drop hundreds of lethal bombs on Japan. Screaming, "Get out of my country!" he crashes his plane into one of the bombers. In the end, Senda stands alone on an empty airfield.

Natsuki recalled, "Mr. Mifune was great, both as an actor and as a person. All actors in Japan were trying to catch up with him. All of the young actors would go to whichever stage he was working and stare at him, including me."[83]

Though he was top-billed, Mifune's role is relatively small. As in most of his war pictures, Mifune offers his great screen presence and little else. He does what he can to keep his pilots alive to fight another day, but his men gradually realize the hopelessness of it all, and they have their own agenda about how and when they'll die. The script gives Mifune little to do other than to act intensely worried, grimacing with concern as the squadrons take off, perhaps never to return.

The picture, by design, isn't about Mifune's character anyway; rather, the focus is on the three squadron leaders and their adventures, which play as lively if innocuous set pieces. Rather shrewdly, the film is tailor-made for its cast of contract leading players: Makoto Sato, then at the height of his popularity via the studio's "Independent Gangsters" series, enacts the lighter-weight, comic sequences (his squadron includes the extremely talented comic actor Kiyoshi Atsumi, several years away from debuting as "Tora-san"); Yosuke Natsuki, known almost exclusively as an action hero, handles the picture's more conventional, tough-guy set pieces; and Yuzo Kayama, Toho's fastest-rising star, carries the weight of the story's moral dilemmas and its romantic subplot.

Due to the popularity of his "Young Guy" films—college-based, song-filled romantic comedies—Kayama was usually paired outside the series with the woman who played his girlfriend in these films, Yuriko Hoshi. She turns up here as the sister of one of Kayama's men. Trying to reach Senda's air base, Taka's transport plane is attacked, and losing fuel, Taka is forced to throw everything he can out of the plane, including the dead bodies of men killed during the attack, among them Hoshi's brother. Later, she shows up at the base to inquire about her brother's death, and when Taka tells her he was forced to dump his body, she's horrified.

Attack Squadron! was immensely popular, even more so than *Storm Over the Pacific*; only Kurosawa's *High and Low* made more money for Toho that year. But Matsubayashi saw an unpleasant shift with this picture. "My Navy films were very popular, but by the time I made *Attack Squadron!* I was concerned that the battle scenes were beginning to dominate the human story. I had been a part of war, and for me to make money on films that showed only the action made me question what I was doing. I felt guilty about it. Was I making a trivial piece of entertainment out of such a serious and deadly part of history? And so, popular as they were, I walked away, rejecting all offers to do more."[84]

EIGHTEEN

HEAVEN AND HELL

Kurosawa's next film, *High and Low*, was based on *King's Ransom*, an "87th Precinct Mystery" novel by Ed McBain (a.k.a. Evan Hunter), published by Simon & Schuster in 1959. The breezy pulp novel concerns a rich shoe executive, Douglas King, faced with a moral dilemma. While engineering a major financial deal, which will give him controlling interest in his company, King receives a telephone call from a man claiming to have kidnapped his son. But the kidnapper has made a mistake. Instead of King's boy, the man grabbed the chauffeur's son. Nevertheless, the kidnapper demands that King pay the ransom anyway, threatening to kill the boy if he doesn't. If King pays, he'll lose his entire fortune. Detectives Steve Carella, Meyer Meyer, and other continuing characters in the 87th Precinct stories track the kidnapper down (though his two accomplices escape), the boy is rescued, and King's money is recovered.

In 1961, *87th Precinct* came to American television as an hourly series produced by MCA/Universal for NBC and starring the underrated Robert Lansing as Carella, Norman Fell as Meyer Meyer, and Ron Harper and Gregory Walcott as the other detectives. (In a few episodes, Gena Rowlands appeared as Lansing's deaf-mute wife.) McBain was directly involved with the series, writing many of its episodes. The series ran just one season, but among the stories McBain adapted was *King's Ransom*, which aired on February 19, 1962, with a well-cast Charles McGraw as Douglas King, Nancy Davis (Reagan) as his wife, John McLiam as the chauffeur, and Charles Aidman, Virginia Vincent, and Tony Carbone as the kidnappers.

Kurosawa hadn't seen the television episode before acquiring the property. Toho had already purchased the film rights, in the summer of 1961, when Charles E. Tuttle, a bookseller and publisher based in Tokyo and Rutland, Vermont, brought Toho and McBain together. Through McBain's agent, Scott Meredith, the rights were sold for $5,000.[1] Kurosawa's film of *King's Ransom* is faithful to McBain's story, but with significant changes, expanding upon its attributes while adding intriguing elements not in the book.

High and Low is one of Kurosawa's finest films. It is a masterpiece of structure, rich in characterization, with genuinely harrowing suspense. Moreover, it grapples with issues far beyond the average pulp novel. It is clever, even ingenious at times, and technically marvelous. It also provided Mifune with one of his best and most overlooked performances.

The story is transplanted to the Yokohama home of wealthy Kingo Gondo (Mifune), an executive director and production head who runs the factory of National Shoes. Gondo meets with three company executives (Jun Tazaki, Nobuo Nakamura, and Yunosuke Ito). They ask Gondo to join them in ousting the company's president, whose shoes and leadership are increasingly old-fashioned. They propose a new line of shoes much cheaper to produce and therefore more profitable. Gondo, who has spent most of his life at the company, is outraged by the shoddiness of the product they show him. As Gondo's assistant, Kawanishi (Tatsuya Mihashi), looks on, Gondo refuses to go along with the scheme, chastising the executives for their lack of integrity. Gondo throws them out, surprising Reiko (Kyoko Kagawa), his wife.

Reiko and Kawanishi quickly realize that Gondo is up to something. Gondo places several calls, arranging some kind of business deal. As he does so, his young son, Jun (Toshio Egi), runs in, dressed in a Western-style sheriff's outfit, "shooting" his friend Shinichi (Masahiko Shimzu), the son of Gondo's chauffeur (Yutaka Sada), with a toy rifle. When Shinichi puts on the cowboy gear and it's Jun's turn to play the outlaw, Gondo encourages him to be ruthless, prompting Reiko to comment, "He takes after you. He likes violent games." Reiko then says that, like Gondo, Jun is "getting worse" and becoming increasingly cutthroat.

Gondo explains that by mortgaging the house and borrowing an enormous amount of money he has raised ¥50 million (about $139,000), enough to acquire a controlling interest in National Shoes. "I've bet my whole fortune on this," he says, and tells Kawanishi to book a flight to Osaka to close the deal.

Suddenly the phone rings. Gondo answers, and a man at the other end says that he has kidnapped Gondo's son, demanding ¥30 million for his return. The kidnapper warns Gondo not to call the police. Gondo and Reiko are frantic, and Gondo says he'll do anything to get his son back. Kawanishi reaches for the phone to call the police but Gondo stops him. Just then, Jun strolls in. "Is this some kind of joke?!" Gondo says, incredulous.

At that point they realize: Shinichi, the chauffeur's son, was wearing Jun's cowboy outfit. "Even I got them mixed up," exclaims Reiko. Aoki, the chauffeur, is horrified. Gondo calls the police, in spite of the kidnapper's threat. Gondo insists the kidnapper will have to give Shinichi up; surely he can't be expected to pay now.

The police arrive, led by Chief Detective Tokura (Tatsuya Nakadai) and a huge bald man, Chief Detective "Bos'n" Taguchi (Kenjiro Ishiyama), with detectives Nakao (Takeshi Kato) and Arai (Isao Kimura) in support. Gondo keeps insisting that the kidnapper will turn over Shinichi when he realizes his mistake, but Tokura isn't so sure. Reiko explains that Aoki is a widower and that Shinichi is his only child. The detectives begin setting up phone-tracing equipment.

The kidnapper calls back, having realized he grabbed the wrong boy, but he still demands that Gondo pay the ransom. "You're a fool to pay," he says, "but you must. You don't have the guts to kill him." The detectives are impressed by the kidnapper's cool demeanor and ingenuity. As Aoki agonizes over his son's safety, Gondo is beside himself over the absurdity of his situation and how the kidnapper obviously wants to humiliate him.

The kidnapper calls again, putting Shinichi briefly on the phone. "Whether he lives or dies," he tells Gondo, "depends on you." Click. The detectives try to trace the call, but the kidnapper is never on the line long enough. Hearing his son's voice, Aoki begs his employer to save Shinichi. Bowing fervently, Aoki drops to his knees and bursts into tears. Gondo decides to postpone the deal until morning. Picking up his son, he goes to bed.

The next morning Gondo tells the detectives that he is still determined not to pay and tries to justify his decision by explaining that if he does, he'll lose everything he has. Reiko begs her husband to pay anyway. Gondo gives his check to Kawanishi to close the deal, but the assistant refuses. Kawanishi says it's a no-win situation. If Gondo doesn't pay, the kidnapper might kill the boy and the negative publicity surrounding it would hurt National Shoes. Gondo doesn't believe Kawanishi. He accuses the assistant of betraying him. Kawanishi admits that indeed he has: when he saw Gondo weaken, he decided to protect himself and told the other executives everything to save his own skin.

Tokura tries to console Gondo. "You have the right to protect your own life," he says, asking Gondo to say he'll pay when the kidnapper calls back, if only to buy the detectives some time.

Then Aoki enters the room, apologizing for begging him the night before. "Please don't worry about my son," he says in a heartbreaking monologue. Reiko bursts into tears and runs out of the room. Off-camera Jun, seeing his mother weeping, cries, too. Aoki walks out of the room, then collapses on the stairway.

Under immense pressure and weighing all his options, Gondo finally decides to pay. The kidnapper calls again with instructions for the payoff. He demands the money be placed in two briefcases less than 7 cm thick and tells Gondo to board the bullet train. Asking for further instructions, the kidnapper says only, "Get on and you'll see."

The detectives wonder what the kidnapper will do. He couldn't make the exchange on the train; that would be too dangerous. It wouldn't make sense for him to make the exchange at a station, either. Knowing the kidnapper will have to destroy the unusual-looking cases, the detectives plan to hide two tracing devices within their linings. One is a powder that gives off a foul odor when wet; the other gives off pink smoke if burned. Gondo asks Reiko to bring him his old tool bag. Years ago, Gondo says, when he was an apprentice, shoemakers used to make cases, too. As the detectives copy down serial numbers off the bills, Gondo hides the tracing devices in the cases himself. Sitting cross-legged on the floor, he says, "I'm starting over already."

With a sudden, abrupt wipe we cut to the bullet train roaring toward Osaka the next day. Gondo nervously sits with his entire fortune on his lap. The detectives, pretending to be passengers, are sitting nearby, while others search the train for Shinichi. But the boy is nowhere to be found. Watching the shoe executive, Tokura tells Bos'n, "That Gondo is all right."

Bos'n agrees. "I didn't like him at first," he says. "I usually waste no love on the rich."

Gondo is paged. A telephone call awaits him in another car. This he had not expected. He nervously goes to answer the phone, as Tokura and Bos'n follow. Gondo is to go to the lavatory, and from there he will be able to see Shinichi as the train crosses the Sakawa River. He is then to open the lavatory window—which opens exactly 7 cm—and throw the money out as the train reaches the opposite bank. The detectives are stunned at the kidnapper's ingenuity. Gondo is wide-eyed in disbelief at what he's just done. Tokura positions his men from one end of the train to the other to take pictures of the kidnapper and his accomplices as the train passes. The detectives rush about the train as it barrels toward the river. Gondo sees Shinichi, the train crosses the river, and Gondo's fortune goes out the window.

Another wipe and we see, in the distance, Gondo rushing toward Shinichi, the shoe executive overcome with emotion. The detectives are moved by the scene as well, and even Bos'n is teary-eyed. Tokura says, "Now let's get him," and the film begins its second act.

In the sweltering heat detectives Arai and Nakao investigate pay telephones within sight of Gondo's home. Looking at the white mansion looming over them, one of them admits, "This house gets to you, as if it's looking down at you." As they walk on, we see a polluted canal, reminiscent of the sump in *Drunken Angel* and the polluted lot in *Ikiru*. In its reflection we see a man on the other side, walking. It's the kidnapper (Tsutomu Yamazaki). He enters his tiny studio apartment, the window of which looks straight up to Gondo's house. He studies the newspapers for articles on the kidnapping, including one about the huge public support of Gondo's sacrifice. He hears an announcer on the radio personally addressing him, saying that, thanks to the kidnapper, Gondo has become a hero.

The second hour of the film deals with the search for the kidnapper. When the kidnapper burns the cases, Gondo and the detectives see the colored smoke (in this otherwise black-and-white film the smoke is tinted pink) rising from a smokestack. This and other clues eventually lead the detectives to the kidnapper, a medical intern named Takeuchi.

After his capture, Takeuchi is sentenced to death. He asks to see Gondo, and they meet in a small room with glass and wire mesh separating them. Takeuchi asks Gondo if he's pleased with the verdict, that the man who ruined him is going to die. Takeuchi wants Gondo to hate him, but Gondo cannot. "Why do we have to hate one another?" he asks. Takeuchi says that his apartment was freezing cold in the winter, stiflingly hot in the summer, and that Gondo's house looked like heaven from below. His only comfort was the thought of making a fortunate man unfortunate. Trembling, Takeuchi says, "I don't want you to think I died crying and afraid. My hands don't tremble because I'm nervous. It's from being in solitary so long. Just being outside that cell makes them tremble. I'm not afraid of death or hell. My life has been like hell since I was born. But if I had to go to heaven, I'd really tremble." He laughs, puts his head in his hands, then suddenly jumps up, grabbing at the mesh and screaming. Guards rush in to take him away as a metal wall slides down, leaving Gondo, his back to the camera, as the film fades out.

This remarkable last scene exemplifies the degree to which Kurosawa expanded upon McBain's novel. American critics of the time thought *High and Low* little more than an expertly made crime thriller. While no one can deny Kurosawa's technical brilliance, his detractors argued that Kurosawa's form far outweighs his content, that his Eastern Westerns and "sukiyaki" thrillers, while cinematically adroit, remain fundamentally empty exercises in style. This is reflected even in contemporary overviews of the director's legacy. Consider *Sight and Sound*'s thuddingly dismissive obituary, which stated: "Let's be frank: as a thinker, Kurosawa is of very little interest."[2] The last scene of *High and Low* is proof positive of just the reverse.

In this final scene, Mifune and Yamazaki are separated by a glass partition. Because of the glass, reflections of Mifune can be seen in shots of Yamazaki and, in reverse angles, reflections of Yamazaki in shots of Mifune, as if the two characters are merging. In his book on the director, Donald Richie wrote that the images are figuratively and literally merging: "We know they are not one—they are good and evil; they are opposite poles. This is what we have been led to believe, this is what we *must* believe. Yet, here, Kurosawa is showing us something entirely different. He is suggesting that, despite everything, good and evil are the same, that all men are equal."[3]

That's not exactly right, though more than in virtually any of Kurosawa's other films, the ending of *High and Low* is open to interpretation. Rather than good and evil being the same, Kurosawa is saying that each of us is capable of both good and evil, that we choose to be good or bad, or both for that matter. What's important about the reflections in the glass isn't that they become one. (And despite what Richie says, the reflections don't actually move toward each other in the manner he describes in his analysis.) Kurosawa does this to illustrate the thin line, literally and figuratively, that separates them. More precisely, what's shown is how much of Takeuchi is buried within Gondo, and of Gondo within Takeuchi. The great sadness of this scene is Gondo's realization that he's rather like the kidnapper himself. On a certain level, they are one and the same. Choice rather than circumstance is all that separates them. Takeuchi believed his hate is what kept him alive, when in fact it proved his undoing. Gondo, on the other hand, made difficult, agonizing choices in a random, chaotic world where choice is the only thing he has.

In the end, Kurosawa says, money and poverty, heaven and hell are meaningless. The film finishes with a shot of Gondo facing the closed shutter, his face reflected in the glass—Gondo confronting himself. Though the film ends in a vaguely hopeful way (suggesting that Gondo has recognized the ugliness within him), it nonetheless concludes on a deeply sad, existential note.

Despite his wealth, despite his cockiness, Gondo never forgets his past. He is a fair boss to his workers (seen when Bos'n interviews a factory worker, played by Eijiro Tono). When Gondo asks his wife to fetch his tool kit, so that he may hide the dye packs in the two briefcases, he knows exactly where the tool kit is, even though he hasn't used it in years. One can easily imagine Gondo fifteen years earlier, when he was the kidnapper's age, living in a similar slum, looking up at a house very much like his own.

As the film opens, Gondo is on the verge of descending into immorality (exemplified by his attempt at a ruthless takeover of National Shoes and much like the characters who populate *The Bad Sleep Well*), but he chooses—with much difficulty—to embrace the good, despite the consequences. Takeuchi has rejected the good within himself; he chooses to be evil. Gondo, however, was himself once part of the same world as Takeuchi, but he chose to work his way out of it, or so he thinks. In fact, Gondo's very humanity hangs in the balance. Both men were born into a world of poverty, both "victims of society," as it were. Rather than good and evil being the same, Kurosawa is saying that one's roots, one's financial status are irrelevant. More than that, he is suggesting that being a victim is itself irrelevant, because, in a sense, Takeuchi is as much a victim of society as Gondo is a victim of Takeuchi's blackmail. Conversely, Kurosawa says, responsibility is everything. He is literally endorsing the theme that in a chaotic world man is measured by the choices he makes, a theme that appears in most of his best work, from *Rashomon* through *Ikiru* and *Seven Samurai*, continuing more or less to the end of his career.

Kurosawa might have ended *High and Low* with Gondo expressing sympathy for Takeuchi, but the director's genius is that he refuses to let Gondo (or us) off so easily, and this is the most remarkable aspect of the picture. As Richie notes, the final scene puts Gondo through a last important test. In one respect he has lost everything to the kidnapper. But now, facing him, he cannot bring himself to hate, even though Takeuchi very much wants to be hated. He doesn't ask for Gondo's sympathy, and Gondo's pain isn't over the loss of his fortune, or that the circumstances in which he played a major role now condemn a man to death. Quite the contrary—Gondo realizes that he must accept responsibility for the very man who brought him ruination. By extension, he must accept the chaos that is the world today and must demand of himself a humanity he never thought possible.

This conclusion is the very opposite of McBain's, whose novel ends with capitalist King, his money recovered, happily closing his stock deal and ready to take over National Shoes. The television version, which McBain scripted, goes even further. The coda shows the lead detective reading the financial page of the newspaper, as if to follow in King's footsteps.

High and Low is a film about responsibility. In the first hour of the picture, Gondo must weigh his responsibility to himself and to his family and other, peripheral characters. By the end of the film, this responsibility extends to Takeuchi and, by extension, to mankind itself.

When Shinichi is first kidnapped, Reiko admits to feeling responsible for the kidnapping, which at first seems like an odd thing to say. She is referring to the fact that the two boys exchanged clothes, which is why the kidnapper grabbed the wrong child, yet she had nothing to do with that. Nonetheless, she feels responsible for the kidnapping and, unlike Gondo, is ready to pay the ransom without hesitation, regardless of who was kidnapped.

In both the novel and the film, Gondo argues that it's easy to decide to pay when it isn't your fortune you're throwing away. It's not the amount of the ransom that's important but rather—and Kurosawa is careful to emphasize this—how this money is absolutely everything he has that makes Gondo's final decision to pay all the more believable, compelling, and true.

This aspect of *High and Low* is rather like one in Atom Egoyan's acclaimed film *The Sweet Hereafter* (1997), about a small town coming to terms with a bus accident in which nearly all the town's children have drowned. The film is a study of the randomness of tragedy, and how desperate parents who survived them are to find meaning and explanation in a life-shattering event that has, ultimately, no purpose. Kurosawa's film operates in much the same way. Gondo's first reactions upon learning that the kidnapper grabbed the wrong boy are disbelief, then anger. How can he be expected to pay now? "It's ridiculous" and "It's absurd," he insists. And that is precisely the point. The kidnapper has no personal grudge against Gondo, other than his wealth. If Gondo's house hadn't been looming over his apartment, he would have chosen someone else. "Why me?" Gondo keeps demanding. But it is a pointless question. *High and Low* is a film about the randomness of fate, playing heavily on coincidence. (This coincidence is best seen when the detectives, tailing the kidnapper they've now identified, witness something almost unbelievable. The detectives spot Gondo, his money gone, wandering the streets of Yokohama, and Takeuchi sees him looking at the display case of a shoe store. The kidnapper casually walks up to Gondo and asks him for a light. Gondo, unaware of the identity of the man who has approached him, just as casually obliges.) Gondo had mistakenly assumed his wealth would act as a kind of buffer, only to learn that money can protect him from the chaotic, random world we live in no more than it can protect him from cancer.

In Japan, *High and Low* was called "Heaven and Hell" (Tengoku to jigoku), a far more evocative title. The English name Toho gave it is much less true to the scenario's meaning and complexity. In point of fact, the film is filled with references to heaven and hell, as Kurosawa contrasts "heaven" (Gondo's luxurious house, literally above, like heaven) with "hell" (seedy Yokohama) throughout. In one of his calls to Gondo, the kidnapper tells him, "It's hot as hell down here. An inferno. 105 degrees." Later, at the prison, the kidnapper says that looking up at Gondo's house was like looking up at heaven. At the same time, the screenplay and direction constantly blur the lines between this heaven and hell, just as they blur the lines between Gondo and Takeuchi. Gondo's heaven is corrupted by the wolf-like treachery of the three shoe executives, his disloyal assistant, his creditors ready to pounce on him. (One of the creditors, wearing sunglasses and a tacky suit, appears to be a *yakuza*, suggesting that Gondo borrowed money from the mob.) Conversely, Yokohama-as-hell is blurred by the presence of the detectives hard at work on Takeuchi's trail. And the general vibrancy of the city's nightclubs, with their bright neon, dancing soldiers on leave, etcetera, serve to create a hell that is, in part at least, seductive.

High and Low is one of the most beautifully structured of all Kurosawa's films. While the story is McBain's, the film is pure Kurosawa, reflective of a writer-director at the peak of his powers. He neatly divides the film into two acts—the kidnapping and negotiations, followed by a stylistic about-face for the rescue, investigation, and resolution.

The first half is tense and emotional, the second cool and methodical. The first hour takes place virtually in one room of Gondo's luxurious, air-cooled, modernist house and is filmed like a one-act play; the last hour is set all over the sweltering city, or in large, sweaty conference rooms and a Dante-esque "drug alley," and shot first in a semidocumentary style, and later in a film-noirish look, as if seen through a heroin addict's eyes. The two parts are separated by the thrilling payment of the ransom on the bullet train.

A testament to the skill of Kurosawa, his writing team, and the actors involved is that the hour spent in Gondo's living room is never dull. Indeed, just the reverse: the tension mounts steadily, with every line of dialogue building a deeper understanding of its characters. Kurosawa blocks his actors superbly; they move about the room naturally, and his compositions are artistic even here—each frame is composed like a painting, with emotion expressed through the blocking of the actors in relation to one another.

At the same time, Kurosawa employs several clever devices to keep the narrative moving. When the police arrive, disguised as department-store deliverymen to avoid suspicion from the prying eyes of Takeuchi, there is no explanation for their appearance. Kurosawa respects his audience and knows a few simple shots of them is enough. The kidnapper phones Gondo, who picks up the receiver. Kurosawa wipes to everyone listening to the taped conversation a few minutes later, thus avoiding unnecessary action.

After the confined action in Gondo's living room, the abrupt wipe to the speeding bullet train (the soundtrack abruptly cutting to its screaming horn) sets this brilliant set piece on its thrilling way. In contrast to the long takes at Gondo's house and its theaterlike drama, the power of the starkly cinematic action aboard the train is greatly enhanced. The scene is photographed mostly with hand-held cameras as the detectives race from car to car, the editing is taut, and the end result is breathtaking. The train sequence runs under five minutes, yet is one of the most exciting five minutes in world cinema.

With the investigation, the film adopts a more leisurely pace, but interest never flags. The legwork of the detectives is logical and believable, and once again tension mounts with the discovery of each clue. As in *He Walked by Night* (1948), the identity of the kidnapper is revealed early on, at the beginning of the second half. His identity isn't what's important but rather how the detectives' hard work slowly but surely will lead them to him. As with *Stray Dog*, these scenes are rooted in the French *policier* neorealist school of noir, as seen in American films like *Boomerang!* (1947) and *The Naked City* (1948).

Here the film takes another marvelous turn, into Chinatown and the noirish "dope alley," with its urban vision of "hell." This sequence is so beautifully realized that it teeters on the edge of being too stylish for its own good, because it contrasts so starkly with the semidocumentary look of the investigation scenes. But it's entirely believable and ultimately blends into the picture's whole, and its frank depiction of drug abuse is unsettling.

More obvious to Japanese than to Western audiences is that Mifune's working-class features function in tandem with his performance to make clear that Gondo has worked his way up the corporate ladder, that he's part of the nouveau riche. He lives in a world of ostentatious luxury (chauffeur, maids, a Mercedes). Kurosawa trades off the broadly physical parts Mifune usually played by giving him a role that is almost entirely internal. In McBain's novel, Douglas King himself nabs the kidnapper. Gondo plays no role in Takeuchi's capture. Kurosawa denies us this because it's not only unnecessary but would have worked against that final, brilliant scene.

In the beginning, as Gondo wheels and deals his takeover of National Shoes, Mifune plays him with cocky confidence; he is a man who enjoys keeping his wife and assistant in the dark about his plans. His meeting with the executives (also in McBain's novel) is important because it shows Gondo as a basically decent and honest man, while at the same time setting up the red herring that the shoe company executives might have been behind the kidnapping.

Repeatedly, Gondo refuses to pay the ransom. As Aoki, Reiko, and Kawanishi move about him, urging him to pay or not to pay, Mifune wonderfully expresses Gondo's growing desperation to have those around him understand and accept the reasons for his decision. He's a logical, reasonable man who finds himself in an illogical, unreasonable situation. In one scene that exemplifies both Mifune's abilities as an actor and Kurosawa's attention to blocking, Mifune suddenly pulls open the drapes, and then realizes he cannot leave them open (for the kidnapper might see the detectives). Irritated, he jerks them back into position—the kidnapper has taken such complete control over Gondo's life that he cannot open the curtains in his own house. Here Mifune through subtle gestures and Kurosawa through his direction of the scene perfectly express Gondo's frustrations. Also, when Gondo showers just prior to deciding to pay the ransom, Mifune looks like a man violently scrubbing the ruthlessness from his soul. Receiving the phone call from Takeuchi aboard the bullet train, as he prepares to throw his fortune literally out the window, Mifune acutely expresses his character's sense of disbelief and, finally, the horror and realization of what has happened to him. The money gone, he splashes water on his face, looking like a man about to be ill.

Later, as the detectives update Gondo about their investigation, he puts up a brave front, always grateful for every bit of news, every yen that is recovered. But Mifune reveals the devastation just beneath his smiles and cordiality. The actor's ability to express this subtext was never given a better showcase than in *High and Low*.

Like Kikuchiyo in *Seven Samurai*, the role of Gondo was one very close to the actor who plays him. Like Mifune, Gondo lived in relative poverty and became one of Japan's wealthiest men. Like Gondo, Mifune never forgot his past, nor did he ever really assimilate into the elite world which he occupied. Nonetheless, both men surrounded themselves with luxury. Though Mifune disdained servants, he, like Gondo, owned an expensive foreign car (Mifune's was an MG) and lived in a luxurious, air-cooled house with his wife and children. And like Gondo, Mifune was passionate and deeply devoted to his work.

Gondo is also a stand-in for Kurosawa, a man equally rich, a man who, like Mifune, had a male son (Mifune had two), and for Kurosawa the film was an expression of the frustration he felt toward the leniency kidnappers received in Japan—indeed, a friend's son had once been abducted. In fact, one of the major changes Kurosawa made from McBain's novel, and one of the reasons Kurosawa wanted to do the film in the first place, was the contrast between Japanese and American penalties for kidnapping. In the novel, the kidnappers risk "the chair" for their actions. As *Film Daily* reported, "Kurosawa . . . is out to make a point. He has two [sic] young sons himself and considers the penalty for kidnapping too light in Japan, where kidnappers can get as little as three years in prison if the child is not killed."[4]

Preproduction began on July 20, 1962, when Kurosawa started casting those roles he hadn't filled during the writing phase. Appearing in his first Kurosawa film was a shy, twenty-six-year-old actor named Tsutomu Yamazaki, as Takeuchi, the kidnapper. Yamazaki had made his film debut in Kihachi Okamoto's *The Spook Cottage* (Daigaku sanzokutachi, 1960), and prior to *High and Low* had done several films for Shiro Toyoda. He also appeared in *My Daughter and I* (Musume to watashi, 1962), a film directed by Kurosawa's former assistant Hiromichi Horikawa. Kurosawa's decision to cast him may have been at Horikawa's suggestion.

> When I auditioned for the role [Yamazaki remembered], I had to sit in a waiting room all by myself and couldn't stop shaking. I heard a theory that the quantity of adrenaline that an actor secretes due to tension prior to a performance is more than the fatal dose for a nor-

mal person. (I'm not sure whether this is true or not.) Anyway, I was really tense and felt like vomiting that day. To be honest, I was too shy to look into anybody's eyes in those days. If this big director looks at me, I'll die, I thought. I shouldn't have come here. Should I leave without auditioning? When he finally called me in, he asked, "Did you learn your lines?" There were five or six of his main crew around him. I couldn't look up. "Yes," I said, keeping my head down. "Okay, let's get started! I'll be your reading partner. Do it as you like." Oh, my God, I thought! It's getting worse—now he's my reading partner. I can't not look at him. At the other end of the five-foot table, Mr. Kurosawa slowly took off his glasses and sat down. My eyes must have been ugly and impure, but his own eyes slowly and warmly looked back. He was prompting me in a non-judgmental manner. Naturally, my tension decreased. For the first time, I was able to look into someone's eyes while I read my lines. . . . My problem was solved, and at the same time I passed the audition. I'll never forget his soft eyes. I did it thanks to them.[5]

Shooting began with the film's first act, in Gondo's house, on September 2. "The 'Gondo Palace' was supposed to be at the top of a hill, a luxurious house," said actor Takeshi Kato. "The living room of the house was built at the biggest stage at Toho. I was very surprised at the set, especially the backdrop. The story was set in Yokohama, and outside the windows miniatures were made of the city and, amazingly, for night scenes, lights would come on and there was a moving train. It was so precise. I was able to see the Yokohama Bridge, the bay, and lights in the ships, too. However, when we shot scenes through the window during daytime, scenes when the drapes were open, we went to Yokohama, where a second living-room set was built, and we'd shoot those scenes there to enable us to see the real Yokohama below. I didn't think it was necessary to make the miniatures at Toho, because we never really shot them."[6]

During the filming of those scenes, Mifune discussed Kurosawa's methods with *Film Daily*'s George E. Eagle. "It's hard work," he said. "[Kurosawa's] a very painstaking person in a profession that demands painstaking work. It's Kurosawa's practice to have the actors play their parts at their own will, freely. Kurosawa tells [us] what he thinks is proper. Basically, he has his actors play freely and then supervises the acting if he thinks it's necessary. Directors usually start with the script treatment and a rehearsal of dialogue, but in this picture Kurosawa started with standing action."[7]

Nine days later, the interiors aboard the Kodama Super Express train were filmed. "Before the Shinkansen ["New Super Express"], the Kodama Super Express was the fastest train in Japan," Kato said. "Now it takes about three hours to get to Osaka, but in those days it took about six. The rehearsal took place in a train that was in storage, but we were able to get a real train for shooting; it ran from Tokyo to Odawara for one day. I remember right before Odawara there is a famous river where we shot the scene where the money is dropped. As soon as the train left Tokyo, we began shooting the interiors—all the passengers were extras, and there were a lot of them. In that sequence where the kidnapper is waiting under the bridge, where Mr. Mifune is going to drop the money as the detectives run to various points on the train, I was at the very end of the train—we shot all of that simultaneously. We couldn't make any mistakes. Mr. Kurosawa was with Mr. Mifune, and there was a camera under the bridge, and each detective had two cameras following him. Basically, all the cameramen at Toho worked that day; the other productions were shut down.

"The only problem was that when we passed the bridge, the camera following me didn't work. Mr. Kurosawa, of course, didn't know that at the time, and he was all smiles afterward. The main cameraman following me was [Mikio] Naruse's regular cameraman, and when he reported what happened, I still can't forget the expression on Mr. Kurosawa's face. Usually, for most directors it's okay when a B camera gets the action where the A camera does not, but not with Mr. Kurosawa. So on a different day we shot my scenes again. Fortunately, we needed only the back of the train [laughs]."[8]

With the new year, Kurosawa's crew moved to the story's Yokohama exteriors, where drug addicts littered filthy alleyways. "[*High and Low* was] set in the summertime, and all of us wore short sleeves, but the film took a year to make," said Kato. "I'll never forget the scene where Mr. Mifune and the kidnapper met by coincidence in Yokohama. We were supposed to go on location. It was a very important scene, but by then it was already January. That's why we couldn't do it outside. We gave up shooting on location and shot it at the studio, so the crew and all the pedestrians could wear summer clothes. In Japan, January 10 is supposed to be the coldest day of the year, but on that day we were wearing short-sleeved shirts and were sprayed to look like we were sweating!"[9]

Yutaka Sada (b. 1911), excellent as Aoki the chauffeur, had appeared in bit parts at Toho, going back at least as far as 1954. Prior to *High and Low*, he had appeared in many of Kurosawa's films, memorably as the weak son in *Record of a Living Being*, but after that his roles in Kurosawa's films prior to *High and Low* were little more than bit parts. Like Ikio Sawamura of *Yojimbo*, Sada was incredibly prolific, popping up in virtually everything Toho made. His mousy screen persona suited a wide range of genres and he was always in demand.

For Sada, *High and Low* was a once-in-a-lifetime experience. "Nothing will be left if *High and Low* is taken from my life," he wrote. "With this film, I think I have left something for my children."[10]

Amid the stellar cast, Sada was clearly bottom man on the totem pole. Shy and unassuming, he was very much like the characters he played and thus perfectly cast as a lowly servant in the most awkward of situations.

It was difficult because I thought I'd be able to act better. I eventually realized how hard it is to act and that I didn't know what I was doing. I didn't know where to look. . . . I had a difficult time and could barely breathe.

The hardest part was shooting on Eno Island. There was the scene where Aoki was looking for the [kidnapper and his two accomplices] with his son, and then I was found and scolded by Mr. Isao Kimura and Bos'n. No matter how hard I tried, I just couldn't say my lines correctly. I think we spent days on that scene because I couldn't get my lines right. Since the area where we shot it was on a slope, light reflectors would move when the wind kicked up. Mr. Kurosawa scolded not only me but the lighting assistants. It was so hard for me being a burden to other people. We had to stop shooting because of the weather, because it would get cloudy in the midst of my poor acting. The shooting was canceled for three or four days, and the longer the schedule was delayed, the worse I felt.

Since I was born in the Meiji period, I never learned to drive a car. [In preparation for my role,] I went to a driving school for the first time, but there were no cars with the steering wheel on the left side like the Mercedes used in the film. I was responsible for the child in the car when I drove. I was scared of driving, even though we had a real driver hidden below us to pull the emergency brake in case anything happened. I always thought about apologizing to Mr. Kurosawa and all of his crew.[11]

However, Kurosawa saved most of his wrath for sixty-year-old Kenjiro Ishiyama (1903–76), so memorable as Bos'n, his film debut. According to Kato, "Mr. Ishiyama was an actor Mr. Kurosawa had wanted to use before,

as one of the bosses in *Yojimbo*. He belonged to a very famous 'fighting' theater group [which staged historic duels] called Shinkoku-geki, and he was a
very experienced actor. He acted in the group every month, so his schedule
was packed, and every time Mr. Kurosawa asked him to play a role he had
to refuse. Finally, for *High and Low*, he decided to do the film and quit
Shinkoku-geki. I was the one who was scolded in *The Bad Sleep Well*, but
he was the one scolded on *High and Low*. I really empathized with Mr.
Ishiyama's feelings, because we really didn't know what to do when Kurosawa scolded us. I don't know why Mr. Kurosawa didn't like him, but gradually his bald head and red face began to turn very pale. I was so sorry for
him. I had gone through it, so I really understood his feelings. But the final
result was great."[12]

Kyoko Kagawa concurs. "Every time [Ishiyama] was being scolded by
Mr. Kurosawa I didn't know what to do except wait quietly off to the side,"
she said. "But once the film was accomplished, the character was outstanding."[13]

After *High and Low*, Ishiyama subsequently appeared in many of Toho's
films, often playing heavies in their salaryman comedies, such as *The Crazy
Cats Go to Hong Kong* (Honkon kureejii sakusen, 1963), *You Can Succeed, Too*
(Kimimo shussega dekiru, 1964), and *Las Vegas Free-for-All* (Kureejii ogon
sakusen, 1967). His other credits include *Kwaidan* (1964), in which he had
a small role; Hiroshi Inagaki's *Kojiro* (Sasaki Kojiro, 1967); and the Mifune
films *The Emperor and a General* (Nippon no ichiban nagai hi, 1967), *Admiral
Yamamoto* (1968), and *The Militarists* (Gunbatsu, 1970). But after *High and
Low*, he never again worked with Kurosawa.

Though Yutaka Sada and Kenjiro Ishiyama endured the brunt of Kurosawa's temper, Takeshi Kato recalled one day during production reminiscent of his own trials on *The Bad Sleep Well* and the exacting, demanding
lengths Kurosawa went to in his drive for perfection. "I still remember
when we were in Yokohama, there was a scene of [Isao Kimura and me]
walking along the river," said Kato. "The first day we went to the river Mr.
Kurosawa said, 'The water isn't dirty enough,' and he went up and poured
dirt and black paint in it to make the river look dirtier. But he still didn't
like how it looked and walked off the set that day. It's unbelievable, thinking about it now. The next day the crew arrived early, trying to make it look
dirtier. Finally, when we shot it, we were talking along the river, and as
soon as I started to say my lines as usual, Mr. Kurosawa scolded me. This
went on over and over. Finally, he switched my lines with Mr. Kimura's. As
soon as we did the next take, Mr. Kurosawa said, 'Okay' [laughs]. I had a

hard experience. I almost gave up, and wondered why I wasn't fired."[14] But Kurosawa must have liked something about Kato's performance, because he asked him back more than twenty years later for a small role in *Ran*.

Production wrapped on January 30, 1963. Two weeks later, the film was test-screened, and it opened on March 1 to tremendous popular and critical response. *High and Low* became the highest-grossing Japanese film that year, earning ¥460,200,000 (about $1.3 million), even more than *Yojimbo* and *Sanjuro*.

The film made its American debut the week of John F. Kennedy's assassination, in November 1963, at the Toho Cinema, New York. The company specifically opened it there in hopes of finding an American buyer, and their plan worked. Within a month of its premiere, Toho closed a deal with Walter Reade–Sterling, which distributed the film on a wider, though still modest, basis.[15]

American reviewers praised *High and Low*'s technical aspects, but didn't know what to make of the film's social conscience within the context of a "lesser genre," the crime thriller. They found Kurosawa's direction exquisite, but wondered why so skilled a filmmaker would waste his time on such triviality.

Stanley Kauffmann's review echoed his comments on *Sanjuro*: "His new film . . . never flags in interest and is flawlessly executed; but I have no satisfactory idea why, at this stage of his career, he wanted to make it. . . . It is just a story of a kidnapping, with some light psychological and social trim now in vogue in detective novels. We see how the police finally found the kidnapper. That is all. . . . *High and Low* begins, drives on, and ends. No more; no resonance of any kind, if we disregard the jacket-blurb guff about Good and Evil on every mystery story." Kauffmann then very slightly contradicted himself: "There are two scenes in this picture, despite its limitations, that I do not expect ever to forget. The first is a visit to a 'dope den,' done like an elongated misty nightmare. The second is the final scene: when Mifune and Yamazaki confront each other in prison. . . . Although this is not one of Mifune's more demanding roles, it further substantiates his power and versatility."[16]

Newsweek's amusing review poked fun at all the foreign filmmakers turning to American-style crime thrillers as source material.

> One must credit Kurosawa at the very least with setting a new vogue. [In his forthcoming film,] Resnais presumably will make a film about a man who thinks he may have committed a crime;

Fellini, a man planning to commit a crime; Antonioni, the crook who has lost his gun and wanders around looking for it; Bergman, the gangster who has a religious vision; Satyajit Ray will show the flowers blooming behind the hide-out. Kurosawa? The paradoxes of morality, social conscience, and melodrama have been his hallmarks, anyway, and they adapt themselves quite easily to a story about kidnapping. . . . But Mifune is only Gondo . . . and while he has a chance to sputter and yell a couple of times, there isn't much for him do. . . . The way [Kenjiro] Ishiyama scratches that great football field of a forehead is an authentic piece of business, one of those little mannerisms which give the stamp of banal and absolute reality to the great crime films of such journeymen as Howard Hawks, John Huston, Carol Reed, and Alfred Hitchcock.[17]

Variety's "Hawk," reviewing the film at the Venice Film Festival, disliked the picture's length and didn't know what to make of its unique structure: "A tighter film, concentrating and balancing police activity and human conflicts, would have given this added distinction in arty circles. As is, it's a finely tooled item, made by a master craftsman. Acting by all hands, but especially the three principals, is able, camerawork is tops, as are all other technical details."[18]

In contrast, Howard Thompson, reviewing the film in *The New York Times*, loved it: "Let's give fervent thanks for 'High and Low,' one of the best detective thrillers ever filmed. . . . Here is one import—for suspense fans and students of moviecraft—that simply must be seen. . . . The result is a sizzling, artistic crackerjack and a model of its genre, pegged on a harassed man's moral decision, laced with characterizations and tingling detail and finally attaining an incredibly colorful crescendo of microscopic police sleuthing."[19]

Dale Munroe of the *Hollywood Citizen-News* agreed, saying:

Seldom does one discover a motion picture which so brilliantly combines the elements of stark suspense and psychological drama, coupled with an intimate analysis of one man's innate humanity, as does Akira Kurosawa's "High and Low." . . . In a sense director Kurosawa has given his world audience two films for the price of one. . . . The concluding sequence . . . is a masterpiece of irony combined with compassion and searing sadness. Kurosawa has succeeded in weaving a filmic tapestry deserving to be preserved in the "Louvre" of motion picture triumphs. . . . Every facet of this film is superior. The acting is outstanding. Mifune delivers a magnificently etched performance. His integrity packs a wallop that radiates power during each minute of footage in which he appears. . . . Kurosawa has created a superlative work of cinematic art, combining the practical with the artistic; the sordid with the beautiful; the banalities of life with those things which make life meaningful. It is an exciting, emotional, unforgettable experience.[20]

In 1993, Universal announced it had acquired the remake rights to *High and Low* for director Martin Scorsese, and that David Mamet would adapt the screenplay.[21] At one point there was speculation that Steve Martin (an odd choice, to put it mildly) would play the Mifune role, but probably due to a number of similar kidnapping films being made around this same time (notably Ron Howard's *Ransom* with Mel Gibson), the Scorsese *High and Low* lingered in development. In 2001, the project was revived, with Scorsese now co-producer, and Walter Salles (*Central Station*) slated to direct an adaptation by Jeff King (*The Lion's Game*).

In writing about Kurosawa's film, Martin Scorsese points out: "By losing everything, Gondo gains in the end. As he visits Takeuchi the kidnapper in prison, their faces are superimposed through the glass dividing them. Both are condemned to pay a price: that of being human. There is one shot in the film that, for me, synthesizes Kurosawa's mastery of the art: the pink smoke rising from the chimneys, a crucial signal which will lead to the kidnapper. The decision to utilize a few seconds of color in a black and white film and its amazing results—in both dramatic and aesthetic terms—reveals the painter and the poet present in all of Kurosawa's works."[22] (Steven Spielberg's 1993 film *Schindler's List* uses a similar device, perhaps inspired by Kurosawa's film.)

Tsutomu Yamazaki, seeing the film at the Sydney Film Festival nearly thirty years after it was released, felt his performance was less than adequate. "Of course, I enjoyed seeing it and finding it still fresh and interesting, but I couldn't look at the scenes I was in," he recalled. "Here was a skinny and pale young man so obviously tense onscreen. His lines had no rhythm, his movements weren't natural at all—his performance was really bad. I crouched down in my seat, wiped sweat from my brow, and felt great embarrassment, which continued the next morning when I drank, thinking about it."[23] Yamazaki is wrong. As Takeuchi he is entirely natural and believable, and every bit as unnerving and tortured as Mifune. Indeed, the fact that Yamazaki is acting is all but invisible, as if Kurosawa had scooped him up from the litter-strewn streets of Yokohama.

Yutaka Sada, on the other hand, wrote the following in 1993, when he was eighty-two years old: "Since [*Seven Samurai*] I've been in all of his films, but I consider myself a failed student of the Kurosawa school. *High and Low* is my sole memorial."[24]

With the Tokyo Olympics now just a year and a half away, Kurosawa's previous interest in filming the games waned. His staff had submitted a budget that struck the Organizing Committee and Toho as outrageously excessive. He wanted a huge crew of cameramen and cameras to cover the event, and this became one of the primary sticking points in the project. If he wasn't going to have his way, then he wouldn't touch it. Kurosawa officially backed out three weeks into *High and Low*'s release, on March 21, 1963, which caused some embarrassment when Toho had to scramble to find a replacement for him. Kon Ichikawa was chosen in the end, but his approach to the material was much the same. According to Toho publicity materials, Ichikawa employed some "1,031 cameras, 232 lenses, 400,000 feet of film stock, 164 cameramen, and almost 500 persons in supervision, lighting, recording, film processing, editing and music." The dazzling film, one of the best documentaries of its kind, was released in 1965 as *Tokyo Olympiad* (Tokyo Orinppiku).* It is worth noting that Kurosawa, even after the critical and commercial success of a film as powerful as *High and Low*, could easily secure the resources for a film planned and co-produced within his own company but was unable to obtain financing for a production made largely outside his influence, even at the height of his career.

Changing finances led to a new home for the Kurosawas. During the production of *High and Low*, the director moved his family for the third time since his engagement to Yoko—and they would continue to relocate every decade or so until their deaths. In April 1962 they vacated their large, traditional Japanese home for one in Matsubara, 2-chome, in Setagaya, which

*In fact, Toho released four features documenting the games: *Road to the Tokyo Olympics* (Tokyo Orinppiku eno michi, 1963), *Tokyo Olympiad*, *Tokyo Olympiad (International Version)* (Tokyo Orinppiku [Kaigi ban], 1965), and *Tokyo Olympic Games—Impressions of the Century* (Orinppiku Tokyo taikai—Seki no kando, 1966).

mixed Japanese traditional and modern Western styles. The house was huge by Japanese standards: more than 3,600 square feet on three levels.[25]

Kazuko was getting older, and Hisao was attending Seijogakuen University, majoring in economics. He was also gaining minor fame as a folk musician. His group, Broadside Four, had a hit song with "Young People" ("Wakamonotachi"), and the Kurosawa home was frequently visited by other folk singers, from Japan and abroad, including Peter, Paul & Mary.

The fame and material wealth the family enjoyed came at a price, which was all too apparent following *High and Low*'s release. Shortly after it opened, the film actually triggered an increase in the number of kidnappings in Japan, and Kurosawa himself began receiving telephone calls from people threatening to kidnap his daughter. He did not take the threats too seriously, but as a precaution began having nine-year-old Kazuko driven to and from school.[26]

"He usually didn't answer the phone himself," Kazuko said, "but one day I saw him answer the phone and, as I was listening, I heard him say, 'Don't say such an unreasonable thing!' He said it quietly, but I could feel the tension in his voice." She found out later that the call was from a man who threatened to blow up the Number 2 Hatsukari train if Kurosawa didn't bring a sackful of money to the station immediately. " 'Anything could happen,' the man told him. Police came to trace the call, telling my father that if the man calls back to keep him on the line as long as possible. It was almost like a TV drama." Or *High and Low*. Detectives stayed at the home the entire day, and one was sent to the Hatsukari line to meet the man, who never showed up. Kurosawa was beside himself with worry until the train completed its run. "Years later, when I was an adult, he told me, 'Kidnapping is the most heinous, unforgivable of crimes. With *High and Low* I wanted to inspire tougher sentences on kidnappers. Instead, I was criticized for their increase.' "[27]

For Mifune, 1963 marked the beginning of a four-year period of professional expansion. During this time he would form his own production company and actively market his services abroad, earning the kind of money unthinkable at any of the Japanese majors, where even big stars like Mifune typically earned less than $5,000 per picture.

More than in any other period in his life, Mifune was consumed by his work. Beyond spending time with his family, little else interested him. "I don't watch television," he said. "My television is too old to watch. . . . I'm not interested in baseball or sumo wrestling. I see a little bit of boxing." Asked how he spent his free time, Mifune joked, "Nothing special. I get naked and cut the grass around my house or clean my boat."[28]

Just as Hollywood's biggest stars scrambled to form their own production companies in the late 1940s, the early sixties saw the same revolution happening within the Japanese film industry. In December 1962, Nikkatsu star Yujiro Ishihara formed Ishihara Promotion, which led to his being cast in an all-star foreign production, the comedy *Those Magnificent Men in Their Flying Machines* (1965). Barely two weeks after the opening of *Attack Squadron!*, on January 17, Mifune called a press conference at Toho's main office to announce that he was following suit. Mifune Productions had been in the works since the previous spring. (The company was legally formed in July 1962.) It was a risky venture, and Sachiko, Kurosawa, and Senkichi Taniguchi all advised Mifune against it.

Taniguchi recalled Mifune wanting to go independent "five or six years after joining Toho." Both Kurosawa and Taniguchi, however, were opposed to the idea of Mifune leaving the company. "He wanted to leave because he didn't agree with the studio's policies," Taniguchi said. "We disagreed with him. Of course, directors are supposed to be selfish when considering an actor's future. I didn't want him to leave because I thought I might not ever be able to use him again. However, directors usually watch over the beautiful actors and actresses. No one pays any attention to rough-looking actors like Mifune, but I thought he could be a really great actor in his middle age if we educated him. That's why I disagreed with his decision. 'You should stay at Toho a little longer. You're not ready to go independent yet,' I told him. His wife felt the same way. One of the reasons they ultimately separated is that she didn't agree with his decision to leave Toho.

"I wrote a long letter to Mifune explaining why he shouldn't leave. I guess he had her read it. After she read it, she knew I was on her side and she respected me more. But he went independent anyway."[29]

The founding of Mifune Productions Co., Ltd., may have had more to do with pressure from within Toho than with Mifune's desire to have more freedom with his own career. Shiro remembered, "One day one of the executives at Toho called my father and told him to come to the studio. They told him that Toho was no more, that they were going to close the studio and essentially not make any more films except for Godzilla movies and war pictures. They suggested he should create his own production company, like Mr. Kurosawa's, and my father decided to go along with them. Then Toho said they would lend him money to make the films. If the films he made were successful, they would split the profits 50–50."[30]

This meant that Mifune would, for the first time, assume a large financial risk on some of the films in which he starred. If Mifune produced a hit, he would have to share the earnings with Toho, and if it flopped, he could end up owing Toho money to cover the loss. But the deal also provided him certain latitudes he had not had before, such as appearing in outside films of his own choosing, including foreign productions that wouldn't require Toho's financial involvement.

Mifune, Nagamasa Kawakita (president of Towa, which distributed foreign films in Japan), and Toho producer Sanezumi Fujimoto were Mifune Productions' founders. Shiro Mifune said Kawakita "was a very intelligent person. He could speak Chinese and German and many other languages, and he spent his life introducing good Japanese films to the world."[31]

Kazuto Ohira went even further, saying, "Kawakita was the most intelligent person in the Japanese film industry. He spoke English, French, German, and Chinese, and imported a lot of European films. He was essential to Toho for their business in Europe. He had produced [the Japanese-Italian co-production of] *Madame Butterfly* (1955). Until the day he died, Kawakita worked hard at getting Kurosawa and Mifune's films exposure throughout Europe."[32]

At their January 17 press conference, a beaming Mifune and Fujimoto announced that the new firm's first production would be *Legacy of the 500,000* (Gojuman-nin no isan), to be co-produced with Takarazuka, one of Toho's filmmaking subsidiaries. It would be released by Toho later that spring, soon after the premiere of *High and Low*. Mifune would not only star but direct the film as well. Ryuzo Kikushima would write the script. Mifune, still sporting his mustache from *Chushingura*, said filming would begin at Takarazuka Studios on February 15, 1963.[33]

But first he and Fujimoto flew to Honolulu to announce the construction of a Toho theater there, then together flew on to New York for the January 22 opening of the Toho Cinema in Manhattan, where *The Bad Sleep Well* officially premiered. Kazuto Ohira, who had managed the Toho La Brea in Los Angeles, was put in charge of the company's newest American theater.

"[Actor] Akira Takarada and [actress] Mitsuko Kusabue came and sang 'Maria' and 'One Fine Day.' Mifune appeared [via satellite] on [the Japanese TV network] TBS, on their morning show. He flew in a helicopter over New York City, reporting back to Japan."[34]

The Toho Cinema's exhibition policies were quite different from the La Brea's. The La Brea ran double features, short subjects, and newsreels. More prestigious pictures topped the bill, to appeal directly to white audiences as well as Asian ones, while a program picture ran at the bottom of the bill for homesick Japanese immigrants. The Toho Cinema, by contrast, didn't run program pictures; there was no substantial Japanese-American audience in New York to see them. Both theaters ran Japanese-made cultural short subjects (also with English subtitles), but only the La Brea ran newsreels. In Los Angeles the other Japanese movie houses typically ran films from only one studio, but the Toho Cinema exhibited quality films from the other majors, notably Toei and Nikkatsu, as well as independent films.

While both Japanese and Americans embraced Toho's Los Angeles theater, Ohira discovered he had his work cut out for him in Manhattan. "In New York, the Japanese were not welcome," he said flatly. Advertising was another problem. Funds sent from Japan had to be approved by the Japanese Treasury Department, which created reams of red tape. In Los Angeles, only the biggest films were advertised in mainstream newspapers, and Ohira relied on L.A.'s Japanese-language newspapers, which had much lower ad rates, to sell the La Brea's releases. In New York there were no Japanese-language newspapers at all. "I had a difficult time with the Toho Cinema's advertising because we had no budget. I think we were sent only about $1,000 per month for advertising."[35]

Upon Mifune's return from New York, he set to work on *Legacy of the 500,000*. Mifune was not the first Japanese film actor to turn director. Prior to *Legacy of the 500,000*, actor Shin Saburi had made at least five films, beginning with *Reprieve* (Shikko yuyo, 1950), which beat out *Rashomon* on *Kinema Jumpo*'s "Best Ten" list that year. So Yamamura, Mifune's co-star in *My Wonderful Yellow Car* (1953), directed at least two films, *The Crab-Canning Ship* (Kanikosen, 1953) and *The Black Tide* (Kuroi ushio, 1954), the latter placing just behind *Seven Samurai* on *Kinema Jumpo*'s "Best Ten" list. The great actress Kinuyo Tanaka, star of the Mifune film *Engagement Ring* (1950) and Mizoguchi's *The Life of Oharu* (1952), became Japan's first woman director in 1953. She directed six features through 1962, including *Love Under the Crucifix* (Ogin sama, 1960), remade in 1978 as *Love and Faith* (Ogin sama) starring Mifune.

Mifune claimed later that he didn't want to direct *Legacy* in the first place. "The ones I wanted weren't available."[36] It is more likely that he simply couldn't afford any A-list directors. As he said at the time, "I have no experience. For the time being, I'm [my company's] president and its maid. If I was just one of the actors, all I'd have to do was act but, obviously, I have so many things to do. I have to go to meetings, location scouting overseas, and direct. It's hard work."[37]

Therefore, Mifune's decision to direct the picture himself may have had less to do with ambition than with the expense of hiring a director with whom he felt comfortable, not to mention his compulsion to do everything himself. In late 1961, Mifune was asked if he had any interest in directing. "No way!" he responded emphatically. "I don't think one man can do so many things. I'd better stick to one."[38]

Taniguchi, directing Mifune that same year in *Samurai Pirate* (Dai to-zoku), claimed in 1999 he was completely unaware of the picture's exis-tence, which seems unlikely. "I have never seen the film and never even heard of it before," he said. "[Mifune] was having financial problems, wasn't he? . . . I heard his financial troubles were so bad that he was sweep-ing his own studio, but I never heard of this film."[39]

Legacy of the 500,000 begins with an explanatory pre-credit sequence. In 1942, while the Japanese Army occupied the Philippines, 10,000 gold coins were minted and shipped from Japan to stabilize Filipino currency. In 1944, the Allies recaptured Manila, and General Yamashita's Area Army fled into the mountains of northern Luzon, where it was wiped out. The gold was lost.

The titles begin, and for the first and only time in the black-and-white movie, à la *High and Low*, color brilliantly appears in the form of one of these gold coins. The story begins twenty years later, in present-day Japan, where businessman Mitsuru Gunji (Tatsuya Nakadai) approaches crayon company executive Takeichi Matsuo (Mifune), a former major and the last surviving person who knows where the treasure is hidden.

Gunji kidnaps Matsuo, sending him off to the Philippines aboard the *Kibo-maru*, captained by Mitsuru's brother, Keigo (Tatsuya Mihashi), a for-mer naval lieutenant. Also on board are Igarashi (Sachio Sakai), who is Gunji's driver; Tsukuda (Tsutomu Yamazaki), Gunji's bodyguard; and Ya-sumoto (Yoshifumi Tajima), the ship's engineer.

Secretly entering the Philippines, the five pretend to be Japanese-Americans working for the U.S. Army as they make their way into the back country. At other times they claim to be Chinese merchants. Along the way they meet a mysterious Asian (Satoshi "Tetsu" Nakamura), who is tailing them on behalf of mysterious foreigners. As they inch closer to the trea-sure, Matsuo decides that the gold, minted as it was from the compulsory donation of personal jewelry, should be returned to the Japanese people. Haunted by his knowledge of the gold, Matsuo believes returning it is the only way the souls of the 500,000 soldiers who died in the Philippines can rest easy.

When the band reaches the hiding place, they find the treasure gone. Gunji's men decide to leave Matsuo there to die, but he is rescued by Yamazaki (Yoshio Tsuchiya), a Japanese soldier who stayed in the Philippines to live with an Igorot native girl (Mie Hama). Yamazaki found the treasure and moved it for safekeeping. Now in possession of the gold, Matsuo uses Gunji's men to try to return the gold to the Japanese people.

But—and it is here that the picture gradually but completely unravels—as they make their escape on a raft, Yamazaki is speared (unconvincingly) by his native wife and dies. Later, Tsukuda stabs Keigo. Tsukuda, Igarashi, and Yasumoto decide to steal the gold, leaving their boss and Matsuo behind. They have a change of heart, but as they return, Keigo dies of his wounds. The four survivors make their way through the jungle, reaching the beach where the *Kibo-maru* is moored. But as they approach the ship, the four are met by gunfire. The foreigners, tipped off by the mysterious Asian man, want the gold for themselves and gun the four men down.

The abrupt end of *Legacy of the 500,000* makes it one of the most inexplicable and least satisfying films of Mifune's starring career. *Legacy* is no masterpiece, but it is a competent thriller until the final reel, when the script falls apart so thoroughly as to bring down everything that came before it.

As the film's star, Mifune is on camera most of the time. For these scenes especially, he relied on his chief assistant director, Shigekichi Takamae. Takamae's services proved so valuable Mifune generously put his name alongside his on the director's title card, a practice common in Japanese films of the 1930s and 1940s but rare by 1963.

The film's interiors were shot at Takarazuka Studios, Toho's subsidiary located near Osaka. The quieter, more remote stages took some of the pressure off the actor-director, even though Takarazuka's facilities were primitive compared to Toho's.

Mifune was among friends, actors he liked and had worked with before—Tatsuya Nakadai, Tatsuya Mihashi, Yoshio Tsuchiya. Kurosawa's staff wanted to help Mifune in his directorial debut. Most of the crew from *High and Low* eagerly offered their services. Besides screenwriter Ryuzo Kikushima, Mifune enlisted the aid of art director Yoshiro Muraki, cinematographer Takao Saito, script supervisor Teruyo Nogami, and sound engineer Fumio Yanoguchi. Another assistant director, Mikio Komatsu, who had worked with Mifune on the actor's debut film, *Snow Trail*, also lent a hand.

The crew found Mifune quite a contrast to Kurosawa. Mifune went to great lengths to keep everyone happy. He himself served his cast and crew coffee each morning, and at his own expense took them and their families to a nearby hot springs resort after wrapping the film.

On March 4, 1963, barely a month after Mifune had completed his work on *High and Low*, production for *Legacy* began in the Philippines. Among the first footage shot was the scene where Mifune and the gangsters are "rescued" by the Asian man (Tetsu Nakamura) when the group is stopped by the Philippine police. Tatsuya Mihashi recalled that everyone, including the actors, pitched in to help. Yoshifumi Tajima and Tsutomu Yamazaki worked in the wardrobe department. Nakamura, fluent in Japanese and English, worked as a translator, Sachio Sakai was put in charge of the Jeep, and Mihashi did historical research on the guns and other hardware used in the picture. During the scene of Mifune digging up the gold, Tajima held light reflectors while Sakai served everyone juice. None of this extra work was ordered by Mifune. Inspired by their actor-director, everyone simply pitched in to help where they could.[40]

As it had in Mexico, Mifune's tact paid off in the Philippines, and he got on well with the Filipinos who supplemented the Japanese contingent. He was, however, concerned that the locations didn't look all that different from those he could have found in Japan. As soon as he finished shooting his scenes, Mifune would ride off in a Jeep, scouring the countryside for the next suitable, singularly "Filipino-looking" site. According to Mihashi, Mifune would drive back onto the set and say, "Hey! Let's move!" and off they would dash to the next location.[41]

Shooting in the Philippines wrapped at the end of the month, and the unit returned to Japan to shoot the escape on the raft and the scenes with Mie Hama, which were shot in Oboke, in Tokushima Prefecture.

This was Hama's first major role in a Mifune film, and she found that "unlike the characters he plays in his films, deep down he's a very delicate, sensitive person. . . . [Nevertheless] it was somewhat tense working with him." Hama trained diligently with the spear, but never learned how to throw it properly; this is a detriment to the scene where she kills her Japanese husband. Yamazaki's death was ultimately achieved by a painfully unconvincing jump cut. "I guess I never would have been much of an athlete," Hama admitted.[42]

During the production, Mifune celebrated his forty-third birthday with a party he threw for his cast and crew. During the revelry he badly cut the middle finger of his right hand on a beer bottle. For the sake of continuity, he had to remove the bandages for the rest of the shoot.

More than most actors, Mifune needed to stay in character during filming. But with the added duties of producer-director, that proved impossible. And in trying so hard to please everyone all the time, he listened to everyone's ideas and was too flexible where he should have been single-minded. His enthusiasm and concern had him working long hours. He was the first to rise in the morning, surprising his crew by waking them at 6:00 a.m. every day of production. In spite of all this, shooting went smoothly, and even weather problems did not prevent Mifune from finishing the picture ahead of schedule.

As an action film, the picture is little more than competent. The photography, performances, and score are notably good, but Kikushima's script falls markedly short of its ambitions. While the picture has certain resemblances to a Kurosawa film, Kikushima had written his scenario without the benefit of a Kurosawa or Oguni to play devil's advocate. The final scenes are weak and play as if they were written on the spot. Of course, Mifune, who had never written a script in his life, may have felt unqualified to question Kikushima's narrative and filmed the inadequate screenplay as written. (According to Mifune, Kurosawa edited much of the film without credit, but even he couldn't save the picture.)

Legacy of the 500,000 was moderately successful at the box office, but a critical flop when it opened in Japan less than two months after *High and Low*. The picture debuted in the United States the following summer. By then, Toho had clearly lost all faith in the film, double-billing it with an Akira Takarada–Yumi Shirakawa comedy about mixed marriages, *Wall-Eyed Nippon* (Yabuni-rami Nippon, 1964). The American critics were singularly unimpressed. "Perhaps Kurosawa could have carried [the picture] off, a hackneyed tale about a search for buried money, though it's doubtful," said the *Los Angeles Times*'s Kevin Thomas. "Mifune strives for the irony of *The Treasure of the Sierra Madre*, but the tone of his film is closer to *King Solomon's Mines*. . . . Mifune tries to make of this routine adventure a symbolic statement about greed by showing that Nakadai's selfish motives are the same ones that start wars. But the plot becomes preposterous once Mihashi's boat reaches its destination. With restless, probing camerawork, many zoom shots and wipes, *The Legacy* often resembles the bravura style of Kurosawa's films, minus the coherence and impact."[43]

In retrospect, Mifune said of the venture, "Unfortunately, I never had the budget that allows for [Kurosawa's level of] perfection. . . . I [wanted] to grow and improve as an actor, and I was less than happy with [the film]. I decided [from then on] to let the producer produce, the director direct, and the actor act."[44]

Mifune spent the rest of 1963 escaping the pressures of acting in *High and Low* and directing himself in *Legacy of the 500,000*. He starred in an Arabian Nights–style adventure called *Samurai Pirate* (Dai tozoku). Mifune plays Sukezaemon, a roguish pirate shipwrecked in a strange, Middle Eastern–looking kingdom (though its narrative is set deep in the South Seas). The sets and costumes are vaguely, alternately, Chinese, Indian, and Arabic, but inhabited by a Japanese cast, giving the picture a geographically bizarre, out-of-sync feel. This was not lost on Japanese moviegoers, who thought it as absurd as moviegoers everywhere else did, though for domestic audiences this incongruity was also the heart of its appeal. Japanese actors rarely played other ethnicities, and the industry almost never made period films set outside Japan and mainland China. The concept of such pictures was simply alien to them.

Most of the film consists of standard, rather stodgy palace intrigue, with the usual cast of characters—scheming premier (Tadao Nakamaru), ailing king (Takashi Shimura, wasted in a cameo part), captive princess (Mie Hama), and a voluptuous maiden (Akiko Wakabayashi). The film works best in its humorous moments, especially in the series of encounters Sukezaemon has with an intimidating palace guard (Jun Tazaki), who demonstrates his toughness by biting off, with much verve, the head of a frog with his bare teeth.

Tazaki (1913–85) had worked with Mifune on two earlier swashbucklers, *Pirates* (1951) and *Rebels on the High Sea* (1956). He played the heavy in both *The Last Gunfight* and *Man Against Man*, both 1960, and was one of the slimy shoe executives in *High and Low*. With his authoritative, gruff voice and intense eyes, Tazaki closely resembled Mifune, and directors would, on occasion, play off this similarity. The two were often cast as likeminded warriors with deep respect for each other, sadly resigned to find themselves fighting on opposite sides. In *The Boss of Pick-pocket Bay* (Kureji no musekinin Shimizu minato, 1966), a Crazy Cats *jidai-geki* comedy, stars Hitoshi Ueki and Kei Tani find themselves trapped in a gambling den surrounded by *yakuza*. A *yojimbo* rushes in; it is Jun Tazaki, dressed in Mifune's costume from *Sanjuro*. The actor's resemblance to Mifune proved so striking that, for a second or two, audiences thought they were actually seeing Mifune. Tazaki's specialty, however, was playing gang bosses in crime films, generals in war movies and sci-fi epics, and similar roles in other genres. Like Takashi Shimura, Bokuzen Hidari, and Ko Nishimura, Tazaki was in almost constant demand for such parts, appearing in as many as ten pictures a year. He died in 1985, shortly after playing one of the generals in Kurosawa's *Ran*.

Adding to the film's limited fun is comic actor Ichiro Arishima (1916–87) as Mifune's sidekick, an ancient but lusty wizard. As much a staple of Toho's salaryman comedies as Tazaki was to its crime films and war movies, Arishima turned up constantly as harried middle-management types, though he is best remembered in Japan as Yuichi Tamura's perennially flustered father in Toho's "Young Guy" films. In *Samurai Pirate*, Arishima's wizard provides the film's few flashes of broad comedy, the highlight being a duel with a cackling old witch (Hideyo "Eisei" Amamoto in drag).

Samurai Pirate's other star was Eiji Tsuburaya, who received co-director billing for what amounted to a smattering of visual effects. Tsuburaya didn't hit it off with Taniguchi the way he had with Ishiro Honda and Shue Matsubayashi, and this may account for both the unambitious scale and uncharacteristically mediocre execution of the special effects.

Largely because of the reputation of Messrs. Tsuburaya and Mifune, *Samurai Pirate* did shockingly well at the box office, earning ¥245 million (about $700,000), making it the tenth most popular domestic film that year. Of Mifune's four 1963 films, only *Legacy* failed to crack the Top Ten.

With its gaudy action and special effects, *Samurai Pirate* was deemed exploitable enough to be picked up for U.S. release by American International Pictures (AIP), a company whose chief market was the drive-in trade. AIP was famous for (even proud of) its ability to dream up titles and ad campaigns before the pictures were actually made. Never reluctant to mislead the public in the name of box office, AIP thought the title *Samurai Pirate* a bit tame. They toyed with the idea of calling their newly acquired film *The 7th Wonder of Sinbad*, obviously hoping that this new name would confuse audiences into thinking they'd be seeing a Ray Harryhausen stop motion spectacular. However, AIP settled on *The Lost World of Sinbad*, releasing it on a double bill with another acquisition from Toho, Ishiro Honda's sci-fi fantasy *Atragon* (Kaitei gunkan, 1963). That the picture has nothing whatsoever to do with Sinbad was, for AIP, beside the point.

AIP primed the film for its American release by boasting of its Trophy of the Five Continents award for Best Specialized Film, which Toho received at the closing ceremonies of the International Film, TV, and Documentary Association's tenth annual conclave in Milan, Italy.[45]

Like *I Bombed Pearl Harbor*, *The Lost World of Sinbad* received a much wider release than any of Mifune's films for Kurosawa, though, like Mifune's war movie, it was badly dubbed into English. "The Japanese production . . . is strictly for patrons of this kind of film," said *The Hollywood Reporter*, which, like most reviewers, mistakenly believed that the Sinbad angle had originated in the Japanese script. "For them it should be a satisfying entry. The Toho production has some humor, and even its [top] star, Japan's outstanding movie personality, Toshiro Mifune, as Sinbad. . . . This is lightweight stuff for Mifune, but he gives it his usual intensity, heavy scowls and grinding of teeth. The rest of the cast is good, and the dubbing is excellent. Color photography is good and the special effects are amusingly and intriguingly done."[46]

AIP quickly sold *Sinbad* to television syndication. Ironically, more Americans were introduced to Toshiro Mifune through this tacky picture than through all his Kurosawa films combined.

NINETEEN

RAIN

"I had something special in mind when I made [*Red Beard*] because I wanted to make something . . . so magnificent that people would just have to see it."[1]
—Akira Kurosawa

In 1963, Kurosawa would begin production on *Red Beard* (Akahige, 1965), the film that would propel his critical and commercial reputation to its zenith. The film was expensive—$700,000—nearly ten times the cost of an average Japanese feature and produced over two long years, an unprecedented extravagance at a time when film industry insiders were beginning to see the writing on the wall. Audiences were staying home to watch free television, tastes were changing, and the kinds of movies Toho and the other major studios were making simply could not compete with the splashier product Hollywood had to offer. Toho might, for instance, produce amusing little spy films (such as their "International Secret Police" series starring Tatsuya Mihashi), but in terms of production they were dwarfed by the James Bond movies that had inspired them. When it came to excess, Hollywood had no peer.

Indeed, the Bond films ushered in a wave of hipper, poppier Western influences that drew crowds away from the mannered *jidai-geki* samurai adventures and genial salaryman comedies of the past decade. Beyond the gargantuan 007 craze—bigger in Japan than in any other part of the world save America—1965 saw these influences strike the island nation with tidal-wave force, from the arrival of the miniskirt to the explosion of *ereki*, American and British–influenced pop music led by electric guitars wailing derivative riffs.

Younger filmmakers, heavily influenced by the French New Wave, began turning out films as far removed from the old masters as Godard was from John Ford. In terms of content, Kurosawa probably thought *Red Beard*'s narrative of self-realization, its criticism of the class system while championing selflessness in aiding the downtrodden, would be fashionable and appealing to the mod generation. Yet *Red Beard* was, in many ways, the culmination of a style on the way out.

Set in nineteenth-century Edo, the film is a clash between old and new. It tells the story of a young, conceited doctor, Yasumoto (Yuzo Kayama), sent by his father to visit a hospital-clinic for the poor. Here conditions are a far cry from the luxuries he enjoyed during his Dutch-influenced training in Nagasaki, and he is appalled by the dregs of human misery he finds. Paying his respects to the intimidating head of the clinic, Dr. Kyojo Niide, nicknamed "Red Beard" (Mifune), the vain Yasumoto is shocked to learn that he has been assigned there as an intern. Through his wealthy family and various connections, Yasumoto had expected an assignment in the Imperial Court. Feeling the post far beneath his abilities, Yasumoto does everything in his power to incur the wrath of Red Beard and win his dismissal.

Gradually, however, Yasumoto begins to understand that in spite of Red Beard's stern manner, he is in fact a man of immense wisdom. It is Red Beard's belief that the only life worth living is one devoted to helping others. Despite the misery of poverty, illness, and death, it is kindness, Red Beard suggests, that ultimately begets kindness, just as evil begets evil.

In the film's second act, Yasumoto is given his first real patient, a physically abused twelve-year-old girl, Otoyo (Terumi Niki), rescued by Red Beard from a syphilis-infested whorehouse. Ill in mind as well as body, the young girl steadfastly refuses to take her medication. Yasumoto calls on Red Beard for advice and watches in amazement as the wiser, older doctor patiently allows the young girl to splatter him with spoonful after spoonful of gently offered medicine before she finally, reluctantly, swallows it down. Later, the young girl, still not accepting the kindness of the clinic's staff, rebels in much the same manner as Yasumoto had earlier in the story.

In the film's most important moment, Yasumoto breaks down, weeping in the realization of the cruel world he lives in, a world that would transform an innocent young girl into a bitter misanthrope. Only through a hatred and distrust of everything around her can Otoyo survive such an unbearable existence.

But Yasumoto's tears and unceasing kindness, inspired by Red Beard's treatment, gradually work on Otoyo. As she recovers, she's moved to help out at the clinic and becomes a much-loved part of the staff, a surrogate daughter, even, to the cleaning women, and she in turn cares for Yasumoto when he becomes ill from overwork. Otoyo also befriends an even younger child, a poor boy, Choji (Yoshitaka Zushi), who has been stealing food from the clinic to feed his family.

In the end, Yasumoto's residency at the clinic is completed, but at his wedding he surprises his intended bride and his family with the news that, in spite of a recent appointment to the shogun's court, he has decided to remain at the clinic.

The picture had its roots in a novel of the same name by Shugoro Yamamoto (which reminded Kurosawa of Dostoevsky's *The Insulted and Injured*), though the finished film bears little resemblance to the novel. Kurosawa intended to adapt the story for his longtime assistant director Hiromichi Horikawa, whom Toho had promoted to full director in 1955. But Kurosawa became increasingly drawn to its characters and opted to direct the film himself, just as he had done on *Sanjuro*, also based on a Yamamoto novel.

The script was finished in early July 1963, almost exactly four months after the premiere of *High and Low*. Kurosawa, Kikushima, and Oguni were joined this time by Masato Ide (1920–89), who had come to Toho in the mid-1950s after eight years in the administrative and production-planning branches of Shintoho. He wrote Mifune's *A Man Among Men* (1955), based on an idea by Kikushima, and immediately prior to starting work on *Red Beard*, he had co-written *Tatsu*, the Mifune-Inagaki film that had been one of Toho's biggest hits.

Several of *Red Beard*'s assistant directors, upon reading Kurosawa's adaptation (co-written with Ryuzo Kikushima, Hideo Oguni, and Masato Ide), said that at the time they thought the project a direct response to the state of Japan's declining film industry, something that would pry Japanese homebodies away from their TV sets, something that audiences would indeed just have to see.[2]

On July 15, Kurosawa returned to Toho for the first time since wrapping *High and Low*. The director was full of enthusiasm and the following day hired Asakazu Nakai (a Kurosawa veteran going back to *No Regrets for*

Our Youth) and Takao Saito to shoot the picture. Another longtime veteran, Yoshiro Muraki, was brought in to handle the production design. The rest of the month Muraki and his staff did extensive research on clinics similar to the one in the script, modeling *Red Beard*'s on the Koishikawa Nursing Home, built in 1722. Several weeks later the researchers uncovered copies of the nursing home's original blueprints, and information about its layout was incorporated into the film. The exterior set of the hospital would be built on the backlot area known as the "Open Farm" and previously used on both *Yojimbo* and *Sanjuro*. (In fact, several buildings used in *Sanjuro* can be glimpsed beyond the clinic's fence.)

In late July and early August, Kurosawa began casting the picture. Toshiro Mifune and *Sanjuro* co-star Yuzo Kayama were set from the start. Although Mifune would be top-billed and his austere face would dominate posters and ad campaign, the film would really belong to Kayama. Ultimately, the crux of the film isn't Red Beard's dispensing of wisdom but rather Yasumoto's self-realization through compassion and selflessness, a fulfillment no less significant than Watanabe's in *Ikiru*.

Yuzo Kayama was Toho's fastest-rising star of the 1960s. Like Mifune a decade before him, he had become one of the studio's biggest money earners almost overnight, following his debut in 1960 (opposite Mifune in Senkichi Taniguchi's *Man Against Man*). When he played the leader of the inept samurai in *Sanjuro*, Kayama was already red hot, more so than even Mifune, who had, by the mid-1960s, become an icon. Mifune remained bankable, certainly, but Kayama was getting all the attention.

In 1962, the same year *Sanjuro* was released, Kayama had the plum role of Lord Asano in Hiroshi Inagaki's all-star *Chushingura* and made the first of the Toho's "Young Guy" ("Wakadaisho") movies. These were wholesome, entertaining features that the studio cranked out twice a year into the early 1970s. Kayama starred as clean-cut college student Yuichi Tanuma, a young man adept at any sport, a talented pop singer, and an all around swell guy. The series attracted hordes of teenage girls, drawn to Kayama's incredible good looks yet modest persona, while young men, aspiring to be Yuichi in the same way they aspired to be James Bond, watched in envy as any number of Toho starlets swooned over him.

The series' popularity was also due in no small way to its travelogue aspects. In nearly every film Yuichi's athletic competitions sent him to exotic locales—Hawaii, Tahiti, Rio. He skied in the Alps, fenced in Hong Kong, ran the New York Marathon, and always found time to sing catchy pop tunes to girlfriend Yuriko Hoshi (and, later in the series, Wakako Sakai). As

Hoshi said in 1996, "At the time, it was very difficult for Japanese people to travel outside of Japan so, in a way, audiences were able to live out their dreams through the series." If older audiences stayed away, at least they had no qualms about sending their children to these escapist films, for Yuichi was admirably respectful of his father (Ichiro Arishima), grandmother (Choko Iida), and various college professors, and as steadfast as Lord Asano himself. Kayama played the role well into his mid-thirties, and revived the character twice, most recently in a 1992 Japanese teleseries.

Kurosawa was extremely fortunate in getting Kayama. In 1963, the year *Red Beard* went into production, Kayama had starred in six features for Toho, and in 1966, the year after *Red Beard*'s release, another half dozen. Through the "Young Guy" features, Kayama also became a huge *ereki* star. Toho cashed in on Kayama's recording career via a concert movie, *At the Nichigeki: The Yuzo Kayama Show — Young Guy Sings* (Nichigeki [Kayama Yuzo Sho] Yori uta wakadaisho), with Kayama awkwardly, if charmingly, crooning more than a dozen tunes to a theater full of screaming teenage girls. Kayama symbolized a transitional phase for his generation in much the way Frankie Avalon and Annette Funicello did for American teenagers: hipper than the immediate postwar, Eisenhower generation, but also a far cry from those coming of age amid Woodstock and Vietnam. And as *Red Beard* would be Kayama's first film in a year, Kurosawa and Toho were assured a presold audience.

Filling the other roles proved challenging, though. Kurosawa sent out press releases promoting a nationwide search for some parts, including the key roles of Otoyo and Choji. He sent several assistants to Tokyo-based theatrical companies, and by September 1963, eight-year-old Yoshitaka Zushi was hired, partly because his natural personality seemed to match Choji's so well, and partly because his size suggested a boy much younger than Zushi actually was. At eight Zushi was already a seasoned veteran, having been born into a family of child actors who frequented Takarazuka Film Studios. His break came in 1963, when he appeared as a terminally ill boy in Kaneto Shindo's *Mother* (Haha), which Kurosawa had seen at a preview screening. After *Red Beard*, Zushi appeared in a wide range of films and television series. He played a central role in Kurosawa's *Dodes'ka-den*, and later appeared in *Dreams* and *Madadayo*.

Terumi Niki, who played Otoyo, was hired a few days later, and the director turned his attention to what proved the two most difficult roles to cast: Masae, Yasumoto's intended bride, and a madwoman who nearly murders Yasumoto during the film's first act. Kyoko Kagawa, who appeared in

Kurosawa's *The Lower Depths*, *The Bad Sleep Well*, and *High and Low*, was cast against type to play the beautiful but insane woman. After her years of portraying gentle, devoted young daughters and later gentle, devoted wives (including Mifune's wife in both *The Bad Sleep Well* and *High and Low*), Kurosawa took a chance when he tapped her to play a man-killer.

"I was very surprised when the offer came," Kagawa said at the time. "In the beginning I couldn't allow my character's madness to be apparent to the audience. I had to make them sympathetic to my character, so that they'd understand and relate to Kayama's feeling sorry for me.

"I visited psychiatric wards to see patients. I couldn't find any good role models for the character, but I did visit a small clinic and watched a conversation between a doctor and one of his patients, and was struck by how childlike their conversation was. It was strange. The patient spoke normally, but what she said just didn't make any sense. I went back several more times and tried to re-create the image I had of that woman who on the outside looked normal but inside was mentally ill."[3]

Tsutomu Yamazaki, as a mysterious, dying man who is to the other patients what Red Beard is to his staff, was also a surprising choice. His rugged, working-class looks had until now brought him mostly thankless gangster parts, though his multilayered performance as the kidnapper in *High and Low* was beginning to change that. His delicate role in *Red Beard* proved a formidable one for the young actor, and he gained a lot from Kurosawa's intensive rehearsals. His roles here and in *High and Low* established Yamazaki as a major talent. He remains one of Japan's most-sought-after thespians, and his subsequent roles in several films for Juzo Itami (the husband in *The Funeral*, the truck driver/noodle expert in *Tampopo*) won him much deserved praise.

Following a lavish party on December 9, 1963, *Red Beard* began shooting. That same week Kurosawa accompanied his mentor, director Kajiro Yamamoto, as well as contemporaries Yasuki Chiba and Keisuke Kinoshita, to the funeral of Yasujiro Ozu, who had died on his sixtieth birthday, December 12, 1963. Everyone in the industry mourned his passing; however, unlike Kurosawa's, Ozu's genius was slower to be recognized in the West.

By that same week in early December 1963, the role of Masae had still not been cast. In desperation, Kurosawa sent his assistant directors to scour local high schools to look for prospects, quite aware that any woman appearing opposite Yuzo Kayama would likely gain instant stardom. Hanging around local schoolyards at seven in the morning did make them nervous, however: after the uproar created by *High and Low*, Kurosawa's assistant directors worried that they might be mistaken for kidnappers and arrested. Ultimately, Masae was played by a Toho "New Face," Yoko Naito.

Because the clinic in the film was modeled on one that would already have been one hundred years old when the story begins, Kurosawa became obsessed with the film's accuracy, insisting that everything to the tiniest detail appear authentic and aged, from the century-old roof tiles he had placed on his outdoor sets to the bedding that was slept on for six months prior to shooting. When an old farmer in Akita, in southern Japan, learned about the crew's difficulty in finding the right period clothes, he sent forty authentic wardrobes he had stored in a barn. After the actors were fitted for their costumes, Kurosawa encouraged them to wear and wash them as much as possible before the production commenced.

All this effort was seen as the means to a "new type of film," as one assistant director put it. "In order to make it, we have to educate ourselves about essential historical facts,"[4] he wrote. A chest in Red Beard's office was painted, stripped, and repainted several times until the director was satisfied. When Kurosawa saw the finishing touches being put on the open set of the hospital, he declared, "We have to make [it] look older. It has to look like one that has seen wind and rain for many years. The gate and the fence are too beautiful."[5] Kurosawa himself went to Toho's lumberyard and started picking out the oldest available wood. He and his crew rebuilt the hospital's main gate that day, aging it with every means they could think of. "It looks older now," the director finally declared. "After it rains two or three times, it'll look much better."[6]

Surprisingly, Kurosawa uses his mammoth sets only fleetingly. As Donald Richie rightly points out, "By constricting three-fourths of the picture to interiors, and by using this magnificent set only several times, he brought a kind of life to the entire film which a single set—no matter its grandeur—could not. The opposite effect occurs in a picture such as *The Fall of the Roman Empire* [1964] where one feels: one more shot of that expensive forum and I'm going to scream. The *Red Beard* set is really real in part because it is so little emphasized."[7]

Mifune's bushy red beard would likewise have to be really real and similarly lived in. Mifune began growing it three months before shooting began, and spent many hours conferring with Kurosawa over its length and color. As *Red Beard* would be shot in black and white, Kurosawa's fussing over the shade of Mifune's whiskers seemed, to some, a trivial, grossly disproportionate concern. Various tests were filmed with dyes made of tea powder, but none photographed to the director's satisfaction. Kurosawa and Mifune clashed over this, especially when Mifune dyed the beard on his own without telling anyone, and matters became even more confused when someone suggested that Red Beard should have gray hair integrated with the red. Hydrogen peroxide was used next, but Mifune's facial hair was so thick it made the dying process interminably long and damaged his beard. Finally, they decided to use an oil-based bleach. It smelled terrible, but Mifune opted to grin and bear it rather than face another month of headache-inducing tests.

Despite the difficulties getting that beard right, Mifune was consumed with his character. "He's an interesting man," said the actor of Red Beard. "He has the body of a man in his forties, but his wisdom is like that of someone in their sixties or seventies. Nobody really knows how old he is. He's ageless."[8]

As 1963 drew to a close, Mifune visited the backlot and was overheard telling Yuzo Kayama, "We'll have to do a really good job against this incredible set."[9] A few days later, a hundred members of the press were given a tour of Kurosawa's expansive, extraordinarily detailed set. The cast, in full costume, were carefully positioned for publicity shots. Nothing on this scale had ever been attempted in Japan. Journalists left the studio in a state of awe. "I was surprised when I looked behind the set for the first time," Yamazaki said. "It wasn't a flat. A roof, walls in three dimensions were built. It's incredible."[10]

On December 21, 1963, *Red Beard* began filming, with one of the love sequences between Tsutomu Yamazaki and Miyuki Kuwano, seen in flashbacks as Yamazaki's Sahachi lies dying at Red Beard's clinic. "[On the first day,]" Kurosawa said, "I gathered everyone, cast and staff together, and I played them the last movement of Beethoven's Ninth—the 'An die Freude' part, you know. I told them that this was the way that the audience was supposed to feel when they walked out of the theater and it was up to them to create this feeling."[11] By now, Kurosawa's cast and crew knew they were a part of something very special.

"People say he takes a long time to make a film," Mifune had commented, "but we're taking it one scene at a time. We could shoot the entire film in a few weeks, but Kurosawa rehearses with all of the equipment and crew for two or three days for one scene and then shoots it all at once, usually in one day. Then he moves on to something new—that's the way he works."[12]

Kurosawa was lucky with the weather, shooting scenes involving snowfall in January and February (skies remained clear and he resorted to artificial flakes), and when he had wrapped those, shooting continued through spring. Kirk Douglas visited the set and, like the cast and crew, was tremendously impressed with both the size of the production and the director's dedication and boundless enthusiasm.

The scenes with Yasumoto and the madwoman were filmed in mid-July, and as with Mifune's beard, Kurosawa paid considerable attention to the use of color for this sequence. He had Kagawa wear an intensely blue eye shadow and, using the braids in her hair, had the skin around her eyes stretched tightly back, like a face-lift gone bad, giving her a subtly off-kilter look. "When I saw the makeup I was afraid of myself!" Kagawa remarked.[13]

Kurosawa's obsession with color in a black-and-white film paid off in subtle ways: one American friend of mine first saw *Red Beard* in the early 1980s. When he took a friend to see the film in revival some months later, and remembering being impressed by Kurosawa's use of color, he was disappointed to find the theater was running a black-and-white print. Only later did he realize what Kurosawa had done—he had been subconsciously persuaded into believing that he had seen a color film.

Shooting continued throughout 1964, the first year since 1959 that Kurosawa did not have a new film in release. But Kurosawa's name appeared in theaters and in the news throughout the year. During *Red Beard*'s production, no fewer than three adaptations of his work turned up on movie screens: Sergio Leone's *A Fistful of Dollars*; Martin Ritt's Western remake of *Rashomon*, *The Outrage*; and *Jakoman and Tetsu*, an authorized redo of the 1949 film of the same name that Kurosawa had written for Mifune with director Senkichi Taniguchi. This version, notably less successful, was directed by genre director Kinji Fukasaku at Toei and starred matinee idol Ken Takakura (in the Mifune role) and Tetsuro Tamba. The following year, Nikkatsu director Seijun Suzuki remade the Kurosawa-Taniguchi–scripted *Escape at Dawn* (1950) as *The Story of a Prostitute* (Shunpuden).

Meanwhile, Toho's own matinee idol, Yuzo Kayama, took Kurosawa's growing faith in him very seriously. "Of course, I cannot work on any other films once I've started on Mr. Kurosawa's film," Kayama said. "I get tired. People say we have a lot of free time because we shoot only one scene a day and take Sundays off. But the truth is, it's very hard work. I've worked harder on this film than all my other films combined. When I don't meet his expectations, I get mad at myself and feel I'm not good enough for the part—I hope this feeling encourages me to grow as an actor. My experiences on my previous pictures just don't apply on this film. I just have to put that away and just instinctively do everything I can think of—that he can draw this out of me impresses me."[14]

Years later, Kayama looked back on his performance with an intensely critical eye. "I used to watch my acting [in earlier films] objectively thinking, Why am I doing this, and hate myself when I was instructed about how to play a scene. . . . I became Noboru Yasumoto naturally in each situation. I think [Kurosawa] is a genius controlling an actor's emotions. He can surprise you when he needs to. For example, there was the scene where I watched Otoyo and Choji from behind the hanging futons. No matter how many times Choji tried, he couldn't get it right during rehearsals. I understood that the director was thinking about controlling him with an almost psychic power. When he knew it was the right time to go for a take, his eyes changed. Even I got excited. Choji played the scene perfectly on the first take. The director held him up in his arms and said, 'Okay!' I was impressed by that."[15]

Though Kayama's early scenes with Mifune were confined to small clinic rooms, Kurosawa frequently used up to five cameras at once. "When he does that I can no longer pay attention to the camera," Mifune said. "I'm not able to play to any one camera. Anyway, the actors have to play their characters completely, just like in rehearsal. It's very tense."[16] He also echoed Kayama's commitment to the director. "That's why I can't work on another film simultaneously. But some people are busy [with many assignments], and come to us after shooting another film and it's different somehow. I think that's something [Kurosawa] doesn't like."[17]

Mifune devoted himself completely to *Red Beard*. Unlike Kayama, he's not in the picture for long stretches and could have appeared in other films simultaneously, certainly in "guest star" type roles, but he didn't. Mifune appeared in only one film in 1964, Hiroshi Inagaki's *Whirlwind* (Shikon-mado—Dai tatsumaki), a special-effects–filled *jidai-geki* released on January 3. His part was shot before *Red Beard* went into production, and before he grew his beard for Kurosawa. Somegoro Ichikawa and Yosuke Natsuki were *Whirlwind*'s stars. Mifune's role in this average but colorful *jidai-geki* is small, along the lines of his guest turn in *Chushingura*, and most of the time his face is hidden behind a wicker mask. But even Mifune proved no match for Eiji Tsuburaya's special effects, which include the burning of Osaka Castle (stock footage from *Daredevil in the Castle*) and the whirlwind of the title, a black tornado that gave the one in *The Wizard of Oz* a run for its money.

"Although Mifune is top-billed," noted *Variety*'s "Robe," "he's actually seen in what amounts to a bit more than a cameo role. However, even the brief glimpses of the fantastic Japanese actor are worthwhile as he disdains using a sword during the few action scenes in which he participates, whipping his way through his many assailants with nothing more than a short stick until, near the end, he meets an opponent worthy of a bit of sword-play. Mifune easily dominates every scene in which he appears."[18]

Both Mifune and Kayama worked to the point of exhaustion during the production of *Red Beard*, and Kurosawa himself was hospitalized for several weeks in late May after struggling with illness and exhaustion for months.

Despite this, Mifune's performance is exactly what it should be: he expresses profound wisdom with a minimum of dialogue, and his presence is felt throughout the narrative, even during his long absences. Significantly, the film does not attempt a saintly portrayal in the manner of Dr. Gillespie (the wise sage of *Dr. Kildare*); Red Beard has moments where he is subversive, even criminal, when left no other choice. In the film's only action sequence, Red Beard uses his knowledge of anatomy to dislocate the bones of several thugs who try to prevent his rescue of Otoyo from the brothel. "Dr. Red Beard . . . is possessed by, consumed by, a rage for good," Donald Richie wrote of the character. "He will do anything to get at it, even . . . things that he considers bad. . . . He does more than merely devote himself to the good; he devotes himself to a fight against bad. . . . This is why the picture is not sentimental. To simply feel for, sympathize with, weep over—this is sentimental because it is so ridiculously disproportionate to what is needed. But to gird the loins and go out and do battle, to hate so entirely that good is the result: this is something else."[19] The aftermath of this scene, in which Red Beard admonishes himself as a dozen *yakuza* thugs lie on the ground with their wrenched limbs pointing every which way, is funny because Red Beard's regret is so genuine.

Minoru Nakano recalled, "The fight between the thugs and Red Beard was originally planned as a sword battle. But since it was the story of a doctor, and it would have been very unusual for a doctor to be carrying such a weapon, [fight choreographer Ryu Kuze] and Mr. Kurosawa concluded that the doctor would have known all about the different bones in the body and how to break them, and this is how he is able to defeat the *yakuza* without the benefit of a sword."[20]

Yoshio Tsuchiya, in his last film for Kurosawa, and Tatsuyoshi Ehara, who, like Kayama, was a regular in the "Young Guy" films, are cast as fellow interns. Kurosawa deftly understates these not-insignificant parts, using their opposing views of Red Beard and life at the clinic to parallel Yasumoto's conflicting emotions, one of many such parallels in this beautifully constructed film. Ehara can't wait to leave; at one point he tells Kayama, "The patients are all slum people, they're full of fleas—they even smell bad. Being here makes you wonder why you ever wanted to become a doctor."

Tsuchiya's doctor, by contrast, is a devoted disciple of Red Beard, though it's implied he's rather less talented than Yasumoto. Tsuchiya is excellent throughout, always looking utterly exhausted, as if his passion and drive will make up for any shortcomings he may have as a physician.

Kurosawa crammed his epic with as many great actors as he could find. Besides stock company regulars like Takashi Shimura, Kamatari Fujiwara, and Akemi Negishi, the director cast Haruko Sugimura, the respected stage actress from *No Regrets for Our Youth*, as the selfish, evil brothel mistress. She, like Chishu Ryu, who plays Yasumoto's father, was a regular in Ozu's films. Ryu's wife is played by the luminous Kinuyo Tanaka, an actress most associated with the great films of Kenji Mizoguchi, including *The Life of Oharu* (1952), *Ugetsu* (1953), and *Sansho the Bailiff* (1954). No performance in the picture is less than excellent. Even the child actors, Terumi Niki and Yoshitaka Zushi, are astonishing.

Some critics, like film theorist Joan Mellen, complained that "the seeds of Kurosawa's decline were already apparent in *Red Beard*," in part, she wrote, because of its perceived absence of conflict. Specifically, Kurosawa's title character dispenses wisdom without the self-discovery of, say, Takashi Shimura's government worker in *Ikiru*. "*Red Beard* contains a didactic quality absent from Kurosawa's finest works. . . . And the wide-screen, grand-shot compositions and the virtuosity of Kurosawa's use of the telephoto lens function to conceal the film's failure to realize its point of view beyond the level of homiletic preaching. By 1965 Kurosawa seemed committed to the dangerous path of the artist who relies on a body of received truths that a master, as a surrogate for the director, imparts to an eager disciple."[21]

The truth, however, is that many of the director's best films use this premise, including *Seven Samurai*. Probably many of Kurosawa's advocates were unprepared for Mifune's shift into the *sensei* (teacher) role. Had the film been made ten years earlier, it's likely Takashi Shimura or Denjiro Okochi might have played Red Beard to Mifune's young doctor. And while Kurosawa ingeniously uses Mifune's great screen presence to intimidate young Dr. Yasumoto, his realization is indeed a process of self-actualization and comes not through any didactic teachings of Red Beard. The film is Yasumoto's story, not Red Beard's.

And despite his pretty-boy, "Young Guy" image, Kayama's performance is very good, notably better than his work for other directors. For Japanese audiences in 1965, Yasumoto's initial selfishness was even more surprising and off-putting with clean-cut Kayama in the role. "Young Guy" would never have been so self-absorbed.

Indeed, the role closely echoed Kayama's own frustrations about the acting business. "I was Yasumoto and Kurosawa was Red Beard. I used to think about quitting acting. I thought it was stupid to laugh [in films] when I didn't want to laugh at all. And then I met [Kurosawa] on *Sanjuro* for the first time and worked again for him on *Red Beard*. As Yasumoto says, 'I will stay at the clinic no matter what.' I decided then, 'I will stay at the studio.' It has been thirty years since then, but like a blink in the history of the universe."[22]

Kayama's long commitment to the film made Toho uneasy, for it kept their hottest star off movie screens for nearly two years. After shooting had been completed, there was a mad rush to produce as many starring vehicles for him as possible. But the flood of Kayama vehicles during the mid-sixties was not at all uncommon for a leading player of his status. Partly this was due to the prolific nature of the Japanese studio system. The studios themselves, in an effort to control their contract stars, perpetuated the common notion that if actors were out of the spotlight, even for six or nine months, the public was ready to replace them with any number of new faces waiting in the wings.

This could not have been lost on Mifune, for the making of *Red Beard* coincided with a critical period in his own international and domestic marketability. After seventeen years under contract to Toho, he officially went freelance just as *Red Beard* was wrapping production. Remember that Mifune was risking his personal fortune in a small but expensive film studio of his own, also in Seijo and literally minutes from Toho. The studio was only in the planning stages, but Mifune had several of his own productions in the works, and he could not appear in any of those until *Red Beard* had finished.

Kurosawa's seeming ambivalence about Mifune's dedication to *Red Beard* created a rift, especially when the film, originally scheduled for a fifty-day shoot, stretched to more than a year. This put Mifune in a financial quandary. Whether he worked on the film two months or two years, his fee stayed the same. Desperate for income, he signed to do a television commercial for a pharmaceutical firm, but still had that beard. Kurosawa, feeling the beard was, in essence, partly his, didn't want Mifune to do it.

Not only did *Red Beard* represent a huge investment for both Toho and Kurosawa Production, it also kept Mifune and Kayama out of Toho's theaters for nearly two years. To placate the studio, Kurosawa rushed a second Mifune-Kayama vehicle into production while *Red Beard* entered its postproduction stage. It was a scene-for-scene remake of Kurosawa's 1943 directorial debut, *Sanshiro Sugata*, and something he had been working on, on-and-off, for about two years. In fact, it had originally been planned as Kurosawa's next film after *High and Low*.

"By the time *Red Beard* was completed," said Mifune, "it had met with quite a few costly delays. Therefore, *Sanshiro Sugata*, which was one of Kurosawa's first successes, was remade in order to recoup some of the initial expense of *Red Beard*."[23]

Sanshiro Sugata was a co-production between the director's own Kurosawa Production and Toho's B-picture subsidiary, Takarazuka Motion Picture Co., Ltd. Kurosawa adapted his old script and edited the film, though the picture was directed by Seiichiro Uchikawa, a former assistant. Uchikawa was hired for his willingness to follow Kurosawa's orders and shoot the film as quickly as possible. Kayama starred in the title role, while Mifune played Denjiro Okochi's part, judo instructor Shogoro Yano. Additional cast members of *Red Beard* appeared in the film, including Tsutomu Yamazaki and Takashi Shimura (also in the original version, in a different role), while Masaru Sato, Tomoyuki Tanaka, and others were culled for the production end.

Though the film went on to win the Catholic International Prize in Rio, most found the results tremendously disappointing, and few were fooled into believing this version of *Sanshiro Sugata* could be anything more than a quickie remake. Everyone involved seemed rather embarrassed by the picture, including Kurosawa, whose name was uncharacteristically buried in the credits. Successful when it opened on May 29, 1965, barely a month after *Red Beard*'s wide release, it quickly disappeared, is rarely revived, and has never been available for home video in Japan. In the United States *Sanshiro Sugata* was released to Toho-owned theaters that August as *Judo Saga*, where it received little attention and fell into almost instant obscurity. Kevin Thomas of the *Los Angeles Times* knew a turkey when he saw one, despite Kurosawa's name on the credits. He called the film "a mistake of epic proportions, for this picture is bad in a big way. . . . Kurosawa, in attempting to raise questions about one's obligations to one's self and to others, by extension also shows that the sacrifice art demands of the artist may be so total as to be destructive. Unfortunately, Uchikawa is unable to express these ideas with any vitality or imagination. It is ironic that Kurosawa, whose films are characterized by their sweeping movement and bold composition, should have such a static protégé—one so devoid of a sense of style or tempo. For two and a half hours we are treated to a series of dull tableaus so stagy that continuity is all but destroyed and progression non-existent. . . . As his teacher Shogoro Yano, the inventor of judo, Toshiro Mifune performs with his customary authority in this small role, a sort of special guest star appearance."[24]

Like the director's previous few films, Japanese coming-attraction trailers for *Red Beard* were dominated not only by Kurosawa's name in gigantic type but also by images of Kurosawa on-camera, on the set with Mifune, and supervising the scoring of Masaru Sato's music. Sato's lovely score was recorded in four-track magnetic stereo, a luxury very few Japanese features could afford. (Kurosawa's superb use of this directional, discrete sound system was lost on American audiences, who have to date heard only monophonic soundtracks, even in the current U.S. home video versions.)

Red Beard opened on April 3, 1965, on a limited, roadshow basis, going into wide release three weeks later, when it was paired with a 25-minute documentary about the Emperor's grandson, *Pretty Hironomiya* (Kawaii Hironomiya-sama). The two films played to packed theaters for months, and *Red Beard* easily became the year's biggest hit.

Japanese and American audiences responded to the film quite differently. In Japan it won the Asahi Cultural Prize after it was completed but before it was even released, and it subsequently earned best-film awards in the Mainichi Film Competition and at NHK. It picked up the Tokyo Roei Million Pearl Award and won *Kinema Jumpo*'s Best Film and Best Director Prizes. In Moscow *Red Beard* was given the Film Union Prize and Toshiro Mifune the Best Actor Award. He also won his second Best Actor Award at the Venice International Film Festival. In its announcement of Kurosawa as Best Director, *Kinema Jumpo* noted: "Akira Kurosawa has always depicted mankind's love and truth in his films. He has made a dynamic drama in *Red Beard*, a magnificent and exciting creation rich with humanism. His perfectionism carries through to every single shot. His work is full of passion and excitement. This is a film made by the leader of Japan's film industry, a man who has led it with great generosity."[25] (When Kurosawa and Mifune died, memorial books published in Japan were dominated by more images and articles on *Red Beard* than any other film in their respective canons, including *Rashomon*, *Ikiru*, and *Seven Samurai*.)

Despite its unprecedented domestic success, *Red Beard* proved a tough sell to American audiences. Nine months after its premiere, Toho finally released *Red Beard* on their own, premiering it at the Toho La Brea Theater in Los Angeles on January 11, 1966, immediately following the Japanese-American New Year's holiday. Kevin Thomas was one of the few Western critics to recognize the film's significance:

"The greatness of *Red Beard* is something more than the sum of its parts. It is a film not only to be seen but also to be felt. . . . [The premise] sounds mawkish and maudlin, and certainly it could easily come out as soap opera in lesser hands. But Kurosawa has the ability to make of this material a tough-minded affirmation of life in the face of an existence so brutal and harsh as to be often untenable. Consequently, he approaches here the spirit of Dostoevsky, his favorite author. . . . [It] is a film of breathtaking beauty, extraordinary emotional impact and profound significance. It is still another masterpiece . . . from one of the greatest directors of all time."[26]

In his book, Donald Richie likened the movie to writers as varied as Dickens and Camus. "The film is both compassionate and hard-boiled," he wrote, "because Kurosawa's concern, like Red Beard's, is the opposite of indulgent. The film can carry its extraordinary weight of sentiment . . . because it can carry us so far beyond the confines of our daily hells."[27]

But the majority of American critics, by now used to the swift-paced excitement of *Yojimbo*, *Sanjuro*, and *High and Low*, were put off by *Red Beard*'s deliberate pacing, its vignette-style storytelling. Many likened it to an arty *Ben Casey* or *Dr. Kildare*. Few understood the picture's merits or ambitions.

It was three years before *Red Beard* received anything like national exposure; Frank Lee International released the film to the art-house circuit in January 1969 with, as *Time* wrote, "only a whisper of publicity."[28] *Time* found the film "an Oriental *Pilgrim's Progress*." *Variety*'s "Hawk" condescendingly called it "hokum lifted to the highest denominator." Like so many Western critics baffled by its intent and pacing, "Hawk" suggested Kurosawa "[took] a season of 'Doctor Kildare' TV skeins, [threw] in a half dozen classic Hollywood hospital perennials, and [did] them all up with great taste and flair." He also suggested that "much of the film's initial footage could be elegantly elided for major effect."[29]

Tony Velella, writing for the *Motion Picture Herald*, while giving the picture a "Very Good" rating, concurred, suggesting that "*Red Beard* could have used a lot less time to be presented," and found its length "unneeded and bothersome."[30]

What Kurosawa strived for and achieved in *Red Beard* would be lost in his subsequent work. Films like *Dersu Uzala*, and especially *Kagemusha* and *Ran*, would be unrelentingly grim and pessimistic, but in the 1990s, renewed critical acceptance and other factors would lead Kurosawa back to the kind of optimistic, meditative work that *Red Beard* predicts. Mifune would never again appear in a film as great. With very few exceptions, his subsequent roles don't even come close.

Japanese audiences continue to embrace the film like no other. They may concede the historical significance of *Rashomon*, the greatness of *Ikiru* and *Seven Samurai*, but *Red Beard* struck a deeply personal chord that continues to resonate in Japan as strongly as that of any of Kurosawa's best films. Despite continuing American indifference, *Red Beard* is a masterpiece, in many ways his finest work. In the end Kurosawa was right: in Japan at least, *Red Beard* remains the film you just *have* to see.

Kurosawa received recognition of another sort that August when Donald Richie's groundbreaking book, *The Films of Akira Kurosawa*, was published by the University of California Press. Although a Japanese-language edition would not appear until the late 1970s, Kurosawa read a translated copy and was immensely pleased with Richie's thoughtful, informed essays, even where Richie's opinion differed from his own. Compared to most Japanese-film critics of the period, Richie's astute readings of Kurosawa's films were a revelation. Mifune paid Kurosawa an intelligent and heartfelt tribute in the book's preface, flatly stating: "Kurosawa has this quality, this ability to bring things out of you that you never knew were there. . . . When you see his films, you find them full of realizations of ideas, of emotions, of a philosophy which surprises you with its strength, even shocks you with its power. You had not expected to be so moved, to find within your own self this depth of understanding."[31] Mifune then made an astonishing statement: "I have never as an actor done anything that I am proud of other than with him."[32] Tellingly, this testimonial was removed from later editions of the book, when Mifune and Kurosawa had long been estranged.

Shortly after *Red Beard*'s release, Mifune stated, "An actor is not a puppet with strings pulled by the director. He is a human being with seeds of all emotions, desires, and needs within himself. I attempt to find the very center of this humanity and explore and experiment." Asked about working with Kurosawa, Mifune called his experiences "wonderful! But painstaking. He is such a perfectionist that he will reshoot an entire scene if a single chopstick is out of place."[33]

After *Red Beard* was completed, Mifune often entertained reporters with anecdotes frequently exaggerated or at odds with the facts. In one such example he claimed, "I recall an incident which occurred during the shooting of 'Sanjuro.' Several special-effects men were assigned to create artificial camellias. They worked diligently for an entire week, but Kurosawa's only comment was 'And what am I supposed to do with that?' With a crew he then scoured the countryside until he found the perfect camellia.

Pointing to the flower he said, 'That's the one I want,' ordered them to up-root the tree, haul it back to the studio, and re-plant it on the set. They did!"[34]

Yet, despite their many differences during the making of *Red Beard*, Mifune had by no means lost respect for Kurosawa. "As far as I'm concerned, Kurosawa is *the* director," Mifune said, "though there are many good ones."[35]

With *Red Beard* and *Sanshiro Sugata* finished, Mifune needed an extended vacation from Kurosawa. After the Japanese premiere of *Red Beard*, he flew to Honolulu, then to New York, where the Toho Cinema premiered *Samurai Assassin* (Samurai), Mifune's second co-production with Toho following the disastrous release of *Legacy of the 500,000*. Produced immediately after the filming of *Red Beard*, *Samurai Assassin* was actually released first, for the New Year's 1965 holiday audience, three months prior to the unveiling of Kurosawa's epic.

Mifune took no chances this time, choosing a straightforward samurai action–political thriller, loading it with an all-star cast and a reliable director he'd worked with before, Kihachi Okamoto.

Based on the complex, real-life 1860 assassination of a shogunate's counselor, Naosuke Ii, the film follows a skillful and ambitious *ronin*, Tsuruchiyo Niiro (Mifune), who joins the band of imperialist assassins (led by Yunosuke Ito), hoping the event will catapult him into a high-paying, prestigious position. The film offers Mifune an offbeat, complex role; what at first appears to be a simple variation of *Yojimbo* (early on, Mifune's character is suspected of spying for the other side) evolves into an interesting portrait of an emotionally scarred man, one who is ultimately the very opposite of his Sanjuro.

Unbeknownst to him, Niiro is the son of a high-ranking government official who, while financially supportive, has kept him at a distance because Niiro's mother (Haruko Sugimura) was a prostitute. Cared for by a kindly merchant (Eijiro Tono) sworn to secrecy, Niiro becomes a promising samurai and falls in love with a young woman (Michiyo Aratama). The woman's father (Takashi Shimura), however, unaware of Niiro's true parentage, will not allow his daughter to marry this lowly warrior. Plans for the assassination are postponed for several weeks. Niiro meets the manager of an inn who bears a remarkable resemblance to his lost love (also played by Aratama), awakening deeply repressed feelings. As the merchant tells her, Niiro is a man spiraling out of control, "like a rolling stone, rolling down a steep hill."

Director Okamoto's period films rarely equaled his best work; his *jidai-*

geki often come off as middling Kurosawa riffs, but *Samurai Assassin* is an exception, a solidly structured and original work, and his best in the genre. Instead of black humor, the hallmark of Okamoto's best films, the director and screenwriter Shinobu Hashimoto employ a darker sense of irony. The climax, the assassination by Mifune of the shogunate counselor who we—but not Mifune—have learned is his father, is a tour de force, an apocalyptic bloodbath of editing, scoring, and swordplay choreography (again by the great Ryu Kuze) against blizzardlike conditions in front of a magnificent set, beautifully photographed by Hiroshi Murai. The image of Mifune triumphantly prancing in the snow as he carries off the prized, dismembered head of his father on a spear is deeply sad and unsettling. His blind determination is emphasized by Okamoto's excellent use of numerous close-ups of Mifune.

Also good is Niiro's relationship with another samurai suspected of betrayal, the scholarly Einosuke Kurihara (Keiju Kobayashi), who, like Lord Ii, sees the Meiji Restoration as inevitable. Niiro longingly watches Kurihara's ordinary family life (personified by an ideal wife, well played by Kaoru Yachigusa) and finds peace only during his visits there. The film's supporting cast make the most of its guest roles, notably Sugimura as Niiro's mother, Susumu Fujita as Niiro's martial-arts instructor, Takashi Shimura as Aratama's father, and Eijiro Tono as Niiro's sensitive, adopted father. All were, of course, members of Kurosawa's stock company.

Beyond Mifune, the film belongs to Yunosuke Ito (1919–80) as the slimy leader of the assassins. The distinctive-looking Ito, with his long face, ruddy features, and prominent lower lip, gives one of his best performances. He's entirely believable playing a man so ruthless he uses Niiro to kill Kurihara (only to later learn that Kurihara wasn't the spy, either) and knowingly allows Niiro to assassinate his own father. Ito tangled with Mifune before in *Stray Dog* and *High and Low*, and would again in films to come, but never more memorably than here.

The film's only flaw, a necessary one to keep track of the convoluted events, is the narration by Tatsuyoshi Ehara as Ito's samurai historian, which intrusively offers a play-by-play of the assassination itself. Okamoto makes up for this by using Ehara's comments to book-end the film, coupled with identical camera angles of opening umbrellas carried by wandering assassins in the falling snow, and he also uses this historical account to harshly criticize the samurai code, Okamoto's main interest in the genre. (In a nice touch, Ehara's account ends up in an icy river, never to be read.)

The film is well structured, cut by the director with numerous but rewarding flashbacks, as well as several excellent, stand-alone set pieces, such as Okamoto-regular Hideyo "Eisei" Amamoto's stalking of Yachigusa's sister, Ito's bloody execution of the real traitor (Akihiko Hirata), and Niiro's first meeting with Kurihara.

After the long, arduous production of *Red Beard*, *Sanshiro Sugata*, and *Samurai Assassin*, Mifune was warmly received in New York and, for the first time, was beginning to escape Kurosawa's shadow. In Los Angeles, the Toho La Brea held a special "Mifune Night" in conjunction with *Samurai Assassin*'s premiere there. When the picture ended, Mifune went onstage and demonstrated some new swordplay techniques choreographer Ryu Kuze had devised for the film. The audience went wild, and more than a thousand fans rushed him for autographs. Afterward, he met with friends and Hollywood professionals at the Cherry Blossom Inn, a restaurant above the Toho La Brea, which became a regular stop whenever Mifune was in town.

The same could not be said for Toho's New York branch. In June 1965, the Toho Cinema closed its doors. According to *The Hollywood Reporter*, "Management states the project has fulfilled the purpose originally planned to obtain a good indication of American taste and interest to assist in future production of Japanese films, and the company will now concentrate on distribution of films from Nippon."[36]

Kazuto Ohira, who returned to Japan one year before its closing, said, "We had so-so box office. In the long term, the good films were profitable. And because they were more commercial, the special-effects films and Kurosawa's movies were bought up for release in Canada, South America, Australia, and Africa. I returned to Japan with vivid memories of American audiences lining up at the La Brea and the Toho Cinema."[37]

While Mifune was in Hollywood, John Frankenheimer, who had directed in quick succession *The Manchurian Candidate*, *Birdman of Alcatraz* (both 1962), and *Seven Days in May* (1964), approached Mifune to appear in the director's forthcoming Cinerama epic about the Formula One circuit, *Grand Prix*. By the time he reached New York on May 18, Mifune had had a second offer, this one from David Weisbart and 20th Century-Fox to play a "redskin scalp-grabber," Chief Crazy Horse, in *The Day Custer Fell*.[38] Mifune was then asked by producer Joseph Levine to appear opposite Peter O'Toole in *Will Adams*, a biopic about the first Caucasian samurai. *Variety* reported that Mifune was "intensely interested in making one or all," but any decision would have to be based on the finished script, and none of them had been written yet.[39] After appearing on a television panel with Charlton Heston and Tony Curtis, Mifune talked to columnist Louella Parsons through his interpreter, actress Miiko Taka. Asked about *The Day Custer Fell*, Taka told Parsons, "After all the dramas he's made, the idea strikes him as funny."[40]

"I really wanted the part of General Custer, but my eyes were the wrong color!" joked Mifune. "No, seriously, I was originally asked to consider the part of Sitting Bull, but I preferred the Chief Crazy Horse role. This was agreeable to all concerned; however, the project was shelved. So, it was not until I met with John Frankenheimer, and was taken by his enthusiasm for *Grand Prix*, and his eagerness to have me in the picture, that I finalized my agreements for my first English-language film."[41] In *Grand Prix* Mifune would play a Japanese automobile executive based on Soichiro Honda, whose company entered the Formula One racing circuit in 1964. Mifune's character agrees to sponsor a down-on-his-luck race-car driver, played by James Garner.

Mifune then accompanied a print of *Samurai Assassin* to the Mar del Plata Film Festival in Argentina, where the film was Japan's official entry, stopping in New York on his way there. While in the Big Apple, Mifune was interviewed by *The New York Times*'s Howard Thompson, who wrote: "Mifune suggested the alert, introspective businessman he indeed is. He sat in his hotel suite, neatly attired in a pin-stripe suit and conservative tie, and thoughtfully weighed questions before replying. . . . His hands are a striking combination of muscularity and sensitivity."[42]

Vincent Canby wrote that, for his own interview, Mifune "didn't seem ill at ease, only distant and removed, a creature of another exotic time and place plopped, temporarily, into a setting of impersonal, corn-colored hotel décor. . . . He sipped his coffee delicately and chain-smoked his Philip Morris filter-tips, listening vaguely to the interpreter and the journalist, paying no attention to the television screen in the corner on which something like Bonzo [sic] the Clown was mugging frantically."[43]

Writer Wayne Warga, who interviewed Mifune during this same period, had a different view, describing him as being as "glib and animated as a kid with a new toy" and spending much of that interview demonstrating a studio cobweb-making machine he picked up in Hollywood. "Mrs. Mifune," Warga added, "who is chic, composed and very quiet, sat on the sofa and watched with one of those he's-got-another-doodad expressions. 'You can expect a lot of cobwebs in my next picture,' " Mifune quipped. " 'Also, while I'm here, I am buying a tape recorder and a camera to help restore the balance of trade.' "[44]

Mifune did not leave the Mar del Plata Film Festival empty-handed; *Samurai Assassin* won the Special Reporter's Award. The film also got good reviews in America. *Variety*'s "Robe" enjoyed the film with reservations: "Toshiro Mifune and a samurai plot go together like Lunt and Fontanne or Laurel and Hardy. Some of the results are superb, some are only very good. *Samurai Assassin* belongs to the latter group."[45]

Dale Munroe of the *Hollywood Citizen-News* also had high praise for the actor: "Swords and Toshiro Mifune are becoming almost as familiar to cosmopolitan Americana as baseball and bubble gum. . . . Japan's greatest star attraction is once again the robust, determined he-man warrior seeking a path of honor and glory. . . . He is incapable of making a bad movie."[46]

For the remainder of 1965 and into 1966, Mifune took an undemanding role in Seiji Maruyama's war movie *Retreat from Kiska* (Taiheiyo kiseki no sakusen—Kisuka, 1965), and co-produced and starred in *Fort Graveyard* (Chi to suna, 1965), a wartime thriller and his second film that year for director Kihachi Okamoto. He also flew to Argentina and Moscow, accepting awards for his performance in *Red Beard*, and posed, happily clean-shaven, for a magazine spread, sipping coffee alone at a café, relaxing aboard his yacht, shooting *Fort Graveyard*, and appearing before the press at the opening of his new studio. Publicly, Mifune was very much a man's man—he enjoyed riflery and was named vice-chairman of the "Cultured People's Rifle and Target Club."[47]

Privately, Mifune's life when he wasn't working was more subdued than the fan magazines suggested. He valued his time out of the spotlight at his home in Seijo-machi, located in Setagaya near Toho Studios. "We live quietly, too," Mifune said. "Socially, we mingle quite a bit with movie people, but with other groups as well."[48] When he wasn't working, the actor still liked to dabble in still photography and fishing, but little else—working was his life.

By now, he was also receiving fan mail from abroad, especially the United States. "I don't really know [America]," Mifune admitted, "only through your films. One thing they don't ask for is money. They know no Japanese has any."[49]

Retreat from Kiska was Toho's big war movie of 1965, and a thankful if temporary departure from the formula pictures this genre were fast becoming. The film recounted the daring naval maneuver of 1943 in which more than 5,000 Japanese soldiers were miraculously rescued from the Aleutians. With some 36,000 American troops just 150 miles away and closing in, the rescue mission was one of the big surprises of the war—

when American troops arrived at Kiska, they found the island completely deserted.

Kiska, though, was never theatrically released in the United States. The picture bypassed Toho's theater circuit, and the studio licensed the picture to Henry Saperstein's United Productions of America (UPA) in February 1966. At the time, Saperstein was actively working with Toho. He had gotten into the Japanese market co-financing and providing American actors for such Toho monster movies as *Monster Zero* (Uchu daisenso, 1965), *Frankenstein Conquers the World* (Furankenshutain tai chitei kaiju Baragon, 1965), and *War of the Gargantuas* (Furankenshutain no kaiju—Sanda tai Gaira, 1966).

Saperstein wanted to release the film nationally, but couldn't muster any interest, and it didn't appear in America at all until 1973. It skipped a theatrical release altogether and instead was dubbed into English and syndicated for local television.[50] The picture premiered on KNBC in Los Angeles on August 24, 1973, the thirtieth anniversary of the famous retreat, introduced by Japanese-American actor James Shigeta, who praised the dubbing job for its use of actors of Japanese descent in lieu of the usual practice of hiring Occidental actors adopting Charlie Chan–like voices.[51] The picture also aired on a local television station in San Francisco, but soon after disappeared from view, never to return.

Predictably, Mifune stars as the commander who engineers the operation. "His worried caution," the *Los Angeles Times* said, "is a startling change from the damn-the-torpedoes heroics of most war films. . . . 'Retreat from Kiska' is not, by purely cinematic standards, a great movie, but it is, as Shigeta makes clear, a welcome and stimulating shift of view which takes on fresh relevance in the context of present-day Southeast Asia and the bombing of Cambodia, now ceased."[52]

Fort Graveyard, a seriocomic World War II movie, was the sixth and final film in Toho's "Independent Gangster" series, whose films were sardonic instead of reverential like Toho's Navy films, rooted in black humor and irony in place of finely crafted re-creations of historic battles. The series began after Kihachi Okamoto's *Desperado Outpost* (1959), which featured Mifune in a guest-star role and turned out to be a surprise hit. The next year Okamoto directed *Westward Desperado* (Dokuritsu gurentai nishi-e, 1960). This was followed by *Operation Enemy Fort* (Yamaneko sakusen, 1962) and *Outpost of Hell* (Dokuritsu kikanjutai imada shagekichu, 1963), both directed by Senkichi Taniguchi; and *Operation Mad Dog* (Norainu sakusen, 1963), directed by Jun Fukuda. Makoto Sato appeared in all the films (playing a different character in each one), but because Sato had never transcended his near-star status, the films usually were supported with bigger names: Yuzo Kayama, Yosuke Natsuki, and Tatsuya Mihashi among them. As a film series, the "Independent Gangster" films were on the wane by 1965. The fourth one was produced by one of Toho's subsidiaries, Takarazuka Eiga, and *Fort Graveyard* would be a co-production between Toho and Mifune Productions. Okamoto's return and Mifune's name, as well as those of co-stars Tatsuya Nakadai and Reiko Dan, gave the film a certain pedigree.

The story takes places near the end of the war. Mifune stars as Sergeant Kosugi, who, after striking a superior officer, is transferred to the collapsing Chinese front, where he's ordered by tyrannical Captain Sakuma (Nakadai) to train a marching band for battle. As Kosugi trains his men, whose ranks include a cook (Sato) and a gravedigger (Yunosuke Ito), he finds time for romance with Reiko Dan, playing the hackneyed "prostitute with a heart of gold." Naturally, Mifune whips these young men into shape. In the end, everyone dies in a suicide mission trying to recapture a Chinese stronghold.

Given Mifune's wartime experiences, where he trained young men sent to certain death, his own ties to China, and Okamoto's daring penchant for mixing comedy and tragedy simultaneously, *Fort Graveyard* sounded like a winner. But it wasn't. Considered among the worst of the series, *Fort Graveyard* was a bomb, mainly due to Kan Saji and Okamoto's script, one overflowing with clichés. The picture received downright hostile reviews when it opened in the United States for a brief run the following year. "Casting [Mifune, Ito, Dan, Nakadai, and Sato] in a hunk of junk like 'Fort Graveyard,'" said the *Los Angeles Herald-Examiner*, "is like having Jason Robards, Marlon Brando, Eli Wallach, Audrey Hepburn, and George Peppard in a beach party movie. Worse, in fact, because 'Fort Graveyard' doesn't even have the intelligence and consistency of these unassuming films. . . . Mifune accomplishes feats of daring that even John Wayne would be embarrassed to claim. He charges point-blank at a machine gun nest firing directly at him, but receives not a scratch. He knocks out five men with one sweeping blow of his rifle butt. He sustains colossal wounds, but keeps on fighting for the cause."[53]

"Once the unit enters combat," added the *Hollywood Citizen-News*, "the clichés and unbelievable battle scenes tear down whatever dramatic mood had been achieved in the first part of the film."[54]

Even Kevin Thomas thought the film "thoroughly terrible. It is an overlong [131 minutes], overdone pretentious bore. . . . That the presence of

Mifune—not to mention Kurosawa regulars Tatsuya Nakadai and Yunosuke Ito—cannot be said to be sufficient reason for seeing this picture is an indication of how bad it is." Thomas also had a few words of advice for Mifune: " 'Fort Graveyard' is the third movie . . . that Mifune has produced himself in connection with Toho. Since all three have been duds, let's hope he confines himself to being merely the great star he is."[55]

Mifune next moved from World War II melodramas back into *jidai-geki* and *chambara* for his next two pictures. This became his pattern for the next several years, alternating between *jidai-geki* spectacles, which he usually produced, and heroic leaders in Toho war movies. With few exceptions, Mifune played stock characters in these movies who, while often physically demanding, became more and more alike. Indeed, his admirals and generals weren't that much different from the samurai leaders he played. And while the next dozen or so films were well produced, even lavish with their large casts, elaborate costumes, and beautiful cinematography, they were, on the whole, empty-headed action films markedly lacking the rich characterizations that stretched Mifune's skills in even his weakest collaborations with Kurosawa.

Director Hiroshi Inagaki had been directing films for more than three decades, and his 1964 film, *The Rabble* (Garakuta), had been billed by Toho, with only a bit of exaggeration, as his one hundredth feature. By the time he made *Rise Against the Sword* in 1966, the *jidai-geki* genre Inagaki worked in almost exclusively was on the way out. Nevertheless, both he and Mifune would continue cranking them out into the early 1970s. Inagaki, though, seemed to sense the end was near. He said at the time, perhaps only half-jokingly, "I still want to be able to enjoy the smell of film when I'm older and have to work as a security guard."[56]

Rise Against the Sword is based on a true story, with Mifune starring as a sixteenth-century farmer-turned-warrior. Abare Goemon (Mifune) leads a grass-roots army of peasants known as the Kaga into rebellion against samurai oppression. The ambitious Lord Asakura (Akihiko Hirata), following Goemon's victories, tries to enlist his aid in fighting a rival clan. Goemon refuses, and the lord craftily uses conflicts within Goemon's family (including the great actress Nobuko Otowa as Mifune's wife) against him.

"Mifune gives a performance of incredible vigor, rigidity and violent energy," reported the *San Francisco Chronicle*. "It is one-dimensional, yet reveals breadth almost subliminally; it is vicious yet hints of compassion; it is bloodthirsty but just in a time when there was no ACLU or county sheriff. Of all actors in the world, Mifune is probably capable of the most domineering presence. . . . 'Rise Against the Sword' is simply a historical film of battle and conflict, well done."[57]

> Only the films of Kurosawa are more eagerly anticipated . . . than the samurai movies of veteran director Hiroshi Inagaki [wrote the *Los Angeles Times*'s Kevin Thomas]. They're packed with action and palace intrigue, they move like lightning, and they're played to the hilt. They're so much fun, they're entertaining even if the thread of their plots is lost from time to time in a maze of complications. After 37 years in the business, Inagaki reveals as much verve as ever in "Rise Against the Sword." . . . There's nothing new about this story . . . yet Inagaki and Mifune tackle it with such zest you would never know that both have done it countless times before. . . . None of this unfolds with the slightest bit of subtlety—indeed, Mifune has never been more flamboyant—yet it is engrossing because Inagaki, like DeMille, is a great storyteller who likes to tell a story for its own sake. . . . Sophisticates may snicker at Mifune's awesome invincibility. Still, the Duke of Marlborough could not have greeted his Duchess with greater lusty passion than the magnificent Mifune does the ever-enchanting Nobuko Otowa.[58]

Mifune then put in a guest appearance in Kihachi Okamoto's violent *chambara* film *The Sword of Doom* (Daibosatsu toge, 1966). Okamoto was directing the film on probation. He had then just shot what was certainly one of the best films of his career, *The Age of Assassins* (Satsujin kyo jidai), a brilliant, hilarious black comedy starring Tatsuya Nakadai and, in a deliciously theatrical performance, Hideyo Amamoto. But the film's weird visual style and jet-black humor—a style and humor along the lines of Tony Richardson's *The Loved One*—was too extreme for the studio: they refused to release it. "The producer [Tomoyuki Tanaka] and everyone at the studio said it was about ten years ahead of its time," Okamoto remembered. "After that [Tanaka and producer Sanezumi Fujimoto] wouldn't let me write any of my films—I could only direct someone else's script. That's why I did *Samurai Assassin* and *The Sword of Doom*; I didn't write them."[59]

The Sword of Doom is set in the 1860s and stars Nakadai as Ryunosuke Tsukue, a vicious and outcast samurai. Working as a hired assassin, killing for the sheer art of killing, Tsukue is haunted by a mysterious avenger, the brother of a man he brutally killed in a fencing duel. The brother, Hyoma Utsuki (Yuzo Kayama), is now working as an assistant fencing instructor at the school of Toranosuke Shimada (Mifune), and his identity unknown to Tsukue, the two face off in an impromptu match in which Utsuki is defeated. When Shimada and Utsuki learn of Tsukue's identity, Shimada sets Tsukue on a rigid training program in anticipation of the inevitable showdown. When the group Tsukue works for botches an assassination attempt, an outraged Shimada cuts them down in a spectacular swordfight as Tsukue watches from the sidelines. As Shimada's moral opposite, Tsukue is troubled not only by Shimada's skill—he's the only swordsman who might actually defeat him—but also by his comment "The sword is the soul. Study the soul to study the sword." Eventually Tsukue's madness catches up with him. Alone in a room with a young courtesan (Yoko Naito), whose grandfather he had senselessly murdered sometime earlier at Daibosatsu Pass (the film's title in Japan), Tsukue's mind snaps, his demons propelling him into total madness, just as his own men turn on him. In another superbly staged swordfight, in which Tsukue battles what seems like at least fifty *ronin*, he meets his (apparent) bloody end as the picture comes to its abrupt, freeze-framed conclusion.

Because of its (now fashionable) nihilist approach and incredible swordplay action, *The Sword of Doom* is today commonly regarded as Okamoto's best film. The action scenes were markedly explicit for their day, extremely well choreographed, and photographed in stark black and white by Hiroshi Murai. As always, Okamoto's eye for wide-screen composition is excellent, his choice of camera angles and his blocking of actors never better.

But *The Sword of Doom* is no masterpiece. Despite its impressive set pieces, it isn't half the film *The Age of Assassins* or *Samurai Assassin* are, nor is it even up to the level of Okamoto's best crime and war pictures (especially *Human Bullets* [Nikudan], 1968). Shinobu Hashimoto's uncharacteristically choppy script is confused and disjointed, jerking from one subplot to another, promising much but delivering little. Perhaps Hashimoto and Okamoto were drawn to the psychotic killer Nakadai had played in *Yojimbo*—although Nakadai's *Yojimbo* character is more a juvenile delinquent, while Tsukue is an obsessed soul spiraling into full-blown madness—and wanted to explore the psyche of such a man but, in the end, came up empty. Nakadai's deadpan, glassy-eyed performance and Hashimoto's script offer no insight into this bloodthirsty wanderer whose remorseless cruelty ends simply when the picture does, with a pretentious frame of Tsukue frozen in time, apparently at the moment of death.

The script builds toward not one but two climactic duels, between Tsukue and Utsugi, and Tsukue and Shimada—neither of which ever happen. The characters simply disappear toward the end of the picture, never to be heard from again. Perhaps Okamoto and Hashimoto thought they were being clever in cheating audiences of their expectations by having Tsukue killed by his own, equally cruel men. Perhaps it was their intention to have Shimada merely contrast Tsukue and simply "haunt" him, but the result is confusing rather than satisfying. Tsukue's relationship with the assassins, led by Tadao Nakamaru and Kei Sato, is never clear, and Mifune's sudden appearance at their failed assassination attempt comes out of nowhere, as if for no other reason than to give Mifune something to do.

Mifune's part is small, and the implied face-off between him and Nakadai in the film's advertising is simply a cheat. Subplots involving Kayama, Naito, Michiyo Aratama (as the wife of the samurai murdered by Nakadai, whom she then marries out of financial desperation), and Ko Nishimura (as Naito's shady but sympathetic guardian) similarly go nowhere.

Okamoto recalled the differences between directing Nakadai and Mifune: "Basically, I direct actors the same way, but Nakadai has a theater background so, for instance, Nakadai can joke around with someone on the set, then when we're shooting be totally in character. In Mifune's case, he wasn't a stage actor before becoming a movie star so he had to be in character all the time, from the beginning of the day until the end of the shoot. In that way Mifune was more tense to work with, and Nakadai was a little more relaxed."[60]

"Teaming [Mifune and Nakadai] is, to a samurai film," said *Variety*, "the equivalent of having John Wayne and Lee Marvin in the same cast. If the script is good, the result is a Nipponese variation on a John Ford Western; if the script is fair, as in this instance, there's still plenty of action and enough gore to satisfy even a first-year medical student. Only color could have made it more impressive but Hiroshi Murai's black and white camerawork is skillfully used to make the wholesale mayhem acceptable."[61]

Kevin Thomas, who never seemed to care much for Okamoto's work, called the picture "hopelessly confusing despite subtitles. Adding to the burden is its assumption of the audience's considerable knowledge and interest in Japanese history and dueling practices. So, if you don't qualify, you're likely to find it a bloody bore. Not helping matters is Kihachi Okamoto's static, old-fashioned direction. . . . Perhaps a parallel between [Nakadai's] brutal career and the break-up of feudalism in the Japan of the 1860's is implied, but one would have to speak Japanese to be certain of this. There are some exciting though gory duels, but they are scant compensation for the rampant plot intricacies."[62]

Though dismissed at the time, today *The Sword of Doom* is considered one of the classics of the genre. (In Japan, however, it's still regarded as only fair; Japan's *Cinema Club*, for instance, on a four-star scale, gave *The Sword of Doom* just two stars—average.) But Bruce Eder, in his liner notes for the film's American laserdisc release, said: "If Akira Kurosawa is the John Ford of Japan's samurai dramas, then . . . Kihachi Okamoto is the samurai film's Sam Fuller." While the case could certainly be made that Okamoto's crime and war films have the gritty, pulpy feel of Fuller's films, Okamoto's samurai action films are, by and large, weaker than his work in other genres. Eder argued: "If [the film] seems superficial, it's supposed to be—Okamoto is less interested in philosophy than in entertainment."[63] In fact the reverse is true. *Sword of Doom* is by no means intended as superficial entertainment; rather, it is a failed if ambitious attempt at something more. Okamoto aspired to make films on the level of Kurosawa's, and to some degree Toho tried to mold him in that direction. But while all these films— *The Sword of Doom, Kill!* (Kiru, 1968), *Samurai Assassin*—are well crafted, they never reach Kurosawa's level, and *The Sword of Doom*, for all its impressive ballet-like violence, is a far cry from Okamoto's best work, which nearly always mixes whistling-in-the-graveyard humor with unspeakable tragedy. *The Sword of Doom*, by contrast, is humorless and, except for its well-crafted mayhem, devoid of entertainment. For years, it was the only Okamoto film available on home video in the United States. The lack of other, better Okamoto films to compare it with, combined with its impressive swordplay, chiefly account for its bloated reputation in America.

As for the picture's vaguely ambiguous freeze-frame ending, Okamoto said, "We were going to make a sequel, but the company predicted that if we did a series of films they would not be successful, so the idea was abandoned."[64]

TWENTY

SEKAI NO MIFUNE—
MIFUNE OF THE WORLD

Mifune signed on to his second American film—and his first leading role in such—in May 1966. The film, to be called *Hell in the Pacific*, was a World War II drama about two soldiers, one Japanese, the other American, stranded on a remote island in the South Pacific. Mifune had been approached before with similar projects. "M-G-M producer Jack Cummings met Mifune in the spring of 1962," recalled Kazuto Ohira. "M-G-M invited Mifune to make a film about a battle on an isolated island between Japanese and American soldiers, but at that time Toho didn't go along with the project. A few years later the film was made as *Hell in the Pacific*."[1] The current picture would be co-produced by the American Broadcasting Company (ABC), through their subsidiary, Selmur Productions, and Henry Saperstein's United Productions of America (UPA). The head of Selmur, Selig J. Seligman, was executive producer of the TV show *Combat*, the still-in-production Vic Morrow series set during World War II. *Combat* was tremendously popular in Japan, so going one step further and producing a like-minded feature film was a natural move. Toho had a change of heart and came on board with Tomoyuki Tanaka. Together they would serve as co-executive producers. The project had been put together by Saperstein, who had co-produced films with Toho before and who had recently acquired the American rights to *Retreat from Kiska*.[2]

But problems began almost immediately. Saperstein said he envisioned a modest co-production, made in Hawaii for less than a million dollars.

"Along came ABC and Cinerama," Saperstein said in 1994. "They wanted to get into the deal and guaranteed network play. I made a stupid mistake: I agreed to go along with them. They immediately became pigs and didn't want Toho in the deal as a partner."[3] Within three months of the initial announcement, Toho was out of the picture.

Another problem was the lack of a firm commitment from actor Lee Marvin, who was pegged to play the unnamed American soldier. Marvin, eager to work with Mifune, had a unique connection in the Kurosawa-Mifune story: he was simultaneously being considered for the starring role in what was to have been Akira Kurosawa's first American film, *Runaway Train*. In the meantime, though, Marvin was busy filming *The Dirty Dozen* for Robert Aldrich and *Point Blank* for John Boorman, and this helped push *Hell*'s schedule out of whack. Preproduction dragged on through 1966 and 1967.

With his production company struggling to stay afloat, Mifune had to keep working. And with the start date on *Hell in the Pacific* clearly a long way off, he launched two new films for Mifune Productions: *The Adventures of Takla Makan* (Kiganjo no boken), to be co-produced with Toho, and *The Mad Atlantic* (Doto ichiman kairi), his company's first fully funded production. The two films were to be shot at Mifune's brand-new studio and on location on the opposite side of the world. *The Mad Atlantic* would be filmed in and around the Canary Islands, while *The Adventures of Takla Makan* would be shot, in part, in Iran.

The Mad Atlantic would go into production first. Mifune spent the last few weeks of December 1965 prepping the film in Madrid, while Jun Fukuda, its director, flew ahead to scout locations. Most of both pictures would actually be shot in Tokyo, but Mifune wanted enough location footage to give them the international look he felt would increase their marketability abroad. He allotted two weeks of filming with Fukuda off the Canary Islands for *The Mad Atlantic*, and the director recalled how refreshing it was to film there instead of in the crowded streets of Tokyo that he was used to. "The Japanese don't understand filmmaking very much," he said. "Whenever I work outside Japan, I get jealous about how film conscious the rest of the world is. When we were shooting *The Mad Atlantic*, the police stopped traffic for half a day for us—that would never happen in Japan."

Soft-spoken Jun Fukuda (1923–2000), a deeply tanned, leathery faced, chain-smoking man, had been Hiroshi Inagaki's chief assistant director on the *Musashi Miyamoto* trilogy, but *The Mad Atlantic* would be the only time he would direct Mifune himself. A second-stringer at Toho, Fukuda excelled in thrillers like *Witness Killed* (Ankokugai gekimetsu meirei, 1962) and *The Weed of Crime* (Ankokugai no kiba, 1964), but he had also made a number of "Young Guy" movies with Yuzo Kayama, a series Fukuda himself didn't much care for. "The producer, Sanezumi Fujimoto, liked my action films," he recalled, "and his way of rewarding me was to give me the more prestigious, more popular 'Young Guy' assignments. They were very big films, and I couldn't very well say no!"[4] Producer Tomoyuki Tanaka liked Fukuda, too, and began rewarding him with big, splashy Godzilla films, which Fukuda enjoyed even less.

"I had known Mr. Fukuda since he was an assistant director," said actor Yosuke Natsuki. "We'd talk to each other about anything and everything. I worked on almost all his films. He was nervous, jumpy at the studio. . . . I was worried about him because he put so much of himself into his work."[5]

A superb craftsman whose work is often no less thrilling and frequently better than that of more famous contemporaries like Seijun Suzuki, Fukuda himself dismissed his films out of hand. For a man who lived through the Golden Period of the late 1940s and 1950s, working as a director in the decay of the 1960s was an immense letdown. "I think my films are terrible," he once wrote, later stating in an interview, "Movies are a hundred years old, and I have been in the film industry for half that time, and as I look back, I wonder what I've done. I guess I don't speak very confidently."[6]

Confident or not, Fukuda was, like Toshio Sugie before him, capable of producing excellent work, often making gold purses out of sow's ears in virtually any genre. He must also have been terribly efficient shooting on location abroad, which is probably why Mifune hired him and why Toho relied on him for most of the rest of his career.*

In Madrid, Mifune was visited by Albert R. "Cubby" Broccoli and Harry Saltzman, producers of the wildly popular Bond movies, who tried to get him to play "Tiger" Tanaka, head of the Japanese secret service, in their next 007 film, *You Only Live Twice* (1967). Toho was providing not only production assistance but two of their busiest leading ladies, Mie Hama and Akiko Wakabayashi. Mifune no longer had to accede to Toho's wishes and turned down the role. *The Mad Atlantic* and *Takla Makan* would keep him busy through spring, he wanted to do Frankenheimer's *Grand Prix*, and who

---

*Among the films Fukuda shot outside Japan were *Young Guy in Hawaii* (Hawai no wakadaisho, 1963), *Son of Godzilla* (Gojira no musuko, 1967), and *Young Guy on Mt. Cook* (Nyu Jiirando no wakadaisho, 1969).

knows what Kurosawa had in store for him after *Runaway Train?* The role in the Bond movie eventually went to Tetsuro Tamba.

Praising Spain's technical support, which enabled him to wrap filming there three days early, Mifune flew to Teheran for a week of shooting on *Takla Makan* out in the desert.[7]

The Mad Atlantic was a story about tuna fishermen. In Japan it was advertised with the line "Hooligans of the Sea Exhibit Their Power and Spirit to the Atlantic Ocean!" obviously touting the novelty of a Japanese production filmed on the other side of the world. But except for the obvious visual appeal of the Canary Islands, the film might just as well have taken place in Yokohama Harbor. Mifune plays Murakami, a deskbound tuna man who returns to sea as the captain of the *Azuma-maru*, one of the company's many trawlers working off the African and Spanish coasts. Murakami encounters the expected resentment and trepidation from the tough crew when he replaces their beloved captain. He then proceeds to work them to the point of exhaustion, resulting in one man severely injuring his arm. Returning to port to get the man to the hospital, Murakami learns of the hostility between the crew of the *Azuma-maru* and a Spanish trawler, whose crew believe the Japanese had once sabotaged their fishing nets. Murakami gradually wins his men's respect after he engineers a large haul of tuna. But just as the ship has netted its biggest catch ever, Murakami receives an SOS from a Spanish yacht caught in a hurricane. The *Azuma-maru* is the only vessel within reach. Despite protests from the crew, Murakami orders the net lines cut and they brave fierce storms to rescue the yachtsmen.

Later they return to the site where they had cut their nets with little hope of ever retrieving them. However, the Spanish tuna fishers, having heard of Murakami's brave act, are holding the net for them. In the end, Murakami thanks the Spaniards for "the great friendship they have shown."[8]

Of *The Adventures of Takla Makan*, a garish costume film, director Senkichi Taniguchi said, "I made it for kids. I wanted to make a kids' movie and the company wanted to make it. It was one of those very rare films where everything goes smoothly."[9] The story, set in the distant past, concerns a Japanese adventurer, Osami (Mifune), and a priest, Ensai (Tadao Nakamaru), searching for Buddha's ashes. The two travel the Silk Road and reach a strange kingdom lorded over by an evil king (Tatsuya Mihashi), a scheming chamberlain (Akihito Hirata), and Gojaka, the Black Thief (Makoto Sato).

In the tradition of Republic Studios escapist serials of the 1940s, *Takla Makan* is little more than a series of action set pieces and an escape-recapture formula. It is practically a remake of *Samurai Pirate*. Both films have fantasy elements and *Arabian Nights*–inspired settings, and both feature Ichiro Arishima as a wizard, Hideyo Amamoto as a witch, Makoto Sato as a heavy, and Mie Hama and Akiko Wakabayashi as damsels in distress. The main difference between the two films was that *Samurai Pirate*'s early scenes were set at sea, whereas *Takla Makan* is in the desert.

Conditions in Iran were primitive, and the unit Mifune had sent there was a small one because of the expense involved. So small, in fact, that Mifune himself doubled as a lighting assistant, while co-stars Tadao Nakamaru and Makoto Sato pitched in as well, assisting the crew on various odd jobs.

Taniguchi had directed Mifune in his first film and now, almost twenty years later, was working for Japan's biggest star. Had Mifune changed? "Not at all," Taniguchi contended. "Mifune, Kurosawa, and I never changed. I really liked Mifune's personality. I was able to tell him anything. I guess he respected me a little, but he did not hide anything from me. I fell in love with his personality. I think if Kurosawa had not had the talent, Mifune might have continued doing pictures with me."[10] Despite their closeness early on and the many films they did together, Taniguchi and Mifune did not associate much after *Takla Makan*. Once shooting was completed, they rarely spoke, and Taniguchi didn't see Mifune at all in the years before the actor's death.

When the unit returned to Tokyo, art director Hiroshi Ueda began work on the film's castle set, built on a hill in Sakuragaoka near the studio. "When I designed it, I took the cultures of the Middle East and Southern Asia into consideration, combining them with the color scheme of the Chinese," he said. The castle, all five stories of it, took nearly three months to build, at a cost of ¥20 million (about $56,000).[11] (The expensive set was later rented out for use in television productions.)

Takla Makan's odd mishmash of Middle Eastern and Asian styles—cast members wear turbans and ride on camels—was even stranger to Japanese eyes than the more overtly fantasy-driven *Samurai Pirate* had been. For all the energy that went into making it, the picture is as ridiculous as a Jon Hall–Maria Montez Technicolor extravaganza. The film is appealing, but chiefly in its strangeness. Mifune throws himself into every action scene, but many of these are downright silly. In one scene, for example, Mifune battles a big stuffed bird that hovers above him without flapping its wings, obviously swinging from wires.

After the 1963 *Samurai Pirate*, Taniguchi was determined to avoid the tension he had endured between himself and special-effects director Eiji

Tsuburaya. This time Tsuburaya was not directly involved in the picture and did not take a co-director credit. The film's opticals are limited to composite shots of Ichiro Arishima sleeping underwater and Mifune's beheading the witch. The best effect is one dating back to the dawn of movies, a simple jump cut in which the witch, disguised as a princess (Yumi Shirakawa), reveals her true self in a flash of lightning.

Mifune had gambled that by shooting *The Mad Atlantic* and *Takla Makan* on the other side of the world he could broaden his appeal outside of Japan, especially in America, while giving Japanese audiences something different from the usual program picture. But when a movie with *Red Beard*'s pedigree was having trouble finding a wider, more international audience, the two Mifune films didn't have a chance. Despite the drive-in treatment given to *The Lost World of Sinbad*, at least it got released—*Takla Makan* was barely shown anywhere, and Japanese critics were thoroughly unimpressed. According to Taniguchi, "When it was released, people thought, Oh, it's for kids, and they were disappointed by it. But I heard that it made a lot of money."[12]

The Mad Atlantic, more ambitious and less ridiculous, nonetheless garnered even more tepid reviews. As Kevin Thomas pointed out, "None of the pictures Japan's top star Toshiro Mifune has made for his own company has been very good—to put it mildly. The latest . . . is no exception. But at least its extravagant melodramatics and unrestrained sentimentality make it lots more fun than its predecessors."[13]

As *The Adventures of Takla Makan* and *The Mad Atlantic* went into release, Mifune went before John Frankenheimer's 70mm cameras for his guest part as James Garner's automobile mogul–savior in *Grand Prix*. Principal photography began on May 22, 1966, with locations all over Europe, including racing sequences in Monte Carlo, Italy, France, Belgium, Germany, and Holland. By the time Mifune was filming his American debut, the actor said he had already turned down sixty overseas offers. "There are two reasons why it has taken me so long to make an English-language film," he explained. "First, there was not the opportunity because up till four years ago I was under contract to Toho, which insisted on the Japanese rights to any foreign films I might make. Second, I unfortunately didn't find the right script, either. I feel Japan is still not understood well abroad, and I didn't want to play in anything I'd regret later."[14]

As with *The Important Man*, Mifune learned his lines phonetically, with the help of tape-recorded dialogue and assistance from his interpreter, Masaaki Asukai, who also had a small role as Mifune's interpreter in the picture. The production was not only pricy but technically complex, with huge second-unit crews using twenty-three cameras shooting some 850,000 feet of racing footage, all on expensive Super Panavision 70 stock. Footage of the races was then integrated with photography of the leading players.[15] Production on the film took four months, wrapping in September, although Mifune's scenes were probably done in only a few weeks.

"I can't really compare [Frankenheimer's] methods to those of Kurosawa," Mifune told the media. "But they are similar in their professionalism. He kept saying, 'Very good, once more.' I started calling him that, and it became a joke in the company."[16]

Grand Prix left an indelible impression on the actor, one that would be reflected in many of the films he would subsequently produce, and the experience solidified his negative view of the Japanese studio system of the 1960s. "I was extremely impressed by the devotion and efficiency of the crew of 'Grand Prix,' which was made up of people from all over Europe and America. This has left me with the feeling all the more that the Japanese film industry has become one big assembly line with people working for nothing but their paychecks."[17]

It took nine separate teams of editors to piece the film together. There was talk of moving the release date to the summer of 1967, but several other racing films in the works forced Frankenheimer, Cinerama, and MGM to get the film out by the end of the year. The postproduction madness to meet the film's mid-December premiere pushed the film's cost to $10 million, but for Frankenheimer the expense was worth it. "There have been no compromises," he said. "Nothing has been spared. I think I've actually saved four months of ordinary delays by using an accelerated program. I haven't had to go through channels or red tape. . . . By getting the film out in December instead of the following June, you save half a year's bank interests on the production loans."[18]

During filming, Frankenheimer was troubled by Mifune's clipped English. It was clear to the director that Mifune's delivery was not only thickly accented but that he didn't understand the words he was saying, and his performance suffered. Unhappy with the results, Frankenheimer had Mifune reloop his lines in Los Angeles that October. But just as the film was going into release, the director opted to redub Mifune entirely with voice actor Paul Frees, who had already looped him once before, in the Americanized *I Bombed Pearl Harbor* (1960). Mifune speaks Japanese in his first scene in the film, but the rest of the time, whenever he speaks English, it is Frees's voice we hear, and with it Mifune's performance is all but lost.

"Toshiro Mifune is a painstaking actor," Frankenheimer commented at the time. "He learned all his English lines phonetically, but I had to dub him afterwards. It was an excellent dubbing job, in speech and recording. Most people think it was Mifune. Actually, when the film opened in New York he did speak his first [English] scene. That was his voice. But then I changed it and put in the dubbed voice in the first part, too, to make it all a whole."[19]

It's unfortunate that with the dubbing Mifune's performance is all but lost, as there are intriguing facets to the character. Mifune's automotive mogul, Izo Yamura, is an honest, no-nonsense businessman who, during the Occupation, lost his home to an American general and his family. By the time he got his house back, Yamura says, "it had flowered wallpaper, three new bathrooms, and four new closets. Americans, I think, are overdevoted to bathrooms and closets." Indeed, all his scenes with Garner are well written and fully dimensional, but they're also fatally compromised by the obvious dubbing.

Mifune spent the last few months of the year promoting *Grand Prix* and his role in it, unaware that much of his performance was about to be cast aside. In New York that September, he gave a surprisingly candid interview to Ronald Gold of *Variety*. By now he was blasting the Japanese studio system, saying, "The Japanese film industry is on a suicide course. It hasn't reached bottom yet, but it probably will have to before conditions improve." He complained that Japan was behind, following "the pattern of the U.S. industry by about ten years," saying only independents like himself were working to avoid total disaster. The studios, he argued, "are doing absolutely nothing to improve their situation," cranking out in-house program pictures which, said the actor, get worse every year. His biggest complaint, though, was that the studios—obviously meaning Toho in particular—were failing to make inroads in the world market the way Italy, Britain, Spain, and the rest of Europe were. Instead, they were "sticking firmly to a double-feature policy and concentrating almost entirely on 'cutting costs,' " with the average feature budget in Japan now down to around $80,000. "Yes, the big five all have branches overseas and pretend that they're interested in foreign sales; but they're not making pictures that are good enough." Mifune felt Japan should follow Hollywood's lead and invest large capital in "big" pictures that would pry audiences around the world away from their television sets.[20]

In retrospect, Mifune's notions about large-scale filmmaking were naïve, but not uncommon within the industry. By 1966, Hollywood's (and, to a lesser extent, Europe's) penchant for epic productions was already beginning to have disastrous effects on the studios that financed them. An expensive Hollywood film of the 1950s might have cost $3–4 million, but by the 1960s several dozen films were being made for $10 million and up; Fox's *Cleopatra* (1963), at $42 million the priciest film of its time, nearly bankrupted the studio. When their *The Sound of Music* (1965), another expensive title, became a gargantuan hit, they followed it with a half-dozen megaflops, including *Doctor Dolittle* (1967) and *Star!* (1968), films that brought the studio to its knees for a second time.

Mifune also criticized the studios for catering to "the current craze for violence and near-pornographic sex," a rather ironic statement, as Ronald Gold noted, considering how his last few films had been advertised. *Fort Graveyard* had been sold with the line "Here is the front line of Hell. I'll be killed unless I kill them first!" *Takla Makan*, a decidedly tame film, nonetheless went one step further with its advertising: "On horseback, he kills and kills with his sword! See Mifune's lightning-fast killing skill!"

The actor also expressed a bitterness that, while he was under contract to Toho, they had rejected loan-out bids from foreign studios. According to Gold, "He'd been willing to accept offers when he was working for [them], but the company had asked for 'unreasonable' prices for the loanout." Mifune even disclosed that his salary on *Grand Prix*, a role that required no more than a few weeks' shooting on his part, earned him more than the two years he had spent on *Red Beard*.[21] However, Mifune was quick to add, he and Kurosawa were still hoping to do another film together soon.

That December, *Grand Prix* opened to impressive grosses and mixed reviews. "John Frankenheimer has given MGM a hot box office runner in 'Grand Prix,' " said *Variety*. "He has also placed a pace-setter for the Academy's technical award sweepstakes . . . with [a] personal drama that is sometimes introspectively revealing, occasionally mundane, but generally a most serviceable framework. The real stars of 'Grand Prix,' however, are the cameramen."[22]

Arthur Knight was more critical, stating: "The wide-screen Cinerama process would seem the ideal medium on which to project the thrills of this asphalt jungle. But, somehow, even though there are well over three hours of *Grand Prix*, nothing seems to happen."[23]

Mifune received scant praise for his American debut. Overdubbed and lost among an all-star cast (including Garner, Yves Montand, and Antonio Sabato), he played second fiddle to the racing sequences. (Ultimately, so did everyone else.) *Grand Prix* was a big picture, surely, but Mifune's role in it was not.

Nonetheless, *Grand Prix* proved popular all over the world. In the United States the film ran nearly a year in its limited roadshow version (in 70mm Cinerama) before opening in wide release in 35mm 'scope the following summer. In one theater alone, Pacific's Cinerama Dome in Los Angeles, the picture earned more than $1.1 million over 43 weeks. Domestic rentals on the $7 million picture totaled $9.3 million.[24]

Mifune was at this time in preproduction on *Rebellion* (Joiuchi—Hairyozuma shimatsu, 1967), his company's sixth feature, again co-produced with Toho. His plans were to shoot *Rebellion* and then he and Kurosawa were to begin work on their fifteenth film together, a joint production between their two companies.[25] Just what this project might have been was not, apparently, decided—if plans to work together had actually been discussed at all.

Rebellion, meanwhile, offered Mifune one of his last great roles. The picture was directed by Masaki Kobayashi (1916–96), who had been making films since the early 1950s. At Shochiku he helmed the mammoth *Human Condition* trilogy, an epic, nine-hour adaptation of Jumpei Gomikawa's novel *Ningen no joken*, about a soldier struggling to maintain his humanity amid Japan's occupation and subsequent defeat in China. Kobayashi brought to the films, made over four years (1958–61), his own wartime experience, which mirrored that of the story's tragic hero in many respects. He won the Silver Prize of San Giorgio at the Venice Film Festival. The picture not only established Kobayashi as a major figure in Japanese film, it also made a star of Tatsuya Nakadai, then languishing, for the most part, in Toho comedies and melodramas. After directing Keiko Kishi in *The Inheritance* (Karami-ai, 1961), Kobayashi had made what is probably his best film, *Harakiri* (Seppuku, 1962), an extraordinary picture that criticized Japan's feudal system as uncompromisingly as *The Human Condition* had Japan's atrocities in Manchuria. The film featured yet another landmark performance by Nakadai, who also appeared in Kobayashi's *Kwaidan* (Kaidan, 1964), a hypnotic, highly stylized horror anthology adapted from Lafcadio Hearn's *Kwaidan: Stories and Studies of Strange Things*. Partly because of its perceived "Japaneseness" and exotic (i.e., non-Western) telling, the film became a tremendous hit abroad, though much less so in Japan. Kobayashi left Shochiku for Toho (which distributed though only partly financed *Kwaidan*), but he soon learned Toho was reluctant to bankroll the pictures he wanted to make, and the co-financing of Mifune's company was needed to produce *Rebellion*.

In fact, most of the interiors were shot on Mifune's new 500-square-meter soundstage, built at a cost of ¥140,000,000 (about $400,000), with money he had earned on *Grand Prix*. The stage was financed by Trissen Enterprises, an offshoot of Mifune Productions; Mifune and Nikkatsu star Yujiro Ishihara (and his wife) made up its board of directors. Other investors in the company included a large fishing company and a pharmaceutical firm.[26] A ceremony to open the stage was held on December 15, 1966, and *Rebellion* would be the first film shot there.[27]

"My studio will be available to independent directors like [Hiroshi] Teshigahara, [Kaneto] Shindo, and [Susumu] Hani," Mifune said. "The Japanese industry is on the decline—attendance dropped 14 percent last year. The good pictures are not coming out of the old monopolistic majors anymore."[28]

From the start, Mifune garnered a reputation as a meticulous caretaker of his pride and joy. "He was very sensitive about everything," said Shiro. "He liked things very neat and clean, even the toilets."[29]

"Once he established Mifune Productions," said long-time friend Tomio Sagisu, "he would clean the bathrooms himself. He would clean the gate. For instance, in the bathrooms the windows would open on both sides; he didn't like it if they weren't opened evenly. He wanted ashtrays in the center of the table. After someone had smoked, he'd pick up the ashtray, empty it, wash it, and immediately put it back in the center of the table. When he invited me to restaurants in Seijo, we'd be given chopsticks wrapped in paper. Everybody would tear open their chopsticks, and Mifune would grab the paper and put it in his pockets to throw away later. He never threw away rubber bands; he had a special box where he saved them. He used scraps of newspapers to write memos. I think all of this was due to his hard experiences during the war. His personality was like that."[30]

Mifune was relieved to finally be able to shoot films on his own lot, rather than rely on Toho or the availability of stages at Takarazuka or Tokyo Eiga. Up until now, *The Legacy of the 500,000* was the only film Mifune had produced that made a profit. The reason for this, Mifune said, was the high distribution rates Toho charged. "Also," Mifune said, "I was charged $700,000 by Toho for making *Samurai Assassin* at their studio. I know it didn't cost that much. It was a big success at the box office, yet I lost money myself."[31]

"The studio isn't big, but it's really functional," Mifune said in a brief article he wrote for *Kinema Jumpo*. "It has the tallest stage of all the Japanese studios, something I'm really proud of. . . . I'm experimenting by producing [*Rebellion*] with a small but great crew. Mifune Productions is coproducing it with Toho and we're responsible for making it within the budget Toho gives us."[32]

In addition to his upcoming film projects, he announced plans to appear in a television film. While films were in steady decline, TV production was soaring, and unlike in America, even the biggest film stars were making the transition. Mifune was no exception. He couldn't afford to be a TV snob, especially when his studio would reap the benefits of the pervasive medium. In 1968 his first starring role came with *Five Masterless Samurai*, a series of six one-hour programs that featured another of Toho's biggest film-stars-turned-TV-actor, Akira Takarada.

With *Rebellion* in preparation, Mifune took time out to appear at the Tokyo premiere of *Grand Prix*, held at the Toho-owned Teikoken Cinerama Theater in Tokyo. Co-stars Jessica Walter and Antonio Sabato, among others, joined Mifune onstage. Partly due to Mifune's much-anticipated role in the epic production, the theater broke advance sales records by the time the film went into its official roadshow release the following day.[33]

Rebellion, meanwhile, provided Mifune with a character he had never played before, a middle-aged family man with adult children, albeit an eighteenth-century samurai, and a henpecked husband at that. His character, Isaburo Sasahara, is an expert swordsman and vassal of Lord Matsudaira (Tatsuo Matsumoto), and as the film opens, he and another vassal, longtime friend Tatewaki Asano (Nakadai), demonstrate their skill, cutting up a scarecrow in the grassy borderlands. It is a time of relative peace, or so it seems.

Matsudaira wants Sasahara to take in one of the lord's former mistresses, Ichi, who bore the lord a son, and have her marry Sasahara's oldest son, Yogoro (Go Kato). Sasahara is not happy about this—he had married a woman (Michiko Otsuka) twenty years earlier for the sake of the clan and has been unhappy ever since. But the lord's request is really a demand, and when he modestly tries to decline, he's reprimanded and the marriage takes place anyway.

However, Ichi (Yoko Tsukasa) turns out to be the ideal wife for Yogoro, and Sasahara couldn't be happier. Ichi, unlike many a lord's mistress, was not the ambitious or jealous troublemaker they had expected. She became a mistress against her wishes; she had a fiancé until the lord decided he wanted her, and the fiancé's family quickly gave her up for the sake of *their* clan. As time passes, Yogoro and Ichi have a child, a little girl named Tomi. Sasahara, happy at last through the bliss of his son and daughter-in-law, decides to retire.

But Matsudaira dies, leaving Ichi's son as heir-apparent. Now it is decided that Ichi, in her new position as mother of the lord's son, cannot remain married to Yogoro, a mere vassal, and she is told to renounce her marriage and return to the castle. This is finally too much to bear. Yogoro and Ichi refuse. Isaburo, too, refuses to give her up. Suga, Sasahara's wife, in allegiance with a younger son, Bunzo (Tatsuyoshi Ehara), pressure Ichi to return. Other leaders within the clan, knowing they, too, will be punished if she's not returned, pressure her also. But Ichi, with Sasahara's backing, will not submit, even if it means the ruination of the family. As Yogoro begins to break down under the strain, Sasahara takes charge. Meanwhile, Suga and Bunzo, working with members of the clan, kidnap Ichi and whisk her to the castle. Tomi, all but abandoned, is given a nursemaid (Etsuko Ichihara) to breast-feed her.

Sasahara has had enough and does something nearly unthinkable. He sends a letter demanding Ichi's return; otherwise, he will expose the lord's tyranny to the Edo government. Instead, Isaburo and Yogoro are ordered to commit suicide. They refuse and prepare for battle. Because of Sasahara's supreme swordplaying skill, Tatewaki urges a peaceful settlement. An offer of confinement in the castle is presented if either Yogoro gives her up or Ichi renounces her marriage. It is refused. Taken to Sasahara's home, Ichi realizes the hopelessness amid all the pretense; she grabs a nearby spear and commits suicide. Sasahara and Yogoro battle the lord's guards, and Yogoro is killed.

Sasahara decides to take Tomi to Edo to expose the corruption. He is stopped at the border by his old friend Tatewaki. They duel, and Tatewaki is killed. Dozens of riflemen gun down Sasahara. The nursemaid, witness to these events, finds Tomi and carries her away.

Rebellion is a companion piece to *Harakiri* in that both films condemn the Tokugawa system with its notions of honor and duty, its pretenses and formalities. At every step Mifune is formally asked to submit to a request that is really a command. Once he and his family have finally found genuine happiness, he tries everything he can to circumvent the feudal tradition against them, but in the end there's simply no way around it. *Harakiri* and *Rebellion* were not the first films to subvert the notion of feudal honor, but Kobayashi's focus and uncompromising vision sharply contrast the kind of *jidai-geki* programmers being cranked out of studios like Toei and Daiei at the time. These and films like *Yojimbo* and *Samurai Assassin* signaled a change in the genre, much as American Westerns were re-examining their foundations in films like *Ride the High Country* (1962), *The Professionals* (1966), and *The Wild Bunch* (1968).

Rebellion is a bleak film, but that is not to say it is without humor or compassion. Carefully balancing out the tragedy, Kobayashi and screen-writer Shinobu Hashimoto show us the genuine if fleeting happiness in the Sasahara family. Ichi's kindness extends even to her cruel mother-in-law; when she becomes head of the household, she refuses to show disrespect to her. Sasahara is a loving grandfather, and these scenes—unfairly criticized as talky—have a genuine humanity and are a contrast to the horrible events to follow. The film, like *Harakiri*, also has moments of brilliant black humor. After Isaburo sends his demands to the castle, Kiku, the nursemaid, arrives to find the Sasahara house ready for battle. When she looks in confusion at the overturned tatami, Sasahara explains, matter-of-factly, it's so they won't slip on all the blood to come.

Later, when Sasahara confronts Tatewaki at the border and they sadly realize they'll have to fight one another, Tatewaki stops to find a comfortable place to put the infant Tomi during the fight. Having found a small patch of open land, he then gently bounces Tomi on his lap before commencing with the duel. He urges Sasahara to lose, for if Tatewaki wins, he promises to raise Tomi himself—better odds than Isaburo and Tomi making it all the way to Edo. For a film as bleak as this, *Rebellion* is also one of surprising tenderness.

Early in the picture, Tatewaki discusses Sasahara's fighting style. He will allow his opponent to push him back, again and again, until finally he lunges forward, which is precisely how he reacts to external pressure in the story. Mifune is extremely good here, making a believable transition from a man who has spent a lifetime toeing the line to a liberated one. Sasahara knows he'll probably die, but he's happy anyway because "for the first time in my life I feel really alive." And Mifune plays him in a determined manner; he's not a samurai seeking vengeance really, he simply refuses to bend any further. There is an unnerving and delicate scene involving Mifune's character: burying his son and daughter-in-law, he holds Tomi over the grave and tells the baby about her dead parents.

Yoko Tsukasa (b. 1934), a beautiful woman rarely used by Toho much beyond window dressing, gives a revelatory performance as the defiant Ichi. While she had appeared in a half dozen films with Mifune, including *All Is Well* (1955), *Samurai Saga* (1959), and *Yojimbo* (1961), this was the only time, outside of her films for Mikio Naruse, she was really given an opportunity to play a fully three-dimensional character. Her expressive eyes display a wide range of emotions, from love to outrage to refusal to be victimized any longer. Sasahara comes to realize that Ichi is stronger than either he or his son. It is ironic that an actress who spent an entire career playing faithful, unquestioning wives should, well after her peak, play one of the strongest, most memorable women in Japanese cinema.

Toru Takemitsu (1930–96), the avant-garde composer as closely linked to Kobayashi as Hayasaka and Sato were to Kurosawa, contributes a haunting score of *biwa* and other traditional Japanese instruments. As in Sato's best work, he uses silence effectively. As Kobayashi said, "The movies I made before I worked with Takemitsu are so full of music. The flow of music tended to become monotonous. But Takemitsu uses music to *slash* the monotony. The way he places the music catches viewers by surprise and makes the director feel, 'How extraordinary! He really brought that scene to life!' "[34]

Particularly surprising is Ichi's attack on Matsudaira's new mistress. Kobayashi cuts a series of swift movements (the lord rising, the ladies-in-waiting rushing out) with freeze frames. There is no dialogue or sound effects, only Takemitsu's music, which uses tempo and style jarringly to counter what is shown onscreen.

The director makes excellent use of high-angle shots, particularly after Ichi and Yogoro are killed in the forecourt, once full of neatly raked sand but now littered with footprints of battle. In these takes, Kobayashi cleverly uses his cast like chess pieces. His tracking, zoom, and telephoto shots are equally well done, and like Takemitsu's music, he uses them sparingly and to great effect.

The film received good reviews in America (where it was also known in some markets as *Samurai Rebellion*), though many critics thought of it as just a better-than-average samurai cut-up. They also mistook Kobayashi's measured pacing as chattiness, an unjust and rather ridiculous complaint.

Variety's "Chie," reviewing the film in Tokyo, said *Rebellion* was "probably . . . the year's best adult Japanese film. . . . [It] represents all the best in the Japanese period film. . . . The film is very talky most of the time. Nothing happens, except talk, for the first hour and 40 minutes, and the screen explodes into the most slashing *chambara* since 'Harakiri.' . . . The film is so absolutely hopeless and is also depressing. . . . The films of Kobayashi never once settle for the sentimental isn't-it-all-too-bad. Instead, the feudal philosophy (still as lively as ever in contemporary Japan) is attacked head-on and if the hero cannot win, then he makes a grand display of his immolation."[35]

H. R. Weiler of *The New York Times* said: "Despite a creakily slow pace and a format that is often close to soap opera, it evolves as a compelling legend by stressing one man's opposition to tyranny in an age when such opposition was unthinkable."[36]

Kevin Thomas called *Rebellion* "Toho's best film this year," while arguing that it "lacks the stark simplicity, the driving tempo of *Harakiri*. . . . The Mondrian-like designs of Japanese architecture and landscapes express the suffocating rigidity of the ritualized existence of the characters. A pluck of the *samisen* punctuates the tension building silently amidst clansman who sit on *tatami* like carved chessmen. . . . [*Rebellion*] stands out in a year when Japanese pictures in general have been way below par."[37]

The British Film Institute agreed, awarding *Rebellion* a prize as "the most original and imaginative film presented at the National Film Theatre during 1967."

After *Rebellion*, Mifune went to work again for Kihachi Okamoto and screenwriter Shinobu Hashimoto, in an ambitious, intriguing film about the final day of the Pacific War, told from inside the collapsing military regime, *The Emperor and a General* (Nippon no ichiban nagai hi, 1967). The film was Toho's most important production of 1967, its thirty-fifth anniversary, but this time there would be none of Eiji Tsuburaya's miniature battleships. The film instead focused on the human drama of Japan's defeat.

Mifune led the all-star cast as the general of the title, Korechika Anami, Minister of the Army, a man who opposes surrender even after the atomic bombs are dropped on Hiroshima and Nagasaki. After a long pre-credits sequence showing the events leading up to *Japan's Longest Day* (the Japanese title), the story opens on August 14, 1945, with Prime Minister Suzuki (Chishu Ryu) receiving the Potsdam Declaration from the Allied Forces proposing Japan's unconditional surrender. Both Suzuki and Foreign Minister Togo (Seiji Miyaguchi) are in favor of accepting its terms. They are opposed by both Anami and Navy Minister Yoneuchi (So Yamamura), who want to fight on, even to the "honorable death of the hundred million," the proposed mass suicide of the Japanese people.

The Emperor, however, opposes the recommendations of Anami and Yoneuchi. He records a message to be broadcast to the Japanese people. A drastic measure on many levels, for by going on the radio and urging Japan's citizens to surrender peacefully, thus ending the war and saving Japan from total destruction, the man regarded as a god by the Japanese people reveals himself as a mere mortal. But the Emperor's own decision fails to sway firebrand members of his government. Dissident Army officers (Toshio Kurosawa [no relation to Akira], Jun Tazaki, Tadao Nakamaru, and Makoto Sato) present a plan to Anami whereby the civilian government would be overthrown and the Emperor isolated from those wanting a peaceful resolution. Anami, however, has a change of heart. He wants to preserve the monarchy and avoid the "honorable death of the hundred million" and will have none of it. Several officers attempt to prevent the broadcast of the Emperor's message anyway, but their efforts to stage a coup fail. The officers are stopped, and Anami commits *seppuku*. As he disembowels himself (graphically—his internal organs steam as they pour from his body), he orders his men to aid in the rebuilding of Japan.

The Emperor and a General won considerable publicity by simply depicting the Emperor himself. Up to that time, no narrative film had ever actually shown a living emperor, and Toho's much-publicized search for the right actor was reported all over the world. The $700,000 film began shooting on March 15, 1967, with the key role yet to be cast.[38] Nearly six weeks into filming, it was announced that the part had been awarded to distinguished Kabuki actor Koshiro Matsumoto (who played Oishi in Inagaki's *Chushingura* and Lord Ii in *Samurai Assassin*).[39] Even so, Matsumoto's face was barely glimpsed onscreen, possibly because the film was carefully scrutinized by the Imperial Household, or because Matsumoto looked almost nothing like the real Hirohito. Nonetheless, the actor was made up on the set, where he stayed until the day's shooting was finished. Toho didn't want Matsumoto walking around the lot dressed as the Emperor. If depicting the Emperor was a publicity stunt, the moment when he tells Japan's leaders to surrender—with many dropping to their knees and bursting into tears—is still extraordinary, both in terms of Okamoto's handling of the scene and for its raw emotion and confessional aspect.

As usual, Toho loaded the picture with practically every man under contract. Yuzo Kayama appeared as the NHK announcer who introduces the Emperor's message. And the cast also included Takashi Shimura, Michiyo Aratama, Takeshi Kato, Yoshio Tsuchiya, Yunosuke Ito, Keiju Kobayashi, Daisuke Kato, and many others.

The film opened on a roadshow basis on August 3, going into general release August 12, right before the anniversary of Japan's defeat. It was well received, placing third on *Kinema Jumpo*'s "Best Ten" list, behind *Rebellion* and Shohei Imamura's *A Man Vanishes* (Ningen johatsu), giving Mifune starring roles in two of the top three films that year, a feat he would not again match.

Reviews in America were mixed. *Variety* complained about the film's length, more than two and a half hours, stating: "Toho has chosen to make a film about an incident which is neither filmic nor epic; the event itself is important but not dramatic; decisions were made through talk, not action, and there is certainly a lot of talk." *Variety*'s "Chie," however, favored its ideology. "This is an 'official' film presenting 'official' history. Though its surface is 'documentary' (a keeping track of minutes worthy of 'Dragnet,' clips of actual newsreels, including some new and horrible material from Hiroshima and Nagasaki, a careful 'emotionless' delivery), the intentions of the film are not. They are nothing less than an elaborate rationale for Japan's having lost the war. This has been needed now for 22 years, and is still as necessary as it was in 1945. A national 'failure' is very hard to live with. [Soichi] Oya [author of the book on which the film is based], Hashimoto, and Okamoto have built up a perfect brief accounting for Japan's surrender. . . . Mifune [lends] enormous dignity in a difficult role."[40]

Kevin Thomas called the film

> a meticulously made 158-minute semi-documentary . . . that is admirably objective as it is ultimately tedious. . . . By the time things pick up with an attempt by a group of fanatic young officers to prevent that record from being played to the nation, boredom has irrevocably set in. The insistence upon being comprehensive when dealing with an occasion of such historic significance is to be applauded, but the fact remains that there were numerous opportunities and ways in which both script and direction could have been considerably more economical—thus heightening suspense and impact—without sacrificing authenticity. If "The Emperor and a General" is disappointing as a whole, it is still a picture of outstanding parts. . . . Also, it has uniformly strong performances, notably Toshiro Mifune. . . . It is effective, too, in showing the need of men to rely upon ritual and ceremony to give their actions meaning in a time of chaos. But most important, it shows how difficult it is to get soldiers who have been whipped into a state of nationalistic frenzy to lay down their arms abruptly.[41]

Meanwhile, *Hell in the Pacific* was finally beginning to come together. Marvin was tied to director John Boorman, who had just directed the actor in the violent cult film *Point Blank* (1967). Marvin brought Boorman into the project, much against Saperstein's wishes. He wanted Robert Altman, but Selmur would have opposed this: Altman had been fired from *Combat*.

Boorman had spent the war years in a British boarding school, years he later recalled in his autobiographical film *Hope and Glory* (1987). After a stint as head of the BBC's documentary division, he made his film debut with *Catch Us If You Can* (a.k.a. *Having a Wild Weekend*, 1965), starring the

English pop band the Dave Clark Five. He then returned to television, making a documentary about D. W. Griffith before his second film, *Point Blank*, launched his career and he was recognized as a major new talent. Boorman was attracted to the proposed film's subject matter, thinking of it as an opportunity to play "a trick on the movie industry by making a silent film—or, at least, seeing if I could."[42]

But Boorman's own ideas for the film soon clashed with Saperstein's. "Bill Ludwig's script was good enough to get Mifune, Toho, and Lee Marvin and ABC's money into it," Saperstein insisted. "Boorman immediately brings his own guy over from England and they rewrite the script together and emasculate it."[43]

That fall it was also announced that screenwriter Shinobu Hashimoto had been "engaged to function as script consultant" on *Hell in the Pacific*.[44] But Boorman, who had already described his work on the script with co-writer Eric Bercovici as a "rather uneasy collaboration," was surprised that Hashimoto wanted to do more than provide the dialogue and details for Mifune's character. "[He] came to me with a proposal for a different version of the story and requested a week to write it. When he presented it to me, I realized that he'd turned it into a comedy in the style of *Yojimbo*. He'd treated everything farcically. It wasn't bad in itself, but it bore no relation to what I wanted. So we continued working on the script and shooting began."[45]

Filming didn't get under way until January 1968, some nineteen months after Mifune first signed on to the film, then took four months to shoot. The script still wasn't ready, and rather than shoot in Hawaii or some other relatively convenient locale, it was decided to film most of *Hell in the Pacific* on the remote Micronesian island of Koror. According to Saperstein, "Boorman didn't want to shoot in Hawaii. He wanted to go 'authentic,' to where the Japanese and Americans actually were. So he picks . . . Palau, where we have to bring our own drinking water and food for the 90-to-120-day shoot. We had to bring *everything*. When you look at the film today, in terms of the physical nature of the location, it could have been done on Catalina Island [near Los Angeles]."[46]

> Mifune immediately created dreadful problems [Boorman recalled]. He was very proud of what he had prepared, but he invariably missed the point of the scenes he was playing. I'd have a word with him and advise him, but he'd make the same mistakes all over again. After three or four days, I realized that Hashimoto had given him

the script which I'd rejected. . . . I wanted to go much further in the scenes where they retrogress, where they begin to behave like animals, but I couldn't persuade Mifune to do it. He believed he was defending the honor of Japan. Just as Marvin wanted to relive his personal experiences, so Mifune wanted to relive the war—with Japan on the winning side. He refused to do anything that might have been considered uncouth; he was determined to retain his honor. In a way, he was right: in that kind of situation, the Japanese are probably far more resourceful and far less likely to go to pieces.[47]

Though Mifune didn't care for his director, he bonded with Lee Marvin as no foreign actor before or since, and they remained friends until Marvin's death. At a Mifune retrospective in 1984, Marvin commended Mifune for his "ultimate professionalism" when the two were accidentally swept out to sea during a take—Mifune had the foresight to carry with him a waterproof pack of cigarettes.[48] Together the two real-life war veterans visited the site of a fierce battle on nearby Peleliu and placed floral wreaths at its memorial.[49]

Saperstein fondly recalled the bonding of the two actors. "Every night after dinner, Lee Marvin—and this is what finally killed him—drank a fifth of Cutty Sark. Every night Mifune, to match him in a challenge, drank a magnum of sake. They both went to bed every night stone drunk; they both were up and on the set every morning at seven, fresh as a daisy, perfect in their lines, and ready to go. You never saw two more consummate professionals work together as they did."[50] When the picture opened in America, Mifune joked that he and Marvin would make another film together called "Wild, Heavy Drinkers."[51]

Mifune's relationship with Boorman was another story. During his first starring role in an American film (he was, at best, a supporting player in *Grand Prix*), Mifune and the director were constantly at odds. "I'd rehearse with him until five in the morning to persuade him to perform one little piece of business," Boorman said. "By the end, he had accepted my arguments. Then, on the set, he would revert to his original idea and would refuse to be budged. Despite his unconditional acceptance of my ideas, he was capable of undoing a whole night's work. And he simply would not give way. But when I was hospitalized during the shoot, and the producers considered engaging another director, Mifune announced that he would refuse to continue the film with someone else."[52]

An article by Wayne Warga in the *Los Angeles Times* reported: "According to several survivors of the location, Mifune candidly informed the director that he was temperamental, unprofessional and would be better off staying in England and making home movies." One unconfirmed report said Mifune became so frustrated he threatened Boorman with a rifle.

But Mifune said, "It wasn't a fight, it was a discussion among creative people, differences about how best to make this film. . . . When I raised my voice—and that's a privilege I have as an actor in my country, and I assure you I use it—it was never toward Lee. Tension between an actor and a director is quite natural; so is it between a director and a producer. In the end, we collaborated."[53]

Of Mifune's conflicts with Boorman Lee Marvin said, "Mifune is beyond professionalism, he's even better than that. What he did off the set was his own business, and I won't discuss that. I admire his talent and abilities tremendously. . . . Let's just say Mifune was displeased and that we were all fed up with living on a ship [a Liberian freighter with a Chinese crew, called *The Oriental*]. . . . Mifune had his troubles with the director, too. I kept out of that. . . . Look, it was a joining together of Occidental and Oriental philosophies which, like in the movie, didn't work out too well. . . . The problems never got resolved, we just kept shooting . . . [but] Mifune, as an actor, is even greater than I had dreamed. You've got to be consumed with your art to do what he did."[54]

In the finished picture, the story is very simple, indeed one far too thin to justify its 103-minute running time. After ditching his plane, Marvin finds himself stranded on a tiny island in the South Pacific. Realizing the island is already occupied by a Japanese soldier, Mifune, he tries to reach the latter's water supply to stay alive. Both live in fear of the other, but neither can bring himself to actually kill his wartime enemy. When Mifune captures Marvin, he ties him up, and the American soldier is seen dragging a giant piece of wood along the beach as the Japanese soldier ponders what to do with him. Marvin escapes and captures Mifune, and the overly symbolic dehumanization starts all over again. Eventually, the two form an uneasy alliance and together build a raft. After many days they reach an island and find a bombed-out base, occupied in turn by Japanese and American forces. Their tenuous friendship is eventually shattered when memories of the war (a *Life* magazine with photographs of dead Japanese soldiers) renew their basic hatred of each other. In the end, they simply walk off, presumably to rejoin their respective armies.

"The film is about two men who were enemies not by choice but by circumstance," Mifune said. "And maybe some of that tension worked on everyone else. The point of the picture is that it is useless for individuals to fight. It was not a statement about World War II; it was a statement about any war anywhere."[55]

As *Hell in the Pacific* wrapped, it received more bad press from a battle over its title, of all things. "The distributor liked the title," argued Selig Seligman, president of Selmur, "because they felt it would bring in conventional audiences. They were afraid an arty title would chase people away. And they were willing to count on word of mouth to help. . . . We stuck with 'Hell in the Pacific' because we want the public to feel it's an action Lee Marvin picture [sic]. From this point of view, the title is right for its misleading quality." Marvin himself countered, "The title is awful." Boorman wanted to call it "The Enemy."[56]

Seligman won out in the end, and producer Henry Saperstein, who had fought with Boorman nearly as intensely as Mifune had, got his revenge. For the American release, he changed the movie's ending. Rather than have Mifune and Marvin simply walk away, during the final moments of their heated argument, Saperstein abruptly inserted stock footage of a bunker exploding—KA-BOOM!—making it appear that a bomb had killed them both. Boorman cried foul; he wasn't even aware of the change until he learned about it in London the following spring. While the director conceded "that contractually he did not have final editing control, [he] contend[ed] he was to be consulted on any changes," and argued that Saperstein's tampering "damaged the picture."[57]

Admittedly, Saperstein's ending is worse, but really, neither conclusion was particularly effective. In the final analysis, *Hell in the Pacific* is a failure, but an interesting one. By sticking so steadfastly to its own gimmick, the script strains credibility. In an effort to maintain some level of universality, for example, we never learn the men's names (they are billed simply as "American Soldier" and "Japanese Soldier"), nor do they make any attempt to learn a single word of the other's language, which just isn't believable. The film starts out well, with Marvin and Mifune discovering each other, and Marvin trying to stay alive, but the middle third of the film is a pretentious mess. Mifune comes off as rather less human than Marvin—no wonder he was in constant battle with Boorman. The picture's *Lord of the Flies*–like attempt to show the regression of its marooned characters into animalistic brutality is constantly undermined by weak stabs at humor, such as Marvin's tiresome and unfunny efforts to have Mifune fetch a stick, dog-style. The film works best when they finally begin working together, and

the scenes aboard the raft are well directed. But the script, quite unbelievably, does not show them demonstrating the slightest curiosity about the
other. Once they reach the bombed-out base and old prejudices bubble to
the surface, the film's artifice is woefully apparent, with Marvin booming
ridiculous dialogue at Mifune ("How come you guys don't believe in
God!?") that is as strained as it is inexplicable, even in a scene where Marvin's character is drunk.

Mifune and Marvin both give sincere and emotionally charged performances, although Marvin's lines are quite bad and Mifune's character is little more than the clichéd Japanese soldier he was trying so earnestly to
avoid. Both are pigheaded and intractable to the point of stopping the film
dead in its tracks. In the end, Boorman and screenwriters Alexander Jacobs
and Eric Bercovici achieved universality at the expense of character and be-
lievability. Boorman, as his work often reflects, chose to ignore these problems, focusing instead on the locale-as-character, the one aspect of the
picture that works well, an antecedent to some of his more successful future films, such as *Deliverance* (1972) and, to a lesser extent, *The Emerald
Forest* (1985). He is helped enormously by Conrad Hall's cinematography,
which is simply marvelous. Hall takes full advantage of the island setting to
create an atmosphere of otherworldly beauty and mystery. Lalo Schifrin's
score, influenced at times by Jerry Goldsmith's unconventional music for
Planet of the Apes (1968), is likewise atmospheric but often obtrusive and
obvious.

Variety's "Murf" nailed the film's faults and attributes:

> The title is a liability, suggesting the very type of film this isn't.
> . . . The desired mood certainly is established and maintained. . . .
> Conrad Hall's terrific Panavision-Technicolor lensing repeatedly
> captures the atmosphere. . . . [But] Mifune's unrestrained grunting
> and running about creates an outdated caricature of an Oriental.
> Marvin, when he finally starts talking, has sardonic lines which
> resemble wise-cracks, intended for onlookers. The subtle humor
> which was meant to exist in the early confrontation becomes over-
> powering and heavy-handed. . . . Net effect [of Schifrin's score] is
> the impression that there have got to be 50 musicians lurking just
> off-camera, and, when Marvin delivers his flip lines, he's talking to
> them, not Mifune. . . . Mifune gets few chances to project three-
> dimensional characterization, though flashes are there. . . . Running
> time evaluation is a dilemma: without the continual restoration of

mood (shattered repeatedly by incidents), film would have fallen apart in its first hour; yet, with the length, the dramatic flaws are made more manifest.[58]

But *Newsweek* thought *Hell in the Pacific* had achieved exactly what it set out to do. "Director John Boorman . . . has skillfully resolved the problems posed by a two-character film in which the principals cannot talk to each other—only at each other. By treating language as so many anguished animal noises, he leaves his two fine actors to convey with the changing topography of their faces the steady hysteria of men cast together without the comfort of mutual trust. . . . They are, to the very end, ordinary, rather mean-minded and ignorant representatives of the human race, capable of generosity only when they have nothing to lose. . . . Nationalism and racial enmity, Boorman is saying, can destroy even relationships built on the most intense interpersonal experience."[59]

Playboy was less impressed: "The message implied hardly requires heavy italicizing, and director John Boorman, for the most part, lets human conflicts unfold in an almost casual manner. . . . Marvin and Mifune exude enough juicy vitality to animate a script that has only slight perception of character and very little dialogue. . . . But instead of a touch of genius that might have resulted in a great film, *Pacific* has a touch of contrivance—as well as a pounding, obtrusive musical score—that pegs it as a solid popular melodrama performed with a high level of competence."[60]

Arthur Knight, calling *Hell in the Pacific* a "stunt film," said: "The arbitrary, artificial restrictions placed upon the motion picture camera militated against the ultimate effectiveness of the movie. . . . Perhaps the implication here is that war reduces men to a brutish animality, but by this time the film might just as well be saying that thirst and hunger turn men into savages. . . . Unfortunately, by presenting a multitude of moral and ethical imponderables, presumably in an attempt at profundity, the picture takes on the quality of parable that never quite makes its point. Its two characters, although presented as men acting on an instinct for self-survival, actually seem more at the mercy of their writer than of their fate."[61]

To qualify for Academy Award consideration, *Hell in the Pacific* opened for one week in Los Angeles, beginning on December 18, 1968.[62] Despite heavy promotion in the trades, the picture failed to win a single nomination. Mifune spent most of the month tub-thumping the picture with his co-star. He flew to Los Angeles on December 11, and then both he and

Marvin flew to New York for press junkets. This was followed by a special screening of the film on December 16 in Los Angeles. Marvin and Mifune also flew to Tokyo for the film's premiere in Japan.[63] While in Southern California, Mifune shopped for camera equipment in Beverly Hills, toured Panavision's facilities, and was the guest of honor at a dinner hosted by Kenneth Hyman of Warner Bros.–Seven Arts. After Ted Richmond's efforts the previous year, Hyman was still trying to sign the actor to appear in their "Eastern Western" called *Red Sun*, which he also asked Mifune to direct. After his experience on *The Legacy of the 500,000*, though, Mifune wasn't eager to go behind the camera again. Sam Peckinpah was mentioned as another possible choice to helm the picture.[64]

Incredibly, *Hell in the Pacific* cost $4.2 million to make, plus another $2 million in prints, advertising, and bank loan interest costs. Mifune's three other 1968 releases had all been large-scale pictures with extensive casts, but *Hell in the Pacific*, essentially about two guys on an island, cost more than the other three pictures combined. The film did mediocre business in America, earning $1.3 million in United States and Canadian rentals, but it did well overseas, adding another $1.9 million. Yet once distribution fees and other costs were taken into account, *Hell in the Pacific* proved to be a colossal bomb, and the film lost more than $4 million.[65]

After shooting had finished on *Hell in the Pacific*, but prior to its release in December 1968, Mifune starred as *Admiral Yamamoto* (Kantai shireichokan—Yamamoto Isoroku, 1968). Essentially a remake of the Ishiro Honda–Eiji Tsuburaya biopic of the naval hero, *Eagle of the Pacific* (1953), *Admiral Yamamoto* was yet another special effects–filled *senso eiga* (war movie), this time with more personal drama, though not much. Directed by *Kiska's* Seiji Maruyama and scripted by Maruyama and Katsuya Suzaki, the film mirrors *Eagle of the Pacific's* biographical approach, adding little more than splashy color and wide-screen images. What looked like an epic was also deceptively cheap. To save money, Toho insisted that Tsuburaya use stock footage from earlier glories: when Yamamoto's forces attack Pearl Harbor, the special effects are lifted from *Storm Over the Pacific*; footage from several other pictures, including the Mifune-starrer *Attack Squadron!*, was also used. This is readily apparent when one watches the picture as the color shifts noticeably between the new and old film, while many of the scenes shot for *Admiral Yamamoto*, with its actors crammed on small sets against obviously painted backdrops, further displayed Toho's waning resources.

As in *Eagle of the Pacific*, *Admiral Yamamoto* opens with the Tripartite Military Alliance between Germany, Italy, and Japan. Even though he is anti-Axis, Yamamoto (Mifune), Vice Minister of the Navy, is appointed Commander in Chief of the Combined Fleet of the Imperial Naval Force.

Yamamoto believes that the only way for Japan to win such a global conflict is to strike an overwhelming blow in the first days of the war. The attack on Pearl Harbor is set into motion. The sneak attack appears to be a glorious victory to everyone but the admiral, who realizes that, having failed to sink America's fleet of aircraft carriers, Japan is already doomed. A week later, Yamamoto takes command of the *Yamato*, the 70,000-ton pride of the Japanese Navy. After a task force commanded by Admiral Doolittle begins to bomb Japan from the aircraft carrier *Hornet*, Yamamoto's Navy suffers a stunning defeat at the Battle of Midway, in which four Japanese aircraft carriers, including the *Akagi* (the ship at the center of *Storm Over the Pacific*) are sunk.

American forces reach Guadalcanal, cutting off resources Japan cannot do without. As Yamamoto had predicted, the war is being lost. Setting up a base in Rabaul, he oversees the evacuation of 12,000 troops. Then, on April 18, 1943, Yamamoto boards a bomber, escorted by six Japanese Zeroes. But a Japanese telegram has been intercepted and Allied planes are ready for him. Flying over Bougainville Island, Yamamoto's plane is fatally damaged, and the admiral, ready to die, can only sit helplessly as the aircraft crashes.

This last sequence is well directed by Eiji Tsuburaya and his special-effects crew. A helpless squadron of Zeroes escorts Yamamoto's plane until seconds before the crash, which occurs behind tall trees and out of view. Maruyama, filming Yamamoto aware that his death is imminent, gives the scene a certain poetry. Although shot in the shoulder, Mifune is stone-faced as the plane goes down. Otherwise, the film plays more like a highlight reel of famous naval battles than an intimate portrait of this complex, Western-educated man, and Toho's English-language synopsis is nothing more than a summary of his career. Mifune himself is hardly more than a prop moved from battle to battle, allowed to offer little expression of Yamamoto's conundrums and inner agonies. There are few glimpses of the private man, merely endless military conferences with the all-star cast.

As Kevin Thomas wrote in the *Los Angeles Times*: "Except for a few notable exceptions since [*Red Beard*] Mifune has been wasting his formidable talent and presence on mediocre ventures such as this. . . . [Yamamoto] is the kind of military man Mifune has played numerous times before. He is tortured by his knowledge of war's folly, but [his] loyalty to the emperor is unshakable. . . . [Maruyama and his screenwriter have] done a solid job but one that is hardly imaginative, and their tossing in of a love interest via a young lieutenant [Toshio Kurosawa] and his girl back home [Wakako Sakai] is a ploy as gratuitous as it is old-fashioned."[66]

Mifune wasn't in Japan when *Admiral Yamamoto* opened. He was in America, at a reception given in his honor at the Beverly Hills Hotel. There he was reunited with his *Hell in the Pacific* co-star, who flew down from the Oregon location for *Paint Your Wagon* just to see him. Clint Eastwood was on hand, as well, and there was apparently no tension over his part in the *Yojimbo*-inspired *A Fistful of Dollars*: Mifune claimed never to have seen any of the Western adaptations of the Mifune-Kurosawa films. *Hell*'s co-producer, Reuben Bercovitch, and even John Boorman paid tribute to Mifune, as well as Warner–Seven Arts producer Ted Richmond, who was still trying to get Mifune to do *Red Sun* for his company.

Despite *Admiral Yamamoto*'s failure to enlighten audiences about the man behind the Pearl Harbor attack, Mifune would go on to play the naval hero several more times in the next few years. "Almost half the 100 pictures I've made in the past twenty-two years have been war movies," Mifune once admitted, while simultaneously arguing the value of these films. "It's important that we make such movies. Most of the war themes demonstrate the uselessness of battle, and the others show the comic aspects."[67] Yamamoto remains one of the most fascinating and durably popular characters in Japanese culture. In 1995, on the fiftieth anniversary of Japan's defeat, a massive, speculative novel was published titled *Deep Blue Fleet*, in which Yamamoto doesn't die in a plane crash but instead goes on to capture Hawaii, grants it independence from the United States, blows up the Panama Canal, then leads Japan's fight against Hitler. The eight-volume novel was a bestseller; three million copies were sold soon after its publication.[68]

Now that Mifune had played Japan's biggest World War II hero, it was only natural that he would portray their biggest naval hero of the Russo-Japanese War—Admiral Heihachiro Togo, Commander in Chief of the Combined Fleet—in *Battle of the Japan Sea* (Nihonkai Daikaisen, 1969), a film released almost one year to the day after *Admiral Yamamoto*. After the Boxer Rebellion, Russia and Japan were at odds over Korea. Using older, outdated vessels, Admiral Togo (Mifune) sends Commander Hirose (Yuzo Kayama) to block the Russian Asiatic Fleet at Port Arthur. Army General Nogi (Chishu Ryu) begins an assault on Port Arthur as well, but the Russian military, using superior weaponry and outnumbering the Japanese troops, strikes a crippling blow. The Baltic Fleet leaves Port Libau on October 20, 1904. Togo is certain that Russian ships are headed for the Japan

Sea. Then, on May 27, 1905, in a shocking victory by the Japanese, Togo uses a maneuver that has become known as the "Togo Turn," devastating the Russian fleet, destroying all but two Russian destroyers and a converted cruiser. Togo's fleet loses just three destroyers. Japan's naval prowess is suddenly recognized as the mightiest in the Pacific and leads to Japan being recognized as a world power by the West.

Once again Mifune, this time sporting a white goatee and graying temples, plays second fiddle to Eiji Tsuburaya's miniature battleships, in what was to be a last hurrah for the genre. Although the Japanese film industry was now in rapid decline, Toho poured money into the picture's effects as they never had before, resulting in visuals rivaled only by *The War at Sea from Hawaii to Malaya* (1942) and *Storm Over the Pacific* (1960). Mifune, though, has little to do.

What praise the film got went to its special effects and to a subplot involving Tatsuya Nakadai as a Paris- and Stockholm-based diplomat who buys military secrets from the Bolsheviks, who use the money from the Japanese to finance the Russian Revolution. The cast, as in all of Toho's war movies, is overflowing with talent. Besides Chishu Ryu and Tatsuya Nakadai, it included such weighty names as Koshiro Matsumoto (playing another Japanese Emperor), Yoshio Inaba from *Seven Samurai*, Susumu Fujita, Yoshio Tsuchiya, Takeshi Kato, and many others.

By the time *Battle of the Japan Sea* reached American shores, Eiji Tsuburaya was dead. "Mr. Tsuburaya died in January 1970," his assistant director, Teruyoshi Nakano, recalled. "He had seemed very tired of late. I think the most difficult time for him was during the production of *Battle of the Japan Sea*. Mr. Tsuburaya was going back and forth between Toho and [his own company] Tsuburaya Productions. He was so busy. He was also handling a big special exhibit for Mitsubishi at Expo 1970 in Osaka. In the middle of everything, he passed away."[69]

The United States did not know about Tsuburaya's death when the picture opened. Kevin Thomas compared *Battle of the Japan Sea*'s "David and Goliath appeal" to the just released *Battle of Britain*: "The enjoyment of this particular blockbuster is dependent specifically on one's knowledge and interest in the Russo-Japanese War and in general upon one's attitude toward the traditional war picture. Those who find such pictures anachronistic in the extreme will regard 'Battle of the Japan Sea' as meticulous a period recreation as it is irrelevant and dull dramatically. . . . The naval battles are quite impressive, there are lots of maps and unusually adequate titles to keep track of intricate logistics and there are a number of scenes of stiff-upper-lipped sentimentality designed to show us what swell guys there were on both sides." Thomas also found the subplot with Nakadai of more interest than Mifune's usual posturing.[70]

Dale Munroe, like Thomas, noticed a certain irony lost in the adaptation of the story, noting that "the Japanese fought the Russians for failing to withdraw from Manchuria following the Boxer Rebellion, yet years later Japan herself invaded Manchuria, giving Russia her opportunity to even old scores. [Nevertheless] a few pertinent facts are clearly illustrated, i.e., the behind-the-scenes wheeling and dealing between the Japanese government and the Bolsheviks. . . . Director Seiji Maruyama and screenwriter Toshio Yasumi are to be credited with bringing to the screen an intelligent, articulate, textbook-style war film. Eiji Tsuburaya's special effects and Hiroshi Murai's cinematography combine to overshadow most of the film's slow spots. Also, *Battle* is exceptionally well-cast; Toshiro Mifune [delivers] another distinguished performance."[71]

Between wars, Mifune put in an appearance in *The Day the Sun Rose* (Gion matsuri, 1968), an epic, all star, historical drama/action film produced independently and released by Shochiku, a studio he hadn't worked with since *The Idiot* in 1951. The film began shooting with director Daisuke Ito (1898–1981), but when he fell ill the picture was taken over by his chief assistant, Tetsuya Yamanouchi (b. 1934), who received a co-director on the finished product. Yamanouchi had a minor career in Japanese films, though he did direct a lively fantasy film for Toei called *The Magic Serpent* (Kai tatsu daikessen, 1966), a children's movie that was a cross between a breathlessly paced Hong Kong period film and a Japanese monster movie, with a plot similar to that of *Star Wars*.

Set in the midst of a sixteenth-century civil war, *The Day the Sun Rose* tells the story of a modest cloth dyer (Kinnosuke Nakamura) who is galvanized by memories of the Kyoto Gion festivals, which were banned at the time. The dyer's memories are stirred by a flute-playing outcast (beautiful Shima Iwashita), and this inspires him to try to unite the various warring factions of farmers, bandits, and laborers and revive the festival. In the course of the nearly three-hour film, Mifune pops up as the leader of the bandits, in a role apparently patterned after his *Yojimbo* character.

The film was a tremendous hit in Japan. Despite this, it has never been released on home video there, possibly due to legal complications arising from its independent status. "While [it] is thoroughly wooden in its acting, staging of crowd scenes, and dialogue," wrote *Cue*, which reviewed a reissue version cut to 123 minutes, "the material with which it deals has interest, at least what we can get through the subtitles. . . . Basically a historical potboiler . . . it does not even resemble a work to be taken seriously."[72]

But Kevin Thomas found the picture "a traditional Japanese period film in its most pristine form—a form that is sadly on the wane. It has the usual cast of thousands, gallons of spilled blood, and miles of gorgeous scenery. At its best, as in this instance, the Japanese period picture becomes in a true sense an epic. . . . It has the dash and vigor to sustain its nearly three-hour length and has glorious battle sequences contrasted with scenes of sublime pastoral splendor in muted color. As for wrestling beauty and bloodshed, Ito was doing that when Arthur Penn was still in knee pants."[73]

Mifune's production company expanded to include a one-hour weekly television series, produced at his Trissen Studios. "The studio is small, one soundstage," Mifune said in January 1969, "but our pictures are big. When a feature goes into production, we send the television series on location to keep it fresh." He continued his one-man campaign to salvage the flagging Japanese film industry, telling *The Hollywood Reporter*'s John Mahoney, "The five major companies . . . have diversified their activities to include bowling alleys, hotels, TV production units, studio facility rentals, theater operation, vast entertainment complexes. As a result, they have become so busy just turning out product to fill their theaters that quality has too frequently lost priority." He added that the studios were neither aggressive nor savvy enough, while distributors like Toho's international division were content with maintaining a regular audience through films like their *Shacho* comedies and failing to hold on to the non-Japanese market that had been established in the 1950s.[74]

As Mifune tried to balance his career between television work, Toho-produced films, those he developed with his own company, and appearances in international productions, other stars like Yujiro Ishihara, Mifune's partner in Trissen Studios, focused their energies on producing and starring in Japanese films specifically with the foreign market in mind. Of course, Mifune had earlier criticized such productions, but in 1968 and 1969 he would join forces with Ishihara on what would be Japan's highest-grossing domestic films of those years, *Tunnel to the Sun* (Kurobe no taiyo, 1968) and *Safari 5000* (Eiko e no 5,000 kiro, 1969).

Tunnel to the Sun was a three-hour, sixteen-minute epic, filmed in a semidocumentary style, based on the true story of the building of a massive tunnel deep in the Japan Alps. The tunnel was needed to move materials in the construction of the Kurobe Dam, the second-largest in the world. It was a massive and dangerous project. Nippon Eiga Shinsha had released three feature-length documentaries about the tunnel's construction be-tween 1958 and 1962. In *Tunnel to the Sun*, Mifune stars as Kitagawa, the engineer put in charge of building the passageway. The tunnel needs to run directly through a fault line, and the risk of cave-ins and flooding is great.

And that's exactly what happens. The two thousand workers face all manner of hazards. Several die as the result of floods and cave-ins, setting up a conflict between the diggers and their supervisors, and all work under Sword of Damocles–like pressure. The conflict between the two groups is exemplified by the relationship between engineer Iwaoka (Yujiro Ishihara) and his father (Ryutaro Tatsumi), who leads the workers' union.

Kitagawa's determination is linked to his daughter, a young girl dying of leukemia. If Kitagawa is helpless in his daughter's medical crisis, then he'll drill a tunnel through an impassable mountain. Iwaoka falls in love with Kitagawa's older daughter, and the two marry. After three years, the tunnel is finally completed. As the workers celebrate, Kitagawa receives a tele-gram that his younger daughter has died.

Tunnel to the Sun was helmed by Kei Kumai, who would direct Mifune in three more films spread out over nearly thirty years. Born in 1930, Kumai worked at Nikkatsu beginning in 1954 and made his directorial debut with *The Long Death* (Teigin jiken—shikeishu, 1964). But it was his second film, *The Japanese Archipelago* (Nihon Retto, 1965), that brought him mainstream attention. The thirty-five-year-old's film received rave reviews, ranking third on *Kinema Jumpo*'s "Best Ten" list behind *Red Beard* and *Tokyo Olympiad*. As Joseph Anderson and Donald Richie note, Kumai's odd, Ping-Pong ca-reer has shifted back and forth between deeply felt, philosophical films like *Long Darkness* (Shinobugawa, 1972), *Sandakan 8* (Sandakan hachiban shokan—Bokyo, 1975), and *Deep River* (Fukai kawa, 1995) and notably less ambitious, more mainstream films like *An Ocean to Cross* (Tempyo no Iraka, 1979). With its mix of spectacle and humanist drama, *Tunnel to the Sun* falls somewhere in the middle; it was well received by Japanese critics and placed fourth on *Kinema Jumpo*'s list of the year's best.

For some reason *Tunnel to the Sun* is rarely revived and, like *The Day the Sun Rose*, has never been released to home video in Japan, despite its great box office and the enduring popularity of Mifune and Ishihara.

The picture cost more than $1 million, making it one of the most ex-pensive Japanese films to date, but when Nikkatsu released it in March 1968, it became the highest-grossing domestic film that year, earning $5 million domestically.[75] Because Nikkatsu owned no theaters in the United States, Toho International handled the American release that fall.

The *Hollywood Citizen-News* was amused that Mifune had moved "from sword to pneumatic drill," but their critic, David Sutherland, didn't like the subplot about Mifune's daughter: "It is at this point that Masato Ide's screenplay takes on some trite philosophical overtones. Mifune desperately asks a rival company's president for much needed power drills. He boldly states that nature (the mountain) can be defeated with brains, money (for equipment), and time. His adversary retorts, 'What about cancer?' . . . 'Tunnel to the Sun' is highlighted by picturesque color photography and by another superb Mifune performance. However, it runs an hour too long and is lacking the intricate-suspenseful plot development which is so characteristic of Japanese cinema."[76]

On the other hand, Kevin Thomas thought it "one of the year's best Japanese pictures. . . . It is a thoroughly satisfying traditional-style drama starring Toshiro Mifune in the best role he's had in a long time." And although he found *Tunnel to the Sun*'s trappings "a familiar source of suspense," overall he found the 198-minute blockbuster "engrossing nonetheless. . . . The film's theme, embodied by Mifune, is that accomplishing the difficult, dangerous task is never more important than the life of the least important laborer. On the other hand, this movie reminds us how rewarding it is for people to commit themselves to undertakings which they consider larger than themselves. For all its considerable suspense, action, and spectacle 'Tunnel to the Sun' is fundamentally a tribute to human dignity."[77]

Japanese critics also welcomed Mifune's return, temporary though it might be, to better, more ambitious projects. *Kinema Jumpo* awarded him Best Actor of 1968 for his work in *Admiral Yamamoto*, *The Day the Sun Rose*, and *Tunnel to the Sun*.

Safari 5000, by contrast, was an international car-racing movie, recalling Ishihara's appearance in the English-language comedy *Those Magnificent Men in Their Flying Machines* (1965), its many subsequent imitators, and, to a lesser extent, *Grand Prix*. Covering the Safari Rally, filmed on location in Europe and Africa, it featured not only Ishihara, Mifune, Tatsuya Nakadai, and Ruriko Asaoka, but also Emmanuele Riva of *Hiroshima mon amour* and Jean-Claude Drouot of *Laughter in the Dark*.

It too cost $1 million, outrageously expensive for a Japanese film but modest compared to films like *Those Magnificent Men in Their Flying Machines*, which cost ten times that. By now there was a glut of splashy, all-star epics, but the novelty of *Safari 5000* made it a hit in Japan if nowhere else. Popular as it was, *Safari 5000* has all but vanished since its release in Japan and was never distributed in the United States.

Mifune also spent much of 1969 returning to the *jidai-geki* and *chambara* genre, appearing in no fewer than three such films. Prior to *Safari 5000*'s release, he starred in what would be director Hiroshi Inagaki's last important film, *Samurai Banners* (Furin kazan, 1969).

A *jidai-geki* densely packed with historical events (aided by numerous animated maps and title cards), *Samurai Banners* is the fictionalized account of Kansuke Yamamoto (Mifune), a brilliant if ruthless and ambitious strategist who finds employment as the most trusted vassal of warlord Shingen Takeda (Kinnosuke Nakamura) in the mid-sixteenth century. Despite blood ties, Yamamoto engineers, like Iago, the fall of an adjacent domain headed by Lord Suwa (Akihiko Hirata). Suwa is married to Takeda's sister. Yamamoto initiates a peace treaty between the two kingdoms, then convinces Takeda to have Suwa murdered. When Yamamoto assumes control of Suwa's castle, he finds Suwa's samurai dead, having committed *seppuku*. Suwa's strong-willed daughter, Princess Yu (Yoshiko Sakuma), refuses to join them in death. Takeda makes her his concubine, though Yamamoto would (unrealistically, given his position) like her for himself. She bears Takeda a son, setting the film's strongest asset—Yamamoto's relationship with Takeda's family—into motion. Yamamoto has fallen in love with Princess Yu and sees the infant prince as the product of his own engineering, through battle and his devotion to her.

As Yamamoto's power continues to grow, he realizes that Takeda's three offspring by his wife (Yoshiko Kuga) are more likely to inherit the warlord's domain than his son by Princess Yu. Yamamoto is torn between his desire to see his "son" rule and his loyalty to and friendship with Takeda. Yu longs to kill Takeda, the man who had her father assassinated, yet she also wants to love Takeda, because he is the father of her child. She also has her own emerging conflicted feelings for Yamamoto.

This royal triangle is played out against spectacular battle scenes: Yamamoto's military savvy results in thirty years of victories. Yamamoto and, to a lesser extent, Takeda want to expand the domain from the east to the west coast of Japan. The triangle is broken when the princess succumbs after an illness and Yamamoto makes a tragic blunder at the Battle of Kawanakajima. Feeling responsible, he leads a desperate charge that saves Takeda's army, but at the cost of his own life.

Like many of Mifune's samurai films from the late 1960s and early '70s, *Samurai Banners* is so dripping in historical events as to limit its appeal— and, at times, its comprehension—to audiences outside Japan. Yet as Donald Richie wrote in *The Japanese Film—Art and Industry*, *Samurai Banners* "is one of the finest of period-pictures, as well as the last authentic example of that genre. Despite its moderate success, Inagaki found himself unable to work after that. [This is not entirely true: Inagaki would go on to produce *The Ambitious* and direct *The Ambush: Incident at Blood Pass*, though his career was virtually over by the following year.] He was considered too old by the new producers, all of whom were much younger, and he had never culti-vated a major philosophical overlook—as had Kurosawa—that could lend his *oeuvre* the destiny that invites critical and scholarly attention."[78]

Richie is correct in stating that *Samurai Banners* symbolized the end of a *jidai-geki* genre, which had moved to television, where complex historical events and palace intrigue were in many ways better suited to a format in which long, complex stories could be played out over months. This luxury could capture the subtleties even a nearly three-hour film like *Samurai Ban-ners* could not, even if it meant losing much of the spectacle due to the lim-ited finances of Japanese TV.

Good as the picture's battle sequences are (which, incidentally, predate Kurosawa's use of brightly color-coded armies in *Ran*), their impact is less-ened by cramming so much intricate history into a story that really concerns three characters and their relationship to one another. The film's producers—Mifune, Inagaki, Tomoyuki Tanaka, and former sound man Yoshio Nishikawa—believed spectacle was what audiences wanted to see, yet spectacle is really secondary in a film like this. Western filmmakers like Franklin Schaffner struggled with the same problem, in films like *Patton* (1970) and *Nicholas and Alexandra* (1972): how to produce an "intimate epic." But all over the world, this genre was dead by the early 1970s. As in Japan, such stories were better suited to television, perhaps best exempli-fied in the West by *I, Claudius*, in which a cast of thousands and epic battles were, in the end, unnecessary.

It's unfortunate then that so much screen time is devoted to Mifune leading his armies into one battle after another, because these scenes inter-rupt the evolution of his intriguing character. In the first hour, he appears to be nothing more than a power-hungry warmonger. Once the princess enters the story, the film comes to life in the complexities of his relation-ship to her. Mifune is very good in these sequences. The moment when he declares himself to be the true "parent" of the newborn prince is mesmer-izing and the kind of scene only an actor of Mifune's presence could have pulled off.

His face deeply etched by a scar running down his forehead into his right eye, mustached, and his head adorned with a spectacular horned helmet, Mifune is as visually striking as he has ever been. Thematically, there are intriguing, contradictory elements to this character, too, in the contrast between his hard-line, ruthless general defined by his bloody battles and his lifelong dreams of everlasting peace in a world of natural beauty (seen in some brilliantly colored cinematography by Kazuo Yamada).

The film was mildly successful in Japan and recognized by critics as a final triumph of the waning *jidai-geki* genre. It made *Kinema Jumpo*'s "Best Ten" list that year, at a time when most critics found such films old-fashioned, outranking the works of Oshima (*Boy* [Shonen]), Shinoda (*Double Suicide* [Shinju ten no Amajima]), and older leftist filmmakers like Tadashi Imai (*The River with No Bridge* [Hashi no nai Kawa {ichi-bu}]) and Satsuo Ya-mamoto (*Vietnam*).

Samurai Banners was first released in the United States as *Under the Banner of Samurai*. Kevin Thomas declared that the film "may well be Inagaki's masterpiece. . . . Beyond creating an entertainment that never flags throughout its near three-hour length, the prime achievement of Inagaki and Shinobu Hashimoto . . . is to demonstrate that by adhering to the conventions of a classic genre you can wrest more meaning from it than by using it to 'make a statement' that will be 'relevant' today."[79]

But *Variety*'s "Mosk" argued: "Even Mifune's unique presence fails to give this many new twists and provide dynamic stature or the poetic insights that marked some earlier Japanese films of this genre. . . . Mifune is spectacular as usual [even] if the film's surface prettiness and melodramatic flourishes, without the deeper classic flair and rightness to make this more than a florid actioner, limit its art potential."[80]

Mifune's second *jidai-geki* of 1969 was *Red Lion* (Akage), another Ki-hachi Okamoto swordplay adventure more in keeping with the director's strengths than *The Sword of Doom*. (Though, for all its faults, *The Sword of Doom* more fully realizes the director's intentions.) *Red Lion* mixed comedy and tragedy, laced with heavy doses of irony, all of which were really Okamoto's forte. Though ambitious, the film fumbles pretty badly in the end. Mifune, however, gives one of his better performances, and this goes a long way to compensate for the picture's shortcomings.

The title refers to the red tassels, resembling a lion's mane, worn by the Emperor's officers during the Meiji Restoration of the late 1860s. As the picture opens, the Emperor's Sekihe troops, led by Sozo Sagara (Takahiro Tamura), are marching toward Edo, spreading word from village to village that 300 years of military dictatorship under the shogunate have come to an end. Gonzo (Mifune), a none-too-bright foot soldier, learns that the forces are approaching the village of his birth. He borrows an officer's red mane and convinces them to give him three days to single-handedly "liberate" the village from feudal rule.

Most of the picture revolves around the chaos Gonzo generates once he arrives. Passing himself off as "head of the army, basically," he releases hostages the local government (led by Yunosuke Ito) had imprisoned after they were unable to pay their steep taxes, and rescues villagers used as slave laborers. He tears up the loan contracts that forced dozens of the town's women into prostitution, promises the villagers that the Emperor will cut taxes in half, and releases tons of rice withheld from the peasants.

Though the townspeople remember Gonzo as something of an illiterate rube (years earlier he fell out of a persimmon tree), they are also poor and desperate enough to believe in him, and a party atmosphere sweeps the village.

The town's merchants and leaders, their power and fortunes waning, enlist a bodyguard, Hanzo (Etsushi Takahashi), to kill the buffoon-turned-hero, hoping to restore some order to the village. Meanwhile, the town is abuzz about a mysterious task force called Mobile Unit One, pro-shogunate warriors ready to fight the imperialist soldiers when they move in.

The film becomes muddled as the Emperor's forces, lacking war funds and envious of Sekihe's popularity with the masses, falsely accuse the Sekihe troops of being impostors, execute them, rescind their promise about reducing the taxes, and, in short, become as hard-line in their authority as the shogunates had been. This subplot, as well as all the screen time devoted to the Mobile Unit One group and the fatalistic Hanzo, becomes almost hopelessly confusing toward the end. Fortunately, one of the villagers offers up the picture's theme: "What changes are the flowers of the official crest, nothing more." The violent climax has the town fighting a hopeless battle against the Emperor's army, which kills Gonzo in a hail of gunfire.

As in many of his best films, Okamoto's style reflected his wartime experiences working at an airplane factory that was targeted by B-29 bombers. Okamoto survived, but hundreds of others, mostly women, died in the attack. "Only half of my classmates survived the war," he said, "and none of my childhood friends survived—I was the only one who came back. I developed this attitude that all this wasn't so much a tragedy as a comedy. You know, everything is so fucked up, everything was so sad it was funny."[81]

To this end, the important and much-acclaimed actress Nobuko Otowa (1924–94) turns up in a pivotal but surprisingly small role as a middle-aged prostitute temporarily freed from bondage by Gonzo. When he's killed, the

Army moves on, and it becomes clear that the peasants will return to their lives of misery, Otowa's prostitute goes mad and begins chanting, "It's okay! It's okay! Never mind!" The rest of the village joins in chanting, "It's okay! It's okay! Never mind!" all knowing they are doomed. The irony of this closing scene has a certain power as the peasants' brief respite comes to its violent, sudden conclusion. Unfortunately, it's also undermined by the confusion that reigns during the picture's second half. This is a common problem in Okamoto's period films, such as *Kill!* (Kiru, 1968). The director is clearly reaching for something more, but his scripts rarely match the level of his ambition. The film's Japanese title, *Akage*, was intended to remind audiences of Kurosawa's *Akahige* (*Red Beard*), though anyone expecting a film of its level would surely have been disappointed.

Adding to the *Red Lion's* failure is the complete lack of subtlety in the performances. Given the nature of his character, that Mifune is so broad is forgivable; that much of the rest of the picture is played on the same level is not. The contrast between the comic and the tragic is interesting, even daring, but the comic elements are overplayed and lose considerable steam as the film progresses. That Okamoto goes out on a stylistic limb is admirable, but *Red Lion* is played at much too high a pitch. A scene where the jubilant peasants fantasize about what to do with their cruel oppressors doesn't work at all. Several normally fine actors—including Yunosuke Ito and Minoru Terada—give atypically poor performances.

Mifune, however, is excellent as a larger-than-life, lusty character far removed from the interchangeable, poker-faced samurai roles that were now dominating his career. The part recalls both Kikuchiyo from *Seven Samurai* and his *Rickshaw Man*, but without the crippling self-loathing. While he may be naïve and inarticulate, he is also innocent, brave, and pure. This purity is best expressed in his scenes with Tomi (Shima Iwashita), his lover, now a prostitute who gave Gonzo up for dead long ago. To save herself she betrays him, only to be awestruck by his purity. Fool though he may be, she realizes that Gonzo is indeed a great man. From the very beginning, in films like *Rashomon*, Mifune had been criticized for his broad style. In this case, it's not scenery chewing but very much in keeping with the character.

Okamoto remembers Mifune staying in character during the shoot: "I don't think he was quite [a Method actor]. He'd enjoy showing off his swordplay skills and stuff like that. Two good examples are *The Emperor and a General* and *Red Lion*. In *Red Lion*, his character was more robust, more alive, more energetic, so he was really loose on the set, really relaxed. But for *The Emperor and a General* he knew his character was going to commit suicide at the end of the film, so he was really quiet on the set and always in character."[82]

Along with Otowa, the film's fine cast includes Bokuzen Hidari, the old farmer from *Seven Samurai*, in a similar role—his last appearance in a Mifune film before his death in 1971. Hideyo Amamoto and Hideo Sunazuka, both regulars in Okamoto's own stock company, have colorful supporting roles as old Dr. Gensai and a shady reporter, respectively.

Technically the film, like all Mifune's pictures from this period, is excellent. *Red Lion* boasts a notably rousing score by Masaru Sato and good camerawork by Kurosawa's regular cinematographer, Takao Saito. Okamoto did a fine job of cutting the film, and his setups and direction of the action sequences are energetic, though, at nearly two hours, *Red Lion* is a trifle long.

In the United States the film received lukewarm reviews. John Goff of *The Hollywood Reporter* said: "Strap a samurai sword to his back, give him a character with fire in his blood and Toshiro Mifune will deliver as much action as is needed to keep a film moving. . . . [His] portrayal from comical character to leader is smooth and subtle. His feelings of desire and hate build well enough to lend credence to his extended death in the final scene. . . . The love scenes between [Mifune and Iwashita] however are not as subtle, well enacted or as careful from any standpoint as the rest of the film."[83]

Kevin Thomas didn't think the picture subtle at all. " 'Red Lion' quickly wears out its welcome by dint of its mercilessly unrelieved flamboyance. It's hard to recall a period Japanese picture played so broadly that it actually lapses into burlesque. Never has Mifune managed so unrestrainedly. The story does build to a cruelly ironic climax, along the way there is lots of action and swordplay staged with energy if not style, but one is pretty bored and exhausted by that time."[84]

Variety's "Whit" found the film confusing: "Picture is far overlength [sic] and carries a confused plot further bogged down by inept subtitles. . . . Star portrays a varied character in which comedy is mixed with customary Japanese expression, scarcely his best performance but still displaying the type of artistry which has won him his reputation."[85]

Mifune immediately followed *Red Lion* with *Band of Assassins* (Shinsengumi, 1969), which he billed as his one hundredth film. This was more or less true—it was actually his hundred and fourth (in order of release), though if one discounts multipart-film appearances, the claim was accurate.

Set in the 1860s, the story concerns fencer Isami Kondo (Mifune), whose eight students travel to Kyoto to defend the Tokugawa shogunate against those who would restore the Emperor to power. Kondo organizes the Shinsengumi, a strictly ordered band of assassins. Co-founder Kamo Serizawa (Rentaro Mikuni), unable to abide by the group's code, tarnishes its reputation when he oversteps the Shinsengumi's parameters of violence. The band uncovers a plot to abduct the Emperor and burn Kyoto, though in the end public opinion leads to the restoration, and in 1868 Kondo is executed.

Band of Assassins is a tired historical drama / *chambara* epic, one of the last gasps of the genre. It was directed by Tadashi Sawashima (b. 1926), a disciple of Masahiro Makino and Kunio Watanabe who specialized in samurai melodramas at Toei's Kyoto studio during the 1950s and '60s, many starring singer Hibari Misora. *Band of Assassins* was his first and last film for Mifune, and his last feature, period.

When the film opened in America in April 1970, reviewers were surprisingly kind, some apparently not wanting to dispute the film's advertising, which billed the film as "Japan's Last 'Wild Bunch,' " Hollywood's *Canyon Crier* going so far as to call it "Mifune's Best." "Samurai are modern men," its critic wrote, "what they experience is what all men experience, and thus it is a pleasure to recognize in the new Mifune film . . . the humanistic philosophy of the acceptance of responsibility for principle—although the result is unhappiness. This is Mifune's 100th film and certainly his best since he left Toho and Kurosawa. . . . This latest film . . . reminds us of [Yamanaka's *Humanity and Paper Balloons*]. We can pay it no greater compliment."[86]

Kevin Thomas called the film "a worthy milestone. Indeed, it is one of the best films Mifune has made since parting with Kurosawa five years ago and by far the best he has produced himself. With his 50th birthday fast approaching, Mifune, perhaps for the first time, is beginning to look a little older yet is ever the virile figure of authority, to be sure." Thomas thought the picture "quite unlike most samurai spectaculars. . . . By the end we've experienced something like 'Butch Cassidy and the Sundance Kid.' "[87]

A less enthusiastic *Hollywood Reporter* said: "It contains enough action and clear cut relationships so that interest flags only occasionally for one without historical and language knowledge. . . . The samurai battles are fast-moving and fascinating in their action staging, well planned by director Tadashi Sawashima, while some of the hari-kiri scenes are actually painful to watch in their deliberate execution. Mifune again gives a strong performance. . . . His brooding countenance lends itself to the part which is one strong man who relies completely on himself."[88]

TWENTY-ONE

FIRE

For Akira Kurosawa, the five years after *Red Beard* were as disaster-plagued as the five years prior had been artistically and commercially prosperous. During the latter half of the 1960s, as the Japanese film industry went deeper into decline, Kurosawa saw that the natural progression of his career would be to make movies outside and independent of Japan, particularly after his exclusive contract with Toho expired in February 1966. Foreign directors, no matter how acclaimed and successful, tend to believe they can somehow transcend their domestic artistic and commercial successes using the bountiful resources available to them in Hollywood—and Kurosawa was not immune to this. That filmmakers ranging from Sergei Eisenstein to John Woo directed work far inferior to that made in their homeland—or foundered altogether—did not dissuade others from the allure of Hollywood. No one can deny that big studios worked with budgets the rest of the world could only dream about. Even in Japan, where films had a polish rivaled only by Hollywood and which had an output second to none (including India), filmmakers often worked in conditions that recalled the rougher, more primitive Hollywood of the 1930s. They used old, overworked cameras, their soundstages had dirt floors, and until the 1950s many of the biggest stars used outhouses like the rest of the crew. More than in any other country, Japanese filmmakers breathed life into their most routine pictures. To their great credit and quite unlike Hollywood, even in their most mindless programmers the Japanese demonstrated a level of craftsmanship unrivaled anywhere else in the world.

By the late 1960s, however, directors like Kihachi Okamoto and Jun Fukuda found working under such conditions wearying, especially since Toho was now giving them even less time and money. Kurosawa, on the other hand, was known the world over and felt the time right to parlay his commercial and critical fame to establish himself as a truly international filmmaker.

Up to this moment, according to Kurosawa, he had received "about sixty other properties offered by film companies in Europe and the [United States]," but turned them all down, later saying through a spokesman that he "was only willing to work on something that was his 'original idea.' "[1] One of the more intriguing of these offers came from actor Peter O'Toole, who asked Kurosawa to direct him in *Will Adams*, a project that had also been pitched to Mifune, about the first Caucasian samurai.[2] The role had obvious appeal for O'Toole, as it was a kind of Eastern *Lawrence of Arabia* (and later the basis of James Clavell's *Shogun*), but Kurosawa demurred, and the film was never made. However, the director attracted the attention of Joseph E. Levine, head of Embassy Pictures, who was to co-produce *Will Adams* for Paramount; Levine wanted to work with Kurosawa even after *Will Adams* fell through.

Kurosawa had read an article by Warren R. Young that had originally appeared in the May 29, 1963, edition of *Life* (later translated in the February 1964 issue of *Bungei Shunshu*) about a runaway train, powered by four coupled locomotives, that had created all manner of havoc in upstate New York between Syracuse and Rochester. "I've been crazy about locomotives since I was a child," Kurosawa said, and from *Sanshiro Sugata* to *High and Low*, he exhibited an adeptness in shooting them.

He received the cooperation of Hedley Donovan, chairman of Time-Life and himself a Kurosawa fan. Donovan conferred with the director and said at a press conference, "My purpose for coming is to meet the Japanese Emperor and the Emperor of the Japanese film industry, Akira Kurosawa." Donovan also helped Kurosawa coordinate American research on the project and obtained the assistance of General Motors, which provided specific details about the train's mechanics.[3]

On June 30, 1966, when Mifune was in Europe making *Grand Prix*, Kurosawa was in New York. At the Four Seasons restaurant he and Levine announced that they would co-produce *Runaway Train*, a fictionalized account of Young's story. More than 150 members of the press were in attendance, a large photograph of the director looming over them. Co-screenwriter Ryuzo Kikushima and the managing director of Kurosawa Production, Tetsu Aoyagi, were also present. Kurosawa and Levine were flush with enthusiasm, so much so that they spoke of plans for a four-picture deal, with all the films to be made in America. *Runaway Train* would be completely financed by Embassy and Levine, who would executive-produce and retain worldwide rights, including Japan. Kurosawa Production would provide a Japanese screenplay and the director's services (he would also act as co-producer and chief editor), though no decision had yet been made whether other members of Kurosawa's usual staff would be involved. The cast would be exclusively American.[4]

Joe Levine was not inexperienced with Japanese films. A former small-time distributor based in Boston, he had made his first big deal when he accepted an offer from two low-budget Hollywood producers to help finance the distribution of a Japanese movie they had acquired: Toho's *Godzilla*. Levine used his money from and experience with this international hit (it was their Americanized version that most of the world saw) to achieve even greater success when, a few years later, he bought the American rights to a two-year-old Italian muscleman movie called *Hercules* (Le Fatiche di Ercole, 1957), the film that launched the sword-and-sandal genre. This time Levine didn't have the gaggle of partners he had had on *Godzilla*, and the several million he made from the film launched a career for him as a minor mogul. He began co-financing European art-house films along with drive-in fare, including *The Tenth Victim* (La Decima Vittima, 1965) and Godard's *Contempt* (Le Mépris, 1963). Levine also began making films within the United States. Many were awful, such as *The Oscar* (1965) and *Stiletto* (1969). But he did produce some of the best films of the late 1960s, including *The Graduate* (1967) and *The Lion in Winter* (1968), and he supported writer-filmmakers like Mike Nichols, Mel Brooks, and Woody Allen. For Levine, helping Kurosawa to emigrate to make an American film was akin to David Selznick's bringing Hitchcock over from England twenty-five years earlier.

Kurosawa was grateful for Levine's support: "I truly appreciate Mr. Levine for accepting my requirements," he said, "and allowing me to direct it from my idea and script." When asked about directing the film in English, Kurosawa said, "I believe there's no problem, working within the film industry. It's like a conductor who is understood by people all over the world who understand his use of the baton, or a painter who expresses his thoughts through one of his paintings. I am sure that I'll be able to make a film that people from all over the world will understand—all I need is a camera and film."[5]

The script for *Runaway Train* was written by Kurosawa, Hideo Oguni, and Ryuzo Kikushima, and was then adapted into English by Sidney Carroll, who co-wrote *The Hustler* (1961) and had recently worked on *A Big Hand for the Little Lady* and *Gambit* (both 1966). "We hired him," Kurosawa wrote later, "because Mr. Levine had recommended him, and we did some checking. He's a talented person. Right after we decided to hire him, Mr. Nagaharu Yodogawa told me over the phone, 'You chose a good one.' He was right."[6]

An undated English-language script from the mid-1970s, credited to Kurosawa, Kikushima, and Oguni (with no translator cited), exists in the collection of the USC Cinema-Television Library. On the surface it is similar to the adaptation that was eventually filmed in 1985 by director Andrei Konchalovsky, but different in many respects. The script is 105 pages of nonstop, breathless action. The main characters are Manny and Buck, two escaped convicts who climb aboard four coupled engines in a train yard. Something goes wrong and the train picks up tremendous speed, eventually reaching 90 miles per hour. The train's engineer has fallen off, the emergency brakes have burned away, and it soon becomes apparent that the two are trapped in the fourth engine of a runaway train. Meanwhile, at the control tower, the line's supervisors try to determine what's going on and how to stop the locomotive. As Manny and Buck try to reach the front engine, engineers scramble to get their own trains out of the runaway's path. Officials consider derailing her before they realize there are people aboard. As it turns out, there is a third person on the runaway, a meek sheet-metal worker named Charlie, who had the misfortune to be on the train when it started moving. An attempt is made to have another engine catch up with the runaway, couple her from behind, and slow her down. But the train is going too fast and it is feared its tremendous speed will tear up an oncoming bridge. Charlie and the two convicts try to unhook the cables between the engines in order to cut power to them one by one, allowing the train to slow down. They manage to power down two of the engines, but the lead car is a different model, a streamliner, which appears inaccessible from the second engine. Their efforts do have one effect—the reduction in speed gets the train across the bridge without its collapsing in the process.

Manny and Buck's identity becomes apparent when their prison clothes are discovered in the train yard. Meanwhile, Manny forces Buck outside to try to unhook the second cable. At the control tower, a plan is hatched to write instructions for the trio in huge letters on boxcars far from the main track.

A second attempt is made to catch the runaway and get an experienced engineer aboard her. Meanwhile, Manny, Buck, and Charlie begin fighting, missing the painted boxcars altogether, but accidentally hit a red button that turns off the power in the second engine. As the other train nears, the convicts continue struggling with each other, hitting the button several times, causing the train to repeatedly slow down and speed up. After a near-collision between the two trains, the rescue attempt is aborted.

Yet another train catches up to the runaway, running alongside her this time, with the engineers holding up a sign with instructions for reaching a door to the lead engine. Manny and Buck, braving the bitterly cold winter wind to get to the lead engine—the only way to reach it is from outside—succeed in cutting all power. The train, still moving with tremendous momentum, barrels into Rochester. A steep grade slows it to a stop, and Buck, Manny, and Charlie jump off. But the train now begins to roll backward. Charlie frantically balances large rocks on the track to brake it, as Buck joins him. The police arrive and the two prisoners are recaptured, without resistance. The train's journey has reached its end.

As Kurosawa noted, "The lead [in the picture] is the train itself. I am still attracted to the sound of the Odakyu Express and I have to stop when I see it. Since the story itself is pretty simple, we can view it from several different aspects. I guess modern people, especially Americans, have a desire to escape from somewhere. I want to entrust this to the train going out of control."[7]

Kurosawa's plan was to give the picture, his first in color, the look of a black-and-white film, with black engines roaring through the white, snow-covered hills of upstate New York. He would use color only for punctuation: the red signal lights the train whizzes past and the control panel used to keep track of the train's movements. Like *High and Low*, *Runaway Train* was obsessed with the intricate machinations (here of "running a railroad") and with the logical measures both experienced railroaders and inexperienced men take.

In this respect, the script is quite similar to one later written by Peter Stone for *The Taking of Pelham One Two Three* (1974), adapted from John Godey's bestseller about the hijacking of a New York subway train. Both screenplays carefully establish the inner workings of the train line, so that once the action is under way, the audience is just a step or two behind at all times.

Runaway Train is a straightforward action thriller, Kurosawa's first such project since *The Hidden Fortress*, although he and his collaborators symbolically tie the runaway train to the escaping convicts. There are references to a song about how train engines, pulling freight a mile long, are prisoners themselves, thus likening the four barreling engines to Manny and Buck. Other characters are prisoners, too. Charlie is a prisoner of his own self-doubts. The men trying to stop the train break out of the prison of bureaucracy. One of the rail workers jokes about escaping to Hawaii. In Kurosawa's script, Manny is little more than a thug, Buck is more philosophical, and, as with Charlie, the experience brings out his strengths. The two eventually take charge from the more fatalistic Manny.

Levine had been negotiating with Kurosawa on the project since November 1965. Tetsuro "Tetsu" Aoyagi (b. 1934), son of longtime Toho director-producer Nobuo Aoyagi, reached terms both by telephone and at Levine's New York office in February 1966. Once an agreement was reached, Kurosawa left for New York, arriving on June 27, and the contracts were signed two days later. On July 4, Kurosawa, Aoyagi, and assistant director Yoichi Matsue met the Japanese press at the VIP room of Narita Airport at 10:00 p.m. The budget of the film was about $5.6 million, a staggering amount of money for Kurosawa—nearly equal to Toho's entire annual budget. It was also reported that the film would be shot in 70mm and released as a roadshow, meaning it would initially be exhibited on a reserved-seat-only basis, then put into general release months later, a common practice for big, prestigious films like *Lawrence of Arabia* (1962), *The Sound of Music* (1965), and *The Greatest Story Ever Told* (1965).[8] "It is going to be a little over two hours," Kurosawa said, "but I'm not going to have an intermission in the middle like other 70mm films because the train won't stop once it starts moving."[9]

Shooting with top-of-the-line equipment held obvious appeal for the director. "If we used a Japanese camera to shoot the runaway train it would break," Kurosawa joked. "Some of the cameras I use in Japan are almost as old as I am. One day an American journalist asked me, 'What kind of camera is this? It looks like a rare antique.' I was mortified."[10] Release prints would be in 70mm as well, and Kurosawa was anxious to experiment with the format's six-track, magnetic stereophonic sound.

Variety reported Lee Marvin, pre–*Hell in the Pacific*, was "understood to be everybody's first choice for the part of the train's lone passenger."[11] (Marvin obviously would have played Manny. Reportedly, Henry Fonda was supposed to have been Charlie.) *Film Daily* added: "[The film] will be shot beginning in October on the actual locations where the incident occurred. In addition, interior scenes will be filmed at a studio in New York or Hollywood. A 16-week shooting schedule is planned. Release in the fall of 1967 is anticipated."[12]

The Runaway Train was a giant step for Kurosawa. It would be his first film in color, produced at six times the cost of *Red Beard*, and he would have to direct an all-English-speaking cast using a script translated into a language he did not understand. Levine, to his credit, was gambling on something unheard of in postwar Hollywood. As *Film Daily* pointed out, Kurosawa would be "the first major foreign filmmaker to shoot a feature in the United States since the late 1930's, when such luminaries as Fritz Lang, Jean Renoir, René Clair and Alfred Hitchcock came to our shores."[13]

Throughout 1966, Kurosawa continued mapping out the picture with Sidney Carroll at Kurosawa Production's small office, located on the fourth floor of the Akasaka (Tokyo) Prince Hotel. Though in Japan, he surrounded himself with English speakers. There was his nephew, Mike Inoue, and at the office he employed an American, Carol Sherman, who had come from Stanford before earning her graduate degree from Tokyo University. Kazuko Seki, his secretary, a Seijo University graduate, had gone to high school in America. And Matsue, his assistant director, had had international film experience already, having studied film in an exchange program in Italy.[14]

Kurosawa confessed he had a lot to learn about the differences between Japanese and American production methods, beginning with the script itself. "I heard that the American crew was very surprised by the first draft because there was no continuity that showed any camera angles," he said. "We can't simply write 'A train moves.' We should put down on paper how many cars the train has, which cars are on camera, where the camera shoots the train from, and so on."[15]

But that winter, as snow began to fall in upstate New York, Kurosawa abruptly canceled his plans to shoot in the fall.

The biggest problem was the script [Kurosawa told *Kinema Jumpo*]. Writer Sidney Carroll was often sick and we hadn't anticipated that. Because of this, we weren't able to discuss the script in depth and we had differing opinions, even by the time he went back to America. The biggest problem was that he asked me to put a message in the film. However, the movie is entirely an action film, isn't it? I felt the theme would flow naturally through the runaway train and there wasn't a need to explain this verbally. . . . Furthermore, I had another problem with the telling of the story. For example, I believed we should spend three minutes on something that takes three minutes, not twenty minutes. . . . But we disagreed. We don't know why the train starts running violently. The people who are in charge of the train have to find a way to stop it. What are they going to do? I believed I should start the movie with something thrilling. I'm not blaming him; we simply didn't have enough time.

By the time Mr. Carroll eventually understood what we really wanted to do and agreed with us, we had taken so much time that he had to leave Japan. . . . Mr. Levine of Embassy Pictures started complaining. We repeatedly made changes and in the end decided to keep the script we wrote in Japan. . . . The film is very important to me, and I thought very deeply about all the problems. Then I decided to postpone for one year. I wanted all the preparations to be perfect before we started shooting. I'm sure that Embassy was surprised when they received my telegram four or five days before I was supposed to leave for America. My decision, I'm sure, was a bombshell to the cast and crew who were waiting for me in America. . . . I know it's a big headache for them, because we've already spent an amount of money equal to the entire budget of *Red Beard*. . . . I've heard rumors that Kurosawa Production and Embassy Pictures disagreed about the budget, but that's not true. . . . Besides, Mr. Levine provided a larger budget than I expected, saying, "Let Kurosawa do whatever he wants."[16]

As late as March 1967, there was still talk of shooting *Runaway Train*. *Variety* reported that Kurosawa "expects to shoot [the film] around Rochester, N.Y., next autumn."[17] By the end of 1968 the project had been "shelved indefinitely. . . . One reason given is Kurosawa's insistence on filming during the winter for authenticity."[18]

Kurosawa thought the snow critical to the picture's success. He added in 1966, "When I got on [one of the trains], I was glad I chose winter, because it was so hot. If we were to shoot in the summertime, we would definitely get sick. Of course, it would be hard to shoot in winter with all of us wearing heavy winter clothes. What are we going to do if the train gets stuck in the snow? It will be a big headache."[19]

The exact reasons for the film's cancellation remain unclear, but the delays in getting started prompted an even bigger offer—and one more trouble-plagued—for Kurosawa to do a film for 20th Century-Fox. The problems he would face there would end his involvement on both films, which were ultimately made without his direct participation.

The script of *Runaway Train* would not be filmed until 1985, and Kurosawa's role in that adaptation would be minimal. Directed by Andrei Konchalovsky, *Runaway Train* was a decent-enough thriller, but little else. With the heavy-handed existentialism that was thrust upon it, there is little to suggest its roots as a Kurosawa project. Jon Voight played the Manny character, and he is uncharacteristically hammy. In fact, the film has several overly theatrical performances, particularly that of Eric Roberts, who is insufferable as Buck, in this version a virtual dimwit. Both manage to chew more scenery than John P. Ryan does as the sadistic prison warden in pursuit of them. This is no mean feat for Ryan, a gloriously hammy character actor who played the warden like Ming the Merciless. Ryan's role was not part of Kurosawa's original script, nor was its lengthy prison sequence, which lifts a scene straight out of *Yojimbo*: Voight makes his escape hidden in a pile of laundry, in a cart pushed by fellow escapee Eric Roberts. One of the prison guards, rather than search the basket, offers to lend Roberts a hand. Kurosawa hated these additions, which he felt broke the script's momentum and pacing.

In adapting the story, screenwriters Djordje Milicevic, Paul Zindel, and Edward Bunker also changed the sex of the railroad worker—Charlie became Sara, played by actress Rebecca DeMornay. This isn't a bad idea, but rather than the three main characters, who admittedly were underdeveloped in Kurosawa's script, expanding, they change into less interesting, more unpleasant figures. The addition of Ryan's character, so obsessed with bringing Voight back that he lowers himself onto the train only to be trapped with Voight as the runaway meets its doom (the train doesn't stop in the 1985 film), is both contrived and absurd.

By spring of 1967, Kurosawa was off in another direction altogether, one that would drag out much longer and end any chances of a career in American films. In late April 1967 it was announced that he would direct the Japanese half of 20th Century-Fox's ambitious retelling of the attack on Pearl Harbor, in a film to be called *Tora! Tora! Tora!*, its title coming from the Japanese code that the sneak attack had been a successful surprise. Based on Gordon Prange's book of the same name, it was to be a follow-up of sorts to Fox's *The Longest Day* (1962), a gargantuan though profitable production (it earned almost $18 million in domestic rentals alone) about the Allied landing at Normandy. Personally produced by Fox head Darryl F. Zanuck, *The Longest Day* was one of the first war movies to re-create a famous battle with detailed, historic accuracy, using many of the actual locations, combined with the almost unprecedented move (for a Hollywood studio anyway) of casting prominent foreign actors in French and German roles in which they spoke their own language, with the dialogue subtitled on American movie screens. *Tora! Tora! Tora!* would go one step further, using not only a Japanese cast but also a Japanese script that told *their* side of the attack as well.

"Kurosawa was very happy in the beginning," according to his nephew Mike Inoue. "He became good friends with Darryl Zanuck. He had great admiration for the directness of Darryl Zanuck, and Zanuck liked him very much."[20]

Both producer Elmo Williams (b. 1913), who had been Zanuck's associate on *The Longest Day*, and Zanuck himself, his own career in jeopardy due to many costly flops, wanted badly to do the picture. Kurosawa's name would bring considerable weight to the project, and the cost of using him would be greatly offset by the reduced cost of filming the Japanese sequences in Japan with a Japanese crew. In Williams's own notes to his crew, dated August 1, 1968, and signed "Elmo," he wrote: "[Kurosawa's] importance to this project is such that we would not be involved in it had he rejected our bid to make his American debut on 'Tora! Tora! Tora!' "[21]

On the surface, Kurosawa's deal appeared very sweet: Kurosawa Production and Fox would be co-producers, even though Fox would be footing nearly all of the $8 million budget, and Kurosawa would receive 10 percent of the net profits. He would shoot the film's interiors at Toei's Kyoto Studios, except for scenes set at the American Embassy and the Imperial Palace, which would be lensed in Tokyo. The exteriors would be filmed in Hokkaido and Kyushu, and he would be involved at some level in filming the attack itself.[22] As with *Runaway Train*, Kurosawa was excited about the opportunity to shoot *Tora! Tora! Tora!* in the 70mm format.*

Originally, the picture was to begin shooting early in 1968, but Kurosawa, working with screenwriters Ryuzo Kikushima and Hideo Oguni (Zanuck and Williams hired Larry Forrester to pen the American half),[23] found the project quite different from anything they had done before, a daunting task for which they felt enormous responsibility, yet one that, as Kurosawa put it, was "almost a duty." They had already been working on the script for three months.

---

*The picture was slated for production in Dimension-150, a 70mm process. Instead, Fox opted to shoot *Patton* in D-150, and *Tora! Tora! Tora!* was ultimately made in 35mm Panavision, with some release prints blown up to 70mm.

"I don't wish to sound arrogant, but I never worked harder than I did on *Tora! Tora! Tora!*," Oguni said. "Kurosawa brought a huge number of reference books and told me to read all of them. And I did read them. And then he told me to remember everything."[24]

They wanted to go beyond the scope of Toho's own films dealing with the raid, notably Kajiro Yamamoto's *The War at Sea from Hawaii to Malaya* (1942), Ishiro Honda's *Eagle of the Pacific* (1953), and Shue Matsubayashi's *I Bombed Pearl Harbor* (1960)—films that, while rich in Eiji Tsuburaya's elaborate and ingenious miniature work, struggled with depicting Japan's militarism and events that would forever alter the lives of everyone in Japan.* After working on the script for more than three months at the hot springs inn in Atami, Kurosawa held a press conference to discuss the work they had done. *Seven Samurai*, with its nearly four-hour running time, had seemed to take forever to write, but *Tora! Tora! Tora!* was taking even longer. By now, Kikushima had come to regard the *ryokan* as a "prison." Kurosawa added, "It's worse than a prison, and I'm not released yet—I'm only here on parole. We have to go back now and finish it."[25]

Donald Richie was given access to the script up to that point. He noted: "If its present form is retained for the finished picture, it seemingly should be an excellent film indeed. Already one can see that it shares much with other Kurosawa films."[26]

Once it was finished, Kurosawa himself seemed pleased. "I face up to the fact of war, telling the whole, true story—hiding nothing—the story from all sides." Both he and Zanuck agreed on the need for historical accuracy, that the real story had more than enough drama on its own. And it was a story, Kurosawa insisted, "for which neither side need apologize."[27]

Meanwhile, Richard Fleischer was signed to direct the American sequences. For Kurosawa, this development must have been a huge disappointment. He had been led to believe that David Lean would supervise the American half. Fleischer was a journeyman, not an auteur. The son of famed animator Max Fleischer, Richard had been an editor on newsreels before directing his first feature in 1946. He was good when working in film noir and crime pictures like *The Narrow Margin* (1952) and the underrated *Ten Rillington Place* (1971), but it was his ability with complex, technically challenging films like *20,000 Leagues Under the Sea* (1954), *The Vikings*

---

*Kurosawa Production submitted the names of several companies to build the many miniatures, but not Eiji Tsuburaya's. Nor was use of the "Toho pool" considered, as Toho wouldn't rent it out unless they had a financial stake in the production.

(on which Elmo Williams had been second unit director, 1958), and Fox's *Fantastic Voyage* (1966), that won him the flip side of *Tora! Tora! Tora!* While Kurosawa struggled with *Runaway Train*, Fleischer had just finished *Doctor Dolittle* (1967); while Kurosawa spent months writing his half of *Tora! Tora! Tora!*, Fleischer was putting the finishing touches on *Che!* (1969), one of the biggest flops—and most notoriously awful films—of its era. Though talented, Fleischer was surely no David Lean.

According to Fleischer, his hiring came at the insistence of Richard Zanuck, vice president of Fox and Darryl's son, who "had no faith in the project but went ahead with it for Darryl's sake. Dick's main proviso, however, was that I direct it."[28]

The script written, Kurosawa anxiously awaited the green light to begin shooting either *Runaway Train* or *Tora! Tora! Tora!*, and yet, in 1967 and most of 1968, he did neither.

As he brooded about Fleischer's hiring, other aspects of preproduction began to cause him grief. For the first time since the real war, Kurosawa endured government red tape due to the need for U.S. Navy cooperation in filming the Pearl Harbor sequences and securing vintage planes and ships for the picture. In August 1967 he went to Hawaii to meet with Williams to discuss shooting there. Kurosawa was annoyed that he required "script approval from the Department of Defense" and became increasingly concerned about how his half of the film would be integrated with Fleischer's work.[29]

Williams's ideas didn't reassure him. Williams gave Kurosawa four months to shoot the Japanese half; only then would Fleischer begin shooting his portion, which, including the battle itself, would take six months.[30] The reason for this was the limited number of surviving or reconstructed planes, which would have to double for both sides. No one—not Kurosawa, not Williams, not Fleischer—knew how it was all going to fit together, and certainly Kurosawa's confidence that it would all somehow mesh cohesively was waning.

After the New Year, Jonas Rosenfield, Jr., vice president of Fox's advertising and publicity department, met with the director to establish an office in Japan to promote that part of the production. Fox was going all-out, allotting $250,000 for production publicity alone. The Japanese could have made several features with that kind of money.[31]

Then came another blow. To save money Williams suddenly decided he wanted to shoot all the film's interiors, including Kurosawa's footage, on the Fox lot in Westwood, California.[32] In the past eighteen months

Williams had flown to Japan a half dozen times to meet with Kurosawa, and had also met him in Hawaii. For Kurosawa, Williams was becoming a nuisance. Then, just as quickly, Williams reversed himself, opting to shoot the Japanese half's interiors at Toei Studio in Kyoto as originally planned.

A larger problem concerned Kurosawa's script. The scenario Richie praised is presumably the same one translated into English and dated June 9, 1967, copies of which can be found at the USC Cinema–Television Library and the Margaret Herrick Library of the Academy of Motion Picture Arts & Sciences. The Kurosawa-Kikushima-Oguni screenplay has many interesting moments, but it is also long—very long. At 401 pages, complete with diagrams of sets, maps, and the like, Kurosawa's script—essentially covering the Japanese half—was timed by Fox at four hours and twenty minutes of screen time.

There are a few American scenes, including several revolving around the prewar activities of President Roosevelt, as well as some interesting prewar anti-Japanese sentiment. One brief scene has average Americans discussing an "expert's theory" that the shape of Japanese eyes makes them poor fliers, while FDR's desire to meet with the Japanese Emperor illustrates the American government's lack of understanding that the Japanese regarded their Emperor as no mere leader but as a god. Kurosawa's purpose was to illustrate the lack of awareness by the American people and its government to Japanese culture and society.

Kurosawa's minutiae regarding every aspect of the story was obviously well researched but simply impractical in a feature film. In his script, the Japanese planes don't even leave for Pearl Harbor until three and a half hours into the story.[33]

Kurosawa's screenplay created a potentially volatile situation for Williams. He and Zanuck agreed that the picture could run no more than three hours, leaving Kurosawa just 90 minutes to tell his part of the story. Williams then began cutting the Japanese script to a manageable length. "Kurosawa will, undoubtedly, scream when he sees that I have thrown out all of the scenes of the political maneuvering between Japanese and Americans during the years 1939 and 1940," Williams predicted in a memo to Richard Zanuck. "This is interesting stuff to read but it is dull material for a motion picture. Fleischer was quick to recognize that. Kurosawa will be slow to see it."[34]

Williams met with Kurosawa in July and October, but Kurosawa didn't like the American dilution of his material. "He complained bitterly about some of the Japanese scenes Larry and I had eliminated when we wrote the final draft," Williams wrote that November to Richard Zanuck.[35] Handwritten notes in a copy of the script available in the special collections library at the USC School of Cinema–Television, probably written by Richard or Darryl Zanuck, indicate that they did in fact like much of what Kurosawa and his writers had done. In a letter to Kurosawa, Williams expressed deep regret for the need to cut so much of it down. Revised versions of the script were written in the fall and early winter of 1967–68. The "Revised Final Shooting Script," dated May 29, 1968, is noteworthy for its author credit: "by Akira Kurosawa, Hideo Oguni, and Ryuzo Kikushima (Japanese Sequences); Larry Forrester and Mitchell Lindemann (American Sequences)," while noting: "This script was re-edited and finalized in conferences with Mr. Darryl Zanuck in Beverly Hills May 27 and 28, 1968, attended by Elmo Williams, Akira Kurosawa, Richard Fleischer, Tetsu Aoyagi."

Never before had Kurosawa been forced to work so closely with producers regarding his writing. Nor had he ever been expected to outline his intentions as the picture's director. In a letter to Tetsu Aoyagi, Williams wrote: "It would help me a great deal, if you and Mr. Kurosawa could put on paper for me Mr. Kurosawa's thoughts on how he intends to direct some of the more difficult scenes."[36]

Meanwhile, Kurosawa's confidence was boosted when it was announced that producer Saul David would remake *The Hidden Fortress* in America as a Western. David had produced Fox's successful *Fantastic Voyage*, but moved to Universal Studios, taking the remake rights with him. Kurosawa didn't hold out much hope for the proposed American version, but it did further the studio's confidence in hiring the Japanese filmmaker for *Tora! Tora! Tora!* As *Variety* noted: "[It] added to the contention that Kurosawa, in making samurai dramas, has fully grasped the essence of western U.S. dramatic themes."[37] (Ultimately, Saul David's adaptation of *The Hidden Fortress* was never made.)

Back in Japan, Kurosawa buried himself in the planning and construction of the exterior sets, wanting the authenticity he had achieved on *Red Beard*, and this time he didn't have to worry about money. A full-size replica of Yamamoto's flagship, the *Nagato*, was constructed at the Ashiya Air Base in Kyushu.* Facing the sea, it measured 660 feet long and 115 feet high. Built mainly out of wood, it had a concrete base and steel girders.[38]

When Fox hired Kurosawa, they may have assumed they would be get-

*The real *Nagato* was one of the few vessels to survive the war. Ironically, it was destroyed by the United States in a 1946 atomic bomb test.

ting Mifune as part of the package. He had already played Yamamoto that same year (in *Admiral Yamamoto*) and had starred in Kurosawa's last ten films. Indeed, Toho's *Admiral Yamamoto* was clearly made in part to cash in on the publicity surrounding the Fox-Kurosawa film, and initially Fox was concerned that Toho's film might diffuse interest in *Tora! Tora! Tora!* It's likely that Kurosawa was not happy to learn that Mifune agreed to appear in Toho's film, and that played a role in Kurosawa's decision against using Mifune in *Tora!* "Although roles will be played by actors out of the director's 'stock company,' " *Variety* reported, "it will not include Toshiro Mifune, as the 'best-known' Japanese actor and the 'best-known' Japanese director have agreed to disagree."[39] How seriously Mifune was considered for the film at this point is not known, and no memos about his possible casting exist in Fox's production files.

Kurosawa then announced a radical casting decision: he not only had no plans to use Mifune, he intended to "cast fifteen prominent Japanese industrialists and business personalities in principal roles," including Takeo Kagiya, president of Takachiho Trading, as Yamamoto; Ban Ando, managing director of Japan Broadcasting Co., as Admiral Onishi; and Yasuyoshi Obata, president of the Fuyo advertising agency, as Ambassador Nomura.

"One of my employees was a friend of Yoichi Matsue," Kagiya said of his casting as the famous admiral. "He heard that they were having a hard time finding the right person to play the role and showed a picture of me to Mr. Kurosawa. Director Kurosawa was happy to find me. I was surprised at the news, because I didn't know anything about it. I decided to meet Mr. Kurosawa and listen to him. He explained what kind of character Yamamoto was and the theme of the movie. He asked me to play the part. I trusted his personality and decided to make my film debut. The deeper our personal relationship went, the more I wanted to work with him."[40]

Fox moved the film's starting date from November 1 to December 7, the twenty-seventh anniversary of the "day of infamy," an obvious and rather impractical move to generate a lot of press. A few days before filming started, Kurosawa signed Tsutomu Yamazaki, so prominent in both *High and Low* and *Red Beard*, as Commander Genda, "architect of the Pearl Harbor raid."[41] Actors Eijiro Tono, Susumu Fujita, Osamu Takizawa, Koreya Senda, and Shogo Shimada were also signed to the picture. The publicity department pointed out that since their expensive battleship set was just that, a set, Kurosawa intended to have the Japanese Zeroes take off from the flight deck of the U.S.S. *Yorktown*. The takeoffs would be at pre-dawn, thus hiding the ship's true identity, but the irony was clear: the *Yorktown* had fought the Japanese in World War II.[42]

What happened once shooting got under way has long been a mystery. However, Fox's production files, which provide a day-by-day account of their version of events, paint a dark and disturbing portrait of an artist unraveling in the face of a triumvirate of obstacles. These documents conclude that Kurosawa was clearly and seriously mentally ill. But Kurosawa's actions during December 1968 were the result of several factors lost on Americans reporting back to Fox's executives: the pressures of working on a multimillion-dollar production in general and the unresolved issues about how his work would be incorporated into the production in particular; his unwillingness or inability to work harmoniously with a Japanese crew with which he had never worked before; and disloyalty and conspiracy in the highest levels of his own company that had a profound and lasting impact on the remainder of his career.

According to a letter from production coordinator Stanley Goldsmith, "In the long preparation for principal photography, we were promised that Mr. Kurosawa would start shooting on December 2. Their constant delay in moving to Kyoto and in starting construction of the first sets caused the concern of both Elmo [Williams] and myself, yet Tetsu [Aoyagi] promised that on December 2nd Mr. Kurosawa would be ready to shoot. They were not able to start shooting on December 2nd because the set was not constructed in time, so later in the day Mr. Kurosawa started rehearsals for Int. Japanese Embassy, scenes 176 and 177. On December 6, Int. Konoye's Residence, Scene 93, Mr. Kurosawa rehearsed for the entire day and he rehearsed the following day, December 7th. Also he continued rehearsals part of the day December 8th, after which he shot the scene which totaled one script page. I strongly suspect a great deal of this long rehearsal was attributed to the fact that Mr. Kurosawa might not have been well because only two actors, plus one extra, were involved."[43]

Another document, "Production Report—Akira Kurosawa's Illness," dated December 31 and unsigned, picks up the production beginning December 9: "Kurosawa went into a rage over the use of a clapper, and proceeded to beat the clapper man over the head with a piece of rolled paper. The clapper man quit. He then turned on the assistant director and hit him with the paper. Following this act, he instructed the assistant director to beat the entire crew over the head. The assistant refused and he, along with two other assistants who refused to strike the other members of the crew, were fired. Tuesday declared as a rest day in order to allow Mr. Kurosawa time to regain composure and for the crew to cool their anger."

December 10: "Akira Kurosawa moved out of the *ryokan* and in with his crew, this to the great displeasure of the crew."

December 11: "We were forced to suspend a shooting call when Mr. Kurosawa did not come into the studio on this day, for he suffered a nervous collapse at 6:00 a.m. and was taken to Kyoto University Hospital for treatment of hypertension. He rested until evening. Our production office was not informed until late in the day. The three assistant directors were told to report on the set after Kurosawa rescinded dismissal."

December 12: "(Kurosawa again fired his three assistant directors and wanted two second unit directors for the next day.) He told Tetsu he wanted our production building torn down and wants Fox to buy half of Toei Studio to keep their actors and personnel away from ours."

December 13: "Kurosawa fired his two new assistants." Two setups were shot on this day, and Tetsu Aoyagi sent for a Dr. Hajime Handa, a "brain specialist," to visit the inn and examine Kurosawa.[44]

December 14: On this day, Kurosawa allegedly issued a set of demands. The handwritten document, translated into English as "Imperative Requirements by Director Kurosawa," states the following: "(1) [not translated]; (2) Give helmets to both Mr. Kurosawa and [Second Unit Director Junya] Sato to be worn in the stages; (3) Whenever Mr. Kurosawa goes to the toilet, please have a guard to escort him; (4) Make his car safely [sic] as much as possible and put bullet-proof glass in the car; (5) It is not in perfect condition to put the light equipments in the set, so try to make it [sic]; (6) Keep the studio clean; (7) We always have to have somebody to keep guard through 24 hours [sic]."[45] On that same day, according to the production report, "Teruko Arimitsu and Stanley Goldsmith visited Dr. Hajime Handa. . . . The doctor, a brain surgeon, said Kurosawa could continue to work, but must not be under pressure or strain. He said Kurosawa is a tyrant and highly excitable so everyone must cater to him. Tranquillizers were prescribed. Elmo Williams notified in Honolulu."[46]

December 15 (9:00 a.m. call): "Mr. Kurosawa arrived and in one hour's time made work unbearable for the crew, who notified Tetsu Aoyagi they could no longer work under the conditions Kurosawa had imposed. . . . Crew held a meeting and was encouraged to write a list of their grievances about Kurosawa's conduct."

December 16: "Tetsu stated Kurosawa's willingness to rehire all crew members who were 'fired' by him. . . . Tetsu calls back Dr. Hajime Handa and Dr. Masashi Murakami, Professor of Psychiatry at Kyoto University Hospital. The doctors waited at Kurosawa's inn for one hour and Kurosawa refused to see them."

December 17: On this day, in front of Elmo Williams, Teruko Arimitsu, and a Mr. Nakasume, "our translator," Kurosawa was read the crew's list of demands by Tetsu Aoyagi. Elmo Williams then met with the crew for three hours. "In the evening Kurosawa came to Toei Studio and entered our production building where he proceeded in a fit of rage to knock out our location auditor's window. He then went to the local police station and requested that he be arrested."

December 18: Elmo Williams read the doctors' reports on the director's condition, while Kurosawa spent the day looking at the rushes thus far.

December 19: "Kurosawa's personal doctor from Tokyo arrived and after examination gave a report to Elmo Williams stating Kurosawa was not in a bad condition and was perfectly capable of completing the assignment. The doctor said Kurosawa shows slight signs of mental tension and tranquillizers were necessary—sedatives should be taken. Elmo Williams and Kurosawa had a meeting in which he promised to comply with the crew's request but refuses to apologize."

On December 20 and 21 there was no filming, but on December 22 shooting resumed on Stage 10. Two scenes were completed in Yamamoto's cabin. The day seemed to go relatively smoothly; shooting began at 10:00 a.m. and wrapped at 7:05 p.m., and one and a quarter pages were shot.

December 23: "Before noon there was another reoccurrence of his condition. In the early afternoon he stopped rehearsing and ordered crew members to repaint the set. The assistant art director requested to quit. Company was unable to shoot. Key crew members met with Elmo Williams and Stanley Goldsmith to state they could not work with Kurosawa any longer. Kurosawa fired the property assistant for not wearing his Kurosawa Company jacket. Kurosawa disregarded all promises to control himself. Tetsu told Elmo he felt Kurosawa was not capable physically to continue the picture."

December 24: "His escapades during the wee hours of the morning included rushing to Toei Studio for two uniformed company guards to remain with him for protection and arousing unit managers at home. He visited the police station and complained about the lack of police on the city streets, then moved from his Japanese inn to the Kyoto Hotel and with the two company guards sent for Tetsu to arrange an immediate meeting with Elmo. Tetsu and Goldsmith met with Kurosawa at 2:00 a.m. in his room at the Kyoto Hotel at which time he told Goldsmith of his hatred for his Japanese crew except for five men who he wanted Goldsmith to teach

English so he could replace the others with an American crew. He also asked Goldsmith to teach his daughter English and warned Goldsmith not to walk the Kyoto streets at night as there was danger lurking about."[47]

That afternoon, Elmo Williams and Tetsu Aoyagi went to see Kurosawa. They discussed Dr. Murakami's report, "and advised him to return to Tokyo for hospital treatment. Elmo then informed Kurosawa he would have to be replaced as director so he could care for his health, thereby relieving him of his duties. Mr. Kurosawa arrived at the studio at 4:30 p.m. and announced to the crew that he would take over the production."

The following day Elmo Williams gave Tetsu Aoyagi Kurosawa's "informal letter of dismissal." "The production record of Mr. Kurosawa," wrote Stanley Goldsmith, "is in twenty-three days of work he has been able to deliver only seven days of shooting, totaling seven and an eighth script pages which cover eighteen scenes, and approximately eight minutes of usable screentime. During the period from December 2nd to December 24th, there were three company rest days."[48]

On Christmas Eve, 1968, the announcement was made public—Kurosawa was out. Officially, producer Elmo Williams told reporters in Kyoto that Kurosawa had *resigned* from the project "due to fatigue," adding that he "deeply regretted it, but it is a matter of health, and that comes first." Doctors attending the announcement said the fifty-eight-year-old director was "extremely tired and needs extensive rest."[49] But Darryl Zanuck initially vetoed Williams's plans a few days later, telling reporters that they'd wait for Kurosawa to "recover."[50]

But before the press conference had even ended, Kurosawa's dreams of a career in American film had come crashing to an end. If he wasn't mentally ill, he was viewed as an unreasonable man unable to work within the American studio system, an irrational autocrat along the lines of other flawed geniuses like Erich von Stroheim and Orson Welles.

Had everything gone smoothly, *Tora! Tora! Tora!* would have been by far the largest, most technically challenging film of Kurosawa's career. Logistically, it was a nightmare, and the strain was enormous. Moreover, Fox withheld information from Kurosawa in an effort to keep him on the picture. In a November 1967 letter to Richard Zanuck, Fox head of production Stan Hough wrote about the need to keep Kurosawa in the dark about the film's tenuous status, and the decision to delay production for another year. "Kurosawa is another problem," he wrote. "His recent cables indicate he sees no reason why the Japanese version can't go forward. Of course, we all know it is impossible to tell him the real reason [i.e., Fox's financial problems and Richard Zanuck's lack of faith in the film]. . . . Both Elmo Williams and I agree that as far as Kurosawa is concerned our only recourse is to try and keep him in the picture if we can."[51] Kurosawa was then pressured to begin filming before he was ready, and he was still uncertain how his material would be incorporated into the finished product.

On his previous film, *Red Beard*, Kurosawa's crew was composed of dozens of people he had worked with for a decade or more. His crews were used to his working methods, and to be assigned to one of his films was seen as both an honor and a stepping-stone to a great career. At Toei, Kurosawa was working with a crew largely unknown to him. Toei was a model of efficiency—the studio was famous for its quickly made, inexpensive films—and Kurosawa's methods were completely alien to their crews. To them *Tora! Tora! Tora!* was just another assignment, and many probably resented being pulled away from directors they were used to working with. When they rebelled, Kurosawa was beside himself. His crews had always been fiercely loyal. Now, far from Tokyo, everyone seemed to be against him.

As Mike Inoue explained further: "For example, when Kurosawa was shooting the scene for Yamamoto's entrance, Kurosawa arranged for a red carpet that went outside the stage and out to the studio gate, and here Yamamoto comes riding in his limousine. Kurosawa thought it was very important to get the actor mentally thinking he was really Admiral Yamamoto. Tetsu Aoyagi, then acting as a coordinator, didn't explain these kinds of things well enough to reassure the American team members, who must have started suspecting that Kurosawa was wasting his precious budget."[52]

In retrospect, Kurosawa was no more demanding than most great artists, especially within an art form where they had to depend on hundreds of people at a time. And what Kurosawa had endured for the last three years would have exhausted the strongest of men, let alone a man nearing sixty. Moreover, there were crueler, more insidious matters at play that were, as yet, unknown to the general public.

"The blame for this catastrophic turn of events lay on both sides," wrote Fleischer, "although Twentieth Century-Fox must carry most of the burden. Kurosawa had always been his own, completely autonomous, boss. Now he had many bosses, all of whom he surely felt were his inferiors, all of whom were tearing away at his autonomy, his dignity. His way of operating was totally unlike anything they were used to. He had a different set of rules: his own. Kurosawa was a master precisely because he went his own way. They made a major mistake in how they treated him. It was folly to try to squeeze him into the Hollywood studio mold. You don't hire Kurosawa to give you just another movie or even behave like just another director."[53]

By late January 1969 there was no question that he would be replaced, but Williams assured reporters when the announcement was made, "We will proceed as quickly as possible to continue filming this production exactly as it was planned and conceived."[54] By the first week of March, just as Kurosawa was to have completed filming, Fox had regrouped and was ready to resume filming of the Japanese half. Williams had hoped the Kurosawa fiasco was behind him. In Tokyo he wanted to talk to Japanese reporters about how he was going to salvage the project. Instead, all they wanted to know were details about Kurosawa. To Williams's growing irritation, the reporters repeatedly asked him why Kurosawa was out, and he repeatedly told them that Kurosawa was unable to continue because of his health. Reporters cited Kurosawa's public concerns about the editing and asserted that he hadn't resigned, he'd been fired. "There was no question but that the man was ill," Williams insisted in a press conference reported in the *Los Angeles Times*.[55] Kurosawa, meanwhile, remained bitter about the project and continued holding his own press conferences, giving his side of events well into 1970. In the midst of all this, Toho reissued both *Red Beard* and *Throne of Blood*, cashing in on all the publicity.

As Kurosawa and Fox staged dueling press briefings, an even darker impact on Kurosawa's future began to emerge. It became known in the early months of 1969 that much of the unraveling of Kurosawa's involvement with *Tora!* was rooted deep within the offices of Kurosawa Production. Some of the details remain cloudy to this day. What is clear is how deeply the corruption within the company impacted Kurosawa professionally and personally, and how sadly it echoed Kurosawa's own *The Bad Sleep Well*.

In a series of articles written by esteemed film critic and *Kinema Jumpo* editor Yoshio Shirai, using information provided by Kurosawa's supporters, many disturbing facts came to light about Tetsu Aoyagi, general manager at Kurosawa Production, and his relationship with Fox. Aoyagi, who had joined Kurosawa Production after a stint in the foreign film division at Toho, and who had been an assistant director under Mikio Naruse and Yuzo Kawashima, was a desperately ambitious man who saw *Tora! Tora! Tora!* as his ticket to large-scale production.

His letters to Williams, written in English, reflect just how ambitious, passionate, and emotionally involved Aoyagi was with *Tora! Tora! Tora!* For example, when Fox expressed concern about the Toho *Admiral Yamamoto*, Aoyagi wrote a desperate-sounding letter to Williams assuring him not to worry. "I am not telling you a dream [sic]," he wrote, "but if we fail to

gross $4,000,000 out of Japan with 'Tora! Tora! Tora!' we will commit
HARAKIRI."[56]

First, the deal with Kurosawa Production was not as sweet as it might
first have appeared. As it turned out, Fox had final cut of the film, including
the Japanese section. And while Kurosawa would be held accountable if the
Japanese half went over-budget and over-schedule, all production decisions
were subject to the approval of Richard Zanuck.

Kurosawa had also signed away all copyright claims on his screenplay.
Although the film was no longer his, Fox continued associating his name
with the film, publicly stating during December and January that Kurosawa's stamp would somehow be retained on the finished project, even if he
was no longer involved. They considered keeping his name in the official
credits, curtly stating, "Since director Kurosawa surrendered his copyright
of the script per the agreement, he has no rights to publicly express his
opinion. . . . We understand that he wishes not to be credited in the titles.
This wish may influence our decision, but we confirm that Fox has the right
to make the final decision." Kurosawa responded in a statement made
through his office: "Even if this is legally true, I reject the use of my name
once the film is no longer mine."[57]

Kurosawa and members of his staff tried to locate the original, complete agreement, but Aoyagi apparently had never provided them with one
and wasn't about to show it to them now. Kurosawa had trusted him im-
plicitly, but Aoyagi was also a producer with little experience, hired mainly
because of Kurosawa's thirty-year friendship with his father, who had been
with Toho since its inception as P.C.L., and because the younger Aoyagi
supposedly spoke excellent English and had managed to secure the deals
for both *Runaway Train* and *Tora! Tora! Tora!*

Kurosawa, meanwhile, called upon his Admiral Yamamoto, businessman
Takeo Kagiya, for help. "I went to the Toei-Kyoto Studio on December 5,"
Kagiya recalled. "I got the sense that there was a lack of excitement to
make the great film Mr. Kurosawa had planned. Later on, I heard that three
of the assistant directors had been fired because of something that had happened between them and [Kurosawa]. Second-Unit Director Junya Sato
was brought back from location in Hokkaido by Fox on the evening of December 12. Fox said, 'Kurosawa will leave the picture and director Sato
will take it over due to Mr. Kurosawa's sickness.' I thought that was
strange. . . . Mr. Kurosawa looked frustrated and shooting was canceled
from December 15 to December 19. The shooting resumed on December 20."[58] A few days after Kurosawa's dismissal, Sato resigned out of loyalty.

According to Kagiya, Kurosawa visited his home on December 25, the day after Fox announced his departure. "Fox doesn't want me to make the film," Kurosawa told him. "I don't understand why [my company is financially] responsible to complete [the Japanese half even though I have been fired]." When Kagiya asked to see the agreement between Fox and Kurosawa Production, the director admitted he had left everything in Aoyagi's hands. Kagiya agreed to help, and when Kurosawa and Aoyagi appeared at his door the next day, Kagiya was struck by Aoyagi's reticence. "I always had the impression of him as an untrustworthy man," Kagiya admitted. He demanded that Aoyagi show him the Fox-Kurosawa contract, but Aoyagi replied, " 'I will be fined $200,000 if I show it to a third party.' 'What are you talking about?' I asked. 'There's no law saying you can't show it to the president of a company. I am telling you on behalf of Mr. Kurosawa—don't fuck with me! I'm being straight with you; show me whatever Mr. Kurosawa asks to see.'

"[Aoyagi] finally said, 'I will bring it over tomorrow,' but he also whispered to me, 'Nobody signed the contract,' as they left. I thought that was strange. The next day, I sent one of my employees to Aoyagi to pick it up. After a while, he came back with the agreement, but only a portion of it—the 7 to 12th clauses of an amendment to the original contract. He said Mr. Aoyagi didn't give him anything else. I then had the feeling that [Mr. Kurosawa] was being cheated and that there was danger lurking around the corner."[59]

Aoyagi wired Fox on December 30 officially canceling the agreement between Kurosawa Production and the American studio, but Kurosawa, seemingly unaware of this, continued to believe that the project might be resumed with him as director. At Kurosawa's behest, Kagiya invited Elmo Williams and the head of Fox's Japan office to his home; they met for two hours. According to Kagiya: "I said, 'Mr. Kurosawa is saying that he would like to make the film per the agreement. If you think he's sick, why not let [Junya] Sato and [assistant director Yoichi] Matsue shoot it. I think this is the only Japanese way to solve the problem.' They didn't even try to listen to me. I asked them, 'Since I couldn't get a copy of the agreement from Mr. Aoyagi, I would like to get one from you.' [They replied,] 'It is in our legal department' and the meeting was over without getting anywhere."[60]

As the ranks of Kurosawa's personal support grew, Kagiya and Kurosawa set up a meeting with Fox's attorneys in Kyoto. According to Kagiya, Aoyagi changed the venue for the meeting, and when Kagiya showed up, Fox's men were nowhere to be found. They were met instead by Aoyagi and Kurosawa Production's executive accountant, Sadahiro Tsubota. Again, Kagiya asked to see the contract, but Tsubota and Aoyagi refused to show it to him. Kagiya later told Kurosawa, "In my entire life I have never had a more unpleasant and baffling experience."

Then, on January 9, while still in Kyoto, Kurosawa sent a telegram directly to Darryl Zanuck saying, "I think it is best that I make the film my own way. If there are financial problems, I am ready to assume the financial risk in order to be able make it." At Kagiya's suggestion, Kurosawa announced that he would, out of his own pocket, put up the money for a $5 million completion bond to let him finish the film.

He left Aoyagi in Kyoto and returned to Tokyo that same day by bullet train, accompanied by Yoichi Matsue. When they tried to contact Aoyagi upon their return, he couldn't be found—Aoyagi had secretly returned to Tokyo that same day. Before the telegram had even reached Zanuck, Aoyagi suddenly called Kurosawa to say Fox's answer to the proposal was definitely no. "Why did the answer to our telegram go to Aoyagi, and by phone?" Kagiya wondered. "Besides, the reply came much too quickly."[61]

Kurosawa was stunned. But bigger shocks were to come. "We found a copy of a telegram at Kurosawa Production later on," Kagiya explained. "It was sent by Aoyagi to [Elmo] Williams and said, 'Neither Kurosawa nor Kagiya is going to buy that kind of [completion bond].' It was obvious that he was trying to circumvent Kurosawa's rehiring."[62] As late as February 1969, Darryl Zanuck was still considering rehiring Kurosawa. He sent Kurosawa a telegram informing him that he was sending Richard Zanuck to Japan to meet with him. However, Aoyagi intercepted the telegram, signing for it on February 10. By the time Kurosawa became aware of the telegram, on February 19, it was too late—Zanuck had flown to Japan, never heard from Kurosawa, and flew back home.

Fox attorney Charles G. Ball responded to the confusion by saying, "I understand that what Tetsu Aoyagi has done is questionable, but Fox has worked with him as the [sole liaison and] managing director of Kurosawa Production."[63]

Shirai also learned that Aoyagi had approached Kurosawa's actors after he was fired. According to him, Aoyagi told the cast that Kurosawa Production would be liable for ¥700,000,000 (about $2 million) in damages if the production was canceled or needed to start over from scratch. According to Tsubota, Aoyagi told Kurosawa the same thing on January 12, in an emergency meeting with accountant Tsubota and co-writer Kikushima. "Aoyagi said, 'We have to pay Fox ¥700,000,000 in damages if we don't do anything,'" Tsubota told *Kinema Jumpo*. "I remember thinking, 'Where does that amount come from?'" The four discussed whether Kurosawa should publicly state he had resigned, even though this wasn't true, or simply break the agreement. "We agreed that Mr. Kurosawa would publicly 're-sign' as director due to his illness," Tsubota said, also denying claims by Fox and Aoyagi that the director was actually suffering from mental illness. "I interpreted [his illness] as fatigue. He was really tired because of the script and casting changes and having a crew that wasn't strong. Mr. Aoyagi said, 'Fox's decision not to use director Kurosawa is firm. There is nothing we can do to change it.' As the accountant, I was concerned about losses we might suffer and agreed he would 'resign' because of illness. I had to avoid paying damages no matter what."[64]

There were claims that Kurosawa said he would take his own life if hit with such a suit from Fox, but Williams and Ball denied that threats of a suit were ever made. However, Fleischer contends that Kurosawa did in fact warn Fox executives that he would commit *seppuku*, and that the matter was kept quiet out of respect for Kurosawa.[65]

Aoyagi never publicly released the budget of the Japanese half (which, according to Fox's records, amounted to $3.2 million), and Kurosawa him-self never knew what the budget was. Fox stated that up to Kurosawa's de-parture, they had wired $100,000 in American currency and an additional ¥100,000,000 (about $300,000). According to Fox's records, about a third of the American currency had been sent on June 24, 1968, but Aoyagi didn't deposit the money into Kurosawa Production's accounts until January 8, 1969, some six months later and *after* Kurosawa had left the project. Asked about this, Aoyagi said, "I didn't receive my fee as script adviser, which should have been paid first, so I was negotiating to change my title from associate producer." But Aoyagi had already received $600,000 from Kurosawa Production on March 23, 1968, as a "producer's fee." Aoyagi continued to claim that he "did not receive compensation on *Tora! Tora! Tora!* from either Fox or Kurosawa Production." Additionally, it was discov-ered that script fees on *Runaway Train* were channeled to executives in the company not involved with the writing of that script.[66]

Kurosawa's team gradually realized the root of *Runaway Train*'s cancella-tion. Aoyagi had made concessions to Embassy Pictures without Kurosawa's consent, including acquiescing to Levine's change of heart about shooting the picture in 70mm. According to one source, Levine simply tired of deal-ing with Aoyagi and gave up.[67]

A short time later, Tetsu Aoyagi, producer-screenwriter Ryuzo Kiku-shima, and executive accountant Sadahiro Tsubota held a press conference in which they announced that, because of Kurosawa's behavior toward them, they had resigned from Kurosawa Production. Yoichi Matsue and Kurosawa's wife, Yoko, were later named to replace them.

Upon Aoyagi's departure, Kurosawa's staff discovered telegrams sent by Aoyagi to Fox that suggested he had conspired with the American studio while still employed by Kurosawa Production. One message, sent from the production office, provided evidence that Aoyagi was even working with Fox to hire Nikkatsu director Toshio Masuda to replace Kurosawa.[68]

Unlike Aoyagi and Kikushima, fifty-five-year-old executive accountant Sadahiro Tsubota actively tried to help the company sort through the mess Aoyagi had wrought. "I have to start by explaining why I joined Kurosawa Production," he said in 1969. "I was an employee in the Accounting Department at Toho's main office starting in 1938. I transferred to Toho Studios [ten years later], and joined Kurosawa Production in 1966. If I had stayed with Toho, I would have been promoted to the chief section. . . . I thought long and hard about leaving the company, but I decided to work for Mr. Kurosawa because I always respected him. I did my best, but then *Tora! Tora! Tora!* happened." Tsubota, who never said a word at the press conference with Aoyagi and Kikushima, was deeply disturbed by their comments, most of which he claimed he had not heard until then. In the months that followed, Tsubota was shocked by revelations about Aoyagi's secret dealings with Fox. For him, Aoyagi's mysterious actions now made sense. "He opened all the mail from foreign countries himself. He gave me the payments from Fox. One day I opened a document from Fox and he panicked. After that, everything started going directly to his office." Tsubota was as hurt by Aoyagi's actions as Kurosawa. "[Aoyagi's] father asked me to look after him," Tsubota said. "To tell the truth, he wasn't the right person to be producing *Tora! Tora! Tora!* He was too selfish. Some of the crew came to me and said, 'Who does he think he is?' . . . He lacked knowledge and experience, though he spoke English very well. [But] I was insecure about the project from the beginning. I decided that I would have [covered for Aoyagi] if he had not been able to do [his job] on his own. Mr. Kurosawa trusted him completely."[69]

Kurosawa believed Aoyagi was fluent in English and therefore capable of interpreting the finer points of Fox's arrangement with Kurosawa Production. However, Aoyagi's English skills were far below the professional standards required for a multi-million dollar international production.[70]

As associate producer of the Japanese half, Aoyagi had signed an agreement whereby he would receive his producer's fee even if the agreement between Fox and Kurosawa Production was canceled. However, neither Kurosawa nor anyone else was afforded the same protection. This fee was to be paid by Kurosawa Production, but after he resigned, Aoyagi requested that the payment be made directly by Fox. Fox severed their ties with

Aoyagi and refused to pay him. Aoyagi even claimed co-authorship of the script and demanded payment for his alleged work.[71]

"It is obvious that he had nothing to do with the script," Shirai wrote in 1969, "but the following clause appears on the top page of the script . . . that Fox is presently using: 'This script is the final draft edited in discussion with Fox President Darryl F. Zanuck, Mr. Elmo Williams, Akira Kurosawa and Tetsu Aoyagi in Kyoto on December 3, 1968. The final (third) draft February 11, 1969.' There are about 30 differences between that script and the one that Kurosawa wrote." Shirai adds that Kurosawa Production agreed that the script had been altered.[72]

But Fox asserted that the studio had in no way conspired with Aoyagi to get rid of Kurosawa. "What Tetsu Aoyagi has done is a mystery," said Fox attorney Charles Ball in early 1969. "There are so many things which simply do not make any sense. . . . Nothing is clear at this point."[73]

Indeed, Elmo Williams had had concerns about Aoyagi as far back as the previous November, when he wrote in his production diary: "Told [Tetsu] this was a Fox production, Fox was putting up all the money, so we expect to be running the show and not the other way around. We realize that Kurosawa Productions [sic] is doing their share, but they have been acting like they're in the driver's seat. If Tetsu doesn't realize this and doesn't stop creating problems, he will be replaced. We have huge problems with this film without having someone around creating them."[74]

Fleischer remembered Aoyagi as a man "with the glibness of a Hollywood press agent. Elmo and I didn't trust him. We had no way of knowing if he was translating us or Kurosawa accurately."[75]

Throughout the scandal, Aoyagi refused to be interviewed and was hostile about Shirai's articles, which pinned much of the blame on his shoulders. He later told Shirai, "I believe writing a splashy story or making one up is third-class journalism and destroys the tradition of *Kinema Jumpo*."[76] Aoyagi later added, "I don't know what to say about the repeatedly one-sided articles. . . . I do not want to get involved in a problem created by people around [Kurosawa], who use his name and do whatever they want to. I do not want to confuse Mr. Kurosawa, as he is about to start work on a new film. You [Shirai] are the only one who says it's unclear. Who worked on *Tora! Tora! Tora!* for the past three years? Kurosawa and I. I am the most knowledgeable person about this film. What I did was follow the decisions made at executive meetings at Kurosawa Production. Mr. Kurosawa attended those meetings. . . . Furthermore, what right does *Kinema Jumpo* have to impel me to testify and appear with [you] as the judge?"[77]

"There were so many details in the contract with 20th Century-Fox," said Hisao Kurosawa. "He hated having to deal with so many details while he was trying to make the film. They wanted too many details during the production, such as the daily production reports. Well, America has its own way of making films, and Japan has its own. It just didn't come together. Especially for someone used to the Japanese way. It's easier now with to-day's generation, but back then it was hard."[78]

In the end, Takeo Kagiya said, "I believe it was a plot by Fox. I think Fox carefully planned it from the start and used Aoyagi. All they wanted was Kurosawa's name and his script."[79]

Toshiro Mifune was approached by Fox on January 15 to replace Kagiya as Admiral Yamamoto. As with Kurosawa, Mifune was himself in the midst of scandal, having suddenly dropped out of two television films and Hideo Gosha's feature *Goyokin* (1969), allegedly due to an ulcer and exhaustion from overwork. Mifune had shot more than half his scenes when he abandoned the remote location on the northern island of Hokkaido, and Gosha was forced to replace Mifune with Kinnosuke Nakamura and reshoot all of Mifune's footage.

During much of the negotiations between Fox and Mifune, the actor was staying at the Sanno Hospital in Akasaka, in Tokyo. Yoshio Nishikawa, managing director of Mifune Productions, said they would take over only "if the issues between Fox and Kurosawa Production are resolved, and if Mr. Kurosawa is satisfied regarding the terms of his departure. If we accept their offer, Mr. Mifune will play Admiral Yamamoto, and shooting will begin in March and expect to finish in sixteen weeks. We would be responsible for hiring the cast and crew, which would be completely different, including the director."[80]

In the midst of negotiations, Mifune put his foot in his mouth. "It is not my intention to hurt Kurosawa," he said at a January 23 press conference regarding Fox's offer, "but his casting of amateurs in *Tora! Tora! Tora!* was as if he had insulted the entire Japanese acting community. If Kurosawa should have the opportunity to make films in the future, no actor will cooperate with him." Mifune quickly recanted his statement, telling the *Weekly Bunshun*, "I didn't mean to attack Kurosawa. I am from the farming country—I talk loudly and rudely, and that leads to misunderstandings. I think . . . the friendship between Kurosawa and myself runs deep. I would gladly act in Kurosawa's [future] films, of course."[81]

Mifune was of two minds regarding Fox's offer. On one hand, he did not wish to anger Kurosawa by involving himself with the picture; on the other hand, if Mifune Productions produced the Japanese version, the financial benefits might be enormous. Fox wanted Mifune, but there was no way they would move sets, costumes, and cameras from Kyoto to Tokyo. After much hedging, Mifune bowed out.

During January and February 1969, Kihachi Okamoto, Masaki Kobayashi, Noboru Nakamura, and Kon Ichikawa were all approached to replace Kurosawa. Out of respect for Kurosawa, all said no.

It took two directors to replace him: Toei's Kinji Fukasaku (b. 1930), who had remade Kurosawa's script of *Jakoman and Tetsu*, and the man in Aoyagi's telegram, Nikkatsu's Toshio Masuda (b. 1927). Both were excellent craftsmen who knew how to work fast and within company guidelines. Fukasaku had worked with Americans before, directing the English-language *The Green Slime* (Gamma sango uchu daisakusen, 1968) at Toei with American, Japanese, and Italian money. Admittedly, *The Green Slime* was no epic, but by now Fox didn't want a masterpiece. They just wanted it done.

Masuda admitted in the film's press kit, "You know what I feel like? I feel like a target. . . . I took the assignment to uphold Japanese honor. We had made commitments on this film to the Americans; we had begun shooting it here. I did not think it right to walk away from the commitment. All of us believed it should be done by a Japanese director, using Japanese actors and technicians and made on Japanese soil."[82]

As part of Kurosawa's settlement with Fox, none of the footage Kurosawa shot, meager though it may have been, was used in the finished film. Allegedly, this film still exists but will probably never be shown publicly. In his autobiography Richard Fleischer maintains, to the contrary, that a scene at the U.S. Embassy was shot by Kurosawa and used in the finished film. However, this is not so.

Fukasaku was assigned the action scenes (mostly process photography and second-unit footage), while Masuda filmed most of the drama Kurosawa was to shoot. Fukasaku remembered: "Kurosawa and the American producer didn't get along. They were looking for other directors in Japan. . . . I had the opportunity to use their front projection system [a process developed by Fox that blended images shot at different times in a manner superior to rear-screen and other commonly used systems] and thought it might be an interesting experience—that was a really important factor in my decision to do it. That was partly what fascinated Kurosawa, too. But after starting production, I learned that Williams hadn't done his research and there wasn't enough electrical power at the studio, and although the stage was huge, [because of the lack of power and subsequent lighting difficulties] we kept having to move the camera closer and closer to the process screen, until there really was only enough room for one fighter plane, almost exactly the same as in the Japanese rear-screen process! I was really pissed, but I couldn't very well quit at that point."[83]

At Williams's March press conference, he assured reporters that Kurosawa's name would remain on the picture as co-writer and that his basic approach to the material would remain unchanged. However, Kurosawa's name appears nowhere on the official credits, even though much of the script was, in fact, his. (Kikushima and Oguni are credited with the Japanese half.) The finished film is virtually identical to the "Revised Final Shooting Script" dated May 29, 1968, and, however reluctantly Kurosawa may have agreed to it, the finished product is at least partly his work, whether his name appeared on the credits or not.

Meanwhile, Kurosawa celebrated his fifty-ninth birthday that March with a private party at the Akasaka Prince Hotel. An exorcism of sorts, it helped him, in part, to rid the debacle of *Tora! Tora! Tora!* from his life forever. The party was even given a name: "Akira Kurosawa—Make a New Film!" Glasses were raised and toasts were proposed. The usual Kurosawa group was there: Teruyo Nogami, Yoichi Matsue. Aoyagi's absence was no doubt a great relief, but the loss of Ryuzo Kikushima, with whom he had collaborated since 1949, hurt Kurosawa deeply. At the press conference announcing his resignation, Kikushima had accused Kurosawa of being neurotic and "impossible to work with."[84] They would never collaborate again.

But one man was there encouraging Kurosawa to forget his troubles and forge ahead, as earnestly as anyone else at the party—Toshiro Mifune. Apparently whatever strain Mifune may have created by appearing in *Admiral Yamamoto* had been erased by his refusal to play that same character for Fox.[85]

In the wake of Kurosawa's departure, Kikushima did minor rewrites on the script, to Fox's specifications. Oguni, however, wanted nothing to do with it. "After [Kurosawa] left the project, I never saw the movie. I heard later that my name was on the credits."[86] But, as Williams had promised, the basic structure and emphasis remained unchanged. Kurosawa's influence could not be wiped away completely. It was Kurosawa who had chosen art director Yoshiro Muraki for the film (he shared an Oscar for his work) and who had cast familiar faces like Eijiro Tono and Susumu Fujita in minor but colorful roles. Cinematographer Takao Saito, whom Kurosawa had hired, was let go, second-unit director Junya Sato resigned, and the company executives were replaced by professional actors. Toru Takemitsu, in what would have been his first score for a Kurosawa film, was replaced by Jerry Goldsmith, who scored the entire picture. But the usually excellent Goldsmith, while creating several haunting cues, filled the Japanese sequences with the very type of "Oriental" clichés that the Japanese filmmakers were trying to avoid.

Tora! Tora! Tora! wound up costing $25.5 million, triple its original budget and more than three times the cost of *The Longest Day*. Many critics, some unfairly reviewing the budget instead of the film, pointed out that Fox had spent far more on *Tora! Tora! Tora!* than the Japanese had on the actual attack. But it's true that Kurosawa's departure resulted in a three-month delay in the production and was a factor in Fox's decision to push the film's release from December 7, 1969, to the following September. It lost a fortune when it finally opened to mixed-to-negative reviews, earning $14.5 million in the United States and Canada.

Except for its unquestionably impressive full-scale destruction effects, *Tora! Tora! Tora!* doesn't look all that different from or more expensive than Toho's own war movies, including *I Bombed Pearl Harbor* and *Admiral Yamamoto*, each made for less than a quarter of the cost of Fox's folly. Given the script's time constraints in telling each side of this complex historical event in the space of about seventy minutes, it seems unlikely that Kurosawa and his writers could have fashioned anything much more enlightening than what's onscreen while keeping factually accurate. Once again, Admiral Yamamoto is seen as little more than a wise leader who predicts Japan's fall long before the attack on Pearl Harbor has begun. *The Longest Day*, despite its all-star cast, managed several interesting character vignettes, but the American characters of *Tora! Tora! Tora!* proved colorless, its script relying far too heavily on ironic mistakes made by virtually everyone in the United States government. After a while, all the viewer can do is sit back and guess which character will screw up next.

Perhaps it was just as well that Kurosawa's name didn't appear on the credits of *Tora! Tora! Tora!* Few today remember that he was ever involved with the film at all; fewer still understand his significant role in the finished product.*

*Conversely, neither Kikushima nor Oguni is credited as a co-writer of the *Runaway Train* script. Credits on the Cannon film read: "Based on a screenplay by Akira Kurosawa." In Japan, Kurosawa's role in the film continues to be a source of speculation, and in 2001, a massive *manga* was published which offered a detailed—if fictionalized—account of the production.

The scandal finished Tetsu Aoyagi's career in Japan. He came to be regarded as a pariah within the Japanese industry, and he would never produce another feature. In a sad, telling letter to Elmo Williams in April 1969, Aoyagi wrote: "Kurosawa and Matsue are still shooting [sic] all kinds of fabricated stories, but now people do not pay attention to them. . . . I have no intention to fight against that stupidity, because I can hardly bring myself down to that low level. Kurosawa can do nothing but appreciate me who had absolutely exclusively worked for him without expecting any return, including monetary things for more than three years. I ignored myself getting bad reputations [sic] by protecting him and Kurosawa Production even when I found out that he did not make any sense. Well, Elmo, I do not want to think nor talk about all the past. All I want to do toward the past is spit on them. . . . I would like to stay in touch with you the rest of my whole life even after the picture is completely over. I will always try to become a motion picture producer like you, and will always remember all what I have learnt from you this time. . . . Please keep writing me."[87]

As for Elmo Williams, who had endured terrible pre-release press on both sides of the Pacific, bad reviews and worse box office, 20th Century-Fox did to him what Hollywood often does to such executives: in 1971 he was appointed head of worldwide production.

TWENTY-TWO

TROLLEY CRAZY

As the war of *Tora! Tora! Tora!* press conferences dragged on into early 1970, Kurosawa began work on a film called *Dodes'ka-den*, yet another adaptation of a Shugoro Yamamoto novel, this time *A Town Without Seasons*. Kurosawa's title for the picture is derived from the sound Japanese trains make as they clickety-clack along their tracks. (In Japan, the equivalent of "clickety-clack" is *gatan goton*, but Kurosawa uses the term *dodesukaden*, a word coined in Yamamoto's novel. Whether *gatan goton* or *dodesukaden*, trains in Japan *really do* make that sound.)

In the five years since Kurosawa's last completed work, *Red Beard*, he had watched his country's film industry collapse around him. The younger generation preferred foreign films, especially those from Hollywood, and the older began staying at home to watch television. The number of theaters showing only Japanese movies dropped by nearly 40 percent between 1965 and 1970, with the number of admissions likewise ebbing.[1] On the other hand, Japanese television couldn't have been healthier. By 1970 television sets were in 95 percent of Japanese homes, and the industry, catering to a public that preferred shows made in Japan, became the world's busiest producer of television programming.[2]

In December 1970, the same year *Dodes'ka-den* was released, Daiei, the company that had produced *Rashomon*, spiraled into bankruptcy and closed its studio. The public had lost interest in Nikkatsu's program of gangster and *chambara* films starring its contracted pop stars, and as production costs rose, the studio heads made a radical decision. The company dramatically reduced its overhead, letting go much of its talent, and, in 1971, switched to Roman porno films. (*Roman poruno*, the name derived from "romance porno," was essentially soft-core pornography, though it evolved into an occasionally artful genre. These films had far less of the stigma attached to them than their American counterparts did. Indeed, many came to be highly regarded by Japanese film critics, and much of the industry's top talent rose through their ranks. Despite what the name suggests, Roman porno has nothing whatsoever to do with ancient Rome.) Shochiku was saved only by the box-office successes of director Yoji Yamada's films, especially the "Tora-san" (*Otoko wa tsuraiyo*, meaning "It's Tough to Be a Man") film series he created. Toei, having for many years catered to current public tastes while shooting its pictures as quickly and cheaply as possible, survived the early 1970s relatively unscathed, but only after a period of massive restructuring.

Toho, by comparison, had become a dinosaur. Its pool of contract talent was enormous, perhaps larger than that of any other studio in the world at the time. The vogues for "Young Guy" romances, salaryman comedies, and Inagaki style *jidai-geki* were over. With the exception of the company's still marginally successful Godzilla movies (which by now had been banished to the kiddie market), every one of Toho's long-running film series—"Young Guy," "Shacho" movies, "Ekimae" ("In front of the Train Station") series, the Crazy Cats comedies—was phased out in 1970 and '71. Toho did take over the still-popular "Zatoichi" series from Daiei after they closed, but this only supported the general feeling within the industry that Toho had completely lost its identity.

Significantly, it had been these inexpensive, once highly profitable films that helped finance Toho's more prestigious, less financially assured projects. Kurosawa's old home was infested with uncertainty, and everyone's future was in doubt. For many directors, including Hiroshi Inagaki, Senkichi Taniguchi, Shiro Toyoda, Ishiro Honda, and others, it was the end of the line.

In the early part of the decade, Toho even considered the unthinkable: joining Nikkatsu in the Roman porno business. "[We] cannot stick to [our] traditional trademark of 'clean and sweet [pictures].' "[3]

In response, Kurosawa, along with directors Masaki Kobayashi, Keisuke Kinoshita, and Kon Ichikawa, formed their own joint company, Club of the Four Knights (*Yonki no kai*), in July 1969. This powerhouse of talent, arguably the four greatest living Japanese directors of the time, was created with the single purpose of producing films that would rejuvenate the flagging industry. It was decided that each man would direct a film in turn and expand their output from there. The four collaborated on a *jidai-geki* story, *Dora-Heita*, which wound up being too expensive a project to produce with their limited resources. Instead, Kurosawa, whose last four films had been enormous hits, proposed *Dodes'ka-den* as their initial offering.

"We have had considerable difficulties in obtaining financial backing for any of our films," Kurosawa said at the time. "We borrowed from a bank and this is the first time they have helped [a] film production. If my film is a success, they will give more, so it must be a success!"[4]

With Ryuzo Kikushima on the outs after siding with Tetsu Aoyagi during the *Tora! Tora! Tora!* scandal, Kurosawa turned to his former assistant director, Yoichi Matsue, now one of the heads of Kurosawa Production to produce *Dodes'ka den*. Matsue was a veritable disciple of the director, and Kurosawa believed he would have none of the producer-director conflicts he had endured on his aborted American films. Without Kikushima to co-write the script with him and Hideo Oguni, Kurosawa brought back one of his most important collaborators, Shinobu Hashimoto, with whom he hadn't worked since *The Bad Sleep Well*. "Since the film industry was in decline," Hashimoto recalls, "we had to make the film with a low budget. It was a difficult period. I remember Mr. Kurosawa was having a hard time with *Tora! Tora! Tora!*, but that he was determined to shoot *Dodes'ka-den* in twenty-eight days—that's what I remember."[5]

Oguni remembered it differently. "We had a great time," he insisted. "Kurosawa fell in love with Shugoro Yamamoto and was confident in adapting it. I said, 'This is going to work but it will decide in the public's mind whether or not you're crazy. Are you confident in yourself?' He said, 'Yes.' . . . It was tough, but we finished the script together in just one week. He was desperate, and I told him over and over, 'No matter how tight the budget is, you have to make this. Prove to them you're not crazy. You can't stop until it's finished. . . . If *Dodes'ka-den* had never been completed, what would people have thought of him? He would have been branded 'crazy' forever."[6]

"We were able to finish the script in about one-third the time we'd anticipated," recalled Kurosawa. "The manager of the *ryokan* where Oguni, Hashimoto, and I hole up and write thought we were leaving because we didn't like his place. We'd finished so quickly that he became very upset and tried to appease us by saying, 'From now on, you will be served only the best foods!' " [laughs].[7]

Composed of a series of vignettes set in a present-day shanty town, the script and subsequent film have no central character. Poor squatters live and work in a vast dump. Residents of this "village" include Roku-chan (Yoshitaka Zushi), an odd-looking teenage boy who lives in a shack with his mother (Kin Sugai). When we first meet them, the mother is praying intensely, and the boy joins her, saying, "Please, Buddha, make my mother smarter." Later we find out it's not the mother who is ill but the boy. He lives under the delusion that he's a train conductor and each morning goes off to work, climbs aboard his imaginary streetcar, and roams around the dump chanting "Dodes'ka-den! Dodes'ka-den!"

We also meet Mr. Shima (Junzaburo Ban), a kind, much loved member of the shanty town cursed with a nervous tic and a horribly abrasive and domineering wife (Kiyoko Tange). And there is the village slut (Yoko Kusunoki), now pregnant with her sixth child. In spite of her open infidelity, her husband, Ryotaro (Shinsuke Minami), is nonetheless a loving and dutiful father to their children, all born of illicit affairs.

Mr. Hei (Hiroshi Akutagawa, who played Hideko Takamine's husband in *The Rickshaw Man*) is a ghostly figure, a shell of a man, more dead than alive, who shuffles through the slum like a zombie, the victim of a mysterious personal tragedy. A beggar (Noboru Mitani) lives in an abandoned car with his little boy (Hiroyuki Kawase), who listens to his father's pipe dreams of building a perfect house for them. Two drunken blue-collar workers (Kunie Tanaka and Hisashi Igawa) swap wives, resulting in a tremendous scandal among the middle-aged women who gather at the village's single water supply, yet the men and their wives seem perfectly content with this alcohol-induced arrangement.

Much less happy is Katsuko (Tomoko Yamazaki), a young woman who lives with her aunt (Imari Tsuji) and uncle (Tatsuo Matsumura). When the aunt is hospitalized, the niece is forced to work nonstop making artificial flowers, doing both her and her aunt's share of the work, while her unpleasant, alcoholic uncle drinks the day away, berating her mercilessly. Lastly, there is an old tinker (Atsushi Watanabe), a poor but wise man respected by everyone in the community.

The script shifts among these sets of characters, most of whom never interact with anyone else. Mr. Shima brings three colleagues home from the office, but his wife is brutishly rude to everyone. When she abruptly leaves to take a bath, Shima's co-workers urge their friend to leave her— not because of her rudeness to them, but out of deep and genuine concern for Shima's own happiness. Shima, in turn, becomes livid. When they were younger, he explains, his wife stuck by him when he was penniless; she even stole rice on his behalf.

Ryotaro's children are reaching the age where they are being teased at school about their mother's promiscuity. They ask Ryotaro whether he is really their father or not. A genuinely loving man, he tells them it's not important what other people think: If you believe I'm your father, then I am.

Mr. Hei is visited by a woman, Ocho (Akiko Naraoka), begging forgiveness. Ocho was Hei's wife. She committed adultery, and Hei has allowed this betrayal to consume his very existence. For several days she stays with him, but though she clearly loves him, he cannot forgive her. Indeed, her love seems deeper and more mature than his.

As the beggar weaves dreams of a perfect house, his son goes from restaurant to restaurant pleading for scraps. The father ignores the warnings of one sympathetic cook about boiling some mackerel. The two get food poisoning and the son dies a painful, lingering death. As the beggar buries his son's ashes, his mind snaps; the boy's grave becomes a giant, imaginary swimming pool at the dream house.

The two workers eventually stumble back to their original wives, still as unconcerned as can be.

While her aunt is away at the hospital, Katsuko is raped by her uncle. She later stabs a teenage delivery boy who tries to befriend her. She attacks him out of fear that the boy, whom she likes, will one day abandon her. She doesn't want him to forget her. The boy survives and has the charges against the girl dropped. When the police begin to suspect she may have been raped by her uncle, the uncle flees, leaving his wife and niece to a presumably better life.

As Kurosawa was putting the finishing touches on the script, the first Japanese retrospective of his career was held in Nagoya on March 6, 1970. Fourteen of his films were shown, and the director gave a public lecture on his craft for the first time.

Preproduction for *Dodes'ka-den* began on March 31, 1970. "Having finished the script," Kurosawa said, "I racked my brains almost to the point of a nervous breakdown about how to direct it. A story about a slum—there's no such place for a location. Then I went out to the Tokyo dump, where I decided to construct outdoor sets, and right in the middle of everything, I made roads, piled up trash, did all sorts of things, and built weird houses. While doing this, I gradually realized what I should do and became decisive. Once the shooting began and Roku-chan's streetcar was running, I was able to work completely at ease."[8]

As he'd done in the past, Kurosawa went public with his needs, requesting that schoolchildren all over Japan send paintings of streetcars to fill Roku-chan's home. "I was greatly impressed by those pictures," he said. "In a relatively short period of time we received about 2,000 pictures. They were colorful, spontaneous, and winsome. I said to my staff, 'Okay, make something better than this.' Consequently, they knew exactly what I wanted and spontaneously painted the sun, the clouds, and other pictures we used. No art direction at all; they just painted."[9]

Shooting began soon thereafter, on April 23, at the dump in Horie-cho, in Edogawa-ku. Yoshitaka Zushi remembers that first day vividly: "Between *Red Beard* and *Dodes'ka-den* so much happened in his life, like *Tora! Tora! Tora!*, and he started to think he wouldn't be able to make films anymore. Then he stood up and established the Club of the Four Knights, but he was still concerned about his ability to make a film. On the first day of the shooting his first film in a long time, he said '*Yoi, sutato!*' [the Japanese equivalent of 'Action!'], but the way he said it wasn't in his usual voice. I looked over and saw that he was weeping."[10]

Because of the limited budget and Kurosawa's desire to re-establish himself within the industry, *Dodes'ka-den* was shot faster than anything he had done in years, despite the fact that this was his first completed film in color. The weather was not much of a factor this time. As Kurosawa explained, "The real weather isn't good for color films. The result is something like Technicolor. . . . I'd rather use color filters on the lights and shoot in cloudy weather. In fact I ignored the weather most of the time, except on rainy days."[11]

Kurosawa left most of the second-unit shooting to his staff of assistant directors. "The swimming pool [which the beggar imagines after his son's death] is the one at Geihinkan in the Meguro section of Tokyo," Kurosawa said. "I told my assistant director [Kenjiro] Omori to shoot the scene; I was busy editing with Nogami and some others. Mitani, who plays the beggar, came to me and pleaded helplessly, 'You're not coming with us?' And I said, 'I can't go to a swank place like that with a filthy bum like you' " [laughs].[12]

After the shooting of the background plates for the opening titles, the film wrapped on June 29, a bit more than two months after it had begun, and a fraction of the time Kurosawa had spent on his last completed film, *Red Beard*. "The final take was finished on a day which had originally been scheduled for rehearsal," added producer Matsue.[13]

Typically, Kurosawa's nighttime editing during production and long, un-interrupted takes hastened the editing phase; Kurosawa had the film ready for its first test screening on July 17. This time, his rush to finish the film was partly due to an invitation he had received to participate in the Moscow International Film Festival, where the film would be shown out of competition that August. "The audiences at the Kremlin Palace of Congresses were highly pleased with the film," said *Variety*, "whose maker 'strove to disclose the inner world of man with all his merits and faults.' [Kurosawa] added that 'an attempt to evoke respect for man has been the leitmotif of my film activities for thirty years.' "[14]

Dodes'ka-den is in one sense a return to familiar themes and ideas, and was criticized by some for failing to offer anything new. The picture is often compared with *The Lower Depths*, also about slum dwellers, and its charac-ters bear some resemblance to those of *Red Beard*. The big difference is that the characters of *Dodes'ka-den* are weak-willed. They do not undergo the kind of metamorphosis the major (and many of the minor) characters do in *Red Beard*; instead, they live in a world of nostalgia, unrealizable dreams, and self-deception. The film becomes an examination of the internal lengths to which people will go to deny the world around them.

To some small extent, *Dodes'ka-den* has its own Red Beard/pilgrim in the form of the old tinker, played by Atsushi Watanabe. Unlike Red Beard, the tinker can effect only small changes. He talks a sickly old man out of suicide and calms a crazed, sword-carrying drunk (Jerry Fujio). Generally, though, in matters of life and death, all he can do is sit on the sidelines and sadly watch events unfold.

Admirably, Kurosawa also takes tremendous risks, and in many ways, the film is quite unlike anything he had made before, at times bordering on the experimental. Kurosawa disliked the effect anamorphic wide-screen lenses had on the color stock available at the time. As director Yasujiro Ozu had done in the late 1950s, Kurosawa shot *Dodes'ka-den* in the old, standard-size ratio, the same one he shot all of his films in through 1957. (In the United States, some home video versions are incorrectly matted to give the picture a slight wide-screen shape, but in Japan the film was defi-nitely shown "standard size.") As Kurosawa noted, "With a standard-size frame the colors are clear, but with CinemaScope the colors are blanche. Also, this time I was filming small houses and small interiors. CinemaScope is much too wide, for example, for the father-son episode in the abandoned car. I would've preferred to use what we call the 'European-size' frame [matted anywhere from 1.66 to 1.75:1], that is, not quite as high as stan-dard size. Depending on the story, 70mm would be fine in the future."[15]

The look he and cinematographers Takao Saito and Yasumichi Fukuzawa achieved is dazzlingly rich and vibrant. Everything, from the sets to the props and costumes, even the very ground the actors walk on, is painted in bright hues that sharply contrast with the dreary, hopeless lives his characters endure. For some exterior scenes, Kurosawa moved his cast and crew to a soundstage so he could incorporate even more radical color schemes, using deeply filtered lights and expressionistic cyclorama backdrops representing brilliant, Van Gogh–like sunrises and sunsets. Everything at the real-life dump was similarly painted with powders, dyes, and paint guns.

One incident particularly impressed Zushi: "The art director tried to make an artificial rainbow by painting colors on a piece of wood. But Kurosawa said, 'It's no good. I'm going to make my own rainbow.' What he did was paint the ground a dark color, sprayed water into the air, and when the camera shot through the sunlight, he got a real rainbow! He even painted the shadows for the houses."[16]

The look of the film is established immediately during the opening titles, which are brightly painted against colorful backdrops and set to enchanting music, whose melodic, childlike motif also contrasts with the shanty town setting. Kurosawa had a falling out with Masaru Sato during the postproduction of *Red Beard* and so turned to Toru Takemitsu. The composer was set to score Kurosawa's version of *Tora! Tora! Tora!* When Kurosawa teamed with Masaki Kobayashi, who had used Takemitsu on all his films since the early 1960s, Takemitsu became the natural choice. Like Stanley Kubrick, Kurosawa usually envisioned classical works for particular projects and implored his composers to write something along similar lines. (And, like Kubrick, Kurosawa later began transposing these pieces directly, rather than go to the trouble of paying a film composer to mimic a particular piece.) According to Donald Richie, for *Dodes'ka-den* Takemitsu was told to use Bizet as his model, something he managed to avoid, coming up with film music as glorious to the ears as its cinematography is to the eyes. Noteworthy is Takemitsu's cue when the beggar's son roams the streets of Tokyo looking for food, in the only sequence set outside the dump's borders. In a more typical Takemitsu style, he supplements Kurosawa's eerie treatment of the city as a frighteningly alien world with a haunting, unearthly cue that suggests an incorporeal music box.

Dodes'ka-den represents a major shift away from the stock company of actors Kurosawa had used repeatedly since the late 1940s. It was his first film since *Ikiru* (1952) without Toshiro Mifune. However, regardless of any rift the two might already have had, there is no obvious role for Mifune in the film. More obvious is the fact that *Dodes'ka-den* is without Takashi

Shimura, Yoshio Tsuchiya, and the many bit players like Ikio Sawamura, Bokuzen Hidari, Yutaka Sada, and the dozens more who regularly populated his movies. (There are exceptions, such as Kamatari Fujiwara and Akemi Negishi, but the shift away from regulars is nonetheless significant.) Kurosawa chose not to use them in spite of the fact that many of these actors were still under contract to Toho (though they soon wouldn't be). And, for the first time, Kurosawa chose to abandon the lengthy rehearsals that had been so integral to his filmmaking process. (Although Zushi remembers rehearsing his role for "four or five months."[17]) This time, the director wanted a freer, more spontaneous feel.

In light of the events that had preceded, there are conflicting accounts of Kurosawa's mood at the time of filming. Matsumura recalls Kurosawa as "very self-centered, very different from other great directors! [laughs]. It's probably easy for him to forget about what he says when he gets pissed off. He'd never take his anger out on the actors playing minor roles, only the major ones. He gets pissed off like a firecracker, but then the next minute he is all smiles."[18]

Before shooting began, Kurosawa was quoted as saying, "The story is ostensibly told in a cold, objective manner; it depicts man's respectability, sorrow and tenderness. I think that I will suffer agony in producing this film."[19] Just as *Dodes'ka-den* was going into release, the director reversed himself. "Never before have I worked with so much relaxation," he said. "So, as you can see from the snapshots of me while working on the set, I was always smiling and never angry. I enjoyed it heartily."[20]

Actor Yoshitaka Zushi agreed, remembering that "during the shooting he was energetic; he had a 'Let's do it!' kind of attitude. When I first met Kurosawa [on *Red Beard*], I was seven years old, but my main memory was that he was very tall; I didn't know that he was a big shot. When I was in high school, I was living in Osaka and I came to Tokyo for some reason, and Mr. Kurosawa called, and I went to see him at the Akasaka Prince Hotel. At that time I realized he was a big, big director, and I got scared, just like a lowly employee going to meet the chairman of the company. There was no audition. I remember that I got the script; I read it, and he asked me if I could do it. Usually a fifteen-year-old would say, 'I don't know.' But I said, 'Yes, I can.' "[21]

Zushi is perfectly cast, bringing to life both his character and his imaginary streetcar. His head shaved to accentuate his large, oversized forehead against his tiny eyes, Zushi's Roku-chan is certainly odd-looking, appearing slightly retarded. (Some reviewers state that the character is literally retarded, though this is not explicitly stated in the film.) Kurosawa costumed him in a jacket and slacks several sizes too small. His sleeves end well before the wrist and his pants just below the knee.

Less successful is the realization of the beggar's son, played by Hiroyuki Kawase. "[He] belonged to the *Gekidan Nihon jido* [an acting school for children]," script supervisor Teruyo Nogami remembered. "I think he was eight years old at the time. His mother brought him to the set and picked him up, but during shooting he quietly waited on the set by himself. He didn't have a script with him but he perfectly remembered all his lines. . . . He was a mysterious boy."[22]

"A mysterious kid," Kurosawa concurred. "He once appeared on the stage as a dead prince in a Sartre play. . . . He's so sharp and intuitive. Whenever I stood up to go over and correct him, he already knew what I was going to say. He would just nod and then make the proper correction in his performance. . . . After the final session I was told he said, 'What would happen to [the beggar] after I die? I wonder if he would die soon since he can't feed himself.' "[23] Kawase didn't have much of a film career after *Dodes'ka-den*. He went on to play the child leads in *Godzilla vs. the Smog Monster* (Gojira tai Hedora, 1971) and *Godzilla vs. Megalon* (Gojira tai Megaro, 1973), then disappeared from movies altogether.

Dodes'ka-den is an uneven film. That it came after the very nearly perfect *Red Beard* makes it seem more flawed than it actually is. And because there is no central character, the picture invites comparison among the vignettes. Some are excellent, others never fully blossom. Certain characters are clearly more developed than others, probably because the film was written so hastily, and this throws the work off balance. The visual style is unique, even daring at times, and the "cheery Hell" approach, while sometimes off-putting, is always original.

Despite the flaws, there are several stories within the film that are beautifully realized. Best are those of the henpecked husband, Mr. Shima, wise old Mr. Tamba, and the wife-swapping Kawaguchi and Masuda. Shima is played by Junzaburo Ban (1901–81), who by 1970 was already the veteran of several hundred films since the onset of his film career in 1927. Primarily a comedian, Ban was one of the stars of Toho's long-running *Ekimae* comedies with Hisaya Morishige and Frankie Sakai (twenty-four films released between 1958 and 1969). But Ban was also a good dramatic actor, and his character—a man full of loyalty for a wife that no longer exists for him—is sensitively played. That he was a comic actor who used his entire body in his performances was probably a factor in his casting. A beautiful example of physical acting are his violent tics, which at times reveal the deep sadness of the character while at other times are simply hilarious in their timing, a subtle balance between the tragic and the absurd. It's also worth noting that this particular sequence was shot in a nine-minute, uninterrupted take. That it doesn't draw attention to itself is a tribute to Kurosawa's skill as a director.

The scenes with Kunie Tanaka and Hisashi Igawa are a relief from the darker aspects of the film. Their sequences are almost always cut in immediately before or after the picture's dreariest moments, and Tanaka and Igawa are quite funny as drunken neighbors who swap wives as if they were borrowing cups of sugar. Tanaka (b. 1932), with his droopy features and lazy eyes, spent most of the 1960s stuck in Toho's "Young Guy" series, as the Reggie-like foil to Yuzo Kayama's Archie. He played the would-be assassin in *The Bad Sleep Well* and was the dopiest of the young samurai in *Sanjuro*. By the end of the decade, directors like Kobayashi, Hiroshi Teshigahara, and Hideo Gosha began casting him in more serious roles. He remains a popular fixture in films today. Igawa (b. 1936) was, like Mifune, born in China and didn't move to Japan until he was ten years old. He studied acting at Haiyu-za, the same theater company Yoshio Tsuchiya attended, before making his film debut in Tadashi Imai's *A Story of Pure Love* (*Junai monogatari*) in 1957. He frequently worked with Masaki Kobayashi and was perhaps cast at his suggestion. Igawa won *Kinema Jumpo*'s Best Actor Prize in 1970 for his role in Yoji Yamada's *Where Spring Comes Late* (*Kazoku*). Igawa would go on to become Kurosawa's most consistent player late in the director's career, appearing in all his films from *Ran* on, as well as the Kurosawa-scripted *Ame agaru* (2000).

Quite interesting, too, if less successful, are the scenes involving the niece and her abusive uncle. In a film so thoroughly unreal in its visual design, the rape of the niece is harrowingly, almost clinically real. The uncle wakes the sleeping girl, telling her, "It's all right. It's normal. Just lie still." Kurosawa films her from above, as she lies in a "field" of artificial flowers, vaguely recalling the end of *Stray Dog*, where Mifune and Isao Kimura, exhausted, collapse in a similar field. This episode is undercut by a clouded point of view. When the niece is arrested, she asks to speak to her uncle in front of the investigators, finally mustering the strength to break free from his control. The scene occurs off-camera, with Kurosawa choosing instead to focus on the uncle's growing panic as the authorities begin catching up with him. The stabbing of the delivery boy is also not shown. We learn of it secondhand when a police officer details the news to her aunt and uncle in a talky though interesting scene. The niece, who has not had a word of dialogue to this point, remains an enigma, and optimism about her future is uncertain by her absence from much of the film.

As he often did, Kurosawa made surprising choices in some of his actors: for the uncle he picked Tatsuo Matsumura, cast against type. A theater actor exclusively during most of the 1950s, Matsumura founded the acclaimed theater troupe *Goju-nin gekijo* in 1952. He didn't make his film debut until 1959, when he was cast in *A Maiden's Prayer* (Otome no Inori). Most of his subsequent film career was spent playing kindly, middle-management types. After *Dodes'ka-den* he played an altogether different uncle in Yamada's "Tora-san" series for several years. "I think I always had a kind of fatherly, salaryman-type look," Matsumura said. "With Kurosawa it was different. In *Dodes'ka-den* he asked me to play a really vicious character. It surprised me when I was asked. Actually, though, I like to play those kinds of parts in films and in the theater. Something like Tony Curtis in *The Boston Strangler*. I always wanted to play intelligent mobsters, but it was difficult finding those types of roles. I was always playing teachers, professors [laughs]. Directors would take one look at me and say, 'No way!' "[24]

Matsumura would work for Kurosawa only one more time, ironically playing the kindly teacher role in which he was usually typecast, in Kurosawa's last film, *Madadayo*, but this part would also be the best of his career.

Of the remaining principals, three simply don't work at all—Mr. Hei, the zombie-like husband, and the beggar and his son—yet are given substantial screen time. The latter pair are one-note characters, the eternal dreamer who shuts out all the misery around him and his wiser, more resourceful son. Kurosawa is clearly sympathetic to these characters, and the cutaways to the house as it is constructed are intended to have a magical air about them, but the effect is strained and unsatisfying. There's also a certain redundancy to these scenes. Roku-chan is similarly living in his own world of fantasy, yet his scenes, which invite the viewer to imagine the trolley along with the boy, have an earnest simplicity the beggar's scenes, for all their elaborate shots of gates and fences and swimming pools, never achieve. Roku-chan, through his imaginary trolley, lives in an alternate reality altogether, while the beggar's retreat into fantasy comes off as irresponsible behavior, resulting in his child's death (the reverse of what happens to the poisoned boy in *Red Beard*).

If the character of Mr. Hei is as closed-mouthed as that of the young niece, his own plight is trivial by comparison. Critics who complained that Kurosawa was reaching back into his past are justified to a certain extent by this role. He recalls the tragic lover played by Tsutomu Yamazaki in *Red Beard*. Where that character is deftly used as a counterpoint/mirror image to Red Beard, Hei is an isolated, uninteresting figure. Technically well done, these scenes have no emotional or intellectual impact, and Hei appears a self-pitying, self-involved fool.

As the old tinker, Tamba, Atsushi Watanabe is one of the film's few fully realized characters, recalling Red Beard and anticipating the old professor at the center of *Madadayo*. This is best represented in a scene where an old man (Kamatari Fujiwara), having lost his health, his family, and his fortune, begs for help committing suicide. The tinker casually obliges him, giving the old man poison. As the old man swallows the poison and wistfully recalls his dead family, killed during the war, the tinker states that if they are, in essence, alive as long as they live in the old man's memories, is it then fair to kill them off? The old man panics and desperately begs for an antidote as the tinker goes from drawer to drawer. At this point the tinker admits that he didn't give him poison at all but an antacid. Stunned by his own foolishness, the old man collapses in disbelief. (Kurosawa regular Fujiwara is very good in this vignette. Though only sixty-five, Fujiwara looks much older due to skilled makeup and the removal of most of his bridgework.) It's a funny, insightful moment, and it's unfortunate that the simplicity of this scene does not more consistently permeate the entire picture.

Seventy-one-year-old Watanabe (1898–1977) had appeared in several Kurosawa films beginning with *One Wonderful Sunday* in 1947. He was memorable as the patient who warns Takashi Shimura about the deception of terminally ill cancer patients in *Ikiru* and as the coffin maker in *Yojimbo*. He had been in films going back to at least 1927 and was with Toho since its inception in the late 1930s.

"I'd wanted Watanabe from the beginning," Kurosawa said, "but I'd heard that he was very old, with very weak legs and almost deaf. And then I saw him on television and he looked perfect! So weather-beaten and imperturbable. He couldn't hear me because my voice is so thick, but he could recognize the voice of my script assistant, [Teruyo] Nogami. Utterly unperturbed, he performed precisely what he was told. Whenever I said, 'Thank you; you must be tired,' he mimed a 'What?' "[25]

For the film's advertising, Kurosawa himself painted elaborate, expressionistic art that barely hinted at what the film was. "He took a long time to do such a strange one," co-screenwriter Hideo Oguni recalled. "I heard that he was concentrating on it so much that he lost a lot of weight."[26]

The Japanese audience was likewise caught off guard, or perhaps turned off, by the film's unexpected tone against its bleak yet colorful setting, which perhaps reminded them of their own difficult postwar years. (The film's dump recalls *Drunken Angel*. And the director's signature sump separates the shanty dwellers from the middle classes, seen at the film's beginning.) Audiences expected another *Red Beard*—what they got was practically a fairy tale.

Dodes'ka-den was met with indifferent box office. It lost money—Kurosawa's first film in fifteen years to do so. Japanese audiences didn't want to be reminded of the dire conditions they had endured immediately after the war. And while such conditions were, for the most part, a thing of the past, a new economic recession was looming. *Dodes'ka-den* was in one sense a reminder of where they had been and where many might be heading if conditions in Japan didn't improve.

The financial failure was especially heartbreaking for Kurosawa, since the film had been so inexpensive to make by his standards. The picture cost just ¥100,000,000 (about $300,000), three times the cost of an average Japanese feature in 1970 but a bargain when compared with the director's last few films. What's more, *Dodes'ka-den* had come in ahead of schedule and *under* budget. But worst of all, its failure quashed any future films for the Club of the Four Knights. Borrowing money to make it, they themselves had put up half the production costs.

Dodes'ka-den was not a complete disaster in Japan. It did make *Kinema Jumpo*'s "Best Ten" list, ranking third behind Yoji Yamada's *Where Spring Comes Late* (Kazoku) and Satsuo Yamamoto's ambitious *Man and War* (Senso to ningen). *Kinema Jumpo* editor Yoshio Shirai said at the time, "Because the actors are relaxed and performing freely, the audience is also relaxed and frequently bursts into uproarious laughter. This is very new for a Kurosawa film. And periodically the audience is very deeply touched. Therefore I think *Dodes'ka-den* is an extremely 'popular' film in the best sense of the word."[27] But Shirai was wrong; *Dodes'ka-den* was not as popular as it should have been.

The film was better received abroad, winning prizes in Australia, the Soviet Union, Yugoslavia, and Belgium. It was warmly received in America as well, ultimately earning a nomination for Best Foreign Film. (*The Emigrants*, Israel's *The Policeman*, and the Soviet-made *Tchaikovsky* were also nominated. They all lost to *The Garden of the Finzi-Continis*.) *The Hollywood Reporter* said:

> Any new Kurosawa film is a cause for celebration, especially after his six-year absence. . . . Kurosawa gets away from any forms of Western filmmaking and into pure cinema which is closer to Ozu or

Mizoguchi than it is to Peckinpah or Leone. . . . What strikes one most in this film is Kurosawa's resolute humanity, and the film comes off with the haunting lyricism of a Brahms symphony. . . . It is hard to imagine a Kurosawa film without the swaggering, scowling Toshiro Mifune, but his absence here is not felt if only for the excellence of the actors used. . . . In each and every frame of "Dodes'ka-den," it is apparent that Akira Kurosawa knows of the human spirit in all its manifestations, fierce and noble, proud and gentle, and most important, spirited and reflective.[28]

Variety's "Mosk" said: "Some may find it old hat but Kurosawa cannily skirts mawkishness and sentimentality for a rousing and beguiling picture of people who live in an environment that they do not rebel against but sometimes try to avoid by dreams or even a passing rage. . . . For his return he has a human comedy which his agile direction keeps alive and adroit despite its deceptively simple theme and locale. . . . [His] talent has raised it from its familiar pattern and it shows him still a discerning director."[29]

Judith Crist dismissed the film as "disappointing," adding: "The Kurosawa touch—of high comic insight, warm human perception—and keen camera eye are intermittently apparent, but the film as a whole is pedestrian and trite, its effects garish rather than surreal. It is his first film in five years; we look forward to his next."[30]

But John Torzilli argued: "*Dodes'ka-den* is a powerful and memorable film, and certainly one of the Japanese master's best. . . . His use of color, though hardly subtle, is a hundred times more effective than all of Antonioni's painted cities and Fellini's bizarre film dreams."[31]

"Probably there were many reasons," Tatsuo Matsumura says of *Dodes'ka-den*'s failure to find an audience. "He was running out of ideas, maybe. The Golden Age of Japanese film had ended. Other media were becoming popular; the Japanese were better off, vacationing in hot spas and all that."[32]

As *Dodes'ka-den* went into release, and before its notably lukewarm reception, Kurosawa had talked about the possibility of adapting another Dostoyevsky novel, *The House of the Dead*. Like *The Idiot*, it would be rewritten with a Japanese setting and was to be shot in 70mm. But the failure of *Dodes'ka-den* halted plans for anything so elaborate.

Kurosawa meanwhile busied himself with his only significant work in television, a documentary about horses, *Song of the Horse* (Uma no uta), which recalled his final work as an assistant director, *Horse* (1941). It aired on August 31, 1970, exactly two months prior to the opening of *Dodes'ka-den*.

When asked by reporters to name his favorite film from his oeuvre, Kuro-sawa always had the same answer: "The next one." Making movies was his life, his raison d'être. Now it looked as if there might never be a next one.

On the morning of December 22, 1971, sixty-one-year-old Akira Kurosawa went to his bathroom, took out his razor, and slashed his own throat six times and his wrists eight.[33] His maid was the first to find him, lying on the bathroom floor in a pool of blood.

"In those days," said Mike Inoue, "Kurosawa Production had very severe financial problems because he couldn't find any studio interested in his making a new film. His budgets were so huge, and Kurosawa was very sad, because everything, his life, was about making movies. [Yoichi] Matsue was running around like a crazy man trying to find extra income, even from a television drama Kurosawa might agree to write and direct, but Kurosawa said, 'I just can't direct a stupid television drama.'

"All this was happening around that time. Kurosawa said to himself if he couldn't keep shooting films, then there was no reason for him to stay on this earth. But that's my assumption; he didn't tell me that. Early in the morning, his maid heard water running very loudly in the bathroom, and she rushed in and there was Kurosawa—he had cut himself all over his neck and wrists, and all the water was running down the [bathtub] drain. Later, he said the reason he had drained the tub was that he did not want his family to see all the bloody water. Luckily, because he did that, she heard him."[34]

The maid woke up Yoko and Kazuko. They wrapped bandages around his wrists and neck as he lay beneath a blanket in the middle of the courtyard hallway, near the family garden.[35] They called for an ambulance, and Kuro-sawa was taken to the hospital. There, doctors reported that he was in seri-ous condition but was expected to live. Yoko made a brief statement in which she acknowledged that her husband had recently seemed depressed about his lack of work.[36] Once safely inside the house, Yoko had a break-down and stayed in bed herself for several days.

"It was real chaos," Inoue said. "A few days later, when I found out that he was going to survive, I went to the hospital. He was very calm; he was awake. I shouldn't have, but I asked the question 'Why did you do it?' You know what my uncle said? 'A man who commits suicide always has a reason he wants to take to his grave, so don't try to dig it up. Don't ask me that question.' That was the end of the conversation. I was ashamed that I asked."

Reporters and colleagues flooded the hospital, but the family allowed few visitors. According to Inoue, "Only his children, his wife, myself, and my wife. Of course, there were other people, and there was a lot of confusion. Maybe Mr. Honda was permitted, but I'm not sure."[37]

Shiro Mifune recalled, "My father was shooting a TV show at the Tamagawa River when he heard about it. He stopped the shooting and ran to Mr. Kurosawa's home." Yoshio Tsuchiya said he spent a great deal of time visiting Kurosawa after he was brought home to recover, and recalled that Mifune later visited Kurosawa at the house. Mifune, Tsuchiya said, was notably ill at ease and left after a short time. "After that," said Shiro, "they didn't have too much contact."[38]

Senkichi Taniguchi, whose relationship with Kurosawa during this time was admittedly cool, was nonetheless shaken by Kurosawa's desperation. "I don't know why he did it. I heard that two or three days earlier a few actors had gone to his house for drinks, and one of them had said something that hurt him. Many people ask me about it. I went to the front of his house and I saw him lying in bed with [bandages around his neck and wrists] but could tell he was okay from the atmosphere around the house. I left without visiting him. I don't know what happened exactly. I just heard that everything was going wrong with him at that time. That's the difference between his personality and mine. He was very sincere and put all his energy into a film. I know how to evade a problem. I never thought about killing myself."[39]

While the suicide attempt was barely mentioned in the West, the Japanese media had a field day. Once Kurosawa returned home, the press continued their siege unabated, climbing fences and positioning reporters and cameramen atop the roofs of Kurosawa's neighbors. After the disaster of *Tora! Tora! Tora!* and now this, Kazuko later joked, "December is not a good month for our family. Very emotional blood runs through our family's veins. Sometimes we're not so rational. He's very good-natured, but also easily hurt. Our family is very sentimental, and sometimes very stupid. He had been at the top for so long, maybe it's difficult for people to understand how he felt. Still, he shouldn't have done it. He's a great man, but he has weaknesses, too. To be truly strong, you have to be sensitive."[40]

Yoshitaka Zushi said, "It hurt us very badly. . . . His family was very supportive, especially his son, Hisao. I think he was able to move on. I don't think it was the box-office failure of *Dodes'ka-den* that led to his attempting suicide, though. I guess that he may have thought he might never be able to make another film, a Japanese film, within the Japanese film industry."[41]

For a Japanese artist to commit suicide when, for whatever reason, he finds himself unable to work, or feels his creativity waning, is not uncommon, nor in Japan is it considered illogical or shameful. Thirteen months earlier, Yukio Mishima had publicly committed *seppuku* as an ultimate protest against Japan's move away from its traditions. And Yasunari Kawabata, author of the famous short story "The Izu Dancer" and the novels *Snow Country* and *Thousand Cranes*—a man considered the dean of Japanese letters—asphyxiated himself in April 1972, just four months after Kurosawa's attempt, when (it was presumed) he decided he was unable to produce work at the level which he had become known for and accustomed to.

Some reports said that after his suicide attempt it was discovered that Kurosawa had been suffering from an undetected ulcer, the discomfort of which might have contributed to his mental state. Inoue, though, denies this. "He was physically healthy but mentally ill, very troubled."[42]

Against everyone's expectations, Kurosawa quickly recovered. He returned to doing what he always did between films. According to his daughter, Kazuko, he would typically get up in the morning to read the newspaper, go back to bed, and not rise until noon. He preferred showers to baths, and on rare occasions, when Kazuko or Yoko would coax him to take a Japanese-style bath, he could never sit in it for very long. And he loved the company of his dogs. Throughout his adult life he kept them—Pomeranians named Poni and Mini, a collie named Sonny, a black cocker spaniel named Putti. He even kept a St. Bernard, Leo, which he entered in dog shows and accorded the luxury of a room-sized cage, complete with fan and ever-running water.[43]

In the years that followed, Kurosawa shut the door completely on this darkest phase of his life. "He never discussed it again," said Inoue. "And I never asked him about it."[44]

TWENTY-THREE

RONIN

In 1970 Toshiro Mifune turned fifty years old. His career as a leading man in Japanese films was waning. As if to prove this, he pitched beer in a series of television commercials. Sapporo had hired him for his manly appeal. The testosterone-driven ads, which must have seemed a self-parody even then, have Mifune stoically sipping brew as he says in voice-over, "Real men just drink, without saying a word." The ad proved enormously successful, running for more than two years. Its slogan became a popular phrase among Japanese men trying to look cool.

He was also becoming a television mainstay. He was a guest star on ANB's *Epic Chushingura* (Dai Chushingura), one of the earliest examples of a yearlong historical drama. Such programs ran fifty-two weeks; the form had the advantages of being able to play out myriad subplots and exhaustive historical details. *Chushingura*, with its historical complexity and dozens of major characters, was a saga tailor-made for such adaptation and enticed stars from the stage, screen, and music worlds to appear in it.

Mifune produced *Ronin of the Wilderness* (Koya no so ronin), in which he starred as Kujuro Toge, yet another variation of his *Yojimbo* character. The program, which aired weekly for two years beginning in 1972, had an exhausting but not uncommon production schedule and precluded Mifune from taking on any film work during that time. Its staff, however, was largely culled from films he had recently made for director Hiroshi Inagaki, a crew that, if not for Mifune, would have been out of work. The series featured Jiro Sakagami and the terrific actress Mieko Kaji, soon to become a major film and pop star in her own right, famous for her subsequent "Female Convict Scorpion" films at Toei. Despite all this, the television programs Mifune produced were sold—by the actor himself—for peanuts. He had undersold himself by acting as his own agent throughout his career, as he was now doing with the entire run of a television series he had produced.

His son Shiro, meanwhile, made his film debut in *Forbidden Affair* (Sono hito wa jokyoshi, 1970), a modern romantic drama of doomed love amid the student protest scene and the kind of film that the older Mifune lamented was taking over his industry. When high school student Ryo Takeuchi (Shiro Mifune) joins protesters opposed to the Japan–U.S. Security Treaty, police crack down on them, and Takeuchi eludes arrest when a young woman, Maki (Shima Iwashita), grabs him and kisses him, pretending to be his lover. Maki turns up as one of his teachers at the high school. He falls in love with her, but initially she resists his advances. When Takeuchi leaves home and his father unwittingly asks Maki to help bring him back, she falls in love with him as well. Maki is arrested for having sex with a minor, and Takeuchi commits suicide to demonstrate his sincere love.

"I was nineteen years old," Shiro recalled, "and Masanobu Deme, one of Mr. Kurosawa's assistant directors, was directing *Forbidden Affair*, and he asked me to appear in his film. At the time I was still a teenager and thought I could do anything, and besides, I was interested in my father's career and wanted to give it a try. My father never said anything either way. My family wasn't in the Kabuki tradition or anything, where the son takes over for generation after generation. My father was just a film actor. He used to say, 'I'm only a radish [hammy] actor.' Making the first one was my decision, and after we finished, I was busy with my school life. Besides, I'm very shy about love scenes and things like that. Then my father ordered me to do the second one, and I did it and wasn't satisfied with myself—I was young and I wanted to refuse."[1]

Shiro's second film was Ken Matsumori's *Morning for Two* (Futari dake no asa, 1971), with Eiji Okada and Ryoko Nakano (later to star opposite Toshiro Mifune in 1978's *Love and Faith*), for Mifune Productions. Shiro then began shooting a film called *Young, Young* (Japanese title: *Kenji*; also known as *Sand Drops*), produced by his father's company. The picture was directed by Masaaki Asukai, the 1964 graduate of the UCLA film school who had worked for Mifune as an interpreter as far back as *Grand Prix*. The film was to be shot entirely in the United States, with an American crew, cast, and equipment. Most of the picture was to be in English, which Shiro, unlike his father, spoke fairly well. The script follows a Japanese student (Shiro Mifune) who becomes acquainted with an American student (Diane Hull) in San Francisco. The two then travel around the country.[2]

"Shiro and Diane meet on a bus," Asukai explained. "He's discovering America, and she's discovering herself. I know it sounds corny, but I interviewed seventy-five girls before picking Diane. It's not easy to find a nineteen-year-old girl who can act. I need a good actress because it's my debut and I don't know what I'm doing! We're shooting entirely in English. I think that's a first for a Japanese company. [We're shooting] in Wyoming, Idaho, San Francisco, Pismo Beach, and Los Angeles."[3]

As a young man, Shiro bore a remarkable resemblance to his father at that age, though he was considerably taller. But by his own reckoning, Shiro was not the actor his father was, and when *Young, Young* was canceled during production, he gave up acting altogether.

The film was canceled, at least in part, because of a falling out between Asukai and Mifune, one similar to that between Kurosawa and Tetsu Aoyagi. "Mr. Asukai used to do the foreign negotiations before my father knew Miiko [Taka]," Shiro said. "But finally Asukai was gone. My father trusted people, but Asukai was . . . doing strange things."[4]

Mifune's naïve trust in the judgment of others out to make a fast yen extended as far away as Germany, where the actor launched one of his costliest failed ventures. "He used to go to Munich to film commercials for Sapporo Beer, because Sapporo and Munich were sister cities," said Shiro. "He went there several times. Before the 1972 Olympic Games in Munich there were no Japanese restaurants there, and his German interpreter suggested opening a restaurant, and so he . . . decided to do it. The construction was started, and all the raw materials were sent over to Munich, as well as Japanese carpenters, and a complete tea ceremony room. But during that time, the laws in Munich changed and the site was rezoned so that restaurants could not be built in that area. My father filed a lawsuit against the City of Munich and spent a lot of money. He said, 'I don't like to give up.' He found another place in Munich, but due to the delays he couldn't get the restaurant open in time for the Olympics. It finally opened in 1975. I went there to help and ended up working there for six years. It was really hard work. The first three years we lost money, but after that, the business picked up. Nevertheless, those first three years I kept calling my father in Tokyo saying we have no money."[5] Like so many other schemes he was talked into, the restaurant ultimately failed, and Mifune lost a small fortune.

He turned fifty on April 1, 1970, and, though in excellent health and still quite handsome, Mifune was beginning to show his age. This was apparent in his first released film of the decade, *Zatoichi Meets Yojimbo* (Zato Ichi to Yojimbo), shot in late 1969. Fighting the inevitable collapse of the Japanese film industry, the man who not too long ago had been Toho's biggest star joined forces with Daiei's most popular actor, Shintaro Katsu. (Katsu's only rival at Daiei, cult actor Raizo Ichikawa, had died the previous July.) As he had in 1968 with Nikkatsu's Yujiro Ishihara, Mifune reckoned that if audiences were reluctant to go to the movies to see one leading man, surely they would plunk down their yen to see two stars for the price of one. Mifune's domestic career was ebbing and he knew it. But he may not have realized that such rudderless pairings had an air of desperation, similar to what Universal Studios attempted with their second cycle of horror films in the 1940s, when Frankenstein met the Wolfman, who met Dracula.

Thus came *Zatoichi Meets Yojimbo*, actually "Zatoichi *and* Yojimbo" in Japan. Under any title, pitting the two icons of *chambara* against each other was simultaneously thrilling and cheap. Nor would it be the end of such measures. Katsu would produce *Zatoichi Meets Yojimbo* for his company, with Mifune nominally a hired hand. Mifune would then return to Tokyo to star opposite Kinnosuke Nakamura in *The Ambitious* (Bakumatsu, 1970), a film produced by Nakamura's production company. Then all three would converge with Yujiro Ishihara in *The Ambush* (Machibuse) for Mifune Productions. All these films were released in the first four months of 1970, and all were tremendous disappointments. *Zatoichi Meets Yojimbo* was the best of the lot, but because expectations ran so high, it was also the biggest letdown.

For many, Shintaro Katsu (1931–97) simply *was* Zatoichi, the blind swordsman, who already had nineteen adventures under his belt.* The series began in 1962 and proved so popular that as many as four Zatoichi movies were released each year. Katsu had been with Daiei since 1954, but for much of his early career he toiled in supporting roles, usually playing heavies. He himself was a stocky man with beady, baggy eyes, protruding ears, and a round face whose features were pushed together like an infant's. It was this childlike, innocent look that Daiei's better directors began tap-

---

*Technically, Zatoichi means "Masseur Ichi," but the author has chosen instead to refer to the character by the more commonly accepted name.

ping into, casting him in villainous and anti-hero roles until he found his niche playing the character that would make him famous. As a blind man living in nineteenth-century Japan, Zatoichi occupied the bottom rung of the social ladder, his standing below even those of the peasants and whores who populate his movies. Zatoichi ekes out his meager living as a wandering masseuse, a common occupation for blind men at the time, but Zatoichi is no ordinary blind man. His lack of sight has enhanced his other senses to a fantastic degree. He is a master swordsman, using his cane sword and wits to stay one step ahead of gangsters who would gladly do him in. Also a gambler: in nearly every Zatoichi movie he stumbles into a gambling den filled with tattooed *yakuza*, meekly asking if he might make a wager. *Yakuza* hoods, thinking they can easily take advantage of his blindness, condescendingly welcome him. Alternately humble and disrespectful, Zatoichi goads the *yakuza* boss into making a large wager as the boss's lackeys try to fix the game. But Zatoichi always outsmarts them, usually with his fantastic swordplay, before politely stumbling out again with a pocketful of *ryo*.

Audiences loved this. Even more than Yoji Yamada's "Tora-san" films, the Zatoichi movies followed a rigid formula they rarely deviated from. Not that it mattered. The films catapulted Katsu to super-stardom in Japan. Daiei, in even worse financial shape than Toho, all but gave him the keys to the studio. He made as many as nine films a year for Daiei, and starred in not one but several continuing film series, notably the "Hoodlum Soldier" pictures, which began in 1965 with *Hoodlum Soldier* (Heitai Yakuza) under the direction of Yasuzo Masumura. A delightful black comedy about Japanese soldiers stationed in China during the later days of the war, Katsu, like Lon Chaney, Jr., before him, played a Lennie-like brute to Takahiro Tamura's George. Daiei even flooded the market with imitation Katsu pictures starring Shintaro's older brother, Tomisaburo Wakayama (1929–92), who later starred in the Katsu-produced "Lone Wolf and Cub" film series of the 1970s.

On paper, *Zatoichi Meets Yojimbo* looked promising. It may have been Mifune's suggestion to hire Kihachi Okamoto, still under contract to Toho, to direct the film. It seemed a good match. Okamoto was best working with material that uncomfortably blurred the darkly comic with the tragic, the very appeal of the best Zatoichi movies. Composer Akira Ifukube had scored nearly half the series, and more than a dozen films starring Mifune. Daiei's star cinematographer, Kazuo Miyagawa, had shot four Zatoichi films, plus *Rashomon* and, significantly, *Yojimbo*. Why then did the film fall apart so badly?

The story has Zatoichi nostalgically returning to a village three years after his last visit, only to find the town has become a gang-infested sewer not unlike the village in *Yojimbo*. Two years earlier a drought had led to famine, and its citizens either left, starved, or resorted to eating rats. The village elder (Kanjuro Arashi) had hoarded food to get his people through the winter, but word of this spread to similarly suffering villages, and he made the mistake of hiring thugs to protect it. The gangsters took over, corrupting the village. A prostitute, Umeno (Ayako Wakao), tells Zatoichi, "Good people die. Only the bad thrive."

One of the gangsters is Sassa, a *yojimbo* (Mifune), who describes himself in even more dire terms: he's "bad-bad." He's offered 100 *ryo* to kill Zatoichi and drunkenly tries to do so. But Zatoichi is too fast for him. In a very funny first meeting, Sassa stabs Zatoichi and the blind man lets out a wail. But he's only taunting Sassa—Zatoichi, quick in his movements, has positioned himself so that Sassa has slid his sword right back into its sheath. They decide to resume their duel another time, and Sassa invites Zatoichi for a drink.

Sassa is employed by Masagoro (Sakatoshi Yonekura), the greedy, disowned son of Eboshiya (Osamu Takizawa), an opportunist silk merchant. Eboshiya, a seemingly kind old gentleman who is worse than the thugs working under him, hires Zatoichi to be his combination masseuse and personal bodyguard. This sets up the film's second act, in which Sassa and Zatoichi create trouble for each other, echoing the edgier taunting between Lee Marvin and Mifune in *Hell in the Pacific*.

The film's primary narrative, and its downfall, is an ordinary struggle between father and son. Eboshiya, in charge of gold shipments, has been skimming off the top, hiding sacks of gold dust. His son becomes aware of this, as does a second, more "respectable" son, Sanaemon (Toshiyuki Hosokawa), who uses a greedy spy (bony-faced Shin Kishida) to get to the gold, hidden in tombstones at the local cemetery.

Zatoichi and Sassa, who is in actuality an Edo government spy, find out about the gold as well but are only incidentally connected to it. Beyond a means to an end, money has never been important to Zatoichi. In this film alone he gives away 200 *ryo* to buy off Umeno's debt to Eboshiya, so that she can run off with Sassa, whom she loves. As for Sassa, only briefly does he toy with the idea of running off with the loot. And so Zatoichi and Sassa's story must share screen time with this glum family melodrama that concludes, as such things are apt to do, with a bloodbath (with a nod to *Treasure of the Sierra Madre*), only the two leads and Umeno surviving.

The film is both a Zatoichi movie in which the *yojimbo* is a supporting character and a Mifune/*Yojimbo* movie in which Zatoichi is brought in for support. Neither character manages to drive the narrative. Zatoichi is a loner; every Zatoichi film ends with the blind man resuming his solitary journey. So, rather than a pair, Katsu and Mifune are no more than occasional rivals jerkily pulled through the story to its predictable climactic duel, one that can end only in a draw.

As a Zatoichi film, *Zatoichi Meets Yojimbo* is a disappointment, a lesser but not awful entry in the series. For Mifune, returning to the kind of role that defined his career, the picture was a failure. As this was a Katsu production with no connection to Kurosawa's company, Mifune couldn't legally play the character from *Yojimbo*, and Sassa is far removed from the scraggly *ronin* he'd played for Kurosawa's cameras. This *yojimbo* is a troubled, drunken informer. He's in love with Umeno but ashamed of the way she sells her body and of her resignation to being a "slave to money." He's a skillful swordsman, but one who allows the hell he occupies to consume him. An interesting premise, but once he's introduced, screenwriters Okamoto and Tetsuro Yoshida don't know what to do with the character. In the end, he resolves to start a new life (what that means is never made clear), yet, when it looks as if he's going to run off with Umeno, the film ends inexplicably with Zatoichi and Sassa walking off in different directions, alone.

And there are other problems. Okamoto, whose direction so enhanced *Samurai Assassin*, gives us more snowy battles, but they pale against his earlier work. He fumbles Zatoichi's comedy scenes with uncomfortable camera angles and abrupt, choppy editing. In retrospect, Akira Ifukube was entirely the wrong choice to write the film's score. It's a heavy, doom-laden affair, unmemorable and devoid of the irony Okamoto's favorite composer, Masaru Sato, might have brought to the film. Perhaps owing to the shaky finances of the period, *Zatoichi Meets Yojimbo* has a cheap air to it, as if its shack-filled village and muted colors (everything is brown, black, or dirty green) were reflections of the crumbling industry itself. Finally, it is the screenplay, a myriad of unused opportunities, misplaced emphasis, and poor structure that brings the whole misguided affair crashing to the ground.

Most critics agreed. The film's American advertising touted it as "roughly the equivalent of Clint Eastwood shooting it out with John Wayne," but as David Shute wrote: "The picture is just a tad too stately for its own good [and] all too well aware of its own 'instant classic' status. The

rather solemn, reverential tone of the picture doesn't fit the central characters, who are two of the mangiest, smelliest anti-heroes who ever slouched
across a movie screen. . . . Both Mifune and Katsu are in good form, however, and their scenes together are the macho ham actor's equivalent of an
arm-wrestling tournament. It's great fun watching them try to out-shrug,
out-scratch and out-belch each other. If the picture were a little peppier, it
would be an unqualified delight."[6]

Kevin Thomas, calling the match-up "as momentous as King Kong going
up against Godzilla," had fewer reservations, calling the film "a handsome,
action-filled movie, expertly directed with both humor and poignancy by
Kihachi Okamoto in what is perhaps his best job to date."[7]

Mifune then put in a guest appearance in actor Kinnosuke Nakamura's
The Ambitious, a mid-nineteenth-century political and class drama, with
Nakamura (who also produced) as a thoughtful samurai wanderer. Mifune's
part in the film, Shojiro Goto, was small. The story revolves around the adventures of Goto and his friend, played by Tatsuya Nakadai. The film is significant mainly as the last work of director Daisuke Ito, the same man who
had left *The Day the Sun Rose* due to illness.

Next came *The Ambush*, which starred not only Mifune, Nakamura, and
Shintaro Katsu but Yujiro Ishihara and stage and film actress Ruriko Asaoka
as well. Once again, Mifune plays a bodyguard, further cheapening his great
Sanjuro from the Kurosawa films. Here Mifune's unnamed *yojimbo* makes
his way through Mikuni Pass in remote Shishu. He has been instructed to
wait at the pass and stops by a teahouse run by Tokubei (Ichiro Arishima)
and his granddaughter, Oyuki (Mika Kitagawa). Living in a barn behind the
teahouse is a "doctor" named Gentetsu (Shintaro Katsu, looking shaggy and
bearded). There is much scheming and double-crossing but little else in
terms of story.

A tedious, uninspired film despite its cast, *The Ambush* was Hiroshi Inagaki's last feature, and reviews were mixed-to-negative. Most dismissed the
picture as another routine Mifune samurai action film; they had become interchangeable of late, particularly with their similar-sounding English titles: *The Ambitious* and *The Ambush*; *The Day the Sun Rose* and *Tunnel to the
Sun*; *Samurai Banners*, *Samurai Assassin*, and *Band of Assassins*; and so forth. *The
Hollywood Reporter* found *The Ambush* "lethargic," adding that the movie, "is
interesting but overly long at 1 hour and 55 minutes. Devotees of Japanese
movies should enjoy both the film and Mifune, though his role is far from
his best."[8]

Boxoffice wasn't thrilled either, calling it "much in the accepted Toshiro

Mifune mold . . . the kind of role he's emoted with effectiveness over the years. . . . It's Mifune melodrama, scenery-chewing of old, complete with snarls and smirks, and to the stateside audience that seemingly dotes on the Mifune cult, there's little to quibble about."[9]

Mifune had a fleeting role in another Ishihara film, *The Walking Major* (Aru heishi no kake, 1970), based on a true story about a Korean War veteran (Dale Robertson) compelled to raise money to rebuild a dilapidated Japanese orphanage. Making bets with U.S. soldiers stationed in Japan, he walks more than 800 miles, from Zama (in Kanagawa Prefecture) to Beppu (Oita Prefecture), several times to raise funds. In spite of his dedication, it takes the intervention of a newspaper publisher (Mifune, his part little more than a cameo) to complete the project. All the while, the soldier's motives are questioned by a television news cameraman (Yujiro Ishihara), who learns that the soldier had accidentally shot a Korean couple, leaving their child an orphan. Over the years, the soldier had visited the decaying orphanage managed by Shige Yamada (Michiyo Aratama). Before the soldier can see the completed building, he's killed in Vietnam. The news cameraman resumes his journey for him, searching for meaning in the American's gesture.

As press material for the film noted, "The Japanese motion picture industry is undergoing drastic changes today. The five major film studios which dominated the Japanese movie industry for a long time are on the wane, giving rise to numerous independent film producers in the latter half of the 1960s. . . . The producers feel that the concept of utilizing foreign film stars and creative talents will give the film an international appeal and will break new ground in Japanese motion picture history."[10]

Despite the appearance in the film of such third-tier names as Frank Sinatra, Jr., and Dina Merrill, *The Walking Major* could no more rescue the film business than an all-star *jidai-geki* like *Band of Assassins* could. At a time when the majors were desperate to keep costs down—some producing features for less than $100,000 and Nikkatsu making Roman porno for as little as $25,000—*The Walking Major*, filmed at a cost of $800,000, was a gamble. Ishihara had rolled the dice with *A Tunnel to the Sun* and *Safari 5,000*, and the risk had paid off. He wasn't so lucky with *The Walking Major*.

Mifune also put in a brief appearance in *The Militarists* (Gunbatsu), Hiromichi Horikawa's examination of Japan's most infamous military leader, Hideji Tojo. The picture begins in 1936 with the Army mutiny and the appointment of Tojo (Keiju Kobayashi) by the Japanese Emperor. Amid growing tension between Japan and the United States, Tojo is urged to make a peaceful settlement by both Admiral Yamamoto (Mifune) and Tojo's assistant, Takei (Goro Tarumi). He responds to this by sending Takei to the front, but can do little to stop the popular admiral after his victory at Pearl Harbor. When the Battle of Midway proves the turning point in the war, Tojo opts to hide the Japanese defeat from the public. Soon after, Yamamoto is killed. A war correspondent, Goro Arai (Yuzo Kayama), realizing the inevitable, presses his editor (Takashi Shimura) to print his story and alert the Japanese people. Goro's actions incur Tojo's wrath, and the reporter, like Takei, is sent to the front to die. After the Americans invade Saipan in the Marianas, Tojo's cabinet begins to crumble. Arai is reproached by a kamikaze pilot (Toshio Kurosawa) for his hypocrisy. Didn't Arai fan the flames of war and increase Tojo's power during the Japanese victories, only to denounce him later? Arai realizes that, had he printed the truth earlier, the war might never have begun.

Toho had a lot of money riding on *The Militarists*, an attempt to combine serious drama with the popular appeal of its epic war films, much as *The Emperor and a General* had four years earlier. It was considered such a big deal that it premiered in Japan on a roadshow basis with release prints in 70mm. For these reasons, probably, Mifune was pressed into recycling a character he had played less than two years earlier.

While the film focused on Tojo, Kevin Thomas admired the fact that the filmmakers "wisely [did] not make him simply the scapegoat for his country's disasters. . . . [The film] makes a special point of the crucial importance of not only the freedom but also the responsibility of the press—and by extension all the media—to tell the truth to people. . . . Its picture of a nation whose leaders are propelling it toward a war impossible for it to win is utterly convincing, and its pertinence for us today scarcely needs underlining."[11]

"Director Horikawa has caught pungent moments of savageness and torment," said *The Hollywood Reporter*. They disliked Yuzo Kayama's acting but had praise for Kobayashi. "Keiju Kobayashi gives a thoughtful performance as Tojo . . . transformed from a self-controlled militarist to a dictatorial viper. . . . In a very brief role, Toshiro Mifune is Admiral Isoroku Amamoto [sic], an enthusiastic but also hesitant advocate of the war. Toshiro Mifune furrows his brow and worries his way through the part."[12]

The *Reporter* also praised the special effects, although most of them, including Yamamoto's death, were culled from stock footage of earlier films. As big a picture as *The Militarists* was, Toho could no longer afford to produce a war film on the scale they used to.

Mifune was busy in 1970, putting in appearances in five films. But after his next, *Soleil rouge* (U.S. title: *Red Sun*), released in Europe in 1971, the actor would be absent from the screen for four years. In the majority of pictures that followed, his parts were limited to guest star roles far beneath his abilities, many weaker than the films he had made in the late 1960s and early '70s.

Mifune's decline is apparent in *Red Sun*, a forgettable Western. It starred Charles Bronson as Link, a train robber whose partner, Gauche (Alain Delon), double-crosses him in the middle of a big heist, stealing the gold and leaving Link for dead. Coincidentally, on that same train is a Japanese ambassador (Tetsu Nakamura) whose gold samurai sword, intended as a gift for the U.S. President, is now part of Delon's booty. The ambassador dispatches one of his samurai, Kuroda (Mifune), to retrieve the sword, and he and Bronson form a reluctant alliance, eventually kidnapping Gauche's girl (Ursula Andress) as leverage against the ruthless gunman.

After the success of Sergio Leone's *A Fistful of Dollars* and its follow-ups, European filmmakers flooded the market with such films, *Red Sun* being just one of dozens released in 1971 alone. Only during this eclectically continental period could a movie about the American West have been filmed in Europe by a British director for Italian, Spanish, and French companies, starring Lithuanian-American, Japanese, Swiss, and French actors.

Mifune had been approached with a fifteen-page outline in Japan by producer Ted Richmond back in 1966. Giving a verbal commitment, Mifune met with Richmond again in Hollywood in early August 1968. The project was allied with Paramount, then moved to a pre–Ted Ashley Warner Bros. In the end, the film was produced by France's Corona Films and distributed in the United States by National General, a second-rate company that never gained a real foothold in the market. Still, the film cost a good deal of money, going a million dollars over budget and ultimately brought in for $4.5 million.[13] Nevertheless, it did extremely well in Europe, largely due to the novelty of Mifune's presence and Bronson's cult status there. (Like Telly Savalas, Bronson was far more popular and enduring in Europe than he ever was in the United States. Alain Delon, a self-confessed fan of Mifune's work, was big in Europe, too, starring with Bronson in *Adieu, L'Ami*.)

The picture was to have been shot in the American West, prompting *Variety* to ask, "Will [Mifune] at last get to act in an American-filmed pic?"[14] But Mifune's income tax situation precluded shooting there—with his tax bracket, he simply could not afford to make money in America. Instead, *Red Sun* was shot in Madrid and Almería, Spain, and on a new soundstage at the Studio de la Victorine in Nice.[15]

Terence Young, director of two of the best James Bond films, *Dr. No* (1962) and *From Russia with Love* (1963), and the most successful, *Thunderball* (1965), was signed onto the project. While he prepped the film, Mifune asked for and got permission to push the starting date ahead from late fall 1969 to early 1970.[16] There were more delays, and shooting didn't actually begin until mid-January 1971. Mifune's commitments to *Red Sun*, and the delays that resulted, may in part explain the mediocre quality of his own film work in Japan during this period.

When the picture was at last ready to begin shooting, Mifune brought with him a tremendous entourage. In addition to his wife and Shiro came his own makeup man, hairdresser, propman, double, and tailor. He also brought enough Japanese food to get him through the 18-week schedule, which was ultimately delayed 18 more days due to rain. Mifune used the time to practice his English with the aid of tape cassettes he'd brought from Japan.[17] If he could, he was going to avoid the embarrassment of being dubbed, as he had been on *Grand Prix*.

Though the principal cast kept largely to themselves, shooting went smoothly, no doubt supported by Young's fluency in English, French, Spanish, and Italian.

The picture opened in Paris, where it was a smash hit. Reviewing an English-language version there, *Variety's* "Mosk" complimented Mifune's enunciation, adding: "[He] is his towering, glowering self in his rich samurai garb. . . . Terence Young has brought off an actionful thatawayer that should have good chances in Europe with playoff and regular possibilities abroad, too. Has zest and intros a Samurai to the old West."[18]

The movie itself is rather ordinary, with Mifune, as if dropped from the sky above, brought in for novelty value alone. Though the plot is based on a historical incident, Mifune is required to play only the Western-imagined stock samurai character. For his part, he doesn't add much, playing his role stoically and stony-faced from beginning to end, perhaps because he was concentrating on his English. He had managed to avoid being dubbed by someone else, but this proved to be a mixed blessing. Gone, fortunately, is the disembodied voice of Paul Frees emanating from Mifune's lips, but his English is thickly accented and difficult to discern at times. What he does say is often singularly un-Japanese ("I think you are one son of a bitch!") and awkward, not even remotely the kind of English a Japanese native would speak. Rather, it sounds like the dialogue an English speaker would put in a Japanese man's mouth, designed to be amusing, not believable.

A bigger problem is that the relationship between Bronson and Mifune never jells. Producer Richmond had wanted Clint Eastwood, but his Spaghetti Western days were already behind him by the time *Red Sun* was made. Bronson acts bemused and slightly contemptuous but little else about Mifune's "exotic" Eastern ways, and Mifune fails to tangibly warm up to him. Bronson is disgusted by Mifune's Japanese cuisine. They spar at one point, and predictably, Bronson's fisticuffs are outmatched by Mifune's martial arts.

Worse, Mifune is required to be cute:

LINK (*Making an excuse after trying to escape*) Goddamn mosquitoes! I can't sleep! There's mosquitoes all over this goddamn place!
KURODA Wrong. One mosquito. (*Kuroda whips out his short sword and cuts the bug down.*) No mosquito.

The one effort at characterization comes when Kuroda tells Link that, with changes in the Japanese government and the end of the feudal system, his breed of samurai warrior will soon be a thing of the past. Retrieving the sword may be his last mission of honor, and this means everything to him. It's a throwaway moment, but it's clear that the picture would have been better with more of this. Perhaps it should have been more elegiac, along the lines of Sam Peckinpah's *Ride the High Country* (1962) or *The Wild Bunch* (1969), and it's a pity Peckinpah wasn't hired to direct. Perhaps if Bronson's character had more depth, the predictable denouement might play better than it does. As it is, *Red Sun* is standard East-meets-West material and no credit to Mifune's career.

When *Red Sun* opened in the United States, with tacky ads screaming "A Meeting of the Far East with Far West That Is Far Out!" critics were unimpressed. *Playboy* called the film "a kind of prank. . . . Although the glittering company provides passable high-geared entertainment, the curious dignity of Mifune's performance persistently suggests that *Red Sun* might have been something more, and measurably better. Even at his most outlandish—striding through Comanche territory in full battle regalia or cutting down mosquitoes in mid-air with his sword—Mifune is a wonder to behold."[19]

The unnamed reviewer for the *Los Angeles Herald-Examiner* grumbled, "The profusion of international names may help the picture in the worldwide film market, but the resulting melting pot looks calculated and artificial. 'But what about the Armenian audience?' I asked myself by the time the film was half over."[20]

"This highly original premise . . . is not as well developed as it could have been," noted Kevin Thomas. "Mifune is the same appealing and digni-fied figure . . . but *Red Sun* does not begin to suggest what a great actor he can be in his native language."[21]

Regardless, *Red Sun* made a fortune in Europe; it ran, off and on, in the-aters there for years—well into the 1980s. As Mifune traveled to Paris for the movie's premiere, he was mulling over several film offers. One was yet another war movie, a biography of General Yamashita. "I don't know," Mi-fune sighed to the *Los Angeles Times*, "I've played so many generals."[22]

Following Kurosawa's suicide attempt, Ted Richmond, *Red Sun*'s pro-ducer, tried to reunite Kurosawa and Mifune for another "Eastern West-ern," a picture to be called *The Longest Ride*. The story concerns a Mexican bandit (presumably to be played by Mifune) trying to get a herd of horses from the American Southwest into Mexico. A script was written by Herb Meadows with, according to Richmond, "the assistance of Kurosawa and Shinobu Hashimoto." (Hideo Oguni was reputed to have worked on the script as well.) The picture was to be shot in Durango, Mexico, beginning in April 1973, but nothing more was ever heard of the project.[23] A second project, which went unnamed, was another Kurosawa-Mifune film. The film was originally going to be shot in Spain, but at Kurosawa's request, the location was switched to, of all places, Minnesota (which would make sense if it were a revised script of *Runaway Train*). Finally, Corona Films was also going to co-produce with Mifune a film to be called *Farewell to the King*, about British and Japanese tensions in Borneo at the end of World War II, and apparently based on a novel of the same name by Pierre Schoendoerf-fer. None of these projects ever came to fruition, though director John Mil-ius adapted Schoendoerffer's novel in 1989.[24]

On the way to Paris for *Red Sun*'s September 1971 premiere, Mifune and Sachiko stopped in Los Angeles, where they visited a few friends at the Cherry Blossom Inn and checked on the progress of the Mifune-produced *Young, Young*.

The trip marked the end of Mifune's marriage to Sachiko. Just six years earlier, the press kit for *Samurai Assassin* had noted of Mifune: "His family consists of Mrs. Sachiko Mifune and two sons, Shiro and Takeo. He had no love affair except with Sachiko who later became his wife. Mifune is indeed an exemplary husband."[25] What may have been true in 1965 was anything but by 1971.

In 1969 a young actress named Mika Kitagawa was cast as one of the prostitutes in *Red Lion*. During that film's production, Kitagawa became friendly with Mifune, who had discovered her in a talent search conducted by his own production company. Soon the two were having an affair. Kitagawa, only twenty-one at the time and nearly thirty years Mifune's junior, would also turn up in small roles in several more Mifune-produced films into the 1970s. Whether Mifune had had affairs prior to Kitagawa is unclear, but as he grew closer to her—especially during the productions of *Red Lion* and *The Ambush*—he became less and less discreet about their relationship.

Soon after Mifune's family returned from Europe and *Red Sun*, Mifune's troubled relationship with Sachiko became front-page news. It was reported that, in a drunken rage, he had fired a gun he owned inside his home. Police were called, Shiro left home, and Mifune's affair with Kitagawa became public knowledge. Sachiko left him and moved in with her parents. He went to their house to apologize, but instead childishly accused *her* of having an affair.

The following June he filed for divorce. *Variety* reported: "The international actor is blamed for squandering money by selling his property without her knowledge."[26] Left unsaid was that a large part of the separation had to do with Miss Kitagawa, who, given Mifune's busy schedule, had simply become a bigger part of his daily life than Sachiko had been in years.

The divorce Mifune wanted and later demanded was a messy affair. Sachiko refused to grant him one and succeeded in forestalling the process indefinitely. Mifune countered by publicly flaunting Kitagawa, hoping to goad his estranged wife into caving in. The tabloids and mainstream press had a field day: Mifune denied he had forged incriminating love letters, but admitted to spray-painting obscenities on the house of his in-laws.[27]

In 1974 Mifune made headlines when he brought Kitagawa instead of his wife to a government function attended by the Japanese Emperor and President Gerald Ford. "The actor was accused in the press of an act of *lèse majesté*, of flaunting his mistress in the imperial presence," wrote Donald Richie.[28]

"As far as I'm concerned, I was already divorced," Mifune countered. "I got an invitation that said Mr. and Mrs. The tables all had name cards and it would have been rude of me to leave an empty place . . . Some American film actresses have had five divorces. Me, only once." The media, he argued, was "always going into people's houses and looking down their toilets. I just don't want them coming in to open the drawers and take out the dirty underwear. Some of them do it without any conscience."[29]

Mifune's public separation and Kurosawa's public suicide attempt paralleled the near-meltdown of their respective careers and their increasingly strained relationship with each other. Whether their acts were symptomatic of their inability to regain control of their careers is difficult to say, but the early 1970s were personal and professional low points for both men. What is clear in retrospect is that Kurosawa would fully rebound; Mifune would not.

Kurosawa's recovery was partly due to the small but intensely loyal crew that remained at his side. Mifune, conversely, had no such support. Reacting to the plague of financial problems that had beset Mifune Productions almost from the beginning, coupled with his personal scandal, many of the actors he had under contract walked out on him.

It was *Scandal* for real.

TWENTY-FOUR

SIBERIA

"Being able to make a film . . . with complete creative control restored my spirits."[1]
—Akira Kurosawa

To Western observers, by 1975 the Japanese film industry had turned its back on Kurosawa, but this was not entirely true. To begin with, Kurosawa was hardly alone. The state of the industry ground the careers of many of his contemporaries—all in their sixties—to a halt: Senkichi Taniguchi, Ishiro Honda, and Hiroshi Inagaki among them. Each director had become specialized in relatively high-budget genres—Inagaki in epic *jidai-geki*, Honda in large-scale fantasy films—but by this time the audiences for those films had declined. Their pictures, like Kurosawa's, were costly by Japanese standards, and though they were popular, their profits had become marginal, when they were profitable at all. Conversely, directors like Kinji Fukasaku and Toshio Masuda made inexpensive yet highly lucrative films; their overall attendance may have been lower, but at least they were safe investments promising large returns.

Kurosawa might have shifted his efforts to television as Ishiro Honda did (as well as directors in other countries whose film industries were flagging, such as Ingmar Bergman and Jacques Tati). But Kurosawa was a filmmaker through and through: his style relied on storytelling techniques that were exclusive to film, and the projects that interested him were far beyond the limited budgets TV production in Japan could provide.

Kurosawa's film career might easily have ended with *Dodes'ka-den*. Then, out of the blue in 1973, he was given carte blanche to make a film of his own choosing. This marked the beginning of a dozen-year renaissance. There had been talk of Kurosawa shooting a film in the Soviet Union as far back as February 1971. When he accompanied *Dodes'ka-den* to the Moscow Film Festival, serious negotiations began, and the official invitation came in the early months of 1973. "I was the first one to receive a call from the Russian Embassy," recalled Mike Inoue. "The man.who called us said there was a problem. 'Movies [in the Soviet Union] are our only entertainment. We have very poor writers and directors, and we decided to ask Mr. Kurosawa a favor and ask him to write a Russian story and direct it for us.' " Inoue then asked for the man's name. "I could hardly believe it! He was a Russian who spoke fluent Japanese! Anyway, Kurosawa agreed to take that job because he had always liked the novels of Dostoevsky and other Russian literature. He had ideas about the script, even before the Russians asked him."[2]

Kurosawa chose a nonfiction work called *Dersu okhotnik*, eventually known in English as *In the Jungles of Ussuri*. It was an autobiographical account by a Russian soldier, Vladimir Arseniev, of his surveying expeditions in the Ussuri region of Siberia in the early 1900s. There he met a hunter named Dersu Uzala, a Mongolian of the Goldi tribe. Dersu lived a simple life, but one that amazed Arseniev. He felt that Dersu's affinity with nature made him a great man. Kurosawa's backers were delighted with his choice. Many were surprised that he was even aware of Arseniev's work, which was famous in Russia but largely unknown outside the Soviet Union.

Indeed, Kurosawa had toyed with adapting *Dersu okhotnik* as far back as his assistant director days. For him the appeal of the material was not unlike that of one of his favorite silent films, Robert Flaherty's *Nanook of the North* (1922), about a primitive yet remarkably resourceful Eskimo who struggled for survival in the Arctic region. After completing *The Idiot* in 1951, Kurosawa enlisted Eijiro Hisaita to help him draft an adaptation. "I never considered filming it in the Soviet Union," Kurosawa said, "so we transposed everyone and everything to Japan. However, the script wasn't very interesting. I found there was no way to make it work with a Japanese setting."[3]

Hisaita agreed: "I changed Dersu into one of the original natives of Hokkaido, the *Oroko*, and wrote it. But it was just impossible to shoot it in Japan, so we didn't go any further with it."[4]

Now, Kurosawa felt, was his chance to do the story right.

"Arseniev is not a professional writer," Kurosawa had said, "but a traveler and explorer, [yet] I respect him as a writer, too. Just [like] his colleagues in Russian literature he is capable of deep penetration into a human heart. His books gave me a chance to contemplate the problems that have always interested me."[5]

A contract between Mosfilm and Kurosawa was signed on March 14, 1973. Toho declined to participate, but a new conglomerate, Nippon Herald, agreed to invest Japanese funds in exchange for the Japanese distribution rights. At a press conference attended by Kurosawa, a Mosfilm spokesman said, according to *Variety*, "Artistic direction of the [film] will be left 100% to Kurosawa's discretion."[6] Moreover, Kurosawa was to shoot the film in 70mm, the large-screen format denied him for *Runaway Train*.

One rumor circulating at the time had Toshiro Mifune being considered for the part of Dersu, but Inoue denies this. "Not true," he said. "That was a Russian film. No Japanese actors were invited. That was a false rumor."[7] However, *Variety* reported that Kurosawa "said tentatively that he hoped to cast Toshiro Mifune in the title role."[8] Yuri Solomin was cast as the Russian officer that summer, while *Variety*'s Moscow bureau was still claiming that Mifune was up for the lead.[9]

Mifune had genuinely wanted to work with Kurosawa again, but according to Shiro, the thought of spending a year or more in Siberia terrified him. He had his company to consider, and *Dersu Uzala* came at a time when the actor was appearing constantly on Japanese television in an effort to get his studio out of the red. "My father . . . was busy with his company's affairs," Shiro remembered. "And of course, Mr. Kurosawa kept asking him to do *Dersu Uzala* but he said he was busy. My father knew Mr. Kurosawa's films took a long time to make, and he knew he could not go to Siberia for more than one year. It was a difficult situation."[10]

Kurosawa, however, was desperate to make another film, so much so that he was willing to brave harsh Siberian winters working with a cast and crew largely made up of people who didn't speak Japanese. That the offer from the Soviets to make *Dersu Uzala* was as much political as aesthetic— they were courting the Japanese to invest capital in the region—was beside the point. Kurosawa was making a new film, and for him that meant everything.

Though he left his family behind, Kurosawa would not be going to the Soviet Union alone. His longtime script supervisor, Teruyo Nogami, whom Kurosawa years ago had affectionately given the nickname "Non-chan," would constantly be at his side. Her assistance would prove so valuable that he would reward her with an associate-director credit. He also brought cinematographer Asakazu Nakai into the production. Nakai had worked with Kurosawa for nearly thirty years, going back to *No Regrets for Our Youth*. He was used to Kurosawa's long production schedules, having endured both *Seven Samurai* and *Red Beard*. Nakai would shoot *Dersu* with two Russians familiar with the Sovscope 70 cameras, Yuri Gantman and Fyodor Dobronravov. Out of the hundred men and women that made up *Dersu*'s crew, only six were Japanese.

Kurosawa's collaborator on the screenplay was Yuri Nagibin, a novelist since 1940 and a screenwriter from 1955. His screenplays, often Communist in nature, alternated between adaptations of his own stories, including *The Night Visitor* (1958)—several based on the lives of composers, including the Dimitri Tiomkin–supervised *Tchaikovsky* (which Nagibin co-wrote, 1972)—and stories set in contemporary Russia. He wrote two novels about Tchaikovsky, *How the Forest Was Bought* and *When the Fireworks Went Out*, and another, *The Memorial Concert*, about Sergei Rachmaninov.[11]

Kurosawa and Nagibin worked with earlier drafts and ideas Kurosawa had developed over the years. In particular, they removed many of the bleak, heavy existential implications of life and death that haunt Dersu. According to critic Peter B. High, much of this was written shortly after the financial failure of *Dodes'ka-den*, when Kurosawa's spirits were at their lowest. Had these scenes not been dropped, the film might have been better, but also extremely bleak.

With Mifune out, Kurosawa cast Maxim Munzuk in the title role. Munzuk had graduated from the Kyzil Drama School in 1945, and soon after became the leading actor and co-founder of the Music and Drama Theatre of Kyzil, the capital of the Tuva Autonomous Soviet Republic. He became a household word to theater fans there, especially after playing the part of Vladimir Lenin in *The Man with the Gun*. For his work in the theater, Munzuk was awarded several honorary titles, including Merited Artist of the Russian Federation and People's Artist of the Tuva Autonomous Republic. He made his film debut in 1959, in a small role in *People of the Blue Rivers*, but otherwise his film career had been spotty. Kurosawa valued him "not as an actor, but as a man, whose temperament and way of life are very close to Dersu. He also likes the mountains, woods, and hunting."[12] Munzuk died in 1999.

For the part of Captain Arseniev Kurosawa turned to Russian actor Yuri Solomin. Solomin was culled from the ranks of the U.S.S.R. Maly Theatre, where he had been awarded the People's Artist of the Russian Revolution Prize. A 1957 graduate of the Shchepkin Drama School, Solomin had made his film debut in a small role in *The Sleepless Night* (1960). He found the experience unrewarding and worked exclusively on the stage for the next several years. By the mid-1960s, his fame had soared, and he was offered roles in many prominent Soviet films, turning down most offers, though he began appearing regularly in television dramas. "Solomin is a very skilled actor and a highly intelligent one," Kurosawa said. "And Arseniev, a military man, was also a scientist and a writer. In this I saw a compliance of the actor's personality with the future film character."[13]

Neither actor was known outside Russia, but this only served to make them more real, more immediate, particularly Munzuk, who all but became the simple, noble hunter.

Prior to leaving for the Soviet Union, Kurosawa received word that seventy-one-year-old Kajiro Yamamoto was seriously ill and confined to his bed. Like that of so many of his contemporaries, Yamamoto's career went into sharp decline after 1960. In 1964 he directed and co-wrote *Samurai Joker* (Hana no o Edo no musekinin), a period Crazy Cats comedy. The film was a success, but at that time the Crazy Cats were at the peak of their popularity. Toho's management felt that their younger directors, men like Kengo Furusawa and Takashi Tsuboshima, were better suited to their style; Yamamoto was old school by contrast. In 1967 he wrote the gently humorous *Youth Belongs to Us!* (Bocchan Shain—Seishun wa ore no Monoda!), about a young salaryman sent to a small town. It was a popular film and Yamamoto wrote the sequel, *Young White Collar—Let's Run!* (Bocchan Shain—De tsuppashire!, 1967), but directed neither. At sixty-five his career was over.

Kurosawa was shocked by Yama-san's appearance. "On his sickbed [he] had lost so much weight that his unusually large nose looked even larger," Kurosawa wrote. Yamamoto asked about the progress of *Dersu*, and the Russian assistant directors, and they spoke fondly of various sukiyaki restaurants even though Yamamoto could now hardly eat at all. "I couldn't help marveling at the characteristic enthusiasm he showed in talking about it so cheerfully. He probably wanted to send me off to Russia with light-hearted memories."[14] It was the last time Kurosawa would see him. Yamamoto died on September 21 of that same year, while Kurosawa was a thousand miles away.

By the time New Year's Eve rolled around, Kurosawa was still in Russia. "Since I didn't have anywhere to go that day, I went to the Filmmakers'

Union," he recalled. "There were some screening rooms and a few restaurants. Some people there threw a party and it was very festive when the clock struck midnight. I envied that environment."[15] For Kurosawa, the atmosphere reminded him of a period in the Japanese industry now lost.

Filming began in February 1974. Kurosawa got on well with the Russian crew, particularly Dobronravov. "Cameraman Fyodor is a funny man and he's trying to learn Japanese," Kurosawa said. "When he heard that Mr. Asakazu Nakai was suffering from constipation, he said, in Japanese, 'Nakai-san having a pain, constipation,' or 'Nakai-san suffering.' He's very clever with words. He kept me laughing the whole time. And he's thoughtful, too. I got a cold twice during filming. He said that I needed more vitamin C and went to the market and bought me some radishes and tomatoes."[16]

Dobronravov and the Soviet crew thought very highly of seventy-three-year-old Nakai, too. For them Nakai had become nearly as much the living legend as Kurosawa, and the camera crew learned much from Nakai's decades of lensing films in Japan.

Both literally and figuratively, conditions were harsh for Nakai and Kurosawa, himself in his mid-sixties. In Siberia the temperature dropped at times to 40 degrees below zero. The colds Kurosawa developed resulted in a leg ailment, and early in the production he suffered from frostbite, the aftereffects of which would plague him for years after *Dersu*'s completion.[17] In addition, concern for his own country's industry troubled him greatly while he was shooting abroad. "I thought about it constantly while I was in Moscow," he said.[18]

As the film neared completion, Kurosawa toyed briefly with having Masaru Sato write the score, but he quickly recognized the need for a Russian composer. He watched a number of Soviet films and conferred with his six-person contingent before settling on Isaak Shvarts. Shvarts's music, both intimate and mournful, is exactly what the film needed.

Kurosawa then began the task of editing the large-frame 70mm film at Mosfilm's studios. He worked with Liuba Fejginova, Andrei Tarkovsky's regular editor, to cut the picture. After the better part of eighteen months in Moscow and Siberia, Kurosawa's first film made outside Japan was completed.

Dersu Uzala is told in flashback, in two parts. The story opens in 1910, as Arseniev searches for the grave of his dearest friend, the hunter Dersu

Uzala. Arseniev first met Dersu in 1902, during a military expedition to the Taiga region. At first, the soldiers regard the illiterate peasant as something of a joke. Dersu speaks pidgin Russian, and in contrast to the tall, hearty Slavs, he is a small, squinty-eyed, barrel-chested Asian, almost elf-like. Dressed in skins and furs, he waddles through the forest like an animal. It soon becomes apparent, however, that Dersu's experience in and knowledge of the Siberian forest far outclass that of the hapless Russians. Arseniev invites Dersu to become their guide, and he proves invaluable. When Arseniev and Dersu are stranded on a remote plain during a blizzard, Dersu saves the captain's life by building a makeshift shelter out of the tall grass that surrounds them.

Five years later, Arseniev returns to Ussuri for another surveying expedition, and is just about to give up hope of ever seeing Dersu again when the two are happily reunited. Dersu again proves a worthy guide, but as the expedition draws to a close, it becomes clear that he is losing his sight. For a hunter such as Dersu, this is catastrophic. He begins to panic, and Arseniev offers to take him into his home. In the city, though, Dersu is miserable. He finds urban life alien and unbearable, and decides to return to the wilderness. Arseniev gives him a high-powered rifle (to compensate for his failing eyesight), but soon after returning to the forest, Dersu falls victim to thieves who steal the rifle and murder him.

Dersu Uzala marked a major turning point in Kurosawa's career. Formerly scornful of and resistant to the media, Kurosawa was now accessible as never before. Though his irascible side would peek through the cracks, he was for the most part gregarious and cheerful. At the same time, his films became increasingly bleak, sullen, mournful. The faith in mankind *Red Beard* and even *Dodes'ka-den* exhibited, in spite of their settings, would evaporate in *Dersu*, *Kagemusha* (1980), and *Ran* (1985). Kurosawa the public persona and Kurosawa the artist seemed at odds with each other.

In response, many of the critics who had championed Kurosawa's work of the 1950s and '60s turned on him. If *Dodes'ka-den* was an interesting failure, they argued, then *Dersu Uzala* was proof positive that Kurosawa was no longer capable of reaching the heights of his earlier work. For them, *Dersu Uzala* was a supreme disappointment.

If *Dodes'ka-den* represented an interlude in Kurosawa's career [wrote Japanese film scholar Joan Mellen], with *Dersu Uzala* the decline in

THE EMPEROR AND THE WOLF 513

Kurosawa's powers truly becomes apparent. In *Dodes'ka-den* Kurosawa used color in an expressionistic and brilliant manner to shield himself from subject matter with which he was no longer willing to engage in creative combat. A similar distancing of the artist from the world he depicts is accomplished in *Dersu Uzala* by means of 70mm wide screen, so large that normal theaters cannot accommodate the film, and by six-track stereophonic sound, which surrounds the audience from rear to side speakers and envelops them in mood at the expense of substance.

Style had become an end in itself. Gone was Kurosawa's intervention in the pain his characters face in everyday life. . . . It is too late for a knowing elder to educate a younger man, because that instruction can no longer be put into practice in the world as it is: this feeling about present-day Japan Kurosawa transports to Russia of the turn of the century. . . . Kurosawa in fact appears to have lost all interest in the living human being beset by his own intransigence, balancing joy and sadness, and forced to face the depleted world as it is. And in abandoning a dynamic sense of character, Kurosawa has produced for the first time in his long and outstanding career a rather lifeless film. Its hollowness is barely concealed by the overwhelming screen size, the sound effects, and the elegiac musical motif mourning [Dersu].[19]

Donald Richie seems to have agreed: "I didn't write the chapters on *Dodes'ka-den* and *Dersu Uzala* [in later editions of *The Films of Akira Kurosawa*]. . . . The fact that I didn't want to or couldn't, to a certain extent, was that the kind of Kurosawa I had known up to *Red Beard* is the kind of man I wrote about, and I didn't want to write about the others. The reason . . . probably, is that I don't approve of the pictures. They stopped interesting me. They're so different."[20]

The decline perceived by scholars and critics originated in Japan. To be sure, like Kubrick, David Lean, and other great filmmakers, Kurosawa had his loyal followers, who championed even the weakest of his films. But for many in Japan, Kurosawa, like Orson Welles, had sold out. He now courted the media to generate publicity he had previously disdained. And in 1976 he did the unthinkable—like Mifune, Kurosawa traded on his fame by appearing in a television commercial. That he did so on his own terms mattered not to them. As he sits stoically, his eyes hidden behind sunglasses, his appearances in a series of ads for Suntory whiskey asked nothing of him but his name and image. But even this much was painful for him. Nevertheless, he felt he had to do it—he needed the money. He had completed only two films in ten years, and until now making movies had been his primary source of income. He was spared the indignity of pitching cheap wine and frozen peas like Welles, but for some his very appearance in ads was disgraceful for an artist as moral as Kurosawa. For him, an afternoon before a television camera somehow had compromised his status as a filmmaker.

While it mattered little to Kurosawa that to continue making films he had to do so in the Soviet Union, some Japanese were insulted. Not to mention that, as an artist, Kurosawa was leaning in a different direction. *Dodes'ka-den* and *Dersu Uzala* bore little resemblance to *Yojimbo* and *High and Low*, and they resented that as well. Kurosawa had become restless in his art, and for the remainder of his career he, like Picasso, constantly experimented. It is understandable, then, that many mistook Kurosawa's ongoing growth as a filmmaker for artistic decline. As Mellen wrote: "[It] was as if his despair had been refined to a cynical surrender to a world he once challenged in disdain. Kurosawa seemed to be flaunting an ultimate alienation, asserting that he no longer considered it worth the effort to struggle; he appeared at home with his despair and with the loss of faith in the artist's ability to transcend the limitations of the present."[21]

Mellen concluded: "The looser, more relaxed personality may actually have concealed a hardening in Kurosawa, a determination to resist feeling deeply, whether in his work or in his life, perhaps because he had been profoundly hurt and betrayed by the Japanese film industry and by a public to which he had for years given his personal and creative all."[22]

Mellen wrote these words in 1979, for the Japanese edition of Richie's *The Films of Akira Kurosawa*. By the early 1990s, Kurosawa's art had again transformed itself into something that clearly refuted such statements, but during the 1970s and '80s, such assessments were not uncommon. As *Dersu Uzala*, *Kagemusha*, and *Ran* won sackfuls of international awards and filled theaters all over the world—including Japan—a contingent of elitist critics, whose influence had grown enormously in the 1970s, became increasingly dismissive when not downright hostile toward the great director in his autumn years. Such treatment was much like the venomous attacks on David Lean upon the release of *Ryan's Daughter* (1970). Invited to a meeting of the National Society of Film Critics in New York, Lean recalled:

[It] was one of the most horrible experiences I have ever had. I remember Pauline Kael meeting me at the door and leading me by the hand to the table where there were ten or twelve critics and they sat me at the head of the table and within seconds they started grilling me in the most unfriendly fashion. One of the most leading questions was, "Can you please explain how the man who directed *Brief Encounter* can have directed this load of shit you call *Ryan's Daughter?*" It really cut me to the heart, and that was Richard Schickel. I think he's a jolly good writer, by the way. And it got worse and worse. . . . I was a fool to stay there, of course. I remember saying to Pauline Kael at the end, "You won't be content until you've reduced me to making a film in black and white and 16mm." And she said, "We'll give you colour."[23]

Kurosawa avoided such head-on collisions, but the print attacks on his so-called decline grew fiercer in direct proportion to the acclaim he had received from many of these same critics years earlier. This climaxed with the release of *Ran* and a cruel dismissal by the *National Review*'s John Simon, who thought the internationally acclaimed *Ran* so bad he didn't bother to review it. Pressed by readers to explain his abstention, Simon wrote: "I didn't review Akira Kurosawa's *Ran* . . . because I find it an almost total failure by a genius in his old age, and tearing it apart would be worse than taking candy from a baby—knocking an old man's crutch out of his hand. . . . Since I am neither a daily reviewer nor a Kurosawa monographer, I can pass over *Ran* in silence. Besides a gesture of regret for his last few films, let that silence also be one of respect for the many that went before."[24]

In part, critics resented Lean and Kurosawa choosing to embrace 70mm, insisting that the format's advantages came at the cost of substance. Lean proved such thinking faulty with *Lawrence of Arabia* (1962), but it is true that most 70mm films were overproduced, empty-headed epics or saccharine musicals. The critics failed to realize that, like Lean, Kurosawa used the format in a manner quite unlike that of other directors. In 70mm, *Dersu Uzala* is more intimate than epic. With it he creates mood not, as Mellen states, at the expense of substance, but to draw his two characters closer together and to heighten the reality of the world they inhabit.

Although *Dersu*'s cast included the captain's wife and son, and various peripheral characters like the soldiers who accompany Arseniev, the film is entirely about Arseniev's friendship with Dersu. The other characters barely exist, and this is by design. The profound effect Dersu will have on Arseniev's life is all-encompassing. When they are reunited in the film's second act, Kurosawa uses his camera not for grandeur, but to express the intimacy of the moment, to capture every unsaid emotion. He uses the six-track, stereophonic sound to envelop Arseniev and his men, and by extension the audience, in the otherworldly forests of Siberia, where they sit by their campfire, fearfully listening to the strange sounds that surround and threaten them until they encounter Dersu.

Kurosawa and cameramen Nakai, Gantman, and Dobronravov also depict the duality of nature. Throughout the film there are indescribably beautiful shots that express the insignificance of man against its awesome power, a common theme in Asian art and philosophy. But Kurosawa does so in ways unlike any film that had come before *Dersu*. The Siberian forest becomes a brilliant, golden sea. Tree branches come alive in gleaming red-orange hues illuminated by the soldiers' nighttime campfire. Arseniev and Dersu gaze at the setting sun and rising moon within the same frame. As Kazuo Miyagawa had done in *Rashomon*, the sun itself is photographed in a manner without precedent. At times it is a threatening red ball that slowly, surely slips into the horizon, while Arseniev and Dersu desperately construct their grass shelter as the deafening, freezing wind whirls around them. Kurosawa isn't distancing himself from the world he depicts, as Mellen asserts; rather, he is putting himself and his audience at the very center of it.

It is true that Kurosawa mourns the death of man's simpler, more harmonious relationship with nature. But *Dersu Uzala* isn't chiefly a film of nostalgic despair, nor does it depict, as Mellen suggests, a world trying too late to absorb the lessons of a man like Dersu. Change is inevitable, Kurosawa concedes, but through Arseniev, Dersu's lessons are not lost. They certainly weren't lost on Kurosawa when he read Arseniev's book in the 1930s, and with *Dersu Uzala*, Kurosawa made Arseniev's cautionary tale accessible to the world.

Dersu, too, is not without humor. One of the film's best scenes, which Mellen considered "far less dramatic than the snowstorm of Part One," is simultaneously frightening and funny. As the soldiers attempt to ford a river, Arseniev's men are thrown overboard, and Dersu is left clinging to a tree stump in the middle of the raging waters. The soldiers try to rescue him, but haven't a clue how. Clinging to branches, his energy waning, Dersu instructs the men to chop down a nearby tree. "No, not that one!" he shouts as the soldiers rush from tree to tree. "Not that one!" instructs Dersu, "*that* one!"

Mellen is presumptuous in assuming that Kurosawa was projecting himself onto Dersu, the wise, misunderstood man, too pure for the modern, civilized world. Dersu is a man so pure that when he asks a man to hold on to his money for him and the man runs off, it never occurs to Dersu that he's been robbed. When Dersu sees Arseniev's wife buying water, the hunter is outraged by the very idea. Certainly Kurosawa never claimed to be that pure or that naïve.

Perhaps it was just as well Mifune didn't portray Dersu. Munzuk looks as if Kurosawa had plucked him out of the Siberian forests, and his acting is invisible. By contrast, Mifune would have been too larger-than-life for the part. (Solomin is likewise excellent, utterly believable as a turn-of-the-century Russian soldier.) At first, Kurosawa makes Dersu an almost mythic figure. He seems to come out of nowhere, rather like, as Mellen suggests, a forest fairy. His past is shrouded in mystery. Asked his age, Dersu responds, "Me live a long, long time." But as the film progresses, his mortality becomes sadly apparent. As Arseniev and Dersu draw closer, the captain learns how Dersu's wife and children died of smallpox. When Dersu shoots a tiger, he considers it a bad omen, experiences nightmares, and becomes irritable. By the time his eyesight begins to fail, his pain has become overwhelming.

Like so much of Kurosawa's work, *Dersu Uzala* is a film where appearances are deceiving. At first Dersu appears the cliché country bumpkin. His idea that the natural elements—fire, wind, rain—are living beings, too, is dismissed as quaint superstition. But Dersu sees what civilized men cannot. He is, as Arseniev describes him, a "beautiful soul" who wastes nothing and is considerate of everyone and everything around him.

As the end of production was drawing near, Chinese officials charged the film with "adding fuel to the Sino-Soviet dispute," claiming that the picture had "anti-China overtones." The charge was absurd, particularly in light of one of the film's more striking characters, an old Chinese man who also finds kinship with Dersu.[25] Kurosawa considered the film apolitical, adding, "There was no clear border between the Ussuri region and China back then, and there were Chinese, Korean and Japanese people in the region. Now there is a problem between China and the Soviet Union. I think I wrote the script with fairness toward both. . . . We should not bring the issue in the story. We'll make the film with the Moscow Film Festival's motto in mind: 'Humanism through film art. Peace and friendship among the nations.' " Still, Kurosawa conceded that depicting the story's Chinese characters proved one of the more difficult challenges when writing the script.[26]

By the time it was finished, *Dersu Uzala* had cost an estimated $4 million, though the exact figure remains impossible to pinpoint due to Russian production and Communist bookkeeping methods far removed from Western standards.[27] *Dersu* premiered in Japan on August 2, 1975, and was far more successful than *Dodes'ka-den* had been five years earlier. The reviews, however, were mixed, and the film was shut out by *Kinema Jumpo*, which gave their Best Foreign Film award to the American film *Harry and Tonto*. The film was screened at the Moscow Film Festival on August 12, 1975, where it subsequently won the festival's top prize, the Gold Medal. By late 1976, it was estimated that more than 20 million Russians had seen the 70mm version, with more screenings in the coming year, after it had been reduced to 35mm for outlying markets.[28]

By the time *Dersu Uzala* was ready to open in the United States, Toho's effort to crack the U.S. distribution-exhibition market was over. Increasingly inferior products and dwindling attendance led to the closing of the Toho La Brea in May 1976, which soon thereafter became a Korean church. Toho then joined forces with Shochiku. They shared operating expenses on another Los Angeles–based theater, the Shochiku-owned Kokusai, alternating releases until that theater closed on October 30, 1986. In Hawaii, Shochiku supported Toho's Nichigeki Theater in Honolulu until it, too, closed.

The end of the La Brea did not directly affect Kurosawa or Mifune, as neither was regularly making films for Toho anymore, but its passing marked the end of an era. As manager Tetsuzo Ueda noted, "The population of first-generation Japanese people, who were our principal customers, has been diminishing every year, and the second generation of Japanese people understand English so well that they are not interested in Japanese pictures."[29] In addition, Japanese-Americans were by this time mirroring the sentiments of moviegoers in Japan: Japanese movies just weren't good anymore. Like the rest of the world, the Japanese were spending their money on Hollywood films.

Dersu Uzala was first shown in the United States at the Samuel Goldwyn Theater in Beverly Hills, California, on a Sunday afternoon, February 8, 1976. The screening was for Academy Award consideration, despite the fact that the film had not yet been released in America. It was projected in its original 70mm, six-track stereo format, with a billed running time of 165 minutes.[30] Seven weeks later, on March 29, *Dersu Uzala* won the Oscar as Best Foreign Film. Because the Academy ruled it a Soviet film, Kurosawa wound up competing with one of his own countrymen, Kei Kumai, whose *Sandakan No. 8* was also nominated. The Associated Press's Naoaki Usui interviewed Kurosawa in Tokyo after *Dersu Uzala* won the coveted prize. "I feel as if I have unloaded a heavy burden that I owed to the Russians," he said. "When I was making the film, the Russians were very generous in helping me, which I really appreciated. And with this award, I feel I can present something in return to them. The appeal I wanted to make in this movie was to conserve nature, which is a worldwide concern today. And I think that is why *Dersu Uzala* won the prize." Kurosawa added that he wished he could have won the award for a film made in Japan, "but I think it is impossible. Japanese producers are not too eager to invest a lot of money and they are also reluctant to produce a controversial movie."[31]

Inoue was of two minds about the victory. "He went with Nogami-san, spent three years over there, and ironically that film received Best Foreign Film. But all the prizes went to the Russian government—he never received a thing!"[32]

The following day, March 30, *Dersu Uzala* was shown at the Los Angeles International Film Exposition (Filmex), again in 70mm and six-track stereophonic sound and likewise billed at 165 minutes.* Kurosawa's use of the wide film format was praised by those who saw it. "The film is brilliantly photographed," said *The Hollywood Reporter*'s Todd McCarthy. "The 70mm work approaches the highest standards of David Lean's work with Freddie Young and the painstaking care is especially evident in the incredible storm scene in which—in every shot—the sun seems to have set slightly more as two men [are] lost, literally, in the middle of nowhere. . . . This is an eloquent film from a mature, resourceful filmmaker."[33] The film was shown, again in 70mm, at the New York Film Festival on October 5.[34]

But *Dersu Uzala* might never have been shown beyond the festival circuit had the picture not been acquired by Roger Corman. A cult director of clever, low-budget genre films, Corman gave up directing in 1970 to form New World Pictures, a company that distributed exploitation movies to the drive-in market. New World's releases of the period included such luridly titled works as *Big Bad Mama* (1974), *Death Race 2000* (1975), and *Eat My Dust!* (1977). In September 1976, Corman announced that he had acquired

---

*It is undetermined whether this was in fact a longer cut of the film or a misprint, with Filmex simply repeating a mistake made by the Academy, which may have incorporated an intermission into the program's running time. The film was shown throughout the world at 141 minutes, except, according to one source, in the Soviet Union, where *Dersu Uzala* ran 181 minutes. (Filmex program. 1976. 44.)

the U.S. and Canadian distribution rights to Kurosawa's film and planned to open *Dersu* the following January.

New World had made a verbal agreement not with the Russians but rather with a group of New York investors who were first in acquiring the U.S. and Canadian rights. They did so not out of love for the film or Kurosawa's oeuvre, but rather as part of a tax shelter scheme. (Copyright on the film's U.S. version is registered to the Churchill Coal Corporation.) Their distribution plans fell through when the U.S. tax laws were abruptly changed. They then made a deal with New World, but the Russians stepped in and, according to New World sales manager Robert Rehme, had "an unrealistic view of what the film was worth in the American market." The Russians wanted a larger advance, and New World refused to budge. Finally, an agreement was reached in which New World would pay the advance they had originally offered, while the Soviets would retain the Canadian rights.[35]

The negotiations were handled by Barbara Boyle, New World's attorney. "It was only because of Roger's belief that the film is so gorgeous and he wanted it so much that we kept checking back on the availability of rights," she said. Corman surprised many by releasing a series of acclaimed foreign films through his company, including Bergman's *Cries and Whispers* (Viskningar och Rop, 1972), Fellini's *Amarcord* (1973), and Truffaut's *The Story of Adele H.* (L'Histoire d'Adèle H., 1975). For Corman the benefit of releasing these movies was twofold: he genuinely admired them and he also knew he could turn a profit. When the market for foreign-language films dwindled in the 1980s, he stopped distributing them.

Dersu Uzala finally opened to the public on December 20, 1977, more than two years after it debuted in Japan. Sadly, New World released Kurosawa's film in 35mm only, with monophonic sound. In America, most 70mm houses were huge theaters tailored for blockbusters; *Dersu Uzala* was an art-house film that didn't fit the bill. Likewise, Corman could not justify the expense of remixing the six-track stereo sound to one of the 35mm stereo formats. Subsequent home video versions have been murky and monophonic. So, except for its initial screenings, Kurosawa's intimate epic has yet to be seen in America as it was intended.

This may account, in part, for the mixed reviews it received. "Visually, *Dersu Uzala* is perhaps less successful than *Jeremiah Johnson* [1972] in evoking the awesome majesty of nature as yet unspoiled by civilization," concluded the *Monthly Film Bulletin*. "*Dersu Uzala* is rescued from the reefs of sentimentality by the direction, as calmly matter-of-fact as the best of John Ford."[36]

Kevin Thomas, though, recognized the problem: "[It is] not in its splendiferous 70mm Oscar-winning form but rather in decidedly murky 35mm," adding, "While there's an undeniable loss of impact with this reduced image, the scope and magnitude of Kurosawa's achievement is evident still, if not so clearly as before."[37]

"*Dersu Uzala* is an uncharacteristic Kurosawa film," said the *Independent Film Journal*, "and even with its Academy Award for best foreign film and Kurosawa's name, its potential is limited even for the art house audience. Although it is difficult not to fall in love with the short little man of nature, it's doubtful that people will be urging their friends to go see it."[38]

The New Republic was recklessly dismissive: "*Red Beard* was excellently made, [though] it suffered from a soapy script. *Dersu Uzala* . . . is very ordinarily-made and has a 1930-type Soviet didactic script. . . . Only one sequence, in which the guide hastily constructs a shelter against an oncoming storm, is shot and edited like Kurosawa of old. The rest is more sad than bad."[39]

The *New West*'s Stephen Farber was no better: "Dersu and the explorer aren't characterized in any depth, and the ideas about the end of an era and the death of the natural man are fearfully simple. Kurosawa has wanted to make this movie for a long time. It's hard to know why. One can't help but feel disappointed that an artist of his stature is so mesmerized by a fourth-grade adventure story."[40]

"The film falters when it reaches what should be the end of its journey and pursues the relationship between the captain and Dersu back in civilization," offered *New York*. "But, ah, those chilling and inhuman snow-filled forests, those vast landscapes that seem to stretch into an infinity of time as well as space. Kurosawa captures this terrain as no one has since Dovzhenko. As with that great silent director, it behooves one simply to overlook the more obvious effects and surrender to the lyrical mood."[41]

The technical compromises and mixed reviews in America were nothing compared to the problems Kurosawa encountered when *Dersu Uzala* premiered in Europe the year before. Kurosawa's relationship with his Soviet benefactors began to sour. Initially, everyone was so delighted with the results, Kurosawa dreamed of making a whole series of films for them. But late in November 1976 a press screening in Rome revealed that *Dersu* had been drastically altered. The following night Kurosawa, having heard the outcry from the Italian press, viewed an Italian print in Milan and was horrified by what he saw.[42]

A few days later Kurosawa was in Frankfurt for the German premiere and charged that Sovexport had lied to EVI, the Italian releasing company.

According to Kurosawa, they had told the Italians the director had agreed to proposed changes for the Italian release. This included cutting the film down to two hours and replacing the music track with their own score. Members of the Italian press were as shocked as co-writer Nagibin, who also attended the press conference, and Kurosawa, who commented, "The Italian version reveals lack of understanding for the Russian film and lack of sympathy for this great Soviet hero."[43]

Sovexport's Italian representative Victor Iijin pleaded ignorance, saying that as far as he knew, the complete *Dersu* was being released. EVI, however, said that they were given approval to bring in Giuseppe Bertolucci (brother of director Bernardo) and Kim Arcalli (co-writer and editor of *1900*) to prepare a shorter Italian version. In the end, all parties ceded to Kurosawa, and the complete *Dersu* was ultimately released there.[44]

By 1976, virtually anything Kurosawa put his name on was likened to American Westerns, and when a Swiss reporter absurdly did so with *Dersu*, the director "shook an angry finger" at him. This anger was symptomatic of his frustrations that, after *Dersu*'s worldwide success, he once again found himself begging for money with which to finance his next picture. He complained that, after spending six months developing *Ran* (a first draft screenplay was completed on March 19, 1976), he had hit a wall of indifference in Japan—no one there was willing to risk the required budget. If he couldn't make films in Japan and wouldn't make films in Russia, he countered, then perhaps he'd do so in the United States, in Italy, Yugoslavia, France, or England.[45]

Just prior to his suicide attempt, Kurosawa had moved out of the large house in Matsubara, far away this time from Toho, into a large condominium in the fashionably hip Ebisu neighborhood of Shibuya. Not that Kurosawa didn't continue his lavish lifestyle. With the constant parties and gatherings of the Kurosawa-gumi, Yoko had become quite a gourmet after her marriage. She passed these skills on to Kazuko, and both were able to create a different meal for every day of the year. The constant *daienkai* and Kurosawa's love of beef resulted in grocery bills more akin to that of a restaurant than a home. By the mid-1970s their monthly butcher bill alone was running upward of ¥1,000,000 (about $5,000). One famous story had it that Yoko was passing her knowledge of cuts of meat along to a favorite butcher, who in turn used the lessons to open his own shop.[46]

At home Kurosawa's relationship with daughter Kazuko—strained during his long absences when his career was in full swing—improved. They went to see movies together, and in May 1976 she married Hiroyuki Kato, the oldest son of Daisuke Kato, the much-loved character actor who had died the previous June. The wedding was attended by two of Kato's cousins, actor Hiroyuki Nagato and Masahiko Sugawa, and his wife, actress Yukiji Asaoka. Kurosawa became a grandfather the following year, when Kazuko gave birth to a son, Takayuki, with another son, Hideyuki, to follow in 1978. "After I had my first child," she wrote, "it was like my parents became different creatures. They really loved being grandparents." The following year, in September, Kazuko moved to Torino, Italy, with her husband, who had gotten a job offer there. She stayed for two years, but made friends who would become a part of the Kurosawa family. Indeed, their bond and the influence of Kazuko's time in Italy made at least one lasting impact: every year at Christmastime the family would share the big Italian meals Kazuko had learned to cook there.[47]

When Kurosawa finished *Dersu Uzala*, Mifune made overtures about the possibility of working with his former *sensei* on a new film. The announcement came in February 1976, while Mifune was in Honolulu. "Mifune . . . did not go into details, but said the film will be targeted for international release."[48] The script, described only as an "epic drama" by *The Hollywood Reporter*, was scheduled to be finished in March and had a twelve-week shooting schedule.[49] *Variety* reported that production on the film would begin that July in Japan and that some location shooting would be done in Russia.[50] But Mifune's plans to work again with Kurosawa would never materialize. Kurosawa's ideas simply did not include Mifune, and the actor never spoke of such discussions again.

"To tell the truth, I don't know what happened," said Senkichi Taniguchi. "Even if the relationship between an actor and a director goes well, they will sometimes fight during such long-term relationships, just like children. . . . Kurosawa never came to me about it because, when it happened, our own relationship was the most distant it had ever been. Both of us were selfish and stubborn, like other directors."[51]

"They stayed in contact with each other," insisted Hisao Kurosawa. "There is a difference, though, in the relationship between an actor and a director and that between a director and an actor. The director directs an actor's performance, which position he wants him to be at, and so forth. Mr. Mifune established his own production company and became busier. They stayed in touch—it was just in a different way."

"You see," Hisao added, "as Mr. Mifune got older he [was reluctant to change his screen persona]. He wanted to be strong, but sometimes you have to change your colors. Just as a beautiful actress cannot be an ingenue all her life. Eventually he'd have to play an old man. But he still wanted to be a tough guy."[52]

"When he was young," Shiro said of his father, "it was okay to work with Kurosawa, but as he got older it got to be too much stress to work with him all the time. Then, I think, my father . . . wanted to work with other directors. Most of the people he worked with came from Mr. Inagaki's group, and they were different from Mr. Kurosawa's staff."[53]

Indeed, Mifune's camaraderie with Inagaki's group was as much a part of his estrangement from Kurosawa as anything else. Mifune had worked with director Hiroshi Inagaki's crew beginning with *Pirates* in 1951, and made twenty-one features with them—compared with the sixteen he did for Kurosawa. When Mifune's first independent feature, *Legacy of the 500,000*, composed of a crew drawn from the Kurosawa-gumi, ended disastrously, he turned to men and women culled from Toho and Inagaki—and he never looked back. When Inagaki was forced into retirement, Mifune felt obligated to keep his longtime colleagues employed on his various TV programs; they were, after all, relationships stretching back twenty years or more.

Mifune's announcement came on the heels of his first feature in three and a half years—*Paper Tiger* (1975), a curious, old-fashioned adventure melodrama filmed in Malaysia. He received second billing playing Kagoyama, the Japanese ambassador to a fictitious Asian nation. Top-billed David Niven plays "Major" Bradbury, newly arrived to tutor Kagoyama's son, Koichi (Kazuhito Ando, billed simply as "Ando"), in English and English history. Political unrest leads to the kidnapping of Koichi and Bradbury by terrorists demanding the release of sixty-five of their comrades in exchange for their return. Bradbury, a chronic liar forever telling a receptive Koichi tall tales about his supposed wartime heroism, confesses to the boy and then effects his escape from the kidnappers.

It's hard to imagine for whom *Paper Tiger* was intended. The film is part *Wee Willie Winkie*, part *High and Low*, part political thriller. Its political assassinations, kidnapping, and terrorist bombing are not exactly the stuff of children's matinees. Yet there are scenes of Koichi's imagination running wild with fantasy sequences of his brave tutor in the trenches during World War II and archly "cute" scenes of the moppet being lectured about the difference in pronouncing "L" and "R." "Okey-dokey, Mr. Bladbuly, sir," says the boy. Only Niven, an underrated actor whose great charm always seemed effortless, could get away with such treacle. He rises well above the material given him, and his final scene, where he comes clean with Kagoyama about his past (he was a schoolmaster during the war, his "war wound," the result of childhood polio), is played with honest sentiment.

Mifune signed on to the film in June 1974, which began shooting the following month in Kuala Lumpur.[54] The picture was directed by Ken Annakin and written by Jack Davies (their *Those Magnificent Men in Their Flying Machines* ten years earlier had featured Mifune's one-time business partner, actor-singer Yujiro Ishihara). Miiko Taka acted as Mifune's interpreter and doubled as his onscreen wife. Mika Kitagawa also accompanied him to Malaysia and had a bit role as the ambassador's secretary. As his scenes were being wrapped, a fire swept through the top floors of the Holiday Inn where the film's production offices were headquartered. This proved a temporary setback, however, and the production crew moved to London on September 5 to finish the picture.[55]

By 1975, neither Niven nor Mifune could be considered box-office draws anymore, nor did the film have much in the way of exploitable elements beyond its picturesque locale. Its nondescript title—confusing to audiences in the wake of *Paper Lion* (1968), *The Paper Chase*, *Paperback Hero*, and *Paper Moon* (all 1973)—didn't help matters, and *Paper Tiger* whimpered rather than roared at the box office. Distribution in the United States was spotty. It opened on the West Coast in November 1975, but in New York was first shown on cable television before opening at Radio City Music Hall the following fall. A few critics admired its old-fashioned charm, but most thought it tepid and unappealing. "A number of people in the Saturday afternoon audience wiped away tears as the melodrama ended," reported *Cue*, "so I suppose it has emotional appeal for certain tastes. Not mine. . . . Nobody, least of all director Ken Annakin, can rescue the picture from contrivance and corn."[56]

Judith Crist disagreed, calling *Paper Tiger* "a first-rate adventure story designed for those who enjoy a smartly told tale that isn't steeped in blood and/or sex. . . . It is old-fashioned entertainment in the best sense."[57]

But *Variety*'s "Mack" thought it "old fashioned in the bad sense of the word. . . . Toshiro Mifune acts like his mind is elsewhere."[58] But it wasn't his mind, it was again his voice. For release in the West, Mifune was dubbed whenever his character speaks English, which is most of the time. As dubbing goes, the looping of *Paper Tiger* is decent enough but still gives Mifune's voice a disembodied effect whenever he opens his mouth. His role in the film is significant, but most of his screen time is spent in plodding scenes that recall *High and Low* (he rushes to the phone several times, confers with the authorities about the investigation, etc.) and, much like his overdressed surroundings, occasionally lapses into hoary Japanese clichés to the strains of Roy Budd's *shamisen*-filled score. As *Variety*'s "Mack" describes it, "Mifune reacts to the kidnapping by pulling out his samurai sword and waving it around in his room."[59]

The picture affords him only one good scene. Where Mifune's character in *High and Low* is anguished over whether to pay the kidnapper's ransom, in *Paper Tiger* he doesn't even have that option. Kagoyama is told by a government official that the President refuses to give in to the terrorists' demands, and he knows this means his son's life might be sacrificed. Mifune puts up a brave, very diplomatic, and very Japanese front. Then he leaves, gets into his limousine, and nearly breaks down.

If *Paper Tiger* afforded Mifune scant opportunity to stretch his acting wings, he had none in *Midway* (1976), his first American movie actually shot in Hollywood. It was a cheap-looking war epic from Universal, a studio then so immersed in TV production that many of its theatrical features had all the style and sheen of its cheaply made, flatly shot television movies. Filming began on May 12, 1975, though Mifune, again playing Admiral Yamamoto, didn't begin work on his part until early July. He was welcomed into the production at a cocktail reception at the Century Plaza Hotel attended by co-stars Charlton Heston, Glenn Ford, Robert Mitchum, and Japanese-American actor James Shigeta, as well as director Jack Smight and producer Walter Mirisch.[60] Miiko Taka was his interpreter. Mifune was starstruck and characteristically modest. "He didn't know the party was for him," Taka admitted to writer James Bacon.[61] On Universal's Stage 22, he posed for publicity photos with another of the film's many guest stars, Henry Fonda, who played Admiral Chester Nimitz. "There is a new generation [in Japan] which can learn a lesson from what happened," Mifune told reporters, plugging the film. "The Japanese are very philosophical about such things." He said he was happy to at last be making a film in Hollywood, though he admitted he was tired of playing the famed admiral yet again.[62]

"I was in Manchuria studying to be a pilot," he told Bob Thomas. "I knew nothing about the defeat at Midway, of course. The news was kept secret, and we learned about it only after the war."[63]

Unlike *Tora! Tora! Tora!*, in which all the Japanese sequences were filmed in Japanese and presented with English subtitles, for *Midway* Mirisch and Smight opted to shoot the Japanese sequences with English dialogue. Mifune was dubbed, and the rest of the Japanese cast were portrayed by seasoned

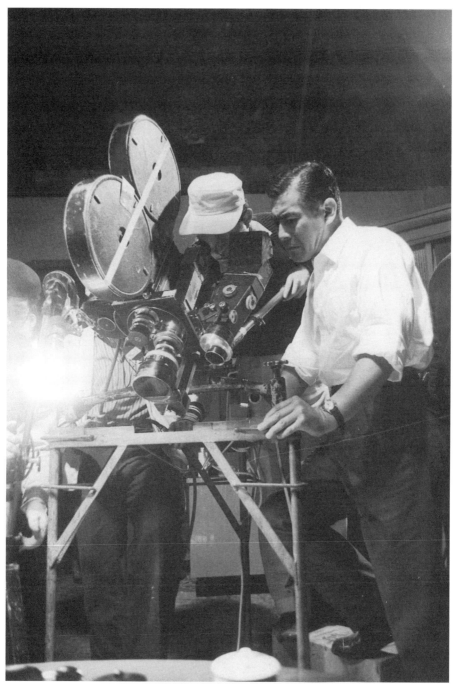

Mifune behind the camera on *Legacy of the 500,000* (1963). (Courtesy of Mifune Productions Co., Ltd.)

Director Mifune confers with script supervisor Teruyo Nogami (left) as Tatsuya Nakadai looks on during production of *Legacy of the 500,000*. (Courtesy of Mifune Productions Co., Ltd.)

Kurosawa and Mifune on the set of *Red Beard* (c. 1965). (Courtesy of and reproduced with the permission of Kurosawa Production K.K. of Yokohama, Japan)

Mifune and Sachiko during *Red Beard*'s production. Note the well-stocked liquor cabinet.
(Courtesy of and reproduced with the permission of Kurosawa Production K.K. of Yokohama, Japan)

Kurosawa enjoys a board game with daughter Kazuko as wife Yoko looks on, at their home in 1964. (Courtesy of and reproduced with the permission of Kurosawa Production K.K. of Yokohama, Japan)

Yuzo Kayama and Mifune on the set of *Red Beard*. (Courtesy of and reproduced with the permission of Kurosawa Production K.K. of Yokohama, Japan)

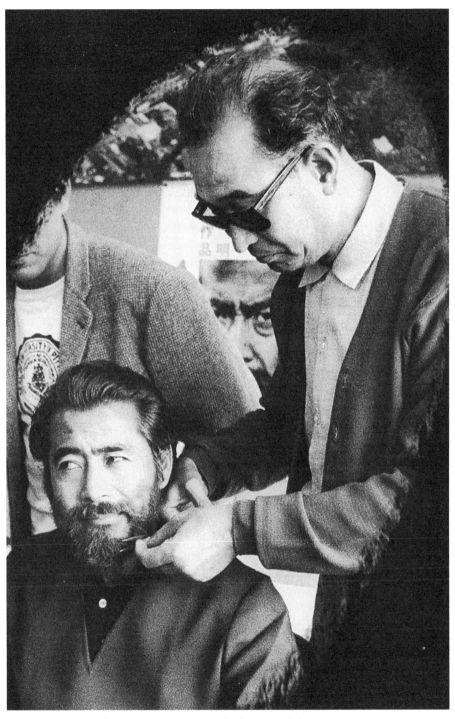

Kurosawa shaves Mifune's whiskers at the end of *Red Beard*'s long production. (Courtesy of and reproduced with the permission of Kurosawa Production K.K. of Yokohama, Japan)

Mifune and wife Sachiko in 1965, shortly after *Red Beard*'s completion, at the Mifune home. (Courtesy of and reproduced with the permission of Kurosawa Production K.K. of Yokohama, Japan)

During preproduction on *Runaway Train* at Kurosawa Production's office at the Akasaka Prince Hotel. Clockwise from center: Kurosawa, managing director Tetsuro "Tetsu" Aoyagi, translator Carol Sherman, secretary Kazuko Seki, and accountant Sadahiro Kubota. (Courtesy of and reproduced with the permission of Kurosawa Production K.K. of Yokohama, Japan)

Mifune at his Seijo studio in 1967. (Courtesy of and reproduced with the permission of Kurosawa Production K.K. of Yokohama, Japan)

The Club of the Four Knights. (L-R) Keisuke Kinoshita, Kurosawa, Kon Ichikawa, and Masaki Kobayashi. (Courtesy of and reproduced with the permission of Kurosawa Production K.K. of Yokohama, Japan)

"Real men just drink, without saying a word." Mifune pitches beer in a July 1970 ad. (Sapporo Breweries Ltd. and Mifune Productions Co., Ltd.)

Kurosawa at a January 21, 1970, press conference regarding his firing from *Tora! Tora! Tora!* held at the Akasaka Prince Hotel. (Courtesy of and reproduced with the permission of Kurosawa Production K.K. of Yokohama, Japan)

Kurosawa in Russia for *Dersu Uzala* (1975). (Courtesy of and reproduced with the permission of Kurosawa Production K.K. of Yokohama, Japan)

Kurosawa with benefactors Serge Silberman, George Lucas, and Francis Ford Coppola on the set of *Kagemusha* (1980). (Courtesy of and reproduced with the permission of Kurosawa Production K.K. of Yokohama, Japan)

Yoshiro Muraki's incredible castle set, built at the base of Mt. Fuji for *Ran* (1985). (Courtesy of and reproduced with the permission of Kurosawa Production K.K. of Yokohama, Japan)

Two icons of Japanese cinema. Mifune and Tora-san (Kiyoshi Atsumi) in Yoji Yamada's *Tora-san Goes North* (1987). (© Shochiku Co. Ltd.)

Three days after his eightieth birthday, Kurosawa is presented an honorary Oscar by admirers George Lucas (left) and Steven Spielberg. (AP Wide World Photos)

Tatsuo Matsumura and Kyoko Kagawa in *Madadayo* (1993). (Courtesy of and reproduced with the permission of Kurosawa Production K.K. of Yokohama, Japan)

Mifune in 1995, when Alzheimer's disease and other health problems had taken their toll.
(Courtesy of Mifune Productions Co., Ltd.)

Kurosawa in France, May 1990. (Courtesy of and reproduced with the permission of Kurosawa Production K.K. of Yokohama, Japan)

Japanese-American actors like Shigeta and John Fujioka. Their American-accented English, coupled with Paul Frees's voice once again emanating from Mifune's lips, is jarringly incongruous. Understandably, Mifune appears ill at ease in his scenes. "It was an agonizing decision," Mirisch claimed. "The problem was that we had 50 minutes of dialogue, much of it expository and technical; to have all that spoken in Japanese with English subtitles would have been too difficult for American audiences."[64]

And, unlike *Tora! Tora! Tora!* and Joseph Levine's forthcoming *A Bridge Too Far* (1977), *Midway* eschewed expensive full-size effects and elaborate miniature destruction in favor of grainy wartime stock footage. The reason was simple: most of its budget had gone to its star-studded cast. Exhibitors who blind-booked the film at premium rates in January 1976, well before it was completed, expected a film as lavish as *Tora! Tora! Tora!* When they realized that *Midway*'s battle scenes had been cobbled together from other sources, they complained to Universal about its cheap look, especially its incorporation of stock footage from a Japanese war movie Walter Mirisch had acquired for "about $96,000."[65] That bevy of footage turned out to be from *Storm Over the Pacific* (a.k.a. *I Bombed Pearl Harbor*), the fifteen-year-old Toho film that featured Mifune as Admiral Yamaguchi. (Co-stars Yosuke Natsuki and Makoto Sato are even visible in one stock shot.) Mirisch claimed there was no other way to shoot the Japanese-effects sequences, but that didn't explain the mountain of recycled footage used for other scenes, which included innumerable snippets lifted from *Tora! Tora! Tora!* and the thirty-two-year-old *Thirty Seconds Over Tokyo*, tinted sepia and used under the opening titles. Exhibitors also grumbled about the 5 percent surcharge shelled out to cover the installation of Universal's booming sound system, Sensurround, which was introduced on *Earthquake* (1975) but had been gathering dust ever since.[66]

Despite bad reviews, *Midway* earned a good deal of money. In its first three weeks the picture grossed $15 million in the United States (it went on to earn $21.6 million), while in Japan it earned more than $1.3 million in its first week in twenty-eight theaters.[67]

Mifune returned to Japan to appear in publisher-turned-producer Haruki Kadokawa's *Proof of the Man*, a $2 million international production starring George Kennedy and featuring Broderick Crawford and the "Samurai" trilogy's Mariko Okada. The picture was directed by Junya Sato. The story concerns the investigation of a young African-American murdered in a hotel. A Japanese detective (Yusaku Matsuda) flies to New York to investigate and is aided by an American policeman (Kennedy).

"I want to make a good entertainment film and not a kind of highbrow, academic one," Kadokawa said. "I know many reviewers wrote that my film is not artistic. But look at the long lines of people who want to see it. I shall let them judge my product."[68] And long lines there were. In Japan, *Proof of the Man* earned $18 million in its first four months, representing 3.7 million admissions, albeit admissions prompted largely by Kadokawa's huge conglomerate machine of hard-sell advertising. Kadokawa was much criticized for his self-named "trinity" approach to marketing: push the best-selling book simultaneously (with the tag line "Read it or see it first?") with the film and its title song. Still, Mifune must have been glad to appear in a hit movie, for it came at a time in Japan when admissions had dropped nearly 50 percent from just ten years earlier.[69]

In January 1977 he flew again to the United States, to appear in *Winter Kills*, an underrated, sometimes surreal black comedy adapted from Richard Condon's book. Loosely based on the Kennedy family, the picture suggests that it was the Kennedy empire itself that had murdered the President and engineered the alleged cover-up that followed. Jeff Bridges stars as the late President's brother, here called Nick Kegan, black sheep of the family. He's a drifter with no political aspirations, much to his father's (John Huston) chagrin. Kegan learns of a conspiracy, and the film plays more like a collection of anecdotes than a continuous narrative, with the young man sent off on a wild-goose chase from one eccentric to the next (all well played by such actors as Sterling Hayden, Anthony Perkins, and Richard Boone). Huston is especially memorable as the Joseph Kennedy character, Pa Kegan, delivering one outrageous and amusing line after another. "Do you get laid?" he asks Bridges at one point. "Do you know how many times your brother was laid while he was in office? One thousand seventy-two—and with a schedule like his!" And when he sends Bridges off in another direction: "Take these brass knuckles, but don't lose them—they have a sentimental value."

Unfortunately, Mifune's talents are wasted as never before. He plays Keith, Huston's butler. (At least that's what he appears to be; publicity materials and the film itself are unclear about this.) As in *Red Sun*, his own voice is heard, though it's even more thickly accented and nearly unintelligible. He appears in only two brief scenes, about one minute apiece. In the first he greets Jeff Bridges upon his initial arrival at the Huston compound, and later he wishes him a good night. It was an insultingly trivial role—one that could have been played by the most inexperienced bit player.

It's difficult to imagine why a performer of Mifune's caliber (and price) would have been flown all the way to America for such an inconsequential part. *Winter Kills* had a troubled production history, nearly as fascinating as the film itself. Preproduction was financed on director William Richert's credit card, and once shooting was under way, the film, partly funded by the mob, was shut down several times; one producer, Leonard Goldberg, was, according to Richert, gunned down on his thirtieth birthday. Robert Sterling, the other producer, Richert says, was subsequently convicted of six felonies and sentenced to forty years.[70] *Winter Kills* sat unfinished for two years before it was restarted in late 1978, when Avco Embassy picked it up for release the following year. Their version was apparently heavily edited and it bombed at the box office. However, the film managed to win over a few prominent critics with its *Manchurian Candidate*–like audaciousness, biting, sardonic dialogue, and sociopolitical implications, and in 1983 *Winter Kills* was afforded a second chance. Director/screenwriter William Richert's cut of the film was rereleased in an extremely limited run through his own company, with different title music, some minor reediting, and a different ending. Then, with just $2.5 million of the film's $8 million paid for, the film vanished yet again. Considering its erratic shooting schedule and multiple release versions, perhaps Mifune's role was originally intended to be meatier. In the United States, only the 1979 version is presently available on home video, and the film was never released in Japan. Although the script's endless, Byzantine conundrums become wearying before it ends, *Winter Kills* also has its moments of brilliance, and that it has become all but forgotten is unfortunate.

Back in Japan, Mifune was never busier. His production staff and contract players had swelled to 235 people, while the actor's hectic schedule included regular appearances in no fewer than five television shows: four samurai, one contemporary.[71] None of these programs—*Ronin in a Lawless Town* (Muhogai no suronin, 1977), *The Spy Appears* (Kakushimetsuke sanjo, 1977), *An Eagle in Edo* (Edo no taka, 1978), and *Hideout in Suite 7* (Kakekomibiru nanagoshitsu, 1979)—made any impact outside the Asian market, when they were sold outside of Japan at all, and have never turned up on home video in Japan.

He also began a seven-year association with Toei, appearing in ten of their releases between 1977 and 1983. By now Toei was the only reliably successful studio in Japan, but its box-office victories came at the cost of alarmingly short shooting schedules and hackneyed, formula scripts catering to undemanding audiences in search of violent action and little else.

Typically, Mifune appeared in guest star parts in these films, which demanded little of him or the contract stars, such as Shinichi "Sonny" Chiba, Koji Tsuruta, Hiroki Matsukata, Bunta Sugawara, who populated them.

Typical among these were *The Godfather: Ambition* (Nihon no don—yabohen, 1977) and its sequel, *The Godfather: Resolution* (Nihon no don—kanketsuhen 1978), two unfortunate attempts to combine the appeal of Francis Coppola's *The Godfather* (1972) with the dying *yakuza* genre. Throughout his career Mifune was famous for his professionalism, giving his all in both good and bad films, but these features sorely tested his resolve. In both pictures, Mifune looks like an impatient airline passenger in the middle of a fifteen-hour flight.

He had better luck in Toei's *The Shogun's Samurai* (Yagyu ichizoku no inbo, 1978), directed by Kinji Fukasaku. The picture was a moderately successful attempt by the studio to return to the kind of traditional samurai pictures that had launched the company in the early 1950s but were dropped over time in favor of more lucrative *chambara* and *yakuza* thrillers. It was for Toei what the war movies had been for Toho in the 1960s: a nostalgic return to an old genre that centered around a classic yet commercially proven story (the Yagyu clan) and could be loaded down with current and aging contract players (Sonny Chiba, Hiroki Matsukata, Tetsuro Tamba) and stage veterans (Isuzu Yamada), who lent the film a degree of prestige.

Kevin Thomas called *Shogun's Samurai* "a superb example of its kind. It has the usual struggle for power, triggering myriad plot complications and much swordplay; authentic settings in ancient palaces (mainly in Kyoto); an emperor's ransom in rich kimonos and antique weaponry, and an immense cast that allows for a sprinkling of veteran screen favorites."[72] Mifune's part as the brother of the title shogun, poisoned in a struggle for power, demanded little of him, but at least he was back working in a genre in which he was more comfortable and confident.

Mifune's name still sold tickets, but he could no longer sell a film on his name alone, nor was he winning awards for these new films. Mifune had to eat, he had to pay his company's bills, so he took work where he could find it. This was something Kurosawa could not understand. Many of his acclaimed actors—Tatsuya Nakadai, Takashi Shimura, Isuzu Yamada—had taken roles beneath their abilities, but they balanced their careers with respectable stage work or in more ambitious NHK television programs. Mifune, by contrast, was frittering away his talents in instantly forgettable endeavors. Most of his films in the 1970s were mediocre; their quality was well below that of the program pictures he made at Toho. And most of his television work consisted of *chambara* and spy shows that were indifferently written and cheaply produced. After his years of building him up as the country's leading actor, Kurosawa felt Mifune had thrown it all away.

Good roles for Mifune were now few and far between. In the midst of the routine films he made at Toei came *Love and Faith* (Oginsama, 1978). The film was directed by Kei Kumai, with whom he had worked on *A Tunnel to the Sun* (1968). The picture would also reunite Mifune with Takashi Shimura for the last time. At seventy-three Shimura still looked vital and little changed from the man Mifune had met on the set of *Drunken Angel* thirty years earlier. In fact, Shimura was battling emphysema, but after *Love and Faith* the actor kept busy, appearing in five more films over the next three years, including a Tora-san picture where he popped up from time to time in the series as Gin Maeda's father, as well as a brief part in *Kagemusha*.

Love and Faith is a historical drama set in the late sixteenth century, centering around Lady Ogin (Ryoko Nakano), the beautiful adopted daughter of Sen Rikyu (Shimura), leading tea master and adviser to warlord Hideyoshi (Mifune). Ogin has long been in love with Lord Ukon (Kichiemon Nakamura) and was engaged to him until the death of her biological father (and the consequent fall of her family's power) prevented their marriage. After a long journey, Ukon returns to Rikyu's home, the prospering seaport of Sakai, and Ogin's passion is rekindled. Ukon, however, has converted to Christianity, just as Hideyoshi's patience with this foreign influence is nearing an end. Ukon rejects her, though her love for him remains unchanged.

Meanwhile, despite the relative peace and prosperity of Japan at this time, Hideyoshi moves to reunify a politically splintered Japan as part of a larger plan to invade China and Korea. This greatly distresses Rikyu and just about everyone else, who see Hideyoshi's stubborn ambitions as extremely foolhardy. Hideyoshi, however, argues that if Japan doesn't invade the Asian mainland, one of the European countries will. Growing influence from outside Japan is seen throughout the picture—Dutch cannons and rifles continually boom in the distance, and Ukon, when we first see him, has brought back not only a new faith but a mandolin to accompany his Christian psalms. (The excellent score was written by Akira Ifukube, at that time moving away from film work.) The picture, surprisingly, does not pass judgment on these influences, or Christianity for that matter.

Ogin's undying love of Ukon incurs the anger of a merchant (Daijiro

Harada) she marries but refuses to bed, and later she rejects Hideyoshi's brutish advances, too. He orders his men to surround Rikyu's house, and after much discussion she decides, with her father's blessing, to commit *seppuku* rather than face arrest and slavery under Hideyoshi. Later, Rikyu openly insults Hideyoshi and commits suicide himself.

Love and Faith is a straightforward though delicate adaptation of Toko Kon's 1927 story. Scripted by Yoshitaka Yoda, Kenji Mizoguchi's longtime collaborator, the film has a certain Mizoguchi flavor and is less ponderous and pretentious than some of director Kumai's more recent work. Kumai's emphatically minimalist style works for the most part here. Filmed in the old standard ratio (not 'scope) and richly photographed by Kozo Okazaki, the film has a lost-in-time look and, despite a certain lavishness, must have seemed rather old-fashioned when it was released.

Ryoko Nakano (b. 1950) is radiant as Ogin. An astonishingly beautiful woman, she has a virginal quality reminiscent of Kaoru Yachigusa, but also an inner strength that makes her performance believable. Despite her glowing presence in this film, she made little impact, and her motion picture career was seemingly confined to the 1970s and early '80s.

Shimura is an excellent Rikyu. Generally, he is very mannered, but the warmth and wisdom of the character come through in several key scenes, particularly as his family spends one last night together before Ogin takes her life. There is also an excellent moment when Hideyoshi informs Rikyu that he has just executed one of the tea master's disciples. Rikyu has been whittling away at a piece of wood and continues doing so as the horrible news is recounted. Finally, he can stand it no more and, shuddering mid-whittle, nearly collapses. For a character so deliberate with every move—much like the tea ceremony itself—this bubbling of emotion is powerful, and Shimura pulls it off with great effect.

Mifune comes and goes as Hideyoshi, playing him as an immature hothead. Unfortunately for Western audiences unfamiliar with Hideyoshi's reign, there is little hint in Mifune's performance of what got Hideyoshi to this position of power in the first place; such details remained primarily confined to the dry narration of historical events peppered throughout the picture.

Ultimately Rikyu's story, while subservient to Ogin's tale of love and faith, is a kind of Japanese *A Man for All Seasons*. The clashes between Mifune and Shimura are generally well done, if not exceptionally so, climaxed by a final tea ceremony soon after Ogin's death in which Hideyoshi continues to oafishly dangle Rikyu's life at every turn. There's a bit of momentary suspense when it first appears that Rikyu may finally cave in. Shimura returns from the kitchen area with a handful of flowers, throws them at Mifune, and laughs broadly, while saying, essentially, "Ah, the hell with it!" Mifune is aghast. In their last film together, thirty years after Mifune's debut in *Snow Trail*, Mifune and Shimura continue to surprise audiences in their scenes together.

There had been prior versions of this same story, notably Kinuyo Tanaka's 1960 film, also called *Ogin-sama* but released in the United States as *Love Under the Crucifix*. That film starred Ineko Arima as Ogin, Osamu Takizawa as Hideyoshi, Ganjuro Nakamura as Rikyu, and Tatsuya Nakadai as Ukon. Nakadai himself later played Rikyu in a television miniseries about the tea master. It's one of the classic roles of Japanese drama, one a great many Japanese actors play at one time or another.

A little more than a decade later, Yoda, Kumai, *and* Mifune covered much of the same territory in *Death of a Tea Master* (Sen no Rikyu—honkakubo ibun, 1989), with Mifune this time playing Rikyu. Based on the novel *Honkakubo Ibun* by Yasushi Inoue, the film is told in flashbacks by Rikyu disciple Honkakubo (Eiji Okuda) twenty-seven years after the tea master's death. The story centers around Honkakubo trying to determine whether Rikyu committed suicide by his own volition, or whether he was compelled to commit *seppuku* by Hideyoshi. This version went on to win the Venice Film Festival's Silver Lion Award, though it received mixed reviews in Japan and the United States. *Variety*'s "Edna" called it a "heavy-handed, academic version . . . [which] moves ponderously along at a snail's pace, preferring to take Rikyu and his life on a metaphoric level rather than a realistic one. . . . Kumai relies heavily on the presence of Toshiro Mifune as Rikyu, but fails to explore the potential of the actor."[73]

Adding to the confusion, that same year director Hiroshi Teshigahara made yet another *Rikyu*, with Rentaro Mikuni in the title role. The flood of Rikyu movies and television programs was due to the four hundredth anniversary of the tea master's death in 1989, with both pictures exploring Rikyu's final days and, ultimately, his place in Japanese history. As Kumai said of his film, it was to suggest "the depth of Rikyu's feelings and thoughts, which has since guided the Japanese toward spirituality and aesthetics through the tea ceremony."[74]

Love and Faith made its stateside debut in Los Angeles about ten months after it opened in Japan, but it got mixed reviews and Toho generated a lot of confusion by releasing it under several titles, including *Love and Faith of Ogin* and *Lady Ogin*. "Young Japanese director Kei Kumai made a big impression Stateside with his last film, *Sandakan No. 8*, which was nominated for the Best Foreign Film Oscar in 1975," noted *Variety*'s "Cart." "[This is the] umpteenth remake of the perennial Japanese epic soap opera 'Love Under the Crucifix' and the results are disappointingly laborious. Despite its name cast, little chance is held out for this one to break out of the normal limited Japanese distribution circuit. . . . Kumai has cast this saga of tragic inevitability impeccably but has paced it ploddingly, bringing little that is sufficiently original or different to justify the lavish production values and excessive running time. . . . It's good to see [Shimura and Mifune] in meaty, full-blown roles again, but unfortunate that the context isn't more exciting."[75]

But Kevin Thomas countered that the film was indeed "a superb new version. . . . In their different ways all three men are of heroic stature, but for all Nakamura's piety and Shimura's pacifism, Nakano is as much a victim of their cruel chauvinism as she is of Mifune, who is at least without pretense. However, by her final act, she has affected them all, particularly Shimura. . . . [He] reminds us what a consummate actor he is, conveying so much in a look of resignation. It's gratifying, too, to see Mifune . . . in a fine, fierce samurai role again. . . . That *Love and Faith* is a splendiferous period re-creation and has a strongly traditional style only underlines its contemporary feminist sensibility. The plight of women has long preoccupied Japan's filmmakers, most notably Kenji Mizoguchi, but Kei Kumai is bringing to the theme fresh, bitterly ironic meaning."[76]

After *Love and Faith*, *1941* was nothing if not a stark change of pace for Mifune. Since *Jaws* (1975) and *Close Encounters of the Third Kind* (1977), director Steven Spielberg had become a leader of the New Hollywood. American studios were as eager to finance his movies as Japanese studios were indifferent toward Kurosawa. *1941* (1979) was a bloated comedy involving West Coast paranoia about a Japanese military assault in the days following Pearl Harbor. Mifune, nearly lost among the all-star cast and overwhelming production, once again found himself portraying a naval officer, here a frustrated submarine captain. He shared his scenes with the accomplished English actor Christopher Lee (as a German accompanying the mission) and broad cowboy character player Slim Pickens (*Dr. Strangelove*) as one "Hollis Wood," Christmas tree vendor. Pickens is very funny as a country bumpkin taken prisoner by the Japanese, who, when their compass breaks, need directions to Hollywood. Mifune's sub commander believes an attack on Tinseltown would demoralize the nation. Among Pickens's belongings they find a toy compass in a box of "Popper Jacks," but out of a sense of patriotism, Hollis bravely swallows it, and his captors force him to drink prune juice in an effort to retrieve it.

Much of Spielberg's film falters under the weight of its lavishness (John Williams's score even features booming cannons), but its creators insist that its excesses were part of the joke. Some of its characterizations, particularly those played by John Belushi and Dan Aykroyd, don't work at all, but the scenes with Mifune are often hilarious. Pickens's broad playing is neatly countered by Mifune and Lee as his intimidating straight men, and the Abbott & Costello–like banter between Mifune and Pickens over Hollis's name is amusing. Mifune had never done this kind of thing before, and he plays it absolutely straight.

"He became very close to Steven Spielberg while making *1941*," according to Tomio Sagisu, "and made up a nameplate with 'Steven Spielberg' in Chinese characters [allowing for a phonetic translation]. On the sets of those foreign films, he'd correct the Kanji, because he couldn't stand inaccuracies like that."[77]

"The script was shot, and then some," co-writer Bob Zemeckis said. "There was a lot more in the way of action and effects and broad comedy. And then what happened was it had to be trimmed into a two-hour movie, and a lot of the thrust of the original story took a secondary position. But I'm still really proud to have written scenes that had Toshiro Mifune, Christopher Lee and Slim Pickens in them."[78]

"The movie didn't come across as a parody," concluded Mifune. "There was a lot of truth in it, maybe too much. Why make a fuss over something that caused a real panic? Spielberg never went through a war. He looked at it with a kind of naïveté."[79]

TWENTY-FIVE

LORDS AND *GAIJIN*

The end of the 1970s found Mifune co-starring in the role for which he is best known by mainstream American audiences: Lord Toranaga in the miniseries of James Clavell's *Shogun*, an epic tale based on the adventures of Will Adams, the first Englishman to reside in Japan. A feature film about Adams had been kicking around since at least the mid-1960s, when, at different times, both Kurosawa and Mifune were approached. As late as the mid-1970s, while Mifune was making *Midway*, co-star Charlton Heston was in discussions about yet another ultimately unfilmed adaptation.

It was not until James Clavell fictionalized Adams's exploits in a novel called *Shogun* (1975) that serious talk began anew. Despite its extreme length (1,207 pages), *Shogun* was an instant bestseller, with four million copies in print by 1979. As the *New York Times* book critic said, "It's almost impossible not to continue to read 'Shogun' once having opened it. Yet it's not only something that you read—you live it."[1]

Like Adams, *Shogun*'s Blackthorne (played in the film by Richard Chamberlain) is a pilot major on a Dutch warship that reaches Japan in the year 1600. There he encounters Portuguese and Jesuit settlers who do not wish to share their tenuous relationship with Lord Toranaga. But Blackthorne immerses himself in Japanese culture, wins the respect of Toranaga, is made a samurai, and falls in love with his interpreter, Mariko. Toranaga, however, is merely using Blackthorne as a pawn in his own lust for power, and in the end Mariko is dead and Blackthorne is marooned, never to return to his homeland.

The enormous success of the television miniseries *Rich Man, Poor Man* (1976) and *Roots* (1977), among the first ABC Novels for Television, convinced NBC and Paramount to co-produce a miniseries of *Shogun*. Toho, the Asahi television network, and Jardine Mathieson, a Hong Kong–based trading company, joined in as co-producers, believing that the work could be reconfigured for theatrical release in Asia. A still different version was prepared for theatrical release in Europe.

According to the author's daughter, Micaela, while writing *Shogun*, Clavell had Mifune in mind when he created Toranaga. "I think Mifune *is* Toranaga," added director Jerry London. "He's a man of great dignity. He was the most prepared actor [during production]. He was always the first one on the set, made up, ready to go. And he understood the part." Mifune helped with the non-professional, Japanese extras, which he had also done with the non-actors playing his sub crew on *1941*. "He was very helpful in the staging of the extras and enthusing them. The extras were a bunch of college kids and he'd get out there and make a speech and get 'em all pumped up."[2]

As Mariko, the producers first cast singer Judy Ong, but she dropped out at the last minute and was replaced by Yoko Shimada, whose background was mainly in Japanese television. Shimada was lovely, but spoke no English, and spent most of the production learning her lines phonetically. This was no easy task: as Blackthorne's interpreter, she had nearly three times as many lines as either Mifune or Chamberlain.

The rest of the Japanese cast consisted of actors who had worked with Mifune before, or had known him from his days as a Toho contract player: comedian Frankie Sakai, Seiji Miyaguchi, Masumi Okada, and Yosuke Natsuki among them. Miiko Taka acted as Mifune's interpreter; she and Mika Kitagawa appeared onscreen in supporting roles.

"Miss Kitagawa was one of the ladies-in-waiting in the palace," said first assistant director Charles Ziarko, "and did a lot more waiting than acting as I recall. Mika was always with Mifune on the set; she rode to and from the locations with him sometimes. For the big earthquake sequence, which was being done outside Kyoto, there were reporters waiting outside the gate because she was in Mifune's limousine, probably as a protective measure so she didn't have to come in by herself. But they didn't pal around [with the rest of the crew between setups] the way people do in Hollywood movies. They were very circumspect."[3]

Shooting began on June 4, 1979, at Toho Studios.[4] Almost immediately the problems started. Just as shooting commenced, Mifune flew to Korea to appear in a cameo role in the Reverend Moon–financed *Inchon!* It was the first of an endless stream of misunderstandings between the American and Japanese crews over their differing working methods. Unlike the American system, Japanese leading players are locked into shooting dates and allowed to take on other roles in other projects for the days they're not scheduled to work. Mifune, at this point needing money wherever he could get it, had accepted an offer to appear in *Inchon!*, and when *Shogun* fell behind schedule, the Americans found themselves without their Toranaga.

Throughout the long production, in fact, Mifune came and went. "Miiko Taka, Toshiro Mifune's liaison and interpreter, came in to inform us that Mifune had a television commitment November 23 to 25," recalled unit production manager Wally Worsley. "We had already changed our schedule because of a previously announced trip to Rome; earlier his office had asked [assistant director Masahiko] Okumura to change the schedule so that Mifune did not work Mondays or Fridays, and I had said no. Now I made it clear that without the star, we would simply have to shut down the picture. Mifune decided against going to Rome."[5]

But the larger problem looming over the production lay in a fundamental friction between the American and Japanese crews. The Japanese crew was egregiously overstaffed. Toho was apparently trying to wring every yen it could get out of the big spenders from Hollywood. The Americans, meanwhile, adamantly refused to adapt themselves to Japanese ways, Blackthorne-style, and the Japanese crew resented their often brutish lack of etiquette and tact.

"The real problem," said Ziarko, "was that Jerry London and the producer, Eric Bercovici [who also worked on *Hell in the Pacific*], treated the Japanese like shit. They treated them as if they were on location in San Diego. They were abusive and foul-mouthed Hollywood people who felt they could be so anywhere they wanted. The Japanese, from the highest to the lowest—they just loathed them."[6]

Privately, London and Bercovici's cavalier disregard for cultural authenticity irked Mifune. "They wanted me to say things to the effect of 'Good morning, sir, and how are we?' or 'Oh, but did you understand that?' when I would have said, 'Get it?' A lot of it was also modern phrasing, not the dialogue used 400 years ago. Other people complied. But I'm a shogun. There's no way I can say that. The shogun has more dignity."[7]

Mifune also objected to London's tendency for multiple takes of Mifune's scenes without clear direction. Ziarko remembers one scene in particular: "We were doing a night scene where Lord Toranaga rides in for something with his troops with a lot of tents and torches waving. He did it perfectly, rode in with a gallop, jumped off his horse—and this is a man who was in his sixties at the time—and the director kept wanting to do it over. Maybe the third or fourth time, as Mifune dismounted, the horse spooked, his foot was caught in the stirrup and he was dragged. Everybody jumped, but he didn't even want to see a doctor. The company sent him to the hospital to be checked over. He wanted to get back into the saddle and do it again. He was the greatest."[8]

"I felt so sorry for a lot of the crew people there," Chamberlain commented. "They said, 'Here we are in the middle of Kyoto and there's nothing to do. I'm so tired of eating McDonald's hamburgers. There's nothing [American] to eat.' And here they are in the midst of this immense treasure chest of the most beautiful, ancient culture, right there, seconds away. I used to jog around the Holiday Inn. Five minutes away were these wonderful temples. If you were there at the right time, you'd see incredible things."[9]

As production dragged on, the American cast and crew soon became aware of Mifune's method of staying in character. "He's quite sweet when he's in his civvies," said Chamberlain. "But the minute he puts his costume on, he is a samurai. He just sits in a corner and growls. And looks *incredibly* forbidding. Wouldn't *dare* go up and talk to him. But he did some of the most astonishing things [with the role]."[10]

"He was not gregarious, but on the other hand he was one of the most professional actors I ever saw in any of the work I ever did," added Ziarko. "He had his little director's chair, he sat by the set, none of this running back to the dressing room and having to be called, and when the setup was ready, he was out of his chair. Absolutely a dream as a professional actor."[11]

For Ziarko, one scene in particular exemplified Mifune's professionalism: "Chamberlain was supposed to be teaching Mifune how to do a hornpipe dance from English culture. And the day we shot it, in the studio, using at least two cameras and possibly three [simultaneously to cover it], we started about 8:30 in the morning and Richard Chamberlain was still kind of working his way through various things he wanted to do. Mifune had already worked out exactly what he was going to do—where he was going to hesitate, where he was going to come on strong, from the first rehearsal in the morning to the master shots; through all of the coverage, his performance never varied an iota. He had it completely locked, without any help from the director, who was no help to anybody."[12]

At his own expense, Mifune treated his co-stars and crew to "a little informal cocktail party," which turned out to be an elaborately catered affair, complete with ship-shaped salmon and ice statues. He later hosted *Shogun's* wrap party, complete with servants in white jackets and gloves.[13]

Mifune's co-star likewise won over the Japanese crew with his professionalism. Unit production manager Wallace Worsley called Chamberlain "the major unifying force on the beleaguered troupe," adding, "It was his presence and example that inspired the heavily stressed Americans to plod on—an attribute that I have rarely seen in all my years in this business. He was unaware . . . that but for him many crew members would have quit the picture before its conclusion."[14]

"[At the end of shooting there] was a flood of tremendous genuine good feeling," Chamberlain said, "and I'm sensitive to that. They had never expressed it to any large degree during the filming. I didn't even know a lot of them spoke English. There had been this distance. And I was so moved to find that they had been fond of me—and also so disappointed that I hadn't known earlier so that we could have made friends."[15]

Throughout filming, several different phone book–size scripts were used. In addition to the bilingual 12-hour miniseries version, a 2½-hour theatrical version was prepared for release in Europe, using alternate takes with added nudity and violence, which also served to simplify the overwhelmingly complex narrative. A third version, which ran 159 minutes, was prepared for theatrical release in Japan. Toho's film of *Shogun* was a disaster. Their cut downplayed Blackthorne's story while playing up its Japanese cast and Japanese-language sequences. When it was released six months after Kurosawa's *Kagemusha*, it was greeted with negative reviews that complained about its historical inaccuracies and confused narrative. The latter complaint was understandable. Even at more than 2½ hours, its story played like a Hollywood serial from the 1940s recut for feature length.

With all its problems, *Shogun* ended up costing $22 million (an astonishing $12 million *over budget*), making it by far the most expensive production in the history of American television. But in spite of everything that had gone wrong, *Shogun* emerged as a kind of television miracle. The miniseries was a sensation, seen by an astonishing 120 million viewers, most of whom had never heard of Toshiro Mifune. It immersed moviegoers who abjectly refused to see movies with subtitles in a fascinating world utterly alien to them. It sparked a flurry of interest in Japan and Japanese culture not seen in America since the early 1950s. And despite its historical lapses, *Shogun* was utterly engrossing.

Chamberlain's sincere performance is nicely balanced by Shimada's delicate beauty. Frankie Sakai's character, Yabu, was especially memorable, and his *seppuku* a dramatic highlight. But above it all was Mifune's towering Toranaga. The stoicism and grunts of Mifune's dreary, clichéd cameos are present, but in *Shogun* the context is altogether different. Behind the fierce poker face is a wholly believable leader craftily maneuvering Blackthorne to his own ends. Toranaga is imposing, witty, treacherous. For all of London's leaden direction, Mifune's role offers a glimpse of what he was capable of in his later years, making one wonder what Kurosawa might have done with him at this stage of his career had their collaborations not come to such an acrimonious end.

Maclean's review was typical. It praised *Shogun* as "rarely anything less than engrossing. Apart from its intrinsic achievement, *Shogun* points to the possibilities of television as a popular medium: are the people who will spend a week with *Shogun* any less lucky than those who waited a long time ago for the next installment of a Dickens novel? Movies can't provide that ongoing pleasure and books, lately, seldom do. . . . *Shogun* doesn't look much like television and, for a change, you wonder how they did it for *only* $22 million. And despite some vein-like flaws in Eric Bercovici's script you look and listen and learn and come away saying *wakarimasu*—I understand."[16]

Deservedly, Mifune was nominated for an Emmy, but was up against co-star Chamberlain and they wound up canceling each other out in the voting (Anthony Hopkins won, instead, for his riveting performance as Hitler in *The Bunker*). Yoko Shimada was nominated as well, but lost to Vanessa Redgrave for her work in Arthur Miller's concentration-camp drama *Playing for Time*. But the series won the award for Best Limited Series against stiff competition: *East of Eden*, *Masada*, *Rumpole of the Bailey*, and *Tinker, Tailor, Soldier, Spy*. And while even more elaborate miniseries were to come, *Shogun* remains the pinnacle of the form.

Shogun was Mifune's last stab at international stardom. Unable to build upon his American success, he spent the next seven years appearing in more guest star cameos in Toei pictures, and made a great many appearances on Japanese television. Between 1980 and 1984 he was in no fewer than eleven television shows, starring in several. He reprised his "Ronin of the Wilderness" character in a short-lived revival series and appeared in *The Crescent-Shaped Wilderness* (Kyukei no koya), a two-hour television film, with Yoko Shimada.

But Mifune's film work during this period was undistinguished. Certainly his frequent absences from *Shogun* to make *Inchon!* did him little good. An epic war drama about General Douglas MacArthur (a wildly miscast Laurence Olivier) and his daring landing at the South Korean port, *Inchon!* featured Mifune in one of its numerous subplots as Saito-san, father of a Korean-Japanese daughter (Karen Kahn) in love with a married Marine major (Ben Gazzara).

The $15–20 million production was announced in March 1978, and it's likely that Mifune came to it via producer Tomoyuki Tanaka, who early on acted as line producer, when much of the film's interiors were to be shot at Toho.[17] (Some sources reported that Mifune's role was added at the insistence of director Terence Young.) Funding for the would-be epic came from the most unlikely of sources, and its bizarre production history proved far more dramatic than the picture that resulted. *Inchon!* was produced by Mitsuharu Ishii, a Japanese newspaper publisher with a film production office in Los Angeles. But Ishii's One Way Productions was really a front for none other than the Reverend Sung Myung Moon, controversial head of the Unification Church. Ishii, with Moon acting as his "spiritual advisor," chose to make a film about MacArthur after plans for a film about the life of Jesus and a proposed epic Elvis Presley vehicle failed to pan out.

When it became known that the film was being financed by the Moonies, the church's publicity machine kicked into overdrive, flooding the media with wild tales of religious visions likening MacArthur to Christ and other bogus claims about the film's supposed divine (and occasionally psychic) guidance from the heavens. The church's involvement, plus the script's virulent anticommunist tone, led to a strike at Toho, its employees refusing to have anything to do with the picture. Toho and Tanaka bowed out, as did director Andrew V. McLaglen, who was replaced by Young, Mifune's *Red Sun* director. Young tried valiantly to piece together a more commercial and coherent war film, but all was in vain.

The production was even more trouble-plagued than *Shogun*. The budget soared when two typhoons and an earthquake destroyed expensive sets, while co-star Jacqueline Bisset's bout of laryngitis halted shooting for an entire week at $200,000 per day.

By the time it premiered, *Inchon!* had cost an astonishing $48 million (of which a reported $35 million came directly from the Unification Church), making it one of the most expensive pictures made up to that time. The May 1981 premiere was a disaster. *Inchon!* went back to the editing room and re-emerged in September 1982 shorn of some 35 minutes (its current 105-minute running time), including all scenes featuring Rex

Reed and the by then deceased David Janssen as journalists. Mifune's scenes were apparently trimmed as well, for he pops in and out of the picture without explanation.

Peter Rainer's review in the *Los Angeles Herald-Examiner* was typical: " 'Inchon' is quite possibly the worst movie ever made for the most amount of money. It's stupefyingly incompetent. . . . Scenes butt into each other like bumper cars and, despite the plethora of superimposed title cards, it's often difficult to figure out where the action is taking place—or why. But even the scenes that appear to have survived intact are howlers." Rainer, like most critics, singled out Olivier's waxworks-like deifying of MacArthur in his review. "Outfitted with a pointy chin, a long, pointy nose, and a slick, shiny pate that resembles Howdy Doody's dome, Olivier . . . is so pasty that, standing under the hot lights, you expect him to melt."[18]

Added *The Village Voice*'s J. Hoberman: "Head covered with a shoe polish toupee, cheeks caked with rouge, eyes mascaraed beyond belief, Olivier subverts the entire project by appearing in the appropriate guise of a broken-down tart. . . . Toshiro Mifune appears as a taciturn ex-samurai (left over from the Japanese occupation?) who inscrutably manages to save the day."[19]

Even the chance of winning lavish prizes (which included a Rolls-Royce Corniche and $100,000 in cash) failed to entice audiences to sit through *Inchon!*[20] The picture bombed all over the world—it made less than $2 million in North America—and was never even released in Japan.

Neither was *The Bushido Blade* (1980), an unfortunate, cheap-looking international enterprise. The film was produced in 1979 by Trident Films in association with Rankin/Bass, which had been co-producing features and television films with Toho and other Japanese companies going back to 1964, and much of *The Bushido Blade* was shot in Japan. The company was best known for animated television specials like *Rudolph, the Red-Nosed Reindeer* and other holiday perennials, but occasionally drifted into live action feature-length production. Rankin/Bass had a major hit with *The Last Dinosaur*, a 1977 television film that scored high ratings on ABC and did respectable business theatrically in Japan. "I became very popular with the network," said producer Arthur Rankin, Jr., "because my films all had special effects in them. I was the only producer using special effects for television movies at this time. I got to make the movies and was having a ball. I always wanted to make a Japanese samurai movie, so I made . . . *The Bushido Blade*."[21]

The film was directed by Tsugunobu Kotani, a Toho director since the late 1960s who had helmed *The Last Dinosaur* and several other Rankin/Bass films. The story concerns the signing of the Kanagawa treaty in 1854. Just as Commodore Matthew Perry (Richard Boone, in his last role) and the shogun's commander, Hayashi (Mifune), are about to sign it, the Japanese gift for the American President, a valuable sword, is stolen. Hayashi dispatches Prince Ido (Shinichi "Sonny" Chiba) to retrieve it, while Perry, against Hayashi's orders, sends out three of his best men. Except for his last scenes, Mifune is once again dubbed by Paul Frees and has almost nothing to do.

The picture itself is little more than a rehash of *Red Sun*, and its script overflows with Japanese cultural clichés. This, combined with some wildly inaccurate depictions of Japanese people (for example, Laura Gemser, screendom's Emanuelle, as a scantily clad half-breed) and their culture, made the film unmarketable in Japan, and *The Bushido Blade* was never released there. It didn't do much better in the United States, where it debuted on cable television before a brief theatrical run in a somewhat longer version (retitled *The Bloody Bushido Blade*). Today the film is all but forgotten.

More typical for Mifune was *Port Arthur* (Nihyakusan-kochi, 1981), the first of two Russo-Japanese War films he made early in the decade. Toho had all but given up on the genre in the early 1970s, but Toei, having had considerable success with their all-star "Japanese Godfather" movies, felt the time was right for a nostalgic return to the form. Featuring elaborate miniatures directed by Teruyoshi Nakano, Eiji Tsuburaya's underfinanced successor at Toho, *Port Arthur* aped Toho's sixties war movies shamelessly, to the point of loading the film down with actors more associated with the rival studio—Mifune, Hisaya Morishige, Makoto Sato, Akihiko Hirata—than their own. Mifune, cast as Emperor Meiji, walked through his role, as did top-billed Tatsuya Nakadai as General Nogi, but the three-hour-plus epic was a popular hit, earning close to $8.5 million at the box office, a record for the studio.[22] Its success inspired *Battle Anthem* (Nihonkai daikaisen—umi yukaba, 1983), which had fewer stars, more stock footage, and less success.

"I had Mifune play Emperor Meiji in one movie and Admiral Heihachiro Togo in [*Battle Anthem*]," said director Toshio Masuda, "convinced these roles had to be played by none other than Mifune. It was his sheer stage presence that infused life into each character he played. The fact that he starred in fewer movies later in his career showed that the Japanese film industry was unable over the years to produce real large-scale movies that were fit for Mifune's caliber."[23]

Mifune spent the second half of the 1970s appearing in one mediocre film after another, but at least he was working. However, the three years Kurosawa had spent on *Dersu Uzala* had taken their toll, and it was said that making the movie had ruined his health. Audie Bock reported that Kurosawa was "gaunt, pale and walking with difficulty, [looking] older than his 68 years. He seemed to have joined the ranks of living institutions of the cinema."[24]

Following *Dersu Uzala*, Kurosawa once again could not get any of his projects off the ground. With the continued popularity of Hollywood films over Japanese and the industry's failure to develop new talent, film production in Japan had become a shadow of its former self. By 1978, Kurosawa and Mifune's old studio released just fourteen features and a few shorts, of which only four could truly be called in-house productions. Toho had virtually become a ghost town, with most of its releases being produced off the lot as independent pickups. Their pool of contract talent was gone, and even its most reliable breadwinner, Godzilla, had been put into semiretirement.

Kurosawa was still being approached with offers to do television. He was even asked early on to direct *Shogun*. "I waited until the book had been translated into Japanese before I responded," Kurosawa said. "When I read it, it seemed so far from historical truth that it would not have been appropriate for me to accept."[25]

Instead, he spent the rest of the seventies writing three scripts of his own: *Ran*; an adaptation of Poe's *Masque of the Red Death*, written in 1977; and *Kagemusha*. All three were period films; Kurosawa was uncharacteristically defeatist at the time about doing something modern. He was probably still smarting after the financial failure of *Dodes'ka-den*. "[While there are] mountains of things I want to say about contemporary Japan," he insisted, "I could never get permission to do it in a contemporary film. Why, if I even tried to make a picture like *Ikiru* today, the Education Minister would squelch it. Those iron-faced bureaucrats don't want to believe that's what they're really like."[26]

Ran, a story he had been developing since the completion of *Dersu*, was the film he most wanted to direct. "I started out to make a film about Motonari Mori, the sixteenth-century warlord whose three sons are admired in Japan as paragons of filial virtue," he said. "What might their story be like, I wondered, if the sons had not been so good? It was only after I was well into writing the script about these imaginary unfilial sons of the Mori clan that the similarities to *Lear* occurred to me. Since my story is set in medieval Japan, the protagonist's children had to be men; to divide the realm among daughters would have been unthinkable."[27]

But of the three scripts, *Kagemusha*, a violent but humorous historical epic, seemed the most bankable, especially in the wake of the money NBC and Paramount were pouring into *Shogun*. Toho agreed to finance *Kage-musha*, then just as quickly backed out. They said Kurosawa's budget—as much as $5.5 million, or about five times the cost of the average feature— was beyond their means.

Disheartened, and thinking he might never be able to make his movie, Kurosawa created nearly 250 paintings and sketches, most measuring 12 x 15 inches, of scenes and characters as he visualized them. "In many of my movies," he said, "when I could not find words to explain to my cast and crew what I wanted, I would make a sketch. But this case was special. I wanted to leave behind some record of my plans."[28]

Kagemusha is based on a true story. "[It's] the only case where a whole clan was killed in one battle," Kurosawa said.[29] "It is at once the portrait of a great man . . . the tragi-comic story of a shadow-man, the 'kagemusha' [shadow warrior]; and, at the same time, the drama of the destruction of a clan."[30] Like *Seven Samurai*, the inspiration for *Kagemusha* came when Kuro-sawa and co-writer Masato Ide were researching sixteenth-century Japa-nese history. They were intrigued by the story of a lord, Shingen Takeda (1521–73), who had employed a *kagemusha*, or double, to impersonate him and confuse his enemies. Coincidentally, Takeda was the same character played by Kinnosuke Nakamura in the Mifune-Inagaki *Samurai Banners* (1969), while *Kagemusha* was set in the same era as *Shogun*. "It's my favorite period," Kurosawa told Audie Bock. "People were straightforward and un-pretentious then. It was a time of great ambitions and great failures, great heroes and equally great scoundrels."[31]

The script by Kurosawa and Masato Ide concerns a condemned thief compelled to become Takeda's *kagemusha* or face crucifixion. After the lord succumbs to a sniper's bullet, Takeda's inner circle vow to keep his death a secret from their enemies for at least three years. The thief assumes his identity, and the truth is known only to a handful of advisers, Takeda's brother and son, and a few bodyguards and pages. Gradually, the thief all but becomes the man he has replaced, and the clan remains remarkably sta-ble during his "reign." Coached by Takeda's look-alike brother (Tsutomu Ya-mazaki), who previously acted as a *kagemusha*, the thief's impersonation fools everyone for months: the lord's concubines, his grandson, and sol-diers. But ultimately, he does not fool the lord's horse. When the thief is thrown, the ruse is unmasked, and the lord's son (Kenichi Hagiwara) as-sumes his father's title. He plunges his dominion headlong into an un-winnable battle, and the entire clan is wiped out. The thief, who by now feels part of the clan in all but blood, joins them in death.

Like *Sanjuro*, *Kagemusha* was a story in which nothing is what it seems: lords are criminals and criminals become lords. The aspirations of the thief, and the heart of the story, go beyond acting the part of the ruler. He literally wants to become him. His confidence grows, he comes to genuinely love his "grandson" and his kingdom. Once he's unmasked and summarily dismissed with a small reward, the money means nothing to him—he wants his family and new identity back.

Among the many prominent directors who fell in love with Kurosawa's films during the 1960s was George Lucas, who was part of the new breed of filmmakers that dominated Hollywood in the 1970s. He, along with Francis Ford Coppola, John Milius, Martin Scorsese, Steven Spielberg, and others, considered themselves disciples of Kurosawa, though their own work bore little resemblance in content or style to Kurosawa's. Still, Lucas had lifted story and character elements from *The Hidden Fortress* into *Star Wars* (1977), and through Coppola obtained an introduction.

When Kurosawa told director George Lucas his story and showed him his artwork, Lucas could scarcely believe investors weren't rushing to back the film. "It was a tragedy. It was like telling Michelangelo, 'All right, you're seventy and we're not letting you paint anymore.' "[32] In July 1978 they met in San Francisco to plan a course of action.

"I contacted Kurosawa and asked him if it was true they didn't have enough money to do it, and he said yes," Lucas remembered. "I said, 'How much do they need in order to finish the movie?' It was two or three million or something like that. So I turned around and went to Laddie [Alan Ladd, Jr.] at Fox, and I told him that I wanted to buy the international rights to the film and pay [the studio] the difference between what they had and what they needed to finish the movie—about two or three million."[33]

Lucas leaned heavily on 20th Century-Fox—the same studio that had produced *Star Wars* and booted Kurosawa from *Tora! Tora! Tora!* a decade earlier—to buy the international rights to *Kagemusha*. By demonstrating their faith in the film, Lucas would shame Toho into financing the balance of the production. Kurosawa's film would surely bring prestige to Fox, but financially they knew the venture was risky at best. Still, they could ill afford to alienate Lucas: Fox desperately wanted to distribute Lucas's *Star Wars* sequel, and Lucas held all the sequel rights.

"This was right after I had done *Star Wars*," Lucas said, "and Laddie was in a great mood at the time, so they said yes, they would do the movie. I then went to Francis [Coppola] and said . . . 'Would you like to be the co-international producer on this picture with me?' "[34]

And so, for the first time in history, an American studio was pressured into buying a film it didn't especially want, to engineer another company into pouring money into a film it did not want to make.

Feature film division president Ladd and Toho president Isao Matsuoka announced the deal on December 20, 1978, with production beginning the following April.[35] Fox agreed to pay Toho $1.5 million up front for the rights to Kagemusha outside Japan, and Toho would fund the balance of the now $6–$7.5 million film. The Japanese studio would have to pay the lion's share of the film's negative cost, but even at just $1.5 million for the remaining world rights, Fox wasn't too sure they would recoup their investment.

For the first time in nearly a decade, Kurosawa was making a Japanese film, and once again he rallied and his health—weakened by the long production of Dersu Uzala—made a remarkable comeback. "He is about 20 pounds heavier," Bock wrote, "suntanned and quick—nearly impossible to keep up with. Obviously, exercising his métier suits him, and he could pass for someone ten years his junior."[36] Now pushing seventy, Kurosawa amazed his crew by pitching in, digging trenches, building fences, and raking gravel. He still held court with his company in the evenings, though even he admitted that the production was exhausting him, joking, "You'll have to forgive me if I'm not very talkative—you see, I've been waging war all day."[37]

His spirits were also bolstered when he turned, yet again, to the Japanese public for assistance. He placed ads to recruit extras, ads that implored the citizens of Japan to help him to revive the Japanese film industry. Fifteen thousand applied.[38] He found this infusion of youth invigorating and spent hundreds of hours drilling his extras and giving some prominent roles. As with Dodes'ka-den, most of the supporting parts went to actors outside Kurosawa's stock company. And as if to confirm his instinct about casting non-professionals in Tora! Tora! Tora!, he picked Masayuki Yui, a business executive with no acting experience, for the key role of Ieyasu Tokugawa. For the part of Takeda's son, the director cast Kenichi Hagiwara, a rock star–turned-actor.

Kurosawa's spirits remained high, despite the fact that Kagemusha proved one of the most trouble-plagued productions of his career. When shooting commenced in June 1979 on location at Himeji Castle, the production was shut down for several days due to an unrelated bomb scare. The following month, director of photography Kazuo Miyagawa, the seventy-one-year-old cinematographer who had shot Rashomon and Yojimbo, was forced to bow out due to vision and other health problems related to diabetes. Much of the film was shot in Hokkaido, the northernmost island of Japan and to most Japanese what Alaska is to Americans. But even there, Kurosawa and his crew had to work hard to avoid letting electrical towers and other symbols of the computer age slip into the frame. In November a typhoon struck the island, and weather delays cost the production $40,000 per day.

But the biggest setback occurred at the very start of production. Kurosawa and Ide had written *Kagemusha* specifically for Shintaro Katsu. His beloved Zatoichi character had made a successful transition from features to series television during the 1970s, and the actor's popularity remained high in Japan. They thought him perfect for the dual role as the lord and his *kagemusha*, for he was a great comic actor and equally adept at drama. Katsu was also cast, in part, because of his good-natured, larger-than-life public persona. For all of his tough-guy roles, Katsu was in essence a pudgy, overindulged baby. He wore shirts as loud as he was in public, and he had an entourage of followers and bodyguards who lit every cigarette and guffawed at every joke. Kurosawa wanted to channel this lusty energy into *Kagemusha*, particularly the early scenes, where the thief is awed and outraged by the task presented him. In turning his thief into a noble lord, Kurosawa saw himself playing Henry Higgins to Katsu's Eliza Doolittle.

Additionally, Katsu's domestic popularity eased Toho's fears about their investment. (Toho released many of Katsu's profitable films and those he produced for brother Tomisaburo Wakayama during the lean seventies.) Compared to Mifune, Katsu was a complete unknown outside Japan, but his Zatoichi films were slowly but surely developing a cult following, and no one doubted, least of all Katsu, that *Kagemusha* could propel him to international stardom. Kurosawa reckoned that Katsu wanted the role badly enough that he'd acquiesce to his demanding direction. But where Mifune was a respectful student, Katsu, as Donald Richie described him, was "an unruly boy seeing how far he could push papa."[39] Katsu was used to having his way with directors, all directors, and this was something Kurosawa hadn't bargained on.

The trouble began on the Toho lot, during dress rehearsals on July 18, 1979. Katsu came to the set with his own camera crew to videotape and immediately assess his performance. He, not Kurosawa, would chart the direction of his character. Actor Jinpachi Nezu, who played one of Takeda's bodyguards, recalled: "It rained that day. I usually go to the studio earlier than most but [Katsu] seemed to have gotten there an hour before I did. When I went to the make-up room, he was already seated in front of the mirror as [wigmaker Junjiro] Yamada put the wig on his head. I thought he seemed excited. I said, 'Good morning.' 'Hey, Nezu!' he said, 'I'm going to videotape the shooting today.' I thought it would mean trouble, but I said only, 'I see.' And then he left for the set."[40]

According to Mike Inoue, Kurosawa heard Katsu's entourage setting up their equipment and asked, " 'What's that noise?' Katsu replied, 'That's my video crew. I make it a rule to do this all the time.' To which Kurosawa responded, 'Well, it may be *your* rule, but you're not permitted to do this. It's very disturbing.' Katsu immediately took off his armor and walked out of the studio. Kurosawa was very quiet as he watched him go. He immediately called Ms. [Teruyo] Nogami and said, 'Call up [Tatsuya] Nakadai to see if he's free.' She called him up, I think that night, and Nakadai said, 'I'm willing to do it.' "[41]

"When I went to put on my armor," Nezu said, "[Katsu] came back. He looked angry and took off his costume. I thought he was going to the bathroom, but I soon realized that something had happened with the taping because he took his wig off and put it on his costume. Then an assistant director came and told me to report to the set. Mr. Kurosawa calmly said, 'Katsu got angry regarding the videotaping and left, but let's review [the scene].' I remember rehearsing with the assistant director for the camera and lights for about an hour after that."[42]

According to Mike Inoue, "Kurosawa then said, 'Where's Katsu?' Someone said he was in his trailer sleeping, and he walked over to his trailer. My uncle later told me, 'Katsu was smiling. He thought I was going to apologize.' Instead he said, 'Katsu, you're discharged.' That was the end of the story. Katsu thought nobody could talk to him like that."[43] Kurosawa walked away. Katsu tried to chase him, but producer Tomoyuki "Yuko" Tanaka held him back. Katsu then attempted to revive the specter of *Tora! Tora! Tora!* by challenging Kurosawa to dueling press conferences, but succeeded only in looking like a pouting child. The public knew Katsu all too well. They weren't surprised that this partnership had so miserably failed. Kurosawa and Katsu were oil and water.

Kurosawa argued, not without reason, that if Katsu was this difficult on the first day of shooting, what would he be like on the last? "There is no need for two directors for the movie," he said.[44] He wasn't kidding.

Mifune was the obvious choice to replace him. He was a far bigger star abroad and could effortlessly fill Katsu's shoes in the role, one not far removed from Sanjuro or Kikuchiyo. The official word was that Mifune was too tied up with other projects to take Katsu's place. But, in reality, he wasn't even asked. As Inoue said, Kurosawa wanted Nakadai before Katsu had even reached his trailer.

"There are a lot of rumors, but the truth is—and I know the facts—they always stayed good friends," Inoue insists. "Kurosawa said, 'Red Beard was the last film I was near him.' He started his own production company, and he said, 'I couldn't find any roles for him after that, but I still owe him for my success.' . . . He always said, 'He was a great actor as long as he was acting in my films. He was a wonderful actor.' "45

But after Katsu, the last thing Kurosawa needed was tension between himself and the actor he hadn't directed in fifteen years, particularly under the intense media scrutiny that followed Katsu's dismissal. Nakadai quickly agreed to take over Katsu's part, but conceded, "It was a difficult decision, because Katsu is a friend of mine. But I did it partly out of a feeling of duty toward Mr. Kurosawa. If I had refused, the whole production would have fallen apart."46 However, despite the seemingly effortless replacement, the production problems continued—Nakadai had commitments that stretched into the fall and couldn't start shooting until then, and he would be needed in almost every scene.

With Katsu fired and Mifune not an option, Nakadai was virtually Kurosawa's only option. Nakadai was one of the few Japanese actors both respected and popular in Japan and in the United States, and one of the very few stars besides Mifune with whom Kurosawa had worked before and who was the right age. Kurosawa's decision may have been influenced by a major retrospective of Nakadai's career in New York shortly before Katsu's firing. Sponsored by the Japan Society, the festival included such Nakadai showcases as Sword of Doom, Yojimbo, Harakiri, and The Human Condition. In the years between High and Low and Kagemusha, he had kept as busy as Mifune, appearing in a mix of prestige and program pictures as well as television dramas. He continued to act on the stage and founded a drama school with his wife, Kyoko Miyazaki, in 1975.

For Nakadai, acting both parts was a challenge. "I had to play both roles with absolutely identical makeup and costumes," he said. "That was very difficult. And Mr. Kurosawa would not permit me to enter into each character from the outside, by means of the way one walked, for example, but insisted that it be done from the inside." Reflecting on working with Kurosawa again after more than fifteen years, the actor noted, "This time he wanted a more internalized interpretation, acting that was simultaneously naturalistic and complex, whereas in *Sanjuro* and *Yojimbo* he was more concerned with movement."[47]

In the face of one disaster after another, Kurosawa maintained a relentless pace, which he attributed, in part, to the experience of his cast and crew. Kurosawa reacted to the loss of the diabetic Miyagawa (who still functioned as a consultant) by replacing him with Takao Saito and Shoji Ueda, the latter a forty-two-year-old former assistant on films like *Sanjuro*. Veteran Asakazu Nakai joined Miyagawa as a consultant. Teruyo Nogami was back, naturally, this time pulling double duty as assistant producer and script supervisor. Besides Nakadai, old-timers like Kamatari Fujiwara were brought in for small roles. And even seventy-four-year-old Takashi Shimura was flown in, despite his being in the advanced stages of emphysema. Kurosawa wanted to give him a bigger role but, he said, "I was afraid he'd break."[48] Perhaps most important, *Kagemusha* marked Kurosawa's professional reunion with one of his oldest colleagues.

Ishiro Honda had directed his last feature, *Terror of Mechagodzilla* (Mekagojira no gyakushu) in 1975—it was his only film after 1970. He spent the first half of the decade directing mindless superhero programs for Toho's television division, but found the work unrewarding. Loyal company man that he was, Honda agreed, against his better judgment, to go along with Toho's plan to re-edit his earlier fantasy films for reissue packages during the seventies, and again later for home video release. For all his work Honda was paid very little money.

Honda and Kurosawa were playing golf one afternoon when Kurosawa invited his old friend to join him on *Kagemusha*. "Why don't we make a film together," Kurosawa said, "just like the old times when we were very young assistant directors?"[49] And that's exactly how it worked out. Honda was only one year younger than Kurosawa, but with his shock of white hair and thin, wrinkled face, he looked much older. And in working on *Kagemusha*, Honda, like Kurosawa, seemed to have the energy of the twenty-five-year-old assistant director he had been four decades earlier.

Honda's function on *Kagemusha*, as well as on all of Kurosawa's subsequent films, was as a kind of chief assistant director. "He advised me about the special-effects scenes and shot supplementary footage as director of B Group," Kurosawa said. "He made an effort to communicate with the crew and teach acting. I was able to concentrate on other things without anxiety thanks to his good work. . . . I learned a lot from him and his movies. He was my mental support."[50]

Tatsuo Matsumura, whom Honda had directed in *King Kong vs. Godzilla* and who worked with him again on Kurosawa's *Madadayo* (1993), described him as "a great person. Very gentle, a real gentleman. He had a warm heart and paid delicate attention to people. I cannot understand why he was always shooting Godzilla movies. . . . He wanted to make movies about ordinary life in Japan. He never said it explicitly, but when the three of us had dinner together, Honda talked about seeing an ordinary, daily life movie and the end of that picture, where there was a quiet, ordinary street scene. He spoke thoughtfully and elegantly about it, and it made a strong impression on me."[51]

"Honda and Kurosawa had shared fifty years together and had become old gentlemen simultaneously," said Honda's widow, Kimi. "The joy of working jointly was everything. Some people have suggested they were brothers even before they were born. It was a very special relationship and very difficult to explain in words. Their feelings just came together; each respected the other's attributes and failings. They were on different tracks, but bound very deeply. They respected each other."[52]

Honda described his contribution this way: "He . . . uses three cameras at the same time, so he sometimes needs me to supervise one of the cameras, especially for scenes featuring a lot of actors. For these scenes, it's difficult for him to follow everything himself. And sometimes I'll give direction to the extras." When asked about his unusual billing, Honda said, "Someone in France asked, 'Why is the director of Godzilla movies working on Kurosawa's films?' Well, Kurosawa seems more relaxed with me on his staff. . . . We have the same way of thinking about life, the war, politics. Also we care about the same things working at the studio."[53]

But Honda's importance on Kurosawa's later films extended far beyond the realm of an assistant director, and he would assume a position not unlike the one Hideo Oguni had years before in the writing stage. Honda didn't play the part of devil's advocate the way Oguni had, but he would quietly make suggestions, and many of his ideas were incorporated in their films together.

To some extent, Honda was also Kurosawa's eyes. The director was increasingly plagued with vision problems, and took to wearing dark sunglasses outdoors and at public appearances where studio lights glared at him. "The light is very bad for my eyes, which are not very good," he explained in 1992.[54]

From *Kagemusha* onward, Honda would be billed alternately as Associate Director or Directorial Adviser. Such billing on any film, anywhere in the world, is unusual. For a filmmaker as notoriously autocratic as Kurosawa, it was unprecedented. According to Kimi, "They discussed what his title should be, but Honda said that there should be only one director, and so he chose 'Directorial Adviser.' 'I don't need the title,' he said. Everybody wondered why he was given this unusual billing; journalists from all over the world asked him, but he said he couldn't explain why—it just was. But his modesty was never false. He hated that. He was never pretentious or competitive."[55]

Toho was glad to have Honda on the film. He brought a stability to the production and was one of the few people Kurosawa would listen to. Honda and Kurosawa were too busy during the 1950s and '60s to spend much time together, but beginning with *Kagemusha*, their joint experience as assistant directors in the thirties, their love of film, and common friends drew them closer than ever before. They became inseparable. Mike Inoue warmly recalled the times he would join his uncle and Honda in Gotemba: "We sometimes had guests visiting the country villa in Gotemba. Mr. Honda and I would share the same bedroom. One morning we were in the kitchen and he and Kurosawa were laughing. I asked, 'What are you laughing about?' And Honda-san said to me, 'Don't you remember? You were talking in your sleep, but I couldn't understand what you were saying because it was all in English. At the end you said, "Thank you very much," so I figured you were making a speech!' Mr. Honda was very important mentally to Mr. Kurosawa, he gave him peace of mind."[56]

Shooting took nine months. As usual, Kurosawa demanded historical accuracy throughout the production, particularly after the liberties *Shogun* had taken. For some scenes, the director secured real sixteenth-century armor and other clothing from Japanese museums and private collections. In a rare departure from historic reality, 10 percent of the riders atop the film's 200 specially trained horses (many flown in from America) were women members of various equestrian organizations. Kurosawa admired these women, saying publicly that they were "more daring than most men."[57] (The heavy samurai armor disguised their sex in the finished picture.) Nearly two months were spent in Hokkaido, on the Yuhara Plain, for the climactic battle. Kurosawa instructed his extras portraying the Takeda clan to "go toward death as if it were a kind of festival."

These men were Buddhists [the director explained]. They believed in the existence of another world. If their life here below was worthy and admirable, they could go to Paradise. Through their choice of clothing . . . they expressed their sensitivity to beauty, their aspiration to a life after death. It's an aestheticism which dates back to the 13th century. When a warrior-chief thought that he might die in battle, he put on his most beautiful costume so that his death might be a thing of beauty. I don't wish to give the impression that war is beautiful. That's an extremely dangerous attitude. When I shot the battle scenes, I concentrated on making them as realistic as possible. But out of that horror—weirdly enough and absolutely involuntary on my part—a beauty emerged. A terrible beauty.[58]

The delays *Kagemusha* incurred prompted Toho president Isao Matsuoka to be markedly frank about the yet-unreleased film: "We are not just nervous, we are extremely nervous. This picture is costing us more than six times what a normal movie does and twice what we've ever spent on a prestige picture. We could practically make a whole movie for what this Hokkaido location alone is costing—$700,000. Of course, these figures sound small by U.S. standards, and Fox has helped us a great deal, but we have to make our money back in Japan."[59]

Articles published in the United States claimed that Kurosawa's film, which ultimately cost around $7 million, was the most expensive Japanese film ever made, but this simply is not true. While *Kagemusha* was in production, publisher Haruki Kadokawa and the Tokyo Broadcasting System (TBS) were spending more than twice that figure ($20 million) on a disaster epic directed by Kinji Fukasaku called *Virus* (Fukkatsu no hi, 1980).

Kurosawa, however, remained undeterred. In fact, he was relaxed, so much so that for the first time in his career, he allowed his cast, crew, and friends to see his rough cut of the film during production.[60] Again and again he proudly told reporters, "Mine is the first Japanese film released worldwide by a major American studio."[61]

Amid countless setbacks, Kurosawa rushed to complete his epic, but simply could not make the scheduled April 13 opening. Toho's theater circuit called upon Nippon Herald, *Dersu Uzala*'s distributor, for a film to run in its place while Kurosawa wrapped postproduction. So, instead of *Kagemusha*, Japanese audiences endured *The Amityville Horror*.

Kagemusha finally premiered at the Yurakuza Theater in Tokyo on April 27, 1980. The 1,200 invitation-only guests represented a cross section of politicians, artists, educators—and filmmakers. A contingent of six Western directors flew to Japan to attend the premiere: Francis Ford Cop-

pola, William Wyler, Irvin Kershner, Arthur Penn, Sam Peckinpah, and Terence Young. James Coburn and Peter Fonda were also there, as well as
Toshiro Mifune. Despite the fact that Kurosawa never even considered him
for what might have been his best role in years, Mifune nevertheless chose
to support the efforts of his estranged *sensei*.[62]

Kagemusha was an enormous hit in Japan and earned back its negative cost
two weeks after it opened. In the first seventeen days of its release, the picture made $10,122,000 at 217 theaters, representing more than 1.7 mil-
lion admissions.[63] Ultimately, it earned approximately $12 million in
Japanese rentals during its initial release. Advance ticket sales were huge,
but the film had no "legs" at the box office. Initially at least, the theaters
were crammed—according to one report, to 98.3 percent of capacity.[64]
Reviews were mixed, but Kurosawa said, "That's because those who did not
like it were expecting something else."[65] *Kagemusha* placed second on
Kinema Jumpo's "Best Ten" list, behind another comeback film, Seijun
Suzuki's perversely noncommercial, self-consciously arty *Zigeunerweisen*.
Tsutomu Yamazaki was awarded Best Supporting Actor.

    Kagemusha was submitted for competition at the thirty-third Cannes
Film Festival. Officials at Cannes offered to screen it out of competition,
thus saving the director any possible embarrassment if it lost, but Kurosawa
insisted on taking his chances. 1980 was a decidedly weak year for films,
and it was a foregone conclusion that Kurosawa's film would win Cannes'
top prize, the Palme d'Or. A rumor spread during the festival that "the fix
was in," that Kurosawa would be handed the prize merely for showing up,
but once the film was screened, a victory seemed not only assured but justified. "As it turned out," wrote Andrew Sarris, "Kurosawa was depending
on his laurels to carry the day. The fierceness and energy of *Kagemusha* . . .
burst through the screen as if it were the visual roar of a young lion. Its dy-
namically pulsating canvas of sixteenth-century Japan derives some of its
inspiration from Shakespeare's chronicle plays, and some from John Ford's
cavalry Westerns, but Kurosawa's personal signature is inscribed on every
physical and spiritual contortion of his characters."[66]

    On May 26, *Kagemusha* was indeed proclaimed winner of the Palme
d'Or. However, as had happened at Cannes the year before, the prize
would be shared with an American film, in this case Bob Fosse's *All That
Jazz*. According to *Variety*, the announcement "was greeted with mild boos,
[as] the Kurosawa film was expected to be the outright winner."[67]

In September, Kurosawa flew to Paris for *Kagemusha*'s opening there on October 1. He held a press conference at the Espace Pierre Cardin to talk about the film and to exhibit the 200-plus paintings and sketches he had made when he thought the film a lost cause. He arrived in New York on September 29, 1980, and *Kagemusha* debuted at the New York Film Festival at Lincoln Center a week later, on October 6. "Kurosawa in person looks like a dignified elder corporate executive," reported Peter Rainer. "Even allowing for cultural differences, he appears remote. . . . At the press conference he expressed his credo: 'I have something I want to say and I know how to say it. I will let nothing get in the way of that.' Asked whether he has seen any films by his benefactors . . . he slowly spins out a list: 'The Godfather,' 'American Graffiti,' 'Apocalypse Now,' 'Star Wars.' Did he like any of them? For the first time in the interview, Kurosawa beams. 'I liked "Star Wars." ' "[68]

Kagemusha was also shown at the San Francisco and San Diego Film Festivals later that same month. Kurosawa flew to Los Angeles, where a luncheon sponsored by the Directors Guild of America (DGA) was held in his honor. Among the guests were George Cukor, Samuel Fuller, John Huston, and Billy Wilder. From Los Angeles he flew to San Francisco for the festival there and met with Lucas and Coppola.[69]

In San Francisco, after a noisy introduction by eight *taiko* drummers, Kurosawa stepped onstage and was greeted by 1,500 festivalgoers, who gave him a two-minute standing ovation. Asked about the importance of the writer on his films, Kurosawa replied, "If you have a first-rate script and you give it to a third-rate director you will get a very good film out of it. If you have a third-rate script and you give it to a first-rate director you'll get a *mess*."[70]

Kagemusha did "spectacular business in its European engagements," according to Emile Buyse, president of 20th Century-Fox International. In its first seven weeks the film earned more than $2 million, in a limited number of theaters, many of which ran the film just three times per day.[71] There was even talk of producing an English-dubbed version, so the film could earn additional money in a sale to network television. The dubbing would cost Fox a mere $50,000, a figure surely to be outweighed by a sale to one of the networks. But by the time *Kagemusha* was released, Fox president Alan Ladd, Jr., was gone, and according to *New West*, "The film was always considered a questionable legacy by the remaining Fox brass."[72]

Their reason was simple. As an "art film," *Kagemusha* had done exceedingly well. But as a $1.5 million investment from a major studio, Kurosawa's film, in the United States at least, lost money. In its first month, in six cities—New York, Los Angeles, San Francisco, Philadelphia, Berkeley, and Boston—the film grossed just under $400,000.[73]

That Kurosawa wound up with a film as good as *Kagemusha* is a testament to his tenacity and love of filmmaking. But the curse that seemed to befall the production, coupled with Kurosawa's own deeply rooted pessimism at this stage in his career, resulted in a bleak and emotionally remote film. *Kagemusha* would be the coldest, least satisfying of his later films.

The film is crushed under the weight of its own intractable formality. The years of conceptual paintings, the arduous research expeditions to castles all over Japan, the insistence on authentic armor and props, completely overwhelm it. Everything from the costumes to the individual shots has been designed to the tiniest detail and predetermined well in advance of production. Every idea is so carefully controlled that the humanity is lost and the film can't escape a mechanical quality. Kurosawa here seems to be self-consciously making an exhaustively structured Kurosawa film. It is a masterpiece of form and style, with every scene single-mindedly an expression of its theme, exploring the director's fascination with Doppelgängers and the dichotomy of reality and illusion. As Donald Richie wrote: "Though always a rigorous director, he has heretofore at least partially hidden his theme. . . . In *Kagemusha*, the film is exclusively about the theme, it *is* the theme."[74]

He also continues to explore his growing fascination with dreams in a beautifully filmed nightmare sequence, in which the thief is haunted amid a swirling pool of colored backdrops by the ghost of Takeda. There are impressive sequences throughout, including stunning telephoto shots of red-orange sunsets, tracking shots out the windows of Suwa Castle, smoke-filled battlegrounds, and fog-shrouded lakes. But otherwise it is an exasperating film to watch.

Kurosawa's next film, *Ran*, would be just as formal, but in dealing with universal issues about the disintegration of family and old age it is infinitely more transcendent. *Kagemusha* gives moviegoers nothing to latch on to. For all his immaturity, Katsu—or, for that matter, Mifune—might have brought to *Kagemusha* the human element so ill-served by Nakadai, whose performance is likewise formal and staid. Replacing Katsu with Nakadai was like replacing Charles Laughton with Laurence Olivier, with a Richard II when a Henry VIII was called for. In scenes written with Katsu in mind, where the thief explodes with incredulity or amusement, Nakadai is quite bad, though most of the fault isn't Nakadai's, it's Kurosawa's. For all of Nakadai's considerable talents, he fails to convey the thief's self-deception that he might actually and permanently be accepted in his role, nor does he adequately express the love he develops for his grandchild and his kingdom. This deep longing was key to making the film work, but Nakadai creates an enigma, not a character.

For all its historical inaccuracies and lapses into soap-opera-ish melodrama, the miniseries version of *Shogun* is at least engrossing, whereas *Kagemusha* keeps its viewers at an emotional distance. Moreover, while *Shogun* flopped in Japan in its truncated version, in America it trounced its far more prestigious competition. That Mifune participated in *Shogun*, for whatever the reason, irked Kurosawa enormously. He ridiculed Mifune and the miniseries, and he never completely forgave him for appearing in it.

During postproduction, Kurosawa also had a falling out with composer Masaru Sato, who had scored all of the director's films from *Throne of Blood* through *Red Beard*. The director had imposed his musical tastes on the composer before, especially during the production of *Red Beard*, and now on *Kagemusha* Kurosawa was doing it again. Sato, rivaled only by Toru Takemitsu and Akira Ifukube as Japan's leading composer of film music and never short of work even as the industry bottomed out, walked out. His replacement was Shinichiro Ikebe, who'd worked in films since the late 1970s and was far more willing to follow Kurosawa's predilection for aping classical composers. But this backfired on Kurosawa, and for the first time, one of his films was provided with an awful score; the fault was Kurosawa's, just as Nakadai's casting had been.

But *Kagemusha* had "comeback" written all over it. Lucas and Coppola had put themselves on the line, and Fox had poured far more into the film than they felt it was worth. Toho had reluctantly invested a comparative fortune, and Kurosawa had invested nearly five years of his life in it. It had to succeed.

And succeed it did. Critics and audiences wanted so badly to like it that they forgave its many shortcomings. The film received more press than any Kurosawa picture that had come before it and earned some of the best notices of his career.

"At the age of 70," wrote David Denby, "Akira Kurosawa has made a stirring and beautiful film that is utterly unlike anything he's done before. Spectacular yet severe, violent yet gravely formal, *Kagemusha* is marked by an overall nobility of style that extends to every gesture, stance, or movement. . . . I would have enjoyed learning more about the shadow—what kind of man he was earlier in his life, how he felt about his imperson-ation—but *Kagemusha* is a study of acts, not motives or feelings. Like many fierce old men, Kurosawa may no longer care very much about feelings, doubts, 'psychology.' Caught up in his mastery of physical movement and filmmaking craft, we may not much care ourselves."[75]

But the *Los Angeles Herald-Examiner* countered this, calling *Kagemusha* "the work of a superb, imagistic moviemaker who no longer engages your heart and mind [the way he] does your eyes. . . . As with many another dream film—like, for instance, 'Apocalypse Now'—too much of its nuance and significance have evaporated or gone awry in the time it took to bring the dream to light."[76]

"The considerable pleasure of *Kagemusha* tends to be of the stately visual variety," said *Time*. "Kurosawa's mood now is autumnal and dispassionate. What really interests him is an imagery that can only be termed timeless: the look of an army on the march, silhouetted against a setting sun or out-lined against a placid shoreline or engaged in night battle on a ground as mysteriously dark as the midnight sky."[77]

"As an elegy for a genre," wrote Kevin Thomas, "an era and a particular kind of hero, 'Kagemusha' is by its very nature an eloquent recapitulation rather than a bold innovation, like 'Rashomon' or 'Seven Samurai,' films that immediately seemed masterpieces. Time will determine where 'Kage-musha' ranks in the Kurosawa canon—and one suspects it will be high—but meanwhile there's no question that with this film we're in the presence of a work by a master."[78]

Kagemusha premiered in Japan with a running time of 179 minutes. This cut was shown at Cannes, but after that, throughout the world, audiences saw only a shorter version running 162 minutes. In May 1980, *Variety* re-ported that the "film will be edited with help from Francis Coppola and George Lucas, [executive] producers of the Japanese [Cannes] entry. . . . As screened at the [festival], 'Kagemusha' ran one minute under three hours and that is the same length as its current release in Japan. But that is con-sidered too long by 20th. It is believed that Coppola and Steven Spielberg (a Lucas and Coppola chum) are currently editing the pic's foreign version in Los Angeles. But at the fest, Kurosawa indicated he would start the edit-ing after the fest with Coppola and Lucas."[79]

However, American Michael Rich, in response to a review that com-plained about the deletions, wrote the following: "I was assistant director on this film and spent over a year working with Kurosawa on its preproduction and production. . . . The true fact of the matter is that Kurosawa himself cut the film from its Japan release length (which was shown at Cannes)—no one else touched *Kagemusha*. Because of its expense and length of production, it was rushed into release in Japan to make back some of Toho's investment as soon as possible. As a result, Kurosawa did not have sufficient time to cut the film to his liking. He considers the longer version a 'rough cut' of the film which unfortunately got shown and has used the intervening summer to prepare a final cut to his approval for the international release version. Contrary to popular film buff belief, it is not always the longer version which is truer to the filmmaker's intentions."[80]

Critic Michael Auerbach responded, in part: "Kurosawa himself has said that the 20 minutes removed from the film were removed specifically because they would be 'incomprehensible to an American audience.' This is quite a value judgment! Even more, it is a peculiarly American point of view. . . . I do think . . . Kurosawa has compromised, understandably, according to the ideas of his executive producers. They did, after all, make it possible to finance the film and they interested a major studio in it."[81]

Whatever the case, all Japanese home video versions of the film continue to clock in at 179 minutes, while all versions outside Japan run nearly 20 minutes shorter, including the version ultimately nominated for an Oscar as Best Foreign Film (it lost to *Moscow Does Not Believe in Tears*). Among the cut footage was Takashi Shimura's brief appearance.

Shimura attended *Kagemusha*'s Japanese premiere, and by all appearances had changed little since the 1950s. But his career was nearly over. He made one final screen appearance, in *Fifth Movement* (Honoo no Daigo Gakusho) and then passed away on January 11, 1982, at the age of seventy-six.

Later, as Kurosawa promoted *Kagemusha* around the world, the director completed his autobiography, *Gama no abura* ("An Oily Toad"; retitled *Something Like an Autobiography* for release in America). The title refers to the old legend that when a toad is placed in a box filled with mirrors, the amphibian, frightened by his own reflection, begins to sweat, and that sweat was said to have medicinal value. Kurosawa found this an apt analogy to how he felt about writing his life story.

The autobiography was serialized in Japan in 1980 and published in book form in Japan and the United States in 1981 and '82. Its timing was excellent. Soon after *Kagemusha*'s release, a major Kurosawa retrospective covering nearly all his films was sponsored by the Japan Society's Film Center in New York City.[82]

With *Kagemusha*, Kurosawa re-established himself as a major force in world film. "We have a Japanese proverb," he said at the time. "You can fall down seven times in the same place, and if you stand up the eighth time you have won."[83]

As Kurosawa moved on to his next project, Mifune was back working for John Frankenheimer, with whom he had made *Grand Prix* fifteen years earlier. *The Challenge* (1982) was produced with American money but filmed for the most part in Kyoto. The picture falls into that peculiar sub-subgenre about displaced Americans who first hate, then embrace Japanese culture, ultimately and improbably gaining acceptance there as equals. These films run the gamut from the intriguing to the terrible. *The Yakuza* (1975), starring Robert Mitchum and Ken Takakura, was one of the better of these, having been made by people with a sincere interest in and knowledge of Japan; Ridley Scott's *Black Rain* (1989), also featuring Takakura and toplining Michael Douglas, was one of the most ludicrous and unpleasant films made by Westerners in Japan. *The Challenge* falls somewhere in between, its lack of success due largely to having been made during a change in management at CBS Theatrical Films, which produced it. When the new management failed to get behind the picture, it didn't stand a chance.

The story follows a down-and-out American boxer, Rick (Scott Glenn), who is offered $500 per day to deliver an antique samurai sword to Osaka. He gets more than he bargained for the minute he climbs into an Osaka taxicab and quickly finds himself immersed in a decades-old blood feud over two family swords: On one side there is the traditional martial-arts *sensei*, Yoshida (Mifune), on the other is his outrageously wealthy brother, Hideo (Atsuo Nakamura, who actually resembles Mifune), ostracized from the family years earlier.

Rick eventually becomes Yoshida's pupil, romances his daughter (Donna Kei Benz), and eventually joins Mifune in a duel to the death in Hisao's James Bondian headquarters (filmed, to good effect, throughout the Kyoto International Convention Center; Mifune's school was shot at Kyoto's Sogokujii Temple). But despite some well-choreographed and audaciously graphic action sequences, supervised by the reliable Ryu Kuze and a young Steven Seagal, the film never once convincingly gets into the heart and soul of the Japanese mystique, nor does the story ever really click, relying as it does on the by now usual, hackneyed American notions of Japanese exoticism. Several of the picture's themes—the ignorant *gaijin* (foreigner) turned Japanese warrior and traditional vs. postwar corporate Japan (Nakamura threatens Glenn with a sword while simultaneously closing a business deal over the phone) being the most dominant—are either overdone or never developed. Frankenheimer remembers "big script problems" when he signed on to do the film, and apparently they were never solved.[84]

Like the swords in *Red Sun* and *The Bushido Blade*, the symbol of Yoshida family tradition is little more than a Maguffin to keep the plot moving. However, there is an effective scene when Mifune explains how the sword—one of two priceless heirlooms—was lost at the end of World War II and traded among American soldiers for cigarettes, then subsequently lost for forty years in America. A search for the sword in the United States by Glenn and Mifune might have been more interesting than this pretentious and not very accurate reflection of supposed traditional Japanese values.

The Challenge symbolized the sad decline of its director, John Frankenheimer, whose career took a nosedive soon after *Grand Prix*. *Seconds*, filmed after *Grand Prix* but released first, was ahead of its time, an extraordinary, deeply disturbing film as good as anything he ever made. But after *The Gypsy Moths* (1969) Frankenheimer seemed to lose his way; his best films of the 1970s (*French Connection II*, *Black Sunday*) were mediocre, his worst films (*99 and 44/100% Dead*, *Prophecy*) awful. The sole exception to this was the American Film Theater's production of *The Iceman Cometh* (1973), a brilliant adaptation of Eugene O'Neill's play. In the 1980s Frankenheimer continued to struggle, cranking out mostly forgettable thrillers like *The Holcroft Covenant* (1985) and *52 Pick-up* (1986), which barely hinted at the real genius he had exhibited in his early work. Frankenheimer admitted to writer Charles Champlin that it was during the making of *The Challenge* that his alcoholism expanded to drinking on the set, which may explain the film's rather lackluster direction. (He went into a detox program after he returned to the United States.[85])

In *The Challenge*, however, we see little of Frankenheimer's talent or, for that matter, much of Mifune's. As Yoshida, the traditional older brother who wants to restore the swords' place of honor, Mifune has little to do but once again stand around glowering fiercely. With his long gray hair, mustache, and goatee, he is as imposing as always, and the sixty-one-year-old actor is admirably athletic in the film's action set pieces, but that's the extent of his superficial performance. As in *Red Sun*, Mifune speaks both Japanese and English in the picture (watching Glenn's swordplay moves, Mifune says, "You stink"). However, according to Frankenheimer, "Mifune was a great help" with the film's authenticity, adding, "As a friend he would constantly take me aside and tell me what was right and wrong from the Japanese aspect. His production company was helpful, too. A lot of the crew we used worked for him."[86]

But Mifune's assistance could not overcome the fundamental problems with the picture's fish-out-of-water clichés, replete with exotic Japanese cuisine sure to turn American stomachs upside down, as well as the predictable scene where American boxer Rick goes up against one of Yoshida's martial-arts students (Kiyoaki Nagai) and is beaten to a pulp. The film's script was written by John Sayles and Richard Maxwell. Sayles, who had just scripted *Battle Beyond the Stars* (1980) for Roger Corman's New World Pictures—a rather blatant steal of *Seven Samurai*—went on to bigger and better things (*Eight Men Out*, *Lone Star*), Maxwell did not (*The Serpent and the Rainbow*, *Shadow of China*). (*Battle Beyond the Stars* was released abroad by United Artists, owners of *Seven Samurai*'s remake rights via *The Magnificent Seven*. This may explain how New World avoided being sued by Toho and Kurosawa.)

Whereas Richard Chamberlain's John Blackthorne has many months—and a miniseries—to immerse himself in the ways of Japan to gain acceptance from Mifune, Scott Glenn's Rick covers the same ground in a matter of weeks, and this simply isn't believable. Glenn's performance, however, is generally good, and he nearly overcomes this scripting flaw.

Glenn, with his drawn, rugged, working-class features, is a good actor and had several plum roles early in his career, in *Urban Cowboy* (1980), *Personal Best* (1982), and especially *The Right Stuff* (1983), where he was excellent as astronaut Alan Shepard. He never caught on, however, despite his talent, and has since alternated between starring roles in little-seen action films and supporting parts in big films like *The Silence of the Lambs* (1991) and *Courage Under Fire* (1996). Although the script of *The Challenge* affords him little to work with—observing Mifune's archery students he asks, "Hey, these guys are pretty good, huh?"—physically he's fine, and he performed nearly all his own stunts.

Glenn, like everyone else, was in awe of Mifune. "It's like being part of an event when you work with [him]. . . . It's no big deal to the people of Kyoto to see actors filming a movie, but because Mifune was in *The Equals* [the film's prerelease title], we'd get over a thousand people just standing around, quietly, to see him. He doesn't speak much English, but he's a force you feel. I think the three greatest action films ever made are *Yojimbo*, *Seven Samurai*, and *Sanjuro*, and they all star Mifune, so you can imagine how I feel working with him. He was very kind to me, like when I was suffering, being buried in that hole [a test Yoshida puts the character through], I'd say 'Please do [the mannerisms you did in] that opening shot of *Yojimbo*,' and he would, just to cheer you up."[87]

Donna Kei Benz (playing Yoshida's daughter) remembered Mifune as "a pretty private man" who kept to himself. "He was very shy, very stoic. He was very much a gentleman, but hard to speak to." Like so many others, Benz remembers him using little English on the set, yet it was also clear he understood much of what was being said.[88]

Benz joined Frankenheimer and Mifune when the film was premiered at the Manila Film Festival. At sixty-two, Mifune may have been old enough to retire, but that didn't stop the festival's judges from declaring him "the sexiest man in movies."

As if to prove this, Mifune became a father for the third time, with the birth of a daughter, Mika. The mother was his mistress, and the press had a field day. Over the next few years, Mifune lavished his new child with attention. "He would take her to kindergarten in Yokohama, and he'd pick her up from school every day," said Tomio Sagisu. "I'm sure he loved her very much."[89]

But as Mifune found a measure of happiness in his new daughter, his film career continued to slide, and *The Challenge* was no help. It bombed at the box office in America, so much so that when it went to cable and syndication, it was given a more exploitable name, *Sword of the Ninja*, and ten minutes were chopped out. It wasn't even released in Japan. If *The Challenge* is remembered at all, it is for reuniting three of the original Seven Samurai: Mifune, Seiji Miyaguchi, and Yoshio Inaba. Regrettably, Miyaguchi and Inaba have almost nothing to do—they're more like extras than featured players—and upon seeing the single shot in the film that puts all three together, one can only imagine what might have been done with these three screen veterans.

More typical among Mifune's film work of the early and mid-1980s was the oddly titled *The Miracle of Joe the Petrel* (Umitsubame Jyo no kiseki, 1984), a gangster film originally intended for cult actor Yusaku Matsuda and director Kinji Fukasaku at Toei. Mifune took over the project with Shiro and produced it for release through Toei. Saburo Tokito starred as Joe, a half Filipino-half Japanese hood on the lam after shooting an Okinawan gang boss. Fleeing to the Philippines in search of his long-lost father, he befriends a nightclub worker (Miwako Fujitani), encountering corrupt Filipino police, hookers, tough-talking gangsters, and Toshiro Mifune, in a brief cameo as a fisherman who whisks Joe to safety aboard his boat.

Kevin Thomas found *The Miracle of Joe the Petrel* "a riveting *yakuza* (gangster) picture of epic scale and surprising emotional impact. . . . [It's] one of those paradoxical films that captures with a rare beauty so much that's ugly and despairing in life."[90]

"[The film] is all form and no content," countered *Variety*'s "Bail," "and serves to recall, without the intended irony, Mark Twain's cautionary remarks about the futility of trying to find any moral in 'Tom Sawyer.' Technically top-notch, the film has the engagingly steamy/sleazy, neon-lit look of a Forties *film noir*. . . . But the plot! . . . The title of the film to the contrary withstanding, the only 'miraculous' thing about [it] is its release."[91]

Just prior to *Joe*'s premiere, Mifune paid a visit on March 5, 1984, to the White House, where he presented an arrow to Vice President George Bush on behalf of the Japan Horseback Archery Association, of which Mifune was an executive board member.

His trip to the White House was just one of many extended visits Mifune made to the United States during the 1980s. In 1983, the first significant retrospective of his career was held in Chicago, and he brought Shiro with him, as well as actress Miiko Taka, now acting as his Los Angeles–based executive assistant. The following year saw even bigger events in Boston (twenty films at the Museum of Fine Arts) and New York (forty films at the Japan Society). He was extensively interviewed, and reporters noted that his schedule was busier than ever.

"Even if I want to retire, how could I?" he asked one reporter. "There are too many other people depending on me, too many mouths to feed. I'm supposed to be an actor, but I have hardly any time to appear in movies. They take too long, and I'm too busy running the company."[92] At the time Mifune had 250 people in his employ.

Between festivals, and while in the Philippines making *Joe the Petrel*, Mifune made a guest appearance in *The Homeland Is Burning* (Sanga moyu), a yearlong, highly controversial NHK television series, starring Koshiro Matsumoto, about Japanese-Americans during World War II. One climactic scene had its characters—who had never lived in Japan—weeping uncontrollably at the very sight of Mt. Fuji.

During shooting, Mifune found time to make appearances at the Boston and New York retrospectives. In the many interviews he gave, he echoed his amazing foreword to Richie's *The Films of Akira Kurosawa*, saying, "Whatever I'm able to do as an actor I learned from him. . . . My best work is all in Kurosawa-*sensei*'s films."

But being so closely linked with Kurosawa, even at a retrospective supposedly honoring himself, was also something he found irksome, even though just thirteen of the forty films shown in New York were directed by Kurosawa. The connection was clearly beginning to wear on Mifune, and he poutingly commented, "Why not call it a Kurosawa series instead? . . . I haven't done much else worth showing."[93]

The New York retrospective, "A Tribute to Toshiro Mifune," was presented by the Japan Film Center throughout March and April 1984. In addition to the expected Kurosawa titles, the series ran such rarely seen Mifune films as *Downtown*, *The Important Man*, *Snow Trail*, and *Sword for Hire*, some classics like *Rebellion* and *The Rickshaw Man*, newer films like *Port Arthur*, and international showcases like *Red Sun* and *Hell in the Pacific*. Francis Ford Coppola, Lee Marvin, Yoko Ono, Mick Jagger, Raul Julia, and Robert De Niro were among those paying him tribute, and critic Stanley Kauffmann noted that Mifune transcended every film he appeared in.

One of the best tributes came from director Terence Young, who said that during the making of *Inchon!* Laurence Olivier was very anxious to meet Mifune because Japanese movie fans and critics kept referring to the British actor as "the Toshiro Mifune of England." A Kurosawa retrospective this certainly was not.

As Peter Grilli put it, "Sixteen films with Kurosawa in the first 15 years of his career and the absence of a single collaboration in the last two decades speak too plainly of rupture. . . . If there is rancor, Mifune has kept it hidden. 'I see *sensei* from time to time, and I often send him scripts for his advice.' "[94] Asked again and again "Why?" Mifune offered up the same answer given by everyone else who had become professionally estranged from Kurosawa: scheduling conflicts. He wasn't suited for *Dodes'ka-den*, he told *Variety*, "couldn't participate" in *Dersu Uzala*, and was unable to appear in *Kagemusha* because of his commitment to do *Shogun* and *Inchon!*[95]

At the climax of the festival, Mifune donned medieval samurai armor once more, something he knew would impress the packed theater as he walked onstage. He also told anecdotes certain to elicit delighted reactions, such as the following tale about *Seven Samurai*: "Remember how I died in the battle, practically naked and face down in the mud? They tell me that after *Seven Samurai* was first shown abroad, at the Venice Film Festival, a European woman coming out of the theater was overheard saying, 'God, what an ass he's got!' "[96] But, despite his cavalier attitude, such events embarrassed him. He disliked watching his own performances and felt uncomfortable at large, formal affairs.

By now many in Japan regarded Mifune's performances as exaggerated and overwrought, much the way Charlton Heston is today viewed by some in America. Yet how could so bad an actor be so fêted outside his homeland? At another New York event, "An Evening with Toshiro Mifune," the actor felt tremendously uneasy watching a clip from *Rashomon*. "Look at what a ham I was!" he exclaimed. "How could I have been so awful?"[97]

And if watching himself was an uncomfortable experience, seeing friends and colleagues now deceased was outright painful. After seeing a clip from *Seven Samurai*, Mifune asked his audience, "Did you notice that scene, after the battle, where one of the three surviving samurai says, 'And we still remain'? What a curious irony—of all seven samurai, it is just those three actors who've since died, and the other four of us who died in the movie are all still alive and working."[98]

Mifune grew increasingly uncomfortable in public, yet he endured such tributes nonetheless; he was forever polite, thanking everyone, including security guards, caterers, and the like, and he felt an obligation to take the time to address his fans individually whenever possible, spending far longer signing autographs than his handlers ever expected him to.

TWENTY-SIX

CLOUDS

"Making *Kagemusha* has renewed the passion I have for filmmaking," Kurosawa said in 1980. "However, all the scripts I have been working on reflect a very pessimistic view of life."[1] At the time of *Kagemusha's* release, Kurosawa was confident that his beloved *Ran* could now finally be made. "All that stood in the way of filming *Ran*," he told *The New York Times*, "[was] inexperience and budgets. Now I have the actors and the horses, the armor and the crew that I need. Potential backers are already getting together."[2]

But once again, help from the Japanese studios was not forthcoming, this in spite of *Kagemusha's* sackful of awards, American studio support, and long lines at the box office in Japan and Europe. *Kagemusha* had made a lot of money, but it was also expensive, and the Japanese majors felt its profit margin too small compared to its cost. Making another historical epic, they reasoned, was too much of a gamble. "Our big problem," Kurosawa countered, "is that the decisions of the movie companies are dictated by the marketing directors."[3] Toho made a preliminary offer to distribute *Ran* in Japan, but refused to finance it.

"It is true the Japanese movie business is going down," admitted Toho president Isao Matsuoka in 1983. "And we are in the bottom line, as we say, of people who go to see the movies." Citing *Ran's* ¥2.4 billion ($10 million) budget, compared to the $1–2 million Toho spent on most of its in-house features, he said, "We will distribute this film . . . but only in Japan. . . . We are not involved in the production, but we are going to invest some money—the minimum amount—the minimum guarantee for distribution. We are negotiating. . . . [But] we cannot invest in the production because it has a huge scale for us." Explaining that Toho could not afford anything above $6 million for an in-house production, Matsuoka added, "What Kurosawa has in mind is the worldwide market. This can't be supported only by the Japanese."[4] The following year Toho would spend more than $10 million on its in-house remake/sequel of *Godzilla*.

Part of the Toho company's reluctance may have been because much of *Ran* would be made on location, away from the studio, and thus could not earn revenue for use of its stages and equipment. In the wake of *Kagemusha*, Kurosawa and his son, Hisao, had established the Kurosawa Film Studio in Yokohama, where much of *Ran*'s interiors would be photographed. It was less a studio than a large, single building, yet it gave Kurosawa more autonomy than he would have making *Ran* at Toho. Kurosawa Film Studio was a good hour's drive from Seijo, but land near Toho and Kurosawa's home had become prohibitively expensive. They invested several million dollars in production equipment, which they then began leasing to other production companies, much like the established majors. Within a few years, trucks bearing the Kurosawa Film Studio logo would be turning up on the lots of Daiei, Shochiku, Toei, and Toho.

At the same time, Hisao's role in his father's activities was increasing. After living briefly in the United States, he returned to Japan, where he tackled a wide range of careers. He married pop singer and film actress Hiroko Hayashi in 1980, and together they parlayed their success and its surrounding publicity into acting assignments. Hisao became a staple of Japanese radio as a disk jockey and program host. He began producing television commercials and, at the suggestion of his cousin Mike Inoue, took a more active role in his father's business interests. *Ran* would be his first direct involvement in one of his father's films; he acted as a production coordinator.

Simultaneously, the Kurosawa-Oguni-Kikushima script of *Runaway Train* was being resurrected. It had been kicking around for fifteen years by the time the first serious rumblings of a production were heard in 1981. Cambridge Film Group, Ltd. (CFG), an organization described in the trades as "an all-encompassing servicing organization for independent producers worldwide," announced plans to film *Runaway Train* in Canada, with CFG, Japan's Nippon Herald, Marlow Productions, and Somerville House of Toronto working in tandem as co-producers. The $5 million production was to be directed by Koreyoshi Kurihara.[5]

The project languished in "development hell" for several more years. By 1983, only Nippon Herald was still with the project, now slated as a co-production among Weinstein/Skyfield Productions, Nippon Herald, and Channel Communications Proprietary, Ltd. of Australia, where the film was now inexplicably scheduled to be lensed. Kurihara was out as director, and the project, now budgeted at $8–9 million, was to be helmed by Russian director Andrei Konchalovsky. Konchalovsky had been approved by Kurosawa upon the recommendation of Francis Coppola soon after the release of *Kagemusha*.[6] But Weinstein/Skyfield was allied with Cannon, the Israeli-owned financer of exploitation films founded by Yoram and Menahem Globus, and the film was produced in North America.

Runaway Train opened to mixed reviews. *Variety*'s "Cart" found it "a sensational picture. Wrenchingly intense and brutally powerful . . . [it] rates as the most exciting action epic since 'The Road Warrior' and, like that film, is fundamentally serious enough to work strongly on numerous levels. . . . The imprint of the renowned Japanese director can be felt throughout."[7]

But *The Village Voice*'s David Edelstein thought it high camp. "What a ride on the *Runaway Train*! Did *Plan 9 from Outer Space* have this much action? Did *Airport '75* address the Cosmos? . . . Jon Voight snarls defiantly, as if he'd just strangled the guy holding the long hook in the wings—the stage belongs to him now, and not even God is going to hustle him off."[8]

For *Ran* to be made, it took the intervention of the French. Serge Silberman, a Polish-born French producer, was approached by Daniel Toscan du Plantier, the general manager of France's leading studio, Gaumont, at the 1982 Deauville American Film Festival. Plantier asked Silberman to produce *Ran* for Gaumont, but after meeting with Kurosawa that same year, Silberman expressed an interest in producing the film for his own company. This was just as well, because at the same time, Gaumont pulled out completely.[9] Silberman had been a movie producer since the mid-1950s, but was best known for financing the later films of director Luis Buñuel, including *The Milky Way* (La Voie lactée, 1969) and *The Discreet Charm of the Bourgeoisie* (Le Charme discret de la bourgeoisie, 1972). After *Ran*, Silberman would oversee Nagisa Oshima's odd *Max mon amour* (1986) to considerably less acclaim.

Silberman had one condition before agreeing to produce *Ran*: "I offered Kurosawa the same contract I had with Buñuel, simply that we had to be in agreement about everything." Kurosawa had never worked this way before, but fortunately he and Silberman discovered that, most of the time at least, they agreed about Kurosawa's approach to the production. "They call me the Emperor," Kurosawa reportedly told him, "but with you I will not be the Emperor." For his part, Silberman worked closely with the director on the screenplay rewrites and on casting, but otherwise stayed largely in the background.[10] Filming was set to begin in July 1983, but in April *Ran* stalled when the French government devalued its currency, and preproduction did not resume until that December.

In addition, Silberman's company was on its own financial roller coaster, and ultimately, he simply didn't have enough money to finance *Ran* alone. Herald Ace, the production arm of foreign film distributor Nippon Herald (they released *Dersu Uzala* in Japan and held the rights to the *Runaway Train* script), stepped in and arranged a $10.5 million loan from Japan's Sumitomo Bank. Silberman's company, Greenwich Films, kicked in another $1 million, and would handle *Ran*'s release outside Japan, with Nippon Herald and Toho distributing it domestically. Fuji-TV lent its support as well in exchange for television rights.[11] The complex arrangement echoed one made for director Koreyoshi Kurahara (late of *Runaway Train*) and his similarly expensive *Antarctica* (Nankyoku monogatari, 1983). "Nippon Herald came up with the financing," said *Variety*. "Toho had the prime theaters. Fuji had a high-powered publicity mechanism of national scope. Thanks to repeated primetime plugolas on Fuji TV, 'Antarctica,'—a simple tale of explorers saving a band of sled dogs marooned in the Antarctic—emerged as a box-office juggernaut."[12] The companies saw *Ran* in similar terms. "Whatever happens," Silberman said of *Ran*'s chances, "I have the satisfaction that after I die *Ran* will still survive."[13] Kurosawa, however, was blunt about the arrangement: "For the money one of them spends [advertising their products] in Japan, I could make more than ten *Rans*."[14]

Despite the complexities of the arrangement, Kurosawa remained optimistic. "I am waiting for the snows to melt on Mt. Fuji so that I can build a castle set on a one-square kilometer site on the slopes," he said. "Battle scenes will be integral to the picture and I intend to purchase about 150 quarter horses for it."[15] He also said that the years spent putting the financing together had given him the opportunity to hone his script and condense its story.[16]

The plot centers on seventy-year-old warlord Hidetora (Tatsuya Nakadai). Like Lear, Hidetora's advancing years are catching up with him, and as the film opens, he is showing his age. In the presence of neighboring lords Fujimaki (Hitoshi Ueki) and Ayabe (Jun Tazaki), Hidetora abruptly abdicates, giving his oldest son, Taro (Akira Terao), complete power over his dominion and his largest castle, with sons Jiro (Jinpachi Nezu) and Saburo (Daisuke Ryu) given the second and third castles. Hidetora wants to live out his remaining years in peace, but his youngest son, Saburo, protests. He accuses his father of recklessness: only through Hidetora's bloody, iron-clad rule has the domain been maintained. To divide the kingdom among sons who have known only ruthless warfare and expect filial loyalty from them, he argues, is wholly impractical. Ironically, it is Saburo's loyalty that Hidetora is incapable of believing in, and he banishes Saburo from the kingdom. Fujimaki, who recognized Saburo's wisdom, invites Hidetora to stay in his kingdom.

Immediately the family ties which Hidetora maintained during his reign begin to crumble. Taro's wife, Lady Kaede (Mieko Harada), whose family was murdered and whose castle was taken by Hidetora, compels her husband to assert his authority over his father when he visits the castle. Insulted by his son's actions, Hidetora leaves, turning to the castle of his second son, Jiro, and his wife, Lady Sue (pronounced "Suu-eh," and portrayed by Yoshiko Miyazaki). Her family was likewise slaughtered by Hidetora, but she, unlike Lady Kaede, is a devout Buddhist and does not hate him. Jiro, however, has received an order from Taro to refuse Hidetora any hospitality, and insulted once more, Hidetora leaves Jiro's castle, vowing never to return.

Hidetora is then deceived into occupying the third castle, where Taro and Jiro's forces attack the old warlord's retinue. His warriors are slaughtered, and his concubines are forced to commit *seppuku*. The castle is set afire, and Hidetora, driven to madness, wanders out like a ghost. Jiro, urged to usurp his brother's rule by vassal Kurogane (Hisashi Igawa), has his own brother shot during the melee.

As Hidetora wanders the plains and the remains of the third castle with his jester, Kyoami (Peter), and retainer Tengo (Masayuki Yui), Lady Kaede seduces Jiro and orders her brother-in-law to have his own wife murdered. Saburo learns of his father's plight and sets out with a large contingent of soldiers to bring him back. Threatened by Saburo's troops, Jiro sends his own force against them, but they are easily routed, while Ayabe takes advantage of their absence from the castle and attacks it. Returning to his besieged fortress, Jiro faces certain death, and Kurogane, disgusted by Lady Kaede's murder of Lady Sue, promptly cuts her down with his sword.

Saburo, meanwhile, is reunited with Hidetora, now almost completely mad. But the reunion is short-lived: Jiro's assassins shoot Saburo dead, and Hidetora collapses over his body and dies.

Prior to shooting *Ran*, Kurosawa staged a press conference to introduce his cast. For projects like *Kagemusha* and *Ran*, the director had begun to embrace media coverage, a stark turnaround from the days when he kicked reporters off the set of *Seven Samurai*. For the *Kagemusha* press conference he introduced the cast as if it were a Kabuki extravaganza. On *Ran* he went even further, with a presentation worthy of Ziegfeld, at his new studio, unveiling his fifteen principals in full makeup and costume. Tatsuya Nakadai would be his Lear, and the rest of the cast was, as in *Kagemusha*, an eclectic mix of stock company regulars (Takeshi Kato, Jun Tazaki), pop stars (Akira Terao), a comedian (Hitoshi Ueki), and a drag queen icon (Peter). Shooting, he said, would take some thirty weeks.[17]

Hitoshi Ueki (b. 1927) had been Toho's top comedy star of the 1960s, appearing in dozens of comedies, always playing the envy of the white-collar workforce, the irresponsible salaryman. Kurosawa cast him as a sixteenth-century general. "Kurosawa wrote the role with me in mind and called my manager," Ueki remembered. "My manager told me that it didn't matter whether I accepted the role or not, but naturally I should be polite and go to see him. We were left in a room alone, and he crossed over to me, shook my hand, and said. 'Thank you very much for accepting my offer' [laughs]. That's it! It was a kind of sudden incident."[18]

Ueki brought to the film some much-needed comic relief, though his character's humor was lost on Western audiences unfamiliar with his screen and television persona, which he carefully incorporated into his role. "Japanese audiences expected something different from me in a Kurosawa film, naturally. And yet I did see the character in my own manner. When I saw myself in the final film, it was kind of weird, and I wondered about the historical accuracy of my performance. And so I asked Mr. Kurosawa if it was okay, and he said, 'Yeah, it's okay.' I came to know how good he was at handling people."[19]

Ueki joined his cast members in horseback riding lessons and the rigor of rehearsing in full costume and makeup. "Rehearsing is like making a sculpture of papier-mâché," Kurosawa said. "Each repetition lays on a new sheet of paper, so that in the end the performance has a shape completely different from when we started. I make actors rehearse in full costume and makeup whenever possible, and we rehearse on the set even though we may have no intention of shooting that day. In costume, the work has an on-stage tension that vanishes whenever we try rehearsing out of costume."[20]

Peter was another unlikely though inspired bit of casting. He had been born Shinnosuke Ikehata in 1952, into a family of traditional Japanese dancers. A popular drag star on Japanese television, Ikehata adapted his stage name after quitting high school in 1967. He became a fixture of variety and talk shows beginning in 1969, and played female, male, and androgynous roles on the stage. He made his film debut in *Funeral Parade of Roses* (Bara no soretsu, 1969), Toshiro Matsumoto's avant-garde feature loosely based on *Oedipus*, which co-starred Yoshio Tsuchiya as his lover, and opposite Shintaro Katsu in *Zatoichi's Fire Festival* (Zatoichi abare hima-tsuri, 1970). He also had a major role in an earlier French-Japanese co-production, Shuji Terayama's *The Fruits of Passion* (Shanghai ijin Shokan, 1980), but his film career had been otherwise sporadic, and he was best known to Japanese audiences as a flamboyant television personality.

Kurosawa liked to call *Ran* his "three-castle film," referring to the trio of fortresses in the story.[21] Real castles were used for some exteriors, but the third castle would have to be built. It alone cost ¥400 million (about $1.6 million) to construct, only to be burned down. Kurosawa was dissatisfied with the modern chemicals used to dye *Kagemusha*'s costumes, so he had designer Emi Wada use sixteenth-century techniques in weaving and dying them, adding another $1 million to the budget.

Shooting on location was more difficult than ever. Rural Japan had all but disappeared during the postwar expansion. Just a few years later, when producer-director Haruki Kadokawa mounted his own *Ran*-like historical epic, *Heaven and Earth* (Ten to chi to, 1990), he shipped his samurai armor and horses to Alberta, Canada, at great expense. He concluded that there simply wasn't anywhere left in Japan that resembled the back country as it had existed hundreds of years ago—Japan was now a country of utilitarian apartment buildings, factories, and television antennas.

Location scouting on *Ran* had begun in 1982, and Kurosawa had hoped to use the same Hokkaido plains utilized in *Kagemusha* but couldn't get permission to shoot there. Instead, *Ran* was filmed mostly in southern Japan, near Mt. Aso in Kyushu, and on the slopes of Mt. Fuji. "There's always something unexpected when you come to this mountain," Kurosawa said of the inactive volcano.[22] Once again, he used some 250 horses (many shipped over from America) and 1,400 extras, and edited his battle footage so expertly that erroneous reports filtered out of Japan that he had used 15,000 horses and 120,000 extras, an outrageous but widely reported claim.[23]

When he planned to shoot a storm sequence in Kyushu, the elements obliged him by delivering a typhoon. "In Japan," he joked, "journalists often call me 'Emperor' because they think I'm so tyrannical. Well, I guess I can now command even the elements!"[24]

Where *Kagemusha* was plagued by production problems, *Ran* was plagued by death. Ryu Kuze, who had choreographed the swordplay in all of Kurosawa's films since *The Hidden Fortress*, could no longer work. "He had to retire halfway through because of a heart condition," said Minoru Nakano.[25] Kuze's condition was worse than he had let on. In January 1985, he died suddenly at the age of seventy-six. His death depressed Kurosawa deeply. Only a few days earlier, Fumio Yanoguchi, Kurosawa's sound man since *Stray Dog*, had collapsed on location, and he died soon thereafter. He was just sixty-seven.

But the biggest blow of all came in January. The previous October, Kurosawa's wife, Yoko, had not been feeling well and, while not especially concerned, went to the hospital for an examination. Kazuko bumped into the doctor who had suggested she be examined. He confided in her just how seriously ill he suspected her mother was. With Kurosawa and Hisao on location for *Ran*, and the doctors reluctant to speak directly to Yoko, Kazuko was burdened with the horrible news: her sixty-three-year-old mother had been given only four months to live. Exactly what illness struck her was never publicly revealed, but Kazuko talked it over with her brother and decided that she would be frank with her father.

"I can remember telling him: it's incurable. There's no hope. She has four months to live." There was a long pause, after which he said only, "*Aa, soka*" ("Well, that's it").[26] On January 27, 1985, shooting was suspended for two weeks so Kurosawa could attend to Yoko. He was wearing his work clothes when he arrived at the hospice where she spent her final days. When she saw his blue jeans, his white cotton gloves half-tucked in his pocket, his cap, Kazuko thought, "This isn't reality. It was almost like shooting a movie. His trailer was parked in the hospice's parking lot, he directed all of us as she lay dying."[27] Just five days later, Yoko passed away.

"I visited his wife at the hospice in Atami when she died," remembered Senkichi Taniguchi. "The place was the best hospice in Japan. I did not know Kurosawa would be at her side. It had been a long time since we last saw one another." But Kurosawa had little to say to his old friend. "The reunion was strained, too."[28]

"For him, she was a good wife, and very supportive," concluded son Hisao, "especially of his filmmaking."[29] Kurosawa instructed his children to prepare a "funeral not like a funeral." So by design it was as lighthearted an affair as possible. Yoko's coffin was surrounded by bright pink flowers, which she had loved, and music from Hisao's old folk band, the Broadside Four, was played.

The deaths of his wife and longtime colleagues might have consumed a man less dedicated to his art. But Kurosawa bravely forged ahead, working more intensely, focusing more deeply on *Ran* than ever before.

"When I think about it now," Kazuko wrote in 1999, "it was good that he returned to *Ran*, because when he said, '*Yoi, staato,*' he was able to forget everything else. . . . As long as he was shooting, he would be all right."[30]

After Yoko's death, Kurosawa immersed himself deeper in the production of *Ran*. It was the culmination of an era that had began twenty years earlier with his fall from grace on *Runaway Train*, *Tora! Tora! Tora!*, and *Dodes'ka-den*. "I think I'm getting closer to making movies that are true cinema," he told reporters at the base of Mt. Fuji.[31] He even ran a rough cut of the film for journalists flown into Tokyo by Silberman.

As the film neared completion, eyebrows were raised when, in March 1985, Silberman confirmed that he, not Kurosawa, had final cut of the film. "I'm not a dictator, but we have to speak a common language," said the Frenchman. "I have the feeling that we are not all that far from one another."[32] Apparently he was right. Their differences, if any, were minor, and postproduction proceeded smoothly, if behind schedule. Kurosawa, meanwhile, revealed that he had regarded *Kagemusha* as little more than a "dry run" for *Ran*, a film he regarded as "more richly conceived, more deeply personal."[33]

And so it is. *Ran* succeeds in every way *Kagemusha* does not, from its tightly woven screenplay to Toru Takemitsu's haunting score. *Ran* is a compelling, devastating portrait of a bloody dynasty's descent into hell. As Donald Richie notes: "*Ran* is not only an allegory of Kurosawa's own life but a parable of all of our lives. From a sometimes sentimental humanism . . . Kurosawa has moved closer to a more precise and honest statement concerning humanity and its predicament. That is what Shakespeare did as well and, in *Lear*, left us a tragedy with little hope but much understanding. In *Ran*, Kurosawa—in Shakespeare-like fashion—has shown us the tragedy of the human dilemma. He has done it with great honesty and so thrills our senses that we can never forget his lesson. To make this statement was perhaps the director's most important reason for creating this extraordinary film."[34]

Ran differs from *Lear* in its emphasis on Hidetora's bloody past as a trigger for his collapse into insanity. "How did Lear acquire the power that, as an old man, he abuses with such disastrous effects?" the director asked. "Without knowing his past, I've never really understood the ferocity of his daughters' response to Lear's feeble attempts to shed his royal power. In *Ran* I've tried to give Lear a history. I try to make it clear that his power must rest upon a lifetime of blood-thirsty savagery. Forced to confront the consequences of his misdeeds, he is driven mad. But only by confronting his evil head-on can he transcend it and begin to struggle again toward virtue."[35]

Three people emerge from *Ran* as major characters. One is Lady Sue, who after witnessing the destruction of her family at Hidetora's hands and being forced to marry his middle son, retreats into Buddhism. There she is able to release her hatred of the warlord and renew her soul. Hidetora, in contrast, cannot look upon her, precisely because she does not hate him. Another is Tsurumaru (Takeshi Nomura), Sue's Gloucester-like brother, his eyes gouged out years earlier by Hidetora after Sue begged him to spare her sibling's life. Like Sue, Tsurumaru tries to embrace Buddhism and release his hate, but finds he cannot. The blind Tsurumaru is left, after Sue's murder, high atop a precipice, alone in the film's haunting, unforgettable final image. He is poised at the edge of a cliff, as if frozen between life and death; an image of the Buddha dropped earlier gazes up at him, as if condemning him to this world of unspeakable horror.

Sue is murdered by her opposite, the scheming Kaede, whose hatred so consumes her that she engineers the destruction of Hidetora's entire clan, finding a kind of infernal bliss as she meets her own bloody end. Kaede is portrayed—marvelously—by Mieko Harada. Born in 1958, Harada made her film debut at sixteen in Miyoji Ieki's *Love in the Spring Wind* (Koi wa midori no kaze naka). She subsequently won the *Kinema Jumpo* Best Actress Award for her work in Kazuhiko Hasegawa's *The Killer of Youth* (Seishun no satsujinsha, 1976). After *Ran*, Harada went on to win virtually every acting honor in Japan, including the Houchi Film Best Supporting Actress Award for her role in Kinji Fukasaku's *House on Fire* (Kataku no hito, 1986) and the Japanese Academy Award as Best Supporting Actress for two roles—in *Akira Kurosawa's Dreams* and Kei Kumai's *Mount Aso's Passion* (Shikibu monogatari, 1990); she also won numerous prizes for her dual role as a mother and her daughter in Hideyuki Hirayama's *Begging for Love* (Riko, 1998). Two years later, she had a prominent supporting part in the Kurosawa-scripted *After the Rain* (Ame agaru, 2000).

On the surface, *Kagemusha* and *Ran* seem rather alike, but Kurosawa saw a fundamental difference: *Kagemusha* is a tale seen through the eyes of one individual, while *Ran* depicts human events as viewed from the heavens. There are no bird's-eye-view camera angles; instead, Kurosawa depicts this heavenly perspective in a series of shots from Hidetora's point of view, as he gazes at stunning cloud formations, as if to show gods weeping and angry at the senseless violence they witness.

Technically, *Ran* is a remarkable achievement. Reviewers singled out the film's haunting battle sequences, which use color-coded banners for the respective troops of the three brothers and Lords Fujimaki and Ayabe. "As regards color and compositions we were guided by Mr. Kurosawa's sketches," said cinematographer Takao Saito. "[He] divided the three brothers into yellow, red, and blue camps, and devised special costumes based on color schemes found in *Noh*. We tried to be faithful to these colors, and also tried to preserve the true qualities of these subjects—the textures of their hair and clothing, etc. We meddled very little with the colors, but we sometimes used color reflectors for character delineation."[36]

The sea of red, yellow, and blue flags lend the film a horrifying splendor. The extremely long lenses capture the charges of the infantry and cavalry in a brightly hued blur of supreme violence. (The film's Japanese posters beautifully replicate this image.) In contrast to the cameras placed amid hoofs of the charging bandits in *Seven Samurai*, Kurosawa purposely keeps his distance, with more painterly compositions. As *The Village Voice*'s David Edelstein described it, "Not even David Lean has Kurosawa's eye for color, for turning landscapes into formidable characters. And he never calls attention to his hand; the artist stands outside the canvas, grieving."[37]

"Mr. Kurosawa does not like wide angle lenses," Saito explained. "He also avoids zooming, though zoom lenses are used most of the time. Instead, the zoom lenses are generally locked down at a specific focal length, very often 75mm." He used the zoom lenses "to assure very precise color balancing." Saito and Kurosawa were by then using Eastman Color film stock "because of its consistency in processing, ease in handling during editing, and the comparative stability of colors and images during storage."[38]

The first battle, between Taro and Jiro's forces against Hidetora's soldiers at the third castle, remains one of the director's most extraordinary moments, a *tour de force*. The seven-minute sequence is without sound effects or dialogue of any kind. Instead, we hear only Takemitsu's haunting Mahler-esque cue, amid flying arrows, pouring blood, dismembered limbs, flapping banners, and, finally, leaping flames and billowing smoke. Any few feet of this nightmarish footage is astonishing in its ghastly if beautiful chaos. Perhaps most memorably, two of Hidetora's concubines stab each other in ritualized suicide amid the battle, collapsing into each other's arms, in a deathly embrace. The influence of this sequence can be seen today in other war movies, like Steven Spielberg's *Saving Private Ryan*, early scenes of which directly lift stylistic elements from *Ran*.

Memorable, too, is the moment when the eerie silence is broken by the sound of gunfire, as Taro is shot dead by Jiro's vassal, followed by Hidetora emerging from the castle as it is engulfed in flames. "Without speaking a word and with a few gestures to rely on, [Nakadai] must convey the disintegration of a great mind and powerful will," Kurosawa noted. "With his castle consumed in flames around him, his soldiers all dead or dying, he must emerge alone through billowing clouds of smoke, staring straight ahead and walk down a long flight of steps, each a foot or so high. I didn't want him to stumble or look down at his feet, but each time I tried to go down those steps myself during rehearsals I had to be helped by two or three people. Since the castle was literally burning, we had only one take to shoot the scene. If he had stumbled, it would have weakened the intensity of the scene but we would have had to accept it. But Nakadai did it perfectly, without a single misstep, staring sightlessly like a sleepwalker or a madman."[39]

Even *Ran*'s tiniest details are executed with intelligence and imagination, from the deep creaking of the castle gates to the blocking of the extras. Kurosawa again lavished attention on every single soldier, but it is the subtle movements and gestures of *Ran*'s rich characters, such as the magnificently staged confrontation between Lady Kaede and Jiro, a masterpiece of choreography in its own right, that sears itself into one's memory. Kaede bows in submission to Jiro, then in the blink of an eye lunges at him with a dagger, threatens to cut his throat as she blackmails him into submission, then just as quickly consummates their agreement with a ferocious and demonic sexual fury, licking Jiro's bloody neck like a panther. The sequence is breathtaking.

Kurosawa justifiably received some of the best notices of his career with *Ran*. "Akira Kurosawa has a secure claim to the title of the world's greatest active director," wrote Richard A. Blake in *America*, "and 'Ran' insures him a place in the pantheon as a peer of Sergei Eisenstein, Abel Gance and D. W. Griffith."[40]

"There are moments in *Ran*," said *American Film*, "when the screen throbs with so much life, so many soldiers on horseback, such extraordinary battles, that one thinks, this is what Tolstoy saw in his mind when he wrote about Napoleon's invasion of Russia in *War and Peace*."[41]

Nakadai, like Kurosawa, received the best Western notices of his career, even though to some degree the character has less impact than the sup-

porting parts, because Kurosawa keeps Hidetora at an emotional arm's
length, muting his reality under mounds of chalky makeup. In America,
Nakadai's work was occasionally undermined by the obvious absence of
Kurosawa's most famous collaborator. "Throughout the film," wrote *Film
Comment*, "it was hard not to think of what a difference Toshiro Mifune
would have made in this role."[42] (Mifune would have made a superb Kurogane, for that matter.) According to director Kaizo Hayashi, Kurosawa
wanted Mifune to play Hidetora, but producer Masato Hara overruled
him. Mifune, argued Hara, was too expensive, so Nakadai was cast in an effort to reduce costs.[43] But this is unconfirmed.

It can be argued that, with its betrayals from within and Hidetora's fall
from grace, *Ran* is autobiographical. "One sees the connection most
clearly," wrote Donald Richie, "in the parallel between the later years of
Kurosawa and those of the warlord Hidetora Ichimonji. . . . Both men have
been, in a sense, dispossessed. Hidetora can find no home, no castle to take
him in. Kurosawa could find no studio, no funding for his films. He was
spurned by his former studio, Toho (Lear's oldest daughter, Goneril, in this
parallel), and ignored by the others. So, he was, like Lear himself, forced to
wander. . . . The causes for the neglect of Kurosawa and his wandering on
the heath are also a bit Lear-like. Like the monarch, the director had a reputation for being dictatorial. . . . In conformist Japan, he who does not accommodate is singled out for dispraise."[44]

Indeed, Kurosawa's humanism, often mislabeled as sentimental, was
never more brusque than it is in *Ran*. On his part Kurosawa admitted, "I resemble Lear in that the studio I always worked for, Toho, has betrayed me.
But I had no such intention in doing this film."[45]

Ran was invited to Cannes, but production didn't wrap until February
1985, one month behind schedule, and for this reason Kurosawa wasn't able
to complete the film in time. Instead, Silberman submitted a film he produced on the making of *Ran*, entitled *AK* (1985) and directed by Chris
Marker (best known for the influential *La Jetée*, 1962). The *cinéma vérité* feature depicts Kurosawa as we have come to know him: smiling among his
crew in his denim cap and blue jeans, giving precise and exceedingly cour-
teous direction to his actors (whom he calls by their character names) and
attending to small details himself, such as waving smoke pots, as if to affect
the direction of the winds. We see the scope of the production, the many
trucks used to haul the equipment and horses and costumes and extras up
the slopes of Mt. Fuji, the fine detail of hand-made costumes that will be
seen only in long shots. We see, and Marker recognizes, the tightly knit in-

ner circle around Kurosawa: Honda, Nogami, Saito, Muraki. There are bit-tersweet images of Fumio Yanoguchi filmed shortly before his death, quietly seated at a tiny wooden table, adjusting sound levels. "We recall how cheer-ful he was," said the film's narrator, "how gentle, how supremely eloquent in his skinny old-cat style." The film was dedicated to his memory. In France, in the wake of enthusiasm generated for *Ran* with *AK*, Cannes officials an-nounced that Kurosawa's film would receive a special showing in Cannes that September, as "a reminder that we had Kurosawa on the schedule."[46]

Instead, *Ran* premiered at the Tokyo International Film Festival on May 31, 1985. Delays in its production had made it a race to the finish, and the first print of the film didn't come out of the lab until May 20.[47] *Ran* opened in 219 theaters across Japan on June 1. Initially, business was even better than for *Kagemusha*, and producer Hara estimated that the film would ultimately earn rentals of around $16 million, $4 million better than *Kage-musha*. But the novelty of a large-scale Kurosawa comeback had worn off. During its seven-week run, *Ran* grossed just over $11.4 million, making it a popular but not very profitable domestic release.[48] It received mixed re-views, but placed second on *Kinema Jumpo*'s "Best Ten" list. Donald Richie, however, contended that it was pressure rather than a consensus that put it there. "There would have been a scandal if it hadn't been ranked," he said.[49] There may be some justification for that argument. The film awarded as "Best Picture" that year was *And Then* (Sorekara), directed by Yoshimitsu Morita, who was as dedicated to market considerations as Kurosawa was not. Kurosawa's dedication to his art could hardly be denied, nor could the acclaim he received outside Japan. But his detractors could deny him the top domestic awards, and withhold them they did, for the rest of his career.

But *Ran* did well in Europe, especially in France, where nearly 400,000 moviegoers saw the film in twenty-two theaters on its opening weekend. Kurosawa flew to Paris for the opening, and to attend an exhibition of some of his production sketches and paintings at the Georges Pompidou Arts Centre. On September 19, Prime Minister Laurent Fabius decorated the Japanese filmmaker with the Order of Arts and Letters at the Hôtel Matignon. The following day Kurosawa tried to enjoy an open-air screening of *Ran* at the Pompidou Centre with 4,000 invitees, but the evening was marred by hecklers who unabatedly interrupted the event with catcalls throughout the screening.[50]

The following week Kurosawa flew to New York to attend *Ran*'s Ameri-can premiere on September 27 at the twenty-third New York Film Festival. Reaction was stupendous, and *Ran* received nearly universal raves. Vincent Canby's review, published that same day in *The New York Times*, was typical:

"Akira Kurosawa's 'Ran' ('Chaos') is a film of the sort that brings to mind Griffith's 'Birth of a Nation,' 'Napoléon Vu par Abel Gance,' and Eisenstein's 'Ivan the Terrible.' Though big in physical scope and of a beauty that suggests a kind of drunken, barbaric lyricism, 'Ran' has the terrible logic and clarity of a morality tale seen in tight close-up, of a myth that, while being utterly specific and particular in its time and place, remains ageless, infinitely adaptable."[51]

Some critics, including Pauline Kael and the aforementioned John Simon, dissented. In *Vanity Fair*, Stephen Schiff ludicrously called Kurosawa "the Gene Autry of Japanese cinema, loping westward with a six-gun in his belt and a song in his throat." Schiff typified *Ran*'s dissenters, calling it "long and boring and beautiful."[52] But they were in the minority. In short order *Ran* won the Best Picture and Best Cinematography prizes from the National Society of Film Critics, the first of many such awards.[53] The setting for the New York premiere could not have been more apropos: Kurosawa arrived just as Hurricane Gloria roared into Manhattan.

But another hurricane was brewing on the other side of the world, in Japan. In spite of the growing rave reviews in the West, many of which pegged *Ran* as Kurosawa's masterpiece, the Japanese chose not to enter *Ran* as their Best Foreign Film entry for the upcoming fifty-eighth annual Academy Awards. Instead, they picked *Gray Sunset* (Haha ichimonme, 1985), a film about a man's battle with Alzheimer's disease, starring Kurosawa stock company actor Minoru Chiaki and directed by Shunya Ito.

American critics and filmmakers were incredulous. They smelled a rat and accused the Japan Movie Producers Association (JMPA), which determines Japan's official entry, of conspiring against the film, pointing their finger directly at Toei mogul Shigeru Okada, who produced *Gray Sunset*, and who headed the Tokyo Film Festival, which Kurosawa had not attended. (These same critics, however, failed to realize that *Ran*'s Japanese producer, Masato Hara, was himself "chief coordinator of the organizing committee" for the festival.) Critics like the *Los Angeles Times*'s Jack Mathews charged that the combination of Kurosawa's disdain for the state of the Japanese film industry, *Ran*'s French participation, and the large budget had all worked against industrywide acceptance. "He snubbed them and now they're paying him back," argued David Owens, assistant director of the film department of New York's Japan Society. "Kurosawa has been outspoken in his criticism of the Japanese film industry and they haven't liked it."[54]

"Okada is a very powerful guy," added producer Tom Luddy, whose *Mishima: A Life in Four Chapters*, co-produced by Lucas and Coppola after *Kagemusha*, was dropped from the Tokyo Film Festival after an ardent campaign by Okada. "He can pretty much get what he wants there." As he later noted, "These people like Okada are very xenophobic and jingoistic. They have a sense of Japan as superior to the outside world and they really don't like foreigners or Japanese who cater to foreigners. So if they feel Kurosawa is grandstanding to the people in Paris or Hollywood then they're going to pay him back for that."[55]

The JMPA pleaded ignorance. Secretary General Susumu Suzuki said the JMPA had asked producer Hara if he intended to submit the film, but he told them that he planned to pursue a nomination as a French entry. But Silberman had assumed it would be submitted from Japan. Had *Ran* been a French nominee, it would, according to the Academy's outdated rules, have to be submitted dubbed into French with English subtitles. "It is all very strange," Silberman said.[56] He tried to submit the film as a French-Japanese co-production, but the Academy said no.

Kurosawa's own U.S. representative, named in a *Los Angeles Times* article as "Tac Watanabe," but probably referring to Tak W. Abe, agreed that it was all a big misunderstanding. Kurosawa didn't snub the Tokyo Film Festival, he said, because he was dealing with the deaths of his wife, Kuze, and Yanoguchi. Nor was the JMPA snubbing him. "Akira is not interested in awards," he said. "He just wants the public to enjoy his work."[57]

"The public has never deserted him, but the media has," said Donald Richie. "For example, everybody saw *Ran*, but it is as though there had been a [Japanese] conspiracy to bad-mouth it. I didn't hear one good thing said about *Ran*. Not from the critics I talked to, not from the people I know. . . . It's really strange, because he is a prophet without honor in his own country."[58]

The Oscar incident only added fire to the argument, by now overstated in the West, that Kurosawa had been rejected by Japanese critics, who regarded his films as too Western and not "Japanese" enough. The fact that his films did huge business in Japan (though were much less profitable) and that his later films still made "Top Ten" lists in Japanese film magazines and newspapers did not dampen the argument. The director himself thought the notion that he was pandering to foreigners absurd. He was an international filmmaker, to be sure, he said, but never at the expense of losing touch with his own national identity. "I would never make a film especially for foreign audiences," he said. "If a work cannot have meaning for a Japanese audience, I—as a Japanese artist—am simply not interested."[59]

"As a very normal part of my education, I have studied not only the Japanese classics but also the Western classics and music," Kurosawa stated in another interview. "There is nothing unusual about this for a person of my generation. But there is some misunderstanding of my work in Japan, probably because contemporary Japanese have not studied their own cultural background to the extent I do for my films. I am trying to get as close as possible to the historical and cultural truth of Japan. I can only say that I am very pleased that this seems to be appreciated outside Japan."[60]

But *Ran* was still eligible for other Oscars, and director Sidney Lumet launched a campaign to get Kurosawa a Best Director nomination. " 'Masterpiece' is an overused term, but I don't think it's overused here," said Lumet. "There are some directors whose films can be justified solely on their sense of beauty, and there are some whose films can be justified solely on their depth of profundity. Kurosawa is the only director who puts the two together."[61]

The campaign worked. Kurosawa was nominated as Best Director, the first Japanese so honored since Hiroshi Teshigahara for *Woman in the Dunes* (Suna no onna, 1964). He was up against John Huston for *Prizzi's Honor*, Peter Weir for *Witness*, Hector Babenco for *Kiss of the Spider Woman*, and Sydney Pollack for *Out of Africa*. Huston became the oldest director ever nominated; at seventy-nine he was three years older than Kurosawa. *Ran* was also the first Japanese film ever nominated for Best Cinematography, and the film would also vie for Best Costume Design, while Yoshiro Muraki and his wife were in the running for their Art Direction. *Gray Sunset*, meanwhile, didn't even make the final list of nominees for Best Foreign Film.

At the same time, *Runaway Train*, having been heavily pushed in trade ads by distributor Cannon, earned several nominations of its own. Jon Voight was nominated for his lead performance, along with Eric Roberts in the supporting category, and editor Henry Richardson. They all lost.

Kurosawa, naturally, would attend the ceremony, and even agreed to hand out the Best Picture prize with Billy Wilder and Federico Fellini. When Oscar night came on March 24, 1986, Fellini was a no-show—he had fractured his leg while shopping in Rome and could not attend. John Huston agreed to take his place, but there was a problem: Huston was in the advanced stages of emphysema and required an almost constant hookup to an oxygen tank.

Ran's cinematography lost to David Watkin's lensing of *Out of Africa*; the Murakis lost to Pollack's film as well, but Emi Wada's costumes prevailed. Kurosawa was a long shot, but that couldn't hide the disappointment of many when Sydney Pollack, generally regarded as the least deserving nominee, took home the award. Kurosawa had little time to contemplate his loss, for he was soon backstage, watching as Huston was wheeled in with his oxygen tank. Kurosawa opted to read his part in the Best Picture presentation in Japanese, with English subtitles, delighting the audience by pronouncing the name of *Out of Africa*'s co-producer as "Si-du-knee Po-rock." "They had the presentation carefully orchestrated so that they could have Huston at the podium first," Wilder recalled, "and then he would have 45 seconds before he would have to get back to his wheelchair and put the oxygen mask on." In sharing their duties, Huston was to open the envelope, pass it to Kurosawa, who would pull the winner's name out, then pass it to Wilder, who would name the winner. According to Wilder, "Kurosawa was not very agile, it turned out, and when he reached his fingers into the envelope, he fumbled and couldn't grab hold of the piece of paper with the winner's name on it. All the while I was sweating it out; three hundred million people around the world were watching and waiting. Mr. Huston only had about ten seconds before he needed more oxygen." Wilder said later he wanted to turn to Kurosawa and say, in the Wilder manner, "Pearl Harbor you could find."[62] *Out of Africa*, a dreary Hollywood epic, won the award, besting *The Color Purple*, *Kiss of the Spider Woman*, *Prizzi's Honor*, and *Witness*. Two nights later, Kurosawa was awarded an honorary membership in the Directors Guild of America (DGA) by John Huston as Oscar-winner Pollack looked on. Asked about the Oscar telecast, Kurosawa was diplomatic: "I wouldn't say I didn't like it, but it was a little long."[63]

Meanwhile, *Ran* was being released in art houses (and a smattering of mainstream theaters) across America. Once again, the press material perversely played up the film's cost, about $11.5 million; as with *Kagemusha*, *Ran* was alleged to be "the most . . . expensive undertaking in Japanese film history." Everyone bought this line, including Donald Richie, but it simply wasn't true. Press materials were correct, however, in one astute observation: "By American standards, *Ran*'s cost . . . is modest, and the visual splendor achieved for the budget nearly unimaginable."[64] Orion Classics had acquired the U.S. rights in May 1985.[65] The distributor declined to state what they had spent licensing the film, but the trades estimated they had paid roughly $500,000.[66]

During production, Kurosawa referred to *Ran* as if it were a culmination of his life's work, vowing to put his remaining strength into its completion. During *Ran*'s American release, Kurosawa turned seventy-six, and many assumed this great masterpiece would surely be his last. But resting on his laurels was the furthest thing from Kurosawa's mind. In the last eleven years of his life he would go on to direct three films and write scripts for two more. After one unfortunate misstep, he would enter a last, remarkable phase of his long career.

TWENTY-SEVEN

WANDERER

During the production of *Ran*, Toshiro Mifune appeared in a little-seen Italian film, *Shatterer* (Shyataraa, 1987), making a guest star appearance as a Japanese businessman in modern-day Sicily. The film was typical of the kind of pictures he was forced to make to meet his bills, to pay for schemes such as the Munich restaurant he'd been suckered into, and to pay the creditors who were maintaining his studio. A routine Mafia thriller directed by Tonino Valerii (*My Name Is Nobody*), *Shatterer* concerns the kidnapping of a Japanese auto executive by the Sicilian mob after the Japanese open a plant there. Insurance company consultant Mifune sends an American detective (Andy J. Forest) to investigate, and he's aided by a Japanese race car driver (Koji Kikkawa, a would-be pop and film star, under contract to Watanabe Productions, which co-produced the film). Mifune appears in three key scenes, looking tired and slightly embarrassed by the material given him. At the climax he graphically dispatches a gun-toting Mafioso and his don with a sword hidden in his cane. Like many of these guest star roles in B movies, where the time and trouble were hardly worth the small fee he himself negotiated, he did *Shatterer* as a personal favor. At least he got to visit Rome.

Despite Mifune's name value and Kikkawa's showy role, the film wasn't even released theatrically in Japan. In 1987 it turned up on Japanese video, where the entire film—including Mifune's phonetic English lines—was dubbed into English and presented with Japanese subtitles. Mifune's stock as an actor was falling rapidly.

He fared little better in Japan, where he was reduced to appearing opposite Priscilla Presley in a television commercial hawking mattresses.[1] And despite an occasional good role in films like *Death of a Tea Master*, Mifune was soon back to making cameos in mediocre movies. Typical among these was *cf Girl* (cf gaaru, 1989), a comedy-melodrama about a team of filmmakers battling *yakuza* and the like in their efforts to make splashy, cutting-edge television commercials. Mifune's brief appearance comes during the last ten minutes of this mediocre effort. During a location shoot in Alberta, Canada, he turns up suddenly, mythlike, in a helicopter and saves the day by enabling the crew to shoot some fine aerial shots. It was the kind of film—a modestly budgeted Japanese movie trying to look like a slick Hollywood one—that Japanese audiences loathed, the kind that was killing the industry and driving audiences toward an exclusive diet of Hollywood pictures.

His career was slipping away; nevertheless, in 1987 Mifune had the unwanted distinction of being Japan's twenty-fifth-highest payer of income tax. That year he owed more than ¥559 million (about $4 million). His income came mostly from the sale of land near Mifune Productions, which caused him considerable embarrassment. "An actor should earn money from his performances," he said. "I feel ashamed of becoming a big taxpayer out of land (sales) rather than through my talent."[2]

In July of that same year, Mifune's onetime partner Yujiro Ishihara died of liver cancer at fifty-two. Fans mourned the Nikkatsu star and *enka* singer much as America had Elvis a decade earlier. And like Elvis's, Ishihara's popularity and cult status actually increased after his untimely death. All the media coverage made Mifune think about his own place as a pop icon. "If I were to die, you wouldn't see all the public mourning [me like you saw] when [Ishihara] died."[3] He dismissed assumptions by Western journalists that he was to the Japanese what John Wayne or Gary Cooper had been in America. "Hardly," he said. "Actors like John Wayne or Gary Cooper represented America to many Americans, but most Japanese don't see me that way. . . . [However,] I really appreciate the fact that Westerners judge me as an actor. The Japanese are more interested in my private life, my divorce, scandal in general."[4]

Sadly, Mifune was right. He was considered by many in the West to be Japan's greatest actor, but this was hardly the case in Japan. Indeed, this dichotomy was far more extreme for Mifune than it ever was for Kurosawa, whose films were still popular in Japan and who was still regarded as a master filmmaker by at least some Japanese critics. Mifune, however, hadn't impressed them much since the 1960s. In their eyes he was an active, familiar presence, but also a has-been who remained lost without Kurosawa. If Mifune wanted adulation, he had to go abroad to find it. In June 1986, he was fêted by the University of California at Los Angeles with the UCLA Medal for "his social contribution as an international film star." He was only the fifth recipient of the award, joining the likes of Nobel Prize winner Bruce Merrifield. The only other actor so honored was Laurence Olivier.[5]

When he returned to Japan, Mifune began work on *Tora-san Goes North* (Otoko wa tsuraiyo—Shiretako bojo), the thirty-eighth of forty-eight "Tora-san" films, a series as enduring a Japanese icon as Godzilla. The Tora-san films are virtually unknown in the West, but in Japan these films, released between 1969 and 1995, consistently entered "Top Ten" lists both with critics and at the box office. They made a ton of money for Shochiku, the studio behind the series: each film cost between $1 and $3 million, yet typically grossed $10 million. Including television and home video earnings, Tora-san raked in approximately $883 million. Godzilla and James Bond may have been around longer, but Tora-san's amazing longevity is matched by its remarkable, one-of-a-kind consistency. The dozen or so principal cast and crew members remained essentially unchanged, and director/chief writer Yoji Yamada helmed all but two of the four dozen films.

In one sense, if you've seen one Tora-san movie, you've seen them all. The stories are virtually the same from film to film. Torajiro Kuruma (Kiyoshi Atsumi), a naïve, middle-aged peddler, returns home to visit his only surviving sibling, his sister Sakura (Chieko Baisho), as well as her husband, Hiroshi (Gin Maeda), their son, Mitsuo (Hidetaka Yoshioka), Tora-san's Aunt Tsune (Chieko Misaki) and Uncle Ryuzo (Masami Shimojo). Tora-san's bumbling tests everyone's patience, but his family are also excited and intrigued by their outrageous black sheep. In every film Tora-san falls in love—a new neighbor, a visiting professor, a doctor, etc.—but it never works out, and by the closing credits he is alone once more, hawking his wares. There's always a subplot involving other family members—later films focused on Tora's troubled teenage nephew—and other series regulars, including Hisao Dazai and Chishu Ryu, make token appearances.

Within this format, the films play in much the manner of a Western or other genre programmer, and the subtle variation within the formula is part of the fun. For detractors of the series, these subtle differences are invisible, and the films are dismissed and even actively disliked by some Japanese reviewers. But their familiarity is also part of the reason they have remained so popular for so long—several generations have literally grown up with Tora-san and his family. Most agree that the films are valentines to a bygone yet still familiar Japan, before its emergence as an economic superpower. "People come to see Tora-san," Kiyoshi Atsumi once told *Variety*, "because they want to see a guy who can no longer be found in Japan."[6]

The Tora-san films are sentimental in the best sense of the word, a deft balance of pathos and humor. Tora-san has been compared favorably to Charlie Chaplin, and Shochiku even called the first film *Tora-san, Our Lovable Tramp* for the international market. Like Chaplin's alter ego, Tora-san is both street-smart and innocent, foolish and wise. Like Laurel and Hardy, he is childlike but never infantile—a very fine line to tread—and like the Little Tramp, he always manages to brush off his sorrows, however heartbroken he may be, in the closing moments (bittersweet acceptance is common in Japanese fiction). Tora-san is a hopeless romantic, but never marries. Sometimes his love is unrequited; sometimes he realizes the relationship would never work out, usually because of class, education, and social differences, and, resigned to his peddler life, he walks away. His would-be girlfriends were nicknamed "Madonnas" in Japan (coined long before the American pop star's rise) and played by leading film actresses, including Machiko Kyo and Kyoko Kagawa.

Tora-san began life as a TV show named *Otoko wa tsuraiyo* ("It's Tough to Be a Man"), which debuted on Fuji-TV in October 1968. In the last episode, Tora-san is bitten by a snake and dies. This so outraged viewers that Shochiku saw a market for a one-shot film (also called *Otoko wa tsuraiyo*), which they released the following August, some five months after the series had ended. Yamada co-wrote but did not direct the third and fourth installments, which deviated somewhat from his vision of the series, and so from that point forward he took full creative control.

In this, the thirty-eighth Tora-san movie, Tora-san goes to Hokkaido, where he meets a surly veterinarian, Junkichi (Mifune), a widower long estranged from his daughter (Keiko Takeshita), who married against her father's will and now, reluctantly, is returning home to face him. Tora-san falls for her, of course, while Junkichi dismisses the obvious advances of Etsuko (Keiko Awaji), owner of the local diner.

"Well, you know, [Mifune] always looked serious and intimidating," said Yamada, "while Tora-san was the very opposite in character. I thought it would be very interesting if they worked together. And in that sense, Tora-san made fun of his image: 'Why do you look so serious?' and 'Why are you yelling all the time?' The idea was to take Mr. Mifune's persona, the strong samurai, and watch it change to a very real human being. I thought that would be very interesting to show. It's like putting John Wayne and Orson Welles in the same story."[7] As if to emphasize this, Yamada and co-writer Yoshitaka Asama gave Mifune's character the name Jun(kichi) Ueno, which, to Japanese ears, sounds like "John Wayne."

Unlike most people who worked with him and knew him, Yamada does not remember Mifune as a shy and reserved man. "I didn't experience that. He wasn't talkative, but he was easily excited and got angry about tiny little things. He was like a small boy and tried to make jokes which weren't funny. Once we realized he was trying to tell jokes, we all tried to laugh."[8]

Chris Hicks's review in the *Desert News* was typical: "Imagine my surprise to find [it] a thoroughly delightful film, loaded with heart and a sweetness that is all too lacking in contemporary American films."[9]

"What's gratifying—but not surprising," commented Kevin Thomas, "is that writer-director Yoji Yamada has created a role ideal for Mifune. . . . The rapport between star and director is such that one can only hope that Yamada will be able to direct Mifune in a film outside the series."[10]

That didn't happen, but the same year Mifune and Yamada went on a vacation to China together. Like Mifune, Yamada had been raised there, and according to him, this "was the only time [Mifune] ever went back. I don't think he especially wanted to go, because he didn't want to see how much of where he was raised had changed. Once he found his old house, he got angry, saying, 'It's not supposed to be like this!' He was in a bad mood the whole time, and never laughed once. His facial expressions were always very serious [laughs]."[11] For almost the entire trip, Mifune stayed in his hotel room.

Mifune had another plum role later that same year, in Kon Ichikawa's odd genre mix *Princess from the Moon* (Taketori monogatari). Based on a centuries-old fairy tale, "Story of a Bamboo-Cutter," *Princess from the Moon* casts Mifune as a poor peasant who finds a baby girl hatched from a golden egg deep in the forests near his home. Childless, he and his wife (Ayako Wakao) adopt the child, who overnight becomes a beautiful teenager (played by pop star Yasuko Sawaguchi). He also parlays the gold of the egg into a fortune, and the now wealthy family moves to the city. Noblemen ask for her hand in marriage, but the girl from another world is beyond their reach.

Ichikawa creates a sumptuous-looking film, but it's marred by an attempt to give this fantasy a sci-fi edge, complete with a *Close Encounters*—esque flying saucer that appears at the climax. As Dan Fainaru noted in his review of the film for the *Jerusalem Post*, "[It's] a nice legend that young audiences could easily enjoy if not for Ichikawa's attempt to replace magic with science fiction and his wavering between sheer imagination and literary special effects designed to create some sort of credibility. . . . Pure, mysteriously wonderful magic might have been better in this case."[12]

Mifune went to New York for the U.S. premiere in September, accompanied by co-star Sawaguchi and Oscar-winning costume designer Emi Wada. The event was also a celebration of Toho's gift of more than fifty films to the Museum of Modern Art's film archives, a donation arranged, in part, by Martin Scorsese.

Mifune returned to America when he visited Seattle in late April 1990 for the premiere of Kei Kumai's *Death of a Tea Master* (Sen no Rikyu—Hongakubo Ibun), and San Francisco for a screening of the film a few days later. There he served as Grand Marshal at that city's Cherry Blossom Festival Parade. (He had previously appeared at least once as Grand Marshal of the Los Angeles Nisei Festival Parade.)

. After appearing in Kumai's film, Mifune was made up in flowing gray hair and beard à la Charlton Heston in *The Ten Commandments*, for his role in Akira Kobayashi's *Demons in Spring* (Haru kuru oni, 1989). Adapted by Ryuzo Kikushima from a novel by Tokuhei Suchi, the film had been a pet project of Kobayashi's for twenty-five years, since his days as one of Nikkatsu's top actor-singers. It is a period fable somewhere in tone and substance between John Ford's *The Hurricane* (1937) and Imamura's *Kurage-jima—Legends from a Southern Island* (a.k.a. *The Profound Desire of the Gods*; Kamigami no fukaki yokubo, 1968), with Mifune top-billed as a village elder in a remote community off the shores of Sanriku. Young lovers (Masaru Matsuda and Sachiko Wakayama), escaping the girl's arranged marriage with another man, have washed ashore. Village custom dictates that they be thrown back into the ocean to appease the gods, but the elder intervenes. However, the village chief (Sakae Takita) orders the man to submit to a series of tests to claim the woman as his bride.

Demons in Spring was barely released in the United States, though Kevin Thomas, referring to director Kobayashi's tenacity, concluded: "It was worth the wait, for 'Demons in Spring' uses the familiar, stylized conventions of the Japanese period picture to create a unique and stunning experience. . . . [It] is an adventure-filled tale well-told, thanks to Kobayashi's skill and passion and to the gifts of screenwriter Ryuzo Kikushima."[13]

But the continued success of Tora-san and realization of projects like *Demons in Spring* were hardly capable of turning around the fortunes of

Japan's film industry. In 1960 its major studios produced nearly 600 features. Thirty years later, one-tenth as many films were being made. Only the most surefire properties were being produced in-house, and Kurosawa was not alone in having to look elsewhere to have projects financed. By 1990, the same fate had befallen Japan's New Wave directors, like Nagisa Oshima, and for the younger generation of filmmakers the situation was, if anything, bleaker. Actor-turned-director Juzo Itami, for example, had to sell his car and mortgage his home to make *The Funeral* (Ososhiki, 1984).[14]

"It's a national problem," Yoji Yamada commented. "If the government subsidized the studios, events like the closing of Shochiku's Ofuna Studios [in 1999] wouldn't have happened. Japanese producers and directors have never requested help from the Japanese government, and that saddens me greatly. Nowadays, American movies dominate all over the world, and if Japan were to receive a percentage of films exhibited in Japan, that money could be used to subsidize our own industry. I think we should be requesting this. . . . When I watch Chaplin's films, I'm speechless. But when the Japanese people today see a film like *The Matrix*, it's different. *The Matrix* is all about marketing, Chaplin's films are about art. I think many Americans would agree. Similarly, I'm not proud of *Pokemon*'s success, its showing in two or three thousand theaters in America. It's just taking up space. But I'm proud of Mr. Ozu's films or Mr. Kurosawa's."[15]

Toshiro Mifune turned seventy in 1990 and took on even fewer film roles than he had in the eighties. From 1950 to 1957, he appeared in forty-eight features, mostly in starring or major supporting roles. In the last seven years of his life, he would be seen in just five.

"When we were young," he said, "there were classics, memorable films, good actors and actresses. Now there are so very few good films. There may be some good people out there trying to make some. I don't want to give up all hope. But I'm very disappointed today. It's the leisure industry to blame, and television. Nobody goes to movies anymore. Three of the big five studios have closed. And just look at the television here—game shows, music shows, quiz shows. It's all a rehash of American television 20 years ago."[16] But as writer David Schweisberg and others have pointed out, Mifune Productions itself turned to television when it had to. For the actor it was a bitter pill to swallow. By now, Mifune had all but accepted his fallen status in Japan and that his contemporary work paled next to his best work of the 1950s and '60s. He could turn up in virtually any part of the world and they'd give him an award and hold a retrospective in his honor. But in his own country he was an old man who, to the young people of Japan, was more familiar as a face on the front page of tabloids or in magazines pitching beer or as a guest star on some TV show.

The Japanese industry which he once dominated was now completely alien to him, and so he shut it out of his life. Only one of his last five movies could truly be considered a Japanese film. "It's in new hands," he said. "I'm asked to give advice on many things—acting, culture, finance—which I know a little about. I can tell you my story, but that's history. I have nothing to say that I feel is inspirational. I lived, I worked, I intend to continue for as long as I want and as long as I can."[17] Quite a contrast to the man who in 1984 asked, "Even if I wanted to retire, how could I?"

He flew back and forth to the United States frequently in the early 1990s, visiting friends in Hawaii and Los Angeles, being fêted by film societies, wearing his *Shogun* costume as grand marshal at a cherry blossom parade in San Francisco, appearing at Japanese-American fund-raisers. He was given a Special Achievement Award at the thirty-ninth Asia Pacific Film Festival "for his contribution to cinema in a career spanning more than four decades." The award was presented to him—in one of his last public appearances—on September 1, 1994, in a theater in Sydney, Australia, the closing night of the festival.[18]

But awards didn't pay bills, and reluctantly he had the stages of Mifune Productions torn down. The land was now far more valuable than the studio that occupied it. Its buildings were bulldozed and condominiums were built on the property. Perversely, Mifune moved into one of its units and made it his last home. The irony that, in his later years, it was through real estate and not films that Mifune made most of his income wasn't lost on him. "I'd never thought I'd be [in the real estate business]. It just shows how far the movie industry has declined. I'm just being logical.[19]

"The company was a great joy," he said. "At our peak there were some 200 people working for me and it was the greatest tragedy to finally have to close the operation."[20]

"[My father] was not a businessman," remarked Shiro. "An actor, but not a businessmen. His dream, because his father was a cameraman, was to have his own studio, but a movie studio is different [from a photography studio]. He later said he made the same mistake as his father: just like his father, he lost everything. His was the type of personality that wanted to do everything himself, but it was too much."[21]

He still drove the black Rolls-Royce he had bought in 1961; back then, there was only one other in Japan, and that belonged to the Japanese Emperor. He referred to it, only half-jokingly, as "[the] hearse they will someday bury me in."[22] In his book of essays *Geisha, Gangster, Neighbor, Nun*, Donald Richie painted a sympathetic but devastating portrait of the man Mifune had become. Though he portrayed him too much the victim of Kurosawa's callousness and not enough the talented but naïve, overly ambitious man of his own misguided making, it is otherwise accurate:

> One of Mifune's problems is that he wants to do the right thing in a world that is plainly wrong. . . . The world does not like nice guys. Not really. They always come in last, says Western wisdom. And Eastern wisdom acts as if they do. They are charming, fun to be with, absolutely trustworthy, and so what? So says the world. Mifune has been cheated in his business dealings, has been victim of fraud and misrepresentation, and, finally, has been misunderstood in the most important emotional relationship he ever had—that with Kurosawa.
>
> Mifune has no drive for perfection, he has a drive for virtue. How otherwise transparent the man is. His office has plaques on the walls, trophies. It is the room of any Japanese business executive. One expects golf clubs or racing-car pictures. His living room has lots of beaded lampshades, an onyx coffee table on gilt legs, an overstuffed chair like a throne, embossed wallpaper, diamond-patterned carpet, ludicrous crystal chandelier. It is all in the ordinary taste (or lack of it) of the newly rich in Japan, but there is nothing in it of Mifune. . . . As I look at him and again he laughs, briefly, looking down at the table, I seem to hear his parents saying what a good boy Toshi-bo is. And I can see Kurosawa, that bad parent, turning away from this good son who loved him.[23]

Mike Inoue recalled one such incident, which had occurred years earlier: "Kurosawa had a big home in Komai City, near Seijo. He always invited actors to have drinks. Mifune was a very heavy drinker, and I still remember the night I drank with [Mifune] and he gave me a big beer glass and said, 'Let's have a drinking contest.' I thought he was going to pour beer, but he put whiskey in it. We started the contest, and the man who lost had to hang himself from the ceiling and sing a song. Both of us were so drunk. He went over to the railroad station, got on the tracks, and yelled, 'Train! Kill me if you can!' The next day, Kurosawa said, 'Let's go fishing,' and I heard behind me someone walking on the gravel. It was Mr. Mifune. My uncle said, 'Mifune is behind us. Never mind. Don't look back.' But I couldn't help it. He was sitting on the gravel, wanting to apologize. I said, 'Uncle, he's bowing so deeply.' 'Never mind,' Kurosawa said, 'leave him alone.' This went on for something like thirty minutes."[24]

Richie, whose own association with Kurosawa waned upon completion of his book *The Films of Akira Kurosawa*, wondered whether any of Kurosawa's personal relationships lasted after he no longer needed someone's services, adding, "He cares desperately about everybody, you know . . . being on his side, and so to that extent it does [extend beyond his current film], but Kurosawa is a splendid, wonderful director and he can talk to you about what the next film is going to be. However, he cannot talk about anything else, nor does he want to. . . . Anybody who is less a master of small talk than he I don't know. In that sense, he's like John Ford or William Wellman. . . . In a way they're divine tinkerers. If you hang around Kurosawa, there's really nothing to talk about unless you're interested in hearing what he's going to do."[25]

For Mifune, adding salt to the wound was the question invariably asked him at every interview: "Are you ever going to do another movie with Kurosawa?" His response was always polite, but often he knowingly skewered his replies with gross misinformation. He told one reporter that the reason he didn't work with Kurosawa after *Red Beard* was that Toho had fired Kurosawa while he, Mifune, was still under contract with them.[26] Asked about *Seven Samurai*, Mifune said, inaccurately, "The producers were ready to fire Kurosawa. In fact, they took the film away from him after he finished it and it became an international success."[27]

When Leonard Klady of the *Toronto Star* interviewed him, Mifune said, "I've [been in] more than 150 films and maybe six with Kurosawa, but those are the ones everyone remembers." But Klady knew better—Mifune had been in sixteen Kurosawa movies (and even more written by him). When he questioned Mifune's count, the actor went and looked them up on his official filmography. Mifune, Klady wrote, "seems bored with the idea of one last film together. [According to Mifune] George Lucas . . . has pushed for such a project but he says nothing proposed has caught his fancy."[28]

"It's not as if we had any kind of argument," Mifune said in 1990. "Indeed, we continued working together behind the scenes. Kurosawa edited the first film I produced [*Legacy of the 500,000*]. And later on, when he was in trouble and came to me for money, I gave him ¥5 million, which at the time was a lot of money."[29]

Without Kurosawa, Mifune's solo efforts continued their rudderless path into the 1990s, when he made some of the better—and some of the worst—films of his career. The first was *Kabuto* (Helmet), an $18 million international production in English and Japanese, eventually released in the United States as *Journey of Honor* (a.k.a. *Shogun Mayeda*). He filmed his brief scenes in April 1990, though the picture wasn't released until 1992. Sho Kosugi starred as Lord Mayeda, who is sent by Shogun Ieyasu (Mifune, playing the same character as Masayuki Yui had in *Kagemusha*) to Spain to buy modern rifles. The film, directed by Gordon Hessler, is a likable if unspectacular old-fashioned adventure reminiscent of swashbucklers from Hollywood's golden age as much as of the sixties' *jidai-geki*. Its battle scenes are undernourished—the Battle of Sekigahara consists of about forty soldiers—and with their staging and cutaways to ominous clouds, they suggest a low-rent version of *Ran*. But the picture is helped considerably by its marvelous cast of supporting players: Norman Lloyd as a sinister Franciscan friar, Christopher Lee as King Philip III, John Rhys-Davies as the Sultan of Morocco. Besides Mifune, sixties Daiei ingenue Miwa Takada appears as Yadogime, Ieyasu's rival. Nijiko Kiyokawa, the Toho starlet of the late 1930s who appeared in several films on which Kurosawa acted as chief assistant director, and who co-starred with Mifune in *Jewels in Our Hearts* (1952), plays Yadogime's counselor.

As critic Jeff Shannon suggests, *Journey of Honor* "[transports viewers] to the innocent, golden age of the Saturday matinee. If the film doesn't always meet today's exacting standards of entertainment . . . it at least flies with the spirit of adventures past, when an adequate yarn and a good hero were enough to satisfy the kid in all of us. . . . To see the still-intimidating Mifune, looking imposingly grand in full Shogun regalia, is to appreciate the affection that 'Journey of Honor' has for a long-gone era of filmmaking that can never truly return."[30]

Immediately after finishing work on *Journey of Honor*, Mifune accepted a supporting role in *Strawberry Road* (Sutoroberi rodo, 1991), a $13.7 million Japanese-American co-production filmed in May, June, and July of 1990. The film was adapted from Yoshimi Ishikawa's 1989 autobiography, which won the Oya Soichi (Japanese Pulitzer Prize), about two brothers who emigrate to California in the 1960s and establish a strawberry farm. The entire film was shot in rural California and New York City, using an American and Japanese crew.[31]

Strawberry Road had no release in the United States, which is unfortunate, for while it bites off a bit more than it can chew, addressing everything from Vietnam War protests to racism and interracial marriage, it has a seductive, heartfelt sincerity. It paints a wide, rich canvas of the lives and loves of several generations of Japanese-Americans. Mifune, still robust at seventy, plays one of the older farmers, who drives around in a weather-beaten pickup truck with his Hispanic wife and child. Former Toho comedian Norihei Miki is another old-timer who never learned to speak English, which lends a real poignancy when he's reunited with a long-lost brother (Noriyuki "Pat" Morita) who, having lived in Texas for more than forty years, can't speak Japanese.*

In the fall of that same year, Mifune appeared in what would be his last major role. He received second billing on *Shadow of the Wolf*, a French and Canadian production he worked on in November and December 1990, though it wasn't released until 1993. It did absolutely nothing for his career. He admitted to making the film mainly as a "favor" to *Red Sun* producer Robert Dorfman, whose son Jacques was directing the picture.[32] Based on the bestselling novel *Agaguk*, the film is a badly written adventure drama about several tribes of Inuit Eskimos. Its advertising likened the picture to *Dances with Wolves* (1990) and *The Last of the Mohicans* (1992). Unfortunately, its script is far more akin to the Raquel Welch–Ray Harryhausen caveman epic *One Million Years, B.C.* (1966). Both films are about a young native who leaves his tribe after a fight with his father, the aging chief, falls in love with a girl from a rival tribe, lives and learns about life at *her* tribe, then returns home a full-fledged warrior and replaces his father as their leader. *Shadow of the Wolf*, however, is set in 1935 and doesn't have dinosaurs.

Mifune plays Kroomak, the aging chief, while an overripe, hot-blooded Lou Diamond Phillips is Agaguk, his son. Mifune once again learned his lines phonetically, and was once again dubbed, this time with a voice straight out of an Italian sword-and-sandal movie. He's also very broad, though downright restrained compared to Phillips, who is perfectly awful. (Jennifer Tilly is even worse as Igiyook, Phillips's Eskimo bride.) As a man who thinks he's more in control of his kingdom than he actually is, Mifune's character with better writing might have offered something Lear-esque. Instead, we first see him tied up and stripped to the waist, chanting incantations, and later bedding a middle-aged Eskimo, complete with exaggerated, dubbed-in grunts.

There is but one mildly interesting scene in the picture when Donald

*According to *Boston Globe* reporter Andy Daibilis, Mifune had been offered Morita's role in *The Karate Kid* but turned it down due to other commitments (Andy Daibilis. Personal interview by Anne Wasserman, December 28, 1999).

Sutherland, playing a sympathetic policeman (his hair and beard inexplicably dyed bright orange), compares cultures with Mifune in the tribe's mammoth igloo. Sutherland, a talented actor all too often wasted in bad films, nearly makes these scenes work, and Mifune's subtle facial expressions almost allow us to forget the awful looping of his performance, though even he overacts for most of the film. The pretentious, outrageous ending has Mifune leaping out of a plane in mid-flight, only to literally turn into a hawk, while Eskimos cheer at the metamorphosis as if at a football rally.

Despite the lavish (somewhere between $22 and $35 million) budget, the movie somehow managed to look and sound cheap, possibly due to an unusually long postproduction period, when it may have been heavily retooled. Maurice Jarre's score is peppered with odd electronic cues suggesting a low-budget horror film. And it opens with a disclaimer assuring viewers that no animals were injured in the production of the film, but they needn't have bothered: anytime Lou Diamond Phillips is supposedly attacked by a wolf or polar bear, it looks as if he's having rugs flung at him. When Phillips has part of his face chewed off by the title mammal, there's no trace of the deep scars he should have; instead, the actor is made up with what appears to be melted cheese. (When he later returns home he wears an odd, *Phantom of the Opera*–esque mask.) The picture does have a campy charm and is undeniably earnest, but in the end, every scene is so overwrought that it simply becomes wearying.

The film received scathing reviews and flopped in the United States. Roger Ebert hated the contrived plot and Mifune's transformation from grumpy ruler to Eskimo martyr. "The notion of making a movie about Eskimo life is a good one, but why did the filmmakers feel obligated to connect it to a lame and unconvincing story about a murder investigation? Are scriptwriters and producers so bankrupt of imagination that only the ancient clichés of crime films can supply them with a story to plug into? Couldn't they imagine their Eskimo characters in enough detail so that their lives would be interesting without the phony suspense of a transplanted Perry Mason episode?"[33]

The Washington Post's Hal Hinson added: "The movie is just bad enough to be considered camp, but still not bad enough to be fun. . . . With a price tag of $31 million, *Shadow of the Wolf* is being called 'the most expensive motion picture in Canadian film history.' Watching it, you have to ask, 'What did they spend all that money on? Dog food?' Certainly, all that expense is not visible on the screen. What is on the screen? Ice. Lots of ice."[34]

Variety said that the dialogue "borders on the laughable . . . [and is] almost a parody of typical Indian dialogue from old movies. . . . Toshiro Mifune lends his imposing presence, but is obviously dubbed."[35] Perhaps the ultimate insult came when Jeff Craig of "Sixty-Second Preview," which exists solely to provide rave reviews for publicists looking for good ad copy, actually gave *Shadow of the Wolf* a mere three stars (***), practically a condemnation.

TWENTY-EIGHT

NOT YET

"I feel that as I'm getting older," Kurosawa said in 1980, "I am more relaxed and move more slowly, and this is reflected in technique. I set up the camera, step back and watch the action flow by."[1]

Many critics saw *Ran* as Kurosawa's last hurrah, and the director himself had, consciously or not, perpetuated the notion that the picture would be his last. Not so, he said once it was completed. "What I meant when I spoke of *Ran* in terms of my life's work was that I now feel I am at a place where I can make a new start in a different direction."[2]

This different direction turned out to be a move toward more intimate, chamberlike drama. For many critics, used to the visceral action of *Seven Samurai* and *Yojimbo* and, more recently, visually stunning historical epics like *Kagemusha* and *Ran*, Kurosawa's shift away from such projects was seen as the indulgences of an old artist finally secure in his position, or, worse, the last gasps of an aging artist whose abilities were drying up. Western critics who pointed angry fingers at the Japanese for supposedly rejecting him for being too Western now accused him of making films too Eastern. In his last works, they said, he pandered to the Japanese, just as the Japanese had accused him of pandering to the West in the 1970s and '80s. Critics mistook the films' intimacy and straightforwardness for simplemindedness. Gone was the visceral action, the historical epics, and in their place came a lean, almost Ozu-like sensibility. Like many artists whose work became more mature—from filmmakers like Alain Resnais to musicians like Charlie Parker—Kurosawa did so at the expense of an audience that didn't want him to change.

Western critics who thought they knew Kurosawa didn't know what to make of these stylistic changes, even though, as Donald Richie wrote, "there is nothing in [them] that earlier pictures had not prepared us for."[3] Nonetheless, many in the West reacted like *LA Weekly*'s Tom Carson, who seemed hopelessly out of touch with Kurosawa's entire oeuvre. "[Kurosawa has] made extraordinary movies in his half-century career, but they aren't famous for their play on ideas. If anything, in the 1950s and early '60s, he was the director who reinvented art house moviegoing as pure visceral sensation—a celebration of action and spectacle for their own cacophonous sake."[4]

The first of these last films, more a link between his two later styles than an example of it, was to be entitled "Such Dreams I Have Dreamed" ("Konna yume wo mita," later changed to *Yume*, or *Dreams*), an anthology based on actual dreams experienced by the director, linked by a concern for man's misuse of and inability to control the natural elements. "A human being is a genius while dreaming," Kurosawa wrote. "Fearless and brave. . . . This was the most important point I had to remember when I attempted to make this film from the eight dreams described in my script. Audacious and fearless expressions were essential to make this motion picture."[5]

For the first time since *The Men Who Tread on the Tiger's Tail* forty-five years earlier, Kurosawa wrote by himself, without a collaborator. Partly this was because he had outlived most of his screenwriters. Eijiro Hisaita had died in 1976, and Ryuzo Kikushima and Masato Ide apparently were ailing and passed away while *Dreams* was in production. Hideo Oguni was in his late eighties, and Shinobu Hashimoto, a comparative youngster at sixty-eight, was nonetheless chronically in poor health and had written just two scripts since directing *Bright Lake* (Maboroshi no mizuumi) in 1982. In 1975, Kurosawa had cautioned Toho employees: "In writing alone there is a danger that your interpretation of another human being will suffer from one-sidedness. If you write with two other people about that human being, you get at least three different viewpoints on him, and you can discuss the points on which you disagree."[6] Now, in 1990, with no one to question his ideas, no one to play the role of devil's advocate, he ran the risk of that very problem himself.

Of course, the hero of *Dreams* was Kurosawa's alter ego, but even so, he ran the risk of being didactic, of indulging himself without a collaborator like Oguni to tell him to start over and try again. Writing alone, Kurosawa penned his script quickly, in just "two months, maybe less."[7]

Kurosawa's people approached Toho about financing this latest project, and once again he walked away empty-handed. Other companies were reportedly approached as well, but still no funding was forthcoming. That his last two films were only moderately profitable was, the director insisted, not the reason. Instead, he laid the blame at the feet of conservative Japanese businessmen. One segment of the film was to depict the destruction of Japan's nuclear power plants and the catastrophic release of radioactive clouds. Modern Japan may unilaterally oppose the nuclear arms race, but, he said, it depends on nuclear power more than any other country in the world save France and West Germany. Kurosawa felt such thinking immensely hypocritical. "We only think we need nuclear reactors because the power companies have convinced us we need to use a lot of electricity in order to live well," he said. "If one company were to back my film, it'd have to worry that any other company it does business with would take offense. . . . They're just too conservative to deal with the subject."[8] So once again Kurosawa had to pitch his idea outside Japan.

"One day," recalled Mike Inoue, "I got a call from my uncle, who said, 'I need your help. Why don't you come over?' Kurosawa told me, 'I received a letter from Steven Spielberg which doesn't make any sense to me.' So I went over to his home and he said that he had written a script called 'Such Dreams I Have Dreamed' and that he had sent a translation of that script to Spielberg for possible financing. I read Spielberg's reply, which said, 'Thank you for sending the synopsis, and if you do a script, please send it to me.' I said, 'Uncle, what did you send to him?' And he said, '[I didn't send a synopsis.] I finished the whole script and sent it to a translation company, and they sent it on.' I read the translation he sent. It was terrible and missing many important nuances from Kurosawa's original Japanese script. I then volunteered to re-translate. It took me over a month to complete my translation as I had to commute to his home frequently to ask him about the nuances he intended to express between the lines. A few days after we sent my translation to Spielberg, we received a fax from him stating that he was highly impressed with this script and offering his help to find a financier. He brought in Warner Brothers who gave us a Negative-Pickup guarantee for the film to be directed by Kurosawa."[9]

The translators Kurosawa hired, it turned out, had done a slapdash job. They also didn't convert the script to the very different American-style format, so Spielberg assumed he was reading a treatment, not a complete screenplay. Inoue took Kurosawa's script home and translated it himself, with the help of Greg Knapp, who had co-written Kinji Fukasaku's *Virus* (a 1980 post-apocalyptic film in which roughly half the dialogue was in English).

Inoue and Kurosawa decided to meet with Spielberg at Universal Studios. When they greeted each other, they kept bowing, and Spielberg refused to sit down before Kurosawa did. The respect was mutual. Perhaps surprisingly, Kurosawa adored Spielberg's films. Donald Richie recalled attending a screening of *Jaws* with him; after the film was over, the director jumped up and talked excitedly about the picture's editing.[10] As their meeting began, Kurosawa lit a cigarette, unaware he was in a non-smoking building. Spielberg's assistants ran around in vain, trying to find him an ashtray. But the day's comedy of errors paid off in the end. Within weeks, Spielberg had arranged a deal with Warner Bros.*

The company announced its intention to purchase worldwide distribution rights of *Dreams* on May 26, 1988.[11] Many assumed Warner Bros. was bankrolling the picture, but it agreed only to a "negative pickup." In other words, the American company committed to buying the completed picture, budgeted at $12 million, but would not finance its production. "*We* raised the money," declared an irritated Hisao, reportedly "miffed by the widespread assumption that the studio simply handed over a pile of greenbacks." The director's Beverly Hills–based subsidiary, Kurosawa Enterprises USA, arranged a fixed-rate European loan from a California bank.[12]

Dreams's production was, like all Kurosawa's last projects, a family affair. Mike Inoue and Hisao acted as its producers, while Kazuko assisted Emi Wada with the film's elaborate wardrobe.

Dreams had long fascinated Kurosawa and had played a major role in his previous three films. He said he had been inspired to keep a journal of his dreams after reading a passage by Dostoyevsky "in which the author said dreams revealed men's deepest thoughts, liberated in sleep." Originally, he hoped to adapt eleven of his most vivid dreams, but was forced to drop three episodes "because technically they were too difficult [to film], or expensive enough to bankrupt the producer."[13]

But this wasn't exactly true. Kurosawa said later that one of these dreams was to have depicted men and women flying through the air, and its opticals would have indeed been expensive to effectively realize. But another, about Buddhist priests protesting temple taxes, was dropped because

*According to both Mike Inoue and Hisao Kurosawa, Spielberg's involvement after that was minimal, at least as far as the production and postproduction of the film in Japan went. The film was released only as "A Steven Spielberg Presentation."

it "lacked international appeal," and the third, "The Wonderful Dream," planned as the final segment, was to have had newscasters announce an outbreak of worldwide peace. That segment, according to Inoue, was dropped because it would have made the film too long, and Warners wanted to get the film in under two hours.[14]

With financing secured, shooting began at Toho Studios on January 10, 1989. It was produced at a leisurely pace and took more than eight months to complete. Beyond its association with Spielberg and George Lucas's ILM, which provided at cost its extensive optical effects, *Dreams* garnered additional publicity with the casting of Martin Scorsese for a segment in which the American director portrays Vincent van Gogh. Scorsese had first met Kurosawa several years earlier in New York, when he asked Kurosawa for help with film preservation issues. "According to my uncle," said Mike Inoue, "on a trip to the United States he had the chance to meet . . . Martin Scorsese. 'That man really impressed me the way that he expresses himself,' my uncle said, 'the tone of his voice. He reminded me of Van Gogh.' So, naturally, when he decided to make 'Such Dreams I Have Dreamed,' he could think of nobody except . . . Scorsese for that role, and Scorsese said, 'Without any question I'll do it.' He acted very well."[15] Filming of the segment began on July 31, 1989, on location in a wheat field in Memanbetsu-cho in Hokkaido.

Dreams had none of the production and personal problems that had plagued Kurosawa on *Kagemusha* and *Ran*, although Hisao Kurosawa described the relationship with Warner Bros. as "not so good. The most difficult issue was that there was a Warner Bros. branch in Japan, which had no rights in the decision-making process, but they reported back to the headquarters. If we had been able to deal with the headquarters directly, it would have been easier."[16] Still, *Dreams* wrapped ahead of schedule, at the end of the summer, giving Kurosawa plenty of time to edit his film and to wait ILM's opticals. He spent much of that fall writing a new script, which was to become *Rhapsody in August*.

Kurosawa also welcomed a great many reporters to his set. As described by Ralph Rugoff,

Kurosawa travels and holds interviews accompanied by an entourage of relatives and producers (most of whom are relatives); all smoke like crazy. Elegant, aristocratic, and refined, he carries himself with an unobtrusive dignity. (Indeed, his humility is astonishing: before removing his jacket, for example, he asks permission of all present.)

He looks twenty years younger than his age; he has beautiful gray hair. His dark glasses, removed only rarely, somehow betray his profound alertness. He misses nothing. Before answering a question, he mulls it over for a long moment with lips pursed, as if turning over an object and carefully inspecting all sides. When he speaks, he gesticulates with fluid gestures, his hands moving with the slow grace of small languid fish. Despite his illustrious career and the red-carpet treatment he's receiving these days, there's absolutely no trace of the prima donna about him.[17]

Early the following spring, Kurosawa received word that, five years after he had lost the Best Director award to Sydney Pollack, the Academy planned to give him an honorary Oscar. Kazuko, Hisao, and Mike Inoue accompanied him to the ceremony that April. George Lucas and Steven Spielberg walked onstage to present the award, the latter calling Kurosawa "a man who many of us believe is our greatest living filmmaker and all of us know as one of the few true visionaries ever to work in our medium." A montage of clips, assembled by *Time* critic Richard Schickel, preceded the presentation of the award, and Kurosawa received a standing ovation as he walked to the stage. He was surprised by a remote television feed from Tokyo, where members of his staff wheeled out a cake and wished him a happy birthday. The American audiences joined Kurosawa's disciples in singing "Happy Birthday" to the eighty-year-old Oscar recipient. "I have to ask if I really deserve it," he said, through a translator. "I'm a little worried because I don't feel that I understand cinema yet." He said, "Thank you," in English, and walked off with his prize to another standing ovation.

As *Dreams* neared its premiere at Cannes on May 10, 1990, anticipation ran high. Audie Bock prepared the English subtitles. "*Dreams* is like nothing that any contemporary director anywhere in the world would think of trying to get away with. It's very personal, it gets into nightmares. It's very much something that people who have an interest in Kurosawa will feel that they have to see."[18]

Very true, but when *Dreams* was finally unveiled, it proved a supreme disappointment. Critics were kind, even apologetic. After *Ran* they were also reluctant to trounce it, and in the United States, partly because Spielberg's name was given nearly equal billing, the film did very well in the first weeks of its release. Renamed *Akira Kurosawa's Dreams* by Warner Bros., the picture earned more in its initial week than had any previous Kurosawa film in the United States. In its first seven days at the 57th Street Playhouse in New York, *Dreams* grossed nearly $80,000 and set a house record.[19]

But, as David Denby said in *New York*, "I love Akira Kurosawa more than any other living director, but I don't understand critics who praise the moralistic *Dreams*." His comments echoed those he had had for *Kagemusha*: "The theme of the movie is the extinction of nature, and the loss of man's humanity with it. But the movie is all theme. . . . Almost nothing is developed, and the preset anecdotal approach seems almost smug."[20]

Kevin Thomas was less harsh: "[*Dreams*] contains some of the most beautiful images ever conceived by the man . . . and it also has a couple of the most ponderous moments of any of his 28 films. Even so, what works far outweighs what doesn't, and this picture is an event for film lovers. Of all the films that have played Los Angeles this year, only Theo Angelopoulos's 'The Traveling Players' can be mentioned in the same breath in regard to level of aspiration and intensity of vision."[21]

Dreams was like no other Kurosawa film in the highly subjective reaction to its individual segments. Never before had there been such a complete absence of consensus. No one seemed to agree: high praise for one segment was countered by sharp criticism for another. Every reviewer had his own favorite.

Observant critics likened *Dreams* to the later films of Buñuel or *Le Petit Théâtre de Jean Renoir* (1971). But while supposedly based on the actual dreams of its director, the picture's fatal flaw is that Kurosawa has distanced himself from the material. The dreams play as if they were written rather than experienced. The work that promises filmed adaptations of actual dreams comes off instead as detached and distant, much along the lines of *Kagemusha*. Perhaps the film might have worked if it were more autobiographical, more personal, but in adapting his dreams cinematically, and in his insistence on imposing on them didactic concerns, Kurosawa robs them of the very essence that would have made them more compelling. In its final form, *Dreams* offers almost no insight on the man or his psychology, or on mankind. Dreams are intensely personal experiences, yet in spite of the fact that the main character is called "I" throughout, rarely does "I" ever seem to be Kurosawa; instead, he is more of an abstract and impartial observer. The eight dreams are expressionistic but impersonal, with "I" rarely a participant in the action. There is nothing in the film as vivid as any of the anecdotes in his autobiography; there are no dreams about Kurosawa's brother, the Kanto earthquake, his marriage, his suicide attempt. Even "The Tunnel," a sequence set shortly after the war, seems detached from his own experiences. Its dreams may be Kurosawa's dreams, but "The Tunnel" is more the autobiography of creative consultant Ishiro Honda than of Kurosawa. Kurosawa never went off to battle, but the "I" of the segment—a soldier wandering through Japan at the war's end, the dark, tragic past of the character—matches Honda's experiences almost to the letter. And "The Blizzard," with its mountaineers, seems more like something springing from the mind of Senkichi Taniguchi.

More important perhaps, the dreams are too literal in both their dialogue and their style when they needed to be more abstract and ambiguous, less preachy.

As Terrence Rafferty wrote in *The New Yorker*: "What Kurosawa calls dreams are more like poetic *tableaux vivants*: meticulous formal elaborations of imagery that could have originated in the mind of someone dreaming. And although Kurosawa's style is unmistakable, we never get the sense that he's truly revealing himself here; the movie has an eerily impersonal quality."[22]

"My film is not like the standard dream sequence that you're used to seeing in movies," Kurosawa explained. "The power of dreams cannot be expressed through music or lighting because dreams don't have those elements. Dreams are one thing and movies are another. The way I look at this is that my dreams are the original material, the original stories. My screenplay is, in a sense, an adaptation for the cinema."[23]

But, as David Denby asserts, *Dreams* is all about theme, and the theme is mankind's sins and, to a lesser extent, harmony with nature. Peach orchards are cut down, nuclear power plants disperse lethal radiation, mountain climbers struggle against the elements. But unlike earlier films that dealt with such issues—*Dersu Uzala*, *Record of a Living Being*, *Snow Trail*—*Dreams* keeps its concerns in the foreground at all times.

The first and last segments come closest to being successfully realized. "Sunshine Through the Rain" has young "I" (Toshihiko Nakano) being told by his mother (Mitsuko Baisho) not to go out into the forest. It is raining yet sunny, and this, she tells him, is when the forest foxes hold their wedding processions. "I" goes out anyway and sees the foxes (sublimely portrayed by choreographed actors in stylized makeup), which see him as well. Upon returning home, his mother refuses to let "I" back into the house, because he disobeyed her and now the foxes have seen him. He must commit *seppuku*, or find the foxes and apologize to them. The segment ends without resolution, as the boy searches for the forest foxes under a brilliant rainbow. Despite appearing more a fantasy anecdote than a dream, "Sunshine Through the Rain" seems the most autobiographical of the segments. The house with the gate, constructed in Gotemba by art director Yoshiro Muraki, is a reproduction of Kurosawa's childhood home in Koshikawa, and the nameplate reads KUROSAWA. The director also provided Baisho with pictures of his mother and instructed the actress how to act like her. Through all this, Kurosawa succeeds in giving the segment a genuinely childlike (but not childish), even magical quality. Unfortunately, the film goes downhill from here.

"The Peach Orchard" depicts another childhood encounter with the spiritual world. Instead of foxes, Japanese dolls come to life to chastise "I" because his family has cut down a precious orchard of peach trees. The episode is compromised by the extremely poor acting of Mitsunori Isaki, the boy portraying "I" in this segment, and overwhelmed by its static though beautiful visuals (particularly Emi Wada's gorgeous costume design). Moreover, it seems redundant and preachy after the beauty of the first episode.

"The Blizzard" is downright excruciating and interminably paced, with "I" and his fellow mountaineers wading through waist-deep styrene foam and salt, an unconvincing substitute for real snow, desperate to reach their mountaintop campsite. Although "The Blizzard," like the other segments, runs approximately 15 minutes, it seems considerably longer and manages to come alive only near the end, with the appearance of Mieko Harada's haunting Snow Woman, who tries unsuccessfully to hypnotize "I" and lead him to an icy death. But this legendary character had been depicted to greater effect in other films, notably in Masaki Kobayashi's *Kwaidan* (Kaidan, 1964), which seems to have directly inspired Kurosawa's approach to this section. The cinematography, makeup, and costume design are exquisite, but nothing is new. Another problem is that we simply do not care for the mountaineers, because they are not developed characters, including Akira Terao's adult "I."

As described by Tom Carson, "Nodding emphatically at everyone else's speeches so we'll register how deep they are, [Terao's "I" is] like a cosmic Bill Moyers."[24] Kurosawa is more interested in creating mood and atmosphere, and since the segment was obviously, painfully filmed on a soundstage—but trying to look otherwise, the very opposite of *Kwaidan*—it comes off as extremely lightweight, especially when compared with the stunning location work on *Snow Trail* and *Dersu Uzala*.

Visually, "The Tunnel" is more successful, particularly when "I" nervously walks through the eerie underground passage. After the vivid use of color in the first two segments, Kurosawa's dominant use of blacks here is impressive. But the makeup of the soldiers that come to haunt him is overdone, and with the exception of the episode's coda, in which "I" is threatened by a (presumably) rabid German shepherd, overtly symbolic of wartime militarism, the segment is again emotionally distant and remote.

"Crows" fails utterly, with its stunt casting of Martin Scorsese as Van Gogh. His beard is overdyed a bright red-orange, like Kool-Aid, and inexplicably he responds to Akira Terao's Japanese in New York–accented English. (According to Terao, the scene was originally longer, and all the dialogue was to have been spoken in French. The change was made at the last minute.[25]) "I" has literally stepped into the world of Van Gogh's paintings, and the HDTV-produced visual effects of "Crows" are unsuccessful. On movie screens especially, these images lose whatever fancy Kurosawa was after, because they never appear to be anything other than video wizardry blurrily transferred to film. The actual sets designed by Yoshiro Muraki and patterned after Van Gogh's *Drawbridge at Arles* are more effective, but in the end "Crows" has all the kitsch of a Disneyland ride.

"Mt. Fuji in Red," which deals with a nuclear-bred holocaust of swirling radioactive clouds and the eruption of the long-dormant volcano, has problems of a different sort. Beyond its didactic preaching, Kurosawa incurred considerable headaches from ILM, George Lucas's special-effects company, over the depiction of Mt. Fuji. The American effects crew failed to understand the deeply personal (and, for some, religious) and singularly Japanese view of its poetic qualities. Part of the fascination with Mt. Fuji for the Japanese is its ever-changing appearance; the sun and clouds cast myriad colors upon it, rendering its slopes almost transcendental. For the Americans, Mt. Fuji was just another mountain, and its eruption looks more like something out of a lost world than a Kurosawa film. But even if the special effects had worked, the segment is awkwardly structured, badly staged, and fails to capture a genuine sense of horror.

"The Demon" is another dreary, Beckett-like post-apocalyptic set piece, marred by silly-looking gargantuan dandelions and an overly made-up Chosuke Ikariya transformed into the title character after being exposed to intense radiation. Ikariya, known to Japanese audiences as one of the leaders of The Drifters, a lowbrow comedy team tremendously popular in the 1960s and '70s, adds to the piece's incongruity.

"Village of the Windmills," in which "I" travels to a town that has abandoned modern technology, fares much better, thanks to its gentle and, in this case, genuine autobiographical basis (a childhood trip to his father's remote Akita village). But even this segment is undermined by the town crier–like delivery of its pro-nature preaching. The sermon nearly works, though, thanks to the casting of eighty-five-year-old Chishu Ryu as the 103-

year-old man. Filmed at a horseradish farm near the Mansui River in Nagano, "Village of the Windmills" has a straightforwardness and delicate theme that makes up—albeit too late—for the segments preceding it. The joyous funeral procession at its conclusion, with beautifully costumed extras marching through the village to the surprising but oddly appropriate strains of Ippolitov Ivanov's "Caucasian Sketches," closes the film—at last—with another moment of beguiling fancy.

The absence of collaborators on the screenplay is keenly felt (although Honda may have co-written with Kurosawa to some extent). The script is preachy and uneven, especially in "Mt. Fuji in Red." "When I look back on his life," observed Shinobu Hashimoto, who co-wrote many of Kurosawa's best scripts, "in the beginning he wrote scripts by himself. Then after the war he would have somebody write the script; then he would go through it and write a final draft. And after that, several writers would get together and write a script from the beginning. And then, finally, he was writing by himself again. He had come full circle."[26] The four scripts he wrote following *Dreams* were all adapted from books Kurosawa loved, and the results would be much better.

For all its faults, *Dreams* is undeniably a beautiful film to look at. Takao Saito and Masaharu Ueda's camerawork is sumptuous and Wada's costumes beautiful and varied. Shinichiro Ikebe's score is much improved from his work on *Kagemusha*. The film did reasonably well in Japan and placed fourth on *Kinema Jumpo*'s "Best Ten" list.

Akira Terao (b. 1947), who appears as Kurosawa in six of the eight episodes, is the son of actor and stage director Jukichi Uno. In 1964, Terao formed a band, played bass at the height of the "Group Sounds" era of Japanese pop, and recorded an album, "Forever, Forever," in 1966. He made his film debut with his father in Kei Kumai's *Tunnel to the Sun* (1968), which starred Toshiro Mifune. While continuing his singing career, Terao first gained prominence in Yoji Yamada's *The Village* (Harakara) in 1975 and subsequently worked with Yamada on several more films; frequently he appears in Japanese television dramas. His place in Japanese pop culture was cemented with the song "Ruby Ring" ("Rubii no yubiwa") in 1981, but Terao was also something of a one-hit wonder. He has never been a box-office draw, but his expressive, weary features and large, sad eyes were effectively used by Kurosawa.

At Cannes, Kurosawa joked with reporters not once but twice, predicting that Japanese audiences would "hate" the film.[27] Journalists laughed, but Kurosawa was not completely happy with the film, either. "I wanted to have more moments of pure and perfect cinema with *Dreams*, but while I did my best, I don't think I got much more than two or three. . . ."[28] He's right. *Dreams* comes alive when Kurosawa is inclined to show rather than tell. It has less dialogue than any other film he directed, yet it seems talkier than most. Kurosawa was disappointed with the picture, but not for long—before *Dreams* was even released, he was working on a new film.

Rhapsody in August received a good deal of attention as Kurosawa's first fully Japanese-produced film since *Dodes'ka-den*. The picture was allied with Shochiku, with which he had not worked since *The Idiot* four decades earlier. *Kagemusha*, *Ran*, and *Dreams* had, more or less, all been successful—but those pictures used the names of George Lucas and Steven Spielberg to make them more palatable, more commercial to Japanese audiences, who now preferred Hollywood movies. The extent of the changes within the industry that had occurred since *Dodes'ka-den* can been seen in the film's financing. *Rhapsody* was produced by Kurosawa Production and financed by Shochiku and Feature Film Enterprise No. 2, an investment partnership composed of no fewer than eighteen companies, including Hakuhodo, Inc., Japan's second-largest advertising firm; Imagica, the film laboratory formerly known as Toyo Developing; and Kawasaki Enterprises, Inc.[29] The project, estimated to cost around $10 million, was announced in May 1990, just prior to Kurosawa's scheduled appearance at the Academy Awards.[30]

"I started with *Rhapsody in August* before I had completely severed myself from *Dreams* and thought it might trouble me," Kurosawa said. "But as I started to come to [the] set, I was soon engrossed in this new film."[31]

In both tone and visual style, *Rhapsody in August* is quite different from anything Kurosawa had made in decades. With its deliberate pacing and low-key, multigenerational familial conflicts, it somewhat resembles the later films of Ozu, though Kurosawa's lifelong concerns and interests are ever-present. Indeed, its framework and many of its issues recall those first introduced in *Record of a Living Being*. Both films have an elderly protagonist haunted by images of the atomic bomb, materialistic children, innocent, impressionable grandchildren, and a visitor from abroad.

The film is based on *In the Stew* (Nabe no naka), the Akutagawa Prize–winning novel by Kiyoko Murata. "I read the original novel while shooting *Dreams*," Kurosawa said, "and thought that the portrayal of the family, which is the core of the story, is wonderful. And the old woman within the family is very special. In the film this grandmother will be very active and the focal point. . . . However, underlying this film is a tragedy called nuclear bombs. It's been 45 years since the end of the war but radioactivity is still killing people. The screenplay touches on that."[32]

Kurosawa adapted the novel into a screenplay in an extraordinarily short time, about fifteen days, in Kyoto.[33] For his script he made a number of changes, most notably shifting the locale to the outskirts of Nagasaki and making the woman's dead husband a victim of the atomic bomb dropped there on August 9, 1945.

The screenplay concerns Kane (pronounced "Kah-nay"), who is portrayed by Sachiko Murase. She is an elderly widow spending the summer with her four grandchildren (Hidetaka Yoshioka, Tomoko Otakara, Mie Suzuki, and Mitsunori Isaki). The children seem very Americanized; all but the youngest wear T-shirts bearing the names of American universities. One set of parents has flown to Hawaii to visit Clark (Richard Gere), a half-Japanese cousin whose father, Kane's brother, is dying. Kane, however, is reluctant to visit this brother she's not seen in decades. At first the children are annoyed by their grandmother's lack of interest in going to Hawaii, and by her old-style, rural existence: she has no TV, no washing machine, and cooks bland meals they don't like. But they love her and, during the course of their stay, enjoy listening to stories about her family, acquiring her appreciation of such simple pleasures as gazing at the moon. Unlike their parents, the children come to embrace Grandma's old-fashioned ways. Eventually, she agrees to go to Hawaii to visit her ailing brother, but only after attending the memorial services for her husband and other victims of the bomb. The children are ecstatic about the trip and send Clark a telegram announcing their arrival.

Three of the children take a bus over the mountains and visit Nagasaki, where Kane's husband, a teacher, died in the blast along with most of his students. They visit his school and see a set of monkey bars, deformed and blackened by the bomb, that serve as a memorial. It dawns on them that perhaps the reason Kane is reluctant to go to Hawaii is that she hates America for dropping the bomb. But when they return, Kane insists, "I neither like nor dislike America." Both Japanese and Americans died, she says. "The war was to blame."

The children's parents (Hisashi Igawa, Toshie Negishi, Choichiro Kawarasaki, and Narumi Kayashima) return from Hawaii, arriving at Grandma's house with dollar signs in their eyes, and mull over their newly found, wealthy relative and his luxurious lifestyle. They talk excitedly about the possibility of going to work at Clark's enormous pineapple plant. But the children recognize that their parents are using Grandma to win Clark over. Clark writes that he's coming to Nagasaki. The parents assume the children's letter offended him by referring to the memorial service. "Americans don't like to be reminded of the bomb," one parent says. They think Clark's coming to Japan to "call the deal off."

But when Clark arrives, he surprises everyone with his genuine concern for Grandma's feelings, and his deeply felt empathy for the victims of Nagasaki. This impresses the children, and the parents feel foolish. But then Clark's father dies, and suddenly he returns to America for the funeral. Learning of her brother's death, Kane feels tremendous guilt for not visiting him earlier. As the forty-fifth anniversary of the bombing approaches, she begins reliving the emotional horror of that terrible day, which her children diagnose as episodic senility. Then, during a cloudburst, Kane runs off. As she stands against the fierce wind and pounding rain, her children and grandchildren race after her.

Sachiko Murase, wonderful as Kane, was born in 1905 and was one of the founders of Haiyu-za, Japan's leading repertory theater. Onstage from the age of nineteen, she was part of Japan's leftist, avant-garde movement and was drawn to the Western realism of Ibsen, Chekhov, and O'Neill. During the war, when the Japanese military closed such theaters, she turned to reading the classics on Japanese radio, but was frequently compelled to read wartime propaganda also. After the war, at the Haiya-za's home in Roppongi, she played both Japanese and Western roles, including Nora in *A Doll's House* and Anya in *The Cherry Orchard*. In 1965 she was awarded the Ministry of Education Outstanding Performance prize for playing a courageous mother in *Japanese Ghosts*, a drama about poison gas manufactured on an island near Hiroshima during World War II. Murase went into semi-retirement in the 1980s, but returned to the stage to star in a play adapted from *In the Stew*, the same novel that served as the basis for *Rhapsody in August*.[34] She had appeared in a smattering of films beginning in the mid-1930s, including *Love in a Teacup* (1953) and the Kurosawa-scripted *Tomorrow I'll Be a Fire-Tree* (1955). She also appeared in films for Mizoguchi and Keisuke Kinoshita, but generally her roles were small. She had a major role in Yoshishige Yoshida's *A Promise* (Ningen no yakusoku) in 1986, but that appears to have been her only major credit since the 1960s.

"When I first read the script," she said, "I wanted to refuse the role . . .

because she is what the Japanese call a 'kettle head.' Bald!" (Exposure to radiation had caused Kane's hair to fall out.) She described Kurosawa as a "gentle man" in his direction of a "difficult and demanding performance. . . . I was shocked to receive the offer from Mr. Kurosawa. I had heard many times that he was a frightening director, but after reading the script, I was impressed by his comprehension of the war and his compassion for the suffering on both sides. To him, each side was as destructive as possible and would do anything to win."[35]

Though not a direct victim of the atomic bomb, Murase had lost her husband of thirty years three decades earlier and identified with Kane's loss. She added, "Being an aged woman, I often fall into the situation of incomprehension. I know the feeling. . . . The way Mr. Kurosawa wanted me to act was, I knew, the right thing to do, but Kane was too good, not like me. I didn't want to be a perfect old lady, but I didn't dare ask him to change it." Asked if her own personality was like that of the lovable Kane, she would say only, "I wonder."[36] Murase died in 1993.

During production, Kurosawa remembered casting the film's other pivotal role: "I met Richard Gere for the first time at a New York party in connection with *Ran*. Then we bumped into each other on several other occasions. When we met at a party to celebrate my receiving an Oscar and my birthday [in Tokyo], I explained to him the role in *Rhapsody* and asked if he was interested. He was overjoyed." Gere's interest in Asia and Lamaism impressed Kurosawa as well; here was an American movie star already versed in the sutra, "perhaps," Kurosawa suggested, "better than some Japanese."[37]

"He was wearing the dark glasses he always wears and had a big smile on his face," Gere recalled. "And in the middle of this party we started jabbering through our interpreter. . . . Of course I agreed to do it. And it turned out to be a short, wonderful experience working with one of the great masters of our time."[38]

Just prior to being offered the role of Kane's nephew, Gere was at the peak of his popularity, having starred opposite Julia Roberts in *Pretty Woman* (1990). "He was making several million dollars a picture at the time," recalled co-producer Mike Inoue, "and we said we couldn't afford to pay that kind of money. Right away he said, 'I'll work free for Kurosawa.' I hated to take advantage of what he said, so I offered a minor sum of money which he kindly accepted. We also offered to pay the expenses of friends he wanted to bring with him to Japan. He brought Cindy Crawford with him. We used to stay in the same inn around the shooting locations and spent wonderful days with them.

"I originally had a terrific Italian makeup guy do some eye pieces," Gere said of the efforts made to convince viewers he was half-Japanese. "But Kurosawa liked the way I looked. However, I had to do *something*. . . . So we fooled around with my eyebrows, cutting them back, reshaping my eyes with extending lines, and flattening out planes. But in the end it's quite a simple makeup job."

After nearly three weeks with a Japanese dialogue coach, Gere joined the production for four weeks beginning on August 6, 1990.[40] "An old friend of mine, Peter Grilli, who grew up in Japan and is totally bilingual, did a tape for me, and I used his inflections and tone. I got so used to [learning my Japanese dialogue that way that] I knew what I was saying, but it sounded—as it was supposed to—like a character who obviously didn't speak Japanese often."[41]

Many Americans criticized Gere's casting. Physically, he doesn't look half-Japanese in the slightest, but otherwise he is quite up to the role, and his Japanese is perfectly adequate for the character. Unlike Martin Scorsese in *Dreams*, Gere gives a relaxed, natural, and sensitive performance.

The film was shot in the spring and summer of 1991, most of it in Chichibu, Saitama Prefecture, where Kane's farmhouse was constructed especially for the film. "I decided to have this set built here rather than using one in the studio because this way I can discover different camera angles," Kurosawa said. "Although there are always weather limitations, freedom of camera angles is much preferred to limited angles in studios. Today, because of the rain yesterday, the ground has a reddish tint. Usually summer soil is white and very bright. That reflects in a farmhouse and creates summer atmosphere. Thus, the feeling of a farmhouse in the strong summer sun will be created. . . . I chose this site because the mountains around here resemble the ones in Nagasaki."[42]

"On the last day of shooting," Gere said, "the cast had a farewell dinner for me in Nagasaki. And Kurosawa had brought photographs of the scenes he'd shot with me. I looked through them and realized we'd really done a lot of work in a very few days. I was leaving the next morning, and when I got up from the table, this giant of a man also got up and gave me a very big bear hug. And I remember how wonderful that felt. Heart to heart. That was my biggest memory of *Rhapsody in August*."[43]

The film received mixed reviews in Japan, but still ranked third on *Kinema Jumpo*'s "Best Ten" list. However, reaction in the United States was less enthusiastic, when not downright hostile. Not since *Red Beard* had a Kurosawa film been so summarily dismissed, so accused of being what it wasn't: didactic, anti-American, if not fascist, sentimental, and dull. Bad reviews killed its chances commercially, and it did mediocre business in the States.

In the end, *Rhapsody in August* is one of Kurosawa's finest yet most misunderstood films. Reviewers mistook its almost minimalist script and deliberate pacing as simplistic rather than straightforward. Quite unlike *Kagemusha* and *Dreams*, where theme dominates all other concerns, *Rhapsody* is much more obliquely stated, set against a complex family drama that more than holds its own. It is gently humorous, ironic, moving, and at all times intriguing.

Most American critics thought differently. Kurosawa was accused of being both overtly and inadequately literal, when in fact he boils down the horror of the atomic bomb to the abstract, to simple images that speak volumes, images wholly believable in their impact on the children. When they visit their dead uncle's school, it's implied that they go there partly out of boredom but are moved, as we are, by the haunting image of that tangled jungle gym—for all its ILM wizardry, the eruption of Mt. Fuji in *Dreams* isn't half as effective. Critics complained that the children's declarations of empathy weren't enough. What they missed was that they speak with the directness and honesty children so often do. They know not the unbridled, selfish materialism and political diplomacy of their parents. (They want to go to Hawaii for the exotic adventure of it, not economic gain.) And while American films had in the 1980s and '90s become deeply cynical, its characters in studio pictures increasingly dark and acerbic, Clark is nothing more or less than a decent man, idealized perhaps, but equally believable in his empathy.

And, unlike in *Dreams*, Kurosawa shows far more than he tells. In sharp contrast to the razzle-dazzle of *Dreams*'s showy opticals, *Rhapsody* offers natural, static shots of blackened statues that survived the bomb. Its survivors, several blinded by the blast, silently lay flowers at the memorial to the dead classmates. In one scene, Kane is visited by an old woman whose husband likewise died in the bombing. They sit together face-to-face for several hours without saying a word. For them, speaking isn't necessary, and this says more than reams of dialogue ever could.

Nor do the children see newsreel footage of charred bodies amid radiated rubble. Instead, Kurosawa shows his audience something equally disturbing and compelling: recalling the blast, Kane likens the explosion over the mountains' rim to an omnipotent, single eye, looming godlike in the distance. During a thunderstorm, as lightning flashes around, Kane relives the terror of the bomb, much like Mifune's Nakajima in *Record of a Living Being*. Instinctively she throws white sheets over her grandchildren, asserting that many survived Nagasaki because they wore white.

Many of *Rhapsody*'s best moments come without comment or explanation. At dusk, when the children return from the Nagasaki memorials, they see Grandma running toward them. But they look at her very differently. Now they have some comprehension of what she has endured. She realizes that they've changed, too. Again there is little dialogue, and the effect is quietly powerful. As survivors of the bomb chant Buddhist sutras, Clark and one of the children observe an army of ants purposefully making a single line in and out of the forest. The camera moves away from the service (though we continue to hear the chanting) as the camera observes the ants climbing up and down a single rose. The film's ambiguous ending, with Kane running through the rain, likewise is unexplained, unresolved.

The surprising affirmation, rather than tragedy, of this final sequence is, like the ant scene, linked to Schubert's *"Heidenröselein,"* the picture's leitmotif. The oldest child (Hidetaka Yoshioka, famous as Tora-san's nephew) is determined to fix his grandfather's harmonium. As he attempts to tune the instrument, he frequently plays excerpts of Schubert's piece, which the children also sing. The lyrics are about the glory of a single rose found in a field that, though it is never explicitly stated, is likened to Kane. Thus, when Kane's umbrella snaps inside out as she stands almost frozen amid the fierce wind and drenching rain, *"Heidenröselein"* bursts from the soundtrack in a chorus of children's voices and full orchestration. All this suggests that her indomitable spirit, like a rose in an empty field, like the ants ascending its stem, will endure insofar as her lessons will be remembered, if not by her own children, then by theirs.

When *Rhapsody* was previewed in March 1991, and the American media began making accusations about the film's so-called anti-American sentiments, Shochiku began getting nervous about reaction in Japan. In a practice fairly common to large-scale Japanese productions, the studio asked fifty of the country's leading corporations, many of whom had financed *Rhapsody*, to push ticket sales to their employees. Shochiku argued that the film had "an important message for international understanding."[44] They also launched a pre-order ticket campaign, in which ¥300 ($2.12) of the ¥1,300 advance ticket price would go to the Japan Bird Protection Association, money used to help birds victimized in oil dumps during the Gulf War. Shochiku hoped to turn over $1.4 million to the association by the end of the summer.[45]

At the Oscars, Kurosawa was approached by representatives from Orion Classics to distribute the film theatrically in America, and a deal was finalized by August 1990. "We've handled three of his films before, so it was a relationship we wanted to continue to cultivate," said Orion acquisitions vice president Marcie Bloom. *Ran* had done reasonably well theatrically in America, and had been Orion's bestselling foreign video title, with 40,000 videotapes sold by 1990. "Shochiku is financing the film, but we had never worked with them before, so Kurosawa introduced us all to each other at Cannes, and we found we were all speaking the same language on this film after all."[46]

In March 1991, *Rhapsody* was screened for non-Japanese journalists in Tokyo. Many reacted with inexplicable outrage. They argued that "the film is no more than pro-Japanese propaganda as it focuses only on the tragedy and suffering of a family victimized by the American bombing. The film neglects any discussion of Japan's involvement in the war. Kurosawa denies that his conception of the film was in any way triggered by any political notions or ambitions, but is simply a sensitive story of one family during a historic period in time."[47]

Not that Kurosawa hadn't anticipated trouble before filming had even started. Shochiku head Toru Okuyama had said the previous summer that the director was worried that "his real intention in making this picture might not be correctly interpreted."[48] He could not have been more accurate.

The absurdly wrongheaded reaction was perhaps a response to the "economic miracle" of Japan and its blockbuster economy, then at its height, and residue from the Reagan-Bush/Thatcher era of conservatism, particularly the misplaced, flag-waving patriotism of the Gulf War. A review in *The Economist* was typical, ludicrously charging that the film "[deals with] the lack of Japanese remorse for the second world war and its feeling of 'victimization' by America. . . . It includes a scene where Richard Gere . . . tearfully asks [Kane's] forgiveness for the United States when he learns that his grandfather [sic] was killed in the bombing of Nagasaki. Some foreign critics have called the film 'fascist.' "[49]

But *The Economist* was dead wrong. No such scene occurs in the film. What dozens of important critics completely misread is a scene where Clark apologizes not on behalf of America for dropping the bomb but rather for his insensitivity in pressing Kane to come to Hawaii on the anniversary of her husband's death and while Nagasaki mourned the deaths of its citizens forty-five years earlier. (Clark does not ask for forgiveness "tearfully," either.) Western critics misinterpreted this sequence, because Clark's actions are very Japanese. He had no way of knowing Kane's husband died in Nagasaki, because her own children withheld that from him. Nevertheless, he, like Gondo in *High and Low*, accepts responsibility for the misunderstanding. At no point does Clark apologize for America dropping the bomb.

The other scene that infuriated conservatives comes earlier, when three of the children visit the Nagasaki memorial site, Peace Park, where beautifully eloquent statues contributed from different countries around the world mourn the dead. One of the children asks why there's no statue from America, and another answers, "America dropped the bomb." This is a statement of fact, yet conservative Americans took umbrage at this. As one character in the film astutely asks, "Do [Americans] resent being reminded of it?" However, in shooting this sequence, Kurosawa did choose to emphasize statues from Communist countries, and in so doing, he makes the only really questionable choice in his direction of the picture, for it compromises what is an otherwise apolitical story.

The film was criticized for its focus on Kane, a victim of the bomb, without addressing Japanese militarism, the bombing of Pearl Harbor, and the atrocities in China. But that's simply not what the movie is about, and to criticize it for this is beside the point. The film isn't about Sino genocide or Pearl Harbor: it's the story of an old Japanese woman and her family. Their concerns are the film's concerns and are personal and immediate by design. The story reflects the suffering endured by many civilian Japanese who had no part in their country's aggressions.

Likewise, instead of the film's being critical of America and Americans, just the reverse is true. Clark is as idealized as Sidney Poitier was in representing black Americans in *Guess Who's Coming to Dinner* (1967). Instead, it is the children's selfish parents who receive the brunt of Kurosawa's criticism. Moreover, as the children begin to comprehend the enormity of the tragedy at Nagasaki, Kurosawa's camera shows other Japanese even more critically. At the Nagasaki memorial they snap their cameras and buy ice cream from vendors, as if it were an amusement park. Extreme telephoto shots of the children wandering through the modern, rebuilt Nagasaki express a kind of bewilderment at how quickly the city and its people have forgotten its terrible place in history.

Against the tide of criticism, Georgia Brown of *The Village Voice* countered: "Given the current climate of mutual paranoia—fueled by [President] Bush's stupid response when questioned about an apology for the atomic bomb ('Not from the president!')—the film will probably rouse some chauvinistic hostility. Maybe when the 50th anniversary of Hiroshima and Nagasaki arrives it will be possible, with the predictable media coverage, to get Americans to admit dropping the bombs was one of the worst acts of terrorism ever perpetrated. Possible. Perhaps not likely, considering the magnitude of guilt, but possible."[50]

However, most Western reviews echoed Peter McGill's in London's *Observer*: "*Rhapsody in August* is perhaps Kurosawa's most embarrassingly insipid and cloying sentimental lapse from his own rigid standards."[51] "The . . . film has scenes of haunting brilliance," added Mark Schilling for *Screen International*, "but its underlying tone is that of a typical Japanese memorial service for the bombing victims: ritualized remembrance, historical one-sidedness. Western audiences . . . may well find his way of presenting it less than compelling."[52]

Vincent Canby saw the criticisms coming: "Long regarded at home and abroad as the least Japanese of great Japanese directors, in part because his work has been so widely hailed outside Japan, Akira Kurosawa has now made his most Japanese film in years and, as might be expected, he has been damned for it. When his new 'Rhapsody in August' was shown out-of-competition at this year's Cannes festival, the critics were inclined to dismiss it for the simplicity of its structure and its moralizing tone. The inference was that Mr. Kurosawa . . . was giving in to age, losing his touch. Not so. The master is as vigorous and complex as ever, though now impatient with the world in which he has been making movies so productively since 1943."[53]

"It is touching to watch," said *Time*'s Richard Schickel, "a bond being created between wise age and innocent youth and wonderful to experience the grace of Kurosawa's art as he explores, with a new simplicity, one of his preoccupying themes: man's inability to control, or even think coherently about, the mighty historical forces he so often and carelessly unleashes."[54]

Henry Sheehan of *LA Weekly* agreed. "It's unfortunate that this rebuke to Japanese reticence should have been misconstrued by some critics as a nationalistic screed. This is a profound and masterful film that rewards careful viewing; rarely has the human part of history been attended so thoughtfully."[55]

Kevin Thomas called *Rhapsody* "the most intimate drama of his career. A film of the utmost simplicity and serene beauty. . . . Yet its gentleness is deceptive, for it is through [the] family that Kurosawa . . . touches upon the eternal themes of war and reconciliation. . . . From the veteran Murase, he elicits a portrayal of the utmost eloquence—and a sturdy, common-sense earthiness. As for Gere, who blends in the film's ensemble easily and speaks almost entirely in Japanese, he has been given a rare opportunity to play a thoroughly decent man of intelligence and sensitivity; it's surprisingly easy to accept him as a Eurasian."[56]

Playboy gave *Rhapsody* 3½ stars, writing: "Japanese director Akira Kurosawa, arguably the greatest living filmmaker, has made *Rhapsody*—his 29th movie—a rueful, conciliatory and quietly humorous family drama. . . . In [his] almost delicate treatment of U.S. guilt and corresponding resentment in Japan, the younger Japanese—who wear American-style T-shirts and seem uniformly Westernized—appear more embarrassed than angry over a past as distant to them as a samurai legend. Only the living relatives remember the terror that *Rhapsody in August* brings back with the haunting beauty of a dark reflection in a lily pond."[57]

But *Variety* thought the first half "surprisingly static" and the film overall "very much an old man's film, [that] almost completely lacks the visual excitement Kurosawa once brought to the cinema. Scene after scene is flatly staged and shot, as characters just sit around and talk. It would be dull were it not for the evident sincerity with which Kurosawa is pushing his message of reconciliation between America and Japan for the past, though it almost seems a redundant message these days."[58]

The film did well in Europe, earning $5 million before it even opened in Japan, where it did respectable business; box-office estimates ran upward of $10 million in rentals.[59]

Kurosawa's next film, *Madadayo* ("Not Yet") would, like *Rhapsody in August*, be financed through a tangled web of Japanese conglomerates. Kurosawa Production would co-produce the $11.9 million film with the reorganized Daiei (his first film for them since *Rashomon* forty-two years earlier), now under the corporate arm of the Tokuma Group, one of Japan's leading publishers of books, music, and computer software. Also involved in the production was the Japanese conglomerate Dentsu, Inc.; Toho agreed to distribute *Madadayo* in Japan, while Daiei retained international rights.[60]

Kurosawa's intentions for the film were stated in its press materials and program: "This motion picture describes the heartwarming and pleasant relationship between Professor Hyakken Uchida and his former students. There is something very precious which has been all but forgotten. The enviable world of warm hearts. I hope that all the people who have seen this motion picture will leave the theater refreshed with broad smiles on their faces."[61] In a 1992 press conference Kurosawa added, "We used to visit our teachers at their homes. What we've lost in education today is the importance of the teacher as a human being quite apart from what he teaches."[62]

Kurosawa regarded the film as a response to the "economic miracle" of contemporary Japan, a concern that *Rhapsody in August* also addresses and that he felt was dehumanizing his countrymen. "It was a better time," he said of the film's war and postwar setting. "Of course, it was also a very hard time, but when I look back on it, human relations were warmer. I have bad memories of Japanese militarism, but teachers and students were closer than they are now."[63]

The works of Hyakken Uchida (1889–1971), a German-language professor-turned-writer, are still popular in Japan for their gentle humor and wry observations on life. Uchida's early novels, *Hades* (Meido) and *The Procession to Ryojun* (Ryojun nyujo-shiki), were noted for their dreamlike imagery. But it was his bestselling *Essays by Hyakken* (Hyakkien zuihitsu) that established him as one of Japan's great writers. Discussing a wide range of subjects, from haiku to locomotives, Uchida became a much-loved, eccentric figure for his simple yet profound insight into the art of living. His later works, including an account of the Tokyo air raids, *Tokyo Burnt Out* (Tokyo shojin), and a collection of essays about his beloved *Nora, My Lost Cat* (Noraya), became instant classics. Uchida's postwar life became the basis of *Madadayo*.

In the role of Uchida, Kurosawa cast seventy-seven-year-old Tatsuo Matsumura. After playing the repulsive uncle in *Dodes'ka-den*, Matsumura had returned to the lovable middle-management and harried-father figures for which he was best known. During the 1970s he became the second of three actors to play Oi-chan, Tora-san's uncle in the long-running film series.

The middle-aged students were played by actors with whom Kurosawa had worked before: Hisashi Igawa, one of the drunks in *Dodes'ka-den* and the selfish son in *Rhapsody in August*; Akira Terao, Kurosawa's alter ego in *Dreams*; and Masayuki Yui, who had played Ieyasu Tokugawa in *Kagemusha* and Tengo in *Ran*. The other key student was portrayed by newcomer George Tokoro (b. 1955), a television comedian and singer-songwriter, who had a hit with "Scenes of Winter Suite: Gamble Rhapsody" ("Gamble kyosokyoku—kumikyoku: fuyu no jokei") and was the author of some thirty books. Hidetaka Yoshioka, the oldest grandchild in *Rhapsody in August*, had a brief role in *Madadayo* as one of Uchida's students, while Yoshitaka

Zushi, the boy in *Red Beard* and *Dodes'ka-den*, turns up in a small part as one of his neighbors.

In the pivotal role of Uchida's wife, Kurosawa cast his favorite actress, Kyoko Kagawa. It was the first time they had worked together since *Red Beard* almost thirty years earlier, and she is luminous in the role. "Not many women appeared in Mr. Kurosawa's films," Kagawa recalled. "In *Madadayo* and *High and Low*, I was virtually the only one. But these were very important roles. I had to watch each male actor very carefully and react, even if I didn't have any lines. That was very challenging. I couldn't stand out, but I also had to make an impression. It was a difficult balance.

"Mr. Kurosawa didn't give us instructions about acting. We had to direct ourselves. He never said, 'Do this' or 'Do that.' He'd watch all the actors and actresses, and if someone's instincts were good, he would run with it. Mr. [Kenji] Mizoguchi would ask me, 'Are you collecting?' which meant reacting to my acting partner. Mr. Kurosawa used to say the reflection or the reaction was very important. Not the details or the format, but if you express your emotion, that's everything. You have to react."[64]

Kagawa recalled a relaxed atmosphere on the set of *Madadayo*. "We went on location to Gotemba, and also shot at Toho. During lunch breaks Mr. Kurosawa told us many wonderful stories, but they were all filled with lessons about acting. Matsumura and I had played a couple before, on television, and this helped our performances, too. We had to listen carefully."[65]

Madadayo's story is even more elemental and straightforward than that of *Rhapsody in August*. The film uses a series of anecdotal essays, like Uchida's writings, in place of a conventional narrative. Uchida retires from teaching but maintains a warm relationship with his former students, who love him dearly. There are gatherings at the teacher's home, in which Uchida regales his students with funny, observant stories lifted from his essays. His students' devotion intensifies as the professor faces a series of crises: his house is destroyed during Allied bombing raids, and he and his wife are forced to live in a tiny shack. Nora, Uchida's beloved cat, disappears, and the students launch a citywide search for the animal. And, of course, the professor gets older and increasingly frail.

One of the challenges Kurosawa faced was in translating Uchida's warm humor, consisting of a form of *rakugo*, a style of Japanese writing that plays on singularly Japanese words or expressions, to the screen. "My translator has been trying hard to find English equivalents for the jokes," Kurosawa said, "but it's very difficult. But I think foreign audiences will understand the humor of Uchida's character—he was a very funny man."[66] Though the precise use of language is lost on non-Japanese speakers, the film's English subtitles make perfectly clear the essence of Uchida's gentle, astute intent.

Madadayo cost $12 million. It was argued, not without some justification, that given its small cast and limited action, the film might have been made much less expensively. Such films in Japan typically cost around $2–3 million. But the care Kurosawa afforded through his extensive rehearsals, his attention to detail in its production, is reflected in the finished film. For a picture that consists mainly of students and their teacher sitting around talking, visually *Madadayo* is a film of immense beauty.

Shooting began in February 1992, with a schedule stretched over fourteen months due to its dependence on the change of seasons for its exteriors.[67] Uchida's postwar shack was built in Gotemba. For scenes showing the other side of the shack, Kurosawa had art director Yoshiro Muraki build a set on a large field of sand on the slopes of Mt. Fuji.[68] Prewar Tokyo streets were re-created on the lot at Toho.

Once again, Kurosawa courted the media during filming, knowing full well the value of press coverage. Three busloads of reporters were brought in to the Gotemba location, and Kurosawa himself conducted a personal tour of the sets of Uchida's burned-out neighborhood. "He is becoming more aware of the importance of marketing, of making money," noted author and reporter Yuichiro Nishimura.[69]

Production wrapped at the end of September, ahead of schedule, and the director held a 90-minute press conference in Tokyo to announce its completion. Asked why he had made three movies in quick succession Kurosawa joked, "I don't have much more time to live. I have to hurry." More seriously he added, "Japanese directors are very poor. We must work to eat. When I finish a film I get very lonely. I want to see the crew again. The doctor says to rest, but I don't like to rest. So I go on." He ignored questions about working again with Mifune and declined to discuss a $500,000 lawsuit he had filed against Toho over residuals from the airings of his films on Wowow, a cable television network. He did, however, offer moral support for fellow director Juzo Itami, whose recent controversial film *Minbo: or The Gentle Art of Japanese Extortion* (Minbo no onna, 1992) had led to a vicious assault on the director by a *yakuza* thug.[70]

Madadayo was greeted with reviews even less enthusiastic than those for *Rhapsody in August*. Mark Schilling, who didn't much care for *Rhapsody*, thought *Madadayo* worse. Schilling's condescending review in *Screen Interna-*

tional was typical of the hostility that greeted the film: "Akira Kurosawa has lost touch not only with his international audience, but with his filmmaking instincts. As though to answer domestic critics who claim that he panders to foreign tastes, Kurosawa has written a script filled with untranslatable puns and awash in a 'typically Japanese'—and unexportable—sentimentality. . . . On the strength of *Madadayo*, it may be time [for Kurosawa] to call it a day."[71]

David Sterritt of *The Christian Science Monitor*, who saw *Madadayo* at Cannes in May 1993, admired Kurosawa's "blend of sincerity and tenacity," but reported that the film's reception there was in marked contrast to that which had greeted *Kagemusha* thirteen years earlier. "Unfortunately, this two-hour-plus drama has enough dull spots—talky speeches, unfunny jokes, painfully slow story developments—to drive unreceptive spectators out of the theater long before it was over . . . and I was tempted to make an early exit when the narrative threatened to bog down altogether on a few occasions."[72]

With *Rhapsody* and *Madadayo*, Kurosawa's style had changed, and critics around the world resented him for it. "It's a kind of unpleasant subject," said Mike Inoue. "You know, I always said to myself, You take a Picasso, his paintings during his younger days. They were pleasing to the eyes of an amateur. But as he got older, he got more abstract—it's very difficult for people who are not experts to judge whether it's a good painting or not. We can say the same thing about Kurosawa's later films. His tastes changed along with his age. *Madadayo* is a heartwarming story, and he thought the audience would leave the theater feeling that way. Japanese audiences that saw the later films went to see a Kurosawa film with a lot of action. In that sense they were disappointed. They didn't see what they expected to."[73]

Many critics misread Kurosawa's treatment, claiming that he was positioning himself in the role of the professor. "I had never really realized myself that it would be seen that way," the director admitted. "I simply wanted to portray a wonderful person. I don't want to teach lessons."[74] In fact, the character is much more like that of Seiji Tachikawa, Kurosawa's own beloved teacher, and in later scenes Uchida bears a physical resemblance to Kajiro Yamamoto. Uchida and the director share many of the same concerns that all men do in their old age, but Kurosawa was hardly the soft-spoken, diminutive Uchida.

Distribution rights for *Madadayo* were quickly sold to France, Brazil, Argentina, Chile, Turkey, and Israel. But despite *Rhapsody in August*'s success in other parts of the world, after its box-office failure in America, *Madadayo* proved a tough sell there. Kurosawa had sadly joined the ranks of Fellini,

Antonioni, and other masters whose later films went unreleased in the United States for years. *Madadayo* was shown at the 1995 San Francisco Film Festival, but was not widely seen and had no official release in the United States prior to its American television premiere on September 3, 1999—one year after Kurosawa's death—on the cable channel Turner Classic Movies.

Kevin Thomas said Kurosawa "could not have made a more fitting finale to one of the greatest careers in the history of cinema. A gentle, humorous contemplation of the inevitability of old age and mortality, 'Madadayo' celebrates the enduring joys of camaraderie and the rewards of kindness. . . . 'Madadayo' flows like a forest stream, and it risks seeming slow and sentimental on the surface when it is in fact leisurely in the most positive sense. So effortlessly does it unfold that you scarcely notice how evocative, even profound, is its impact by the time it's over."[75]

As Kurosawa's swan song, *Madadayo* recalls John Huston's *The Dead* (1987), with its lovely, unadorned delicacy and unabashed warmth. This warmth was misinterpreted as sentimentality by critics who failed to understand that while the professor himself is indeed sentimental—and he admits as much—the audience is allied not with him but with the students. When Uchida is beside himself with worry and depression over his lost cat, the pain audiences experience is that of his students, who worry about the effect the lost cat will have upon their beloved teacher. It is their observations of a great man coming to terms with his own mortality that is the heart of the film.

The students love their professor because he has maintained a childlike innocence; adulthood has not corrupted him. He is eccentric only because he is pure. "He's a child," says his loving wife. "He never grew up." And as Takayama (Hisashi Igawa) says at one point, "His sensitivity and imagination are beyond us."

Like *Rhapsody*, *Madadayo* spurns showy visual devices for the most part, but there are several extraordinary touches throughout. The film's most beautiful sequence—which might be viewed as clichéd in the hands of a lesser director—displays the passage of time, with Uchida and his wife serenely sitting in and about their postwar shack as the seasons change around them. "When I went to Kurosawa Production to get the script," Kagawa remembered, "Mr. Kurosawa said, 'This wife loves this teacher, doesn't she? That's going to be the love scene. This to me expresses their love together.' I realized that even though we were stationary in this series of shots, we had to show the affection between the wife and the husband."[76]

Shooting this scene required months of planning. "We waited for the snow," Kagawa said, "and one day we heard it was going to snow, so we raced to the location. There wasn't a lot of snow, and that was perfect. The second time, around March, we shot fall in the morning and spring in the afternoon; then, in May, we shot the summer."

The result is a love scene perhaps unique in the history of motion pictures.* With no dialogue at all, it eloquently expresses the couple's profound love for each other. Except for Mifune and Kagawa's scenes in *The Bad Sleep Well*, it is without precedent in Kurosawa's work.

The film opens with a long monologue by Uchida to his students about his retirement, and when the students surprise him with a heartfelt testimonial, in which their spokesman (Hidetaka Yoshioka) tells him, "You have taught us many precious things" and describes Uchida as "solid gold," the professor is ashamed of his own emotional reaction. He turns away from his students, the film cuts to a close-up of Uchida in profile, and as he blows his nose, the film cuts to its title card.

"Madadayo" comes from the Japanese version of hide-and-seek. It is a response to *Mo ii kai* ("Are you ready?"). *Mada da yo* ("Not yet"), then, becomes the professor's (and Kurosawa's) refusal to stop creating and surrender to death. This refusal comes in many forms. Like Red Beard, Uchida not only embraces good but stands tall against evil. One sequence involves a *yakuza* gang boss intent on building a three-story house adjacent to Uchida's that will block his view of the sun. Out of respect for the professor and at great personal risk, the land broker changes his mind and refuses to sell the land to the boss. The students, inspired by the respect the broker and the professor have for each other, pool their money and buy the land themselves, thus enabling the broker to send for his faraway family. As in *Red Beard*, kindness is shown to beget kindness.

Neither the students nor the professor want to believe that Nora the cat, lost for many weeks, will never return. Eventually, though, it becomes clear that she isn't coming home. This defeat is twofold: not only did the professor love Nora, but, for the first time, he is forced to confront his own mortality. Eventually another stray cat wanders into the couple's lives, and they name him Kurz. But Kurosawa, in an extremely moving bit of editing, abruptly cuts to tiny tombstones erected for Nora and Kurz many years later, further emphasizing the mortality of all living things.

As the professor tells his amusing stories to the engrossed students, some are dramatized in flashback form. One example involves Uchida's

---

*Buster Keaton uses the same visual concept in *College* (1927), but in a different manner.

buying horsemeat from a butcher, beef being a rarity late in the war. As he buys the meat, a horse on the street stops suddenly, turns its head, and stares accusingly at him. Other scenes show the professor's ingenuity in solving life's little problems. When, amid the rubble of postwar Japan, passersby urinate on a concrete wall just outside the professor's front door, he paints an "incantation" to keep men away. The students walk over to the wall and find that Uchida has drawn a pair of scissors.

The warmth of the film extends to its frequent use of traditional song. Indeed, there is more singing in *Madadayo* than in any other Kurosawa film. These songs, sung by the professor and his students, effectively express their joy of camaraderie while addressing the professor's sentimentality and his mortality. The students hold an annual party for their professor, attended by dozens of former students, now adults of varying age. By design very little happens that furthers the narrative, but this extended sequence (captured with the use of multiple cameras) expresses, as only Kurosawa can, the simple joys of student-teacher relationships, of kinship, of being alive. Like the rest of the film, it is warm and often very funny.

Years later, the professor is an old man, and at what is perhaps the last of these parties, we see the enduring impact he has had. Now the students are themselves older men and have brought to the party their wives, their children, and their grandchildren. Uchida tells the youngest of them, "Please find something you'll really like [as a career] . . . and you'll be happy." An irregular heartbeat sends the professor home in the middle of the festivities, but in the end it doesn't matter: Uchida's wisdom has already been passed on. In this, his last film, Kurosawa has regained a measure of hope for mankind.

Madadayo ends with Uchida dreaming. Unlike anything in *Dreams*, this sequence is beautifully realized. Uchida dreams he is once again a child, playing hide-and-seek in a field. To the playful cries of *"Mo ii kai?"* and *"Mada da yo!"* gold, violet, and yellow-orange clouds swirl Van Gogh–like above him, while Vivaldi's "Spirits of Harmony," from Concerto Nine, is heard on the soundtrack. It is an epilogue of serene beauty.

Matsumura, beyond bearing a striking resemblance to the real Uchida (though his white hair was dyed black for most of the film), is superb. In life Matsumura, a small man even by Japanese standards, projects much of the same wisdom as the professor and is likewise a great raconteur. Comparing Kurosawa's personality with his days on *Dodes'ka-den*, Matsumura joked, "He's still moody. He's not necessarily a perfectionist. But he's got a really sharp eye for everything. That ability precedes his perfectionism."[77]

"Mr. Matsumura had a hard time because of his long lines," Kagawa recalled. "And there was a long scene shot with Mr. Kurosawa's using three cameras simultaneously. But Mr. Kurosawa loved the first take and came from behind the camera clapping his hands. I worked with Mr. Matsumura on a television drama twenty years earlier. We played parents and he was a doctor. He had an open mind and always listened to my opinions. Now, more than twenty years later, we played a couple once again. In the script there was a twenty-year difference between the wife and the husband. In order to show the natural love between them, I felt I shouldn't be nervous playing with him. That's why I was so happy and comfortable."[78]

Despite mixed-to-negative reviews and the lack of timely distribution in America, *Madadayo* remains one of Kurosawa's best films. Like *Ikiru*, *Seven Samurai*, *High and Low*, and *Red Beard*, it may be years before this unaffected yet profound film is appreciated for what it is. Like its much-loved professor, *Madadayo* is solid gold.

TWENTY-NINE

SHADOW OF THE WOLF; AFTER THE RAIN

By the early nineties, it was clear that Toshiro Mifune was a very sick man. The decades of heavy drinking, the packs of Cartier cigarettes, the abuse he put his body through well into his sixties were all catching up to him. In October 1992 he suffered a heart attack, and for the rest of his life was repeatedly hospitalized. But Mifune's heart problems were coupled with a far more serious, far more insidious illness that would eventually rob him of everything. In the mid-1990s, slowly but relentlessly, Mifune's mind was fading away under the grip of Alzheimer's disease.

Tomio Sagisu and Mifune's son Shiro first began noticing symptoms around 1994, three years before his death, but the earliest stages may have appeared as far back as the mid-1980s. Writer James Bailey of the *Tokyo Journal* recalled interviewing Mifune as production wrapped on *Tora-san Goes North* in 1987. Mifune was congenial, but during the course of the interview could not remember the names of the film's director, Yoji Yamada, nor his leading lady, Keiko Awaji, whom he had known for nearly forty years.[1]

Despite failing health, Mifune made two final film appearances, shot four years after his work on *Shadow of the Wolf*. The first was a brief role in Kayo Hatta's sincere, occasionally charming *Picture Bride* (1994), about a Japanese woman shipped off to Hawaii to marry a Japanese immigrant she knows only through a single photograph. The film is set early in the twentieth century. Mifune appears in two short scenes as a *benshi*. The film's cast is adequate, but when Mifune turns up, the picture is infused with a different energy, and for the last time his presence alone lights up the screen like a rocket briefly illuminating the night sky. Hatta admitted writing Mifune "a big fan letter," asking him to appear in her film. "We didn't hear anything for three months, and then all of a sudden he said yes, after we were already filming. He's a living legend, so it's kind of like inviting the queen over and discovering all you have to serve is cheese and crackers."[2]

Picture Bride earned the audience award at the Sundance Film Festival, and was released in the United States by Miramax to good reviews.

Mifune's final screen appearance came in Kei Kumai's little-seen *Deep River* (Fukai kawa, 1995), based on the 1993 novel by acclaimed author Shusaku Endo. The film is an ambitious but muddled religious odyssey about a trio of Japanese travelers in India. One is a widower (Hisashi Igawa) whose wife (Kyoko Kagawa) believed in reincarnation; after her death he goes to India in search of a young girl whose body, he believes, may host the dead wife's spirit. Another is a young woman (Kumiko Akiyoshi), seduced by a Japanese Christian (Eiji Okuda), trying to resolve the fundamental differences between Eastern and Western religious philosophies. Finally, there is a World War II veteran (Yoichi Numata) determined to ease the tormented soul of one of his comrades (Mifune), who on his deathbed confessed to resorting to cannibalism to survive while deep in the Burmese jungle in the waning days of the war.

Mifune appears in two scenes, first at a restaurant and later at a hospital as he lies dying. In the brief time between his appearance in *Picture Bride* and *Deep River*, it is alarmingly clear just how far his health had deteriorated. In these two scenes, filmed in the fall of 1994, Mifune is shockingly gaunt and aged. His loose-fitting wardrobe appears too large for his now bony frame, and tellingly, the intensity of his eyes is gone, replaced by a kind of glassy stare.

"He was obviously not well," Kumai said. "But he became a different person the moment he came on the sets. Mifune was an actor, through and through."[3] *Deep River* had virtually no release in the United States. In Los Angeles it had a single performance at the University of Southern California's Norris Theater in 1998. Reviewing the film, Kevin Thomas called it "a slow-paced, demanding film . . . nonetheless a richly rewarding odyssey."[4]

When Mifune's condition grew worse, Mika Kitagawa, his lover since the late 1960s, abruptly left him. She moved to Saitama and opened a sushi restaurant, and to this day declines interviews about their relationship. "I think she just couldn't take care of my father any longer," Shiro said. "I'm sure there was a lot of mental strain within him."[5]

Ironically, it was Sachiko who remained devoted until the end. She rushed to his side. Shiro recalled, "It was just like they never separated. It all seemed very natural."[6] Mifune quit drinking, and the reunited couple lived quietly, spending much of their time together at Mifune's second home in Aburatsubo. But their happiness was short-lived. Sachiko had contracted leukemia and had considered chemotherapy and surgery to extend her life before doctors discovered she had inoperable pancreatic cancer as well. Together the couple grew weaker and weaker, and on September 15, 1995, Sachiko succumbed, leaving Mifune alone once more. "Even though they were together again for only a short time, I think it was good for her to be with him," said a devastated Shiro.[7] With Sachiko gone, Mifune's health further declined.[8]

In the last year of Mifune's life, it became clear that he would never work again. That same year, however, his children and grandchildren, as if in response, took up acting themselves. Mifune's daughter Mika, now fifteen, made her television debut on an NHK drama, while his grandson, Rikia, made his film debut in a Hong Kong film, *Extreme Crisis* (B Gai waak, 1998), along with his father, Shiro, who had a small role as a scientist.

In January 1997, Mifune's younger brother, Yoshiro, died of cancer. By then, however, Mifune was too ill to attend his brother's funeral, or even to derive much satisfaction in the successes of his children and grandchildren. He needed full-time care and was permanently moved to a hospital in Mitaka. Emaciated, dying, he spent nearly all of 1997 in his fourth-floor hospital ward. Rumors about his condition made headlines and sold tabloids. "When his Alzheimer's was getting worse," said Tomio Sagisu, "many magazines tried to sneak into his room and take his picture. Shiro hated this and tried to protect his father from photographers." Shiro got his father a private room with his own personal caretaker, "but in the end someone snuck in and the magazines got pictures anyway."[9]

Outside the immediate family, only Sagisu and Takashi Shimura's widow were allowed to see him.

Years ago [Sagisu recalled], Mr. Kurosawa was shooting Mifune from far away, and there were some actors between Mifune and the camera. Kurosawa said, "There's somebody wearing glasses, because we're getting a bright reflection. Tell whoever it is to take off his glasses." The assistant director came back saying, "Nobody's wearing glasses"—it was Mifune's eyes. His eyes reflected that strongly. When I visited him for the last time, that spark was gone from his eyes. I found that profoundly sad.

Shiro warned me, "I have to let you know in advance, he probably won't remember you." I took the elevator to the fourth floor where his room was. When the door opened, Mr. Mifune was there in the hall, waiting for me. We shook hands, but his hands were so weak and his eyes so different from his eyes in *Seven Samurai* and other films. He used to have a powerful voice, but when I saw him, he could no longer speak. His mouth would move like he was trying to speak, but nothing was coming out. Slowly, however, he seemed to remember me. He took me to a recreation room and to other places in the ward. He couldn't talk, and nobody understood him, but I understood that he was taking me around because I had visited the hospital so often it was like he was introducing me to everybody as one would a best friend.[10]

"The last time I saw him," said Masako, Takashi Shimura's widow, "he had reached the point where he was unable even to consume liquid food. When I visited him he was bedridden . . . I saw tears in his eyes. Did he want to say something? I wondered."[11]

Toshiro Mifune died on December 24, 1997, survived by his three children. Officially, the cause of death was organ failure. "Around nine o'clock," Sagisu remembered, "Shiro-san called me and said, 'He just passed away.' I was supposed to visit him the next day, and I really regretted that I was not able to see him again. I couldn't stop crying."[12]

"I am deeply saddened and shocked by his passing," Kurosawa said. "I never imagined he would go before me. Strangely, though, I was thinking of him recently, reminding myself I had to go see him soon."[13] "I wanted to see him and tell him, 'You really have done a great job.' There is no actor of his stature anymore."[14] Pressed for an official statement, Kurosawa later added, "I would just like to say to him, 'Thank you and rest in peace.' "[15]

"He was a really kind person, very delicate," said Kazuo Miyagawa. "About four years earlier, when I attended the funeral of Kashiko Kawakita of Toho-Towa, he was already there. When he saw me, he jumped up and gave his seat to me."[16]

The press and old friends and co-workers gathered outside Mifune Productions, but a note on the door said that, in accordance with Mifune's will, the funeral would be private. Actor Kotaro Satomi recalled the first time he had visited Mifune's company, back in the late 1970s. Satomi came to see him early in the morning, and met a man at the gate spraying water on the street in front of the office—it was Mifune. When Satomi asked him why he—the president of the company—was engaged in such a trivial task, Mifune told him, 'Because I get up the earliest.' " Film critic Nagaharu Yodogawa remembered Mifune as "a down-to-earth person—he didn't have a star's arrogance." Yodogawa recalled a screening of *Rashomon* where, after the film was over, he turned to Mifune and told him how great he was. "He blushed and asked, 'Really?' "[17]

On Christmas Day, Mifune's family held a private ceremony in his home. "The actor lay in a coffin topped with a color picture taken in 1983 and placed on a seven-meter-wide funeral dais decked in white flowers," said one report.[18] The following day his body was cremated.

Kurosawa Production joined Toho and what was left of Mifune Productions in paying for an elaborate wake, held on January 24, 1998, at Aoyama Ceremonial Hall. Nearly 5,000 friends and fans came to pay tribute, including Prime Minister Ryutaro Hashimoto, Steven Spielberg, and *Red Sun*'s Alain Delon. Kurosawa himself was too ill to attend, but Hisao read a brief note, in which Kurosawa said, "I was in love with your speedy and delicate acting. You did a great job."[19] The famous shot from *Seven Samurai*, where it is learned that Kikuchiyo is a farmer's son, was used as the centerpiece of the affair.

Mifune left an estate estimated at ¥630,000,000 (about $5.4 million). Consisting mainly of real estate holdings and bank deposits, it was divided among his three children.[20]

Throughout the productions of *Dreams*, *Rhapsody in August*, and *Madadayo*, Kurosawa's love of making films had helped him defy his physical years. But by the time Mifune died, he himself was in very poor health. He aged dramatically after Mifune's death. He was spared senility, but physically his body was winding down. In his mid-eighties Kurosawa suddenly became an old man.

"I still have so many projects I want to do," Kurosawa had said in 1992, during the production of *Madadayo*. His longtime art director Yoshiro Muraki said at the time that the director's next film would probably be a *jidai-geki*, one on a far more intimate scale than *Kagemsuha* or *Ran*. "Kurosawa doesn't have the energy to do something like that again."[21]

During his final years, a variety of non-film-related projects kept him busy. In March 1996 his expressionistic artwork was painted on a fleet of Japanese passenger jets, and he was commissioned, along with Robert Altman and Pedro Almodóvar, by the Swatch company to design a limited-edition wristwatch as part of a line celebrating 100 years of cinema. Kurosawa came up with one he dubbed "Eiga-shi" ("History of Movies"), with a gold-spattered eye on its face and a red-and-blue band with the director's signature. "I found it interesting to express my imagination in this way for once," he said, "like wrist graffiti."[22]

"I have no intention of retiring," Kurosawa said. "There are a lot of films I want to make yet—and time is running out."[23] But after *Madadayo*'s release, he had little choice.

By 1990, Hisao had become president and chief executive officer of Kurosawa's four companies—Kurosawa Production, Kurosawa Film Studio, Kurosawa Enterprises USA, and Kurosawa Office—which revolved around the later feature films but also included the rental studio and its equipment, and the marketing and licensing of Kurosawa's image and work in other media. Hisao became increasingly protective of his father as Kurosawa's health began to decline. "Kurosawa married when he was over thirty," said Mike Inoue, "so his own children were born when he was [already] a . . . famous man. He didn't have too much time to take care of them. In those days Hisao was somewhat resentful of his father, but later when he became more active with Kurosawa's companies, his opinion of his father changed greatly compared with his younger days."[24]

On *Ran* Orion worked closely with Kazuko for the right to merchandise items based on the film. She assisted Emi Wada on *Dreams* and took over as costume designer on *Rhapsody in August* and *Madadayo*. Like Hisao, Kazuko became much closer to her father in his last years, a stark contrast to the days when, so consumed with his work, he couldn't remember her age, what school she attended, or even whether she was single or divorced.

Kurosawa's long decline began shortly before *Madadayo* premiered, when he lost one of his closest friends. With his shock of white hair, Ishiro Honda had always looked older than Kurosawa, even though he was a full year younger. But like Kurosawa, Honda maintained a youthful energy on the sets of their later films, and when he died suddenly of respiratory failure during a routine hospital visit on February 28, 1993, Kurosawa was crushed. "He died of lung cancer," noted Mike Inoue. "Mr. Honda didn't know he had it."[25]

Honda's funeral was held on March 6, six weeks before *Madadayo*'s opening. A large contingent from Kurosawa's staff attended the services. No one, least of all Kurosawa, was surprised to see so many of Honda's colleagues from his salad days at Toho, many of whom had not worked with him in decades. According to the Japan Economic Newswire, Mifune was among the mourners: "[Kurosawa and Mifune] made eye contact and hugged in tears at the funeral for their mutual friend."[26] Kurosawa, without his trademark director's cap, delivered the eulogy in a pained voice.

"There was a strong level of trust between them," remembered Kyoko Kagawa, who attended the service. "Actually, I had worked for Mr. Honda before, on *Mothra* (1961), and he was an A-level director; even so he decided to assist Mr. Kurosawa. That's why I really respected him."[27]

That same year, on December 19, Kurosawa lost his oldest friend, Keinosuke Uegusa. In his eighties, Kurosawa had made three films in four years, but in 1993 all he seemed to be doing was burying friends he had outlived. Many more followed. Hideo Oguni died in February 1996 at the age of ninety-one. In the year of Mifune's death, six more colleagues slipped away: Toho director Kengo Furusawa (at the age of seventy-seven); Yoshiro Muraki's art director wife, Shinobu (seventy-three; they had fallen in love on the set of *Stray Dog*); his former producer Tomoyuki Tanaka (eighty-six); actress Haruko Sugimura (ninety-one); actor Ko Nishimura (seventy-four). Even Shintaro Katsu, who had given him so much grief on *Kagemusha*, was gone: he died of cancer that same year at sixty-five.

Still, Kurosawa pressed on. In July 1993, the same month Kazuko gave birth to a third son, she accompanied her father to Cannes. He had begun writing *The Ocean Is Watching* (Umi wa miteita). The screenplay was based on two stories by Shugoro Yamamoto (the author whose stories were adapted as *Sanjuro*, *Red Beard*, and *Dodes'ka-den*), *Trying to Smell the Flowers* (Nanno hana ka kaoru) and *During the Rainy Season* (Tsuyuno hinuma). It was set in an eighteenth-century seaside brothel and followed the lives of two prostitutes. One is obsessed with money and pretends to be married to a samurai, while the other falls in love with one of her clients. The script included a flood sequence that would have been Kurosawa's most physically demanding set piece since the castle burning in *Ran*. The flood destroys an entire village, and one of the two women, seen on the brothel roof, is swept away in the raging current.[28] He finished his script in December and went so far as to begin casting his new film (it is probable that Mieko Harada would have played one of the prostitutes), and Yoshiro Muraki began sketching set designs, but the film's relatively high budget—estimated at $7.5 to $15 million—scared off Toho, Daiei, and Shochiku, and *The*

Ocean Is Watching never got beyond the planning stage. "We needed a lot of money for its production," said Hisao, "yet it wouldn't be a conventional entertainment film. So he decided, 'Okay, let's write another script.' "[29] (However, Tak Abe, president of Kurosawa Enterprises USA, the Los Angeles–based affiliate of Kurosawa Production, has said that the film may yet get financing and be produced in the next few years.[30])

Kurosawa was awarded the tenth Kyoto Prize in November 1994 and humbly accepted the award, claiming he deserved it only because he had outlived so many of his contemporaries. In interviews he spoke of the need to organize festivals and retrospectives of classic Japanese films. Seeing films of the great masters on videotape and laserdisc was fine, he said, but to be really appreciated they needed to be seen in theaters, on big screens.

In the late 1970s and early '80s, Kurosawa and Yoko had lived in a two-story house at 7 Irima, 3-chome, in Chou-fu, and Seijo Nichichomei in Setagaya. In the spring of 1995, it was time for Kurosawa, now an aging widower better suited to a single-story home, to move once again. Kazuko said that these moves were usually done when Kurosawa was away on location. This time she convinced him to be present so they could move together as a family. However, shortly before moving day, Kurosawa changed his mind about wanting to be there. He was inspired to write a new script and wanted to develop his new idea at a *ryokan* in Kyoto.[31]

In March of 1995 he began work on *Ame agaru* ("After the Rain"), a project more on the scale of *Rhapsody* and *Madadayo*. In May, as he was finishing his script, Kurosawa had a life-changing accident. "He was writing *Ame Agaru* in Kyoto," said Mike Inoue, "and he slipped on a tatami in the morning as he was going to the bathroom, and [was] very badly [injured]." The injury seemed minor at first, but a few days later, his longtime assistant director Takashi Koizumi called Kazuko to let her know that the pain had gotten so bad that Kurosawa had been rushed to the hospital.

The fall had broken the base of his spine. He had a high fever that left him unable to think clearly, and what he said to his family often seemed out of character. This shocked Kazuko—when she had talked to her father from Tokyo by telephone, he sounded fine. She, Mike Inoue, and Hisao decided to move him to a hospital in Tokyo. "He had to stay in bed," said Inoue. "He stayed in a hospital in Kyoto for about ten days, but we all decided to bring him back to Tokyo."[32]

Kurosawa spent most of the summer in the Tokyo hospital. Slowly, his fever subsided, and he had, fortunately, little memory of the extreme pain he had suffered and the long days and nights in the hospital in Kyoto.

Kazuko and Mike Inoue visited him constantly, while Hisao, burdened with the financial responsibilities of running his father's companies, came less often. Kurosawa cherished visiting with his grandchildren, especially the youngest, whom he nicknamed "Chibisuke" (meaning, roughly, "Little One"). "Seeing him was the best medicine," said Kazuko.[33]

"After he left the hospital," Inoue said, "and came back to his home in Seijo-Gakujin, I decided to move closer to him, about ten minutes' driving distance, and would visit him once or twice every week. He was very pleased when he saw my face and would give me a big smile."[34]

A younger man might have recovered, but Kurosawa was eighty-five years old, and this trivial accident abruptly and permanently ended one of cinema's greatest careers. He spent the rest of his life in a wheelchair and, more frequently, in bed. Kazuko provided daily care and cooked all his meals. She commuted to her father's home every day with her children. The strain proved overwhelming. The breaking point came when, desperate to step outside this overwhelming situation, even if only briefly, she decided to treat herself and her children to a meal at a restaurant. "I went . . . to eat *chukasoba* [buckwheat noodles]," she recalled, "and my hands started trembling and wouldn't stop. Somehow I managed to get a bite of noodles into my mouth—but then I couldn't even swallow it. I lost fifty-five pounds, my body would shake, and I couldn't sleep or eat because I was so scared."[35]

The director conferred with Takashi Koizumi about the *Ame agaru* script and would lovingly recount its story to Inoue. Kurosawa once joked that he'd like to die on the set, right in the middle of a shot. But now it was clear that never again would he sit behind a camera. His directing career was over. His last visit to a soundstage came late in 1995, when he appeared in a wheelchair in a television commercial for Panasonic. He later supervised his first and only television commercial in 1997 for Culpis, a soft-drink company, but the actual onstage directing chores were left to others. He was simply too weak to do it himself.

Gradually, he lost even the strength to finish his script of *Ame agaru*. "His condition changed from day to day," Kazuko said. "In that sense, he was like an infant. The tiniest things would make him worse."[36]

To boost his spirits, large parties were held for him at Christmas and on his eighty-eighth birthday (an important occasion in Japanese culture, known as his *beiju*), on March 23, 1998. Kazuko's Shih-tzus, Cyndi (named after Cyndi Lauper, the pop singer) and Apple, reminded Kurosawa of his own beloved dogs, and he still enjoyed the company of grandson

Chibisuke, but his mobility was limited to his wheelchair, and he could barely eat. At the party Apple suddenly collapsed and died. "I thought," wrote Kazuko, "maybe she had died in his place."[37]

"He was not able to write," Inoue continued. "He was totally [incapacitated during] the last six months, his condition was much worse than Hisao let on. But his brain was sharp and he was able to speak."[38] He spent much of his time listening to classical music, yelling at his maid when she failed to put on the correct performance of a particular piece. He watched American sports, which he loved, especially football, baseball, and golf, which he no longer could enjoy himself."

"He had to concern himself with his recovery," said Hisao, "but as he was having to spend so much time in bed, physically he was getting weaker and weaker. He was so full of energy for making films. But the last two years I didn't see that energy in him any longer."[39]

"It was September 6 [1998]," Inoue recalled. "I was going to visit him that day, in the afternoon, and around eleven o'clock I got a call from Takashi Koizumi. He said, 'Hurry, get over here.' When I got there, his eyes were already closed. I put my hand on his forehead and he was still warm—he had just passed away a few minutes earlier. He looked as if he was smiling. I think he must have said to himself, 'I have done everything I wanted to do.' " A stroke was the official cause of death. It had claimed him at 12:45 p.m.

Koizumi rushed to O'hyoi's, a Tokyo wine bar where many of Kurosawa's staff hung out. According to its owner, actor-comedian Shunji Fujiyama, Koizumi spent the evening leaning against a wooden post weeping uncontrollably.

"I think we lost a very great man," Inoue said, unsuccessfully holding back tears. "He had a warm heart. A lot of people called him 'Emperor Kurosawa,' but that was not him."[40]

As television networks around the world broadcast tributes to the director of *Rashomon*, *Seven Samurai*, and *Ikiru*, the discovery of more than 350 pages of heretofore-unknown handwritten script pages was announced. The pages, which included unfilmed scenes for *The Lower Depths* and *The Hidden Fortress*, among others, had been "kept safely by [an] innkeeper in Kawazu, Shizuoka Prefecture."[41] The inn was long gone and the land converted into a parking lot. The innkeeper had died, but her daughter, to whom the pages had been left, recalled how Kurosawa, Hideo Oguni, Shinobu Hashimoto, and Ryuzo Kikushima would visit with her family or toss around a baseball after a full day's work on the script. (There was another connection, too. The innkeeper's daughter's first-grade teacher had been Haruyo Kurosawa, Akira's sister.)[42]

George Lucas responded to Kurosawa's death by giving $1.5 million to the USC School of Cinema–Television, from which Lucas had graduated in 1966, to fund a state-of-the-art digital studio in Kurosawa's name. "[He] was one of film's true greats," he said. "His ability to transform a vision into a powerful work is unparalleled. So it seemed appropriate to name the new digital stage after him. This way, we pay tribute to Kurosawa while at the same time inspiring students to break new ground the way he did."[43]

Back in Japan, the staff of Kurosawa Production worked through their grief by determinedly producing a film of Kurosawa's last script. Financed by Japanese and French companies including, among others, Kurosawa Production, Asmik Ace Entertainment, and 7 Films Cinema, the picture was launched by Hisao Kurosawa almost immediately after his father's death, with the intention of completing it in time for the Venice Film Festival, which would mark the first anniversary of the director's passing. *After the Rain* wound up making its American premiere at the American Film Institute Film Festival in Los Angeles in late October 1999, prior to a Japanese release the following year. (The Festival also included a Danish-made domestic comedy called *Mifune*, in which, as part of a game, one of the characters is compelled to imitate the actor.)

Using notes Kurosawa left behind, Takashi Koizumi, who had worked closely with the director on the scripts for his last series of pictures, finished it for him. Happily, Koizumi, who also directed, neither aped his mentor's style nor felt obligated to impose his own personal stamp. The result is a glorious epilogue, a wonderfully gentle, disarming film very much in keeping with the style and feel of both *Rhapsody in August* and *Madadayo*. In both tone and content, it is very much like Kurosawa's great, underrated *Red Beard*. *After the Rain* also has traces of *The Lower Depths*, *Rashomon*, and *The Men Who Tread on the Tiger's Tail*. The film is preceded by a brief montage of photographs of Kurosawa, and the picture is dedicated to him.

The simple story, set in the early eighteenth century, follows a down-and-out but cheerful *ronin*, Ihei Misawa (Akira Terao), who waits with his wife, Tayo (Yoshiko Miyazaki), at a modest country inn for the rains to lift so they may cross a river and continue their journey. Ihei is not a successful samurai: though he is extremely skilled, his good nature, honesty, and generosity always seem to get him into trouble, and invariably he loses whatever employment opportunities come his way.

In the film's first act, we see various peasants staying at the inn, feeling miserable. Ihei disappears (we later learn he has been prizefighting, something nearly unthinkable for even a desperate samurai to do) in order to buy food and entertainment for everyone at the inn. And by doing so, he brings a rare moment of joy and happiness into their lives. One of the peasants sings a bawdy song, an old woman begins singing another song, a fat man entertains everyone with a dance about picking watermelons, and so on. "This once a year, and I'd happily endure another year of hardship," says one peasant, and the sequence becomes reminiscent of the final scene in *The Lower Depths*. Even the inn's bitter prostitute (Mieko Harada, the calculating Lady Kaede in *Ran*) finds a tiny bit of joy through Ihei's kindness. Ihei's wife, however, is dismayed by her husband's prizefighting, for she knows it can only lead to trouble. While uncomplaining, she remains separate from the festivities.

The following morning, Ihei takes a walk in the forest and stumbles upon two young samurai engaged in a senseless, *Rashomon*-like duel. Seeing the foolishness of it all, he steps in to stop the fight, despite the protests of other samurai nearby, and uses his skill and experience to disarm them. The samurai are outraged, but Lord Shigeaki (Shiro Mifune), having seen all from a distance, is greatly impressed by Ihei's skill and invites him to his castle.

Ihei is delighted to find Shigeaki to be a hearty man of good humor eager to hear about the samurai's adventures. In an extended flashback sequence, Ihei wanders from castle to castle challenging various fencing masters to duels, always yielding during the match. Thus winning, and in "a good mood," they would serve him food and drink and provide traveling money. One day Ihei challenges one of the best fencing masters in Japan, Getten Tsuji (Tatsuya Nakadai). Getten, surprised by Ihei's relaxed demeanor, is caught off guard and, not sure what to do, yields before Ihei has a chance to do so himself. Embarrassed, Ihei confesses the scheme, but Tsuji takes a liking to him anyway and makes him his student. Ihei becomes a master fencer, and Tsuji finds a post for him at another castle, but soon Ihei is dismissed and has lost several other posts since.

This story impresses Shigeaki, and he offers Ihei the position of fencing master at his castle. As a formality of his employment, Ihei is required to give a demonstration to the lord and his samurai. This proves his undoing. Ihei easily wins every challenge, mainly by dodging his opponents' blows, and when Shigeaki himself challenges Ihei, the *ronin*'s moves send the lord tumbling into a muddy pond. Seething with outrage, Shigeaki sends Ihei back to the inn.

With the river now crossable, Tayo has begun packing. Okin, the bitter prostitute, having been touched by Ihei's kindness, gives Tayo some ash—the only thing the poor woman can think to give—to help make Tayo's feet more comfortable for the long journey ahead. Just then, Shigeaki's retainer (Hisashi Igawa) and chamberlain (Hidetaka Yoshioka) arrive to tell Ihei that his appointment has suddenly been revoked, Shigeaki having learned of Ihei's prizefighting. Tayo, moved by Okin's gesture, finally understands her husband's actions and tells off Shigeaki's men, calling them idiots, saying she understands now that it is less important what a man does than why he does it.

As Ihei and Tayo resume their journey, Shigeaki hears of Tayo's comments and, realizing he's losing a very special man, chases after them. By now, however, it is too late: the couple are already high in the mountains overlooking the sea.

"This is a drama about a man and his wife," Kurosawa wrote in his notes for the project. "First, their relationship must be clearly drawn. The wife, who lives for her husband, is content with that. The husband, however, thinks that his wife is unhappy with the poverty in their lives. He is obsessed with the thought of somehow getting ahead in the world and achieving a more comfortable way of life. It is hard for his wife to see him like this; it saddens her, but her husband does not understand."[44]

Reviews, predictably were mixed. Mark Schilling, who had suggested Kurosawa should have retired on the basis of *Madadayo*, was similarly condescending: "The obvious question is whether this homage . . . meets the standards of 'Rashomon,' 'Ikiru,' or 'Shichinin no samurai.' The short answer is 'no.' As narratively unadorned as a folk tale, with an affirmative message as straightforward as its samurai hero is upright, the film will no doubt strike many who know and love Kurosawa's work as Kurosawa and water—and I can't disagree."[45]

After the Rain is a modest yet joyous film of unexpected decency, about self-realization through goodness, the kind of picture one watches with an almost childlike sense of wonder. It is astonishing to consider that Kurosawa, in his mid-eighties, was still growing as a screenwriter-director. Every line of dialogue, every expression and reaction has been carefully considered—the film is impressively straightforward. Made at a time when overtly visceral, desperately postmodern movies from Hollywood dominate the world market—and as mainstream Japanese filmmakers attempt, not very well, to imitate them—Kurosawa, by way of Koizumi, was able to express the wonder of simply being alive.

"If you are only concerned with how you say something, without having anything to say," Kurosawa once said, "then even the way you say it won't come to anything. Besides, technique is there only to support a director's intentions. If he relies solely on the technique his original thought won't appear. Techniques do not enlarge a director, they limit him. Technique alone, with nothing to support its weight, always crushes the basic idea which should prevail."[46]

For those familiar with the Kurosawa canon, there is also something quite touching in seeing such a remarkable film made by the disciples of a departed master. As Koizumi noted when introducing the picture at the AFI festival, the average age of those working for Kurosawa was nearing seventy. The film marked the return, for example, of seventy-one-year-old composer Masaru Sato, who wrote a lovely score. Seventy-five-year-old Yoshiro Muraki once again did the art direction; sixty-seven-year-old Tatsuya Nakadai is delightful in the very funny flashback sequence (filmed in black and white); and eighty-five-year-old Tatsuo Matsumura, the old professor of *Madadayo*, has several nice moments as the oldest of the inn's guests.

I first saw *After the Rain* at the AFI festival with two friends, both longtime fans of Kurosawa. When Shiro Mifune makes his first appearance, he is on horseback in full regalia, including a helmet that obscures his face. As he spoke his first lines, one of my friends let out a laugh—she knew right away who it "was," for coming from this costume was the unmistakable voice of Toshiro Mifune. It was almost a ghostly visitation. After his film debut in Masanobu Dame's *Forbidden Affair* in 1970, the twenty-year-old Mifune appeared in just one more film, Ken Matsumori's *Morning for Two* (1971), making *After the Rain* his first (substantial) film role in twenty-eight years. Instead of pursuing an acting career, he attended Cambridge University for eighteen months, then ran his father's Japanese restaurant, Mifune, in Munich for six years. Like Hisao Kurosawa, Shiro returned to Japan to work for his father's firm, overseeing the Mifune Academy of the Arts, and assumed presidency of Mifune Productions upon his father's death. As Shigeaki, he gives a broad performance, but as he is—by design—imitating his father's distinctive voice and facial expressions, and since the character is himself something of a blowhard, Shiro transcends his limitations as an actor and creates a memorable character.

But the film really belongs to Akira Terao, a talented performer whose acting muscles were rarely flexed in *Ran*, *Dreams*, and *Madadayo* (though his narration of the latter is excellent). As Ihei, Terao gives a gentle, restrained performance. A kind of distant relative of Minoru Chiaki's Heihachi from *Seven Samurai*, Terao, with his long face, deeply tanned features, large, expressive eyes, and wide smile, is perfectly cast. Ihei is a selfless, decent man who automatically thinks of others. Indeed, he doesn't think at all, he simply *does*, and that's why the character works so well. When he spars with one of Shigeaki's men and easily defeats him, Ihei asks, "I'm sorry, did I hurt your hand?" Terao is consistently, believably sincere.

Later, Ihei goes fishing, returning to the inn just as he is called by Shigeaki, and not only does he immediately hand over his catch to the peasants, he proceeds to tell them the tastiest way to prepare it, thus further exemplifying his tireless generosity. In a violent scene in which Ihei is faced with angry samurai—and cuts them down when they attack—Terao also illustrates an important part of Ihei's character—that his humanity evolved, in part, from past experience with the evils of the world, much like Red Beard's.

Lovely Yoshiko Miyazaki (b. 1959) is exquisite as Ihei's wife. She had a small role in *Ran* (her film debut), but was otherwise not part of the Kurosawa stock company. At the age of twenty, while studying law at Kumamoto University, Miyazaki was approached to appear in a magazine spread on college coeds. This led to television commercials and a role on the television show *I'm Fine!* After *Ran*, she appeared in several other films, including one for Kaneto Shindo, and as Akira Terao's second wife in Yoji Yamada's *Tora-san Takes a Vacation* (Otoko wa tsuraiyo—Torajiro no kyujitsu, 1990). Miyazaki is likewise excellent, expressing with the tiniest of gestures a woman who knows her husband's frailties but deeply loves him anyway.

Director Takashi Koizumi (b. 1944) had known Kurosawa since 1970, when he joined the Club of the Four Knights founded by Kurosawa, Kinoshita, Kobayashi, and Ichikawa. He became a self-described disciple of Kurosawa and worked under him as an assistant director on the TV documentary *Song of the Horse*. He traveled with Kurosawa to the Soviet Union for *Dersu Uzala*, and helped Kurosawa and Masato Ide prepare *Kagemusha*. Koizumi subsequently worked on all of Kurosawa's later films as an assistant director and collaborated closely on the scripts as well. During lean periods, he found work as a still photographer on films directed by Ichikawa, Kinoshita, Kozaburo Yoshimura, and others. When *After the Rain* was rapidly put into production following Kurosawa's death, Hisao Kurosawa suggested that Koizumi, who had never directed a feature, take over. His direction is proficient and never intrusive. He uses shots of the river and the rain to good effect, and there are some classic Kurosawa-esque shots involving Shigeaki's mad dash on horseback, filmed with a long telephoto lens. Ultimately, he manages to capture the essence of the script's lesson that, as in *Red Beard* and *Madadayo*, kindness begets kindness. The film expresses the joy of living, and the directions in one of the notes Kurosawa left behind: "It should be a story that, when you have seen it, leaves you feeling cheerful." And so it does.

In February 1999, Nikkatsu announced that it would begin production on *Dora-Heita* ("Alley Cat," which can also be translated as "Playboy"), based on an old script by Kurosawa, with Kon Ichikawa, Masaki Kobayashi, and Keisuke Kinoshita, written in 1969–70 during the Four Knights period. Based on Shugoro Yamamoto's novel *Diary of a Town Magistrate*, the film is a lighthearted tale along the lines of *Sanjuro*, set during the Edo period.

The original idea was to have each of the four filmmakers direct portions of the narrative, but the financial failure of *Dodes'ka-den* quashed any plans for such an expensive picture. By the time *Dora-Heita* was announced for production in February 1999, Kon Ichikawa was the sole survivor. Though by now eighty-five years old, he was chosen to direct.

The story concerns a samurai, Koheita Mochizuki (Koji Yakusho, star of *The Eel* and *Shall We Dance?*), nicknamed "Dora-Heita," who poses as a drunken magistrate while fighting corruption in a small fief. Like Wyatt Earp, Dora-Heita comes to the lawless town on the heels of three earlier magistrates who had mysteriously disappeared. But Dora-Heita's reputation has been carefully engineered by the samurai. When he appears before the district council, his drunkenness and lack of respect outrage them. They're ready to boot him out of town before he produces a personal message from the lord giving him full authority over them. Problems erupt as Dora-Heita's determined mistress, the geisha Kosei (Yuko Asano), arrives, demanding he return to her.

Dora-Heita was reviewed at the Berlin Festival in February 2000 by *Variety*'s David Stratton. "Filmgoers with nostalgic memories for a golden age of Japanese cinema, when Toshiro Mifune played the fastest swordsman in the East in films by Akira Kurosawa and Masaki Kobayashi, will embrace 'Dora-Heita,' a nostalgic throwback to that exciting era. [The film] has many of the elements that made classics like 'Yojimbo,' 'Sanjuro' and 'Rebellion' so rewarding, but noticeably lacks their energy and muscularity. Nevertheless, there's plenty to enjoy in this slyly humorous film from the last surviving veteran of that era, Kon Ichikawa."[47]

The late 1990s were years of devastating loss for the Japanese film industry. The months following Kurosawa's death saw the passing of much-loved film critic Nagaharu Yodogawa, eighty-nine, and eighty-six-year-old Keisuke Ki-noshita, a filmmaker who, while never as internationally successful as Kurosawa, was nonetheless a contemporary whose work at Shochiku mirrored in many ways Kurosawa's. As Yoshio Shirai, the dean of Japanese film critics, put it, "Kinoshita's death after Kurosawa's makes me realize that the century of cinema is over."[48] Shochiku's Ofuna Studios was sold to an adjacent women's college in June 1999. "All I can say is that it's a crying shame," said Masato Tsuchiyama, spokesman for the Shochiku labor union. "This is just another bad example of Japanese *risutora* [company cost-cutting]—only this time they're getting rid of the entire legacy of Japanese film."[49] Toho, Kurosawa and Mifune's home studio for decades, presently charges so much money for use of its stages and equipment that it sits empty most of the year, like a ghost town. At the millennium Toho was making just two in-house films per year, compared with the nearly 100 features they had released yearly during the late fifties.

When Akira Kurosawa and Toshiro Mifune first met on June 4, 1946, they were at the crossroads of their professional lives. Kurosawa was finding his voice as a writer-director, only recently freed from the aesthetic constraints brought about by the war. By 1946, freedom of expression was not only allowed but actively encouraged. The success of his early films and screenplays had given him the artistic latitude he required. Mifune's talent was raw, a diamond in the rough, which Kurosawa molded into something never before seen in Japanese cinema. Together they flourished during the film industry's long-lost Golden Period, a time of tremendous creative growth for films of all types, from brassy B's to myriad great works by Mizoguchi, Ozu, Naruse, Kinoshita, Toyoda, and Imai. And the Kurosawa-Mifune films were among the very best. They enjoyed an international acclaim denied nearly all their contemporaries, which helped their professional rise, contributed to their separation, and drove them into sudden decline.

For Mifune, a shy, sensitive man uncertain of his abilities and uncomfortable with his image, the independence for which he had worked so hard proved his undoing. He was simply too trusting with his business affairs—and more frequently insisted on taking too much responsibility on himself—and this nearly destroyed him. When his marriage eroded, his screen persona came to dominate his public life, while at home he found little solace and much unhappiness. He never came to terms with his own strengths and weaknesses. Despite Kurosawa's many setbacks, it was, ironically, Mifune, with his business interests and prolific career, who was unable late in his career to fully enjoy the rewards he had reaped and richly deserved.

Kurosawa was driven to the point of suicide by two film industries that did not understand him any more than he understood them. But, like so many of his screen heroes, he ultimately refused to give in to despair. Phoenix-like, he enjoyed not one but three comebacks (*Dersu Uzala*, *Kagemusha*, and *Ran*), and became the oldest active director of feature films in the world.

The wall that separated Kurosawa and Mifune was not erected overnight. Like many estranged relationships, it was built brick by brick, over many years and many issues. Mifune would not, could not commit to leading roles in Kurosawa's later films because that was a luxury he could not afford. The artistic benefits of working with Kurosawa were outweighed by the overwhelming business concerns that constantly plagued Mifune. Kurosawa felt betrayed and refused to understand how the actor could appear in inferior films, yet pass on his. Kurosawa made no effort to placate Mifune's needs and Mifune would not acquiesce to Kurosawa's demands. It was a vicious circle left unresolved.

"After [Kurosawa] died," said his nephew, "a lot of people asked me if he had left a will. He didn't have any will—as far as Hisao and I were concerned, his films, his scripts, his storyboards—that was his legacy."[50]

And it is a legacy that shows no sign of fading away. In the years since Kurosawa's death, retrospectives continue to be held all over the world—and documentaries on his life have been produced by the Independent Film Channel, the British Broadcasting Corporation, PBS, and others. His films are enjoying new life on DVD, and several of his most obscure pictures made their home video and television debuts in the years following his death.

"That the Japanese film is known at all in the West is due mainly to the pictures of Akira Kurosawa," Mifune wrote. "That I am known both here and abroad as an actor is also mainly due to him. . . . He taught me practically everything I know, and it was he who first introduced me to myself as an actor. Kurosawa has this quality, this ability to bring things out of you that you never knew were there. It is enormously difficult work, but each picture with him is a revelation. When you see his films, you find them full realizations of ideas, of emotions, of a philosophy which surprises with its strength, even shocks with its power. You had not expected to be so moved, to find within your own self this depth of understanding."[51]

"Films are made up of many elements," Kurosawa said late in his life. "Literary, theatrical, painterly, and musical. But there is something in film that is purely cinematic. When I make films or go to see the films of others, I go in hopes of experiencing this. I'm at a loss to express the quality in words. I hope one day to make a film in which every moment has that power. Until I do I am still only a student."[52]

FILMOGRAPHY

What follows are cast, credits and release information on the films of Akira Kurosawa and Toshiro Mifune. The author has made every effort to be as complete as possible. In the interest of space and their availability elsewhere, credits for some films in which Mifune made cameo appearances, and films based on stories or screenplays by Kurosawa, have been abbreviated.

For their films in Japan, however, especially the films directed by Kurosawa and/or starring Mifune, onscreen credits have been completely translated wherever possible, and supplemented when the information became available. The completeness of credits may then serve as a tool for future research and interest when viewing their films, and is especially important for those viewing subtitled home video or theatrical versions. When cast and crew information is provided at all, almost always it is skimpy at best, and rarely useful.

I have chosen not to break up their work into separate categories. Rather, films are listed by their release date in Japan. Partly this is because so much of their careers intertwined, and partly to serve as an illustration of what each was working on as their careers went off in different directions. I have also integrated Kurosawa's work as an assistant director, on films that he wrote but did not direct, and those adapted from his screenplays for this same reason. Kurosawa and Mifune's names have been underlined to make their participation in each picture easy to locate. This is especially important in Mifune's case as, where possible, I have opted to list the cast in the order in which they are billed onscreen—and for his "guest star" appearance, Mifune's name often came at or near the end.

Credits are presented thusly:

JAPANESE TITLE ("Translation of Japanese Title")
[INTERNATIONAL TITLE]
Crew, including Producer, Director, Screenplay, Story, Director of Photography, Art Director, Lighting, Sound, Music, and additional credits where known.
    Cast: Actor's name (Actor's role).
    Production company (or companies). Releasing company. Sound format (if known to be

stereophonic). Black and white or Color. Screen format. Running time. Release date in Japan.

U.S. version: U.S. title. U.S. distributor. Production credits for U.S. version (e.g., Producer, additional cast, etc.). Running time of U.S. version. MPAA rating (for films released in the United States after January 1, 1968). Earliest known release date in the United States.

Notes: Including awards, sequels, billing discrepancies, etc..

For their assistance in translating and compiling this information, I am especially indebted to Yukari Fujii and Tony Sol.

SHOJO HANAZONO ("Paradise of the Virgin Flowers")
Director, Shigeo Yagura; Screenplay, Chimio Tanaka and Matsue Fukamachi; Director of Photography, Tatsuo Tomonari; Art Director, Masao Tozuka; Sound, Kinjiro Kameyama; Music, Kyosuke Kami; Third Assistant Director, <u>Akira Kurosawa</u>

Cast: Masako Tsutsumi, Hideharu Nakano, Sumie Tsubaki, Satoko Date

A P.C.L. Co., Ltd. Production. A P.C.L. Motion Picture Co., Ltd. Release. Black and white. Standard size. 65 minutes. Released June 11, 1936.

U.S. version: Release, if any, is undetermined.

ENOKEN NO SENMAN CHOJYA ("Enoken's Ten Million")
Director, Kajiro Yamamoto; Story and Screenplay, P.C.L. Literary Division; Director of Photography, Hiromitsu Karasawa; Art Director, Takeo Kita; Sound, Jun Yamaguchi; Music, Shigekazu Kurihara; Chief Assistant Director, Senkichi Taniguchi; Second Assistant Director, Ishiro Honda; Third Assistant Directors, Motoyoshi Oda, Sojiro Motoki, and <u>Akira Kurosawa</u>

Cast: Kenichi "Enoken" Enomoto, Sadaichi Nimura, Mitsuko Hirokawa, Sadaichi Yanagida, Sumie Tsubaki, Teiko Nakamura, Kanta Kontsuki, Kisae Kitamura, Kiyoko Taka, Takeo Kitamura, Enoken Group

A P.C.L. Co., Ltd. Production. A Toho Film Distributing Co., Ltd. Release. Black and white. Standard size. 58 minutes. Released July 21, 1936.

U.S. version: Release, if any, is undetermined.

Notes: Also known as *The Millionaire* and *Enoken, the Millionaire*. The first feature distributed by Toho's newly formed distribution arm. Followed by *Enoken's Ten Million Sequel* (Zoku Enoken no senman chojya, 1936).

ZOKU ENOKEN NO SENMAN CHOJYA ("Enoken's Ten Million Sequel")
Director, Kajiro Yamamoto; Screenplay, P.C.L. Literary Division, based on a departmental story; Director of Photography, Hiromitsu Karasawa; Art Director, Takeo Kita; Sound, Jun Yamaguchi; Music, Shigekazu Kurihara; Third Assistant Director, <u>Akira Kurosawa</u>

Cast: Kenichi "Enoken" Enomoto, Sadaichi Nimura, Mitsuko Hirokawa, Sadaichi Yanagida, Enoken Group

A P.C.L. Co., Ltd. Production. A Toho Film Distributing Co., Ltd. Release. Black and white. Standard size. 53 minutes. Released September 1, 1936.

U.S. version: Release, if any, is undetermined.

TOKYO RAPESODEII ("Tokyo Rhapsody")
Director, So Fushimizu; Screenplay, Ryuji Nagami, based on a story by Takao Saeki; Director of Photography, Akira Mimura; Art Director, Masao Tozuka; Sound, Kinjiro Kaneyama; Music, Masao Koga; Third Assistant Director, <u>Akira Kurosawa</u>

Cast: Ichiro Fujiyama, Sumie Tsubaki, Reiko Hoshi, Satoko Date, Shiro Isono, Teruko Miyano

A P.C.L./Nikkatsu Corp/Teichiku/Production. A Toho Eiga Distribution Co., Ltd. Release. Black and white. Standard size. 68 minutes. Released December 1, 1936.

U.S. version: Release, if any, is undetermined.

SENGOKU GUNTO-DEN—DAI ICHIBU TORAOKAMI ("Saga of the Vagabonds—Part One: Tiger-wolf")
Director, Eisuke Takizawa; Screenplay, Kinpachi Kajihara, based on a story by Jyuro Miyoshi; Director of Photography, Hiromitsu Karasawa; Art Director, Takeo Kita; Music, Kosaku Yamada; Third Assistant Director, <u>Akira Kurosawa</u>

Cast: Chojuro Kawarazaki, Shizue Yamagishi, Kanemon Nakamura, Kunitaro Kawarazaki, Tsuruzo Nakamura, Sachiko Chiba, Zenshin-za Group

A P.C.L./Zenshin-za Production. A Toho Eiga Distribution Corp. Release. Black and white. Standard size. 74 minutes. Released February 11, 1937.

U.S. version: Release, if any, is undetermined.

Notes: Sequel: *Saga of the Vagabonds—Part Two* (Sengoku gunto-den—Dai nibu Akatsuki no zenhin, 1937). Remade as *Saga of the Vagabonds* (Sengoku gunto-den, 1959), with a screenplay by Akira Kurosawa and art direction once again by Takeo Kita.

SENGOKU GUNTO-DEN—DAI NIBU AKATSUKI NO ZENHIN ("Saga of the Vagabonds— Part Two: Forward at Dawn")
Director, Eisuke Takizawa; Screenplay, Kinpachi Kajihara, based on a story by Jyuro Miyoshi; Director of Photography, Hiromitsu Karasawa; Art Director, Takeo Kita; Music, Kosaku Yamada; Third Assistant Director, <u>Akira Kurosawa</u>

Cast: Chojuro Kawarazaki, Shizue Yamagishi, Kanemon Nakamura, Sachiko Chiba, Zenshin-za Group

A P.C.L./Zenshin-za Production. A Toho Eiga Distribution Corp. Release. Black and white. Standard size. 67 minutes. Released February 20, 1937.

U.S. version: Release, if any, is undetermined.

OTTO NO TEISO—HARU KUREBA ("A Husband's Chastity—If Spring Comes")
Director, Kajiro Yamamoto; Screenplay, Kajiro Yamamoto and Chiio Kimura, based on a story by Nobuko Yoshiya; Director of Photography, Mitsuo Miura; Art Director, Kazuo Kubo; Sound, Isamu Suzuki; Music, Shigeru Kiyoda; Second Assistant Director, Ishiro Honda; Third Assistant Director, <u>Akira Kurosawa</u>

Cast: Takako Irie, Minoru Takada, Sachiko Chiba, Sadao Maruyama, Hideko Takamine, Masako Tsutsumi

A P.C.L. Production. A Toho Eiga Distribution Corp. Release. Black and white. Standard size. 85 minutes. Released April 1, 1937.

U.S. version: Release, if any, is undetermined.

Notes: Followed by *A Husband's Chastity—Fall Again* (Otto no teiso—aki futatabi, 1937).

OTTO NO TEISO—AKI FUTATABI ("A Husband's Chastity—Fall Again")
Director, Kajiro Yamamoto; Screenplay, Kajiro Yamamoto and Chiio Kimura, based on a story by Nobuko Yoshiya; Director of Photography, Mitsuo Miura; Art Director, Kazuo Kubo; Sound, Isamu Suzuki; Music, Shigeru Kiyoda; Second Assistant Director, Ishiro Honda; Third Assistant Director, <u>Akira Kurosawa</u>

Cast: Takako Irie, Minoru Takada, Sachiko Chiba, Sadao Maruyama, Hideko Takamine, Masako Tsutsumi

A P.C.L. Production. A Toho Eiga Distribution Corp. Release. Black and white. Standard size. 85 minutes. Released April 21, 1937.

U.S. version: Release, if any, is undetermined.

NIHON JOSEI DOKUHON ("Japanese Women's Textbook")
Directors, Kajiro Yamamoto (Volume 1), Sotoji Kimura (Volume 2), and Toshio Otani (Volume 3); Screenplay, Matakichi Eguchi, Masafusa Ozaki, and Ryuji Nagami, based on two stories by Hiroshi Kikuchi: *Modern Girls Book* and *Modern Wives Book*; Directors of Photography, Akira Miura, Hiroshi Suzuki, and Yoshio Miyajima; Art Directors, Takeo Kita and Teruaki Abe; Sound, Isamu Suzuki, Kinjiro Kaneyama, and So Kataoka; Music, Shigeru Kiyoda; Third Assistant Director (Volume 1), <u>Akira Kurosawa</u>

Cast: (Volume 1) Minoru Takada, Chieko Takehisa. (Volume 2) Ranko Edogawa, Hyo Kitazawa. (Volume 3) Nijiko Kiyokawa

A P.C.L. Production. A Toho Eiga Distribution Corp. Release. Black and white. Standard size. 80 minutes. Released May 21, 1937.

U.S. version: Release, if any, is undetermined.

NADARE ("Avalanche")
Director, Mikio Naruse; Screenplay, Mikio Naruse, based on a story by Jiro Osaragi and a concept by Tomoyoshi Murayama; Director of Photography, Mikya Tachibana; Art Director, Takeo Kita; Sound, Isamu Suzuki; Music, Nobuo Iida; Assistant Directors, Ishiro Honda and <u>Akira Kurosawa</u>

Cast: Noboru Kiritachi, Ranko Edogawa, Hideo Saeki, Yuriko Hanabusa, Sho Asami, Sadao Maruyama

A P.C.L. Production. A Toho Eiga Distribution Corp. Release. Black and white. Standard size. 59 minutes. Released July 1, 1937.

U.S. version: Release, if any, is undetermined.

Notes: Double-billed with *The Clear Weather of Tokaido* (Tokaido ha nihonbare).

ENOKEN NO CHAKIRI KINTA (ZEN)—MAMAYO SANDOGASA · IKIHA YOIYOI ("Enoken's Chikiri Kinta Part 1—Momma, the Hat · The Nice Way")
Producer, Tai Hagiwara; Director, Kajiro Yamamoto; Screenplay, Kajiro Yamamoto, based on his story; Director of Photography, Hiromitsu Karasawa; Art Director, Takeo Kita; Sound, Isamu Suzuki; Music, Shigekazu Kurihara; Second Assistant Director, Ishiro Honda; Third Assistant Director, <u>Akira Kurosawa</u>

Cast: Kenichi "Enoken" Enomoto, Kiyoko Hanajima, Keiko Ichikawa, Naoya Yamagata, Zeko Nakamura, Teiichi Futamura, Kenta Kisaragi, Teiichi Yanagida, Enoken Group

A P.C.L. Production. A Toho Eiga Distribution Corp. Release. Black and white. Standard size. 63 minutes. Released July 11, 1937.

U.S. version: Release, if any, is undetermined.

Notes: Followed by *Enoken's Chikiri Kinta 2* (Enoken no Chakiri Kinta 2, 1937). Double-billed with *White Roses Are in Bloom, But* . . . (Shirobara ha sakedo).

ENOKEN NO CHAKIRI KINTA (GO)—KAERI WA KOWAI, MATEBA HIYORI ("Enoken's Chikiri Kinta Part 2—Returning Is Scary, but the Weather Will Clear If You Wait")
Producer, Tai Hagiwara; Director, Kajiro Yamamoto; Screenplay, Kajiro Yamamoto, based on his story; Director of Photography, Hiromitsu Karasawa; Art Director, Takeo Kita; Sound, Isamu

Suzuki; Music, Shigekazu Kurihara; Second Assistant Director, Ishiro Honda; Third Assistant Director, <u>Akira Kurosawa</u>

> Cast: Kenichi "Enoken" Enomoto, Kanta Isaragi, Keiko Ichikawa, Sadaichi Nimura, Enoken Group
> A P.C.L. Production. A Toho Eiga Distribution Corp. Release. Black and white. Standard size. 61 minutes. Released August 1, 1937.
> U.S. version: Release, if any, is undetermined.
> Notes: Double-billed with *Hill of the South Wind* (Minami kaze no oka).

UTSUKUSHIKI TAKA ("The Beautiful Hawk")
Producer, Masanobu Takeyama; Director, Kajiro Yamamoto; Screenplay, Shinmi Iida, based on a story by Hiroshi Kikuchi; Director of Photography, Akira Mimura; Art Director, Satoshi Chuko; Sound, Yuji Michinari; Music, Tadashi Ota; Chief Assistant Director, <u>Akira Kurosawa</u>

> Cast: Noboru Kiritachi, Hideo Saeki, Chizuko Kanda, Hyo Kitazawa, Sumie Tsubaki, Sho Asami
> A P.C.L. Production. A Toho Eiga Distribution Corp. Release. Black and white. Standard size. 82 minutes. Released October 1, 1937.
> U.S. version: Release, if any, is undetermined.
> Notes: The second half of a double bill headlined by Mikio Naruse's *Learn from Experience* (Kafuko).

CHINETSU ("Subterranean Heat")
Producer, Tei Hagiwara; Director, Eisuke Takizawa; Screenplay, Juro Miyoshi and Eisuke Takizawa, based on a story by Juro Miyoshi; Director of Photography, Akira Mimura; Art Director, Konosuke Yamazaki; Sound, Yuji Michinari; Music, Tadashi Ota; Chief Assistant Director, <u>Akira Kurosawa</u>; Assistant Director, Ishiro Honda

> Cast: Mitsugu Fujii, Chieko Takehisa, Sadao Maruyama, Masako Tsutsumi, Osamu Takizawa, Kumeko Otowa
> A Toho Eiga (Tokyo) Co., Ltd. Production. A Toho Eiga Distribution Corp. Release. Black and white. Standard size. 84 minutes. Released February 1, 1938.
> U.S. version: Release, if any, is undetermined.
> Notes: Double-billed with the documentary *Shanghai*.

TOJURO NO KOI ("Tojuro's Love")
Producer, Michimi Tamura; Director, Kajiro Yamamoto; Screenplay, Shintaro Mimura, based on a story by Kan Kikuchi; Director of Photography, Mitsuo Miura; Art Directors, Kumoyo Komura and Kohei Shima; Sound, Yuji Michinari; Dubbing Supervisor, Akira Kurosawa; Music, Akiro Sugawara (Koto) and Michio Miyagi; Chief Assistant Director, <u>Akira Kurosawa</u>; Assistant Director, Ishiro Honda

> Cast: Kazuo Hasegawa, Takako Irie, Kamatari Fujiwara, Naoyo Yamagata, Osamu Takizawa, Keinosuke Uekusa
> A Toho Eiga (Tokyo) Co., Ltd. Production. A Toho Eiga Distribution Corp. Release. Black and white. Standard size. 121 minutes. Released May 1, 1938.
> U.S. version: Release, if any, is undetermined.
> Notes: Hasegawa's first film for Toho after leaving Shochiku (where he left behind the name Chojiro Hayashi) amid tremendous publicity. Writer Uekusa appears unbilled as an extra. Kurosawa's work as dubbing director was, presumably, unbilled.

TSUZURIKATA KYOSHITSU ("Composition Class")
Producer, Nobuyoshi Morita; Director, Kajiro Yamamoto; Screenplay, Chiio Kimura, based on a story by Masako Toyoda; Director of Photography, Akira Mimura; Art Director, So Matsuda; Music, Tadashi Ota; Chief Assistant Director, <u>Akira Kurosawa</u>

Cast: Hideko Takamine, Musei Tokugawa, Nijiko Kiyokawa, Osamu Takizawa, Masaru Kodaka, Ranko Akagi

A Toho Eiga (Tokyo) Co., Ltd. Production. A Toho Eiga Distribution Corp. Release. Black and white. Standard size. 87 minutes. Released August 21, 1938.

U.S. version: Release, if any, is undetermined.

ENOKEN NO BIKKURI JINSEI ("Enoken's Surprising Life")
Producer, Michimi Tamura; Director, Kajiro Yamamoto; Screenplay, Kajiro Yamamoto, based on his story; Director of Photography, Hiromitsu Karasawa; Art Director, Kazuo Kubo; Lighting, Kaiya Sato; Sound, Isamu Kubo; Music, Shigekazu Kurihara; Chief Assistant Director, <u>Akira Kurosawa</u>

Cast: Kenichi "Enoken" Enomoto, Noboru Kiritachi, Mitsuko Hirokawa, Enoken Group

A Toho Eiga (Tokyo) Co., Ltd. Production. A Toho Eiga Distribution Corp. Release. Black and white. Standard size. 58 minutes. Released December 29, 1938.

U.S. version: Release, if any, is undetermined.

Notes: The second part of a triple bill which included *Pepper Son* (Kosho musuko) and *New Tange Sazen: Monster Sword* (Shinpen Tange Sazen [yoto no maki]).

ENOKEN NO GACHIRO JIDAI ("Enoken's Shrewd Period")
Producer, Michimi Tamura; Director, Hiromitsu Karasawa; Screenplay, Kajiro Yamamoto; Director of Photography, Isamu Suzuki; Art Director, Kazuo Kubo; Sound, Kaiya Sato; Music, Shigekazu Kurihara; Chief Assistant Director, <u>Akira Kurosawa</u>

Cast: Kenichi "Enoken" Enomoto, Noboru Kiritachi, Sadaichi Yamagida, Sadaichi Nimura, Kazuko Enami, Harue Wakahara

A Toho Eiga (Tokyo) Co., Ltd. Production. A Toho Eiga Distribution Corp. Release. Black and white. Standard size. 76 minutes. Released January 11, 1939.

U.S. version: Release, if any, is undetermined.

Notes: Double-billed with *Blizzard Ronin* (Ronin fubuki).

CHUSHINGURA (GO) ("Chushingura [Part Two]")
Producers, Yoshinobu Morita and Nobuo Aoyagi; Director, Kajiro Yamamoto; Screenplay, Shintaro Mimura; Director of Photography, Hiromitsu Karasawa; Art Director, Kohei Shima; Sound, Kenji Maruyama; Music, Nobuo Iida; Chief Assistant Director, <u>Akira Kurosawa</u>

Cast: Denjiro Okochi, Kazuo Hasegawa, Yataro Kurokawa, Ichiro Tsukita, Setsuko Hara, Isuzu Yamada, Toho All-Star Cast

A Toho Eiga (Tokyo) Co., Ltd. Production. A Toho Eiga Distribution Corp. Release. Black and white. Standard size. 89 minutes. Released April 21, 1939.

U.S. version: Release, if any, is undetermined.

Notes: Preceded by *Chushingura (Part One)* (Chushingura [zen]), on which Kurosawa did not work. Recommended by the Ministry of Education. Hideko Takamine is also credited in some sources as appearing in this production, which is highly probable, though it is unknown which part (if not both) she appeared in. Remade by Toho in 1962, which also featured Hara. Double-billed with *Chushingura (Part One)*.

NONKI YOKOCHO ("Easy Alley")
Producer, Kazuo Takimura; Director, Kajiro Yamamoto; Screenplay, Kajiro Yamamoto, based on an idea by Minoru Akita; Director of Photography, Akira Mimura; Art Director, Koko Takahashi; Lighting, Tekero Marukawa; Sound, Yatsuo Matano; Music, Yuji Taniguchi; Chief Assistant Director, <u>Akira Kuroswa</u>

Cast: Kamatari Fujiwara, Heihachiro "Henry" Okawa, Yumiko Togawa

A Toho Eiga (Kyoto) Co., Ltd. Production. A Toho Eiga Distribution Corp. Release. Black and white. Standard size. 85 minutes. Released September 19, 1939.

U.S. version: Release, if any, is undetermined.

Notes: Double-billed with *Rivals* (Enoken no ganbari senjutsu).

ROPPA NO SHINKON RYOKO ("Roppa's Honeymoon")

Producer, Kazuo Takimura; Director and Screenplay, Kajiro Yamamoto; Director of Photography, Yoshio Miyajima; Art Director, Takeo Kita; Lighting, Kyuichiro Kishida; Sound, Isamu Suzuki; Music, Seiichi Suzuki; Chief Assistant Director, <u>Akira Kurosawa</u>

Cast: Roppa Furukawa, Yoshio Kawada, Aiko Mieki, Hamako Watanabe, Nijiko Kiyokawa

A Toho Eiga (Tokyo) Co., Ltd. Production. A Toho Film Distributing Co., Ltd. Release. Black and white. Standard size. 65 minutes. Released January 4, 1940.

U.S. version: Release, if any, is undetermined.

Notes: Double-billed with *Enoken's "Yajikita"* (Enoken no Yajikita).

ENOKEN NO ZANGIRI KINTA ("Enoken's Cropped Kinta")

Producer, Teppei Himuro; Director, Kajiro Yamamoto; Screenplay, Masashi Kobayashi, based on a story by Kajiro Yamamoto; Director of Photography, Takeo Ito; Art Director, Kazuo Kubo; Lighting, Masayoshi Onuma; Sound, Isamu Suzuki; Music, Shigekazu Kurihara; Chief Assistant Director, <u>Akira Kurosawa</u>

Cast: Kenichi "Enoken" Enomoto, Sadaichi Yanagida, Hideko Sasahara

A Toho Eiga (Tokyo) Co., Ltd. Production. A Toho Film Distributing Co., Ltd. Release. Black and white. Standard size. 81 minutes. Released March 27, 1940.

U.S. version: Release, if any, is undetermined.

Notes: Double-billed with *In Case of Wife (Part Two)* (Tsuma no baai [go]).

SONGOKU ("Songoku" [Volume 1])

Producer, Kazuo Takimura; Director and Screenplay, Kajiro Yamamoto; Special Effects, Eiji Tsuburaya; Director of Photography, Akira Mimura; Art Director, So Matsumura; Lighting, Masaki Onuma; Sound, Kenji Murayama; Music, Seiichi Suzuki and Shigekazu Kurihara; Chief Assistant Director, <u>Akira Kurosawa</u>

Cast: Kenichi "Enoken" Enomoto, Ranko Hanai, Akira Kishii, Hideko Takamine, Sadaichi Yanagida, Toshio Kanei

A Toho Eiga (Tokyo) Co., Ltd. Production. A Toho Film Distributing Co., Ltd. Release. Black and white. Standard size. 72 minutes. Released November 6, 1940.

U.S. version: Release, if any, is undetermined.

Notes: Double-billed with *Songoku (Volume 2)*.

SONGOKU ("Songoku" [Volume 2])

Producer, Kazuo Takimura; Director and Screenplay, Kajiro Yamamoto; Special Effects, Eiji Tsuburaya; Director of Photography, Akira Mimura; Art Director, So Matsumura; Lighting, Masaki Onuma; Sound, Kenji Murayama; Music, Seiichi Suzuki and Shigekazu Kurihara; Chief Assistant Director, <u>Akira Kurosawa</u>

Cast: Kenichi "Enoken" Enomoto, Ranko Hanai, Akira Kishii, Hideko Takamine, Sadaichi Yanagida, Toshio Kanei

A Toho Eiga (Tokyo) Co., Ltd. Production. A Toho Film Distributing Co., Ltd. Release. Black and white. Standard size. 67 minutes. Released November 6, 1940.

U.S. version: Release, if any, is undetermined.

UMA ("Horse")

Producer, Nobuyoshi Morita; Director, Kajiro Yamamoto; Screenplay, Kajiro Yamamoto and (uncredited) Akira Kurosawa; Directors of Photography, Hiromitsu Karasawa (*Spring*), Akira Mimura (*Summer and Sets*), Hiroshi Suzuki (*Autumn*), and Takeo Ito (*Winter*); Art Director, Shu Matsuyama; Sound, Tomohisa Higuchi; Music, Shigeaki Kitamura; Second Unit Director and Editor, Akira Kurosawa; Assistant Director, Ishiro Honda; Equestrian Supervisors, Jun Maki and Shoichiro Ozaki

Cast: Hideko Takamine (Ine Onoda), Keita Fujiwara [Kamatari Fujiwara] (Jinjiro Onoda, *her father*), Chicko Takchisa (Saku Onoda), Kaoru Futaba (Grandma Ei), Takeshi Hirata (Toyokazu Onoda, *Ine's brother*), Toshio Hosoi (Kinjiro Onoda, *her youngest brother*), Setsuko Ichikawa (Tsuru Onoda, *her little sister*), Sadao Maruyama (Master Yamashita), Yoshio Kosugi (Zenzo Sakuma), Sadako Sawamura (Kikudo Yamashita), Tsuruko Mano (Madame Sakuma), Soji Kiyokawa (Mr. Sakamoto)

A Toho Co., Ltd. (Tokyo) Production. A Toho Film Distributing Co., Ltd. Release. Black and white. Standard size. 128 minutes. Released March 11, 1941.

U.S. version: *Horse*. Released by R5/S8. English subtitles. 128 minutes. No MPAA rating. Released May 9, 1986.

Notes: Recommended by the Ministry of Education. During the Pacific War, actor Kamatari Fujiwara went by the name Keita Fujiwara.

SEISHUN NO KIRYU ("Wind Currents of Youth")

Producer, Keiji Matsuzaki and Joji Shirota; Director, Shu Fushimizu; Screenplay, Akira Kurosawa, based on "Construction of Love" and "The Life Plan" by Jun Minamikawa; Director of Photography, Takeo Ito; Art Director, Shu Matsuyama; Lighting, Soichi Yokoi; Sound, Shin Ehara; Music, Ryoichi Hattori

Cast: Setsuko Hara, Toshiko Yamane, Houden Onichi, Susumu Fujita, Hyo Kitazawa, Ichiro Ryuzaki, Yuriko Hide

A Toho Eiga Co., Ltd. Production. A Toho Film Distributing Co., Ltd. Release. Black and white. Standard size. 87 minutes. Released February 14, 1942.

U.S. version: Release, if any, is undetermined.

TSUBASA NO GAIKA ("The Triumphant Song of the Wings")

Producer, Sanezumi Fujimoto; Director, Satsuo Yamamoto; Screenplay, Bonhei Sotoyama and Akira Kurosawa; Director of Photography, Taiichi Kankura; Special Effects, Eiji Tsuburaya: Art Director, Tatsuo Kita; Lighting, Kyuichiro Kishida; Music, Ryoichi Hattori

Cast: Joji Oka, Takako Irie, Ranko Hanai, Heihachiro "Henry" Okawa, Seizaburo Kawazu

A Toho Eiga Co., Ltd. Production. A Film Distribution, Inc. Release. Black and white. Standard size. 109 minutes. Released October 15, 1942.

U.S. version: Release, if any, is undetermined. Also known as *A Triumph of Wings* and *Victory Songs of Wings*.

SUGATA SANSHIRO ("Sanshiro Sugata")
[JUDO SAGA]

Producer, Keiji Matsuzaki; Director, Akira Kurosawa; Screenplay, Akira Kurosawa, based on the novel *Sugata Sanshiro* by Tsuneo Tomita; Director of Photography, Akira Mimura; Art Director, Masao Tozuka; Lighting, Masaki Onuma; Sound, Tomohisa Higuchi; Music, Seichi Suzuki; Editors, Toshio Goto and Akira Kurosawa; Assistant Directors, Toshio Sugie, Seki Nakamura; Negative Cutter, Toshio Goto; Script Supervisor, Yukie Kikuchi; Still Photographer, Akira Otani; In Charge of Production, Jin Usami; Judo Instructors, Kinnosuke Sato and Keishichi Ishiguro

FILMOGRAPHY ♟ 659

Cast: Denjiro Okochi (Shogoro Yano), Susumu Fujita (Sanshiro Sugata), Yukiko Todoroki (Sayo Murai), Ryunosuke Tsukigata (Gennosuke Higaki), Takashi Shimura (Hansuke Murai, *Sayo's father*), Ranko Hanai (Osumi Kodama), Sugisaku Aoyama (Tsunetami Iimura), Ichiro Sugai (Mishima, *chief of police*), Yoshio Kosugi (Master Saburo Kodama, *the jujitsu teacher and Osumi's father*), Kokuten Kodo (*Buddhist priest*), Michisaburo Segawa (Wada), Akitake Kono (Yoshima Dan), Soji Kiyokawa (Yujiro Toda), Kunio Mita (Kohei Tsuzaki), Akira Nakamura (Toranosuke Niiseki), Eisaburo Sakauchi (Nemeto), Hajime Hikari (Torakichi)

A Toho Eiga Co., Ltd. Production. A Film Distribution, Inc. Release. Black and white (processed by Toho Developing). Standard size. 97 minutes. Released March 25, 1943.

U.S. version: *Sanshiro Sugata*. Also released as *Judo Saga*. Released by Toho International Co., Ltd. English subtitles. 80 minutes. No MPAA rating. Released April 28, 1974.

Notes: Filmed at Toho Studios, Ltd. (Kyoto). The original Japanese cut was reconstructed and reissued in Japan in 1952; all current prints are taken from this reissue version, not the original release. Running time of reconstructed version: 80 minutes. An English-subtitled version was apparently produced by Toho at about this time and may have received limited exhibition soon thereafter. Kurosawa's first film as director. Remade in 1955 and 1965, the latter version edited by Kurosawa. Followed by *Sanshiro Sugata—Part Two* (Zoku Sugata Sanshiro, 1945). Awards: Sadao Yamanaka Prize; the National Incentive Film Prize (shared with *Torii Kyouemon*, directed by Tomu Uchida); Eiga Hyoren Film Prize (second place).

DOHYOSAI ("Wrestling-Ring Festival")
Director, Santaro Marune; Screenplay, <u>Akira Kurosawa</u>, based on a story by Hikojiro Suzuki; Director of Photography, Kazuo Miyagawa; Art Director, Heikichi Kadoi; Music, Goro Nishi and Kiyoshi Kawamura

Cast: Chiezo Kataoka, Akira Kishii, Haruyo Ichikawa

A Daiei Motion Picture Co., Ltd. Production. A Film Distribution, Inc. Release. Black and white. Standard size. 78 minutes. Released March 30, 1944.

U.S. version: Release, if any, is undetermined.

ICHIBAN UTSUKUSHIKU ("The Most Beautiful")
[THE MOST BEAUTIFUL]
Planning, Motohiko Ito; Producer, Jin Usami; Director and Screenplay, <u>Akira Kurosawa</u>; Director of Photography, Joji Ohara; Art Director, Teruaki Abe; Lighting, Masaki Onuma; Sound, Hisashi Shimonaga; Music, Seichi Suzuki; Music Producer, Hisashi Iuchi; Assistant Directors, Jin Usami and Hiromichi Horikawa; Still Photographer, Taizo Shin; Fife and Drum Band Instructor, Hisa Iuchi

Cast: Takashi Shimura (*Chief Goro Ishida*), Soji Kiyokawa (Soichi Yoshikawa, *Chief of General Affairs Section*), Ichiro Sugai (Ken Shinda, *Chief of Labor Section*), Takako Irie (Noriko Mizushima, *the dorm mother*), Yoko Yaguchi (Tsuru Watanabe, *president of the women workers*), Sayuri Tanima (Yuriko Tanimura, *vice-president of the women workers*), Sachiko Ozaki (Sachiko Yamazaki), Shizuko Nishigaki (Fusae Nishioka), Asako Suzuki (Asako Suzumura), Haruko Toyoma (Masako Koyama), Aiko Masu (Tokiko Hiroda), Kazuko Hitomi (Kazuko Futomi), Shizuko Yamada (Hisae Yamaguchi), Itoko Kono (Sue Okabe), Toshiko Hadori (Toshiko Hattori), Emiko Rei (Chie Shima), Haruko Mii (Haruko Kawai), Minori Toyohara (Minori Yoyota), Eiko Hirayama (Yoshiko Shirayama), Harue Yamashita (Kiyo Mishima), Mineko Mashiro (Mineko Bando), Isuzu Miyakawa (Shizue Miyazaki), Michiko Aikawa (Michiko Ayukawa), Teruko Kato (Teruko Sato), Akitake Kono (*fife and drum band instructor*), Unpei Yokoyama (*dormitory worker*), Chieko Nakakita (*student worker*)

A Toho Co., Ltd. Production. A Film Distribution, Inc. Release. Black and white (processed by Toho Developing). Standard size. 84 minutes. Released April 13, 1944.

U.S. version: Released by R5/S8. English subtitles. Alternate title: *Most Beautifully*. Released 1987.

Note: According to one source, this feature was shot in 16mm. It's also possible that it was shot in 35mm, but that only a 16mm print or negative survived the war.

TENBARE ISHIN TASUKE ("Bravo! Tenbare Ishin")
Producer, Sojiro Motoki; Director, Kiyoshi Saeki; Screenplay, Akira Kurosawa; Director of Photography, Kazuo Yamazaki; Art Director, Yasuhide Kato; Sound, Ryohachi Sugawara; Music, Seiichi Suzuki
    Cast: Kenichi "Enoken" Enomoto, Yukiko Todoroki, Akira Kishii, Musei Tokugawa, Toshiko Hattori, Sadaichi Yanagida
    A Toho Co., Ltd. Production. A Film Distribution, Inc. Release. Black and white. Standard size. 69 minutes. Released January 11, 1945.
    U.S. version: Release, if any, is undetermined.

ZOKU SUGATA SANSHIRO ("Sanshiro Sugata Sequel")
[SANSHIRO SUGATA—PART TWO]
Producer, Motohiko Ito; Director, Akira Kurosawa; Screenplay, Akira Kurosawa, based on the novel *Sugata Sanshiro* by Tsuneo Tomita; Director of Photography, Takeo Ito; Art Director, Kazuo Kubo; Lighting, Choshiro Ishii; Sound, Masaji Kameyama; Music, Seichi Suzuki; Assistant Directors, Jin Usami and Hiromichi Horikawa; Negative Cutter, Yoshie Yaguchi; Script Supervisor, Hachiko Toi; Still Photographers, Jun Yamazaki and Taizo Shin; In Charge of Production, Takehiro Aoki; Judo Instructors, Kinnosuke Sato and Norikazu Takamura; Karate Instructor, Yasuhiro Konishi; Kento Instructor, Tsuneo Horiguchi
    Cast: Denjiro Okochi (Shogoro Yano), Susumu Fujita (Sanshiro Sugata), Ryunosuke Tsukigata (Gennosuke Higaki *and* Teshin Higaki, *his younger brother*), Akitake Kono (Genzaburo Higaki, *his youngest brother*), Yukiko Todoroki (Sayo), Soji Kiyokawa (Yujiro Toda), Masayuki Mori (Yoshima Dan), Seiji Miyaguchi (Kohei Tsuzaki), Ko Ishida (Daisuburo Hidarimonji), Kazu Hikari (Kihei Sekine), Kokuten Kodo (*Buddhist Priest* Saiduchi), Ichiro Sugai (Yoshizo Fubiki), Osman Yusef (American sailor), Roy James, E. H. Eric
    A Toho Co., Ltd. Production. A Film Distribution, Inc. Release. Black and white (processed by Toho Developing). Standard size. 82 minutes. Released May 3, 1945.
    U.S. version: Released by R5/S8. English subtitles. Released 1987. Possibly exhibited by Toho International Co., Ltd. with or without English subtitles as early as 1974. Alternate title: *Judo Saga—II*.
    Notes: Some sources credit Hiroshi Suzuki as Director of Photography. The film was originally released without cast and crew credits. The opening credits on current prints were added after the war at the behest of Kajiro Yamamoto.

TORA NO O FUMU OTOKOTACHI ("Men Who Tread on the Tiger's Tail")
Producer, Motohiko Ito; Director, Akira Kurosawa; Screenplay, Akira Kurosawa, based on the Kabuki play *Kanjincho*; Director of Photography, Takeo Ito; Art Director, Kazuo Kubo; Lighting, Iwaharu Hiraoka; Sound, Keiji Hasebe; Music, Tadashi Hattori; Chorus, Vocal for Chorus; Negative Cutter, Toshio Goto; Script Supervisor, Hachiko Toi; Sound Effects, Ichiro Minawa; Still Photographer, Koichi Shikida; Unit Production Manager, Jin Usami
    Cast: Denjiro Okochi (Benkei), Susumu Fujita (Togashi), Kenichi "Enoken" Enomoto (Kyoryoku, *the porter*), Masayuki Mori (Kamei), Takashi Shimura (Kataoka), Akitake Kono (Ise), Yoshio Kosugi (Shunkawa), Dekao Yoko (Hidachibo), Shubo Nishina [known later as Hanshiro

Iwai] (Lord Yoshitsune), Yasuo Hisamatsu (*messenger of Kajiwara*), Soji Kiyokawa (*messenger of Togashi*)

A Toho Co., Ltd. Production. A Toho Co., Ltd. Release. Black and white (processed by Toho Development). Standard size. 59 minutes. Released April 24, 1952 (see below).

U.S. version: *The Men Who Tread on the Tiger's Tail*. Released by Brandon Films, Inc. English subtitles. 59 minutes. Released February 1960.

Notes: The Noh drama *Ataka* and the Kabuki play *Konjincho* are based on the same story. Completed in September 1945, but release withheld by the Allied Occupation Forces. Alternate titles: *Walkers on the Tiger's Tail*, *They Who Step on the Tail of the Tiger*.

ASU O TSUKURU HITOBITO ("Those Who Make Tomorrow")
Producers, Ryo Takei, Keiji Matsuzaki, Tomoyuki Tanaka, and Sojiro Motoki; Directors, Kajiro Yamamoto, <u>Akira Kurosawa</u>, and Hideo Sekigawa; Screenplay, Yusaku Yamagata and Kajiro Yamamoto; Directors of Photography, Mitsui Miura, Takeo Ito, and Taiichi Kankura; Art Directors, Takeo Kita and Keiji Kitagawa; Lighting, Soichi Yokoi, Iwaharu Hiraoka, and Kenzo Ginya; Sound, Isamu Suzuki and Masatoshi Karahima; Music, Noboru Ito

Cast: Takashi Shimura (*theater manager*), Kenji Susukida (*father*), Masayuki Mori (*driver*), Sumie Tsubaki (*driver's wife*), Chieko Nakakita (*older sister*), Sayuri Tanima (*dancing girl*), Cheiko Takehisa (*mother*), Mitsue Tachibana (*younger sister*), Ichiro Chiba (*light man*), Hyo Kitazawa (*director*), Itoko Kono (*actress*), Masao Shimizu (*section chief*), Yuriko Hamada (*second dancing girl*), Susumu Fujita, Hideko Takamine, Sachiko Mitani, Seizaburo Kawazu (themselves)

A Toho Co., Ltd. Production. A Toho Co., Ltd. Release. Black and white. Standard size. 82 minutes. Released May 2, 1946.

U.S. version: Never released in the United States.

WAGA SEISHUN NI KUINASHI ("No Regrets for Our Youth")
[NO REGRETS FOR OUR YOUTH]
Producer, Keiji Matsuzaki; Director, <u>Akira Kurosawa</u>; Screenplay, Eijiro Hisaita, Keiji Matsuzaki, and Akira Kurosawa; Director of Photography, Asakazu Nakai; Art Director, Keiji Kitagawa; Lighting, Choshiro Ishii; Sound, Isamu Suzuki; Music, Tadashi Hattori; In Charge of Production, Ryo Takei; Chief Director, Hiromichi Horikawa; Assistant Directors, Akitoshi Maeda and Ko Horiuchi; Negative Cutter, Toshio Goto; Script Supervisor, Yukie Kikuchi; Sound Effects, Ichiro Minawa; Still Photographer, Goichi Araki

Cast: Setsuko Hara (Yukie Yagihara), Susumu Fujita (Ryukichi Noge), Denjiro Okochi (Professor Yagihara, *Yukie's father*), Haruko Sugimura (Madame Noge, *Ryukichi's mother*), Eiko Miyoshi (Madame Yagihara, *the professor's wife*), Kokuten Kodo (Mr. Noge, *Ryukichi's father*), Akitake Kono (Itokawa), Takashi Shimura (Police Commissioner "Poison Strawberry" Dokuichigo), Taizo Fukami (*Minister of Education*), Masao Shimizu (Professor Hakozaki), Haruo Tanaka (*student*), Kazu Hikari (*detective*), Hisako Hara (*Itokawa's mother*), Shin Takemura (*prosecutor*), Katao Kawasaki (*servant*), Fusako Fujima (*old woman*), Sayuri Tanima, Itoko Kono, Chieko Nakakita (*ladies*), Ichiro Chiba, Isamu Yonekura, Noboru Takagi, Hiroshi Sano (*students*)

A Toho Co., Ltd. Production. A Toho Co., Ltd. Release. Black and white (processed by Toho Film Laboratory). Standard size. 110 minutes. Released October 29, 1946.

U.S. version: Released by Libra Films. English subtitles. Alternate title: *No Regrets for My Youth*. 110 minutes. No MPAA rating. Released June 6, 1980.

Notes: Apparently first screened in the United States in Los Angeles, in May 1978. Matsuzaki does not receive screen credit as co-screenwriter. Awards: Mainichi Film Contest (Best

Director, Best Screenplay), *Kinema Jumpo* "Best Ten" (placed sixth), Eiga Sekni Film Award (Best Director).

YOTSU NO KOI NO MONOGATARI ("Four Love Stories")
Producers, Keiji Matsuzaki, Sojiro Motoki, and Tomoyuki Tanaka; Directors, Shiro Toyoda, Mikio Naruse, Kenta Yamazaki, and Teinosuke Kinugasa; Screenplay, <u>Akira Kurosawa</u>, Hideo Oguni, Kenta Yamazaki, and Toshio Yasumi; Directors of Photography, So Kawamura, Seiichi Kizuka, Takeo Ito, and Asakazu Nakai; Art Directors, Shu Matsuyama, Esaka, Keiji Kitagawa, and Hirakawa; Lighting, Soichi Tahata, Ito, Kyuichiro Kishida, and Mitsuharu Hirata; Sound, Masatoshi Karahima, Michio Okazaki, Maruyama, and Yaue
    Cast: Ryo Ikebe, Yuriko Hamada, Itoko Kuwano, Akitake Kono, Isao Numasaki, Yoshiko Kuga, Setsuko Wakayama, Kenichi "Enoken" Enomoto, Sadaichi Yanagida, Teiko Nakamura, Takeo Kitamura, Taiko Fukumoto, Shizuko Nagaoka, Mari Hata, Takashi Shimura, Masao Shimizu, Yasuo Hisamatsu, Kenzo Asada, Tokuei Hanazawa, Togo Yamamoto, Yuriko Hide, Fudeko Tanaka, Ko Ishida, Tadashi Okabe, Tamotsu Kawasaki, Isamu Yonekura, Eitaro Shindo, Ichiro Sugai, Choko Iida, Tokuji Kobayashi, Haruko Sugimura, Michiyo Kogure
    A Toho Co., Ltd. Production. Black and white. Standard size. 112 minutes. Released March 11, 1947.
    U.S. version: Release, if any, is undetermined.
    Notes: Ads billed actresses Kuga and Wakayama as "New Faces." Omnibus of love stories in four parts: 1. "First Love" 2. "Separating's Fun, Too" 3. "Love Is Easy" 4. "Love Circus." Kurosawa contributed the script for Toyoda's segment only.

SUBARASHIKI NICHIYOBI ("One Wonderful Sunday")
[ONE WONDERFUL SUNDAY]
Producer, Sojiro Motoki; Director, <u>Akira Kurosawa</u>; Screenplay, Keinosuke Uegusa and Akira Kurosawa; Director of Photography, Asakazu Nakai; Art Director, Kazuo Kubo; Lighting, Kyuichiro Kishida; Sound, Jun Yasue; Music, Tadashi Hattori; Assistant Cameraman, Takao Saito; Chief Assistant Director, Tsuneo Kobayashi; Assistant Director and Negative Cutter, Zenji Koizumi; Script Supervisor, Reiko Kawamura; Sound Effects, Ichiro Minawa; Still Photographer, Yoji Takagi
    Cast: Isao Numasaki (Yuzo), Chieko Nakakita (Masako), Atsushi Watanabe (Yamamoto, *a hoodlum*), Zeko Nakamura (*Japanese dessert shop owner*), Ichiro Namiki and Toppa Utsumi (*street photographers*), Ichiro Sugai (Yamiya, *the black-marketeer*), Masao Shimizu (*manager of dance hall*), Tokuji Kobayashi (*overweight receptionist of apartment*), Shiro Mizutani (*waif*), Aguri Hidaka (*dancer*), Midori Ariyama (Sono, *Yamiya's mistress*), Sachio Sakai (*shady ticket man*), Katao Numazaki (*bakery owner*), Toshi Mori (*apartment superintendent*)
    A Toho Co., Ltd. Production. A Toho Co., Ltd. Release. Black and white (processed by Toho Film Laboratory). Standard size. 107 minutes. Released July 1, 1947.
    U.S. version: Released by FDM. English subtitles. Alternate title: *Wonderful Sunday*. 95 minutes. No MPAA rating. Released June 29, 1982. Reissued by R4/S8 in 1987.

GINREI NO HATE ("To the End of the Snow-Capped Mountains")
[SNOW TRAIL]
Producer, Tomoyuki Tanaka; Director, Senkichi Taniguchi; Screenplay, <u>Akira Kurosawa</u> and Senkichi Taniguchi; Director of Photography, Junichi Segawa; Art Director, Taiji Kawashima; Lighting, Mitsuharu Hirata; Sound, Shoji Kameyama; Music, Akira Ifukube; Editors, Akira Kurosawa and Senkichi Taniguchi; Negative Cutter, Yoshiki Nagasama; Sound Effects, Ichiro Minawa; Still

Photographer, Ikuo Kobayashi; Chief Assistant Director, Jin Usami; Assistant Directors, Kihachi Okamoto, Mikio Komatsu; Production Chief, Noboru Nezu; Special Effects, Toho Technical Division; Assistant Cameramen, Hiroshi Komatsu, Tadashi Sato, Masashi Aramaki; Assistant Lighting, Rokuro Ishikawa, Kozaburo Mikami; Property Master, Shoji Kamiho; Script Supervisor, Yoshie Yaguchi; Second Unit Director of Photography, Takeo Ito; Second Unit Lighting, Kyuichiro Kishida; Second Unit Assistant Cameramen, Yoshio Teshirogi, Takeshi Nakamachi, Jo Aizawa

Cast: <u>Toshiro Mifune</u> (Eijima), Takashi Shimura (Nojiro), Akitake Kono (Honda), Setsuko Wakayama (Haruko), Kokuten Kodo (Haruko's *grandfather*), Fusataro Ishijima (*owner of the Shikanoyu Hotel*), Haruko Toyama (*maid A*), Chizuko Okamura (*maid B*), Toshio Kasai, Ko Ishida (*students*), Eizaburo Sakauchi (*investigation chief*), Taizo Fukami (*chief detective*), Fumio Omachi (*detective*), Kenzo Asada (*reporter*), Nobumitsu Morozuki (Kiuemon), Tokubei Hanazawa, Fumiyoshi Kumagawa, Mitsuo Tsuda (*lumberjacks*)

A Toho Co., Ltd. Production. Black and white (processed by Kinuta Laboratory). Standard size. 88 minutes. Released August 5, 1947.

U.S. version: Release, if any, is undetermined.

Notes: Taniguchi's contributions to the screenplay are uncredited, as is Kurosawa's editing. Toshiro Mifune's screen debut.

SHIN BAKA JIDAI (ZEN) ("The New Age of Fools [Part 1]")
[THESE FOOLISH TIMES]
Producer, Sojiro Motoki; Director, Kajiro Yamamoto; Screenplay, Hideo Oguni; Directors of Photography, Takeo Ito and Susumu Urashima; Art Director, Shu Matsuyama; Lighting, Kazuo Ito and Hyakumi Shima; Sound, Choshichiro Mikami; Music, Yuji Koseki

Cast: Roppa Furukawa, Kenichi "Enoken" Enomoto, Minoru Takada, Aiko Mieki, Ranko Hanai, Atsushi Watanabe, <u>Toshiro Mifune</u>

A Kenichi Enomoto Acting Group/Roppa Group/Toho Co., Ltd. Production. A Toho Co., Ltd. Release. Black and white. Standard size. 77 minutes. Released October 12, 1947.

U.S. version: Release, if any, is undetermined.

Notes: It is undetermined whether Mifune's role, reportedly very minor, is in this film, its sequel, or whether he appears in both.

SHIN BAKA JIDAI (GO) ("The New Age of Fools [Part 2]")
[THESE FOOLISH TIMES II]
Producer, Sojiro Motoki; Director, Kajiro Yamamoto; Screenplay, Hideo Oguni; Directors of Photography, Takeo Ito and Susumu Urashima; Art Director, Shu Matsuyama; Lighting, Kazuo Ito and Hyakumi Shima; Sound, Choshichiro Mikami; Music, Yuji Koseki

Cast: Roppa Furukawa, Kenichi "Enoken" Enomoto, Minoru Takada, Aiko Mieki, Ranko Hanai, Atsushi Watanabe, <u>Toshiro Mifune</u>

A Kenichi Enomoto Acting Group/Roppa Group/Toho Co., Ltd. Production. A Toho Co., Ltd. Release. Black and white. Standard size. 88 minutes. Released October 26, 1947.

U.S. version: Release, if any, is undetermined.

YOIDORE TENSHI ("Drunken Angel")
[DRUNKEN ANGEL]
Producer, Sojiro Motoki; Director, <u>Akira Kurosawa</u>; Screenplay, Keinosuke Uegusa and Akira Kurosawa; Director of Photography, Takeo Ito; Art Director, Shu Matsuyama; Lighting, Kinzo [Kinji] Yoshizawa; Sound, Wataru Konuma; Music, Fumio Hayasaka, performed by the Toho Or-

chestra and Toho Modernnyaz; Song, "Jungle Boogie," lyrics by Akira Kurosawa and music by Ryoichi Hattori; Guitar, Osuke Ito; Assistant Art Director, Yoshiro Muraki; Chief Assistant Director, Tsuneo Kobayashi; Negative Cutter, Akikazu Kono; Script Supervisor, Sumiko Nakao; Sound Effects, Ichiro Minawa; Still Photographer, Masao Soeda

Cast: Takashi Shimura (Dr. Sanada), Toshiro Mifune (Matsunaga), Reizaburo Yamamoto (Okada, *the gang boss*), Michiyo Kogure (Nanae, *Matsunaga's mistress*), Chieko Nakakita (Nurse Miyo), Noriko Sengoku (Gin, *the bar girl*), Shizuko Kasagi (*singer*), Eitaro Shindo (Takahama), Masao Shimizu (*boss*), Taiji Tonoyama (*shop proprietor*), Yoshiko Kuga (*schoolgirl*), Choko Iida (*old servant*), Isamu Ikudata (*punk*), Akira Tani (*yakuza follower*), Sachio Sakai (*guitar player*), Kato Kawasaki (*flower shop proprietor*), Kumiko Kisho (*daughter at flower shop*), Toshiko Kawakubo, Haruko Toyama, Yukie Nanbu, Yoko Sugi (*dancers*), Sumire Shiroki (Anego)

A Toho Co., Ltd. Production. A Toho Co., Ltd. Release. Black and white (processed by Toho Film Laboratory). Standard size. 98 minutes. Released April 27, 1948.

U.S. version: Released by Brandon Films, Inc. English subtitles. 98 minutes. Released January 1960.

Notes: A version running 150 minutes was prepared but never released; the original negatives and all existing prints are of the cut version. Awards: Best Film Award, *Kinema Jumpo* (1948). Selected by the Ministry of Education. Mainichi Film Contest (Japanese Film Prize, Best Cinematography, Best Music), Tokyo Citizen Film Contest (Gold Medal), *Kinema Jumpo* "Best Ten" (first place).

SHOZO ("The Portrait")
Producer, Takeshi Ogura; Director, Keisuke Kinoshita; Screenplay, Akira Kurosawa; Director of Photography, Hiroshi Kusuda; Art Director, Motoji Kojima; Lighting, Ryozo Toyoshima; Sound, Saburo Ono; Music, Chuji Kinoshita; Editor, Yoshi Sugiwara; Chief Assistant Director, Masaki Kobayashi

Cast: Kuniko Igawa, Kuniko Miyake, Mitsuko Miura, Ichiro Sugai, Chieko Higashiyama, Eitaro Ozawa, Kamatari Fujiwara, Yoko Katsuragi, Keiji Sada, Toru Abe

A Shochiku Co., Ltd. Production. A Shochiku Co., Ltd. Release. Black and white. Standard size. 73 minutes. Released August 3, 1948.

U.S. version: Release, if any, is undetermined.

SHIZUKANARU KETTO ("The Quiet Duel")
[THE QUIET DUEL]
Producers, Sojiro Motoki and Hisao Ichikawa; Director, Akira Kurosawa; Screenplay, Senkichi Taniguchi and Akira Kurosawa, based on the play by Kazuo Kikuta; Director of Photography, Shoichi Aisaka; Art Director, Koichi Imai; Lighting, Tsunekichi Shibata; Sound, Mitsuo Hasegawa; Music, Akira Ifukube; Editor, Masanori Tsuji; Still Photographer, Isamu Shima

Cast: Toshiro Mifune (Dr. Kyoji Fujisaki), Takashi Shimura (Dr. Konosuke Fujisaki, *his father*), Miki Sanjo (Misao Matsumoto), Kenjiro Uemura (Susumu Nakada), Chieko Nakakita (Takiko Nakada, *his wife*), Noriko Sengoku (Apprentice Nurse Rui Minegishi), Jyonosuke Miyazaki (Corporal Horiguchi), Isamu Yamaguchi (Patrolman Nosaka), Shigeru Matsumoto (*appendicitis boy*), Hiroko Machida (*Nurse Imai*). Kan Takami (*laborer*), Kisao Tobita (*typhoid boy*), Shigeyuki Miyajima (*officer*), Tadashi Date (*father of appendicitis boy*), Etsuko Sudo (*mother of appendicitis boy*), Seiji Izumi (*policeman*), Masateru Sasaki (*old soldier*), Kenichi Miyajima (*dealer*), Yosuke Kudo (*boy*), Yakuko Ikegami (*gaudy woman*), Wakayo Matsumura (*student nurse*), Hatsuko Wakahara (Mii-chan)

A Daiei Motion Picture Co., Ltd./Film Art Association Production. A Daiei Co., Ltd. Release. Black and white. Standard size. 95 minutes. Released March 13, 1949.

U.S. version: Released by Brandon Films, Inc. English subtitles. Alternate title: *A Silent Duel*. 95 minutes. Released November 1979.

JIGOKU NO KIFUJIN ("The Lady from Hell")
Producer, Tomoyuki Tanaka; Director, Motoyoshi Oda; Screenplay, <u>Akira Kurosawa</u> and Motosada Nishikame; Director of Photography, Shinichiro Nakao; Art Director, Minoru Esaka; Lighting, Kinzo Yoshizawa; Sound, Michio Okazaki; Music, Ryoichi Hattori

    Cast: Michiyo Kogure, Eitaro Ozawa, Ichiro Ryuzaki, Minoru Takada, Takashi Shimura, Shi Tokudaiji, Akitake Kono

    A Toho Co., Ltd./Matsuzaki Production. A Toho Co., Ltd. Release. Black and white. Standard size. 72 minutes. Released March 15, 1949.

    U.S. version: Release, if any, is undetermined.

HARUNO TAWAMURE ("Spring Flirtation")
Producers, Nobuo Aoyagi and Kajiro Yamamoto; Associate Producers, Sojiro Motoki, <u>Akira Kurosawa</u>, and Senkichi Taniguchi; Director and Screenplay, Kajiro Yamamoto; Director of Photography, Kazuo Yamazaki; Art Director, Shu Matsuyama; Lighting, Kiyoyuki Hayasaka; Sound, Masakau Kamiya; Music, Fumio Hayasaka

    Cast: Hideko Takamine, Ureo Egawa, Musei Tokugawa, Jukichi Uno, Masao Mishima, Choko Iida

    A Shintoho Co., Ltd./Film Art Association Production. A Toho Co., Ltd. Release. Black and white. Standard size. 109 minutes. Released April 12, 1949.

    U.S. version: Release, if any, is undetermined.

JYAKOMAN TO TETSU ("Jakoman and Tetsu")
Producer, Tomoyuki Tanaka; Director, Senkichi Taniguchi; Screenplay, <u>Akira Kurosawa</u> and Senkichi Taniguchi, based on the story "Herring Fishery" ("Nishin gyogyo") by Keizo [Tokuzo] Kajino; Director of Photography, Junichi Segawa; Art Director, Tatsuo Kita; Lighting, Arao Wakatsuki; Sound, Masayuki Fujiyoshi; Music, Akira Ifukube

    Cast: <u>Toshiro Mifune</u> (Tetsu), Ryunosuke Tsukigata (Jakoman), Yuriko Hamada, Yoshiko Kuga, Yuriko Hide, Kamatari Fujiwara, Nijiko Kiyokawa, Eitaro Shindo

    A Toho/49 Year Pro Production. A Toho Co., Ltd. Release. Black and white. Standard size. 91 minutes. Released July 11, 1949.

    U.S. version: Release, if any, is undetermined.

    Notes: Remade as *Jakoman to Tetsu* (q.v.), directed by Kinji Fukasaku, and produced at Toei in 1964.

NORA INU ("Stray Dog")
[STRAY DOG]
Producer, Sojiro Motoki; Associate Producers, Akira Kurosawa, Senkichi Taniguchi, and Kajiro Yamamoto; Director, <u>Akira Kurosawa</u>; Screenplay, Akira Kurosawa and Ryuzo Kikushima; Director of Photography, Asakazu Nakai; Art Director, Shu Matsuyama; Lighting, Choshiro Ishii; Sound, Fumio Yanoguchi; Music, Fumio Hayasaka; Assistant Cameraman, Kazuo Yamada; Assistant Art Director, Yoshiro Muraki; Chief Assistant Director, Ishiro Honda; Assistant Director, Zenshu Koizumi; Negative Cutter, Toshio Goto; Script Supervisor, Hachiko Toi; Sound Effects, Ichiro Minawa; Still Photographer, Isei Tanaka; In Charge of Production, Seinosuke Hirai; Choreography, Yoji Ken

    Cast: <u>Toshiro Mifune</u> (Detective Murakami), Takashi Shimura (Chief Detective Sato), Keiko Awaji (Harumi Namaki, *the girlfriend*), Eiko Miyoshi (Madame Namiki, *Harumi's mother*),

Noriko Sengoku (Ogin, *the pickpocket*), Fumiko Homma (*woman of wooden tub shop*), Reikichi Kawamura (Officer Ichikawa), Eijiro Tono (*old man of wooden tub shop*), Yasushi Nagata (Investigation Chief Abe), Katsuhei Matsumoto (*bar owner*), Isao Kimura (Shinjuro Yusa), Teruko Kishi (*pickpocket*), Minoru Chiaki (*girlie show director*), Ichiro [Hajime] Sugai (*owner of Yayoi Hotel*), Gen Shimizu (Police Inspector Nakajima), Hiroshi Yanagiya (*police officer*), Reizaburo Yamamoto (Honda), Hajime Izu (*police officer of the Criminal Identification Section*), Masao Shimizu (Nakamura, *husband of a victim*), Kokuten Kodo (*old landlord*), Yunosuke Ito (*manager of* Bluebird Theatre), Akira Ubukata (*police doctor*), Fujio Nagahama (Sakura Hotel *manager*), Isao Ikukaka (Sei-san, *a hotel worker*), Shiro Mizutani (*punkster*), Eizo Tanaka (*old doctor*), Kazuko Ihonbashi (*Sato's wife*), Haruko Togo (Azuma Hotel *madam*), Haruko Toyama (*Kintaro geisha*), Aso Mie [Mitsue Yasuseki] (*woman at pinball parlor*), Rikie Sanjo (*wife of manager*), Choko Iida (Kogetsu Hotel *manager*).

A Shintoho Co., Ltd./Film Art Association Production. A Toho Co., Ltd. Release. Black and white (processed by Shintoho Developing). Standard size. 122 minutes. Released October 17, 1949.

U.S. version: Released by Toho International Co., Ltd. English subtitles. 120 minutes. Released August 1963.

Notes: Rights acquired by Toho Co., Ltd. in 1959. Remade in 1973 (q.v.). Awards: Ministry of Education Prize; Citizen Film Contest (Silver Prize); Mainichi Film Contest (Best Actor: Takashi Shimura, Cinematography, Music, Art Direction); *Kinema Jumpo* "Best Ten" (third place).

AKATSUKI NO DASSO ("Escape at Dawn")
Producer, Tomoyuki Tanaka; Director, Senkichi Taniguchi; Screenplay, Senkichi Taniguchi and Akira Kurosawa, based on the novel *Shumpuden* ("The Story of a Prostitute") by Taijiro Tamura; Director of Photography, Akira Mimura; Art Director, Shu Matsuyama; Lighting, Masaki Onuma; Sound, Masakazu Kamiya; Music, Fumio Hayasaka

Cast: Ryo Ikebe (Shinkichi Mikami), Yoshiko "Shirley" Yamaguchi (Harumi), Eitaro Ozawa, Hajime Izu, Haruo Tanaka, Setsuko Wakayama, Harue Tone

A Shintoho Co., Ltd. Production, in association with Toho Co., Ltd. A Shintoho Film Distribution Committee Release. Black and white. Standard size. 116 minutes. Released January 8, 1950.

U.S. version: Release, if any, is undetermined. Also known as *Desertion at Dawn*.

Notes: Remade by director Seijun Suzuki at Nikkatsu in 1965, as *The Story of a Prostitute* (Shumpuden).

ISHINAKA SENSEI GYOJYOKI ("Conduct Report of Professor Ishinaka")
[CONDUCT REPORT ON PROFESSOR ISHINAKA]
Producer, Sanezumi Fujimoto; Director, Mikio Naruse; Screenplay, Ryuichiro Yagi, based on a story by Yojiro Ishizaka; Director of Photography, Hiroshi Suzuki; Art Director, Satoshi Chuko; Lighting, Iwaharu Hiraoka; Music, Tadashi Hattori

Cast: Ryo Ikebe, Yuji Hori, Toshiro Mifune, Setsuko Wakayama, Kumiko Kisho, Yoko Sugi, Atsushi Watanabe, Kamatari Fujiwara

A Shintoho Co., Ltd./Fujimoto Production, in association with Toho Co., Ltd. A Shintoho Film Distribution Committee Release. Black and white. Standard size. 98 minutes. Released January 22, 1950.

U.S. version: Release, if any, is undetermined.

DATSUGOKU ("Escape from Prison")
Director, Kajiro Yamamoto
    Cast: Mieko Takamine, Takashi Shimura, Eitaro Ozawa, <u>Toshiro Mifune</u>
    A Film Art Association Production. A Daiei Co., Ltd. Release. Black and white. Standard
size. Running time undetermined. Released 1950.
    U.S. version: Release, if any, is undetermined.

SHUBUN—SUKYANDARU ("Scandal")
[SCANDAL]
Producer, Takashi Koide; Planning, Sojiro Motoki; Director, <u>Akira Kurosawa</u>; Screenplay,
Ryuzo Kikushima and Akira Kurosawa; Director of Photography, Toshio Ubukata; Art Director,
Tatsuo Hamada; Lighting, Masao Kato; Sound, Saburo Omura; Music, Fumio Hayasaka; Chief
Assistant Director, Teruo Hagiyama; Assistant Directors, Keizaburo Kobayashi, Hotaro No-
mura, Yoshiho Nihonmatsu, Yasu Nakahira; Negative Cutter, Yoshi Sugihara; Processing,
Kametaro Kamida; Special Effects, Keiji Kawakami; Equipment, Takamasa Kobayashi; Display,
Fushitaro Moriya; Still Photographer, Kazuzo Kajimoto; Script Supervisor, Hideo Morishita;
Costumes, Bunjiro Suzuki; Hair Stylist, Toku Sakuma
    Cast: <u>Toshiro Mifune</u> (Ichiro Aoye), Yoshiko "Shirley" Yamaguchi (Miyako Saigo), Yoko
Katsuragi (Masako Hiruta), Noriko Sengoku (Sumie), Sakae [Eitaro] Ozawa (Hori), Ta-
kashi Shimura (Attorney Hiruta), Shinichi Himori (Editor Asai), Koji Mi (*cameraman A*),
Ichiro Shimizu (Arai), Fumiko Okumura (*Miyako's mother*), Masao Shimizu (*judge*), Tanie
Kitabayashi (Yasu Hiruta), Sugisaku Aoyama (Dr. Kataoka), Kokuten Kodo (*old man A*), Kichi-
jiro Ueda (*old man B*), Bokuzen Hidari (*drunk*), Taiji Tonoyama (*friend of Aoye*), Junji Masuda
(*news reporter*)
    A Shochiku Co., Ltd. Production. A Shochiku Co., Ltd. Release. Black and white. Standard
size. 105 minutes. Released April 30, 1950
    U.S. version: Released by Shochiku Films of America, Inc. English subtitles. 105 minutes.
Released July 17, 1964. Reissued by Entertainment Marketing in August 1980. Released to
American television by Janus Films on September 24, 1999.
    Note: Onscreen title has Japanese word "Shubun" ("Scandal") followed by a katakana "bor-
rowed word" for "scandal" (see above).

KONYAKU YUBIWA ("Engagement Ring")
[ENGAGEMENT RING]
Producer, Ryotaro Kuwata and Keisuke Kinoshita; Director and Screenplay, Keisuke Kino-
shita; Director of Photography, Hiroshi Kusuda; Art Director, Mikio Mori; Music, Chuji
Kinoshita
    Cast: Jukichi Uno, Kinuyo Tanaka, <u>Toshiro Mifune</u>, Mitsuko Yoshikawa, Nobuko Otowa,
Kenji Usuda, Junji Masuda, Mitsuko Yoshikawa
    A Shochiku Co., Ltd./Kinuyo Tanaka Production. A Shochiku Co., Ltd. Release. Black and
white. Standard size. 96 minutes. Released 1950.
    U.S. version: Release, if any, is undetermined.
    Also known as *Engage Ring* (sic).

JIRUBA NO TETSU ("Tetsu of Jilba")
Director, Isamu Kosugi; Screenplay, <u>Akira Kurosawa</u> and Goro Tanada, based on a story by
Shinzo Kajino; Director of Photography, Kazue Nagatsu
    Cast: Utaemon Ichikawa, Yuriko Hamada

A Toyoko Eiga Co., Ltd. Production. Black and white. Standard size. 89 minutes. Released August 12, 1950.

U.S. version: Release, if any, is undetermined.

RASHOMON ("Rashomon")
[RASHOMON]
Executive Producer, Masaichi Nagata; Associate Producer, Minoru Jingo; Director, <u>Akira Kurosawa</u>; Screenplay, Shinobu Hashimoto and Akira Kurosawa, based on the stories "Rashomon" and "In a Groove" ("Yabu no naka") by Ryunosuke Akutagawa; Director of Photography, Kazuo Miyagawa; Art Director, Shu Matsuyama; Lighting, Kenichi Okamoto; Sound, Daiei Recording Studio; Music, Fumio Hayasaka; Set Decorator, H. Matsumoto

Cast: <u>Toshiro Mifune</u> (Tajomaru, *the bandit*), Machiko Kyo (Masago, *the samurai's wife*), Takashi Shimura (*the woodcutter*), Masayuki Mori (Takehiro, *the samurai*), Minoru Chiaki (*the priest*), Kichijiro Ueda (*the commoner*), Daisuke Kato (*the policeman*), Fumiko Homma (*the medium*)

A Daiei Motion Picture Co., Ltd. Production. A Daiei Co., Ltd. Release. Black and white. Standard size. 88 minutes. Released August 25, 1950.

U.S. version: Released by RKO Radio Pictures, Inc. English subtitles. Prints by Pathé. Simultaneously released English-dubbed in some markets. Released December 26, 1951.

Notes: Also known as *Rasho-mon*. Nagata's name does not appear on original release prints and was added after the film's international success. The dubbed version superimposes shots of the main characters over the Japanese titles. American rights reverted to Daiei after RKO began releasing its product in Japan through Universal. Reissued in America by Edward Harrison in 1957. Remade as *The Outrage* (q.v.). Awards: Venice Film Festival [1951] (Grand Prize); Academy Award (1951; an honorary award as Best Foreign Film)

TATESHI DANPEI ("Fencing Master")
Director, Masahiro Makino; Screenplay, <u>Akira Kurosawa</u>, based on a story by Yukinobu Hasegawa; Director of Photography, Shigeto Miki; Music, Tokuji Okubo

Cast: Utaemon Ichikawa, Ryunosuke Tsukigata, Chiaki Tsukioka

A Toei Co., Ltd. Production. A Toei Co., Ltd. Release. Black and white. Standard size. 103 minutes. Released August 26, 1950.

U.S. version: Release, if any, is undetermined. Also known as *Swordplay Choreographer*.

AI TO NIKUSHIMI NO KANATA E ("Beyond Love and Hate")
[BEYOND LOVE AND HATE]
Producer, Tomoyuki Tanaka; Director, Senkichi Taniguchi; Screenplay, Senkichi Taniguchi and <u>Akira Kurosawa</u>, based on the story "Fugitive" by Kotaro Samukawa; Director of Photography, Masao Tamai; Art Director, Tatsuo Kita; Lighting, Kyuichiro Kishida; Sound, Masayuki Fujiyoshi; Music, Akira Ifukube

Cast: Ryo Ikebe, Mitsuko Mito, <u>Toshiro Mifune</u>, Takashi Shimura, Sakae Ozawa [Eitaro Ozawa], Kichijiro Ueda

A Film Art Association Production. A Toho Co., Ltd. Release. Black and white. Standard size. 107 minutes. Released January 11, 1951.

U.S. version: Release, if any, is undetermined.

EREJII ("Elegy")
[ELEGY]
Producers/Planners, Kazuhei Hoshino and Sojiro Motoki; Director, Kajiro Yamamoto; Screenplay, Hideo Oguni and Kajiro Yamamoto, based on the story "Saint Woman" by Hideo Oguni; Director of Photography, Asakazu Nakai; Art Director, Shu Matsuyama; Lighting, Kyuichiro Kishida; Sound, Masanobu Miyazaki; Music, Urato Watanabe

Cast: Ken Uehara, Mieko Takamine, <u>Toshiro Mifune</u>, Takashi Shimura, Haruna Kaburagi, Kyoko Yoshizawa

A Toho Co., Ltd./Film Art Association Production. A Toho Co., Ltd. Release. Black and white. Standard size. 110 minutes. Released February 24, 1951.

U.S. version: Release, if any, is undetermined.

HAKUCHI ("Idiot")
[THE IDIOT]
Executive Producer, Takashi Koide; Producer, Sojiro Motoki; Director, <u>Akira Kurosawa</u>; Screenplay, Eijiro Hisaita and Akira Kurosawa, based on the novel *The Idiot* (1868–69) by Fyodor Mikhailovich Dostoevsky; Director of Photography, Toshio Ubukata; Art Director, Shu Matsuyama; Lighting, Akio Tamura; Sound, Yoshisaburo Imo; Music, Fumio Hayasaka; Camera Operator, Asakazu Nakai; Chief Assistant Director, Yoshitaro Nomura; Settings, Shohei Sekine and Genzo Komiya; Set Decorator, Ushitaro Shimada; Assistant Editor, Yoshi Sugihara

Cast: Setsuko Hara (Taeko Nasu), Masayuki Mori (Kinji Kameda), <u>Toshiro Mifune</u> (Denkichi Akama), Takashi Shimura (Ono, *Taeko's father*), Chieko Higashiyama (Satoko, *Taeko's mother*), Chiyoko Fumiya (Noriko), Eijiro Yanagi (Tohata), Yoshiko Kuga (Ayako), Minoru Chiaki (Mutsuo Kayama), Kokuten Kodo (Jumpei), Eiko Miyoshi (Madame Kayama), Noriko Sengoku (Takako), Daisuke Inoue (Kaoru), Bokuzen Hidari (Karube), Mitsuyo Akashi (Madame Akama)

A Shochiku Co., Ltd. Production. A Shochiku Co., Ltd. Release. Black and white. Standard size. 180 minutes (premiere engagement only; cut to 166 minutes for subsequent release). Released May 23, 1951.

U.S. version: Released by Shochiku Films of America, Inc. English subtitles. 166 minutes. Released April 30, 1963.

Notes: Kurosawa prepared a 265-minute cut, which apparently was never shown theatrically.

KEDAMONO NO YADO ("The Den of Beasts")
Producer, Koichiro Ogura; Director, Tatsuyasu Osone; Screenplay, <u>Akira Kurosawa</u>, based on the story "The Rose on the Lake" ("Mizumi nobara") by Shinya Fujiwara; Director of Photography, Kiyoshi Kataoka; Art Director, Haruhide Kuwano; Music, Mitsuo Kato

Cast: Takashi Shimura, Keiko Kishi, Koji Tsuruta, Ichiro Arishima

A Shochiku-Kyoto Co., Ltd. Production. A Shochiku Co., Ltd. Release. Black and white. Standard size. 85 minutes. Released June 8, 1951.

U.S. version: Release, if any, is undetermined.

KAIZUKUSEN ("Pirate Ship")
[PIRATES]
Producers, Sojiro Motoki and Hidehisa Kan; Director, Hiroshi Inagaki; Screenplay, Hideo Oguni; Director of Photography, Hiroshi Suzuki; Art Director, Teruaki Abe; Lighting, Shigeru Mori; Sound, Shoji Kameyama; Music, Shiro Fukai

Cast: <u>Toshiro Mifune</u>, Shinobu Asaji, Tomoemon Otani, Jun Tazaki, Hisaya Morishige, Kichijiro Ueda

A Toho Co., Ltd. Production. A Toho Co., Ltd. Release. Black and white. Standard size. 114 minutes. Released July 13, 1951.

U.S. version: Release, if any, is undetermined.

SENGOHA OBAKE TAIKAI ("Postwar Ghost Contest")
[MEETING OF THE GHOST OF APRÈS-GUERRE]
Producer, Sanezumi Fujimoto; Director, Kiyoshi Saeki

Cast: Keiju Kobayashi, Yoko Sugi, <u>Toshiro Mifune</u>

A Fujimoto Production. A Shintoho Co., Ltd. Release. Black and white. Standard size. Running time undetermined. Released 1951.

U.S. version: Release, if any, is undetermined.

Notes: "Après-Guerre," or *apure geru*, refers to the Japanese postwar generation.

KANKETSU SASAKI KOJIRO—GANRYU-TO KETTO ("Conclusion of Kojiro Sasaki—Duel on Ganryu Island")
[KOJIRO SASAKI]
Producers, Nobuyoshi Morita and Shizuharu Miyagi; Director, Hiroshi Inagaki; Screenplay, Motozo Murakami, Kenro Matsuura, and Yumi Fujiki, based on a story by Motozo Murakami; Director of Photography, Tadashi Iimura; Art Director, Takeo Kita; Lighting, Kyuichiro Kishida; Sound, Masanobu Miyazaki; Music, Shiro Fukai

Cast: Tomoemon Otani (Kojiro Sasaki), <u>Toshiro Mifune</u> (Musashi Miyamoto), Hisako Yamane, Shin Tokudaiji, Yuriko Hamada, Kamatari Fujiwara

A Toho Co., Ltd. Production. A Toho Co., Ltd. Release. Black and white. Standard size. 98 minutes. Released October 26, 1951.

U.S. version: Release, if any, is undetermined. Also known as *Kojiro Sasaki III*.

BAKU ROU ICHIDAI ("The Life of a Horse-Trader")
[THE LIFE OF A HORSE-TRADER]
Director, Keigo Kimura: Screenplay, Masashige Narusawa and Keigo Kimura, based on the novel by Masao Nakayama; Director of Photography, Shigeyoshi Mine; Music, Fumio Hayasaka

Cast: <u>Toshiro Mifune</u>, Machiko Kyo, Takashi Shimura, Ichiro Sugai, Bokuzen Hidari

A Daiei Motion Picture Co., Ltd. Production. A Daiei Co., Ltd. Release. Black and white. Standard size. 113 minutes. Released 1951.

U.S. version: Release, if any, is undetermined.

Notes: Filmed at Daiei-Tokyo Studios. Followed by *The Life of a Horse-Trader Sequel* (Zoku Baku rou ichidai, 1953), made without Mifune, and remade by Toei in 1963.

ONNAGOGORO DARE KA SHIRU ("Who Knows a Woman's Heart")
[WHO KNOWS A WOMAN'S HEART]
Producer, Sojiro Motoki; Director, Kajiro Yamamoto; Screenplay, Toshio Yasumi and Kajiro Yamamoto, based on a story by Makoto Hokujo; Director of Photography, Asakazu Nakai; Art Director, Keiji Kitagawa; Lighting, Shigeru Mori; Sound, Hisashi Shimonaga; Music, Urato Watanabe

Cast: Mieko Takamine, Ryo Ikebe, <u>Toshiro Mitune</u>, Kyoko Kagawa, Choko Iida, Masao Shimizu

A Toho Co., Ltd. Production. A Toho Co., Ltd. Release. Black and white. Standard size. 80 minutes. Released December 21, 1951.

U.S. version: Release, if any, is undetermined.

ARAKI SAUEMON—KETTO KAGIYA NO TSUJI ("Sauemon Araki—Duel at the Key-Maker's Corner")
[VENDETTA FOR A SAMURAI]
Producer, Sojiro Motoki; Director, Kazuo Mori; Screenplay, Akira Kurosawa; Director of Photography, Kazuo Yamazaki; Art Director, Shu Matsuyama; Lighting, Kyuichiro Kishida; Sound, Masanobu Miyazaki; Music, Goro Nishi

Cast: Toshiro Mifune (Mataemon Araki), Yuriko Hamada, Takashi Shimura, Akihiko Katayama, Minoru Chiaki, Daisuke Kato, Shin Tokudaiji

A Toho Co., Ltd. Production. A Toho Co., Ltd. Release. Black and white. Standard size. 82 minutes. Released January 3, 1952.

U.S. version: Release, if any, is undetermined. An English-subtitled version was produced by Toho prior to 1955. Also known as *Vendetta of Samurai*.

KIRIBUE ("Foghorn")
[FOGHORN]
Producer, Tomoyuki Tanaka; Director, Senkichi Taniguchi; Screenplay, Toshio Yasumi and Senkichi Taniguchi, based on the novel by Jiro Osaragi; Director of Photography, Masao Tamai; Art Director, Shu Matsuyama; Lighting, Tsuruzo Nichikawa; Sound, Ariaki Hosaka; Music, Ichiro Saito and Nobuo Iida

Cast: Yoshiko "Shirley" Yamaguchi, Toshiro Mifune, Bob Booth, Takashi Shimura, Fuyuki Murakami, Noriko Sengoku

A Toho Co., Ltd. Production. A Toho Co., Ltd. Release. Black and white. Standard size. 99 minutes. Released March 3, 1952.

U.S. version: Release, if any, is undetermined.

Notes: Previously filmed by director Minoru Murata.

SAIKAKU ICHIDAI ONNA ("Saikaku—Life of a Woman")
[THE LIFE OF OHARU]
Executive Producer, Isamu Yoshiji; Producer, Hideo Koi; Director, Kenji Mizoguchi; Screenplay, Yoshikata Yoda and Kenji Mizoguchi, based on the 1686 novel *Koshoku ichidai onna* ("The Woman Who Loved Love") by Saikaku Ihara; Director of Photography, Yoshimi Hirano; Art Director, Hiroshi Mizutani; Music, Ichiro Saito; Historical Consultant, Isamu Yoshi

Cast: Kinuyo Tanaka (Oharu), Tsukue Matsura (Tomo, *Oharu's mother*), Ichiro Sugai (Shinzaemon, *Oharu's father*), Toshiro Mifune (Katsunosuke), Toshiake Konoe (Lord Harutaka Matsudaira), Hisako Yamane (Lady Matsudaira), Jukichi Uno (Yakichi Ogiya), Eitaro Shindo (Kahe Sasaya), Akira Oizumi (Fumikichi, *Sasaya's friend*), Masao Shimizu (Kikuoji), Daisuke Kato (Tasaburo Hishiya), Toranosuke Ogawa (Yoshioka), Hiroshi Oizumi (Manager Bunkichi), Haruyo Ichikawa (Lady-in-waiting Iwabashi), Kikue Mori (Myokai), Yuriko Hamada (Otsubone Yoshioka), Noriko Sengoku (Lady-in-waiting Sakurai), Sadako Sawamura (Owasa), Masao Mishima (Taisaburo Hishiya), Eijiro Yanagi (*counterfeiter*), Chieko Higashiyama (Myokai, *the old nun*), Bokuzen Hidari (*clothes rental shop owner*), Takashi Shimura (*old man*), Benkei Shiganoya (Jihei)

A Shintoho Co., Ltd./Koi Productions Production. A Shintoho Film Distribution Committee Release. Black and white. Standard size. 148 minutes. Released April 3, 1952.

U.S. version: Released by Toho International Co., Ltd. English subtitles. 133 minutes. Released April 20, 1964.

Notes: Some versions run 137 minutes. Awards: Venice Film Festival (Grand Prize).

SENGOKU BURAI ("Vagabonds in a Country at War")
[SWORD FOR HIRE]
Producer, Tomoyuki Tanaka; Director, Hiroshi Inagaki; Screenplay, Hiroshi Inagaki and <u>Akira Kurosawa</u>, based on a serialized novel by Yasushi Inoue, published in *Sunday Mainichi*; Director of Photography, Tadashi Iimura; Art Director, Takeo Kita; Lighting, Tsuruzo Nichikawa; Sound, Shoji Kameyama; Music, Ikuma Dan; Chief Assistant Director, Katsuya Shimizu; Still Photographer, Matsuo Yoshizaki

Cast: <u>Toshiro Mifune</u> (Hayatenosuke Sasa), Rentaro Mikuni (Jurota Tachibana), Danshiro Ichikawa (Yaheiji Kagami), Yoshiko "Shirley" Yamaguchi (Oryo), Shinobu Asaji (Kano), Takashi Shimura, Yoshio Kosugi, Sugisaku Aoyama, Eijiro Higashino [Eijiro Tono], Ryosuke Kagawa, Kokuten Kodo, Kichijiro Ueda, Eiko Miyoshi

A Toho Co., Ltd. Production. A Toho Co., Ltd. Release. Black and white. Standard size. 134 minutes. Released May 22, 1952.

U.S. version: Released by Topaz Film Company. English subtitles with narration by Bob Booth. Released November 15, 1956.

Notes: The version released by Topaz was produced by Toho. Booth frequently appeared in Toho's films of the 1950s (see *Foghorn*, *The Black Fury*).

TOKYO NO KOIBITO ("Tokyo Sweetheart")
[JEWELS IN OUR HEARTS]
Producers, Hisatora Kumagai and Sanezumi Fujimoto; Director, Yasuki Chiba; Screenplay, Toshiro Ide and Fumio Yoshida; Director of Photography, Tadashi Iimura; Art Director, Takeo Kita; Lighting, Masaki Onuma; Sound, Masanobu Miyazaki; Music, Hyoei Hamagami

Cast: Setsuko Hara, <u>Toshiro Mifune</u>, Yoko Sugi, Hisaya Morishige, Murasaki Fujima, Hiroshi Koizumi, Nijiko Kiyokawa, Kazuo Masubuchi

A Toho Co., Ltd. Production. A Toho Co., Ltd. Release. Black and white. Standard size. 97 minutes. Released July 15, 1952.

U.S. version: Release, if any, is undetermined.

Notes: An English-subtitled version was produced by Toho prior to 1955. Also known as *Tokyo Sweetheart*.

IKIRU ("Living")
[DOOMED]
Producer, Sojiro Motoki; Director, <u>Akira Kurosawa</u>; Screenplay, Akira Kurosawa, Shinobu Hashimoto, and Hideo Oguni; Director of Photography, Asakazu Nakai; Art Director, Shu Matsuyama; Lighting, Shigeru Mori; Sound, Fumio Yanoguchi; Music, Fumio Hayasaka, performed by the Cuban Boys, P.C.L. Swingband, and the P.C.L. Orchestra; Assistant Cameraman, Takao Saito; Assistant Art Director, Yoshiro Muraki; Adviser to the Director, Hiromichi Horikawa; Chief Assistant Director, Hisanobu Marubayashi; Assistant Director, Teruo Maru; Negative Cutter, Koichi Iwashita; Script Supervisor, Teruyo Nogami; Sound Effects, Ichiro Minawa; Still Photographer, Masao Soeda; Unit Production Manager, Teruo Maki; Hair Stylist, Sadako Okada; Accountant, Akira Araki

Cast: Takashi Shimura (Kanji Watanabe, *Chief of Citizens Section*), Shinichi Himori (Kimura, *assistant, Citizen's Section*), Haruo Tanaka (Sakai, *assistant, Citizen's Section*), Minoru Chiaki (Noguchi, *assistant, Citizen's Section*), Miki Odagiri (Toyo Odagiri), Bokuzen Hidari (Ohara, *assistant, Citizen's Section*), Minosuke Yamada (Subordinate Clerk Saito), Kamatari Fujiwara (Subsection Chief Ono), Makoto Kobori (Kiichi Watanabe, *Kanji's older brother*), Nobuo Kaneko (Mitsuo Watanabe, *Kanji's son*), Nobuo Nakamura (*deputy mayor*), Atsushi Watanabe (*patient*),

Isao Kimura (*intern*), Masao Shimizu (*doctor*), Yunosuke Ito (*novelist*), Kumeko Urabe (Tatsu Watanabe, *Kiichi's wife*), Kin Sugai, Eiko Miyoshi, Fumiko Homma (*petitioning housewives*), Yatsuko Tanami (*madame of bar*), Yoshie Minami (*the maid*), Kyoko Seki (Kazue Watanabe, *Mitsuo's wife*), Kusuo Abe (*city assemblyman*), Tomo Nagai, (*newspaperman A*), Seiji Miyaguchi (*yakuza boss*), Daisuke Kato (*first yakuza*), Miki Hayashi (*second yakuza*), Fuyuki Murakami (*newspaperman B*), Hirayoshi Aono (*newspaperman C*), Toranosuke Ogawa (*Park Section Chief*), Akira Sera (*worker in General Affairs*), Ichiro Chiba (*policeman*), Akira Tani (*bar owner*), Yoko Kajima (*worker in Sewage Section*), Haruko Toyama, Mie [no other name given] (*woman at dance hall*), Sachio Sakai (*yakuza*). *Special Appearances*: Toshiyuki Ichimura (*pianist*), Harue Kuramoto (*dancer*), Lasa Saya (*stripper*)

A Toho Co., Ltd. Production. A Toho Co., Ltd. Release. Black and white (processed by Toho Developing). Standard size. 143 minutes. Released October 9, 1952.

U.S. version: *Ikiru*. Released by Brandon Films, Inc. English subtitles. Released February 1960.

Note: A Toho 20th Anniversary Production. First exhibited in America March 25, 1956, in Westwood, California, as *Doomed*. Alternate title: *To Live*. Awards: Silver Bear Prize (Berlin International Film Festival, 1954); Art Festival, Minister of Education Award; Mainichi Shimbun Film Concourse, Japanese Film Award: *Kinema Jumpo* "Best One" Prize (1952); Eiga Sekai Award, David O. Selznick Golden Laurel Award (1961), and many others.

GEKIRYU ("A Swift Current")
[SWIFT CURRENT]
Producer, Tomoyuki Tanaka; Director, Senkichi Taniguchi; Screenplay, Motosada Nishikame and Senkichi Taniguchi; Director of Photography, Kazuo Yamada; Art Director, Tatsuo Kita; Lighting, Tsuruzo Nichikawa; Sound, Ariaki Hosaka; Music, Akira Ifukube

Cast: <u>Toshiro Mifune</u>, Asami Kuji, Setsuko Wakayama, Yuriko Tashiro, Setsuko Shimazaki, Masao Shimizu

A Toho Co., Ltd. Production. A Toho Co., Ltd. Release. Black and white. Standard size. 96 minutes. Released October 23, 1952.

U.S. version: Release, if any, is undetermined.

MINATO E KITA OTOKO ("The Man Who Came to Port")
[THE MAN WHO CAME TO PORT]
Producer, Tomoyuki Tanaka; Director, Ishiro Honda; Screenplay, Ishiro Honda and Masashige Narizawa, based on the story "Dance of the Stormy Waves" by Shinzo Kajino; Director of Photography, Taiichi Kankura; Art Director, Tatsuo Kita; Lighting, Shigeru Mori; Sound, Masayuki Fujiyoshi; Music, Ichiro Saito; Still Photographer, Masao Fukuda; Chief Assistant Director, Jun Fukuda; Planning, Yasuaki Sakamoto

Cast: <u>Toshiro Mifune</u>, Asami Kuji, Takashi Shimura, Hiroshi Koizumi, Bokuzen Hidari, Yuriko Tashiro, Kamatari Fujiwara, Shujiro Tomita, Seijiro Onda, Ren Imaizumi, Senkichi Omura, Ren Yamamoto, Soichi "Solomon" Hirose, Masaaki Tachibana, Kenzo Echigo, Sachio Sakai, Teruhiko Suzuki, Yasuhisa Tsutsumi, Shiego Kato, Akira Yamada, Hideo Ihara, Etsuryo Saijo, Nira Kumagai, Akira Sera, Junpei Natsuki, Akira Kichijoji, Yaeko Izumo, Yoko Ueno, Tsuruko Umano, Yutaka Oka, Akira Tani

A Toho Co., Ltd. Production. A Toho Co., Ltd. Release. Black and white. Standard size. 88 minutes. Released November 27, 1952.

U.S. version: Release, if any, is undetermined.

FUKEYO HARUKAZE ("Blow! Spring Wind")
[MY WONDERFUL YELLOW CAR]
Producer, Tomoyuki Tanaka; Director, Senkichi Taniguchi; Screenplay, <u>Akira Kurosawa</u> and Sen-kichi Taniguchi; Director of Photography, Tadashi Iimura; Art Director, Kazuo Ogawa; Lighting, Shigeru Mori; Sound, Choshichiro Mikami; Music, Yasushi Akutagawa

 Cast: <u>Toshiro Mifune</u>, Hisako Yamane, So Yamamura, Fubuki Koshiji, Mariko Okada, Kyoko Aoyama

 A Toho Co., Ltd. Production. A Toho Co., Ltd. Release. Black and white. Standard size. 83 minutes. Released January 15, 1953.

 U.S. version: Release, if any, is undetermined.

 Notes: Double-billed with *My Boss's Youth* (Oyabun no seishin).

HOYO ("The Last Embrace")
[THE LAST EMBRACE]
Producer, Tomoyuki Tanaka; Director, Masahiro Makino; Screenplay, Motosada Nishikame and Haruo Umeda, based on an idea by Toshio Yasumi; Director of Photography, Tadashi Iimura; Art Director, Kazuo Ogawa; Lighting, Tsuruzo Nichikawa; Sound, Yumei Hosaka; Music, Yasushi Akutagawa

 Cast: Yoshiko "Shirley" Yamaguchi (Yukiko Nogami), <u>Toshiro Mifune</u> (Shinkichi), <u>Toshiro Mifune</u> (Hayakawa), Takashi Shimura (Watanabe, *alias Nabesan*), Akihiko Hirata (Yamaoka, *alias Sandaime*), Hiroshi Koizumi (Yoshikawa, *alias Sampei*), Sachio Sakai (Uchimura, *alias Saboten*), Ren Yamamoto (Numaguchi, *alias Kurochan*), Seiji Miyaguchi, Katsumi Tezuka (*gangsters*), Toyoko Takegawa (Madame Natsuko), Yo Shiomi (Mitsutaro)

 A Toho Co., Ltd. Production. A Toho Co., Ltd. Release. Black and white. Standard size. 87 minutes. Released March 11, 1953.

 U.S. version: Release, if any, is undetermined. An English-subtitled version was produced by Toho.

 Notes: Mifune plays a dual role, hence billing above.

HIMAWARI MUSUME ("Sunflower Girl")
[LOVE IN A TEACUP]
Producer, Sanezumi Fujimoto; Director, Yasuki Chiba; Screenplay, Kimiyuki Hasegawa, based on a story by Keita Genji; Director of Photography, Kazuo Yamada; Art Director, Yasuhide Kato; Lighting, Masayoshi Onuma; Sound, Wataru Konuma; Music, Toshiro Mayuzumi

 Cast: <u>Toshiro Mifune</u> (Ippei Hitachi), Ineko Arima (Setsuko Fujino), Hajime Izu (Ryosuke Tanabe), Mayuri Mokusho (Toshiko Shiimura), Sumiko Abe (Eiko Ishii), Keiko Sawamura (Mikiko Iida), Masao Shimizu (Setsuko's father), Sachiko Murase (Setsuko's mother), Daisuke Inoue (Setsuko's brother)

 A Toho Co., Ltd. Production. A Toho Co., Ltd. Release. Black and white. Standard size. 87 minutes. Released March 26, 1953.

 U.S. version: Release, if any, is undetermined.

 Notes: An English-subtitled version was produced. Also known as *Sunflower Girl*.

TAIHEIYO NO WASHI ("Eagle of the Pacific")
[THE EAGLE OF THE PACIFIC]
Executive Producer, Iwao Mori; Producer, Sojiro Motoki; Director, Ishiro Honda; Screenplay, Shinobu Hashimoto; Director of Photography, Kazuo Yamada; Art Directors, Takeo Kita and Gen Akune; Lighting, Masayoshi Onuma; Sound, Masanobu Miyazaki; Music, Yuji Koseki; Spe-

cial Effects Staff Supervisor, Motoyoshi Oda; Special Effects, Eiji Tsuburaya, Akira Watanabe, and Hiroshi Mukoyama

Cast: Denjiro Okochi (Admiral Isoroku Yamamoto), Hiroshi Nihonyanagi (Commander Furukawa), Masao Shimizu (Commander Kashima), Eijiro Yanagi (Premier Admiral Mitsumasa Yonai), Minoru Takada (Prince Fumimaro Konoe), Ichiro Sugai (Admiral Koshiro Oikawa), Takashi Shimura (Colonel A, *staff officer of the Army*), Takamaru Sasaki (Chief of Staff, *Combined Fleet*), Bontaro Miake (Commander of the Task Force), Rentaro Mikuni, Keiju Kobayashi, Hajime Izu (staff officers), <u>Toshiro Mifune</u> (1st Lt. Tomonaga), Toranosuke Ogawa, Minosuke Yamada, Fuyuki Murakami, Heihachiro "Henry" Okawa, Yoshio Kosugi, Koreya Senda, Sachio Sakai, Haruo Nakajima

A Toho Co., Ltd. Production. A Toho Co., Ltd. Release. Black and white. Standard size. 119 minutes. Released October 21, 1953.

U.S. version: Release, if any, is undetermined.

Notes: Includes stock footage from *The War at Sea from Hawaii to Malaya* (1942) and possibly other wartime Toho films.

SHICHININ NO SAMURAI ("Seven Samurai")
[SEVEN SAMURAI]

Producer, Sojiro Motoki; Director, <u>Akira Kurosawa</u>; Screenplay, Akira Kurosawa, Shinobu Hashimoto, and Hideo Oguni; Director of Photography, Asakazu Nakai; Art Director, Shu Matsuyama; Lighting, Shigeru Mori; Sound, Fumio Yanoguchi; Music, Fumio Hayasaka; Music Assistant, Masaru Sato; Assistant Camera, Takao Saito; Assistant Lighting, Mitsuo Kaneko; Assistant Art Director, Yoshiro Muraki; Sound Assistant, Masanao Uehara; Chief Assistant Director, Hiromichi Horikawa; Assistant Directors, Sakae Hirosawa, Masaya Shimizu; Yasuyoshi Tajitsu, and Toshi Kaneko; Negative Cutter, Koichi Iwashita; Script Supervisor, Teruyo Nogami; Sound Effects, Ichiro Minawa; Still Photographer, Masao Fukuda; Production Supervisor, Hiroshi Nezu; Production Assistant, Takeharu Shimada; Accountant, Yuji Hamada; Art Consultants, Seison Maeda and Kohei Ezaki; Property Master, Koichi Hamamura; Costumes, Mieko Yamaguchi (Kyoto Costume); Hair Stylists, Midori Nakajo and Junjiro Yamada; Acting Office, Toshio Nakane; Swordplay Instructor, Yoshio Sugino; Archery Instructor, Ienori Kaneko; Archery Instructor (Horseback), Shigeru Endo

Cast: *The Seven Samurai*: Takashi Shimura (Kambei Shimada, *leader of the Seven Samurai*), <u>Toshiro Mifune</u> (Kikuchiyo, *the would-be samurai*), Yoshio Inaba (Gorobei, *the wise warrior*), Seiji Miyaguchi (Kyuzo, *the master swordsman*), Minoru Chiaki (Heihachi, *the cheerful samurai*), Daisuke Kato (Shichiroji, *Kambei's old friend*), Isao Kimura (Katsushiro Okamoto, *Kambei's young disciple*). *The Peasants*: Keiko Tsushima (Shino), Yukiko Shimazaki (*Rikichi's wife*), Kamatari Fujiwara (Manzo, *Shino's father*), Yoshio Kosugi (Mosuke), Bokuzen Hidari (Yohei), Yoshio Tsuchiya (Rikichi), Kokuten Kodo (Gisaku), Eijiro Tono (*thief*), Kichijiro Ueda (*captured bandit scout*), Jun Tatara (*first coolie*), Atsushi Watanabe (*bun vendor*), Toranosuke Ogawa (*grandfather of Gono family*), Isao Yamagata (*samurai*), Sojin Kamiyama (*blind minstrel*), Gen Shimizu (*samurai who kicks farmers*), Keiji Sakakida (Gosaku), Shimpei Takagi (*bandit chieftain*), Shin Otomo (*bandit second in command*), Shuno Takahara (*samurai with gun*), Hiroshi Sugi (*owner of tea shop*), Sachio Sakai (*second coolie*), Sokichi Maki (*strong-looking samurai*), Ichiro Chiba (*Buddhist priest*), Noriko Sengoku (*wife of Gono family*), Fumiko Homma (*woman farmer*), Masanobu Okubo, Etsuro Nishijo, Minoru Ito, Haruya Sakamoto, Kyoro Sakurai, Kiyoshi Kamota (*samurai*), Senkichi Omura, Takashi Narita (*bandits who escape*), Shoichi "Solomon" Hirose, Choji Uno, Kaneyuki Tsubono, Kyoji Naka, Seiji Sunagawa, Akira Tani, Haruo Nakajima, Akio Kusama, Ryutaro Amami, Jun Mikami (*bandits*), Sanpei Mine, Ippei Kawagoe, Jiro Suzukawa, Junpei Natsuki, Kyoichi Kamiyama,

Kazuo Suzuki, Goro Amano, Akira Kichioji, Koji Iwamoto, Akira Yamada, Kazuo Imai, Eisuke Nakanishi, Toku Ihara, Hideo Otsuka, Hideo Oe, Yasuo Onishi, Megeru Shimoda, Masayoshi Kawabe, Shigeo Kato, Yoshikazu Kawamata (*farmers*), Masahide Matsushita, Kaneo Ikeda (*additional samurai*), Fumiyoshi Kumaya (*Ginsaku's son*), Hiroshi Agetsu (*Gono husband*), Yasuhisa Tsutsumi and Tsuneo Katagiri (*farmers in front of Gono*), Takeshi Seki (*third coolie*), Haruo Toyama (*wife of Gisaku's son*), Tomeko Umayato (*woman farmer in front of Gono*), Matsue Ono, Tazue Ichimanji, Masako Oshiro, Keiko Ozawa, Misao Suyama, Toriko Takahara (*women farmers*), Michiko Uwamoto, Toshiko Nakano, Shizuko Hogashi, Keiko Mori, Michiko Kawabe, Yuko Togawa, Yayoko Kitano (*farmers' wives*), Tatsuya Nakadai, Hisaya Ito (*samurai wandering through town*), Acting Team Kokeshiza, Nihon Sogo Geijutsu-sha

A Toho Co., Ltd. Production. A Toho Co., Ltd. Release. Black and white (processed by Toho Laboratories). Standard size. 206 minutes plus intermission. Released April 26, 1954.

U.S. version: *The Magnificent Seven*. Released by Columbia Pictures Corp. English subtitles. 158 minutes. Released November 1956. According to one source, an English-dubbed version was also available. Complete version apparently screened in Los Angeles in May 1969, then broadcast on PBS-TV in 1972. Theatrically reissued by Landmark Films (later acquired by Avco Embassy Pictures Corp.) in December 1982 running 203 minutes. Reissued post-1982 by Avco Embassy Pictures Corporation, Janus Films, Inc., and Films Incorporated, all running 208 minutes. Running time of home video version: 206 minutes.

Notes: Some Japanese general-release prints run 160 minutes. The acknowledged remake was *The Magnificent Seven* (United Artists, 1960) with Yul Brynner in the Shimura role. Other versions include *Battle Beyond the Stars* (New World, 1980) and *The Seven Magnificent Gladiators* (Cannon Releasing Corp., 1984). Sojin Kamiyama appeared in silent films made in the United States under the name "Sojin." Awards: The Silver Lion of Saint Mark (Venice International Film Festival); Nomination: Best Art Direction–Set Decoration (black and white) (Academy Awards); Nomination: Costume Design [black and white] (Academy Awards).

MIYAMOTO MUSASHI ("Musashi Miyamoto")
[MASTER SWORDSMAN]
Producer, Kazuo Takimura; Director, Hiroshi Inagaki; Screenplay, Tokuhei Wakao and Hiroshi Inagaki, based on the novel *Miyamoto Musashi* (1937–39) by Eiji Yoshikawa and the play by Hideji Hojo; Director of Photography, Jun Yasumoto; Art Director, Makoto Sono; Art Advisor, Kisaku Ito; Lighting, Shigeru Mori; Sound, Choshichiro Mikami; Music, Ikuma Dan; Chief Assistant Director, Jun Fukuda; Editor, Eiji Oi; Special Effects, Toho Technical Division (Eiji Tsuburaya, Director); Unit Production Manager, Hidehisa Kuda

Cast: Toshiro Mifune (Takezo Shimmen, *later* Musashi Miyamoto), Rentaro Mikuni (Matahachi Honiden), Kuroemon Onoe (Priest Takuan), Kaoru Yachigusa (Otsu), Mariko Okada (Akemi), Mitsuko Mito (Oko, *her mother*), Eiko Miyoshi (Osugi, *Matahachi's mother*), Akihiko Hirata (Seijiro Yoshioka), Kusuo Abe (Temma Tsujikaze), Yoshio Kosugi (Tanzaemon Aoki), Daisuke Kato (Toji Gion), Sakae Ozawa [Eitaro Ozawa] (Terumasa Ikeda), Akira Tani (Kawarano-Gonroku), Seijiro Onda (*chief official*), Fumito Matsuo, Masanobu Okubo (*petty officials*), Jiro Kumagawa, Akira Sera, Yasuhisa Tsutsumi (*villagers*), Yutaka Sada, Shigeo Kato, Junichiro Makai (*soldiers*), Kiyoshi Kamota, Michio Sakurai, Kyoro Sakurai (*roving warriors*), Sojin Kamiyama, Kanta Kisaragi (*old men*), Masao Masuda (*woodcutter*)

A Toho Co., Ltd. Production. A Toho Co., Ltd. Release. Eastman Color (processed by Toyo Developing). Standard size. 93 minutes. Released September 26, 1954.

U.S. version: *Samurai (The Legend of Musashi)*. Released by Fine Art Films, Inc. English subtitles with English narration. A Homel Pictures, Inc. Presentation, in association with International Toho Co., Ltd. Producers and Editors, William Holden and Robert B. Homel; English Translation and Assistant to Mr. Homel, Minoru Sakamoto; Editors, Homel and Holden. Narrator, William Holden. 93 minutes. Released November 18, 1955.

Notes: The second Toho feature in color, and the first in the Eastman Color process. Inagaki filmed the same story in 1942. Other versions include *Musashi Miyamoto* (Shochiku, 1944); *Musashi Miyamoto* (Toei, 1954), directed by Yasuo Kuhato and starring Rentaro Mikuni; Tomu Uchida's five-part *Zen and Sword* (1961–65); and *Musashi Miyamoto* (Shochiku, 1973). Reissued and released to home video restored and minus narration by Janus Films, alternately as *Samurai I*, *Samurai I: Musashi Miyamoto*, and *Musashi Miyamoto*. Followed by *Samurai (Part II)* (1955). Awards: Best Foreign Film (Academy Awards, 1955)

SHIOSAI ("The Sound of the Waves")
[THE SURF]
Producer, Tomoyuki Tanaka; Director, Senkichi Taniguchi; Screenplay, Senkichi Taniguchi and Shinichiro Nakamura, based on the novel by Yukio Mishima; Director of Photography, Taiichi Kankura; Art Director, Shu Matsuyama; Lighting, Rokuro Ishikawa; Sound, Yumei Hosaka; Music, Toshiro Mayuzumi

Cast: Akira Kubo (Shinji), Kyoko Aoyama (Hatsue), Yoichi Tachikawa (Jukichi), Keiko Miya (Chiyoko), Toshiro Mifune (Skipper of the *Utashima-maru*), Kichijiro Ueda (Terukichi, *Hatsue's father*), Sadako Sawamura (Tomi, *Shinji's mother*), Daisuke Kato (*Chiyoko's father, the lighthouse keeper*), Eijiro Tono ("Schoolmaster," *a peddler*), Minoru Takashima (Hiroshi, *Shinji's younger brother*), Sue Motobe (*Chiyoko's mother*), Yoshio Kosugi (Jukichi), Ikichi Ishii (Ryuji), Fumiko Homma (*old woman of O-Haru*)

A Toho Co., Ltd. Production. A Toho Co., Ltd. Release. Black and white. Standard size. 96 minutes. Released October 20, 1954.

U.S. version: Release, if any, is undetermined. An English-subtitled version was produced by Toho in the mid-1950s.

Notes: Location filming was done at the Shima Peninsula of Mie prefecture. Remade by director Kenjiro Morinaka at Nikkatsu in 1964, by Shiro Moritani at Toho in 1971, by Katsumi Nishikawa for Toho/Hori Productions in 1975, and by Tsugunobu Kotani for Hori Productions in 1985, all as *The Sound of the Waves* (Shiosai).

MITSUYU-SEN ("Smuggler")
[THE BLACK FURY]
Producer, Sojiro Motoki; Director, Toshio Sugie; Screenplay, Hideo Oguni and Teruaki Miyata, based on an idea by Tatsuo Takano; Director of Photography, Tadashi Iimura; Art Director, Yoshiro Muraki; Lighting, Ichiro Inohara; Sound, Wataru Onuma; Music, Fumio Hayasaka

Cast: Toshiro Mifune (Eiichi Tsuda), Asami Kuji (Emi Tomiura), Machiko Kitagawa (Tamie Matsuo), Shin Tokudaiji (Captain Mitani of the *Fukujin-maru*), Bob Booth (J. Bellgran), Yoshifumi Tajima (Soga), Takamaru Sasaki (Wang Taishing), Nakajiro Tomita (Captain Onishi of the *Kyuryu-maru*), Hideo Saeki (Manager Natsukawa of the *Club Poppy*), Yoshio Tsuchiya

A Toho Co., Ltd. Production. A Toho Co., Ltd. Release. Black and white. Standard size. 114 minutes. Released November 30, 1954.

U.S. version: Release, if any, is undetermined. An English-subtitled version was produced by Toho in 1954–55.

DANSEI NO. 1 ("No. 1 Man")

[A MAN AMONG MEN]

Producer, Sojiro Motoki; Director, Kajiro Yamamoto; Screenplay, Masato Ide, based on an idea by Ryuzo Kikushima; Director of Photography, Kazuo Yamada; Art Director, Gen Akune; Lighting, Tsuruzo Nishikawa; Sound, Choshichiro Mikami; Music, Ikuma Dan

Cast: Koji Tsuruta, <u>Toshiro Mifune</u>, Mariko Okada, Fubuki Koshiji, Yu Fujiki, Shin Tokudaiji

A Toho Co., Ltd. Production. A Toho Co., Ltd. Release. Black and white. Standard size. 95 minutes. Released January 3, 1955.

U.S. version: Release, if any, is undetermined.

Notes: Double-billed with *Diary of the Incredible First Laughing Trip* (Hatsuwarai sokonuke tabi niki).

KIETA CHUTAI ("Vanished Enlisted Man")

Producer, Kazuhei Hoshino; Director and Director of Photography, Akira Mimura; Screenplay, <u>Akira Kurosawa</u> and Ryuzo Kikushima, based on a story by Masato Ide; Art Director, Ichiro Takada; Music, Seitaro Omori

Cast: Ryutaro Tatsumi, Kenichiro Kawamura, Goro Matsuki

A Nikkatsu Corp. Production. A Nikkatsu Corp. Release. Black and white. Standard size. 92 minutes. Released January 14, 1955.

U.S. version: Release, if any, is undetermined.

TENKA TAIHEI ("A World of Peace")

[ALL IS WELL]

Producer, Shiro Horie; Director, Toshio Sugie; Screenplay, Naoyuki Hata, based on a story by Keita Genji; Director of Photography, Taiichi Kankura; Art Director, Yoshiro Muraki; Lighting, Ichiro Inohara; Sound, Wataru Konuma; Music, Nobuo Iida

Cast: <u>Toshiro Mifune</u>, Asami Kuji, Akira Takarada, Yoko Tsukasa, Chishu Ryu, Shuji Sano, Hanayo Toshimi

A Toho Co., Ltd. Production. A Toho Co., Ltd. Release. Black and white. Standard size. 93 minutes. Released January 29, 1955.

U.S. version: Release, if any, is undetermined.

Notes: Followed by *All Is Well, Part 2* (Zoku tenka taihei, 1955).

ZOKU TENKA TAIHEI ("A World of Peace II")

[ALL IS WELL, PART 2]

Producer, Shiro Horie; Director, Toshio Sugie; Screenplay, Dai Ishijima and Toshi Kumano, based on a story by Keita Genji; Director of Photography, Taiichi Kankura; Art Director, Yoshiro Muraki; Lighting, Ichiro Inohara; Sound, Wataru Konuma; Music, Nobuo Iida

Cast: <u>Toshiro Mifune</u>, Asami Kuji, Akira Takarada, Shuji Sano, Chishu Ryu, Hanayo Toshimi, Yoshio Tsuchiya, Yoko Tsukasa

A Toho Co., Ltd. Production. A Toho Co., Ltd. Release. Black and white. Standard size. 78 minutes. Released February 20, 1955.

U.S. version: Release, if any, is undetermined.

OTOKO ARITE ("There Was a Man")

[NO TIME FOR TEARS]

Producer, Goro Kontaibo; Director, Seiji Maruyama; Screenplay, Ryuzo Kikushima; Director of Photography, Masao Tamai; Art Director, Kazuo Ogawa; Lighting, Choshiro Ishii; Sound, Ariaki Hosaka; Music, Ichiro Saito

Cast: Takashi Shimura ("Sparrows" Coach Shimamura), <u>Toshiro Mifune</u> (Yano), Mariko Okada (Michiko), Yu Fujiki (Onishi), Shizue Natsukawa (Kinue), Masao Shimizu, Gen Shimizu, Yoshio Tsuchiya, Katao Kawasaki, Takashi Ito, Daisuke Kato, Seijiro Onda, Michiko Kawa, Keiko Mori, Shunichi Dragon's Diamonds Baseball Team

A Toho Co., Ltd. Production. A Toho Co., Ltd. Release. Black and white. Standard size. 109 minutes. Released May 10, 1955.

U.S. version: Release, if any, is undetermined. An English-subtitled version was produced by Toho in the mid-1950s.

Notes: Recommended by the Ministry of Education.

ZOKU MIYAMOTO MUSASHI—ICHIJOJI NO KETTO ("Musashi Miyamoto Sequel—Duel at Ichijoji Temple")
[DUEL AT ICHIJOJI TEMPLE]
Producer, Kazuo Takimura; Director, Hiroshi Inagaki; Screenplay, Hiroshi Inagaki and Tokuhei Wakao, based on the novel *Miyamoto Musashi* (1937–39) by Eiji Yoshikawa and the play by Hideji Hojo: Director of Photography, Jun Yasumoto; Art Director, Kisaku Ito; Set Decorator, Makoto Sono; Lighting, Shigeru Mori; Sound, Choshichiro Mikami; Music, Ikuma Dan; Choreographers, Tukuho Gosai, Yoshio Sugino; Chief Assistant Director, Jun Fukuda; Editor, Eiji Oi; Unit Production Manager, Boku Morimoto

Cast: <u>Toshiro Mifune</u> (Musashi Miyamoto), Koji Tsuruta (Kojiro Sasaki), Mariko Okada (Akemi), Kaoru Yachigusa (Otsu), Michiyo Kogure (Dayu Yoshino), Mitsuko Mito (Oko), Akihiko Hirata (Seijuro Yoshioka), Daisuke Kato (Toji Gion), Kuroemon Onoe (Priest Takuan), Sachio Sakai (Matahachi Honiden), Yu Fujiki (Denshichiro Yoshioka), Machiko Kitagawa (Kogure), Eiko Miyoshi (Osugi), Eijiro Tono (Baiken Shishido), Kenjim Iida (Jotaro), Akira Tani (Kawara-no-Gonroku), Ko Mihashi (Koetsu Honami), Kokuten Kodo (Old Priest Nikkan), Yoshifumi Tajima (Yoshioka samurai), Keiko Kondo, Hisako Takibana, Ren Yamamoto, Etsuro Nishijo, Ryu Kuze, Ichiro Tetsu, Torahiko Hamada, Yoshio Inaba, Kioro Sakurai, Fumito Matsuo, Minoru Ito, Yasuhisa Tsutsumi, Koji Iwamoto, Ren Imaizumi, Rinsaku Ogata, Sokichi Maki, Kenzo Tabu

A Toho Co., Ltd. Production. A Toho Co., Ltd. Release. Eastman Color (processed by Toyo Developing). Standard size. 104 minutes. Released July 12, 1955.

U.S. version: *Samurai (Part II)*. Released by Toho International Co., Ltd. English subtitles. 104 minutes. Released October 20, 1967. Subsequent international and home video title: *Samurai II: Duel at Ichijoji Temple*.

Notes: Second film of the "Samurai" trilogy. Preceded by *Samurai I: Musashi Miyamoto* (Miyamoto Musashi, 1954) and followed by *Samurai III: Duel at Ganryu Island* (1956). Toho's second-biggest money earner of 1955. In the late 1950s Toho retitled their international version *Bushido*, pairing it with *Samurai III* (q.v.). Double-billed with *Windstorm Harutaro* (Hayate no Harutaro).

ASUNARO MONOGATARI ("Hiba Arborvitae Story")
[TOMORROW I'LL BE A FIRE-TREE]
Producer, Tomoyuki Tanaka; Director, Hiromichi Horikawa; Screenplay and Editor, <u>Akira Kurosawa</u>, based on a story by Yasushi Inoue; Director of Photography, Kazuo Yamasaki; Art Director, Yasuhide Kato; Lighting, Choshiro Ishii; Sound, Hisashi Shimonaga; Music, Fumio Hayasaka

Cast: Akira Kubo (Ayuta, *at 18 years old*), Isao Kimura (Kashima), Yoshiko Kuga (Reiko), Mariko Okada (Saeko), Akemi Negishi (Yukie), Takashi Kubo (Ayuta, *at 12 years old*), Yoichi Tachikawa (Emi), Eiko Miyoshi (*Ayuta's grandmother*), Nobuya Kashima (Ayuta, *at 15 years old*),

Makoto Kobori (*priest*), Tsugio Izumida (Numata), Toshio Takahara (Takeuchi), Munenori Oyamada (Kihara), Nobuo Kaneko (Sayama), Sachiko Murase (landlady), Kumeko Urabe (Tomi).

A Toho Co., Ltd. Production. A Toho Co., Ltd. Release. Black and white. Standard size. 109 minutes. Released October 5, 1955.

U.S. version: Release, if any, is undetermined. An English-subtitled version was produced by Toho in 1955 or 1956.

IKIMONO NO KIROKU ("Record of a Living Being")
[I LIVE IN FEAR——"RECORD OF A LIVING BEING"]
Producer, Sojiro Motoki; Director, <u>Akira Kurosawa</u>; Screenplay, Shinobu Hashimoto, Hideo Oguni, and Akira Kurosawa, suggested by an idea by Fumio Hayasaka and Akira Kurosawa; Director of Photography, Asakazu Nakai; Art Director, Yoshiro Muraki; Lighting, Kyuichiro Kishida; Sound, Fumio Yanoguchi; Music, Fumio Hayasaka and Masaru Sato; Assistant Director of Photography, Takao Saito; Assistant Lighting, Shozo Hada; Assistant Art Director, Oyako Kato; "Cherry Pink Mambo," Music by Hachiro Matsuri; Chief Assistant Director, Hisanobu Marubayashi; Assistant Directors, Samachi Norase, Yasuyoshi Tajitsu, Ken Sano, and Takeo Nakamura; Negative Cutter, Chozo Kobata; Script Supervisor, Teruyo Nogami; Sound Effects, Ichiro Minawa; Still Photographer, Masao Fukuda; In Charge of Production, Hiroshi Nezu; Property Master, Kiyoshi Toda; Costumes, Miyuki Suzuki; Hair Stylist, Sadako Okada; Hair Design, Junjiro Yamada

    Cast: <u>Toshiro Mifune</u> (Kiichi Nakajima), Takashi Shimura (Dr. Harada, *counselor of the Domestic Court*), Minoru Chiaki (Jiro Nakajima, *Kiichi's second son*), Eiko Miyoshi (Toyo Nakajima, *Kiichi's wife*), Kyoko Aoyama (Sue Nakajima, *Kiichi's second daughter*), Haruko Togo (Yoshi Nakajima, *Kiichi's first daughter*), Noriko Sengoku (Kimie Nakajima, *Ichiro's wife*), Akemi Negishi (Asako Kuribayashi, *Kiichi's present mistress*), Yoichi Tachikawa (Ryoichi Sayama, *Kiichi's son by a former mistress*), Kichijiro Ueda (Mr. Kuribayashi, *Asako's father*), Eijiro Tono (*the old man from Brazil*), Yutaka Sada (Ichiro Nakajima, *Kiichi's first son*), Kamatari Fujiwara (Okamoto), Ken Mitsuda (Judge Araki), Atsushi Watanabe (Ishida, *a factory worker*), Kiyomi Mizunoya (Satoko, *Kiichi's first mistress*), Gen [Masao] Shimizu (*chief of mint factory*), Toranosuke Ogawa (Hori), Nobuo Nakamura (*psychologist*), Bokuzen Hidari (*landowner*), Yoshio Tsuchiya (*worker at factory following fire*), Akira Tani (*first man in custody*), Kokuten Kodo, Fumiko Homma (*family members of workers*), Kazuo Kato (Susumu, *Harada's son*), Yoshiko Miyata (Tamiya, *secretary of the court*), Toyoko Okubo (*Susumu's wife*), Kyoro Sakurai (*worker at factory*), Senkichi Omura (*second man in custody*)

A Toho Co., Ltd. Production. A Toho Co., Ltd. Release. Black and white (processed by Toho Developing). Standard size. 103 minutes. Released November 22, 1955.

U.S. version: *I Live in Fear*. Released by Brandon Films, Inc. English subtitles. Also released as *Record of a Living Being*. Alternate title: *What the Birds Knew*. Current 35mm and television prints do not have an English-subtitled translation of the title, which may account for the confusion over the film's correct English name. 103 minutes. Released January 25, 1967. An English-subtitled version had been produced by Toho in 1955 or 1956.

Notes: Sato completed Hayasaka's score following the latter's death.

MIYAMOTO MUSASHI KONKETSUHEN——KETTO GANRYU SHIMA ("Musashi Miyamoto Conclusion——Ganryu Island Duel")
[MUSASHI AND KOJIRO]
Producer, Kazuo Takimura; Director, Hiroshi Inagaki; Screenplay, Tokuhei Wakao and Hiroshi Inagaki, based on the novel *Miyamoto Musashi* (1937–39) by Eiji Yoshikawa and the play by Hideji Hojo; Director of Photography, Kazuo Yamada; Art Director, Kisaku Ito; Lighting, Tsu-

ruzo Nishikawa; Sound, Masanobu Miyazaki; Music, Ikuma Dan; Assistant Art Director, Hiroshi Ueda; Chief Assistant Director, Jun Fukuda; Editor, Hirokazu Iwashita; Special Effects, Toho Special Effects Group; Production Manager, Hideyuki Suga

Cast: Koji Tsuruta (Kojiro Sasaki), <u>Toshiro Mifune</u> (Musashi Miyamoto), Kaoru Yachigusa (Otsu), Michiko Saga (Omitsu), Mariko Okada (Akemi), Takashi Shimura (Sado Nagaoka, *the court official*), Minoru Chiaki (Sasuke, *the boatman*), Takamaru Sasaki (*Omitsu's father*), Daisuke Kato (Toji Gion), Haruo Tanaka (Kumagoro, *horse dealer and "tough guy"*), Kichijiro Ueda (Priest Ogon), Kokuten Kodo (*old priest*), Ikio Sawamura (*innkeeper*), Nakajiro Tomita, Sonosuke Sawamura, Minosuke Yamada, Soji Kiyokawa, Masako Sakurai, Yutaka Oka, Tominosuke Hayama, Kumeko Otowa, Yaeko Izumo, Fumiko Homma, Etsuro Nishijo, Katao Kawasaki, Fumito Matsuo, Ren Yamamoto, Fuminori Ohashi, Haruko Toyama, Jiro Kumagaiya, Hideo Shibuya, Katsumi Tezuka, Keiichiro Katsumoto, Hirotoshi Tsuchiya, Masao Masuda, Yu Agetsu, Senkichi Omura, Shoichi "Solomon" Hirose

A Toho Co., Ltd. Production. A Toho Co., Ltd. Release. Eastman Color (processed by Toyo Developing). Standard size. 105 minutes. Released January 1, 1956.

U.S. version: *Samurai (Part III)*. Released by Toho International Co., Ltd. English subtitles. 105 minutes. Released 1967. In the late 1950s Toho retitled their international version *Bushido*, pairing it with *Samurai II* (q.v.). Subsequent international and home video title: *Samurai III: Duel on Ganryu Island*. Released 1967.

Notes: Third film of the "Samurai" trilogy. Includes footage from *Samurai II. Bushido* was a title given to a package that included *Samurai II*, and this version was presented in two parts. This international version may also have been optically converted to Toho Scope; it was apparently never released in the United States.

KUROOBI SANGOKUSHI ("Black Belt Sangokushi")
[RAINY NIGHT DUEL]
Producer, Tomoyuki Tanaka; Director, Senkichi Taniguchi; Screenplay, Takero Matsuura, Iwao Yamasaki, and Senkichi Taniguchi, based on a story by Akira Shimomura; Director of Photography, Tadashi Iimura; Art Directors, Takeo Kita and Yoshiro Muraki; Lighting, Ichiro Inohara; Music, Akira Ifukube

Cast: <u>Toshiro Mifune</u> (Masahiko Koseki), Shin Saburi (Masazumi Amaji), Akio Kobori (Shiro Katahara), Kyoko Kagawa (Shizue Amaji), Mariko Okada (Kikuko Kamo), Asami Kuji (Oyo), Akihiko Hirata (Shunsuke Iba), Hideo Saeki (Hachiro Iba), Yu Fujiki (Kotetsu), Haruo Tanaka (Joji, *the coolie procurer*)

A Toho Co., Ltd. Production. A Toho Co., Ltd. Release. Black and white. Standard size. 96 minutes. Released January 29, 1956.

U.S. version: Release, if any, is undetermined. Toho produced an English-subtitled version in late 1955 or early 1956.

Notes: Double-billed with *I Saw the Killer* (Kiyatsu wo no gasuna).

ANKOKUGAI ("The Underworld")
[THE UNDERWORLD]
Producer, Sojiro Motoki; Director, Kajiro Yamamoto; Screenplay, Tokuhei Wakao, based on a story by Ryuzo Kikushima; Director of Photography, Seiichi Endo; Art Director, Gan Akune; Lighting, Tsuruzo Nishikawa; Sound, Shoichi Fujinawa; Music, Ikuma Dan; Chief Assistant Director, Jun Fukuda; Editor, Yoshitani Kuroiwa; Unit Production Manager, Kazuo Baba

Cast: Koji Tsuruta (Takao Shoji), Kyoko Aoyama (Yumiko), Akemi Negishi (Natsue), Hiroshi Koizumi (Yumiko's fiancé), Takashi Shimura (Tsunejiro Furuya), Seiji Miyaguchi, Minosuke Yamada, Seijiro Onda, Yutaka Oka, Sachio Sakai, Masamiku Sugiyama, Junichiro Mukai, Kyoro Sakurai, Tsurue Ichimonji, Senkichi Omura, Mitsuo Tsuda, Katao Kawasaki, Akira Sera, Matsue Ono, Katsumi Tezuka, Shin Yoshida, Akira Yamada, Etsuro Nishijo, Haruya Sakamoto, Ren Koizumi, Koji Iwamoto, Ryutaro Amami, Shoichi "Solomon" Hirose, Jun Mikami, Koji Sawa, Oeko Kuroiwa, Akemi Uno, Haruo Nakajima, Reiko Wakasui, Michiko Kawa, Isamu Takahashi, Takuya Yuki • Toshiro Mifune (Chief Inspector Kumada)

A Toho Co., Ltd. Production. A Toho Co., Ltd. Release. Black and white (processed by Toho Development). Standard size. 99 minutes. Released February 26, 1956.

U.S. version: Release, if any, is undetermined.

Notes: The first of many Toho-produced "Ankokugai" thrillers, which include *The Big Boss* (Ankokugai no Kaoyaku, 1959), *The Last Gunfight* (Ankokugai no taiketsu, 1960), *Blueprint of Murder* (Ankokugai no dankon, 1961), *Witness Killed* (Ankokugai gekimetsu meirei, 1961) and *The Weed of Crime* (Ankokugai no kiba, 1962). Double-billed with *The Wife of a University Student* (Okusama wa daigakusei).

AIJO NO KESSAN ("Settlement of Love")

[SETTLEMENT OF LOVE]

Producers, Sanezumi Fujimoto and Jin Usami; Director, Shin Saburi; Screenplay, Toshiro Ide, based on the story *Kono jyunen* ("For These Last Ten Years") by Hidemi Ima; Director of Photography, Kazuo Yamada; Art Directors, Takeo Kita and Kiyoshi Shimizu; Lighting, Choshiro Ishii; Sound, Masanobu Miyazaki; Music, Ikuma Dan

Cast: Setsuko Hara, Keiju Kobayashi, Toshinobu Sawaki, Toshiro Mifune, Kaoru Yachigusa, Yuriko Hamada, Shin Saburi

A Toho Co., Ltd. Production. A Toho Co., Ltd. Release. Black and white. Standard size. 116 minutes. Released March 28, 1956.

U.S. version: Release, if any, is undetermined.

TSUMA NO KOKORO ("A Wife's Heart")

[A WIFE'S HEART]

Producers, Sanezumi Fujimoto and Masakatsu Kaneko; Director, Mikio Naruse; Screenplay, Toshiro Ide; Director of Photography, Masao Tamai; Art Director, Satoshi Chuko; Lighting, Choshiro Ishii; Sound, Masayuki Fujiyoshi; Music, Ichiro Saito

Cast: Hideko Takamine, Toshiro Mifune, Keiju Kobayashi, Akemi Negishi, Yoko Sugi, Machiko Kitagawa, Chieko Nakakita, Ranko Hanai, Sadako Sawamura, Eiko Miyoshi, Minoru Chiaki, Daisuke Kato, Haruo Tanaka, Yoshio Tsuchiya, Toyoji Shimozawa, Michiko Kawa, Haiyoko Kitano, Fumiko Homma, Yoko Tsukasa

A Toho Co., Ltd. Production. A Toho Co., Ltd. Release. Black and white. Standard size. 101 minutes. Released May 3, 1956.

U.S. version: Release, if any, is undetermined.

Notes: Tsukasa's participation in cast is unconfirmed. Double-billed with *Blue Buds* (Aoi me).

NARAZU MONO ("Blackguard")

[SCOUNDREL]

Producer, Tomoyuki Tanaka; Director, Nobuo Aoyagi; Screenplay, Takeshi Kimura and Haruyuki Nakata, based on the story "Takurin Dining Room" (Takurin meshiba) by Takemi Sasaki; Director of Photography, Seiichi Endo; Art Directors, Takeo Kita and Gan Akune; Lighting, Tsuruzo Nishikawa; Sound, Yoshio Nishikawa; Music, Masaru Sato

Cast: <u>Toshiro Mifune</u>, Mariko Okada, Yumi Shirakawa, Takashi Shimura, Minoru Chiaki, Yoichi Tachikawa, Nijiko Kiyokawa

A Toho Co., Ltd. Production. A Toho Co., Ltd. Release. Black and white. Standard size. 95 minutes. Released May 10, 1956.

U.S. version: Release, if any, is undetermined.

Notes: Double-billed with *Norihei's College Affair—The Happy Family* (Norihei no uwaki daigaku—Yukai na kazoku).

SHUJINSEN ("Prison Ship")
[REBELS ON THE HIGH SEA]

Producer, Shiro Horie; Director, Hiroshi Inagaki; Screenplay, Hiroshi Inagaki and Takeo Murata, based on a story by Kazuo Kikuta, adapted from *Hokokumura no hanashi* ("The Story of the Hokokumura Ship"); Director of Photography, Tadashi Iimura; Art Directors, Takeo Kita and Teruaki Abe; Lighting, Tsuruzo Nishikawa; Sound, Yoshio Nishikawa; Music, Yoshio Nikita

Cast: <u>Toshiro Mifune</u>, Kichijiro Ueda, Jun Tazaki, Mariko Okada, Hiroshi Koizumi, Yoshio Kosugi

A Toho Co., Ltd. Production. A Toho Co., Ltd. Release. Black and white. Standard size. 109 minutes. Released August 8, 1956.

U.S. version: Release, if any, is undetermined.

Note, Double-billed with *A Young Lady On Her Way* (Ojosan tojo).

KUMONOSU-JO ("Castle of the Spider's Web")
[THRONE OF BLOOD]

Producers, Sojiro Motoki and Akira Kurosawa; Director, <u>Akira Kurosawa</u>; Screenplay, Hideo Oguni, Shinobu Hashimoto, Ryuzo Kikushima, and Akira Kurosawa, based on the play *Macbeth* by William Shakespeare; Director of Photography, Asakazu Nakai; Art Director and Costume Design, Yoshiro Muraki; Lighting, Kyuichiro Kishida; Sound, Fumio Yanoguchi; Music, Masaru Sato; Assistant Cameraman, Takao Saito; Assistant Art Director, Yoshifumi Honda; Assistant Lighting, Shogo Hada; Assistant Sound, Masanao Uehara; Chief Assistant Director, Mimachi Norase; Assistant Directors, Shoya Shimizu, Yasuyoshi Tajitsu, Ken Sano, Yoshimitsu Sakano, Michio Yamamoto; Negative Cutter, Chozo Obata; Script Supervisor, Teruyo Nogami; Sound Effects, Ichiro Minawa; Still Photographer, Masao Fukuda; Production Supervisor, Hiroshi Nezu; Accountant, Ikemichi Hashimoto; Art Supervisor, Kohei Ezaki; Special Effects Supervisor, Eiji Tsuburaya; Special Effects, Toho Special Effects Group; Property Master, Koichi Hamamura; Costumes, Taiki Mori (Kyoto Costume Co., Ltd.); Hair Stylists, Yoshiko Matsumoto and Junjiro Yamada; Horseback Riding Instructors, Ienori Kaneko and Shigeru Endo

Cast: <u>Toshiro Mifune</u> (Taketori Washizu), Isuzu Yamada (Lady Asaji Washizu, *his wife*), Takashi Shimura (Noriyasu Odagura), Akira Kubo (Yoshiteru Miki), Yoichi Tachikawa (Kunimaru Tsuzuki), Minoru Chiaki (Yoshiaki Miki), Takamaru Sasaki (Kuniharu Tsuzuki), Kokuten Kodo (*military commander*), Kichijiro Ueda (*miscellaneous worker of Washizu*), Eiko Miyoshi (*old woman at the castle*), Chieko Naniwa (*old ghost woman*), Nakajiro Tomita (*second military commander*), Yu Fujiki, Sachio Sakai, Shin Otomo, Yoshio Tsuchiya, Senkichi Omura (*Washizu samurai*), Yoshio Inaba (*third military commander*), Takeo Obugawa (*Miki party member*), Akira Tani, Ikio Sawamura (*miscellaneous soldiers of Washizu*), Yutaka Sada (*Washizu samurai*), Seijiro Onda (*second Miki party member*), Shinpei Takagi, Masao Masuda (*additional commanders*), Akifumi Inoue, Asao Koike, Kyoro Sakurai, Kaneyuki Tsubono (*servants*), Takeshi Kato (*guard killed by Washizu*), Kin Takagi and Higuchi [first name undetermined] (*Tsuzuki guards*), Shiro Tsuchiya, Takaeo Matsushita, Jun Otomo (*commanders*), Fuminori Ohashi (*samurai*), Isao Kimura, Seiji Miyaguchi, Nobuo Nakamura (*phantom samurai*), Gen Shimizu

A Toho Co., Ltd. Production. A Toho Co., Ltd. Release. Black and white (processed by Toho Developing). Standard size. 110 minutes. Released January 15, 1957.

U.S. version: *Throne of Blood*. Released by Brandon Films, Inc. English subtitles. English adaptation, Donald Richie. 105 minutes. Released November 22, 1961.

Notes: Selected by the Ministry of Education. Reissued in Japan February 2, 1970. Double-billed with *A Town of Starry Skies* (Hoshizora no machi).

ARASHI NO NAKA NO OTOKO ("The Man in the Storm")
[A MAN IN THE STORM]
Producer, Tomoyuki Tanaka; Director, Senkichi Taniguchi; Screenplay, Senkichi Taniguchi, Kenro Matsuura, and Takeo Murata; Director of Photography, Kazuo Yamada; Art Director, Yasuhide Kato; Lighting, Tsuruzo Nishikawa; Sound, Wataru Konuma; Music, Urato Watanabe

Cast: Toshiro Mifune (Saburo Watari), Kyoko Kagawa (Akiko), Akio Kobori (Tsujido), Akemi Negishi (Okon), Jun Tazaki (karate expert), Midori Isomura, Akihiko Hirata, Yoshio Kosugi

A Toho Co., Ltd. Production. A Toho Co., Ltd. Release. Black and white. Standard size. 95 minutes. Released February 5, 1957.

U.S. version: Released by Toho International Co., Ltd. English subtitles. 95 minutes. No MPAA rating. Released August 1969.

Notes: Toho produced an English-dubbed version of this title. Its release, if any, is undetermined.

KONO FUTARINI SACHI ARE ("Be Happy, These Two Lovers")
[BE HAPPY, THESE TWO LOVERS]
Producer, Shiro Horie; Director, Ishiro Honda; Screenplay, Zenzo Matsuyama; Director of Photography, Hajime Koizumi; Art Director, Tatsuo Kita; Lighting, Soichi Yokoi; Sound, Ariaki Hosaka; Music, Yoshinao Nakata

Cast: Hiroshi Koizumi, Yumi Shirakawa, Keiko Tsushima, Toshiro Mifune, Kamatari Fujiwara, Takashi Shimura, Shizue Natsukawa, Yuriko Ei, Tamae Kiyokawa, Takeo Oikawa, Hirota Kisaragi, Yoshifumi Tajima, Sumiko Koizumi, Yu Fujiki

A Toho Co., Ltd. Production. A Toho Co., Ltd. Release. Black and white. Standard size. 97 minutes. Released February 19, 1957.

U.S. version: Release, if any, is undetermined.

YAGYU BUGEICHO ("Yagyu Secret Scrolls")
[YAGYU SECRET SCROLLS (PART I)]
Producer, Tomoyuki Tanaka; Director, Hiroshi Inagaki; Screenplay, Hiroshi Inagaki, Tomoyuki Tanaka, and Takeshi Kimura, based on the serialized novel *Yagyu Bugeicho* (1956–59) by Kosuke Gomi; Art Directors, Takeo Kita and Hiroshi Ueda; Director of Photography, Tadashi Iimura; Music, Akira Ifukube; Recording, Yoshio Nishikawa

Cast: Toshiro Mifune (Tasaburo), Koji Tsuruta (Senshiro), Yoshiko Kuga (Yuhime), Mariko Okada (Rika), Denjiro Okochi (Lord Yagyu), Kyoko Kagawa (Oki), Senjaku Namamura (Matajuro), Hanshiro Iwai (Iyemitsu), Jotaro Togami (Jubei), Akihiko Hirata (Tomonori), Eijiro Tono (Fugetsusai), Nobuko Otowa, Akio Kobori, Koshiro Matsumoto

A Toho Co., Ltd. Production. A Toho Co., Ltd. Release. Agfa Color (processed by Tokyo

Laboratory Ltd.). Standard size. 109 minutes. Released April 14, 1957 (roadshow version) and April 23, 1957 (general release).

U.S. version: Released by Toho International Co., Ltd. English subtitles. Sequel: *Secret Scrolls (Part II)* (1958). Also known as *Yagyu Secret Scrolls*. 109 minutes. Released October 11, 1967.

Notes: General release version double-billed with *Here Is Tokyo, Mother* (Tokyo dayo okasan).

KIKEN NA EIYU ("A Dangerous Hero")
[A DANGEROUS HERO]
Producer, Masakatsu Kaneko; Director, Hideo Suzuki; Screenplay, Eizo Sugawa, with additions by Mikiyuki Hasegawa; Director of Photography, Asakazu Nakai; Art Director, Hyoei Hamagami; Lighting, Ichiro Inohara; Sound, Shoichi Fujinawa; Music, Yasushi Akutagawa

Cast: Shintaro Ishihara, Yoko Tsukasa, Eitaro Ozawa, Takashi Shimura, Tatsuya Nakadai, Toshiro Mifune

A Toho Co., Ltd. Production. A Toho Co., Ltd. Release. Black and white. Standard size. 94 minutes. Released July 30, 1957.

U.S. version: Release, if any, is undetermined.

Notes: Double-billed with the documentary featurette *Kurobe Gorge* (Kurobe Kyokoku).

DONZOKO ("The Lower Depths")
[THE LOWER DEPTHS]
Producer, Akira Kurosawa; Associate Producers, Tomoyuki Tanaka and Sojiro Motoki; Director, Akira Kurosawa; Screenplay, Hideo Oguni and Akira Kurosawa, based on the play *The Lower Depths* (*Nadne*, 1902) by Maxim Gorky; Director of Photography, Kazuo Yamasaki; Art Director, Yoshiro Muraki; Lighting, Shigeru Mori; Sound, Fumio Yanoguchi; Music, Masaru Sato; Assistant Cameraman, Takao Saito; Assistant Lighting, Katsumi Murakami; Assistant Art Director, Jun Sakuma; Chief Sound Assistant, Mimachi Norase; Sound Assistant, Shoichi Yoshizawa; Assistant Directors, Yasuyoshi Tajitsu, Yoshimitsu Sakano, and Toshi Kaneko; Negative Cutter, Chozo Kobata; Script Supervisor, Teruyo Nogami; Sound Effects, Ichiro Minawa; Still Photographer, Masao Fukuda; Production Supervisor, Hiroshi Nezu; Production Assistance, Mitsugu Narita; Property Master, Koichi Hamamura; Costumes, Yoshiko Samejima (Kyoto Costume); Hair Stylists, Yoshiko Matsumoto and Junjiro Yamada; Acting Office, Yuichi Yoshitake

Cast: Toshiro Mifune (Sutekichi, *the thief*), Isuzu Yamada (Osugi, *the landlady*), Kyoko Kagawa (Okayo, *her sister*), Ganjiro Nakamura (Rokubei, *Osugi's husband*), Minoru Chiaki (*the ex-samurai*), Kamatari Fujiwara (*the actor*), Akemi Negishi (Osen, *the prostitute*), Nijiko Kiyokawa (Otaki, *the candy-seller*), Koji Mitsui (Yoshisaburo, *the gambler*), Eijiro Tono (Tomekichi, *the tinker*), Haruo Tanaka (Tatsu), Eiko Miyoshi (Asa, *Tomekichi's wife*), Bokuzen Hidari (Kahei, *the priest*), Atsushi Watanabe (Kuna), Kichijiro Ueda (Shimazo, *the police agent*), Yu Fujiki (Unokichi), Fujitayama (Tsugaru)

A Toho Co., Ltd. Production. A Toho Co., Ltd. Release. Black and white (processed by Tokyo Laboratory Co., Ltd.). Standard size. 124 minutes. Released September 17, 1957 (roadshow version), and October 1, 1957 (general release).

U.S. version: Released by Brandon Films, Inc. English subtitles. 125 minutes. Released February 9, 1962.

Notes: Other versions include Jean Renoir's *The Lower Depths* (1936). Toho produced an English-dubbed version. Its release, if any, is undetermined.

SHITAMACHI ("Downtown")

[DOWNTOWN]

Producer, Sanezumi Fujimoto; Director, Yasuki Chiba; Screenplay, Ryozo Kasahara and Seiya Yoshida, based on a story by Fumiko Hayashi; Director of Photography, Rokuro Nishigaki; Art Director, Satoshi Chuko; Lighting, Mitsuo Kaneko; Sound, Wataru Konuma; Music, Akira Ifukube

 Cast: Isuzu Yamada, <u>Toshiro Mifune</u>, Haruo Tanaka, Jun Tatara, Keiko Awaji, Chieko Murata, Harunori Kametani

 A Toho Co., Ltd. Production. A Toho Co., Ltd. Release. Black and white. Standard size. 57 minutes. Released October 29, 1957 (roadshow version), and November 5, 1957 (general release).

 U.S. version: Released by Brandon Films. English subtitles. 57 minutes. Released 1966.

 Notes: Released with the animated short *The Top-Heavy Frog* (Fukusuke). General release version double-billed with *Men of Toho-ku* (Tohoku no zummutachi).

NICHIRO SENSO SHORI NO HISHI—TEKICHU ODAN SANBYAKU RI ("Three Hundred Miles Through Enemy Lines")

[ADVANCE PATROL]

Executive Producer, Masaichi Nagata; Director, Kazuo Mori; Screenplay, <u>Akira Kurosawa</u> and Hideo Oguni, based on a story by Hotaro Yamanaka and their screenplay *Three Hundred Miles Through Enemy Lines* (Tekichu odan sanbyaku ri); Director of Photography, Michio Takahashi; Art Director, Tomo Shimogawara; Music, Seiichi Suzuki

 Cast: Kenji Sugawara, Yoshiro Kitahara, Hideo Takamatsu

 A Daiei (Tokyo) Motion Picture Co., Ltd. Production. A Daiei Co., Ltd. Release. Black and white. Daiei Scope. 85 minutes. Released December 28, 1957.

 U.S. version: Release, if any, is undetermined.

YAGYU BUGEICHO—NINJUTSU ("Yagyu Secret Scrolls—Ninjitsu")

[YAGYU SECRET SCROLLS—NINJITSU (PART II)]

Producer, Tomoyuki Tanaka; Director, Hiroshi Inagaki; Screenplay, Hiroshi Inagaki, Tomoyuki Tanaka, Takeshi Kimura, and Takuhei Wakao, based on the serialized novel *Yagyu Bugeicho* (1956–59) by Kosuke Gomi; Director of Photography, Asakazu Nakai; Art Directors, Takeo Kita and Hiroshi Ueda; Sound, Yoshio Nishikawa; Music, Akira Ifukube

 Cast: Koji Tsuruta (Senshiro), <u>Toshiro Mifune</u> (Tasaburo), Nobuko Otawa (*princess*), Yoshiko Kuga (Yuhime), Mariko Okada (Rika), Denjiro Okochi (Lord Yagyu), Senjaku Namamura (Matajuro), Jotaro Togami (Jubei), Hanshiro Iwai (Iyemitsu), Kyoko Kagawa (Oki), Akihiko Hirata (Tomonori), Akio Kobori, Koshiro Matsumoto

 A Toho Co., Ltd. Production. A Toho Co., Ltd. Release. AgfaColor. Toho Scope. 105 minutes. Released January 3, 1958.

 U.S. version: Released by Toho International Co., Ltd. English subtitles. 105 minutes. No MPAA rating. Released May 22, 1968.

 Notes: Also released in Japan as *Soryu hiken*. A sequel to *Secret Scrolls (Part I)* (1957). Double-billed with *Three Generations of Company Presidents* (Shacho sandaiki).

TOKYO NO KYUJITSU ["Tokyo Holiday"]

(HOLIDAY IN TOKYO)

Producer, Shiro Horie; Director, Kajiro Yamamoto; Screenplay, Toshiro Ide and Kajiro Yamamoto; Director of Photography, Ichiro Yamazaki; Art Director, Hyohei Hamagami; Lighting, Tsuruzo Nishikawa; Sound, Choshichiro Mikami and Masanobu Miyazaki; Music, Hachiro Matsui

Cast: Yoshiko "Shirley" Yamaguchi, Kaoru Yachigusa, Asami Kuji, Yoko Tsukasa, Akira Takarada, Keiju Kobayashi, Hiroshi Koizumi, Ken Uehara, Ryo Ikebe, Chisako Hara, Chikage Ogi, Daisuke Kato, Kyoko Kagawa, Reiko Dan, Akira Kubo, Mitsuko Kusabue, Kingoro Yanagiya, Fubuki Koshiji, Ichiro Arishima, Michiyo Aratama, Keiko Awaji, Kyoko Aoyama, Kyoko Anzai, Izumi Yukimura, Toshiro Mifune, Norihei Miki, Mariko Miyagi, Yumi Shirakawa, Hisaya Morishige

A Toho Co., Ltd. Production. A Toho Co., Ltd. Release. Western Electric Mirrophonic Recording (encoded with Perspecta Stereophonic Sound). Eastman Color. Toho Scope. 90 minutes. Released April 15, 1958.

U.S. version: Release, if any, is undetermined.

Notes: Double-billed with *Fighting Is Fun, Too* (Kenta no tanoshi).

MUHOMATSU NO ISSHO ("Wild Matsu, the Rickshaw Man")
[MUHOMATSU, THE RIKISHAW MAN] (SIC)
Producer, Tomoyuki Tanaka; Director, Hiroshi Inagaki; Screenplay, Mansaku Itami and Hiroshi Inagaki, based on the story by Shunsaku Iwashita; Director of Photography, Kazuo Yamada; Art Director, Hiroshi Ueda; Lighting, Ichiro Inohara; Sound, Yoshio Nishikawa and Hisashi Shimonaga; Music, Ikuma Dan; Chief Assistant Director, Teruo Maru; Editor, Yoshitami Kuroiwa

Cast: Toshiro Mifune (Matsu, *the Rickshaw Man*), Hideko Takamine (Yoshiko Yoshioka, *the widow*), Hiroshi Akutagawa (Kotaro Yoshioka, *the officer*), Chishu Ryu (Shigezo Yuki, *the boss*), Choko Iida (*the innkeeper*), Haruo Tanaka (Kumakichi), Jun Tatara (*theater employee*), Kenji Kasahara (*Toshio Yoshioka as an adult*), Kaoru Matsumoto (*Toshio Yoshioka as a child*), Nobuo Nakamura, Ichiro Arishima, Chieko Nakakita, Seiji Miyaguchi, Bokuzen Hidari, Kokuten Kodo, Yoshio Tsuchiya, Kichijiro Ueda, Yoshio Kosugi, Ikio Sawamura, Senkichi Omura

A Toho Co., Ltd. Production. A Toho Co., Ltd. Release. Agfa Color. Toho Scope. 103 minutes. Released April 22, 1958.

U.S. version: Released by Toho International Co., Ltd. English subtitles. 103 minutes. Release date undetermined. Also known as *The Rikishaw Man* (sic).

Notes: Awards: Golden Lion of Saint Mark (Venice International Film Festival, 1958).

YAJIKITA DOCHU SUGOROKU ("Yaji and Kita's Travel Journey")
[THE HAPPY PILGRIMAGE]
Producers, Sanezumi Fujimoto and Shiro Yamamoto; Director, Yasuki Chiba; Screenplay, Ryozo Kasahara, based on *Dochu Hizakurige* (1802) by Iku Tohensha; Director of Photography, Rokuro Nishigaki; Art Director, Takeo Kita; Lighting, Soichi Yokoi; Sound, Shoichi Fujinawa and Hisashi Shimonaga; Music, Yuji Koseki

Cast: Keiju Kobayashi, Daisuke Kato, Ryo Ikebe, Nobuko Otowa, Keiko Awaji, Akira Takarada, Izumi Yukimura, Mitsuko Kusabue, Norihei Miki, Toshiro Mifune, Reiko Dan

A Toho Co., Ltd. Production. A Toho Co., Ltd. Release. Eastman Color. Toho Scope. 119 minutes. Released April 29, 1958.

U.S. version: Release, if any, is undetermined. Also known as *Yaji and Kita on the Road*.

KEKKON NO SUBETE ("All About Marriage")
[ALL ABOUT MARRIAGE]
Producer, Masakatsu Kaneko; Director, Kihachi Okamoto; Screenplay, Ishio Shirasaka; Director of Photography, Asakazu Nakai; Art Director, Gan Akune; Lighting, Toshio Takashima; Sound, Masanao Uehara and Hisashi Shimonaga; Music, Seiichi Bawatari

Cast: Izumi Yukimura, Michiyo Tamaki, Michiyo Aratama, Ken Uehara, Tatsuya Nakadai, Tatsuya Mihashi, Reiko Dan, Shinji Yamada, Murasaki Fujima

A Toho Co., Ltd. Production. A Toho Co., Ltd. Release. Black and white. Standard size. 84 minutes. Released May 26, 1958.

U.S. version: Release, if any, is undetermined. A 35mm English-subtitled print is currently held at the Pacific Film Archive.

Notes: Okamoto's first film as director. According to Japanese film expert Michael Jeck, Toshiro Mifune has a small, uncredited role in this romantic musical as a fey acting instructor.

JINSEI GEKIJO—SEISHUN HEN ("THEATER OF LIFE—YOUTH VERSION")
[THEATER OF LIFE]
Producer, Ichiro Sato; Director, Toshio Sugie; Screenplay, Ryuji Shiina and Toshio Yasumi, based on the novel by Shiro Ozaki; Director of Photography, Taiichi Kankura; Art Director, Shinobu Muraki; Lighting, Toshio Takashima; Sound, Toshiya Ban and Masanobu Miyazaki; Music, Yoshiyuki Kozu

Cast: Ryo Ikebe, Hisaya Morishige, Takashi Shimura, Mitsuko Kusabue, Hisako Takibana, Eijiro Tono, Yoichi Tachikawa, Toshiro Mifune

A Toho Co., Ltd. Production. A Toho Co., Ltd. Release. Color. Toho Scope. 111 minutes. Released November 23, 1958.

U.S. version: Release, if any, is undetermined.

Notes: A remake of Tomu Uchida's 1936 film, *Theater of Life* (Jinsei gekijo—seishun hen) based on the same novel, and subsequently filmed, also as *Theater of Life*, by Tai Kato (Shochiku, 1972) and Kinji Fukasaku (q.v., Toei, 1983).

KAKUSHI TORIDE NO SAN-AKUNIN ("Three Bad Men in a Hidden Fortress")
[THE HIDDEN FORTRESS]
Producers, Sanezumi Fujimoto and Akira Kurosawa; Director, Akira Kurosawa; Screenplay, Ryuzo Kikushima, Hideo Oguni, Shinobu Hashimoto, and Akira Kurosawa; Director of Photography, Kazuo Yamasaki; Art Director, Yoshiro Muraki; Lighting, Ichiro Inohara; Sound, Fumio Yanoguchi; Music, Masaru Sato; Assistant Cameraman, Takao Saito; Assistant Art Director, Shinko Kato; Assistant Lighting, Sei Arai; Sound Assistant, Yoshiro Miyamoto; Sound Mixing, Hisashi Shimonaga; Chief Assistant Director, Mimachi Yanagase; Assistant Directors, Yasuyoshi Tajitsu, Yoshimitsu Sakano, Kan Sano, Yoichi Matsue, Masahiro Takase; Negative Cutter, Chozo Kobata; Script Supervisor, Teruyo Nogami; Sound Effects, Ichiro Minawa; Still Photographer, Masao Fukuda; Production Supervisor, Hiroshi Nezu; Production Assistant, Takuyuki Inoue; Accountant, Koichi Noguchi; Art Supervisor, Kohei Ezaki; Special Effects, Toho Special Effects Group; Property Master, Koichi Hamamura; Costumes, Masahiro Kato (Kyoto Costume); Hair Stylists, Yoshiko Matsumoto and Junjiro Yamada; Acting Office, Yuichi Yoshitake; Choreography, Yoji Ken (Nichigeki); Swordplay Instructor, Yoshio Sugino; Horseback Riding Instructors, Ienori Kaneko and Shigeru Endo

Cast: Toshiro Mifune (General Rokurota Makabe), Misa Uehara (Princess Yuki), Minoru Chiaki (Tahei), Kamatari Fujiwara (Matakishi), Takashi Shimura (General Izumi Nagakura), Susumu Fujita (Heiei Tadokoro), Eiko Miyoshi (*old lady-in-waiting*), Toshiko Higuchi (*girl bought from slave trader*), Yu Fujiki (*barrier guard*), Yoshio Tsuchiya (*samurai on horse*), Kokuten Kodo (*old man in front of sign*), Takeshi Kato (*fleeing, bloody samurai*), Koji Mitsui (*guard*), Toranosuke Ogawa (*magistrate of the bridge barrier*), Kichijiro Ueda (*slave trader*), Nakajiro Tomita, Yoshifumi Tajima (*potential slave buyers*), Ikio Sawamura (*gambler*), Senkichi Omura (*soldier*), Sachio Sakai and Akira Tani (*captured foot soldiers*), Makoto Sato (*Yamada foot soldier*), Yutaka Sada (*guard at bridge barrier*), Yoshio Kosugi, Haruo Nakajima, Senkichi Omura (*Akisuki soldiers waiting for the fog to lift*), Takeo Oyabigawa (*guard at pass barrier*), Tadao Nakamaru (*young man*), Niyoshi Kumaya (*Yamana foot soldier*), Shoichi "Solomon" Hirose (*Yamana soldier*), Etsuro Nishijo, Masayoshi

Nagashima (*Yamana samurai*), Fuminori Ohashi (*samurai who buys horse*), Shin Otomo, Minoru Ito, Haruo Suzuki, Shigemasa Kanazawa, Hiroyoshi Yamaguchi, Haruya Sakamoto (*samurai on horseback*), Kazuo Hikita (*Yamana foot soldier*), Ryu Kuze (*Akitsuki soldier*), Ichiro Chiba (*Yamana foot soldier*), Rinsaku Ogawa (*second young man*), Nichigeki Dancing Team (*female dancers*)

A Toho Co., Ltd. Production. A Toho Co., Ltd. Release. Western Electric Mirrophonic Recording (encoded with Perspecta Stereophonic Sound). Black and white (processed by Tokyo Laboratory, Co. Ltd.). Toho Scope. 139 minutes. Released December 28, 1958.

U.S. version: Released by Toho International Co., Ltd. English subtitles. Screened in San Francisco in November 1959, probably at 139 minutes. Released October 6, 1960, 126 minutes. Reissued in 1962 at 90 minutes. Theatrical reissue and home video version restored. Alternate title: *Three Bad Men in a Hidden Fortress*.

Notes: The characters and story were the uncredited (though later acknowledged) basis for *Star Wars* (20th Century-Fox, 1977). Toho's only film to crack the Top Ten money earners of 1958, ranking fourth overall. Double-billed with the documentary *The Story of a Baseball Team* (Kyojingun monogatari). Awards: Berlin International Film Festival [1959] (Silver Bear, Best Director); the International Film Critics Prize (1959), Blue Ribbon Prize (Best Film, 1958), *Kinema Jumpo* "Best Ten" (second place). Toho also produced an English-dubbed version. Its release, if any, is undetermined.

ANKOKUGAI NO KAOYAKU ("Boss of the Underworld")
[THE BIG BOSS]
Producer, Tomoyuki Tanaka; Director, Kihachi Okamoto; Screenplay, Motosada Nishigame and Shinichi Sekizawa; Director of Photography, Asakazu Nakai; Art Director, Iwao Akune; Lighting, Shigeo Mori; Sound, Norio Tone and Hisashi Shimonaga; Music, Akira Ifukube; Songs: Music by Konnosuke Hameguchi and Lyrics by Senichi Sekizawa, performed by Akira Takarada; Assistant Cameraman, Susumu Takebayashi; Editor, Yoshitani Kuroiwa; Special Effects, Toho Special Effects Group; Unit Production Manager, Toshio Kitamura

Cast: Koji Tsuruta (Ryuta Komatsu), Akira Takarada (Mineo Komatsu, *his brother*), Yumi Shirakawa (Junko), Keiko Yanagawa (Yoko), Mitsuko Kusabue (Rie), Seizaburo Kawazu, Yosuke Natsuki, Mickey Curtis, Haruo Tanaka, Makoto Sato, Akihiko Hirata, Kokuten Kodo, Fumiko Homma, Michio Yokoyama, Sonomi Nakajima, Rumiko Sasa, Miki Hayashi, Sachio Sakai, Hideyo Amamoto [Eisei Amamoto], Ren Yamamoto, Haruya Kato, Shin Otomo, Akira Sera, Ikio Sawamura, Nadao Kirino, Yutaka Nakayama, Koji Ueno, Koji Iwamoto, Katsuji Ichikawa, Hiroshi Takaragi, Shoichi "Solomon" Hirose, Tadao Nakamaru, Ren Koizumi, Ed Keane • Toshiro Mifune (Kashimura, *the mechanic*)

A Toho Co., Ltd. Production. A Toho Co., Ltd. Release. Western Electric Mirrophonic Recording (encoded with Perspecta Stereophonic Sound). Fujicolor (processed by Toyo Developing). Toho Scope. 101 minutes. Released January 15, 1959.

U.S. version: Release undetermined, possibly by Toho International Co., Ltd. in subtitled format.

Notes: Double-billed with *Temptation on Glamour Island* (Gurama-to no yuwaku).

ARU KENGO NO SHOGAI ("Life of an Expert Swordsman")
[SAMURAI SAGA]
Producer, Tomoyuki Tanaka; Director, Hiroshi Inagaki; Screenplay, Hiroshi Inagaki, based on Edmond Rostand's *Cyrano de Bergerac*; Director of Photography, Kazuo Yamada; Art Director, Yoshiaki Ito; Lighting, Masahichi Kojima; Sound, Yoshio Nishikawa; Music, Akira Ifukube; Still Photographer, Matsuo Yoshizaki; Chief Assistant Director, Teruo Maru

Cast: <u>Toshiro Mifune</u> (Heihachiro Komaki), Yoko Tsukasa (Lady Ochii, *a.k.a. Princess Chiyo*), Akira Takarada (Jutaro [Jurota] Karibe), Keiko Awaji (Nanae), Seizaburo Kawazu (Nagashima), Kamatari Fujiwara (Rakuzo, *the sake seller*), Akihiko Hirata (Akaboshi), Eiko Miyoshi (Okuni), Sachio Sakai, Yoshifumi Tajima, Akira Tani, Yutaka Sada, Senkichi Omura, Hideyo Amamoto [Eisei Amamoto]

A Toho Co., Ltd. Production. A Toho Co., Ltd. Release. Eastman Color. Toho Scope. 111 minutes. Released April 28, 1959.

U.S. version: Distributor undetermined, probably Toho International Co., Ltd., in subtitled format. No MPAA rating.

Notes: Double-billed with *Foxes and Badgers* (Kitsune to tanuki).

SENGOKU GUNTO-DEN ("The Story of Robbers of the Civil Wars")
[SAGA OF THE VAGABONDS]
Producers, Sanezumi Fujimoto and Kazuo Nishino; Director, Toshio Sugie; Screenplay, <u>Akira Kurosawa</u>, based on a 1937 screenplay by Sadao Yamanaka and an original story by Juro Miyoshi; Director of Photography, Akira Suzuki; Art Director, Takeo Kita; Music, Ikuma Dan

Cast: <u>Toshiro Mifune</u> (Rokuro Kai), Koji Tsuruta (Taro Toki), Yoko Tsukasa (Tazu), Misa Uehara (Princess Koyuki), Takashi Shimura (Saemon Toki, *Taro's father*), Minoru Chiaki (Jibu), Akihiko Hirata (Jiro Hidekuni, *Taro's brother*), Seizaburo Kawazu (Hyoe Yamana, *Jiro's vassal*). Yoshio Kosugi, Kenzo Tabu, Akira Tani, Ren Yamamoto, Sachio Sakai, Yoshifumi Tajima, Shin Otomo, Tadao Nakamaru

A Toho Co., Ltd. Production. A Toho Co., Ltd. Release. Western Electric Mirrophonic Recording (encoded with Perspecta Stereophonic Sound). Agfa Color. Toho Scope. 115 minutes. Released August 9, 1959.

U.S. version: Released by Toho International Co., Ltd. English subtitles. 115 minutes. Released November 23, 1960. Advertised as *The Vagabonds*.

Notes: Double-billed with *New Third-Grade Executive* (Shin santo juyaki).

TATESHI DANPEI ("Fencing Master")
Director, Harumi Mizuho; Screenplay, <u>Akira Kurosawa</u>, based on a story by Yukinobu Hasegawa; Director of Photography, Hiroshi Imai; Art Director, Shigeru Kato; Music, Nakaba Takahashi

Cast: Raizo Ichikawa, Michiko Saga, Ganjuro Nakamura

A Daiei (Kyoto) Motion Picture Co., Ltd. Production. A Daiei Co., Ltd. Release. Color. Daiei Scope. 85 minutes. Released September 30, 1959.

U.S. version: Release, if any, is undetermined.

Notes: A remake of *Tateshi danpei* (1950).

DOKURITSU GURENTAI ("Independent Gangsters")
[DESPERADO OUTPOST]
Producer, Tomoyuki Tanaka; Director and Screenplay, Kihachi Okamoto; Director of Photography, Yuzuru Aizawa; Art Director, Gan Akune; Lighting, Tsuruzo Nishikawa; Sound, Shin Tokai and Hisashi Shimonaga; Music, Masaru Sato; Unit Production Manager, Masao Suzuki; Chief Assistant Director, Susumu Takebayashi; Editor, Yoshitami Kuroiwa

Cast: Makoto Sato (Sergeant Okubo, *alias Araki, the war correspondent*), Izumi Yukimura (*prostitute*), Misa Uehara (*sister of bandit chieftain*), Tadao Nakamaru (*aide-de-camp*), Ichiro Nakatani (*squad leader*), Yosuke Natsuki, Tatsuyoshi Ehara, Michiro Minami, Mickey Curtis, Chieko Nakakita, Michiyo Yokoyama, Toki Shiozawa, Akira Sera, Ikio Sawamura, Akira Tani, Ren Yamamoto, Sachio Sakai, Yutaka Nakayama, Nadao Kirino, Kenji Kasahara, Yukiyoshi Uemura, Akira

Yamada, Koji Iwamoto, Yasuyuki Tsutsumi, Koji Uno, Akira Wakamatsu, Toshio Miura, Hiroshi Takagi, Yusuzo Ogawa, Hirokaru Okado, Riki Nakayama, Jerry Fujio, Shigeo Tazuka, Yukihiko Gondo, Haruo Suzuki • Koji Tsuruta (*bandit chieftain*) and <u>Toshiro Mifune</u> (*battalion commander*)

A Toho Co., Ltd. Production. A Toho Co., Ltd. Release. Western Electric Mirrophonic Recording (encoded with Perspecta Stereophonic Sound). Black and white (processed by Kinuta Laboratory). Toho Scope. 109 minutes. Released October 6, 1959.

U.S. version: Release, if any, is undetermined.

Note: First feature of the 6-film "Independent Gangsters" series (1959–64), all starring Sato. Followed by *Westward Desperado* (Dokuritsu gurentai nishi e, 1960). Double-billed with *Young Lover* (Wakai koibitotachi).

NIPPON TANJO ("Birth of Japan")
[THE THREE TREASURES]
Producers, Sanezumi Fujimoto and Tomoyuki Tanaka; Director, Hiroshi Inagaki; Special Effects Director, Eiji Tsuburaya; Screenplay, Toshio Yasumi and Ryuzo Kikushima, based on the legends "Kojiki" and "Nihon Shoki," and the origin of Shinto; Director of Photography, Kazuo Yamada; Art Directors, Kisaku Ito and Hiroshi Ueda; Lighting, Shoshichi Kojima; Sound, Yoshio Nishikawa and Hisashi Shimonaga; Music, Akira Ifukube; Assistant Director, Teruo Maru; Editor, Hitoshi Hira; In Charge of Production, Katsutaro Kawakami; Still Photographer, Matsuo Yoshizaki; Choreographer, Enjaku Kiyokata. *Toho Special Effects Group*: Director of Photography, Sadamasa Arikawa; Art Director, Akira Watanabe; Lighting, Kyuichiro Kishida; Matte Process, Hiroshi Mukoyama; Optical Photography, Shuzaburo Araki

Cast: <u>Toshiro Mifune</u> (Prince Yamato Takeru), Yoko Tsukasa (Princess Tachibana), Kyoko Kagawa (Princess Miyazu), Koji Tsuruta (*younger* Kumaso), Takashi Shimura (*elder* Kumaso), Kumi Mizuno, Misa Uehara, Kinuyo Tanaka, Nobuko Otowa, Haruko Sugimura, Akira Kubo, Akira Takarada, Ganjuro Nakamura, Eijiro Tono, Akihiko Hirata, Ko Mishima, Hisaya Ito, Jun Tazaki, Takashi Shimura, Kichijiro Ueda, Yoshio Kosugi, Kozo Nomura, Yu Fujiki, Michiyo Tamaki, Keiko Muramatsu, Kakuko Murata, Chieko Nakakita, Bokuzen Hidari, Minosuke Yamada, Akira Sera, Hajime Izu, Yoshifumi Tajima, Fuyuki Murakami, Akira Tani, Junichiro Mukai, Ikio Sawamura, Senkichi Omura, Yutaka Sada, Ryu Kuze, Kyoro Sakurai, Nadao Kirino, Mitsuo Tsuda, Shin Otomo, Katsumi Tezuka, Masayoshi Nagashima, Shoichi "Solomon" Hirose, Shiro Tsuchiya, Fumito Matsuo, Yasuhisa Tsutsumi, Masao Masuda, Jiro Kumagaya, Tadashi Okabe, Koji Uemura, Yasuhiro Shigenobu, Haruya Sakamoto, Rinsaku Ogata, Izumi Akimoto, Hiroyoshi Yamaguchi, Akira Kitano, Akira Yamada, Hiroyuki Wakita, Hideyo Amamoto, Koji Iwamoto, Yoshiko Ieda, Midori Kishida, Michiko Kawa, Misako Asuka, Toshiko Higuchi, Teruko Mita, Harumi Ueno • Keiju Kobayashi, Daisuke Kato, Norihei Miki, Ichiro Arishima, Kingoro Yanagiya, Kenichi "Enoken" Enomoto, Taro Asahiyo, Koji Tsuruta • Setsuko Hara

A Toho Co., Ltd. Production. A Toho Co., Ltd. Release. Agfa Color (processed by Tokyo Laboratory, Ltd.). Toho Scope. 182 minutes. Released November 1, 1959.

U.S. version: Released by Toho International Company, Ltd. English subtitles. Some engagements advertised as *Age of the Gods*. 112 minutes. Released December 20, 1960.

Notes: An English-dubbed version was produced by Toho. Its release, if any, is uncertain. Billed as Toho's 1,000th production. Toho's biggest money earner of 1959, ranking second overall.

ANKOKUGAI NO TAIKETSU
[THE LAST GUNFIGHT]
Producer, Tomoyuki Tanaka; Director, Kihachi Okamoto; Screenplay, Shinichi Sekizawa; Art Director, Iwao Akune; Lighting, Tsuruzo Nishikawa; Music, Masaru Sato

Cast: <u>Toshiro Mifune</u> (Detective Saburo Fujioka), Koji Tsuruta (Tetsuo Maruyama), Yoko Tsukasa (Sally), Seizaburo Kawazu (Kyuzaburo Oka), *The Oka Gang*: Tadao Nakamaru (Shibata), Sachio Sakai (Ofudokichi), Jiro Makino (Tanba), Koji Iwamoto (Tomita), Keiko Muramatsu (Benichiyo, *Shibata's lover*). *The Kozuka Gang*: Jun Tazaki (Otokichi Kozuka), Makoto Sato (Yata), Yutaka Nakayama (Tako). *The Killers*: Akihiko Hirata (Susumu Tendo, *the killer*), Hideyo Amamoto [Eisei Amamoto] (Ichino), Akira Wakamatsu (Nikawa), Hiroshi Takagi (Mita), Mickey Curtis (Sugino). *Kojin Police Station*: Yoshio Kosugi (Chief Officer Okubo), Ichiro Nakaya (Tsugiseki Mochizuki), Yosuke Natsuki (Officer Miake), Fuyuki Murakami (Chief of the Metropolitan Police Department), Yasuhisa Tsutsumi (Section Chief of the Metropolitan Police Department), Ren Yamamoto (Iwaimura, *reporter for the Tocho News*), Akemi Kita (Mari, *a part-time prostitute*), Kaoru Hama (Hiromi, *a stripper*), Akira Naoki (Matsuo), Ikio Sawamura (Yata, *an entertainment broker*), Miki Hayashi (Politician Numata), Shiro Tsuchiya (*big shot*), Akira Tani (Boyaki Jogo), Akira Sera (Naki Jogo), Yuataka Sada (*owner of Miyoshino*)

A Toho Co., Ltd. Production. A Toho Co., Ltd. Release. AgfaColor. Toho Scope. 94 minutes. Released January 3, 1960.

U.S. version: Release, if any, is undetermined. An English-dubbed version was produced by Toho. Double-billed with *The Five Jolly Thieves* (Tenka no odorobo—Shiranami gonin otoko).

THE MAGNIFICENT SEVEN

Executive Producer, Walter Mirisch; Associate Producer, Lou Morheim; Producer and Director, John Sturges; Screenplay, Walter Newman, Walter Bernstein [uncredited] with additions by William Roberts, based on the screenplay of *Seven Samurai*, written by Shinobu Hashimoto, Hideo Oguni, and <u>Akira Kurosawa</u>; Director of Photography, Charles Lang, Jr. Art Director, Edward Fitzgerald; Sound, Jack Solomon and Rafael Esparza; Music, Elmer Bernstein; Editor, Ferris Webster; Assistant Directors, Robert E. Relyea and Jamie Contreras; Unit Production Manager, Chico Day; Wardrobe, Bert Henrikson; Script Supervisor, John Franco; Dialogue Coach, Thom Conroy; Makeup, Emile LaVigne and Daniel Striepke; Special Effects, Milt Rice; Property Master, Sam Gordon; Set Decorator, Rafael Suarez; Production Supervisor, Allen K. Wood; Sound Effects Editor, Del Harris

Cast: Yul Brynner (Chris), Eli Wallach (Calvera), Steve McQueen (Vin), Horst Bucholtz (Chico), Charles Bronson (O'Reilly), Robert Vaughn (Lee), Brad Dexter (Harry Luck), James Coburn (Britt), Vladimir Sokoloff (*the old man*), Rosenda Monteros (Petra), Jorge Martinez de Hoyas (Hilario), Whit Bissell (Chamlee), Val Avery (Henry), Bing Russell (Robert), Rico Alaniz (Sotero), Robert Wilke (Wallace), Pepe Hern, Natatvad Vacio, Mario Navarro, Danny Bravo, John Alonzo, Enrique Lucero, Alex Montoya

A Mirisch Co., Inc./Alpha Production. A United Artists Release. Color by De Luxe. Panavision. 126 minutes. Released 1960.

Notes: Released in Japan on May 3, 1961, as *Koya no Shichinin* ("Seven Men of the Wilderness"), where it became the top-grossing imported film that year. Followed by *Return of the Seven* (1966), also with Brynner; *Guns of the Magnificent Seven* (1969); *The Magnificent Seven Ride!* (1972); and a television series. Filmed on location in Cuernavaca and Estudios Churobusco, Mexico. Screen credits acknowledge "This picture is based on the Japanese film *Seven Samurai*, Toho Company, Ltd." None of that film's writers are credited.

KUNISADA CHUJI ("Chuji Kunisada")
[THE GAMBLING SAMURAI]

Producer, Sanezumi Fujimoto; Director, Senkichi Taniguchi; Screenplay, Kaneto Shindo; Director of Photography, Rokuro Nishigaki; Art Director, Takeo Kita; Lighting, Choshiro Ishii;

Sound, Wataru Konuma; Music, Masaru Sato; Assistant Director, Teruo Maru; Continuity, Fumie Fujimoto; In Charge of Production, Hiroshi Nezu

Cast: <u>Toshiro Mifune</u> (Chuji Kunisada), Daisuke Kato (Enzo Niko), Michiyo Aratama (Toku, *Funakichi's lover*), Yosuke Natsuki (Sentaro Itabashi), Yu Fujiki (Gentetsu Shimizu), Susumu Fujita (Magistrate Jubei Matsui), Eijro Tono (Kansuke), Kankuro Nakamura (Kantaro, *at six years old*), Kumi Mizuno (Kiku, *Chuji's sister*), Ko Mishima (Yosaku), Yoshio Kosugi (Tokisaburo), Senkichi Omura (Yoshi, *Tokisaburo's servant*), Tetsuro Tamba (Fumizo Mitsuki), Minosuke Yamada (Uemon), Yusuke Minami (Tokimatsu Yamamura), Jiryou Kumagaya (Seiichiro Nakajima), Mutoshi Yanami (Matahachi), Junichiro Mukai (Seishichiro), Kyoro Sakurai (Sadashiro), Hideyo Amamoto (Tomimatsu), Koji Iwamoto (Mintaro), Akira Yamada (Gorozo), Ren Yamamoto (Isuke), Sachio Sakai (Tamazo), Masao Oda (Niuemon, *a farmer*), Yutaka Sada (*farmer*)

A Toho Co., Ltd. Production. A Toho Co., Ltd. Release. Western Electric Mirrophonic Recording (encoded with Perspecta Stereophonic Sound). AgfaColor. Toho Scope. 101 minutes. Released March 29, 1960.

U.S. version: Released by Toho International Co., Ltd. English subtitles. 93 minutes. Released September 27, 1960. Reissued in March 1975.

Notes: Double-billed with *Salaryman Success Story • Conclusion—Bridegroom Manager No. 1* (Sarariiman shusse taikoki • Kanketsuhen—Hanamuko bucho No. 1)

HAWAII • MIDDOWEE DAIKAIKUSEN—TAIHEIYO NO ARASHI ("Hawaii • Midway Battle of the Sea and Sky—Storm in the Pacific Ocean")
[THE STORM OF THE PACIFIC]
Producer, Tomoyuki Tanaka; Director, Shue Matsubayashi; Special Effects Director, Eiji Tsuburaya; Screenplay, Shinobu Hashimoto and Takeo Kunihiro; Director of Photography, Kazuo Yamada; Art Directors, Takeo Kita and Kiyoshi Shimizu; Lighting, Shoshichi Kojima; Sound, Yoshio Nishikawa and Masanobu Miyazaki; Music, Ikuma Dan; Assistant Director, Yasuyoshi Kazane; Sound Effects, Ichiro Minawa; Editor, Koichi Iwashita; In Charge of Production, Katsutaro Kawakami; Still Photographer, Matsuo Yoshizaki. *Toho Special Effects Group*: Director of Photography, Sadamasa Arikawa; Lighting, Kyuichiro Kishida; Art Director, Akira Watanabe; Matte Processing, Hiroshi Mukoyama; Optical Photography, Shuzaburo Araki

Cast: Yosuke Natsuki (Lt. Koji Kitami), Makoto Sato (Lt. Matsuura), Misa Uehara (Keiko, *Koji's sweetheart*), Keiju Kobayashi, Tatsuya Mihashi, Hiroshi Koizumi, Akira Takarada, Seizaburo Kawazu, Ken Uehara, Susumu Fujita, Takashi Shimura, Aiko Mimasu, Kenichi "Enoken" Enomoto, Akihiko Hirata, Tadao Nakamaru, Yoshio Tsuchiya, Ko Mishima, Hisaya Ito, Hiroshi Tachikawa, Jun Tazaki, Yoshio Kosugi, Sachio Sakai, Ren Yamamoto, Tetsu Nakamura, Senkichi Omura, Yutaka Sada, Shin Otomo, Fuyuki Murakami, Yoshifumi Tajima, Shunichi Segi, Kendo Yashiki, Jun Funado, Yutaka Oka, Nadao Kirino, Akira Oka, Koji Ishikawa, Ko Mishima, Haruo Nakajima, Hiroshi Sekita, Daisuke Kato • <u>Toshiro Mifune</u> (Admiral Yamaguchi), Ryo Ikebe, Koji Tsuruta (Lt. Tomonari)

A Toho Co., Ltd. Production. A Toho Co., Ltd. Release. Western Electric Mirrophonic Recording (encoded with Perspecta Stereophonic Sound). Eastman Color (processed by Toyo Laboratory, Ltd.). Toho Scope. 118 minutes. Released April 26, 1960.

U.S. version: *I Bombed Pearl Harbor*. Released by Parade Releasing Organization. English-dubbed. A Hugo Grimaldi Production. A Riley Jackson and Robert Patrick Presentation. Executive Producers, Riley Jackson and Robert Patrick; Producer/Director/Editor, Hugo Grimaldi; Music and Sound Supervisor, Gordon Zahler; Music, Walter Greene; Sound, Ryder Sound Services, Inc. Voice Characterizations, Paul Frees, others unidentified. Prints by Technicolor. Westrex Recording System. 98 minutes. Released November 29, 1961. Released simultaneously in subtitled format by Toho International Co., Ltd., as *Storm Over the Pacific*.

Notes: Toho apparently also produced an English-dubbed version of its own. Its release, if any, is undetermined. Daisuke Kato appears unbilled. Double-billed with *New Third Class Executive—Fortune Teller Version* (Shin santo juyaku—Atarumo hake no maki).

OTOKO TAI OTOKO ("Man Against Man")
[MAN AGAINST MAN]

Director, Senkichi Taniguchi; Screenplay, Ichiro Ikeda and Ei Ogawa; Director of Photography, Rokuro Nishigaki; Art Director, Yoshiro Muraki; Lighting, Tsuruzo Nishikawa; Sound, Shuichi Fujinawa; Music, Masaru Sato; Chief Assistant Director, Ken Matsumori

Cast: <u>Toshiro Mifune</u> (Kaji), Ryo Ikebe (Kikumori), Takashi Shimura (Chotaro Masue), Yuzo Kayama (Toshio Masue), Jun Tazaki (Boss Tsukamoto), Akihiko Hirata (Torimi), Yumi Shirakawa (Mineko Nishijo), Akemi Kita (Harumi), Yuriko Hoshi (Natsue), Yutaka Sada (Wada), Shoichi "Solomon" Hirose (Genpachi), Yoshifumi Tajima (Taro), Ikio Sawamura (Santa), Sachio Sakai (Shinchan), Shin Otomo (Kitagawa), Ren Yamamoto (Igarashi), Nadao Kirino (Tsuchiya), Tadao Nakamaru (Machida), Hideyo Amamoto (killer), Yoshio Tsuchiya (Detective Yoshizawa), Michiko Kawamoto (Tome, *the maid*), Fumito Matsuo (*doctor*)

A Toho Co., Ltd. Production. A Toho Co., Ltd. Release. Western Electric Mirrophonic Recording (encoded with Perspecta Sterophonic Sound). Eastman Color. Toho Scope. 116 minutes. Released August 14, 1960.

U.S. version: Released by Toho International Co., Ltd. English subtitles. Apparently reissued in Japan at 90 minutes. 116 minutes. Released March 17, 1961.

Notes: Yuzo Kayama's film debut. Toho also produced an English-dubbed version of this title. Double-billed with *The Country Doctor* (Fundoshi isha).

WARUIYATSU HODO YOKU NEMERU ("The Worse You Are the Better You Sleep")
[THE BAD SLEEP WELL]

Producers, Tomoyuki Tanaka and Akira Kurosawa; Director, <u>Akira Kurosawa</u>; Screenplay, Hideo Oguni, Eijiro Hisaita, Akira Kurosawa, and Shinobu Hashimoto, suggested by an unproduced screenplay by Mike Y. Inoue; Director of Photography, Yuzuru Aizawa; Art Director, Yoshiro Muraki; Lighting, Ichiro Inohara; Sound, Fumio Yanoguchi; Music, Masaru Sato; Assistant Cameraman, Takao Saito; Assistant Lighting, Sei Arai; Assistant Art Director, Jun Sakuma; Sound Assistant, Masanao Uehara; Sound Mixing, Hisashi Shimonaga; Chief Assistant Director, Shiro Moritani; Assistant Directors, Yoshimitsu Sakano, Kiyoshi Nishimura, Yoichi Matsue, Kazuko Kawakita; Assistant Editor, Reiko Kaneko; Script Supervisor, Teruyo Nogami; Sound Effects, Ichiro Minawa; Still Photographer, Masao Fukuda; Production Supervisor, Hiroshi Nezu; Production Assistant, Hidehiko Eguchi; Property Master, Koichi Hamamura; Costumes, Shoji Kurihara (Kyoto Costume); Hair Stylists, Tomoko Asami and Junjiro Yamada; Transportation, Ginzo Osumi

Cast: <u>Toshiro Mifune</u> (Koichi Nishi), Masayuki Mori (Public Corp. Vice President Iwabuchi), Kyoko Kagawa (Keiko Nishi, *his daughter*), Tatsuya Mihashi (Tatsuo Iwabuchi, *his son*), Takashi Shimura (Public Corp. Administrative Manager Moriyama), Ko Nishimura (Public Corp. Contract Chief Shirai), Takeshi Kato (foreign car dealer Itakura, *the real Koichi Nishi*), Kamatari Fujiwara (Public Corp. Assistant to the Chief Wada), Chishu Ryu (Public Prosecutor Nonaka), Seiji Miyaguchi (Prosecutor Okakura), Koji Mitsui (*reporter A*), Ken Mitsuda (President of Public Corp.), Nobuo Nakamura (*legal adviser*), Susumu Fujita (*detective*), Koji Minamibara (Prosecutor Horiuchi), Gen Shimizu (Miura, *managing director of the construction company, who commits suicide*), Yoshifumi Tajima (*reporter B*), Yoshio Tsuchiya (*officer worker*),

Somesho Matsumoto (Hatano, *president of the construction company*), Kyu Sazanka (Kaneko, *executive director of the construction company*), Kin Sugai (Mrs. Wada), Natsuko Kahara (Mrs. Furuya), Nobuko Tashiro (Mrs. Moriyama), Atsuko Ichinomiya (Mrs. Ariyama), Toshiko Higuchi (Wada's *daughter*), Jun Kondo (*reporter D*), Yutaka Sada (*wedding receptionist*), Ikio Sawamura (*taxi driver*), Hisa Yakomori (*reporter C*), Kunie Tanaka (*would-be assassin*), Kyoro Sakurai (*prosecutor*), Ryoji Shimizu (*worker in management section of Public Corp.*), Soji Ikukata, Shiro Tsuchiya (*construction company employees*), Kyoko Ozawa (*Iwabuchi maid*), Akemi Ueno (*receptionist at safety deposit box rentals*), Hiromi Iwabuchi (*second Iwabuchi maid*)

A Kurosawa Production Co., Ltd./Toho Co., Ltd. Production. A Toho Co., Ltd. Release. Western Electric Mirrophonic Recording (encoded with Perspecta Stereophonic Sound). Black and white (Eastman stock; processed by Kinuta Laboratory). Toho Scope. 151 minutes. Released September 19, 1960 (roadshow version), and October 1, 1960 (general release).

U.S. version: Premiered at a special screening at UCLA on October 5, 1962, 151 minutes (?). Released by Toho International Co., Ltd. English subtitles. Released January 22, 1963. 135 minutes. Reissued by Janus Films. Reissue and home video version restored.

Notes: Announced by Toho as *The Rose in the Mud*. Inoue, upon whose story the film is based, is not given official credit. General release version double-billed with *The Approach of Autumn* (Aki tachinu).

SARARIIMAN CHUSHINGURA ("Salaryman Chushingura")
[THE MASTERLESS 47]
Producer, Sanezumi Fujimoto; Director, Toshio Sugie; Screenplay, Ryozo Kasahara, based on an idea by Yasuo Ihara; Director of Photography, Taiichi Kankura; Art Director, Yoshiro Muraki; Lighting, Mitsuo Kaneko; Sound, Choshichiro Mikami; Music, Yoshiyuki Kozu; Still Photographer, Kazuhiko [Isei] Tanaka

Cast: Hisaya Morishige (Yoshio Oishi), Daisuke Kato (Jyusaburo Onodera), Keiju Kobayashi (Heitaro Teraoka), Yoko Tsukasa (Keiko), Reiko Dan (Konami), Sonomi Nakajima (Yasuko Hosobe), Mitsuko Kusabue (Saiko), Michiyo Aratama (Geisha Kayoji), Akira Takarada (Kohei Hayano), Yosuke Natsuki (Riki Oishi), Tatsuya Mihashi (Sadagoro), Asami Kuji (Ritsuko Oishi), Eijiro Tono (Gonosuke Kira), Ichiro Arishima (Kube Ono), Kyu Sazanka (Koichi Bannai), Takashi Shimura (Honzo Kadokawa), Eijiro Yanagi (Naoyoshi Ashikaga), Shin Otomo (Hara), Kiyoshi Kodama (Okano), Tatsuyoshi Ehara (Isogai), Yu Fujiki (Akagaki), Mutoshi Yanami (Takebayashi), Ikio Sawamura (Kurabayashi), George Riker (Henri Richard), Kingoro Yanagiya (*owner of Yamashita, a soba restaurant*), Ryo Ikebe (Takuni Asano) • Toshiro Mifune (Kazuo Momoi).

A Toho Co., Ltd. Production. A Toho Co., Ltd. Release. Color. Toho Scope. 101 minutes. Released December 25, 1960.

U.S. version: Release, if any, is undetermined.

Notes: Billed as "Toho's 100th Salaryman Movie." The 13th of 40 "Shacho" comedies. Followed by *The Masterless 47 Part II* (Zoku • Sarariiman Chushingura, 1961). Double-billed with *Sazae-san and Aunt Apron* (Sazae-san to epuron obasan).

OSAKAJO MONOGATARI ("The Story of Osaka Castle")
[DAREDEVIL IN THE CASTLE]
Producer, Tomoyuki Tanaka; Director, Hiroshi Inagaki; Screenplay, Hiroshi Inagaki and Takeshi Kimura, based on the novel by Genzo Murakami; Director of Photography, Kazuo Yamada; Art Director, Hiroshi Ueda; Lighting, Seishichi Kojima; Sound, Yoshio Nishikawa; Music, Akira Ifukube; Chief Assistant Director, Masahiro Takase; Still Photographer, Matsuo Yoshizaki. *Toho Special Effects Group*: Director, Eiji Tsuburaya; Photography, Sadamasa Arikawa and Mototaka

Tomioka; Art Director, Akira Watanabe; Lighting, Kyuichiro Kishida; Matte Process, Hiroshi Mukoyama; Optical Photography, Taka Yuki and Yukio Manoda

Cast: <u>Toshiro Mifune</u> (Mohei), Kyoko Kagawa (Ai), Yuriko Hoshi (Senhime), Yoshiko Kuga (Kobue), Isuzu Yamada (Yodogimi), Yosuke Natsuki (Chomonshu Kimura), Jun Tazaki (Teikabo Tsutsumi), Danko Ichikawa (Saizo Muin), Akihiko Hirata (Hayatonosho [Hayato] Susukida), Takashi Shimura (Katagiri), Koedako Kuroiwa (Nobuo), Tetsuro Tamba (Sadamasa Ishikawa), Tadao Nakamaru (Hyogo), Ryusuke Kagawa (Michiiku Itamiya), Yu Fujiki (Danuemon Hanawa), Seizaburo Kawazu (Harunaga Ono), Susumu Fujita (Katsuyasu Sakakibara), Hanshiro Iwai (Hideyori Toyotomi), Sachio Sakai (Kai Hayami), Yoshio Kosugi (Gidayu Fujimoto), Kichijiro Ueda (Jinbei, *owner of the equipment shop*), Chieko Nakakita (Kyoku, *of Yae*), Haruko Togo (*Ono woman*), Hideyo Amamoto (*interpreter*), Junichiro Mukai (Kumoi), Shoji Ikeda (Chusho Nanjo), Shiro Tsuchiya (Tosho Horita), Akira Tani (*rice shop owner*), Shin Otomo (*Itamiya manager*), Katsumi Tezuka (Shuma Ono), Senkichi Omura, Ikio Sawamura, Koji Uno, Yasuhisa Tsutsumi, Haruo Nakajima, Hans Horneff, Bill Bassman, Toshiko Nakano, Osman Yusef.

A Toho Co., Ltd. Production. A Toho Co., Ltd. Release. Western Electric Mirrophonic Recording (encoded with Perspecta Stereophonic Sound). Eastman Color. Toho Scope. 95 minutes. Released January 3, 1961.

U.S. version: Released by Frank Lee International, Inc. English subtitles. Alternate title (?): *Devil in the Castle*. 95 minutes. Released June 6, 1961.

Notes: Toho produced an English-dubbed version of this title. Its release, if any, is undetermined. Reiko Dan and her role come from *Kinema Jumpo*'s credits, but her name does not appear in the onscreen titles, so her participation is unconfirmed. Actor Danko Ichikawa is today known as Sarunosuke Ichikawa. Double-billed with *Blueprint of Murder* (Ankokugai no dankon).

ZOKU SARARIMAN CHUSHINGURA ("Salaryman Chushingura Sequel")
[THE MASTERLESS 47—PART II]
Producer, Sanezumi Fujimoto; Director, Toshio Sugie; Screenplay, Ryozo Kasahara, based on an idea by Yasuo Ihara; Director of Photography, Taiichi Kankura; Art Director, Yoshiro Muraki; Lighting, Mitsuo Kaneko; Sound, Choshiro Mikami; Music, Yoshiyuki Kozu; Still Photographer, Kazuhiko Tanaka

Cast: Hisaya Morishige (Yoshio Oishi), Daisuke Kato (Jyusaburo Onodera), Keiju Kobayashi (Heitaro Teraoka), Yoko Tsukasa (Keiko), Reiko Dan (Konami), Sonomi Nakajima (Yasuko Hosobe), Mitsuko Kusabue (Saiko), Michiyo Aratama (Geisha Kayoji), Akira Takarada (Kohei Hayano), Yosuke Natsuki (Chikara), Tatsuya Mihashi (Sadagoro), Asami Kuji, (Ritsuko), Eijiro Tono (Gonosuke Kira), Ichiro Arishima (Kube Ono), Kyu Sazanka (Koichi Bannai), Takashi Shimura (Honzo Kadokawa), Kiyoshi Kodama (Okano), Tatsuyoshi Ehara (Isogai), Yu Fujiki (Akagaki), Mutoshi Yanami (Takebayashi), Ikio Sawamura (Kurabayashi), Kingoro Yanagiya (*owner of Yamashita, a soba restaurant*), Toki Shiozawa (*hostess A*), Ayumi Sonoda (*geisha A*) • <u>Toshiro Mifune</u> (Kazuo Momoi)

A Toho Co., Ltd. Production. A Toho Co., Ltd. Release. Color. Toho Scope. 110 minutes. Released February 25, 1961.

U.S. version: Release, if any, is undetermined.

Notes: The 14th "Shacho" feature. Followed by *Playboy President* (Shacho dochuki, 1961). Double-billed with *Sanshiro Sebiro—Man Needs Courage* (Sebiro Sanshiro—Otoko wa dokyo).

YOJINBO ("Bodyguard")
[YOJIMBO]
Executive Producers, Tomoyuki Tanaka and Ryuzo Kikushima; Associate Producer and Director, <u>Akira Kurosawa</u>; Screenplay, Ryuzo Kikushima and Akira Kurosawa; Director of Photogra-

phy, Kazuo Miyagawa; Art Director and Costumes, Yoshiro Muraki; Lighting, Choshiro Ishii; Sound, Hisashi Shimonaga and Choshichiro Mikami; Music, Masaru Sato; Assistant Cinematographer, Takao Saito; Assistant Lighting, Shoji Kaneko; Assistant Art Director, Yoshifumi Honda; Assistant Sound, Zen Shida; Mixer, Masanobu Miyazaki; Production Supervisor, Hiroshi Nezu; Assistant Production Supervisor, Shigeru Nakamura; Chief Assistant Director, Shiro Moritani; Assistant Directors, Masanobu Deme, Yasuhiro Yoshimatsu, and Yoshikumi Wada; Assistant Editor, Reiko Kaneko; Script Supervisor, Teruyo Nogami; Sound Effects, Ichiro Minawa; Still Photographer, Masao Fukuda; Property Master, Koichi Hamamura; Costumer, Masahiro Kato (Kyoto Isho); Hair Stylists, Yoshiko Matsumoto and Junjiro Yamada; Transportation, Ginzo Osumi; Swordplay Instructor, Yoshio Sugino; Swordplay Technique, Ryu Kuze; Choreography, Hiroshi Kanesu

Cast: <u>Toshiro Mifune</u> (Sanjuro Kuwabatake), Tatsuya Nakadai (Unosuke), Yoko Tsukasa (Nui), Isuzu Yamada (Orin), Daisuke Kato (Inokichi, *Unosuke's older brother*), Seizaburo Kawazu (Seibei, *Orin's husband*), Takashi Shimura (Tokuemon, *the sake maker*), Hiroshi Tachikawa (Yoichiro, *Orin and Selbei's son*), Yosuke Natsuki (*the rebellious son who longs for a short and exciting life*), Eijiro Tono (Gonji, *the sake seller*), Kamatari Fujiwara (Tazaemon, *the silk merchant and head of the village*), Ikio Sawamura (Hansuke, *the corrupt official*), Atsushi Watanabe (*coffin shop owner*), Susumu Fujita (Homma, *the cowardly but wise* yojimbo), Kyu Sazanka (Ushitora, *Tokuemon's gang boss*), Ko Nishimura (Ronin Kuma), Takeshi Kato (Ronin Kobuhachi), Ichiro Nakaya (*first samurai*), Sachio Sakai (*first foot soldier*), Akira Tani (Kame), Namigoro Rashomon (Kannuki, *the giant* yojimbo), Yoshio Tsuchiya (Kohei, *the unlucky gambler*), Gen Shimizu (Magotaro), Jerry Fujio (ronin *whose arm is cut*), Yutaka Sada (Matsukichi), Shin Otomo (Kumosuke), Shoichi "Solomon" Hirose (*Ushitora follower*), Hideyo Amamoto (Yahachi), Shoji Oki (Sukeju), Fuminori Ohashi (*second samurai*), Hiroshi Yoseyama (*farmer*), Senkichi Omura (*traveler*), Fumiko Homma (*ex-wife of farmer*), Ryusuke Nishio, Naoya Kusama, Nadao Kirino, Jun Otomo (*Seibei followers*), Shinpei Takagi, Sho Kusama, Yasuzo Ogawa, Hiroshi Takagi (*Ushitora followers*), Junichiro Kukai, Fumiyoshi Kamagaya (*Seibei followers*), Ichiro Chiba (*second foot soldier*), Haruya Sakamoto (*Ushitora follower*), Rinsaku Ogata (*Seibei follower*), Fumio Kogushi (*Ushitora follower*), Yoko Terui, Hiromi Mineoka, Michiko Kawa (*women at Seibei's house*)

A Kurosawa Production Co., Ltd./Toho Co., Ltd. Production. A Toho Co., Ltd. Release. Western Electric Mirrophonic Recording (encoded with Perspecta Stereophonic Sound). Black and white (processed by Kinuta Laboratory, Ltd.). Toho Scope. 110 minutes. Released April 25, 1961.

U.S. version: *Yojimbo the Bodyguard* and *Yojimbo.* Released by Seneca International, Ltd. Released in both English-subtitled and English-dubbed format. Released September 13, 1961. Home video versions subtitled.

Notes: Toho's biggest money earner of 1961, ranking third overall. 1964's *Per un pugno di dollari (For a Fistful of Dollars:* U.S. title: *Fistful of Dollars)* was an unauthorized remake over which Kurosawa sued. *Zatoichi Against Yojimbo* (1970) featured Mifune in a similar role. Later remade as *Last Man Standing* (1996). Awards: Best Actor—Toshiro Mifune (Venice International Film Festival, 1961); Silver Prize (Tokyo Residents Film Contest); Screenplay Prize (Screenwriters Association); *Kinema Jumpo* "Best Ten" (second place). Double-billed with *Playboy President* (Shacho dochuki).

GEN TO FUDO-MYO ("Gen and Fudo-Myo")
[THE YOUTH AND HIS AMULET]
Producer, Hiroshi Inagaki; Director, Hiroshi Inagaki; Special Effects Director, Eiji Tsuburaya; Screenplay, Toshiro Ide and Zenzo Matsuyama, based on the story by Shizue Miyaguchi; Director of Photography, Kazuo Yamada; Music, Ikuma Dan; *Toho Special Effects Group*: Photography,

Teisho Arikawa, Motonari Tomioka; Matte Photography, Yukio Manoda, Taka Yuki; Matte Process, Hiroshi Mukoyama; Art Director, Akira Watanabe; Lighting, Kyuichiro Kishida; Assistant Director, Teruyoshi Nakano

Cast: Toru Koyanagi (Gen), Hisako Sakabe (*his sister*), Toshiro Mifune (Fudo-Myoh), Chishu Ryu, Yosuke Natsuki, Minoru Chiaki, Nobuko Otowa, Mie Hama, Yoshio Kosugi, Bokuzen Hidari, Kenzo Tabu, Akira Tani, Yutaka Sada, Ikio Sawamura, Noriko Sengoku, Kin Sugai

A Toho Co., Ltd. Production. A Toho Co., Ltd. Release. Black and white with color insert (processed by Tokyo Laboratory Ltd.). Toho Scope. 102 minutes. Released September 17, 1961.

U.S. version: Released by Toho International Co., Ltd. English subtitles. 102 minutes. Released March 1963.

Notes: Recommended by the Ministry of Education. Double-billed with *Achan's Baby Gang* (Achan no bebii gyangu).

ANIMAS TRUJANO (EL HOMBRE IMPORTANTE)
[THE IMPORTANT MAN]
Executive Producer, Pascual Aragones; Producer and Director, Ismael Rodriguez; Screenplay, Ismael Rodriguez and Vincente Orona, Jr., based on the novel *La Mayordomia* by Rogelio Barriga Rivas; Director of Photography, Gabriel Figueroa; Art Directors, Eduardo Fitzgerald and Pablo Galvan; Music, Raul Lavista; Costume Design, Consuelo Mugica; Unit Production Manager, Alberto A. Ferrer; Assistant Director, Mario Llorca; Editor, Jorge Bustus

Cast: Toshiro Mifune (Animas Trujano), Columa Dominguez [Rodriguez] (Joana, *his wife*), Flor Silvestre (Catarina), Pepito Romay (Pedrito), Titina Romay (Dorotea), Antonio Aguilar (Tadeo), Eduardo Fajardo (El Español), Amado Zumaya (Compadre), Jose Chavez (Brujo), Luis Aragon (Tendero), Juan Carlos Pulido (Belarmine), Jaime J. Pons (Carrizo), David Reynoso (Criton)

A Peliculas Rodriguez Production. An Azteca Release. A Mexican production in Spanish. Black and white. CinemaScope. 104 minutes. Released (in Mexico) January 10, 1962.

U.S. version: Released by Lopert Picture Corp., through United Artists. Apparently released in both Spanish with English subtitles and English-dubbed format. 100 minutes. Released July 18, 1962.

Notes: Released in Japan by Toho Co., Ltd. and Toho-Towa as *Kachi aru otoko* ("The Worthy Man") with Japanese subtitles, running 100 minutes, on November 3, 1961. Filmed in Tlacolula, Cuilapan de Guerrero, El Tule, Xoxocotland, Zaachila, Lorna Larga (Oaxaca, Mexico). Awards: Academy Award Nomination (Best Foreign Language Film—1961), Best Foreign Language Film (Golden Globe, Foreign Press Association); Best Picture (San Francisco Film Festival); Silver Plaque (Turin International Film Festival), Palenque Head Award (Mexican Review of Festivals), Mexican Press Gold Medal, Mexican Producers and Distributors Gold Medal, Screen Actors Guild of Mexico Diamond Pendant.

TSUBAKI SANJURO ("Sanjuro Tsubaki")
[SANJURO]
Producers, Tomoyuki Tanaka and Ryuzo Kikushima; Associate Producer and Director, Akira Kurosawa; Screenplay, Ryuzo Kikushima, Hideo Oguni, and Akira Kurosawa, based on the story *Hibi Heian* ("Peaceful Days") by Shugoro Yamamoto; Directors of Photography, Fukuzo Koizumi and Takao Saito; Art Director/Costumes, Yoshiro Muraki; Lighting, Ichiro Inohara; Sound, Wataru Konuma; Music, Masaru Sato; Assistant Cameraman, Kazutani Hara; Assistant

Art Director, Tsuneo Shimura; Assistant Lighting, Isao Hara; Sound Assistant, Jin Sashida; Mixing, Hisashi Shimonaga; Chief Assistant Director, Shiro Moritani; Assistant Directors, Masanobu Deme, Yoichi Matsue, Yoshikuni Wada; Assistant Editor, Reiko Kaneko; Script Supervisor, Teruyo Nogami; Sound Effects, Ichiro Minawa; Still Photographer, Masao Fukuda; Production Supervisor, Hiroshi Nezu; Production Assistance, Shigeru Kishima; Property Master, Shoji Jinko; Costumes, Shoji Kurihara (Kyoto Costume); Hair Stylists, Yoshiko Matsumoto and Junjiro Yamada; Transportation, Isamu Miwano; Swordplay Instructor, Ryu Kuze

Cast: Toshiro Mifune (Sanjuro Tsubaki), Tatsuya Nakadai (Hanbei Muroto), Keiju Kobayashi (Kimura, *the captured samurai in closet*), Yuzo Kayama (Iiro Izaka, *leader of the nine young samurai*), Reiko Dan (Chidori), Takashi Shimura (Kurofuji), Kamatari Fujiwara (Takebayashi), Takako Irie (Mrs. Mutsuta, *the chamberlain's wife*), Masao Shimizu (Kikui, *the superintendent*), Yunosuke Ito (Mutsuta, *the chamberlain*). *Young Samurai:* Akira Kubo (Morishima, *the younger brother*), Hiroshi Tachikawa (Kawahara), Yoshio Tsuchiya (Hirose), Kunie Tanaka (Yasukawa), Tatsuyoshi Ehara (Sekiguchi), Akihiko Hirata (Terada), Kenzo Matsui (Yata), Tatsuhiko Hari (Morishima) · Toranosuke Ogawa (Sandyu, *of the Kobuto family*), Sachio Sakai (Ashigaru), Toshiko Higuchi (Koiso), Yutaka Sada (*Kikui samurai*), Shin Otomo

A Kurosawa Production Co., Ltd. / Toho Co., Ltd. Production. A Toho Co., Ltd. Release. Western Electric Mirrophonic Recording (encoded with Perspecta Stereophonic Sound). Black and white (Eastman stock; processed by Kinuta Laboratory). Toho Scope. 95 minutes. Released January 1, 1962.

U.S. version: Released by Toho International Co., Ltd. English subtitles. 95 minutes. Released June 14, 1962.

Notes: A sequel, of sorts, to *Yojimbo* (1961). This was Toho's biggest money earner of 1962, ranking second overall. Awards: The *Mainichi* Japanese Film Prize, Blue Ribbon Award (Best Picture), Screenwriters Association Award (Best Screenplay), *Kinema Jumpo* "Best Ten" (fifth place), Asia Film Festival (Best Cinematography and Best Sound Recording). Double-billed with *Shimizu Port Salaryman* (Sarariiman Shimizu Minato).

DOBUROKU NO TATSU (Home-Brewed Tatsu")
[TATSU]
Producer, Tomoyuki Tanaka; Director, Hiroshi Inagaki; Screenplay, Masato Ide and Toshio Yasumi, based on the novel by Yoshio Nakae; Director of Photography, Kazuo Yamada; Art Director, Hiroshi Ueda; Lighting, Masashichi Kojima; Sound, Yoshio Nishikawa; Music, Kan Ishii; Chief Assistant Director, Masahiro Takase; Still Photographer, Matsuo Yoshizaki

Cast: Toshiro Mifune (Tatsu), Tatsuya Mihashi (Shaguma, *the foreman*), Chikage Awashima (Umeko, *the madam*), Junko Ikeuchi (Shino Shimokita), Ichiro Arishima (Oiwake), Yoshio Tsuchiya (Kida), Sonomi Nakajima (Nonko), Jun Tazaki (Kakibetsu), Soji Kiyokawa (Choba), Ryosuke Kagawa (Boss), Chieko Nakakita (Otaka), Yoshio Kosugi (Onishika), Sachio Sakai (Marumatsu), Kozo Nomura (Maisaka), Yoshifumi Tajima (Numajiri), Shoji Oki (Idehama), Ren Yamamoto (Urakawa), Sachiyuki Kamimura (*unprofessional A*), Yasuzo Ogawa (*unprofessional B*), Fuminori Ohashi (Shaguma *follower A*), Junichiro Mukai (Shaguma *follower B*), Jun Kuroki, Eisuke Nakanishi, Minoru Ito, Hiroyoshi Yamaguchi (*guards*), Akira Tani (*shop owner*), Kiyoko Tsuji (Matsueda), Toki Shiozawa (Utako)

A Toho Co., Ltd. Production. A Toho Co., Ltd. Release. Agfa Color. Toho Scope. 115 minutes. Released April 29, 1962.

U.S. version: Released by Toho International Co., Ltd. English subtitles. 115 minutes. Released November 22, 1962.

Note: Toho produced an English-dubbed version of this title. Its release, if any, is undetermined. Toho's third biggest money earner of 1962, ranking eighth overall. Double-billed with *Three Gentlemen from Tokyo* (Shacho Yokoki).

CHUSHINGURA—HANA NO MAKI YUKI NO MAKI ("Chushingura—Part One: Flowers Part Two: Snow")
[CHUSHINGURA]
Producers, Sanezumi Fujimoto, Tomoyuki Tanaka, and Hiroshi Inagaki; Director, Hiroshi Inagaki; Screenplay, Toshio Yasumi, based on the 1748 Kabuki play cycle *Kanadehon Chushingura* by Izumo Takeda, Senryu Namiki, and Shoraku Miyoshi; Director of Photography, Kazuo Yamada; Art Director, Kisaku Ito; Lighting, Shoshichi Kojima; Sound, Yoshio Nishikawa; Music, Akira Ifukube; Assistant Art Director, Hiroshi Ueda; Mixing, Hisashi Shimonaga; Choreography, Kiyokata Seruwaka; Editor, Hirokazu Iwashita; Swordplay Choreography, Ryu Kuze; Production Manager, Shotaro Kawakami; Still Photographer, Matsuo Yoshizaki; Chief Assistant Directors, Teruo Maru and Masahiro Takase. *Toho Special Effects Group*: Director, Eiji Tsuburaya

Cast: Koshiro Matsumoto (Chamberlain Kuranosuke Oishi) · Yuzo Kayama (Lord Naganori Asano), Tatsuya Mihashi (Yasubei Horibe), Akira Takarada (Gunpei Takada), Yosuke Natsuki (Kinemon Okano), Makoto Sato (Kazuemon Fuwa), Tadao Takashima (Jyujiro Kan), Seizaburo Kawazu (*Asano official*), Takashi Shimura (Hyobu Chishaka), Daisuke Kato (Kichiemon Terasaka), Keiju Kobayashi (Awajinokami Wakisake), Ryo Ikebe (Chikara Tsuchiya, *Kira's next-door neighbor*) · Setsuko Hara (Riku Oishi, *the chamberlain's wife*), Yoko Tsukasa (Aguri Asano), Reiko Dan (Okaru, *Kichiemon's sister*), Yuriko Hoshi (Otsuya, *the carpenter's sister*), Yumi Shirakawa (Ume), Kumi Mizuno (Saho, *a spy and Samurai Shiota's sister*), Mie Hama (*woman refugee*), Nami Tamura (*undetermined*), Yoko Fujiyama (Miyuki, *the Asano maid*), Junko Ikeuchi (Ofumi, *of the tea shop*), Keiko Awaji (Otoki, *Hanbei's wife*), Mitsuko Kusabue (*undetermined*), Michiyo Aratama (*undetermined*) · Hisaya Morishige (Hanbei, *owner of the secret headquarters*) · Frankie Sakai (Heigoro, *a carpenter*), Norihei Miki (Toshibei, *the male geisha*), Kingoro Yanagiya (Otokichi, *of the tatami shop*), Yoshitomi "Keaton" Masuda (Tachu Matsubara), Mutoshi Yanami (Tokuzo, *of the Ueki Shop*), Toru Yuri (Nonta, *Heigoro's cousin*), Toshiaki Minami (Denpachi, *Heigoro's cousin*), Kyu Sazanka (Debashu Yanagisawa), Ichiro Arashima (Lord Denpachiro Tamura) • Hiroshi Koizumi (Gengo Otaka), Yu Fujiki (Yushichi Takebayashi), Akira Kubo (Lord Date), Akihiko Hirata (Yajuemon Okajima), Kenji Sahara (*Asano samurai*), Hiroshi Tachikawa (Aminori Uesugi), Tatsuyoshi Ehara (Daigaku Asano), Tadao Nakamaru (Heihachiro Kobayashi), Sachio Sakai (Shusui Kishima, *a spy*), Yoshio Tsuchiya (Matanosho Shoita, *Saho's brother*), Kamatari Fujiwara (Kyubei, *the innkeeper*), Jun Tazaki (Kiken Murakami), Susumu Fujita (Yosubei Kajikawa), Ken Uehara (Seikanji, *of the Chunagons*) • Jun Funato (Sanjyuji Kaizuka), Kiyoshi Kodama (*undetermined*), Hisaya Ito (Sezaemon Oishi), Kozo Nomura (*undetermined*), Ko Mishima (*undetermined*), Kunio Otsuka (*undetermined*), Ren Yamamoto (*Asano samurai*), Hideyo Amamoto (Takano, *of the Chunagons*), Nadao Kirino (*undetermined*), Heihachiro "Henry" Okawa (Katafu Kanse), Shigeki Ishida (Rishichi), Akira Tani (*undetermined*), Yoshifumi Tajima (*undetermined*), Ikio Sawamura (*tatami maker*), Yoshio Kosugi (Yahei Hattori, *Yasubei's tough father*) • Sonomi Nakajima (Otama, *of the drinking place*), Machiko Kitagawa (Okyo, *the bathing guard*), Keiko Yanagawa, Mieko Beni, Misako Asuka, Hiromi Mineoka, Yaeko Izumo (*all undetermined*), Haruko Togo (Okyo, *Sasaya's wife*), Atsuko Ichinomiya (Otomi, *Kyubei's wife*), Chieko Nakakita (Ofude) · Ryosuke Kagawa (Souemon Hara), Soji Kiyokawa (Matazaemon Fujii), Unpei Yokoyama (Matsuemon, *Heigoro's uncle*), Haruya Kato, Yoji Misaki (*both undetermined*), Gen Shimizu (Gensuke Koga), Jotaro Togami (Ikaku Shimizu), Sadako Sawamura (Tomiko, *Konosuke's wife*), Kiyoko Tsuji, Kumeko Otowa, Teruko Mita, Noriko Sakabe, Naoko Sakabe (*all undetermined*), Senkichi Omura (*concerned citizen at collapsed bridge*), Shin Otomo, Yutaka Nakayama, Mitsuo Tsuda, Keiichiro Katsumoto, Hiroshi Agetsu, Haruo Suzuki, Jun Kuroki, Kanso Uni, Koji Iwamoto, Katsumi Tezuka, Akio Kusama, Kaneyuki Tsubono, Kosuke Uruki, Rinsaku Ogata, Hiroshi Sekita, Hiroyoshi Yamaguchi, Masaki Shinohara, Ryuichi Hosokawa, Saburo Kadowaki, Tadashi Okabe, Akira Yamada, Junpei Natsuki, Koichi Sato, Kenzo Echigo, Jiro Mitsuaki (*all undetermined*), Ichiro Chiba (Yanagihara, *of the Dainagons*), Shoji Ikeda, Junichiro Mukai (*both undetermined*) • Somegoro Ichikawa (*undetermined*), Mannosuke Nakamura (Sanpei Kanno), Matagoro Nakamura (Mokichi Tokugawa), Shigetsuru Nakamura (Kurobei Ono), Korazo Ichikawa (Kansuke Chikamatsu), Kichijuro Nakamura (*undetermined*), Danshiro Ichikawa (Gengoemon Kataoka), Danko Ichikawa (Matsunosho Oishi), Chusha Ichikawa (Lord Yoshinaga Kira) • <u>Toshiro Mifune</u> (Genba Tawaraboshi)

A Toho Co., Ltd. Production. A Toho Co., Ltd. Release. Eastman Color (processed by Tokyo Developing). Toho Scope. 208 minutes (plus intermission). Released November 3, 1962.

U.S. version: Released by Toho International Co., Ltd. English subtitles and English narration. Narrator, Michael Higgins. 108 minutes (later cut to 100 minutes for release in New York). Released October 10, 1963. Reissued by Berkeley Cinema Guild (Beverly Films) in 1966 running 207 minutes. Producer, Edward Landberg; Subtitles, Herman G. Weinberg. Also known as *Chushingura: 47 Samurai*. Reissued by East-West Classics subtitled and running 208 minutes. The otherwise excellent letterboxed video version is missing entr'acte, and possible overture, intermission and exit music as well. Subtitles, Steve Barger; Subtitles Editor, Audie Bock.

Notes: For this title, the credits are listed as they appear onscreen, even though some of the actors' roles are undetermined. This has been done here so that the reader may note the complex billing order of talent which, for this picture, represented virtually everyone under contract to the studio at this time. A Toho 30th Anniversary Production. Toho's fourth biggest money earner of 1962, ranking tenth overall. Eiji Tsuburaya's special-effects group contributed forced-perspective sets and miscellaneous opticals, without credit. Co-billed with the documentary featurette *Kurobe Gorge Part III* (Oinaru Kurobe).

TAIHEIYO NO TSUBASA ("Wings of the Pacific")
[ATTACK SQUADRON!]
Producer, Tomoyuki Tanaka; Director, Shue Matsubayashi; Special Effects Director, Eiji Tsuburaya; Screenplay, Katsuya Suzaki; Director of Photography, Takeshi Suzuki; Art Director, Takeo Kita; Lighting, Chushiro Ishii; Sound, Shin Watarai; Music, Ikuma Dan, Editor, Yoshitami Kuroiwa; Assistant Director, Koji Kajita. *Toho Special Effects Group*: Photography, Teisho Arikawa, Mototaka Tomioka; Art Director, Akira Watanabe

Cast: <u>Toshiro Mifune</u> (Lt. Colonel Senda), Yuzo Kayama (Captain Shiro Taki), Takashi Shimura (*admiral*), Yosuke Natsuki (Captain Nobuo Ataka), Makoto Sato (Teppei Yano), Yuriko Hoshi, Ryo Ikebe, Kiyoshi Atsumi, Ko Nishimura, Susumu Fujita, Jun Tazaki, Akihiko Hirata, Yoshifumi Tajima, Yoshio Kosugi, Senkichi Omura, Hideo Sumazanka, Ichiro Nakaya, Seiji Miyaguchi, Tadao Nakamaru, Seizaburo Kawazu, Masao Shimizu, Nadao Kirino, Ren Yamamoto, Yutaka Nakayama, Ko Mishima, Katsumi Tezuka, Kozo Nomura, Akira Wakamatsu, Shoichi Hirose, Wataru Omae, William Schoolinger, Jack Davis

A Toho Co., Ltd. Production. A Toho Co., Ltd. Release. Eastman Color. Toho Scope. 101 minutes. Released January 3, 1963.

U.S. version: Released by Toho International Co., Ltd. English subtitles. Released February 1, 1975. Home video: Combat Video/Video City Distributing in 1988 as *Kamikaze*. English-dubbed. 101 minutes.

Note: Toho produced an English-dubbed version. Its release, if any, or if this dubbed version is the same as the U.S. home video version, is undetermined. The home video version is panned-and-scanned, with some of the worst telecine work ever done; the entire film appears to have been mastered showing only the extreme left side of the image. Toho's second biggest money earner of 1963, ninth overall. Double-billed with *Travel Stories of a Company President* (Shacho manyuki).

TENGOKU TO JIGOKU ("Heaven and Hell")
[HIGH AND LOW]
Producers, Tomoyuki Tanaka and Ryuzo Kikushima; Associate Producer and Director, <u>Akira Kurosawa</u>; Screenplay, Hideo Oguni, Eijiro Hisaita, Ryuzo Kikushima, and Akira Kurosawa, based on the novel *King's Ransom* (1959) by Ed McBain (i.e., Evan Hunter), translated and published in Japan by Hayakawa Shobo; Directors of Photography, Asakazu Nakai and Takao Saito; Art Director, Yoshiro Muraki; Lighting, Hiromitsu Hori; Music, Masaru Sato; Sound, Fumio Yanoguchi; Assistant Cameraman, Kazutami Hara; Assistant Art Director, Jun Sakuma; Assistant Lighting, Fukahiro Akike; Sound Assistant, Jin Sashida; Sound Mixing, Hisashi Shimonaga; Chief Assistant Director, Shiro Moritani; Assistant Directors, Masanobu Deme, Yoichi Matsue, and Kenjiro Omori; Assistant Editor, Reiko Kaneko; Script Supervisor, Teruyo Nogami; Sound Effects, Ichiro Minawa; Still Photographer, Masao Fukuda; Production Supervisor, Hiroshi Nezu; Production Assistance, Shigeru Kishima; Costumes, Miyuki Suzuki (Kyoto Costume), Hair Stylists, Yoshiko Matsumoto and Junjiro Yamada; Transportation, Ginzo Osumi; Acting Office, Yuichi Yoshitake

   Cast: <u>Toshiro Mifune</u> (Kingo Gondo), Tatsuya Nakadai (Chief Detective Tokura), Kyoko Kagawa (Reiko Gondo, *Kingo's wife*), Tatsuya Mihashi (Kawanishi, *Gondo's secretary*), Isao Kimura (Detective Arai), Kenjiro Ishiyama (Chief Detective "Bos'n" Taguchi), Takeshi Kato (Detective Nakao), Takashi Shimura (*chief of the investigation section*), Jun Tazaki (Kamiya, *National Shoes publicity director*), Nobuo Nakamura (Ishimaru, *National Shoes design department director*), Yunosuke Ito (Baba, *National Shoes executive*), Tsutomu Yamazaki (Ginjiro Takeuchi, *the kidnapper*), Minoru Chiaki (*first reporter*), Eijiro Tono (*National Shoes factory worker*), Masao Shimizu (*prison warden*), Yutaka Sada (Aoki, *the chauffeur*), Masahiko Shimazu (Shinichi Aoki, *the chauffeur's son*), Toshio Egi (Jun Gondo, *Kingo's son*), Koji Mitsui (*second reporter*), Kyu Sazanka (*first creditor*), Susumu Fujita (*chief of the first investigating section*), Kamatari Fujiwara (*cook at the junkyard*), Yoshio Tsuchiya (Detective Murata), Kazuo Kitamura (*third reporter*), Gen Shimizu (*chief physician*), Akira Nagoya (Detective Yamamoto), Jun Hamamura (*second creditor*), Masao Orita (*first executor at the tax office*), Ko Nishimura (*third creditor*), Yoshifumi Tajima (*chief prison officer*), Koji Shimizu (*fish market office worker*), Hiroshi Unanzan (Detective Shimizu), Yoshisuke Makino (Detective Takahashi), Jun Kondo (*detective*), Tomo Suzuki (Detective Koike), Senkichi Omura (*"patient" who gives kidnapper note*), Kazuo Kato (*worker at identification center*), Ikio Sawamura (*trolley man at Yokohama Station*), Kin Sugai (*woman drug addict*), Keiko Tomita (*murder victim*), Isamu Onoda (*male drug addict*), Seiichi Taguchi (Detective Nakamura), Takeo Matsushita (*second executor at the tax office*), Kiyoshi Yamamoto (Detective Ueno), Kenji Kodama (Detective Hara), Minoru Ito (*detective*), Kazuo Suzuki (*detective disguised as drug addict*), Kozo Nomura (*detective*)

   A Kurosawa Production Co., Ltd./Toho Co., Ltd. Production. A Toho Co., Ltd. Release. Three-Dimensional Magnetic Stereophonic Sound (Perspecta Stereophonic Sound for general release). Black and white, with Eastman Color insert (stock by Eastman; processed by Kinuta Laboratory). Toho Scope. 143 minutes. Released March 1, 1963.

   U.S. version: Released by Toho International Co., Ltd. English subtitles. Subtitles, Herman G. Weinberg. Alternate titles: *Heaven and Hell* and *The Ransom*. 142 minutes. Released November 26, 1963. Reissued by Continental/Walter Reade–Sterling. Subtitles for reissue versions: Audie Bock.

Notes: A Toho 30th Anniversary Production. Toho (and Japan's) highest grossing Japanese film of 1963. Includes stock music from *The H-Man* (1958). Toho produced an English-dubbed version. Its release, if any, is undetermined. Recommended by the Ministry of Education. Double-billed with *Travel Stories of a Company President Sequel* (Zoku Shacho manyuki). Awards: The Edgar Allan Poe Prize, the *Mainichi* Film Award (Best Japanese Film and Best Screenplay), NHK Film Festival (Best Film and Best Director), the Tokyo Union Film Award (Million Pearl Prize), Kawasaki Citizen Film Competition (Best Film), *Sakai Weekly* (Silver Star Prize for Best Director), Screenwriters Association Award (Best Screenplay), the Golden Laurel Prize (1964).

GOJUMAN-NIN NO ISAN—LEGACY OF THE 500,000 ("The Legacy of the 500,000")
[LEGACY OF THE 500,000]
Producers, Sanezumi Fujimoto and Tomoyuki Tanaka; Associate Producer, Toshiro Mifune; Director, <u>Toshiro Mifune</u>; First Assistant Director, Shigekichi Takemae; Screenplay, Ryuzo Kikushima; Director of Photography, Takao Saito; Art Director, Yoshiro Muraki; Lighting, Hiromitsu Mori; Sound, Fumio Yanoguchi; Music, Masaru Sato; Assistant Director, Mikio Komatsu; Script Supervisor, Teruyo Nogami; Still Photographer, Masao Fukuda; Editor, Shuichi Anbara

Cast: <u>Toshiro Mifune</u> (Takeichi Matsuo, *Chief, General Affairs Sec. of Tozai Crayon* Co.), Tatsuya Mihashi (Keigo Gunji, *captain of the* Kibo-maru), Tsutomu Yamazaki (Tsukuda, *Keigo's henchman*), Mie Hama (*Igorot native*), Yuriko Hoshi (Masako Matsuo, *Takeichi's daughter*), Yoshio Tsuchiya (Yamazaki), Sachio Sakai (Igarashi, *Gunji's driver*), Yoshifumi Tajima (Yasumoto), Tetsu Nakamura (*Asian man*), F. J. Horning (*foreigner with cigar*), Evie King (*his wife*), Teddy Akauiri (*man*), Keiko Yamada (*woman at bakery*), Terry (*police officer at Paigo*), Michio Hayashi (Clark) • Tatsuya Nakadai (Mitsura Gunji, *Keigo's brother and president of the Kyokuyo Trading Co.*)

A Takarazuka Motion Picture Co., Ltd./Mifune Productions Co., Ltd. Production. A Toho Co., Ltd. Release. Black and white, with color insert. Toho Scope. 97 minutes. Released April 28, 1963.

U.S. version: Released by Toho International Co., Ltd. English subtitles. 97 minutes. Released June 12, 1964. An English-dubbed version was also produced.

Notes: The first feature of Mifune Productions, and Mifune's only film as director. The on-screen title is as it appears above. Mifune has stated that Akira Kurosawa worked on the film as an uncredited editor. Double-billed with *Company President Travels Abroad* (Shacho gaiyuki).

DAI TOZOKU ("The Great Thief")
[SAMURAI PIRATE]
Producers, Tomoyuki Tanaka and Kenichiro Tsunoda; Director, Senkichi Taniguchi; Special Effects Director, Eiji Tsuburaya; Screenplay, Takeshi Kimura and Shinichi Sekizawa; Director of Photography, Takao Saito; Music, Masaru Sato; Sound, Toho Recording Centre; Sound Effects, Hisashi Shimonaga, Toho Sound Effects Group. *Toho Special Effects Group*: Art Director, Akira Watanabe; Photography, Sadamasa Arikawa, Mototaka Tomioka; Lighting, Kyuichiro Kishida; Matte Process, Hiroshi Mukoyama; Optical Photography, Taka Yuki, Yukio Manoda; Assistant Director, Teruyoshi Nakano

Cast: <u>Toshiro Mifune</u> (Sukezaemon Naya, *alias "Luzon"* [Sinbad]), Makoto Sato (Black Pirate), Jun Funato (Ming, *the Prince of Thailand*), Ichiro Arishima (Sennin the Wizard), Mie Hama (Princess Yaya), Kumi Mizuno (Miwa), Akiko Wakabayashi (Yaya's *maid*), Mitsuko Kusabue (Sobei), Tadao Nakamaru (the Premier), Jun Tazaki (Itaka Tsuzuka of the Royal Guards), Takashi Shimura (King Raksha), Hideyo Amamoto (*witch*), Yutaka Sada (*governor*), Senkichi Omura (*ped-*

dler), Eishu Kin (*giant*), Little Man Machan (*dwarf*), Hideo Sumazuka, Masanari Nihei (*bandits*), Tetsu Nakamura (*chief archer*), Yoshio Kosugi (*captain of Thai ship*), Nadao Kirino (*member of Luzon's crew*), Masashi Oki, Yutaka Nakayama, Nakajiro Tomita, Tadanori Kusagawa, Junichiro Mukai, Yasuhisa Tsutsumi, Kozo Nomura, Hiroshi Hasegawa, Hidezu Kane, Haruo Suzuki, Masako Shibaki, Akira Shimada, Rokumaru Furukawa, Chiyoko Tanabe, Toru Ibuki, Shoji Ikeda

A Toho Co., Ltd. Production. A Toho Co., Ltd. Release. Eastman Color (processed by Tokyo Laboratory, Ltd.). Toho Scope. 96 minutes. Released October 26, 1963.

U.S. version: *The Lost World of Sinbad.* Released by American International Pictures. English-dubbed. A James H. Nicholson & Samuel Z. Arkoff Presentation. English-language version, Titra Sound Studios; Prints by Pathé. Wide-screen process billed as Colorscope. Onscreen credits misidentify co-screenwriter Sekizawa as director of photography. Retitled *Samurai Pirate* after initial engagements, then switched back to *The Lost World of Sinbad.* Announced by AIP as *7th Wonder of Sinbad.* Double-billed with *War of the Zombies* (AIP, 1965). 95 minutes. Released March 17, 1965.

Notes: Toho produced an English-dubbed version. Its release, if any, is undetermined. Toho's third biggest money earner of 1963, tenth overall. Double-billed with *Crazy Free-for-All—Go to Hell! Irresponsibles* (Kureejii sakusen—Kutabare! Musekinin).

SHIKONMADO—DAI TATSUMAKI ("Shikonmado—Big Tornado")
[WHIRLWIND]
Producer, Tomoyuki Tanaka; Director, Hiroshi Inagaki; Special Effects Director, Eiji Tsuburaya; Screenplay, Hiroshi Inagaki and Takeshi Kimura, based on the novel *Shikonmado* by Norio Nanjo: Director of Photography, Kazuo Yamada; Music, Akira Ifukube: Chief Assistant Director, Akihiro Takase. *Toho Special Effects Group*: Photography, Sadamasa Arikawa, Mototaka Tomioka; Matte Photography, Yukio Manoda, Taka Yuki; Matte Process Work, Hiroshi Mukoyama; Art Director, Akira Watanabe; Lighting, Kyuichiro Kishida; Assistant Director, Teruyoshi Nakano

Cast: Somegoro Ichikawa (Jubei), Yosuke Natsuki, Makoto Sato, Yuriko Hoshi (Kozato), Kumi Mizuno (*witch*), Mitsuko Kusabue, Yoshiko Kuga, Akira Kubo, Akihiko Hirata, Sachio Sakai, Yoshio Kosugi, Ren Yamamoto, Akira Tani, Somesho Matsumoto • Toshiro Mifune (Lord Akashi)

A Takarazuka Motion Picture Co., Ltd. Production. A Toho Co., Ltd. Release. Eastman Color (processed by Tokyo Laboratory, Ltd.). Toho Scope. 108 minutes. Released January 3, 1964.

U.S. version: Released by Toho International Co., Ltd. English subtitles. 108 minutes. Released July 26, 1968.

Notes: Includes stock footage of the burning of Osaka Castle from *Daredevil in the Castle* (1961, q.v.). Double-billed with *A Company President's Gentleman Story* (Shacho Shinshiroku)

JYAKOMAN TO TETSU ("Jakoman and Tetsu")
[JAKOMAN AND TETSU]
Director, Kinji Fukasaku; Screenplay, Akira Kurosawa and Senkichi Taniguchi, based on a story by Shinzo Kajino; Director of Photography, Makoto Tsuboi; Art Director, Teruo Kondo and Shuichiro Nakamura; Music, Masaru Sato

Cast: Ken Takakura (Tetsu), Tetsuro Tamba (Jakoman), Isao Yamagata, Kumeko Urabe, Hizuru Takachiho

A Toei (Tokyo) Co., Ltd. Production. A Toei Co., Ltd. Release. Black and white. Toeiscope. 99 minutes. Released July 11, 1964.

U.S. version: Release, if any, is undetermined.

Notes: A remake of *Jakoman and Tetsu* (1949).

THE OUTRAGE

Producer, A. Ronald Lubin; Director, Martin Ritt; Screenplay, Michael Kanin, based on the screenplay *Rashomon* by Shinobu Hashimoto and <u>Akira Kurosawa</u>, the stories "Rashomon" and "In a Groove" (*Yabu no naka*) by Ryunosuke Akutagawa, and the play *Rashomon* (1959) by Fay and Michael Kanin; Director of Photography, James Wong Howe; Art Directors, George W. Davis and Tambi Larsen; Music, Alex North; Associate Producer, Michael Kanin; Set Decorators, Henry Grace and Robert E. Benton; Special Visual Effects, J. McMillan Johnson and Robert R. Hoag; Editor, Frank Santillo; Assistant Director, Daniel J. McCauley; Costume Design, Don Feld; Makeup Supervisor, William Tuttle; Hair Stylist, Sydney Guilaroff

Cast: Paul Newman (*Juan Carasco, the bandit*), Laurence Harvey (*the husband*), Claire Bloom (*the wife*), Edward G. Robinson (*the con man*), William Shatner (*the preacher*), Howard Da Silva (*the prospector*), Albert Salmi (*the sheriff*), Thomas Chalmers (*the judge*), Paul Fix (*the Indian*)

A KHF/Martin Ritt Production. A Metro-Goldwyn-Mayer Release. Black and white. Panavision. 97 minutes. Released October 8, 1964.

Notes: Onscreen credits read "based on the Japanese Daiei film (sic) *Rashomon* by Akira Kurosawa and the play . . ." with no mention of co-screenwriter Hashimoto. A computer-colorized version was produced for television release.

PER UN PUNGO DI DOLLARI ("For a Fistful of Dollars")

[FISTFUL OF DOLLARS]

Producers, Arrigo Columbo and Giorgio Papi; Director, Bob Robertson [Sergio Leone]; Screenplay, Bob Robertson [Sergio Leone], Duccio Tessari, Victor A. Catena, and Jaime Comas, from a story by Toni Palombi and Sergio Leone; Director of Photography, Jack Dalmas [Federico G. Larraya] and Massimo Dallamano; Art Director, Carlo Simi; Sound, Elio Parcella and Edy Simson; Music, Dan Savio [Ennio Morricone]; Title Animation, Luigi Lardani; Editor, Roberto Cinquini; Set Decorator, Sigfrido Burman; Assistant Director, Frank Prestland; Production Managers, Franco Palaggi and Günter Raguse; Special Effects, John Speed

Cast: Clint Eastwood (Joe), Marianne Koch (Marisol), John Wells [Gian Maria Volonte] (Ramon Rojo), Wolfgang Lukschy (John Baxter), Sieghardt Rupp (Esteban Rojo), Antonio Prieto (Benito Rojo), Pepe Calvo (Silvanito), Margarita Lozano (Consuela Baxter), Daniel Mann (Julian), Benito Stefanelli (Rubio), Richard Stuyvesant (Chico), Bruno Carotenuto (Antonio Baxter), Josef Egger (Piripero), Enrico Maria Salerno (*voice characterization for Clint Eastwood*), Carla Calo, Raf Baldassarre, Antonio Vico, Johannes Siedel

A Jolly Films/Constantin Film/Ocean Film Production. A UNIDIS Release. An Italian/German/Spanish co-production. Color (prints by Technicolor). Techniscope. 100 minutes. Released (in Europe) November 1964.

U.S. version: Released by United Artists. English dialogue. Released January 18, 1967.

Notes: The film was an uncredited remake of *Yojimbo* (1961), screenplay by Ryuzo Kikushima and <u>Akira Kurosawa</u>. Released in West Germany in 1965 as *Für eine Handvoll Dollars* and in Spain as *Por un puñado de dolares*. Released in Japan on December 25, 1965, as *Koya no Yojimbo* ("Bodyguard of the Wilderness").

SAMURAI ("Samurai")

[SAMURAI ASSASSIN]

Producers, Tomoyuki Tanaka and Reiji Miwa; Associate Producer, <u>Toshiro Mifune</u>; Director, Kihachi Okamoto; Screenplay, Shinobu Hashimoto, based on the book *Samurai Japan* (*Samurai Nippon*) by Jiromasa Gunji; Director of Photography, Hiroshi Murai; Art Director, Iwao Akune; Lighting, Tsuruzo Nishikawa; Sound, Yoshio Nishikawa; Music, Masaru Sato; Mixing, Hisashi

Shimonaga; Chief Assistant Director, Yuzuo [Michio?] Yamamoto; Special Effects, Minoru Izumi; Editor, Yoshitami Kuroiwa; Line Producer, Masao Suzuki; Fight Choreographer, Ryu Kuze

Cast: <u>Toshiro Mifune</u> (Tsuruchiyo Niiro), Keiju Kobayashi (Einsouke Kurihara), Michiyo Aratama (Okiku *and* Kukuhime), Yunosuke Ito (Kenmotsu Hoshino), Eijiro Tono (Seigoro Kisoya), Tatsuyoshi Ehara (Ichigoro Hayama), Tadao Nakamaru (Shigezo Inada), Kaoru Yachigusa (Mitsu), Haruko Sugimura (Tsuru), Nami Tamura (Yae), Shiro Otsude (Kaname Kojima), Yoshio Inaba (Keijiro Sumita), Akihiko Hirata (Sohei Masui), Hideyo Amamoto (Matazaburo Hagiwara), Ikio Sawamura (Tatsukichi Bisenya), Chotaro Togin (Seiichi Morikawa), Yasuzo Ogawa (*ronin*), Masanari Nihei (*ronin*), Toshio Kurosawa (Katsunoshin Itamura), Yoshifumi Tajima (*samurai*), Koraizo Ichikawa (Shuzen Nakano), Nadao Kirino (*samurai*), Junichiro Mukai (*samurai*), Hiroshi Iwamoto (*ronin*), Naoya Kusakawa (*man with sharp eyes*), Yasuhisa Tsutsumi (*manager of Sumoya*), Fujio Tsuneda (*ronin*), Hiroshi Hasegawa (*ronin*), Mitsugu Terashima (Chuzaemon Nishikawa), Takashi Shimura (Narihisa Ichijo), Susumu Fujita (Tatewaki Todo), Shikaku Nakamura (Gengobei Nosaka), Chusha Ichikawa (Sahetoku Matsudaira), Kazuo Suzuki (*samurai*), Hiroshi Sekita (*ronin*), Yasushi Yamamoto. Yurie Hidaka, Fujio Tsuneta, Kita Nagama, Kan Hosei · Koshiro Matsumoto (Lord Naosuke Ii)

A Toho Co., Ltd./Mifune Productions Co., Ltd. Production. A Toho Co., Ltd. Release. Black and white (processed by Kinuta Laboratory). Toho Scope. 121 minutes. Released January 3, 1965.

U.S. version: Released by Toho International Co., Ltd. English subtitles. 121 minutes. Released March 18, 1965. Home Video: 1998 by Samurai Cinema, a division of AnimEigo, Inc. English subtitles. Video versions letterboxed. Executive Producer and Subtitling Director, Robert J. Woodhead; Translator, Shin Kurokawa; Dialogue Checker, Natsumi Ueki; Cultural Consultant, Hisayo Klutz.

Notes: Title apparently changed for U.S. release to avoid confusion with Hiroshi Inagaki's *Samurai* (Miyamoto Musashi, 1954). Double-billed with *Fire Gents' Trick Book* (Shacho Ninpocho).

AKAHIGE ("Red Beard")
[RED BEARD]
Producers, Tomoyuki Tanaka and Ryuzo Kikushima; Associate Producer and Director, <u>Akira Kurosawa</u>; Screenplay, Masato Ide, Hideo Oguni, Ryuzo Kikushima, and Akira Kurosawa, based on the novel *Akahige shinryotan* ("Akahige Consultation Story") by Shugoro Yamamoto; Directors of Photography, Asakazu Nakai and Takao Saito; Art Director, Yoshiro Muraki; Lighting, Hiromitsu Mori; Sound, Shin Watari; Music, Masaru Sato; Assistant Cameraman, Kazutami Hara; Assistant Art Director, Nozomi Fukusako; Assistant Lighting, Fumiyoshi Hara; Sound Assistant, Zen Sashida; Mixing, Hisashi Shimonaga; Chief Assistant Director, Shiro Moritani; Assistant Directors, Masanobu Deme, Yoichi Matsue, and Kenjiro Omori; Assistant Editor, Reiko Kaneko; Script Supervisor, Teruyo Nogami; Sound Effects, Ichiro Minawa; Still Photographer, Masao Fukuda; Unit Production Manager, Hiroshi Nezu; Production Assistant, Shigeru Kishima; Property Master, Akio Nojima; Costumes, Yoshiko Samejima (Kyoto Costume); Hair Stylists, Yoshiko Matsumoto and Junjiro Yamada; Transportation, Yoshio Sekine; Acting Office, Yuichi Yoshitake

Cast: <u>Toshiro Mifune</u> (Dr. Kyojio "Akahige" ["Red Beard"] Niide), Yuzo Kayama (Dr. Noboru Yasumoto), Tsutomu Yamazaki (Sahachi), Reiko Dan (Osugi), Miyuki Kuwano (Onaka), Kyoko Kagawa (*madwoman*), Tatsuyoshi Ehara (Genzo Tsugawa), Terumi Niki (Otoyo), Akemi Negishi (Okuni), Yoshio Tsuchiya (Dr. Handayu Mori), Eijiro Tono (Goheiji), Takashi Shimura (Tokubei Izumiya), Chishu Ryu (Mr. Yasumoto, *Noboru's father*), Haruko Sugimura

(Kin, *the madam*), Kinuyo Tanaka (Madame Yasumoto, *Noboru's mother*), Eijiro Yanagi (*the mad-woman's father*), Koji Mitsui (Heikichi), Ko Nishimura (*chief retainer*), Nobuo Chiba (Matsudaira), Kamatari Fujiwara (Rokusuke, *the dying man*), Ken Mitsuda (Genpaku Amano, *Masae's father*), Yoko Fujiyama (Chigusa, *Masae's sister*), Yoko Naito (Masae), Reiko Nanao (Otoku), Imari Tsuji (Okatsu), Akiko Nomura (Ofuku), Sue Mitobe (Otake), Yoshitaka Zushi (Choji), Kin Sugai (Choji's *mother*), Michiko Araki (*woman owner of brothel*), Bokuzen Hidari (*patient A*), Atsushi Watanabe (*patient B*), Yasuzo Ogawa (*businessman*), Yutaka Sada, Ikio Sawamura, and Fumiko Homma (*residents*), Miyoko Nakamura (Okoto), Shoko Kazami (Masae's *mother*), Chisato Aoki, Kyoko Kurisu, Yukiko Yanagishita, Toshiko Fukai (*prostitutes*), Keiko Tomita (*girl on street*), Taiko Shoji, Shoichi "Solomon" Hirose, Hiroyoshi Yamaguchi (*thugs*), Masanobu Okubo (Choji's *father*), Fujio Tsuneta, Tasuo Araki, Hiroshi Tanaka, Toru Ibuki, Mitsuga Uni, Hiroto Kimura, Shu Komuro, Ryu Kuze (*more thugs*)

A Kurosawa Production Co., Ltd./Toho Co., Ltd. Production. A Toho Co., Ltd. Release. Four-track magnetic stereophonic sound. Black and white (Eastman stock; processed by Kinuta Laboratories). Toho Scope. 185 minutes plus intermission. Released April 3, 1965 (roadshow version) and April 24, 1965 (general release).

U.S. version: Released by Toho International Co., Ltd. English subtitles. 185 minutes. Released January 1966. Reissued by Frank Lee International in December 1968.

Notes: General release version issued in Perspecta Stereophonic Sound. The last film of record in Perspecta Stereophonic Sound. In general release *Red Beard* was shown with the short subject *Kawii Hironomiya-sama* ("Pretty Hironomiya"). Reissued in Japan February 2, 1970, uncut and part of a double bill that included *Throne of Blood*.

SUGATA SANSHIRO ("Sanshiro Sugata")
[JUDO SAGA]
Producers, Akira Kurosawa and Tomoyuki Tanaka; Director, Seiichiro Uchikawa; Screenplay, Akira Kurosawa, based on the novel(s) *Sugata Sanshiro* (1942–4) by Tsuneo Tomita and the screenplays *Sugata Sanshiro* (1943) and *Sanshiro Sugata—Part 2* (1945) by Akira Kurosawa; Director of Photography, Fukuzo Koizumi; Art Director, Hiroshi Mizutani; Lighting, Kazuo Shimomura; Sound, Koji Onmi; Music, Masaru Sato; Production Supervisor, Hiroshi Nezu; Still Photographer, Daizo Tai

 · Cast: Yuzo Kayama (Sanshiro Sugata), Tsutomu Yamazaki (Genshiro), Eiji Okada (Gennosuke *and* Tesshin), Takashi Shimura (Mishima), Bokuzen Hidari (*priest*), Daisuke Kato (Hansuke Murai), Yumiko Kokonoe (Sayo, *Hansuke's daughter*), Tatsuhiko Namisato (Daisaburo Hidarimonji), Kinji Matsueda (Yoshimaro Dan), Hiroshi Aoyama (Toranosuke Shinkai), Yoshiro Aoki (Yujiro Toda), Kenji Kodama (Kohei Tsuzaki), Yoji Arisawa (Nemoto), Toshiro Chiba (Torakichi), Choko Iida (*old lady*), Takamaru Sasaki (Inuma), Yunosuke Ito • Toshiro Mifune (Shogoro Yano)

A Kurosawa Production Co., Ltd./Takarazuka Motion Picture Co., Ltd. Production. A Toho Co., Ltd. Release. Black and white. Toho Scope. 158 minutes. Released May 29, 1965.

U.S. version: Released by Toho International Co., Ltd. English subtitles. 158 minutes. Released August 27, 1965.

Notes: A remake of *Sanshiro Sugata* (1943) and *Sanshiro Sugata—Part 2* (1945). One source also credits Kurosawa as editor. Remade again by director Kunio Watanabe for Shochiku as *Sanshiro Sugata* (Sugata Sanshiro, 1970), and by Kihachi Okamoto for Toho as *Sanshiro Sugata* (Sugata Sanshiro, 1977). Double-billed with *Japan's Number One Flatterer* (Nippon ichi no gomasuri otoko).

TAIHEIYO KISEKI NO SAKUSEN · KISKA ("Miraculous Military Operation in the Pacific Ocean, Kiska")
[RETREAT FROM KISKA]
Producers, Tomoyuki Tanaka and Yasuyoshi Tami; Director, Seiji Maruyama; Special Effects Director, Eiji Tsuburaya; Screenplay, Katsuya Suzaki and (English-language sequences) Walter Black, based on the story *Taiheiyo kaisen saidai no Kiseki* ("The Most Miraculous Battle in the Pacific Ocean") by Masataka Chihaya; Director of Photography, Rokuro Nishigaki; Art Director, Takeo Kita; Lighting, Tsuruzo Nishikawa; Sound, Yoshio Nishikawa; Music, Ikuma Dan; Still Photographer, Matsuo Yoshizaki; Editor, Ryohei Fujii. *Toho Special Effects Group*: Photography, Sadamasa Arikawa and Mototaka Tomioka; Matte Photography, Yukio Manoda, Taka Yuki; Matte Process Work, Hiroshi Mukoyama; Art Director, Akira Watanabe; Lighting, Kyuichiro Kishida; Assistant Director, Teruyoshi Nakano

Cast: <u>Toshiro Mifune</u> (Omura), So Yamamura (Kawashima), Makoto Sato (Commander Amano), Tadao Nakamaru (Kunitomo), Susumu Fujita (Akitani), Jun Tazaki (Akune), Ko Nishimura (*staff officer*), Takashi Shimura (*president of the Military Command*), Akihiko Hirata (Dr. Kudo), Akira Kubo (Tawara), Jun Funato (*undetermined*), Yoshio Tsuchiya (Terai), Susumu Kurobe (Kato), Sachio Sakai (Kojima), Ren Yamamoto (*branch chief*), Masanari Nihei (*undetermined*), Yutaka Sada (Sano), Hisaya Ito (Captain Kiso), Yoshio Inaba (Tamai), Kiyoshi Kodama (Fukumoto), Shin Otomo (*staff officer of the Five Squadron Institute*), Akira Yamada (*officer*), Shoichi "Solomon" Hirose (Yamashita), Junichiro Mukai (*staff officer*), Tadashi Okabe (*second staff officer*), Nadao Kirino (*officer*), Yutaka Oka (Miyamoto), Hiroshi Hasegawa (*air defense chief*), Yasuhisa Tsutsumi (*chief accountant*), Shigeki Ishida (Matsubara), Kunio Otsuka (Shigeki), Wataru Omae (*communications officer*)

A Toho Co., Ltd. Production. A Toho Co., Ltd. Release. Stereophonic sound. Black and white. Toho Scope. 105 minutes. Released June 19, 1965 (roadshow version) and July 4, 1965 (general release).

U.S. version: Never released theatrically. Released directly to television by UPA Productions of America. English-dubbed. Syndicated August 24, 1973.

Notes: General release version double-billed with *Comedy—Finance in Front of the Train Station* (Kigeki Ekimae kinyu).

CHI TO SUNA ("Blood and Sand")
[FORT GRAVEYARD]
Producer, Tomoyuki Tanaka; Associate Producer, <u>Toshiro Mifune</u>; Director, Kihachi Okamoto; Screenplay, Kihachi Okanoto and Kan Saji, suggested by the story "Kanashiki Syonen" ("Sorrowful Battle Diary"); Director of Photography, Rokuro Nishigaki; Art Director, Iwao Akune; Lighting, Tsuruzo Nishikawa; Sound, Yoshio Nishikawa; Music, Masaru Sato; Still Photographer, Taizo Shin; Editor, Yoshitami Kuroiwa

Cast: <u>Toshiro Mifune</u> (Sergeant Kosugi), Makoto Sato (Inuyama), Reiko Dan (Oharu, *a.k.a.* Kin Sun Ho), Yunosuke Ito (Mochida), Tatsuya Nakadai (Sakuma), Hideyo Amamoto (Shiga), Toru Ibuki (Sanpo), Akira Nagoya (Nezu), Hiroshi Hasegawa (Nakano), Kenzaburo Osawa (Harada), Katsumi Nezu (Oga), Tsutomu Hiura (Yoshino), Koichi Nakamura (Ueki), Shinnusuke Awachi (Seki), Hiroshi Miyao (Yabe), Akio Ito (Wataru), Akira Nichikawa (Tsuboi), Fujio Seki (Saito), Toyoyuki Kimura (Okawa), Kazuhiro Kanai (Inomata), Hiroshi Toshiyasu (Saeki), Shigeru Kinami (Chin), Shinji Mitsuta (Obara), Keiichi Taki (Sugiyama), Koji Uno (Inamoto), Shigeo Kato (Deguchi), Nadao Kirino (*terminator*), Toku Ihara (*guerrilla A*), Kazuo Suzuki (*guerrilla B*), Shin Ibuki (Hachiro), Ikio Sawamura (*Chinese worker A*), Koji Kosugi (*Chinese worker B*), Kyoko Mori (*comfort woman A*), Tamami Urayama (*comfort woman B*), Mihiko Kawa (*comfort woman C*)

A Toho Co., Ltd./Mifune Productions Co., Ltd. Production. A Toho Co., Ltd. Release. Black and white. Toho Scope. 131 minutes. Released September 18, 1965.

U.S. version: Released by Toho International Co., Ltd. English subtitles. 131 minutes. Released May 13, 1966.

Notes: The seventh and final film in the "Independent Gangsters" series. Double-billed with *Comedy—Local Train Line* (Kigeki kakuekiteisha).

ABARE GOEMON ("Wild Goemon")
[RISE AGAINST THE SWORD]
Producer, Tomoyuki Tanaka; Director, Hiroshi Inagaki; Screenplay, Hiroshi Inagaki and Masato Ide; Director of Photography, Kazuo Yamada; Art Director, Hiroshi Ueda; Lighting, Seiichi Ono; Sound, Yoshio Nishikawa; Music, Kan Ishii; Still Photographer, Taizo Shin; Editor, Koichi Iwashita

Cast: <u>Toshiro Mifune</u> (Abare Goemon), Nobuko Otowa (Osasa, *his wife*), Makoto Sato (Yatouta, *his brother*), Ryo Tamura (Masato, *his second brother*), Yuriko Hoshi (Princess Azusa), Ko Nishimura (Uncle Etanba), Akihiko Hirata (Asakura), Daisuke Kato (Budeuemon Hattori), Gen Shimizu (Kesho Yada), Takamaru Sasaki (Goro Shiro), Ikio Sawamura (Yasubei), Yoshifumi Tajima (Shozaemon Ube), Kichijiro Ueda (Kaniuemon), Junichiro Mukai (Kokichi, *of the Omi-ya store*), Susumu Kurobe (Jyuro Kamiho), Mayumi Ozora (Ayame), Hideyo Amamoto (Heiroku), Yoshio Kosugi (Gonji), Ren Yamamoto (Sukeichi), Yasuo Araki (Heikichi), Naoya Kusakawa (Matahachi), Sachio Sakai (Shigeju), Keiji Sakakida (Sanzo), Wakako Tanabe (Chiyo), Toki Shiozawa (Tamai), Nakajiro Tomita (Sachibei), Shoji Ikeda (*senior in Kaga*), Akira Kichioji (*old priest*)

A Toho Co., Ltd. Production. A Toho Co., Ltd. Release. Black and white. Toho Scope. 99 minutes. Released January 15, 1966.

U.S. version: Released by Toho International Co., Ltd. English subtitles. 99 minutes. Released November 25, 1966.

Notes: Double-billed with *Comedy—The Art Gods in Front of the Train Station* (Kigeki Ekimae benten).

DAIBOSATSU TOGE ("Daibosatsu Pass")
[THE SWORD OF DOOM]
Producers, Sanezumi Fujimoto, Masayuki Sato, and Kaneharu Minamizato; Director, Kihachi Okamoto; Screenplay, Shinobu Hashimoto, based on the novel by Kaizan Nakazato; Director of Photography, Hiroshi Murai; Art Director, Shu Matsuyama; Lighting, Tsuruzo Nishikawa; Sound, Shin Tokai; Music, Masaru Sato; Still Photographer, Jun Yamazaki; Negative Cutter, Yoshitami Kuroiwa

Cast: Tatsuya Nakadai (Ryunosuke Tsukue), Yuzo Kayama (Hyoma Utsuki), Michiyo Aratama (Ohama), <u>Toshiro Mifune</u> (Toranosuke Shimada), Yoko Naito (Omatsu), Tadao Nakamaru (Isamu Kondo), Ichiro Nakaya (Bunnojo Utsuki), Ko Nishimura (Shichibei, *Omatsu's "uncle"*), Hideyo Amamoto (Lord Shuzen Kamio), Kamatari Fujiwara (Omatsu's *grandfather*), Kei Sato (Kamo Serizawa), Yasuzo Ogawa (Yohachi), Ryosuke Kagawa (Dansho Tsukue), Atsuko Kawaguchi (Okinu), Kunie Tanaka (Senkichi), Takamaru Sasaki (Ishinsai Nakamura), Akio Miyabe (Toshizo Ogata), Kinnosuke Takamatsu (*old pilgrim*)

A Takarazuka Motion Picture Co., Ltd./Toho Co., Ltd. Production. A Toho Co., Ltd. Release. Black and white. Toho Scope. 119 minutes. Released February 25, 1966.

U.S. version: Released by Toho International Co., Ltd. English subtitles. 119 minutes. Released July 1, 1966.

Notes: A proposed sequel was never made. Double-billed with *5 Gents on the Spot* (Zoku shacho gyojoki).

KIGANJO NO BOKEN ("Adventures in Kigan Castle")
[THE ADVENTURES OF TAKLA MAKAN]
Producer, Tomoyuki Tanaka; Associate Producer, <u>Toshiro Mifune</u>; Director, Senkichi Taniguchi; Screenplay, Kaoru Mabuchi [i.e., Takeshi Kimura], based on the story "Hashire Merosu" ("Run, Merosu!") by Osamu Dazai; Director of Photography, Kazuo Yamada; Art Director, Hiroshi Ueda; Lighting, Shu Norihiro; Sound, Yoshio Nishikawa; Music, Akira Ifukube; Assistant Producer, Hiroshi Nezu; Mixer, Hisashi Shimonaga; Negative Cutter, Yoshitami Kuroiwa; Assistant Directors, Susumu Takebayashi and Yoichi Matsue; Assistant Camera, Kazutami Hara; Still Photographer, Minori Ishitsuki; Production Assistant, Hidehiko Eguchi

 Cast: <u>Toshiro Mifune</u> (Osami), Tatsuya Mihashi (*the king*), Makoto Sato (Gorjaka), Tadao Nakamaru (Ensai), Mie Hama (*innkeeper's daughter*), Akiko Wakabayashi (*chamberlain's daughter*), Yumi Shirakawa (Princess Izato), Akihiko Hirata (*chamberlain*). Masashi Taiki (Sundara), Jun Tazaki (*innkeeper*), Ichiro Arishima (*old wizard*), Hideyo Amamoto (*old witch*), Minoru Takada (*old king in Kotan*), Sachio Sakai (*guide*), Susumu Kurobe (*military leader*), Shigeki Ishida (*pastor chief*), Akiyoshi Haruta, Hiroshi Hasegawa (*chief guard*), Shante Zaberi (*Priest A*), E. M. Aziz (*Priest B*), Toshio Kurosawa, Naoya Kusakawa, Ren Yamamoto, Ikio Sawamura, Jun Kuroki

 A Mifune Productions Co., Ltd./Toho Co., Ltd. Production. A Toho Co., Ltd. Release. Color (processed by Tokyo Laboratory, Ltd.). Toho Scope. 104 minutes. Released April 28, 1966.

 U.S. version: Released by Toho International Co., Ltd. English subtitles. Alternate titles: *Adventure of the Strange Stone Castle, Adventure in the Strange Castle*, and *Adventure in Taklamakan*. 100 minutes. No MPAA rating. Released February 14, 1968.

 Notes: Filmed in Iran near Isfahan, and at Toho Studios, Ltd. (Tokyo). Double-billed with *Comedy—The Manga in Front of the Train Station* (Kigeki Ekimae manga).

DOTO ICHIMAN KAIRI ("10,000 Miles of Stormy Seas")
[THE MAD ATLANTIC]
Executive Producer, <u>Toshiro Mifune</u>; Producers, Tomoyuki Tanaka and Koichi Sekinaka; Director, Jun Fukuda; Screenplay, Ei Ogawa, Jun Fukuda, and Shinichi Sekizawa; Director of Photography, Takao Saito; Art Director, Hiroshi Ueda; Lighting, Koshu Mori; Sound, Yoshio Nishikawa; Music, Masaru Sato; Assistant Directors, Yoichi Matsue and Julio Sempere; Camera Operator, Kazutami Hara; Negative Cutter, Ryohei Fujii; Still Photographer, Minori Ishitsuki

 Cast: <u>Toshiro Mifune</u> (Heihachiro Murakami), Tatsuya Mihashi (Isaku Yano), Makoto Sato (Aoki), Ryo Tamura (Tsuda), Mie Hama (Yoko Togawa), Akihiko Hirata (Nozaki), Tadao Nakamaru (Iwata), Sachio Sakai (Kawabe), Ikio Sawamura (Kaga), Akira Hitomi (Yasuhara), Yasuzo Ogawa (Nemoto), Kazuo Suzuki (Minami), Tsutomu Hiura (Kojima), Akiyoshi Kasuga (Ema), Shintaro Nakaoka (Maehara)

 A Mifune Productions Co., Ltd. Production. A Toho Co., Ltd. Release. Black and white. Toho Scope. 101 minutes. Released July 13, 1966.

 U.S. version: Released by Toho International Co., Ltd. English subtitles. 101 minutes. No MPAA rating. Released November 22, 1967.

 Notes: Filmed on location in Las Palmas, Canary Islands. Double-billed with *Zero • Fighter—Great Air Battle* (Zero • Faitaa—Daikusen), with *Mad Atlantic* occupying the lower half of the bill.

GRAND PRIX
Executive Producers, Kirk Douglas, James Garner, and John Frankenheimer; Producer, Edward Lewis; Director, John Frankenheimer; Screenplay, John Frankenheimer and Robert Alan

Arthur, with additional dialogue by William Hanley; Director of Photography, Lionel Lindon; Art Director, Richard Sylbert; Sound, Franklin Milton, Roy Charman, and Harry Warren Tetrick; Music, Maurice Jarre; Supervising Film Editor, Fredric Steinkamp; Editors, Henry Berman, Stewart Linder, and Frank Santillo; Assistant Directors, Enrico Isacco, Roger Simons, Stephen Isovesco, and Sam Itzkowitch; Sound Editor, Gordon Daniels; Special Effects, Milt Rice and Robert Bonning; Makeup, Giuliano Laurenti and Alfio Meniconi; Costume/Hairstyles/Makeup Supervisor, Sydney Guilaroff; Racing Advisors, Phil Hill, Joakim Bonnier, and Richie Ginther; Visual Consultant and Title Design, Saul Bass

Cast: James Garner (Pete Aron), Eva Marie Saint (Louise Fredrickson), Yves Montand (Jean-Pierre Sarti), <u>Toshiro Mifune</u> (Izo Yamura), Brian Bedford (Scott Stoddard), Jessica Walter (Pat Stoddard), Antonio Sabato (Nino Barlini), Françoise Hardy (Lisa), Adolpho Celi (Agostini Manetta), Claude Dauphin (Hugo Simon), Enzo Fiermonte (Guido), Genevieve Page (Monique Delvaux Sarti), Jack Watson (Jeff Jordan), Donald O'Brien (Wallace Bennett), Jean Michaud (*father of killed boys*), Albert Remy (*Monte Carlo surgeon*), Rachel Kempson (Mrs. Stoddard), Ralph Michael (Mr. Stoddard), Alan Fordney, Anthony Marsh, and Tommy Franklin (*sportscasters*), Phil Hill (Tim Randolph), Graham Hill (Bob Turner), Bernard Cahier (*journalist*), Bruce McLaren (Douglas McClendon), Richie Ginther (John Hogarth), Evan Evans [Frankenheimer] (Mrs. Randolph), Bernard Chier (Victor), John Bryson (Dave), Arthur Howard (Claude), Alain Gerard (*American boy*), Tiziano Feroldi (*Monza doctor*), Gilberto Mazzi (Rafael), Raymond Baxter (*BBC interviewer*), Eugenio Dragoni (*Ferrari official*), Maasaki Asukai (*Japanese interpreter*), Peter Ustinov (*press photographer*), Joakim Bonnier, Bob Bondurant, Ludovico Scariotti, Jack Brabham, Dan Gurney, Lorenzo Bandini, Mike Spence, Dennis Hulme, Joseph Siffert, Chris Amon, Michael Parkes, Jochen Rindt, Juan Mañuel Fangio, Giuseppe "Nino" Farina, Louis "The Debonair" Chiron, Jean Pierre Beltoise, Ken Costello, Skip Scott, Jo Schlesser, Jim Russell, Peter Revson, Peter Frere, Tony Lanfranchi, Guy Ligier, Andre Pillette, and Teddy Pillette (*drivers*), Carey Loftin, Tom Bamford, and Max Balchowski (*stunt drivers*), Paul Frees (*voice characterization for Toshiro Mifune*)

A Douglas & Lewis Production, in association with Joel Productions, Inc., John Frankenheimer Productions, and Cherokee Productions. A Metro-Goldwyn-Mayer Release. A U.S. Production. Westrex six-track magnetic stereophonic sound. Metrocolor. Super Panavision 70. Presented in 70mm Super Cinerama. 179 minutes (plus overture and intermission). Released December 21, 1966.

Notes: According to most reports, Mifune's own voice was heard at the film's premiere, then replaced by voice actor Paul Frees for both the roadshow and general release of the picture.

JOIUCHI—HAIRYOZUMA SHIMATSU ("Rebellion—Receive the Wife")
[REBELLION]
Producers, Tomoyuki Tanaka and <u>Toshiro Mifune</u>; Director, Masaki Kobayashi; Screenplay, Shinobu Hashimoto, based on the story *Hairyozuma shimatsu* by Yasuhiko Takiguchi; Director of Photography, Kazuo Yamada; Art Director, Yoshiro Muraki; Lighting, Yasuo Konishi; Sound, Shigenosuke Okuyama; Music, Toru Takemitsu; Editor, Hisashi Sagara

Cast: <u>Toshiro Mifune</u> (Isaburo Sasahara), Yoko Tsukasa (Ichi Sasahara), Go Kato (Yogoro Sasahara), Tatsuyoshi Ehara (Bunzo Sasahara), Etsuko Ichihara (Kiku), Isao Yamagata (Shobei Tsuchiya), Tatsuya Nakadai (Tatewaki Asano), Shigeru Koyama [Shigeru Kamiyama] (Geki Takahashi), Michiko Otsuka (Suga Sasahara), Tatsuo Matsumura (Masakata Matsudaira), Masao Mishima (Sanzaemon Yanase), Jun Hamamura (Hyoemon Shiomi), Emi Yamada (*his wife*), Takamaru Sasaki (Kenmotsu Sasahara), Hideo Fukuhara (Sahei), Noriko Kawajiri (Nui), Tetsuko

Kobayashi (Otama), Hisano Yamaoka (*mother of Sannjo Kasai*), Tomoko Hito (Yoshino), Yoshio Aoki (Takazo Komiya)

A Toho Co., Ltd./Mifune Productions Co., Ltd. Production. A Toho Co., Ltd. Release. Black and white. Toho Scope. 128 minutes. Released May 27, 1967 (roadshow version), and June 3, 1967 (general release).

U.S. version: Released by Toho International Co., Ltd. English subtitles. 120 minutes. Released December 1967.

Notes: A Toho 35th Anniversary Production. General release version double-billed with *Five Gents Prefer Geisha* (Zoku shacho sen ichiya).

NIPPON NO ICHIBAN NAGAI HI ("The Longest Day of Japan")
[THE EMPEROR AND A GENERAL]
Producers, Sanezumi Fujimoto and Tomoyuki Tanaka; Director, Kihachi Okamoto; Screenplay, Shinobu Hashimoto, based on the book *Nihon no ichiban nagai hi* (1965) by Soichi Oya; Director of Photography, Hiroshi Murai; Art Director, Iwao Akune; Lighting, Tsuruzo Nishikawa; Sound, Shin Tokai; Music, Masaru Sato; Editor, Yoshitami Kuroiwa

Cast: <u>Toshiro Mifune</u> (Korechika Anami, *Minister of the Army*), So Yamamura (Yoneuchi, *Minister of the Navy*), Takashi Shimura (Shimomura, *Minister of the Board of Information*), Yuzo Kayama (Morio Tateno of NHK), Koshiro Matsumoto (Emperor Hirohito), Michiyo Aratama (Yuriko Hara), Seiji Miyaguchi (Foreign Minister Togo), Matsuhiro Toura (Matsumoto, *Vice-Minister of Foreign Affairs*), Chishu Ryu (Prime Minister Suzuki), Yoshio Kosugi (Okada, *Minister of Public Welfare*), Etsushi Takahashi (Commander Ida), Takao Inoue (Commander Takeshita), Tadao Nakamaru (Commander Hatanaka), Toshio Kurosawa (Lt. Commander Hatanaka), Takeshi Kato (Chief Secretary Sakomizu), Kyuzo Kawabe (Interpreter Kihara), Tatsuyoshi Ehara (Private Secretary Kawamoto), Koji Mitsui (*old writer on political affairs*), Yoshio Tsuchiya (staff Fuwa), Shogo Shimada (Mori, *Division Commander of the Imperial Guard Division*), Yunosuke Ito (Rear Admiral Toshio Nonaka), Hirayoshi Aono (Grand Chamberlain Fujita), Keiju Kobayashi (Chamberlain Tokugawa), Daisuke Kato (Yabe), Jun Tazaki (Colonel Kozono), Akihiko Hirata (Lt. Colonel Sugahara), Nobuo Nakamura (Minister Kidouchi), Yu Fujiki (Major Seike), Makoto Sato (Major Koga), Akira Kubo (Major Ishihara), Kenjiro Ishiyama (General Tanaka), Susumu Fujita (Colonel Haga), Hiroshi Koizumi (Nobukata Wada), Kiyoshi Kodama (Chamberlain Toda), Torahiko Hamada (Chamberlain Mitsui), Tadashi Fukuro (Chamberlain Irie), Ichiro Nakaya (1st Lieutenant Kuroda), Tadasaburo Wakayama (Mizutani, *Chief of General Staff*), Yasushi Yamamoto (*corporal*), Kanta Mori (Major-General Takashima), Toru Ibuki (staff Itagaki), Seishiro Hisano (*battalion commander*), Yasuzo Ogawa (*policeman*), Yoshifumi Tajima (Colonel Watanabe), Goro Morino (Ohashi), Shigeki Ishida (Arakawa), Susumu Tatsuoka (Minister of the Imperial Household), Ryuji Kita (Hasunuma, *chief aide-de-camp to His Majesty*), Akiji Nomura (Major Nakamura), Kazuo Kitamura (Sato), Fuyuki Murakami (Matsuzaka, *Minister of Justice*), Hyo Kitazawa (Hirose, *Minister of Finance*), So Iwatani (Marshal Sugiyama), Masao Imafuku (Marshal Hata), Eisei Amamoto (Captain Sasaki), Shigeru Kamiyama (Kato), Jun Hamamura (Kakei), Kaku Oze (Wakamatsu), Naoya Kusakawa (Engineer Osatomo), Keikichi Taki (Major Tsukamoto), Hiroshi Tanaka (Major Kobayashi), Yutaka Sada (Keisaku Sano), Tadayoshi Ueda (Komonta Sano), Hiroyuki Katsube (Lt. Colonel Shiraishi), Akio Mayabe (staff Inatome), Ginzo Sekiguchi (Chamberlain Okabe), Hiroshi Sekita (staff Kamino), Hisashi Igawa (*gendarmerie lieutenant*), Junnosuke Suda (Takeji Takahashi), Shin Otomo (*Chief of the Bureau of Military Affairs*), Sachio Sakai (*chief of the general crew at Atsugi Air Base*), Akira Kichoji (Umezu, *Chief of General Staff*), Haruo Yamada (Toyoda, *president of military headquarters*), Ryosuke Kagawa (Ishiguro, *Minister of Agriculture and Forestry*), Ushio Akashi (Hiranuma, *President of the Privy Council*), Isao Tamagawa (Captain Arao), Hiroshi Nihonyanagi (Onishi, *vice president of military headquarters*), Toru Takeuchi (Naval Surgeon Kobayashi)

A Toho Co., Ltd. Production. A Toho Co., Ltd. Release. Black and white. Toho Scope. 157 minutes. Released August 3, 1967 (roadshow version), and August 12, 1967 (general release).

U.S. version: Released by Toho International Co., Ltd. English subtitles. Alternate title: *Japan's Longest Day*. 157 minutes. No MPAA rating. Released March 26, 1968. An "international soundtrack" version was also produced.

Notes: A Toho 35th Anniversary Production. Recommended by the Ministry of Education. General release version double-billed with the documentary featurette *The Crown Prince and Consort Visit South America* (Kotaishi Dohirodenka no Nanbei Gohomon).

KUROBE NO TAIYO ("The Sands of Kurobe")
[TUNNEL TO THE SUN]
Producers, Akira Nakai, <u>Toshiro Mifune</u>, and Yujiro Ishihara; Director, Kei Kumai; Screenplay, Masato Ide and Kei Kumai, based on a story by Sojiro Motoki; Director of Photography, Mitsuji Kanau; Art Directors, Masao Yamazaki, Masayoshi Kobayashi, and Hiroshi Yamashita; Sound, Tetsuo Yasuda; Music, Toshiro Mayuzumi; Costume Design, Makoto Ikeda; Editor, Mutsuo Tanji; Assistant Directors, Mizuho Doi, Toshi Aoki, and Hideo Miyau; Production Manager, Hideo Tomohisa

Cast: <u>Toshiro Mifune</u> (Kitagawa), Yujiro Ishihara (Iwaoka), Osamu Takizawa (Otagaki), Takashi Shimura (Ashimura), Shuji Sano (Hirata), Jukichi Uno (Mori), Ryutaro Tatsumi (Genzo), Isao Tamagawa (Sayama), Takeshi Kato (Kunikida), Sumio Takatsu (Ono), Eijiro Yanagi (Fujimura), Akira Yamauchi (Tsukamoto), Akira Terao (Kenichi), Eimei Nitani (Odagiri), Masahiko Naruse (Kumada), Fumie Katayama (Yuki), Tomoe Hiiro (Makiko), Aki Kawaguchi (Makiko), Mieko Takamine (Kayo), Tanie Kitabayashi (Kiku), Kinzo Shin (Takemoto), Shinsuke Ashida (Kurosaki), Eiji Okada (Yoshino), Nagatake Shoji (Ohashi), Keisuke Yukioka (Seyama), Toshinosuke Nagao (Kurasawa), Joji Hidehara (Yamaguchi), Mizuho Suzuki (Senda), Sayuri Kishido (Hazumi), Takashi Koshiba (Shibata), Gisuke Makino (Takahashi), Shuji Otaki (Dojo), Norio Mineda, Sonosuke Niki, Kenji Shimamura (*miners*), Taketoshi Naito (*doctor*), Tatsuhei Shimokawa (Abe), Tsuneo Arakawa, Jushiro Hirata, Yuzo Harumi, Yu Izumi, Hyoe Enoki, Hiroshi Chiyoda, Akio Muto (*additional miners*), Yuichi Sato (Takagi), Takashi Nomura (Takeyama), Jun Miyazaki (Tokuda), Keiji Ishizaki, Yoshinobu Ogawa, Masao Uchikura, Katsumasa Yamayoshi, Daisuke Oumi (*workers*), Masayoshi Miyasaka (Kihara), Aiko Mimasu (*restaurant madame*), Masao Shimizu (*geology professor*)

A STAR Production, in association with Mifune Productions Co., Ltd. and Ishihara Productions Co., Ltd. A Nikkatsu Corp. Release. Eastman Color. CinemaScope. 196 minutes (plus intermission). Released March 1, 1968.

U.S. version: Released by Toho International Co., Ltd. 196 minutes (also released at 136 minutes). English subtitles. Released October 2, 1968.

KANTAI SHIREICHO-KAN—YAMAMOTO ISOROKU ("Combined Fleet Admiral Isoroku Yamamoto")
[ADMIRAL YAMAMOTO]
Producer, Tomoyuki Tanaka; Director, Seiji Maruyama; Special Effects Director, Eiji Tsuburaya; Screenplay, Katsuya Suzaki and Seiji Maruyama; Director of Photography, Kazuo Yamada; Art Director, Takeo Kita; Sound, Yoshio Nishikawa; Music, Masaru Sato; Editor, Ryohei Fujii; Sound Effects, Toho Sound Effects Group; Mixing, Toho Recording Centre. *Special Effects Unit*: Photography, Sadamasa Arikawa; Optical Photography, Yukio Manoda and Sadao Iizuda; Art Director, Akira Watanabe; Lighting, Kyuichiro Kishida; Assistant Director, Teruyoshi Nakano

Cast: <u>Toshiro Mifune</u> (Admiral Isoroku Yamamoto), Yuzo Kayama (1st Lieutenant Ijuin), Yoko Tsukasa (Sumie Kimura), Toshio Kurosawa (1st Lieutenant Kimura), Makoto Sato

(Genda), Daisuke Kato (*chief of press section*), Masayuki Mori (Prime Minister Konoe), Wakako Sakai (Tomoko Yakuki), Koshiro Matsumoto (Minister Yoneuchi), Kenjiro Ishiyama (Commander Momotake), Eijiro Yanagi (Nagano), Seiji Miyaguchi (Ito), Susumu Fujita (Kurita), Fuyuki Murakami (Air Force Commander Iwakeini), Kazuo Nakaya (Staff Officer Tsuji), Ryutaro Tatsumi (Boatman Kitaro), Yoshio Inaba (Chief of Staff Ugaki), Yoshio Tsuchiya (Staff Officer Kuroshima), Akihiko Hirata (Staff Officer Watanabe), Masaaki Tachibana (Staff Officer Arima), Yu Fujiki (Staff Officer Fujii), Kenji Sahara (*staff officer of Information Section*), Yoshifumi Tajima (*air force officer*), Junichiro Mukoi (Fukutome), Tadashi Okabe (Tomioka), Ryuji Kita (Minister of the Navy Oikawa), Masao Imafuku (Minister of the Army Hata), Toru Abe (Chief of Staff Soka), Hisaya Ito (*staff officer of Navigation*), Naoya Kusakawa (*staff officer of Machines*), Rinsaku Ogata (Captain Hayakawa), Hideo Mineshima (Major General Yamaguchi), Akira Kubo (1st Lieutenant Takano), Ryo Tamura (Sub-Lieutenant Mikami), Tatsuji Ehara (Sub-Lieutenant Morisaki), Shinsuke Awaji (Ohmori), Hiroyuki Ohta (Nogami), Toru Ibuki (*first Army staff officer*), Susumu Kurobe (*second Army staff officer*), Tatsuya Nakadai (*narrator*)

A Toho Co., Ltd. Production. A Toho Co., Ltd. Release. Eastman Color. CinemaScope. 128 minutes. Released August 14, 1968.

U.S. version: Released by Toho International Co., Ltd. English subtitles. 131 minutes. Released December 27, 1968.

Notes: Footage was later incorporated into *Midway* (Universal, 1976). Recommended by the Ministry of Education. Double-billed with *Imaginary Paradise* (Kuso tengoku).

GION MATSURI ("Gion Festival")
[THE DAY THE SUN ROSE]
Directors, Daisuke Ito and Tetsuya Yamanouchi; Screenplay, Hisayuki Suzuki and Kumio Shimizu, based on the story "Gion matsuri" (1968) by Katsumi Nishiguchi; Planning, Daisuke Ito; Cooperation, Kyoto Prefecture (Kyoto)

Cast: Kinnosuke Nakamura (Shinkichi), <u>Toshiro Mifune</u> (Kuma), Shima Iwashita (Ayame), Yunosuke Ito (Akamatsu), Takahiro Tamura (Sukematsu), Takashi Shimura (Tsuneemon), Eitaro Ozawa (Kadokura), Kunie Tanaka, Tomoo Nagai, Orie Sato, Hisako Takibana, Kamatari Fujiwara, Masami Shimojo, Ryosuke Kagawa, Shinsuke Mikimoto, Tsutomu Shimomoto, Kiyoshi Atsumi, Ken Takakura, Katsuo Nakamura, Eitaro Matsuyama, Shiro Otsuji • Kinya Kitaoji • Hibari Misora

A Nihon Eiga Fukko Kyokai Production, in association with Shochiku Co., Ltd. A Shochiku Co., Ltd. Release. Eastman Color. Shochiku GrandScope. 168 minutes. Released November 23, 1968.

U.S. version: Released by Shochiku Films of America, Inc. English subtitles. 168 minutes. No MPAA rating. Released February 12, 1969.

Notes: The highest-grossing Japanese film of 1968. Yamanouchi replaced Daisuke Ito as director, though they shared the director credit. Reissued in the United States in 1973 running 123 minutes.

HELL IN THE PACIFIC
Executive Producers, Selig J. Seligman and Henry G. Saperstein; Producer, Reuben Bercovitch; Director, John Boorman; Screenplay, Alexander Jacobs and Eric Bercovici, based on a story by Eric Bercovici; Director of Photography, Conrad Hall; Art Directors, Anthony D.G. Pratt and Masao Yamazaki; Lighting, Harry Sunby; Sound, Toru Sakata; Music, Lalo Schifrin; Editor, Thomas Stanford; Production Managers, Lloyd E. Anderson, Harry F. Hogan, and Isao Zeniya; Assistant Director, Yoichi Matsue; Script Supervisor, John Franco; Production Assistant, B. C.

"Doc" Wylie; Property Masters, Frank A. Wade and Kesataka Sato; Set Decorator, Makoto Kikuchi; Technical Adviser, Masaki Asukai; Technical Assistance, Trissen Enterprise, S.A. (Tokyo); Camera Operator, Jordan Croenweth; Key Grip, Arthur Brooker; Communications. Bertil Hallberg; Special Effects, Joseph Zomar and Kunishige Tanaka; Makeup, Shigeo Kobayashi; Recording Supervisors, Gordon E. Sawyer and Clem Portman; Assistant Editor, Neil Travis; Sound Effects, Frank E. Warner; Music Editor, James Henrikson; Sound, Samuel Goldwyn Studios (Hollywood)

> Cast: Lee Marvin (*the American soldier*), <u>Toshiro Mifune</u> (*the Japanese soldier*)

> A Selmur Pictures Corp./Henry G. Saperstein Enterprises, Inc. Production. A Cinerama Releasing Corporation (CRC) Release. A U.S./Japanese co-production in English and Japanese (with no subtitles). Stereophonic sound. Eastman Color (prints by Technicolor). Panavision. 103 minutes. MPAA rating: G. Released (U.S.) December 18, 1968.

> Notes: Released by Shochiku Co., Ltd. December 21, 1968 as *Taiheiyo no jigoku* ("Hell in the Pacific"). Presented in Panavision 70 (70mm, blown up from 35mm Panavision) in Japan. Filmed on location on Koror and other Palau islands, Micronesia, Mifune Productions (Tokyo), and Samuel Goldwyn Studios (Hollywood). The film has a different ending for its U.S. release (running time is virtually identical); both versions are included in current U.S. home video releases.

FURIN KAZAN ("Wind-Fire-Forest-Mountain")
[SAMURAI BANNERS]
Producers, <u>Toshiro Mifune</u>, Tomoyuki Tanaka, Yoshio Nishikawa, and Hiroshi Inagaki; Director, Hiroshi Inagaki; Screenplay, Shinobu Hashimoto and Takeo Kunihiro, based on the novel *Furin kazan* (1955) by Yasushi Inoue; Director of Photography, Kazuo Yamada; Art Director, Hiroshi Ueda; Lighting, Sachiro Sato; Sound, Shoichi Fujinawa; Music, Masaru Sato; Chief Assistant Director, Teruo Maru; Assistant Director, Toshikazu Tanaka; Mixing, Hisashi Shimonaga; Editor, Yoshihiro Araki; Optical Effects, Saburo Doi; Special Effects, Cho Chiku; In Charge of Production, Shoichi Koga; Set Decoration, Takatsu Movie Decoration; Costumes, Kyoto Costumes; Makeup, Ya Yamada; Special Thanks, Haramichi City (Fukushima Prefecture), Somanomaoi Committee; Swordplay Choreography, Ryu Kuze and Yokai Nana (Mifune Productions); Tessen Group Shizuo Kanze; Archery, the Greater Japan Mountain Archery Society

> Cast: <u>Toshiro Mifune</u> (Kansuke Yamamoto), Yoshiko Sakuma (Princess Yufu), Kinnosuke Nakamura (Shingen Takeda), Yujiro Ishihara (Kenshin Uesugi), Katsuo Nakamura (Nobusato Itagaki), Kankuro Nakamura (Katsuyori Takeda), Ganemon Nakamura (Mobukata Itagaki), Masakazu Tamura (Nobushige Takeda), Mayumi Ozora (Princess Okoto), Umenosuke Nakamura, Ken Ogata, Masami Harukawa, Haruko Togo, Keiko Sawai, Yoshiko Kuga, Akihiko Hirata, Yoshio Tsuchiya, Akira Kubo, Ichiro Nakaya, Sachio Sakai, Nakajiro Tomita, Tetsuro Sagawa, Kichijiro Murata, Junichiro Mukai, Ryosuke Kagawa, Masao Shimizu, Ryunosuke Yamazaki, Jotaro Togami, Koji Nambara, Ryo Shimura, Ryunosuke Tsukigata, Naraimon Nakamura

> A Mifune Productions Co., Ltd. Production. A Toho Co., Ltd. Release. Color (processed by Tokyo Laboratory, Ltd.). CinemaScope. 165 minutes plus intermission. Released February 1, 1969 (roadshow version).

> U.S. version: *Under the Banner of Samurai*. Released by Toho International Co., Ltd. English subtitles. 165 minutes. No MPAA rating. Released June 24, 1969. Home video version released as *Samurai Banners*.

> Notes: Recommended by the Ministry of Education.

EIKO E NO 5,000 KIRO ("5,000 Kilometers to Glory")
[SAFARI 5000]
Producers, Yujiro Ishihara, Seiichiro Sakaeda, and Akira Nakai; Director, Koreyoshi Kurahara; Screenplay, Nobuo Yamada, based on the story by Gozo Kasahara; Director of Photography, Mitsuji Kanau; Art Director, Yoshinaga Yoko; Music, Toshiro Mayuzumi

Cast: Yujiro Ishihara, Tatsuya Nakadai, Toshiro Mifune, Ruriko Asaoka, Juzo Itami, Emmanuele Riva, Jean-Claude Drouot

An Ishihara Promotion Production. A Shochiku Co., Ltd. Release. Color. 177 minutes. Released July 19, 1969.

U.S. version: Release, if any, is undetermined.

Notes: The highest-grossing Japanese film of 1969. Filmed on location in Africa and Europe.

NIHONKAI DAISUKAISEN ("Great Battle of the Japan Sea")
[BATTLE OF THE JAPAN SEA]
Producer, Tomoyuki Tanaka; Director, Seiji Maruyama; Special Effects Director, Eiji Tsuburaya; Screenplay, Toshio Yasumi; Director of Photography, Hiroshi Murai; Art Director, Takeo Kita; Lighting, Toshio Takashima; Sound, Noboru Yoshioka; Music, Masaru Sato; Still Photographer, Iwao Yamazaki; Negative Cutter, Yoshitami Kuroiwa; Sound Track Album, CBS/Sony Records. *Toho Special Effects Group*: Photography, Mototaka Tomioka and Yoichi Manoda; Matte Process Photography, Yoshiyuki Norimasa; Art Director, Noriyoshi Inoue; Matte Compositions, Hiroshi Koyama; Wire Manipulation, Fumio Nakadai; Assistant Director, Teruyoshi Nakano

Cast: Toshiro Mifune (Admiral Heihachiro Togo), Tatsuya Nakadai (Major Genjiro Akashi), Yuzo Kayama (Commander Hirose), Chishu Ryu (General Maresuke Nogi), Susumu Fujita (Uemura), Mitsuko Kusabue (Mrs. Tetsu), Ryutaro Tatsumi (Gonbei Yamamoto), Koshiro Matsumoto (*the Emperor*), Toshio Kurosawa (Maeyama, *the first soldier*), Yoko Tsukasa (*undetermined*), Akira Kubo (Matsui), Makoto Sato (*gunnery chief of security*), Akihiko Hirata (Staff Officer Tsunoda), Yoshio Tsuchiya (Staff Officer Akiyama), Kenji Sahara (*sub-chief*), Yoshifumi Tajima (Ijichi), Hiroshi Koizumi (Kurino), Jun Tazaki (Shimaji Hashiguchi), Takeshi Kato (Chief of Staff Officer Kato), Atsushi Higashiyama (Sugino), Keiji Higashiyama (Dr. Fujimoto), Shoji Matsuyama (Matsu), Jun Funato (Staff Officer Yamaoka), Eijiro Yanagi (Hirofumi Ito), Masao Shimizu (Tozuka), Torn Yasube (Suchi), Gen Shimizu (Narikawa), Ryuji Kita (Kataoka), Mikita Mori (Chief of Staff Officer Ijichi), Toshiyuki Takahashi (Nagata), Shin Takioka (Laoru Inoue), Takamaru Sasaki (Consultant Kuki), Yoshio Inaba (Chief of Staff Officer Shimamura), Ken Mitsuda (Ariaki Yamagata), Yutaka Sada, Kazuo Suzuki, Wataru Omae, Chotaro Togin, Seishiro Kuno, Yutaka Oka, Fumiko Homma, Ted Gunther, Jacob Shapiro, Harold S. Conway, Hans Horneff, Osman Yusef, Peter Williams, Andrew Hughes

A Toho Co., Ltd. Production. A Toho Co., Ltd. Release. Hyper Stereo Three-Dimensional Sound. Eastman Color. CinemaScope. 128 minutes. Released August 1, 1969 (roadshow version) and August 13, 1969 (general release).

U.S. version: Released by Toho International Co., Ltd. English subtitles. 128 minutes. MPAA rating: G. Released October 28, 1970.

Notes: The last film featuring special effects personally directed by Eiji Tsuburaya. General release version double-billed with *Konto55—Weakness of the Human Race* (Konto55 go—Jinrui no daijakuten).

AKAGE ("Red Hair")
[RED LION]
Producers, <u>Toshiro Mifune</u> and Yoshio Nishikawa; Director, Kihachi Okamoto; Screenplay, Kihachi Okamoto and Sakae Hirosawa; Director of Photography, Takao Saito; Art Director, Hiroshi Ueda; Lighting, Sachiro Sato; Sound, Masamichi Ichikawa; Music, Masaru Sato; Mixing, Hisashi Shimonaga; Chief Assistant Director, Yoshikazu Tanaka; Negative Cutter, Yoshihiro Araki; Makeup, Shigeo Kobayashi; Swordplay Choreography, Ryu Kuze; Unit Production Manager, Eiichi Yamazaki

    Cast: <u>Toshiro Mifune</u> (Gonzo), Shima Iwashita (Tomi), Etsushi Takahashi (Hanzo), Minoru [No] Terada (Sanji, *the wallet collector*), Nobuko Otowa (*aging prostitute*), Yuko Mochizuki (*undetermined*), Jitsuko Yoshimura (*undetermined*), Kaai Okada (*undetermined*), Shigeru Koyama (Staff Chief Aragaki), Hideyo Amamoto (Dr. Gensai), Tokue Hanasawa (Komotora), Shin Kishida, Hideo Sunazuka, Bokuzen Hidari, Goro Mutsu, Daigo Kusano, Nakajiro Tomita, Fujio Tokita, Jun Hamamura, Sachio Sakai, Ren Yamamoto, Hiroshi Hasegawa, Shoji Nomura, Mika Kitagawa, Kawako Noguchi, Ayako Suda, Chie Iwasaki, Sue Mitobe, Yutaka Nakayama, Takeo Chii, Nobusuke Achiba, Mamora Sawanobori, Akio Kinoshita, Tomiyuki Kimura, Shoichiro Maruoka, Shoji Uno, Shoji Yoshida, Kinuyo Sado, Kazuko Asari, Yoko Ishido, Aiko Sarami, Yoko Toyoda, Kimie Shimazu, Shigeko Kawamura, Yumiko Taniguchi, Jun Majima, Michi Matsubara, Toriko Takahara, Yoshie Kihei, Hiroshi Tanaka, Hiroyoshi Yamaguchi, Koji Asakawa, Hiroto Kimura, Hajime Tanaka, Shigeo Kato, Yoshihiro Mito, Hiroyuki Umabe, Junichi Ito, Yokai Nana, Ichiro Nakaya (narrator) · Yunosuke Ito (magistrate), Takahiro Tamura (Sozo Sagara)

    A Mifune Productions Co., Ltd. Production. A Toho Co., Ltd. Release. Eastman Color (processed by Tokyo Laboratory, Ltd.). CinemaScope. 115 minutes. Released October 10, 1969.

    U.S. version: Released by Toho International Co., Ltd. English subtitles. 116 minutes (possibly released at 106 minutes). No MPAA rating. Released December 17, 1969. Reissued to home video at its original length.

    Notes: Double-billed with *Konto55—I Am a Ninja's Great-Great Grandson* (Konto55 go— Oro wa ninja no mago no mago).

SHINSENGUMI ("Shinsen Group")
[BAND OF ASSASSINS]
Producers, <u>Toshiro Mifune</u>, Yoshio Nishikawa, and Hiroshi Inagaki; Director Tadashi Sawashima; Screenplay, Kenro Matsura; Director of Photography, Kazuo Yamada; Art Director, Hiroshi Ueda; Lighting, Sachiro Sato; Sound, Masamichi Ichikawa; Music, Masaru Sato; Still Photographer, Ko Iidaka; Editor, Yoshihiro Araki

    Cast: <u>Toshiro Mifune</u> (Isami Kondo), Keiju Kobayashi (Toshizo Hijikata), Kinya Kitaoji (Soshi Okita), Rentaro Mikuni (Kamo Serizawa), Yoko Tsukasa (Tsune), Yuriko Hoshi (Otaka), Ganemon Nakamura (Yasubo Katsu), Junko Ikeuchi (Oyuki), Kinnosuke Nakamura (Fujita Arima), Umenosuke Nakamura (Keisuke Yamaminami), Yumiko Nogawa (Oume), Takahiro Tamura (Koshitaro Ito), Katsuo Nakamura (Kisaburo Kawai), Mita Kitagawa (Kaori), Shinsuke Okimoto (Hachiro Shoga), Ichiro Nakaya (Moribe Tani), Ryohei Uchida (Nishiki Shinmi), Ryunosuke Yamazaki (Sanosuke Harada), Kinzo Shin (Honmeido), Kazuya Okuri (Naouemon Teshiro), Hiroshi Tanaka (Shinpachi Nagakura), Shinnosuke Ogata (Heisuke Todo), Seishiro Kuno (Gennosuke Inoue); Kiyoshi Taiki (Goro Hirayama), Hiroto Kimura (Shigesuke Hirama), Kyosuke Ugami (Jo Yamazaki), Jotaro Togami (Teizo Miyabe), Eijiro Soma (Ninmaro Yoshida), Yoshijiro Murata (Shuzo Ishizaka), Shin Tsuda (*executive*), Naoki Yamazaki (Tokutaro Ikeda)

    A Mifune Productions Co., Ltd. Production. A Toho Co., Ltd. Release. Eastman Color.

CinemaScope. 122 minutes. Released December 5, 1969 (roadshow version), and January 1, 1970 (general release).

U.S. version: Released by Toho International Co., Ltd. English subtitles. 122 minutes. No MPAA rating. Released April 15, 1970.

Notes: General release version double-billed with *Bravo! Young Guy* (Burabo! Wakadaisho).

ZATOICHI TO YOJINBO
[ZATOICHI MEETS YOJIMBO]

Producer, Shintaro Katsu; Director, Kihachi Okamoto; Screenplay, Kihachi Okamoto and Tetsuro Yoshida, based on a character created by Kan Shimozawa; Director of Photography, Kazuo Miyagawa; Art Director, Yoshinobu Nishioka; Lighting, Gengon Nakaoka; Sound, Taro Hayashido; Music, Akira Ifukube; Editor, Toshio Taniguchi; Chief Assistant Director, Chuza Nakanishi; Assistant Directors, Haruo Ueda, Akikazu Ota; Sound Effects, Cho Kurashima; Still Photographer, Eiichi Otani; Continuity, Mitsuko Matsuda; Administration, Shoichi Hattori; Publicity, Toshigi Tomoeda; In Charge of Production, Masanori Shinda

Cast: Shintaro Katsu (Zatoichi), Ayako Wakao (Umeno, *the prostitute*), Osamu Takizawa (Yasuke Eboshiya, *the silk merchant*), Sakatoshi Yonekura (Boss Masagoro, *his son*), Shin Kishida (Kuzuryu), Kanjuro Arashi (Hyoroku, *the village elder*), Toshiyuki Hosokawa (Sanaemon, *Eboshiya's second son*), Shigeru Kamiyama (Jinzaburo Wakiya), Minoru Terada, Hideo Sunazuka, Daigo Kusano, Fujio Tsuneda, Gen Kimura, Hiroshi Tanaka, Hiroto Kimura, Ryutaro Itsumi, Yuji Hamada, Kazu Echikawa, Ken Kuroki, Junshiro Araseki, Yoko Netsuda, Suyama Productions, Kenmokukai Co., Ltd. • <u>Toshiro Mifune</u> (Sassa, *the yojimbo*)

A Katsu Production. A Daiei Co., Ltd. Release. Eastman Color (processed by Toyo Developing). Daiei Scope. 116 minutes. Released January 15, 1970.

U.S. version: Released by Daiei International Films, Inc. English subtitles, Cinetype; Subtitles Editor, Audie Bock. 116 minutes. No MPAA rating. Released July 17, 1970.

Notes: Kihachi Okamoto was still under contract to Toho at the time of filming. Filmed at Daiei-Kyoto Studios. The 20th "Zatoichi" feature, followed by *Zatoichi's Fire Festival* (1970). Originally released in the United States with the line "Not Seen in Ten Years!" and advertised as *Zatoichi vs. Yojimbo*. Reissued November 22, 1971, by Bijou of Japan, Inc. Reissued (date undetermined) by R5/S8. Eastern Hemisphere rights later acquired by Toho Co., Ltd.

BAKUMATSU ("The Ambitious")
[THE AMBITIOUS]

Producer, Kinichiro Ogawa; Associate Producer, Kinnosuke Nakamura; Director, Daisuke Ito; Screenplay, Daisuke Ito, based on a story by Ryotaro Shiba; Director of Photography, Kazuo Yamada; Art Director, Toshikazu Ito; Lighting, Haruo Nakayama; Sound, Hiroo Nozu; Music, Masaru Sato; Assistant Art Director, Junichi Yamada; Still Photographer, Kazumari Suzuki; Negative Cutter, Yoshihiro Araki

Cast: Kinnosuke Nakamura (Ryoma Sakamoto), <u>Toshiro Mifune</u> (Shojiro Goto), Keiju Kobayashi (Yoshinosuke Saigo), Tatsuya Nakadai (Shintaro Nakaoka), Sayuri Yoshinaga (Oryo), Katsuo Nakamura (Chojiro Kondo), Noboru Nakaya (Hanheita Takeichi), Eitaro Matsuyama (Umanosuke Shinmiya), Shigeru Kamiyama (Kaishu Katsu). Shinsuke Mikimoto (Kogoro Katsura), Akihiko Kataoka (Toranosuke Nakahira), Terumi Niki (Mitsukazu Nakadaira), Tsutomu Yamagata (Hiroe Yamada), Ryuichi Nagashima (Tabun Iegami), Kentaro Ozato (Unosuke Urashima), Hiroshi Aoyama (Bensai), Shogen Shinda (Shoji Sawaki), Manabu Yamamoto (Ukichi Sensa), Jo Okuda (Hidemi Shinda), Hiroshi Tanaka (Kisuke Deishi), Isemu Fukumoto (Denjiro Jodo), Senzo Hashimoto (Kinba Yasuoka), Hirosuke Ota (Tarotsugu Mikami), Shinnosuke

Ogata (Jutaro Chiba), Tayoko Ueda (Mari), Toshiaki Amata (Yataro Shinagawa), Yoshitaro Asawaka (Muta), Takashi Yasuda (Kuo), Akira Naiai (Ikuhisa), Shintaro Ehara (Shinzo Sankichi), Shiro Otsuji (Saiichi), Chiemi Eri (Oman), Keiko Akata (Ofuku), Hiromi Takano (Ochiyo), Atsushi Watanabe (Kan), Saburo Sawai (Ichinosuke Fuse), Tokinosuke Nakamura (Koshitaro Ito), Ryosuke Kagawa (Fujikichi), Keiko Kagawa (Otome)

A Nakamura Pro Production. A Toho Co., Ltd Release. Eastman Color. CinemaScope. 121 minutes. Released February 14, 1970 (roadshow version), and February 28, 1970 (general release).

U.S. version: Released by Toho International Co., Ltd. English subtitles. 120 minutes. No MPAA rating. Released August 26, 1970.

Notes: Recommended by the Ministry of Education. General release version double-billed with *Five Gents and a Kuniang* (Zoku Shacho gaku ABC)

MACHIBUSE ("Ambush")
[THE AMBUSH: INCIDENT AT BLOOD PASS]
Producers, <u>Toshiro Mifune</u> and Yoshio Nishikawa; Director, Hiroshi Inagaki; Screenplay, Kyu [Yumi] Fujiki, Hideo Oguni, Hajime Takaiwa, and Ichiro Miyakawa; Director of Photography, Kazuo Yamada; Art Director, Hiroshi Ueda; Lighting, Yukio Sato; Sound, Masamichi Ichikawa; Music, Masaru Sato; Assistant Directors, Teruo Maru and Osamu Yasui; Editor, Yoshihiro Araki; Sound Effects, Sadamasa Nishimoto; Assistant Cameraman, Nobuaki Murano; Lighting Assistant, Naoyuki Doi; Assistant Sound, Nao Kobayashi; Assistant Art Director, Hikokozaburo Takayama; Set Design, Yoshio Yoshida; Set Decoration, Kasataka Sato; Makeup, Shigeo Kobayashi; Costumes, Makoto Ikeda; Script Supervisor, Fumie Fujimoto; Swordplay Choreography, Ryu Kuze and Yokai Nana (Mifune Productions); Special Thanks, Kawanaka Jindaiko Drum Corps, Shinoi Preservation Society; Line Producer, Mamoru Kumada; Rerecording, Toho Dubbing Theatre

Cast: <u>Toshiro Mifune</u> (*the yojimbo*), Yujiro Ishihara (Yataro), Ruriko Asaoka (Okuni), Shintaro Katsu (Gentetsu), Kinnosuke Nakamura (Heima Ibuki), Chusha Ichikawa, Ichiro Arishima, Mika Kitagawa, Yoshio Tsuchiya, Jotaro Togami, Chicko Nakakita, Ryunosuke Yamazaki, Seishiro Hisano, Yasuo Araki, Hiroshi Tanaka, Hirohito Kimura, Yutaka Sada, Shinsuke Achiba, Yuzuro Sawanobori, Shunichi Okita, Kazuo Suzuki, Koji Kaminishi, Yasuji Uraki, Ken Echigo, Minoru Ito, Yukihiko Gondo, Koji Kakiki, Isamu Arai, Kazotoshi Yoshiyama, Toshio Endo, Shigeyoshi Yokota, Mitsuyuki Oshima, Kimizuka Masazumi, Kengo Nakayama [later Kenpachiro Satsuma], Yoshiharu Takahashi

A Mifune Productions Co., Ltd. Production. A Toho Co., Ltd. Release. Eastman Color (processed by Tokyo Laboratory, Ltd.). CinemaScope. 117 minutes. Released April 29, 1970.

U.S. version: Released by Toho International Co., Ltd. English subtitles. Also known as *The Ambush*. 117 minutes. No MPAA rating. Released December 18, 1970. Home video version reissued as *Ambush at Blood Pass*.

Notes: Double-billed with *Sexy Comic—Strange Friends* (Oiroke Konikku—Fushigina nakama).

ARU HEISHI NO KAKE ("One Soldier's Gamble")
[THE WALKING MAJOR]
Producer, Yujiro Ishihara; Directors, Koji Senno, Nobuaki Shirai, and Keith Eric Burt

Cast: Dale Robertson (Captain Clark J. Allen), Yujiro Ishihara (Hiroshi Kitabayashi), Frank Sinatra, Jr. (James Dickson), Dina Merrill (Kelly Allen), Michiyo Aratama (Mother Yamada), Keith Larsen (Captain White), Ruriko Asaoka (Setsuko Takiguchi), <u>Toshiro Mifune</u> (Tadao Kinugasa), Arihiro Fujimura (Frank Choe), Yuriko Ishihara (Kyoko), Mayumi Nagisa (*village girl*), Linda Purl (Rose Allen), Keith Larsen, Jr. (Danny Allen), Marshie Patton (Carol White)

An Ishihara International Production. A Shochiku Co., Ltd. Release. Color. CinemaScope. Running time undetermined. Released June 6, 1970.

U.S. version: Release, if any, is undetermined.

Notes: Recommended by the Ministry of Education and the Japan Film Society. Actor Keith Larsen is also listed as director according to some sources.

GEKIDO NO SHOWASHI—GUNBATSU ("A Turning Point of Showa History— The Militarists")
[THE MILITARISTS]
Producers, Sanezumi Fujimoto and Hiroshi Haryu; Director, Hiromichi Horikawa; Screenplay, Ryozo Kasahara; Director of Photography, Kazuo Yamada; Art Directors, Iwao Akune and Shigekazu Ikuno; Lighting, Choshiro Ishii; Sound, Shin Watarai; Music, Riichiro Manabe; Chief Assistant Director, Masashi Matsumoto

Cast: Keiju Kobayashi (Premier Tojo), Yuzo Kayama (Goro Arai), Toshiro Mifune (Admiral Isoroku Yamamoto), So Yamamura, Tatsuya Mihashi, Toshio Kurosawa (*kamikaze pilot*), Goro Tarumi (Takei), Kenjiro Ishiyama, Toho All Stars

A Toho Co., Ltd. Production. A Toho Co., Ltd. Release. Hyper Stereo Three-Dimensional Sound. Eastman Color. Super Panavision 70. 133 minutes. Released August 11, 1970 (roadshow version), and September 12, 1970 (general release).

U.S. version: *Gunbatsu (The Militarists)*. Released by Toho International Co., Ltd. English subtitles. 133 minutes. No MPAA rating. Released March 10, 1971.

Notes: Possibly filmed in 35mm CinemaScope and blown up to 70mm; Toho's records are unclear. General release version double-billed with *A Simple, Simple Clerk—Mr. Sunset* (Hira hira shain—Yuhi-kun).

TORA! TORA! TORA! [*UNCOMPLETED JAPANESE SEQUENCES*]
Director, Akira Kurosawa; Associate Producer, Tetsuro "Tetsu" Aoyagi; Second Unit Director, Junya Sato; Screenplay, Akira Kurosawa, Hideo Oguni, and Ryuzo Kikushima; Director of Photography, Takao Sato; Art Director, Yoshiro Muraki; Sound, Noboru Watari; Music, Toru Takemitsu; Technical Advisers, Minoru Genda and Yasuji Watanabe; Second Unit Directors of Photography, Hiroshi Segawa and Tadashi Sato; Unit Production Manager, Masahiro Oba; First Assistant Director, Yutaka Osawa; Assistant Art Director, Tsukasa Kondo; Aviation Advisor, Kameo Sonokawa; Aircraft Modification, Kisaku Kobayashi; Key Grip, Koji Hirata; Hair and Makeup, Junjiro Yamada; Wardrobe, Kyoto Isho Co., Ltd.; Props, Kozu Props Co., Ltd.; Property Master, Masuji Ogawa; Special Effects (mechanical), Kunio Kunisada; Set Construction, Tadao Kudo; Production Controller, Sadahiro Kubota; Production Accountant, Ryohachi Tsuboya; Production Supervisor (for 20th Century-Fox), Stanley Goldsmith

Cast: Takeo Kagiya (Admiral Isoroku Yamamoto), Hiroshi Iwamiya (Lt. Syogo Masuda), Kunio Nagai (Nagao Kita), Yasuyoshi Obata (Ambassador Kichisaburo Nomura), Yoshiaki Kaimasu (Hankyu Sasaki), Ban Ando (Admiral Onishi), Tsuguto Kitano (Admiral Yamaguchi), Hanji Aoki (Rear Admiral Shigeru Takutomi), Tajuro Nande (Seiichi Ito), Yoshio Miyoshi (Admiral Ugaki), Yoshio Katagiri (Ambassador Kurusu), Daisaku Goto (Jujiro Wada), Kohei Hatta (Toshihide Maejima), Kazushige Hirasawa (Shigenori Togo), Sabaru Kazusa (Shigeru Fujii), Koreya Senda (Prime Minister Konoe), Tsutomu Yamazaki (Minoru Genda), Eijiro Tono [billed as Eijiro Higashino], Susumu Fujita, Osamu Takizawa, Shogo Shimada

A 20th Century-Fox Film Corp./Kurosawa Production Co., Ltd. Production. Eastman Color. Panavision. Unfinished (see below).

Notes: Shooting began in December 1969 but halted and Kurosawa was fired. Shooting resumed without his participation (see below). Hiroshi Teshigahara was named as Co-Second Unit Director, and Kazuo Miyagawa as Director of Photography, but both dropped out before filming began. Of the professional cast, only Senda had begun filming his role when shooting was halted.

TORA! TORA! TORA!

Executive Producer, Darryl F. Zanuck; Executive in Charge of Production, Richard D. Zanuck; Producer, Elmo Williams; Associate Producers of Japanese Episodes, Otto Lang, Masayuki Tagaki, and Keinosuke Kubo; Director (U.S.), Richard Fleischer; Directors (Japan), Toshio Masuda and Kinji Fukasaku; Second Unit Director, Ray Kellogg; Screenplay (American and Bridging Sequences), Larry Forrester; Screenplay (Japanese Sequences), Akira Kurosawa, Hideo Oguni, and Ryuzo Kikushima, based on the books Tora! Tora! Tora! (1969) by Gordon W. Prange and The Broken Seal: Operation Magic and the Secret Road to Pearl Harbor (1967) by Ladislas Farrago; Music, Jerry Goldsmith; Director of Photography (U.S.), Charles F. Wheeler; Directors of Photography (Japan), Shinsaku Himeda, Masamichi Sato, and Osami Furuya; Art Directors, Jack Martin Smith, Yoshiro Muraki, Richard Day, and Taizo Kawashima; Sound Recording, James Corcoran, Murray Spivack, Douglas O. Williams, Theodore Soderberg, Herman Lewis, and Shin Watari; Set Decorators, Walter M. Scott, Norman Rockett, and Carl Biddiscombe; Orchestration, Arthur Morton; Makeup Supervision, Daniel J. Striepeke; Makeup, Layne "Shotgun" Britton; Wardrobe Supervision, Courtney Haslam; Wardrobe, Edward Wynigear; Editors, James E. Newcom, Pembroke J. Herring, Toshio Masuda, and Inoue Chikaya; Assistant Directors, David Hall, Elliott Shick, and Hiroshi Nagai; Unit Production Managers, William Eckhardt, Jack Stubbs, Stanley H. Goldsmith, and Masao Namikawa; Special Photographic Effects, L. B. Abbott, Art Cruickshank, and Howard Lydecker; Mechanical Effects, A. D. Flowers, Glen E. Robinson; Script Supervisor, Duane Toler; Air Operations, Lt. Col. Arthur P. Wildern, Jr., USAF (Retd.), Capt. George Watkins, USN, and Jack Canary, Department of Defense Project Officer and Naval Coordinator, Commander E. P. Stafford, USN; Production Coordinators, Maurice Unger and Theodore Taylor, Technical Advisers, Kameo Sonokawa, Kuranosuke Isoda, Shizu Takada, Tsuyoshi Saka, Konrad Schreier, Jr., Commander Minoru Genda, and Robert Buckhart; Aerial Photography, Vision Photography, Inc.; Titles, Pacific Title; Director of Photography (Second Unit), David Butler; Supervising Sound Editor, Don Hall, Jr.; Supervising Music Editor, Leonard A. Engel; Unit Publicists, Ted Taylor and Hal Sherman; Still Photographers, Sterling Smith, Malcolm Bullock, Doug Kirkland, and Tamotsu Yato; Camera Operator, Jack Whitman, Jr.; Assistant Cameraman, Tom Kerschner; Camera Operators (Second Unit), Michael Butler and Tony Butler; Assistant Cameraman (Second Unit), John Fleckstein; Gaffer, Bill Huffman III; Gaffer (Second Unit), Don Knight; Key Grip (Second Unit), Chuck Record; Chief Pilot, Dave Jones; Construction Supervisor, Ivan Martin; Miniature Construction Supervisor, Gail Brown; Army Affairs Coordinator, Col. B. H. Watson, USA; Story Consultants, Rear Admiral Yasuji Watanabe, Retd. and Rear Admiral Shigeru Fukutomi; Japanese Aircraft Consultant, Kanoe Sonokawa; Production Auditor, Gaines Johnston; Cooperation, U.S. Department of Defense, U.S. Navy, U.S. Army, U.S. Air Force, U.S. Embassy in Japan, Japanese Imperial Navy, Japanese Imperial Government

Cast: Martin Balsam (Admiral Husband E. Kimmel), Jason Robards (Lt. General Walter C. Short), So Yamamura (Admiral Isoroku Yamamoto), Joseph Cotten (Secretary of War Henry L. Stimson), Tatsuya Mihashi (Commander Minoru Genda), E. G. Marshall (Lt. Colonel Rufus G. Bratton), Takahiro Tamura (Lt. Commander Mitsuo Fuchida), James Whitmore, Sr. (Admiral William F. "Bull" Halsey), Eijiro Tono (Vice Admiral Chuichi Nagumo), Wesley Addy (Lt. Commander Alvin D. Kramer), Shogo Shimada (Ambassador Kichisaburo Nomura), Frank Aletter

(Lt. Colonel Thomas), Koreya Senda (Crown Prince Fumimaro Konoye), Leon Ames (Secretary of the Navy Frank Knox), Junya Usami (Admiral Zengo Yoshida), Richard Anderson (Captain John Earle), Kazuo Kitamura (Foreign Minister Yosuke Matsuoka), Keith Andes (General George C. Marshall), Edward Andrews (Admiral Harold R. Stark), Neville Brand (Lt. Kaminsky), Leora Dana (Mrs. Kramer), Asao Uchida (General Hideki Tojo), George Macready (Secretary of State Cordell Hull), Norman Alden (Major Truman Landon), Walter Brooke (Captain Theodore S. Wilkinson), Rick Cooper (Lt. George Welch), Evlen Havard (Doris Miller), June Dayton (Ray Cave), Jeff Donnell (Cornelia), Richard Erdman (Colonel Edward F. French), Jerry Fogel (Lt. Commander William W. Outerbridge), Shunichi Nakamura (Kameto Kuroshima), Carl Reindel (Lieutenant Kenneth M. Taylor), Edmon Ryan (Rear Admiral Patrick N.I. Bellinger), Hisao Toake (Ambassador Saburo Kuruso), Susumu Fujita (Yamaguchi), Harlan Warde (officer on General Marshall's staff), Robert Karnes (*Navy admiral*), Francis De Sales (*Admiral Stark's aide*), Berry Kroeger (*Army general*), G. D. Spradlin (*Navy officer*), Meredith "Tex" Weatherby (Ambassador Grew), Harold S. Conway (*first interpreter*), Mike Daneen (*second interpreter*), Paul Frees (*English-language voice characterization for Nomura*), Jamie Farr (*miscellaneous voice characterizations*), Hisashi Igawa (*pilot*), Bontaro Miyake, Ichiro Reuzaki, Kazuko Ichikawa, Hank Jones, Karl Lukas, Ron Masak, Kan Nihonyanagi, Toshio Josokawa

An Elmo Williams and Richard Fleischer Production. A 20th Century-Fox Film Corp. Release. Stereophonic sound. Fujicolor (prints by Toei Chemistry Co., Ltd., and De Luxe) Panavision (exhibited in Panavision 70 in some markets). 143 minutes plus overture and intermission. MPAA rating: G. Released September 23, 1970.

Notes: Kurosawa is not credited as co-screenwriter per his request, though much of the Japanese sequences were in fact co-written by him. A U.S./Japanese co-production in English and Japanese. Filmed at Twentieth Century-Fox Studios (Century City), Toei-Kyoto Studios (Kyoto), Shochiku Studios (Kyoto), and on location in Hawaii, Washington, D.C. (USA), and Ashiya, Kagoshima Bay, Kyushu, Osaka, and Tokyo (Japan). Longtime special-effects artist Howard Lydecker died during shooting. Footage incorporated into *Midway* (Universal, 1976), *Pearl* (Warner Bros. Television, 1978), *From Here to Eternity* (Columbia Television, 1979), and other features and television programs. Contractually, this or *Patton* (Fox, 1970) was to be shot in the 70mm process D-150, but in the end Fox shot the George C. Scott biopic in 70mm instead, shooting *Tora! Tora! Tora!* in 35mm Panavision.

Japanese version: *Tora! Tora! Tora!* The Japanese version bills Masuda and Fukasaku as directors, with Fleischer as "Director of American Sequences," and includes three scenes cut from American version. New scenes include Kiyoshi Atsumi as first cook, and Eitaro Matsuyama as second cook, and Hiroshi Akutagawa's role has been expanded.

DODESUKADEN ("Clickity-Clack")
[DODES'KA DEN]
Executive Producers, Akira Kurosawa, Keisuke Kinoshita, Kon Ichikawa, and Masaki Kobayashi; Producers, Akira Kurosawa and Yoichi Matsue; Director, <u>Akira Kurosawa</u>; Screenplay, Akira Kurosawa, Hideo Oguni and Shinobu Hashimoto, based on the novel *Kisetsu no nai machi* ("The Town Without Seasons") by Shugoro Yamamoto; Directors of Photography, Takao Saito and Yasumichi Fukuzawa; Art Directors, Yoshiro Muraki and Shinobu Muraki; Lighting, Hiromitsu Mori; Sound, Fumio Yanoguchi; Music, Toru Takemitsu; Assistant Cameraman, Daisaku Omura; Assistant Lighting, Shinji Kojima; Assistant Art Director, Tsuneo Shimura; Sound Assistant, Mamoru Yamada; Mixing, Toho Dubbing Theatre; Chief Assistant Director, Kenjiro Omori; Assistant Directors, Yoshishiro Kawasaki, Koji Hashimoto, and Nobumitsu Takizawa; Assistant Editor, Reiko Kaneko; Script Supervisor, Teruyo Nogami; Sound Effects,

Ichiro Minawa; Still Photographer, Naomi Hashiyama; Production Assistance, Shoichi Koga, Shoji Nakayama; Property Master, Akio Nojima; Costumes, Miyuki Suzuki (Kyoto Costume); Hair Stylists, Sakae Nakao and Shozo Takahashi; Transportation, Isamu Miwano; Acting Office, Etsuo Yamamoto

Cast: Yoshitaka Zushi (Roku-chan), Kin Sugai (Okuni, *Roku-chan's mother*), Toshiyuki Tonomura (Taro Sawagami, *Roku-chan's brother*), Shinsuke Minami (Ryotaro Sawagami), Yuko Kusunoki (Misao Sawagami, *Ryotaro's wife*), Junzaburo Ban (Yukichi Shima), Kiyoko Tange (*Shima's wife*), Michio Hino (Okawa, *Shima's colleague*), Keiji Furuyama (Matsui, *Shima's colleague*), Tatsuhei Shimokawa (Nomoto, *Shima's colleague*), Kunie Tanaka (Hatsutaro Kawaguchi), Jitsuko Yoshimura (Yoshie Kawaguchi, *his wife*), Hisashi Igawa (Masuo Masuda), Hideko Okiyama (Tatsu Masuda, *his wife*), Tatsuo Matsumura (Kyota), Imari Tsuji (Otane Watanaba, *his wife*), Tomoko Yamazaki (Katsuko Watanaba, *his niece*), Masahiko Kametani (Okabe), Hiroshi Akutagawa (Mr. Hei), Akiko Naraoka (Ocho), Noboru Mitani (*beggar*), Hiroyuki Kawase (*beggar's son*), Akemi Negishi (*attractive wife*), Hideaki Ezumi (*detective*), Minoru Takashima (*policeman*), Kazuo Kato (*roadside painter*), Michiko Araki (*restaurant proprietess*), Toki Shiozawa (*waitress*), Shoichi Kuwayama (*Western-style restaurant owner*), Hiroshi Kiyama (*sushi shop proprietor*), Koji Mitsui (*owner of foodstand*), Jerry Fujio (Yoshi), Masahiko Tanimura (Mr. So), Atsushi Watanabe (Mr. Tamba), Kamatari Fujiwara (*old man*), Sanji Kojima (*thief*), Kayoko Sono (*wife of Kuman-mine*), Yoshiko Maki (*second wife*), Toshiko Sakurai (*third* wife), Toriko Takahara (*fifth wife*), Matsue Ono (*fourth wife*), Reiko Niimura (*first wife*), Akira Hitomi (*first man calling out to Misao*), Kanji Ebata (*second man calling out to Misao*), Masahiko Ichimura (*third man calling out to Misao*), Masanari Nihei (*fourth man calling out to Misao*), Shin Ibuki (*fifth man calling out to Misao*), Satoshi Hasegawa (Jiro Sawagami), Kumiko Ono (Hanako Sawagami), Tatsuhiko Yanashisa (Shiro Sawagami), Mika Oshida (Umeko Sawagami), Keiji Sakakida (*sake shop proprietor*), Kiyotaka Ishii (*Kumanbachi's first child*), Mihoko Kaizuka (*Kumanbachi's second child*), Tsuji Imura (Mrs. Watanaka)

A Yonki no kai/Toho Co., Ltd. Production. A Toho Co., Ltd. Release. Eastman Color (processed by Tokyo Laboratory Ltd.). Standard size. 140 minutes. Released October 31, 1970 (roadshow version).

U.S. version: Released by Janus Films, Inc. in subtitled format. 140 minutes. No MPAA rating. Released June 9, 1971. Some U.S. home video versions are incorrectly cropped to 1.66:1.

Notes: Donald Richie's *The Films of Akira Kurosawa* lists the running time at 244 minutes. This is apparently a typo, as the running times listed in Japanese sources from the time also give its length at 140 minutes. Awards: Academy Award Nomination as Best Foreign Film, the Moscow International Film Festival (Soviet Filmmaker Alliance Special Prize), the Belgrade International Film Prize (1974), the Belgium International Film Prize (1975).

FUTARI DAKE NO ASA ("Morning for Two")
Producers, <u>Toshiro Mifune</u>, Toshikazu Nakada, and Norihiko Yamada; Director, Ken Matsumori; Screenplay, Hiroshi Nagano; Director of Photography, Takao Saito; Art Director, Hiroshi Ueda; Lighting, Kojiro Sato; Sound, Nobuyuki Tanaka; Music, Akihiko Sato

Cast: Yusuke Okada, Shiro Mifune, Ryoko Nakano, Osamu Terada, Kyoko Enami, Daisuke Kato

A Mifune Productions Co., Ltd./Toho Co., Ltd. Production. A Toho Co., Ltd. Release. Color. CinemaScope. 91 minutes. Released April 1, 1971.

U.S. version: Release, if any, is undetermined.

SOLEIL ROUGE ("Red Sun")
[RED SUN]
Executive Producer, Robert Dorfmann; Producer, Ted Richmond; Director, Terence Young; Screenplay, Denne Bart Petitclerc, William Roberts, and Lawrence Roman, based on a story by Laird Koenig; Director of Photography, Henri Alekan; Art Director, Henry Alarcom; Sound, William R. Sivel; Music, Maurice Jarre; Music Publisher, Eden Roc; Supervising Film Editor, Lou Combardo; Editor, Johnny Dwyre; Costume Design, Tony Preo; Special Effects, Karl Baumgartner; Executive Assistant for Toshiro Mifune, Masaki Asukai; Second Unit Cinematographer, Raymond Picon-Borel; Production Manager, Serge Lebeau and Julio Vallejo; Continuity, Joan Davis; First Assistant Directors, Christian Raoux and Ricardo Huerta; Makeup, Alberto de Rossi

    Cast: Charles Bronson (Link), Ursula Andress (Cristina), <u>Toshiro Mifune</u> (Kuroda), Alain Delon (Gauche), Capucine (Pepita), Bernabe Barta Barri (Paco), Guido Lollobrigida (Mace), Anthony Dawson (Hyatt), John Hamilton (Miguel), Georges Lycan (Sheriff Stone), Luc Merenda (Chato), Tetsu Nakamura [Satoshi Nakamura] (*Japanese Ambassador*), Jules Pena (Pappie), Mónica Randall (Maria), Hiroshi Tanaka (*second samurai*), Jo Nieto, John B. Vermont.

    A Films Corona (Paris) Production, in association with Oceania Films (Rome). A Robert Dorfmann Presentation. A French/Italian/Spanish co-production. A Filmes Lugomundo Release. Color (prints by Eastmancolor and Technicolor). VistaVision size (1.85:1). 112 minutes. Released September 1971.

    U.S. version: Released by National General Films. English soundtrack. 112 minutes. MPAA rating: PG. Released July 26, 1972.

NORA INU ("Stray Dog")
[STRAY DOG]
Producer, Shigerni Sugizaki; Director, Azuma Morisaki; Screenplay, Azuma Morisaki, based on a screenplay by <u>Akira Kurosawa</u> and Ryuzo Kikushima; Director of Photography, Kenichi Yoshikawa; Art Director, Noritoshi Sato; Music, Masaru Sato

    Cast: Tetsuya Watari (Detective Murakami), Shinsuke Ashida (Chief Detective Sato), Machiko Nakashima (Harumi Namai), Keiko Matsuzaka (*Sato's daughter*), Noriko Sengoku

    A Shochiku Co., Ltd. Production. A Shochiku Co., Ltd. Release. Color. Shochiku Grand-Scope. 104 minutes. Released September 29, 1973.

    U.S. version: Released by Shochiku Films of America, Inc. English subtitles. 104 minutes. No MPAA rating. Released March 1974.

    Notes: A remake of *Stray Dog* (1949), which also featured Sengoku. One source lists Kazuo Miyagawa as Director of Photography.

DERUSU UZARA ("Dersu Uzala")
[DERSU UZALA]
Producers, Nikolai Sizov and Yoichi Matsue; Director, <u>Akira Kurosawa</u>; Screenplay, Akira Kurosawa and Yuri Nagibin, based on the book *Dersu, okhotnik* (in English, *In the Jungles of Ussuri*) by Vladimir K. Arseniev; Associate Directors, Teruyo Nogami and Vladimir Vasiliev; Directors of Photography, Asakazu Nakai, Yuri Gantman, and Fyodor Dobronravov; Art Director, Yuri Raksha; Sound, O. Burkova; Music, Isaak Shvarts; Associate Editor, Liuba Fejginova; Production Manager, Karlen Korshikov; Interpreter, Lev Korshikov; Assistant to the Director, Takashi Koizumi

    Cast: Maxim Munzuk (Dersu Uzala), Yuri Solomin (Captain Vladimir K. Arseniev), Svetlana Danilichenko (*his wife*), Dima Kortishev (Vova Arsenieva), Schemeikl Chokmorov (Yan Rao), Vladimir Kremena (Turtwigin), A. Pyatkov, M. Bichkov, B. Khorulev

A Mosfilm/Atelier-41 Production. A Herald-Eiga Release. A Soviet/Japanese coproduction in Russian. Six-track magnetic stereophonic sound. Sovcolor. Sovscope 70. 141 minutes. Released August 2, 1975.

U.S. version: Released by New World Pictures, Inc., in association with Sovexport Film, Gerald J. Rappaport and Satra Films, and Special Projects Corporation. A Roger Corman Presentation. English subtitles. No MPAA rating. 141 minutes. Released December 20, 1977.

Notes: Filmed at Mosfilm Studios (Moscow) and on location in Siberia, R.S. F.S.R. First screened in the United States in 1975 to qualify for Academy Award consideration. An English-dubbed version was also made available. Reissued by Kino International Corp. Released in the Soviet Union as *Dersu Uzala* in 1976, running 181 minutes plus intermission (Part One: 90 minutes; Part Two: 91 minutes). Toho is often erroneously billed as co-producer. Awards: Academy Award, Best Foreign Language Film (1975); Gold Medal, Moscow Film Festival (1975); French Cinema Critics, Best Film and Best Actor [Maxim Munzuk] (1977); Southern California Motion Picture Council, Golden Halo (1978).

PAPER TIGER

Producer, Euan Lloyd; Director, Ken Annakin; Screenplay, Jack Davies; Director of Photography, John Cabrera; Production Designer, Herbert Smith; Sound, George Stephenson; Music, Roy Budd, performed by the National Philharmonic Orchestra of London; Song: "My Little Friend," Music by Roy Budd, Lyrics by Sammy Cahn, Performed by the Ray Conniff Singers; Art Directors, Peter Scharff and Tony Reading; Editor, Alan Pattillo; Dubbing Editor, Geo. Brown; Dubbing Mixer, Gerry Humphreys; Assistant to the Producer, Chris Chrisafis; Production Supervisor, David Anderson; Unit Production Managers, Hen Gee Shaw and Wolfgang von Schiber; Assistant Directors, Ian Goodard, John Copeland, and Tony Braun; Stunt Coordinator, Bob Simmons; Special Effects, Kit West and Erwin Lange; Ando's Voice Coach, Victor Kohn; Script Supervisor, Sally Ball; Makeup, Uschii Borsche and Klaus Winter; Property Master, Tommy Raeburn; Costume Designer, John Furniss

Cast: David Niven ("Major" Bradbury), Toshiro Mifune (*the ambassador*), Hardy Kruger (Muller), Ando (Koichi, *the ambassador's son*), Irene Tsu (Talah), Jeff Corey (Mr. King), Ivan Desny (*foreign minister*), Kurt Christian (Harok), Miiko Taka (Madame Kagoyama), Patricia Donahue (Mrs. King), Ronald Fraser (Sergeant Forster), Jeannine Siniscal (*foreign minister's girl*), Mika Kitagawa (*ambassador's secretary*), Eric Soh (Panthet), Sallah Joned (Sokono), Mustara Maarod (Marco), Gatz Shariff (*chief of police*), Takeo Okuyama (*chargé d'affaires*), David Khoo (Mok), Norkomalasari (Ruby), Rainer Penkert (*army colonel*), Timothy Moores (Staples), Tony Braun (*TV cameraman*), Paul Neuhaus (*Army sergeant*)

A Euan Lloyd/Shalako Enterprises, Inc. Production. A Joseph E. Levine Presentation. A MacLean & Co. Film. An Avco Embassy Release. A British Production. Eastman Color (prints by Technicolor). VistaVision size (Spherical Panavision). 99 minutes. MPAA rating: PG. Released (U.S.) November 5, 1975.

Notes: Released in some markets outside the United States in October 1975. Released in Panavision 70 in some markets. Released in Japan by Towa. Filmed in Kuala Lumpur. Mifune is dubbed for the American release.

MIDWAY

Producer, Walter Mirisch; Director, Jack Smight; Screenplay, Donald Sanford; Director of Photography, Harry Strading, Jr.; Art Director, Walter Tyler; Sound, Robert Martin and Leonard Peterson; Music, John Williams; Editors, Robert Swink and Frank J. Urioste; Set Decorator, John Dwyer; Unit Production Manager, William Gray; First Assistant Director, Jerome Siegel; Second Assistant Director, Richard Hashimoto; Script Supervisor, Bob Forrest; Technical Advisor, Vice Admiral Bernard M. Strean, U.S.N. (Ret.); Special Effects, Jack McMaster; Optical Effects and Titles, Universal Title; Sensurround Created by MCA; Special Thanks, United States Navy, and the officers and men of the U.S.S. *Lexington*

Cast: Charlton Heston (Captain Matt Garth), Henry Fonda (Admiral Chester W. Nimitz), James Coburn (Captain Vinton Maddox), Glenn Ford (Rear Admiral Raymond A. Spruance), Hal Holbrook (Commander Joseph Rochefort), Toshiro Mifune (Admiral Isoroku Yamamoto), Robert Mitchum (Admiral William F. Halsey), Cliff Robertson (Commander Carl Jessop), Robert Wagner (Lt. Commander Ernest L. Blake), Robert Webber (Rear Admiral Frank J. "Jack" Fletcher), Ed Nelson (Admiral Harry Pearson), James Shigeta (Vice Admiral Chuichi Nagumo), Christina Kokubo (Haruko Sakura), Monte Markham (Commander Max Leslie), Biff McGuire (Captain Miles Browning), Kevin Dobson (Ensign George Gay), Glenn Corbett (Lt. Commander John Waldron), Gregory Walcott (Captain Elliott Buckmaster), Edward Albert (Lt. Tom Garth, *Matt's son*), Noriyuki "Pat" Morita (Rear Admiral Ryunosuke Kusaka), Dale Ishimoto (Vice Admiral Moshiro Hosogaya), Dabney Coleman (Captain Murray Arnold), Erik Estrada (Ramos), Phillip R. Allen (Lt. Commander John S. "Jimmy" Thach), Conrad Yama (Commander Minoru Genda), Dennis Rucker (Ensign Mansen), Paul Frees (*voice characterization for Admiral Yamamoto*), John Fujioka, Ken Pennell, Clyde Kusatsu, Tom Selleck, Sab Shimono, Robert Ito, Yuki Shimada, Seth Sakai, Kurt Grayson, Alfie Wise, Beeson Carroll, John Bennett Perry, Steve Kanaly, Kip Niven, Michael Richardson, James Ingersol

A Walter M. Mirisch Production. A Mirisch Corporation Presentation. A Universal Pictures Release. Sensurround. Eastman Color (prints by Technicolor). Panavision. 132 minutes. MPAA rating: PG. Released 1975.

Notes: Jack Smight replaced John Guillermin as director. Includes stock footage from *Storm Over the Pacific* (q.v.), *Tora! Tora! Tora!* (q.v.), and *Thirty Seconds over Tokyo* (1944). Susan Sullivan appears with Heston and Kokubo in the expanded television version. Miiko Taka reportedly also appears in the expanded version.

NINGEN NO SHOMEI ("Proof of the Man")
[PROOF OF THE MAN]
Executive Producer, Haruki Kadokawa; Producers, Simon Tse and Toru Yoshida; Associate Producer, Milton Moshlak; Director, Junya Sato; Screenplay, Zenzo Matsuyama, based on the novel by Seiichi Morimura, published by Kadokawa Publishing; Director of Photography, Shinsaku Himeda; Art Director, Shuichiro Nakamura; Lighting, Hideo Kumagaya; Sound, Senichi Benitani; Music, Yuji Ono; Theme song composed by Yaju Nishijo and performed by Jo Yamanaka; Editor, Jun Nabeshima; Costume Design, Junko Kasuga; Still Photographer, Mitsuo Kato; Unit Production Manager, Eiji Takeda. *New York Crew*: Director, Simon Tse; Director of Photography, So Neglin; Assistant Director, Alex Hopsis; Unit Production Manager, Leland Haas; Art Director, Dave Moran; Sound, Mike Tromer.

Cast: Mariko Okada, Yusaku Matsuda, George Kennedy, Toshiro Mifune, Koji Tsuruta, Hajime Hana, Broderick Crawford, Jo Yamanaka, Koichi Iwaki, Keiko Takeshita, Ryoko Sakagushi, Junko Takazawa, Shelly [no other name given], Janet Hata, Bunjaku Han, Isamu Natsuyagi, Koji Wada, Hideo Murata, Mizuho Suzuki, Toru Negishi, Takeo Chii, Shuji Otaki, Robert Aljohns, Gajiro Saito, E. H. Eric, Hiromitsu Suzuki, Theresa Merritt, Kei Taguchi, Tadahiko Kudano, Hiroshi Kondo, Koji Kawamura, Tetsuya Yamaoka, Koji Kawaii, Shigeru Tsuyuki, Ayako Mikami, Hikari Yamanaka, Akito Ishii, Seiichi Morimura, Rick Jason, Yuji Konno, Junko Tamura, Mineko Nishikawa, Hiroshi Ogawa, Kinji Fukasaku, Hiroyuki Nagato, Tanie Kitabayashi, Junzaburo Ban, Michiko Hoshi

A Haruki Kadokawa Films, Inc. Production, in association with ProSer Co. (PSI). A Toei

Co., Ltd. Release. A Japanese/U.S. co-production in English and Japanese. Color (processed by Toyo Developing). VistaVision size (spherical Panavision). 132 minutes. Released 1977.

U.S. version: Release, if any, is undetermined.

Notes: Filmed on location in New York City, Tokyo, and at Nikkatsu Studios.

NIHON NO DON—YABOHEN ("Japanese Godfather—Ambition")
[THE GODFATHER: AMBITION]
Executive Producer, Shigeru Okada; Producers, Goro Hikabe and Mitsuru Taoka; Director, Sadao Nakajima; Screenplay, Koji Takada, based on a story by Koichi Iguchi; Director of Photography, Toshio Masuda; Art Director, Yoshikazu Sano; Lighting, Etsuaki Masuda: Sound, Shigeji Nakayama; Music, Toshiro Kuro and Harumi Ibe, performed by the Tokyo Orchestra; Editor, Koji Horiike; Assistant Directors, Toshiyuki Fujiwara and Kazushige Saito; Script Supervisor, Sho Ishida; Equipment, Mikito Miura; Costume Design, Fumio Nishida; Backgrounds, Saburo Nishimura; Still Photographer, Kenji Nakayama; Makeup, Toshio Tanaka; Hair Stylist, Taeko Nakazawa

Cast: Shin Saburi, Hiroki Matsukata, Kyoko Kishida, Etsushi Takahashi, Midori Kanazawa, Akira Nishikino, Masato Hoshi, Saiyoko Nimiya, Maki Orihara, Akira Orita, Masaru Shiga, Maki Tachibana, Kyoko Nami, Hiroko Okamoto, Emma Hitomi, Maya Hiromi, Nobiko Sawa, Takashi Noguchi, Yasuhiro Suzuki, Ryo Nishida, Masataka Iwao, Daisuke Iwaji, Shoji Irimura, Kinji Nakamura, Joshua Rome, Shuichiro Moriyama, Yusef Toruko, Torahiko Hamada, Yoshifumi Tajima, Kunieyasu Atsumi, Asao Uchida, Emiko Higashi, Akitomo Nogami, Tomio Fujimura, Sengoro Shigeyama, Kanjuro Arashi, Kei Sato, Fumio Watanabe, Hosei Komatsu, Asao Koike, Takuya Fujioka, Nobuo Kaneko, Mikio Naruse, Eitaro Ozawa, Bunta Sugawa • Toshiro Mifune

A Toei Co., Ltd. Production. A Toei Co., Ltd. Release. Color. Toeiscope. 140 minutes. Released 1977.

U.S. version: Release, if any, is undetermined.

Notes: A sequel to Conflicts Between Yakuza—The Godfather (Yakuza senso—Nihon no don, 1977), which did not feature Mifune. Followed by The Godfather—Resolution (Nihon no don—kanketsuhen, 1978).

YAGYU ICHIZOKU NO INBO ("Intrigue of the Yagyu Clan")
[THE SHOGUN'S SAMURAI]
Director, Kinji Fukasaku; Screenplay, Tatsuo Nogami, Hiro Matsuda, and Kinji Fukasaku; Director of Photography, Toru Nakajima; Art Director, Norimichi Igawa; Music, Toshiaki Tsushima

Cast: Shinichi "Sonny" Chiba, Kinnosuke Yorozuya, Tetsuro Tamba, Hiroaki Matsukata, Teruhiko Saigo, Sue Shiomi, Isuzu Yamada, Etsushi Takahashi, Toshiro Mifune, Yoshio Harada, Sen Yano

A Toei Co., Ltd. Production. A Toei Co., Ltd. Release. Color. 130 minutes. Released 1978.

U.S. version: Released by Toei Co., Ltd. English subtitles. 130 minutes. No MPAA rating. Released December 7, 1984.

INUBUE ("Dog Flute")
[SHAG]
Executive Producer, Toshiro Mifune; Producers, Joichi Tanaka and Mitusuru Ito; Director, Sadao Nakajima; Screenplay, Ryuzo Kikushima and Takero Kaneko, based on an original story by Yoshiyuki Nishimura (published by Tokuma Shoten); Director of Photography, Takao Saito; Art Director, Hiroshi Ueda; Lighting, Naoyuki Doi; Sound, Shin Miyanaga; Music, Asei

Kobayashi; Editor, Yoshihiro Araki; Assistant Director, Yoshito Nakajima; In Charge of Production, Toru Moriya; Still Photographer, Minori Ishizuki

Cast: Bunta Sugawara (Shiro Akitsu), Wakako Sakai (Junko Akitsu), Mika Matsushita (Yoshiko Akitsu), Kinya Kitaoji (Detective Konishi), Keiko Takeshita (Noriko Norime), <u>Toshiro Mifune</u> (*captain*), Raita Ryu (Detective Hashikawa), Mizuho Suzuki (Controller Ohara), Go Wakabayashi (Detective Sato), Kazuo Kitamura (*section manager of Ishii Design*), Shin Kishida (Masao Ikeda), Keiko Matsu (Yoko Yano), Hideharu Otaki (Section Manager Usami), Takewaki Murano (Dr. Ono), Yoko Akino (*nurse*), Jiro Sakagami (*taxi driver*), Asao Koike (*police inspector*), Takeshi Kato (Instructor Hamada), Hiroshi Katsuno (Mikio *in cargo ship*), Junzaburo Ban (*old man*), Junkichi Orimoto (*Head of Matsumoto*), Mitsuo Hamada (*plainclothes officer*), Rina Takase (*woman officer*), So Yamamura (*head of Maritime Safety Agency*), Masaya Takahashi (*deputy manager*), Kumiyasu Atsumi (Watanabe), Shigeru Kamiyama (Maekawa), Tamio Kawachi (*chief navigator*), Akira Orita (correspondent Nogami), Yoshio Harada (Kanji Mitsueda), Akio Tanaka (Odawara), Kyoko Kishida (*narrator*)

A Mifune Productions Co., Ltd. Production. A Toho Co., Ltd. Release. Color. Standard size. 139 minutes. Released April 1, 1978.

U.S. version: Released by Toho International Co., Ltd. English subtitles. 139 minutes. No MPAA rating. Released January 12, 1979.

OGINSAMA ("Lady Ogin")
[LOVE AND FAITH]
Producers, Tsuneyasu Matsumoto, Kyoko Oshima and Muneo Shimojo; Director, Kei Kumai; Screenplay, Yoshitaka Yoda, based on an original story by Toko Kon; Director of Photography, Kozo Okazaki; Art Director, Takeo Kimura; Music, Akira Ifukube; Editor, Tatsuji Nakashizu; Costumes, Mitsukoshi Department Store; Tea Ceremony Supervisor, Urasenke [no other name given]

Cast: Ryoko Nakano (Ogin), Kichiemon Nakamura (Ukon Takayama), Takashi Shimura (Rikyu Sen), <u>Toshiro Mifune</u> (Taiko Hideyoshi), Atsuo Nakamura (Soji Yamagami), Daijiro Harada (Mozuya), Eiji Okada (Ankokuji), Ko Nishimura (Sojin Kamiya)

A Takarazuka Motion Picture Co., Ltd. Production. A Toho Co., Ltd. Release. Color. Standard size. 153 minutes. Released June 3, 1978 (roadshow version), and June 24, 1978 (general release).

U.S. version: Released by Toho International Co., Ltd. English subtitles. Alternate titles: *Love and Faith of Ogin, Ogin Her Love and Faith, Love and Faith: Lady Ogin.* 150 minutes. No MPAA rating. Released March 1979. Later reissued at 115 minutes.

Notes: May have been released in stereophonic sound for its roadshow release.

NIHON NO DON   KANKETSUHEN ("Japanese Don—Conclusion")
[THE GODFATHER: RESOLUTION]
Director, Sadao Nakajima; Screenplay, Koji Takada, based on a story by Koichi Iboshi; Director of Photography, Toshio Masuda; Music, Toshiro Mayazumi

Cast: Toshinobu Sawaki, <u>Toshiro Mifune</u>, Chiezo Kataoka, Bunta Sugawara, Naoto Otani, Ko Nishimura, Shin Saburi

A Toei-Kyoto Co., Ltd. Production. A Toei Co., Ltd. Release. Color. Wide screen. 131 minutes. Released 1978.

U.S. version: Release, if any, is undetermined.

AKO-JO DANZETSU ("Last of the Ako Clan")
[THE FALL OF AKO CASTLE]
Director, Kinji Fukasaku; Screenplay, Koji Takada, based on his story; Directors of Photography, Yoshio Miyajima and Hanjiro Nakazawa; Music, Toshiaki Tsushima
     Cast: Kinnosuke Yorozuya, Shinichi "Sonny" Chiba, Tsunehiko Watase, Masaomi Kondo, Toshiro Mifune, Kyoko Enami, Kasho Nakamura, Shinsuke Mikimoto
     A Toei-Kyoto Co., Ltd. Production. A Toei Co., Ltd. Release. Color. Toeiscope. 159 minutes. Released 1978.
     U.S. version: Release, if any, is undetermined.

TONO EIJIRO NO MITO KOMON ("Eijiro Tono's 'Mito Komon' ")
[LORD INCOGNITO]
Producers, Shunichi Nishimura, Go Toshin, Naoyuki Sugimura, and Seiichi Mori; Director, Tetsuya Yamauchi; Screenplay, Akiko Hamura, based on her story; Director of Photography, Toshio Masuda; Music, Chuji Kinoshita
     Cast: Eijiro Tono, Kotaro Satomi, Shinya Owada, Ichiro Nakatani, Gentaro Takahashi, Toru Abe, Muga Takewaki, Toshiro Mifune
     A Toei-Kyoto Co., Ltd. Production. A Toei Co., Ltd. Release. Color. Wide Screen. 88 minutes. Released 1978.
     U.S. version: Release, if any, is undetermined.

WINTER KILLS
Executive Producers, Leonard J. Goldberg and Robert Sterling; Producer, Fred Caruso; Director, William Richert; Screenplay, William Richert, based on the novel by Richard Condon; Director of Photography, Vilmos Zsigmond; Art Director, Robert Boyle; Sound, Chris Newman; Music, Maurice Jarre; Casting, Robert de Mora; Editor, David Bretherton; Associate Producer, John Starke; Unit Production Managers, Bill Venegas and Ira Loonstein; First Assistant Director, Pete Scoppa; Camera Operator and Additional Photography, John Bailey; Art Director, Norman Newberry; Set Decorator, Arthur Seph Parker; Construction Coordinator, Bill Maldonado; Special Effects, Augie Lohman; Transportation Captain, Mickey McAteer; Casting, Ross Brown and Hank McCann; Gaffer, Rick Martin; Key Grip, Bob Moore; Accounting, Zeiderman, Oberman & Associates; Auditor, Selma Brown; Production Illustrators, Harold Michelson and Joseph Hurley; Second Unit Director, Jim Arnet; Production Secretary, Shari Leibowitz; Makeup, Del Acevedo; Hair Stylist, Kathy Blondell; Script Supervisor, Hannah G. Scheel; Rerecording, Buzz Knudson, Robert Glass and Bud Grenzback; Sound Editing, Gomillion Sound, Inc.; Sound Effects Editor, Norvall Crutcher; Music Editor, Jeff Carson, La Da Productions; Location Manager, Mark Hurwitz; Property Master, Sam Gordon; Second Assistant Director, William P. Scott; Assistant Director, Chris Saldo; Assistant to William Richert, Cathy Nonas; First Assistant Cameraman, Mike Genne; Second Assistant Cameraman, Johnny Walker; Assistant Editors, José Antonio Torres and Suzanne Fenn; Assistant Property Master, Ted Mossman; Costumers, Donald Vargas, Mina Mittelman Short, and Vicki Sanchez; Wardrobe Assistant, Betty De Stefano; Construction Foreman, Clay Johnson; Painter Foreman, Ray Villalobos; Propmaker Foreman, Bruce Wineinger; Best Boy, Arthur J. Boyle; Dolly Grip, Tim Ryan; Second Best Boy, Dan Marzolo; Electrical, Fred R. Muncey and John C. Kirk; Still Photographer, Jack Shannon; Boom Operator, Morley Harris; Extra Casting, Sally Perle & Associates; Craft Services, Ron Weber; Transportation Captain, Gene Clinsesmith; Title Design, Don Record; Title Design Photography, Wilson Hong; Publicity, Blowitz & Canton, Robert Rodney

Cast: Jeff Bridges (Nick Kegan), John Huston (Pa Kegan), Anthony Perkins (John Ceruti), Eli Wallach (Joe Diamond), Sterling Hayden (Z. K. Diamond), Dorothy Malone (Emma Kegan, *Nick's mother*), Tomas Milian (Frank Mayo), Belinda Bauer (Yvette Malone), Ralph Meeker (Gameboy Baker), <u>Toshiro Mifune</u> (Keith), Richard Boone (Keifitz). With David Spielberg (Miles Garner), Brad Dexter (Captain Heller One), Michael Thoma (Ray Doty), Ed Madsen (Captain Heller Two), Irving Selbst (Irving Mentor), Chris Soldo (Jeffreys), Robert Courleigh (*First Mate of T.K.*), Peter Brandon (*doctor*), Joe Spinell (Arthur Fletcher), Ira Rosenstein (*orderly on T.K.*), Kyle Morris (John Kullers), Phil Lito (*police driver*), Barbara Richert (*woman cyclist*), Jake Hughes (*child on cycle*), Peter Bough, Eloise Hardt (*secretaries*), Gladys Hill (Rosemary), Kim O'Brien and Candice Rialson (*blond girls*), Bill P. Wilson (*admiral*), Lloyd Catlett (Z. K. Dawson guard), Michael Bond (*flight engineer*), Helene Fagen (*stewardess*), Peter Kilman (*pilot*), Gianni Russo (*co-pilot*), Peter Koshel (*cop at Casino Latino*), Lissette (*Cuban singer*), Robert Boyle (*desk clerk*), Sidney Lanier (Raymond, *the butler*), Helen Curry (*black maid*), Derrick Lynn-Thomas (*maître d'*), Jesse Veliz (*Cuban man in Havana*), Robert Wolcott (*shoeshine boy*), Robert Moresco (*intern*), Agneta Eckemyr, Tisa Farrow (*nurses*), Billie Allen (*receptionist*), Joe Ragno (*doorman*), Loutz Gage (*butler*), Camilla Sparv, Andrea Claudio, Erin Gray, Susan Walden, Rebecca Grimes, Jennifer Keith, and Amanda Jones (*beautiful women*), Berry Berenson (*morgue attendant*), Tim Culbertson (*security guard*), Regis Mull (*cop with Keifitz*), Elizabeth Taylor (Lola)

A Leonard J. Goldberg–Robert Sterling Production (Winter Gold Productions, Ltd.), in association with Daniel H. Blatt. A Frank Aries Presentation. An Avco Embassy Pictures Release. Color. Panavision. 97 minutes. MPAA rating: R. Released 1979.

Notes: Never released in Japan. Elizabeth Taylor appears unbilled. Reissued in 1983 by Invisible Studio, with alternate main title music, some minor reediting, and a different ending.

KINDAICHI KOSUKE NO BOKEN ("The Adventures of Kosuke Kindaichi")
[THE ADVENTURES OF KOSUKE KINDAICHI]
Producer, Haruki Kadokawa; Director, Nobuhiko Obayashi; Screenplay, Koichi Saito and Kensho Nakano, based on a story by Seishi Yokomizu; Director of Photography, Daisuku Kimura; Music, Katsumi Kobayashi

Cast: Iko Furuya, Kunie Tanaka, Noboru Nakatani, Miyuki Kumagaiya, Chionosuke Azuma, Hideko Yoshida, Rinichi Yamamoto, <u>Toshiro Mifune</u>

A Haruki Kadokawa Office Production. A Toei Co., Ltd. Release. Color. Wide screen. 113 minutes. Released 1979.

U.S. version: Release, if any, is undetermined.

OMITSU DOSHIN O EDO SOSAMO ("Secret Detective Investigation—Net in Big Edo")
Producer, Tokumaru Kiniho, Takeshi Motomura, Kiyosumi Ogawa, and Saburo Naito; Associate Producer, <u>Toshiro Mifune</u>; Director, Akinori Matsuo; Screenplay, Hide Ogawa and Tetsu Koto; Director of Photography, Kazuo Yamada; Art Director, Taizo Kawashima; Lighting, Senyoshi Shimada; Sound, Toshimi Katagiri; Music, Hiroki Tamaki

Cast: Hiroki Matsukata, Tetsuro Sagawa, Sanae Tsuchida, Rino Takase, Takeya Nakamura, Keiko Orihara, <u>Toshiro Mifune</u>

A Channel Tokyo 12/Mifune Productions Co., Ltd. Production. A Toho Co., Ltd. Release. Color. Standard size. 85 minutes. Released December 1, 1979.

U.S. version: Release, if any, is undetermined.

Notes: A Channel Tokyo 12 15th Anniversary Production. Possibly a theatrical release of an episodic teleseries.

1941

Executive Producer, John Milius; Producer, Buzz Feitshans; Director, Steven Spielberg; Screenplay, Robert Zemeckis and Bob Gale, based on a story by Robert Zemeckis, Bob Gale, and John Milius; Director of Photography, William A. Fraker; Art Director, Dean Edward Mitzner; Music, John Williams; Editor, Michael Kahn; Associate Producers, Michael Kahn and Janet Healy; Executive in Charge of Production, John Wilson; Unit Production Managers, Chuck Myers and Herb Willis; First Assistant Directors, Jerry Ziesmer and Steve Perry; Second Assistant Director, Chris Soldo; Special Effects Supervisor, A. D. Flowers; Miniature Supervisor, Gregory Jein; Costumes, Deborah Nadoolman; Supervising Art Director, William F. O'Brien; Matte Paintings, Matthew Yuricich; Assistant Film Editor, Daniel Todd Cahn; Visual Effects Supervisor, Larry Robinson; Optical Consultant, L. B. Abbott; Blue Screen Consultant, Frank Van Der Veer; Miniature Lighting, Robin Leyden; Casting, George Jensen; Set Decorator, John Austin; Set Design, Henry Alberti, Dan Gluck, Greg Pickrell, Carlton Reynolds, Virginia L. Randolph, William Skinner; Mixer, Gene S. Cantamessa; Music Editor, Ken Wannberg; Music Scoring Mixer, Marion Klein; Orchestrations, Herbert Spencer; Supervising Sound Effects Editor, Fred J. Brown; Makeup Supervisor, Bob Westmoreland; Hairstyles, Susan Germaine; Script Supervisor, Marie Kenney; Stunt Coordinator, Terry Leonard; Construction Coordinator, Mickey Woods; Additional Director of Photography, Frank Stanley; Camera Operator, Dick Colean; Choreography, Paul De Rolf; Property Master, Sammy Gordon; Songs: "Down by the Ohio" and "Daddy," performed by the Andrews Sisters; Optical Effects, Van Der Veer Photo Effects; Sound, Todd-AO; Titles, Denis Hofman-Freeze Frame

Cast: Dan Aykroyd (Sergeant Tree), Ned Beatty (Ward Douglas), John Belushi (Wild Bill Kelso), Lorraine Gary (Joan Douglas), Murray Hamilton (Claude), Christopher Lee (Von Kleinschmidt), Tim Matheson (Birkhead), Toshiro Mifune (Commander Mitamura), Warren Oates (Maddox), Robert Stack (General Stilwell), Treat Williams (Sitarski), Nancy Allen (Donna), Lucille Bensen (Gas Mama), Jordan Brian (Macey), John Candy (Foley), Elisha Cook, Jr. (*the patron*), Eddie Deezen (Herbie), Bobby DiCicco (Wally), Dianne Kay (Betty), Perry Lang (Dennis), Patti LuPone (Lydia Hedberg), Penny Marshall (Miss Fitzroy), J. Patrick McNamara (DuBois), Frank McRae (Ogden Johnson Jones), Steve Mond (Gus), Slim Pickens (Hollis Wood), Wendie Jo Sperber (Maxine), Lionel Stander (Angelo Scioli), Dub Taylor (Mr. Malcomb), Ignatius Wolfington (Meyer Mishkin), Christian Zika (Stevie), Joseph P. Flaherty (*USO m.c.*), David Lander (Joe), Michael McKean (Willy), Susan Backlinie (*Polar Bear Club swimmer*), E. Hampton Beagle (*phone man*), Deborah Benson, Audrey Landers, Kerry Sherman, Maureen Teefy, Carol Ann Williams, Jenny Williams (*USO girls*), Don Calfa (*telephone operator*), Dave Cameron, John R. McKee, Dan McNally, Rita Taggart (*reporters*), Vito Carenzo (*Vito of the Shore Patrol*), Mark Carlton, Paul Cloud, Jack Thibeau, Galen Thompson (*Stilwell aides*), Gary Cervantes (*zoot suiter*), Luis Contreras (*zoot suiter*), Carol Culver, Marjorie Gaines, and Trish Garland (Anderson sisters), Lucinda Dooling (Lucinda), Gray Frederickson (Lieutenant Bressler), Brian Frishman (*USO goon*), Sam Fuller (*interceptor commander*), Dian and Denise Gallup (*twins*), Barbara Gannen, Diane Hill (*interceptor assistants*), Brad Gorman, Frank Verroca, John Volstad (*USO nerds*), Jerry Hardin (*map man*), Bob Houston (*Maddox's soldier*), John Landis (Mizerany), Ronnie McMillan (Winowski), Richard Miller (Officer Miller), Akio Mitamura (Ashimoto), Antoinette Molinari (Mrs. Scioli), Walter Olkewicz (Hinshaw), Mickey Rourke (Reese), Whitney Rydbeck (Daffy), Donovan Scott (*kid sailor*), Hiroshi Shimizu (Ito), Geno Silva (Martinez), Andy Tennant (Babyface), Elmer the Dummy (Elmer)

An A-Team Production for Universal Pictures and Columbia Pictures. A Universal Pictures Release. Stereophonic sound. Color (prints by Technicolor and Metrocolor). Panavision (Panavision 70 for some engagements). 118 minutes. MPAA rating: PG. Released December 19, 1979.

Notes: Filmed at The Burbank Studios and Metro-Goldwyn-Mayer Studios. Includes footage from *Dumbo* (RKO, 1941). Expanded to 146 minutes for release on laserdisc and DVD.

INCHON!

Producer, Mitsuharu Ishii; Director, Terence Young; Special Advisor, Sun Myung Moon; Screenplay, Robin Moore and Laird Koenig, based on a story by Robin Moore and Paul Savage; Director of Photography, Bruce Surtees; Art Directors, Shigekazu Ikuno and Pierluigi Basile; Sound, David Hildyard and Yoji Hiyoshi; Music, Jerry Goldsmith; Associate Director, Sung Ku Lee; Associate Producer, Matsusaburo Sakaguchi; Production Supervisor, Guy Luongo; Supervising Editor, Gene Milford; Editorial Consultant, Bill Cox; Editors, John W. Holmes, Peter Taylor, Dallas Sunday Puett, Michael J. Sheridan; Unit Production Manager, Brad H. Aronson; First Assistant Director, Gianni Cozzo; Supervising Sound Editor, Gordon Daniel; Sound Editors, Greg Dillon, James Fritch, Ed Sandlin, Andrew Herbert, Martin Tomson; Supervising Music Editor, Len Engel; Orchestrations, Arthur Morton; Location Production Managers, Roberto Cocco, Young Sil Park, Minoru Kurita; Location Managers, Frank Ernst, Se Hyung Lee; Production Auditor, Robert F. Kocourek; Production Coordinator, Kiyotaka Ugawa; Associate Production Manager, Toni Ermini; Assistants to the Producer, Robert M. Standard, Kyung Do Park, Kayo Inoue, Takehiro Ono, Kazuhiro Horimoto, Hiroko Otsuka; Casting Director, Jack Baur; Assistant Film Editors, Franca Silvi, George Martin; Production Assistants, Sean Ferrer, Miko Brando, Assistants to the Director, Eva Chun, Katinka Revedin; Script Supervisors, Yvonne Axworthy, Francesca Roberti (Second Unit); Dialogue Coach, Juliet Nissen; Laurence Olivier's Dialogue Coach, Robert Easton; Military Advisor, General Samuel Jaskilka, USMC (Ret.); U.S. Eighth Army Korea Liaison Officers, Lt. Commander Freeman Neish (Ret.), Major Arthur Jungwirth; ROK Armed Forces Liaison Officer, Major Sang Don Park; Camera Operators, Rick Neff, Cesare Allione, Otello Spila, Yonero Murata, Duk Chin Kim; Still Photographers, Akira Nakayama and Sergio Strizzi; Unit Publicist, Lou Dyer; Set Decorators, Kyoji Sasaki, Francesco Chianese, Ho Kil Kim; Property Master, Graham Summer. Special Effects Unit: Supervisors, Fred Cramer, Kenneth Pepiot; Production Manager, Dennis Hall; Design, Geoff Drake; Cameramen, Alex Thompson, Robert Cuff, Bunzo Hyodo; Gaffers, Charles Holmes, Kazuo Shimomura, Jung Nam Cha; Key Grip, Charles Saldana; Stunt Coordinators, Ed Stacey, Remo De Angelis; Arms and Weapons Specialist, Carl G. Schmidt; Action Vehicles Supervisor, Woodrow McLain; Extras Coordinators, Major Greg Vito Anders (U.S.) and Do Soon Im (Korea); Ms. Bisset's Costumes, Donfeld; Military Wardrobe Costumer, Jules Melillo; Civilian Wardrobe Costumer, Gloria Musetta; Korean Wardrobe Costumer, Haei Yoon Lee; Wardrobe Accessories, Jae Shik Pak; Wardrobe Assistants, Susan Moore, Maya Ryan; Makeup, Gianni Morosi, Nilo Jacoponi; Laurence Olivier's makeup, Peter Robb King; Ms. Bisset's makeup, Chuck Craft; Hairdresser, Giancarlo De Leonardis; Ms. Bisset's hair styles, Darby Hoppin; Postproduction, 20th Century-Fox Film Corp. and Gomillion Sound, Inc.; Supervising Mixers, Theodore Soderberg and Don MacDougall; Mixers, Paul Wells, Douglas Williams, David Dockendorf, John Mackl; Main Title Design, Michael Salisbury; Main Titles, Kaleidoscope Films, Ltd., and Cinema Research Corp.; Main Title Cinematography, William Fraker

Cast: Laurence Olivier (General Douglas MacArthur), Jacqueline Bisset (Barbara Hallsworth), Ben Gazzara (Major Frank Hallsworth), Toshiro Mifune (Saito-san), Richard Roundtree (Sergeant August Henderson), Nam Goon Won (Park), Dorothy James (Jean MacArthur), Lydia Lei (Mila), John Pochna (Lieutenant Alexander Haig), Gabriele Ferzetti (*Turkish brigadier*), Karen Kahn (Lim), James Callahan (General Almond), Anthony Dawson (General Collins), Peter Burton (Admiral Sherman), William Du Pree (*Turkish sergeant*), Grace Chan (Ab Cheu), Nak Hoon Lee (Jimmy), Kwang Nam Yang (President Rhee), Il Woong Lee

(*North Korean commissar*), Yung Hoo Lee (*Barbara's driver*), Mickey Knox (Admiral Doyle), Richard McNamara, Gordon Mitchell (*GHQ officers*), Robert Spafford (Admiral Lawson), Franco Ressel (*officer aboard* Mt. McKinley), Ji Sook Choe (*smallest*), Joon Sook Choe (*small*), Hye Yun Choo (*middle*), Hyun Joo Kwak (*big*), Jung Sook Hong (*biggest*), Ed Flanders (*voice characterization of President Harry S. Truman*), the Little Angels (*orphans*), Phil Chong (*stuntman*)

A One Way Productions, Inc. Production, in association with the Unification Church. An MGM/UA Release. Dolby Stereo. Color (prints by Deluxe and Technicolor). VistaVision size (spherical Panavision). 105 minutes. MPAA rating: PG. Released September 17, 1982.

Notes: A U.S./Korean co-production in English. Premiered in Washington, D.C., in May 1981 at 140 minutes. Scenes featuring David Janssen and Rex Reed were cut after the premiere. Never released in Japan. Young replaced Andrew V. McLaglen as director.

THE BUSHIDO BLADE
Executive Producer, Jules Bass; Producer, Arthur Rankin, Jr.; Director, Tsugunobu "Tom" Kotani; Screenplay, William Overgard; Director of Photography, Shoji Ueda; Art Director, Toyokazu Ohashi; Lighting, Kazuo Shimomura; Sound, Yuji Hiyoshi; Music, Maury Laws, arranged and conducted by Kenjiro Hirose; Editor, Yoshitami Kuroiwa; Associate Producers, Benni Korzen and Masaki Iizuka; Postproduction Executive, Robert O. Cardona; Editorial Consultant, Anne V. Coates; Production Manager, Kinshiro Okubo; First Assistant Director, Koichi Nakajima; Sound Editor, Ian Crafford; Sound Rerecording, Paul Carr; Swordplay Choreography, Ryu Kuze; Postproduction Secretary, Barbara Hilse; U.S. Navy Coordinator, Commander William North, USN

Cast (in alphabetical order): Richard Boone (Commander Matthew Calbraith Perry), Shinichi "Sonny" Chiba (Prince Ido), Frank Converse (Captain Lawrence Hawk), Laura Gemser (Tomoe), James Earl Jones (*imprisoned harpooner*), Mako (Emjiro), Timothy Murphy (Midshipman Robin Burr), Michael Starr (Bos'n Gave Johnson), Tetsuro Tamba (Lord Yamato), Toshiro Mifune (Shogun's Commander Hayashi), William Ross (*aide to Commander Perry*), Iwae Arai (*guide*), Mayumi Asano (Yuki), Kin Omai (Sumo)

A Trident Films, Ltd. Production, in association with Rankin/Bass Productions. An Aquarius Releasing Corp. Release. A British/U.S. Production. Color. VistaVision size (spherical Panavision). 104 minutes. MPAA rating: R. Released 1981 (see below).

Notes: Filmed in 1979 at Toho Studios (Tokyo) and completed in London, England. First exhibited in the United States on cable television as *The Bushido Blade*, running 92 minutes, then released theatrically in a longer version retitled *The Bloody Bushido Blade*. Apparently never released in Japan, as it does not appear in any of Mifune's filmographies. Richard Boone's last feature. Chiba is billed as "Sonny Chiba."

KAGEMUSHA ("The Shadow Warrior")
[KAGEMUSHA: THE SHADOW WARRIOR]
Producers, Akira Kurosawa and Tomoyuki Tanaka; Director, Akira Kurosawa; Directorial Adviser, Ishiro Honda; Assistant Producer and Script Supervisor, Teruyo Nogami; Production Advisers, Shinobu Hashimoto and Takao Saito; Screenplay, Akira Kurosawa and Masato Ide; Directors of Photography, Takao Saito and Shoji Ueda; Photography Consultants, Kazuo Miyagawa and Asakazu Nakai; Art Director, Yoshiro Muraki; Lighting, Takeji Sano; Sound, Fumio Yanoguchi; Music, Shinichiro Ikebe, conducted by Kotaro Saito and performed by the New Japan Philharmonic Orchestra, with the cooperation of Tokyo Concerts; Assistant Cameraman, Tamio Matsuo; Assistant Art Director, Aki Saburagi; Assistant Lighting, Satoshi Kurikihara; Assistant Sound Recording, Mamoru Yamada (Toho Recording Centre); Chief Assistant Director,

Fumiryo Okada; Assistant Directors, Hideyuki Inoue, Takao Okawara, Takashi Koizumi; Assistant Editor, Yoshihiro Iwatani; Negative Cutter, Tome Minami; Sound Effects, Ichiro Minami (Toho Sound Effects Group); Still Photographer, Naomi Hashiyama; Unit Production Managers, Toshiaki Hashimoto and Akira Fujita; Scene Shifter, Masa Furugawara; Property Master, Hatsumi Yamamoto; Costumes, Seiichiro Hagakusawa (Kyoto Costume); Hair Stylists, Yoshiko Matsumoto, Junjiro Yamada, and Shigeo Tamura; Transportation, Isamu Miwano; Special and Optical Effects, Toho Special Effects Group; Acting Office, Hiroaki Honda; Instructors (samurai etiquette), Ryu Kuze; (horseback riding), Tamihei Shirai and Toshi Hasegawa

 Cast: Tatsuya Nakadai (Shingen Takeda *and his double, the kagemusha*), Tsutomu Yamazaki (Nobukado Takeda, *Shingen's brother*), Kenichi Hagiwara (Katsuyori Takeda, *Shingen's son*), Jinpachi Nezu (Sohachiro Tsuchiya, *Shingen's bodyguard*), Shuji Otaki (Masakage Yamagata, *Takeda Clan general, fire battalion leader*), Daisuke Ryu (Nobunaga Oda, *Shingen's enemy*), Masayuki Yui (Ieyasu Tokugawa, *Shingen's enemy*), Mitsuko Baisho (Oyunokata, *Shingen's concubine*), Kaori Momoi (Otsuyanokata, *Shingen's concubine*), Hideo Murata (Nobuharu Baba), Takayuki Shiho (Masatoyo Naito), Koji Shimizu (Katsusuke Atobe), Noboru Shimizu (Masatane Hara), Sen Yamamoto (Nobushige Oyamada), Shuhei Sugimori (Masanobu Kosaka), Kota Yui (Takemaru Takeda, *Shingen's grandson*), Yasuhito Yamanaka (Ranmaru Mori), Kumeko Otowa (*Takemaru's nurse*), Tetsuo Yamashita (Nagahide Tanba), Takashi Ebata (*monk*), Hiroshi Shimada (Jingoro Hara), Toshiaki Tanabe (Kugutsushi), Yoshimitsu Yamaguchi (*salt vendor*), Hidekazu Kanetsubo (Okura Amari), Yugo Miyazaki (Matahachi Tomono), Norio Matsui (Tadaji Sakai), Yasushi Doshinda (Susei Ishikawa), Nori Sone (Heihachiro Honda), Akihiko Sugisaki (*Noda foot soldier*), Francesco Selk, Alexisander Keilus (*missionaries*), Rihiko Shimizu (Kenshin Uesugi), Takashi Shimura (Gyobu Taguchi), Kamatari Fujiwara (*Shingen's doctor*), Naruto Iguchi, Masatsugu Kuriyama, Niro Yabuki, Takashi Watanabe, Toshimitsu Kato, Paul Okawa, Senkichi Omura, Yasutoshi Urata

 A Kurosawa Production Co., Ltd./Toho Pictures, Inc. Production, in association with 20th Century-Fox Film Corp. A Toho Co., Ltd. Release. Dolby Stereo. Eastman Color (processed by Toyo Developing). VistaVision size (spherical Panavision). 179 minutes. Released April 26, 1980.

 U.S. version: Released by 20th Century-Fox Film Corp. English subtitles. Producers, Francis Ford Coppola and George Lucas; Assistant Producer, Audie Bock; Subtitle Supervisor, Donald Richie. Prints by DeLuxe. 162 minutes. MPAA rating: PG. Released October 11, 1980.

 Notes: Filmed on location at Himeji Castle, Kumamoto Castle, in Kyoto, the Yuhara Plain in Hokkaido, Gotemba, and at Toho Studios. Takashi Shimura's role was cut from the American version. Steven Spielberg is often erroneously credited as co-producer of the international version. Awards: Palme d'Or (Cannes Film Festival, 1980).

NIHYAKUSAN-KOCHI ("203 Plateaus")
[PORT ARTHUR]
Executive Producer, Shigeru Okada; Producers, Kiyoshi Koda, Kanji Amao, Tsuneo Sato; Director, Toshio Masuda; Screenplay, Kazuo Kasahara; Director of Photography, Masahiko Iimura; Art Director, Hiroshi Kitagawa; Sound, Hiroyoshi Munakata; Music, Naozumi Yamamoto and Masashi Sada; Songs: "Sakimori no uta" and "Seiya," Music and lyrics by Masashi Sada; Editor, Kiyoaki Saito; Special Effects Director, Teruyoshi Nakano

 Cast: Tatsuya Nakadai (General Nogi), Teruhiko Aoi (Takeshi Koga), <u>Toshiro Mifune</u> (Emperor Meiji), Hisaya Morishige (Hirobumi Ito), Shigeru Koyama (Aritomo Yamagata), Masako Natsume (Sachi Matsuo), Masayuki Yuhara (Kikumatsu Umetani), Kentaro Kaneko (Shigeru

Amachi), Tetsuro Tamba (General Kodama), Makoto Sato, Yoshio Inaba, Akio Hasegawa, Yoko Nogiwa, Akihiko Hirata, Sen Yano

A Toei Co., Ltd. Production. A Toei Co., Ltd. Release. Color. ToeiScope. 185 minutes. Released August 2, 1980.

U.S. version: Released by Shochiku Films of America, Inc. English subtitles. 185 minutes (some sources give U.S. running time at 155 minutes). No MPAA rating. Released March 20, 1981.

SHOGUN

[SHOGUN]

Executive Producer, James Clavell; Producer, Eric Bercovici; Associate Producers, Kerry Feltham and Ben Chapman; Director, Jerry London; Screenplay, Eric Bercovici, based on the novel by James Clavell; Director of Photography, Andrew Laszlo; Art Director, Joseph R. Jennings; Music, Maurice Jarre; Production Executive, Frank Cardea; Editors, James T. Heckert, William Luciano, Donald R. Rode, Benjamin H. Weissman, and Jerry Young; Unit Production Managers, Ben Chapman and Wallace Worsley; First Assistant Directors, Charles Ziarko and Phil Cook; Casting, Maude Spector and Tatsuhiko Kuroiwa; Set Decorator, Tom Pedigo; Foreign Production Coordinator, Chris Bartlett; Construction Coordinator, Al De Gaetano; Special Effects, Robert Dawson; Sound Editor, Howard Beals; Music Editor, John LaSalandra; Music Recordist, Gerry Ulmer; Camera Operator, Chuy Elizondo; Gaffer, Sal Orefice; Key Grips, Ken Johnson and Vern Matthews; Dialogue Coach, Luca Bercovici; Script Supervisor, Larry K. Johnson; Special Consultant, Fred Ishimoto; Sound Mixer, John Glascock; Stunt Coordinator, Glenn R. Wilder; Production Accountant, Don Henry; Auditor, J. Steven Hollander; Property Master, Marty Wunderlich; Painter, Ed Charnock; Interpreter/Consultant, Chiho Adachi; Assistant to Eric Bercovici, Anna Mills; Assistant to James Clavell, Valerie Nelson; Title Design, Phill Norman; Title Optics, Westheimer Co.; Recording, Glen Glenn Sound. *Japanese Crew*: Art Director, Yoshinobu Nishioka; Costume Designer, Shin Nishida; Unit Production Managers, Shinji Nakagawa, Kazuo Shizukawa, and Keisuke Shinoda; Adviser to Jerry London, Umeo Minamino; Assistant Director, Masahiko Okumura; Set Decorator, Shoichi Yasuda; Makeup, Masato Abe; Wardrobe, Toshiaki Manki; Construction Department, Hideo Yoshioka; Script Supervisor, Chiyo Miyakoshi; Stunt Coordinator, Shinpachi Miyama; Production Services and Consultation, Tohokushinska Film Co., Ltd., and Banjuro Hemura. "We gratefully acknowledge the cooperation and assistance furnished by Himeji Castle (Himeji City, Japan). . . . The vessel *The Golden Hinde* was photographed in this production."

Cast: Richard Chamberlain (John Blackthorne), <u>Toshiro Mifune</u> (Toranaga), Yoko Shimada (Mariko), Frankie Sakai (Yabu), Alan Badel (Father Dell'Aqua), Michael Hordern (Friar Domingo), Damien Thomas (Father Alvito), John Rhys-Davis (Vasco Rodrigues), Vladek Sheybal (Captain Ferriera), George Innes (Johann de Vinck), Leon Lissek (Father Sabastio), Hideo Takamatsu (Buntaro), Yuki Meguro (Omi), Nobuo Kaneko (Ishido), Edward Peel (Pieterzoon), Eric Richard (Maetsukker), Steven Ubels (Roper), Stewart MacKenzie (Croocq), John Carney (Ginsel), Ian Jentle (Salamon), Neil McCarthy (Spillbergen), Morgan Sheppard (Specz), Seiji Miyaguchi (Muraji), Toru Abe (Hiromatsu), Mika Kitagawa (Kiku), Shin Takuma (Naga), Hiroshi Hasegawa (*galley captain*), Akira Sera (*old gardener*), Hyoei Enoki (Jirobei), Miiko Taka (Kiri), Midori Takei (Sono), Ai Matsubara (Rako), Yumiko Morishita (Asa), Hiromi Senno (Fujiko), Rinichi Yamamoto (Yoshinaka), Yuko Kada (Sazuko), Masumi Okada (Brother Michael), Yosuke Natsuki (Zataki), Takeshi Obayashi (Urano), Yoshio Kitsuda (Kyoko), Masashi Ebara (Suga), Setsuko Sekine (Genjiko), Atsuko Sano (Lady Ochiba), Orson Welles (*narrator*)

A Paramount Television/Paramount Pictures Corp. and NBC Entertainment Production, in association with Toho Co., Ltd., Asahi National Broadcasting Co., Ltd., and Jardine Matheson Co., Ltd. Color. Standard size (photographed with Panavision cameras and lenses). A Toho Co., Ltd. Release. 159 minutes. Released November 8, 1980.

U.S. version: (*James Clavell's*) *Shogun*. Never released theatrically in the United States. Broadcast over the National Broadcasting Company, Inc. Network (NBC), over five nights, September 15 to 19, 1980. 580 minutes (Parts 1 & 5 running 159 minutes; 2–4 running 93 minutes apiece). Released as a feature elsewhere, with some sequences not in the television version. Additionally, a separate home video feature version was released in the United States, this one running 125 minutes.

Notes: A U.S./Japanese co-production in English and Japanese. Filmed at Toho Studios, Ltd. (Tokyo), Daiei-Kyoto Studios, and Shochiku Studios (Kyoto), and on location in Himeji City (Japan), Hakkone Castle, and completed at Paramount Studios (Hollywood, California). The onscreen title begins with the Kanji character "Sho" followed by the word "Shogun" in Romanji, then ends with the Kanji character "Gun" so, technically, the title reads *Sho Shogun Gun*.

THE CHALLENGE

Executive Producer, Lyle Poncher; Producers, Robert L. Rosen and Ron Beckman; Director, John Frankenheimer; Screenplay, Richard Maxwell and John Sayles; Director of Photography, Kozo Okazaki; Art Director, Yoshiyuki Ishida; Sound, John Glassock; Music, Jerry Goldsmith; Editor, John W. Wheeler; Unit Production Managers, Alan Levine (U.S.) and Kijuro Ota (Japan); First Assistant Directors, Hisao Nabeshima and Mike Abe; Second Assistant Directors, Masaichi Shirai, Toshinori Hirayanagi, and Etsu Totoku; Casting, Patricia Mock (U.S.) and Hisao Nabeshima (Japan); Camera Operator, Michael A. Benson; First Assistant Cameraman, Richard Meinardus; Assistant to John Frankenheimer, Max Whitehouse; Production Adviser, Wai Kwan Hung; Script Supervisor, June Samson; Special Effects, Roger Hanson; Makeup, Bob Dawn and Yukio Ueda; Hair Stylist, Masato Abe; Set Decorator, Koichi Sasaki; Property Master, Kyoji Sasaki; Sword and Stunt Coordinator, Ryu Kuze; Martial Arts Coordinator, Steve [Steven] Seagal; Assistant Stunt Coordinator, Hiroyoshi Yamaguchi; Gaffer, Kazuo Shimomura; Key Grip, Koichi Haruta; Unit Publicist, Lou Dyer; Still Photographer, Don Smetzer, Costume Design, Etsuko Yagyu; Men's Costumer, Hiroshi Hamazaki; Women's Costumer, Masatoshi Utsumi; Location Auditor, Robert Monosmith; Location Manager, Toshiro Suzuki; Post Production Sound, Compact Sound Services, Inc.; Rerecording Mixers, John T. Reitz, David E. Campbell, and Joe D. Citarella; Music Editor, Bob Takagi; Supervising Sound Editor, Robert Henderson; Sound Editor, Alan Murray; Looping Editor, Kack A. Finlay; Assistant Editor, Steve Polivka; Main Title Design and Special Visual Effects, Private Stock Effects, Inc.; Special thanks, Mifune Productions, Kyoto International Convention Center

Cast: Scott Glenn (Rick), <u>Toshiro Mifune</u> (Yoshida), Donna Kei Benz (Akiko Yoshida, *his daughter*), Atsuo Nakamura (Hideo Yoshida, *his brother*), Calvin Jung (Ando), Clyde Kusatsu (Go), Sab Shimono (Toshio Yoshida, *Yoshida's son*), Kiyoaki Nagai (Kubo), Kenta Fukasaku (Jiro), Shogo Shimada (Yoshida's *father*), Yoshio Inaba (*instructor*), Seiji Miyaguchi (*old man*), Miiko Taka (Yoshida's *wife*), Akio Kameba (*boxer*), Hisashi Osaka (*knifeman*), Yuko Okamoto (*TV monitor girl #1*), Tae Matsuda (*TV monitor girl #2*), Pat McNamara (*fight promoter*), Pamela Brown (*girl in gym*), Roy Andrews (*hanger-on*), Henry Celis (Jorge), Kazunaga Tsuji (Hashimoto), Kusuo Kita (*thug*), Naoto Fujita (Tanaka), Masao Hisanori (Oshima), Ryuji Yamashita (Toshio Yoshida *as a child*), Toshio Chiba (*customs officer*), Minoru Sanada (*porter*), Shigehiro Kino (*van driver*), Katsutoshi Nakayama (*taxi driver*), Matsutoshi Ishikawa (*thug's driver*), Eriko Sugita (*woman in bar #1*), Munehisa Fujita (*man in bar*), Sanaye Nakahara (*cashier*), Kanata Uyeno (*waitress*), Katsumi Shirono, Noboru Ishihara, Masaru Sakurai, Toshio Matsushima,

Takashi Totsuka, Kazuo Arai, Mitsuyuki Oshima, Yoshio Otake, Hiroyuki Yuasa, Kanichi Hayashi, Akiyoshi Arima, Masuji Fujiwara, Roku Yoshinaka, Tsuneo Ito, Haruo Matsuoka, Michio Harada, Kenji Ono, Takafumi Tanaka, Hiroshi Oike, Yuichi Yoneda, Seiji Nishio, Yoshifumi Tsuboike, Yoshikazu Yoshimoto, Kazunori Asano, Takashi Okamura, Shigeji Aoki (*stunts*)

A Poncher-Rosen-Beckman Production for CBS Theatrical Films. An Embassy Pictures Release. A U.S. production filmed in Los Angeles and on location in Kyoto. Eastman Color. Vista-Vision size (spherical Panavision). 108 minutes. MPAA rating: R. Released (U.S.) July 23, 1982.

Notes: Never released theatrically in Japan. Released directly to Japanese home video, running 112 minutes. An alternate version, produced for American commercial television release, was retitled *Sword of the Ninja*, and runs 97 minutes.

SEIHA ("Conquest")
[CONQUEST]
Director, Sadao Nakajima; Screenplay, Sadao Nakajima, based on a story by Keiki Shimoda; Director of Photography, Tatsuo Suzuki; Music, Naozumi Yamamoto

Cast: <u>Toshiro Mifune</u>, Mariko Okada, Tomisaburo Wakayama, Bunta Sugawara, Akira Nishikino, Koji Tsuruta, Kumiko Akiyoshi, Kei Nakai, Kentaro Shimizu, Takashi Noguchi

A Toei-Kyoto Co., Ltd. Production. A Toei Co., Ltd. Release. Color. Wide screen. 142 minutes. Released 1983.

U.S. version: Release, if any, is undetermined.

JINSEI GEKIJO ("Theater of Life")
[THEATER OF LIFE]
Directors, Kinji Fukasaku, Junya Sato, and Sadao Nakajima; Screenplay, Kinji Fukasaku, Junya Sato, and Sadao Nakajima, based on the novel by Shiro Ozaki; Directors of Photography, Shohei Ando, Hiroyuki Namiki, and Kiyoshi Kitasaka; Music, Masato Kai

Cast: Keiko Matsuzaka, Toshiyuki Nagashima, Kie Nakai, Hiroaki Matsuzaka, Aiko Morishita, Hideo Murota, Morio Kazama, Ko Nishimura, <u>Toshiro Mifune</u>, Kantaro Suga, Yuriko Mishima, Takashi Noguchi, Kinji Nakamura, Mitsuru Hirata, Tomisaburo Wakayama

A Toei Co., Ltd. Production. A Toei Co., Ltd. Release. Color. Toeiscope. 138 minutes. Released 1983.

U.S. version: Release, if any, is undetermined.

Notes: A remake of Toho's film, also filmed by Shochiku in 1973.

NIHONKAI DAIKAISEN—UMI YUKABA ("Big Battle of the Japan Sea—So Goes the Sea")
[BATTLE ANTHEM]
Director, Toshio Masuda; Screenplay, Kazuo Kasahara; Director of Photography, Masahiko Iimura; Music, Harumi Ibe; Special Effects Director, Teruyoshi Nakano

Cast: <u>Toshiro Mifune</u>, Tadashi Yokouchi, Hiroyuki Okita, Junko Mihara, Tetsuro Tamba, Mikijiro Hira, Guts Ishimatsu, Toshitaka Ito, Makoto Kaketa, Eiko Nagashima, Masahiko Tanimura, Shin Takuma, Sayoko Ninomiya

A Toei Co., Ltd. Production. A Toei Co., Ltd. Release. Color. 131 minutes. Released 1983.

U.S. version: Release, if any, is undetermined.

UMITSUBAME JYO NO KISEKI ("The Miracle of Joe the Petrel")
[THE MIRACLE OF JOE THE PETREL]
Producer, Kazuyoshi Okuyama; Director, Toshiya Fujita; Screenplay, Toshiya Fujita, Fumio Ko-

nami, and Eiichi Uchida, based on a story by Ryuzo Saki; Director of Photography, Tatsuo Suzuki; Art Director, Masateru Mochizuki; Sound, Senichi Beniya; Music, Ryudo Uzaki; Editor, Osamu Inoue; Production Assistant, Hisao Nabeshima; Assistant Director, Takao Nagaishi; Planning, Toshiro Mifune; Associate Planning, Shiro Mifune

Cast: Saburo Tokito (Joe), Miwako Fujitani (Yoko), Kentaro Shimizu (Sawaii), Midori Satsuki (Michi), Yoshio Harada (Yanamine), Toshiro Mifune (*fisherman*), Sen Hara, Imari Tsuji, Kunie Tanaka

A Mifune Productions Co., Ltd. Production. A Shochiku-Fuji Co., Ltd. Release. Color. VistaVision size. 134 minutes. Released May 25, 1984.

U.S. version: Released by Shochiku Films of America, Inc. English subtitles. 134 minutes. No MPAA rating. Released November 16, 1984.

Notes: Also known as *The Stormy Petrel* and *The Miracle of Joe Petrel*.

SEIJO DEN SETSU ("Legend of the Holy Woman")
Producer, Kazuyoshi Okuyama; Planning, Kiyoshi Higuchi; Director, Toru Murakawa; Screenplay, Chitani Shiota; Director of Photography, Rokuo Nagamura; Art Director, Shigemori Shigeta; Lighting, Sachiro Sato; Sound, Senichi Benitani and Yasuo Hashimoto; Music, Francis Ray; Editor, Haru Inoue; Assistant Director, Takeyoshi Takeuchi

Cast: Hiromi Go, Shima Iwashita, Miyuki Ono, Koichi Iwaki, Toshiro Mifune

A Shochiku-Fuji Production. A Shochiku Co., Ltd. Release. Color. VistaVision size. 122 minutes. Released March 2, 1985.

U.S. version: Release, if any, is undetermined.

RAN ("Chaos")
[RAN]
Executive Producer, Katsumi Furukawa; Producers, Serge Silberman and Masato Hara; Director, Akira Kurosawa; Screenplay, Akira Kurosawa, Hideo Oguni, and Masato Ide, loosely based on the play *King Lear*, by William Shakespeare; Director of Photography, Takao Saito; Art Directors, Yoshiro Muraki and Shinobu Muraki; Director Counselor, Ishiro Honda; Costumes, Emi Wada; Music, Toru Takemitsu, performed by the Sapporo Symphony Orchestra and conducted by Hiroyuki Iwaki; Sound Recording, Fumio Yanoguchi and Shotaro Yoshida; Sound, Toho Recording Centre and Paris Studio Billancourt (Paris); General Production Manager, Ully Pickardt; Production Managers, Teruyo Nogami, Seikichi Iizumi, Satoro Izeki, and Takashi Ohashi; Production Coordinator, Hisao Kurosawa; First Assistant Directors, Fumiaki Okada and Bernard Cohn; Second Assistant Directors, Takashi Koizumi, Ichiro Yamamoto, Okihiro Yoneda, Kyoko Watanabe, Vittorio Dare Ole, and Kunio Nozaki; Camera Assistants, Yoshinori Sekiguchi, Noboru Asono, Kiyoshi Anzai, Satoru Suzuki, Shigeo Suzuki, Mazakazu Oka, Kosuke Matsushima, Hidehiro Igarashi, and Nobuyuki Kito; Gaffer, Takeharu Sato; Electricians, Koji Choya, Koichi Kamata, Tetsuo Sawada, Yoshio Iyama, Makoto Sano, Yuichi Oyama, Shintaro Tazaki, and Mutsuo Komine; Sound Assistants, Takenori Misawa, Hideo Takeichi, Takayuki Goto, and Soichi Inoue; Final Mixing, Claude Villand; Editing Assistants, Ryusuke Otsubo, Hideto Aga, and Hajime Ishihara; Set Decorators, Tsuneo Shimura, Osami Tonsho, Mitsuyuki Kimura, Jiro Hirai, and Yasuyoshi Ototake; Makeup, Shoichiro Ueda, Tameyuki Aimi, Chihako Naito, and Noriko Takamizawa; Visoria Professional Makeup by Christian Dior; Hairdressers, Yoshiko Matsumoto and Noriko Sato; Wardrobe Assistants, Akira Fukuda, Noriko Taguchi, and Kazuko Numata; Still Photographers, Daisaburo Harada and Yoshio Sato; Still Photograph Processing, Central Color (Paris); Unit Managers, Masayuki Motomochi and Tsutomu Sakurai; Production Assistants, Masahiko Kumada and Ko Nanri; Accountant, Takeo Suga; Titles, Den

Film Effect (Tokyo) and Les Films Michel François (Paris); Panaflex Cameras and Equipment, Panavision and Sanwa Cine Equipment (Tokyo)

Cast: Tatsuya Nakadai (Lord Hidetora Ichimonji), Akira Terao (Taro Ishimonji), Jinpachi Nezu (Jiro Ichimonji), Daisuke Ryu (Saburo Ichimonji), Mieko Harada (Lady Kaede), Yoshiko Miyazaki (Lady Sue), Masayuki Yui (Tengo), Kazuo Kato (Ikoma), Peter (Kyoami, *the jester*), Hitoshi Ueki (Fujimaki), Jun Tazaki (Lord Ayabe), Norio Matsui (Ogura), Hisashi Igawa (Kurogane), Kenji Kodama (Shirane), Toshiya Ito (Naganuma), Takeshi Kato (Hatakeyama), Takeshi Nomura (Tsurumaru)

A Serge Silberman Production for Greenwich Film Production, S.A. (Paris)/Herald Ace, Inc. (Tokyo)/Nippon Herald Films, Inc. A Serge Silberman and Katsumi Furukawa Presentation. A Toho Co., Ltd. Release. A Japanese-French co-production. Dolby Stereo. Eastman Color (processed by Imagica and Eclair). VistaVision size (spherical Panavision). 161 minutes. Released June 1, 1985.

U.S. version: Released by Orion Classics. English subtitles. Subtitles, Anne Brav, Cinetitres—L.T.C. 161 minutes. MPAA rating: R. Released September 27, 1985.

Notes: Filmed at Kurosawa Film Studio (Yokohama), Toho Studios (Tokyo), and on location at Himeji Castle (Himeji), Kumamoto Castle (Kumamoto), Nagoya Castle (Nagoya), and the cities of Gotemba, Kokonoe, Aso, and Shonai. Released in France on September 18, 1985, by AAA, where some prints were blown up to 70mm. Awards: Academy Award—Best Costume Design (Emi Wada).

RUNAWAY TRAIN

Executive Producers, Robert Whitmore, Henry Weinstein, and Robert A. Goldstein; Producers, Menahem Golan and Yoram Globus; Director, Andrei Konchalovsky; Screenplay, Djordje Milicevic, Paul Zindel, and Edward Bunker, based on "Boso kikansha," an unproduced script by Akira Kurosawa, Hideo Oguni, and Ryuzo Kikushima; Director of Photography, Alan Hume; Art Director (Production Designer), Stephen Marsh; Sound, Susumu Tokunow; Music, Trevor Jones; Editor, Henry Richardson; Associate Producer, Mati Raz; Executive in Charge of Production, Sue Baden-Powell; Unit Production Manager, Christopher Pearce; First Assistant Director, Jack Cummins; Second Assistant Director, Nancy King; Casting, Robert MacDonald; Production Coordinator, Mary McLaglen; Auditor, Marc S. Fischer; Art Director, Joseph T. Garrity; Assistant Art Directors, Patrick E. Tagliaferro and Stephen Homsy; Set Decorator, Anne Kuljian; Set Dresser, Susan Emshwiller; Camera Operator, Michael Frift; First Assistant Camera, Simon Hime and Tommy Magglos; Second Assistant Camera, Mark Dawson; Second Camera Operators, Alan Caso and Julio Macat; Loader, Paul Laufer; Boom Operator, Ken Beauchene; Train Sound Effects, Ken Johnson; Location Managers, Phil Christon and Larry Litton; Script Supervisors, Rina Sternfeld and Connie Barzaghi; Casting Associate, Perry Bullington; Makeup/Hair Supervisor, Mony Mansano; Hair Stylist, Dee Mansano; Makeup, Lily Benyair; Costume Design, Kathy Dover; Key Costumer, Jackie Johnson; Property Master, Robin Miller; Property Assistant, Stephen Schwartz; Gaffer, Bobby Bremmer; Best Boy Electric, Stephen Crawford; Electricians, Ray Bilger, John Zumpano, Warren Fox, Michael La Violette; Key Grip, Dwight Campbell; Dolly Grip, Colin Manning; Best Boy Grip, Dwight LaVers; Grips, Kevin Wadowski, Greg Tavenner, and Paul Ayers; Special Effects, Keith Richins and Rick Josephson; Assistant Special Effects, Wayne Walser, Steve Cates, and Eric Piper; Additional Editor, Peter Weatherley; First Assistant Editors, Peter Dansie and Roy Helmrich; Second Assistant Editors, Keith Corder, Paul Elman, Clement Barclay, and Dan Engstrom; Sound Editor, Jim Roddan; Dialogue Editor, Martin Evans; ADR Editor, Nigel Galt; Electronic Sound Effects Creator, Alan Howarth; Electronic Sound Effects Editor, Michael Hart; Assistant Sound Editors, Roy Burge and Peter Culverwell; Storyboard Artist, Alan Munro; Head Scenic Artist, Kelly Deco; Scenic Artists (Alaska), Gary Schoeneck and Jay Burkhart; Set Painters, Dave Clark, Catherine Dixon, and Lisa Finkbohner; Lead Art Department Assistant Christine Volz; Lead Carpenter, Michael Wymore; Assistant Set Dressers, Kara Lindstrom and Dorree Cooper; Construction Coordinator, Phil Peters; DGA Trainee, Christine Larson; Production Secretaries, Sharon Morov and Marilyn Maney; Assistant to Andrei Konchalovsky, Anita Dreike; Production Assistant, Jay Scherrick; Animal Wrangler, Brian McMillan; Railroad Consultant, Norman Pomeroy; Still Photographers, Gale M. Adler and Richard Foreman; Unit Publicity, Howard Brandy; Video Assistant Technician, Raymond Hirsch; Video Playback, Intervideo; Extras Casting, Charlie Messenger; Transportation Coordinator, James P. Jones; Transportation Captain, Ted Mehous: Drivers, Joe "Stinky" Killian, James Jones, Sr., Edward Flotard, Bruce Hauer, Mike Davis, Larry Shepard, and John Yarborough; Honeywagon Driver, Robert Skogerboe; Set Nurses, Lynda Donelson and Saskia Lodder; Craft Service, Sasha Dillon. *Alaska Second Unit*: Second Unit Director, Max Kleben; First Assistant Director, Michael Pariser; Production Coordinator, Kassie O'Connell; Director of Photography, Don Burgess; Camera Operator, Tom Priestley, Jr.; First Assistant Camera, Tony Guadioz; Construction Coordinator, Mick Strawn; Set Decorator/Props, Peter Borck; Lead Carpenter, Mike Carr; Location Auditor (Alaska), Peter Manos; Script Supervisor, Rina Sternfeld; Sound Mixer, Neal Thomas; Special Effects, Bob Riggs, Tassilo Baur, and Ray Brown; Wardrobe/Makeup/Hair, Owen Garner III; Helicopter Pilots, Harry Hauss, Soren Jensen, and Rick Holley; Key Grip, Rick Sands; Best Boy Grip, Geoffrey Griffin; Grips, Steve Grnya, Tony Jefferson, and Scott Sproule; Art/Special Effects Assistants, Phil Davidson, Douglas Schwartz, and Colin MacRae II; Railroad Coordinator, Ted Hewitt; Production Assistants, Zachary Spoon, Mark Jones, Laura "Smitty" Smith, Amy J. Hall, Sean Toohey, Jim Bachelor, and Heather Buchanan; Production Secretary, Carol Howerton; Cook, Dennis Rose; Assistant Cook, Lynn Harrison; First Aid, William Weppler and Jim Bauman; Set Construction, Steve Serrurier & Associates and Five Star Set Services; Cameras, Joe Dunton Cameras of America; Production Equipment and Facilities, Keylite PSI; Crash Sequence, Ermanno Biamonte, Cannon Visual Effects Department; In Charge of Development, Weinstein/Skyfield-Polymuse, Inc.; Titles, Camera Effects, Ltd.; Opticals, G.S.C./Optical Film Effects; Postproduction Facilities and Rerecording, Pinewood Studios; Mixer, John Hayward; Music Recording and Mixing, C.T.S. Studios (Wembley), Paul Hulme; Special thanks, Alaskan Film Commission, Alaskan Railroads, Montana Film Commission, B.A.P. Railroads, and the People of Whittier; Stunt Coordinator, Loren Janes

Cast: Jon Voight (Manny), Eric Roberts (Buck), Rebecca DeMornay (Sara), Kyle T. Heffner (Frank Barstow), John P. Ryan (Ranken), T. K. Carter (Dave Prince), Kenneth McMillan (Eddie MacDonald), Stacey Pickren (Ruby), Walter Wyatt (Conlan), Edward Bunker (Jonah), Reid Cruikshanks (Al Turner), Michael Lee Gogin (*short con*), Norton E. "Hank" Worden (*old con*), John Otrin (*cat con*), Norman Alexander Gibbs (*queen con*), Dennis Ott, Don Pugsley, John Fountain (*guards*), Wally Rose (*announcer*), Daniel Trejo (*boxer*), Big Yank (*trainer*), Tom "Tiny" Lister (*black guard*), Dana Belgarde (*prison guard*), Diane Erickson (Sue Majors), Larry John Meyers (Pulasky), Don McLaughlin (Foreman Cassidy), Vladimir Bibic (Fireman Wright), William Tregoe, Jr. (Rogers), Loren Janes (*engineer Eastbound 12*), Robert M. Klempner (Cushman), Carmen Filpi (*signal maintainer*), David Stompro (Jonson), Harris D. Smith (Willard), Phillip Earl (*first crewman*), Tom Keenan (*second crewman*), Tony Epper (*hit man*), Jerry Brainum (*bodybuilder*), Duey Thomasick (*emergency worker*), Charlie Messenger (*yardworker*), Russel Solberg, Terry Jackson, Jean Makahni, John Clay Scott, Bob Terhune, Mike Johnson, Chick Hicks, Stefan Gudju, John Casino, Dick Durock, Carl Nick Ciafalio, Doc Duhane (*stunts*)

A Golan-Globus Production for Northbrook Films. A Cannon Films Release. A U.S./Israeli co-production in English. Stereophonic sound. Color (processed by Rank Film Laboratories, Denham, England). VistaVision size. 112 minutes. Released December 20, 1985.

Notes: Dedicated "to the memory of Rick Holley," who died in a helicopter crash during production. Kikushima and Oguni are not credited as co-writers of the screenplay basis. Released in Japan as *Boso kikansha* ("Runaway Train") by Shochiku-Fuji on June 7, 1986.

GENKAI TSUREZURE BUSHI ("Song of Genkai Tsurezure")
Director, Masanobu Deme, Screenplay, Kazuo Kasahara, Kikuma Shimoizaka, Go Haito, based on a story by Kenko Yoshida; Director of Photography, Masahiko Imura; Music, Masaru Hoshi and Mark Gordonberg

Cast: Sayuri Yoshinaga, Aki Yashiro, Moriyo Kazama, Yusuke Okada, Ken Iwabuchi, <u>Toshiro Mifune</u>, Sentaro Bushimi

A Toei Co., Ltd. production. A Toei Co., Ltd. Release. Color. Wide screen. 135 minutes. Released 1986.

U.S. version: Release, if any, is undetermined.

SHATARAA ("Shatterer")
[SHATTERER]
Executive Producer, Shin Watanabe; Producer, Asao Kumada; Associate Producer, Francesco Martino De Carles; Director, Tonino Valerii; Screenplay, Yasuo Tanami, Ernesto Gastaldi, and Tonino Valerii, based on a story by Ernesto Gastaldi and Tonino Vallerii; Director of Photography, Giulio Albonico; Art Director, Stefano Ortolani; Sound, Roberto Alberghini; Music, Tot Taylor; Song: "Endless Sunset (Let It Be Forever)," published by Watanabe Music Publishing Co., Ltd.; Planning Associates, Komei Fujii and Toshiro Murayama; Editor, Antonio Siciliano; Production Supervisor, Massimo Ferraro; Production Organization (Japan), Yuichi Ino; Costume Design, Francesca Panicali; Unit Production Manager, Mario Di Biase; Set Decorator, Livia Del Priore; First Assistant Director, Walter Italici; Stunt Coordinator, Franco Salamon; Continuity, Francesca Ghiotto; Second Assistant Director, Mario Miyakawa; Production Assistants, Simona Mattei, Rosella Ferraro, Patrizia Pierucci; Boom Men, Marco Di Biase, Antonio Pantano; Car Rally Consultant, Romano Fazio; Camera Operator, Marco Onorato; Assistant Cameramen, Andrea Busiri Vici, Pietre Clemente; Still Photographer, Gianfranco Saus; Property Masters, Andriano Tiberi, Luciano Argento; Makeup, Rosario Prestupino; Hair Stylist, Teodora Bruno

Cast: Koji Kikkawa, Andy J. Forest, Marina Suma, Orazio Orlando, Mimmo Palmera, Salvatore Billa, Beatrice Ring, Daniela Novak, Tano Cimarosa • <u>Toshiro Mifune</u>, Dalila Di Lazzaro With Greta Vaillant, Nando Muroio, Noboru Homma, Maria Miyakawa, Lorenzo Flaherty, Francesio Torrisi, Giovanni Pazzafini, Elio Bunadonna, Riccardo Parrotti, Tommaso Palladino

A Uanchi Corporation, S.r.L. (Rome) Production. A Watanabe Production/Film Select (Geneve) Presentation. A Toho Co., Ltd. Release. A Japanese-Italian co-production. Stereo. Color (processed by Cinecitta, S.p.A.). VistaVision size. 110 minutes. Released June 13, 1987.

Notes: U.S. version: Release, if any, is undetermined. Released to Japanese home video in 1987 with the entire film dubbed into English with Japanese subtitles. Details of Italian release undetermined. Also known as *The Sicilian Connection*.

OTOKO WA TSURAIYO—SHIRETAKO BOJO ("It's Tough to Be a Man—Shiretako Longing")
[TORA-SAN GOES NORTH]
Producer, Kiyoshi Shimazu; Planning, Shuichi Kobayashi; Director, Yoji Yamada; Screenplay, Yoji Yamada and Yoshitaka Asama, based on characters created by Yoji Yamada; Director of Photog-

raphy, Tetsuo Takaba; Art Director, Mitsuo Degawa; Lighting, Yoshifumi Aoki; Sound, Isao Suzuki; Music, Naozumi Yamamoto; Songs: "Otoko wa tsuraiyo," Music by Naozumi Yamamoto and Lyrics by Hoshino Kei; "Shiretako bojo," Music and Lyrics by Hisaya Morishige; Mixing, Takashi Matsumoto; Editor, Iwao Ishii; Still Photographer, Munehira Hasegawa; Chief Assistant Director, Keiji Igarashi; Costumes, Shochiku Wardrobe

Cast: Kiyoshi Atsumi (Torajiro "Tora-san" Kuruma), Toshiro Mifune (Junkichi Ueno), Keiko Awaji (Etsuko), Keiko Takeshita (Rinko), Chieko Baisho (Sakura Suwa, *Tora-san's sister*), Gin Maeda (Hiroshi Suwa, *her husband*), Masami Shimojo (Ryuzo Kuruma, *Tora's uncle*), Chieko Misaki (Tsune Kuruma, *Tora's aunt*), Hisao Dazai (Umetaro, *the printing shop president*), Chishu Ryu (Gozen-sama, *the temple priest*), Gajiro Sato (Genko), Hidetaka Yoshioka (Mitsuo Suwa, *Tora-san's nephew*), Keiroku Seki, Issei Ogata, Takashi Kasano, Kimihiro Hieizumi, Masato Akazuka, Masayuki Yui, Nagatoshi Sakamoto, Kazuhiko Kasai, Sayoko Makino, Midori Kawai, Rumiko Ishikawa, Rie Kurayama, Tatsuko Amano, Yasuharu Shinohara, Shinobu Ohara, Kei Suma, Jun Miho

A Shochiku Co., Ltd. Production. A Shochiku Co., Ltd. Release. Color (processed by Tokyo Developing). Panavision. 107 minutes. Released August 15, 1987.

U.S. version: Released by Shochiku Films of America, Inc. English subtitles. 107 minutes. No MPAA rating. Released January 11, 1990.

Notes: The 38th "Tora-san" feature. Filmed on location in Shibamata (Tokyo) and in Shari-cho, Rihaku-cho, and Nakarotsu-cho, Hokkaido.

TAKETORI MONOGATARI ("The Tale of Taketori")
[PRINCESS FROM THE MOON]
Executive Producers, Tomoyuki Tanaka and Shigeaki Hazama; Producers, Masaru Kakutani, Hiroaki Fujii, and Junichi Shinsaka; Director, Kon Ichikawa; Screenplay, Ryuzo Kikushima, Mitsuyoshi Ishigami, Kon Ichikawa and Shinya Hidaka; Director of Photography, Setsuo Kobayashi; Music, Kensaku Tanigawa; Costume Design, Emi Wada; Special Effects Director, Teruyoshi Nakano

Cast: Toshiro Mifune (Taketori), Ayako Wakao (Tayoshime, *his wife*), Yasuko Kawaguchi (Kaya, the Princess Kaguya), Koji Ishizaka (Mikado), Kiichi Nakai (Minister of the Military), Koasa Shumetei (Minister of Culture). Takatoshi Takeda (Minister of Finance), Megumi Odaka (Akeno), Katsuo Nakamura, Shiro Ito, Fujio Tokita, Takeshi Kato, Kyoko Kishida, Hirokazu Yamaguchi, Jun Hamamura, Pen Idemitsu, Michiyo Yokoyama, Hirokazu Inoue, Miho Nakano

A Toho Pictures, Inc./Fuji Television Network Production. A Toho Co., Ltd. Release. Dolby Stereo. Color. VistaVision size. 121 minutes. Released September 26, 1987.

U.S. version: Released by Toho International Co., Ltd. English subtitles. 121 minutes. No MPAA rating. Released September 14, 1987.

HARU KURU ONI ("Demons In Spring")
[DEMONS IN SPRING]
Producer, Kazuo Inoue; Director, Akira Kobayashi; Screenplay, Ryuzo Kikushima, based on the novel by Tokuhei Suchi; Director of Photography, Yoshikatsu Suzuki; Art Directors, Yoshiro Muraki and Kazuhiko Fujiwara; Lighting, Mitsuo Onishi; Music, Masaru Sato

Cast: Toshiro Mifune, Masaru Matsuda, Sachiko Wakayama, Sakae Takita, Keiko Tsushima, Teruaki Mochizuki, Hajime Hana

An Arrow Production. A Shochiku Co., Ltd. Release. Color. 137 minutes. Released 1989.

U.S. version: Released by Shochiku Films of America, Inc. English subtitles. 137 minutes. No MPAA rating. Released October 13, 1989.

SEN NO RIKYU—HONKAKUBO IBUN ("Sen no Rikyu—Honkakubo's Student Writings")
[DEATH OF A TEA MASTER]
Executive Producer, Sueaki Takaoke; Producer, Kazunobu Yamaguchi; Director, Kei Kumai; Screenplay, Yoshitaka Yoda, based on the novel *Honkakubo ibun* by Yasushi Inoue; Director of Photography, Masao Tochizawa; Art Director, Takeo Kimura; Sound, Yukio Kubota; Music, Teizo Matsumura; Editor, Osamu Inoue; Chief Assistant Director, Kazuo Hara

    Cast: Eiji Okuda (Honkakubo), Toshiro Mifune (Rikyu), Kinnosuke Yorozuya (Uraku), Go Kato (Oribo), Shinsuke Ashida (Hideyoshi), Eijiro Tono, Taketoshi Naito, Tsunehiko Kamijo, Taro Kawano, Teizo Muta

    A Seiyu, Ltd. Production. A Toho Co., Ltd. Release. Color. VistaVision size. 107 minutes. Released October 7, 1989.

    U.S. version: Released by Metropolis Films. 107 minutes. No MPAA rating. Released June 1, 1990.

    Notes: Awards: Venice Film Festival (Silver Lion).

CF GAARU ("cf Girl")
Executive Producers, Kuniyoshi Matsuhashi, Yoshio Sato, and Kazuo Ota; Planning, Ritsuko Kakita and Kazumasa Fujia; Producers, Mitsuo Fujita, Kazuo Kishimoto, and Noriyasu Ogami; Director, Izo Hashimoto; Screenplay, Hiromichi Nakamura and Nizo Hashimoto, based on a story by Takashi Kitajima; Director of Photography, Katsumi Eshimi; Art Director, Masateru Morozuki; Lighting, Noriyuki Ankochi; Sound, Maki Honda; Music, Masanori Sera and Ichiro Haneda; Editor, Yoshio Kudano; Chief Assistant Director, Ichiro Yamamoto; Action Sequences Director, Reijiro Adachi; Unit Production Manager, Takashi Yamaguchi

    Cast: Masanori Sera, Kumi Nakamura, Ginji Gao, Soki Takaoka, Yuko Asano, Keizo Nagazuka, Ann Lee Sugano, Hideo Murota, Toshiro Mifune, Masumi Okada

    A Garrent Company Production, in association with Agent 21/Toshiba Eiza Soft Corp./Mitsui Busan Sekiu Corp. A Toei Co., Ltd. Release. Color. VistaVision size. 98 minutes. Released 1989.

    U.S. version: Release, if any, is undetermined.

    Notes: Filmed in Japan and on location in Alberta, Canada.

YUME ("Dreams")
[AKIRA KUROSAWA'S DREAMS]
Producers, Hisao Kurosawa, Mike Y. Inoue; Director, Akira Kurosawa; Screenplay, Akira Kurosawa; Creative Consultant, Ishiro Honda; Directors of Photography, Takao Saito and Masaharu Ueda; Art Directors, Yoshiro Muraki and Akira Sakuragi; Sound, Kenichi Benitani; Music, Shinichiro Ikebe; Costume Designer, Emi Wada; Chief Assistant Director, Takashi Koizumi; Production Manager, Teruyo Nogami; Production Coordinator, Izuhiko Suehiro; Associate Producers, Allan H. Liebert, Seikichi Iizumi; Technical Cooperation, Sony; Photography Collaborator, Kazutami Hara; Sound Effects, Ichiro Minawa and Masatoshi Saito; Set Decorator, Koichi Hamamura; Casting Assistant, Yasunori Suzuki; Unit Managers, Kunio Niwa, Masahiko Kumada; Choreographer, Michiyo Hata; Piano Player, Ikudo Endo; Assistant Directors, Okihiro Yoneda, Naohito Sakai, Tsuyoshi Sugino, Kiyoharu Hayano, Toru Tanaka, Vitorio Dalle Ore; Assistant Cameramen, Yoshinori Sekiguchi, Toshio Wattanabe, Hidehiro Igarashi, Hiroyuki Kitazawa, Hiroshi Ishida, Kazushi Watanabe, Shigeo Suzuki, Kosuke Matsushima, Mitsu Kondo, Hiroshi Hattori; Lighting Technicians, Yukio Choya, Tadatoshi Kitagawa, Makoto Sano, Tetsuo Sawada, Miyanobu Inori, Hisanori Furukawa, Isao Yasui, Hideho Ioka, Hiromasa Yonahara; Lighting Rigging, Kenzo Masuda, Yukio Tanaka; Sound Assistants, Soichi Inoue, Masahito Yano,

Noriaki Minami; Grips, Isamu Miwano, Satoshi Tsuyuki, Sadanu Takahara, Yuichi Horita; Art Assistants, Kyoko Heya, Nariyuki Kondo, Yasuyoshi Ototake; Set Construction, Ichio Utsuki, Kazuharu Tsuboi; Props, Satoshi Ota, Yuzuru Sakai, Nami Ishida, Yoshiaki Kawai; Wardrobe, Kazuko Kurosawa, Akira Fukuda, Yoko Nagano, Mitsuru Otsuka; Assistant Editors, Ryusuke Otsubo, Hideto Aga, Yosuke Yafune; Negative Cutters, Tome Minami, Noriko Meharu; Makeup Artists, Shoshichiro Ueda, Tameyuki Aimi, Norio Sano; Hairdressers, Sakai Nakao, Yumiko Fujii; Still Photographer, Daizaburo Harada; Production Publicity, Yasuhiko Higashi; Mountain Climbing Adviser, Tadao Kanzeki; Dance Instructor, Tokiko Mochizuki; Transportation, Takashi Takei, Kimihiko Tsurugaya, Toru Ikegaki, Keisuke Utsumi, Yasuhisa Serizawa, Masaharu Komatsuki; In Charge of Location Site (Gotemba), Magosaku Osada, Shizuo Osada; Production Accountants, Shuji Matsumoto, Hiroko Idetsu; Production Assistants, Shushin Hosoya, Satoshi Shimozawa, Kazutoshi Wadakura; Recording Studio, Toho Recording Centre; Raw Stock, Kodak Japan; Art Department, Toho E-B; Props, Takatsu Soshoku Bijutsu; Explosives, Ohira Special Effects; Hair Styles and Wigs, Yauada Katsura; Wardrobe, Tokyo Isho; Sound Effects, Toyo Onkyo Kauove; Music Production, Tokyo Concert; Sound Equipment, Tisman Service; Camera Equipment, Sanwa Cine-Equipment Rental Co., Ltd.; Lighting Equipment, Lee Colortran International; Vehicles, Nippon Shomei, Film Link International; Background Music, Ippolitov-Ivanov; *In the Village*, from *Caucasian Sketches Suite for Orchestra*, Op. 10; Conducting Moscow Radio Symphony Orchestra, Vladimir Fedoseev; HDTV Technology, Sony PCL; Photo-Composite Process, Akio Suzuki, Mikio Inoue, Mutsuhiro Harada, Yoshiya Takahashi; EBR Process, Tonio Onata, Takaya Takizawa; HDTV Coordinator, Tetsuji Maezawa; Composite Technology, Den-Film-Effects; Special Effects Unit (Japan) Visual Effects, Minoru Nakano; Technical Editor, Michihisa Miyashige; Optical Photography, Takashi Kobayashi, Takashi Kawabata; Optical Camera Operators, Makoto Negishi, Takabuni Hirata; Matte Painting, Takshuiro Miyaguchi. Visual Effects (U.S.), Industrial Light & Magic, a Division of LucasArts Entertainment Company. ILM Visual Effects Unit: Supervisors, Ken Ralston, Mark Sullivan; Producer, Peter Takeuchi; Art Director, Claudia Mullaly; Model Supervisor, Barbara Affonso; Optical Supervisor, Bruce Veccitto; Editor, Michael Gleason; Coordinator, Jil Sheree Bergin; Camera Operators, Terry Chostner, Selwyn Eddy III; Assistant Camera Operators, Randy Johnson, John Gazdik, Robert Hill; Matte Camera Operators, Jo Carson, Wade Childress, Paul Huston, Charles Canfield; Assistant Matte Camera Operator, Nancy Morita; Matte Painters, Yusei Useugi, Caroleen Green; Matte Assistant, Jonathan Crowe; Modelmakers, Brian Gernand, E'ven Stromquist, Randy Ottenberg, Wesley Seeds, Marge McMahon; Optical Lineup, Peggy Hunter, Dave Karpman, Lori Nelson, Thomas Tosseter; Optical Camera Operators, Jon Alexander, Jeff Doran; Postproduction Coordinator, Susan Adele Colletta; Rotoscope Artist, Barbara Brennan; Stage Supervisor, Brad Jerrell; Head Electrician, Tim Morgan; Electrician, David Murphy; Chief Pyro Technician, Charles Ray; Pyro Technician, Reuben Goldberg; Cloud Tank, Craig Mohegan

Cast: *Sunshine Through the Rain*: Mitsuko Baisho (*mother of "I"*), Toshihiko Nakano ("I" *as a young child*); *The Peach Orchard*: Mitsunori Isaki ("I" *as a boy*), Mie Suzuki (*"I's" sister*); *The Blizzard*: Akira Terao ("I"), Mieko Harada (*the snow fairy*), Masayuki Yui, Shu Nakajima, Sakae Kimura (*members of the climbing team*); *The Tunnel*: Akira Terao ("I"), Yoshitaka Zushi (*Private Noguchi*); *Crows*: Akira Terao ("I"), Martin Scorsese (*Vincent Van Gogh*); *Mt. Fuji in Red*: Akira Terao ("I"), Toshie Negishi (*child-carrying mother*), Hisashi Igawa (*power station worker*); *The Weeping Demon*: Akira Terao ("I"), Chosuke Ikariya (*the demon*); *Village of the Watermills*: Akira Terao ("I"), Chishu Ryu (*103-year-old man*). *Also* Mugita Endo, Ryujiro Oki, Masaru Sakurai, Masaaki Sasaki, Keiki Takenouchi, Kento Toriki, Shu Nakajima, Tokuju Nasuda, Masuo Amada, Sakae Kimura, Shogo Tomomori, Ryo Nagasawa, Akisato Yamada, Tetsu Watanabe, Ken Takemura, Yasuhiro Kajimoto,

Makoto Hasegawa, Nagamitsu Satake, Satoshi Hara, Yasushige Turuoka, Shigeru Edaki, Hideharu Takeda, Katsumi Naito, Masaaki Enomoto, Norio Takei, Eiji Iida, Koji Kanda, Hideto Aota, Kazue Nakanishi, Rika Miyazawa, Mika Edaki, Mayumi Kamimura, Sayuri Yoshioka, Teruko Nakayama, Sachiko Nakayama, Toshiya Ito, Takashi Ito, Motoyuki Higashimura, Yasuhito Yamanaka, Haruka Sugata, Noriko Hayami, Ayaka Takahashi, Yuko Ishiwa, Sachiko Oguri, Masayo Mochida, Miki Kado, Ikeya Sakiko Yamamoto, Mayumi Ono, Yumiko Miyata, Aya Ikaida, Megumi Hata, Asako Hirano, Chika Nishio, Yuko Harada, Tomomi Yoshizawa, Kunido Ishizuka, Maumi Yoda, Hatsue Nishi, Michiko Kawada, Machiko Ichihashi, Yumi Ezaki, Chika Yanabe, Mayuko Akashi. Fujio Tokita, Michio Hino, Michio Kida, Ayako Honua, Haruko Togo, Reiko Nanao, Shin Tonomura, Junpei Natsuki, Shigeo Kato, Saburo Kadowaki, Goichi Nagatani, Shizuko Azuma, Yoshie Kihira, Yukie Shimura, Setsuko Kawaguchi, Kemeko Otowa, Machiko Terada, Umiko Takahashi, Harumi Fuji, Hiroko Okuno, Mon Ota, Akitoku Inaba, Kou Ishikawa, Tatsunori Takuhashi, Yoshiko Maki, Hiroko Maki, Ryoko Kawai, Miyako Kawana, Miyuki Egawa, Megumi Sakai, Yoko Hayashi, Yuko Matsumura, Takashi Odajima, Mitsuru Shibuya, Koichi Imamura, Wasuke Izumi, Sachio Sakai, Torauemon Utazawa, Yukimasa Natori, Tadashi Okumura, Kenzo Shirahana, Masato Goto, Sumimaro Yochini, Juichi Kubozono, Masami Ozeki, Yasuyuki Iwanaga, Akira Tashiro, Koichi Kase, Kenji Fujita, Hiroto Tamura, Osamu Yayama, Yuji Sawayana, Mitsuji Tsuwako, Masatoshi Miya, Maiko Okamoto, Nana Yanakawa, Yuka Kojima, Shizuka Isami, Mai Watanabe, Sayuri Kobayashi. Hayakawa Productions, Himawani Theatre Group, Inc., Motoko Inagawa Office, Tanbe Dojo, Kokugakuin University Mizutamakai

An Akira Kurosawa USA, Inc. Production. A Steven Spielberg Presentation. A Japanese/U.S. co-production in Japanese and English. Released by Warner Bros., Inc. Dolby Stereo. Eastman Color (processed by Imagica, prints by Technicolor). VistaVision size (spherical Panavision). 120 minutes. Released May 25, 1990.

U.S. version: Released by Warner Bros., Inc. English subtitles, Donald Richie and Tadashi Shishido. 120 minutes. MPAA Rating: PG. Released August 24, 1990.

Notes: "Thanks to the Akira Kurosawa Film Society." Actors whose roles are not specified are grouped on screen as above.

STRAWBERRY ROAD—SUTOROBERI RODO ("Strawberry Road")
[STRAWBERRY ROAD]
Executive Producer, Shinjiro Kayama; Producers, Junichi Mimura and Tomohiro Kaiyama; Planning, Koichi Murakami; Director, Koreyoshi Kurihara; Screenplay, Nobuo Yamada, based on Yoshimi Ishikawa's autobiography; English Dialogue Supervisor, Bill Schwartz; Director of Photography, Katsuhiro Kato; Art Director, Kazuhiko Fujiwara; Sound, Senichi Beniya and Minoru Nobuoka; Music, Fred Karlin; Theme Song, Shoko Haneda; Editor, Hikaru Suzuki; Line Producer (U.S.), Dennis Bishop; Chief Assistant Director, Hiroyuki Momozawa; Production Office, Shunji Fujiwara, Yo Ishikawa, Teru Onodera

Cast: Ken Matsudaira (Hisa Ishii), Mako (Frank Machida), Mariska Hargitay (Jill Banner), Toshiro Mifune (Taoka), Norihei Miki (*old man on the hill*), Tsutomu Ishibashi (Akira Ishii), Shigehide Kawahira (George), Noriyuki "Pat" Morita (*old man's brother*), Mao Taiichi (*old man's younger brother*), Junko Sakurada, Mari Natsuki

A Fuji Television Network/Tokyo Hoei Television Co., Ltd. Production, in association with Makeo Productions, in English, Japanese, and Spanish. A Toho Co., Ltd. Release. Dolby Stereo. Color. VistaVision size (spherical Panavision). 117 minutes. Released April 27, 1991.

U.S. version: Release, if any, is undetermined.

Notes: Filmed on location in Los Angeles and Monterey, California, and New York City.

HACHIGATSU NO RAPUSODI ("Rhapsody in August")
[RHAPSODY IN AUGUST]
Executive Producer, Toru Okuyama; Producer, Hisao Kurosawa; Associate Producers, Mike Y. Inoue and Seikichi Iizumi; Director, Akira Kurosawa; Screenplay, Akira Kurosawa, based on the novel *Nabe no naka* ("In the Cauldron") by Kiyoko Murata, published by Bungei Shunju, Ltd.; Creative Consultant, Ishiro Honda; Directors of Photography, Takao Saito and Masaharu Ueda; Art Director, Yoshiro Muraki; Lighting, Takeji Sano; Sound, Kenichi Benitani; Music, Shinichiro Ikebe; Costume Design, Kazuko Kurosawa; Production Manager, Teruyo Nogami; Production Coordinator, Izuhiko Suehiro; Chief Assistant Director, Takashi Koizumi; Unit Manager, Masahiko Kumada; Sound Effects, Ichiro Minawa and Masatoshi Saito; Title Calligraphy, Ryosetsu Imai (Sekishin-kai); Nagasaki Dialect Instructor, Ryusuke Otsubo; Japanese Dialogue Adviser for Richard Gere, Peter Grilli; Assistant Directors, Okihiro Yoneda, Naohito Sakai, Toru Tanaka, and Vittorio Dalle Ore; Assistant Cameramen, Yoshinori Sekiguchi, Shigeo Suzuki, Hidehiro Igarashi, Hiroyuki Kitazawa, Masahiko Hayashi, Hiroshi Ishida, and Motonobu Kiyoku; Lighting Technicians, Yukio Choya, Tadatoshi Kitagawa, Makoto Sano, Tetsuo Sawada, Miyanobu Inori, Shintaro Tazaki, Hisanori Furukawa, and Isao Yasui; Lighting Rigging, Kenzo Masuda and Yukio Tanaka; Sound Assistant, Soichi Inoue; Grips, Isamu Miwano, Kazuo Shikayama, Satoshi Tsuyuki, and Hiromatsu Toyoyama; Art Assistants, Tsuneo Shimura, Kyoko Heya, Tsoyoshi Shimizu, and Yasuyoshi Ototake; Set Construction, Ichiro Utsuki, Kazumaru Tsuboi, Katsuji Maruyama, Junichiro Konnai, Takeshi Koshimizu, and Tadao Shibuya; Set Director, Koichi Hamamura; Props, Satoshi Ota, Koichi Nonaka, Mami Ishida, and Tetsuji Tatsuta; Wardrobe, Yoko Nagano and Mitsuru Otsuka; Assistant Editors, Ryusuke Otsubo and Masaru Muramoto; Negative Cutter, Tome Minami; Makeup, Shoshichiro Ueda, Tameyuki Aimi, and Norio Sano; Hair Stylists, Sakai Nakao and Yumiko Fujii; Still Photographer, Daizaburo Harada; Unit Publicist, Naotaka Kacho; Casting Assistant, Tsuyoshi Sugino; "Ants March" Adviser, Ryohei Yamaoka (Kyoto University of Industrial Art & Textile); Organ Tuning, Kenji Kanai; Transportation, Hiroto Kurokawa, Haruo Nakajima, and Ken Ogata; Production in Gotemba, Magosaku Osada and Shizuo Osada; Production Accountants, Shuji Matsumoto and Hiroko Idetsu; Head Production Assistant, Shushin Hosoya; Production Assistants, Satoshi Shimozawa, Kazutoshi Wadakura, Kimihiko Tsurugaya, and Toshiaki Kimura; Production Services, Toho Studios, Toho Sound Creative Studio; Raw Stock, Hoei Sangyo Co., Ltd., and Fuji Photo Film Co., Ltd.; HDTV Technology, Sony PCL; Titles, Den Film-Effects and Sekishin-Kai; Art Department Services, Toho E.B.; Props, Takatsu Soshoku Bijitsu; Hairdresser and Wigs, Yamada Katsura; Wardrobes, Tokyo Isho; Sound Effects, Toyo Onkyo Kamome; Music Production, Tokyo Concerts, Avaco Creative Studio; Sound Equipment, Tisman Service; Camera Equipment, Sanwa Cine-Equipment Rental Co., Ltd.; Lighting Equipment, Kurosawa Film Studio, Lumo Lighting, The Light Maker Company, and S.F. Filter; Coordination in Hawaii, U International Corp.; Vehicles, Nippon Shomei; Music: *Haiden-Roslein* by Franz Schubert; Chorus by Hibari Jido Gasshodan, *Stabat Mater, rv. 621* by Vivaldi; Countertenor, James Bowman with the Academy of Ancient Music, directed by Christopher Hogwood. Feature Film Enterprises II: Nippon Investment & Finance Co., Ltd., Bandai Co., Ltd., Daiwa Finance Co., Ltd., the Daiwa Real Estate Co., Ltd., Hakuhodo, Inc., Imagica Corp., Kawasaki Enterprises, Inc., Maruko, Inc., Nikkodo Co., Ltd., Shochiku Co., Ltd., Shochiku Daiichi Kogyo Co., Ltd., Shochiku-Fuji Co., Ltd., Sogo Housing Co., Ltd., Sumitomo Corp., Tokai Corp., Universal Finance Corp., Yusen Accounting & Finance Co., Ltd.; Thanks: Kurosawa Film Studio, Tokyo Jem Trading Corp., Japan Tobacco, Inc., Suntory, Kokusai Shomei Co., Ltd., Koto Electric Co., Ltd., Honda Airways Co., Ltd., Max Factor, Three Oaks Co., Ltd., Shonan Animal Production, Inc., Japan Underwater Films Co., Liberty House, Chichibu City, Gotemba City, Nagasaki Prefecture, Nagasaki

City, Traffic Department of Nagasaki Prefecture, Lucky Motor's Corp., Minami-Oura Primary School (Nagasaki City), Amagi-Yugashima Town, The Japan Peace Museum, Kazuhiro Sawa; Special Thanks, Eric Roth

Cast: Sachiko Murase (Kane), Hidetaka Yoshioka (Tateo), Tomoko Otakara (Tami), Mie Suzuki (Minako), Mitsunori Isaki (Shinjiro), Hisashi Igawa (Tadao), Toshie Negishi (Yoshie), Choichiro Kawarasaki (Noboru), Narumi Kayashima (Machiko) • Richard Gere (Clark). *With* Matsue Ono, Kappei Matsumoto, Yoshiko Maki, Noriko Homma, Natsuyo Kawakami, Kumeko Otowa, Michio Kida, Shizuko Azuma, Sachio Sakai, Yoshie Kihira, Junpei Natsuki, Setsuko Kawaguchi, Shigeo Kato, Hiroko Maki, Goichi Nagatani, Wasuke Izumi, Sakae Koike, Torauemon Utazawa, Saburo Kadowaki, Yukie Shimura, Tomi Iwasawa, Haruko Uesugi, Teru Oki, Masako Oka, Ei Ogata, Kinu Ono, Mura Kariya, Yukie Sugisaki, Kimi Toshita, Chiyono Nakayama, Ise Maruyama, Tai Yamaguchi, Ayao Imada, Tsuyo Kataoka, Hiroko Kamaya, Akio Sakita, Takatoshi Shimohira, Tomo Takano, Fumi Takeshita, Yoshiko Tsuji, Tadashi Tomonaga, Kiyoshi Nakamura, Satoko Hayashi, Masahito Hirose, Mieko Yasunaga, Akiji Maeda, Katsuji Yoshida, Hideko Yoshiyama, Haruo Yoshihara, Chiyoko Yoshihara, Koji Wada, and the participation of Gekidan Haiyuza, Himawari Theatre Group, Inc., Hayakawa Production, Seinen-Gekijo, Gekidan Tohai, Tanba Dojo, Fantasy Art Nagasaki

A Kurosawa Production Co., Ltd. Production, in association with Feature Film Enterprise II and Shochiku Co., Ltd. A Shochiku Co., Ltd., Release. Dolby Stereo. Fujicolor (processed by Imagica). VistaVision size (spherical Panavision). 98 minutes. Released May 25, 1991.

U.S. version: Released by Orion Classics. English subtitles. Released in Dolby Stereo in the United States. 98 minutes. MPAA rating: PG. Released December 16, 1991.

Notes: Filmed at Toho Studios, Kurosawa Production, and on location in Chichibu, Gotemba, Amagi-Yugashima, and Nagasaki.

KABUTO ("Helmet")
[JOURNEY OF HONOR]
Executive Producers, Hiroshi Tsuchiya and Toshiaki Hayashi; Producer, Sho Kosugi; Director, Gordon Hessler; Screenplay, Nelson Gidding, based on a story by Sho Kosugi and Nelson Gidding; Director of Photography, John Connor; Art Director, Adrian Gorton; Music, John Scott; Music performed by the Hungarian State Opera Orchestra; Yugoslavian Line Producer, Milos Antic; Line Producer, Benni Korzen; Editor, Bill Butler; Casting, Caro Jones; Casting (U.K.), Hubbard Casting; Associate Producer, Second Unit Director and Unit Production Manager, Gene Kraft; Still Photographer, Peter Kernot; Supervising Sound Editor, Mike LeMare; Sound Effects Editor, David Lewis Yewdall; Music Editor, Richard Allen; Negative Cutter, Gary Burritt; Stunt Coordinator, John Stewart. *Japan*: Associate Producers, Susumu Mishima and Kenichiro Fujiyama; Production Manager, Kunio Niwa; First Assistant Director, Yoshihiro Hagiwara; Choreographer, Hiroshi Kuze

Cast: Sho Kosugi (Mayeda), David Essex (Don Pedro), Kane Kosugi (Yorimune), Christopher Lee (King Philip), Norman Lloyd (Father Vasco), Ronald Rickup (Captain Crawford), John Rhys-Davies (El Zaidan), Polly Walker (Cecilia), Dylan Kussman (Smitty) and Miwa Takada (Yadogimi), Nijiko Kiyokawa (*counselor*), Toshiro Mifune (Lord Ieyasu Tokugawa). *With* Yuki Sugimura (Chiyo Mayeda), Ken Sekiguchi (Ishikawa), Naoto Shigemizu (Nakamura), Yuji Sawayama (*East Army general*), Toni Sosie (Dutch), Savic Milutin (*first pistolier*), Radevic Miomir (*second pistolier*), Shinsuke Shirakura (Daisuke Mayeda, *ages 13–14*), Dusko Yujnnovic (Ibrahim), Stevan Minja (Salim), Ljubomir Skiljevic (*taskmaster*), John Stewart (*first sailor*), Dragomir Stanojevic-Kameni (*second sailor*), Bora Stojanovic (*royal chamberlain*), Tadashi Ogiwara (Mayeda's *double*), Yuji Sawayama (Yorimune *stand-in*), Osamu Yayama (*samurai in Edo castle*),

Kenji Miura (*interpreter for* Ieyasu), Manami Mitani (*interpreter for* Yodogimi), Hidekazu Utsumi, Tadashi Ogasawara (*pages*), Akira Hoshino, Kenji Yasunaga, Shogo Ikegami, Junichiro Hayama, Yoshiaki Iguchi (*Ieyasu retainers*), Toshimi Yamaguchi, Tadashi Ogiwara, Satoru Fukasaku, Yuki Nasaka, Kazuhiro Taketoshi, Takashi Odajima (*samurai guards*), Don Pedro Colley (*narrator*)

A Sanyo Finance Co., Ltd./Sho Kosugi Corp./Sho Productions, Inc. Production. A Pocket Pictures Release. Dolby Stereo. De Luxe Color (processed by Technicolor). Panavision. 107 minutes. Released 1992.

U.S. version: Never released theatrically in the United States. Released directly to television and home video by MCA Home Video, Inc. In English and Japanese with English subtitles. 107 minutes. MPAA rating: PG-13. Released 1992.

Notes: A Japanese production in English and Japanese. Filmed in 1990 in Japan and on location in Yugoslavia. Alternate international title: *Shogun Mayeda*.

SHADOW OF THE WOLF

Executive Producer, Charles L. Smiley; Producer, Claude Léger; Director, Jacques Dorfman; Screenplay, Evan Jones, David Milhaud, and Rudy Wurlitzer, based on the novel *Agaguk* by Yves Thériault; Director of Photography, Billy Williams; Art Director, Wolf Kroeger; Music, Maurice Jarre; Editor, Catherine Trouillet; Set Decoration, Jim Erickson; Costume Design, Olga Dimitrov and Joseph A. Porro; Makeup, Nathalie Trépanier; Production Supervisor, Mychèle Boudrias; Unit Production Manager, Mario Nadeau; Visual Effects Supervisor, Ray McMillan

Cast: Lou Diamond Phillips (Agaguk), Toshiro Mifune (Kroomak, *his father*), Jennifer Tilly (Igiyook), Bernard-Pierre Donnadieu (Brown), Donald Sutherland (Henderson), Nicholas Campbell (Scott), Raoul Trujillo (Tulugak), Qalingo Tookalak (Tulugak), Jobie Arnaituk (Nayalik), Tamussie Sivuarapik (Korok), Harry Hill (McTavish), David Okpik (Pualuna), Patricia Eshkibok (Parted Hair), Earl Danylux (Hatchet Jack), Glenn Verdon (Stebbins), Lucie Kadjulik (*first old woman*), Lydia Phillips (*second old woman*), Jean-Michel Dorthan (*first sailor*), Gordon Masten (*second sailor*), Richard Zeman (*policeman*), Alacie Tukalak (Arnattiaq), Sheena Larkin (Mrs. McTavish), Frederic Duplessis (Tayarak, *as a newborn*), Sam Simpson (Tayarak, *one month old*), Estafania Chew (Tayarak, *at six months*), Alunngirk Airo (Tayarak, *at three years*), Lizzie Sivuarapik (*woman in igloo*), Bart Hanna Kappianak (*drum player*), Mary Iqaluk and Nellie Iqaluk (*throat singers*)

An Eiffel Productions/Films A2/Le Studio Canal +/Transfilm/Vision International Production. A Canadian-French co-production. A Triumph Releasing Corp. Release. Stereophonic sound. Color (processed by Laboratories Éclair). Super 35 (release prints anamorphic). 112 minutes. MPAA rating: PG-13. Released March 5, 1993.

Notes: Never released theatrically in Japan. Released directly to home video. Released in Europe in 1992.

MADADAYO ("Not Yet")

[MADADAYO]

Executive Producers, Yo Yamamoto and Yuzo Irie; General Producers, Yasuyoshi Tokuma and Gohei Kogure; Associate Producer, Seikichi Iizumi; Producer, Hisao Kurosawa; Director, Akira Kurosawa; Directorial Adviser, Ishiro Honda; Screenplay, Akira Kurosawa, based on the literary works of Hyakken Uchida (published by Fukutake Publishing Co., Ltd.); Directors of Photography, Takao Saito and Masaharu Ueda; Art Director, Yoshiro Muraki; Lighting, Takeji Sano; Sound, Hideo Nishizaki; Music, Shinichiro Ikebe; Production Coordinator, Izuhiko Suehiro; Production Manager, Teruyo Nogami; Costume Design, Kazuko Kurosawa; Assistant Director, Takashi Koizumi

Cast: Tatsuo Matsumura (Professor Hyakken Uchida), Kyoko Kagawa (*his wife*). *His students*: Hisashi Igawa (Takayama), George Tokoro (Amaki), Masayuki Yui (Kiriyama), Akira Terao (Sawamura *and narrator*), Takeshi Kusaka (Kobayashi), Asei Kobayashi (Kameyama), Hidetaka Yoshioka (*student*), Yoshitaka Zushi (*neighbor*), Mitsura Hirata, Nobuto Okamoto, Tetsu Watanabe, Mikihiro Hiaizumi, Norio Matsui, Murohide Sugizaki, Ken Takemura, Hiroyoshi Takenouchi, Motohiro Shimaki, Masaaki Sasaki, Nobuyoshi Masuda, Masayoshi Nagasawa, Shu Nakahan, Yoshimitsu Shindo, Ryujiro Shin, Tatsuya Ito, Naoto Shigemizu, Masuo Amada, Minoru Hirano, Kozo Nomura, Kazuhiko Sasai, Toshi Sasaki, Norimasa Nattori, Fumihiko Tsuburaya, Hiroshi Nagatsubaki, Tatsuya Sakaguchi, Yoshio Nakahira, Sensaburo Makimura, Yasuji Mita, Katsumi Cho, Norinobu Kodama, Yomaru Yokichi, Mikuni Toyama, Sumimaru Yoshimi, Junichi Tsubota, Makoto Dainenji, Shinji Bando, Kojiro Hayasaka, Masahiko Tanimura, Toshihiko Nakano

A Daiei Co., Ltd./Dentsu, Inc./Kurosawa Production Co., Ltd. Production, in association with Tokuma Shoten Publishing Co., Ltd. A Toho Co., Ltd. Release. Dolby Stereo. Color. Vista-Vision size. 134 minutes. Released April 17, 1993.

U.S. version: Premiered September 3, 1999, on the Turner Classic Movies cable television network with English subtitles. Subsequently released theatrically by Winstar Cinema on September 1, 2000, with English subtitles.

Note: The last films of both Akira Kurosawa and Ishiro Honda.

PICTURE BRIDE
Executive Producers, Cellin Gluck, Diane Mei Lin Mark; Producer, Lisa Onodera; Director, Kayo Hatta; Screenplay, Kayo Hatta and Mari Hatta, based on a story by Kayo Hatta, Mari Hatta, and Diane Mei Lin Mark; Director of Photography, Claudio Rocha; Art Director, Paul Guncheon; Sound, Susan Moore-Chang; Music, Cliff Eidelman; Editors, Mallory Gottlieb and Lynzee Klingman; Costume Design, Ada Akaji; Chief Assistant Director, Emmett J. Dennis III; Second Unit Director, Tim August

Cast: Yuki Kudo (Riyo), Cary-Hiroyuki Tagawa (Kanzaki), Tamlyn Tomita (Kana), Akira Takayama (Matsuji), Yoko Sugi (Aunt Sode), Christianne Mays, Jason Scott Lee • <u>Toshiro Mifune</u> (*the benshi*)

A Thousand Cranes Filmworks and Miramax Production, in association with Cecile Co., Ltd. A Miramax Films Release. A U.S. production in English and Japanese with Japanese subtitles. Ultra-Stereo. Color (processed by Foto-Kem). VistaVision size. 98 minutes. Released May 5, 1995.

Notes: Released in Japan in 1996.

FUKAI KAWA ("Deep River")
[DEEP RIVER]
Executive Producers, Koji Imai and Hide Matsunaga; Planning, Michikazu Masaoka; Producer, Masayuki Sato; Director, Kei Kumai; Screenplay, Kei Kumai, based on the novel by Shusaku Endo; Director of Photography, Masao Tochizawa; Art Director, Takeo Kimura; Lighting, Tadaaki Shimada; Sound, Yukio Kubota; Music, Teizo Matsumura; Editor, Osamu Inoue; Second Unit Director, Kazuo Hara; Associate Producers, Kazuyuki Kuwayama and Ashim Samanta; Unit Production Manager, Yuji Sasaki; Committee Director, Hiroshi Nakahara

Cast: Kumiko Akiyoshi (Mitsuko), Eiji Okuda (Otsu), Hisashi Igawa (Isobe), Kyoko Kagawa (*his wife*), <u>Toshiro Mifune</u> (Tsukada), Kin Sugai (*his wife*), Yoichi Numata (Kiguchi), Tetta Sugimoto (Enam), Hiroyuki Okita (Sanjyo), Maki Shirai (*his wife*)

A Shigato Film Producers Production, in association with Aradhana Films. A Toho Co., Ltd. Release. Color. VistaVision size. 130 minutes. Released June 24, 1995.

U.S. version: Received limited distribution in the United States with English subtitles in March 1998.

Notes: Filmed, in part, on location in India and France. Toshiro Mifune's final film appearance.

LAST MAN STANDING

Executive Producers, Sara Risher and Michael De Luca; Producers, Walter Hill, Arthur Sarkissian, and Ralph Singleton; Director, Walter Hill; Screenplay, Walter Hill, based on the screenplay of *Yojimbo*, by Ryuzo Kikushima and Akira Kurosawa; Director of Photography, Lloyd Ahern; Art Director, Gary Wissner; Sound, Lee Orloff; Music, Ry Cooder; Editor, Freeman Davies; Casting, Mary Gail Artz and Barbara Cohen; Costume Design, Dan Moore; Associate Producer, Ralph S. Singleton; First Assistant Director, Jeffrey Wetzel; Second Assistant Director, Jeffrey Okabayashi; Stunt Coordinator and Second Unit Director, Allan Graf; Executive in Charge of Production, Ted Zachary; Camera Operators, Robert LaBonge and Michael Chavez; Set Decorator, Gary Fettis; Property Master, Rick Young; Script Supervisor, Marilyn Bailey; Makeup Supervisor, Gary Liddiard; Hair Supervisor, Dorothy Fox

Cast: Bruce Willis (John Smith), Bruce Dern (Sheriff Ed Galt), William Sanderson (Joe Monday), Christopher Walken (Hickey), David Patrick Kelly (Doyle), Karina Lombard (Felina), Ned Eisenberg (Fredo Strozzi), Alexandra Powers (Lucy Kolinsky), Michael Imperioli (Giorgio Carmonte), Ken Jenkins (Captain Tom Pickett), R.D. Call (Jack McCool), Leslie Mann (Wanda), Patrick Kilpatrick (Finn), Luis Contreres (Commander Ramirez), Raynor Scheine (*gas station attendant*), Tiny Ron (Jacko the Giant), John Paxton (*undertaker*), Michael Cavalieri (Berto), Hannes Fritsch (Santo), Michael Strasser (docker), Matt O'Toole (Burke), Lin Shayne (*madam*), Larry Holt (*border patrolman*), Allan Graf (*convoy driver*), Cassandra Gava (*barmaid*), Randy Hall (*Doyle thug*), Jimmy Ortega, Tom Rosales (*Ramirez bodyguards*), Dean Rader-Duval (Donnie), Michael Prozzo (Roca), Chris Doyle, Jim Palmer (*brothel thugs*)

A New Line Cinema Production. A New Line Cinema Release. A U.S. Production in English. Stereophonic sound. Color. Super 35. 101 minutes. MPAA rating: R. Released September 20, 1996.

AME AGARU ("After the Rain")
[AFTER THE RAIN]

Executive Producer, Hisao Kurosawa; Producer, Masato Hara; Associate Producers, Kayo Yoshida and Elie Chouraqui; Director, Takashi Koizumi; Screenplay, Akira Kurosawa, based on a short story by Shugoro Yamamoto; Director of Photography, Shoji Ueda; Photography Consultant, Takao Saito; Art Director, Yoshiro Muraki; Lighting, Takeharu Sano; Sound, Kenichi Benitani; Music, Masaru Sato; Costumes, Kazuko Kurosawa; Assistant to Takashi Koizumi, Teruyo Nogami; Assistant Director, Yasunori Suzuki; Line Producer, Tsutomu Sakurai; Editor, Hideto Aga; Assistant Director, Yasunori Miyazaki

Cast: Akira Terao (Ihei Misawa), Yoshiko Miyazaki (Tayo Misawa, *his wife*), Shiro Mifune (Lord Nagai Izuminokami Shigeaki), Fumi Dan (Okugata, *Lord Shigeaki's wife*), Hisashi Igawa (Kihei Ishiyama, *the senior retainer*), Hidetaka Yoshioka (Chamberlain Gonnojo Sakaibara), Takyuki Kato (Hayato Naito, *a page*), Mieko Harada (Okin, *the prostitute*), Tatsuo Matusmura (Sekkyo-Bushi Jii, *the old man at the inn*), Tatsuya Nakadai (Tsuji Gettan)

An Asmik Ace Entertainment/Kurosawa Production Co., Ltd./7 Films Cinema (France) Production. A Toho Co., Ltd. Release. A Japanese-French co-production. Dolby SR stereophonic sound. Color. VistaVision size. 91 minutes. Released January 22, 2000.

U.S. version: Not released in the United States at the time this book went to press.

Notes: Premiered at the Venice Film Festival—Tribute to Akira Kurosawa, on September 5, 1999. U.S. premiere at the American Film Institute Film Festival on October 25, 1999. The onscreen title is subtitled *When the Rain Lifts.*

DORA-HEITA ("Alley Cat")
Executive Producer, Masaya Nakamura; Producer, Yoshinobu Nishioka; Director, Kon Ichikawa; Screenplay, Kon Ichikawa, <u>Akira Kurosawa</u>, Keisuke Kinoshita, and Masaki Kobayashi, based on the novel *Diary of a Town Magistrate* by Shugoro Yamamoto; Director of Photography, Yukio Isohata; Art Director, Yoshinobu Nishioka; Sound, Iwao Otani; Music, Kensaku Tanikawa; Associate Producers, Naoto Sarukawa, Minoru Sakai, and Kazuo Tsuruma; Editor, Chizuko Osada; Chief Assistant Director, Yoshihumi Ogasawara

Cast: Koji Yakusho (Koheita Mochizuki, *aka* Dora-heita), Yuko Asano (Kosei), Bunta Sugawara (Nadahachi), Ryudo Uzaki (Giyoro Senba), Tsurutaro Kataoka (Hanso Yasukawa), Saburo Ishikura, Renji Ishibashi, Tsuyoshi Ujiki, Isao Bito, Shuji Otaki, Shigeru Koyama, Takeshi Kato, Noboru Mitani, Masane Tsukayama, Kyoko Kishida, Nekohachi Edoya

A Dore-Heita Projects/Nikkatsu Corp./Yomiko Advertising Co./Mainichi Broadcasting System Production, in association with Eizo Kyoto Film Co., Ltd. A Toho Co., Ltd. Release. DTS Stereo. Color. VistaVision size. 110 minutes. Released May 13, 2000.

U.S. version: First exhibited in the United States on September 13, 2001. (Originally slated for Sept. 11, it was rescheduled due to the World Trade Center attack.) International rights controlled by Nikkatsu Corp.

Notes: Adapted from a 1969 screenplay, which was intended to be co-directed by its authors. Japanese title can also be translated as "Playboy."

AKIRA KUROSAWA'S UNPRODUCED SCREENPLAYS

DARUMA-DERA NO DOITSUJIN
("A German at Daruma Temple")

SHIZUKANARI ("All Is Quiet")

YUKI ("Snow")

MORI NO SENICHIA ("A Thousand and One Nights in the Forest")

JAJAUMA MONOGATARI ("The Story of a Bad Horse")

DOKKOI KONO YARI ("The Lifted Spear")

SAN PAGUITA NO HANA ("The San Pajuito Flower")

UTSUKUSHIKI KOYOMI ("Beautiful Calendar")

DAISAN HATOBA ("The Third Harbor")

TOSHIRO MIFUNE TELEVISION APPEARANCES

Toshiro Mifune made numerous television appearances through the 1970s and '80s. Only *Ronin of the Wilderness* was available on home video in Japan when this book went to press, though several have aired in the United States in television markets with large Japanese populations, such as Honolulu, San Francisco, and Los Angeles. This list of programs was made available through the generosity of Shiro Mifune and Mifune Productions Co., Ltd.

FIVE MASTERLESS SAMURAI (Gonin no nobushi, 1968)
With Akira Takarada. Six one-hour episodes. Aired on NET.

EPIC CHUSHINGURA (Dai Chushingura, 1971)
With an all-star cast. 52 one-hour episodes. ANB.

KOYA NO SO RONIN ("Ronin of the Wilderness")
(Credits for Pilot) Producers, Yusuzo Katsuda and Yoshio Nishikawa; Associate Producer, Toshiro Mifune; Director, Misuo Murayama; Teleplay, Yoshio Tsuda; Director of Photography, Kazuo Yamada; Art Director, Hikosaburo Takayama; Lighting, Naoyuki Doi; Sound, Hisao Onu; Music, Shunsuke Kikuchi; Editor, Yoshihiro Araki; Special Effects, Toho Effects Group; Assistant Director, Akihiro Kashima

    Cast: Toshiro Mifune (Kujuro Toge), Shun Oide (Konosuke Aiu), Jiro Sakagami (Jirokichi), Mieko Kaji (Ofumi), Yuko Hamada (Bitsu), Shoji Taiki (Ichinosuke Sekine), Akira Kumi (Kai Horita), Shinjiro Ehara (Shimpachi Ikuta), Minoru Terada (narrator), Ryutaro Itsumi, Yuzo Hayakawa, Akiyoshi Kasuga

    A NET/Mifune Productions Co., Ltd. Production. Color (processed by Toyo Laboratories). Standard size. 104 one-hour episodes aired on ANB during the 1972 season.

    U.S. version: Release, if any, is undetermined.

YOJIMBO OF THE WILDERNESS (Koya no yojimbo, 1973)
With Yosuke Natsuki. 5 one-hour episodes. ANB (see below).

THE SWORD, THE WIND, AND THE LULLABY (Ken to kaze to komoriuta, 1976)
With Atsuo Nakamura. 27 one-hour episodes. NET.

RONIN IN A LAWLESS TOWN (Muhogai no suronin, 1977)
With Mayumi Ogawa. 23 one-hour episodes. ANB.

THE SPY APPEARS (Kakushimetsuke sanjo, 1977)
With Toru Emori. 5 one-hour episodes. TBS.

AN EAGLE IN EDO (Edo no taka, 1978)
With Kunie Tanaka. 38 one-hour episodes. ANB.

HIDEOUT IN SUITE 7 (Kakekomibiru nanagoshitsu, 1979)
With Hiroshi Katsuno. 11 one-hour episodes. CX.

SEKIGAHARA (Sekigahara, 1981)
With Go Kato. 1 seven-hour drama. TBS.

BUNGO'S DETECTIVE NOTES (Bungo torimonocho, 1981)
With Sakae Takita. Three-part, one-hour drama. ANB.

THE TEN BATTLES OF SHINGO (Shingo juban shobu, 1981)
With Tomoyuki Kunihiro. Two-part, two-hour program. CX.

MY DAUGHTER! FLY ON THE WINGS OF LOVE AND TEARS (Musumeyo! Ai to namida no tsubasa de tobe, 1981)
With Yuko Tanaka. Two-hour television film. YTV.

THE CRESCENT-SHAPED WILDERNESS (Kyukei no koya, 1981)
With Yoko Shimada. Two-hour television film. NET.

THE RONIN'S PATH (Suronin makaritoru, 1982)
With numerous guest stars. 5 two-hour episodes. CX.

THE HAPPY YELLOW HANDKERCHIEF (Shiawase no kiiroi hankachi, 1982)
With Bunta Sugawara. Two-hour television film. TBS.

THE BRAVE MAN SAYS LITTLE (Yusha ha katarazu, 1983)
With Tetsuro Tamba. One eight-hour drama. NHK.

THE RONIN'S PATH, VOLUME V (Suronin makaritoru, Vol. V, 1983)
With Go Wakabayashi. One-hour television film. CX.

RONIN—SECRET OF THE MYSTERIOUS VALLEY (Suronin makyosashodani no himitsu, 1983)
One-hour television film. CX.

SOSHI OKITA, BURNING CORPSE OF A SWORD MASTER (Moetechiru hono no kenshi Soshi Okita, 1984)
With Toshihiko Tahara. One-hour television film. NET.

THE BURNING MOUNTAIN RIVER (Sanga moyu, 1984)
With Koshiro Matsumoto, Toshiyuki Nishida, Kenji Sawada, Reiko Ohara, Yoko Shimada, Yumi Takigawa, Daijiro Tsutsumi, Yoshie Kashiwabara, Takuzo Kawatani, Kyohei Shibata, Ken Watanabe, Saburo Shinoda, Pink Izumi, Kazuko Kato, Satomi Tezuka, Agnes Chan, Kiyoshi Kodama, Koji Tsuruta, Keiko Tsushima, Toshiro Mifune. 51 episodes running on NHK 1/8/84–12/23/84, based on the book *Futatsu no sokoku* by Toyoko Yamazaki.

NOTES

INTRODUCTION

1. NHK Japanese television newscast, September 1998.
2. "Milestones," *Time*, September 21, 1998.
3. NHK Japanese television newscast, September 1998.
4. Ibid.
5. Ibid.
6. Ibid.
7. Akira Kurosawa, *Something Like an Autobiography* (New York: Vintage Books, 1983), xi.
8. Michael Atkinson, "The Last Samurai," *The Village Voice*, January 13, 1998.
9. Clyde Haberman, "New York Salutes Japan's John Wayne," *The New York Times*, March 4, 1984, 1.
10. Kevin Thomas and Kenneth Reich, "Toshiro Mifune, Acclaimed Japanese Film Star, Dies," *Los Angeles Times*, December 25, 1997, A24.
11. Peter Grilli, "Civil Samurai," *Film Comment*, July 1984, 67.
12. Stephen Hunter, "Toshiro Mifune: A World-Class Talent," *The Washington Post*, December 27, 1997, F26.
13. Thomas and Reich, "Toshiro Mifune, Acclaimed Japanese Film Star, Dies."
14. *Seven Samurai*. Criterion DVD audio commentary.
15. *The* (London) *Times*, quoted in Hunter, "Toshiro Mifune: A World-Class Talent."
16. Kurosawa, *Something Like an Autobiography,* 161.
17. Beverly Beyette, "Toshiro Mifune Takes Up the Samurai Role Again," *Los Angeles Times*, August 12, 1983, 18.
18. Ibid.
19. Haberman, "New York Salutes Japan's John Wayne," 15.
20. John Kobal, *The Top 100 Movies* (New York: New American Library), 1988.
21. Bill Warren. Personal interview, October 13, 1994.
22. Donald Richie. Personal interview by James Bailey, 1990.
23. Richard Corliss, "An Explosive Talent," *Time*, January 12, 1998.

1: FRAGMENTS
1. Akira Kurosawa, *Something Like an Autobiography* (New York: Vintage Books, 1983), 6–7.
2. Ibid.
3. Ibid., 8.
4. Koishikawa-ku no longer exists under that name. Today this area is called Bunkyo-ku and is located near what is now known as Ichomei.
5. Kurosawa, *Something Like an Autobiography*, 18.
6. Ibid., 50.
7. Ibid., 52.
8. Ibid., 52–54.
9. Ibid., 76.
10. Ibid., 71.
11. Ibid., 78.
12. Joseph L. Anderson and Donald Richie, *The Japanese Film—Art and Industry* (Expanded Edition) (Princeton University Press, 1982), 23.
13. Ibid.
14. Kurosawa, *Something Like An Autobiography*, 85–86.
15. Shuko Mifune, *Minami Manshu shashincho* (Views of Southern Manchuria) (Tsingtao, China: Mifune Shashinkan, 1910).
16. Shuko Mifune, *Santo meisho shashincho* (Beautiful Scenes of Santo Prefecture Collection) (Sainan, China: Dairen Bijutsu Insatsusha, 1929).
17. Shiro Mifune. Personal interview, December 10, 1999.
18. Tomio Sagisu. Personal interview, December 9, 1999.
19. Ibid.

2: P.C.L. AND YAMA-SAN
1. Joseph L. Anderson and Donald Richie, *The Japanese Film—Art and Industry* (Expanded Edition) (Princeton University Press, 1982), 81–87.
2. The name is derived from two Kanji characters: *To*, short for Tokyo, and *takara*, short for Takarazuka, which can also be read as *ho*.
3. Akira Kurosawa, *Something Like an Autobiography* (New York: Vintage Books, 1983), 89.
4. Ibid., 90.
5. Michihiro Imata, Kunihiro Susumu, and Akira Kurosawa Kenkyukai-hen, eds., *Kurosawa Akira yume no ashiato* (Akira Kurosawa's Footsteps of Dreams) (Tokyo: Kyodo Tunshin-sha, 1999), 48.
6. Shinbi Iida, "Kurosawa," English translation of undated article reprinted from *Kinema Jumpo*, c. 1960s.
7. Kurosawa, *Something Like an Autobiography*, 93.
8. Senkichi Taniguchi. Personal interview, October 3, 1999.
9. Takamaro Shimaji, ed., *Kurosawa Akira Dokyumento* (Akira Kurosawa Document) (Tokyo: *Kinema Jumpo* Special Edition, May 1974), 137.
10. Kurosawa, *Something Like an Autobiography*, 97–98.
11. Shimaji, ed., *Kurosawa Akira Dokyumento*, 137.
12. Kurosawa, *Something Like an Autobiography*, 100.
13. Shimaji, ed., *Kurosawa Akira Dokyumento*, 137.
14. Kurosawa, *Something Like an Autobiography*, 95.
15. Taniguchi interview.
16. Ibid.

17. Ibid.
18. Kurosawa, *Something Like an Autobiography*, 103.
19. Taniguchi interview.

3: TREADING THE TIGER'S TAIL

1. "Obituary of Toshiro Mifune, Japanese Film Actor Internationally Known," *The Daily Telegraph*, December 27, 1997.
2. Vernon Scott, "A Nippon Clark Gable," *Los Angeles Herald-Examiner*, December 26, 1968.
3. Tomio Sagisu. Personal interview, December 9, 1999.
4. Shiro Mifune. Personal interview, December 15, 1999.
5. Akira Kurosawa, *Something Like an Autobiography* (New York: Vintage Books, 1983), 111.
6. Takamaro Shimaji, ed., *Kurosawa Akira Dokyumento* (Akira Kurosawa Document) (Tokyo: *Kinema Jumpo* Special Edition, May 1974), 137.
7. Kurosawa, *Something Like an Autobiography*, 106.
8. Shinbi Iida, "Kurosawa," English translation of undated article reprinted from *Kinema Jumpo*, c. 1960s.
9. Joseph L. Anderson and Donald Richie, *The Japanese Film—Art and Industry* (Expanded Edition) (Princeton University Press, 1982), 102.
10. Vincent Canby, "Film: 'Horse,' from Japan," *The New York Times*, May 9, 1986.
11. "Horse," *The Village Voice*, May 16, 1986.
12. Kurosawa, *Something Like an Autobiography*, 121.
13. Ibid., 145.
14. Mike Y. Inoue. Personal interview, December 12, 1999.
15. Kurosawa, *Something Like an Autobiography*, 118–19.
16. Ibid., 120.
17. Ibid., 121.
18. Tomoyuki Tanaka, "The Origins of *Sanshiro Sugata*," Liner notes for the Japanese laserdisc release, 1993.
19. Kurosawa, *Something Like an Autobiography*, 122.
20. Masahiro Makino, *Eiga tosei—chi no maki* (The Film Business—From the Ground Up), in Michihiro Imata, Kunihiro Susumu, and Akira Kurosawa Kenyukai-hen, eds. *Kurosawa Akira yume no ashiato* (Akira Kurosawa's Footsteps of Dreams) (Tokyo: Kyodo Tunshin-sha, 1999), 66.
21. Kurosawa, *Something Like an Autobiography*, 123.
22. Translation of this name is uncertain. Honda may be referring to *Mikio* Komatsu, who was an assistant director at Toho around that time.
23. Shimaji, ed., *Kurosawa Akira Dokyumento*, 137.
24. Akira Mimura, "Location Diary of *Sanshiro Sugata*," *Shin Eiga*, April 1943.
25. Ibid.
26. Kurosawa, *Something Like an Autobiography*, 127.
27. Mimura, "Location Diary of *Sanshiro Sugata*."
28. Kurosawa, *Something Like an Autobiography*, 126.
29. Ibid., 131.
30. The film is also preceded by an apology from Toho for losing the footage.
31. Joy Gould Boyum, "A Blend of Bloodletting and Beauty," *The Wall Street Journal*, April 23, 1973.
32. Judith Crist, "The Yakuza film . . ." *New York*, April 29, 1974.
33. "Akira Kurosawa's rarely . . ." *The New Yorker*, May 19, 1990.

34. Kevin Thomas, " 'Judo' Screens at Festival," *Los Angeles Times*, May 10, 1974.
35. Kurosawa, *Something Like an Autobiography*, 132.
36. Ibid., 133.
37. Ibid., 134.
38. Ibid., 135, 137.
39. Donald Richie, *The Films of Akira Kurosawa* (Revised Edition) (Berkeley, CA: University of California Press, 1984), 24.
40. Mitsuhiro Yoshimoto, *Kurosawa* (Durham, N.C.: Duke University Press, 2000), 89.
41. Toru Nishiguchi, ed., *Kurosawa Akira—Bungei besatsu tsuito tokushu Kurosawa Akira kawade yume muku* (Akira Kurosawa—Bungei Special Memorial Issue, Kawade Dreams) (Tokyo: Kawade shubo shin-sha, 1998), 83.
42. Kurosawa, *Something Like an Autobiography*, 136.
43. Richie, *The Films of Akira Kurosawa*, 24.
44. Kyoko Hirano, *Mr. Smith Goes to Tokyo—Japanese Cinema Under the American Occupation, 1945–1952* (Washington: Smithsonian Institution Press, 1992), 26.
45. Yoshie Yaguchi, "Circumstances in Japan." Liner notes for the Japanese laserdisc release, 1993.
46. Hirano, *Mr. Smith Goes to Tokyo*, 215.
47. Kurosawa, *Something Like an Autobiography*, 138.
48. Ibid., 21–22.
49. Mike Y. Inoue. Personal interview, December 12, 1999.
50. Kurosawa, *Something Like an Autobiography*, 140.
51. Ibid., 145.
52. Hirano, *Mr. Smith Goes to Tokyo*, 28.
53. Kurosawa, *Something Like an Autobiography*, 145.
54. Hirano, *Mr. Smith Goes to Tokyo*, 29.
55. Ibid.
56. Nishiguchi, *Kurosawa Akira*, 83.
57. Ibid., 87.
58. Ibid., 86.
59. Ibid., 84.
60. Richie, *The Films of Akira Kurosawa*, 34.
61. Ibid., 34–35.
62. Kon Ichikawa, "A Severe Film." Liner notes for the Japanese laserdisc release, 1993.
63. John McCarten, "The Current Cinema," *The New Yorker*, January 16, 1960.
64. "Anby," "The Men Who Tread on the Tiger's Tail," *Weekly Variety*, January 27, 1960.
65. Inoue interview.

4: NEW FACES OF 1946

1. Donald Richie. Personal interview by James Bailey, 1990.
2. Kyoko Hirano, *Mr. Smith Goes to Tokyo—Japanese Cinema Under the American Occupation, 1945–1952* (Washington: Smithsonian Institution Press), 1992, 216.
3. Ibid.
4. Masahiro Ogi, "Kurosawa Akira zensakuhin o kataru" (Akira Kurosawa Discusses His Films), in *Sekai no eiga sakka* (Three Filmmakers of the World) (Tokyo: *Kinema Jumpo-sha*, 1970), 115–16.
5. Tomio Sagisu. Personal interview, December 9, 1999.
6. Shiro Mifune. Personal interview, December 16, 1999.

7. Sagisu interview.

8. Toshiro Mifune. Liner notes for the Japanese laserdisc release of *Seven Samurai*, August 25, 1993.

9. Sagisu interview.

10. Leonard Klady, "Obituaries—Toshiro Mifune," *Weekly Variety*, January 5, 1998.

11. Akira Kurosawa, *Something Like an Autobiography* (New York: Vintage Books, 1983), 160.

12. Ibid.

13. Yoshio Tsuchiya, "Superstar's Personality Shone on Screen," *Daily Yomiuri*, December 26, 1997.

14. Takamaro Shimaji, ed., *Kurosawa Akira Dokyumento* (Akira Kurosawa Document) (Tokyo: *Kinema Jumpo* Special Edition, May 1974), 196.

15. Ibid.

16. Kurosawa, *Something Like an Autobiography*, 148–49.

17. Hiromichi Horikawa, "No Regrets." Liner notes for Japanese laserdisc release, 1993.

18. Haruko Sugimura, "About That Time." Liner notes for the Japanese laserdisc release.

19. Horikawa, "No Regrets."

20. Sugimura, "About That Time."

21. Kurosawa, *Something Like an Autobiography*, 149.

22. Donald Richie, *The Films of Akira Kurosawa* (Revised Edition) (Berkeley, CA: University of California Press, 1984), 37.

23. Hirano, *Mr. Smith Goes to Tokyo*, 183.

24. Joseph L. Anderson and Donald Richie, *The Japanese Film—Art and Industry* (expanded edition) (Princeton University Press, 1982), 398–99.

25. Horikawa, Hiromichi. Liner notes for the Japanese laserdisc release, 1993.

26. Sugimura, Haruko. Liner notes for the Japanese laserdisc release, 1993.

27. Noriaki Yuasa. Personal interview, February 1996.

28. Hirano, *Mr. Smith Goes to Tokyo*, 195.

29. Ibid., 196.

30. Joan Mellen, "Postwar Japan on Film—The Dark Side of Affluence," *The New York Times*, April 22, 1979, 19.

31. Kevin Thomas, "Two Films Open Japanese Series," *Los Angeles Times*, May 23, 1978, IV:14.

32. Vincent Canby, "Screen: Two Discoveries from Japan at Thalia," *The New York Times*, June 6, 1980.

33. Tom Allen, "Akira Kurosawa's . . ." *The Village Voice*, June 9, 1980.

5: THREE GANGSTERS, A DAY OUT, AND CAYENNE PEPPER

1. Kyoko Hirano, *Mr. Smith Goes to Tokyo—Japanese Cinema Under the American Occupation, 1945–1952* (Washington: Smithsonian Institution Press, 1992), 222–23.

2. Akira Kurosawa, *Something Like an Autobiography* (New York: Vintage Books, 1983), 151.

3. Ibid.

4. Senkichi Taniguchi. Personal interview by telephone, October 3, 1999.

5. Ibid.

6. "Obituary of Toshiro Mifune, Japanese Film Actor Internationally Known," *The Daily Telegraph*, December 27, 1997, 25.

7. Taniguchi interview.

8. Kihachi Okamoto. Personal interview, June 28, 1997.

9. Liner notes for the Japanese laserdisc release, 1995.

10. Akira Ifukube. Personal interview, December 18, 1994.

11. Kurosawa, *Something Like an Autobiography*, 161.

12. Taniguchi interview.

13. Kurosawa, *Something Like an Autobiography*, 154–55.

14. Chieko Nakakita, "The Time of *One Wonderful Sunday*." Liner notes for the Japanese laserdisc release, 1993.

15. Kurosawa, *Something Like an Autobiography*, 152.

16. Ibid., 153.

17. Donald Richie, *The Films of Akira Kurosawa* (Revised Edition) (Berkeley, CA: University of California Press, 1984), 46.

18. Vincent Canby, "Film: 'One Wonderful Sunday,' Japanese in Defeat," *The New York Times*, June 29, 1982.

19. J. Hoberman, "The Sound of One Hand Clapping," *The Village Voice*, July 6, 1982.

20. Richie, *The Films of Akira Kurosawa*, 47.

21. Kurosawa, *Something Like an Autobiography*, 156.

22. Ibid., 156, 157.

23. Ibid., 162.

24. "Takashi Shimura's Story," in Michihiro Imata, Kunihiro Susumu, and Kurosawa Akira Kenkyukai-hen, eds., *Akira Kurosawa's Footsteps of Dreams* (Tokyo: Kyodo Tunshin-sha, 1999), 107.

25. Richie, *The Films of Akira Kurosawa*, 49.

26. Toshiro Mifune. Liner notes for the Japanese laserdisc release of *Seven Samurai*, August 25, 1993.

27. Kurosawa, *Something Like an Autobiography*, 160.

28. Ibid., 162.

29. Kuniharu Akiyama, "*Drunken Angel* and Memo Regarding Fumio Hayasaka." Liner notes for the Japanese laserdisc release, 1993.

30. "Fumio Hayasaka's Story," in Imata et al., eds., *Akira Kurosawa's Footsteps of Dreams*, 110.

31. "Anby," "Drunken Angel," *Weekly Variety*, February 3, 1960.

32. Hirano, *Mr. Smith Goes to Tokyo*, 223–24.

33. Kurosawa, *Something Like an Autobiography*, 165.

34. Hirano, *Mr. Smith Goes to Tokyo*, 225–29.

35. Kurosawa, *Something Like an Autobiography*, 164–68.

6: STRAY DOGS

1. Akira Kurosawa, *Something Like an Autobiography* (New York: Vintage Books, 1983), 168.

2. Ibid.

3. Ibid., 170.

4. Donald Richie, *The Films of Akira Kurosawa* (Berkeley, CA: University of California Press, 1965), 55.

5. Kurosawa, *Something Like an Autobiography*, 172.

6. Akira Ifukube. Personal interview, December 18, 1994.

7. Takamaro Shimaji, ed., *Kurosawa Akira Dokyumento* (Akira Kurosawa Document) (Tokyo: *Kinema Jumpo* Special Edition, May 1974), 112.

8. Vincent Canby, "Film: 'The Quiet Duel' by Akira Kurosawa," *The New York Times*, November 25, 1983.

9. Senkichi Taniguchi. Personal interview, October 3, 1999.

10. Richie, *The Films of Akira Kurosawa*, 58.

11. Kurosawa, *Something Like an Autobiography*, 159.

12. Ibid., 173.
13. Ibid., 175–76.
14. Ishiro Honda, "Memories of *Stray Dog*." Liner notes for the Japanese laserdisc release, 1993.
15. Michihiro Imata, Kunihiro Susumu, and Akira Kurosawa Kenkyukai-hen, eds., *Akira Kurosawa's Footsteps of Dreams* (Tokyo: Kyodo Tunshin-sha, 1999), 120.
16. Ibid., 123.
17. Richie, *The Films of Akira Kurosawa*, 63.
18. Imata et al., eds., *Akira Kurosawa's Footsteps of Dreams*, 122.
19. Ibid., 117.
20. Keiko Awaji, "I Was a Child at the Time." Liner notes for the Japanese laserdisc release, 1993.
21. Kurosawa, *Something Like an Autobiography*, 176.
22. "Seven Bullets," *Newsweek*, March 9, 1964.
23. Ronald Gold, "Stray Dog," *Motion Picture Herald*, April 15, 1964.
24. "Cat and Mouse Games: The Detective in Film," Pacific Film Archive program notes, June 1989.
25. Henry Sheehan, "Stray Dog," *LA Weekly*, December 6, 1991.
26. Herman Pevner, "New Version of 'Stray Dog' at Kokusai Theatre," *Hokebei Mainichi*, June 20, 1974.

7: A NEW DECADE

1. Senkichi Taniguchi. Personal interview, October 3, 1999.
2. Shiro Mifune. Personal interview, December 10, 1999.
3. Ibid., December 16, 1999.
4. Kyoko Hirano, *Mr. Smith Goes to Tokyo—Japanese Cinema Under the American Occupation 1945–1952* (Washington: Smithsonian Institution Press, 1992), 89.
5. Ibid., 87–95.
6. "Nagisa Oshima, Interview with Japanese Film Director," *UNESCO Courier*, July–August 1995, 60.
7. Akira Kurosawa, *Something Like an Autobiography* (New York: Vintage, 1983), 177.
8. Ian Buruma, "Haunted Heroine," *Interview*, September 1989, 126.
9. Takamaro Shimaji, ed., *Kurosawa Akira Dokyumento* (Akira Kurosawa Document) (Tokyo: Kinema Jumpo Special Edition, May 1974), 84.
10. Kevin Thomas, "Two Great Directors Contrasted at Kabuki," *Los Angeles Times*, June 23, 1964.
11. "Robe," *Weekly Variety*, August 20, 1980.
12. Vincent Canby, "From Kurosawa," *The New York Times*, August 26, 1980.
13. Richie, *The Films of Akira Kurosawa*, 66.

8: GATE TO THE WORLD

1. Shinobu Hashimoto. Personal interview, December 15, 1999.
2. Ibid.
3. Akira Kurosawa, *Something Like an Autobiography* (New York: Vintage Books, 1983), 181.
4. Donald Richie, "*Rashomon* and Kurosawa," in *Rashomon—A Film by Akira Kurosawa* (New York: Grove Press, 1969), 222.
5. Hashimoto interview.
6. Kurosawa, *Something Like an Autobiography*, 182.

7. Akira Kurosawa, "A Film Murder Without a Clue," *Rashomon* press book, c. 1952.

8. Richie, "*Rashomon* and Kurosawa," 222.

9. Eiji Funakoshi. Personal interview, January 26, 1996.

10. "SR Goes to the Movies—An Almost Forgotten Art," *The Saturday Review*, January 19, 1952.

11. Donald Richie, *The Films of Akira Kurosawa* (Revised Edition) (Berkeley, CA: University of California Press, 1984), 77.

12. Ray Falk, "Japan's 'Rasho Mon' Rings the Bell," *The New York Times*, October 21, 1951.

13. Kurosawa, *Something Like an Autobiography*, 184.

14. Kazuo Miyagawa, "An Actor Who Used His Entire Body," in *Toshiro Mifune—The Last Samurai*, ed. Finichisya (Tokyo: Mainichi-Shinbun-sha, 1998), 42.

15. "Machiko Kyo—Dedicated Actress," *Asia Scene*, March 1957.

16. Ibid., 47.

17. Kurosawa, *Something Like an Autobiography*, 183.

18. Richie, *The Films of Akira Kurosawa*, 79–80.

19. "Japanese Film Wins Grand Prize in Venice," *Hollywood Citizen-News*, September 11, 1951.

20. Shinobu Hashimoto. Personal interview, December 15, 1999.

21. Kurosawa, *Something Like an Autobiography*, 188.

22. "Mosk," "Rasho Mon (Into the Woods)," *Weekly Variety*, September 19, 1951.

23. "Prize Film to Show," *Los Angeles Daily News*, December 6, 1951.

24. "RKO Snares Jap Film for Subtitled Release," *Weekly Variety*, December 12, 1951.

25. Richard B. Jewell, with Vernon Harbin, *The RKO Story* (New York: Arlington House, 1982), 224.

26. Kurosawa, "A Film Murder Without a Clue."

27. Bosley Crowther, *The New York Times Film Reviews, 1913–1968*, ed. George Amberg (New York: The New York Times & Arno Press, 1970), 268–69.

28. William Whitsbait, "The Movies—'Rashomon' at the Rialto," *The New Statesman and Nation*, March 15, 1952.

29. Ed Sullivan, "Behind the Scenes," *Hollywood Citizen-News*, January 22, 1952.

30. "A Stunning Work of Art," *Newsweek*. From the *Rashomon* pressbook, c. 1952.

31. "The Current Cinema—What Happened in Those Woods?" *The New Yorker*, December 29, 1951.

32. The otherwise tasteful pressbook encouraged theater owners, in an effort to promote the film, to display "war souvenirs" brought back by veterans.

33. Mason Wiley and Damien Bona, *Inside Oscar—The Unofficial History of the Academy Awards* (New York: Ballantine, 1987 edition), 217.

34. " 'Rashomon' Megger Being Honored by Jap Industry," *The Hollywood Reporter*, May 19, 1952.

35. *Rashomon* (New York: Playbill, 1958), 31.

36. James F. Davidson, "Memory of Defeat in Japan: A Reappraisal of Rashomon," in *Rashomon—A Film by Akira Kurosawa*, 209–21.

37. J. Hoberman, "To Tell the Truth," *The Village Voice*, March 3, 1998.

38. Howard Thompson, "Toshiro Mifune: Tokyo Dynamo," *The New York Times*, April 11, 1965.

9: MISSTEP

1. *Time Out*, May 9, 1990, 18.

2. From "People Who Talk About Kurosawa," in Michihiro Imata, Kunihiro Susumu, and Akira Kurosawa Kenyukai-hen, eds. *Kurosawa Akira yume no ashiato* (Akira Kurosawa's Footsteps of Dreams) (Tokyo: Kyodo Tunshin-sha, 1999), 140.

3. "Kajiro Yamamoto's Story," in Imata et al., eds., *Akira Kurosawa's Footsteps of Dreams*, 48.
4. Ray Falk, "Introducing Japan's Top Director," *The New York Times*, January 6, 1952.
5. Donald Richie, *The Films of Akira Kurosawa* (Revised Edition) (Berkeley, CA: University of California Press, 1984), 85.
6. Ibid., 82.
7. Takamaro Shimaji, ed., *Kurosawa Akira Dokyumento* (Akira Kurosawa Document) (Tokyo: *Kinema Jumpo* Special Edition, May 1974), 89.
8. Brendan Gill, "Magnificent Seven," *The New Yorker*, May 4, 1963.
9. Kauffmann, Stanley, "A Cold Season," *The New Republic*, May 11, 1963.
10. "A Japanese Homer Nods," *Time*, May 17, 1963, 117.
11. Kevin Thomas, "Kurosawa's 'The Idiot' Called Artistic Flop," *Los Angeles Times*, September 16, 1964, 9.
12. Richie, *The Films of Akira Kurosawa*, 85.
13. Falk, "Introducing Japan's Top Director."
14. Yoshio Tsuchiya. Personal interview, December 20, 1994.
15. Gerald Peary, "Talking with the Late Toshiro Mifune," *Boston Phoenix*, January 22, 1998.

10: TO LIVE
1. *Rashomon* pressbook, RKO Radio Pictures, c. 1952.
2. Takamaro Shimaji, ed. *Kurosawa Akira Dokyumento* (Akira Kurosawa Document) (Tokyo: *Kinema Jumpo* Special Edition, May 1974), 110–14.
3. Shinobu Hashimoto. Personal interview, December 15, 1999.
4. Shimaji, ed., *Kurosawa Akira Dokyumento*, 110–14.
5. Hashimoto interview.
6. "Teruyo Nogami's Story." Liner notes from the Japanese laserdisc release, 1993.
7. "Takashi Shimura's Story," in Michihiro Imata, Kunihiro Susumu, and Akira Kurosawa Kenyukai-hen, eds., *Kurosawa Akira yume no ashiato* (Akira Kurosawa's Footsteps of Dreams) (Tokyo: Kyodo Tunshin-sha, 1999), 158.
8. Ibid.
9. Ibid., 160.
10. Miki Odagiri, "My Treasured *Ikiru*." Liner notes for the Japanese laserdisc release, July 25, 1993.
11. "Kin Sugai's Story," in Michihiro Imata, Kunihiro Susumu, and Akira Kurosawa Kenyukai-hen, eds., 158.
12. Edwin Schallert, "Japan's 'Doomed' Stirs Spectacular Interest," *Los Angeles Times*, May 27, 1956.
13. *Ikiru* pressbook, c. 1960.
14. Bosley Crowther, *The New York Times Film Reviews, 1913–1968*, ed. George Amberg (New York: The New York Times & Arno Press, 1970), 333–34.
15. Margaret Harford, "Lonely Old Man Is Hero of 'Ikiru' Tale," *Los Angeles Mirror*, October 21, 1960.
16. "Ikiru," *Time*, February 15, 1960, 85.
17. James Powers, "Japanese 'Ikiru' of Limited Appeal," *The Hollywood Reporter*, October 20, 1960.
18. Charles Stinson, "Japan Drama 'Ikiru' Deeply Touching Work," *Los Angeles Times*, October 24, 1960.
19. Arthur Knight, "Season in the Sun," *The Saturday Review*, February 13, 1960.
20. "A Japanese Apocalypse," *Time*, September 21, 1962, 90.

11: THE MAGNIFICENT SEVEN

1. Shinobu Hashimoto. Personal interview, December 15, 1999.

2. Ibid.

3. Ibid.

4. Masaaki Tsuduki, *Kurosawa Akira to Shichinin no samurai—Eiga no naka no eiga tanjo dokyumento* (Akira Kurosawa and Seven Samurai—Document of the Film Behind the Birth of the film) (Tokyo: Asahi Sonotama, 1999), 31.

5. Hashimoto interview.

6. Toshiro Mifune. Liner notes for the Japanese laserdisc release of *Seven Samurai*, August 25, 1993.

7. Tsuduki, *Akira Kurosawa and Seven Samurai*, 31.

8. Hashimoto interview.

9. Tsuduki, *Akira Kurosawa and Seven Samurai*, 53.

10. "Hideo Oguni," in Takamaro Shimaji, ed. *Kurosawa Akira Dokyumento* (Akira Kurosawa Document) (Tokyo: *Kinema Jumpo* Special Edition, May 1974), 110.

11. Hashimoto interview.

12. Donald Richie, *The Films of Akira Kurosawa* (Revised Edition) (Berkeley, CA: University of California Press, 1984), 97.

13. Tsuduki, *Akira Kurosawa and Seven Samurai*, 60.

14. Yoshio Tsuchiya, "Superstar's Personality Shone on Screen," *Daily Yomiuri*, December 26, 1997.

15. Minoru Chiaki, "Memories of Mifune-san," in *Toshiro Mifune—The Last Samurai*, ed. Finichisya (Tokyo: Mainichi-Shinbun-sha, 1998), 37.

16. Richie, *The Films of Akira Kurosawa*, 103.

17. Tsuduki, *Akira Kurosawa and Seven Samurai*, 110.

18. Richie, *The Films of Akira Kurosawa*, 222.

19. Tatsuo Matsumura. Personal interview, January 27, 1996.

20. Michael Jeck. Audio commentary for the DVD of *Seven Samurai*.

21. Keiko Tsushima, "What I Remember." Liner notes for the Japanese laserdisc release, 1993.

22. Yoshio Tsuchiya. Personal interview, December 20, 1994.

23. Ibid.

24. Yoshio Tsuchiya, *Kurosawa-san—Kurosawa Akira tono subarashiki hibi* (Mr. Kurosawa—Wonderful Days with Akira Kurosawa) (Tokyo: Shincho-sha, 1999), 90.

25. Ibid., 162.

26. Ibid.

27. "Bokuzen Hidari," *Kinema Jumpo*, September 1960.

28. Noriaki Yuasa. Personal interview, July 21, 1999.

29. Tsuduki, *Akira Kurosawa and Seven Samurai*, 59.

30. Ibid., 64.

31. Ibid., 76.

32. Ibid., 143.

33. Ibid., 157.

34. Ibid., 158.

35. Ibid.

36. Ibid.

37. Kyoko Hirano, *Mr. Smith Goes to Tokyo—Japanese Cinema Under the American Occupation 1945–1952* (Washington: Smithsonian Institution Press, 1992), 232.

38. Tsuduki, *Akira Kurosawa and Seven Samurai*, 160.

39. Ibid., 197.
40. Ibid.
41. Ibid., 194.
42. Ibid., 212.
43. Tsuchiya interview.
44. Tsuduki, *Akira Kurosawa and Seven Samurai*, 27.
45. Ibid.
46. Peter Grilli, "Civil Samurai," *Film Comment*, July 1984, 66.
47. Tsuduki, *Akira Kurosawa and Seven Samurai*, 97–98.
48. Ibid., 27.
49. Hashimoto interview.
50. Kazuko Kurosawa, *Papa Kurosawa Akira* (Tokyo: Bungei Shunju, 2000), 16.
51. Yoshio Tsuchiya, *Kurosawa-san*, 90.
52. Kurosawa, *Papa Kurosawa Akira*, 18.
53. Ibid., 23.
54. "Epic," *The New York Times*, June 6, 1954.
55. "Mosk." "Shichinin No Samurai (The Seven Samurai)," in *Variety Film Reviews 1954–1958* (New York and London: Garland Publishing, Inc., 1983).
56. "Showing 'Seven Samurai,' " *The Hollywood Reporter*, January 28, 1955.
57. "Col. Organizes New Dept. for Handling Foreign Tongue Pix," *The Hollywood Reporter*, August 15, 1955.
58. Hashimoto interview.
59. "Gun-Gallopers—In Japan and the Old South," *Cue*, November 24, 1956.
60. "The Current Cinema—East Is West," *The New Yorker*, December 1, 1956.
61. "The Magnificent Seven," *Time*, December 10, 1956.
62. Bosley Crowther, *The New York Times Film Reviews, 1913–1968*, ed. George Amberg (New York: The New York Times & Arno Press, 1970), 308–9.
63. Bosley Crowther, "Eastern Western—Kurosawa's 'The Magnificent Seven' Follows Format of Cowboy Films," *The New York Times*, November 25, 1956.
64. Arthur Knight, "SR Goes to the Movies—The Japanese Do It Again," *The Saturday Review*, December 1, 1956.
65. "Actor Quinn Sues Brynner over Film Deal," *Los Angeles Times*, February 3, 1960.
66. Anthony Quinn, with Daniel Paisner, *One Man Tango* (New York: HarperCollins, 1995), 263.
67. Kevin Phinney, "Kurosawa Sued by MGM over Sequel," *The Hollywood Reporter*, December 8, 1991, 4, 70.
68. Shimaji, ed., *Kurosawa Akira Dokyumento*, 110–114.
69. *Daily Variety*, January 12, 1962.
70. "The Magnificent Seven," *Films in Review*, December 1956.
71. "Classics Pay Off at Japanese B.O.," *Weekly Variety*, October 22, 1975.
72. "Foreign News—Tokyo," *The Hollywood Reporter*, March 14, 1978.
73. Dan Cox, "MGM, Kurosawa Settle 'Seven'," *Daily Variety*, January 13, 1994.
74. Dianna Waggoner, "In Homage to the Master, George Lucas and Francis Coppola Unleash Their Clout for Kurosawa," *People*, c. 1980.
75. Cox, "MGM, Kurosawa Settle 'Seven.' "
76. David Chute, " 'Seven Samurai' Conquers Anew," *Los Angeles Herald-Examiner*, January 8, 1983, B:1.
77. Richie, *The Films of Akira Kurosawa*, 103.
78. Kevin Thomas, "Full-Length 'Samurai' at the Nuart," *Los Angeles Times*, January 7, 1983, 6:4.

12: THE GOLDEN AGE
1. Joseph L. Anderson and Donald Richie, *The Japanese Film—Art and Industry* (Expanded Edition) (Princeton University Press, 1982), 91.
2. *Samurai* press kit, c. 1955.
3. Ibid.
4. Jun Fukuda. Personal interview, February 2, 1996.
5. "D.A.," " 'Samurai' Colorful Film Take of Medieval Japan," *Los Angeles Times*, November 21, 1955.
6. John McCarten, "Hand Me My Sword and My Saddle," *The New Yorker*, January 29, 1956.
7. Bosley Crowther, "Just an Ol' Samurai," *The New York Times*, January 22, 1956.
8. "Brog," *Daily Variety*, November 16, 1955.
9. Akira Kubo. Personal interview, January 25, 1996.
10. Anderson and Richie, *The Japanese Film*, 282.
11. Toho Films promotional booklet (Los Angeles, Toho International, c. 1957).
12. Yu Fujiki. Personal interview, January 24, 1996.
13. Toho Films brochure (Los Angeles or Tokyo, c. 1957).
14. Fujiki interview.

13: I LIVE IN FEAR
1. Eric Talmadge, "Obuchi Visits Nuclear Accident Site," Reuters, October 6, 1999.
2. "A Member of the Family," Haruko Togo, in the Toho Video laserdisc insert, 1993.
3. "Music of the Stars" and "My Master Fumio Hayasaka," for the Toho Video laserdisc insert, 1993.
4. Mike Inoue. Personal interview, December 10, 1999.
5. Donald Richie, *The Films of Akira Kurosawa* (Revised Edition) (Berkeley, CA: University of California Press, 1984), 109.
6. Inoue interview.
7. *Cue*, January 28, 1967.
8. "Anby," *Weekly Variety*, September 18, 1963.
9. "J.M.," *Newsweek*, February 6, 1967.
10. Loren G. Buchanan, *Motion Picture Herald*, March 15, 1967.
11. Judith Crist, New York *World Journal Tribune*, January 12, 1967.
12. "A Blow to the Head," Nagisa Oshima, in the Toho Video laserdisc insert, 1993.
13. Kevin Thomas, " 'Samurai, Part III' Arrives at Toho," *Los Angeles Times*, April 13, 1967.
14. "Robe," "Samurai—Part III," *Weekly Variety*, November 15, 1967.

14: TWO PLAYS
1. Shinobu Hashimoto. Personal interview, December 15, 1999.
2. "Interview with Hideo Oguni," in Takamaro Shimaji, ed., *Kurosawa Akira Dokyumento* (Akira Kurosawa Document) (Tokyo: *Kinema Jumpo* Special Edition, May 1974), 110.
3. Jack F. Jorgens, *Shakespeare on Film* (Bloomington, IN: Indiana University Press, 1977), 153.
4. Donald Richie, *The Films of Akira Kurosawa* (Revised Edition) (Berkeley, CA: University of California Press, 1984), 120.
5. Takeshi Kato. Personal interview, December 11, 1999.
6. Ibid.
7. "Takeshi Kato's Story," in Michihiro Imata, Kunihiro Susumu, and Akira Kurosawa Kenkyukai-hen, eds., *Akira Kurosawa's Footsteps of Dreams* (Tokyo: Kyodo Tunshin-sha, 1999), 188.

8. Akira Kubo. Personal interview, January 25, 1996.

9. Michio Yamamoto. Personal interview, January 31, 1996.

10. Peter Grilli, "Civil Samurai," *Film Comment*, July 1984, 66.

11. Minoru Chiaki, "The Horse Master Was Confused, Too." Liner notes for the Japanese laserdisc release, 1993.

12. Kyoko Kagawa. Personal interview, December 15, 1999.

13. Shimaji, ed., *Kurosawa Akira Dokyumento*, 85.

14. Bosley Crowther, *The New York Times Film Reviews 1913–1968*, ed. George Amberg (New York: The New York Times & Arno Press, 1970), 3290.

15. "Kurosawa's *Macbeth*," *Time*, December 1, 1961, 76.

16. "Hideo Oguni," in Shimaji, ed., *Kurosawa Akira Dokyumento*, 110.

17. Kyoko Kagawa. Personal interview, December 15, 1999.

18. Ibid.

19. Yu Fujiki. Personal interview, January 24, 1996.

20. "Takao Saito's Story," in Imata et al., eds., *Akira Kurosawa's Footsteps of Dreams*, 196.

21. Richie, *The Films of Akira Kurosawa*, 128, 130.

22. Kagawa interview.

23. Kyoko Kagawa, "Rehearsals for *The Lower Depths*." Liner notes for the Japanese laserdisc release, 1993.

24. Richie, *The Films of Akira Kurosawa*, 125.

25. Geoffrey Warren, " 'Lower Depths' Fine Japanese Film Play," *Los Angeles Times*, May 2, 1962.

26. "Foreign—The Lower Depths," *Show Business Illustrated*, March 1962.

27. Flavia Wharton, "The Lower Depths," *Films and Filming*, March 1962, 176.

28. *A Tribute to Toshiro Mifune* (New York: The Japan Society, 1984), 13.

29. Joseph L. Anderson and Donald Richie, *The Japanese Film—Art and Industry* (Princeton University Press, 1982), 281.

30. Juliette Gambol, "Toshiro Mifune—An Interview," *Cinema*, Winter 1967, 29.

15: 100 PERCENT ENTERTAINMENT

1. "I Made a 100% Amusement Film," *Die Verborgene Festung*. European program for *The Hidden Fortress*, c. 1958.

2. "Hideo Oguni," in Takamaro Shimaji, ed., *Kurosawa Akira Dokyumento* (Akira Kurosawa Document) (Tokyo: *Kinema Jumpo* Special Edition, May 1974), 110–14, 110.

3. "I Made a 100% Amusement Film."

4. Joseph L. Anderson and Donald Richie, *The Japanese Film—Art and Industry* (Princeton University Press, 1982), 251.

5. Ibid., 254.

6. "I Made a 100% Amusement Film."

7. Ibid.

8. Misa Uehara, "Becoming Yukihime." Liner notes for the Japanese laserdisc release, 1993.

9. *Die Verborgene Festung*. European program for *The Hidden Fortress*, c. 1958.

10. Uehara, "Becoming Yukihime."

11. Ibid.

12. Fuji TV television appearance, April 4, 1981.

13. Masaru Sato. Personal interview, January 27, 1996.

14. Ibid.

15. Minoru Nakano. Personal interview, December 18, 1994.

16. "The Hidden Fortress," *Esquire*, August 1961.
17. Margaret Harford, " 'Hidden Fortress' Legend of Samurai," *Los Angeles Mirror*, October 10, 1960.
18. Selma Wilcox, "Good Story Far Inside 'The Hidden Fortress,' " *Hollywood Citizen-News*, October 8, 1960.
19. Dianna Waggoner, "In Homage to the Master, George Lucas and Francis Coppola Unleash Their Clout for Kurosawa," *People*, c. 1980.
20. Fuji TV television appearance, April 4, 1981.
21. Schlesinger, "Kurosawa's Hidden Fortress."
22. J. Hoberman, "Star Warriors," *The Village Voice*, July 10, 1984.
23. Donald Richie, *The Films of Akira Kurosawa* (Revised Edition) (Berkeley, CA: University of California Press, 1984), 135.
24. Mike Y. Inoue. Personal interview, December 12, 1999.
25. James Powers, "Far-East Western Has General Appeal," *The Hollywood Reporter*, November 25, 1960.
26. Frank Mulcahy, " 'Vagabonds' Japanese Version of Horse Opera," *Los Angeles Times*, November 29, 1960.
27. S. A. Desick, " 'The Vagabonds' Shows Japan Master with Color," *Los Angeles Examiner*, November 26, 1960.
28. A. C. Pinder, "Japan Produces a $1,000,000 Spectacle," *Motion Picture Herald*, October 24, 1959.
29. "Tube," *Daily Variety*, December 21, 1960.
30. S. A. Desick, " 'Treasures' Epic Japanese Film," *Los Angeles Examiner*, December 26, 1960, 3:19.

16: WIND
1. Elliott Stein, "The Private Eye and the Rising Sun," *The Village Voice*, c. late 1980s?
2. Shue Matsubayashi. Personal interview, January 27, 1996.
3. Shinobu Hashimoto, "Something Sad and Big," *Kinema Jumpo*, March 1960, 81.
4. Matsubayashi interview.
5. *I Bombed Pearl Harbor* press kit, c. 1960.
6. "Japan Hails Movie About Pearl Harbor," UPI, April 23, 1960.
7. "Tube," *Weekly Variety*, November 29, 1961.
8. Kay Proctor, " 'Pearl Harbor' Japanese Film," *Los Angeles Examiner*, November 30, 1961.
9. Ibid.
10. Charles Stinson, "Japan's 'Pearl Harbor' Technically Well Made," *Los Angeles Times*, December 1, 1961.
11. "Tube," *Weekly Variety*.
12. Margaret Harford, "Nippon Version of Pearl Harbor; Goldbrickers on Italian Front," *Los Angeles Mirror*, November 30, 1961.
13. Matsubayashi interview.
14. Mike Y. Inoue. Personal interview, December 12, 1999.
15. Takamaro Shimaji, ed., *Kurosawa Akira Dokyumento* (Akira Kurosawa Document) (Tokyo: Kinema Jumpo Special Edition, May 1974), 102–7.
16. Ibid.
17. Inoue interview.
18. "Akira Kurosawa—*The Bad Sleep Well* to Begin Shooting," *Kinema Jumpo*, March 1960.
19. Masaru Sato. Personal interview, January 27, 1996.

20. Donald Richie, *The Films of Akira Kurosawa* (Berkeley, CA: University of California Press, 1965), 143.
21. Kyoko Kagawa. Personal interview, December 15, 1999.
22. Ibid.
23. Ibid.
24. Tatsuya Mihashi, "Tatsuya Mihashi's Story." Liner notes for the Japanese laserdisc release, 1993.
25. Takeshi Kato. Personal interview, December 11, 1999.
26. Shiro Mifune. Personal interview, December 16, 1999.
27. Tomio Sagisu. Personal interview, December 9, 1999.
28. Kagawa interview.
29. Ko Nishimura, "An Explanation of the 'Surprised Actor.'" Liner notes for the Japanese laserdisc release, 1993.
30. Charlton Heston, *The Actor's Life—Journals 1956–1976* (New York: E. P. Dutton, 1976), 91.
31. Charlton Heston, *In the Arena* (New York: Boulevard Books, 1995), 520.
32. Nishimura, "An Explanation of the 'Surprised Actor.'"
33. Bosley Crowther, "Four New Films Are Imitations," *The New York Times*, February 6, 1963.
34. Stanley Kauffmann, "From Bad to Worse," *The New Republic*, January 26, 1963.
35. Fritz Blocki, "New Melodrama Well Made in Japan," *Hollywood Citizen-News*, March 16, 1963.
36. Kevin Thomas, "High Finance Theme of New Film Tragedy," *Los Angeles Times*, February 16, 1963.
37. "Gentlemen of Japan," *Time*, January 25, 1963.
38. Francis Ford Coppola, *The Bad Sleep Well*. Liner notes for the Japanese laserdisc release, 1993.
39. Hideo Sekiguchi, "The Japanese Film in America," *Kinema Jumpo*, c. 1962.
40. Kazuto Ohira. Personal interview, March 14, 2000.
41. Ibid.
42. Margaret Harford, "Japan's Top Star Visits Us," *Los Angeles Mirror*, August 5, 1960, 2:6.
43. Ohira interview.
44. Philip K. Scheuer, "Exports Up 30%, Japan's Head Says," *Los Angeles Times*, June 18, 1962.
45. Yuriko Hoshi. Personal interview, January 29, 1996.
46. A. H. Weiler, "Daredevil in the Castle," *The New York Times*, February 25, 1969.
47. Geoffrey Warren, "Japanese 'Daredevil' in Fairbanks Tradition," *Los Angeles Times*, July 4, 1961.
48. "Robe," "Daredevil in the Castle," *Daily Variety*, March 5, 1969.

17: MULBERRIES, CAMELLIAS, AND CACTI
1. Teruyo Nogami, "The Shooting Spot," in Michihiro Imata, Kunihiro Susumu, and Akira Kurosawa Kenkyukai-hen, eds., *Akira Kurosawa's Footsteps of Dreams* (Tokyo: Kyodo Tunshin-sha, 1999), 205.
2. Minoru Nakano. Personal interview, December 18, 1994.
3. Masaru Sato. Personal interview, January 27, 1996.
4. Ibid.
5. George E. Eagle, "Japanese Western?—Not This Time," *Film Daily*, July 30, 1963.
6. "Yoko Tsukasa's Story," in Imata et al. eds., *Akira Kurosawa's Footsteps of Dreams*, 224.
7. "Toshiro Mifune's Story," in ibid., 234.

8. "The Shooting Spot," in ibid., 228.
9. "Shiro Moritani's Story," in ibid., 225.
10. "The Shooting Spot," in ibid., 228.
11. Tatsuya Nakadai, "Meeting." Liner notes for *Yojimbo*'s Japanese laserdisc release, 1993.
12. Ibid.
13. "The Shooting Spot," in Imata et al., eds., *Akira Kurosawa's Footsteps of Dreams*, 230.
14. Nakadai, "Meeting."
15. Yosuke Natsuki. Personal interview, March 11, 1997.
16. Isuzu Yamada, "Isuzu Yamada's Story," in Imata et al., eds., *Akira Kurosawa's Footsteps of Dreams*, 230.
17. Takamaro Shimaji, ed., *Kurosawa Akira Dokyumento* (Akira Kurosawa Document) (Tokyo: *Kinema Jumpo* Special Edition, May 1974), 130.
18. Takao Saito, "Takao Saito's Story," in Imata et al., eds., *Akira Kurosawa's Footsteps of Dreams*, 224.
19. Shimaji, ed., *Kurosawa Akira Dokyumento*, 130.
20. Bosley Crowther, *The New York Times Film Reviews, 1913–1968*, ed. George Amberg (New York: The New York Times & Arno Press, 1970), 362–63.
21. "SR Goes to the Movies," *The Saturday Review*, September 15, 1962.
22. Dorothy Masters, "Samurai Routs Foes in Saga of Violence," New York *Daily News*, date undetermined.
23. S. A. Desick, " 'Yojimbo' Is Action Packed," *Los Angeles Examiner*, September 14, 1961.
24. Geoffrey Warren, " 'Yojimbo' Exciting New Japanese Drama," *Los Angeles Times*, September 15, 1961, III: 7.
25. "A Japanese Apocalypse," *Time*, September 21, 1962.
26. " 'Yojimbo' Preem in K.C.," *The Hollywood Reporter*, May 2, 1962.
27. Sato interview.
28. Christopher Frayling, *Sergio Leone—Something to Do with Death* (London: Faber & Faber, 2000), 118–19.
29. Ibid., 124–25.
30. Ibid., 147.
31. *The Hollywood Reporter*, December 28, 1964.
32. Frayling, *Sergio Leone*, 148.
33. Ibid.
34. "Rome," *The Hollywood Reporter*, December 22, 1965.
35. "Filmers of 1st Italo 'Dollars' Want Cut of 'A Few More,' " *Daily Variety*, March 29, 1966.
36. Francesca Avinola, "New Line Plans Remake of Kurosawa Classic," *Screen International*, November 13, 1992.
37. Ibid.
38. Anita M. Busch, "Willis Near Deal for 'Gundown,' " *Daily Variety*, June 1, 1995, 1.
39. Andy Seiler, "Loner's Story Stands the Test of Time," *USA Today*, September 20, 1996, W26.
40. "Toshiro Mifune to Make Mexican Film," *Kinema Jumpo*, February 1961.
41. *Kinema Jumpo*, ca. 1961.
42. Raul Fernando V. Jimenez, "Wrap-up of Sunday Events," *InfoLatina S.A. de C.V.*, March 24, 1997.
43. Emilio García Riera, ed., *Historia Documental del Cine Mexicano*, Vol. 11.
44. Toshiro Mifune, "Working in a Foreign Film for the First Time," *Kinema Jumpo*, December 1961, 39.
45. James Powers, " 'Animas Trujano' Fine Arty Film," *The Hollywood Reporter*, December 15, 1961.

46. Margaret Harford, " 'The Important Man' Speaks Right Out," *Los Angeles Times*, July 21, 1962, III:8.
47. "Best Actor—Toshiro Mifune," *Kinema Jumpo*, March 1962.
48. "*Kinema Jumpo* Award Speeches," *Kinema Jumpo*, March 1962, 67.
49. "Close-up: Toshiro Mifune," *Kinema Jumpo*, May 1961.
50. *Kinema Jumpo*, August 1962.
51. "Tube," "Sanjuro," *Weekly Variety*, June 20, 1962.
52. "Keiju Kobayashi's Story," in *Akira Kurosawa's Footsteps of Dreams*, 234.
53. "Reiko Dan's Story," in *Akira Kurosawa's Footsteps of Dreams*, 237.
54. Yoshiro Muraki, "I'm Not Sad if the Film Is Shot Beautifully." Liner notes for the Japanese laserdisc release, 1993.
55. "A Japanese Apocalypse," *Time*, September 21, 1962.
56. Muraki, "I'm Not Sad if the Film Is Shot Beautifully."
57. Akira Kubo. Personal interview, January 25, 1996.
58. Minoru Nakano. Personal interview, December 18, 1994.
59. Philip K. Scheuer, "Exports Up 30%, Japan's Head Says," *Los Angeles Times*, June 18, 1962.
60. "Toho Group Coming Here," *The Hollywood Reporter*, June 6, 1962.
61. "Tube," "Sanjuro."
62. Stanley Kauffmann, New York *Herald-Tribune*, May 25, 1963.
63. James Powers, " 'Sanjuro' Is Superb," *The Hollywood Reporter*, June 21, 1962.
64. Bosley Crowther, "Movie Question Is to Dub or Not," *The New York Times*, May 15, 1963.
65. Judith Crist, "Sanjuro," New York *Herald-Tribune*, May 8, 1963.
66. "Japanese 'Sanjuro' Remake for Quinn," *Weekly Variety*, February 24, 1965.
67. Amy Dawes, "Allyn Adds Three Projects Following 'Cousins' Release," *Daily Variety*, June 6, 1989.
68. " 'Tatsu' Is Scheduled for Toho," *Hollywood Citizen-News*, November 17, 1962.
69. Kevin Thomas, "Tatsu Review," *The Los Angeles Times*, November 22, 1962.
70. "ELGEE," "Japanese Films Come Long Way," *Hollywood Citizen-News*, November 23, 1962.
71. Shue Matsubayashi. Personal interview, January 27, 1996.
72. Howard Thompson, "Toshiro Mifune: Tokyo Dynamo," *The New York Times*, April 11, 1965.
73. Yuriko Hoshi. Personal interview, January 29, 1996.
74. Yu Fujiki. Personal interview, January 24, 1996.
75. Akira Ifukube. Personal interview, December 18, 1994.
76. "Japanese Film Makers Seek U.S. Acceptance," *Motion Picture Exhibitor*, October 16, 1963.
77. Arnold Babbin, "Samurai Clash on Toho Screen," *Hollywood Citizen-News*, October 11, 1963.
78. "Wear," "Chushingura," *Daily Variety*, October 2, 1963.
79. "Slapdash Samurai," *Newsweek*, October 14, 1963.
80. Bosley Crowther, "Screen: 'Chushingura,' " *The New York Times*, October 4, 1963.
81. "Landberg Serves Samurai Buffs Full '47 Ronin,' " *Weekly Variety*, October 6, 1965.
82. "Reassembled from Unsuccessful Cuts, 'Chushingura' Case Is Precedental," *Weekly Variety*, January 11, 1967.
83. Yosuke Natsuki. Personal interview, March 11, 1997.
84. Matsubayashi interview.

18: HEAVEN AND HELL

1. "Rights and Permissions," *Publishers Weekly*, August 28, 1961.
2. "Kurosawa, Akira, 1910–98," *Sight and Sound*, October 1998, 3.

3. Donald Richie, *The Films of Akira Kurosawa* (Revised Edition) (Berkeley, CA: University of California Press, 1984), 170.

4. George E. Eagle, "Japanese Western?—Not This Time," *Film Daily*, July 30, 1963.

5. Tsutomu Yamazaki, "Heaven and Hell." Liner notes for the Japanese laserdisc, 1993.

6. Takeshi Kato. Personal interview, December 11, 1999.

7. George E. Eagle, "Japanese Western?"

8. Kato interview.

9. Ibid.

10. Yutaka Sada, "The Anniversary of My Life." Liner notes for the Japanese laserdisc, 1993.

11. Ibid.

12. Kato interview.

13. Kyoko Kagawa. Personal interview, December 15, 1999.

14. Kato interview.

15. "Toho's N.Y. Showcase in First American Distrib Deal; Sets 'High & Low,' " *Weekly Variety*, December 18, 1963.

16. Stanley Kauffmann, "Japanese Drama, Domestic Japery," *The New Republic*, November 23, 1963.

17. "Mysterious East," *Newsweek*, November 25, 1963, 106.

18. "Hawk," "Tengoku To-Jigoku [sic]," *Weekly Variety*, September 4, 1963.

19. Howard Thompson, " 'High and Low': A Classic by Kurosawa," *The New York Times*, November 27, 1963.

20. Dale Munroe, " 'High and Low' Outstanding Film," *Hollywood Citizen-News*, February 21, 1964, A-6.

21. "Scorsese Developing Kurosawa Remake," *Weekly Variety*, May 24, 1993.

22. Martin Scorsese. Liner notes for *High and Low*'s Japanese laserdisc release, 1993.

23. Yamazaki, "Heaven and Hell."

24. Sada, "The Anniversary of My Life."

25. Kazuko Kurosawa, *Papa Kurosawa Akira* (Tokyo: Bungei Shunju, 2000), 29.

26. Ibid., 30.

27. Ibid., 32.

28. *Kinema Jumpo*, 1963.

29. Senkichi Taniguchi. Personal interview, October 3, 1999.

30. Shiro Mifune. Personal interview, December 9, 1999.

31. Ibid.

32. Kazuto Ohira. Personal interview, March 14, 2000.

33. Nagamasa was a Sinophile who had produced films in China during the Japanese Occupation.

34. Ohira interview.

35. Ibid.

36. Thompson, "Toshiro Mifune: Tokyo Dynamo."

37. *Legacy of the 500,000* theater program, 1963.

38. Ibid.

39. Taniguchi interview.

40. Tatsuya Mihashi, "Diary of the Philippines Location," in the *Legacy of the 500,000* theater program.

41. Ibid.

42. Mie Hama. Personal interview, January 31, 1996.

43. Kevin Thomas, "Mifune Feature Heads Japanese Double Bill," *Los Angeles Times*, June 18, 1964.

44. Juliette Gambol, "Toshiro Mifune—An Interview," *Cinema*, Winter 1967.
45. "AIP's 'Sinbad' Wins Award in Milan," *Film Daily*, January 6, 1965.
46. James Powers, "Japanese 'Sinbad' Okay Adventure," *The Hollywood Reporter*, March 17, 1965.

19: RAIN
1. Donald Richie, *The Films of Akira Kurosawa* (Revised Edition) (Berkeley, CA: University of California Press, 1984), 171.
2. Nobukazu Uekusa, ed., *Kurosawa Akira to Kinoshita Keisuke—Subarashiki kyosho* (Akira Kurosawa and Keisuke Kinoshita—Wonderful Superstars) (Tokyo: *Kinema Jumpo* Temporary Edition, 1998), 132.
3. Ibid., 186–89.
4. Ibid., 134.
5. S. Ohashi, ed., *Kurosawa Akira • Mifune Toshiro—Futari no Nihon-jin* (Akira Kurosawa • Toshiro Mifune—Two Men of Japan) (Tokyo: Kinema Jumpo-sha, 1964 [reprinted 1997]), 136.
6. Ibid.
7. Richie, *The Films of Akira Kurosawa*, 181.
8. Uekusa, *Kurosawa Akira to Kinoshita Keisuke—Subarashiki kyosho*, 94.
9. Ohashi, ed., *Kurosawa Akira • Mifune Toshiro—Futari no Nihon-jin*, 100.
10. Richie, *The Films of Akira Kurosawa*, 182.
11. Ohashi, *Kurosawa Akira • Mifune Toshiro—Futari no Nihon-jin*, 95.
12. Ibid.
13. Kyoko Kagawa. Personal interview, December 15, 1999.
14. Ohashi, *Kurosawa Akira • Mifune Toshiro—Futari no Nihon-jin*, 98.
15. Yuzo Kayama, "Noboru Yasumoto was Myself." Liner notes for the laserdisc release, 1993.
16. Ohashi, *Kurosawa Akira • Mifune Toshiro—Futari no Nihon-jin*, 95.
17. Ibid.
18. "Robe," "Whirlwind," *Daily Variety*, July 31, 1968.
19. Richie, *The Films of Akira Kurosawa*, 175.
20. Minoru Nakano. Personal interview, December 18, 1994.
21. Richie, *The Films of Akira Kurosawa*, 184.
22. Kayama, "Noboru Yasumoto was Myself."
23. Juliette Gambol, "Toshiro Mifune—An Interview," *Cinema*, Winter 1967, 29.
24. Kevin Thomas, " 'Judo Saga' Delivers Low Blow to Kurosawa's Reputation," *Los Angeles Times*, August 31, 1965.
25. "Winner of the Best Japanese Film Award—Director Akira Kurosawa," *Kinema Jumpo*, January 1966.
26. Kevin Thomas, " 'Red Beard' Breathtaking Film Classic by Kurosawa," *Los Angeles Times*, January 14, 1966, IV:8.
27. Richie, *The Films of Akira Kurosawa*, 177.
28. "New Movies—Epic Vision," *Time*, January 17, 1969.
29. "Hawk," "Akahige (Red Beard)," *Weekly Variety*, September 8, 1965.
30. Tony Velella, "Red Beard," *Motion Picture Herald*, January 8, 1969.
31. Donald Richie, *The Films of Akira Kurosawa* (Berkeley, CA: University of California Press, 1965), 9.
32. Ibid.
33. Ohashi, ed., *Kurosawa Akira • Mifune Toshiro—Futari no Nihon-jin*, 94.

34. Gambol, "Toshiro Mifune—An Interview," 26.

35. Howard Thompson, "Toshiro Mifune: Tokyo Dynamo," *The New York Times*, April 11, 1965.

36. "Toho Gives Up NY Cinema," *Hollywood Reporter*, June 1, 1965.

37. Kazuto Ohira. Personal interview, March 14, 2000.

38. Mike Connolly, "Rambling Reporter," *Hollywood Reporter*, February 23, 1965.

39. "Mifune Weighing Offers to Do 3 Hollywood Films," *Daily Variety*, March 19, 1965.

40. Louella Parsons, "Louella Parsons," *Los Angeles Herald-Examiner*, August 18, 1965.

41. Gambol, "Toshiro Mifune—An Interview," 29.

42. Thompson, "Toshiro Mifune: Tokyo Dynamo."

43. Vincent Canby, "Mifune Under Ice," *The New York Times*, November 6, 1966.

44. Wayne Warga, "Mifune: Rather Create Than Fight," *Los Angeles Times*, December 30, 1968, 1, 24.

45. "Robe," *Variety*, March 18, 1965.

46. Dale Munroe, "Mifune Swordplay Featured at Toho," *Hollywood Citizen-News*, May 7, 1965, A-8.

47. David R. Schweisberg, "Toshiro Mifune: Japan's Most Celebrated Actor," *UPI*, July 18, 1996.

48. Ibid.

49. Thompson, "Toshiro Mifune: Tokyo Dynamo."

50. "UPA's 'Kiska' Feature," *Weekly Variety*, June 27, 1973.

51. Charles Champlin, "World War II From the Japanese Side," *Los Angeles Times*, August 24, 1973, IV:23.

52. Ibid.

53. Gene Youngblood, " 'Fort Graveyard' Is Exactly What It Is," *Los Angeles Herald-Examiner*, May 14, 1966.

54. Arnold Babbin, " 'Graveyard' Script Runs Cliché Gamut," *Hollywood Citizen-News*, May 16, 1966.

55. Kevin Thomas, "Japan's 'Ft. Graveyard' Only a Deadly Bore," *Los Angeles Times*, May 14, 1966.

56. "Rise Against the Sword," *Kinema Jumpo*, January 1966.

57. "J.L.W.," "Another Great Saga of Japan," *San Francisco Chronicle*, March 23, 1967.

58. Kevin Thomas, " 'Sword' Is in Best Action Tradition," *Los Angeles Times*, November 24, 1966.

59. Kihachi Okamoto. Personal interview, June 28, 1997.

60. Ibid.

61. "Robe," "The Sword of Doom," *Weekly Variety*, April 12, 1967.

62. Kevin Thomas, " 'The Sword of Doom' Is Sanguinary Bore," *Los Angeles Times*, July 2, 1966.

63. Bruce Eder, *The Sword of Doom*. Liner notes for the laserdisc release, The Voyager Company, 1995.

64. Okamoto interview.

20: SEKAI NO MIFUNE—MIFUNE OF THE WORLD

1. Kazuto Ohira. Personal interview, March 14, 2000.

2. "Mifune to Do U.S. World War II Film," *Daily Variety*, May 10, 1966.

3. Henry G. Saperstein. Personal interview, January 12, 1994.

4. Jun Fukuda. Personal interview, February 2, 1996.

5. Yosuke Natsuki. Personal interview, March 11, 1997.

6. Fukuda interview.

7. "Toshiro Mifune Claims 2 Bids from U.S. Prods," *Weekly Variety*, February 16, 1966.

8. Hy Hyberger, "Mifune in Modern Role: 'Mad Atlantic' at Toho Nov. 22," *The Canyon Crier*, November 16, 1967.
9. Senkichi Taniguchi. Personal interview, October 3, 1999.
10. Ibid.
11. Toshiaki Sato. Liner notes for the Japanese laserdisc release, c 1995.
12. Taniguchi interview.
13. Kevin Thomas, "The Mad Atlantic," *Los Angeles Times*, November 22, 1967.
14. Kevin Thomas, " 'Grand Prix' a Milestone in Mifune's Movie Career," *Los Angeles Times*, October 10, 1966.
15. Nick Spanos, " 'Grand Prix' a Production Race That Went to the Wire," *Los Angeles Times*, January 3, 1967, 14.
16. Thomas, " 'Grand Prix' a Milestone in Mifune's Movie Career."
17. Ibid.
18. Nick Spanos and A. D. Murphy, " 'Grand Prix' Costs Now Over $7 Mil; 9 Cutting Teams at Work on MGM Pic," *Daily Variety*, November 8, 1966.
19. Gerald Pratley, *The Cinema of John Frankenheimer* (London: A. Zwemmer, Ltd., 1969), 161.
20. Ronald Gold, "Toshiro Mifune Wonders: Can Films of Japan Get Off Suicide Course?," *Weekly Variety*, October 5, 1966.
21. Ibid.
22. Terrence Rafferty, *The New Yorker*, September 10, 1990.
23. Arthur Knight, "SR Goes to the Movies—Two Losers and Ten Best," *The Saturday Review*, January 14, 1967.
24. " 'Grand Prix' Gross Tops Mil in Cinerama Dome Run," *Daily Variety*, October 23, 1967.
25. Ibid.
26. Hy Hyberger, "Toshiro Mifune . . . Master of the Mirror of Yamato," *The Canyon Crier*, October 13, 1966, 8.
27. "Mifune Stage Opens," *Kinema Jumpo*, February 1967, 120.
28. Juliette Gambol, "Toshiro Mifune—An Interview," *Cinema*, Winter 1967, 29.
29. Shiro Mifune. Personal interview, December 16, 1999.
30. Frank Mulcahy, " 'Vagabonds' Japanese Version of Horse Opera," *Los Angeles Times*, November 29, 1960.
31. Thomas, " 'Grand Prix' a Milestone in Mifune's Movie Career."
32. Toshiro Mifune, "The Ideal Way to Produce a Film," *Kinema Jumpo*, March 1967.
33. "*Grand Prix* Premiere," *Kinema Jumpo*, March 1967.
34. *Music for the Movies—Toru Takemitsu*, dir. Charlotte Zwerin. Distributed by Alternate Current, 1994.
35. "Chie," *Weekly Variety*, June 28, 1967.
36. H. R. Weiler, *The New York Times*, October 26, 1968.
37. Kevin Thomas, " 'Rebellion' on Screen at Toho," *Los Angeles Times*, December 28, 1967.
38. "Title Role Not Cast but 'Emperor' Rolls in Japan," *Weekly Variety*, March 18, 1967.
39. "Japan Emperor to Be Shown in Toho Pic," *Weekly Variety*, April 26, 1967.
40. "Chie," "Nippon no ichiban nagai hi (The Emperor and a General)," *Weekly Variety*, September 13, 1967.
41. Kevin Thomas, " 'Emperor' War Saga at the Toho," *Los Angeles Times*, March 27, 1968.
42. Michel Ciment, *John Boorman* (Boston: Faber and Faber, Inc., 1986), 89.
43. Henry G. Saperstein. Personal interview, January 14, 1994.
44. "Hashimoto to Advise on Script for 'Pacific,' " *Film Daily*, November 21, 1967.
45. Ciment, *John Boorman*, 89, 91.
46. Saperstein interview.

47. Ciment, *John Boorman*, 89, 91.
48. Peter Grilli, "Civil Samurai," *Film Comment*, July 1984, 66.
49. " 'Hell in the Pacific' Matches Two Former Combat Foes," *Film Daily*, December 10, 1968, 5.
50. Saperstein interview.
51. Army Archerd, "Lee Marvin and Toshiro Mifune . . ." *Daily Variety*, August 5, 1968.
52. Ciment, *John Boorman*, 89, 92.
53. Wayne Warga, "Mifune: Rather Create Than Fight," *Los Angeles Times*, December 30, 1968, 24.
54. Hy Hyberger, "It Must Have Been Hell Making 'Hell in the Pacific,' " *The Canyon Crier*, December 19, 1968.
55. Warga, "Mifune: Rather Create Than Fight."
56. "Tuser," " 'Hell in the Pacific' Title Has Hot Pros, Cons," *Film Daily*, December 18, 1968.
57. "Razing of 'Hell' Burns Boorman," *Daily Variety*, April 28, 1969.
58. "Murf," "Hell in the Pacific," *Weekly Variety*, December 11, 1968.
59. Paul D. Zimmerman, "Two on the Turf," *Newsweek*, February 24, 1969.
60. *Playboy*, February 1969.
61. Arthur Knight, "SR Goes to the Movies," *The Saturday Review*, December 14, 1968.
62. " 'Hell in Pacific' Sets Academy-Qualifying Date," *The Hollywood Reporter*, November 21, 1968.
63. "Marvin, Mifune Set for 'Hell' P.A. Tour," *Film Daily*, December 10, 1968.
64. John Mahoney, "Toshiro Mifune Here—Finds Excellent Camera Equipment," *The Hollywood Reporter*, January 23, 1969.
65. "ABC's 5 Years of Film Production Profit & Losses," *Daily Variety*, May 31, 1973, 8.
66. Kevin Thomas, " 'Admiral Yamamoto' on Screen at Toho La Brea," *Los Angeles Times*, December 27, 1968.
67. Vernon Scott, "A Nippon Clark Gable," *Los Angeles Herald-Examiner*, December 26, 1968.
68. Phillippe Pons, "A Sanitized View of History," *World Press Review*, November 1995, 42.
69. Teruyoshi Nakano. Personal interview by Steve Ryfle and Stuart Galbraith IV, January 25, 1996.
70. Kevin Thomas, "Mifune Featured in 'Battle of Japan,' " *Los Angeles Times*, October 30, 1970, IV: 18.
71. Dale Munroe, "Battle of the Japan Sea," *The Canyon Crier*, November 9, 1970.
72. "W.W.," "The Day the Sun Rose," *Cue*, September 10, 1973.
73. Kevin Thomas, " 'Day the Sun Rose' at Kabuki Theater," *Los Angeles Times*, March 12, 1969.
74. Mahoney, "Toshiro Mifune Here—Finds Excellent Camera Equipment."
75. Ibid.
76. David Sutherland, "Mifune Picture at Toho LaBrea," *Hollywood Citizen-News*, October 5, 1968.
77. Kevin Thomas, " 'Tunnel to the Sun' at the Toho La Brea," *Los Angeles Times*, October 3, 1968.
78. Donald Richie, "A Terminal Essay," in *The Japanese Film—Art and Industry* (Expanded Edition) (Princeton University Press, 1982), 474.
79. Kevin Thomas, "Civil War Theme of 'Samurai,' " *Los Angeles Times*, June 25, 1969, IV: 17.
80. "Mosk," "Furin Kazan (Samurai Banners)," *Daily Variety*, July 30, 1969.
81. Kihachi Okamoto. Personal interview, June 28, 1997.
82. Ibid.
83. John Goff, "Toho's 'Red Lion' Good Samurai Action Feature," *The Hollywood Reporter*, December 18, 1969.

84. Kevin Thomas, " 'Red Lion' Has Theme of Military Dictatorship," *Los Angeles Times*, December 24, 1969.
85. "Whit," "The Red Lion," *Daily Variety*, December 18, 1969.
86. "Band of Assassins: Mifune's Best," *The Canyon Crier*, April 20, 1970.
87. Kevin Thomas, " 'Band' a Mifune Milestone," *Los Angeles Times*, April 16, 1970.
88. John Goff, "Mifune Stars, 'Band of Assassins,' " *The Hollywood Reporter*, April 14, 1970, 3, 8.

21: FIRE

1. "Boyish Locomania Detours Kurosawa to Embassy Track," *Weekly Variety*, July 6, 1966.
2. Mike Connolly, "Mike Connolly: U.S.," *The Hollywood Reporter*, December 11, 1964.
3. Yoshio Shirai, "Director Kurosawa's Launch into the World," *Kinema Jumpo*, July 1966, 12.
4. "Boyish Locomania Detours Kurosawa to Embassy Track."
5. Shirai, "Director Kurosawa's Launch into the World."
6. Akira Kurosawa, "The Conception of 'Runaway Train'—My Ambitions Before My Trip to America," *Kinema Jumpo*, September 1966, 12–13.
7. Ibid.
8. Shirai, "Director Kurosawa's Launch into the World."
9. Kurosawa, "The Conception of 'Runaway Train.' "
10. Ibid.
11. "Boyish Locomania Detours Kurosawa to Embassy Track."
12. "Kurosawa First U.S. Pic for Levine-San," *Film Daily*, July 1, 1966.
13. Ibid.
14. "At Kurosawa Production for 'Runaway Train,' " *Kinema Jumpo*, September 1966, 11.
15. Kurosawa, "The Conception of 'Runaway Train.' "
16. Akira Kurosawa, "My Faith and Art of Films—A Discussion About the Postponement of *Runaway Train*," *Kinema Jumpo*, January 1967, 41–43.
17. *Weekly Variety*, March 29, 1967.
18. "Illness Forces Kurosawa out of 20th-Fox's 'Tora,' " *Weekly Variety*, December 25, 1968.
19. Kurosawa, "The Conception of 'Runaway Train.' "
20. Mike Y. Inoue. Personal interview, December 10, 1999.
21. *Tora! Tora! Tora!* production notes, August 1, 1968.
22. Elmo Williams, "For the Crew." Notes attached as supplement to Revised Final Shooting Script, August 1, 1969.
23. "Japanese Director on Nippon Part of 20th's 'Tora,' " *Daily Variety*, April 28, 1967.
24. "Hideo Oguni," in Takamaro Shimaji, ed., *Kurosawa Akira Dokyumento* (Akira Kurosawa Document) (Tokyo: *Kinema Jumpo* Special Edition, May 1974).
25. Donald Richie, "Japan-Yank Co-Op on 'Pearl Harbor'; Both Gov'ts to Get Look at Script," *Weekly Variety*, May 15, 1967.
26. Ibid.
27. Stuart Griffin, "U.S.–Japan Team to Film 'Pearl Harbor,' " *Los Angeles Times*, November 25, 1967.
28. Richard Fleischer, *Just Tell Me When to Cry—Encounters with the Greats, Near-Greats and Ingrates of Hollywood* (London: Souvenir Press, 1993), 273.
29. "Pearl Harbor Raid for 'Tora' Poses Logistical Problem," *Daily Variety*, August 4, 1967.
30. "Dual 'Tora' Helming to Take 10 Months," *The Hollywood Reporter*, October 23, 1967.
31. "250G Production Publicity Budget for 20th's 'Tora,' " *Daily Variety*, March 7, 1968.
32. Bill Ornstein, "All Interiors 20th's 'Tora' Shifted to Studio's Local Lot," *The Hollywood Reporter*, April 23, 1968.
33. *Tora, Tora, Tora* screenplay by Akira Kurosawa, Ryuzo Kikushima, and Hideo Oguni, June 9, 1967.

34. Elmo Williams, Letter to Richard Zanuck, June 23, 1967.
35. Elmo Williams, Letter to Richard Zanuck, November 7, 1967.
36. Elmo Williams, Letter to Tetsu Aoyagi, September 26, 1967.
37. "David to Re-Do Kurosawa Plot as U.S. Western," *Weekly Variety*, June 12, 1968.
38. "Battleship Replica to Be 'Tora!' Set," *Daily Variety*, August 19, 1968.
39. Robert B. Frederick, "Former Foes Reenact Pearl Harbor; Fox Problems: Ships 'n' Planes of '41," *Weekly Variety*, October 16, 1968.
40. Yoshio Shirai, "Testimony of Takeo Kagiya," *Kinema Jumpo*, 1969.
41. " 'Tora' for Yamazaki," *Daily Variety*, November 29, 1968.
42. "Yorktown to Simulate Japanese 'Tora' Vessel," *Daily Variety*, December 4, 1968.
43. Stanley Goldsmith, Letter to Stan Hough (Fox), January 1, 1969.
44. "Production Report—Akira Kurosawa's Illness," December 31, 1968.
45. Handwritten document, attributed to Akira Kurosawa, December 14, 1969.
46. "Production Report—Akira Kurosawa's Illness."
47. Ibid.
48. Stanley Goldsmith, Letter to Stan Hough (Fox), January 1, 1969.
49. "Illness Forces Kurosawa out of 20th-Fox's 'Tora,' " *Weekly Variety*, December 25, 1968.
50. "20th's 'Tora' to Await Kurosawa's Recovery," *Daily Variety*, December 31, 1968.
51. Stan Hough, Memo to Richard Zanuck, November 9, 1967.
52. Inoue interview.
53. Fleischer, *Just Tell Me When to Cry*, 285.
54. "Illness Forces Kurosawa out of 20th-Fox's 'Tora.' "
55. Don Shannon, " 'Tora!' Director Kurosawa Replaced by Two Unknowns," *Los Angeles Times*, March 6, 1969.
56. Tetsu Aoyagi, Letter to Elmo Williams, April 11, 1968.
57. Yoshio Shirai, "*Tora! Tora! Tora!*—Details of the Discussions and Agreement between Kurosawa Production and Fox," *Kinema Jumpo*, 1969, 31–34.
58. Yoshio Shirai, "Testimony of Takeo Kagiya."
59. Ibid.
60. Inoue interview.
61. Shirai, "Testimony of Takeo Kagiya."
62. Ibid.
63. Ibid.
64. Shirai, "*Tora! Tora! Tora!*"
65. Shirai, "Testimony of Sadahiro Tsubota," *Kinema Jumpo*, 1969, 28–31.
66. Richard Fleischer. Personal interview, October 10, 2000.
67. Yoshio Shirai, "Details of the Financial Problems Appear at Last—How Much Money Was Spent on *Tora! Tora! Tora!* Until its Cancellation," *Kinema Jumpo*, 1969, 30–33.
68. Inoue interview.
69. Shirai, "*Tora! Tora! Tora!*"
70. Yoshio Shirai, "Testimony of Sadahiro Tsubota."
71. Inoue interview.
72. Shirai, "*Tora! Tora! Tora!*"
73. Ibid.
74. Ibid.
75. Elmo Williams, Production diary, week of November 18–22, 1968.
76. Fleischer, *Just Tell Me When to Cry*, 275.
77. Shirai, "*Tora! Tora! Tora!*"

78. Yoshio Shirai, "Expressions of Mr. Aoyagi's Thoughts and the Matter of *Three Bad Men in a Hidden Fortress*," *Kinema Jumpo*, 1969, 36–37.

79. Hisao Kurosawa. Personal interview, December 13, 1999.

80. Shirai, "Testimony of Takeo Kagiya."

81. "Fox Asks Mifune Productions: *Tora! Tora! Tora!*," *Asahi Shinbun*, January 18, 1969.

82. "Crisis in the Golden Combination—Akira Kurosawa and Toshiro Mifune," *Weekly Bunshun*, February 10, 1969.

83. *Tora, Tora, Tora* press kit, Twentieth Century Fox, ca. 1970.

84. Kinji Fukasaku. Personal interview, January 27, 1996.

85. Michiko Yoshii, "Mystery Shrouds Kurosawa Case; Someone Isn't Telling the Truth," *Yomuri*, January 30, 1969.

86. "Kurosawa Production Restarting—Director Kurosawa Begins a New Project," *Kinema Jumpo*, 1969, 32–34.

87. "Hideo Oguni," in Shimaji, ed., *Kurosawa Akira Dokyumento*, 110–14.

88. Tetsu Aoyagi, Letter to Elmo Williams, April 28, 1969.

22: TROLLEY CRAZY

1. Stuart Galbraith, *The Japanese Filmography* (Jefferson, NC: McFarland & Co. 1995), 467–72.

2. Joseph L. Anderson and Donald Richie, *The Japanese Film—Art and Industry* (expanded edition) (Princeton University Press, 1982), 451.

3. "Ah So, Toho Goes Porno to Stay Abreast of B.O.," *Weekly Variety*, December 5, 1972.

4. Hy Hyberger, "'Dodes'ka-den': Kurosawa's Masterpiece," *The Canyon Crier*, June 14, 1971, 8.

5. Shinobu Hashimoto. Personal interview, 1999.

6. "Hideo Oguni," in Takamuro Shimaji, ed., *Kurosawa Akira Dokyumento* (Akira Kurosawa Document) (Tokyo: *Kinema Jumpo* Special Edition, 1974), 110–14.

7. "Dodeskaden Spectrum," trans. Haruji Nakamura and Leonard Schrader, *Cinema*, Spring 1972, 14.

8. Ibid.

9. Ibid., 15.

10. Yoshitaka Zushi. Personal interview, December 10, 1999.

11. "*Dodes'ka-den* and Akira Kurosawa's Secret of the New World of Film" ("*Dodesukaden to Kurosawa Akira no atarashii eizo sekai no himitsu*"), *Kinema Jumpo*, September 1970.

12. "Dodeskaden Spectrum," 16.

13. Ibid., 14.

14. "Shuns Fests, but Kurosawa to Russ," *Weekly Variety*, August 11, 1970, 2, 61.

15. "Dodeskaden Spectrum," 16.

16. Zushi interview.

17. Ibid.

18. Tatsuo Matsumura. Personal interview, January 27, 1996.

19. "Introduction," *Dodesukaden*. Program from the Toho La Brea Theatre, 1971.

20. "Dodeskaden Spectrum," 15.

21. Zushi interview.

22. Teruyo Nogami, "Location References," in Michihiro Imata, Kunihiro Susumu, and Akira Kurosawa Kenyukai-hen, eds., *Kurosawa Akira yume no ashiato* (Akira Kurosawa's Footsteps of Dreams) (Tokyo: Kyodo Tunshin-sha, 1999), 277.

23. "Dodeskaden Spectrum," 15–16.

24. Matsumura interview.
25. "Dodeskaden Spectrum," 16.
26. "Hideo Oguni's Story," in Imata, et al., *Akira Kurosawa's Footsteps of Dreams*, 276.
27. "Dodeskaden Spectrum," 15.
28. Douglas Jones, "New Kurosawa Film Unlike Any Previous," *The Hollywood Reporter*, June 8, 1971.
29. "Mosk," "Dodes'ka-den," *Weekly Variety*, December 9, 1970.
30. Judith Crist, *New York*, October 11, 1971.
31. John Torzilli, " 'Moved' is the Word," *The Canyon Crier*, June 14, 1971, 8.
32. Matsumura interview.
33. Lloyd Shearer, "Director's Decline," *Parade*, February 6, 1972.
34. Mike Y. Inoue. Personal interview, December 12, 1999.
35. Kazuko Kurosawa, *Papa Kurosawa Akira* (Tokyo: Bungei Shunju, 2000), 60.
36. "Kurosawa Cuts Wrists; Hospitalized," *Los Angeles Times*, December 23, 1971.
37. Inoue interview.
38. Shiro Mifune. Personal interview, December 10, 1999.
39. Senkichi Taniguchi. Personal interview, October 3, 1999.
40. Kurosawa, *Papa Kurosawa Akira*, 60.
41. Zushi interview.
42. Inoue interview.
43. Kurosawa, *Papa Kurosawa Akira*, 24.
44. Inoue interview.

23: *RONIN*

1. Shiro Mifune. Personal interview, December 10, 1999.
2. "Toshiro Mifune Prod. Rel. Soon in US," *Weekly Variety*, July 28, 1971.
3. Kevin Thomas, "Mifune Visits as Producer," *Los Angeles Times*, September 17, 1971, IV:24.
4. Shiro Mifune. Personal interview, December 16, 1999.
5. Ibid.
6. David Chute, " 'Zatoichi Meets Yojimbo' in Megastar Ham Samurai Epic," *Los Angeles Herald-Examiner*, July 15, 1983.
7. Kevin Thomas, "Swordsman in 'Zatoichi,' " *Los Angeles Times*, July 17, 1970.
8. John Goff, *The Hollywood Reporter*, April 14, 1970, 3–8.
9. "Machibuse," *Boxoffice*, October 18, 1971.
10. *The Walking Major* press materials, 6.
11. Kevin Thomas, " 'Gunbatsu' at Toho La Brea," *Los Angeles Times*, March 11, 1971.
12. Rochelle Reed, "Japan's 'Gunbatsu' Feature Traces Pacific War's Start," *The Hollywood Reporter*, March 5, 1971.
13. "Rob't Dorfman to Roll $3,600,000 'Sun' in Spain," *Weekly Variety*, January 13, 1971.
14. "Mifune's American Acting Career Due," *Weekly Variety*, October 16, 1968.
15. " 'Red Sun' Sets Spain Filming," *The Hollywood Reporter*, January 29, 1970.
16. "Terence Young Directing 'Sun,' " *The Hollywood Reporter*, July 31, 1969.
17. *Red Sun* press kit, c. 1972.
18. "Mosk," *Weekly Variety*, September 29, 1971.
19. *Playboy*, July 1972.
20. *Los Angeles Herald-Examiner*, July 26, 1972.
21. Kevin Thomas, *Los Angeles Times*, July 27, 1972, 4:28.
22. Thomas, "Mifune Visits as Producer."
23. "Westward, Who?" *The New York Times*, November 19, 1972.

24. "Mifune Back to Pic Prod. with 3 Films," *Weekly Variety*, November 1, 1972.
25. *Samurai Assassin* program (Los Angeles: Toho La Brea Theater), c. 1965.
26. "Tokyo," *Weekly Variety*, June 28, 1972.
27. James Bailey, "Toshiro Mifune," *Northwest*, December 1987, 26.
28. Donald Richie, *Geisha, Gangster, Neighbor, Nun—Scenes from Japanese Lives* (Tokyo: Kodansha International, 1987), 57.
29. UPI International, July 14, 1986.

24: SIBERIA
1. Dianna Waggoner, "In Homage to the Master, George Lucas and Francis Coppola Unleash Their Clout for Kurosawa," *People*, c. 1980.
2. Mike Y. Inoue. Personal interview, December 12, 1999.
3. Akira Kurosawa, "I Dreamed of *Dersu Uzala* for 30 Years," in Michihiro Imata, Kunihiro Susumu, and Akira Kurosawa Kenkyukai-hen, eds., *Kurosawa Akira yume no ashiato* (Akira Kurosawa's Footsteps of Dreams) (Tokyo: Kyodo Tunshin-sha, 1999), 12–18.
4. Soji Sato, "Testimony of a Scenario Writer—Interview with Eijiro Hisaita," in Takamaro Shimaji, ed., *Kurosawa Akira Dokyumento* (Akira Kurosawa Document) (Tokyo: *Kinema Jumpo* Special Edition, May 1974).
5. *Dersu Uzala* press kit, c. 1976.
6. "Kurosawa to Direct 'Uzala' for Mosfilm," *Weekly Variety*, April 11, 1973.
7. Inoue interview.
8. "Kurosawa to Direct 'Uzala' for Mosfilm."
9. "Moscow," *Weekly Variety*, August 8, 1973.
10. Shiro Mifune. Personal interview, December 10, 1999.
11. *Dersu Uzala* press kit.
12. Ibid.
13. Ibid.
14. Akira Kurosawa, *Something Like an Autobiography* (New York: Vintage Books, 1983), 96.
15. Kurosawa, "I Dreamed of *Dersu Uzala* for 30 Years," 12–13.
16. Ibid.
17. Hazel Guild, "Kurosawa Slaps Soviets for Cutting Jointly Made Film," *Weekly Variety*, November 17, 1976.
18. Kurosawa, "I Dreamed of *Dersu Uzala* for 30 Years."
19. Joan Mellen, "Dersu Uzala," in Donald Richie, *The Films of Akira Kurosawa* (Revised Edition) (Berkeley, CA: University of California Press, 1984), 197.
20. Donald Richie. Personal interview by James Bailey, 1990.
21. Mellen, "Dersu Uzala," 196.
22. Ibid.
23. Kevin Brownlow, *David Lean* (New York: St. Martin's Press, 1996), 586.
24. John Simon, "Readers have written . . ." *National Review*, September 12, 1986.
25. "Soviet Film Fuels Dispute with China," *Los Angeles Times*, February 11, 1976.
26. Kurosawa, "I Dreamed of *Dersu Uzala* for 30 Years."
27. Guild, "Kurosawa Slaps Soviets."
28. Ibid.
29. "Japanese Film Showcase Will Close End of Mo.," *Daily Variety*, May 21, 1976.
30. Academy of Motion Picture Arts and Sciences. Best Foreign Film Screening Program, February 2, 1976.
31. Naoaki Usui, "Kurosawa Award Repays Debt," *Los Angeles Times*, April 2, 1976, IV:20.
32. Inoue interview.

33. Todd McCarthy, "Filmex Review—*Dersu Uzala*," *The Hollywood Reporter*, March 30, 1976.

34. New York Film Festival program, 1976.

35. Joseph McBride, "Red Tape Delays U.S. Distrib'n of Russ-Japan Oscar Winner," *Daily Variety*, May 15, 1977.

36. Tom Milne, "Dersu Uzala," *Monthly Film Bulletin*, January 1978.

37. Kevin Thomas, "Kurosawa Hero as Mountain Man," *Los Angeles Times*, December 20, 1977, IV:14.

38. "J.T.," "*Dersu Uzala* . . . The Hunter," *Independent Film Journal*, February 3, 1978.

39. "*Dersu Uzala*," *The New Republic*, February 4, 1978.

40. Stephen Farber, "As in 1900 . . . ," *New West*, January 16, 1978, 90.

41. "Akira Kurosawa's *Dersu Uzala*," *New York*, February 13, 1978.

42. "Sovexport Film Avoids Fuss," *Weekly Variety*, December 1, 1976.

43. Guild, "Kurosawa Slaps Soviets."

44. "Sovexport Film Avoids Fuss."

45. Guild, "Kurosawa Slaps Soviets."

46. Kazuko Kurosawa, *Papa Kurosawa Akira* (Tokyo: Bungei Shunju, 2000), 197.

47. Ibid.

48. "Mifune, Kurosawa to Make Another Film," *Weekly Variety*, February 19, 1976.

49. "Kurosawa, Mifune Set to Produce Feature," *The Hollywood Reporter*, March 9, 1976.

50. "The new Akira Kurosawa . . .," *Daily Variety*, March 9, 1976.

51. Senkichi Taniguchi. Personal interview, October 3, 1999.

52. Hisao Kurosawa. Personal interview, December 13, 1999.

53. Mifune interview.

54. "Toshiro Mifune Signs to Co-Star in 'Paper Tiger,' " *The Hollywood Reporter*, June 18, 1974.

55. " 'Tiger' Prod'n Offices Gutted in Malay Blaze," *Daily Variety*, August 30, 1974.

56. "W. W." (William Wolf), "Maudlin Melodrama," *Cue*, October 2, 1976.

57. Judith Crist, "Equally rare is . . . ," *The Saturday Review*, November 29, 1975.

58. "Mack," "Film Review—Paper Tiger," *Daily Variety*, November 7, 1975.

59. Ibid.

60. Dorothy Manners, "Producer Walter Mirisch . . . ," *Los Angeles Herald-Examiner*, July 3, 1975.

61. James Bacon, "All the big stars . . . ," *Los Angeles Herald-Examiner*, June 30, 1975.

62. " 'Midway': A Secret in Japan, Ending with Mifune's Admiral," *Weekly Variety*, July 9, 1975.

63. Bob Thomas, "Mifune Interviewed at Midway Site," *Rafu Shimpo*, July 3, 1975, 1.

64. "Mifune's Dialogue Will Be in English," *Rafu Shimpo*, July 3, 1975, 1.

65. "Non-Original 'Midway' Footage Has Some Theatermen Grumbling," *The Hollywood Reporter*, June 9, 1976, 5.

66. Ibid.

67. Lee Grant, "East Side," *Los Angeles Times*, July 17, 1976.

68. Shigehiko Togo, " 'The Young Invaders' Devours Tokyo: A Yen to Film," *The Washington Post*, February 26, 1978, F1.

69. Ibid.

70. Larry Ketchum, "Director William Richert," *Hollywood Drama-Logue*, March 10, 1983, 1, 14.

71. Ibid.

72. Kevin Thomas, "Existential 'Shogun's Samurai,' " *Los Angeles Times*, December 6, 1984.

73. "Edna," "Venice Film Fest Reviews," *Weekly Variety*, September 20, 1989, 31, 34.

74. John Hartl, "Toshiro Mifune—Quiet Gestures, Smaller Presence Seemed Fitting for the

'Samurai,' Who Stepped Out of Character for Seattle Appearance," *Seattle Times*, April 27, 1990, E1.

75. "Cart," *Daily Variety*, April 9, 1979.

76. Kevin Thomas, " 'Love and Faith' a Stately Tragedy," *Los Angeles Times*, March 16, 1979.

77. Tomio Sagisu. Personal interview, December 9, 1999.

78. Paul Attanasio, "Bob Zemeckis, Zooming Ahead—the Hot New Director, Romancing the Past with his Mentor Steven Spielberg," *The Washington Post*, July 3, 1985, 1.

79. UPI International, July 14, 1986.

25: LORDS AND *GAIJIN*

1. William Grimes, "James Clavell, Best-Selling Storyteller of Far Eastern Epics, Is Dead at 69," *The New York Times*, September 8, 1994, 19.

2. Elizabeth Barks and Paul Bernstein, eds., *The Making of James Clavell's Shogun* (New York: Delta, 1980), 75.

3. Charles Ziarko. Personal interview, October 18, 1999.

4. Barks and Bernstein, *The Making of James Clavell's Shogun*, 111.

5. Wally Worsley and Sue Dwiggins Worsley, Charles Ziarko, ed., *From Oz to E.T.—Wally Worsley's Half-Century in Hollywood* (Lanham, MD: Scarecrow Press, 1997), 169.

6. Ziarko interview.

7. UPI International, July 14, 1986.

8. Ziarko interview.

9. Barks and Bernstein, *The Making of James Clavell's Shogun*, 200.

10. Ibid., 76.

11. Ziarko interview.

12. Ibid.

13. Barks and Bernstein, *The Making of James Clavell's Shogun*, 76.

14. Worsley, Worsley, and Ziarko, *From Oz to E.T.*, 159.

15. Barks and Bernstein, *The Making of James Clavell's Shogun*, 205.

16. Lawrence O'Toole, "Prime-time Samurai," *Maclean's*, September 1980.

17. Dale Pollock, "English-Language 'Inchon' to Be Totally Financed by Japanese Investment Funds," *Daily Variety*, March 27, 1978, 1, 2.

18. Peter Rainer, " 'Inchon': A Retreat from Quality Filmmaking," *Los Angeles Herald-Examiner*, September 17, 1982, D4.

19. J. Hoberman, "Postcards from Cannes," *The Village Voice*, June 1, 1982.

20. "$1 Mil Sweepstakes Launches 'Inchon,' " *The Hollywood Reporter*, September 17, 1982.

21. Rick Goldschmidt, *The Enchanted World of Rankin/Bass* (Issaquah, WA: Tiger Mountain Press, 1997), 163.

22. " 'Port Arthur' War Recall Rentals Near $8,500,000 for Toei Co.," *Weekly Variety*, October 15, 1980.

23. "Loss of 'Accidental' Actor Mourned," Asahi News Service, December 26, 1997.

24. Audie Bock, "Japan's Kurosawa Is Staging His Comeback in Epic Style," *The New York Times*, April 27, 1980.

25. Peter Rainer, "No Compromises for Kurosawa, Godard at New York Film Festival," *Los Angeles Herald-Examiner*, October 6, 1980, B:4.

26. Bock, "Japan's Kurosawa Is Staging His Comeback in Epic Style."

27. Peter Grilli, "Kurosawa Directs Cinematic 'Lear,' " *The New York Times*, December 15, 1985, 17.

28. Tom Buckley, "Kurosawa at the Drawing Board," *The New York Times*, October 3, 1980, C18.

29. "Kurosawa's Latest Gets Fox Distribbing, Coppola Editing Aid," *Weekly Variety*, May 21, 1980, 7.
30. "Production Information." *Kagemusha* press kit, 20th Century-Fox, 1980, 4.
31. Bock, "Japan's Kurosawa Is Staging His Comeback in Epic Style."
32. Ibid.
33. Michael Schumaker, *Francis Ford Coppola—A Filmmaker's Life* (New York: Crown, 1999).
34. Ibid.
35. "Fox Acquires World Rights to 'Kagemusha,' " *Daily Variety*, December 21, 1978.
36. Bock, "Japan's Kurosawa Is Staging His Comeback in Epic Style."
37. Ibid.
38. "Tokyo," *The Hollywood Reporter*, March 8, 1979.
39. Donald Richie, *Geisha, Gangster, Neighbor, Nun—Scenes from Japanese Lives* (Tokyo: Kodansha International, 1987), 150.
40. Jinpachi Nezu. Liner notes for the Japanese laserdisc release. Interviewed July 26, 1993.
41. Mike Y. Inoue. Personal interview, December 12, 1999.
42. Nezu interview.
43. Inoue interview.
44. Nancy Hata, "Kurosawa Fires Star," *Screen International*, August 25, 1979.
45. Inoue interview.
46. Bock, "Japan's Kurosawa Is Staging His Comeback in Epic Style."
47. *Kagemusha* press kit.
48. Bock, "Japan's Kurosawa Is Staging His Comeback in Epic Style."
49. David Milner, "Ishiro Honda Interview," *Cult Movies*, No. 9, 1992, 50.
50. Akira Kurosawa. Personal interview, March 13, 1996.
51. Tatsuo Matsumura. Personal interview, January 27, 1996.
52. Kimi Honda. Personal interview, January 27, 1996.
53. Ishiro Honda, *Honda Ishiro—Godzilla and My Life* (Tokyo: Jitsugyo-no-Nihon-sha), 1994.
54. Charles Fleming, "Kurosawa 'Not Yet' Done—Great Director Addresses Media on Variety of Topics," *Daily Variety*, October 2, 1992, 38.
55. Kimi Honda interview.
56. Inoue interview.
57. *Kagemusha* press kit.
58. Ibid.
59. Bock, "Japan's Kurosawa Is Staging His Comeback in Epic Style."
60. Ibid.
61. Dianna Waggoner, "In Homage to the Master, George Lucas and Francis Coppola Unleash Their Clout for Kurosawa," *People*, c. 1980.
62. Fox press release, April 28, 1980.
63. "Strong 'Kagemusha,' " *The Hollywood Reporter*, May 27, 1980.
64. " 'Kagemusha' Draws Heavy," *The Hollywood Reporter*, May 13, 1980.
65. Rainer, "No Compromises for Kurosawa."
66. Andrew Sarris, "Kurosawa's Comeback," *The Saturday Review*, September 1980, 18.
67. Roger Watkins, " 'Kagemusha' and 'Jazz' Share Top Cannes Fest Nod," *Daily Variety*, May 27, 1980, 1, 8.
68. Rainer, "No Compromises for Kurosawa."
69. "Akira Kurosawa to Visit U.S. for 'Kagemusha' Premieres," Press release from 20th Century-Fox, October 1, 1980, 1–2.
70. Sheila Benson, "Kurosawa in Film Fest Spotlight," *Los Angeles Times*, October 16, 1980, 2.

71. "Box Office Samplings," *The Hollywood Reporter*, November 28, 1980.

72. Karen Stabiner, "Cannes Winner Is Loser at Fox," *New West*, December 1, 1980, 5.

73. " 'Kagemusha' Hits 395G in 6 Cities," *Daily Variety*, November 13, 1980.

74. Donald Richie, *The Films of Akira Kurosawa* (Revised Edition) (Berkeley, CA: University of California Press, 1984), 210.

75. David Denby, "An Old Man's Dream of Glory," *New York*, October 27, 1980, 71.

76. Michael Sragow, "A Master Fails to Win Our Hearts and Minds," *Los Angeles Herald-Examiner*, October 17, 1980, D7.

77. Richard Schickel, "Shadow Warrior," *Time*, October 13, 1980, 108.

78. Kevin Thomas, " 'Kagemusha' Elegy for a Period," *Los Angeles Times*, October 12, 1980.

79. "Kurosawa's Latest Gets Fox Distribbing, Coppola Editing Aid."

80. Michael Rich, "Letters—Crossing Swords over Kagemusha," *UCLA Daily Bruin*, October 27, 1980, 1.

81. Ibid.

82. Greg Mitchell, "Kurosawa: A Retrospective," *The Nation*, October 24, 1981.

83. Waggoner, "In Homage to the Master."

84. Charles Champlin, *John Frankenheimer—A Conversation* (Burbank, CA: Riverwood Press, 1994), 161.

85. Ibid., 163.

86. Roderick Mann, "Director in Love—with Japan," *Los Angeles Times*, July 21, 1981.

87. Robert Osborne, "On Location," *The Hollywood Reporter*, September 21, 1981.

88. Donna Benz Goodley. Personal interview by telephone, October 17, 1999.

89. Tomio Sagisu. Personal interview, December 9, 1999.

90. Kevin Thomas, " 'Miracle of Joe': A Gangster Epic," *Los Angeles Times*, November 16, 1984.

91. "Bail," "Umi Isubame Joe No Kiseki," *Weekly Variety*, June 6, 1984.

92. Peter Grilli, "Civil Samurai," *Film Comment*, July 1984, 66.

93. Ibid.

94. Ibid.

95. Frank Segers, "Details, but None of Mifune's Stature, Are Lost in Translation," *Daily Variety*, May 11, 1983.

96. Grilli, "Civil Samurai," 67.

97. Ibid., 66.

98. Ibid.

26: CLOUDS

1. "Like good French wine . . . ," *Newsweek*, June 2, 1980.

2. Audie Bock, "Japan's Kurosawa Is Staging His Comeback in Epic Style," *The New York Times*, April 27, 1980.

3. William Wolf, "Japanese Master Looks Ahead," Gannett News Service, c. October 1985.

4. Frank Segers, "Toho Topper—Japan No Monopoly," *Daily Variety*, May 4, 1983.

5. John Austin, "Cambridge Group Will Invest $40 Mil in 12 Pictures a Year," *The Hollywood Reporter*, March 3, 1981, 25.

6. Ray Loynd, "Int'l Flavor for Planned $8–9 Mil 'Runaway Train,' " *Daily Variety*, July 19, 1983, 1, 24.

7. "Cart," "Runaway Train," *Daily Variety*, December 6, 1985, 3, 12.

8. David Edelstein, "Loco Motives," *The Village Voice*, December 17, 1985, 90.

9. Lenny Borger, "Kurosawa's New Epic to Roll in Spring," *Daily Variety*, February 1984, 6.

10. "Latest Kurosawa Film Planned for July Start; Set Shoot Sans Toho," *Weekly Variety*, May 4, 1983.

11. "Kurosawa Completes 'Ran' Cast: 30-Week Lensing Begins June 1," *Weekly Variety*, May 9, 1984.

12. "Complex Nippon Herald Package, Toho in Tow, for Kurosawa Pic," *Weekly Variety*, March 7, 1984.

13. "*Ran*—A Decade in the Making," Japanese press materials, c. 1985.

14. Wolf, "Japanese Master Looks Ahead."

15. "Japan's Kurosawa resumes 'Ran' helming," *The Hollywood Reporter*, December 28, 1983.

16. Mayo Issobe, " 'Chaos' Climaxes Kurosawa's Career," *The Japan Times*, May 15, 1985.

17. "Kurosawa Completes 'Ran' Cast."

18. Hitoshi Ueki. Personal interview, January 30, 1996.

19. Ibid.

20. Peter Grilli, "Kurosawa Directs Cinematic 'Lear,' " *The New York Times*, December 15, 1985, 17.

21. "*Ran*—A Decade in the Making."

22. "Kurosawa Nearly Done with 'Life's Work,' " *Rafu Shimpo*, December 6, 1984.

23. "*Ran*: The Production." From the *Ran* press kit, 1985.

24. Grilli, "Kurosawa Directs Cinematic 'Lear.' "

25. Minoru Nakano. Personal interview, December 18, 1994.

26. Kazuko Kurosawa, *Papa Kurosawa Akira* (Tokyo: Bungei Shunju, 2000), 86.

27. Ibid., 87.

28. Senkichi Taniguchi. Personal interview, October 3, 1999.

29. Hisao Kurosawa. Personal interview, December 13, 1999.

30. Kurosawa, *Papa Kurosawa Akira*, 87.

31. "Kurosawa Nearly Done with 'Life's Work.' "

32. Frank Segers, "Kurosawa's 'Ran' Finally Finished; Producer Has Final Cut Approval," *Weekly Variety*, March 6, 1985.

33. "*Ran*: The Production."

34. Donald Richie, "Chaos Reigns," *Connoisseur*, October 1985, 109.

35. Grilli, "Kurosawa Directs a Cinematic 'Lear,' " 1.

36. Bob Fisher, "The Japanese Method for *Ran*," *American Cinematographer*, July 1986, 76.

37. David Edelstein, "In the Realm of the Sensei," *The Village Voice*, December 24, 1985, 80.

38. Kurosawa, *Papa Kurosawa Akira*, 87.

39. Grilli, "Kurosawa Directs Cinematic 'Lear,' " 17.

40. Richard A. Blake, "The End Time," *America*, March 29, 1986, 249.

41. Gerald Peary, "Akira Kurosawa—Japan's Existential Cowboy Looks West and Thinks East," *American Film*, April 1989, 82.

42. Kaizo Hayashi. Personal interview, January 28, 2001.

43. Elliott Stein, "The 23rd New York Film Festival," *Film Comment*, November–December 1985, 60.

44. Richie, "Chaos Reigns," 108.

45. Joseph McLellan, "Kurosawa, the Battles & the Vision," *The Washington Post*, February 3, 1986, B4.

46. Kirk Ellis, "Kurosawa Premiere of 'Ran' Set for Sept.," *The Hollywood Reporter*, May 20, 1985.

47. "Conjecture Rife Re: 'Ran' Run at Tokyo," *Weekly Variety*, May 22, 1985.

48. Richard Gold, "Orion Classics Tries to Tap Wide Audience for Kurosawa's 'Ran,' " *Daily Variety*, December 13, 1985, 6.

49. Donald Richie. Personal interview by James Bailey, 1990.

50. " 'Ran' Bows Boffo at Paris Theaters," *Weekly Variety*, September 25, 1985.

51. Vincent Canby, "Film: Kurosawa's 'Ran,' " *The New York Times*, December 20, 1985.

52. Stephen Schiff, "*Ran* Amok," *Vanity Fair*, January 1986, 95.

53. Sheila Benson, "Critics Name 'Ran' Best Film," *Los Angeles Times*, January 3, 1986, 1.

54. Jack Mathews, "Snub and Be Snubbed as 'Ran' Misses Oscar Bid," *Los Angeles Times*, December 11, 1985, 1.

55. Edward Guthmann, " 'Ran' Gets Big Runaround for the Oscars," *Datebook*, February 2, 1986, 24.

56. Susan Chira, "How Kurosawa's 'Ran' Missed a Shot at Oscar," *The New York Times*, December 19, 1985.

57. "You First, No You First," *Los Angeles Times*, December 20, 1985.

58. Richie interview.

59. Peary, "Akira Kurosawa—Japan's Existential Cowboy."

60. McLellan, "Kurosawa, the Battles & the Vision."

61. Mathews, "Snub and Be Snubbed," 4.

62. Ed Sikov, *On Sunset Boulevard—The Life and Times of Billy Wilder* (New York: Hyperion, 1998), 578.

63. Mason Wiley and Damien Bona, *Inside Oscar—The Unofficial History of the Academy Awards* (New York: Ballantine Books, 1987), 679.

64. "*Ran*—A Decade in the Making."

65. "Orion Classics Gets Kurosawa 'Ran' Pic," *The Hollywood Reporter*, May 13, 1985.

66. Gold, "Orion Classics Tries to Tap Wide Audience for Kurosawa's 'Ran.' "

27: WANDERER

1. James Bailey, "Toshiro Mifune," *Northwest*, December 1987, 26.

2. "Land Sales Behind the High Income of Most Top Tax Payers," source undetermined, May 1, 1987.

3. Bailey, "Toshiro Mifune."

4. Ibid.

5. "Japanese Actor Mifune Awarded UCLA's Honorary Medal," Kyodo News Service, June 23, 1986.

6. *Shochiku* publicity materials. Circa 1990.

7. Yoji Yamada. Personal interview, December 14, 1999.

8. Ibid.

9. Chris Hicks, "Tora-san Goes North," *Desert News*, March 31, 1989.

10. Kevin Thomas, " 'Tora-san Goes North,' Ideal Role for Mifune," *Los Angeles Times*, December 25, 1987, 6:14.

11. Yamada interview.

12. Dan Fainaru, "Bring Your Own Magic," *The Jerusalem Post*, November 21, 1989.

13. Kevin Thomas, "A Compelling Fable in 'Demons in Spring,' " *Los Angeles Times*, October 31, 1989, F13.

14. "The Hard Sell—Japanese Cinema in a Slump," *The Economist*, April 20, 1991, 92.

15. Yamada interview.

16. David R. Schweisberg, "Toshiro Mifune: Japan's Most Celebrated Actor," UPI, July 18, 1996.

17. Leonard Klady, "Japan's Top Star Brings His Skill to Canada's $25 Million Inuit Movie," *Toronto Star*, November 20, 1990.

18. Don Groves, "Mifune to Be Honored at Asia Pacific Film Fest," *Daily Variety*, August 23, 1994, 14.
19. Schweisberg, "Toshiro Mifune."
20. Klady, "Japan's Top Star Brings His Skill to Canada's $25 Million Inuit Movie."
21. Shiro Mifune. Personal interview, December 9, 1999.
22. Schweisberg, "Toshiro Mifune."
23. Donald Richie, *Geisha, Gangster, Neighbor, Nun—Scenes from Japanese Lives* (Tokyo: Kodansha International, 1987), 58.
24. Mike Y. Inoue. Personal interview, December 12, 1999.
25. Donald Richie. Personal interview by James Bailey, 1990.
26. John Hartl, "Toshiro Mifune—Quiet Gestures, Smaller Presence Seemed Fitting for the 'Samurai,' Who Stepped Out of Character for Seattle Appearance," *The Seattle Times*, April 27, 1990, E1.
27. Klady, "Japan's Top Star Brings His Skill to Canada's $25 Million Inuit Movie."
28. Ibid.
29. "National Gallery's 'Passionate' Show," *Newsbank*, June 1990.
30. Jeff Shannon, " 'Journey' Is Old-Time Epic Fun," *The Seattle Times*, August 14, 1992, 23.
31. Hy Hollinger, "Japanese Team Shoots Feature Pic, for First Time Mainly in States," *Weekly Variety*, June 20, 1990, 23.
32. Klady, "Japan's Top Star Brings His Skill to Canada's $25 Million Inuit Movie."
33. Roger Ebert, *Chicago Sun-Times*, March 5, 1993.
34. Hal Hinson, *The Washington Post*, March 6, 1993.
35. Todd McCarthy, *Daily Variety*, March 5, 1993.

28: NOT YET
1. Tom Buckley, "Kurosawa at the Drawing Board," *The New York Times*, October 3, 1980, C18.
2. William Wolf, "Japanese Master Looks Ahead," Gannett News Service, c. October 1985.
3. Donald Richie, *The Films of Akira Kurosawa* (Revised Edition) (Berkeley, CA: University of California Press, 1984), 223.
4. Tom Carson, "The Sleep of Reason—Akira Kurosawa Gets Caught Napping," *LA Weekly*, August 31, 1990, 31.
5. Akira Kurosawa, Production notes, 1990.
6. Akira Kurosawa, "Some Random Notes on Filmmaking," in *Something Like an Autobiography*, (New York: Vintage Books, 1983), 194.
7. James Bailey, "The Edge of Dreamland," *Los Angeles Times*, August 26, 1990.
8. Ibid.
9. Mike Y. Inoue. Personal interview, December 12, 1999.
10 Donald Richie. Personal interview by James Bailey, 1990.
11. Jane Galbraith, "Kurosawa's Next Pic Due from WB, Amblin," *Daily Variety*, May 27, 1988.
12. Bailey, "The Edge of Dreamland."
13. "Cannes Film Fest Notes," *The Hollywood Reporter*, May 11, 1990.
14. Bailey, "The Edge of Dreamland."
15. Inoue interview.
16. Hisao Kurosawa. Personal interview, December 13, 1999.
17. Ralph Rugoff, "Kurosawa," *Interview*, September 1990, 14.
18. Frank Segers, "Kurosawa Brings 'Dreams' to Cannes," *Weekly Variety*, May 2, 1990, S-22.
19. " 'Dreams' Best U.S. Bow for Kurosawa," *Weekly Variety*, September 10, 1990.
20. David Denby, "Sand Man," *New York*, September 17, 1990, 58.

21. Kevin Thomas, "Beautiful Dreamer," *Los Angeles Times*, August 24, 1990, F1.
22. Terrence Rafferty, "The Current Cinema—High and Low," *The New Yorker*, September 10, 1990, 101.
23. Rugoff, "Kurosawa."
24. Carson, "The Sleep of Reason."
25. Akira Terao. Personal interview, December 11, 1999.
26. Shinobu Hashimoto. Personal interview, December 15, 1999.
27. Bailey, "The Edge of Dreamland."
28. "Cannes Film Fest Notes."
29. Teri Ritzer, "Shochiku Backing New Kurosawa Pic, 'Fortune,' 'Heaven,' " *The Hollywood Reporter*, May 14, 1990, 1, 26.
30. "Kurosawa Waxing 'Rhapsody' with Shochiku Coin," *Weekly Variety*, May 16, 1990.
31. *Rhapsody in August* production notes, 1991.
32. Japanese production notes for *Rhapsody in August*, 1991.
33. Jonathan Cott, "Light in August—Kurosawa Dreams Again," *Elle*, December 1991, 112.
34. Christine Chapman, "At 86, a Japanese Actress Finds Life a 'Rhapsody,' " *The New York Times*, January 26, 1992, 19.
35. Ibid.
36. Ibid.
37. Japanese production notes.
38. Cott, "Light in August."
39. Inoue interview.
40. Will Tusher, "Gere Moves Indie Outfit to Tri-Star," *Daily Variety*, August 8, 1990, 22.
41. Cott, "Light in August."
42. *Rhapsody in August* production notes.
43. Cott, "Light in August."
44. "The Hard Sell—Japanese Cinema in a Slump," *The Economist*, April 20, 1991, 92.
45. Mark Schilling, "Bird Benefit Helps Boost Rhapsody in Tokyo Debut," *Screen International*, June 21, 1991.
46. John Voland, "Kurosawa to Play 'Rhapsody' in Orion Classics Output Deal," *The Hollywood Reporter*, August 20, 1990, 1, 24.
47. Bill Hersey and David Wilson, "Debate Heats Up over Kurosawa's Latest Project," *The Hollywood Reporter*, March 26, 1991.
48. Frank Segers, "Kurosawa Pic to Address Japan–U.S. Friction," *Weekly Variety*, June 13, 1990, 4.
49. "The Hard Sell."
50. Georgia Brown, "Review of Rhapsody in August," *The Village Voice*, December 16, 1991.
51. Peter McGill, "Prophet Honoured in His Own Country," *The Observer*, March 17, 1991, 19.
52. Mark Schilling, "Rhapsody in August," *Screen International*, May 29, 1991, 2-2.
53. Vincent Canby, "Kurosawa, Small in Scale and Blunt," *The New York Times*, December 20, 1991, B6.
54. "R.S.," "Learning to Accept History," *Time*, January 27, 1992.
55. Henry Sheehan, "Film Picks of the Week—Rhapsody in August," *LA Weekly*, December 27, 1991.
56. Kevin Thomas, "War, Reconciliation in Kurosawa's 'Rhapsody,' " *Los Angeles Times*, December 23, 1991, F1.
57. Bruce Williamson, "Movies," *Playboy*, January 1992.
58. "Strat," "Hachigatsu no Kyohshikyoku (Rhapsody in August)," *Weekly Variety*, May 20, 1991.

59. "Kurosawa's 'August' Rhapsodic in Japan," *Daily Variety*, May 29, 1991.
60. Mark Schilling, "Daiei Aboard for New Kurosawa Co-production," *Screen International*, February 7, 1992.
61. Akira Kurosawa. Notes from the Japanese press kit, 1993.
62. Leslie Helm, "Is Kurosawa Ready to Stop Making Films? Not Yet . . . ," *Los Angeles Times*, June 24, 1992, F7.
63. Mark Schilling, "Tokyo," *Screen International*, June 5, 1992.
64. Kyoko Kagawa. Personal interview, December 15, 1999.
65. Ibid.
66. Schilling, "Tokyo."
67. Ibid.
68. Helm, "Is Kurosawa Ready to Stop Making Films?"
69. Ibid.
70. Charles Fleming, "Kurosawa 'Not Yet' Done—Great Director Addresses Media on Variety of Topics," *Daily Variety*, October 2, 1992, 38.
71. Mark Schilling, "Madadayo," *Screen International*, April 30, 1993.
72. David Sterritt, "When Subtle Outweighs Strident," *The Christian Science Monitor*, May 20, 1993, 13.
73. Inoue interview.
74. James Sterngold, "Kurosawa, in His Style, Plans His Next Film," *The New York Times*, February 1, 1992.
75. Kevin Thomas, " 'Madadayo' Opens Salute to Kurosawa," *Los Angeles Times*, September 3, 1999.
76. Kagawa interview.
77. Tatsuo Matsumura. Personal interview, January 27, 1996.
78. Kagawa interview.

29: SHADOW OF THE WOLF; AFTER THE RAIN

1. James Bailey, "Memories of a Pair of Film Giants, Now Dead," *Tokyo Weekender*, February 20, 1998.
2. Laura Chapin, "Picture Bride Pays Off," UPI, May 2, 1995.
3. "Loss of 'Accidental' Actor Mourned," Asahi News Service, December 26, 1997.
4. Kevin Thomas, "Screening Room—A Quintet of Charmers," *Los Angeles Times*, March 26, 1998.
5. "Shiteru tsumori—Mifune Toshiro" (Everything You Always Wanted to Know About Toshiro Mifune). TV program, NTV, aired January 24, 1999.
6. Ibid.
7. Ibid.
8. *Yomiuri Shimbun*, "Sachiko Mifune," September 20, 1995.
9. Tomio Sagisu. Personal interview, December 9, 1999.
10. Ibid.
11. "Shiteru tsumori—Mifune Toshiro."
12. Sagisu interview.
13. "Loss of 'Accidental' Actor Mourned."
14. "Movie Legend Mifune Embodied Japanese Spirit, Captivated World," *The Nikkei Weekly*, December 29, 1997.
15. Richard Corliss, "An Explosive Talent," *Time*, January 12, 1998.
16. Kazuo Miyagawa, "An Actor Who Used His Entire Body," in *Toshiro Mifune—The Last Samurai*, ed. Finichisya (Tokyo: Mainichi-Shimbun-sha, 1998), 98.

17. "Mifune Remembered by Film World," *Daily Yomiuri*, December 26, 1997.

18. "Family Bids Mifune Farewell in Private Gathering," Kyodo News Service, December 25, 1997.

19. "Fans, Cinema Greats Mourn Mifune in Japan," Agence France Presse, January 24, 1998.

20. "Japanese Actor Mifune Left $5.4 Million to His Children, Says Tax Office," Agence France Press, December 17, 1998.

21. Leslie Helm, "Is Kurosawa Ready to Stop Making Films? Not Yet . . . ," *Los Angeles Times*, June 24, 1992, F7.

22. Quoted from the insert included with the Swatch "Eiga-shi," c. 1994.

23. Mark Schilling, "Tokyo," *Screen International*, June 5, 1992.

24. Mike Y. Inoue. Personal interview, December 12, 1999.

25. Ibid.

26. Japan Economic Newswire, September 7, 1998.

27. Kyoko Kagawa. Personal interview, December 15, 1999.

28. "Japanese Director Akira Kurosawa was Planning Demimonde Movie," Reuters, September 9, 1998.

29. Hisao Kurosawa. Personal interview, December 13, 1999.

30. Tak Abe. Personal interview, October 28, 1999.

31. Kazuko Kurosawa, *Papa Kurosawa Akira* (Tokyo: Bungei Shunju, 2000), 201.

32. Inoue interview.

33. Kurosawa, *Papa Kurosawa Akira*, 203.

34. Inoue interview.

35. Kurosawa, *Papa Kurosawa Akira*, 207.

36. Ibid.

37. Ibid., 210.

38. Inoue interview.

39. Hisao Kurosawa interview.

40. Inoue interview.

41. Jonathan Watts, "Kurosawa Scripts Discovered," *The Hollywood Reporter*, September 15, 1998.

42. Nobuo Hori, "*The Hidden Fortress* Was Written Here," in Michihiro Imata, Kunihiro Susumu, and Akira Kurosawa Kenkyukai-hen, eds., *Akira Kurosawa's Footsteps of Dreams* (Tokyo: Kyodo Tunshin-sha, 1999), 205.

43. "Homage to Akira Kurosawa," *Trojan Family Magazine*, Winter 1999, 61.

44. Akira Kurosawa, "From Akira Kurosawa's Notes," *Ame Agaru* press materials, 1999.

45. Mark Schilling, "Cinematic Storm Ends with Light Rain," *The Japan Times*, January 11, 2000.

46. Donald Richie, *The Films of Akira Kurosawa* (Revised Edition) (Berkeley, CA: University of California Press, 1984), 42.

47. David Stratton, "Dora-Heita," *Weekly Variety*, March 6, 2000.

48. "Japan Loses Another Film Director," Agence France Presse, December 30, 1998.

49. Ken Kawashima, "Final Curtain Looms Over a National Movie Shrine," Asahi News Service, April 20, 2000.

50. Inoue interview.

51. Richie, *The Films of Akira Kurosawa*, Preface.

52. Tom Buckley, "Kurosawa at the Drawing Board," *The New York Times*, October 3, 1980, C18.

SELECTED
BIBLIOGRAPHY

Allyn, John. *Kon Ichikawa: A Guide to References and Resources*. Boston: G. K. Hall, 1985.

Amberg, George, ed. *The New York Times Film Reviews, 1913–1968*. New York: The New York Times & Arno Press, 1970.

Anderson, Joseph L. and Donald Richie. *The Japanese Film—Art and Industry* (Expanded Edition). Princeton University Press, 1982.

Andrew, Dudley and Paul Andrew. *Kenji Mizoguchi: A Guide to References and Resources*. Boston: G. K. Hall, 1981.

Barks, Elizabeth and Paul Bernstein, ed. *The Making of James Clavell's Shogun*. New York: Delta, 1980.

Barrett, Gregory. *Archetypes in Japanese Film: The Religious Significance of the Principal Heroes and Heroines*. Selinsgrove, PA: Susquehanna University Press, 1985.

Black and White, eds. *Japanese Film 1955–1964—Showa sanjyu nendai no hito shiriizu* (Japanese Film 1955–1964—Showa 30's Age of Hit Series). Tokyo: Kabushiki Gaisha Neko Publishing, 1999. Two volumes.

Bock, Audie. *Japanese Film Directors*. Tokyo, New York, and San Francisco: Kodansha International, 1978.

Brownlow, Kevin. *David Lean*. New York: A Wyatt Book for St. Martin's Press, 1996.

Carr, Robert E. and R. M. Hayes. *Wide Screen Movies: A History and Filmography of Wide Gauge Filmmaking*. Jefferson, NC: McFarland & Co., 1988.

Champlin, Charles. *John Frankenheimer—A Conversation*. Burbank, CA: Riverwood Press, 1994.

Ciment, Michel. *John Boorman*. New York: Faber & Faber, 1986.

Cowie, Peter, ed. *World Filmography*. London: Tantivy Press, 1977. Two volumes.

Cremin, Stephen. *The Asian Film Library Reference to Japanese Film 1998*. London: The Asian Film Library, 1998. Two volumes.

Endo, Tsumiyoshi, ed. *Toho/Eiga Posutaa gyararii* (Toho/Movie Poster Gallery). Tokyo: Toho Kabushiki-Gaisha, 1995.

Finichisya, ed. *Toshiro Mifune—The Last Samurai*. Tokyo: Mainichi-Shinbun-sha, 1998.

Fleischer, Richard. *Just Tell Me When to Cry—Encounters with the Greats, Near-Greats and Ingrates of Hollywood*. London: Souvenir Press, 1993.

Frayling, Christopher. *Sergio Leone—Something to Do with Death*. New York: Faber & Faber, 2000.

Galbraith, Stuart, IV. *The Japanese Filmography, 1900–1994*. Jefferson, NC: McFarland & Co., 1996.

———. *Monsters Are Attacking Tokyo! The Incredible World of Japanese Fantasy Films*. Los Angeles: Feral House, 1998.

Goldschmidt, Rick. *The Enchanted World of Rankin/Bass*. Issaquah, WA: Tiger Mountain Press, 1997.

Goodwin, James, ed. *Perspectives on Akira Kurosawa*. New York: G. K. Hall & Co., 1994.

Heston, Charlton. *In the Arena*. New York: Boulevard Books, 1995.

———. *The Actor's Life—Journals 1956–1976*. New York: E. P. Dutton, 1976.

Hirano, Kyoko. *Mr. Smith Goes to Tokyo—Japanese Cinema Under the American Occupation, 1945–1952*. Washington: Smithsonian Institution Press, 1992.

Honda, Ishiro. *Honda Ishiro—Gojira to waga eiga jinsei* (Ishiro Honda—Godzilla and My Movie Life). Tokyo: Jitsugyo-no-Nihon-sha, 1994.

Imata, Michihiro, Kunihiro Susumu, and Akira Kurosawa Kenkyukai-hen, eds. *Kurosawa Akira yume no ashiato* (Akira Kurosawa's Footsteps of Dreams). Tokyo: Kyodo Tunshin-sha, 1999.

Isemura, Yoshifumi and Hiroshi Nakamitsu, ed. *Cinema Club 1994–2000* Tokyo: Pia Corp., 1993–2000.

Jewell, Richard B., with Vernon Harbin. *The RKO Story*. New York: Arlington House, 1982.

Jorgens, Jack F. *Shakespeare on Film*. Bloomington, IN: Indiana University Press, 1977.

Kaplan, Mike, ed. *Variety Presents The Complete Book of Show Business Awards*. New York & London: Garland Publishing, 1985.

Katz, Ephraim. *The Film Encyclopedia*. New York: Cromwell, 1979.

Krafsur, Richard P., ed. *The American Film Institute Catalog of Motion Pictures: Feature Films, 1961–1970*. New York: Bowker, 1976.

Kuroda, Toyoji, ed. *UniJapan Film* and *Japanese Film*. Tokyo: UniJapan Film, 1960–1999.

Kurosawa, Akira. *Something Like an Autobiography*. New York: Random House, 1982.

Kurosawa, Kazuko. *Papa Kurosawa Akira*. Tokyo: Bungei Shunju, 2000.

Lent, John A. *The Asian Film Industry*. London: Christopher Helm, Publishers, 1990.

Mellen, Joan. *Voices from Japanese Cinema*. New York: Limelight, 1979.

———. *The Waves at Genji's Door—Japan Through Its Cinema*. New York: Pantheon, 1976.

Mifune, Shuko. *Minami Manshu shashincho* (Views of Southern Manchuria). Tsingtao, China: Mifune Shashinkan, 1910.

Miyamoto, Haruo, ed. *Tsuito Mifune Toshiro otoko* (Toshiro Mifune: Memorial to the Man). Tokyo: Asahi Shimbun-sha, 1998.

———. *Kurosawa Akira—Dakyo naki eiga jinsei* (Akira Kurosawa—An Uncompromised Life in Film). Tokyo: Asahi Shimbun-sha, 1998.

Nishiguchi, Toru, ed. *Kurosawa Akira—Bungei besatsu tsuito tokushu Kurosawa Akira kawade yume muku* (Akira Kurosawa—Bungei Special Memorial Issue, Kawade Dreams). Tokyo: Kawade shubo shin-sha, 1998.

Noguchi, Masanobu, ed. *Mifune Toshiro—Saigo no samurai* (Toshiro Mifune—The Last Samurai). Tokyo: Mainichi-sha, 1998.

———. *Kurosawa Akira no sekai* (The World of Akira Kurosawa). Tokyo: Mainichi Shimbun-sha, 1998.

Nolletti, Anthony Jr. and David Desser, eds. *Reframing Japanese Cinema: Authorship, Genre, History*. Bloomington, IN: Indiana University Press, 1992.

Ohashi, S., ed. *Kurosawa Akira—Sono sakuhin to kao* (Akira Kurosawa—His Work and His Face). Tokyo: Kinema Jumpo-sha, 1963 (reprinted 1997).

———. *Kurosawa Akira • Mifune Toshiro—Futari no Nihon-jin* (Akira Kurosawa • Toshiro Mifune—Two Men of Japan). Tokyo: Kinema Jumpo-sha, 1964 (reprinted 1997).

Perkins, Dorothy. *Encyclopedia of Japan—Japanese History and Culture, from Abacus to Zori*. New York and Oxford: Roundtable Press/Facts on File, 1991.

Pratley, Gerald. *The Cinema of John Frankenheimer*. London: A. Zwemmer, Ltd., 1969.

Quinn, Anthony, with Daniel Paisner. *One Man Tango*. New York: HarperCollins, 1995.

Quirk, Lawrence J. *The Films of William Holden*. Secaucus, NJ: Citadel Press, 1973.

Richie, Donald. *Geisha, Gangster, Neighbor, Nun—Scenes from Japanese Lives*. Tokyo: Kodansha International, 1987.

———. *The Films of Akira Kurosawa*. Berkeley, CA: University of California Press, 1965.

———. *The Films of Akira Kurosawa* (Revised Edition). Berkeley, CA: University of California Press, 1984.

———. *Ozu*. Berkeley, CA: University of California Press, 1974.

——— (consulting editor) and Robert Hughes (general editor). *Rashomon—A Film by Akira Kurosawa*. New York: Grove Press, 1969.

Riera, Emilio Garcia, ed. *Historia Documental del Cine Mexicano* (vol. 11). Date and publisher undetermined.

Sato, Tadao. *Currents in Japanese Cinema*. Trans. Gregory Barrett. New York: Harper & Row, 1982.

Schumaker, Michael. *Francis Ford Coppola—A Filmmaker's Life*. New York: Crown. 1999.

Shimaji, Takamaro, ed. *Kurosawa Akira Dokyumento* (Akira Kurosawa Document). Tokyo: *Kinema Jumpo* Special Edition, May 1974.

———. *Kinema Jumpo Zokan—Nihon eiga Sakuhin zenshu* (Kinema Jumpo Special—A Complete Compilation of Japanese Film). Tokyo: Kinema Jumpo-sha, 1973 (14th edition, 1995).

Sikov, Ed. *On Sunset Boulevard—The Life and Times of Billy Wilder*. New York: Hyperion, 1998.

Silver, Alain. *The Samurai Film*. Woodstock, NY: Overlook Press, 1977.

Slide, Anthony. *The American Film Industry*. Westport, CT: Greenwood, 1986.

———. *The International Film Industry*. Westport, CT: Greenwood, 1989.

Suzuki, Atsushi, ed. *Wakadaisho garafitei* (Young Guy Graffiti). Tokyo: Kadokawa Shoten, 1995.

Svenson, Arne. *Screen Series: Japan*. New York: A. S. Barnes & Co., 1971.

Tsuchiya, Yoshio. *Kurosawa-san—Kurosawa Akira tono subarashiki hibi* (Mr. Kurosawa—Wonderful Days with Akira Kurosawa). Tokyo: Shincho-sha, 1999.

Tsuduki, Masaaki. *Kurosawa Akira to Shichinin no samurai—Eiga no naka no eiga tanjo dokyumento* (Akira Kurosawa and Seven Samurai—Document of the Film Behind the Birth of the Film). Tokyo: Asahi Sonotama, 1999.

Tsushinsha, Jiji, ed. *Japanese Motion Picture Almanac 1957*. Tokyo: Promotion Council of the Motion Picture Industry of Japan, Inc., 1957.

Uekusa, Nobukazu, ed. *Kurosawa Akira to Kinoshita Keisuke—Subarashiki kyosho* (Akira Kurosawa and Keisuke Kinoshita—Wonderful Superstars). Tokyo: *Kinema Jumpo* Temporary Edition, 1998.

Variety Film Reviews, 1905–1992. New York and London: Garland, 1989–1994.

Variety Obituaries, 1905–1986. New York and London: Garland, 1989.

Wiley, Mason and Damien Bona. *Inside Oscar—The Unofficial History of the Academy Awards*. New York: Ballantine, 1987 edition.

Worsley, Wally, Sue Dwiggins Worsley, and Charles Ziarko, eds. *From Oz to E.T.—Wally Worsley's Half-Century in Hollywood*. Lanham, MD: Scarecrow Press, 1997.

Yamazaki, Masaki, ed. *Kurosawa Akira—Sono sekai* (Akira Kurosawa—His World). Hochi Shimbun-sha, 1998.

Yoshimoto, Mitsuhiro. *Kurosawa—Film Studies and Japanese Cinema*. Durham, NC: Duke University Press, 2000.

I,NDEX

Permissions Acknowledgments